OFFICIAL ORGAN OF THE RADIATION RESEARCH SOCIETY

RADIATION RESEARCH

MANAGING EDITOR: TITUS C. EVANS

Volume 19, 1963

Academic Press • New York and London

Made in the United States of America

CONTENTS OF VOLUME 19

NUMBER 1, MAY 1963

CALVIN HANNA AND JAMES E. O'BRIEN. Lens Epithelial Cell Proliferation and Migration in Radiation Cataracts 1

TORE SANNER AND ALEXANDER PIHL. Kinetics of Enzyme Inactivation by Ionizing Radiation 12

ALEXANDER PIHL AND TORE SANNER. X-Ray Inactivation of Papain in Solution 27

JAY S. ROTH AND SYLVIA HILTON. The Effect of Whole-Body X-Irradiation on the Distribution of Acid Deoxyribonuclease and β-Galactosidase in Subcellular Fractions of Rat Spleen 42

G. SILINI, S. HORNSEY, AND D. K. BEWLEY. Effects of X-Ray and Neutron Dose Fractionation on the Mouse Testis 50

D. L. DEWEY. The X-Ray Sensitivity of *Serratia marcescens* 64

A. KATHERINE RUPKEY, RUTH GOLD, ROBERTS RUGH, AND S. C. WANG. Effects of Drugs Alone, or Combined with Refrigeration, in Protecting Female Mice against X-Irradiation-Induced Sterility 88

S. H. COHN, S. W. LIPPINCOTT, E. A. GUSMANO, AND J. S. ROBERTSON. Comparative Kinetics of Ca^{47} and Sr^{85} in Man 104

W. A. ARMSTRONG, R. A. FACEY, D. W. GRANT, AND W. G. HUMPHREYS. A Redetermination of the Salicylic Acid Yield in the Aqueous Calcium Benzoate Dosimeter 120

FRED SNYDER AND EDGAR A. CRESS. Bone Marrow Lipids in Rats Exposed to Total-Body Irradiation 129

RICHARD D. PHILLIPS, DONALD J. KIMELDORF, AND DAVID C. L. JONES. The Relative Potency of Fast Neutrons and 250-Kvp X-Rays in the Guinea Pig 142

J. W. CONKLIN, A. C. UPTON, K. W. CHRISTENBERRY, AND T. P. MCDONALD. Comparative Late Somatic Effects of Some Radiomimetic Agents and X-Rays 156

R. A. DEERING. Mutation and Killing of *Escherichia coli* WP-2 by Accelerated Heavy Ions and Other Radiations 169

Abstracts 179

NUMBER 2, JUNE 1963

RONALD M. HUMPHREY, WILLIAM C. DEWEY, AND ANN CORK. Relative Ultraviolet Sensitivity of Different Phases in the Cell Cycle of Chinese Hamster Cells Grown *in Vitro* 247
ROBERT RUGH AND MARLIS WOHLFROMM. Age of the Mother and Previous Breeding History and the Incidence of X-Ray-Induced Congenital Anomalies 261
SIDNEY O. BROWN, GEORGE M. KRISE, AND HENRY B. PACE. Continuous Low-Dose Radiation Effects on Successive Litters of the Albino Rat 270
MARTIN LIPKIN, HENRY QUASTLER, AND FRANK MUGGIA. Protein Synthesis in the Irradiated Intestine of the Mouse 277
ANDRÉ D. GLINOS. Protein Composition and Growth-Promoting Activity of the Serum after Whole-Body X-Irradiation at Different Ages 286
EDWARD P. RADFORD, JR., VILMA R. HUNT, AND DWYN SHERRY. Analysis of Teeth and Bones for Alpha-Emitting Elements 298
TAKEHIKO TSUCHIYA, JUN-ICHIRO HAYAKAWA, SUSUMU MURAMATSU, AND HIDEO ETŌ. Radiosensitivity and Thyroid Function in Mice 316
FREDERICK D. MALKINSON, MELVIN L. GRIEM, DAVID M. PHILLIPS, AND PETER H. MORSE. Cysteamine Protection of X-Ray-Induced Dysplasia in Mouse Hair 324
DOROTHY C. PETERSON AND HOWARD L. ANDREWS. The Role of Ozone in Radiation Avoidance in the Mouse 331
HOWARD CURTIS AND CATHRYN CROWLEY. Chromosome Aberrations in Liver Cells in Relation to the Somatic Mutation Theory of Aging 337
V. N. SHUBIN AND P. I. DOLIN. The Method of a Competitive Scavenger in Radiation Chemistry 345
J. A. KNIGHT AND FRED SICILIO. Radiolysis Products from the X-Irradiation of 2,2,4,6,6-Pentamethylheptane 359
H. M. RUBINSTEIN AND H. PERIKH. Effect of X-Ray on Antigen Metabolism in the Rabbit 368
DOMINIC J. RASO. Scattering of Gamma Rays in Laminar Media 384
MARTHA D. BERLINER. The Action of Monochromatic Ultraviolet Radiation on Luminescence in *Armillaria mellea* 392
MARY-LOUISE ROTHSCHILD AND WILLIAM T. TSUKAMOTO. Hydrogen Peroxide Yields from Cobalt-60 Gamma Irradiation of Alkaline Solutions 402
ANNOUNCEMENT 408

NUMBER 3, JULY 1963

D. N. SLATKIN, C. R. JANSEN, E. P. CRONKITE, AND J. S. ROBERTSON. Extracorporeal Irradiation of Blood: Calculations of the Radiation Dose 409
MIKIO SHIKITA AND BUN-ICHI TAMAOKI. Influence of X-Irradiation on Zinc-65 Uptake of Testes in Mice 419
M. DRAKULIĆ AND E. KOS. Effect of Some Metabolites and Antimetabolites

on the Breakdown of Deoxyribonucleic Acid and on the Colony-Forming Ability of *Escherichia coli* B after Gamma Irradiation. I. Effect of Citrate, Glutamate, Succinate, Versene and Magnesium Ions 429
E. Kos and M. Drakulić. Effect of Some Metabolites and Antimetabolites on the Breakdown of Deoxyribonucleic Acid and on the Colony-Forming Ability of *Escherichia coli* B after Gamma Irradiation. II. Effect of Phosphorylated Derivatives of Adenosine and Pyrophosphate 439
Lawrence E. Detrick, Harrison Latta, Harvey C. Upham, and Ruth McCandless. Electron-Microscopic Changes across Irradiated Rat Intestinal Villi 447
G. L. Kochanny, Jr., A. Timnick, C. J. Hochanadel, and C. D. Goodman. Radiation Chemistry Studies of Water as Related to the Initial Linear Energy Transfer of 11-Mev to 23-Mev Protons 462
Jean R. Maisin and David G. Doherty. Comparative Chemical Protection to the Intestinal and Hematopoietic Systems of Whole-Body X-Irradiated Mice 474
L. H. Smith and O. Vos. Radiation Sensitivity of Mouse Lymph Node Cells Relative to Their Proliferative Capacity *in Vivo* 485
M. L. Randolph. First-Collision Doses Produced by Fast Neutron Fluxes of Wide Energy Distributions 492
M. H. Biavati, W. Rosenzweig, H. H. Rossi, I. Miyanaga. The Dependence of RBE in the Energy of Fast Neutrons. III. Evaluations of Radiation Quality 512
Richard A. McGrath. X-Ray-Induced Incorporation of Tritiated Thymidine into Deoxyribonucleic Acid of Grasshopper Neuroblast Chromosomes 526
Yosh Maruyama. The Effect of AET (β-Aminoethylisothiuronium) on Thyroid Function in the Rat 538
J. Liebster, J. Kopoldova, and A. Babicky. Radiation-Induced Carboxylation Reactions of Aliphatic Amino Acids and Monocarboxylic Acids 551
J. L. Weeks, G. M. A. C. Meaburn, and S. Gordon. Absorption Coefficients of Liquid Water and Aqueous Solutions in the Far Ultraviolet 559

Number 4, August 1963

James S. Beck. Effects of X-Irradiation on Cell Differentiation and Morphogenesis in a Developing Beetle Wing 569
J. A. V. Butler and A. B. Robins. Effects of Certain Metal Salts on the Inactivation of Solid Trypsin by Ionizing Radiation 582
J. S. Lee, A. W. Anderson, and P. R. Elliker. The Radiation-Sensitizing Effects of *N*-Ethylmaleimide and Iodoacetic Acid on a Radiation-Resistant *Micrococcus* 593
Clifford W. Gurney and Diana Hofstra. Assessment of Actinomycin and Radiation Damage of Stem Cells by the Erythropoietin Tolerance Test 599

W. R. Bruce, M. L. Pearson, and Helen S. Freedhoff. The Linear Energy Transfer Distributions Resulting from Primary and Scattered X-Rays and Gamma Rays with Primary HVL's from 1.25 mm Cu to 11 mm Pb 606
Willie W. Smith, Ilo M. Alderman, Carol A. Schneider, and Jerome Cornfield. Effect of Pretreatment with Colchicine or a Colchicine Derivative on Hemopoiesis in Irradiated Mice 621
R. J. M. Fry, S. Lesher, A. Sallese, and E. Staffeldt. The Generation Cycle of Duodenal Crypt Cells of Mice Exposed to 220 Roentgens of Cobalt-60 Gamma Irradiation per Day 628
C. H. Cheek, V. J. Linnenbom, and J. W. Swinnerton. The Effect of Acidity on the Hydrogen Yield in Gamma-Irradiated Aqueous Solutions 636
Betty Rosoff, Stanton H. Cohn, and Herta Spencer. I. Cesium-137 Metabolism in Man 643
Stanton H. Cohn, Betty Rosoff, Ernest A. Gusmano, and Herta Spencer. II. Long-Term Cs^{137} Turnover in Man as Measured by a Whole-Body Counter 655
A. O. Smoot and J. L. Van Lancker. Effect of Partial Hepatectomy on Nucleic Acid Metabolism of Regenerating Thymus 659
Robert A. Goepp and Frank Fitch. Prevention of Death in Mice after Lethal Irradiation of the Head 670
E. W. Hahn and J. W. Howland. Modification of Irradiation Response of Female Rats by Population Density 676
Yukio Sugino, Eugene P. Frenkel, and Richard L. Potter. Effect of X-Radiation on DNA Metabolism in Various Tissues of the Rat. V. DNA Metabolism in Regenerating Thymus 682
Eugene P. Frenkel, Yukio Sugino, Ronald C. Bishop, and Richard L. Potter. Effect of X-Radiation on DNA Metabolism in Various Tissues of the Rat. VI. Correlative Morphologic and Biochemical Changes during the Regeneration of the Thymus 701
Announcements 717
Author Index 718
Subject Index 720

RADIATION RESEARCH 19, 1–11 (1963)

Lens Epithelial Cell Proliferation and Migration in Radiation Cataracts[1]

CALVIN HANNA[2] AND JAMES E. O'BRIEN[3]

Department of Pharmacology, University of Vermont Medical College, Burlington, Vermont

INTRODUCTION

Lens cataracts produced by ionizing radiation have been carefully studied in both man and animal by histological and clinical methods. A paper by Evans *et al.* (*1*) gives excellent histological and clinical descriptions of three arbitrary stages in the development of cataracts in the mouse lens after neutron and X-irradiation. Although there are some species differences to be considered, the division of cataract development into these arbitrary stages, as given by these authors, is helpful in discussing the movement of cells after irradiation. In general, stage I consists of a disorganized but recognizable lens bow, with abnormal, swollen cortex fibers, a "pseudoepithelium" under the posterior capsule (in the mouse), subcapsular vacuoles, and posterior pole-punctate opacities. Stage II is a continuation of stage I. The lens bow pattern is further disorganized, and the cortex fibers are enlarged and disorganized with subcapsular vacuoles and punctate opacities generally throughout the cortex but concentrated at the poles. Stage III is characterized by complete disorganization of the epithelial and cortex cells, and, in the very advanced stages, by spreading cytolysis of both the new and old fibers, and a complete opacification.

Since the germinative zone is considered to be the most radiosensitive area of the lens epithelium, the majority of investigators now believe that the cells in this area are the locus of the primary radiation injury and that this injury initiates the cataractous changes. The postulated sequence of events (*2*) is that the primary damage to the germinative cells of the lens epithelium results in abortive attempts by these cells to differentiate into normal lens fibers. The damaged cells may be

[1] The study was supported in part by funds made available by a Senior Research Fellowship SF-156(C.H.) and Grant B-2847 from the U.S. Public Health Service, and by a Grant-in-Aid from the Bob Hope Fight for Sight Fund of the National Council to Combat Blindness, Inc., New York City.

[2] Present address: Department of Pharmacology, University of Arkansas Medical Center, Little Rock, Arkansas.

[3] Present address: St. Francis Hospital, Hartford, Connecticut.

completely unable to elongate or, at best, may form swollen fibers in the equatorial region. In some species the degenerate cells will eventually migrate to the posterior pole. The last two stages of opacity formation would be a continuation of the first stage, with the disorganization of the lens cortex becoming more generalized and more extreme as a result of the continued faulty differentiation of epithelial cells.

The sequence of histological changes in an irradiated lens has been described by a number of investigators. However, the movement of epithelial cells could only be inferred from this sequence of cataractous changes. With the use of autoradiographic techniques (*3, 4*) and tritium-labeled thymidine which is incorporated into deoxyribonucleic acid (DNA), it is possible to follow the movement of these labeled cells into the lens. This report is concerned with the movement of lens epithelial cells followed in this manner after γ-irradiation in rats and mice. For the most part, the events occurring in stages I and II of cataract formation were studied.

METHODS AND MATERIALS

Rats and mice were irradiated with 2400 r of γ-rays from a Co^{60} source (*5*) at the rate of 40 r/min. To accomplish this, the animals were anesthetized with 42 mg of pentobarbital sodium per kilogram and placed in plaster of Paris molds behind a 12-inch lead shield, with the left eye exposed. To study DNA synthesis and cell movement, an anterior chamber injection of 5 μc of thymidine–tritium (Schwarz Bio Research, 3 c/mM) was made, and the animals were killed from 2 hours to 4 months later, as indicated in the text. The lenses were removed and subjected to autoradiographic analysis.

The number of cells labeling per sagittal plane section (5 μ thick) and the number of grains found per cell were taken as indicators of the magnitude of nucleic acid synthesis. The change in position of labeled cells with time was taken as an indication of cell movement. Both the degree of labeling and the cell movement rate were altered experimentally. The number of labeled cells was increased by galactose feeding for 2½ days (*6*). The rate of cell movement was accelerated over that of the adult by using very young animals.

At sacrifice the eyes were enucleated, fixed in formalin, and paraffin-embedded. Sections of each eye were placed on glass slides, deparaffinized, hydrated, and painted with Kodak NTB_3 liquid emulsion. After an exposure period of 10 to 14 days, the slides were developed for 4 minutes in Kodak D-19 developer at 20°C, rinsed for 15 seconds in distilled water, cleared for 8 minutes in Kodak Acid Fixer, and rinsed in running water for 10 minutes. The tissue sections were stained with hematoxylin and eosin (*3*). Each eye section was examined by using the oil immersion objective of the light microscope. The mean labeling rate for each eye studied was determined as the average number of labeled cells found by counting twenty sections 5 μ thick.

RESULTS

Effect of Radiation on Labeling Activity

Thymidine–tritium was injected intraocularly 2 hours before sacrifice in this section. A group of adult rats were killed in pairs 12, 19, 24, 48, and 72 hours after irradiation. Only in the 12-, 19- and 24-hour animals was there a decrease in the labeling intensity per cell (grain count). The quantitative extent of the decrease in intensity of the label is difficult to measure because the autoradiographic technique itself is only semiquantitative.

The number of lens epithelial cells undergoing DNA synthesis in the adult rat and mouse gradually increased, starting between 7 and 14 days postirradiation, so that by 1 month the number labeled had increased about 50%. This was in stage I of the cataract formation, and lens epithelial cell damage in the equator region was evident, with an occasional large cell developing. When these large cells in the germinative zone did undergo DNA synthesis, the labeling was much more intense than the labeling that occurred in adjacent cells. The position of the labeled cells in the irradiated lenses remained in the pre-equatorial germinative region at 1 month.

When stage II of the radiation cataract was reached (6 to 12 weeks after irradiation), the number of labeled cells approached almost twice that of the shielded control lens (Fig. 1). The position of the label was generally in the germinative zone, with a few labeled cells scattered toward the anterior pole. At this stage of cataract formation the former pattern of the lens bow became disorganized and sometimes unrecognizable (Fig. 2).

The above study was repeated with weanling rats (24 to 29 days old) because in these animals the initial frequency of labeling is higher (*4*), the mitotic index is higher (*7*), and the radiation cataract develops earlier than in the adult rats (*7*). The results of these experiments were similar to those found with the adult rat except that the initial labeling frequency was higher (Fig. 1) and the stages of cataract formation progressed faster.

Radiation cataract development in the mouse was similar to that found in the rat, as were the changes in area and rate of lens epithelial DNA synthesis. However, in the mouse, groups of cells migrate toward the posterior pole with cataract development to form plaques of cells. These plaques of cells did not label when thymidine–tritium was used.

Cell Movement After Irradiation

The migration of labeled cells from the pre-equatorial germinative zone, around the lens equator, and to the point where these cells enter the lens substance was slow in the adult rat. In 12 weeks approximately one-half of this distance was

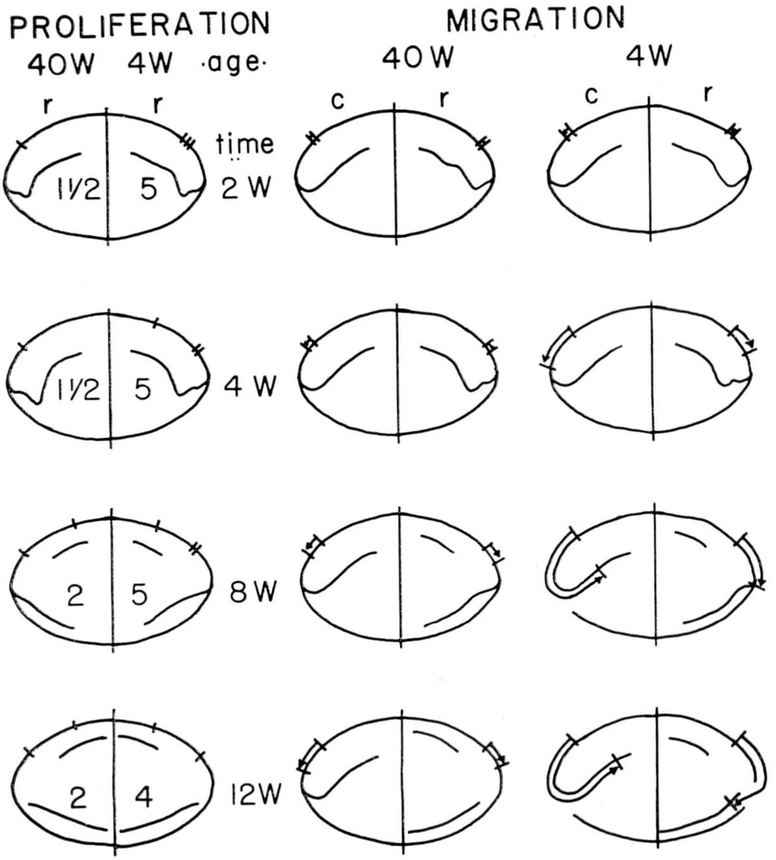

FIG. 1. Graphic representation of the labeling rate and cell movement in lens sections after 2400 r of γ-radiation. Results are for each of two albino rats, Wistar strain. The left-hand column representing lenses is for the 40- and 4-week-old (*W*) rat. The numbers in the lens are for the number of labeled cells found for each full section, and the position of these cells is represented by a dash mark. The column under "time" is the weeks these animals were killed postirradiation. Shown in the center column are the left control eye (*c*) and the right irradiated eye (*r*) of 40-week-old rats. The label was injected 1 day prior to irradiation, and the subsequent position of the labeled cell at sacrifice is indicated by an arrow. The right column is for similar data on the 4-week-old rat.

covered; the effect of irradiation was to decrease this rate slightly (Fig. 1). Although epithelial cells were migrating at a slow rate after irradiation, other changes in the lens were taking place at a much faster rate. By 1 to 2 weeks there was a noticeable displacement of lens nuclei in the lens bow region. This displacement progressed steadily into stage II, where the lens bow became quite disrupted and sometimes difficult to recognize. This region had the histological appearance sug-

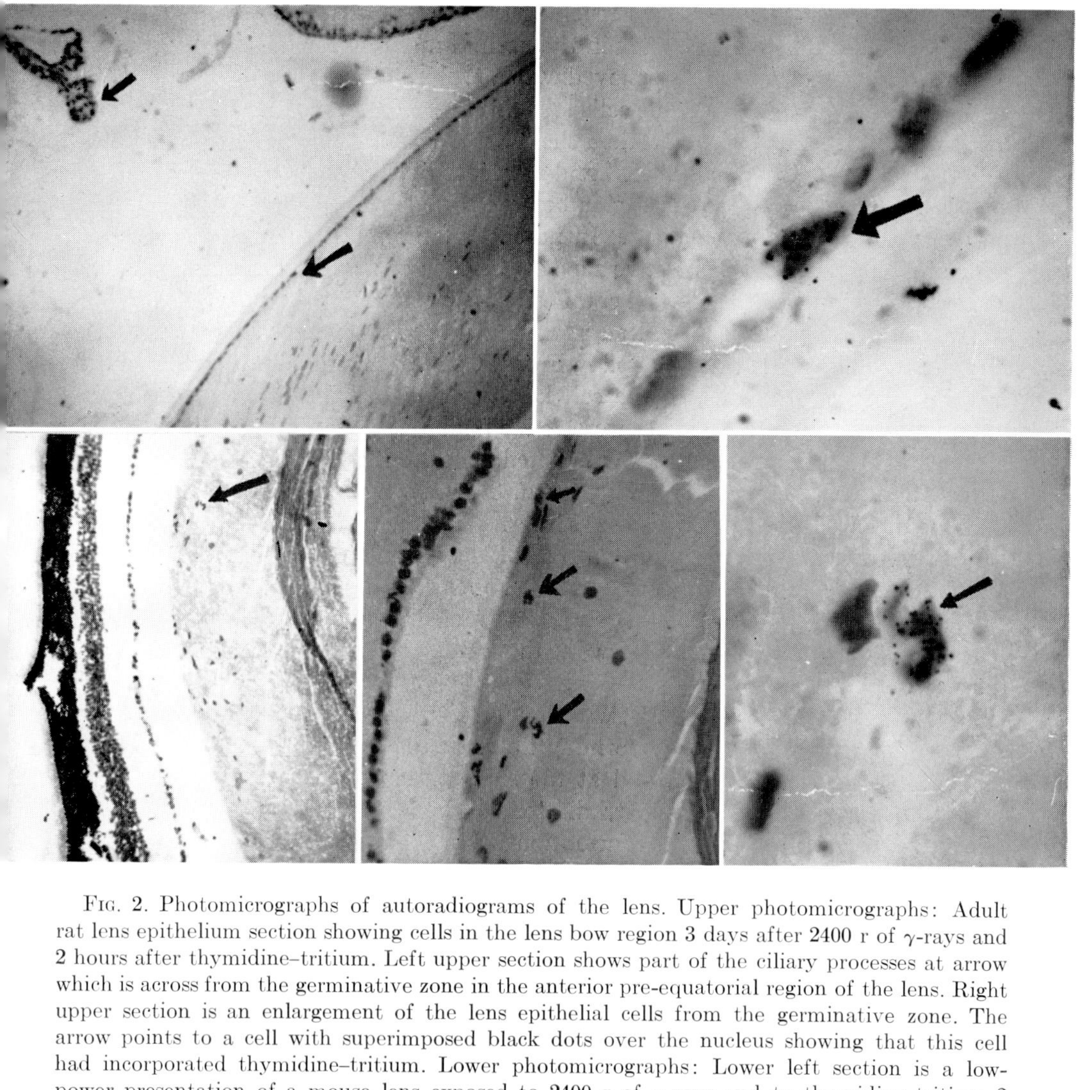

FIG. 2. Photomicrographs of autoradiograms of the lens. Upper photomicrographs: Adult rat lens epithelium section showing cells in the lens bow region 3 days after 2400 r of γ-rays and 2 hours after thymidine–tritium. Left upper section shows part of the ciliary processes at arrow which is across from the germinative zone in the anterior pre-equatorial region of the lens. Right upper section is an enlargement of the lens epithelial cells from the germinative zone. The arrow points to a cell with superimposed black dots over the nucleus showing that this cell had incorporated thymidine–tritium. Lower photomicrographs: Lower left section is a low-power presentation of a mouse lens exposed to 2400 r of γ-rays and to thymidine–tritium 2 months before sacrifice. This section shows the remains of a lens bow and abortive lens fibers under low magnification. The arrow indicates an area that was further magnified and presented in the center photomicrograph. Arrows in the center picture from left to right indicate two abortive fibers, each with a labeled nucleus. To the far right is the area where the epithelial cells normally enter the lens substance and form the lens bow. A further enlarged section from the center slide shows in detail the labeling of the nucleus of the abortive fiber.

gesting that an epithelial cell, on reaching the stage of new fiber formation, could not enter deep into the lens cortex in the normal manner. Furthermore in these irradiated lenses, the labeled cells moved with a pattern different from that in the control lenses. The germinative zone cells label in stage II, and most of the labeled cells move only a short distance and then the label is lost. Histologically this gives the appearance of death of the labeled and associated cells because of the broadening spaces between the cells in this region beginning about three or four epithelial cells posterior to the germinative zone. In no case of the adult rat was a labeled cell which had been in the germinative zone at the time of irradiation found in the lens cortex at a time when the clinical cataract was visible.

The initial rate of cell migration in these studies was increased by using weanling rats (29 days old) as indicated in Fig. 1. Cell death and loss of cell label after irradiation were problems, so the cell labeling rate was increased further in the young rats as follows: The rats were fed a high galactose diet (*6*) for 2½ days, after which thymidine–tritium was injected, and then they were irradiated 2 days later. The rats were sacrificed in groups of 3 (1 of which had been on a galactose diet) at 1, 2, 3, 4, 6, 8, 12, and 16 weeks later.

Cells in the lens epithelium of the irradiated eyes moved noticeably more slowly than the cells in the corresponding shielded eyes (Fig. 1). Histological changes in the irradiated lens of the young animals progressed more rapidly than in the adult lens. During stage I, as early as 1 week there was both a forward and a backward displacement of nuclei in the lens bow region. By 3 weeks the displacement in the lens bow increased in magnitude, with an accompanying vacuole formation at the subcapsular ends of the newly forming fibers in the cortex. By 4 to 8 weeks the clinical cataract was visible, and at the same time cells which had been in the germinative zone at the time of irradiation reached the point in the lens bow, now disrupted, where new lens fiber formation begins. These cells then migrated subcapsularly toward the posterior pole by 12 weeks (Fig. 1). In the young rat, lens epithelial cells in the germinative zone at the time of irradiation moved slowly around the lens equator and entered the lens cortex region after the radiation cataract was in the advanced stages of opacity.

In the above experiments on cell migration, the cell labeling took place 24 to 48 hours before irradiation; therefore, these studies do not exclude the possibility that cells formed after irradiation may move at a different rate. This possibility was studied on 29-day-old rats irradiated as above except that the labeling was carried out later as follows: (1) labeled at 1 week and killed 2, 3, and 4 weeks later; (2) labeled at 2 weeks and killed 3, 4, 5, and 6 weeks later; and (3) labeled at 3½ weeks and killed 4½, 5½, and 6½ weeks later. The results of these experiments showed that the movement of labeled lens epithelial cells was slowed by irradiation, that the germinative zone remained across from the ciliary processes, and that cell death was taking place as evidenced by the loss of labeled cells as compared to the control shielded eye.

Mice were used in place of rats, and the above studies were repeated. The effect of radiation on the migration of lens epithelial cells in the mouse was similar to that seen in the rat with the following exception. Labeled lens epithelial cells migrated from the germinative zone, around the equator, and then subcapsularly toward the posterior pole to form plaques. The plaques contained many cells with abnormally shaped nuclei, some of which retained their label from the germinative zone (Fig. 2). These plaques, as indicated by the position of the label, are first formed by the newly developing lens fibers and later by cells which were irradiated when in the germinative zone.

DISCUSSION

These experiments have some inherent problems. The rate of movement of newly formed lens epithelial cells changed with age (*4*), making it necessary to make all comparisons with the shielded eye of the same animal. Also, the cell deaths in stage II, which occur after the new cells have moved several cell lengths, decreased the number of labeled cells that could be found. Finally, a galactose diet could not be used after irradiation to increase the cell labeling rate because of the unknown effect of this diet on the development of radiation cataracts. These problems could make it more difficult to interpret the results, since any one of these factors could make the cell movement rate appear different from what it really was.

Studies on the irradiated eyes of young mice were interesting in that the final movement of the labeled epithelial cells after irradiation differed in some respects from that of the adult rat. The cells moved normally at first, but as stage I progressed toward stage II the cells labeled at the time of irradiation did not enter deep into the lens cortex. Instead, their movement was restricted to the subcapsular area as they migrated toward the posterior pole. In some cases plaques were formed from these pseudoepithelial cells. These nucleated cells retained the thymidine–tritium label even though their nuclei were sometimes distorted in shape (Fig. 2). In these experiments the control right eye did not show signs of radiation damage during periods up to 8 months.

The opinions of the majority of later investigators concerning the role of the lens epithelium in the formation of radiation cataracts agree with the early observations and statements of Rohrschneider (*8*). His postulated sequence of events, leading to the formation of a cataract, have been summarized by Pirie (*9*) as follows: (1) "The damaged epithelial cells form damaged lens fibers, misshapen and opaque to light." (2) "These get pushed, by subsequent cell divisions, around under the lens capsule to the posterior pole where they constitute the cataract." Since adequate cell tracer techniques were not available until recently, information on the rate of movement of the individual lens epithelial cells was not known when this proposal was originally made. Results presented in this paper, where the movement of epithelial cells was followed, help to clarify the sequence of events leading to the formation of a cataract.

The first part of the current view on radiation cataract formation concerns the role played by the cells from the irradiated germinative zone which form lens fibers that are "misshapen and opaque to light." In young rats and mice, cell tracer studies indicated that these irradiated cells move into the bow region at a slower rate than normal, that they migrate toward the posterior pole, and that they do not lose their nuclei and do not form true lens fibers. In the mouse these cells stay just under the capsule and may migrate to the posterior pole in large enough numbers to form plaques. Owing to the slow migration of the lens epithelial cells in the adult rat, details on the fate of these cells are not known as yet.

The second part of the current view on radiation cataract formation was tested directly by using cell tracer studies in both the rat and the mouse. In the adult rat lens the epithelial cells did not move from the pre-equatorial germinative zone to the area of the lens bow at a sufficient rate to account for the early changes observed in the lens bow region of the cortex after 2400 r of γ-radiation. Epithelial cell movement in young mice and rats occurred at a rate fast enough for those cells dividing around the time of irradiation to reach the lens bow region about a month after irradiation. However, by this time the cataract was already well advanced (stage III). The studies of von Sallmann (*7*) indicate that postirradiation there is a long period of increase in mitosis that follows the initial short period of inhibition of mitosis. This increase in mitotic index, if it could be translated into cell migration, has been taken by some investigators to mean that damaged cells would be pushed into the lens and to the posterior pole at an accelerated rate (*2*). Such an assumption does not take into consideration other events taking place, such as cell death and gradual destruction of the lens bow, or the question of whether increased cell division necessarily means faster lens fiber formation. In measuring epithelial cell movement postirradiation, with autoradiographic techniques, a net decrease was found in the rate at which cells entered the lens cortex at the equator. This was evidenced by signs of cell death, reflected in a lower cell count in the equatorial region (*7*). Histologically it appeared that, because of the increased spaces between the epithelial cells after irradiation, the cells in the equatorial region possibly entered the bow by a process other than by being pushed in as a result of pressure from the new cells formed in subsequent cell divisions. In a study on galactose cataract formation the induction of a marked increase in the rates of labeling and mitosis of the lens epithelial cells by placing rats on a galactose diet for 10 days did not result in the cells' being pushed into the lens at a faster rate (*6*). Instead, the greatly increased number of lens epithelial cells piled up under the anterior capsule, and this situation was not alleviated in 10 days by returning the rats to a normal diet. As a further example, in radiation cataracts von Sallmann (*7*) reported a small increase in the mitotic rate of the mouse lens which lasted for 1 month, whereas in the dog there was a much greater increase in mitotic rate, reaching twenty-two times the normal rate at its peak, and lasting 16 weeks. Clinical lesions of the lens were seen in the mouse in 3 months, but only a small percentage of the dogs showed even minimal clinical effects at the end of 4 months. However, 4 months after irradiation, microscopic examination of the eyes in both animals showed lesions of the cells on the surface of the lens, and of the lens fibers.

There are signs of radiation damage directly to the lens fibers that have not been explained by recent investigators. One of these is the early occurrence of changes in the young nucleated lens fibers, such as the backward and forward displacement of the lens bow which appears as early as 5 to 7 days after 2400 r of γ-radiation in the rat and rabbit (*7*). Also, soon after irradiation there is a swelling of lens fibers accompanied by the formation of vacuoles. Later the angle of insertion of the fibers becomes less acute (*7*), and this is followed in stage II by disruption of the lens fibers in the cortex and evidence of cell death in the subcapsular lens epithelial cells over the anterior surface. Thus the latent period between irradiation and the appearance of the lens opacity could be due to the direct effect of ionizing radiation on the lens fibers, especially those newly differentiating fibers, in the cortex region.

Radiation damage to lens epithelial cells in the germinative zone is seen as an early effect on the proliferation rate and on nuclear structures during mitosis (*7*). Abnormal fibers have developed in the lens bow region, and abnormality has spread from there toward the poles several months before these epithelial cells enter the cortex. It is possible that, normally, epithelial cells contribute energy and metabolites for the proper differentiation of developing fibers (*10*). Thus, when the epithelial cells are damaged, the developing fibers likewise are affected. Another possibility is that radiation affects fibers directly in some way which blocks cell differentiation.

The use of cell tracer techniques could in itself alter some of the results, owing to the possibility of internal radiation produced by the thymidine–tritium label (*11*). Further experiments along this line may make it possible to irradiate internally only certain nuclei, and this will allow a greater clarification of the relative importance of the lens epithelial cells versus the lens fibers in the developing cataract.

In addition, thymidine–tritium could be used to trace individual cells from different areas of the lens at the time of radiation. For example, this has been done with stromal and endothelial cells in the adult cornea (*12*, *13*) and with lens epithelial cells at the anterior pole (*14*) where these cells undergo DNA synthesis and were labeled with thymidine-tritium after wounding. Thus, a way may be found to label nucleated lens fibers selectively and to follow their movement after irradiation.

The studies reported here indicate that the lens fibers show radiation damage at a time before it is possible for those germinative zone epithelial cells in the DNA synthesis stage at the time of irradiation to reach the cortex. Further, the study shows the path into the cortex taken by the epithelial cells postirradiation. This information is incorporated into a revised postulated sequence of events to account for the developing radiation cataract as follows: The early damage is most marked in those lens epithelial cells from the germinative zone to the point of entrance into the lens substance and in the young nucleated lens fibers. The damaged cells forming fibers fail to elongate properly. The nuclei of the younger fibers then begin moving toward the posterior pole of the lens, while the nuclei of the older fibers move a lesser distance toward the anterior pole. In time the pattern of nuclei in the lens bow region becomes unrecognizable with disrupted and swollen fibers. Cells from the germinative zone normally migrate slowly, but this movement is further slowed by cell damage and cell death after irradiation. On reaching the former lens bow region, these cells enter the lens and migrate toward the posterior pole. The process of lens fiber disorganization continues in the cortex, and this may eventually involve the whole lens, giving a complete cataract.

SUMMARY

The left eyes of young and adult mice and rats were exposed to 2400 r of γ-radiation from a Co^{60} source administered at the rate of 40 r/min. The right eyes of the animals served as controls. Thymidine–tritium is incorporated into the deoxyribonucleic acid (DNA) in the synthesis phase of cell division. The number of epithelial cells labeled per section of lens and the number of grains found per cell were taken as a measure of nucleic acid synthesis. The change in position of labeled cells with time was taken as an indication of cell movement.

Initially, the grain count per cell decreased temporarily and then remained near the control level after irradiation. Frequency of cell labeling remained constant for several weeks and then increased moderately. The germinative zone remained in the normal pre-equatorial position even though there was considerable cell damage evident in the epithelium and cortex regions of the lens.

Cells from the germinative zone in the adult rat moved slowly after irradiation. These labeled cells were not found to enter the lens cortex until after the cataract was well advanced or complete. In younger animals cell migration was fast enough so that labeled cells moved into the lens and migrated toward the posterior pole sometimes before the cataract was complete. In the mouse these labeled cells migrated toward the posterior pole just under the lens capsule to form plaques. Lens fiber damage in all cases was well advanced before cells in the zone of DNA synthesis at the time of irradiation migrated and reached the area of opacity in the lens cortex.

Previous work on radiation cataract formation has been critically reviewed, and a postulated sequence of events leading to the cataract has been put forth. In this sequence of events, damage to the newly forming lens fibers at the time of irradiation is seen as directly leading to the cataract.

ACKNOWLEDGMENTS

I wish to acknowledge the help of Dr. Edgar Riley for aid in preparing the manuscript and Dr. Titus C. Evans for making photomicrographs of the lens sections.

RECEIVED: April 3, 1962

REFERENCES

1. T. C. EVANS, R. D. RICHARDS, and E. F. RILEY, Histologic studies of neutron- and X-irradiated mouse lenses. *Radiation Res.* **13,** 737–750 (1960).
2. S. DUKE-ELDER, *Text-Book of Opthalmology,* Vol. 6, p. 6567, C. V. Mosby Company, St. Louis, 1954.
3. C. HANNA and J. E. O'BRIEN, Cell production and migration in the epithelial layer of the cornea. *Arch. Ophthalmol.* **64,** 536–539 (1960).
4. C. HANNA and J. E. O'BRIEN, Cell production and migration in the epithelial layer of the lens. *Arch. Ophthalmol.* **66,** 103–107 (1961).
5. D. J. SMITH, R. C. PARKER, C. HANNA, and H. E. CURLEY, Subacute and late cardiovascular sequelae to low doses of gamma radiation. *Am. J. Physiol.* **197,** 725–729 (1959).
6. C. HANNA and J. E. O'BRIEN, Studies on galactose cataract formation utilizing thymidine-tritium. *Arch. Ophthalmol.* **64,** 708-711 (1960).
7. L. VON SALLMANN, Experimental studies on early lens changes after roentgen irradiation. I. Morphological and cytological changes. *Arch. Ophthalmol.* **45,** 149–164 (1951).
8. W. ROHRSCHNEIDER, Experimentelle Erzeugung von Röntgenstrahlenkatarakt, *Strahlentherapie* **31,** 596–599 (1929); Experimentelle Untersuchungen über die Veränderungen normaler Augengewebe nach Röntgenbestrahlung: Veränderungen der Linse, der Natzhaut und des Sehnerven nach Röntgenbestrahlung. *Arch. Ophthalmol.* **122,** 282 (1929); Über die Wirkung der Röntgenstrahlen auf das Auge, *Strahlentherapie* **38,** 665 (1930).
9. A. PIRIE, In *The Structure of the Eye* (G. K. Smelser, ed.), pp. 259–272, Academic Press, New York, 1961.
10. E. F. RILEY, R. D. RICHARDS, and P. J. LEINFELDER, Recovery of X-irradiated rabbit lenses. *Radiation Res.* **11,** 79–89 (1959).
11. W. L. HUGHES, In *The Kinetics of Cellular Proliferation* (F. Stohlman, Jr., ed.), pp. 83–94, Grune and Stratton, New York, 1959.
12. C. HANNA and J. E. O'BRIEN, Thymidine-tritium labeling of the cellular elements of the corneal stroma. *Arch. Ophthalmol.* **66,** 362–365 (1961).
13. N. L. MILLS and A. DONN, Incorporation of tritium-labeled thymidine by rabbit corneal endothelium. *Arch. Ophthalmol.* **64,** 443–447 (1960).
14. C. V. HARDING, C. FELDHEER, and B. D. SRINIVASAN, *The Structure of the Eye* (G. K. Smelser, ed.), pp. 273–276, Academic Press, New York, 1961.

RADIATION RESEARCH 19, 12–26 (1963)

Kinetics of Enzyme Inactivation by Ionizing Radiation[1]

TORE SANNER[2] AND ALEXANDER PIHL

Norsk Hydro's Institute for Cancer Research, Montebello, Oslo, Norway

INTRODUCTION

When enzymes are irradiated in dilute aqueous solution, the rate of inactivation will usually decrease with increasing radiation dose. This is due to the fact that inactivated enzyme molecules compete with the active ones for the agents formed from water (*1*). In most studies the data more or less closely fit a straight line when the remaining enzyme activity is plotted versus the radiation dose in a semilogarithmic plot (*2, 3*). On this basis it has been assumed that, in general, enzymes are inactivated as an exponential function of the dose (*3*). Accordingly, deviations from straight lines in such plots have frequently been disregarded.

Several authors have derived theoretical equations predicting an exponential dose-inactivation relationship, using the assumption that inactivated and active enzyme molecules destroy the agents from water at the same rate (*1, 4–11*). In fact, it can be shown that strictly exponential dose inactivation can be obtained only when the above assumption holds true.

Recent experiments in this laboratory have shown that the SH enzymes glyceraldehyde-3-phosphate dehydrogenase (GAPDH),[3] alcohol dehydrogenase (ADH), and papain (*12–14*) are inactivated by X-rays in a definitely nonexponential fashion. The data suggested the possibility that in these instances the active enzyme molecules react more readily with the active agents from water than do the inactivated ones. This led us to re-examine the kinetics of enzyme inactivation from this point of view.

The present analysis of enzyme inactivation in solution by ionizing radiation is an extension of previous theoretical treatments (*1, 4–11*). The approach is more general than the previous ones in so far as no assumption is *a priori* made concerning the relative ability of active and inactivated enzyme molecules to deacti-

[1] Work supported by Division of Radiological Health, Bureau of State Service, U.S. Public Health Service.

[2] Fellow of the Norwegian Cancer Society.

[3] The following abbreviations are used: GAPDH, glyceraldehyde-3-phosphate dehydrogenase: ADH, alcohol dehydrogenase, PCMB, *p*-chloromercuribenzoate.

vate radicals formed from water. The analysis has brought to light several points of general interest for the understanding of the significance of factors operating in radiation inactivation of enzymes in solution.

MATERIALS AND METHODS

Crystalline GAPDH and ADH were prepared from rabbit muscle (*15*) and from yeast (*16*), respectively. Crystalline papain was prepared from granular *Papaya latex* (Wallerstein Company, New York) (*17*). The assay of the enzymes was carried out as previously described (*12, 14*).

The water used in the irradiation experiments was obtained by double distillation from glass equipment and passage through a mixed-bed ion-exchange column. The enzymes were dissolved in 0.067 *M* phosphate buffer, pH 7.40, and irradiated in Erlenmeyer flasks placed in crushed ice. The enzymatic measurements were carried out immediately after the exposure. All solutions were equilibrated with air. The irradiation was carried out with an X-ray machine (Stabilipan, Siemens). The irradiation factors were 220 kv, 4 to 20 ma, and 0.5 mm Cu. The dosimetry was carried out with a ferrous system (*18*).

The SH determinations were carried out by the method of Boyer (*19*) as previously described (*20*).

RESULTS

Dose-Inactivation Relationship. Theoretical Analysis

In the following treatment, ordinary chemical reaction kinetics have been used. The approach is analogous to that used by Okada (*8*).

In the derivations the following reactions will be considered (list of symbols, see below):

During irradiation, radiation products (X) are formed from water:

$$H_2O \xrightarrow[\sim]{I} \text{Hel.} \tag{1}$$

The radiation products consist of a number of species (X_2, $X_2 \cdots X_j$) which inactivate the enzyme in question with different rate constants (k_{01}, $k_{02} \cdots k_{0j}$). Since our information on the nature of the active agents is incomplete, and since it does not seem feasible at the present time to determine the individual rate constants, we have chosen, in agreement with previous authors (*8–10*) to develop the equations in terms of a single active "radical." This procedure is valid if the enzyme inactivation is due predominantly to one active species, which may well be the case with certain enzymes. The procedure also seems justified when two or more species contribute to the total inactivation, if their relative efficiency is constant during the inactivation and is independent of the initial enzyme concentration. The radicals are deactivated in reactions with the active enzyme (E) which thereby becomes inactivated:

$$E + X \xrightarrow{k_0} E_{\text{inact}} \tag{2}$$

Radicals disappear in reactions with the active enzyme not leading to enzyme inactivation:

$$E + X \xrightarrow{k' - k_0} E \tag{3}$$

Radicals disappear in reactions with radiation-inactivated enzyme:

$$E_{\text{inact}} + X \xrightarrow{k_1} E_{\text{inact}} \tag{4}$$

Radicals disappear in reactions with contaminating substances (F):

$$F + X \xrightarrow{k_1'} F \tag{5}$$

Radicals disappear in reactions with protective substances (P):

$$P + X \xrightarrow{k_2} P \tag{6}$$

List of Symbols:

E = the concentration of active enzyme.
E_0 = the initial concentration of active enzyme.
y = the concentration of enzyme inactivated by irradiation.
X = the concentration of active species, "radicals." See text above.
F = the concentration of a contaminant in the enzyme preparation (e.g., inactive enzyme or other proteins). F is thus by definition proportional to E_0.
P = the concentration of other protective substances (e.g., added substances). P is independent of E_0.
k_0 = the rate constant for the inactivation of enzyme by radicals.[4]
k' = the rate constant for the inactivation of radicals by the active enzyme (E).
k_1 = the rate constant for the inactivation of radicals by the inactivated enzyme (y).
k_1' = the rate constant for the inactivation of radicals by contaminating substances (F).
k_2 = the rate constant for inactivation of radicals by protective substances (P).
I = the number of radicals (in moles per liter) formed per unit time.
D = the radiation dose in roentgens.

[4] This rate constant, as well as the other ones listed below, refer to the reactivity of X. In cases where X represents two or more species, the rate constants represent the weighted average of the actual rate constants involved.

α = proportionality factor converting dose in number of radicals (in moles per liter) to roentgens ($It = D\alpha$).

t = time.

The rate of inactivation of the enzyme is given by equation 7. The rate of change

$$\frac{dE}{dt} = -k_0XE \tag{7}$$

in the concentration of the radicals is given by equation 8. The term $-k_2XP$ includes all processes whereby radicals disappear, except those involving the enzyme and contaminating substances in the enzyme preparation.[5]

$$\frac{dX}{dt} = I - k'XE - k_1X(E_0 - E) - k_1'XF - k_2XP \tag{8}$$

From equation 8 it follows that

$$X = \frac{I - (dX/dt)}{k'E + k_1(E_0 - E) + k_1'F + k_2P} \tag{9}$$

Since the rate of change in X, dX/dt, presumably is small compared to the rate of formation of radicals (I), dX/dt can be set equal to zero (a steady state is as-

$$\frac{dE}{dt} = -\frac{k_0I \cdot E}{k'E + k_1(E_0 - E) + k_1'F + k_2P} \tag{10}$$

sumed to exist). Substituting then for X in equation 7 gives equation 10. Since y is the concentration of enzyme inactivated by irradiation, we have equation 11.

$$E = E_0 - y \tag{11}$$

On substitution for E in equation 10, and on integration from $t = 0$ to $t = t$, equa-

$$It = \frac{1}{k_0}\left[(k' - k_1)y + (k_1E_0 + k_1'F + k_2P)\ln\frac{E_0}{E_0 - y}\right] \tag{12}$$

tion 12 results. Since $It = \alpha D$, equation 12 can be rearranged to give equation 13.

$$D\alpha = \frac{k' - k_1}{k_0}y + \frac{k_1E_0 + k_1'F + k_2P}{k_0}\ln\frac{E_0}{E_0 - y} \tag{13}$$

Equation 13 gives the relationship between the dose and the extent of inactivation. It is seen that the equation contains a linear and a logarithmic term. If the assumption is made that the active and the inactivated enzyme remove free radi-

[5] Recombination of radicals might be expected to give rise to a term of the form $-kX^2$. A second-order recombination should increase strongly with the dose rate. Since this has not been found experimentally (*11, 21*), second-order recombination of radicals has been disregarded in this paper.

$$D\alpha = \frac{1}{k_0}\left[(k_1E_0 + k_1'F + k_2P)\ln\frac{E_0}{E_0 - y}\right] \tag{14}$$

cals at the same rate ($k' = k_1$), equation 13 reduces to equation 14, which can be written as equation 15,

$$E = E_0 e^{-[k_0 D\alpha/(k_1E_0+k_1'F+k_2P)]} = E_0 e^{-KD} \tag{15}$$

where

$$K = \frac{k_0\alpha}{k_1E_0 + k_1'F + k_2P} \tag{16}$$

Equation 15, which predicts an exponential dose-inactivation curve, is equivalent to the equations derived by previous authors (*1, 4–11*).

With the aid of equation 13, theoretical dose-inactivation curves can be constructed. In Fig. 1, a family of curves is shown, demonstrating the effect of in-

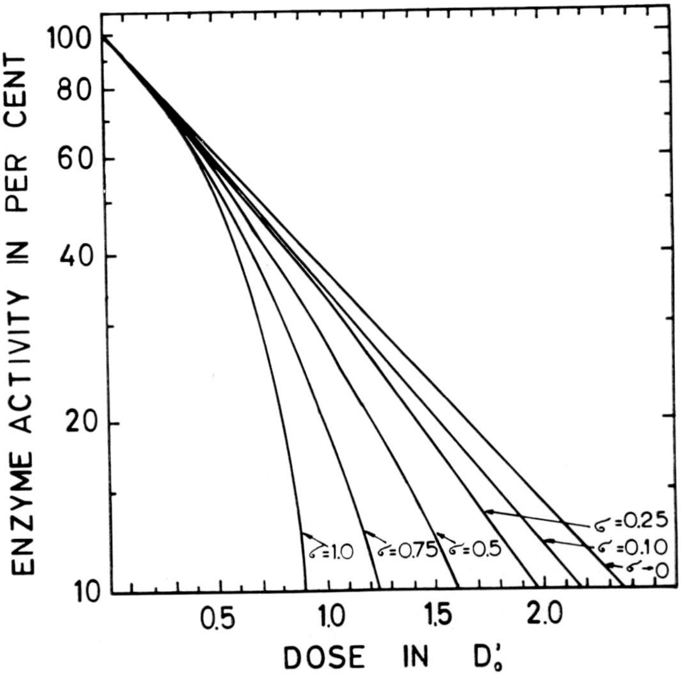

FIG. 1. Theoretical dose-inactivation curves calculated for different yields. The curves were calculated with the aid of equation 13, by assuming that $(k' - k_1)/k_0 = 1$, and that $F = 0$ and $P = 0$. The initial ionic yield under these circumstances is denoted ($\sigma = (k_0/k')$. The dose is expressed in terms of D_0', which is the dose that would be required to inactivate the enzyme completely if the rate of inactivation remained equal to the initial one. The absolute value of D_0' varies inversely with σ.

creasing yield of inactivation on the shape of the curves. These were calculated on the assumption that the enzyme possesses only one active group and that the inactivation of the enzyme is due exclusively to a radiochemical alteration of this group. Each collision between an active group and a radical leading to deactivation of the latter is assumed to result in alteration and inactivation of the active group. The altered group is assumed not to inactivate radicals. These assumptions imply that $(k' - k_1)/k_0 = 1$.

It can be seen that with increasing yield the dose-inactivation curves deviate to an increasing extent from straight lines in semilogarithmic plots. This is due to the fact that with increasing yield, i.e., when k_0 increases relative to the other rate constants, the logarithmic term of equation 13 will assume decreasing significance relative to the linear one.

Application of Theory to Experimental Data

Attempts were made to see whether equation 13 could describe our experimental data on SH enzymes when reasonable assumptions were made regarding the numerical value of the parameters $(k' - k_1)/k_0$ and α. The procedure used and the fit of the theoretical curves to the experimental values will be illustrated for papain and ADH.

In Fig. 2 the results for papain are demonstrated. Here α was taken to be 3×10^{-9}

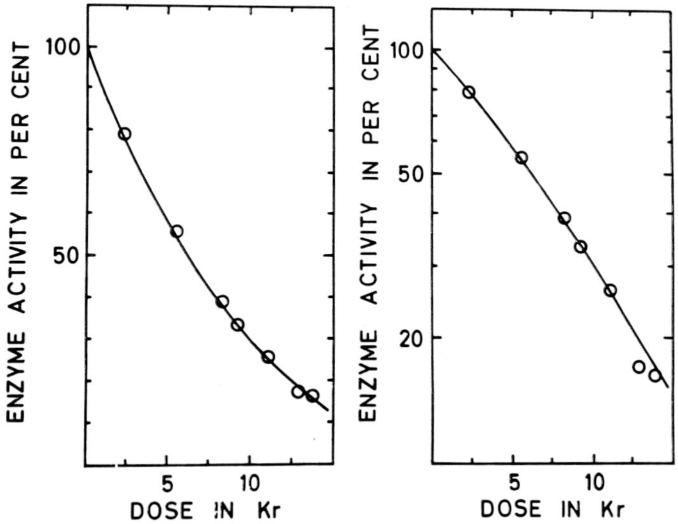

FIG. 2. The X-ray inactivation of papain. Papain (1.2×10^{-5} M) was irradiated in 0.067 M phosphate buffer, pH 7.40, at 0°C at a dose rate of 1850 r/min. Catalase in a concentration of 3.6 μg/ml was present during the irradiation. The papain preparation contained 0.50 SH group per molecule. The experimental values are indicated by circles, and the fully drawn lines represent theoretical curves.

mole of active radicals per liter per roentgen. In this case $(k' - k_1)/k_0$ was set equal to 1. The validity of these assumptions will be considered in the Discussion.

It follows that equation 13 can now be written

$$D\alpha = y + Q_1 \ln \frac{E_0}{E_0 - y} \tag{17}$$

where

$$Q_1 = \frac{k_1 E_0 + k_1' F + k_2 P}{k_0} \tag{18}$$

Since papain consists of a mixture of active enzyme molecules having one SH group and inactive molecules with no free SH group (*22*), E_0 was set equal to the concentration of titratable protein SH groups.

The theoretical values were obtained by choosing for a given Q_1 a set of values for y and calculating the corresponding D values. The value of Q_1 was chosen by successive approximations to give the best fit to the experimental data. It is apparent from Fig. 2 that very close agreement between the theoretical curve and the experimental data was obtained.

In Fig. 3, corresponding data are given for ADH. In the particular preparation used, 19 SH groups were titrated which presumably inactivate radicals at closely the same rate. Since it was found that the enzyme inactivation could be accounted for predominantly by destruction of the SH groups, and since all SH groups had to be destroyed to inactivate the enzyme completely, the ratio $(k' - k_1)/k_0$ was set equal to 19. Figure 3 shows that the curve calculated on this assumption follows closely the experimental dose-inactivation curve.

Yield of Inactivation

If the active and the inactive enzyme molecules remove radicals at different rates, this may have important consequences with regard to the observed parameters of radiosensitivity.

Since the yield of inactivation will usually decrease during irradiation, owing to the fact that inactivated enzyme molecules will compete with the active ones for the radicals, the initial yield is clearly the parameter of interest.

In general the initial ionic yield can be defined by equation 19, where D_0' is the radiation dose required to inactivate completely the enzyme if the rate of inactiva-

$$\frac{M}{N} = -\left(\frac{dE}{\alpha\, dD}\right)_{D=0} = \frac{E_0}{\alpha D_0'} \tag{19}$$

tion were to remain equal to the initial rate. When the inactivation is exponential, D_0' is equal to D_{37}, as will be shown below.

The significance of the initial ionic yield can be discussed with reference to equa-

$$-\left(\frac{dE}{\alpha\, dD}\right)_{D=0} = \frac{E_0}{\alpha D_0'} = \frac{k_0 E_0}{k' E_0 + k_1' F + k_2 P} \tag{20}$$

tion 20, which is obtained from equation 10 by introducing $E = E_0$ and $I\,dt = \alpha\,dD$. It follows from equation 20 that the observed initial yield will be a true indicator of the radiosensitivity of an enzyme only when the irradiated solution contains no other substance than active enzyme, capable of inactivating radicals. Under these circumstances ($F = 0$, $P = 0$), $M/N = k_0/k'$. The parameter k_0/k', which is the true ionic yield, σ, is a measure of the intrinsic radiosensitivity; σ signifies the probability that a radical which becomes inactivated by the enzyme will concurrently inactivate the enzyme.

The experimental determination of the initial ionic yield involves an estimation of D_0'. This parameter can be derived from an experimental dose-inactivation curve, either graphically or by derivation of an equation fitted to the data.

It follows from equation 20 that

$$D_0'\alpha = \frac{1}{k_0}(k' E_0 + k_1' F + k_2 P) \tag{21}$$

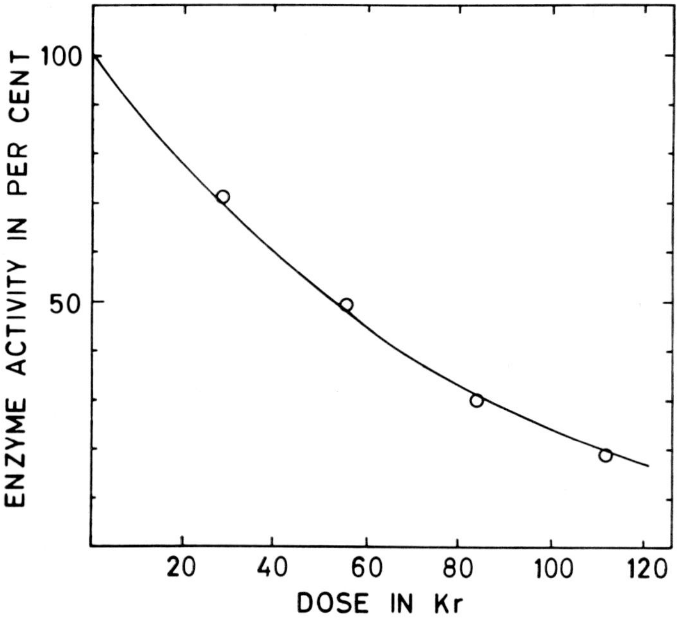

FIG. 3. The X-ray inactivation of ADH. The enzyme (4.92×10^{-6} M) was irradiated in 0.067 M phosphate buffer, pH 7.40, at 0°C, at a dose rate of 1850 r/min. The preparation contained 19 SH groups per molecule. Notation as in Fig. 2.

From equation 15 it follows that, when the inactivation is strictly exponential ($k_1 = k'$), the D_{37}, i.e., the dose required to reduce the activity to $1/e$ or 37% of the initial one, is equal to D_0'. It should be clear that D_{37} is a useful parameter only when the dose-inactivation curve is exponential.

The true ionic yield can be determined also when protective substances have been added ($P \neq 0$) and in some cases even when contaminating substances are present ($F \neq 0$), as will be shown below. Hutchinson and Ross (*10*) have demonstrated that, for substances which are inactivated exponentially with the dose, a straight line will be obtained when the D_{37} dose is plotted against the solute concentration. The authors obtained the yield of inactivation of various solutes from the slope of the curves and demonstrated that the intercepts on the ordinate were proportional to the amount of added protector, as predicted. It is of interest to point out that if D_{37} is replaced by the general parameter, D_0', this approach can be used even when the inactivation is nonexponential. Thus, equation 21 can be written as equation 22, where $k_1'F/E_0$ by definition is constant. This equation predicts that, if D_0' is plotted against E_0, a straight line should be obtained. It follows

$$D_0' = \frac{1}{\alpha}\left[\frac{(k' + k_1'F/E_0)E_0}{k_0} + \frac{k_2P}{k_0}\right] \tag{22}$$

from equation 22 that, when $F = 0$, σ can be directly obtained from the slope of the curve. When $F \neq 0$, σ is not proportional to the reciprocal of the slope. However, if F can be estimated, σ can be calculated from the slope, as will be illustrated with papain as an example.

Since the papain preparation (E_0^{tot}), as pointed out above, consists of a mixture of active enzyme molecules (E_0^{SH}) having one active SH group and inactive molecules having no free SH group, F can be obtained by titration of the SH content of the enzyme. If

$$E_0^{\text{SH}} = \beta E_0^{\text{tot}} \tag{23}$$

then

$$F = (1 - \beta)E_0^{\text{tot}} \tag{24}$$

The assumption is made that the inactive enzyme protein inactivates radicals with the same rate as the radiation-inactivated enzyme ($k_1' = k_1$). By substituting in equation 22 for E_0^{SH} and for F, equation 25 is obtained. It follows from equation

$$D_0' = \frac{1}{\alpha}\left[\frac{\beta k' + (1 - \beta)k_1}{k_0} E_0^{\text{tot}} + \frac{k_2P}{k_0}\right] \tag{25}$$

25 that the slope of the curves in Fig. 4 is equal to

$$\frac{1}{\alpha}\left[\frac{\beta k' + (1 - \beta)k_1}{k_0}\right].$$

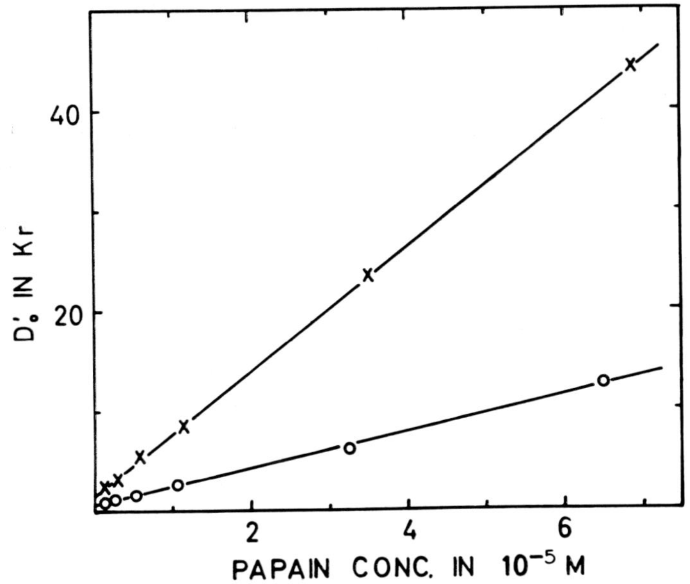

FIG. 4. The D_0' dose for papain as a function of the enzyme concentration. Increasing concentrations of papain were irradiated in 0.067 *M* phosphate buffer, pH 7.40, at 0°C. For each enzyme concentration, D_0' was obtained from a dose-inactivation curve. The papain preparation contained 0.40 SH group per molecule. ×——×, cysteine added before measurement of activity; dose rate 850 r/min. ○——○, no cysteine present during measurement of enzyme activity; dose rate 240 r/min.

In this particular experiment β was 0.40. When the assumption was used that $(k' - k_1)/k_0 = 1$, σ was found to be 0.88 in the absence and 0.40 in the presence of cysteine, respectively. The corresponding observed yields were 1.84 and 0.53.

The above data suggested the possibility that the error in the observed ionic yield, due to F, may primarily be of importance when the observed ionic yield is high. In order to study this question the quantitative significance of F was studied experimentally in the case of papain and GAPDH. F was varied by blocking an increasing fraction of the SH groups with PCMB. Figure 5*A* demonstrates that in the case of papain, D_0', which is an inverse function of the ionic yield, decreases with increasing F. In the case of GAPDH, which is inactivated with a low ionic yield, no detectable effect of F on D_0' was found (Fig. 5*B*).

The reason F influences D_0' markedly only when the observed ionic yield is high can be seen from equation 26 (derived from equation 25) and from equation 27:

$$D_0'\alpha = -\frac{k' - k_1}{k_0} F + Q_2 \qquad (26)$$

where

$$Q_2 = \frac{k'}{k_0} E^{\text{tot}} + \frac{k_2 P}{k_0} \qquad (27)$$

It follows that, since k'/k_0 is the inverse value of σ, Q_2 will be relatively small when σ is high, and the first term, which includes F, will be relatively important. If, on the other hand σ is small, Q_2 will dominate, relative to the first term, and variations in F will influence D_0' only to a limited extent.

The above considerations explain the unexpected finding that the observed yield for ADH was independent of the specific activity of the enzyme (*12*).

"Effective Radicals"

Okada (*8*) has calculated, for certain concentrations of deoxyribonuclease, the fraction of the total number of radicals that react with the enzyme. This fraction, the "effective radicals," was found to increase with increasing enzyme concentration. It is of some interest to point out that the change in the fraction of "effective radicals" with the enzyme concentration is actually proportional to the well-known concurrent changes in the yield of inactivation. Thus, the fraction of radicals, ρ,

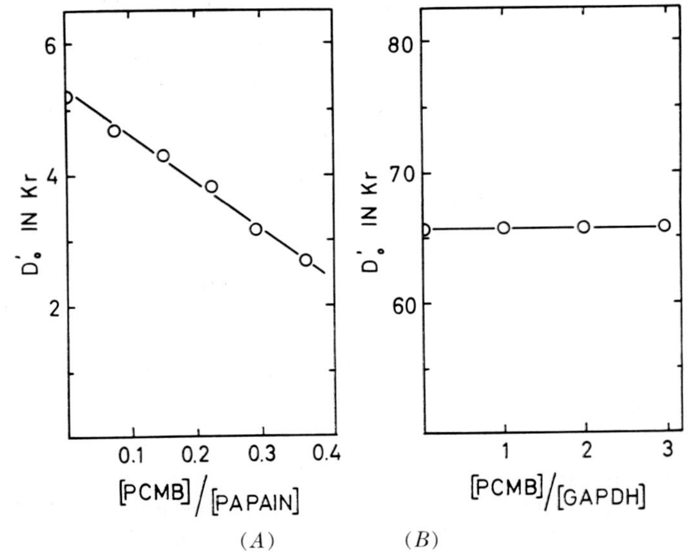

FIG. 5. The effect of SH blocking on D_0' for papain and GAPDH. The enzymes were incubated in 0.067 *M* phosphate buffer, pH 7.40, at 0°C with increasing concentrations of PCMB for 40 minutes. The D_0' was determined in each case from a dose-inactivation curve. The papain was irradiated in a concentration of 2.27×10^{-5} *M*, at a dose rate of 240 r/min. The preparation contained 0.40 SH group per molecule. GAPDH was irradiated in a concentration of 5.00×10^{-6} *M*, at a dose rate of 1850 r/min. The enzyme contained 10.0 SH groups per molecule.

which becomes inactivated in reactions with the enzyme, is by definition

$$\rho = \frac{D_0'\alpha - (k_2P/k_0)}{D_0'\alpha} \tag{28}$$

By substituting for D_0' by means of equation 21, equation 29 is obtained. Equation 29 can be rearranged to give equation 30, where Q_3 is a constant.

$$\rho = \frac{(1/k_0)(k'E_0 + k_1'F)}{(1/k_0)(k'E_0 + k_1'F + k_2P)} \tag{29}$$

$$\rho = \frac{k_0E_0}{k'E_0 + k_1'F + k_2P} \cdot \frac{k' + (k_1'F/E_0)}{k_0} = \frac{M}{N} \cdot Q_3 \tag{30}$$

DISCUSSION

The present work emerged from an attempt to explain the exceptionally high yield of inactivation found for papain and the nonexponential dose-inactivation curves observed for this and for other SH enzymes (*12–14*).

The basic difference between the above analysis and previous kinetic treatments of enzyme inactivation is that the possibility is included that active enzyme molecules may remove radiation-induced radicals faster than do the inactivated ones. The consequence of such a difference will readily be appreciated. During irradiation the concentration of active enzyme molecules will decrease. If the active enzyme molecules remove radicals faster than do the inactivated ones, the concentration of radicals will necessarily increase during the exposure. The decrease in the concentration of active enzyme will therefore in part be counteracted by the concurrent increase in the concentration of radicals, with the consequence that the inactivation will be greater than corresponding to an exponential function of the dose.

Significant differences between the active and the inactivated enzyme molecules in their ability to dissipate radiation energy require the active site of the enzyme to be preferentially attacked by the radicals, which implies that the yield of inactivation is high. Accordingly, the theoretical dose-inactivation curves (Fig. 1) demonstrated that, with increasing yield of inactivation, the dose-effect curves will deviate to an increasing extent from linearity in a semilogarithmic plot.

In the case of papain, evidence has been presented here (Fig. 5) and previously (*14*) that the inactivated enzyme molecules remove free radicals less efficiently than do the active ones having a reactive intact SH group. This seems to explain adequately the fact that the dose-effect curve for this enzyme deviates markedly from linearity in a semilogarithmic plot. Definite deviations from straight lines in such plots found in previous papers (*8, 23, 24*) may have the same explanation. However, in most enzyme studies reported, low ionic yields have been found, and under these circumstances detectable deviations from exponential inactivation will ordinarily not be expected.

Special circumstances account for the finding that the SH enzymes ADH and GAPDH are both inactivated in a definitely nonexponential way in spite of the fact that their over-all ionic yields of inactivation are low (about 0.02) (*12, 13*). In the case of ADH this is in part due to the fact that the enzyme has many SH groups, each of which is inactivated with a rather high ionic yield. Furthermore, all the SH groups must be destroyed in order to inactivate the enzyme completely. This implies that there is in fact a significant difference between the active enzyme molecules and the completely inactivated ones with respect to their ability to deactivate radiation-induced radicals. In the case of GAPDH a special factor is operative. This enzyme has 10 to 11 SH groups (*25, 26*), whereas the enzyme activity is completely abolished when only 3 of the SH groups have been destroyed by irradiation (*13*). Therefore the inactivation curve of the enzyme corresponds to only the first three-tenths of the curve for the destruction of the SH groups.

In the practical application of equation 13 to our experimental data, assumptions were made with regard to the numerical value of the term $(k' - k_1)/k_0$ and of the constant α. In the case of papain, $(k' - k_1)/k_0$ was set equal to 1. This assumption implies that all reactions between radicals and the active group lead to inactivation of the enzyme, and that this is the only process whereby the enzyme is inactivated. Studies of the role of the single active SH group for the enzyme activity (*22, 27*) and of the disappearance of the SH group after irradiation (*14*) provide evidence that this assumption is essentially valid in the case of papain. For α the value 3×10^{-9} was used. This implies that 3×10^{-9} mole of ion pairs is formed per liter per roentgen (*3*), and the further assumption that per ion pair only one species is of significance in the inactivation of the enzyme. Our previous data on the yield on inactivation of papain support the latter assumption (*14*).

The fact that theoretical curves could be successfully fitted to the experimental data obviously does not constitute proof of the validity of the explanations proposed. However, it is of considerable interest that a relationship between the parameters $(k' - k_1)/k_0$ and α is provided by equation 26. This fact permits a determination of α to be made on the basis of the experimental data for papain given in Fig. 5*A*, if a value is chosen for $(k' - k_1)/k_0$. By using the value of 1 for this parameter, α was found to be 2.9×10^{-9}. This result reveals a remarkable internal consistency of the treatment. Also, it should be stressed that the general conclusions drawn from the equations derived are not based on a knowledge of the numerical value of $(k' - k_1)/k_0$ and α.

SUMMARY

A general kinetic analysis of enzyme inactivation in solution by ionizing radiation has been carried out. In the treatment the possibility is included that active and inactive enzyme molecules may deactivate radiation-induced radicals at different rates. The analysis has proved capable of explaining several experimental observations which were difficult to reconcile with previous treatments.

The treatment reveals that, if the active enzyme molecules remove the agents formed from water more rapidly than do the radiation-inactivated ones, deviations from exponential dose-inactivation curves will occur. This may explain such deviations found in the literature. Significant deviations will ordinarily be expected only when the yield of inactivation is high. The almost linear dose-inactivation relationship previously found for papain can be adequately explained on this basis. Special circumstances are responsible for the finding that alcohol dehydrogenase from yeast and rabbit muscle glyceraldehyde-3-phosphate dehydrogenase exhibit nonexponential dose-inactivation curves, in spite of the fact that their over-all yields of inactivation are low.

A procedure is given for determining experimentally the true yield of inactivation when contaminating and protective substances are present. It follows from the analysis that the presence of inactive enzyme molecules in the preparation prior to the exposure will affect the yield of inactivation only when the active and inactive enzyme molecules differ in their ability to deactivate radicals. The very high observed yield of inactivation previously found in the case of papain can in part be ascribed to the presence in the preparation of inactive enzyme molecules. For enzymes which are inactivated at low yields, the true yield of inactivation will be nearly equal to the observed yield at high enzyme concentration.

RECEIVED: June 7, 1962

REFERENCES

1. W. M. DALE, W. J. MEREDITH, and M. C. K. TWEEDIE, Mode of action of ionizing radiations on aqueous solutions. *Nature* **151,** 280–281 (1943).
2. W. M. DALE, The effect of X-rays on enzymes. *Biochem. J.* **34,** 1367–1373 (1940).
3. Z. M. BACQ and P. ALEXANDER, *Fundamentals of Radiobiology,* 2nd ed., Pergamon Press, London, 1961.
4. J. WEISS, Radiochemistry of aqueous solutions. *Nature* **153,** 748–750 (1944).
5. W. M. DALE, L. H. GRAY, and W. J. MEREDITH, The inactivation of an enzyme (carboxypeptidase) by X- and α-radiation. *Phil. Trans. Roy. Soc. (London)* **242A,** 33–62 (1949).
6. M. G. ALDER and H. EYRING, An approach to the kinetics of radiation-induced decomposition of certain organic molecules in solution. *Nucleonics* **10,** No. 4, 54–57 (1952).
7. D. E. LEA, *Actions of Radiations on Living Cells,* 2nd ed., Cambridge University Press, London, 1956.
8. S. OKADA, Inactivation of deoxyribonuclease by X-rays. II. The kinetics of inactivation in aqueous solution. *Arch. Biochem. Biophys.* **67,** 102–112 (1957).
9. L. AUGENSTINE, Indirect inactivation of macromolecules in solution by ionizing radiation. A method of analysis. *Radiation Res.* **10,** 89–111 (1959).
10. F. HUTCHINSON and D. A. ROSS, Some kinetics of the indirect effect of ionizing radiation on aqueous solutions. *Radiation Res.* **10,** 477–489 (1959).

11. J. A. V. Butler, A. B. Robins, and J. Rotblat, The inactivation of α-chymotrypsin by ionizing radiations. *Proc. Roy. Soc.* **256A,** 1–14 (1960).

12. R. Lange, A. Pihl, and L. Eldjarn, The inactivation of SH enzymes by X-rays. *Intern. J. Radiation Biol.* **1,** 73–79 (1959).

13. R. Lange and A. Pihl, The mechanism of X-ray inactivation of phosphoglyceraldehyde dehydrogenase. *Intern. J. Radiation Biol.* **2,** 301–308 (1960).

14. A. Pihl and T. Sanner, X-Ray inactivation of papain in solution. *Radiation Research* in press.

15. S. F. Velick, Glyceraldehyde-3-phosphate dehydrogenase from muscle. In *Methods in Enzymology* (S. P. Colowick and N. O. Kaplan, eds.), Vol. I, pp. 401–411, Academic Press, New York, 1955.

16. E. Racker, Alcohol dehydrogenase from baker's yeast. In *Methods in Enzymology* (S. P. Colowick and N. O. Kaplan, eds.), Vol. I, pp. 500–503, Academic Press, New York, 1955.

17. J. R. Kimmel and E. L. Smith, Crystalline papain and benzoyl-L-argininamide. *Biochem. Prep.* **6,** 61–67 (1958).

18. J. Baarli and P. Borge, The application of the ferrous-ferric system for routine measurements. *Acta Radiol.* **47,** 203–209 (1957).

19. P. D. Boyer, Spectrophotometric study of the reaction of protein sulfhydryl groups with organic mercurials. *J. Am. Chem. Soc.* **76,** 4331–4337 (1954).

20. T. Sanner and A. Pihl, The alleged splitting of thioesters by *p*-chloromercuribenzoate. *Biochim. Biophys. Acta* **62,** 171–172 (1962).

21. F. Hutchinson, Reduced yield in dilute solutions irradiated at very high dose rates. *Radiation Res.* **9,** 13–23 (1958).

22. B. J. Finkle and E. L. Smith, Crystalline papain: Number and reactivity of thiol groups; chromatographic behaviour. *J. Biol. Chem.* **230,** 669–690 (1958).

23. K. B. Augustinsson, G. Jonsson, and B. Sparrman, Effects of ionizing radiation on arylesterase and cholinesterase. *Acta Chem. Scand.* **15,** 11–15 (1961).

24. R. J. Shalek and T. L. Gillespie, The influence of oxygen upon the radiation damage of lysozyme. In *Radiation Biology and Cancer* (A Collection of Papers Presented at the Twelfth Annual Symposium on Fundamental Cancer Research, Houston, Texas, 1958) pp. 41–50, University of Texas Press, Austin, 1959.

25. S. F. Velick and E. Ronzoni, The amino acid composition of aldolase and D-glyceraldehyde phosphate dehydrogenase. *J. Biol. Chem.* **173,** 627–639 (1948).

26. A. Pihl and R. Lange, The interaction of oxidized glutathione, cystamine monosulfoxide, and tetrathionate with the —SH groups of rabbit muscle D-glyceraldehyde 3-phosphate dehydrogenase. *J. Biol. Chem.* **237,** 1356–1362 (1962).

27. T. Sanner and A. Pihl, Studies on the active site of papain and the mechanism of papain activation by thiols. *J. Biol. Chem.* **238,** 165–177 (1963).

RADIATION RESEARCH **19**, 27–41 (1963)

X-Ray Inactivation of Papain in Solution[1]

ALEXANDER PIHL AND TORE SANNER[2]

Norsk Hydro's Institute for Cancer Research, Montebello, Oslo, Norway

INTRODUCTION

Protein SH groups are known to play an important role in numerous biological processes, and their possible participation in the development of radiobiological damage has been widely discussed, particularly with reference to SH enzymes. Comparatively little is actually known, however, about the radiosensitivity of protein SH groups and of SH enzymes. The data available from radiation studies of a few enzymes (*1–7*) hardly warrant general conclusions.

Previously we have found (*3–5*) that muscle glyceraldehyde-3-phosphate dehydrogenase and alcohol dehydrogenase from yeast are inactivated by X-rays with low ionic yields (about 0.02). The low radiosensitivity of these enzymes was shown to be due in part to the fact that they possess many SH groups, several of which must be destroyed before the enzyme activity is abolished.

The purpose of the present investigation was to investigate the factors influencing the radiosensitivity of protein SH groups and SH enzymes. Protein SH groups are known to exhibit widely different chemical reactivity, a fact usually ascribed to steric factors. It seems possible that these differences may reflect different susceptibility of the SH groups to the attack by radiation products from water. Since the low radiosensitivity of glyceraldehyde-3-phosphate dehydrogenase and alcohol dehydrogenase is parallelled by a low chemical reactivity of their SH groups (*8, 9*), it seemed desirable to study the radiosensitivity of protein SH groups having high chemical reactivity. For this purpose the proteolytic enzyme papain was selected. The active molecules of papain possess a single SH group which is essential for the enzyme activity and which is known to be highly reactive (*10*).

It will be demonstrated here that the active SH group of papain is highly radiosensitive. This group is attacked preferentially by the active agents from water with the consequence that papain is inactivated with an exceptionally high yield.

[1] Work supported by Division of Radiological Health, Bureau of State Service, U.S. Public Health Service.

[2] Fellow of the Norwegian Cancer Society.

Also it will be shown that the SH group can be protected to a remarkable extent by reversible blocking with a cysteamine residue.

MATERIALS AND METHODS

Enzyme

Crystalline papain was prepared from granular *Papaya latex* (Wallerstein Co., New York) according to the method of Kimmel and Smith (*11*). The procedure was followed closely with the exception that sodium chloride was replaced by sodium sulfate in the recrystallizations. The enzyme was recrystallized three times before use.

The enzyme activity was assayed by measuring the liberation of ammonia from α-benzoyl-L-arginine amide at 40°C and pH 6.56. The reaction mixture (total volume 1.5 ml) contained in 0.04 *M* phosphate buffer: substrate, 75 μmoles; citrate, 30 μmoles; EDTA, 7.5 μmoles; and papain, 0.005 to 0.015 mg of protein nitrogen per milliliter. Where indicated, 7.5 μmoles of cysteine was added. The enzyme was added last. Samples (200 μl) were taken for analysis after incubation for 10, 20, 30, and 40 minutes. The first-order rate constant, k_1, was calculated for each sample, and the average value was used as a measure of the activity. The specific activity, C_1 (*12*), measured in the presence of cysteine, varied in the different preparations from 1.3 to 1.6.

Analytical Methods

The ammonia liberated was measured by the Conway microdiffusion technique (*13*). The enzyme concentration was determined by the method of Lowry *et al.* (*14*). The procedure was calibrated by micro-Kjeldahl analyses. A molecular weight of 20,700 was used for papain, and the nitrogen content was taken to be 16.1% (*12*). The SH determinations were carried out by the method of Boyer (*15*) as previously described (*16*). Hydrogen peroxide was determined by the titanium sulfate method (*17*).

Irradiation Conditions

The enzyme was dissolved in ice-cold 0.067 *M* phosphate buffer, pH 7.40, and irradiated in Erlenmeyer flasks, surrounded by crushed ice. The measurement of the enzymatic activity was carried out immediately after exposure, and the activity was expressed in per cent of that of the unirradiated control which was identically treated. The solutions were equilibrated with air unless otherwise indicated. When the irradiations were carried out in a nitrogen atmosphere, the following procedure was used: The enzyme crystals were dissolved in a small amount of water from which the oxygen had been removed by vigorous boiling under flushing with nitrogen. A small volume (100 μl) of the concentrated enzyme solution was injected through the rubber stopper of the irradiation vessel into the buffer solution (10 ml), which had been deoxygenated as described above.

In all experiments here reported the water used had been double-distilled from glass equipment and passed through a mixed-bed ion-exchange column. Later experiments carried out with water distilled three times from glass equipment gave identical results.

The irradiations were carried out with an X-ray machine (Stabilipan, Siemens). The irradiation factors were 220 kv, 4 to 20 ma, and 0.5 mm Cu. The dosimetry was carried out with a ferrous system (*18*).

RESULTS

Previous studies of crystalline papain have been complicated by the fact that the preparations obtained were active only after addition of reducing substances or when subjected to reducing procedures (*10*). In the present investigation crystalline papain was used which was active without any special pretreatment or additions. The preparations contained 0.40 to 0.55 SH groups per molecule. There is reason to believe that each active enzyme molecule contains one free SH group (*19*) and that hence the preparations consisted of a mixture of active and inactive enzyme molecules. Since it has been proposed (*10*) that the active SH group of papain is present in the form of a thioester, it was found necessary to reinvestigate the chemical state of the papain SH group to aid the interpretation of the results reported here. This study, which is reported elsewhere (*20, 21*), provided no evidence in support of the view that the enzyme SH group is present in a special configuration or state. Furthermore, it is relevant to the present results that kinetic studies provided evidence that the activating effect of cysteine is largely due to the fact that the added thiol participates in the catalytic mechanism by increasing the rate of splitting of the enzyme–substrate complex. The data indicated that in our preparations only a minor fraction of the inactive enzyme molecules were present in a state (papain—SS—papain, papain—S—metal which could be reduced to papain—SH by thiol addition.

Dose-Effect Relationship

In Fig. 1 the inactivation of papain as a function of the radiation dose is demonstrated. It is apparent that the inactivation is considerably smaller when cysteine is added after irradiation. Since the activity of the irradiated samples is expressed in per cent of that of the identically treated unirradiated control, this phenomenon cannot be due to the activating effect of cysteine mentioned above. The data therefore demonstrate a reversal of the radiation effect which will be denoted here the reactivating effect, as opposed to the activating effect of cysteine mentioned above. Since the activity of papain is proportional with its content of free SH groups, both when measured in the presence (*19*) and in the absence of thiols (*20, 21*), the

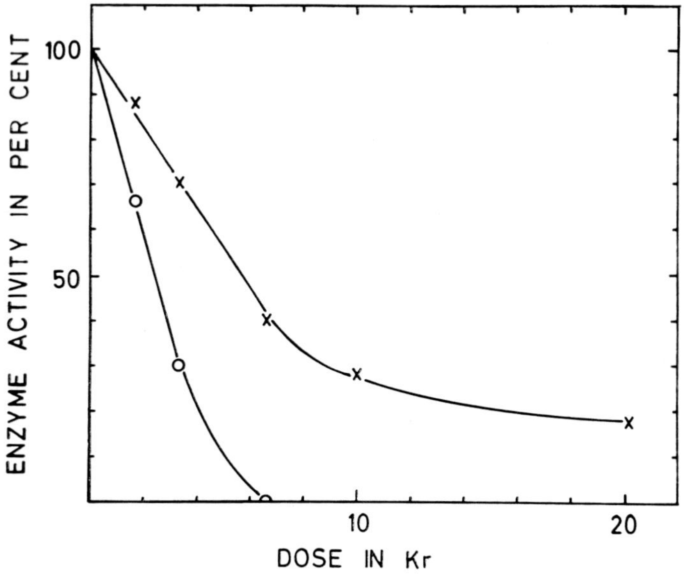

FIG. 1. The X-ray inactivation of papain. Papain (1.35×10^{-5} *M*) was irradiated in 0.067 *M* phosphate buffer, pH 7.40, at 0°C at a dose rate of 840 r/min. The papain preparation contained 0.50 SH group per molecule. ○——○, no cysteine present during measurement of enzyme activity; ×——×, cysteine added before measurement of enzyme activity.

reactivating effect of cysteine here observed must be due to a reduction of enzyme SH groups oxidized by the radiation. It should be noted that the SH enzymes glyceraldehyde-3-phosphate dehydrogenase and alcohol dehydrogenase cannot be reactivated by addition of thiols after the exposure (*4*).

The data in Fig. 1 demonstrate the interesting fact that the inactivation is initially a linear function of the dose. Similar findings have been made with glyceraldehyde-3-phosphate dehydrogenase and alcohol dehydrogenase (*4, 5*). The probable explanation of this linear dose-effect relationship will be discussed below.

It is apparent from Fig. 1 that the inactivation curve for reactivated papain levels off at about 30% remaining activity. On further irradiation the enzyme activity decreases only at a very slow rate. This finding suggests that one of the irradiation products of the enzyme SH group which can be reduced by cysteine is rather resistant to further radiation changes. Most likely this radiation product is the intermolecular disulfide, papain—SS—papain. Chemical evidence is available that papain, in contrast to many other proteins, may form such disulfides (*21*).

Ionic Yield and Enzyme Concentration

The yield of inactivation has been expressed in this paper as the initial ionic yield (M/N). This was calculated from the formula

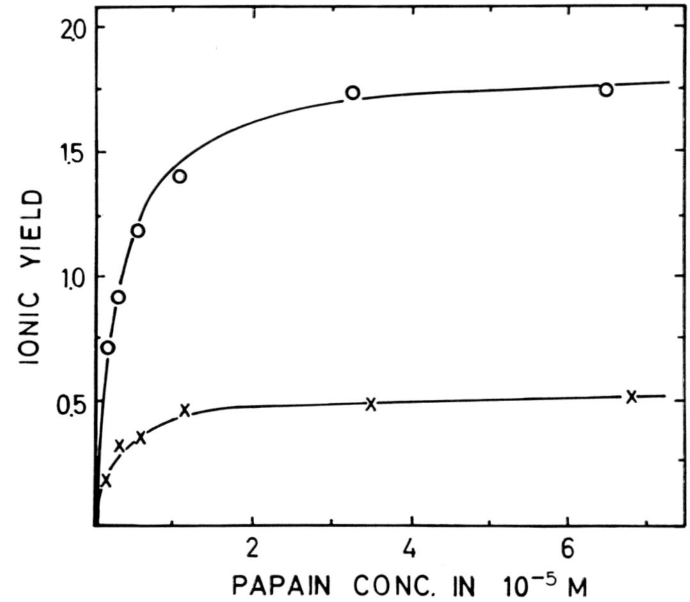

FIG. 2. The ionic yield as a function of the enzyme concentration. Increasing concentrations of papain were irradiated in 0.067 *M* phosphate buffer, pH 7.40, at 0°C. The ionic yield was obtained on the basis of complete dose-inactivation curves, as described in the text. The papain preparation contained 0.40 SH group per molecule. ○——○, no cysteine present during measurement of enzyme activity; dose rate 240 r/min. ×——×, cysteine added before measurement of enzyme activity; dose rate 840 r/min.

$$M/N = E_0/\alpha D_0' \tag{1}$$

where E_0 is the molar concentration of the enzyme, D_0' (*22*) is the radiation dose, in roentgens, required to inactivate the enzyme completely if the rate of inactivation remained equal to the initial rate; and α is a proportionality factor which is taken to be equal to 3×10^{-9}/r, since 1 r is assumed to give 3×10^{-9} mole of ion pairs per liter (*23*). The ionic yields calculated on this assumption are equal to one-third of the *G* values. The D_0' was derived graphically from the experimental dose-inactivation curves. It can be shown that, when the inactivation is an exponential function of the dose, D_0' is equal to D_{37} (*22*).

In Fig. 2 the observed ionic yield as a function of the enzyme concentration is demonstrated. It can be seen that the curves for the unreactivated and for the cysteine-reactivated enzyme reach the plateau at about the same enzyme concentration. The corresponding maximum yields obtained are exceptionally high. This is due to several factors which will be discussed below and in the subsequent paper (*22*).

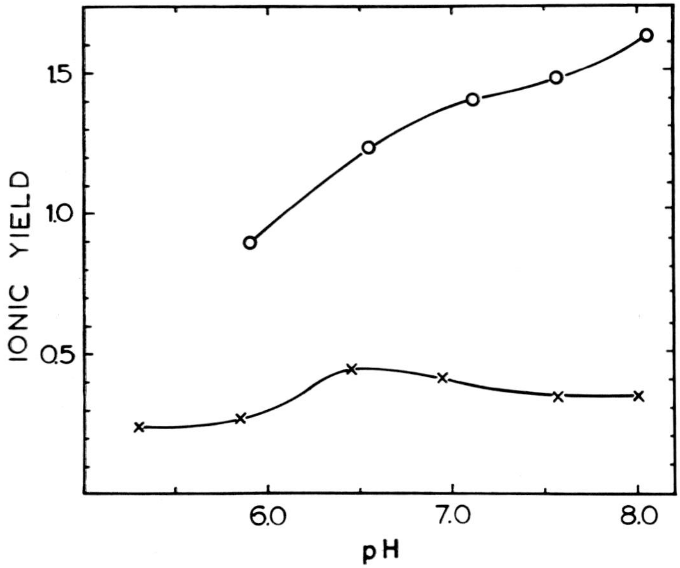

FIG. 3. The ionic yield as a function of pH. Papain was irradiated at 0°C in 0.067 *M* phosphate buffer at varying pH. The papain preparation contained 0.50 SH group per molecule. ○——○, no cysteine present during measurement of enzyme activity; papain concentration 1.60×10^{-5} *M*; dose rate 240 r/min. ×——×, cysteine added before measurement of enzyme activity; papain concentration 1.10×10^{-5} *M*; dose rate 840 r/min.

Effect of pH

The effect of pH on the yield of inactivation is shown in Fig. 3. It is apparent that, when the activity is measured in the presence of cysteine, pH has no significant effect on the yield. On the other hand, the yield for unreactivated papain shows a marked increase with increasing pH. It has been observed that the oxidation of cysteine to cystine increases with increasing pH (*24*). One possible explanation of the data in Fig. 3 would be that the oxidation of papain—SH to papain—SS—papain may show a similar pH dependence.

Role of Hydrogen Peroxide

Previous experiments have demonstrated that papain is highly sensitive to hydrogen peroxide (*21*). The effect of catalase addition and of anoxia on the X-ray inactivation of papain was therefore studied.

In Fig. 4 is shown the dose-inactivation curve obtained when the irradiation was carried out in the presence of catalase. Also under these circumstances a nonexponential dose-inactivation curve was obtained. The data in Table I demonstrate that the presence of catalase reduced the ionic yield in air by approximately 50% (dose rate 967 r/min). The results further indicate that, when the action of

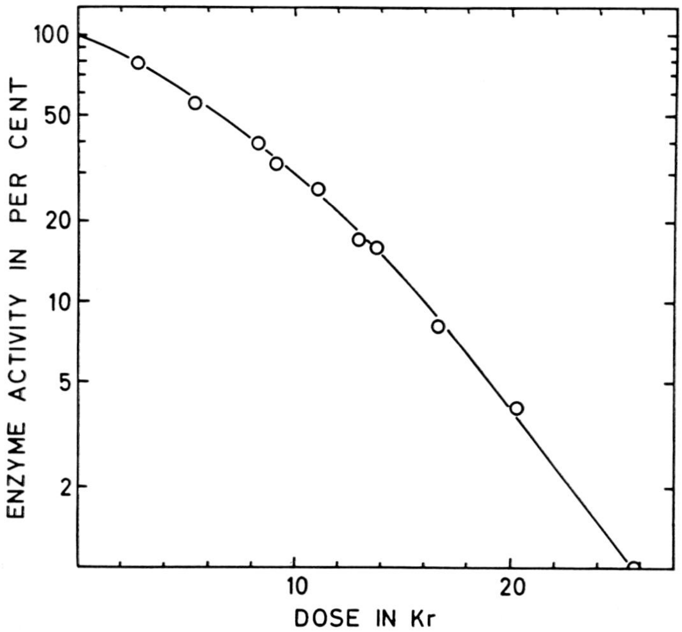

FIG. 4. The dose-inactivation curve in the presence of catalase. Papain (1.2×10^{-5} M) was irradiated in 0.067 M phosphate buffer, pH 7.40, at 0°C at a dose rate of 1850 r/min. Catalase in a concentration of 3.6 μg/ml was present during the irradiation. The papain preparation contained 0.50 SH group per molecule. The enzyme activity was measured in the absence of cysteine.

TABLE I

EFFECT OF NITROGEN AND OF CATALASE ON INACTIVATION OF PAPAIN

(The papain, 0.90×10^{-5} M, was irradiated in 0.067 M phosphate buffer, pH 7.40, at 0°C. The ionic yields were calculated from complete dose-inactivation curves. The enzyme activity was measured in the absence of cysteine. The enzyme preparation contained 0.50 SH group per molecule. Dose rate 967 r/min.)

Conditions		*Ionic yield*
Papain, no addition	Air	0.79
Papain, catalase added[a]	Air	0.41
Papain, no addition	Nitrogen	0.44
Papain, catalase added[a]	Nitrogen	0.37

[a] 1.2 μg/ml.

hydrogen peroxide is eliminated by catalase, the ionic yield is approximately the same in air as in nitrogen.

Since papain is inactivated by hydrogen peroxide at a comparatively slow rate (*21*), radiation-induced hydrogen peroxide might be expected to cause dose-rate

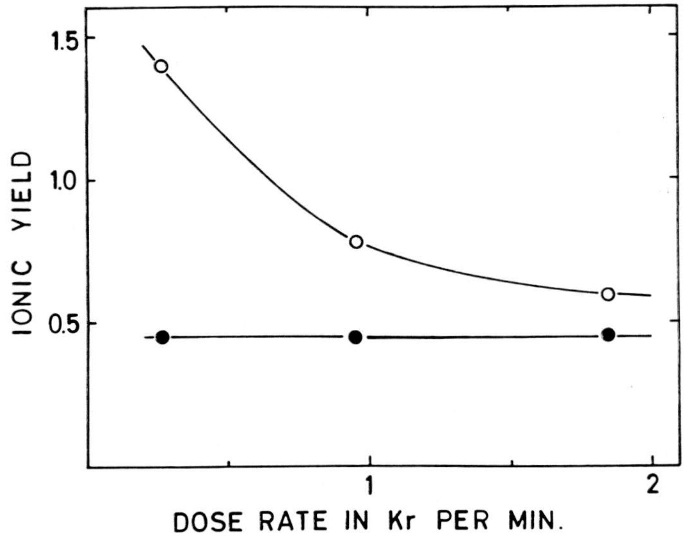

FIG. 5. The ionic yield as a function of the dose rate. Papain (2.52×10^{-5} *M*) was irradiated in 0.067 *M* phosphate buffer, pH 7.40, at different dose rates. The papain preparation contained 0.50 SH group per molecule. The enzyme activity was measured in the absence of cysteine. ○——○, no catalase added; ●——●, catalase present during irradiation (1.2 μg/ml).

effects as well as aftereffects. These expectations were borne out by the experiments demonstrated in Figs. 5 and 6. It is apparent that there is a considerable dose-rate effect, which disappears when the irradiation is carried out in the presence of catalase (Fig. 5). Hydrogen peroxide evidently is of particular significance at low dose rates. The data in Fig. 6 demonstrate that the aftereffect, which is likewise abolished by catalase, lasts for approximately 20 minutes at 0°C. It can be seen that the absolute aftereffect was in all cases approximately 15%, although the radiation dose and the initial inactivation varied by a factor of 3. This finding indicates that the maximum aftereffect is independent of the degree of the initial X-ray inactivation. A simple explanation of this finding might be that, whereas the hydrogen peroxide concentration will increase with the X-ray dose, the active enzyme, the second component in the bimolecular reaction, will concurrently decrease.

Role of SH Group Destruction

In view of the fact that papain may be extensively degraded or modified without loss of its enzyme activity as long as its active site remains intact (*25*), the high yield of inactivation observed here suggested that the active agents formed from water attack primarily the active site of the enzyme. In order to study this point the enzyme inhibition was correlated with the concomitant destruction of SH

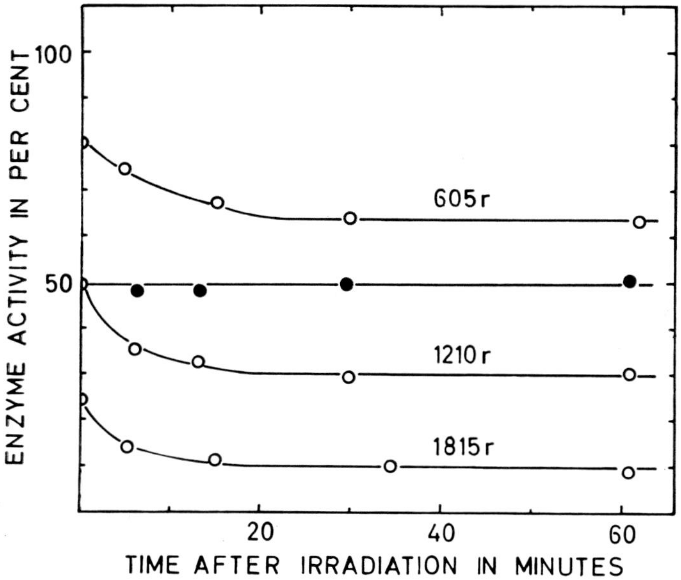

FIG. 6. The aftereffect. Papain (1.10×10^{-5} *M*) was irradiated in 0.067 *M* phosphate buffer, pH 7.40, at 0°C with the doses indicated (dose rate 240 r/min). The enzyme activity was measured in the absence of cysteine at different times after the end of the exposure. The irradiated samples were kept at 0°C. The papain contained 0.40 SH group per molecule. ○——○, no catalase added; ●——●, catalase (1.2 μg/ml) added immediately after the end of the exposure.

groups. A high dose rate was chosen (1770 r/min), since under these conditions the role of hydrogen peroxide in the enzyme inactivation is relatively small (Fig. 5). The data demonstrate (Fig. 7) that under these conditions approximately 85% of the enzyme inactivation can be accounted for by destruction of the active SH group.

Protection by Blocking of SH Groups

The SH group of papain reacts readily with cystamine monosulfoxide to give the mixed disulfide (papain—SSR) and with tetrathionate to give the protein–sulfenyl thiosulfate derivative (papain—$SS_2O_3^-$) (*20, 21*). The radiosensitivity of papain modified in this way and by PCMB treatment was compared with that of native papain. The modified enzyme preparations were obtained as follows: Papain (5×10^{-5} *M*) was incubated at 0°C in 0.067 *M* phosphate buffer, pH 7.40, for 1 hour with a threefold molar excess of the reagents. After incubation the reaction mixtures were dialyzed for 20 hours at 4°C against 0.0067 *M* phosphate buffer.

In Fig. 8 the X-ray inactivation of native papain (papain—SH) is compared with that of papain—SSR. In both instances cysteine was added after the exposure. The data demonstrate that the papain—SSR is very radioresistant compared

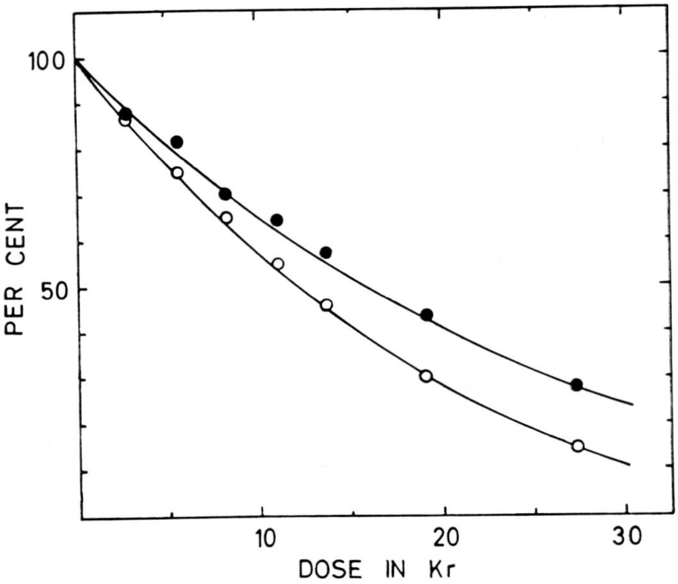

FIG. 7. The radiation-induced enzyme inhibition and SH group destruction. Papain (5.30×10^{-5} M) was irradiated in 0.067 M phosphate buffer, pH 7.40, at 0°C at a dose rate of 1770 r/min. The papain preparation contained 0.55 SH group per molecule. ○——○, enzyme activity (measured in the absence of cysteine); ●——●, titratable SH content.

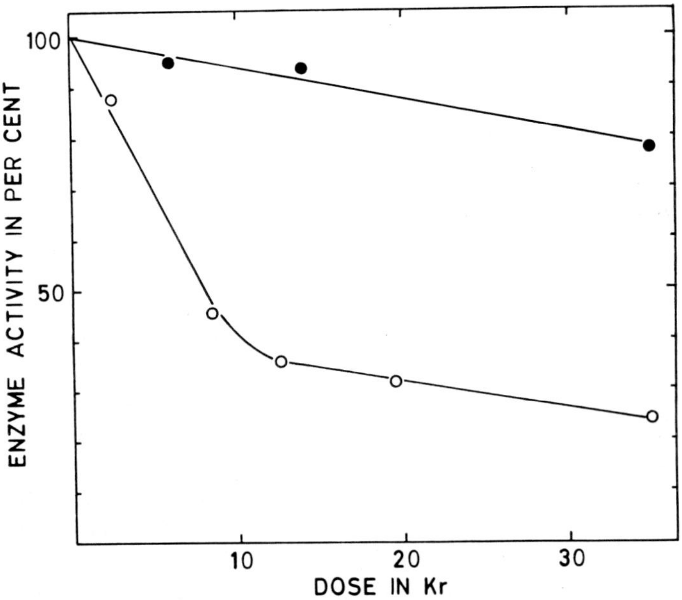

FIG. 8. The protection of papain by mixed disulfide formation. Native papain (papain—SH) and modified enzyme (papain—SSR) in a concentration of 1.50×10^{-5} M were irradiated in 0.067 M phosphate buffer, pH 7.40, at 0°C at a dose rate of 870 r/min. The enzyme activity was measured after addition of cysteine. The unmodified papain contained 0.40 SH group per molecule. ○——○, papain—SH; ●——●, papain—SSR.

TABLE II

PROTECTION OF PAPAIN BY BLOCKING OF ITS REACTIVE SH GROUP

(The enzyme preparations, 1.50×10^{-5} *M*, were dissolved in 0.067 *M* phosphate buffer, pH 7.40, and irradiated at a dose rate of 870 r/min. In each case the ionic yield was calculated from a complete dose-inactivation curve. The enzyme activity was measured after addition of cysteine. The native enzyme contained 0.40 SH group per molecule.)

Preparation	*Observed ionic yield*	
	No addition (*M/N*)	*Catalase added*[a] (*M/N*)
Papain—SH, native	0.33	0.22
Papain—SSR	0.04	0.04
Papain—$SS_2O_3^-$	0.04	0.04
Papain—SHg  COO⁻	0.04	0.04

[a] 1.2 μg/ml.

with the native enzyme. It is of interest to observe that the rate of inactivation of papain—SSR corresponds closely to that of papain—SH after the curve has leveled off. The results are compatible with the view that irradiation of papain—SH results in part in the formation of papain—SS—papain which is rather radioresistant.

The data in Table II show that blocking of the active enzyme SH group with a cysteamine, a thiosulfate, or a PCMB residue provides strong protection against X-ray inactivation. The protection corresponded to dose-reduction factors of 8.2 and 5.5, in the absence and in the presence of catalase, respectively.

DISCUSSION

Two facts which may be of radiobiological significance are established in this paper. In the first place, it is shown that a protein SH group and an SH enzyme may be highly radiosensitive. Secondly, the results demonstrate that such a radiosensitive enzyme may be effectively protected in solution by covering of its SH group with a cysteamine residue. This finding is of interest in view of the suggestion by Eldjarn and Pihl (*26–28*) that the protective action of sulfur compounds *in vivo* may in part be due to mixed disulfide formation with biologically important SH groups.

The present results demonstrate that papain differs strikingly from the SH enzymes previously studied in this laboratory. Whereas papain is inactivated with the highest yield so far reported for any enzyme, and whereas it can be extensively reactivated after exposure, glyceraldehyde-3-phosphate dehydrogenase and alcohol dehydrogenase are inactivated at low yields and cannot be reactivated by cysteine after irradiation (*3–5*).

The finding of a nonexponential dose-inactivation curve for papain and the high ionic yield observed prompted us to undertake a general kinetic treatment of enzyme inactivation in solution by ionizing radiation. The analysis, which is given in detail in the subsequent paper (*22*), seems to provide the explanation for some of the unusual effects here observed. Thus, the nearly linear dose-inactivation curves found can be satisfactorily explained if the active agents formed attack preferentially the active site of the enzyme and if the reaction product deactivates the active agents less efficiently than does the intact enzyme (*22*). Under such conditions the concentration of active agents will increase during the exposure. The results presented indicate that the above conditions prevail in the case of papain. Thus, the data show that the SH group is selectively attacked, and they indicate that one of the reaction products is the protein disulfide, which is rather stable. It should be emphasized that the deviation of the dose-inactivation curves from linearity in semilogarithmic plots cannot be accounted for by an accumulation of hydrogen peroxide, inasmuch as a definitely nonexponential dose-inactivation curve was found also when the action of hydrogen peroxide was eliminated by the presence of catalase during the irradiation.

The unusually high radiosensitivity of papain is due to the concerted action of several factors. In the first place, the enzyme has only a single SH group, the destruction of which is fatal to the enzyme activity. It is demonstrated here that the enzyme inactivation can be accounted for almost entirely by destruction of this SH group which is highly radiosensitive. The fact that the SH group is very susceptible to hydrogen peroxide is an important factor in this regard.

A factor contributing substantially to the high observed ionic yield in this particular case is the fact that the papain preparations contained inactive enzyme molecules. In the subsequent paper (*22*) a procedure is given for the determination of the true ionic yield, i.e., the initial yield of inactivation in the absence of any interfering substances. It can be shown (*22*) that the deviation of the observed ionic yield from the true one, due to the presence of inactive enzyme in the preparation, will be significant only when the observed ionic yield is very high. It was found that the true ionic yield, at a dose rate of 240 r/min, was 0.88 as compared with the observed yield of 1.84. However, under conditions where the observed ionic yield is below 0.5, the presence of inactive protein in the enzyme preparation will only slightly influence the yield. The value here found for papain in the presence of catalase is therefore close to the true one.

It was pointed out above that, when the action of hydrogen peroxide was eliminated by catalase, the ionic yield of inactivation of papain was approximately the same in air as in nitrogen (ionic yield about 0.40, corresponding to a G value of 1.2). In air the active radicals under these conditions are $OH\cdot$ and O_2^-, whereas in nitrogen the radicals present are $OH\cdot$ and $H\cdot$. Since $OH\cdot$ radicals are formed with a G value of about 2.1, in air as well as in nitrogen (*29*), the observed enzyme inactivation could conceivably be accounted for by the action of OH· radicals alone. It can be calculated, however, that in this event no less than 50% of the radicals which become deactivated in collisions with the macromolecule would have to react with the single SH group in order to account for the enzyme inactivation. This value seems highly improbable in view of the fact that OH· radicals are extremely reactive and would be expected to react readily with many other groups on the protein surface. It seems more likely that the O_2^- and H· radicals are the most important radical species in the oxidation of the enzyme SH groups in oxygen and in nitrogen, respectively. These radicals are known to be less reactive and hence more selective in their reactions. Evidence is available from studies of small molecular thiols that the H· and O_2^- radicals can oxidize SH groups (*30*).

The interesting conclusion emerges from this study that one particular chemical group on the surface of a macromolecule may be destroyed by ionizing radiation in a highly specific way. In view of the established importance of SH groups in cellular processes, this finding can hardly be disregarded.

Our present and previous studies of SH enzymes (*4, 8, 9, 21*) indicate that there is a good correlation between radiosensitivity and chemical reactivity of protein SH groups. Hence, those SH groups which are most susceptible to radiation damage may be the ones which are most likely to react with protective compounds and thereby become blocked and efficiently protected.

SUMMARY

Crystalline papain was found to be the most radiosensitive enzyme so far studied. The dose inactivation was nonexponential, and for low dose rates it approached a linear function. The enzyme inactivation could be accounted for almost entirely by a radiochemical oxidation of its single essential SH group. The enzyme could be partly reactivated by cysteine addition after the exposure. The data indicate that in part intermolecular protein disulfides were formed which were rather resistant to further radiochemical oxidation.

The observed ionic yield decreased strongly with increasing dose rate, and the inactivation showed a pronounced aftereffect. These effects were shown to be due to the action of radiation-induced hydrogen peroxide. In the presence of catalase the yield of inactivation was the same in air as in nitrogen ($G = 1.2$).

Blocking of the active SH group with a cysteamine residue reduced the enzyme inactivation by X-rays by factors of 8.2 and 5.5, in the absence and in the presence of catalase, respectively.

RECEIVED: June 7, 1962

REFERENCES

1. E. S. G. BARRON, S. DICKMAN, J. A. MUNTZ, and T. P. SINGER, Studies on the mechanism of action of ionizing radiations. I. Inhibition of enzymes by X-rays. *J. Gen. Physiol.* **32,** 537-552 (1949).

2. E. S. G. Barron and P. Johnson, Studies on the mechanism of action of ionizing radiations. XI. Inactivation of yeast alcohol dehydrogenase by X-irradiation. *Arch. Biochem. Biophys.* **48,** 149–153 (1954).
3. A. Pihl, R. Lange, and L. Eldjarn, The alleged susceptibility of sulphydryl enzymes to ionizing radiation. *Nature* **182,** 1732–1733 (1958).
4. R. Lange, A. Pihl, and L. Eldjarn, The inactivation of SH enzymes by X-rays. *Intern. J. Radiation Biol.* **1,** 73–79 (1959).
5. R. Lange and A. Pihl, The mechanism of X-ray inactivation of phosphoglyceraldehyde dehydrogenase. *Intern. J. Radiation Biol.* **2,** 301–308 (1960).
6. S. E. Lewis, E. D. Wills, and A. Wormall, Inactivation of urease by X-rays. *Intern. J. Radiation Biol.* **3,** 647–656 (1961).
7. E. A. Dickens and B. Shapiro, The mechanism of action of AET. III. The effect of gamma radiation on the viscosity and the enzymatic activity of urease solutions. *Radiation Res.* **15,** 594–603 (1961).
8. A. Pihl and L. Eldjarn, The formation and biological role of mixed disulphides. *Colloq. 4th Intern. Congr. Biochem. Vienna 1958* **13,** 43–62 (1958).
9. A. Pihl and R. Lange, The interaction of oxidized glutathione, cystamine monosulfoxide, and tetrathionate with the —SH groups of rabbit muscle D-glyceraldehyde 3-phosphate dehydrogenase. *J. Biol. Chem.* **237,** 1356–1362 (1962).
10. E. L. Smith and J. R. Kimmel, Papain. In *The Enzymes* (P. D. Boyer, H. Lardy, and K. Myrbäck, eds.) 2nd ed., Vol. 4, pp. 133–173, Academic Press, New York, 1960.
11. J. R. Kimmel and E. L. Smith, Crystalline papain and benzoyl-L-argininamide. *Biochem. Prep.* **6,** 61–67 (1958).
12. J. R. Kimmel and E. L. Smith, Crystalline papain. I. Preparation, specificity, and activation. *J. Biol. Chem.* **207,** 515–531 (1954).
13. E. J. Conway (ed.), *Microdiffusion Analysis and Volumetric Error,* 4th ed., Crosby Lockwood & Son, London, 1957.
14. O. H. Lowry, N. J. Rosebrough, A. L. Farr, and R. J. Randall, Protein measurement with the Folin phenol reagent. *J. Biol. Chem.* **193,** 265–275 (1951).
15. P. D. Boyer, Spectrophotometric study of the reaction of protein sulfhydryl groups with organic mercurials. *J. Am. Chem. Soc.* **76,** 4331–4337 (1954).
16. T. Sanner and A. Pihl, The alleged splitting of thioesters by *p*-chloromercuribenzoate. *Biochim. Biophys. Acta* **62,** 171–172 (1962).
17. G. M. Eisenberg, Colorimetric determination of hydrogen peroxide. *Ind. Eng. Chem.* **15,** 327–328 (1943).
18. J. Baarli and P. Borge, The application of the ferrous-ferric system for routine measurements. *Acta Radiol.* **47,** 203–209 (1957).
19. B. J. Finkle and E. L. Smith, Crystalline papain: Number and reactivity of thiol groups; chromatographic behavior. *J. Biol. Chem.* **230,** 669–690 (1958).
20. A. Pihl and T. Sanner, The state and reactivity of the essential SH-group of papain. *Fifth Intern. Congr. Biochem. Moscow 1961* (Abstract, No. 5.122).
21. T. Sanner and A. Pihl, Studies on the active site of papain and the mechanism of papain activation by thiols. *J. Biol. Chem.* **28,** 165–171 (1963).
22. T. Sanner and A. Pihl, Kinetics of enzyme inactivation by ionizing radiation. *Radiation Research* in press.
23. Z. M. Bacq and P. Alexander (eds.), *Fundamentals of Radiobiology,* 2nd ed., Pergamon Press, London, 1961.
24. S. L. Whitcher, M. Rotheram, and N. Todd, Radiation chemistry of cysteine solutions. *Nucleonics* **11,** No. 8, 30–33 (1953).

25. R. L. HILL and E. L. SMITH, Isolation and characterization of an enzymically active fragment of papain. *J. Biol. Chem.* **235,** 2332–2339 (1960).
26. L. ELDJARN and A. PIHL, On the mechanism of chemical protection against ionizing radiation. The interaction of cysteamine and cystamine with proteins. In *Progress in Radiobiology* (J. S. Mitchell, B. E. Holmes, and C. L. Smith, eds.), pp. 249–257, Oliver & Boyd, Edinburgh, 1956.
27. L. ELDJARN and A. PIHL, Mechanisms of protective and sensitizing action. In *Mechanisms in Radiobiology* (M. Errera and A. Forssberg, eds.), Vol. 2, Chapter 4, pp. 231–296, Academic Press, New York, 1960.
28. A. PIHL and L. ELDJARN, Pharmacological aspects of ionizing radiation and of chemical protection in mammals. *Pharmacol. Revs.* **10,** 437–474 (1958).
29. C. J. HOCHANADEL and S. C. LIND, Radiation chemistry. *Ann. Rev. Phys. Chem.* **7,** 83–106 (1956).
30. E. J. HART and R. L. PLATZMAN, Radiation chemistry. In *Mechanisms in Radiobiology* (M. Errera and A. Forssberg, eds.), Vol. 1, Chapter 2, pp. 93–257, Academic Press, New York, 1961.

RADIATION RESEARCH **19**, 42–49 (1963)

The Effect of Whole-Body X-Irradiation on the Distribution of Acid Deoxyribonuclease and β-Galactosidase in Subcellular Fractions of Rat Spleen[1]

JAY S. ROTH[2] AND SYLVIA HILTON

Institute of Cellular Biology, University of Connecticut, Storrs, Connecticut

INTRODUCTION

It has been shown (*1*) that 700 r of whole-body X-irradiation causes a 100% increase in the specific activity of acid ribonuclease (RNase) in spleen 16 hours postirradiation. At 64 hours, the specific activity has returned to control values. Despite this, there was a continued shift in the RNase from the particulate fractions to the supernatant fraction. It was suggested that, as a result of X-irradiation, spleen lysosomes fragmented *in vivo*, releasing RNase to the supernatant fraction. To explore this possibility further, the effect of 700 r of whole-body X-irradiation on some spleen acid hydrolases (*2*) was determined. The enzymes studied were β-glucuronidase, acid phosphatase, and phosphoprotein phosphatase. However, the greatest portion (50 to 70%) of these three enzymes in normal spleen was found in the supernatant fraction, in contrast to their distribution in normal liver, in which only 10 to 15% occurs in this fraction.

Since a report has been published that acid deoxyribonuclease (DNase) in the supernatant fraction increases after X-irradiation (*3, 4*), it seemed of interest to investigate this enzyme further and to compare the results with those already obtained. In previous work, described above, RNase and other acid hydrolases had been studied at different times in completely different experiments, and therefore in this report a lysosomal enzyme that might be expected to behave differently from DNase was chosen for study, namely, β-galactosidase.

MATERIALS AND METHODS

Care and Irradiation of Animals

Male Wistar-derived rats of the Charles River strain, weighing about 300 to 400 gm, were utilized. The rats were given 700 r of whole-body X-irradiation from a

[1] This research was supported by grants from the U.S. Atomic Energy Commission Contract AT(30-1)2337 and the National Cancer Institute, National Institutes of Health C-5264C1.

[2] Senior Career Investigator, National Cancer Institute, National Institutes of Health.

200-kv therapy machine operating at 15 ma with 0.25 mm Cu and 1 mm Al filters. The dose rate was approximately 100 r/min at 25 cm. The irradiated and control animals were treated similarly and as previously described (*1*). Assays were performed at 16 and 64 hours postirradiation.

DNase Activity

DNase was assayed by a method developed in our laboratory, which is a modification of the method of Schneider and Hogeboom (*5*). To a reaction mixture consisting of 1 ml of 0.1 *M* methyl arsenate buffer, pH 5.5, and 1 ml of tissue extract plus water, 1.0 ml of 0.1% DNA is added at zero time. The mixture is incubated for 30 minutes at 37°C, and then 3.0 ml of a 1 *N* solution of HCl in 76% ethanol, containing 0.5% lanthanum chloride, is added. The precipitate is filtered through 9-cm circles of Whatman No. 42 filter paper, and the funnels are covered with watch glasses to prevent evaporation of the alcohol. The optical density of the filtrate at 260 mμ is determined immediately. Blanks are run by incubating tissue sample without DNA, precipitating, and adding DNA immediately afterward. In later experiments, it was found that the use of 10% $HClO_4$ as a precipitant, followed by standing in the cold for 10 to 15 minutes and centrifugation, gave somewhat more consistent results as well as considerably higher DNase activities. The amounts of homogenate and fractions used were: homogenate, 0.05 and 0.1 ml; nuclei, 0.2 and 0.4 ml; mitochondria, 0.1 and 0.2 ml; microsomes, 0.2 and 0.4 ml; supernatant, 0.25 and 0.50 ml. In general, with these quantities of fractions, enzyme activity was proportional to the amount used. The fractions were prepared as described previously (*6*).

β-Galactosidase Assays

The method of Sellinger and coworkers was utilized (*7*), with *o*-nitrophenyl-β-D-galactoside.

Nitrogen Determinations

Aliquots of the homogenate and of each fraction were assayed for nitrogen content by a micro-Kjeldahl method.

o-Nitrophenyl-β-D-galactoside was a product of Sigma laboratories, and DNA (salmon sperm) was obtained from CalBiochem.

RESULTS

The Effect of 700 R of Whole-Body X-Irradiation on Acid DNase in Rat Spleen

Table I presents the data for the distribution of acid DNase in subcellular fractions of rat spleen of irradiated rats and pair-fed controls. The controls for both 16 and 64 hours postirradiation were averaged, since there were no significant differences among them. Consideration of the data in Table I indicates the following facts:

TABLE I

ACID DEOXYRIBONUCLEASE DISTRIBUTION IN SUBCELLULAR FRACTIONS OF SPLEEN OF IRRADIATED AND CONTROL RATS

(700 r whole-body X-irradiation[a])

Fraction	*Control, avg. range (8 experiments)*	*16 hours postirradiation avg. range (4 experiments)*	*64 hours postirradiation avg. range (4 experiments)*
Homogenate	100%	100%	100%
Nuclei	25.8 (14.1–35.9)	15.9 (13.4–20.9)	17.9 (10.5–27.7)
Mitochondria	30.6 (17.7–42.5)	26.9 (23.0–32.4)	27.3 (18.3–37.0)
Microsomes	10.7 (8.4–16.1)	13.1 (11.6–15.9)	13.3 (9.7–17.6)
Supernatant	32.5 (29.0–39.6)	44.2 (40.6–52.9)	41.5 (36.2–46.4)
Average recovery of activity =	105% (85–127)	102% (86–128)	101% (92–109)

[a] Including, however, one experiment (assayed at 64 hours) in which animals were given 840 r of whole-body γ-irradiation with Co^{60}.

1. The distribution of DNase activity in pair-fed controls did not differ significantly from values determined in fed stock animals. Data for the latter, as well as some observations on the determination of DNase activity, will be presented elsewhere.

2. Sixteen hours postirradiation there was a significant decrease in the percentage of DNase activity in the nuclear fraction and an increase in the supernatant fraction, but no significant change in the mitochondrial or microsomal fraction. At 64 hours, there were no further significant changes in DNase distribution compared to that at 16 hours.

3. Specific DNase activities are given in Table II. At 16 hours after irradiation, homogenate specific activity had increased by 59%. Increases were noted in all the fractions, with the greatest rise in microsomal and supernatant fractions—in both cases, over 100%. At 64 hours postirradiation, increases were observed in the DNase specific activity of homogenate, nuclear, microsomal, and supernatant fractions, when compared to controls. There was, however, a modest decline in the activity of the mitochondrial fraction specific DNase activity at this time.

So that more valid interpretations of the changes taking place may be made, the nitrogen content in the various fractions from control and irradiated animals is given in Table III. These values are similar to those previously determined (*1, 2*). For those experiments reported, nitrogen recoveries ranged from 93 to 107% and averaged close to 100%. There is a considerable shift of nitrogen from the nuclear fraction, primarily to the supernatant and mitochondrial fractions at both time periods. Since an increase in the percentage of the DNase activity in supernatant fraction is observed, this suggests that one of the effects of radiation is to

TABLE II

Specific Acid Deoxyribonuclease Activity[a] in Subcellular Fractions of Spleen of Irradiated and Control Rats

(700 r whole-body X-irradiation[b])

Fraction	*16 hours postirradiation*[c]			*64 hours postirradiation*[c]		
	Control (specific activity)	*X-ray (specific activity)*	*Change (%)*	*Control (specific activity)*	*X-ray (specific activity)*	*Change (%)*
Homogenate	1362 (1155–1935)	2167 (1650–2790)	+59	1731 (1184–2860)	2475 (1980–3200)	+30
Nuclei	840 (545–1260)	1156 (960–1550)	+38	1217 (447–2760)	1575 (860–2070)	+30
Mitochondria	2365 (1800–2790)	3648 (2930–5320)	+54	3860 (1930–6040)	3431 (2360–4300)	−11
Microsomes	874 (637–1050)	2032 (1650–2580)	+132	1417 (800–2530)	1964 (1272–2610)	+28
Supernatant	1533 (1110–2280)	3127 (2670–3610)	+104	2061 (1450–3460)	2925 (2400–3680)	+42

[a] Specific activity is expressed as the optical density increment per milligram of nitrogen at 30 minutes $\times 10^3$.

[b] One experiment, 840 r of γ-irradiation from Co^{60}.

[c] Average and range for four experiments.

TABLE III

Nitrogen Distribution in Subcellular Fractions of Spleen of Irradiated and Control Rats

(700 r whole-body X-irradiation[a])

Fraction	*Control*[b] (%)	*16 hours postirradiation*[c] (%)	*64 hours postirradiation*[d] (%)
Homogenate	100	100	100
Nuclei	41.2 (34.2–44.0)	32.6 (26.9–40.0)	24.9 (23.6–27.7)
Mitochondria	15.1 (12.4–18.6)	17.6 (16.8–19.5)	20.5 (18.3–22.3)
Microsomes	13.9 (12.0–15.2)	15.5 (13.0–17.9)	14.7 (11.5–17.6)
Supernatant	29.7 (26.9–33.0)	33.9 (29.8–37.4)	38.7 (34.8–42.8)
Recovery (%)	101 (96–105)	97 (93–101)	100 (94–107)

[a] One experiment, 840 r of γ-irradiation from Co^{60}.

[b] Eight experiments. Controls for 16 and 64 hours postirradiation were combined.

[c] Four experiments.

[d] Five experiments.

transfer particulate bound DNase from the nuclear to the supernatant fraction. Another explanation is that radiation has altered the cell population in the spleen, favoring cells with a distribution of DNase different from that in normal spleen cells.

The large increases in enzyme specific activity noted in mitochondrial, microsomal, and supernatant fractions 16 hours after irradiation, even though the percentage of nitrogen in these fractions has risen, give the impression that enzyme activation or synthesis may be occurring. This is considered further in the discussion.

It is of interest to observe that the distribution of DNase in control rat spleen varies somewhat from that of RNase, and also from the distribution of DNase in liver (*5, 8*).

Since the assay utilized in this report employs a fairly long incubation (30 minutes) at 37°C in a hypotonic solution, conditions favoring disruption of lysosomes, the results presented are probably total activities (see ref. *10*) and are comparable to RNase distributions measured under the same conditions (*1*).

The recovery in the fractions, in most experiments, of close to 100% of the homogenate activity suggests, furthermore, that there is no inhibitor present for acid DNase in rat spleen.

Effect of 700 R of Whole-Body X-Irradiation on β-Galactosidase in Rat Liver and Spleen

The distribution of β-galactosidase in control and X-irradiated spleen is presented in Table IV. The results are similar to those obtained with phosphoprotein phosphatase (*2*). It is apparent that, as with this latter enzyme, the major portion of β-galactosidase in spleen is found in the supernatant fraction, in contrast to liver, in which only 10% of the enzyme occurs in this fraction. Furthermore, 700 r of whole-body X-irradiation had no significant effect on the distribution of the enzyme, and there was only a small increase in specific activity.

No significant changes were noted in the distribution or specific activity of β-galactosidase in livers of rats given 700 r of whole-body X-irradiation.

TABLE IV

DISTRIBUTION OF β-GALACTOSIDASE IN THE SPLEENS OF RATS GIVEN 700 ROENTGENS OF WHOLE-BODY X-IRRADIATION AND PAIR-FED CONTROLS

Fraction	*16 hours postirradiation*[a]		*64 hours postirradiation*[b]	
	Control (%)	*X-ray* (%)	*Control* (%)	*X-ray* (%)
Nuclei	6.3	4.9	6.8	4.5
Mitochondria	16.0	17.6	17.2	13.9
Microsomes	10.8	11.0	8.9	11.1
Supernatant	67.1	66.4	67.0	70.5

[a] Four experiments.

[b] Three experiments.

DISCUSSION

A considerable literature exists on the effects of X-radiation on lymphatic tissues, including spleen. As this literature has recently been reviewed by Goutier (*9*), only those points pertinent to the present work will be considered.

It appears to be well established that total-body X-irradiation causes a marked increase in the specific acid DNase activity of spleen 6 to 24 hours or more after irradiation (*11–13*). Douglass and Day (*14*) and Okada and co-workers (*12*) have shown, however, that total organ DNase does not change. Douglass and Day suggested (*14*) that the retention of splenic DNase may be a manifestation of a change in the cellular population with survival of those cells that contribute most to DNase activity. Support for this view was offered by Gordon *et al.* (*15*), who found that radiosensitive lymphocyte centers contain little acid DNase activity.

Consideration of spleen weights and their total nitrogen content in this report (data not given) indicates that at 16 hours postirradiation there is a 14.5% increase in the total DNase activity compared to that in controls. Thus, at least some of the increased specific DNase activity observed in the particulate fractions and supernatant 16 hours after irradiation represents net increased enzyme activity.

It appears that a possible source for this could be from the breakdown of lysosomal particles *in vivo*, with some, or all, of the released DNase appearing in the supernatant fraction. Increases in the specific activity observed in the particulate fractions (Table II) might be explained on the basis of absorption of some of the released DNase on the particles in these fractions.

On the other hand, since the assay system used, as already mentioned, probably determines total acid DNase activity, the 14.5% increase in total organ activity might represent increased synthesis of acid DNase after irradiation.

Further experiments are under way to determine unequivocally whether total (bound and free) acid DNase is being measured, as well as experiments to ascertain whether mitochondrial fractions prepared from X-irradiated spleens would show a smaller percentage of bound enzyme (in intact particles) than controls. Information of this nature would be necessary to decide whether the small increase in total organ activity here observed after irradiation represents (1) increased synthesis of enzyme or (2) increased susceptibility of spleen lysosomes from irradiated animals to breakage during isolation and assay.

The unexpected finding that most of the β-galactosidase, as well as some other lysosomal enzymes in spleen (*2*), is obtained largely in the supernatant fraction is of interest, but it interferes with studies of the effect of X-radiation on the subcellular distribution of these enzymes, Greenbaum *et al.* (*16*) have shown that the distribution of acid RNase in mammary gland varies tremendously, depending on the method of tissue homogenization. Thus, use of a conventional Potter-Elvehjem homogenizer gave more than 70% of the enzyme in a nonsedimentable form, whereas with an Emanuel-Chaikoff homogenizer over 70% of the acid RNase was sedimentable by centrifugation at 16,000 × g for 20 minutes. However, homogenization in our laboratory of rat spleen with an Emanuel-Chaikoff homogenizer, although it gave a higher percentage of acid DNase in the nuclear fraction, was also accompanied by a considerably increased nitrogen content of this fraction, which could be attributed to an increased number of unbroken cells.

SUMMARY

The distribution of acid DNase activity in spleen subcellular fractions of rats given 700 r of whole-body X-irradiation was determined 16 and 64 hours postirradiation and compared to that in pair-fed controls. In the controls, the percentage distribution in nuclei, mitochondria, microsomes, and supernatant fraction was 25.8%, 30.6%, 10.7%, and 32.5%, respectively. Sixteen hours after irradiation this had changed to 15.9%, 26.9%, 13.1%, and 44.2% for the same fractions, respectively. There was no further significant change at 64 hours. Considerable increases in specific acid DNase activity were measured in the homogenate and all fractions 16 hours post irradiation; smaller changes were observed at 64 hours. At 16 hours postirradiation, evidence was obtained for a small net increase (14.5%) in total spleen DNase activity, compared to that in controls, and it was suggested that this increase might be caused by either increased enzyme synthesis or increased susceptibility of spleen lysosomes from irradiated animals to breakage during isolation and assay.

In spleen of control animals, 67% of the β-galactosidase activity was found in the supernatant fraction, and 700 r of whole-body X-irradiation did not significantly alter the distribution of this enzyme in subcellular fractions at either 16 or 64 hours postirradiation.

RECEIVED: June 29, 1962

REFERENCES

1. J. S. ROTH and H. J. EICHEL, The effect of total-body X-irradiation on the distribution of ribonuclease activity in subcellular fractions of rat spleen. *Radiation Res.* **11,** 572–581 (1959).
2. J. S. ROTH, J. BUKOVSKY, and H. J. EICHEL, The effect of whole-body X-irradiation on the activity of some acid hydrolases in homogenates and subcellular fractions of rat spleen. *Radiation Res.* **16,** 27–36 (1962).
3. R. GOUTIER, M. GOUTIER-PIROTTE, and P. CICCARONE, Effects of total-body X-irradiation on rat spleen and liver deoxyribonucleases. *Intern. J. Radiation Biol., Suppl.* 93–102 (1960).
4. E. GOUTIER-PIROTTE and A. THONNARD, Action immédiate des rayons X sur la liason desoxyribonucléase acide-granule cytoplasmatique de la rate du rat. *Biochim. Biophys. Acta* **22,** 396–397 (1956).
5. W. C. SCHNEIDER and G. H. HOGEBOOM, Intracellular distribution of enzymes. X. Desoxyribonuclease and ribonuclease. *J. Biol. Chem.* **198,** 155–163 (1952).
6. H. J. EICHEL, Intracellular localization of enzymes in spleen. I. Reduced diphosphopyridine

nucleotide cytochrome *c* reductase, cytochrome *c* oxidase and succinic dehydrogenase in the rat and guinea pig. *J. Biophys. Biochem. Cytol.* **3,** 397–412 (1957).
7. O. Z. Sellinger, H. Beaufay, P. Jacques, A. Doyen, and C. de Duve, Tissue fractionation studies. 15. Intracellular distribution and properties of β-*N*-acetylglucosaminidase and β-galactosidase in rat liver. *Biochem. J.* **74,** 450–456 (1960).
8. G. de Lamirande, C. Allard, and A. Cantero, Intracellular distribution of desoxyribonucleodepolymerase in normal rat liver, liver tumor, and liver of animals fed *p*-dimethylaminoazobenzene. *Can. J. Biochem. Physiol.* **32,** 35–40 (1954).
9. R. Goutier, The effect of X-rays on nucleic acid biosynthesis and on the activity of nucleases in mammalian cells. *Progr. Biophys. Biophys. Chem.* **11,** 53–77 (1961).
10. C. de Duve, Lysosomes, a new group of cytoplasmic particles. In *Subcellular Particles* (T. Hayashi, ed.), p. 128, Ronald Press, New York, 1959.
11. V. M. Fellas, I. Meschan, P. L. Day, and C. D. Douglass, Effect of total-body X-irradiation on deoxyribonuclease activity of rat spleen. *Proc. Soc. Exptl. Biol. Med.* **87,** 231–233 (1954).
12. S. Okada, E. R. Gordon, R. King, and L. H. Hempelmann, The effect of X-ray exposure on deoxyribonuclease II activity in lymphoid tissues. *Arch. Biochem. Biophys.* **70,** 469–476 (1957).
13. N. B. Kurnick, B. W. Massey, and G. Sandeen, The effect of radiation on tissue deoxyribonuclease. *Radiation Res.* **11,** 101–114 (1959).
14. C. D. Douglass and P. L. Day, Effect of various doses of total body X-irradiation on total amount of deoxyribonuclease II in rat spleen. *Proc. Soc. Exptl. Biol. Med.* **89,** 616–617 (1955).
15. E. R. Gordon, E. Gassner, S. Okada, and L. H. Hempelmann, Deoxyribonuclease II activity in lymphoid tissues of rats. *Radiation Res.* **10,** 545–551 (1959).
16. A. L. Greenbaum, T. F. Slater, and D. Y. Wang, Lysosomal-like particles in the rat mammary gland. *Nature* **188,** 318–320 (1960).

RADIATION RESEARCH 19, 50–63 (1963)

Effects of X-Ray and Neutron Dose Fractionation on the Mouse Testis

G. SILINI,[1] S. HORNSEY, AND D. K. BEWLEY

Experimental Radiopathology Research Unit and Radiotherapeutic Research Unit, Hammersmith Hospital, London, England

INTRODUCTION

Since the early work of Schinz and Slotopolsky (*1*), Sartory *et al.* (*2*), and Ferroux *et al.* (*3*), it was recognized that the effect of fractionated irradiation on male germinal tissue was somewhat unusual in that fractionation could, under some experimental conditions, increase rather than decrease the radiobiological damage to the testis, as compared to skin damage. This is at variance with a number of experiments carried out on somatic tissue (*4, 5*) or on the whole animal (*5, 6–12*). On the other hand, observations have been reported of a lack of effect of dose splitting on testicular injury by ionizing radiations (*13, 14*) or even of recovery of this tissue under schedules of very protracted fractionation (*14, 15*).

During recent years some important observations have been made on the timing of the maturation processes of the male germinal epithelium in rodents, and survival data have been obtained for some of the cell types in the testis (*16–21*). Some of these data may be fitted by curves of the Type C form, according to the classification of Gunter and Kohn (*22*) (usually referred to as "multihit curves"), and some recovery effects have been described in somatic cells having survival curves of this type (*23–25*).

We thought it of interest to reinvestigate the problem in the light of these new findings, using both high-energy X-rays and fast neutrons. The latter part of our research also had the intention of gaining background information on the effects of neutron fractionation, in view of the possible application of the neutron beam to tumor radiotherapy.

MATERIALS AND METHODS

Animals

The animals used in the experiment were male albino mice of a non-inbred strain known as "TO." The mice were obtained from a dealer and kept in our laboratory

[1] On leave of absence from Divisione Biologica, Comitato Nazionale per l'Energia Nucleare, Rome. Research Fellowship of the International Atomic Energy Agency, Vienna.

for an acclimatization period of at least 2 weeks before irradiation. They usually received the first dose of radiation when about 9 weeks old. After irradiation the mice were kept in groups of 5 or less to a cage and given pellet food and water ad libitum.

Biological Technique

The biological test of damage applied in this experiment was the weight loss of the testes after irradiation (*26*, *27*). After sacrifice of the animal by dislocation of the cervical column, the testes were dissected free of the epidydimides, and the wet weight of both organs was recorded to the nearest milligram. In the present paper the average weight loss of the two testes has been expressed as a percentage, the control value being the average of all control nonirradiated mice, irrespective of their age or weight. Under our experimental conditions, the standard error of the biological technique for the smaller experimental groups consisting of 5 mice each was of the order of 10% or less.

Statistical Methods

A randomization method was used to allot the animals to each experimental group and to choose the animals to be sacrificed at any fixed day within each group. Five animals out of a total of 545 used in the experiment were discarded from the final calculations because they had only a single testis. In order to reduce the spread of the experimental points, standard deviations were calculated for any single experimental group, and the values outside ±2 standard deviations were discarded from the group. New means and standard deviations were finally worked out on the remaining values. This procedure was applied on only five groups of animals out of a total of seventy-two experimental groups.

The statistical analysis of the data was carried out by a standard regression method, each experimental point being weighted according to the number of animals (*28*). The general formula for this analysis was

$$Y = a + b \log X$$

where Y = percentage of weight loss; a = intercept of the regression line with the ordinate scale; b = slope of the regression; X = dose of radiation. The parallelism between X-ray and neutron dose-effect curves was tested in preliminary calculations, and the slopes were found to be not significantly different. The common slope b was estimated from the experimental points of both lines, which amounts to taking a weighted average of the individual slopes.

Radiation Characteristics and Irradiation Techniques

The X-rays were generated by a linear accelerator running at 8 Mv, and the neutrons by a beam of 15-Mev deuterons from the M.R.C. cyclotron falling on an external beryllium target. The neutron spectrum is shown in Fig. 1; it extends from

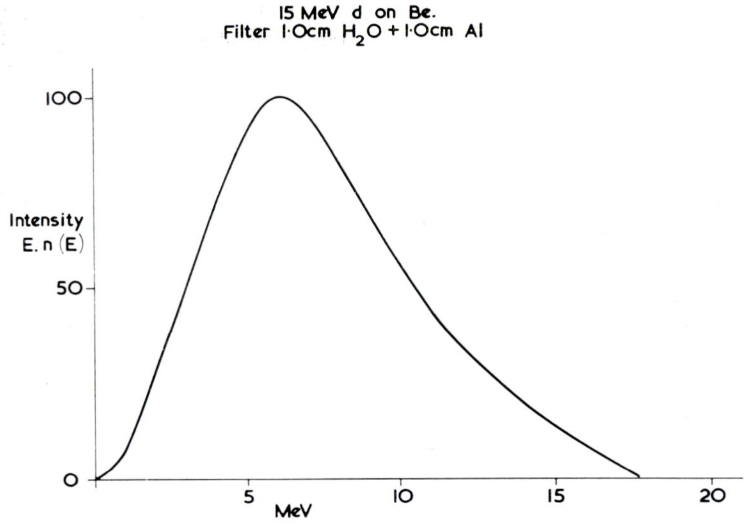

FIG. 1. Energy spectrum of the neutron beam used in the experiments

zero to about 17 Mev, with a peak at 6 Mev. This spectrum is that measured at Pittsburgh by Cohen and Falk (*29*) and has been slightly adjusted to allow for the different filtration.

The mice were contained in a flat Perspex box, partitioned into a number of cells ($3 \times 3 \times 10$ cm). The animals were total-body irradiated, and 16, 20, or 25 of them were exposed together on each occasion. The box was placed across the radiation field, at 230-cm focal distance with X-rays and 150 cm with neutrons. With the X-ray beam, 1.7 cm of Perspex was placed in front to give electronic equilibrium.

The radiation dose was measured by an ionization chamber placed in the middle of the central cell, which did not contain a mouse. The chamber (2.5 cm long and 8 mm in diameter) was air-filled, and its wall was made of conducting plastic having the composition CH; the same chamber was used to measure both X-ray and neutron doses. The chamber was connected by a cable to a meter which integrated the dose during the irradiations. The chamber was calibrated against a Baldwin-Farmer chamber for X-rays (*30*) and against a pair of homogeneous chambers for neutrons. It has also been compared with the neutron-measuring chambers of the M.R.C. unit at Harwell, by the kind cooperation of Mr. F. S. Williamson. The comparison with Harwell has served as the basis of our neutron dosimetry, since the Harwell chambers have been compared with others in the United States (*31*).

The dose rate was about 19 rads/min in soft tissue for both radiations. The exposure was not quite uniform over all the cells in the box. The greatest difference from the central dose was 20% with neutrons and 8% with X-rays. The doses quoted are mean values averaged over the cells used. This variation is no doubt responsible for some of the scatter in the observed weight losses. No correction has been applied for attenuation of the neutrons in passing through the mice, as this was less than 5%. The γ-ray contamination of the neutron beam was about 5%, and these γ-ray doses have been ignored in view of the high RBE of the neutron beam.

The use and dosimetry of the fast neutron beam from the M.R.C. cyclotron will be described in greater detail by one of us (DKB) in a forthcoming article in the British Journal of Radiology.

The experiment may be summarized as follows: The animals received various doses of radiation (X-rays or neutrons) in a single dose or in two equal fractions given 4 or 7 days apart. They were sacrificed at various times between 20 and 39 days after the first dose, and the changes observed in testis weight were taken as an indication of the radiation effects.

RESULTS

Single-Dose Irradiations

Within the limits of our experimental error, the maximum weight loss for any dose of X-rays or neutrons occurred from 26 to 28 days after irradiation. In one case (after a dose of 108.5 rads of X-rays) the minimum testis weight was observed at about 3 weeks, and in this case the curve representing the weight changes with time was very flat between 21 and 28 days (Figs. 2 and 3).

For purpose of computing the RBE of different radiations, the experimental values usually taken are those at 28 days after irradiation. The average weight loss of the testes at this time (as a percentage of the control weight) for animals given various single doses of X-rays or fast neutrons is plotted in Fig. 4. The RBE of fast neutrons against X-rays at 28 days after irradiation was found to be 4.85 ± 0.31 (σ).

Similar calculations were made by taking the values at the time of the maximum observed weight loss, instead of the values at 28 days (Fig. 5). In these conditions the RBE was found to be 4.53 ± 0.26 (σ).

A χ^2 analysis was performed to test for the linearity and the parallelism of the dose-effect curves of the two radiations. The very high probabilities corresponding to the lowest χ^2 values obtained ($P = 0.92$ for the 28 days end point and $P = 0.93$ at the time of the maximum damage) show that the experimental data as plotted in Figs. 4 and 5 can reasonably be interpolated by a straight line and that the two sets of data referring to X-rays and neutrons may be regarded as parallel.

Fractionated Irradiations

The number of mice necessary to obtain complete weight-time curves in the case of dose-fractionation experiments would have been exceedingly high, and it

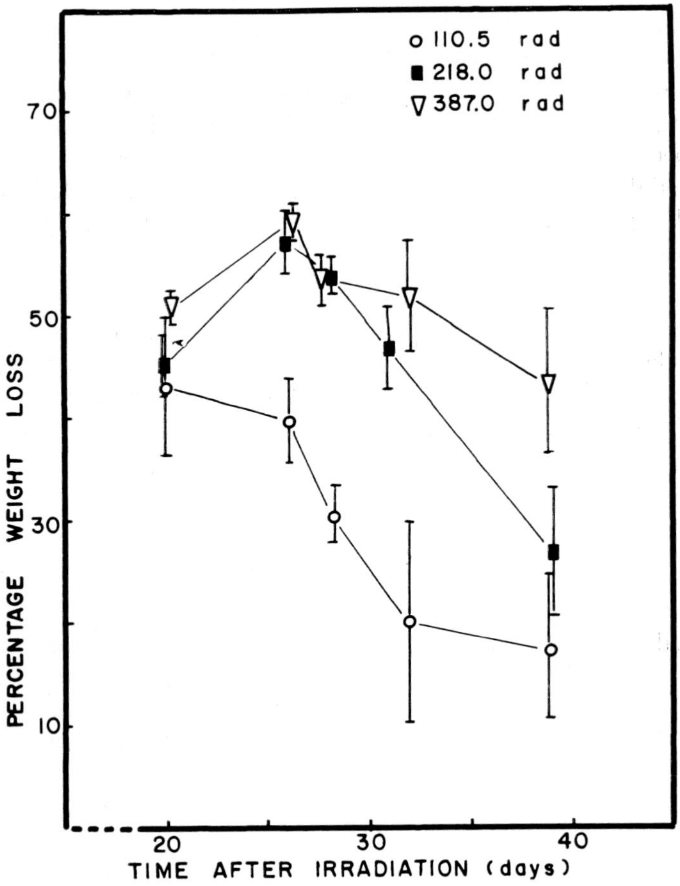

FIG. 2. Changes of testis weight in animals irradiated with various single doses of X-rays. Mean values and standard errors.

was therefore decided to sacrifice the animals at three fixed times, namely: (1) 28 days after the delivery of the first fraction; (2) 28 days after the second fraction; (3) an intermediate time which was chosen at 30 days after the first fraction for mice irradiated at 4-day intervals and at 32 days for mice irradiated at 7-day intervals. The results are presented in Tables I and II and may be summarized as follows:

1. The maximum weight loss was observed in general 28 days after the first fraction, irrespective of the interval between first and second fraction (see Table I, column VI).

2. After this time (28 days) the weight of the testes tended to increase, although

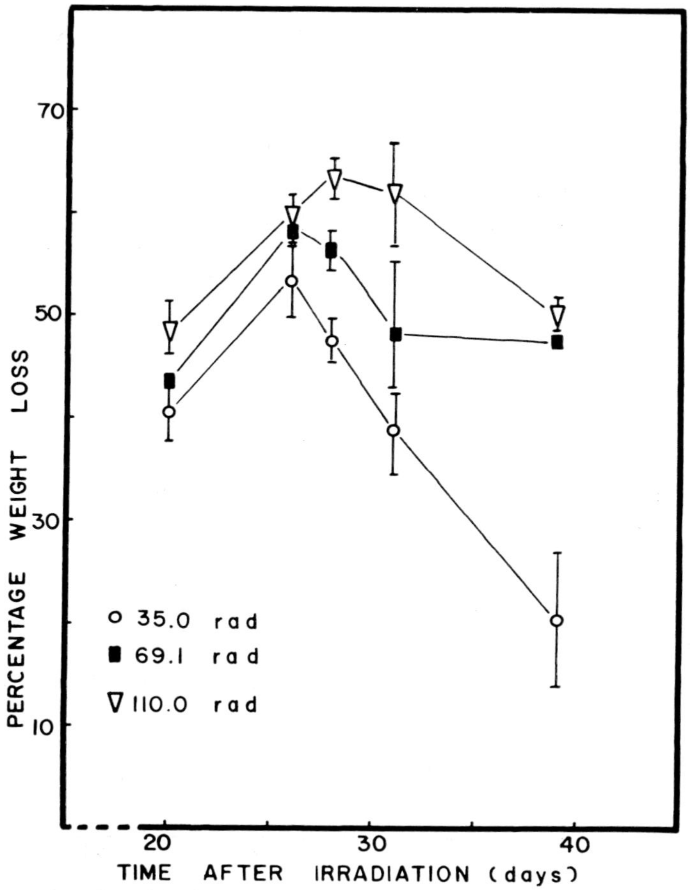

FIG. 3. Changes of testis weight in animals irradiated with various single doses of fast neutrons. Mean values and standard errors.

the actual values were not significantly different from the maximum observed weight loss.

3. The values of the maximum weight loss for animals given the total dose in two fractions were not significantly different from those observed after single-dose irradiations.

4. After 7-day fractionation the testis weights tended to be slightly higher than those obtained after the 4-day schedule. These differences cannot be proved to be statistically significant (i.e., $P > 0.05$), but they may suggest some degree of repair when the two radiation fractions were delivered 7 days apart.

5. As shown in Table II (columns VII and VIII), the RBE values of fast neutrons

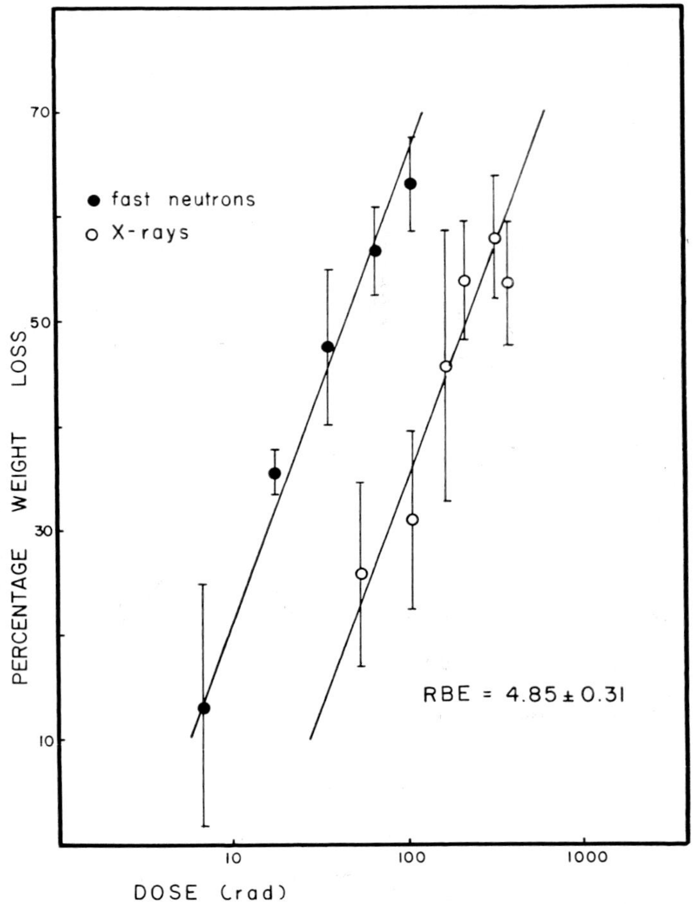

FIG. 4. Dose-effect curves for testis weight loss in animals irradiated with single doses of fast neutrons and X-rays; 28 days end point. Mean values and standard deviations.

against X-rays found after single-dose irradiation did not differ from those obtained when the doses were fractionated.

DISCUSSION

Many of the results described in the present paper may be regarded as common features in experiments in which this biological test of damage has been applied and therefore need not be discussed. For example, the present findings confirmed the occurrence of maximum weight loss at about 4 weeks after irradiation, which is related to the renewal time of the seminiferous epithelium (*26*, *32*). They also

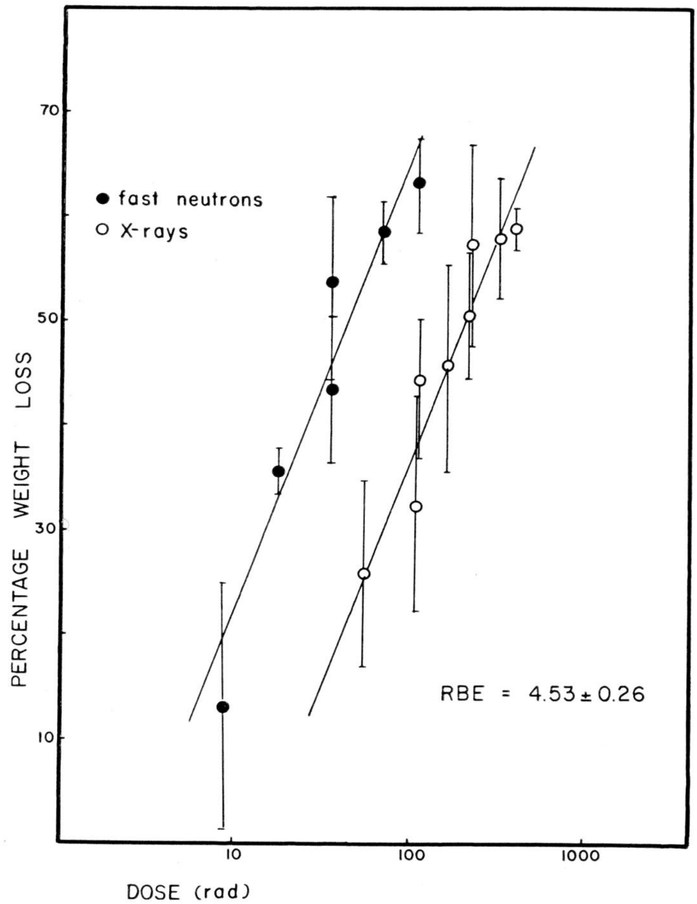

FIG. 5. Dose-effect curves for maximum testis weight loss in animals irradiated with single doses of fast neutrons and X-rays. Mean values and standard deviations.

showed that weight loss was exponentially related to radiation dose (*32*) and that the X-ray and neutron dose-effect curves are parallel (*33*).

The fact that the RBE values reported here are somewhat lower than others previously obtained (*34*) may be accounted for by differences in the LET of the neutron beams. In this connection it should be noted that the mean energy of the neutrons used in the present experiments (6 Mev) was higher than in other cases (*34*), which would tend to yield lower RBE values. Dosimetric differences may also have been of some importance.

The observations that maximum damage occurs at 28 days after the delivery of

TABLE I

MAXIMUM TESTIS WEIGHT LOSS FOR SINGLE AND FRACTIONATED DOSES OF X-RAYS AND FAST NEUTRONS

I First fraction dose (rads)	*II* Time interval between fractions (days)	*III* Second fraction dose (rads)	*IV* Total dose (rads)	*V* Maximum weight loss (percentage ± S.D.)	*VI* Observation time (days)
			X-rays		
109.5	—	—	109.5	43.3 ± 15.2	20
54.4	4	53.7	108.1	40.5 ± 9.2	30
54.4	7	54.4	108.8	39.3 ± 4.8	32
218.0	—	—	218.0	57.2 ± 7.6	26
108.5	4	107.2	215.7	57.7 ± 7.5	28
108.5	7	108.5	217.0	48.7 ± 7.1	28
325.5	—	—	325.5	58.0 ± 3.1	28
162.7	4	161.1	323.8	59.8 ± 6.8	30
162.7	7	162.7	325.4	63.0 ± 7.9	28
			Fast neutrons		
17.7	—	—	17.7	35.6 ± 2.2	28
8.6	4	8.8	17.4	28.5 ± 12.0	28
8.6	7	8.8	17.4	28.5 ± 13.0	28
35.0	—	—	35.0	53.5 ± 8.0	26
17.7	4	17.6	35.3	55.8 ± 7.8	28
17.7	7	17.6	35.3	53.5 ± 8.0	28
69.1	—	—	69.1	58.5 ± 2.9	26
35.7	4	35.2	70.9	61.5 ± 9.4	28
35.3	7	35.4	70.7	61.0 ± 8.3	28

TABLE II

STATISTICAL VALUES OF IMPORTANCE FOR THE REGRESSION ANALYSIS, RBE VALUES, AND STANDARD DEVIATIONS

I Number of dose fractions	*II* Interval between fractions (days)	*III* Day of observation	*IV* Intercept of neutron curve, a_n	*V* Intercept of X-ray curve, a_x	*VI* Common slope, *b*	*VII* RBE	*VIII* S.D. of RBE
1	—	28	−23.3978	−53.7019	44.1765	4.85	0.31
1	—	Maximum damage	−21.4043	−48.8154	43.2920	4.53	0.26
2	4	28	−36.1045	−77.3544	54.7788	5.66	0.44
2	4	30	−44.0454	−78.5264	56.2496	4.10	0.38
2	4	32	−65.9920	−110.6077	66.3899	4.70	0.29
2	7	28	−53.7125	−105.7527	65.6672	6.19	0.47
2	7	32	−33.4287	−62.0624	48.5342	3.89	0.30
2	7	35	−46.3943	−68.5359	49.7426	2.78	0.29

the first fraction, irrespective of whether the second fraction is given 4 or 7 days later, and that appreciable recovery does not occur when the dose is split into two fractions are also not new. The schedule of fractionation, the dose rate, and the total time interval were comparable to those reported by others (*13, 14*), but no satisfactory explanation has been offered to date. This is most probably attributable to the lack of information about survival constants and population kinetics of the cell population involved. Since these earlier studies were reported, new data have become available, and it seems possible now to interpret in more detail the mechanisms of damage and recovery occurring in the irradiated testis.

The points we should like to develop in this discussion are based on experimental facts that may be summarized as follows:

1. All testicular modifications, both histological and gross (e.g., weight loss), seen four weeks after irradiation are caused primarily and perhaps exclusively (at least within the dose range of 100 to 300 r of X-rays) by the killing effect of radiation on spermatogonia (*16, 26, 35, 36*).

2. Changes in testis weight are due to an arrest in the repopulation processes of the germinal epithelium by the most undifferentiated and sensitive cells, at a time when differentiation from spermatocytes into spermatids and spermatozoa is not interrupted (*26*).

3. The time of the maximum observed weight loss in organs other than testis is strongly dependent on the dose of radiation (*37, 38*), owing to the fact that at any one time damage and recovery processes are occurring simultaneously in the same organ. In the case of testis weight the maximum loss is generally observed at 28 days within wide dose ranges (80 to 1000 r) (*32*). At this time, owing to discharge and inactivation of the more differentiated cells and to killing of intermediate and type-B spermatogonia, the weight of the testis reflects the response of the type-A population.

Let us now consider a simple model for the case of fractionated irradiation. If an initial dose of, say, 100 rads of X-rays were delivered to the testis, then the survival data available for spermatogonial cells (*17*) predict that this dose will reduce the surviving fraction of intermediate and type-B spermatogonia to about 1% of the original population. The effect of this depletion of undifferentiated cells will appear, according to our data, after 28 days, with a weight loss of the testes of about 36%, compared to the normal control weight. The type-A spermatogonia being more resistant, about 30% of the original population will survive, and these cells will in due course replace the cell population of the organ. At a time when a second radiation fraction of equal size is delivered, let us consider two extreme cases: (I) The population of intermediate and type-B spermatogonia inactivated by the first dose has been completely replaced through division and differentiation of type-A cells; (II) no replacement of the inactivated cells has occurred, and the number of survivors from the first dose remains unchanged.

In case I the result of a second fraction of 100 rads will be quantitatively similar to that of the first fraction; namely, 28 days after the delivery of the second dose the weight loss of the testes will again be 36% of the control. It is interesting to point out that the possibility of a complete recovery has been experimentally demonstrated (*39*).

In case II a second dose of 100 rads will reduce the number of intermediate and type-B spermatogonia to about 1×10^{-4} of the original population. Owing to the exponential form of the weight-loss curve, the loss caused by the second fraction will not be twice that caused by the first, but only about 49% of the control weight. For the reasons pointed out in (3) above, the time of the maximum observed weight loss will occur 28 days after the first dose. In this case, the effect of delivering to the testis two fractions of 100 rads each will not be different from the effect of a single dose of 200 rads. This will hold until the time interval between the two doses will be long enough to allow an appreciable number of type-A spermatogonia to divide and differentiate again into intermediate and type-B cells.

Under the experimental conditions already described, the second case was found to be true, which points to the conclusion that no replacement of intermediate and type-B cells has occurred within the time interval of 7 days. After doses of the same order of magnitude (100 to 300 r), these are in fact the results of cytological analysis of the irradiated mouse testis (*18*); namely, although the number of type-A spermatogonia increases at 5 days, no appreciable differentiation into intermediate and type-B occurs before day 7.

This schematic picture is likely to be complicated for lower initial doses, so that, for the same time interval, one should expect some degree of recovery at low dose levels. A more detailed analysis of our data, carried out for the low-dose experiments, suggests in fact the existence of such possibility. According to this working model, data on cell population renewal and dose-inactivation curves should allow a prediction of the minimum time within which two doses should be delivered in order to observe recovery phenomena.

All the preceding discussion is based on the assumption that recovery processes are brought about only through cell division, but this may not be the only possible case. The survival curves obtained for type-B and intermediate spermatogonia are of the form usually referred to as multihit, with extrapolation numbers of the order of 2 (*17*). On somatic mammalian cells exihibiting survival curves of this shape, some peculiar recovery phenomena have been demonstrated *in vitro* (*23*, *24*) and *in vivo* (*25*). Such recovery occurs before the first postirradiation division and consists in the reappearance of the shoulder of the survival curves during the time interval between two radiation fractions. It seems worth pointing out that no appreciable recovery which could be referred to this mechanism has been observed in our system.

An aspect of these experiments which may be of some practical importance is concerned with the possible changes in the neutron RBE under dose-fractionation schedules. Comparable experiments on testis are not available, and the experiments carried out with other test systems have given contradictory results. Melville *et al.* (*46*), looking at lethality in mice exposed to paired doses of γ-rays or neutrons, found no difference in the recovery rate between the two radiations, which would suggest no change in RBE. Similar findings were reported by Sproul (cited by Sacher, *11*) in mice. Vogel *et al.* (*40*) found evidence for a slower recovery after neutrons than after γ-rays in mice, and recently Fowler *et al.* (personal communication), using the neutron beam from the cyclotron at Hammersmith Hospital, were able to show a difference in the RBE of neutrons against X-rays for single and fractionated treatments, with erythema in pig skin as the indicator.

Under the experimental conditions described in the present paper, the neutron RBE did not change with fractionation, but further research is needed at lower radiation doses and under more prolonged schedules of fractionation in order to draw any definite conclusion.

SUMMARY

1. Male albino mice were irradiated with single and fractionated doses of 8-Mev X-rays or fast neutrons, and the radiation damage to the testes was assessed from the weight loss of the organs.

2. An RBE of neutrons against X-rays of 4.85 ± 0.31 (σ) was found at 28 days after single-dose irradiations.

3. Splitting of the doses into two equal fractions given 4 or 7 days apart did not result in any significant change of the RBE value.

ACKNOWLEDGMENTS

We are indebted to Dr. B. Vitale, Institute of Physics, University of Rome, and to Dr. R. Miller, Biostatistics Department, Stanford University, for much help and advice offered during the course of the statistical analysis.

Received: July 5, 1962

REFERENCES

1. H. R. Schinz and B. Slotopolsky, Experimenteller betrag sur frage der Röntgenallergie. *Acta Radiol.* **7,** 365–404 (1926).

2. A. Sartory, R. Sartory, and J. Meyer, Phénomènes apportés par l'irradiation sur le tissu cutanè et sur la glande génital male du lapin en fonction du mode d'application du rayonnement. *Compt. rend. acad. sci.* **192,** 447–449 (1931).

3. R. Ferroux, C. Regaud, and N. Samssonow, Comparison des effects produits sur les testicules du lapin, au point de vue de la sterilization de l'epithélium séminal, par un même dose de rayons X, selon qu'elle a été administrée sous fractionnement ou bien fractionée et étalée dans le temps. *Comp. rend. soc. biol.* **128,** 173–176 (1938).

4. W. A. Rambach, J. A. D. Cooper, H. L. Alt, H. H. Vogel, J. W. Clark, and D. L. Jordan, The effects of single and multiple doses of Co^{60} gamma-radiation and fission neutrons on the incorporation of Fe^{59} into the rat erythropoietic system. *Radiation Res.* **10,** 148–166 (1959).

5. L. J. COLE, P. C. NOWELL, and J. S. ARNOLD, Late effects of X-radiation. The influence of dose fractionation on life span, leukemia, and nephrosclerosis incidence in mice. *Radiation Res.* **12,** 173–185 (1960).
6. G. S. MELVILLE, F. P. CONTE, M. SLATER, and A. C. UPTON, Acute lethality of mice as influenced by the periodicity of paired exposures to fast neutrons or X-rays. *Brit. J. Radiol.* **30,** 196–199 (1957).
7. R. H. MOLE, Quantitative observations on recovery from whole-body irradiation in mice. *Brit. J. Radiol.* **30,** 40–46 (1957).
8. H. I. KOHN and R. F. KALLMAN, Acute X-ray lethality studies with the hamster. The LD_{50}, death rate, and recovery rate. *Radiation Res.* **6,** 137–147 (1956).
9. H. I. KOHN and R. F. KALLMAN, The influence of strain on acute X-ray lethality in the mouse. II. Recovery rate studies. *Radiation Res.* **6,** 329–338 (1957).
10. H. I. CURTIS and K. GEBHARD, The relative biological effectiveness of fast neutrons and X-rays for life-shortening in mice. *Radiation Res.* **9,** 278–284 (1958).
11. G. A. SACHER, Reparable and irreparable injury: A survey of the position in experiment and theory. In *Radiation Biology and Medicine* (W. D. Claus, ed.), pp. 283–313, Addison-Wesley Publishing Company, Reading, Massachusetts, 1958.
12. J. B. STORER, Rate of recovery from radiation damage and its possible relationship to life shortening in mice. *Radiation Res.* **10,** 180–196 (1959).
13. H. I. KOHN and R. F. KALLMAN, The effect of fractionated X-ray dosage upon the mouse testis. I. Maximum weight loss following 80 to 240 r given in 2 to 5 fractions during 1 to 4 days. *J. Natl. Cancer Inst.* **15,** 891–899 (1955).
14. H. I. NUZHDIN, N. I. SHAPIRO, M. D. POMERANTZEVA, and N. N. KITZNETZOVA, Comparative study of the effectiveness of a single and fractionated X-raying of the mouse testis. *J. Gen. Biol. U.S.S.R.* **20,** 216–229 (1959).
15. E. LORENZ, W. E. HESTON, A. B. ESCHENBRENNER, and M. K. DERINGER, Biological studies in the tolerance range. *Radiology* **49,** 274–285 (1947).
16. E. F. OAKBERG, Sensitivity and time of degeneration of spermatogenic cells irradiated in various stages of maturation in the mouse. *Radiation Res.* **2,** 369–391 (1955).
17. E. F. OAKBERG, Gamma-ray sensitivity of spermatogonia of the mouse. *J. Exptl. Zool.* **134,** 343–356 (1957).
18. E. F. OAKBERG, Initial depletion and subsequent recovery of spermatogonia of the mouse after 20 r of gamma-rays and 100, 300, and 600 r of X-rays. *Radiation Res.* **11,** 700–719 (1959).
19. E. A. JONES, Number of spermatogonia after X-irradiation in the adult rat. *Intern. J. Radiation Biol.* **2,** 157–170 (1960).
20. E. F. OAKBERG and R. L. DI MINNO, X-Ray sensitivity of primary spermatocytes of the mouse. *Intern. J. Radiation Biol.* **2,** 196–209 (1960).
21. B. R. NEBEL, C. J. MURPHY, and H. J. LINDER, Autoradiographic study with tritiated thymi- *Res.* **13,** 126–136 (1960).
22. S. E. GUNTER and H. I. KOHN, The effects of X-rays on the survival of bacteria and yeast. *J. Bacteriol.* **71,** 571–581 (1956).
23. M. M. ELKIND and H. SUTTON, X-Ray damage and recovery in mammalian cells grown in culture. *Nature* **184,** 1293–1295 (1959).
24. M. M. ELKIND and H. SUTTON, Radiation response of mammalian cells grown in culture. I. Repair of X-ray damage in surviving Chinese hamster cells. *Radiation Res.* **13,** 556–593 (1960).
25. S. HORNSEY and G. SILINI, Recovery of tumor cells cultured *in vivo* after X-ray and neutron irradiation. *Radiation Res.* **16,** 712–722 (1962).

26. A. B. ESCHENBRENNER, T. WANG, and E. MILLER, Preliminary report: the value of mouse testes for biological dosimetry of ionizing radiation. U.S. Atomic Energy Commission Report ANL-4451, pp. 39–41 (1950).
27. A. B. ESCHENBRENNER, E. MILLER, and E. LORENZ, Quantitative histologic analysis of the effect of chronic whole-body irradiation with gamma-rays on the spermatogenic elements and interstitial tissue of the testes of mice. *J. Natl. Cancer Inst.* **9,** 133–147 (1948).
28. C. W. EMMENS, *Principles of Biological Assay,* Chapman and Hall, London, 1948.
29. B. COHEN and C. E. FALK, *(d,n)* reactions with 15 MeV deuterons. II. Neutron energy spectra and yields. *Phys. Rev.* **84,** 173–178 (1951).
30. G. R. NEWBERG and D. K. BEWLEY, The performance of the Medical Research Council's 8-MeV Linear Accelerator. *Brit. J. Radiol.* **28,** 241–251 (1955).
31. G. J. NEARY and F. S. WILLIAMSON, A simple method of fast neutron dosimetry for use in radiobiology, and an intercomparison with some methods used in the United States. In *Selected Topics in Radiation Dosimetry,* pp. 463–471, International Atomic Energy Agency 1961.
32. H. I. KOHN and R. F. KALLMAN, Testes weight loss as a quantitative measure of X-ray injury in the mouse, hamster and rat. *Brit. J. Radiol.* **27,** 586–591 (1954).
33. J. B. STORER, P. S. HARRIS, J. E. FURCHNER, and W. H. LANGHAM, The relative biological effectiveness of various ionizing radiations in mammalian systems. *Radiation Res.* **6,** 188–288 (1957).
34. G. J. NEARY, R. J. MUNSON, and R. H. MOLE, *Chronic Radiation Hazards,* Pergamon Press, New York, 1957.
35. C. REGAUD and A. LACASSAGNE, Effets histophysiologiques des Rayons de Roentgen et de Becquerel-Curie sur les tissus adultes normaux des animaux supérieurs. *Arch. inst. radium* **1,** 1 et seq. (1927).
36. E. F. OAKBERG, Degeneration of spermatogonia of the mouse following exposure to X-rays and stages in the mitotic cycle at which death occurs. *J. Morphol.* **97,** 39–54 (1955).
37. R. F. KALLMAN and H. I. KOHN, The reaction of the mouse thymus to X-rays measured by changes in organ weight. *Radiation Res.* **2,** 280–293 (1955).
38. R. F. KALLMAN and H. I. KOHN, The reaction of the mouse spleen to X-rays measured by changes in organ weight. *Radiation Res.* **3,** 77–87 (1955).
39. A. B. ESCHENBRENNER and E. MILLER, Effect of roentgen rays on the testis. Quantitative histological analysis following whole-body exposure of mice. *A.M.A. Arch. Pathol.* **50,** 736–749 (1950).
40. H. H. VOGEL, J. W. CLARK, and D. L. JORDAN. "Recovery" after fission neutrons: Paired equal doses with varying time intervals. (Abstract) *Radiation Res.* **7,** 458 (1957).

RADIATION RESEARCH 19, 64–87 (1963)

The X-Ray Sensitivity of *Serratia marcescens*

D. L. DEWEY

British Empire Cancer Campaign, Research Unit in Radiobiology, Mount Vernon Hospital, Northwood, Middlesex, England

INTRODUCTION

Bacteria have many advantages when used as a tool for investigating the biological effects of ionizing radiations. The small size of bacteria coupled with the ease and low cost of growing high concentrations in a small space results in the ability to measure the fraction surviving radiation over many powers of 10 and still obtain sufficient survivors to maintain statistical accuracy. Consequently, the sensitivity to radiation under standard conditions can be determined with great precision.

The use of bacteria also eliminates gross oxygen gradients and concentration gradients of other metabolites inevitably present in organized tissue. Thus the effects of protectors and sensitizers can be studied at the cellular level. The modifying influences of organized tissue can be studied later in the knowledge of what already happens at the cellular level. This paper deals only with the factors that modify the radiosensitivity of bacteria.

METHOD

Bacteria

The strain of *Serratia marcescens* originally obtained from Miss Mahoney of University College, London, has been maintained for many years in this laboratory. For experiments the bacteria were grown in test tubes containing nutrient broth (made from tablets CM2 Oxo Limited, 16, Southwark Bridge Road, London, S.E.1.). The test tubes were incubated for 24 hours at 25°C in air without shaking. After irradiation, samples were placed in plastic petri dishes, and 12 ml of nutrient agar (CM4 Oxo Limited) kept liquid at 48°C was poured in. The petri dishes were incubated for 48 hours at 25°C or at room temperature if it was near 25°C. No difference could be detected between results obtained with glass or plastic petri dishes.

Irradiation

The experiments extended over 5 years and employed three X-ray installations operating at 200 kv. For a few experiments at higher dose rates, 250 kv was em-

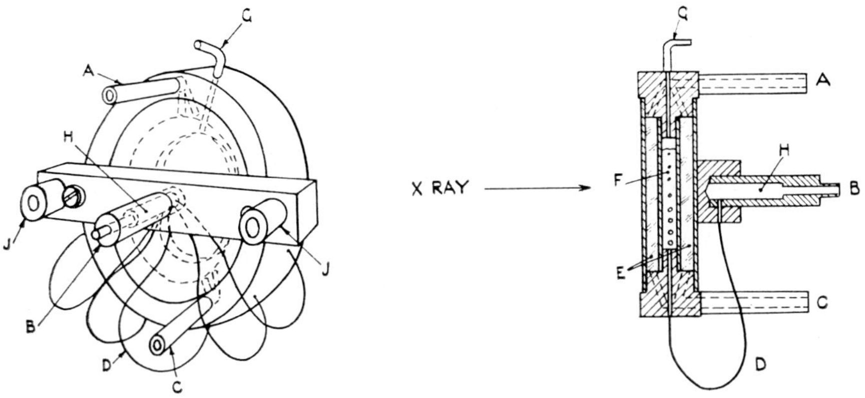

FIG. 1. The irradiation cell consists of an inner water-jacketed chamber constructed from Perspex (Lucite). See text for details.

ployed. In all cases a 1.6 mm Al filter was added. The exposure rate was 800 to 3200 r/min. The irradiation vessel, shown in Fig. 1, consisted of a Perspex (Lucite) block machined and drilled to form the irradiation cavity 3 mm thick and 30 mm in diameter, in the center of a water jacket. Gas entered through five nylon tubes each of which was first treated to make the gas flow uniformly from all five tubes. The treatment consisted in putting a 0.05-mm wire down the length of the tube and filling the end 10 mm with wax. After the wax cooled, the wire was pulled out.

The gas under test was connected to the nipple (*B*) and passed through the cotton wool plug (*H*), then via the five nylon bubbling tubes (*D*) into the cavity (*F*) containing the sample to be X-rayed. After bubbling through the test sample, the gas left through the hollow plug (*G*). This plug was removed to replace or remove the test sample. The water, which was circulated continuously, entered at *C* and left at the highest point to sweep out any trapped air bubbles which might otherwise permit a nonuniform X-ray dose in the cell. The apparatus was fixed at *J* to a jig attached to the X-ray set to ensure exactly reproducible geometry.

When the bacteria were irradiated in gases at high pressure, 0.2 ml of the bacterial suspension was placed in an ultraviolet-sterilized nylon planchette, 2 mm deep. The planchette was placed in a cavity 4 cm in diameter, in a stainless-steel block 9 cm in diameter. The cavity was covered with a 1-cm aluminum disk held in place on a gasket with a stainless-steel O ring and held down with eight ⅜-inch B.S.F. high-tensile bolts, each tightened to a tension of 40 foot-pounds. The vessel was flushed with the gas required and then taken up to a pressure 10% higher than that finally required. The whole apparatus was then agitated for a few minutes to cause a ripple on the liquid surface and thereby increase the rate of equilibration, after which the pressure was lowered to the required value. After irradiation the chamber was evacuated to avoid foaming of the otherwise supersaturated suspension.

Dosimetry

The exposure rate was measured by ionization chambers mounted in a jig so that they were located on the axis of the beam at a fixed distance from the target, where it was conveniently low and could be accurately measured. The dose received by the bacterial suspensions was then estimated with the help of relevant physical parameters by an inverse square calculation. This method was cross-checked by using ferrous sulfate in a ceresin wax-lined Lucite container having geometry similar to that of the bacterial irradiation chamber.

Gases

All gases except nitric oxide were obtained from British Oxygen Gases Limited. The specification of the oxygen-free nitrogen supplied was less than 10 parts per million (ppm); by retesting and selecting the best cylinders available, an upper limit of 4 ppm of oxygen was obtained.

The nitric oxide was first made by the action of acetic acid on sodium nitrate in a pre-evacuated system; then nitrogen was added under pressure to obtain the required dilution. A glass vessel was used so that any change in color of the gas due to an air leak would be immediately noticed. The positive pressure in the vessel was used to drive the gas through the radiation cell. Later a sample of nitric oxide was obtained from the United States through the courtesy of Dr. E. L. Powers. The same experimental results were obtained with nitric oxide from both sources.

Oxygen Tension Measurements

When bacteria were being irradiated under anoxic conditions, the carrier gas, after passing through the irradiation chamber, was put through a Hersch cell (*1*) so that any errors in oxygen tension (such as a leak) would be immediately noticed. Rubber tubing was found to be so permeable to oxygen as to cause a significant change in the oxygen tension of the solution. To avoid this error a flexible grade of nylon tubing (Portland Plastics Limited) was used throughout. The biggest oxygen leak was found to be in the pressure reduction valve on most double-valve cylinder heads.

Chemicals

The glycerol was added to the standard buffer at a concentration such that, when 1 ml of bacterial suspension was added to 9 ml of glycerol in buffer, the resulting glycerol concentration was as stated in the diagrams. The glycerol and ethylene glycol in buffer solutions were sterilized by heat.

N-Ethylmaleimide and ethyl alcohol in high concentrations are toxic to bacteria, and no further sterilization was used. The liquid was diluted in sterile buffer until the required concentration was obtained.

Cysteine was made up as a strong solution in water neutralized to the required pH by adding a few drops of 5 *N* KOH, then diluted in buffer and sterilized by heat.

Experimental Procedure

The bacteria were diluted in buffer, and 2 ml of the diluted suspension was transferred to the irradiation chamber. When irradiations were at 2°C, the buffer used for diluting was precooled to about 10°C to avoid possible killing by sudden cold shock (*2*). The chamber was pregassed at 25 ml/min for 20 minutes, 0.1 ml of cell suspension was withdrawn as a control unirradiated sample, and gassing was continued for 5 minutes before the irradiation which was delivered in a time calculated from the previously measured dose rate and monitored by an ionization chamber built into the back of the irradiation chamber.

Immediately after the irradiation of second 0.1-ml sample was withdrawn, and, after a further 5 minutes of equilibrium, a second X-ray dose was delivered and a third sample taken. The samples added to 9 ml of buffer were serially diluted by repeated transferring of 1 ml into 9 ml of buffer with very thorough mixing. A fresh sterile pipet was used for every dilution. When dilution by a large factor was required, the error in successive dilutions was cumulative. Thus each dilution must be made with a high degree of precision. Corrections were applied for loss of fluid, both during the sterilizing procedure and during the time the tube was left to cool after sterilizing. When nonvolatile substances were being sterilized they were made correspondingly more dilute on the assumption that only water would evaporate. For the very high dilutions every tube, including the cotton wool plug, was weighed empty and again just before use in order to determine the exact dilution obtained, and when this deviated from 1 in 10 the appropriate correction was made mathematically.

By adding liquid agar at 48°C to the suspension and agitating to obtain thorough mixing, the bacterial colonies were mixed throughout the bulk of the agar, and larger numbers per petri dish could be accurately counted. The counting was done after 48 hours of incubation by clipping a wire on the edge of the dish to make electrical contact with the agar. The other probe of a high-impedence electromechanical counting device was poked into each colony in turn, thus operating the counter, and also mechanically marking the colony to prevent it's being counted twice. The plates usually contained between 100 and 1000 colonies and were nearly always repeated in triplicate to get high statistical counting accuracy.

RESULTS

The effect of 200-kv X-rays on the survival of *Serratia marcescens* is shown in Fig. 2*A*. This figure covers many powers of 10 and is necessarily reproduced on a small scale. An enlarged view of the area in the enclosed square is shown in Fig. 2*B*. In oxygen, the log surviving fraction is strictly proportional to dose over many

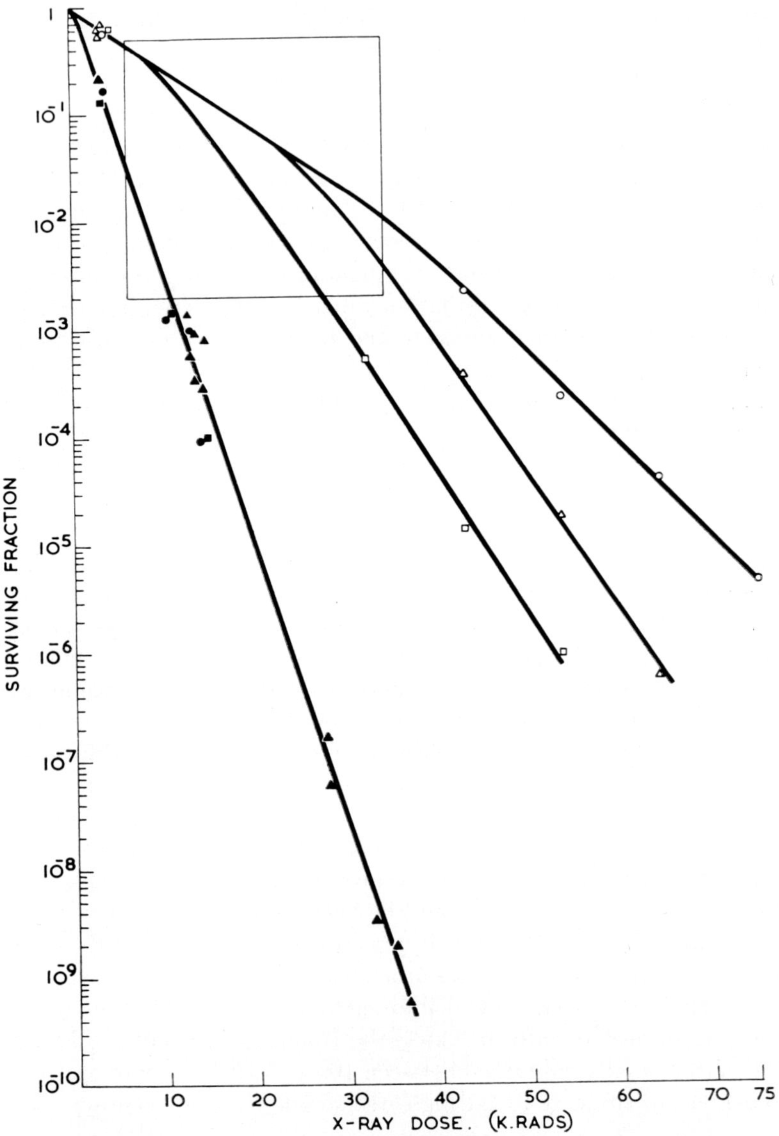

FIG. 2A. Loss of colony-forming ability of *Serratia marcescens* after 200-kv X-rays at 2000 r/min. An enlarged drawing of the area inside the square is shown in Fig. 2B. For symbol explanations see Fig. 2B.

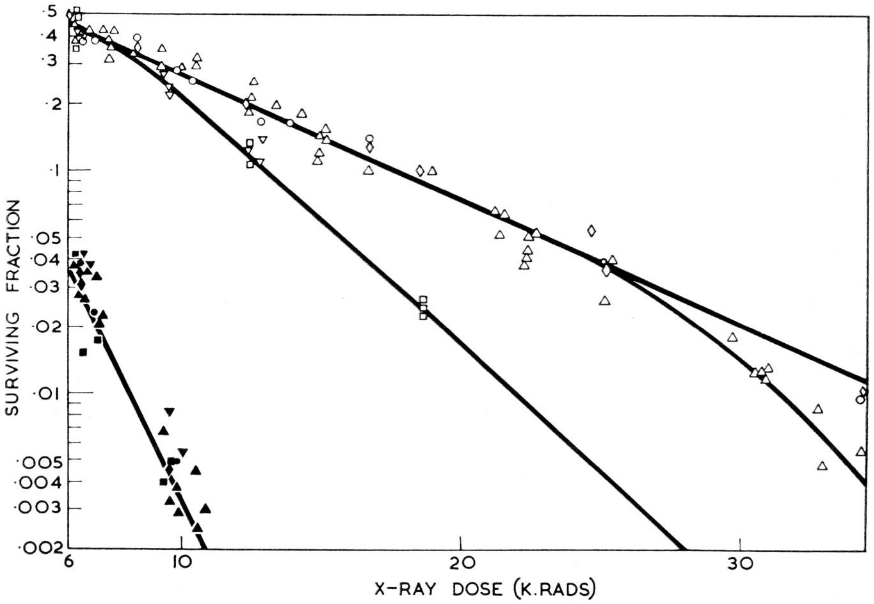

FIG 2*B*. An enlarged view of the enclosed area of Fig. 2*A* (the dose axis has also been enlarged one and one-half times the surviving fraction axis). X-Rayed in nitrogen: at 2°C ○; at 10°C ◇; at 20°C △; at 30°C ▽; at 37°C □. X-rayed in oxygen at the same temperatures: solid symbols.

powers of 10 except that the extrapolation number is 1.3. In nitrogen the log surviving fraction is proportional to dose only over a limited range, depending on temperature, between one-half and two powers of 10, after which the curve bends down and after about four powers of 10 straightens out to a new slope. The initial slope extrapolates to 1.0, and the oxygen–nitrogen dose ratio is 4.6. At 20°C the final slope in nitrogen etxrapolates back to about 1000 and has an oxygen nitrogen dose ratio of about 1.9. The amount of oxygen required to give half the maximum effect was calculated for the initial temperature-independent part of the curve by irradiating the bacteria while gassed with oxygen–nitrogen mixtures which gave roughly the required slope. Then, by substituting in the equation

$$\frac{S}{S_n} = \frac{m(O_2) + K}{(O_2) + K}, \qquad (3)$$

the value of K was, after correction for the different solubility of oxygen in water, independent of temperature. The number of experiments in which the value of K came between certain values is plotted as a histogram in Fig. 3. The most probable value is an oxygen concentration of between 3 and 4 μM/liter.

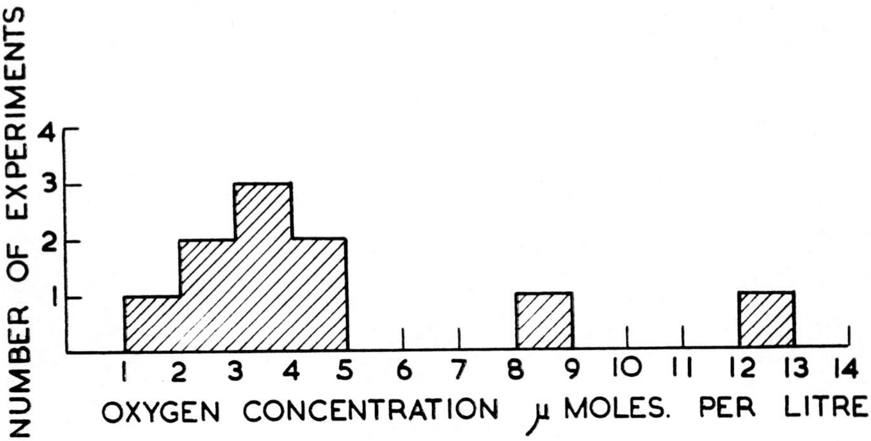

FIG. 3. The oxygen concentration at which the radiosensitivity is half-way between the aerobic and anaerobic values.

In order to make a description of the effect of protectors and sensitizers less cumbersome, the radiation effects illustrated in Figs. 2*A* and 2*B*, will be arbitrarily divided into a number of types of damage. Nitrogen damage is that which is observed at low doses in nitrogen and is independent of temperature. Oxygen damage is that extra damage observed in oxygen; it is also independent of temperature. A third type of damage, called here postirradiation damage for reasons that are explained later, is the additional temperature-dependent damage observed at high doses in nitrogen. It is measured at any given dose by extrapolating the initial straight line in nitrogen and noting the difference between survival on the extrapolated line and the actual survival obtained at the same dose. There may well be an extra temperature-independent type of damage included in the above.

The effect of nitric oxide on radiosensitivity in the strict absence of oxygen is shown in Fig. 4. Although nitric oxide sensitizes *Serratia marcescens* to radiation damage, the effect is not quantitatively the same as was found by Howard-Flanders for *Shigella flexneri*. With *Serratia marcescens* much higher concentrations are required to obtain the same enhancement ratio, and the log surviving fraction is not proportional to dose. This phenomenon is most easily explained by assuming the presence of all three types of damage and by assuming that nitric oxide does not have the additional power that oxygen has of protecting against postirradiation damage.

The effect of glycerol on the radiosensitivity of *Serratia marcescens* has already been reported for the initial part of the survival curve in oxygen (*4*), nitrogen, and nitric oxide, and protection was obtained in all cases. Figure 5 shows an extension of these observations to higher doses where the survival curve in nitrogen is

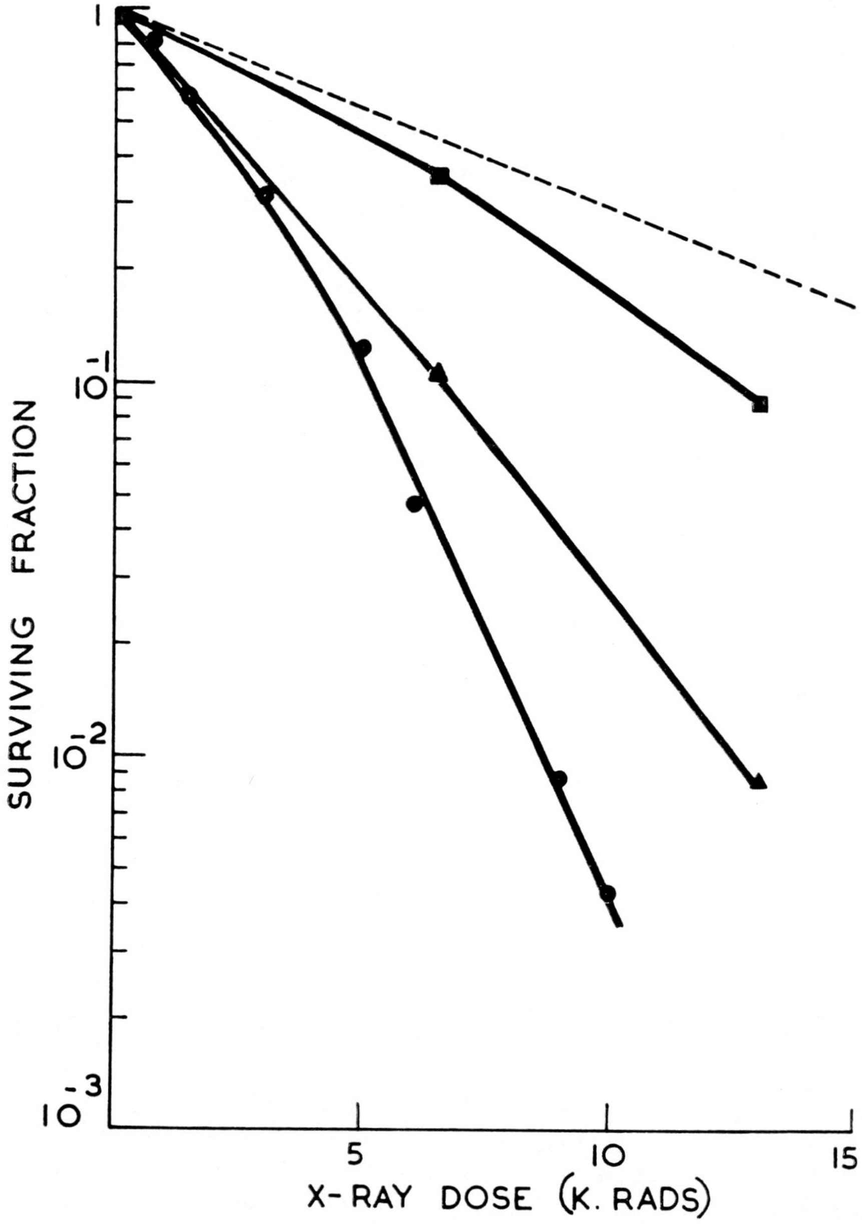

FIG. 4. Loss of colony-forming ability of *Serratia marcescens* after 200-kv X-rays at 20°C at 800 r/min in nitric oxide. ● 10% nitric oxide; ▲ 5% nitric oxide; ■ 2% nitric oxide. The dotted line is the anoxic curve from Fig. 2, included for reference.

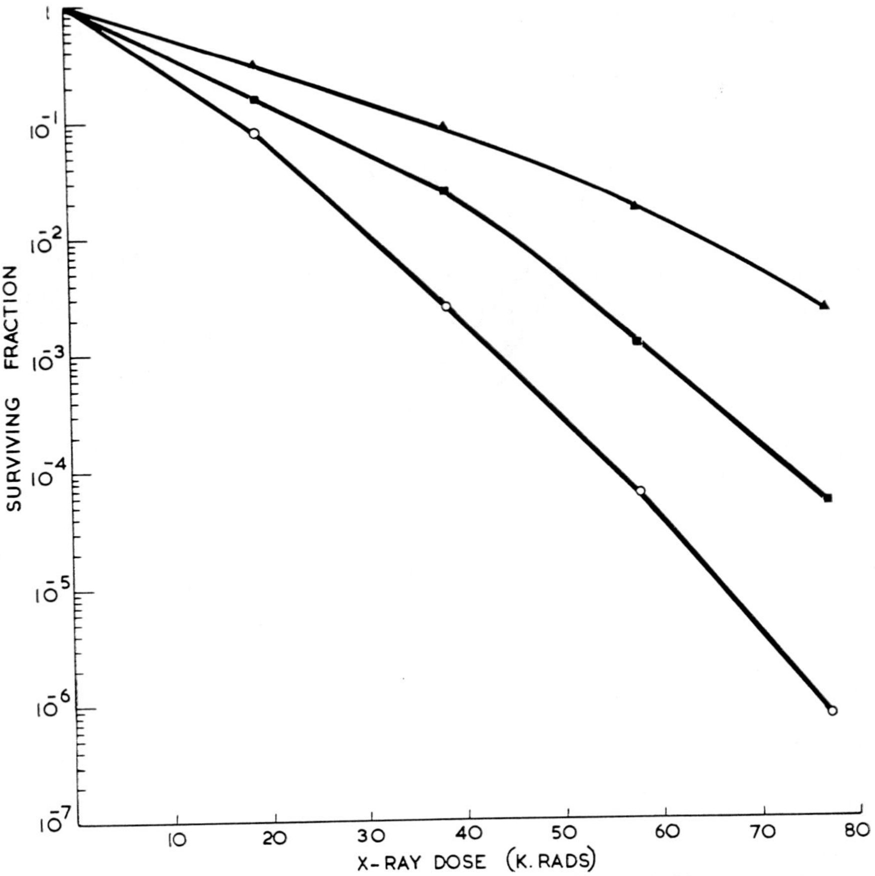

FIG. 5. Loss of colony-forming ability of *Serratia marcescens* after 250-kv X-rays at 2°C. ○ in nitrogen; ■ in nitrogen and 2 *M* dimethyl sulfoxide; ▲ in nitrogen and 2 *M* glycerol.

nonlinear (see Fig. 2*A*). The glyceral line is also nonlinear and can be roughly superimposed on the nitrogen line by a dose-reduction factor of 2. Thus glycerol does not abolish the additional lethal effect at higher doses in nitrogen (postirradiation damage). Epxeriments on the survival of *Serratia marcescens* after exposure to ultraviolet light, where there is no oxygen effect, showed that *M* glycerol was completely without effect. Figure 5 also shows the protective effect of dimethyl sulfoxide against X-irradiation in nitrogen. Although substantial protection was obtained, the amount was not so great as with glycerol at the same concentration. In the presence of oxygen the protective effect of dimethyl sulfoxide was practically the same as that of glycerol when the concentrations of both were 1. But, as in the case of nitrogen, 2 *M* dimethyl sulfoxide was not so effective as 2 *M* glycerol. A

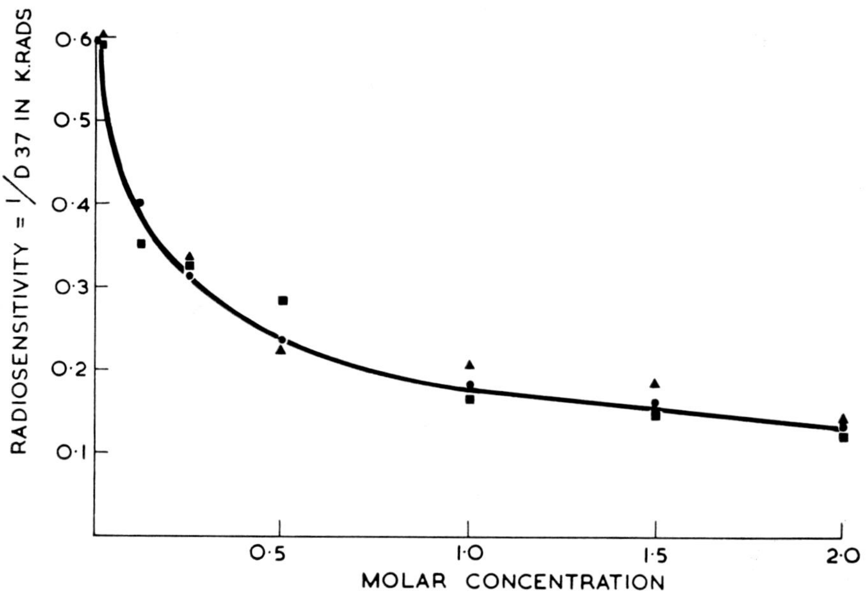

FIG. 6. The effect of the concentration of various protectors on the sensitivity of *Serratia marcescens* to 200-kv X-rays at 20°C in oxygen. ● glycerol; ▲ ethylene glycol; ■ ethyl alcohol.

mixture containing *M* glycerol and *M* dimethyl sulfoxide gave the same degree of protection against aerobic irradiation as 2 *M* glycerol.

Ethylene glycol and ethyl alcohol closely resemble glycerol in that they protect equally well at equal molar concentrations in the presence of oxygen. Figure 6 shows the effect of these three compounds when plotted as the reciprocal of the slope of the survival curve in oxygen against the concentration of protector. The D_{37} was obtained from the slope of the regression line through each set of points as determined by mean square analysis, excluding any points from doses less than 3 krad which might influence the results due to the extrapolation number. All three compounds were found to protect in nitrogen. These experiments were being done when the survival in nitrogen was first found to be not an exponential. The experiments were terminated before enough results had accumulated to determine the equivalence of these compounds in nitrogen.

N-Ethylmaleimide has already been reported to sensitize *Escherichia coli* to γ-rays irradiated in both nitrogen and oxygen (*5*), whereas other bacteria were sensitized when irradiated in nitrogen but not in oxygen (*6*). The effect of this compound on *Serratia marcescens* in nitrogen is shown in Fig. 7. The effect is clearly sensitization but not a simple dose-modifying factor. The change in shape is analogous to the effect of increasing the temperature as shown in Fig. 2. When 0.001 *M* cysteine was added to the bacteria in *N*-ethylmaleimide before irradiation in nitro-

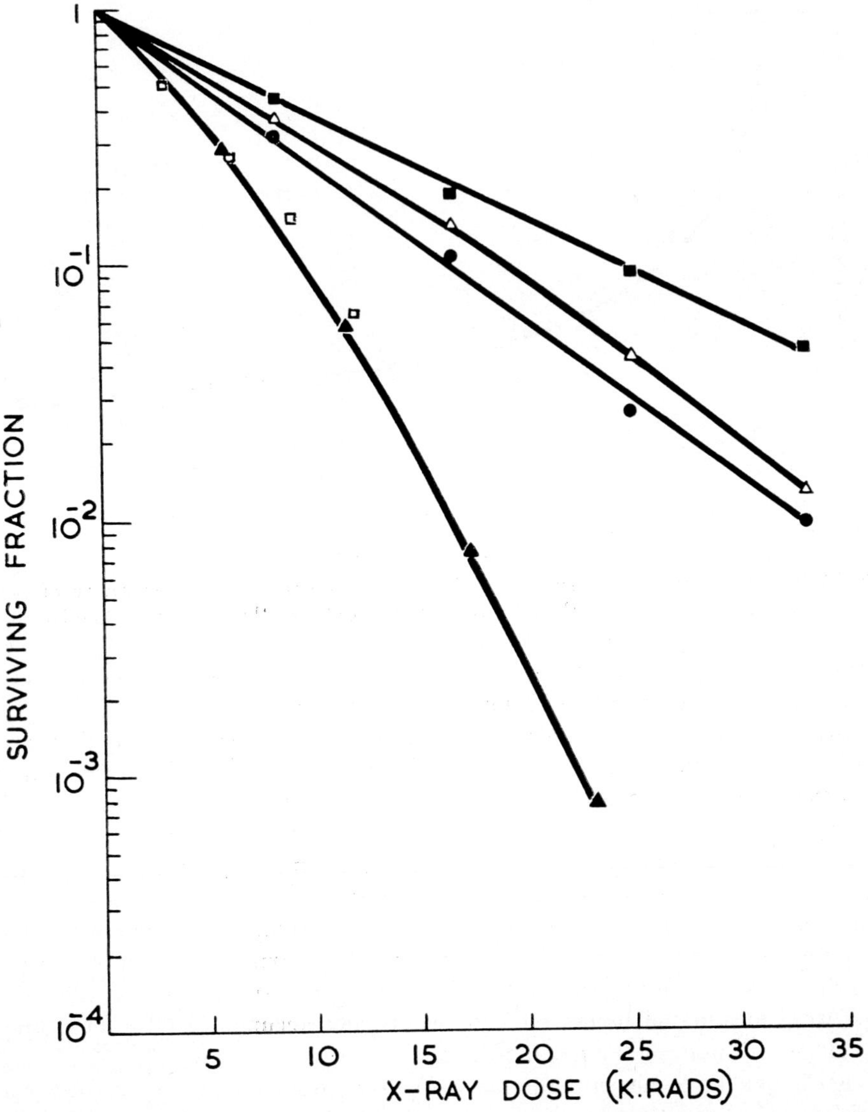

FIG. 7. Loss of colony-forming ability of *Serratia marcescens* after 200-kv X-rays at 20°C in nitrogen. ▲ 0.3 m*M* *N*-ethylmaleimide present during irradiation; ● 0.3 m*M* *N*-ethylmaleimide added immediately after irradiation; ■ 0.3 m*M* *N*-ethylmaleimide added for 15 minutes, then cysteine added to final concentration of 1 m*M* before irradiation; △ control, no *N*-ethylmaleimide, X-rayed at 20°C; □ control, no *N*-ethylmaleimide, X-rayed at 40°C.

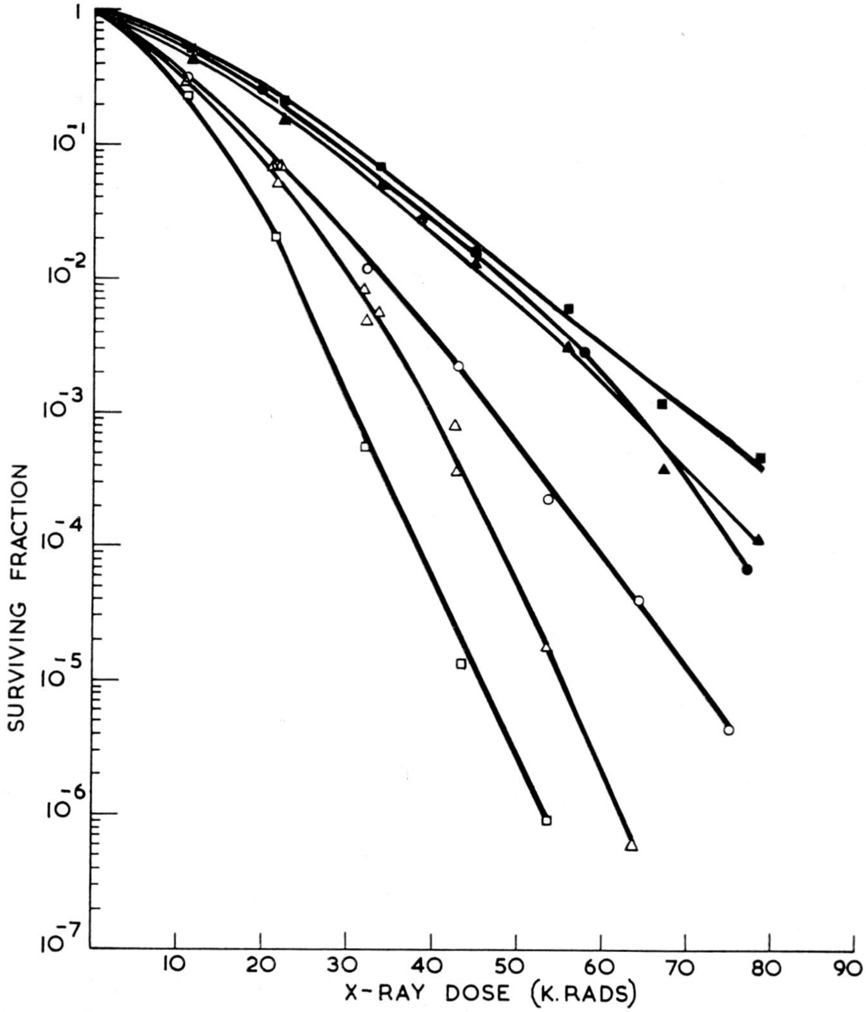

FIG. 8. Loss of colony-forming ability of *Serratia marcescens* after 200-kv X-rays at 2000 r/min in nitrogen. □ irradiated at 37°C; △ irradiated at 20°C; ○ irradiated at 2°C; ■ irradiated in 100 m*M* cysteine at 37°C; ▲ irradiated in 100 m*M* cysteine at 20°C; ● irradiated in 100 m*M* cysteine at 2°C.

gen, the sensitizing effect was abolished and replaced by the protective effect of the cysteine. The log survival of bacteria irradiated in the presence of cysteine in nitrogen is still not straight, but the temperature effect found in the absence of cysteine was abolished (Fig. 8). Thus the addition of cysteine demonstrates that the temperature dependence and the curvature in nitrogen could be two separate

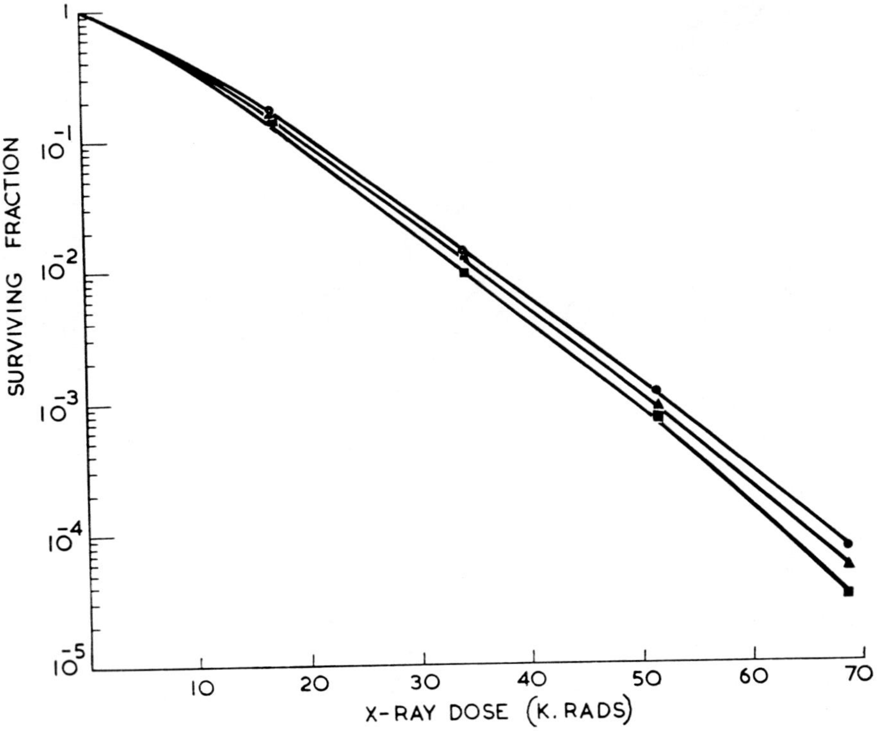

FIG. 9. The effect of small concentration of oxygen on the loss of colony-forming ability of *Serratia marcescens* after 250-kv X-rays at 3200 r/min at 0°C. ■ oxygen concentration in the gas phase is 200 ppm; ▲ 50 ppm; ● 20 ppm.

phenomena. Cysteine protects against nitrogen damage and some but not all of the postirradiation damage.

When the bacteria were irradiated in the absence of oxygen, the same line was obtained irrespective of whether the anoxia was obtained by gassing the suspension with nitrogen, hydrogen, or *nitrous* oxide. (The sensitizing effect shown in Fig. 4 was with *nitric* oxide.) Great care was required to check that the gases were in fact oxygen-free. The effect of small traces of oxygen in the carrier gas is shown in Fig. 9. In this case the carrier gas was nitrogen, and the oxygen was added by diffusion by inserting various lengths of rubber tubing in the gas line. When the oxygen concentration was reduced below 20 ppm, no further protection was obtained at the dose rate used, presumably because the radiochemical removal of the trace of oxygen remaining was fast in comparison with the bubbling efficiency of the cell. The oxygen removed radiochemically has already been shown to be also removed with respect to its damage ability for this organism (*7, 8*).

At zero oxygen concentration the radiosensitivity of *Serratia marcescens* has one

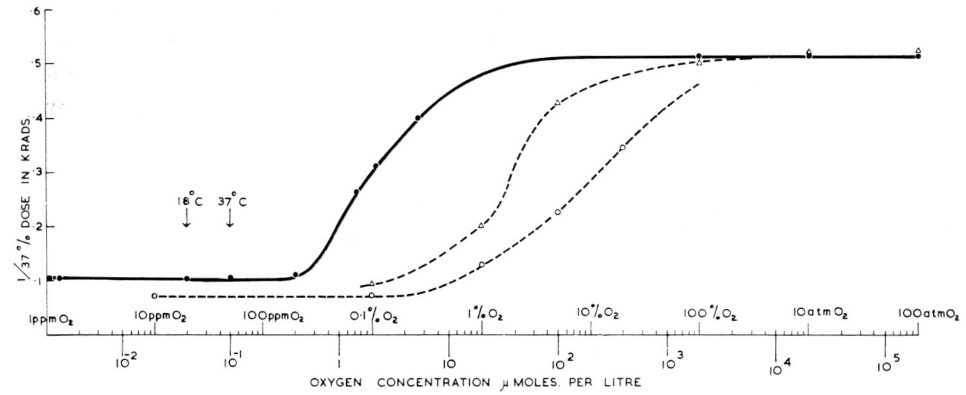

FIG. 10. The effect of oxygen concentration on the radiosensitivity of *Serratia marcescens* after 250-kv X-rays at 2°C. ● No additions; ○ 100 m*M* cysteine at pH 7; △ 100 m*M* cysteine at pH 5.

value (considering only the initial straight part of the survival curve), and at high concentrations the sensitivity has another value independent of the oxygen concentration up to the highest value measured—100 atm. The relation between sensitivity and oxygen concentration between these values is shown in Fig. 10. The oxygen concentration range at which the respiration rate of this strain of bacteria becomes dependent on oxygen tension was kindly measured by Dr. I. S. Longmuir using a gold polarographic electrode. The arrows in Fig. 10 are the concentrations of oxygen at which the respiration rate falls to half its maximum at 16.3°C and at 37°C. The half-value for radiosensitivity, unlike respiration, is not dependent on temperature.

Also in Fig. 10 are plotted the results of an experiment designed to find out what proportion of the radiation protection afforded by cysteine in an aerobic system is due to the oxygen-scavenging properties of cysteine which will produce local anoxia, and how much is due to the type of protection obtained in the anaerobic system. When the oxygen concentration was low, a high degree of protection was obtained. As the oxygen concentration was increased, the degree of protection fell to zero at about 1 atm, but unfortunately at these high oxygen concentrations the autoxidation of cysteine was so rapid it was not certain whether any of the protective compound remained at the time of irradiation. When cysteine is gassed with oxygen for any length of time, the autoxidation product, cystine, being very much less soluble, comes out of solution. The control unirradiated bacterial suspension often contained a smaller number of organisms than expected when a precipitate of cystine was present. It is possible but not proved that cystine coming out of solution inside the bacterium may cause mechanical damage and the death of the cell.

To avoid many of the complications associated with the autoxidation of cysteine, many of the experiments were repeated at pH 5. The pH was obtained by changing the relative concentrations of the components used in the phosphate buffer, and the over-all concentration was increased tenfold to compensate for the loss of buffering capacity of phosphate at this pH. The bacteria were not damaged when suspended in buffer at this pH, and a test run in 100% oxygen without cysteine showed that the radiosensitivity was unaltered.

The rate of autoxidation of cysteine is very much less at pH 5 (*9*). As a result it was possible to take the suspension up to 100 atm of oxygen without much precipitate being formed. In Fig. 10 the difference between pH 5 and pH 7 is partly but may not be completely due to anoxia. An attempt was made to measure the actual concentration of oxygen in solution during the gas equilibration procedure. A sample of the fluid was rapidly mixed with a small quantity of strong acid to stop further autoxidation. The total oxygen content of the sample was measured in the Hersch cell (*1*). When the solution was bubbled with air, the dissolved oxygen concentration was found to be only 80% of the control containing no cysteine. When 5% oxygen in nitrogen was used as the gas phase, on adding cysteine 70% of the control value was observed. The oxygen concentration measured was that of a macroscopic sample; the intracellular concentration could be very different. During irradiation in the presence of cysteine, the radiochemical conversion to cystine in aerated solution has a G value of 74 (*10*). If it is assumed that one atom of oxygen is consumed per molecule of cysteine converted, then this reaction alone would render an ungassed previously aerated solution at 2°C anoxic in 3.2 minutes at the dose rate of 3.2 kr/min used in those experiments. The rate of autoxidation in the absence of irradiation at pH 7 varies slightly depending on catalysis by trace contaminants but is very similar to the radiochemical conversion rate. At pH 5 the autoxidation rate is greatly reduced and radiochemical conversion becomes the main oxygen-depleting factor.

Many substances profoundly modify the amount of biological damage caused by X-rays. It is of fundamental importance to know whether all these chemicals act in the same way or whether there is more than one mechanism by which X-ray damage can be altered. To obtain more information about possible different pathways of action, various different combinations of substances were added to see if the effect of one was added to the other or, if the same mechanism was involved, to see if maximum effect by one compound would block any further effects caused by adding a second compound. Such an additional effect already mentioned is oxygen and glycerol, as greater protection is obtained by adding glycerol to the fully anaerobic system. The *N*-ethylmaleimide and oxygen effects are not additive —although *N*-ethylmaleimide sensitizes the anoxic system, no further sensitization is obtained in an aerobic system. Neither is the effect of adding one in the presence of the other the same as adding more of the other. Many active compounds cannot be tried together, as they rapidly react with each other; for example, nitric oxide rapidly combines with oxygen to form products toxic to the biological material. Cysteine inactivates *N*-ethylmaleimide, and oxygen autoxidizes cysteine. Glycerol and *N*-ethylmaleimide however, do not interact. Glycerol (*M*) in nitrogen protects *Serratia marcescens* by a factor of 2, and 0.3 m*M* *N*-ethylmaleimide sensitizes by a similar amount except that it slightly alters the shape of the survival curve. Both compounds together more or less cancel out, giving a survival curve very similar to the control containing neither compound. Similarly glycerol and cysteine separately both protect the bacteria when irradiated under anoxic conditions. When glycerol and cysteine were added together, the protection was greater than that obtained with either alone, but it was very much less than the product of the two protective factors which would be expected if the mechanism of action of these two compounds were completely independent.

The survival curve of bacteria X-rayed under anoxic conditions was found to be dose rate-dependent. The curve for bacteria irradiated at 20°C at 3200 r/min was very similar to that obtained at 2°C and 2000 r/min. If 3200 r/min at 2°C was used, the survival at high doses was even higher than that obtained with 2000 r/min at the same temperature. These findings are compatible with the possible accumulation of toxic products generated by X-rays in the buffer used as suspending medium. To investigate this possibility the bacteria were irradiated at 3200 r/min at 2°C, and a sample was withdrawn as soon as possible after the end of the irradiation (about 20 seconds). The temperature was then raised to 30°C, and further samples were taken at intervals. The results, shown in Fig. 11, demonstrate that this treatment has no effect on unirradiated cells, yet after anoxic doses of 55 krad the surviving fraction falls to one-tenth of its initial value in just over an hour. In control experiments in which sterile medium was diluted in buffer and irradiated anaerobically, bacteria added just after irradiation were inactivated in a similar manner to the irradiated survivors. When bacteria were added to pure distilled water after the water had received an anaerobic dose of 55 krad, no inactivation was observed (Fig. 12). When the bacteria were centrifuged, twice washed with distilled water, further diluted with distilled water, and then irradiated anaerobically with 55 krad, the initial surviving fraction was the same as with the standard procedure of diluting in buffer. The samples taken at later intervals after the temperature was raised to 30°C showed that the survival also fell off with time, indicating that the external medium was not necessary for the effect.

All these results were obtained in strict nitrogen anoxia. Nitrogen was bubbled continuously through the irradiation chamber before, during, and after irradiation. When the gas was changed to air or oxygen immediately after irradiation, the aftereffect was completely abolished. Oxygen (5%) in nitrogen was the same as air, but a small postirradiation inactivation was still observed when the nitrogen was changed to 0.1% oxygen immediately after irradiation.

DISCUSSION

In considering the problem imposed by the postirradiation toxicity in *Serratia marcescens*, any statements about hit numbers or about oxygen dose-reduction fac-

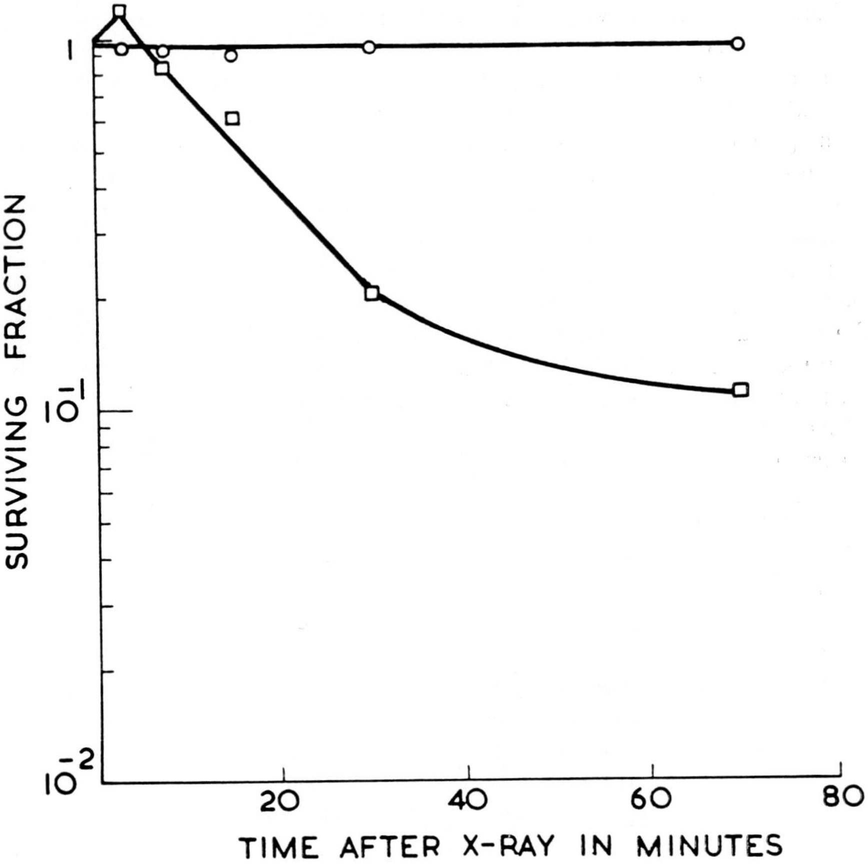

FIG. 11. The loss of colony-forming ability of *Serratia marcescens* with time at 30°C. □ After a single dose of 55 krad of 250-kv X-rays at 20°C in nitrogen; ○ Control treatment as above, but no X-rays.

tors must be made with severe reservations. However, in nitrogen the first part of the survival curve is a straight line through the origin, the slope of which is independent of temperature and dose rate. If the slope of this part of the curve is compared with the slope for aerobic irradiation, then the oxygen/nitrogen ratio is 4.6, which is considerably higher than the majority of values reported for other bacteria, plants, and mammalian cells. Howard-Flanders (*11*) lists thirty-eight published values ranging from 1 (no oxygen effect) to a maximum of 3.5. For *Serratia* the extrapolation number in oxygen is 1.3, and for the first part of the nitrogen line 1.0. These numbers are significantly different, but the interpretation is difficult; for example, although the cells are not dividing when irradiated, they were taken

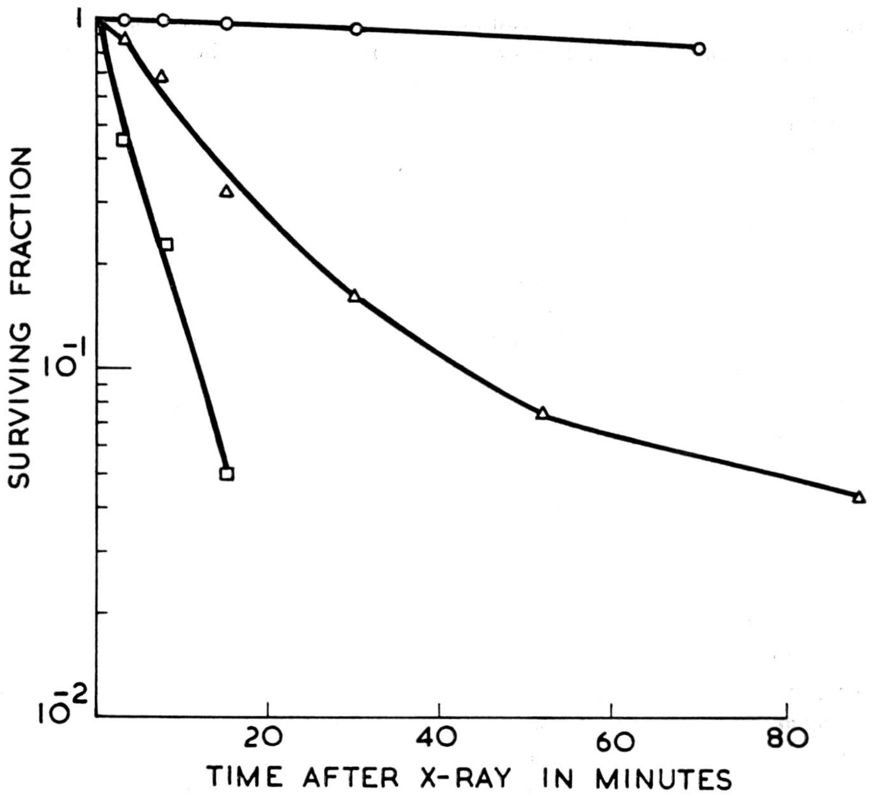

FIG. 12. The loss of colony-forming ability of *Serratia marcescens* with time at 30°C after a single dose of 55 krad of 250-kv X-rays at 2°C in nitrogen; △ bacteria first well washed in distilled water; □ bacteria added to irradiated growth medium; ○ bacteria added to irradiated distilled water.

from a nonsynchronized population. During division it is logical to assume that the radiobiological target duplicates before the physical separation of the two daughter cells. Thus the technique of measuring survival may give an extrapolation number in excess of the number of targets per cell. The error may be immeasurably small or may be influenced by changing the equilibrating gas especially if this causes partial synchronization. There could also be an additional effect in cells taken from a nonsynchronized population: If a small proportion of the cells in a particular phase of the cell cycle were very much more sensitive to irradiation, these would virtually be eliminated from the population by the initial part of the dose, and a spuriously low extrapolation number would be observed. The main cause of the deviation from a straight line in nitrogen is presumably due to the postirradiation toxicity effect, which will start during the irradiation. If the toxicity builds up to a steady state and is additive to radiaion damage, then the final part of the survival curves in nitrogen would be expected to be straight. The effect of oxygen in abolishing the postirradiation damage would account for the absence of any bend in the oxygen line.

The major effect of oxygen is to make the cells more sensitive to radiation. A number of plausible explanations for this effect have already been advanced. Explanations based on whether the cells are respiring or not at the time of irradiation or on the state of intracellular oxidation-reduction systems seem unlikely, as the oxygen concentration for half the maximum radiation effect is considerably different from the concentration required for half the maximum respiration. Thus it is possible to select an oxygen concentration at which the cells are respiring at near-maximum rate and yet show near anoxic sensitivity. Furthermore the concentration for half-maximum respiration is temperature-dependent, whereas that for radiosensitivity is not.

Nitric oxide resembles oxygen in that it is paramagnetic. It has been reported to be as effective as oxygen in sensitizing *Shigella flexneri* to radiation (*12*). However, with *Serratia marcescens* the effect of nitric oxide was found to have two important differences from the effect of oxygen—a much higher concentration was required to give full effect, and the survival curve was not a straight line. The need for a higher concentration could always be accounted for by postulating a lower efficiency of reaction, but the curved line in nitric oxide is best explained by assuming a second function of oxygen not shared by nitric oxide in abolishing the postirradiation damage observed at high doses.

The effects of glycerol, ethyl alcohol, and ethylene glycol are so similar that it is probable that they all act by the same mechanism. The magnitude of the protection of glycerol against radiation damage is the same as that observed by Erikson and Szybalski (*13*) using human cells in culture. The protective effect of glycerol is also very marked in haploid yeast and has been interpreted as being due to dehydration (*14*), although Manney *et al.* (*15*), by studying the time scale of water removal, have shown that protection cannot be attributed simply to the removal of cellular water. Webb and Powers (*16*) showed that glycerol protection in *Staphylococcus aureus* and spores of *Bacillus megaterium* follows closely that of the Langmuir adsortpion isotherm. In *Serratia marcescens* the high concentrations required, 0.9 M for half the maximum effect, suggests that they are competing with something also present in a high concentration. Another plausible explanation is scavenging H and OH radicals. The initial spur concentration of these primary radicals is also thought to approach 1 M (*17*). The finding of Alper (*18*) that glycerol also protects bacteria against α-ray damage is not inconsistent with the mechanism of action being the scavenging primary radicals. Alcohols are known to scavenge OH radicals with high efficiency (*19*) and also to scavenge H radicals rather more slowly (*20, 21*). The protective action of glycerol remained unaltered when nitrogen was replaced by 100% nitrous oxide which will convert H into OH radicals. This result would be expected because of the slow rate of the latter reaction (*22*) by comparison to the speed with which OH and H are removed by other mechanisms. The protective effect of glycerol in oxygen is considerably greater than in nitrogen. If the α-ray result is interpreted to mean that the H and OH radicals are rapidly scavenged, this would give an equal protective factor in nitrogen and oxygen. But the glycerol may have another protective effect in the aerobic system in addition to primary scavenging. This extra effect could be efficient removal of the additional radicals formed in the presence of oxygen or possibly combination with damaged biological sites, preventing oxygen from making such damage permanent. It is interesting to note that Hotz (*23*) found 100% glycerol to be less effective than glycerol–water mixtures in protecting the plaque-forming ability of coliphage T_1. Glycerol (75%) gave the maximum effect. This again points to the mechanism being via an interaction between glycerol and water or their irradiation products.

The effect of *N*-ethylmaleimide is quite different from that of oxygen or glycerol. The sensitizing effect in nitrogen of 0.3 m*M* *N*-ethylmaleimide irradiated at 20°C could be almost reproduced by irradiating in the absence of *N*-ethylmaleimide at 40°C. A further point of difference is that it does not sensitize *Serratia marcescens* gassed with oxygen where there is no temperature effect. Furthermore, cysteine, which abolishes the anaerobic temperature effect, also abolishes the sensitization by *N*-ethylmaleimide. The over-all results deduced from the information in Fig. 10 for the effect of cysteine on the radiosensitivity of *Serratia marcescens* was protection in nitrogen but no effect in a sufficiently oxygenated medium. This is different from the results reported by Kohn and Gunter (*24*), who, using the pH 5 technique, showed that cysteine protected *E. coli* B/r by about the same amount in both oxygen and nitrogen. The discrepancy may well be a species difference, as Bridges (*25*) showed that *E. coli* B/r was sensitized by *N*-ethylmaleimide in both oxygen and nitrogen, whereas with *Serratia* *N*-ethylmaleimide sensitizes only in an anoxic system. At high doses in oxygen slight protection was observed. Thus there is considerable circumstantial evidence that the mechanisms of action of cysteine and *N*-ethylmaleimide involves a common pathway. The fact that the temperature effect can by simulated immediately after irradiation points to the action as being via some long-lived radical or other active species. This species must be rapidly inactivated by oxygen and also probably requires a certain minimum concentration depending on temperature before any damage is observed. The observed effect is the break in the curve at about 30 krad in nitrogen at 20°C or 18 krad at 37°C. The concentration of oxygen required to prevent this type of damage is not small compared with that required to give the conventional oxygen effect; for, if it were, then at a concentration in the gas phase of a few hundred parts of oxygen per million a slightly steeper initial slope would be expected, and this would continue in a straight line crossing the anoxic curve. The results shown in Fig. 9 demonstrate that this is not so. Furthermore the small deviation from the anoxic line at low oxygen concentrations corresponds very closely to that expected from the Alper-Howard-Flanders formula (*3*).

Cysteine protects not only against the temperature effect of the postirradiation type of damage but also against nitrogen damage. The protection against nitrogen damage is demonstrated by the difference in slope of the initial part of the curve in nitrogen with and without cysteine. No protection is obtained against oxygen damage at very high oxygen concentrations. The measured inactivation in oxygen is the sum of the nitrogen and the oxygen damage; thus a change in the observed slope would be expected because of the protection against nitrogen damage. The amount would be small, however, because of the much larger magnitude of oxygen damage. Calculation shows that a 6% change in slope of the oxygen line should be observed. The scatter between repeat samples of bacteria irradiated in cysteine in oxygen was for some unexplained reason greater than for control experiments in oxygen alone. The resulting slope of the best line through the points is as yet accurate only to about 10%. Thus no deductions can be made from the experimental results concerning the magnitude of nitrogen damage in the presence of oxygen.

The K value for oxygen in the presence of cysteine is approximately 30 μM, much higher than without cysteine, even though at pH 5 very little autoxidation would be expected. This can be interpreted as being due either to anoxia caused by the sum of the residual autoxidation at this pH and the radiochemical scavenging of oxygen, or else to protecting of damaged sites in competition with oxygen.

The major effect of N-ethylmaleimide is sensitization of the temperature effect of the postirradiation damage. Thus where there is no temperature effect, as in *Serratia marcescens* in oxygen, then N-ethylmaleimide does not sensitize. Bridges (*25*) reported that N-ethylmaleimide had no action on a *Pseudomonas* when added after irradiation. The results shown in Fig. 7 demonstrate a very small but definite sensitization after irradiation. The difficulty of adding anoxic substances to anoxic irradiated solutions immediately after irradiation is considerable. Gassing the bacterial suspension with as little as 0.1% oxygen after irradiation was found to stop all postirradiation damage after a few minutes. Adding possible protectors directly after irradiation is not yet a reliable way of measuring the postirradiation protection.

By adhering to the strict nitrogen anoxia throughout, the toxic chemical or possibly long-lived radical concentration was built up to such an extent by irradiating the bacterial growth medium that bacteria added after irradiation were rapidly inactivated. The reason for the higher rate of inactivation by adding the bacteria afterward (see Fig. 12) is probably due to the high concentrations of organic constituents in the medium. Normally the bacterial suspension is considerably diluted before irradiation.

The general shape of the survival curves in Fig. 2—namely, a curved line in nitrogen and a straight line in oxygen—is very similar to the survival curves for bacteriophages reported by Bachofer and Pottinger (*26*). In their system bacteriophage in dilute suspension when gassed with nitrogen or hydrogen had a survival curve with a pronounced curvature. When oxygen was used during irradiation the survival curve started along the same line and continued straight so that, at high doses, the phage were protected by oxygen. Butler *et al.* (*27*), studying the radiosensitivity of chymotrypsin at pH 3, found an analogous heat-sensitive postirradiation effect. Oxygen also protects chymotrypsin against radiation damage (*28*). Another striking resemblance between the *Serratia marcescens* postirradiation damage and enzymes in dilute solution is shown by the work of McDonald (*29*), who found that the inactivation of trypsin was continued after the end of irradiation, and that the effect was increased at a higher temperature (and was more rapid after larger doses). Thus components o the bacterial cell are known to be inactivated in a manner now shown to kill the cell itself; but the fact that enzymes behave in this way is not proof that bacteria are killed by damage to their enzymes. Mucopolysaccharides (*30*) and DNA (*31*) also show similar postirradiation effects.

SUMMARY

1. *Serratia marcescens* has been irradiated with 200-kv and 250-kv X-rays under a number of conditions of temperature, dose rate, and pH.

2. The log surviving fraction was plotted against dose so that the slope and hit number of the inactivation curve could be measured in every case.

3. The effect of bubbling the bacterial suspension with the following gases was noted: oxygen, nitrogen, nitric oxide, nitrous oxide, and hydrogen.

4. The effect of the following substances at various concentrations in solution was also noted: glycerol, ethanol, ethylene glycol, cysteine, dimethyl sulfoxide, and *N*-ethylmaleimide.

5. Various combinations of physical conditions, gases, and chemicals were investigated.

6. In a plot of the log surviving fraction against dose, the survival curve in oxygen was found to be a straight line over many powers of 10. In nitrogen the survival curve was not straight.

7. Three types of damage were deduced: damage observed by small doses in nitrogen, additional damage in oxygen, and a temperature-dependent postirradiation damage observed at high doses in nitrogen.

8. Oxygen protects against postirradiation damage. Glycerol and other alcohols protect against damage in both oxygen and nitrogen. *N*-Ethylmaleimide sensitizes the postirradiation type of damage. Cysteine protects against damage in nitrogen and the postirradiation damage but not against damage in oxygen.

ACKNOWLEDGMENTS

I am particularly grateful to Dr. Gray for continuous help and encouragement during the course of this work; also to Mr. J. Steadman and Miss J. Liddon for technical assistance including about 2×10^6 colony counts. Help with the dosimetry from Dr. J. W. Boag and Dr. R. Steele is also gratefully acknowledged.

RECEIVED: July 9, 1962

REFERENCES

1. D. L. DEWEY and L. H. GRAY, The use of the "Hersch Cell" for measurement of oxygen in biological material. *J. Polargraphic Soc.* **7,** 1–11 (1961).
2. G. G. MEYNELL, The effect of sudden chilling on *Escherichia coli. J. Gen. Microbiol.* **19,** 380–389 (1958).
3. T. ALPER and P. HOWARD-FLANDERS, Role of oxygen in modifying the radiosensitivity of *E. coli* B. *Nature* **178,** 978–979 (1956).
4. D. L. DEWEY, Effect of glycerine on the X-ray sensitivity of *Serratia marcescens. Nature* **187,** 1008–1010 (1960).
5. B. A. BRIGGS, Sensitization of *Escherichia coli* to gamma-radiation by *N*-ethylmaleimide. *Nature* **188,** 415–415 (1960).
6. B. A. BRIDGES, The effect of *N*-ethylmaleimide on the radiation sensitivity of bacteria. *J. Gen. Microbiol.* **26,** 467–472 (1961).
7. D. L. DEWEY and J. W. BOAG, Modification of the oxygen effect when bacteria are given large pulses of radiation. *Nature* **183,** 1450–1451 (1959).
8. D. L. DEWEY and J. W. BOAG, Inaktivierung von Bakterien mittels einzelner Elektronenimpulse, *Z. Naturforsch.* **15b,** 372–374 (1960).
9. L. H. GRAY, A method of oxygen assay applied to a study of the removal of dissolved oxygen by cysteine and cysteamine. In *Progress in Radiobiology* (J. S. Mitchell, B. E. Holmes, and C. L. Smith, eds.), pp. 267–278, Oliver & Boyd, Edinburgh, 1956.
10. E. J. HART and R. L. PLATZMAN, Radiation chemistry. In *Mechanisms in Radiobiology* (M. Errera and A. Forssberg, eds.), Vol. 1, pp. 93–257, Academic Press, New York, 1961.
11. P. HOWARD-FLANDERS, Physical and chemical mechanisms in the injury of cells by ionizing radiations. *Advances in Biol. Med. Phys.* **6,** 553–603 (1958).
12. P. HOWARD-FLANDERS, Effect of nitric oxide on the radiosensitivity of bacteria. *Nature* **180,** 1191–1192 (1957).
13. R. L. ERIKSON and W. SZYBALSKI, Molecular radiobiology of human cell lines. 1. Comparative sensitivity to X-rays and ultraviolet light of cells containing halogen-substituted DNA. *Biochem. Biophys. Res. Communs.* **4,** 258–261 (1961).
14. T. H. WOOD, Inhibition of cell division. *Radiation Res. Suppl.* **1,** 332–346 (1959).
15. T. R. MANNEY, T. BRUSTAD, and C. A. TOBIAS, Effects of glycerol and of anoxia on the radiosensitivity of haploid yeasts to densely ionizing particles. University of California Report UCRL-10181, pp. 1–22 (1962).
16. R. B. WEBB, and E. L. POWERS, Glycerol and water effects in bacterial spores and vegetative cells. *Second Intern. Congr. Radiation Res. Abstr.* 42 (1962).
17. E. J. HART, Radiation chemistry of water. *Nucleonics* Special Report, pp. 45–58 (October 1961).
18. T. ALPER, The dependence of chemical protective action on oxygen, as studied with bacteria. *Brit. J. Radiol.* **35,** 361 (1962).
19. J. H. BAXENDALE, The flash photolysis of water and aqueous solutions. *Radiations Research* **17,** 312–326 (1962).
20. J. H. BAXENDALE and G. HUGHES, The X-irradiation of aqueous methanol solutions. Part 1. Reactions in H_2O. *Z. physik. Chem.* (*Frankfurt*) **14,** 306–322 (1958).
21. G. E. ADAMS, J. H. BAXENDALE, and R. D. SEDGWICK, Some radical and molecular yields in the γ-irradiation of some organic liquids. *J. Phys. Chem.* **63,** 854–858 (1959).

22. F. S. DAINTON and D. B. PETERSON, Forms of H and OH produced in the radiolysis of aqueous systems. *Proc. Royal Soc.* **A267,** 443–463 (1962).
23. G. HOTZ, Die kombinierte Schutzwirkung von Cysteamin und glycerin bei rontgenbestrahlten T1-Phagen. *Z. Naturforsch.* **17b,** 37–42 (1962).
24. H. L. KOHN and S. E. GUNTER, Cysteine protection against X-rays and the factor of oxygen tension. *Radiation Res.* **13,** 250–255 (1960).
25. B. A. BRIDGES, The chemical sensitization of *Pseudomonas* species to ionizing radiations. *Radiation Res.* **16,** 232–242 (1962).
26. C. S. BACHOFER and M. A. POTTINGER, Oxygen protection against ionizing radiations. *Science* **119,** 378–379 (1954).
27. J. A. V. BUTLER, A. B. ROBINS, and J. ROTBLAT, The inactivation of α-chymotrypsin by ionizing radiations. *Proc. Roy. Soc.* **A256,** 1–14 (1960).
28. L. K. MEE, Properties of enzymes after irradiation. *Brit. Empire Cancer Campaign Ann. Rept.* **36,** 318–319 (1958).
29. M. R. MCDONALD, The effects of X-rays on dilute solutions of crystalline trypsin: continued inactivation after termination of irradiation. *Brit. J. Radiol.* **27,** 62–63 (1954).
30. H. B. LAMBERTS, Actions of ionizing radiations. 4. Mucopolysaccharides. *Brit. Empire Cancer Campaign Ann. Rept.* **39,** 67–68 (1961).
31. P. ALEXANDER and H. MOROSON, Degradation of DNA by oxidising agents. *Brit. Empire Cancer Campaign Ann. Rept.* **37,** 63–64 (1959).

RADIATION RESEARCH **19**, 88–103 (1963)

Effects of Drugs Alone, or Combined with Refrigeration, in Protecting Female Mice against X-Irradiation-Induced Sterility[1]

A. KATHERINE RUPKEY, RUTH GOLD, ROBERTS RUGH, AND S. C. WANG

Departments of Pharmacology, Radiobiology and School of Public Health, College of Physicians and Surgeons, Columbia University, New York, New York

INTRODUCTION

Protection of animals and tissue against the lethal and sterilizing effects of X-irradiation has been the object of numerous studies. Depressing body temperature before and during exposure has successfully protected newborn and adult mammals against otherwise lethal doses of whole-body irradiation (*1–4*). Parkes (*5*) demonstrated that ovarian transplants irradiated at −79°C "took" better than those irradiated at room temperature.

Certain drugs by themselves—cystamine (Becaptan disulfide) and cysteinamine (β-mercaptoethylamine)—have been shown to possess protective value in at least delaying the onset of sterility in mice (*6, 7*), as well as in reducing their sensitivity to lethal doses of X-irradiation (*8*). Hope (*9*) points out that all radioprotective drugs effective in mice share the characteristic of lowering body temperature, although hypothermia without accompanying anoxia is not protective. Kuskin *et al.* (*10*) demonstrated that neuroplegic drugs such as Hydergine, chlorpromazine, or promethazine, and "lytic cocktails" of these drugs, provided slight protection against lethal X-irradiation dosages. However, in spite of their ability to inhibit temperature-regulating mechanisms and bodily defense mechanisms (*11*), these drugs did not appear to enhance the protective action of refrigeration alone (*10*) when given prior to cooling.

This experiment was designed to ascertain whether Hydergine, chlorpromazine, promethazine, reserpine, urethan, and "lytic cocktails," alone or in combination with refrigeration, protect female mice against sterility induced by whole-body irradiation at dose levels of 25 r, 50 r, 100 r, and 150 r.

[1] This investigation was carried out under a contract with the U. S. Air Force, AF41(657)296, and also by a grant from the National Institute of Neurological Diseases and Blindness, B31(C).

MATERIALS AND METHODS

Experimental Methods

Virgin CF-1 female mice 10 to 12 weeks old and weighing approximately 25 to 30 gm each at the time of X-irradiation were used.The animals were divided into groups of 20. Each group received intraperitoneal injections of one of the drugs or cocktails listed below, or of physiological saline. Ten animals from each group were kept at room temperature (rectal temperature varied from about 37°C for the normal untreated controls to about 31°C for the drug-treated animals), and the other 10 were cooled in a refrigerator freezer to 20°C to 23°C rectal temperature. When the 10 cooled animals' temperatures reached the desired level, which generally took 20 to 60 minutes depending on the drug used, all 20 mice in the group were given a whole-body exposure of 25 r, 50 r, 100 r, or 150 r of X-irradiation, 5 at a time in a perforated circular plastic cage. For each drug or mixture of drugs, a total of approximately 80 mice was used. Irradiation was administered through dual X-ray tubes, each at a distance of 67 cm from the animals. Other physical constants for X-irradiation were: 184 kvp, 30 ma for each tube, 0.28 mm Cu and 0.50 mm Al filtration, HVL 0.6 mm Cu, and dose rate 50 r/min in air.

The drugs and their dosages, for each of the four irradiation levels, were: Hydergine, 0.3 mg/kg (1×) and 0.6 mg/kg (2×); chlorpromazine, 23 mg/kg (1×) and 45 mg/kg (2×); promethazine, 23 mg/kg (1×) and 45 mg/kg (2×); urethan, 0.6 gm/kg; resperine, 3.3 mg/kg—one group X-irradiated 1 hour after injection (1h) and another X-irradiated 16 hours after injection (16h); lytic cocktails: Hydergine (1×)—chlorpromazine (1×), Hydergine (1×)—promethazine (1×), and chlorpromazine (1×)—promethazine (1×). Physiological saline solution was used as the control. All dosages were given in 1 ml of saline solution.

After irradiation, the mice were earmarked for identification, returned to their cages, 5 per cage, and placed in the animal room, where they received water and food ad libitum. Five weeks were allowed for recovery from drug pretreatment and for deaths due to irradiation and handling.[2] All deaths were recorded. At the end of this period a male was placed in each cage and allowed to remain throughout a 40-week observation period. If in any cage no positive pregnancy occurred after 4 weeks, a new male was introduced to guard against the possibility of male sterility. Twice a week observations for deaths, pregnancies, and litters were made and recorded. The young were discarded to allow for optimum frequency in breeding. The mother or mothers of each litter or litters were determined by noting the absence of pregnancy after it had been recorded at the previous observation. When

[2] Deaths occurred during various times of the observation period. Deaths within the first 24 hours are largely due to the drug pretreatment and/or refrigeration. Deaths within the first 30 days might be accounted for by irradiation and/or intercurrent diseases. Occasionally mice were injured or killed through fighting among themselves. Only mice that survived the entire 20-week periods were included for statistical analysis.

more than one litter had been dropped and it was impossible to tell how many young should be assigned to individual mothers, an average was used.

The entire procedure was repeated 7 months later to increase the group size to about 40 females each (approximately 20 in each subgroup) and to compensate for any effect of temperature and humidity on fertility or breeding, since it was impossible to maintain constant atmospheric conditions in the animal room.

Methods of Analysis

Results were tabulated for normal females, for untreated controls, and for each type of pretreatment at each of the four irradiation dose levels. Percentage of pretreatment at each of the four irradiation dose levels. Percentage of fertility and average litter size were calculated for each of ten consecutive 4-week periods. A unit of 4 weeks was chosen after 4 months of observation of normal mice when it was calculated that, on the average, each mouse would have approximately one litter in this time period. Percentage of fertility for each 4-week period was calculated by dividing the number of mice having at least one litter in that period by the number of females present at the beginning of the period. The average litter size for the period was obtained by dividing the total number of young by the total number of litters delivered. At 50 r of irradiation there were some marked differences between the untreated controls and some of the pretreated groups. These data are graphically represented (Fig. 1, *A–N*) and statistically analyzed. For the other levels of irradiation the data were graphically represented only when marked differences were observed (Fig. 2, *A–D*).

Since the above 4-week by 4-week description does not readily lend itself to statistical testing, indices were sought which measure at least roughly the average fertility of each pretreatment group. The measures adopted here, to be defined below, were based on two 20-week periods rather than on the entire 40 weeks of observation. It was clear that the percentage fertility was not uniform throughout the entire 40 weeks; therefore, it was felt that averaging over the entire period might cover up some essential differences between some of the groups.

For each group of mice the following two measures of fertility were compared:

1. Average number of litters per mouse (ANL) over the first 20 weeks (ANL-1) and over the second 20 weeks (ANL-2) was defined as the total number of litters delivered by those mice in the group which survived the entire 20 weeks in question divided by the number of such mice. To compare two such averages, a normal test was used (see *12*, p. 119). A difference between two such averages was considered significant at approximately the 1% or 2% level if it was larger than 2.58 or 2.33 times its estimated standard error, respectively.

2. Average litter size (ALS) for the first 20 weeks (ALS-1) and for the second 20 weeks (ALS-2) was calculated by dividing the total number of young delivered of mice in the group which survived the entire 20 weeks in question by the total

number of litters produced by such mice. The comparisons of two such means were made by the Student *t*-test, except for comparisons involving the ANL-1 of the normals. For the latter comparisons, the average of the normal group was considered as a universe value for the first 20-week period (see *12*, p. 115). In all cases significance at levels of 1% or 2% was again indicated. It should be noted that the symbol ALS is used for average litter size only when calculated over these extended time periods.

In judging the efficacy of pretreatment at a particular irradiation level, any of these measures for the pretreatment group may be simultaneously compared with the corresponding measure for the normals, controls, and cooled controls. Since each individual comparison is made at a level of significance of at most 2%, the combined significance level is at most 6%. This means that the probability of declaring

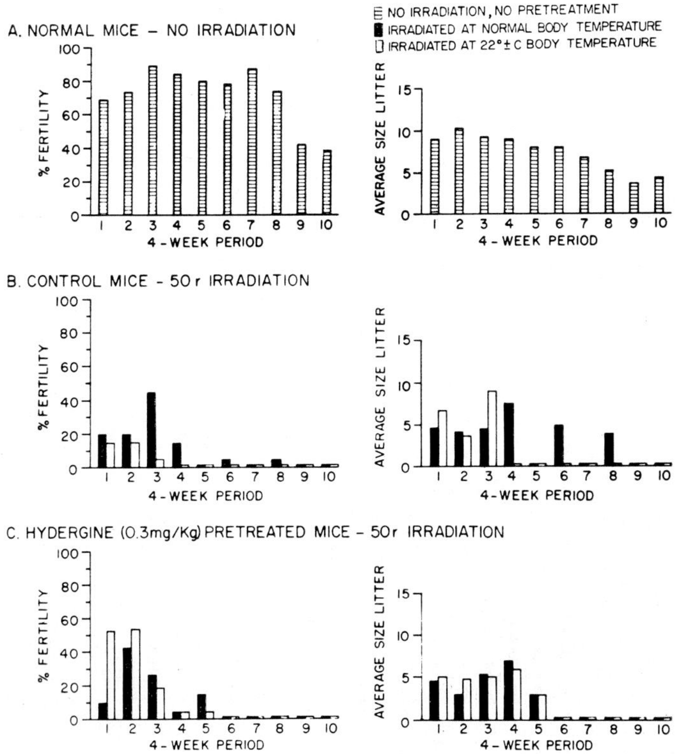

FIG. 1 A–C

FIG. 1. Percentage fertility and average size of litter in each 4-week period for representative groups at 50-r irradiation level. (Slight elevations on the abscissae indicate 0% of fertility, or no litter delivered.)

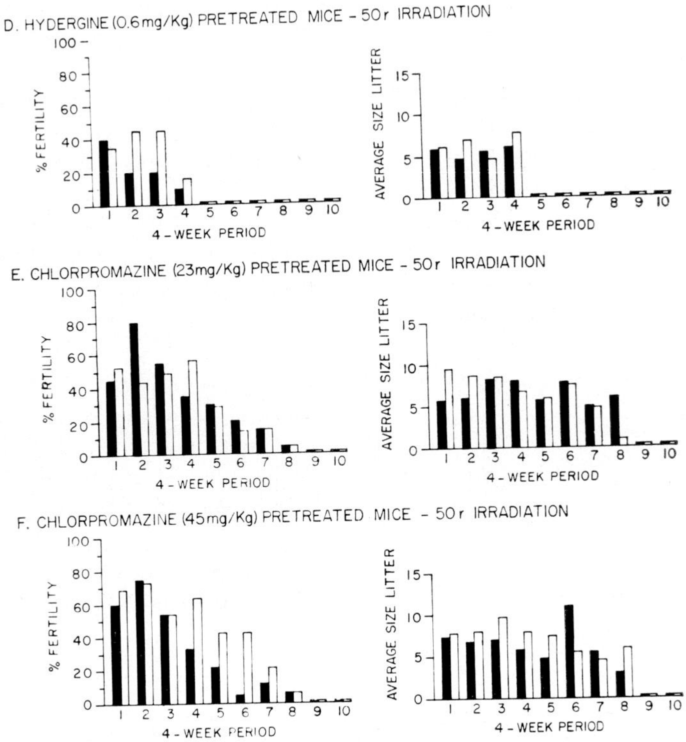

Fig. 1 D–F

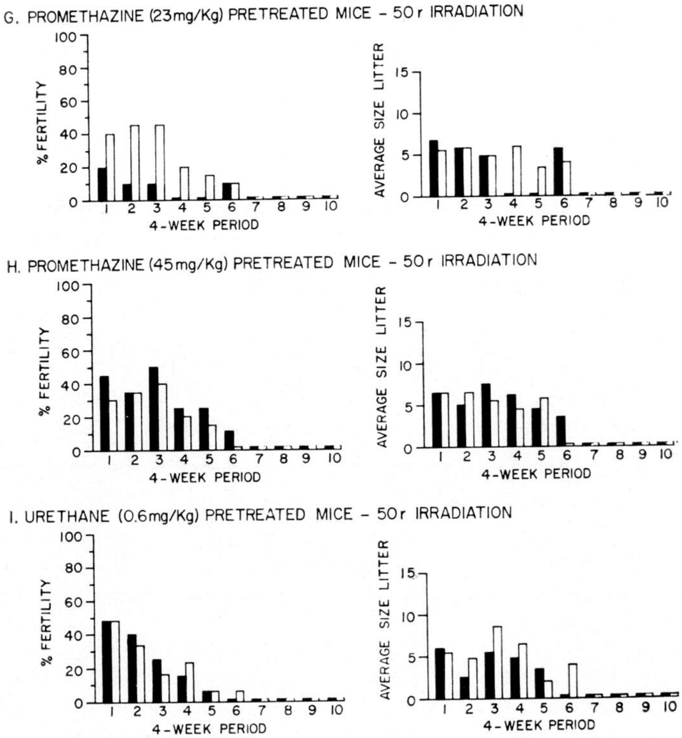

Fig. 1 G–I

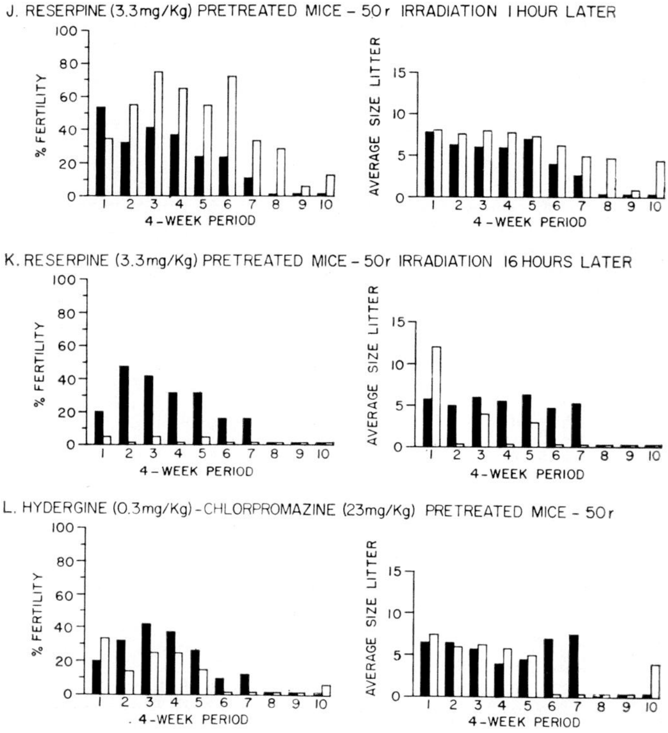

Fig. 1 J–L

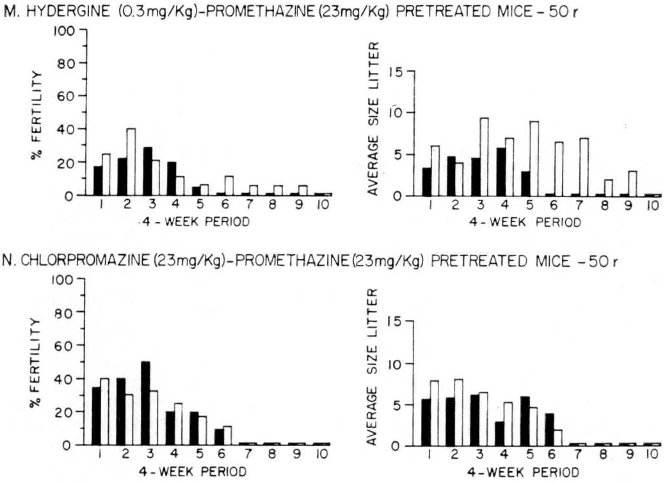

Fig. 1 M–N

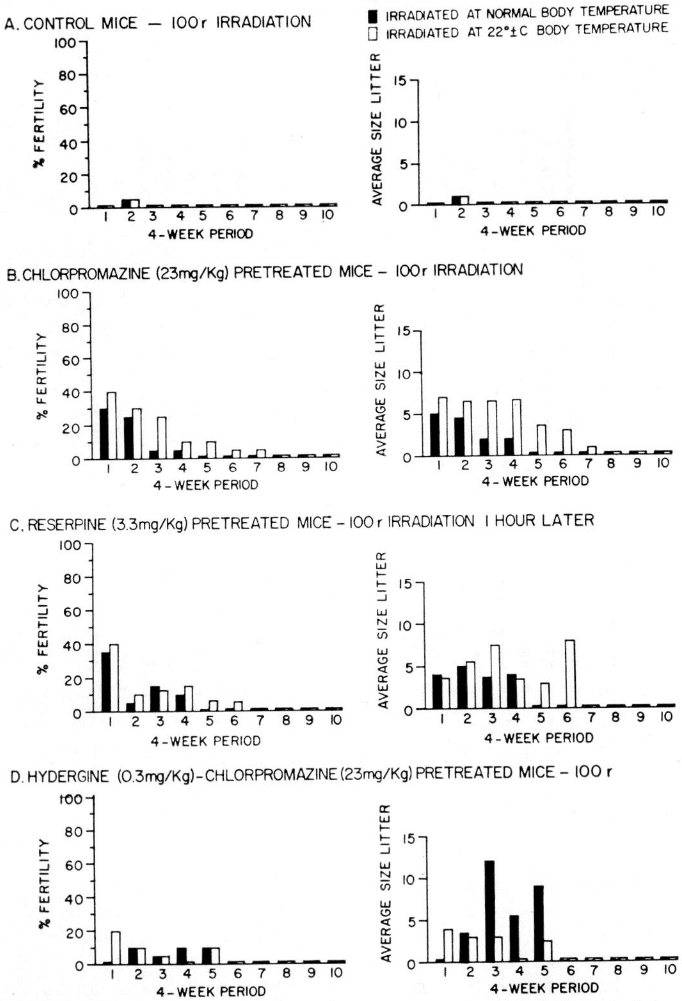

FIG. 2. Percentage fertility and average size of litter in each 4-week period for representative groups at 100-r irradiation level.

at least one of the differences significant when in fact they are all zero is at most 6%.

RESULTS

Mice receiving no irradiation (normal mice). Percentage fertility in this group of 45 normal animals ranged from 69% to 89% through the eighth 4-week period (animals approximately 48 weeks old), and dropped off to 43% and 39% in the ninth and tenth periods (see Fig. 1*A*). The average size of litter ranged from 6.7 to

10.1 (individual range 1 to 17) over the first seven periods and then dropped off to 5.1, 3.8, and 4.6 in the eighth, ninth and tenth periods, respectively. Over the first 20 weeks the ANL-1 was 4.6 (Table I), and in the second 20-week period the ANL-2 dropped to an average of 3.6 per mouse (Table II). The corresponding ALS-1 was 9.0 (Table III), and ALS-2 was 6.0.

TABLE I

AVERAGE NUMBER OF LITTERS PER MOUSE OVER FIRST 20-WEEK PERIOD OF MATING (ANL-1) AFTER 50 ROENTGENS OF X-IRRADIATION

Treatment	*C (denotes cooling)*	*Number of mice observed*	*Number of litters delivered*	*Average number of litters per mouse over 20 weeks (ANL-1)*	*Estimated standard deviation*	*Significance of average[a] compared with:*		
						Normal	*Control*	*Control cooled*
Normal (no irradiation)		45	209	4.64	1.45	—	1%	1%
Control		20	24	1.20	1.40	1%	—	2%
	C	20	7	0.35	0.49	1%	2%	—
Hydergine, 0.3 mg/kg (1×)		19	20	1.05	1.55	1%	ns	ns
	C	21	24	1.14	1.01	1%	ns	1%
Hydergine, 0.6 mg/kg (2×)		20	18	0.90	0.79	1%	ns	1%
	C	15	18	1.20	1.52	1%	ns	ns
Chlorpromazine, 23 mg/kg (1×)		20	56	2.80	1.94	1%	1%	1%
	C	21	51	2.43	1.66	1%	2%	1%
Chlorpromazine, 45 mg/kg (2×)		19	48	2.53	1.50	1%	1%	1%
	C	19	67	3.53	2.12	ns	1%	1%
Promethazine, 23 mg/kg (1×)		20	9	0.45	0.69	1%	ns	ns
	C	20	36	1.80	1.57	1%	ns	1%
Promethazine, 45 mg/kg (2×)		20	41	2.05	1.90	1%	ns	1%
	C	20	30	1.50	1.43	1%	ns	1%
Urethan, 0.6 gm/kg		18	27	1.50	1.04	1%	ns	1%
	C	18	23	1.28	1.71	1%	ns	ns
Reserpine, 3.3 mg/kg (1h)		19	38	2.00	2.19	1%	ns	1%
	C	19	63	3.32	1.80	1%	1%	1%
Reserpine, 3.3 mg/kg (16h)		19	42	2.21	2.11	1%	ns	1%
	C	21	3	0.14	0.36	1%	1%	ns
Hydergine (1×) and chlorpromazine (1×)		19	33	1.74	1.73	1%	ns	1%
	C	19	24	1.26	1.37	1%	ns	1%
Hydergine (1×) and promethazine (1×)		20	21	1.05	1.47	1%	ns	ns
	C	18	21	1.17	1.65	1%	ns	ns
Chlorpromazine (1×) and promethazine (1×)		20	36	1.80	1.99	1%	ns	1%
	C	19	29	1.53	2.01	1%	ns	2%

[a] ns = no significance, and 1% and 2% = significance at 1% and 2% levels, respectively. See Methods for tests used.

TABLE II

AVERAGE NUMBER OF LITTERS PER MOUSE OVER SECOND 20-WEEK PERIOD OF MATING (ANL-2) FOR SELECTED GROUPS AFTER 50 ROENTGENS OF X-IRRADIATION

Treatment	*C (denotes cooling)*	*Number of mice observed*	*Number of litters delivered*	*Average number of litters per mouse over 20 weeks (ANL-2)*	*Estimated standard deviation*	*Significance of average compared with:*		
						Normal	*Control*	*Control cooled*
Normal (no irradiation)		38	135	3.55	1.43	—	1%	1%
Control	C	19	2	0.11	0.46	1%	—	ns
		19	0	0.00	—	1%	ns	—
Chlorpromazine, 23 mg/kg	C	18	9	0.50	0.92	1%	ns	ns
(1×)		20	7	0.35	0.67	1%	ns	2%
Chlorpromazine, 45 mg/kg	C	16	5	0.31	1.01	1%	ns	ns
(2×)		18	14	0.78	1.11	1%	2%	1%
Reserpine, 3.3 mg/kg (1h)	C	18	6	0.33	0.59	1%	ns	2%
		16	26	1.63	1.50	1%	1%	1%
Reserpine, 3.3 mg/kg (16h)	C	19	6	0.32	0.58	1%	ns	2%
		19	0	0.00	—	1%	ns	ns

[a] ns = no significance, and 1% and 2% = significance at 1% and 2% levels, respectively. See Methods for tests used.

TABLE III

AVERAGE SIZE OF LITTERS OVER FIRST 20-WEEK PERIOD OF MATING (ALS-1) FOR SELECTED GROUPS AFTER 50 ROENTGENS OF X-IRRADIATION

Treatment	*C (denotes cooling)*	*Number of litters delivered*	*Total number of young*	*Average litter size (ALS-1)*	*Estimated standard deviation*	*Significance of average compared with:*		
						Normal	*Control*	*Control cooled*
Normal (no irradiation)		209	1878	8.99	2.84	—	1%	1%
Control	C	24	119	4.96	0.60	1%	—	ns
		7	40	5.71	1.06	1%	ns	—
Chlorpromazine, 23 mg/kg	C	56	375	6.70	0.37	1%	ns	ns
(1×)		51	391	7.67	0.43	1%	1%	ns
Chlorpromazine, 45 mg/kg	C	48	314	6.54	0.34	1%	2%	ns
(2×)		67	547	8.16	0.39	ns	1%	ns
Reserpine, 3.3 mg/kg	C	38	247	6.50	0.38	1%	ns	ns
(1h)		63	473	7.50	0.30	1%	1%	ns

[a] ns = no significance, and 1% and 2% = significance at 1% and 2% levels, respectively. See Methods for tests used.

Mice receiving 25 r of X-irradiation. The calculations on the various measures of fertility are not presented in detail because of the lack of striking differences among the various groups at this low irradiation level. However, some differences between groups were statistically significant. For example, the ANL-1 and ANL-2 for the noncooled controls were significantly lower than the corresponding values for the normal mice.

In the pretreatment groups receiving this level of X-irradiation, only chlorpromazine (2×) showed a consistent effect as measured by the ANL in that both ANL-1 and ANL-2 were significantly higher than the corresponding values observed for the noncooled as well as for the cooled controls.

Mice receiving 50 r of X-irradiation. Figure 1 graphically depicts the percentage fertilities and average size of litter in each 4-week period for normal mice, for controls irradiated at 50 r, and for each pretreatment group irradiated at this level, with and without refrigeration. The ANL-1 figures for all groups are shown in Table I, and the ANL-2 and ASL-1 of groups showing significant differences in Tables II and III, respectively. ANL-1, ANL-2, and ALS-1 figures were analyzed statistically for all groups. Tests were not done for ALS-2 because of the small numbers of litters.

Control mice irradiated at normal body temperature, when compared with normal mice, showed a marked decrease in percentage fertility—range 15% to 45%—in the first four of the 4-week periods. From the fifth through the tenth periods, all mice were sterile except for the delivery of one litter each in the sixth and eighth periods. When control mice were cooled, percentage fertility ranged from 5% to 15% in the first three periods, and all mice were sterile thereafter (Fig. 1*B*). With the ANL taken as an index, 50 r of irradiation decreased the average from 4.6 (normal) to 1.2 (noncooled) and 0.4 (cooled) over the first 20 weeks (Table I), and from 3.6 (normal) to 0.1 (noncooled) and 0.0 (cooled) over the second 20 weeks (Table II). These irradiated control figures were significantly lower than those for normal mice. Also the control ANL-2 figures, whether irradiated at normal body temperature or cooled to 22°C, were significantly different from one another. However, the ANL-1 for cooled controls was significantly lower than that of noncooled controls. The ALS-1 and ALS-2 for each control group were also smaller than the corresponding measures for normal mice—5.0 (noncooled) and 5.7 (cooled) compared with 9.0 (normal) (Table III), and 4.5 and 0.0 compared with 6.0. The ALS-1 for both control groups was significantly lower than for the normal. The differences between noncooled and cooled controls were not significant.

Of all pretreatment groups, only the ANL-1 of chlorpromazine (2×) with cooling approached that of normal mice (3.5 compared with 4.6) in that these two numbers are not significantly different (Table I). Chlorpromazine (1×) and (2×), both alone and with cooling, and reserpine (1h) with cooling were the only groups with ANL-1's significantly higher than those of noncooled controls. Reserpine

(16h) with cooling had an ANL-1 significantly lower than that of noncooled controls. The low ANL-1 figure for the cooled control group made detailed presentation of these results meaningless.

Over the second 20 weeks (Table II), only mice pretreated with chlorpromazine (2×) and cooling and with reserpine (1h) and cooling showed ANL-2 figures significantly higher than those of both control groups, and those which received chlorpromazine (1×) with cooling or reserpine (1h) and (16h) alone showed figures significantly higher than the cooled but not the noncooled controls.

Mice pretreated with chlorpromazine (1×) with cooling, chlorpromazine (2×) alone and with cooling, and reserpine (1h) with cooling were the only groups to show an ALS-1 significantly greater than controls irradiated at normal body temperature (Table III). No pretreatment group had an ALS-1 significantly different from that of the cooled controls.

Mice receiving 100 r of X-irradiation. All control mice receiving this dose of irradiation, with and without cooling, were sterile throughout the entire observation period except for 1 mouse in each group having one litter (size, 1 young each) in the second 4-week period. The ANL-1 for both control groups was 0.1, compared with 4.6 for normal mice.

Groups of mice pretreated with chlorpromazine (1×) alone and with cooling and reserpine (1h) alone and with cooling showed the highest percentage fertilities over the longest period of time, when compared with all other groups irradiated at this level (Fig. 2, *B* and *C*). Pretreatment with each of the two drugs alone allowed for 30% and 35% fertility, respectively, in the first period, falling off to 5% and 10% in the fourth period, and an ANL-1 of 0.7 for both types of pretreatment. When cooling was also employed, the groups showed 39% and 40% fertility in the first period, with fertility continuing through the sixth and seventh periods (only two litters delivered at this irradiation level after the first 20 weeks). The only other pretreatment that afforded some protection but not so pronounced as by chlorpromazine (1×) and reseprine (1h) was the Hydergine—chlorpromazine cocktail.

Mice receiving 150 r of X-irradiation. All control mice receiving this high dose of whole-body irradiation were sterile throughout the period of observation. Reserpine (1h) alone was the only pretreatment group in which there was 10% fertility in the first period, and 1 mouse (which did not have a litter in the first period) continued to have litters of 3 young or more through the third period. Reserpine (1h) with cooling was the only group in which 4 different mice had litters of 3 or more (two having litters in the first period and two in the second 10% each period). Other groups pretreated with chlorpromazine (2×) alone and with cooling, reserpine (16h) with cooling, the Hydergine–chlorpromazine cocktail with cooling, and the chlorpromazine–promethazine cocktail with cooling showed 10% to 15% fertilities with litters of 3 or more in either the first or second 4-week period.

DISCUSSION

Under the conditions of our study, radioprotection is taken to mean a delay in the onset of sterility due to X-irradiation and/or a lesser reduction in litter size in the mice that remain fertile than occurs in unprotected mice. It should be noted that, although our findings generally confirmed those of Rugh and Wolff (*13*), our results on the average litter size during the fertile period differ from theirs. Whereas they observed fertility to be an all-or-none phenomenon, we noted that average litter sizes of irradiated mice were significantly smaller than those of normal mice, and that pretreatment with refrigeration and/or drugs sometimes not only delayed sterility but also increased the average litter size compared with animals receiving no pretreatment. Our findings are best considered under two major headings: (1) the effect of hypothermia produced by refrigeration alone, on X-irradiation-induced sterility in female mice; and (2) the effect of drug pretreatment, either alone or combined with refrigeration, on sterility caused by X-irradiation.

1. Our results indicate that at the 100-r and 150-r levels the effect of X-irradiation was so severe that it was not altered by refrigeration. At the 50-r level, hypothermia induced by refrigeration alone did not protect female mice from the sterilizing effect of X-irradiation and, if anything, might have further sensitized the animal. In the first 20-week period, the average number of litters per mouse was significantly smaller than that with animals irradiated at normal body temperature. However, average litter size was slightly increased, although not at a significant level. At the 25-r level, refrigeration prior to X-irradiation afforded some protection against sterility in at least the first 5 to 25 weeks after exposure. Average litter size was significantly larger than in mice irradiated at normal body temperature but was not significantly different from that in normal, unexposed mice. The average number of litters per mouse was also not significantly different from normal and was higher than for noncooled irradiated mice, although not at a significant level. In the second 20 weeks of mating, however, the average number of litters per mouse over the 20-week period was somewhat lower than that for noncooled controls, although the average litter size was still larger than that of noncooled controls. These were not significant differences but indicated a trend which might support Guthrie (*14*) in his assertion that radioprotection delays the premature aging of the ovaries.

Hypothermia has been an effective radioprotective agent in delaying death in survival studies. Hornsey (*4*), Kuskin *et al.* (*10*), Storer and Hempelmann (*3*), and Hajdukovic (*15*), among others, have presented evidence that the LD_{50} and $LD_{50(30)}$ are considerably increased when animals are refrigerated before X-irradiation. To our knowledge, there has not yet been any report of an attempt to apply this principle to a study concerned with the sterility resulting from whole-body X-irradiation. Parkes (*5*) worked on ovarian grafts and found that they "took" better and had a longer survival time when irradiated at a temperature of −79°C. However, in histological examinations he found no ova and could therefore draw no conclusions as to whether they would be afforded any protection in these extreme conditions.

It is interesting that refrigeration alone did not exert a radioprotective effect at sterilizing dose levels, except perhaps at the 25-r level, in the face of such strong evidence for its effectiveness at lethal dose levels. An explanation or evaluation of this apparent contradiction awaits the determination of the mechanism of protective action of refrigeration. It is to be noted here that animals were hyperactive for a long period of time in the process of refrigeration. Undoubtedly the sympathoadrenal system is activated as part of the defense mechanism on exposure to stress. Whether this is beneficial or detrimental to the irradiated animal is difficult to foretell.

2. Our results demonstrate that, of all types of pretreatment with drugs alone, chlorpromazine and reserpine clearly showed the most consistent radioprotective effect in female mice, especially those receiving 50 r and 100 r of X-irradiation. This is seen both in delaying the onset of sterility and in increasing the litter size during the fertile period as compared with unprotected irradiated mice. The use of a double dose of chlorpromazine, 45 mg/kg (2×), however, was not consistent in improving fertility. At the 50-r and 100-r levels the single dose level, 23 mg/kg (1×), was generally more effective, although at the 25-r level, chlorpromazine, 45 mg/kg (2×), was more effective at least in respect to average number of litters per mouse. At 100 r, reserpine, 3.3 mg/kg, was most effective when the animals were X-irradiated only 1 hour (1h) after injection when compared with a 16-hour (16h) delay between injection and irradiation. This observation, however, was not supported at 25-r and 50-r levels, where differences in reaction were small.

Cooling in combination with chlorpromazine, 45 mg/kg (2×), and reserpine, 3.3 mg/kg (1h), seems further to increase the radioprotective effect of the drugs in both measurements of fertility (except ALS-2 pretreated with chlorpromazine, 45 mg/kg) at the 50-r level. At effective dose levels both alone and with cooling, these drugs were among the few that permitted the delivery of any litters at the 150-r irradiation level and gave the most effective protection at the 100-r level. There was, however, no clear-cut pattern of enhanced protection when cooling was administered in conjunction with the drug.

Other types of pretreatment exerted some protective effect at specific irradiation levels (for instance, the Hydergine-chlorpromazine cocktail at 100 r and the chlorpromazine-promethazine cocktail at the 25-r level), but their performance was not consistent enough to merit detailed consideration. The effect of cooling in combination with other specific drugs was also not consistent, and therefore no generalization could be drawn concerning its over-all effectiveness.

Drugs have been demonstrated to be effective against both lethal and sterilizing doses of X-irradiation. Mandl (7) demonstrated that pretreatment with β-mercaptoethylamine (cysteinamine) partially prevented the rapid decrease of primordial oöcytes due to X-irradiation, and Rugh and Wolff (*6*) showed that both cystamine and cysteinamine delayed the onset of sterility in mice which received 50 r of X-irradiation.

Kuskin *et al.* (*10*) used some of the same drugs we have, both alone and in combination with refrigeration, in a study of the survival rate. They concluded that the refrigeration and not the drug administered was the main factor in increasing the survival rate. On the other hand, Hydergine, chlorpromazine, or promethazine in combination with cooling did substantially increase the survival percentage when compared with the survival rate of all cooled groups together, indicating drugs afforded additional protection. It is is difficult to account for our results by this explanation, since even in the case of reserpine (1h) at 50 r, where a combination of the drug and cooling did considerably increase fertility in both respects as compared with the drug alone, the drug alone was still more effective than cooling alone. In our study, the drug pretreatment alone was often as effective and sometimes more effective than the drug combined with refrigeration. Kuskin *et al.* (*10*) also found a slight protective value in the drugs alone and attributed this to the small drop in body temperature effected by Hydergine, chlorpromazine, reserpine, and lytic cocktails.

The primary concern of these experiments was to determine whether the drugs used, either alone or in combination with refrigeration, would act as protective agents against sterilizing X-irradiation dosages. A great deal more work must be done to determine the nature of damage as well as the mechanism of action of the protection afforded. Proposed hypotheses of reducing tissue sensitivity to the damaging effects of X-rays include subsequent lowering of metabolic rate due to hypothermia (*4, 8, 15, 16*) and hypoxia (*2, 3, 9, 17, 18*), or combinations of these factors. It would be difficult to say through which of these mechanisms the drugs used in this study operate. It has been suggested that X-irradiation causes sterilization through destroying the maturing ova (*19*), reducing the number of primary follicles (*13, 20*), inducing premature aging of the ovaries (*14*), or producing hormonal imbalance which results in the production of ovarian tumor (*21*). Protection against X-irradiation sterility could conceivably be achieved through amelioration of one or more of these effects of X-irradiation.

It should be noted that the litters produced by any of the irradiated mice may carry X-irradiation effects of both genetic and developmental significance, but this was not investigated. The only conclusion is that productive time and litter size during this period were increased or extended by certain types of pretreatment.

SUMMARY AND CONCLUSION

Female CF-1 mice were irradiated over the whole body surface at 25 r, 50 r, 100 r, or 150 r. These mice were pretreated with Hydergine, 0.3 mg/kg and 0.6 mg/kg; chlorpromazine, 23 mg/kg and 45 mg/kg; promethazine, 23 mg/kg and 45 mg/kg; urethan 0.6 gm/kg; reserpine, 3.3 mg/kg; various combinations of these drugs; and physiological saline solution as control. One-half of these pretreated groups were additionally cooled by refrigeration.

Our results indicate that, of all types of drug pretreatment, chlorpromazine and reserpine clearly showed the most consistent radioprotective effect on fertility, especially at the level of 50 r and 100 r of X-irradiation. Refrigeration appears to afford additional radioprotection. The radioprotection is evidenced by increases both in rate of fertility and in litter size during the fertile period.

ACKNOWLEDGMENT

We wish to express our gratitude to Dr. Agnes P. Berger of the School of Public Health for her suggestions on the statistical treatment of the data.

RECEIVED: August 27, 1962

REFERENCES

1. L. H. HEMPELMANN, T. T. TRUJILLO, and N. P. KNOWLTON, JR., The effect of lethal doses of X-rays on chilled and thyroidectomized animals. *Nuclear Sci. Abstr.* **3,** 46 (1949).
2. A. LACASSAGNE, Chute de la sensibilité aux rayons X chez la souris nouveau-née en état d'asphyxie. *Compt. rend. acad. sci.* **215,** 231 (1942).
3. J. B. STORER and L. H. HEMPELMANN, Hypothermia and increased survival rate of infant mice irradiated with X-rays. *Am. J. Physiol.* **171,** 341–348 (1952).
4. S. HORNSEY, Protection from whole-body X-irradiation afforded to adult mice by reducing the body temperature. *Nature* **178,** 87 (1956).
5. A. S. PARKES, Radiation sensitivity of ovarian tissue at −79°C. *Nature* **176,** 1216–1217 (1955).
6. ROBERTS RUGH and JOAN WOLFF, Evidence of some chemical protection of mouse ovary against X-irradiation sterilization. *Radiation Res.* **7,** 184–189 (1957).
7. A. M. MANDL, The effect of β-mercaptoethylamine on the sensitivity of oöcytes to X-irradiation. *Proc. Roy. Soc.* **B150,** 72–77 (1959).
8. H. M. PATT, D. E. SMITH, E. B. TYREE, and R. L. STRAUBE, Further studies on modification of sensitivity to X-rays by cysteine. *Proc. Soc. Exptl. Biol. Med.* **73,** 18 (1950).
9. D. B. HOPE, Radio-protective substances and hypothermia. *Brit. J. Radiol.* **31,** 339 (1958).
10. SONDRA M. KUSKIN, S. C. WANG, and ROBERTS RUGH, Protective effect of artificially induced 'hibernation' against lethal doses of whole body X-irradiation in CF_1 male mice. *Am. J. Physiol.* **196,** 1211 (1959).
11. H. LABORIT, *Resistance et soumission en physiobiologis. "L'hibernation artificielle"*, Masson, Paris, 1954.
12. W. J. DIXON and F. J. MASSEY, JR., *Introduction to Statistical Analysis,* McGraw-Hill Book Company, New York, 1957.
13. ROBERTS RUGH and JOAN WOLFF, X-Irradiation sterilization of the female mouse. *Fertility and Sterility* **7,** 546 (1956).
14. M. J. GUTHRIE, Tumorigenesis in ovaries of mice after X-irradiation. *Cancer* **11,** 1226–1235 (1958).
15. S. HAJDUKOVIC, Modification de la radiosensibilité du rat par hypothermie profonde. *Acta Radiol.* **44,** 249 (1955).
16. B. M. ALLEN, O. A. SCHJEIDE, and L. B. HOCHWALD, The influence of temperature upon the

destruction of hematopoietic cells of tadpoles by X-irradiation. *J. Cellular Comp. Physiol.* **38,** 69 (1951).

17. J. B. KAHN, JR., Modification of sensitivity to X-radiation by morphine sulfate. *Proc. Soc. Exptl. Biol. Med.* **78,** 486 (1951).
18. A. HOLLAENDER, W. K. BAKER, and E. H. ANDERSON, Effect of oxygen tension and certain chemicals on the X-ray sensitivity of mutation production and survival. *Cold Spring Harbor Symposia Quant. Biol.* **16,** 315–326 (1951).
19. L. B. RUSSELL and W. L. RUSSELL, The sensitivity of different stages in oögenesis to the radiation induction of dominant lethals and other changes in the mouse. In *Progress in Radiobiology* (J. S. Mitchell, B. E. Holmes, and C. L. Smith, eds.), pp. 187–195, Oliver & Boyd, Edinburgh, 1956.
20. E. F. OAKBERG, Irradiation damage to animals and its effect on their reproductive capacity. *J. Dairy Sci. Suppl.* **43,** 54–67 (1960).
21. J. FURTH, Relation of pregnancies to induction of ovarian tumors by X-rays. *Proc. Soc. Exptl. Biol. Med.* **71,** 274–277 (1949).

RADIATION RESEARCH 19, 104–119 (1963)

Comparative Kinetics of Ca^{47} and Sr^{85} in Man[1]

S. H. COHN, S. W. LIPPINCOTT, E. A. GUSMANO,
AND J. S. ROBERTSON

Medical Research Center, Brookhaven National Laboratory, Upton, New York

INTRODUCTION

In studies of skeletal metabolism, the radionuclide Sr^{85} is frequently employed as a tracer for calcium on the basis that the chemical similarity of these two elements produces correspondingly similar metabolic responses. In certain processes, however, the two elements are handled discriminatively. For example, there is preferential absorption of calcium over strontium by the intestinal wall, and preferential elimination of Sr over Ca by the kidneys. Further, some evidence has been adduced which indicates that discrimination may also occur at the level of bone. Although this has not been established conclusively, crystallographic studies do indicate that Sr cannot easily substitute for Ca in the bone lattice because of the size of the Sr ion (*1*).

The conditions under which Sr may be used as a tracer in order to characterize Ca metabolism in bone remains to be determined more precisely. Such a study necessitates a delineation of both the qualitative and the quantitative differences in the skeletal metabolism of Ca and Sr. The problem may be divided into two parts. The first situation is the short-term study (up to approximately 30 days) which is characterized by the rapid equilibration of Sr and Ca among blood, soft tissue, and bone, and by the subsequent rapid loss of Ca and Sr from bone which must follow the loss from the body. This study is the subject of the present paper. The second is the long-term study, which is characterized chiefly by the very slow loss of Ca and Sr from bone that occurs in remodeling as a result of resorption, and by slow exchange between bone and plasma. This long-term study is the subject of a separate paper (*2*).

Measurements of whole-body retention of Sr^{85} and Ca^{47} were made with a whole-body gamma spectrometer. Simultaneous measurements of the tracers made on the excreta and on samples of plasma yielded data necessary for the determination of the skeletal accretion rate and exchange capacity. The kinetics of skeletal metabo-

[1] Research supported by the U.S. Atomic Energy Commission.

lism could then be characterized in terms of accretion, exchange, biological loss (resorption and "long-term" exchange), and excretion.

METHODS

Six patients with different clinical conditions reflecting various degrees of skeletal involvement were studied. A brief description of the patients and their conditions is presented in Table I. These patients were all ambulatory. They remained on the metabolic ward for the duration of the study.

Administration of Tracers

A saline solution (pH = 5) of 20 μc of high specific activity $Ca^{47}Cl_2$ and 5 μc of $Sr^{85}Cl_2$ was administered by intravenous injection.

Collection and Treatment of Plasma and Urine

Blood samples (10 ml) were collected at 4, 12, and 24 hours, and on days 2, 3, 4, 5, 7, and 10 after administration of the tracers. Twenty-four-hour urine and stool samples were collected from each patient for the 10 days after administration of the isotopes.

Radioactive Assay

Plasma samples were counted in a deep-well NaI (T1) scintillation counter used in connection with a 100-channel pulse-height analyzer. Urine and stool samples were diluted up to a constant volume and counted under the 8 × 4-inch crystal detector in the whole-body counter. All samples were counted with a standard under

TABLE I
CLINICAL DESCRIPTION OF PATIENTS

Patient	*Sex*	*Age*	*Weight (kg)*	*Diagnosis*	*Skeletal survey*
FOR	F	73	55.4	Essential hypertension	Minimal osteoarthritis in cervical and dorsal spine; otherwise normal for age period
QUI	F	53	45.4	Scleroderma	Minimal to moderate osteoarthritis vertebrae, distal phalanges of hands show some minimal osteoporosis; otherwise normal
FUH	M	30	58.6	Chylous ascites	Normal for age period
MAC	F	58	52.6	Multiple myeloma	Extensive involvement of skeleton with myelomatous lesions
BEE	F	66	74.4	Multiple myeloma	Skeletal involvement is minimal to moderate
LER	M	56	58.8	Multiple myeloma	Minimal skeletal involvement

identical geometry. Appropriate corrections were made for the Compton contribution of the Ca^{47} to the Sr^{85} photopeak activity.

Whole-Body Counting Technique

The whole-body retention of Sr^{85} and Ca^{47} was measured in the BNL whole-body gamma spectrometer. The patients were counted daily for the first 10 days, then approximately twice a week for the following 20 days. Details of this whole-body counter, its calibration, and counting statistics have been presented (*2, 3*). After the first few days subsequent to administration of Sr^{85}, the whole-body retention measurements agreed within a few per cent with the retention values derived from the excretion data of 6 patients for periods up to 52 days (*2*).

Principles of Isotope Technique

The mathematical device developed by Bauer *et al.* (*4, 5*) to determine skeletal accretion rate and exchange capacity was employed. (For definition of accretion and exchange used in Bauer's formulation, see final paragraph of Appendix.) Two assumptions underlie the theory on which the technique is constructed. First, it is assumed that the Ca^{47}/Ca^{40} ratio of the exchangeable bone fraction (E) and of the plasma come rapidly into equilibrium. Second, it is assumed that the Ca^{47} and the Ca^{40} are deposited in slowly exchanging bone by the process of accretion, in the same proportions that they simultaneously occur in plasma. At sufficiently short intervals after administration, the amount of Ca^{47} that is resorbed can be ignored, as resorption at this time occurs in areas other than those of bone formation.

The total amount of Ca^{47} in skeleton at any time after administration can be expressed in the following way:

$$Ca^{47}{}_T = Ca^{47}{}_E + Ca^{47}{}_A \tag{1}$$

where

$Ca^{47}{}_T$ = total Ca^{47} in body (skeleton).
$Ca^{47}{}_E$ = amount of Ca^{47} in rapidly exchanging compartment.
$Ca^{47}{}_A$ = amount of Ca^{47} in slowly exchanging compartment.

$$Ca^{47}{}_E = ES \tag{2}$$

where

S = specific activity of plasma.
E = amount of Ca in rapidly exchanging compartment as measured by Ca^{47}.

$$Ca_A^{47}(t) = A \int_0^t S(t)\, dt \tag{3}$$

where

A = accretion rate of Ca as measured by Ca^{47}.

t = interval of time between Ca^{47} administration and observation.

$\int_0^t S(t)\,dt$ = integrated specific activity of plasma from $t = 0$ to time (t).

The formulas above apply equally for Sr^{85}. The integrated specific activity of the plasma

$$\left(\int_0^t S(t)\,dt\right)$$

was obtained graphically (by use of a planimeter) from the plotted data. Specific activity values, $S(t)$, were taken from the plotted data after the curves were smoothed by hand. The value of $Ca^{47}{}_{T'}$ was derived from the curves of retention of the whole body.

Observations made at two different time intervals after administration (5 and 10 days) yielded two equations with two unknowns, A and E, which could then be solved simultaneously. An interval of 5 days after administration for the first reading in this computation increases the probability of equilibration of the tracer in the exchangeable compartment. It is assumed that the accretion rate and the exchange capacity in this computation are constant over the time period under consideration.

RESULTS

Plasma Clearance

There is a rapid initial fall in the levels of Sr^{85} and Ca^{47} in the plasma, reflecting the mixing of the tracers and equilibration with a large, exchangeable Ca space. The exchangeable compartment, which is in equilibrium with the plasma, consists of the extravascular space, soft tissue, and the exchangeable compartment of the bone itself. The activity of each tracer in this space achieves a maximum and then declines. Over the period from 2.5 days to 10 days after administration, the plasma clearance data can be approximated with a single exponential term. The values of the rate constants for this exponential term for Sr^{85} and Ca^{47} obtained from each of the patients are presented in Table II. The average value for Sr^{85} disappearance was 0.241 day^{-1}, and 0.171 day^{-1} for Ca^{47}. As can be seen, the level of Sr in the plasma falls more rapidly than does that of Ca. The mean value for the net rate of loss of plasma Sr^{85} is in good agreement with the figure of 0.253 day^{-1} obtained as the mean value for 5 patients by Bauer and Ray (*6*).

TABLE II

NET RATE OF LOSS OF Ca^{47} AND Sr^{85} FROM PLASMA, FROM WHOLE BODY, AND VIA URINE

Tracer		*Plasma, 2–10 days*	*Urine, 2–10 days*	*Whole body*		*Renal clearance, 5–10 days*
				2–10 days	*10–30 days*	
		(fraction per day)				*(liters/day)*
Ca^{47}						
LER		0.222	0.231	0.0375	0.0140	2.46
BEE		0.174	0.185	0.0209	0.0301	3.06
QUI		0.177	0.163	0.0298	0.0315	2.22
MAC		0.132	0.181	0.0381	—	2.48
FUH		0.163	—	0.0394	0.0234	—
FOR		0.160	0.158	0.0210	0.0178	2.22
	$\bar{x}$ =	0.171	0.184	0.0311	0.0234	2.49
Sr^{85}						
LER		0.257	0.276	0.0624	0.0099	5.88
BEE		0.218	0.216	0.0417	0.0298	8.46
QUI		0.269	0.252	0.0737	0.0167	10.00
MAC		0.307	0.209	0.0537	—	8.55
FUH		0.166	—	0.0481	0.0166	—
FOR		0.230	0.240	0.0525	0.0150	8.24
	$\bar{x}$ =	0.241	0.238	0.0554	0.0176	8.22

Urinary and Fecal Excretion

The mean values of the net rates of urinary excretion of Sr^{85} and Ca^{47} in the 6 patients (as approximated by a single exponential) over the period 5 to 10 days after administration were 0.238 and 0.184 day^{-1}, respectively, (see Table II). These values are quite close to those for plasma Sr^{85} and Ca^{47} disappearance in these patients after equilibration (Table II).

Renal clearance, C, may be computed as follows:

$$C = \frac{\%\text{ dose in urine/24 hours}}{\%\text{ dose in plasma/liter}}$$

The ratio of the mean renal clearance rates for the patients, (C_{Sr}/C_{Ca}) was found to be 3.3 (see Table II). This value is very close to the mean value of 3.5 reported by Barnes *et al.* (*7*).

The mean values of the urinary excretion of Sr^{85} and Ca^{47} for all 6 patients for the first 10 days after adminstration were 39.8% and 17.2% of the administered dose, respectively. Corresponding values of 38.9% and 14.3% were obtained in a study of 7 patients over 12 days by Spencer *et al.* (*8*). In the present study the Sr^{85}/Ca^{47} urinary excretion ratio was 1.5, comparing well with the ratio of 1.7 reported by Spencer *et al.* (*8*).

The corresponding mean values for the fecal excretion of Sr^{85} and Ca^{47} for the first 10 days were 13.0% and 11.7% of the administered dose, respectively. Spencer *et al.* reported corresponding figures of 13.9% and 10.5%. Fecal excretion of Sr was only slightly greater than that of Ca; the discrimination observed in urinary excretion does not occur in fecal elimination.

The patients in both studies were of the same age group but manifested a variety of clinical conditions. Although there is a spread of values within each group, it is interesting to note the similarity of the mean values for the parameters measured in the two groups. This agreement would appear to indicate that the skeletal metabolism was not grossly affected by the particular clinical manifestations observed in the patients.

Uptake by Skeleton

The calculated accretion rate and exchange capacity of the patients (expressed in plasma units) are shown in Table III. The data are expressed in plasma units, since these tend to correct the data for differences in body weight.

Sr^{85} and Ca^{47} used as tracers yield very similar values for the accretion rate and exchange capacity for each patient. In only two patients, QUI and BEE, was there a significant difference in the exchange capacity for Sr^{85} and Ca^{47}, and in patient BEE the accretion rates were also significantly different. In all the other cases, the E and A values check quite closely whether derived from Sr measurements or from Ca measurements. On this basis it would appear that the skeletal uptake of Sr and Ca is quite similar during the first 10 days.

TABLE III

SKELETAL ACCRETION RATES AND EXCHANGE CAPACITIES MEASURED WITH SR^{85} AND CA^{47}

Patient	*Exchange capacity* (*plasma units*[a])		*Accretion rate* (*plasma units*[a])	
	Ca^{47}	Sr^{85}	Ca^{47}	Sr^{85}
FOR	21.5	21.7	1.77	1.90
QUI	24.1	30.2	1.91	1.79
MAC	28.3	27.5	1.95	1.70
FUH	19.5	21.2	1.87	1.74
BEE	21.9	30.8	2.25	2.74
LER	19.9	20.4	1.53	1.42

[a] Plasma unit = [100 × body weight (kg)/20] mg.

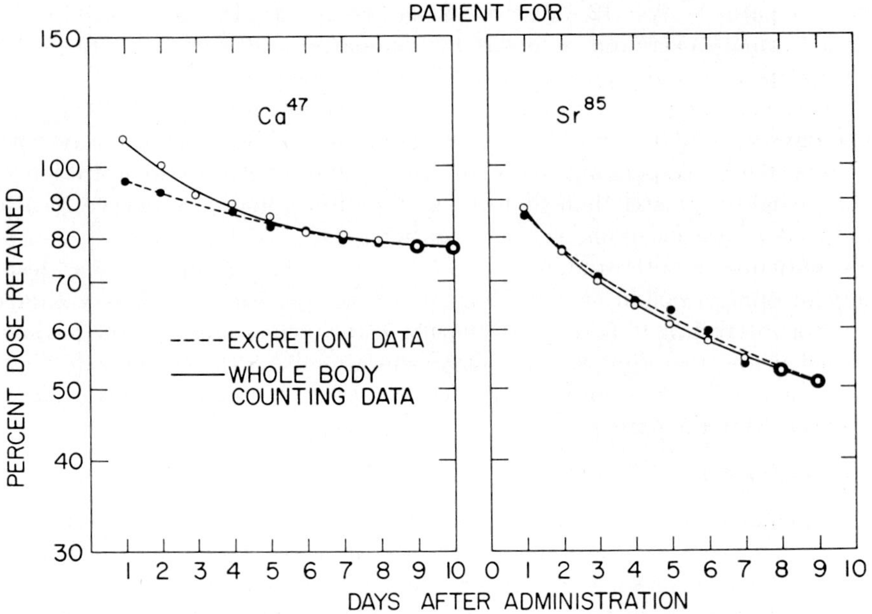

FIG. 1. Whole-body retention of Sr^{85} and Ca^{47} determined by excretion analysis and by whole-body counting.

Total-Body Retention

The whole-body retention of Sr^{85} and of Ca^{47} in a typical patient (patient FOR), as determined both by analysis of excretion data and by whole-body counting, is shown in Fig. 1. Comparison of the Sr and Ca curves indicates that Sr retention drops more rapidly during the first 10 days. This result reflects the preferential renal excretion of Sr.

The whole-body counting data were calibrated against the retention value on day 10 determined from the excretion data. This procedure is made necessary by the difference in values obtained by the two different methods (*3*). The normalized Sr^{85} retention curves from the excretion data and from the whole-body counting data are quite similar in the period day 1 to day 10, but the curve of Ca^{47}, obtained from whole-body counting data, is higher than that obtained from the excretion data for the first few days. The apparent higher retention of Ca^{47} indicated by the whole-body count can be explained in terms of a greater percentage of Ca^{47} in the plasma and soft tissues as compared to Sr^{85} during this initial stage. Such a distribution of Ca^{47} would result in an altered counting geometry and hence a higher counting efficiency. Since the calibration of the whole-body counter was invalid for the first 4 days, the excretion data retention values were used for this early time period.

The retention curves can also be described as the sum of two major exponential components over the 30-day period, exclusive of the initial rapid component representing mixing. From 3 to 10 days the rate of loss of activity, as measured by the whole-body counting technique, is considered to reflect the loss of the tracer from the readily exchangeable compartment via renal excretion. From 10 to 30 days the levels of readily exchangeable Ca and Sr are low, and renal excretion is primarily of the tracers resulting from bone resorption and long-term exchange processes of bone.

The rate constants describing the loss of Sr^{85} and Ca^{47} from the whole body for each patient for the periods 2 to 10 days and 10 to 30 days are presented in Table II. The values obtained for the rate constants of the initial component (2 to 10 days) would indicate that the mean initial loss of Sr^{85} from the body was 1.8 times that of Ca^{47}. The mean values of the rate constants of the secondary component (10 to 30 days) for Sr^{85} and Ca^{47} are 0.0176 day^{-1} and 0.0234 day^{-1}, respectively (see Table II). The rate constant for Ca^{47} in each of the 6 patients was larger than that for Sr^{85} over the period 10 to 30 days (Table II). Differential retention of Sr and Ca can also be expressed in terms of the whole-body Sr/Ca ratio.

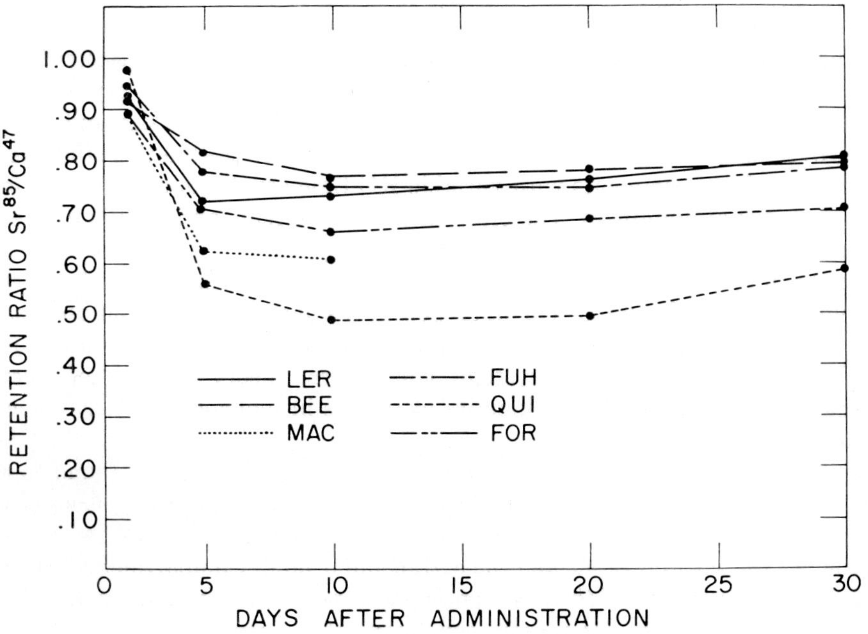

FIGURE 2

FIG. 2. Retention ratio of strontium/calcium determined by whole-body counting

Values for this ratio in the individual patients over the 30-day period are shown in Fig. 2.

DISCUSSION

As has been pointed out by Neuman and Neuman (*9*), studies of the kinetics of uptake and incorporation of Sr^{85} into bone by analysis of the composite exponential curves not only are difficult but have serious limitations. Since a composite curve may be represented by several combinations of exponential terms, and, further, because these exponential terms do not correspond to particular physiological or kinetic entities, this analytic approach has not been satisfactory. On the other hand, the derived functions, accretion (A) and exchange (E), provide a satisfactorily quantitative measure of the kinetics of uptake and incorporation of the radionuclides into bone.

Since no appreciable difference was observed in the skeletal accretion rate or exchange capacity, as determined from the Sr^{85} and Ca^{47} measurements over the first 10 days, it is concluded that the skeletal uptake of the two elements is essentially the same. It should be noted that the method used for calculating E and A assumes a rapid exchange and, further, a uniform distribution of the Ca^{47} and the Sr^{85} within a given compartment. Further, the E and A values obtained represent lumped or average rates and volumes of distribution.

A model of the kinetic metabolic system can be set up on an electronic analog computer. This procedure was followed in the present study, as experimentation with such a model affords insights on the roles of compartment size and flow rates in the over-all metabolic response. The analog computer used in this study consists essentially of compartments with variable RC time constants used in conjunction with operational amplifiers. The electronic analog circuit and details of the computer analysis procedure have been discussed (*10*).

The technique of analysis consists in adjusting the parameters of the electronic system to match the biological data points displayed on an oscilloscope. This curve-fitting process is essentially a method for solving the differential equations which describe the biological system. The general theory and use of electronic analogs for the analysis of the kinetics of tracers in biological systems have been discussed (*11–13*).

A four-compartment system, shown schematically in Fig. 3, was found to represent the Sr–Ca metabolic system adequately in the present study. Compartment I represents the plasma, and compartment II represents the readily exchangeable fraction of the skeletal tissue and the extracellular fluid. Compartments III and IV both represent portions of the skeleton, defined metabolically. This is an open system, with outflow from the plasma compartment I, corresponding to the urinary excretion.

The tracer is introduced into compartment I, the plasma compartment. The exchange rate between compartments I and II is such that they come into rapid

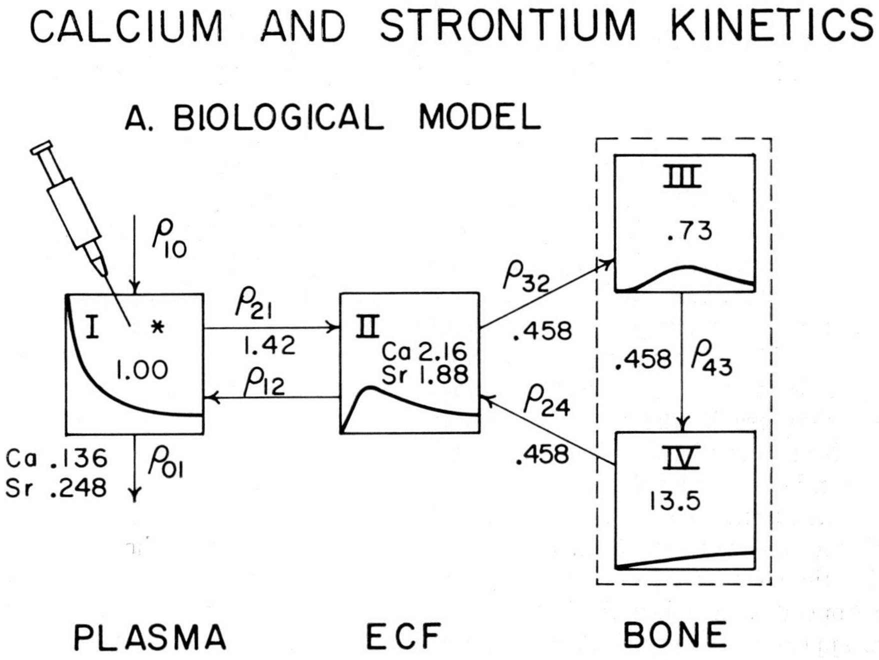

FIG. 3. Compartment model for strontium and calcium kinetics. Compartment I represents the amount of calcium or strontium in the plasma. Compartment II represents the calcium or strontium in extracellular fluid and readily exchangeable bone. Compartments III and IV represent calcium or strontium in different portions of bone having relatively long exchange time constants. The numbers in the boxes are relative masses of the substances traced, as derived from the analog computer parameters. The flow rates, ρ, are similarly designated by the numbers beside the arrows and are in units of relative mass per day. For both the compartment sizes and the flow rates, unit mass is taken as the amount in the plasma.

equilibrium with each other. Although compartments III and IV both have relatively long time constants, that of compartment III is somewhat shorter. The tracers feed back to compartment II from compartment IV. The flow rate of this feedback is designated ρ_{24} in Fig. 3. This flow rate may be considered to correspond to the diminution rate which balances the inflow or accretion rate plus augmentation rate (*14*) (see Appendix). The flow rates into compartments III and IV may be thought of as apposition and augmentation, respectively.

Figure 4 shows two sets of experimental data of patient FOR for both Sr^{85} and Ca^{47}: the whole-body retention (points fitted by curve *E*) and the plasma specific activity (points fitted by curve *A*). These curves were generated by the analog computer, as shown in the photographs of the oscilloscope screen. The remaining curves in Fig. 4 represent the relative specific activities of Sr^{85} incorporated into the rapidly exchanging bone (curve *B*) and into the very slowly exchanging bone compartments (curves *C* and *D*). The figures within the boxes of Fig. 3 represent relative masses of the compartments for Sr and Ca as derived from computer analysis. The flow rates between compartments (ρ) are expressed in units of relative mass per day.

The plasma Ca^{47} specific activity data for patient FOR are shown in Fig. 5, along with the fitted computer curve (curve *A*). It was found in the computer study that the curve for the Ca plasma clearance could be formally transformed to match the Sr clearance data simply by changing the rate of urinary excretion. (An even better fit could be obtained by decreasing the size of compartment II from 2.16 to 1.88, in addition to changing ρ_{01} as illustrated in curve *B* of Fig. 5.) Although the computer admittedly presents one solution selected from a number of possible solutions, this finding nevertheless strongly suggests that the preferential excretion of Sr over Ca (rather than transfer to other compartments) accounts for the differences in the plasma clearance for Sr^{85} and Ca^{47}, and consequently may also account for the differences in whole-body retention as previously noted.

It can be concluded from the similarity in the values of accretion and exchange calculated from Ca^{47} and Sr^{85} data that both elements undergo accretion into bone with the same rate constant. (Accretion as used here includes those processes by which the elements are taken up by the skeleton—apposition and augmentation; see Appendix.) Further, the initial exchange process and surface binding by bone also appear to be very similar for the two elements. The small differences in the relative retention of Ca and Sr observed from 10 days onward expressed quantitatively in terms of rate constants for loss of the tracer from bone may reflect the different modes of Sr and Ca binding in the crystal lattice. It has been shown, for example, by X-ray diffraction studies (*15*) that surface phenomena can account totally for Sr fixation in the skeleton and, further, that only a limited amount of Sr can replace Ca in the apatite lattice. Engström (*1*) suggests that Sr first becomes adsorbed on the surface of the apatite crystal and is eventually fixed by epitaxy.

Another way to illustrate the differential retention is by means of the whole-body Sr/Ca ratios (Fig. 2). The mean Sr/Ca ratio for whole-body retention at 10 days was 0.67, a value in good agreement with that obtained by Spencer *et al.* (*8*) at 12 days after administration. This ratio is also similar to the ratio of 0.75 for Ca/Sr in various bones of a rat obtained by Likens *et al.* (*16*). At all times during the 30-day period studied there is more Ca^{47} tracer than there is Sr^{85} tracer; presumably the ratio holds for skeletal tissues as well. Similar results for the Sr/Ca ratio were obtained for all the patients. A slightly increased value of the Sr/Ca ratio observed at 30 days, as compared to the 10-day value, indicates again a somewhat slower rate of loss of Sr by the body as compared to Ca at this time. This increased Sr/Ca ratio takes on additional significance when the preferential renal excretion of Sr over Ca is considered.

Evidence for *in vivo* Sr–Ca skeletal discrimination is reported by Likens *et al.*

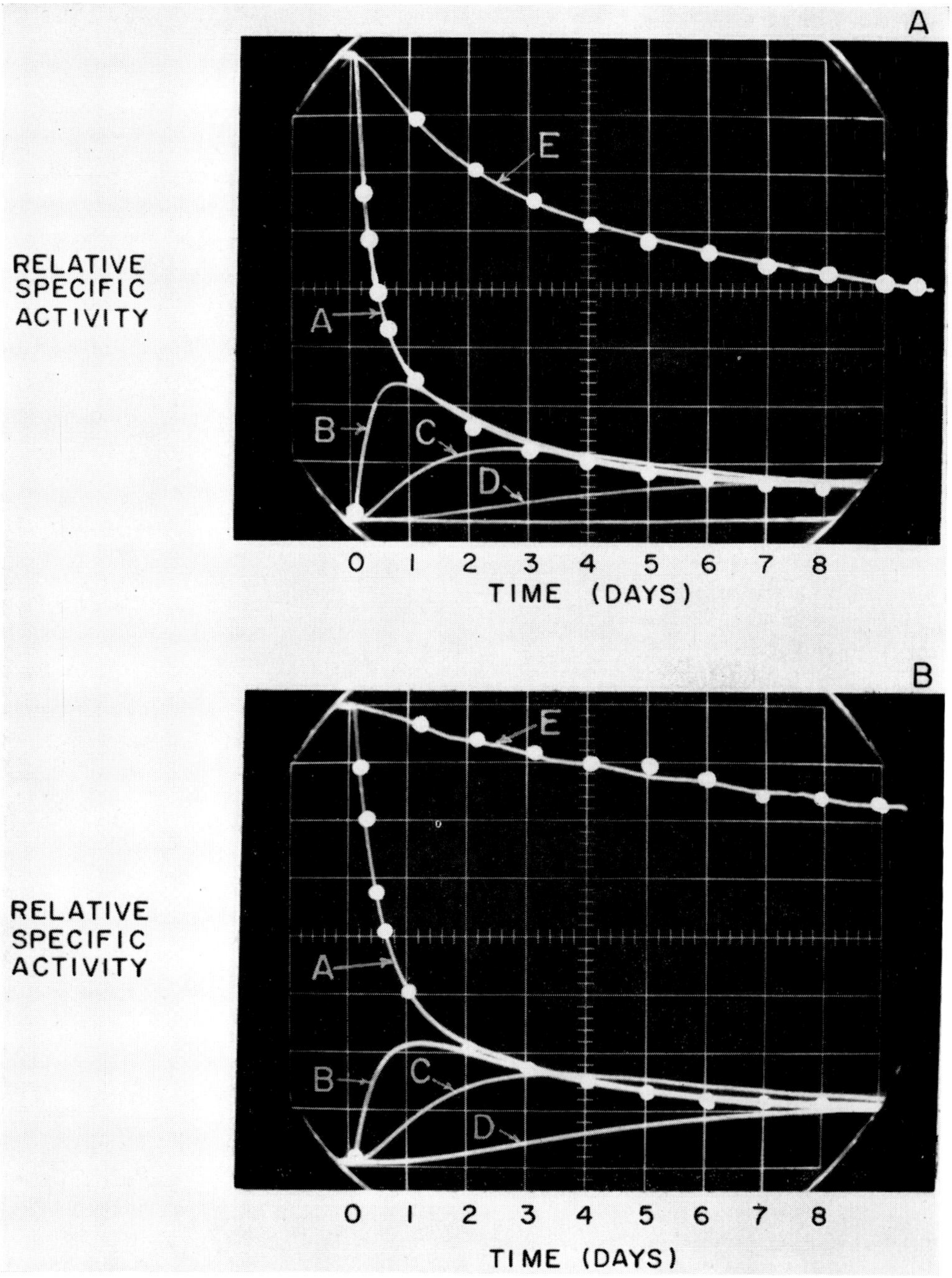

FIG. 4. Computer-derived curves of compartment model for: (*A*) Sr^{85} and (*B*) Ca^{47}. Computer oscillograph showing the fitting of the plasma specific activity data, compartment I, by curve *A* and total-body activity data by curve *E*. Curve *B* represents the derived curve of relative specific activity in compartment II. Curves *C* and *D* represent the relative specific activity in compartments III and IV, respectively.

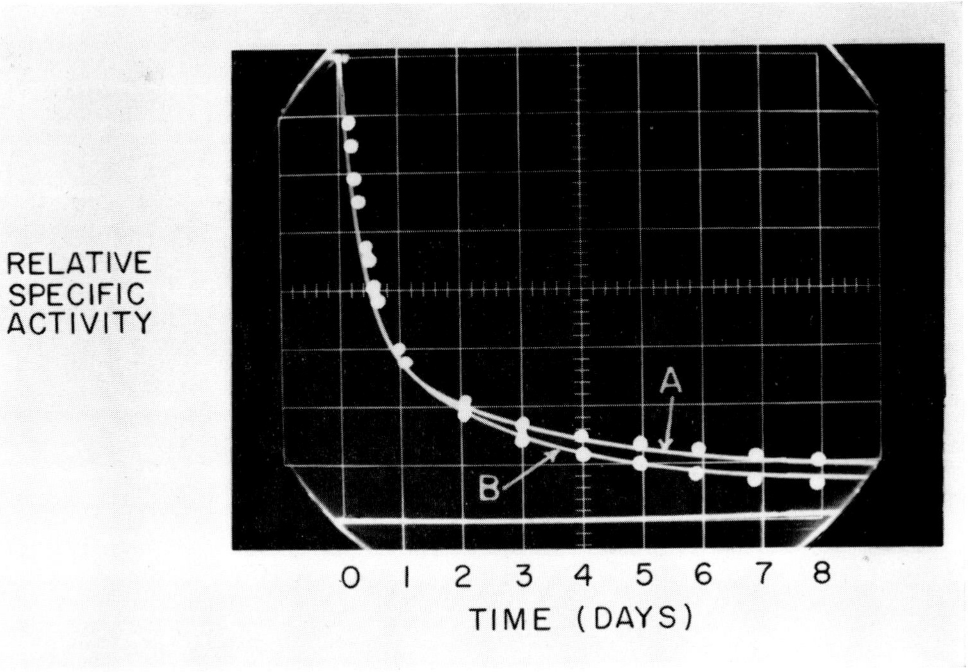

FIG. 5. Comparative plasma specific activities of Sr^{85} and Ca^{47}. The curves are fitted to the plasma Sr^{85} data (curve B) and Ca^{47} data (curve *A*).

(*16*). The preferential release of radioactive Sr from bone in the rat skeleton is postulated as a compensating adjustment which accounts for the sustained ratio of Sr/Ca = 1 in the plasma during the first 24 hours after administration (*16*). This was not observed here, as the Sr/Ca ratio in the plasma fell continuously throughout the experiment. The data in the present study indicate that in the period 10 days to 30 days Sr is released more slowly than Ca.

The rate of loss of Sr from the skeleton has at least one component with a very long time constant, as determined in a previous study of Sr^{85} turnover in patients (*2*); this is not apparent in the present data. Marshall (*17*) also points out that the "long-term" exchange of the diffuse activity deposited in adult bone has a very long time constant and is of considerable magnitude when compared to loss by direct resorption. In fact, it has been customary in the past to describe osseous tissue in terms of a large "non-exchangeable fraction" and a smaller "labile exchangeable fraction." However, it would appear that, from the point of view of its metabolism, bone must be considered to be composed of a number of compartments, which have time constants that vary continuously from very small values to extremely high values (*2*). Thus, the analog model obtained in this study was found to reproduce satisfactorily experimental data for the short term under consideration but would not predict the long-term behavior. It is obvious, of course, that the value of the analog analysis is in direct proportion to the precision with which the various components of the system are represented, and the accuracy with which their relationships are portrayed.

The difficulty of making long-term predictions of Sr and Ca kinetics on the basis of this short-term study can also be seen from the fact that the sum of all the compartment sizes, when converted into absolute values, yields a total Ca content of only 8 gm (based on a Ca content of 250 mg in compartment I). Thus, less than 1% of the total body calcium is involved in the short-term Sr–Ca kinetics. Within this 1%, the longest turnover time found is 30 days. From other studies it is clear that one or more additional large compartments with very long turnover times (years) are required for a complete description of Ca and Sr kinetics, but these compartments and rates are not reflected in the short-term data. The model proposed by Bauer and Ray (*6*), when similarly interpreted, also does not account for the bulk of the body Ca. The bulk of the calcium stores has too slow a turnover rate to feed back into the plasma the tracers incorporated into bone during the short experimental period.

SUMMARY

The kinetics of skeletal metabolism of Sr^{85} and Ca^{47} in man over a 30-day period are characterized in terms of accretion, exchange, and biological loss (resorption and long-term exchange). From a kinetic point of view, bone must be considered to be composed of a number of compartments with time constants ranging from minutes to years. To represent the data in the present study, a four-compartment model of the kinetic metabolic system, as developed on an analog computer, was found to be adequate. Computer analysis yielded estimates of compartment sizes and flow rates between compartments. The models derived from the Ca^{47} and Sr^{85} data differ from each other only in the greater rate of urinary excretion of Sr^{85} and in the slightly smaller size of the readily exchangeable extracellular compartment of Sr^{85} compared to that of Ca^{47}.

Initially the skeletal accretion rate and exchange capacity are very similar for Sr and Ca. Differences in the retention begin to appear only after 10 days, when the metabolic response is characterized chiefly by binding of Ca and Sr tracers in the crystal lattice and long-term exchange. The data suggest that identical roles in skeletal metabolism for Ca and Sr tracers over long periods of time cannot be postulated on the basis of the metabolic similarities observed in the short interval after administration. The difficulty in making long-term predictions on Sr and Ca kinetics from this short-term study lies in the fact that the kinetic model represents less than 1% of the total body calcium. The amount of metabolically active Ca with which this single tracer injection of radioactive Ca or Sr interacts is very small indeed; the vast body Ca store with its very slow turnover rate is not reflected in the model.

APPENDIX

The following definitions of terms used in this paper are largely adopted from Marshall *et al.* (*14*). The terms apply equally to calcium and strontium.

ACCRETION—the process involving net transfer of calcium atoms to a volume of bone.

EXCHANGE—the process involving equal rates of transfer of calcium atoms to and from a volume of bone.

SHORT-TERM EXCHANGE—exchange processes with time constants less than a week. Labeled calcium atoms will be in equilibrium in most tracer experiments.

LONG-TERM EXCHANGE—exchange processes with time constants greater than a week. Labeled calcium atoms will not be in equilibrium in most tracer experiments.

TIME CONSTANT OF AN EXCHANGE PROCESS—the number of calcium atoms available for this exchange in a given volume divided by the rate of transfer of calcium atoms. The time constant is also the reciprocal of the turnover rate constant.

APPOSITION—accretion involved in new bone formation which results in an increased mineral volume as observed microscopically.

AUGMENTATION—gross uptake in a specified volume of existing bone mineral of calcium atoms which remain much longer than a week.

DIMINUTION—the gross loss from a specified volume of bone mineral of calcium atoms which have resided there much longer than a week.

EPITAXY—the oriented growth of one crystalline substance on a substrate of a different crystalline substance.

SPECIFIC ACTIVITY—per cent dose of Ca^{47} or Sr^{85} per milligram of Ca^{40}. An average stable calcium plasma concentration of 10 mg % was used in all calculations for conversion of concentration data to specific activity.

RELATIVE SPECIFIC ACTIVITY—the above specific activity normalized by taking the initial plasma concentration Ca^{47} or Sr^{85}, or the initial whole-body counting rate as unity.

In terms of these definitions of Marshall, the following quantitative relation may be expressed for the skeleton:

$$\text{Accretion} = \text{Apposition} + \text{augmentation} - \text{diminution}$$

Also in terms of Marshall's definitions above, the quantity A measured and defined mathematically by Bauer *et al.* (*4*) is:

$$A = \text{Apposition rate} + \text{augmentation rate}$$

or

$$A = \text{Accretion rate} + \text{diminution rate}$$

and the exchangeable fraction, E, refers to short-term exchange.

The quantities A and E, as derived in this study, are not affected by the diminution rate for the skeleton as a whole.

ACKNOWLEDGMENTS

We wish to express our gratitude to Drs. C. Jansen, S. Fine, and K. Rai for their assistance in carrying out this study, and to Mr. M. Stravino for his technical assistance.

RECEIVED: August 17, 1962

REFERENCES

1. A. ENGSTRÖM, *Bone and Radiostrontium*, p. 78, John Wiley & Sons, New York, 1958.
2. S. H. COHN, H. SPENCER, J. SAMACHSON, and J. S. ROBERTSON, The turnover of Sr^{85} in man as determined by whole-body counting. *Radiation Res.* **17,** 173–185 (1962).
3. S. H. COHN, S. W. LIPPINCOTT, E. P. CRONKITE, and P. G. REIZENSTEIN, Application of whole-body gamma spectrometry to clinical tracer studies. In *Symposium on Whole Body Counting*, pp. 469–480, International Atomic Energy Agency, Vienna, 1962.
4. G. C. H. BAUER, A. CARLSSON, and B. LINDQUIST, Evaluation of accretion resorption and exchange reactions in the skeleton. *Kgl. Fysiograf. Sällskap. Lund. Föhr.* **25,** 3–18 (1955).
5. G. C. H. BAUER, A. CARLSSON, and B. LINDQUIST, Bone salt metabolism in humans studied by means of radiocalcium. *Acta Med. Scand.* **158,** 143–150 (1957).
6. G. C. H. BAUER and R. D. RAY, Kinetics of strontium metabolism in man. *J. Bone Joint Surg.* **40A,** 171–186 (1958).
7. D. W. BARNES, M. BISHOP, G. E. HARRISON, and A. SUTTON, Comparison of the plasma concentration and urinary excretion of strontium and calicum in man. *Intern. J. Radiation Biol.* **3,** 637–646 (1961).
8. H. SPENCER, M. LI, J. SAMACHSON, and D. LASZLO, Metabolism of strontium^{85} and calicum^{45} in man. *Metabolism* **9,** 916–925 (1960).
9. W. F. NEUMAN and M. W. NEUMAN, *The Chemical Dynamics of Bone Mineral*, p. 119, University of Chicago Press, Chicago, 1958.
10. J. S. ROBERTSON and S. H. COHN, Conference on multi-compartment analysis of tracer experiments: Use of an analogue computer in studies of strontium and calcium metabolism in man. *Trans. N. Y. Acad. Sci.* in press.
11. G. L. BROWNELL, R. V. CAVICCHI, and K. E. PERRY, An electrical analogue for analysis of compartmental biological systems. *Rev. Sci. Instr.* **24,** 704–710 (1953).
12. J. R. MACDONALD and E. G. PERRY, An electrical analogue for analysis of tracer distribution kinetics in biological systems. *Radiation Res.* **6,** 585–601 (1957).
13. J. S. ROBERTSON, The use of analogue computers in the kinetic analysis of compartmented systems. *Trans. N. Y. Acad. Sci.* **23,** 506–512 (1961).
14. J. H. MARSHALL, R. E. ROWLAND, and J. JOWSEY, Microscopic metabolism of calcium in bone. V. The paradox of diffuse activity and long-term exchange. *Radiation Res.* **10,** 258–270 (1959).
15. J. E. GLAS and C. LAGERGREN, Strontium fixation in the mineral phase of bone. *Biochem. Biol. Sper.* **1,** 25–28 (1961).
16. R. C. LIKENS, A. S. POSNER, M. L. KUNDE, and D. L. CRAVEN, Comparative metabolism of calcium and strontium in the rat. *Arch. Biochem. Biophys.* **83,** 472–481 (1959).
17. J. MARSHALL, Microscopic metabolism of calcium in bone. In *Bone as a Tissue*, p. 144, McGraw-Hill Book Co., New York, 1960.

RADIATION RESEARCH **19**, 120–128 (1963)

A Redetermination of the Salicylic Acid Yield in the Aqueous Calcium Benzoate Dosimeter

W. A. ARMSTRONG, R. A. FACEY, D. W. GRANT, AND
W. G. HUMPHREYS

Defence Research Chemical Laboratories, Defence Research Board, Ottawa, Canada

INTRODUCTION

A sensitive chemical dosimeter based on the fluorometric analysis of the salicylic acid formed in irradiated aqueous calcium benzoate solutions has been developed (*1, 2*). Since recent experience with the dosimeter suggested that *G*(salicylic acid) or *G*(Sal) values previously reported (*1, 2*) for Co^{60} γ-radiation were slightly high, a re-examination of the system was carried out to determine corrected values and to find possible sources of error.

EXPERIMENTAL PROCEDURE

Materials

Triply-distilled water (one distillation from alkaline $KMnO_4$) was used to make all solutions and preparations. All chemicals were reagent grade unless otherwise stated.

Calcium benzoate was prepared by dissolving 50 gm of benzoic acid (Hopkin and Williams P.V.S. grade) in 800 ml of water containing 16 gm of sodium hydroxide. To this solution was added, slowly with stirring, 50 ml of an aqueous solution containing 30 gm of calcium chloride. The precipitated calcium benzoate was filtered, washed with a small amount of water, and recrystallized twice from water. The crystals were dried at 50°C for a few hours. Weight-loss measurements on heating indicated the crystallized calcium benzoate to be the monohydrate.

Salicylic acid from Eastman Kodak was recrystallized twice from water and dried at 60°C overnight. All salicylic acid solutions were made by appropriate dilution of a single 10^{-3} *M* stock solution.

Potassium benzoate was recrystallized from 95% ethanol and dried overnight at 80°C.

All other chemicals were used without further purification.

Glassware was cleaned, unless otherwise stated, by immersion for a few minutes in fresh chromic acid, followed with repeated rinsings with singly-, doubly-, and triply-distilled water. Irradiation and storage vessels were given an additional cleaning by steam from boiling triply-distilled water just prior to use.

Irradiation Technique

Cobalt-60 γ-irradiations were carried out with dose rates of about 2.3 and 21 rads/min from a 200-curie source. A Müller constant-potential machine was used for X-irradiations at dose rates from 11 to 24 rads/min. X-Radiations were: (1) 250 kvcp, 0.9 gm/cm^2 Cu and 0.13 gm/cm^2 Al filters, effective energy 105 kev; (2) 100 kvcp, 0.4 gm/cm^2 Al filter, effective energy 30 kev; (3) 50 kvcp, no filtration except 0.3 gm/cm^2 Be from window of X-ray tube, effective energy 12 kev (HVL 45.9 mg/cm^2 Al).

When Co^{60} γ-rays and 250-kvcp X-rays were employed, 3.3-ml and 5.0-ml aliquots of solution, respectively, were irradiated in Pyrex tubes (inner diameter 10 mm, outer diameter 12 mm) clamped at right angles to the direction of the beam. In the 100-kvcp and 50-kvcp X-ray experiments, 5.0-ml aliquots were irradiated from above in Pyrex petri dishes (inner diameter 5 cm) covered with Saran plastic sheet (½ thou) to prevent evaporation. The solutions in the latter series of experiments were gently agitated on a horizontal shaker (50 cycles/min) during irradiation to provide mixing and thereby minimize the local depletion of solute at the surface.

Dosimetry

Dosimetry was done with the well-established aqueous ferrous sulfate method (*3*). However, for X-irradiations the sulfuric acid concentration was reduced to 0.1 *N* in order to minimize photoelectric absorption by the sulfur. The dose computations were made by using the following values for $\epsilon^{\circ C}_{m\mu}$, the molar extinction coefficient of Fe(III), and G(FeIII), the ferric ion yield:

$$\epsilon^{24}_{304} = 2181 \text{ in } 0.8\ N\ H_2SO_4\ (4);\quad \epsilon^{24}_{224} = 4559 \text{ in } 0.1\ N\ H_2SO_4\ (4)$$

$$G(\text{FeIII}) = 15.5 \text{ for } Co^{60}\ \gamma\text{-rays, } 14.6 \text{ for 250-kvcp X-rays, } 13.9 \text{ for 100-kvcp X-rays, and } 13.0 \text{ for 50-kvcp X-rays.}$$

The small effect of acidity on the ferric ion extinction coefficient at 224 mμ (*4*) has been neglected. Density corrections were applied to the ferrous sulfate dose rates to yield the dose rates in the calcium benzoate solutions. Simple density corrections could lead to slightly high ($\not> 2\%$) doses in the case of the 100-kvcp and 50-kvcp X-irradiations, but a more precise estimate seemed unwarranted on account of the uncertainty in the values of G(FeIII).

Fluorescence Measurement Technique

Fluorescence measurements were made in 1-cm quartz cells by means of a Bowman-Aminco spectrophotofluorometer with a xenon lamp and slit programme No. 3. The excitation and fluorescence wavelengths employed were 290 and 400 mμ, respectively. For reproducible results at low doses it was essential to handle the optical cells with tongs and to transfer solutions in and out of the cells with pipets. By making alternate fluorescence measurements of aliquots (1 to 2 ml) of irradiated solutions (and unirradiated "blanks") and appropriate standard salicylic acid–calcium benzoate solutions, errors due to lamp output fluctuations were minimized. The average of five measurements for each irradiated sample, "blank," and "standard" was used to calculate the concentration of salicylic acid $[\mathrm{Sal}]_R$ in an irradiated sample:

$$[\mathrm{Sal}]_R = \frac{I_R - I_B}{I_S - I_B} \cdot [\mathrm{Sal}]_S$$

where I_R, I_B, and I_S are the respective fluorescence intensities due to irradiated sample, "blank," and "standard," and $[\mathrm{Sal}]_S$ is the salicylic acid concentration in the "standard."

RESULTS AND DISCUSSION

Purity of Salicylic Acid

In the previous studies it was tacitly assumed that the twice-recrystallized acid was pure. However, small amounts of fluorescent impurities could make a disproportionate contribution to the fluorescence and thereby yield erroneous values of $[\mathrm{Sal}]_R$. For this reason a qualitative analysis of the recrystallized acid by paper chromatography was attempted. Two solvent systems were used—*n*-butanol saturated with 5 N NH_4OH, and methyl ethyl ketone–water–diethylamine (921:77:2). No substance other than salicylic acid was detected on any chromatograms with ultraviolet light, ultraviolet light and hydrogen peroxide (*5*), diazotized *p*-nitroaniline, and diazotized sulfanilic acid as detection agents. Upper impurity limits were estimated to be 0.1% from *m*-hydroxybenzoic acid, 0.1% for *p*-hydroxybenzoic acid, 0.2% for benzoic acid, and 1% for phenol. However, titration with standard alkali indicated the recrystallized acid to be 98.7% pure.

Attempts to dry the acid further by prolonged heating at 50°C did not change the titer appreciably. Sublimation *in vacuo* of the recrystallized acid yielded a product which was 99.4% pure on the basis of titration. From the relative fluorescence intensities of the sublimed and recrystallized samples it was evident that intensely fluorescent impurities were not present. All $G(\mathrm{Sal})$ values reported in this paper have been calculated on the assumption that the salicylic acid used to make the standard solutions was 98.7% pure.

Stability of "Standards" and "Blanks"

A comparison of the absorption bands and fluorescence intensities of a number of 10^{-4} *M* salicylic acid solutions, made by dilution of the appropriate stock solutions prior to measurement, demonstrated the stability of the 10^{-3} *M* stock solutions over a period of many months.

The stability of two samples each of 4×10^{-8} *M*, 2×10^{-7} *M*, and 10^{-6} *M* salicylic acid in 10^{-3} *M* calcium benzoate was studied fluorometrically. The fluorescence of each aging sample was measured relative to the fluorescence of a corresponding sample made on the day of measurement. Appropriate corrections for changes in the "blank" were included. The 10^{-6} *M* and 2×10^{-7} *M* "standards" were unchanged (within estimated experimental error of $\pm 1\%$) after 7 weeks. Although both 4×10^{-8} *M* "standards" appeared to suffer significant decrease (15%) in fluorescence in the same period, the increase observed in the "blank" (67%) considerably reduced the accuracy of these measurements. Since the "blank" reading for fresh 10^{-3} *M* calcium benzoate solutions is usually equivalent to a salicylic acid concentration less than 2×10^{-9} *M*, "blank" errors are relatively insignificant in the more concentrated standard solutions. Although all calcium benzoate solutions studied exhibited a "blank" increase on standing, the variable nature of the change is suggestive of contamination of the solutions with prolonged use.

The stability studies show that 10^{-6} *M* and 2×10^{-7} *M* "standards" are reliable for many weeks, but 4×10^{-8} *M* "standards" should not be used for more than 1 week. For the present *G*(Sal) determinations, "standards" and calcium benzoate solutions were never used for more than a few days.

Photochemical and Temperature Effects

"Standards" and irradiated solutions were left for relatively long periods of time in the cell compartment of the fluorometer to determine if ultraviolet illumination would produce significant photochemical change. The fluorescence of each solution was measured periodically against an appropriate "standard" (to monitor fluctuations in lamp output) which had not been continuously illuminated. The fluorescence of two "standards" (4×10^{-8} *M* and 10^{-6} *M* salicylic acid in 10^{-3} *M* calcium benzoate) and two irradiated 10^{-3} *M* calcium benzoate solutions given 110 rads and 2000 rads was found to decrease about 3% in 30 minutes with increasing illumination time. However, it is doubtful whether there is any photochemical change, because the fluorescence of "standards" left in the cell compartment with the shutter down to exclude ultraviolet radiation also exhibited a similar decrease. The latter effect is probably due to a rise in the sample temperature to about 32°C. Photochemical and temperature effects can be neglected as far as the present measurements are concerned.

Postirradiation Effects

Although no postirradiation effect over a period of 24 hours had been observed previously in irradiated calcium benzoate solutions (*2*), it was decided to repeat the experiments over longer periods of time. In order to prevent inadvertent contamination of solutions after irradiation, the fluorescence measurements were carried out directly on the samples in their quartz irradiation vessels. As usual, the measurements were adjusted to allow for any changes in lamp output detected by appropriate monitor "standards." The results (Table I) show that a slow postirradiation increase in fluorescence occurred in the case of the samples which had received 100 or 1450 rads. The results at the lowest dose are too scattered to show any trend. The effect cannot be considered a source of error in either the present or previous investigations, since measurements on each sample were always made within a period of a few hours after exposure to radiation.

Shape of the Salicylic Acid Concentration–Dose Plots at Low Doses

As in previous studies (*1*, *2*) G(Sal) was determined from the slope of the plot of salicylic acid concentration against dose. The salicylic acid concentration was determined by using only one "standard" corresponding to the middle of the dose range studied. In most experiments the best straight line through the experimental points yielded a small intercept on the concentration axis. There are several possible reasons for an intercept; (*a*) an erroneous determination of the intensity of the "blank"; (*b*) the fact that fluorescence of salicylic acid is not an exact linear function of its concentration; (*c*) nonlinearity of the meter scale of the spectrophotofluorometer; and (*d*) impurity effects. An error in the "blank" has the effect of rotation of the line about an axis corresponding to the standard concentration, since at this point $(I_R - I_B)/(I_S - I_B)$ is independent of I_B. However, the intercept cannot be wholly attributed to "blank" errors, because intercepts were never observed on the dose axis. Although possibilities (*b*) and (*c*) could be checked, it seemed preferable to determine G(Sal) under conditions where $I_S \approx I_R$, so that errors due to (*a*), (*b*), and (*c*) are virtually eliminated. In the majority of results

TABLE I

Postirradiation Effects in 10^{-3} *M* Calcium Benzoate Solutions

Irradiated solution	*Fluorescence (arbitrary units) at:*												
	0.2 hr	*0.5 hr*	*1.25 hr*	*1.5 hr*	*2.0 hr*	*4.5 hr*	*21 hr*	*27 hr*	*45 hr*	*70 hr*	*120 hr*	*144 hr*	*312 hr*
1 (16 rads)	100.0	99.3					105.0		98.5	98.8			
2 (100 rads)	100.0		98.8		101.0	99.9		101.7	100.7		105.9	107.0	113.0
3 (1450 rads)	100.0		98.8	98.8	100.0			102.9	104.5		109.1		

to be reported, $I_S = I_R \pm 10\%$, and all standards lay within the range $I_S = I_R \pm 30\%$. Impurities may be present on the glass walls of the irradiation vessels, in the calcium benzoate, or in the water used for making the solutions. However, unless the nature of the impurities is known, it is impossible to predict their effect on the radiolysis. One approach to the problem is to determine whether the results are sensitive to changes in cleaning techniques and reagents.

Effect of Cleaning Technique on G(Sal)

At moderate doses G(Sal) values are reproducible and independent of cleaning technique, but at low doses the G(Sal) values are widely scattered (Table II). Since all irradiation vessels cleaned with methods A_1 to A_4 had been cleaned at one time with chromic acid, it is possible that variable trace amounts of chromic acid were adsorbed on all vessel walls (*6*). For this reason G(Sal) values were also determined in ampules which had never been in contact with chromic acid. In these cases the cleaning procedure adopted (B_1) was to soak the ampules overnight in an HNO_3–H_2SO_4 mixture (1:3). Even at low doses technique B_1 yielded fairly reproducible G(Sal) values, in excellent agreement with the values for moderate doses (Table II). Thus the use of chromic acid as a cleaning agent would seem to be undesirable when low dose measurements are required. It should be noted that most G(Sal) determinations had been completed before the studies with cleaning method B_1 were instituted. Nevertheless, the excellent reproducibility of the results and their independence on dose (Table III) indicate that with doses of 40 rads and above any effects due to trace amounts of chromic acid are unimportant.

Effect of Source of Benzoate on G(Sal)

Four ampules containing 2×10^{-3} *M* potassium benzoate were given a Co^{60} γ-dose of 56 rads. The average value determined for G(Sal) was 0.639 ± 0.01,

TABLE II

EFFECT OF CLEANING TECHNIQUE ON G(SAL)

Cleaning agent	*G(Sal)*[a,b]		
	16 rads	*158 rads*	*283 rads*
Chromic acid (A_1)[c]	$0.68_2 \pm 0.03_6$		$0.63_6 \pm 0.01_5$
Boiling HNO_3 (A_2)	$0.70_5 \pm 0.06_1$		$0.62_9 \pm 0.00_4$
Boiling HNO_3 + HF (A_3)	$0.63_5 \pm 0.06_4$		$0.64_1 \pm 0.00_2$
Alcoholic NaOH (A_4)	$0.60_0 \pm 0.02_0$		$0.63_6 \pm 0.00_6$
HNO_3–H_2SO_4 (B_1)	$0.64_4 \pm 0.02_3$	$0.64_7 \pm 0.00_3$	

[a] For 10^{-3} *M* calcium benzoate solutions irradiated with Co^{60} γ-rays at a dose rate of 2.26 rads/min.

[b] Mean values with standard deviations.

[c] Normal procedure (experimental section).

TABLE III

DEPENDENCE OF G(SAL) ON PHOTON ENERGY AND CALCIUM BENZOATE CONCENTRATION

Incident radiation	*Effective energy (Mev)*	*Calcium benzoate concentration (M)*	*G(Sal)*[a]				$G(10^{-3}M)/G(10^{-4}M)$
			Low dose[b] *mean value*	*Middle dose*[c] *mean value*	*High dose*[d] *mean value*	*Over-all mean value*	
Co^{60} γ-rays	1.25	10^{-3}	$0.66_1 \pm 0.01_5$	$0.64_1 \pm 0.01_8$	$0.65_6 \pm 0.01_7$	$0.65_5 \pm 0.01_8$	1.1_0
Co^{60} γ-rays	1.25	10^{-4}		$0.59_5 \pm 0.00_7$		$0.59_5 \pm 0.00_7$	
250-kvcp X-rays	0.105	10^{-3}			$0.57_7 \pm 0.00_9$	$0.57_7 \pm 0.00_9$	1.1_3
250-kvcp X-rays	0.105	10^{-4}		$0.50_8 \pm 0.00_8$	$0.51_5 \pm 0.00_8$	$0.51_2 \pm 0.00_9$	
100-kvcp X-rays	0.030	10^{-3}			$0.51_5 \pm 0.00_7$	$0.51_5 \pm 0.00_7$	1.1_2
100-kvcp X-rays	0.030	10^{-4}		$0.47_1 \pm 0.00_4$	$0.44_8 \pm 0.00_3$	$0.46_0 \pm 0.01_2$	
50-kvcp X-rays	0.012	10^{-3}		$0.45_5 \pm 0.01_4$		$0.45_5 \pm 0.01_4$	1.1_2
50-kvcp X-rays	0.012	10^{-4}		$0.40_5 \pm 0.00_8$		$0.40_5 \pm 0.00_8$	

[a] Errors are standard deviations of the mean values.
[b] 40 to 60 rads.
[c] 150 to 300 rads.
[d] 900 to 2400 rads.

which is in good agreement with the results obtained with 10^{-3} *M* calcium benzoate (Tables II and III). Since the pH of the solutions is different, namely 6.3 and 7.3 for the calcium and potassium salts, respectively, the experiments are not strictly comparable. However, the study of Loebl *et al.* (*7*) indicates only a small dependence of salicylic acid yield on pH in this range.

Effect of Benzoate Concentration and Photon Energy on G(Sal)

In earlier experiments (*1*), 10^{-4} *M* calcium benzoate solutions were used in order to ensure low "blanks." However, recent experience with the dosimeter has shown that low "blanks" (2 to 3 rads) can be obtained even with concentrations as high as 10^{-3} *M*. Since it is preferable to work within a range of concentration where *G*(Sal) is independent of concentration, it is now established practice in this laboratory to use a calcium benzoate concentration of 10^{-3} *M* in the dosimeter. However, experiments were carried out with 10^{-4} *M* calcium benzoate as well as with 10^{-3} *M* solutions in order to check both previous determinations by the authors (*1*) and the determinations made independently in this laboratory by Wilson and Carruthers (*8*). The photon-energy range studied has also been extended to facilitate comparison with the latter authors.

The results (Table III) indicate that *G*(Sal) is 12% ± 2% higher for 10^{-3} *M* than for 10^{-4} *M* calcium benzoate solutions. Although this ratio is in excellent agreement with the ratio which can be derived from previous results (*1, 2*), the absolute values for *G*(Sal) are different. For 10^{-3} *M* and 10^{-4} *M* solutions the Co^{60} γ-ray values for *G*(Sal) of 0.65_5 and 0.59_5 (Table III), respectively, are about 6% lower than those determined previously (*1, 2*). Although specific reason(s) for the difference cannot be designated, certain points are worthy of comment. As the purity of the salicylic acid was not determined in previous studies, these results are probably at least 1% high. Furthermore, the previous *G*(Sal) value for 10^{-4} *M* calcium benzoate solutions (*1*) was derived from slopes of [Sal]–dose plots over the range 10 to 120 rads, a method which could lead to a high *G*(Sal) value on account of the enhanced salicylic acid concentrations at low doses (method A_1, Table II). The actual technique of fluorescence measurement employed previously (*1*) involved measurement of two "standards" immediately before and immediately after measurements were made on a series of irradiated solutions. This method cannot be relied on to compensate for lamp fluctuations as accurately as the present method involving a number of alternate measurements for each sample and "standard." It has also been noted that the technique of "matching" samples and "standards" minimizes a number of possible errors.

The results with 10^{-4} *M* calcium benzoate solutions (Table III) are all lower than the corresponding results of Wilson and Carruthers (*8*), who determined *G*(Sal) to be 0.64 for Co^{60} γ-rays, 0.57 for 250-kvcp rays, 0.52 for 100-kvcp X-rays, and 0.52 for 50-kvcp X-rays. The differences are too great to be explained by their use of higher values for *G*(FeIII). It is significant that they employed Pyrex tubes throughout as irradiation vessels. At low photon energies the filtration by the Pyrex walls would produce a "hardening" of the beam incident on the solutions, and, since *G*(Sal) is more energy-dependent than *G*(FeIII), this would lead to higher measured values for *G*(Sal). This effect may explain the limiting value for *G*(Sal) reported by Wilson and Carruthers. However, it does not explain the differences noted for Co^{60} γ-radiation and 250-kvcp X-irradiation where similar irradiation vessels were used.

If we take into account the random errors inherent in the ferrous sulfate and calcium benzoate techniques (standard deviations in Table III) and systematic errors due to inaccuracies in *G*(FeIII), $\epsilon_{Fe(III)}$, and the purity of salicylic acid, it is reasonable to assume that the *G*(Sal) values (Table III) are probably accurate to about ±5% for Co^{60} γ-rays and about ±8% for the X-rays.

SUMMARY

G(salicylic acid) or G(Sal) has been determined for 10^{-3} M and 10^{-4} M aqueous calcium benzoate solutions irradiated with Co^{60} γ-rays, 250-kvcp X-rays, 100-kvcp X-rays, and 50-kvcp X-rays. The G(Sal) values for Co^{60} γ-rays of 0.65_5 (10^{-3} M) and 0.59_5 (10^{-4} M) are about 6% lower than previously determined values. Possible sources of error in the measurements have been examined and discussed. For the measurement of low doses (16 rads), the use of chromic acid for cleaning irradiation vessels has been shown to yield irreproducible results.

RECEIVED: August 29, 1962

REFERENCES

1. W. A. ARMSTRONG and D. W. GRANT, A highly sensitive chemical dosimeter for ionizing radiation. *Nature* **182,** 747 (1958).
2. W. A. ARMSTRONG and D. W. GRANT, The aqueous benzoate system as a sensitive dosimeter for ionizing radiations. *Can. J. Chem.* **38,** 845–850 (1960).
3. J. WEISS, A. O. ALLEN, and H. A. SCHWARZ, Use of the Fricke ferrous sulphate dosimeter for gamma-ray doses in the range 4 to 40 kr. *Proc. 1st Intern. Conf. Peaceful Uses Atomic Energy, Geneva, 1955* **14,** 179–181 (1956).
4. K. SCHARF, and R. M. LEE, Investigation of the spectrophotometric method of measuring the ferric ion yield in the ferrous sulfate dosimeter. *Radiation Res.* **16,** 115–124 (1962).
5. D. W. GRANT, A new method for the detection of some aromatic acids, *J. Chromatog.* in press.
6. H. P. DIBBS, Adsorption of chromic acid on silica. *Can. J. Chem.* **40,** 565–566 (1962).
7. H. LOEBL, G. STEIN, and J. WEISS, Chemical actions of ionizing radiations on aqueous solutions. VIII. Hydroxylation of benzoic acid by free radicals produced by X-rays. *J. Chem. Soc.* **1951,** 405–407.
8. R. WILSON and J. A. CARRUTHERS, Measurement of bone-marrow dose in a human phantom for Co^{60} γ-rays and low-energy X-rays. *Health Phys.* **7,** 171–177 (1962).

RADIATION RESEARCH **19**, 129–141 (1963)

Bone Marrow Lipids in Rats Exposed to Total-Body Irradiation

FRED SNYDER AND EDGAR A. CRESS

Medical Division, Oak Ridge Institute of Nuclear Studies,[1] Oak Ridge, Tennessee

INTRODUCTION

An elevation in total lipids of bone marrow of irradiated rabbits was first reported by Dietz and Steinberg (*1*) and by Bernheim *et al.* (*2*); neither group identified the lipid classes involved. Histologic evidence in man also indicates that fat accumulates in irradiated marrow. A specific chemical inquiry has been made to evaluate the relationship of these lipid changes to current problems associated with irradiation and bone marrow transplantation. We are investigating two aspects of the problem: (1) the mechanism by which the fat accumulates; and (2) the influence of the elevated lipid on the repopulation of normal marrow cells. This report describes some of the chemical and biological factors associated with the fat accumulation in bone marrow of irradiated animals.

METHODS

Female and male CFN rats were irradiated with 200, 800, or 2000 r (4.08 r/min average tissue dose and 4.83 r/min air dose from cesium-137 sources) in the total-body irradiation facility (*3*) at the Oak Ridge Institute of Nuclear Studies. The rats were allowed free movement in a Lucite box (72 cm long, 30 cm wide, 15 cm high; the sides were 1 cm thick, and the ends 0.6 cm thick) during the irradiation. The range in tissue dose delivered was ±10% as measured with a Victoreen condenser r-meter with a high-energy 25-r ionization chamber in rat phantoms filled with 60% rice and 40% sodium bicarbonate. This chamber had been matched against a sister chamber that had been calibrated with a National Bureau of Standards source.

The animals were sacrificed by decapitation at 1, 2, 3, 7, 8, 14, 42, 45, and 86 days after irradiation. The femurs were removed, and the bone was freed of tissue. The ends of the femur were cut off with the aid of a postmortem saw, and the marrow was aspirated from the marrow cavity under nitrogen pressure into a container used for freeze-drying tissue. In all cases bone marrows (about 20 to 40

[1] Under contract with the U. S. Atomic Energy Commission.

mg of marrow per femur) from a number of rats were pooled. In some cases the wet marrow was extracted directly three times with 2:1 (v/v) chloroform–methanol. Other samples were dried in a freeze-dry apparatus before extraction. The lipid extraction under either condition gave the same results. The total lipid extract was dialyzed against a large volume of distilled water to remove water-soluble substances according to the procedure of Folch (*4*). The purified lipids were fractionated and analyzed by methods described in a later section of this report. In some animals plasma was collected for measurements similar to those performed on the marrow.

Separation of Neutral Lipids and Phospholipids on Silicic Acid Microcolumns

Microcolumns patterned after those described by Freeman *et al.* (*5*) were used to separate the neutral lipids and phospholipids. Three hundred milligrams of 300-mesh silicic acid (Bio-Rad) was placed in 5-ml serological pipets that were plugged on one end with a small wad of glass wool. The silicic acid was washed with 20 ml of chloroform, and 10 mg of the lipid (in 1 ml of $CHCl_3$) was applied to the column. Once the solvent level reached the column surface, 20 ml of $CHCl_3$ was used to elute the neutral lipids from the column. When the last volume of $CHCl_3$ reached the surface of the column, 20 ml of methanol was added to elute the phospholipids. The flow rate was maintained at 0.5 ml/min under nitrogen pressure. Fatty acid ester linkages (*6*), glycerol (*7*), and the phosphorus (*8*) content of the two fractions were determined.

Thin-Layer Chromatography

Thin-layer chromatography (TLC) (*9*), with Silica Gel G as the adsorbent, was used to evaluate qualitative changes in the lipids of marrow and also as a preparative procedure for gas–liquid chromatography analysis. Iodine vapor, 2,7′-dichlorofluorescein (0.2% in ethanol), or concentrated H_2SO_4 was used to visualize the separated compounds. When H_2SO_4 was to be used, the silica was suspended in 50% ethanol and applied as a thin layer on an aluminum plate identical in dimensions to the glass plate. Some plates were used to prepare triglycerides for further analysis; up to 18 mg of triglyceride was collected on a single glass plate for the analysis of fatty acids and ester linkages. The developed chromatogram was supported above a funnel, and a Teflon spatula was used to scrape the triglyceride areas into a test tube. The triglycerides were eluted from the Silica Gel G with chloroform–methanol (2:1), and the eluate was filtered through a Büchner funnel.

Preparation of Methyl Esters

Transmethylation of the triglycerides was accomplished by heating the filtered chloroform eluate with 5 ml of methanol containing 2% H_2SO_4 for 1 hour at 75°C. After cooling, water was added, and the mixture was immediately neutralized with $NaHCO_3$. The esters were extracted four times with equal volumes of petroleum ether, a Vortex mixer being used to facilitate the extraction, and the solvent was evaporated under nitrogen. The esters were redissolved in an appropriate volume of petroleum ether for injection into the gas chromatograph.

Gas–Liquid Chromatography

The methyl esters of the fatty acids were separated on a 6-foot column of ethylene glycol succinate (16%) on Chromosorb W (100 to 140 mesh) in a Beckman GC 2A gas chromatograph. This packing material was purchased from Applied Science Laboratories. Other conditions were as follows: column temperature, 190°C; helium flow rate, 70 cc/min; inlet heater, 275°C; and current setting for filaments of thermoconductivity cell, 250 ma. Retention times were determined for fatty acid standards obtained from the Hormel Institute and Applied Science Laboratories.

Histology

Histologic sections of the control and irradiated marrow were prepared by Dr. Anton Lindner, the University of Oklahoma Medical Center, Oklahoma City, Oklahoma.

RESULTS

Biological Results

The time curve for the increase in bone marrow lipid of the rat is shown in Fig. 1. Peak values occur about 1 week ($P < 0.001$) after the 800-r exposure and only slowly decrease with time. Total lipids appear to increase as a function of dose according to the equation $y = bx^a$, since the log of lipid versus log of dose when plotted graphically gives a linear relationship (Fig 2). Figure 3 shows that the marrow lipid content increases as the water decreases. However, this increase is not due simply to dehydration, because the ratio of lipid to nonlipid solids was 0.2 for controls, 0.4 for 200-r treated rats, and 1.8 and 2.2 for two groups of 800-r treated rats 1 week after exposure. Table I shows the variations in water, lipid, and residue values of control and 800-r (8 days after total-body irradiation) rats. The changes in all three compartments after irradiation are highly significant ($P < 0.001$). The increase in total marrow lipids is also correlated quite closely with the increase in fat cells seen in histologic sections (Fig. 4).

The effect of total-body irradiation on bone marrow lipids of other species was determined. In these measurements, conditions were arbitrarily chosen to be identical to those used for the rat. The results in Table II indicate that only the rat showed the marked elevation of marrow fat. The dog, pig, and monkey show a *decrease* in total lipids of marrow after irradiation; however, the small number of animals used does not justify a statistical evaluation of the decrease. A more complete comparison of other species should include a thorough study of other time periods, doses, and marrow sites. On the other hand, the marrow lipid response in the rat appears to be typical of what is seen in histologic sections of marrow obtained from irradiated patients.

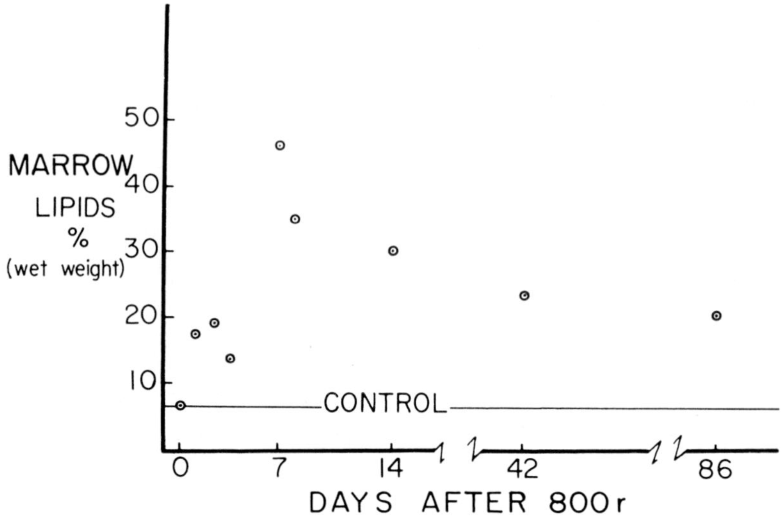

FIG. 1. Total lipids of bone marrow (wet weight) after 800 r of total-body irradiation. Each value represents pooled samples from the following number of rats: 0 day = 182 rats (range 5.5 to 9.3% for seven pooled groups); 1 day = 4 rats; 2 days = 8 rats; 3 days = 8 rats; 7 days = 8 rats; 8 days = 65 rats (range 33.1 to 46.3% for five pooled groups); 14 days = 8 rats; 42 days = 4 rats; 86 days = 4 rats. The probability for chance occurrence was less than 0.001 when the test of significance was applied to the difference between the mean of the control group and the 800-r (8-day) rats.

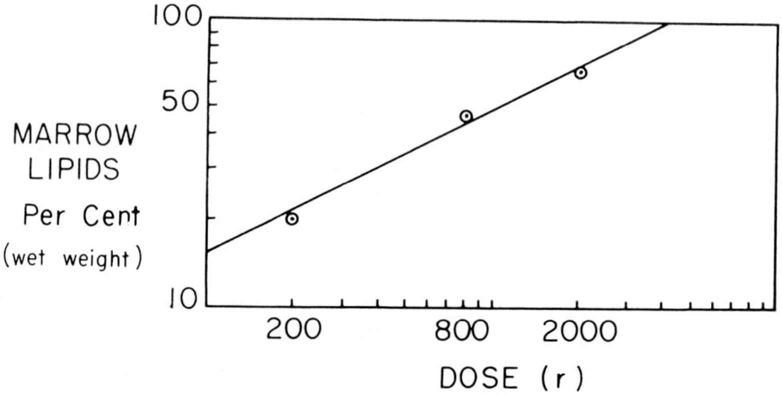

FIG. 2. The effect of dose (total-body irradiation) on total lipids of bone marrow (wet weight). The ordinate and abscissa are logarithmic scales. 200 r = 12 rats; 800 r = 65 rats; 2000 r = 4 rats. All animals were sacrificed 8 days after receiving total-body irradiation.

Chemical Results

The major lipid component of both control and irradiated marrow is triglycerides. Table III shows that the increase in total lipids after irradiation is due entirely to

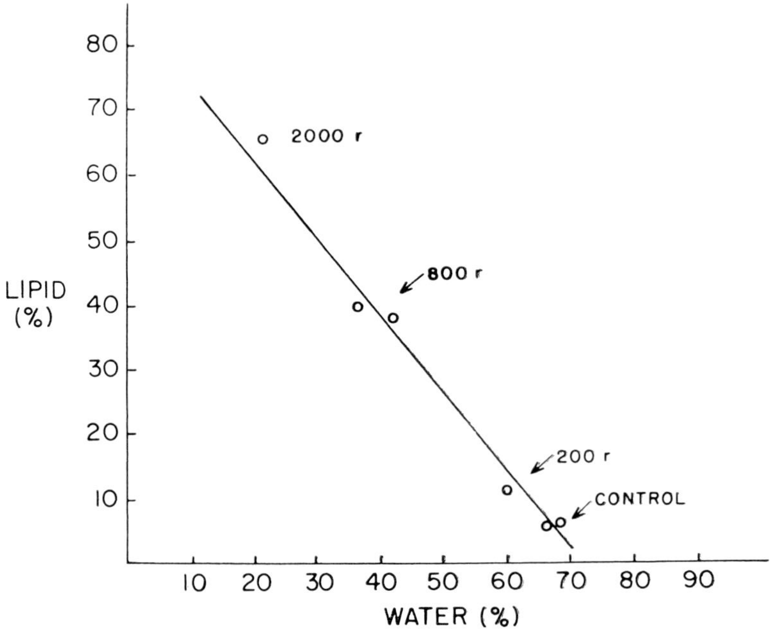

FIG. 3. The effect of total-body irradiation on the relationship of water and lipid content of bone marrow. Each value represents pooled samples from the following number of rats: control = 182 rats; 200 r = 20 rats; 800 r = 65 rats; 2000 r = 4 rats. All rats were sacrificed 8 days after receiving total-body irradiation.

TABLE I

COMPOSITION OF RAT FEMUR MARROW 8 DAYS AFTER 800 ROENTGENS OF TOTAL BODY IRRADIATION[a]

	Number of rats	*Lipid* (%)	*Water* (%)	*Residue*(%)
Controls	182	7.2 ± 1.4 (7)	65.6 ± 1.0 (5)	27.9 ± 1.0 (5)
8 days after 800 r of total-body irradiation	65	38.4 ± 5.6 (4)	39.0 ± 6.7 (3)	22.3 ± 1.2 (3)

[a] The numbers preceded by ± are standard deviations. The numbers in parentheses represent the number of pooled groups used for the determination of the mean value. The lipid expressed on the basis of dry weight was 19.0 ± 2.2% for the control groups and 63.1 ± 4.5% for the irradiated groups. The probability of chance difference between the control group and the irradiated group for lipid, water, and residue compartments was less than 0.001 when the test of significance was applied.

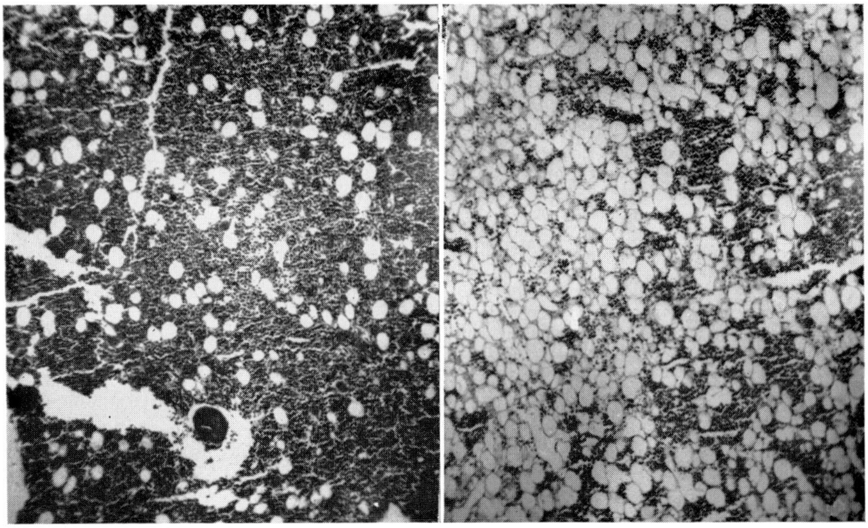

FIG. 4. Histologic sections of femur marrow from control (left) and irradiated (8 days after 800 r) rats (right). The sections were stained with hematoxylin and eosin.

TABLE II

EFFECT OF 800 ROENTGENS OF TOTAL-BODY IRRADIATION ON BONE MARROW TOTAL LIPIDS 8 DAYS AFTER EXPOSURE

Species	*Sex*	*Age*	*Marrow source*	*Lipids (%)*[a]	
				Control	*800 r*
Rat	Female	70–90 days	Femur	7.2 (182)	38.4 (65)
Rat	Male	70–90 days	Femur	3.5 (25)	36.9 (25)
Rabbit	Female	Adult	Femur	35.3 (2)	42.6 (2)
Dog	Female	Adult	Humerus and tibia	60.2 (2)	55.0 (2)
Monkey (*Tamarinus nigricollis*)	Female	Adult	Femur	2.2 (1)	0.7 (2)
Pig	Female	Adult	Humerus	83.3 (1)	54.8 (1)

[a] The numbers in parentheses represent the number of animals.

triglycerides. Other minor components in the marrow as indicated by thin-layer chromatography (Fig. 5) are cholesterol, phospholipids, and traces of fatty acids and glyceryl ethers. Cholesterol esters were not found in bone marrow lipids. The presence of glyceryl ethers in the marrow lipids are indicated by the thin-layer chromatogram shown in Fig. 6. The material used for the chromatography in Fig. 6 represents only those marrow lipids that run below and including cholesterol in the system used for the chromatogram shown in Fig. 5. A preparative TLC plate

TABLE III

THIN-LAYER CHROMATOGRAPHY ANALYSIS OF RAT BONE MARROW TOTAL LIPID EXTRACT

	Control	*800 r*[a]
Per cent of total esterified fatty acids as triglyceride	85	91
Triglyceride, μg/mg marrow	53	384
Phosphorus, μg/mg total lipid extract	5.94	0.85
Phosphorus, μg/mg bone marrow	0.35	0.32

[a] 8 days after total-body irradiation.

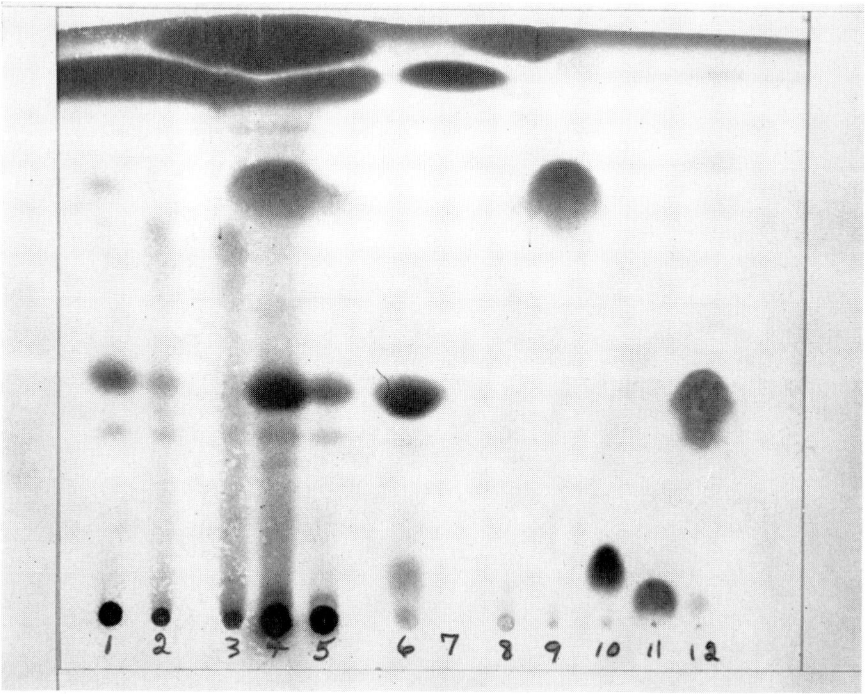

FIG. 5. Thin-layer chromatogram of bone marrow, adipose tissue, plasma, and liver lipids: (1) control marrow, (2) 800-r marrow, (3) perirenal fat, (4) plasma lipids, (5) liver lipids, (6) cholesterol, (7) triolein, (8) cholesterol stearate, (9) oleic acid, (10) batyl alcohol, (11) monopalmitin, (12) 1,3-dipalmitin. The thin layer of silica was applied to an aluminum plate and after chromatography was visualized by spraying with concentrated H_2SO_4 and heating. The origin is located immediately above the numbers. The solvent front containing the cholesterol esters shows a continuous black line representing impurities in the solvent; the esters of cholesterol are distinguished from these impurities by a color change (red-blue) that the sterols exhibit upon reaction with H_2SO_4 and initial heat. Under no circumstances have we ever seen this color change or a spot corresponding to cholesterol esters when bone marrow lipids have been separated by TLC.

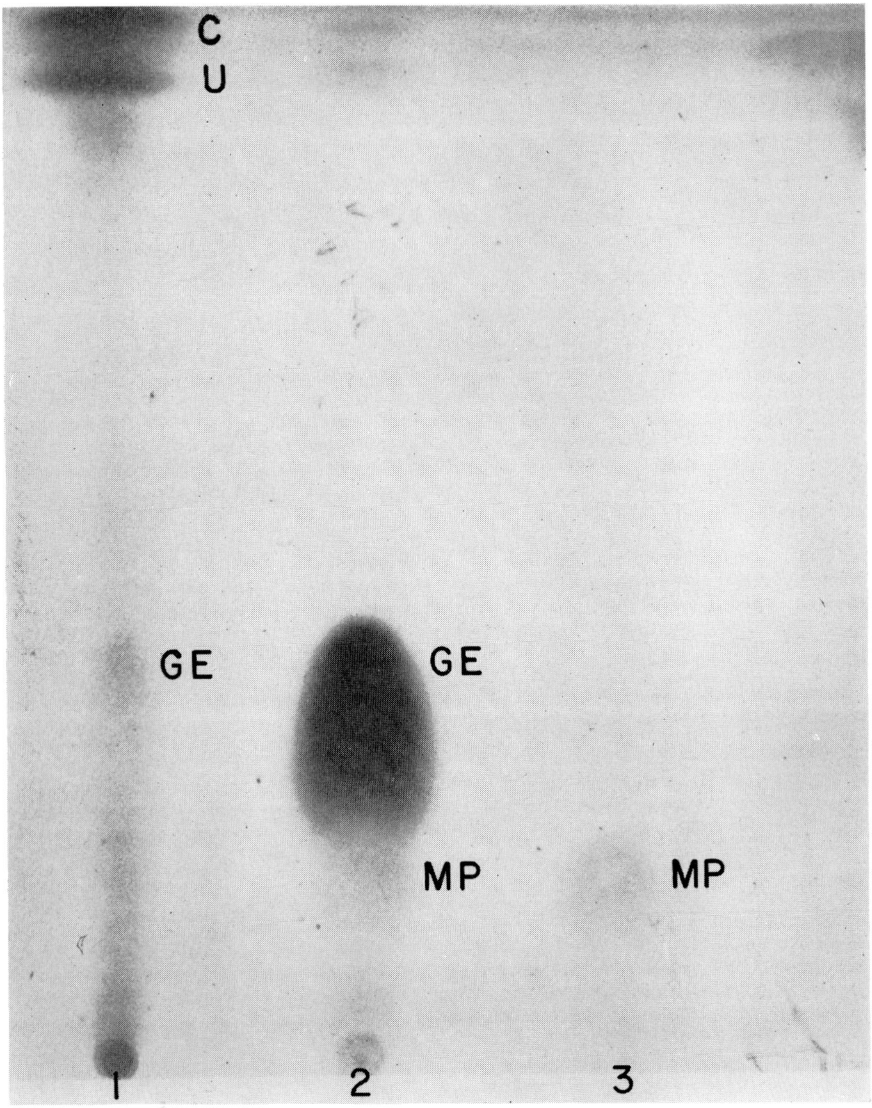

FIG. 6. Thin-layer chromatogram (Silica Gel G) of (1) 800-r femur marrow; (2) batyl alcohol, selachyl alcohol, chimyl alcohol, and monopalmitin, and (3) monopalmitin. GE = glyceryl ether. MP = monopalmitin. C = cholesterol. U = unidentified. The thin layer of silica was applied to an aluminum plate and after chromatography was visualized by spraying with concentrated H_2SO_4 and heating. The origin is located immediately above the numbers.

of marrow lipids was separated in a solvent system of Skelly Solve F, diethyl ether, and acetic acid (80:20:1); the components below and including the cholesterol were recovered from the plates as described earlier and rechromatographed (Fig. 6) in the Skelly Solve F–diethyl ether–methanol (80:20:5) system.

The C-16 and C-18 fatty acid pattern of bone marrow triglycerides is like that found in the triglycerides of liver and perirenal fat. Palmitic and oleic acids were the major fatty acids (accounting for about 80% of the total) present in the triglyceride fractions isolated (Fig. 7). Moreover, the 800-r irradiation did not alter the relative amounts of these acids in the triglycerides of the femur marrow.

Figure 8 demonstrates that essentially no change in the triglycerides occurs in the plasma. However, a considerable increase in the plasma phospholipids occurs within 1 day after total-body irradiation, and the phospholipids remain elevated for at least 45 days after exposure.

DISCUSSION

It has been demonstrated by thin-layer chromatography that the composition of the lipid in normal rat bone marrow is qualitatively similar to that found in perirenal fat. This finding confirms other observations made with less-sensitive techniques (*10*) that showed bone marrow lipids to be chemically indistinguishable from other adipose fat. The largest lipid component of control and irradiated rat marrow was triglyceride, and of this fraction palmitic and oleic acids accounted for about 80% of the constituent fatty acids. These data indicate that the bone marrow fatty acid composition from rats and man (*11*) are similar.

In these studies on rats, irradiation was shown to increase the triglycerides of the marrow cavity at the expense of water. The reciprocal relationship of water and lipid in the marrow confirms the earlier work of Dietz and Steinberg (*1*). The accumulation of triglycerides may result from an increased biosynthesis, for Altman *et al.* (*12*) have shown that bone marrow homogenates from irradiated rabbits do synthesize fatty acids from acetate at a considerably higher rate than those from controls. The role of oxidation and mobilization also must be considered; however, the absence of any change in the neutral glycerides of plasma suggests that transport of glycerides as such from other sites is not an important factor. An initial investigation of plasma-free fatty acids revealed little change in this pool at 1, 3, 5, and 8 days after 800 r of total-body irradiation. The possibility that a humoral agent may be a responsible factor for at least part of the lipid response is suggested by preliminary evidence which shows lipids of the femur to increase after irradiation of only the head; however, additional experiments are required for more definitive proof. The marked influence of hormones on lipid metabolism has been well documented in literature.

The response to irradiation is much more apparent in areas of marrow that are normally highly cellular, with little fat. In support of this statement, our data show

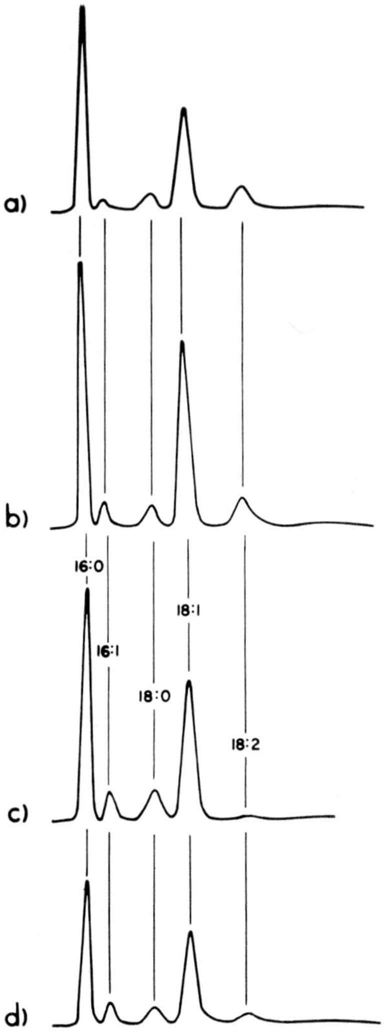

FIG. 7. The effect of 800 r of total-body irradiation on the C-16 and C-18 fatty acid composition of bone marrow triglycerides. The per cent fatty acid in control and in 800-r marrow, respectively, is 16:0 (34.8%, 33.1%); 16:1 (9.1%, 7.4%); 18:0 (9.0%, 8.9%); 18:1 (42.7%, 45.6%); 18:2 (2.1%, 3.9%). (*a*) Control marrow; (*b*) irradiated marrow; (*c*) control liver; (*d*) control adipose tissue.

a much more striking change in the marrow of rat femurs than the changes observed by Dietz and Steinberg (*1*) and by Bernheim *et al.* (*2*) in the marrow of rabbits. Table II shows that the femurs of rabbits are not very active hematopoietically as compared to those of rats, but instead contain a high amount of fat.

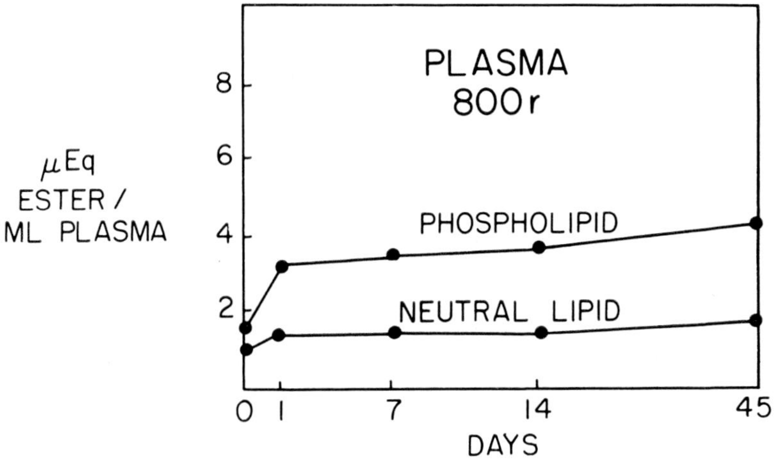

FIG. 8. The effect of 800 r of total-body irradiation on the esterified fatty acids of plasma. Each value represents a pooled sample from the following number of rats: 0 days = 8 rats; 1 day = 4 rats; 7 days = 8 rats; 14 days = 8 rats; 45 days = 4 rats. Measurement of the glycerol content in these samples gave essentially the same curves.

Of the minor lipid components found in bone marrow, the glyceryl ethers are perhaps the most interesting as related to irradiation effects because of their dramatic stimulatory effect on hematopoiesis. The early work of Marberg and Wiles (*13*) with yellow marrow was the first to indicate that the nonsaponifiable fraction of marrow lipids had a hematopoietic stimulating factor present. More recently, protection by glyceryl ethers against the leukopenia in irradiated subjects was reported by Edlund (*14*) and by Brohult and Holmberg (*15–17*). Quantitation of glyceryl ethers in human bone marrow revealed that they constituted about 0.2% of the total lipids (*18*). The protection against irradiation death by other lipids has also received attention (*19*) and further substantiates the involvement of lipids in irradiation injury.

The present study describes the factors involved in the accumulation of triglyceride in irradiated bone marrow cells; however, it does not offer answers concerning the mechanism involved. Metabolic studies of specific marrow cells and their lipid fractions as separated by thin-layer chromatography are expected to answer some of the fundamental questions raised by this report.

SUMMARY

Thin-layer chromatography has been used to demonstrate that bone marrow lipids of rats are primarily triglycerides; gas–liquid chromatography of the fraction revealed that palmitic and oleic acids account for more than 80% of the fatty acids. Minor lipid components present in the control and irradiated marrow are glyceryl ethers, cholesterol, fatty acids, and phospholipids. Cholesterol esters were not found. Total-body irradiation (800 r) increases the femur marrow triglyceride fraction approximately six times by 1 week after irradiation, and it remains elevated for many weeks. The relationship between dose and increase in marrow triglycerides appears to fit the equation $y = bx^a$. The water and lipid content of bone marrow bear a reciprocal relation to each other, while both water and residue are significantly reduced in the irradiated femur marrow.

ACKNOWLEDGMENTS

We are indebted to Dr. Anton Lindner, The University of Oklahoma Medical Center, Oklahoma City, for the histologic examination of the bone marrow, to Dr. F. Comas for helping with the dosimetry measurements, and to Nelson Stephens and Charles Dickinson for technical assistance.

RECEIVED: September 10, 1962

REFERENCES

1. A. A. DIETZ and B. STEINBERG, Chemical composition of irradiated bone marrow. *Arch. Biochem. Biophys.* **23**, 222–228 (1949).
2. F. BERNHEIM, A. OTTOLENGHI, and K. M. WILBUR, Studies on bone marrow lipid in normal and irradiated rabbits. *Radiation Res.* **4**, 132–138 (1956).
3. A. C. MORRIS, JR., Measurements in a total-body irradiation facility. *Intern. J. Appl. Radiation Isotopes* **11**, 108–113 (1961).
4. J. FOLCH, M. LEES, and G. H. S. STANLEY, A simple method for the isolation and purification of total lipides from animal tissues. *J. Biol. Chem.* **226**, 497–509 (1957).
5. N. K. FREEMAN, F. T. LINDGREN, Y. C. NG, and A. NICHOLS, Serum lipide analysis by chromatography and infrared spectrophotometry. *J. Biol. Chem.* **227**, 449–464 (1957).
6. F. SNYDER and N. STEPHENS, A simplified spectrophotometric determination of ester groups in lipids. *Biochim. Biophys. Acta* **34**, 244–245 (1959).
7. E. VAN HANDEL, Suggested modifications of the micro determination of triglycerides. *Clin. Chem.* **7**, 249–251 (1961).
8. W. D. HARRIS and P. POPAT, Determination of the phosphorus content of lipids. *J. Am. Oil Chemists' Soc.* **31**, 124–127 (1954).
9. H. K. MANGOLD, Thin-layer chromatography of lipids. *J. Am. Oil Chemists' Soc.* **38**, 708–727 (1961).
10. J. D. EVANS and M. J. OPPENHEIMER, Effect of bleeding on rabbit marrow polyunsaturated fatty acids. *Am. J. Physiol.* **181**, 509–512 (1955).
11. P. K. LUND, D. M. ABADI, and J. C. MATHIES, Lipid composition of normal human bone marrow as determined by column chromatography. *J. Lipid Res.* **3**, 95–98 (1962).
12. K. I. ALTMAN, J. E. RICHMOND, and K. SALOMON, A note on the synthesis of fatty acids in bone marrow homogenates as affected by X-radiation. *Biochim. Biophys. Acta* **7**, 460–465 (1951).
13. C. M. MARBERG and H. O. WILES, Granulocytopoietic fraction of yellow bone marrow. *Arch. Internal Med.* **61**, 408–429 (1938).
14. T. EDLUND, Protective effect of *d,l*-alpha-octadecylglycerol-ether in mice given total body X-irradiation. *Nature* **174**, 1102 (1954).
15. A. BROHULT and J. HOLMBERG, Alkoxyglycerols in the treatment of leucopaenia caused by irradiation. *Nature* **174**, 1102–1103 (1954).
16. A. BROHULT, Alkoxyglycerol-esters in irradiation treatment. In *Advances in Radiobiology* (G. C. de Hevesy, A. G. Forssberg, and J. D. Abbatt, eds.), pp. 241–247, Oliver & Boyd, Edinburgh, 1957.

17. A. Brohult, Effects of alkoxyglycerols and especially selachyl alcohol on the bone marrow in connexion with irradiation treatment and in leukaemia therapy. *Nature* **181,** 1484–1485 (1958).

18. B. Hallgren and S. Larsson, The glyceryl ethers in man and cow. *J. Lipid Res.* **3,** 39–43 (1962).

19. J. K. Ashikawa, The lipid syndrome in mammalian radiobiology with emphasis on postirradiation protection of animals with lipids. U.S. Atomic Energy Commission Report UCRL-9592, pp. 1–147 (1961).

RADIATION RESEARCH 19, 142–155 (1963)

The Relative Potency of Fast Neutrons and 250-Kvp X-Rays in the Guinea Pig[1]

RICHARD D. PHILLIPS, DONALD J. KIMELDORF, AND DAVID C. L. JONES

U. S. Naval Radiological Defense Laboratory, San Francisco, California

INTRODUCTION

Fast neutrons have been shown to be approximately twice as effective as 250-kvp X-rays in terms of acute (30-day) lethality in many small mammals (*1*). A possible explanation for the potency ratio being greater than unity may reside in differential mechanisms with respect to lethality. The gastrointestinal tract appears to be a system in which the extent of damage may be dependent on the type of radiation employed (*2, 3*). The study of neutron potency in a species in which gastrointestinal damage is not pronounced after exposure to X-rays offers an opportunity to test the value of this hypothesis. The guinea pig is believed to qualify in this respect, primarily on the basis of indirect evidence regarding gastrointestinal function after X-irradiation. In a study by Smith *et al.* (*4*), there was little or no change in body weight during the first week after X-irradiation. Newsom and Kimeldorf (*5*) reported very little change in food consumption in guinea pigs for the first 3 days after a midlethal exposure to X-rays, which also suggested minimal gastrointestinal damage.

The present study was done to determine the 30-day lethality response of guinea pigs exposed to fast neutrons or 250-kvp X-rays, and to assess the relative potency of the two types of radiation with respect to gastrointestinal injury.

METHODS

Young adult male guinea pigs of the Hartley strain were used. The animals were obtained immediately after weaning from a specific pathogen-free stock bred at the Dugway Proving Grounds, Utah. The animals were maintained in individual cages

[1] This study was supported through funds provided by the Bureau of Medicine and Surgery, and the Defense Atomic Support Agency. The opinions and assertions contained herein are the private ones of the authors and are not to be construed as official or as reflecting the views of the Navy Department.

and fed Purina guinea pig chow (vitamin C supplemented) and water ad libitum. During the first week after delivery of the animals, Trisulmeth (Trico) tablets (containing 0.167 gm of sulfadiazine, 0.167 gm of sulfamerazine, and 0.167 gm of methazine) were added to the water bottles of the animals. During a 3-week pre-experimental holding period the animals were weighed three times weekly; no animals with abnormal growth curves were noted.

Animals were distributed into groups for neutron, X-ray, or sham exposure (control) on the basis of comparable means and variances in body weight. Whole-body neutron and X-ray exposures were done on the same day, and the geometry for exposure was the same for both types of radiation. To gain a more homogeneous exposure, each animal was placed in the exposure field with a lateral surface toward the beam, and the exposure was interrupted at half the total dose in order to present the contralateral surface to the entering beam.

The 60-inch cyclotron of the University of California Crocker Laboratory was used as the source of fast neutrons. The neutron and γ-ray characteristics of this source have been described previously (*6*). Neutrons were provided by bombarding a thick beryllium target with 12-Mev protons. The neutron energy distribution approximates that of the fission process. Dosimetry was accomplished by sulfur threshold detectors utilizing the $S^{32}(n,p)P^{32}$ reaction. From the cross section of this reaction and the knowledge of the neutron spectrum, it is possible to calculate the total neutron flux and the resultant first-collision neutron tissue dose according to the method described by Tochilin *et al.* (*7*).

X-Ray exposures were made with a 250-kvp unit, operated at 15 ma, with a 0.5 mm Cu and 1 mm Al filter (HVL, 1.28 mm Cu). The dose rate was 24 to 29 r/min as measured by a Victoreen chamber. A factor of 0.97 was used to convert the roentgen dose, measured in a paraffin phantom, to rad dose.

RESULTS

Lethality

A study was done to determine the relative potency of fast neutrons with respect to 250-kvp X-rays for lethality in the guinea pig. Of the 375 animals used in this study, 138 were exposed to neutrons, 177 were exposed to X-rays, and 60 were sham-exposed controls. The lethality studies were made concurrently for neutrons and X-rays, and all animals were housed in the same room, thus assuring identical environmental conditions. Animals were checked daily for deaths.

The time distributions of deaths after neutron and X-ray exposures are summarized in Table I. The patterns after either type of radiation in the lethal range were essentially the same. There were no deaths before day 7 in the neutron-exposed groups, and no deaths before day 9 in the X-ray-exposed groups. Even when the neutron exposure dose was twice the dose required to produce a 100%

TABLE I

DISTRIBUTION OF DEATHS WITH TIME POSTIRRADIATION AND MEAN SURVIVAL TIMES

Dose (rads)	N	*Number dead on postirradiation day:*												Mean survival time (days)
		1–6	7	8	9	10	11	12	13	14	15	16–23	24–30	
							Neutrons							
119	18	—	—	—	—	—	—	—	1	—	—	1	—	15
132	18	—	—	—	—	—	1	1	—	1	—	—	—	13
140	18	—	—	—	—	—	—	1	1	1	1	—	—	13
144	8	—	—	—	—	—	—	1	—	—	—	2	—	17
152	18	—	1	—	1	—	1	1	2	1	—	1	—	12
161	18	—	—	1	4	2	1	1	3	—	1	—	—	11
172	8	—	—	—	—	1	2	1	—	—	—	—	1	14
175	8	—	—	—	—	—	1	2	—	2	—	—	—	12
221	8	—	—	—	—	1	4	2	—	—	—	1	—	12
323	8	—	—	—	2	5	—	1	—	—	—	—	—	10
431	8	—	3	3	1	1	—	—	—	—	—	—	—	8
							X-rays							
150	7	—	—	—	—	—	—	—	—	1	—	1	1	17
200	8	—	—	—	—	—	—	2	1	—	—	—	—	12
225	30	—	—	—	1	—	2	—	2	2	—	1	—	11
250	7	—	—	—	—	1	2	1	1	—	—	—	—	11
275	18	—	—	—	1	4	2	1	1	—	—	1	—	11
300	26	—	—	—	1	3	3	—	1	—	1	3	1	12
350	25	—	—	—	—	4	4	—	2	—	—	4	—	13
375	30	—	—	—	2	6	5	3	5	1	—	—	—	11
400	26	—	—	—	1	6	6	2	—	4	—	2	—	12

lethality response, no deaths occurred before day 7. Most of the deaths occurred 9 to 16 days after exposure in the lethal range with both types of radiation. As seen in Table I, the mean survival times within each radiation type in the lethal range were fairly consistent, and no obvious trends with dose were present. There was a small decrease in the mean survival time after exposure to neutrons in the supralethal range (323 and 431 rads), but even at these high exposure doses no deaths occurred before day 7. The pooled mean survival times of groups exposed to 250-kvp X-rays and fast neutrons in the lethal range were 12.2 and 13.3 days, respectively.

Table II presents the estimates of the $LD_{50(30)}$ values and slopes of the regression lines for both types of radiation as calculated by an analysis of quantal response using a log dose transformation.[2] The $LD_{50(30)}$ for animals exposed to fast neutrons was 155 rads, with a 95% fiducial probability that the value lies between

[2] B. E. Vaughan and A. K. Davis, to be published.

TABLE II

ESTIMATES OF PARAMETERS OF THE DOSE-RESPONSE RELATIONSHIP OF GUINEA PIGS EXPOSED TO FAST NEUTRONS OR 250-KVP X-RAYS

Parameters	*Radiation type*	
	Neutrons	*X-rays*
$LD_{50(30)}$	155 rads	273 rads
Fiducial limits ($P \leq 0.05$)	149–164 rads	233–306 rads
Number of animals	138	177
Number of dose groups	10	9
Analysis of quantal response:		
Regression coefficient ± S.E.	6.0 ± 1.0	1.7 ± 0.4
G	0.11	0.21
χ^2	4.67	7.17
df	8	7

149 and 164 rads. The $LD_{50(30)}$ for animals exposed to 250-kvp X-rays was 273 rads, with 95% fiducial probability limits of 233 and 306 rads. Thus, in terms of relative potency with respect to the $LD_{50(30)}$, fast neutrons were 1.8 times as effective as 250-kvp X-rays.

Food and Water Consumption

Food consumption measurements were made to determine the extent, if any, of depression in food consumption in the guinea pig as an index of radiation damage to the gastrointestinal system. Water consumption measurements were made concurrently with the food consumption measurements as a further elaboration of the consummatory response of guinea pigs to radiation damage.

Consumption measurements were made over a 22-hour period per day, and all values are expressed in grams. There was essentially no food spillage by the guinea pigs, and no correction was required. Water consumption was measured by placing jars under the water bottle spouts to collect the spillage and subtracting this amount from the change in water bottle weight. A thin layer of heavy mineral oil was placed in each jar to prevent evaporation of collected spillage.

Food and water consumption measurements were made on 131 animals prior to radiation. These animals were then distributed into six groups ($N = 18$ per group) for radiation exposure and two control groups ($N = 11$ and 12 per group) on the basis of comparable means and variances in food and water consumption scores and in body weight. One control and three experimental groups were used for each of the two types of radiation. The three doses for neutron exposure were 132, 152, and 161 rads, which resulted in 30-day survival rates of 83%, 53%, and 41%, respectively. The doses for X-ray exposure were 225, 350, and 400 rads,

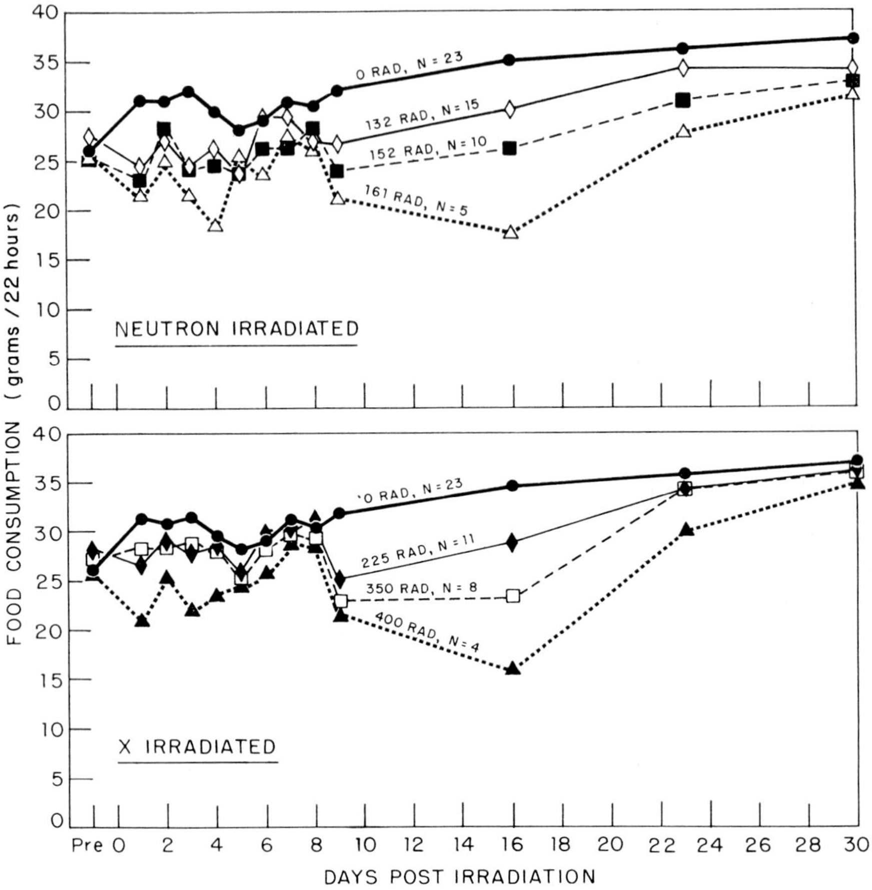

FIG. 1. Food consumption of neutron and X-irradiated survivors and controls. Average standard deviation for preirradiation values was 3.5 gm per 22-hours sample.

which resulted in 62%, 33%, and 25% survivals, respectively. Food and water consumption measurements were made daily for the first 9 days and on days 16, 23, and 30 after exposure. The two control groups did not differ from each other and were combined for purposes of data presentation.

The food consumptions of neutron and X-irradiated survivors and controls are shown in Fig. 1. The preirradiation mean values and variances were similar in all eight groups, with means ranging from 25.7 to 28.3 gm per 22-hour sample and standard deviations ranging from 2.1 to 4.9 gm. Relative to controls, there was only a slight depression in food consumption of irradiated animals during the first week after exposure. A more impressive depression, apparently dose-dependent, occurred during the second week. The response patterns were similar after both types of radiation. However, in the X-irradiated groups there appeared to be a more evident trend toward recovery to the level of controls within the 30-day period of observation. The food consumptions of neutron and X-irradiated nonsurvivors (not shown) did not differ from those of survivors at comparable doses during the first week after radiation exposure. After this period, the food consumption values of the irradiated non-survivors continued to decrease until death.

There was one major difference between the neutron- and X-ray-exposed groups with respect to food consumption after radiation exposure. The dose of X-rays required to produce a given decrease in food consumption during the second week after X-irradiation was approximately twice the dose required to bring about an equivalent decrease after neutron exposure. It is important to note that no marked depression in food consumption occurred during the first week when gastrointestinal damage would be expected to be apparent. Even at the highest dose, food consumption never decreased appreciably below 50% of control values.

Water consumption values of neutron- and X-irradiated survivors and controls are shown in Fig. 2. The preirradiation means for the eight groups ranged from

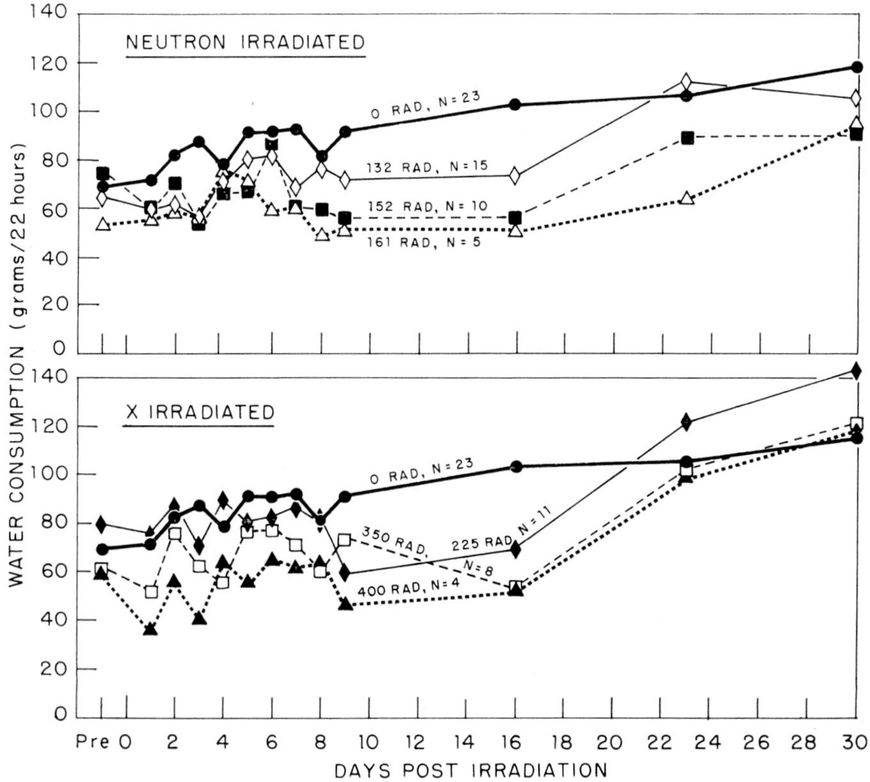

FIG. 2. Water consumption of neutron and X-irradiated survivors and controls. Average standard deviation for preirradiation values was 20.7 gm per 22-hour sample.

53.0 to 70.9 gm per 22-hour sample, with an average standard deviation of 20.2 gm. The pattern of water consumption after irradiation was similar to that of food consumption. During the first week after radiation exposure, the water consumption of irradiated survivors did not differ significantly from controls. There was a mild depression during the second week, which appeared to be dose-dependent. The patterns were generally similar after either type of radiation, except that recovery was apparent by day 23 postirradiation in the X-ray groups but only partially complete by day 30 in the neutron groups. The water consumption of irradiated nonsurvivors (not shown) resembled that for the irradiated survivors until day 9 postirradiation, at which time it decreased sharply until death. It is of special interest to note that no polydipsia occurred after either type of radiation.

Body Weight

Body-weight patterns after irradiation are of considerable importance, since moderate or severe early gastrointestinal damage presumably would be reflected by a decrease in body weight during the first week after exposure. Body weights were measured on the same animals in which food and water consumption measurements were made. Animals were weighed three times weekly for at least 3 weeks prior to exposure and on the day preceding exposure. After irradiation, weights were measured daily for the first 9 days, then at 2- or 3-day intervals up to 30 days postirradiation. The body weights of the two control groups did not differ and were combined for purposes of data presentation.

The body weights of survivors after exposure to neutrons and X-rays are shown in Fig. 3. The preirradiation means of the neutron-irradiated survivors ranged from 377 to 393 gm, with an average standard deviation of 44.5 gm. The range of the preirradiation means for the X-irradiated survivor groups was 379 to 400 gm, with an average standard deviation of 39.9 gm. The body weights of survivors were only slightly less than those of controls for the first 9 days after exposure. After day 9 postirradiation, the differences in body weight became more pronounced, with a definite ordering with respect to dose. The body weights of neutron- and X-irradiated nonsurvivors (not shown) were similar to those of the survivors for the first 14 days after exposure, but continued to decrease until death.

In irradiated groups, the marked depression in body weight which occurred in the second week postirradiation corresponded in time to the previously described depression in food and water consumption. The body-weight depression differed from the depression of food and water consumption in that recovery to control values was approached for food and water consumption, whereas the body weight in irradiated groups was markedly less than in controls 30 days after exposure. The irradiated groups appeared to be running parallel to the controls in a dose dependent fashion.

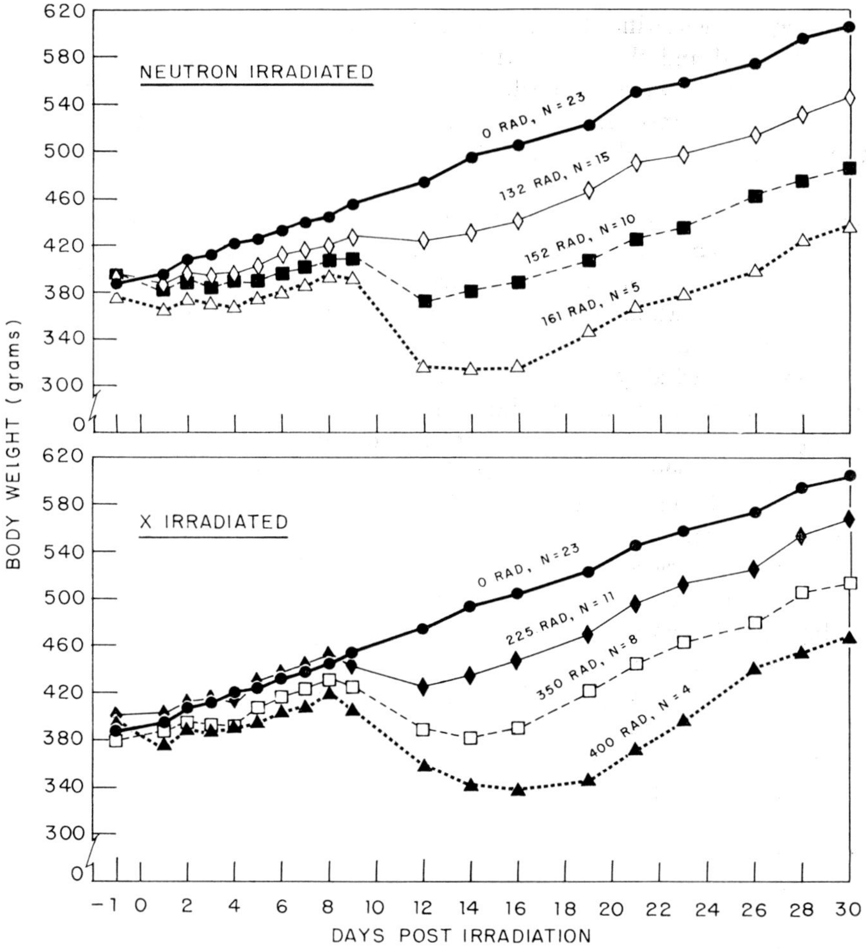

FIG. 3. Body weights after exposure to neutrons or X-rays. The average standard deviation for preirradiation means was 44.5 gm for the neutron-irradiated groups and 39.9 gm for the X-irradiated groups.

Pathology

A study was designed to determine the extent of gastrointestinal pathology evident after exposure to lethal doses of X-rays or neutrons. The first study consisted of 22 guinea pigs distributed into three experimental groups (6 animals per group) and a control group (4 animals). The experimental animals were exposed to either 200 or 400 rads of X-rays, or 190 rads of neutrons, and the controls were sham-exposed. Animals from each group were sacrificed on days 1, 3, 5, 7, 9, and 10 after exposure. Two controls were sacrificed on the first day after sham exposure, and the other two were sacrificed on the tenth day. Immediately after sacrifice, organs of the abdominal and thoracic cavities were examined for lesions. Stomachs, intestines, and cecums were removed, slit open, rinsed free of food matter in physiological saline, examined grossly, and then fixed in formalin–acetic acid–alcohol solution. Paraffin-embedded sections were cut at 4 microns and stained with hematoxylin and eosin.

The gross pathology findings for the gastrointestinal tract were negative for all doses at all time points except for massive hemorrhages in the walls of the stomachs on day 10 after exposure. Hemorrhages were also noted in other tissues on day 10 postirradiation (i.e. lungs, urinary bladder, testes) in all three radiation groups. Tissues of the controls were not remarkable.

There were remarkably few changes despite the potential hazard of the doses in terms of lethality. Essentially no damage was seen in the small intestines in either the X-ray-exposed groups or the neutron-exposed group. Other than an active mucus secretion, no change was seen in the large intestines of the radiation-exposed groups. Cecums were also examined, and no pathologic changes were noted. During the first 7 days after exposure, no abnormal histologic changes were noted in the stomachs. There were a few mucosal petechiae of the pylorus on day 9 in the animals exposed to 400 rads of X-rays, but no ulcers or mucosal erosions. On the tenth day after exposure there were massive intramural hemorrhages of the stomach in all groups. In none of these cases was there evidence of mucosal ulcerations or erosions. Body weight and food consumption measurements were also made on all animals daily, until sacrifice, with only minimal depressions in body weight and food consumption noted during the first week after exposure.

In view of the lack of discernible gastrointestinal damage after either X-ray or neutron doses in the lethal range, a study was designed to examine the effects of massive radiation doses on the gastrointestinal system of the guinea pig. Twenty-four animals (average weight 804 gm) were distributed into two experimental groups (10 animals per group) and one control group (4 animals) on the basis of weights in a balanced design. One experimental group was exposed to 2000 rads of X-rays, and the other to 958 rads of neutrons. Controls were sacrificed on day 6 postirradiation. One of the animals exposed to 2000 rads of X-rays died 1 hour after exposure. The cause of death was unknown, but the clinical symptoms of rigidity and tremors suggested a neurological type of radiation death. The number of animals per time point in the neutron-irradiated group was 1 animal each at hours 3 and 12 and on days 5 and 6, and 2 animals each on days 2, 3, and 4. The number of animals per time point in the X-irradiated group was 1 animal each at hours 3 and 12 and on days 2 and 5, with 2 animals each on days 1 and 3, and 3 animals on day 4 postirradiation. Animals were autopsied immediately after sacrifice and examined as described for the lower dose study.

The only grossly observable gastrointestinal lesions found were in the pyloric area of the stomach. These corresponded to the histological findings to be described below. No lesions were found in the other organs of the thoracic and abdominal cavities at autopsy.

The mucosa of the small intestine was intact after either type of radiation at all time points tested. There was some swelling of the villi and mucosal epithelium, but no ulceration or erosion was noted. The mucosa of the large intestine also remained intact. After 2000 rads of X-rays, little change in the gastric mucosa was seen during the 5 days postexposure. There were mild lesions of gastric glands and mild vascular congestion. The degree of damage to the stomach in animals exposed to 958 rads of neutrons, although not impressive, was greater than the damage after 2000 rads of X-rays. For the first 2 days after the supralethal neutron exposure, there were some dilated glands in the stomach, with a few degenerated gland cells, but no mucosal damage. On the third and fourth day after exposure, moderate areas of superficial ulcers of the pylorus were found. These pyloric ulcers were focal and did not extend to the submucosa but were simply areas of mild erosion.

Daily food consumption and body-weight measurements were also made on the same animals. The results are summarized in Fig. 4. There was a sharp decrease in food consumption in both irradiated groups for the first day after exposure to about 55 to 65% of the preirradiation food consumption levels. Food consumptions in both irradiated groups remained about level for 3 days after exposure, and then a second sharp decrease occurred on day 4 postirradiation. The food consumption curves of both irradiated groups were very similar and demonstrated that the rad dose required to produce a given decrease in food consumption after X-irradiation was approximately twice the dose required to bring about an equivalent decrease after neutron exposure, even after massive doses. There was approximately a 10% decrease in body weight over the first 5 days postexposure. As was the case for food consumption, the weight curves of the two radiation groups were very similar. It may be concluded that food consumption and body weight can be depressed to some extent in guinea pigs during the first few days if massive radiation doses are used.

DISCUSSION

The gastrointestinal syndrome, as recognized in other species, is characterized during the first week after radiation exposure by denudation of the gastrointestinal tract, early deaths, changes in food and water consumption, and a decreased body weight. In the present study, the pathology findings indicated essentially no damage to the gastrointestinal mucosa after doses of either neutrons or X-rays in the lethal range. There were no deaths during the first week after either neutron or X-irradiation. There was no remarkable change in food consumption, water consumption, or body weight during the first week after either type of radiation. Therefore, on the basis of morphology, time pattern of deaths, and indices of function, it can be concluded that the gastrointestinal syndrome is not a major factor in the guinea pig after either neutron or X-irradiation and is relatively unimportant

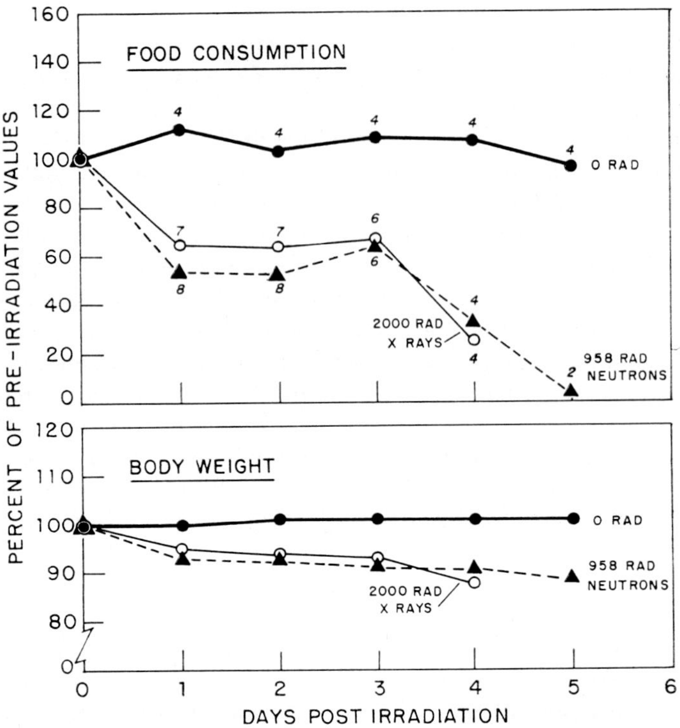

FIG. 4. Food consumption and body weight after exposure to 958 rads of neutrons or 2000 rads of X-rays. The N, which is indicated above the data points, is decreasing owing to serial sacrifice for histopathology studies.

in contributing to death. Although fast neutrons are about twice as potent as 250-kvp X-rays in terms of the $LD_{50(30)}$, this greater potency cannot be accounted for by greater damage to the gastrointestinal tract.

The deaths after neutron or X-irradiation occurred primarily during the second week after exposure, with no animals dying during the first week postirradiation. The most prominent feature found at autopsy during the time period of maximum mortality was hemorrhage. A similar time pattern of death and hemorrhagic state has been described by Newton and Ter-Pogassian (*8*) after γ-irradiation (Co^{60}) of guinea pigs. It has also been demonstrated by Congdon *et al.* (*9*) that injection of bone marrow protects guinea pigs from radiation-induced lethality. Rosenthal (*10*) reported a coagulation defect in guinea pigs after doses of radiation in the LD_{10} to LD_{100} range; hemorrhages were most prominent in the 9- to 13-day period after exposure and were closely related to thrombocytopenia. These factors tend to establish the importance of hematopoietic damage as the major factor leading to radiation deaths in guinea pigs. It appears that the greater potency of neutrons compared to X-rays for lethality in the guinea pig may be explicable on the basis of greater radiation damage to the hematopoietic system.

Although neither neutrons nor X-rays produce gastrointestinal damage in the guinea pig when radiation exposure is in the lethal range, the potential for gastrointestinal damage in the guinea pig does exist. Some mucosal damage was seen at supralethal doses (five times the LD_{100}) of X-rays or neutrons. The guinea pig is not unique with respect to a high threshold for gastrointestinal damage by ionizing radiation. Conard *et al.* (*11*) have reported that the X-ray dose required to produce gastrointestinal injury in dogs is several times as great as the $LD_{50(30)}$. However, the potency of neutrons with respect to lethality in dogs is not greater than that of X-rays. Alpen *et al.* (*2*) obtained a potency ratio of 0.9 for neutrons as compared to 250-kvp X-rays for 30-day lethality in dogs. Rats and mice (*3, 12*), however, have an enhanced sensitivity to neutron irradiation when 30-day death is the end point measured and exhibit severe gastrointestinal damage at doses only slightly higher than the $LD_{50(30)}$.

Three categories have been observed regarding the ratio of neutron to X-ray potency with respect to lethality and gastrointestinal involvement after doses in the lethal range. The guinea pig has a potency ratio of about 2 for lethality and no gastrointestinal injury. The dog has a potency ratio of approximately 1 for lethality and no gastrointestinal injury. Rats and mice have a potency ratio of about 2 for lethality and exhibit severe gastrointestinal injury. It is of special interest that rats still have a neutron potency ratio of 2 for lethality when the gastrointestinal tract is shielded (*13*). Thus, it appears that the increased sensitivity of guinea pigs and rats to neutrons is not explicable on the basis of gastrointestinal damage.

SUMMARY

The 30-day lethality response in Hartley strain guinea pigs was determined for fast neutrons and 250-kvp X-rays. The $LD_{50(30)}$ for animals exposed to neutrons was 155 rads, whereas for animals exposed to X-rays it was 273 rads. Most deaths occurred 9 to 16 days after irradiation, and no deaths occurred before day 7 postirradiation with either neutrons or X-rays. Morphological examination indicated no marked gastrointestinal damage in the guinea pig after either neutron or X-ray exposure in the lethal range. The most frequent finding at autopsy was hemorrhage. Only minimal gastrointestinal damage was seen after supralethal exposures of neutrons or X-rays.

Body weight, food consumption, and water consumption were also determined for 30 days after irradiation. There was a mild depression in these three measurements during the first week after exposure, and a marked decrease in all three measurements 9 to 16 days after irradiation. The relative potency of neutrons with respect to X-rays was greater than unity for depressions in these three measurements. Food and water consumption values of survivors returned to control values by 30 days postirradiation. Body weight, however, remained less than that in controls for at least 30 days in a dose-dependent fashion. No evidence of a post-irradiation polydipsia was found.

The gastrointestinal syndrome is essentially absent in the guinea pig after either neutron or X-irradiation; thus, it is presumed to be relatively unimportant as a factor contributing to death. The higher potency of fast neutrons compared to 250-kvp X-rays for lethality in the guinea pig cannot be accounted for by a greater damage to the gastrointestinal tract. It is suggested that this greater potency of neutrons for lethality in the guinea pig may be explicable on the basis of radiation damage to the hematopoietic system.

ACKNOWLEDGMENTS

We are grateful to V. J. Rosen, Jr., M.D., for the histopathologic diagnoses summarized in this study.

RECEIVED: September 20, 1962

REFERENCES

1. J. B. STORER, P. S. HARRIS, J. E. FURCHNER, and W. H. LANGHAM, The relative biological effectiveness of various ionizing radiations in mammalian systems. *Radiation Res.* **6,** 188–288 (1957).
2. E. L. ALPEN, O. S. SHILL, and E. TOCHILIN, The effects of total-body irradiation of dogs with simulated fission neutrons. *Radiation Res.* **12,** 237–250 (1960).
3. A. C. UPTON, E. P. CONTE, G. S. HURST, and W. A. MILLS, The relative biological effectiveness of fast neutrons, X-rays, and gamma rays for acute lethality in mice. *Radiation Res.* **4,** 117–131 (1956).
4. W. W. SMITH, I. B. ACKERMAN, and F. SMITH, Body weight, fasting and forced feeding after whole body X-irradiation. *Am. J. Physiol.* **168,** 382–390 (1952).
5. B. D. NEWSOM and D. J. KIMELDORF, Species differences in altitude tolerance following X-irradiation. *Am. J. Physiol.* **198,** 762–764 (1960).
6. E. TOCHILIN and G. D. KOHLER, Neutron beam characteristics from the University of California 60-inch cyclotron. *Health Phys.* **1,** 332–339 (1958).
7. E. TOCHILIN, S. W. ROSS, B. W. SHUMWAY, G. D. KOHLER, and R. GOLDEN, Cyclotron neutron and gamma ray dosimetry for animal irradiation studies. *Radiation Res.* **4,** 158–173 (1956).
8. W. T. NEWTON and M. TER-POGASSIAN, Median lethal dose for guinea pigs of Co^{60} gamma irradiation. *Radiation Res.* **13,** 298–304 (1960).
9. C. C. CONGDON, D. UPHOFF, and E. LORENZ, Modification of acute irradiation injury in mice and guinea pigs by injection of bone marrow: A histopathologic study. *J. Natl. Cancer Inst.* **13,** 73–107 (1952).
10. R. L. ROSENTHAL, Relationship among hematopoiesis, blood coagulation, hemorrhage and mortality in the guinea pig after total body X-irradiation. *Blood* **10,** 510–527 (1955).
11. R. A. CONARD, E. P. CRONKITE, G. BRECHER, and C. P. A. STROME, Experimental therapy of the gastrointestinal syndrome produced by lethal doses of ionizing radiation. *J. Appl. Physiol.* **9,** 227–233 (1956).
12. M. N. SWIFT, S. T. TAKETA, E. TOCHILIN, and B. W. SHUMWAY, Comparison of mortality

following partial-body irradiation of rats with fast neutrons and X-rays. *Radiation Res.* **9,** 191 (1958).

13. M. N. SWIFT and S. T. TAKETA, Comparative mortality following partial and whole body irradiation of rats with fast neutrons and X-rays. *U.S. Naval Radiological Defense Laboratory Report* USNRDL-TR-456 (August 18, 1960).

RADIATION RESEARCH 19, 156–168 (1963)

Comparative Late Somatic Effects of Some Radiomimetic Agents and X-Rays

J. W. CONKLIN, A. C. UPTON, K. W. CHRISTENBERRY, AND T. P. McDONALD

Biology Division, Oak Ridge National Laboratory,[1] Oak Ridge, Tennessee

INTRODUCTION

Mutagenic (*1*) and carcinogenic (*2–10*) effects of the radiomimetic chemicals methylbis(β-chloroethyl)amine, or nitrogen mustard (HN2), and triethylene melamine (TEM) are well established. It was the purpose of this study to investigate other late somatic effects of these compounds in comparison with those of X-rays.

MATERIALS AND METHODS

Ten-week-old female RF/Up strain mice were subjected to a dose of HN2, TEM, or whole-body X-rays approximating the $LD_{50(30)}$ days (Table I). A 0.1% solution of HN2 was prepared in sterile 0.9% saline and injected promptly into a tail vein. The TEM was prepared as a 0.03 to 0.04% solution in 0.9% sterile saline and injected intraperitoneally. Whole-body X-irradiation in doses of 85 to 90 rads/min was given from a source operated at 250 kvp with HVL 0.44 mm Cu and 3.0 mm Al filter at a TSD of 93.7 cm. The mice were within an exposure cage already described (*11*). Those surviving 30 days were observed until death for delayed somatic effects. They were grouped 10 per cage and allowed free access to Purina laboratory chow and drinking water. All animals were necropsied, and histological sections were examined when necessary for diagnosis. Some of the mice in each treatment group were examined periodically with a Zeiss-Slit lamp for lens opacities by means of a procedure (*12*) and grading system (*13*) previously reported.

RESULTS

Survival

The life span of 30-day survivors was shortened in all treated groups (Fig. 1). The mean ages at death were as follows: combined X-ray groups, 396 days; combined TEM groups, 508 days; combined HN2 groups, 561 days; and controls, 638

[1] Operated by Union Carbide Corporation for the U.S. Atomic Energy Commission.

TABLE I

THIRTY-DAY SURVIVAL IN RELATION TO TYPE OF TREATMENT

Agent	*Dose*	*Number of mice*	*30-day survivors*	
			Number	*Per cent*
HN2	3.7 mg/kg	140 } 270	93 } 160	66 } 59
HN2	4.5 mg/kg	130	67	51
TEM	3.0 mg/kg	130	76	58
TEM	3.5 mg/kg	110 } 360	42 } 157	38 } 44
TEM	4.0 mg/kg	120	39	32
X-ray	500 r	120	106	88
X-ray	550 r	120 } 360	86 } 259	72 } 72
X-ray	600 r	120	67	56
Control	—	130	130	100

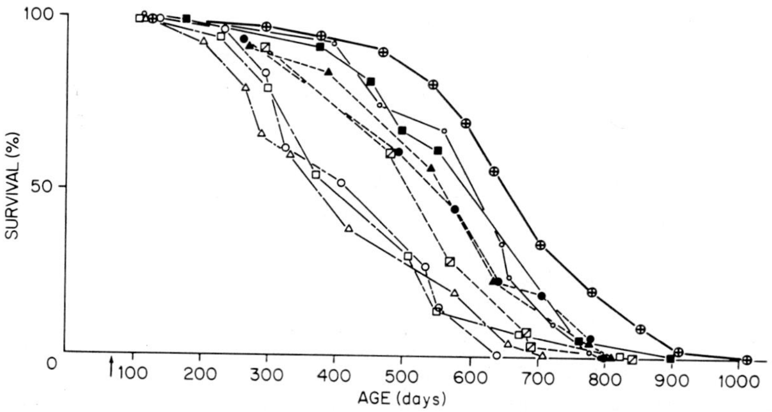

FIG. 1. Influence of HN2, TEM, and X-rays on long-term survival. The arrow denotes age at time of treatment. The curves are based on 30-day survivors only. ■ HN2, 3.7 mg/kg; ○ HN2, 4.5 mg/kg; ● TEM, 3.0 mg/kg; ▲ TEM, 3.5 mg/kg; ⊠ TEM, 4.0 mg/kg; □ X-ray, 500 r; △ X-ray, 550 r; ○ X-ray, 600 r; ⊕ control.

days. Even when all animals with a detectable neoplasm were not considered, there was similar reduction in survival (Fig. 2), except that the TEM curve was shifted even further to the left. Analyzed by Seal's method (*14*), the curve for age-specific death rate in each of the treated groups was similar in slope to that of the controls but displaced upward (Fig. 3).

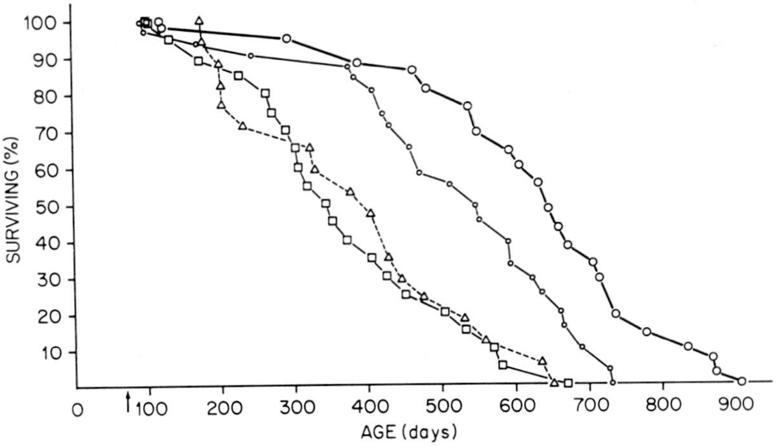

FIG. 2. Influence of HN2, TEM, and X-rays on long-term survival of mice dying without detectable neoplastic disease. The arrow denotes age at time of treatment. ○ HN2, 3.7 to 4.5 mg/kg; △ TEM, 3.0 to 4.0 mg/kg; □ X-ray, 500 to 600 r; ◯ control.

Leukemias

The incidence of thymic lymphoma was increased by X-rays and TEM at all dose levels but by HN2 only at the lowest dose level (Table II). The two groups of HN2-treated animals were, therefore, heterogeneous in regard to the incidence of this disease, but no evidence of a "cage effect" was noted in the cage distribution of neoplasms in any group. The age-specific incidence of thymic lymphoma was increased dramatically within the first year by X-rays and TEM (Fig. 4), making this the earliest of the neoplasms noted.

Myeloid leukemia was observed in all groups (Table II). Except in the TEM group, the mean age at death with myeloid leukemia was reduced to about the same extent as the mean age at death from all causes (Fig. 5). Likewise, the age-specific death rate of mice with myeloid leukemia (Fig. 6) was increased in all treated groups, although there were no significant effects on the over-all incidence of the disease.

Other forms of leukemia were less numerous in each treated group than in the controls (Table II), and the mean age at death for these diseases was reduced to about the same extent in the treated groups as the mean age at death from all causes (Fig. 5).

Other Neoplasms

Lung tumors were greatly increased in frequency by HN2 and TEM but decreased in frequency by X-rays (Table III). These changes in incidence may be correlated with changes in age-specific death rate (Fig. 7); i.e., since lung tumors occurred relatively late in life (Fig. 5), their increased total incidence in the HN2

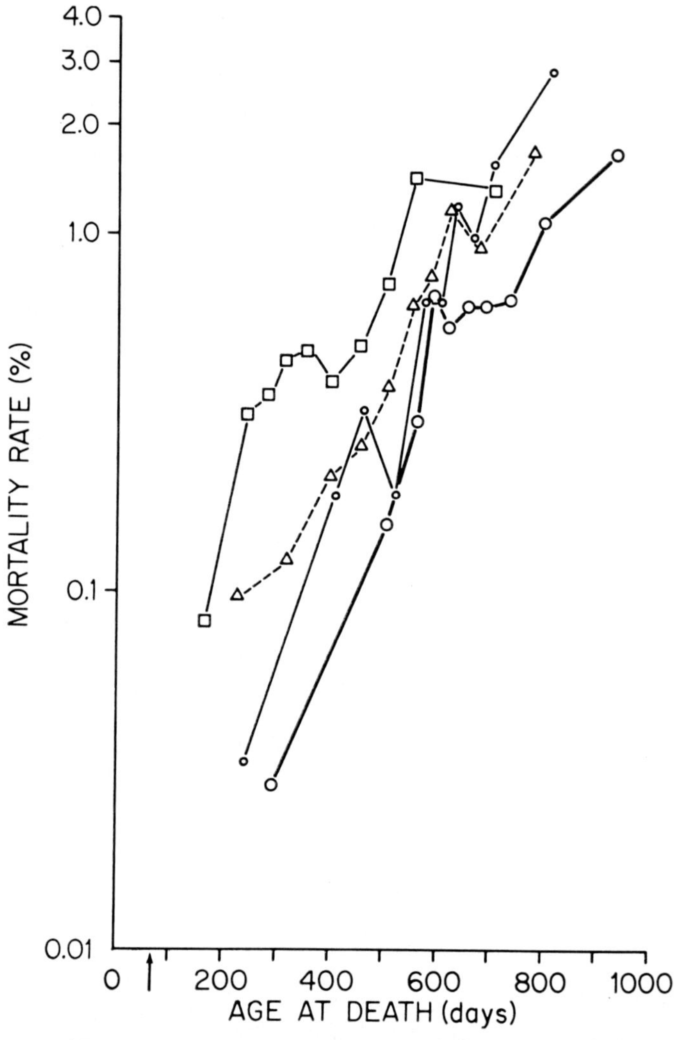

FIG. 3. Influence of HN2, TEM, and X-rays on age-specific death rate in mice dying from all causes. The arrow denotes age at time of treatment. ○ HN2, 3.7 to 4.5 mg/kg; △ TEM, 3.0 to 4.0 mg/kg; □ X-ray, 500 to 600 r; ○ control.

and TEM groups is consistent with their greatly increased age-specific rate in these groups. In the X-ray group, on the other hand, the age-specific death rate for lung tumor was increased less than the age-specific death rate for all causes combined. Hence, oncogenic effects of radiation on the lung, if any, were overshadowed by other effects leading to early mortality. Histologically, the pulmonary tumors, con-

TABLE II

INFLUENCE OF TREATMENT ON OCCURRENCE OF LEUKEMIA

Agent	*Dose*	*Number of mice*	*Thymic lymphoma*		*Myeloid leukemia*		*Other leukemias*	
			Incidence (%)	*Mean age* (%)	*Incidence* (%)	*Mean age* (*days*)	*Incidence* (%)	*Mean age* (*days*)
HN2	3.7 mg/kg	91 }158	9	402	12 }9	513 }511	16	609
HN2	4.5 mg/kg	67	0	—	6	506	46	568
TEM	3.0 mg/kg	69	16	319	9	605	34	569
TEM	3.5 mg/kg	39 }146	15 }16	477 }360	5 }6	404 }557	33 }31	556 }563
TEM	4.0 mg/kg	38	16	318	3	576	21	555
X-ray	500 r	97	26	318	9	325	14	456
X-ray	550 r	85 }242	30 }26	283 }307	6 }7	308 }320	16 }16	447 }446
X-ray	600 r	60	22	335	7	324	18	432
Control	—	114	5	605	3	615	39	646

sisting almost exclusively of alveolar adenomas, appeared similar in all treatment groups.

There were tumors of the ovary in all groups, but these were more frequent among the treated mice, especially those of the TEM group (Table III). The age-specific death rate for the disease also was increased (Fig. 8), the extent of the increase appearing better correlated with the increase in incidence than with the increase in age-specific death rate for all causes combined (Fig. 3). As in the case of lung tumors, therefore, oncogenic effects on a specific organ did not parallel effects on the over-all life span of the animal population. Microscopically, the ovarian tumors comprised a mixture of types and were indistinguishable from those which have been described in irradiated mouse ovaries (*12*).

Nonneoplastic Lesions

Nephrosclerosis was observed in all groups of animals but was rarely detectable grossly. Its low incidence even in the X-ray group (Table III) and its late occurrence (Fig. 5) exclude it as a major cause of life-shortening in this study. Other diseases occasionally encountered are listed in Table III.

All mice surviving 600 days of age showed lens opacities, but these developed earlier in the treated animals than in controls (Fig. 9). Only in the X-irradiated group was there significantly greater severity of lens opacity than that which ultimately occurred in the controls.

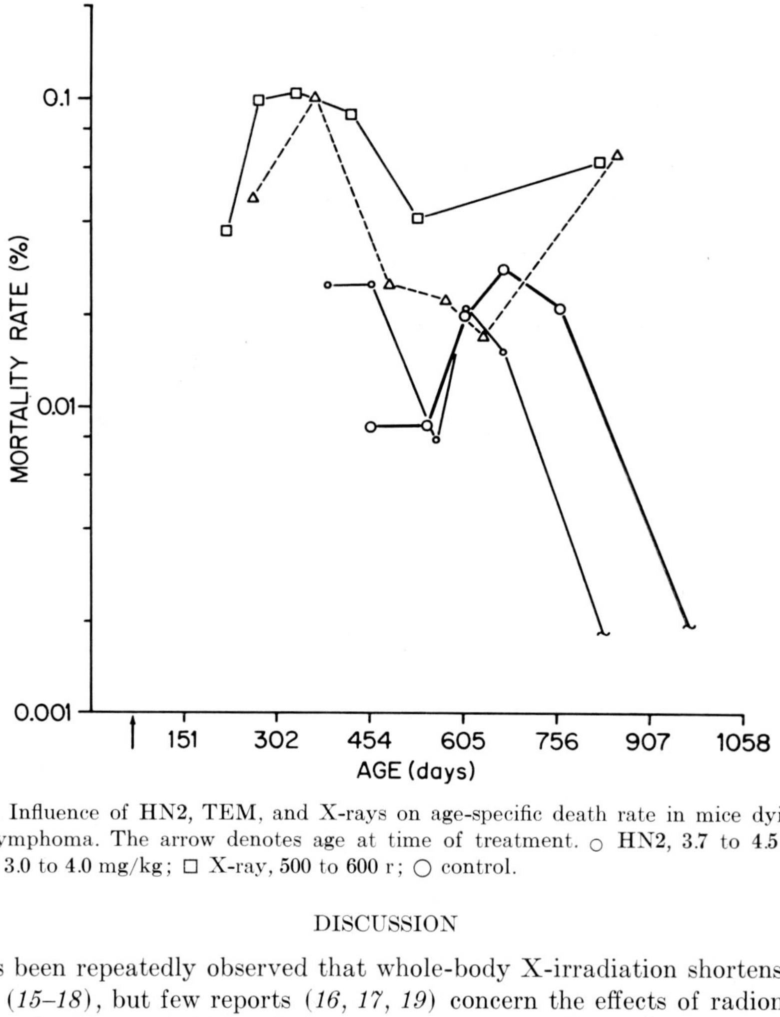

FIG. 4. Influence of HN2, TEM, and X-rays on age-specific death rate in mice dying from thymic lymphoma. The arrow denotes age at time of treatment. ○ HN2, 3.7 to 4.5 mg/kg; △ TEM, 3.0 to 4.0 mg/kg; □ X-ray, 500 to 600 r; ○ control.

DISCUSSION

It has been repeatedly observed that whole-body X-irradiation shortens life in rodents (*15–18*), but few reports (*16, 17, 19*) concern the effects of radiomimetic agents on the life span. Although Curtis *et al.* (*17, 20*) reported no life-shortening by HN2 in mice, Alexander and Connell (*19*) observed pronounced life-shortening by the nitrogen mustard Chlorambucil and by Myleran in the same species. From our results, HN2, as compared with X-rays and TEM, is only weakly effective in shortening life under the conditions employed. However, from experiments in progress, fractionated doses of HN2 appear as effective as fractionated doses of Myleran for life-shortening in RF mice (Conklin and Upton, unpublished data). These discrepancies in results reported by different observers may, therefore, reflect differences in susceptibility among their different strains of mice or differences in their

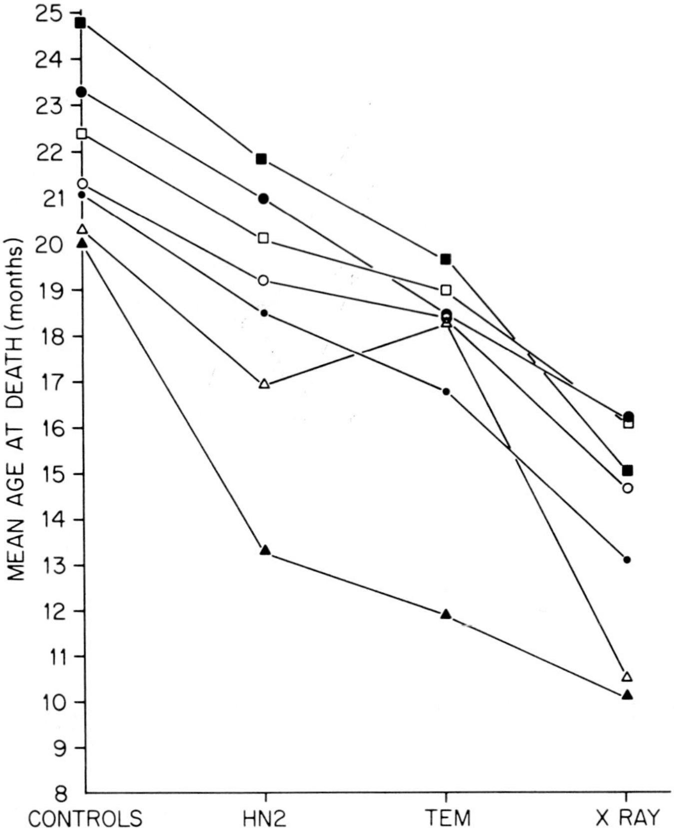

FIG. 5. Mean age at death in relation to treatment and diagnosis. △ myeloid leukemia; ▲ thymic lymphoma; ○ other leukemias; □ lung tumor; ● ovary tumor; • all diagnosis; ■ nephrosclerosis.

methodology. In any event, it is clear that radiomimetic chemicals can under certain circumstances simulate radiation in over-all effects on longevity.

The carcinogenic effects of HN2 and TEM observed in the lung are consistent with earlier observations (*2*, *4–6*, *8*, *9*), as is the reduced incidence of pulmonary tumors in the irradiated mice (*12*). The correlation between these effects and changes in the age-specific death rate for the disease attests to the importance of the induction period in relation to the life span. However, the interrelation of these parameters—incidence, induction period, and life span—remains to be elucidated.

The tumorigenic action of TEM and HN2 on the ovary is noteworthy, for it further demonstrates the broadly radiomimetic action of these two agents. Compared with effects on the lung, however, the effects on the ovary illustrate the variations between agents in the response elicited from different organs.

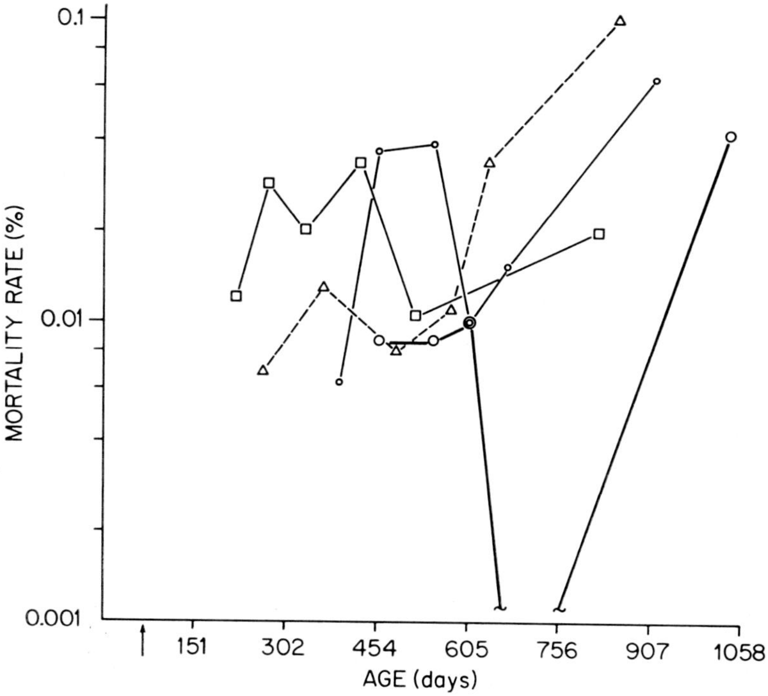

FIG. 6. Influence of HN2, TEM, and X-rays on age-specific death rate in mice dying from myeloid leukemia. The arrow denotes age at time of treatment. ○ HN2, 3.7 to 4.5 mg/kg; △ TEM, 3.0 to 4.0 mg/kg; □ X-ray, 500 to 600 r; ◯ control.

Regarding the lens, the two chemicals were only weakly radiomimetic and differed in this respect from other alkylating agents which are more strongly cataractogenic, such as Myleran (*21*) and 4-(*p*-dimethylaminostyryl) quinoline (K. W. Christenberry, unpublished data).

Although it is tempting to infer from the foregoing that the radiomimetic chemicals HN2 and TEM act through molecular mechanisms common to those of ionizing radiation, this interpretation is speculative (*22*). Furthermore, the variations among these agents in their effects on different organs remain to be explained. Whether these variations reflect differences in uptake and concentration in different cells and organs or variations in mode of action needs to be determined. Available data on organ distribution (*23–25*) fail to resolve this question; hence this problem calls for more refined studies.

SUMMARY

1. Young adult RF female mice were subjected to midlethal doses of nitrogen mustard (HN2), triethylene melamine (TEM), and whole-body X-rays, and the

TABLE III

MAJOR DISEASES IN RELATION TO TREATMENT

Diagnosis	HN_2		TEM		X-ray		Controls	
	Incidence (%)	Mean age at death (days)	Incidence (%)	Mean age at death (days)	Incidence (%)	Mean age at death (days)	Incidence (%)	Mean age at death (days)
Adrenal								
Tumor	—	—	—	—	0.4	801	—	—
Colon								
Colitis	—	—	—	—	1	110	—	—
Megacolon	1	592	—	—	1	669	1	740
Tumor	—	—	1	507	—	—	—	—
Heart								
Abscess	—	—	1	581	2	419	—	—
Endocarditis, subacute bacterial	1	684	—	—	2	394	2	740
Left auricle, thrombosis	2	336	1	474	2	658	8	714
Intestine								
Enterocolitis,								
Ulcerative, acute	—	—	1	411	0.4	489	3	646
Ulcerative, chronic	3	474	1	465	2	446	2	582
Intussusception	1	565	1	533	1	404	—	—
Volvulus	—	—	1	572	2	517	1	638
Kidney								
Abscess	2	648	1	571	4	417	4	478
Cystic disease	1	522	1	303	—	—	1	688
Hydronephrosis	—	—	—	—	0.4	152	—	—
Nephrosclerosis	8	662	6	596	6	458	12	752
Pyelonephritis	1	637	—	—	0.4	499	—	—
Tumor	—	—	1	772	—	—	—	—
Lung								
Abscess	1	552	—	—	3	294	—	—
Bronchitis	—	—	—	—	—	—	2	634
Pneumonia	—	—	1	329	—	—	—	—
Tumor	59	609	52	574	8	488	20	678
Lymph nodes								
Hemorrhage	—	—	—	—	0.4	467	—	—
Mammary gland								
Tumor	1	549	1	629	—	—	—	—
Ovary								
Abscess	1	762	1	651	0.4	692	1	694
Atrophy	—	—	1	461	—	—	—	—
Cystic disease	1	759	1	704	—	—	—	—
Tumor	13	634	58	560	37	490	7	704
Peritoneum								
Abscess	4	464	3	384	1	291	2	603
Ascites	1	715	1	624	0.4	476	2	631

TABLE III—*Continued*

Diagnosis	*HN₂*		*TEM*		*X-ray*		*Controls*	
	Incidence (%)	*Mean age at death* (*days*)	*Incidence* (%)	*Mean age at death* (*days*)	*Incidence* (%)	*Mean age at death* (*days*)	*Incidence* (%)	*Mean age at death* (*days*)
Portal vein								
Anteroposition	1	737	5	455	2	460	5	559
Skin								
Tumor	1	565	—	—	—	—	—	—
Spleen								
Abscess	—	—	—	—	2	490	1	854
Leukemoid reaction	3	484	5	520	1	462	—	—
Thorax								
Hydrothorax	1	729	1	582	0.4	489	3	608
Uterus								
Abscess	—	—	1	563	—	—	1	811

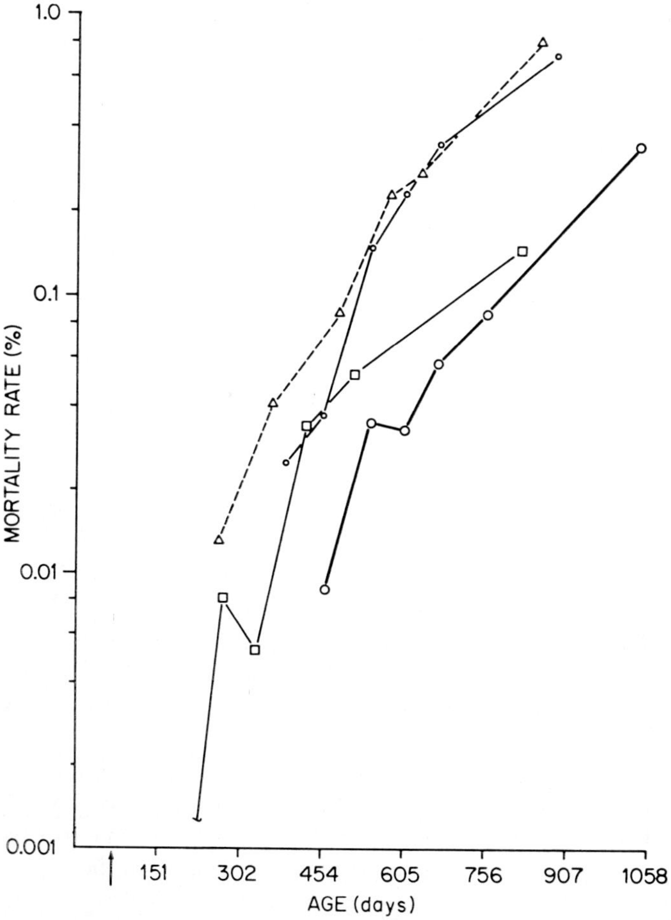

FIG. 7. Influence of HN2, TEM, and X-rays on age-specific death rate in mice dying with pulmonary tumors. The arrow denotes age at time of treatment. ⌒ HN2, 3.7 to 4.5 mg/kg; △ TEM, 3.0 to 4.0 mg/kg; □ X-ray, 500 to 600 r; ○ control.

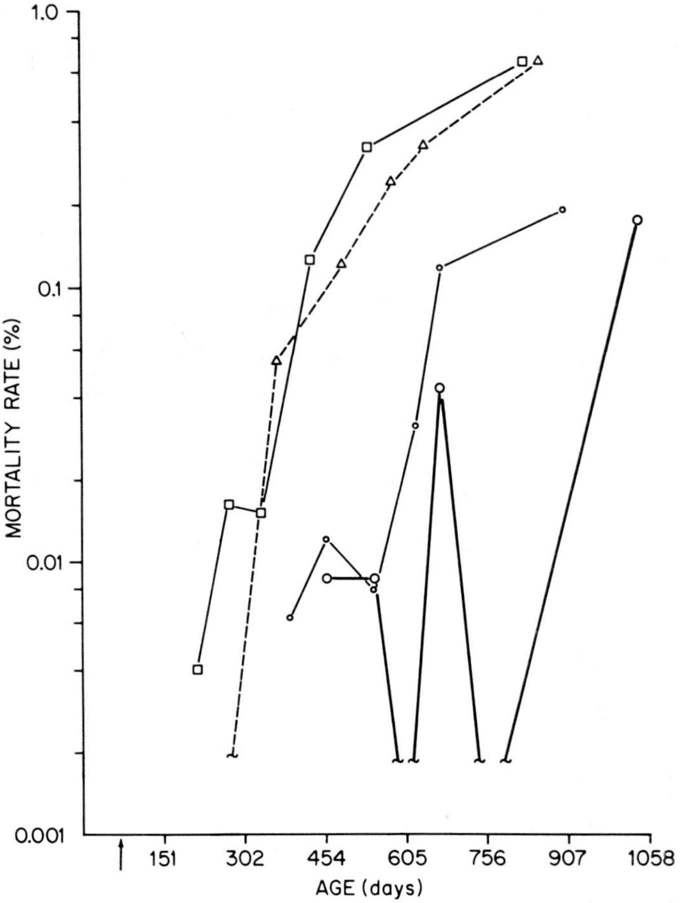

FIG. 8. Influence of HN2, TEM, and X-rays on age-specific death rate in mice dying with ovarian tumors. The arrow denotes age at time of treatment. ○ HN2, 3.7 to 4.5 mg/kg; △ TEM, 3.0 to 4.0 mg/kg; □ X-ray, 500 to 600 r; ○ control.

survivors were observed throughout the remainder of their lives for effects on longevity and on the incidence of late-occurring diseases.

2. The life span was shortened by all treatments. The mean survival time in the various groups was as follows: X-rays, 396 days; TEM, 508 days; HN2, 561 days; and controls, 638 days.

3. The reduction in longevity was not attributable to the induction of neoplasia but was correlated with an increase in the age-specific death rate from diseases of all types. However, the increase varied in degree from one disease to another. Hence, the effects were not equivalent to premature aging in the simplest sense.

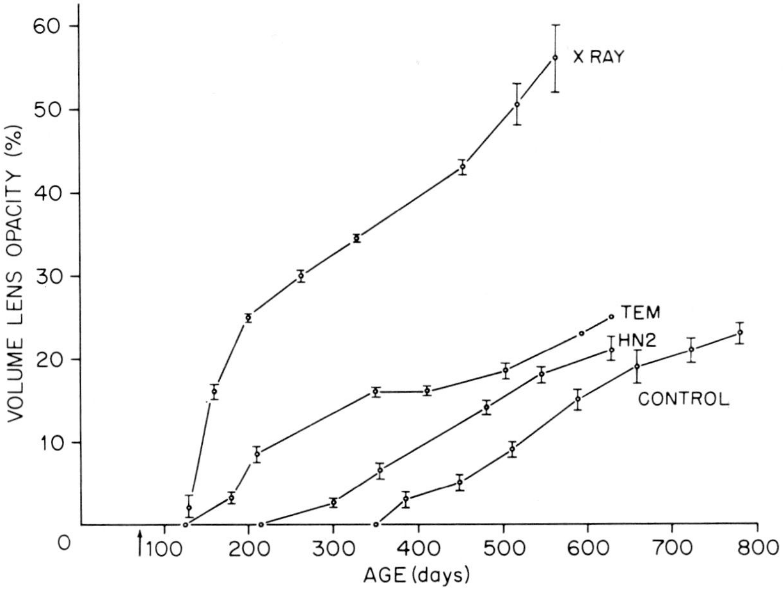

FIG. 9. Influence of HN2, TEM, and X-rays on age-specific development of lens opacities in mice. The arrow denotes age at time of treatment. HN2, 3.7 to 4.5 mg/kg; TEM, 3.0 to 4.0 mg/kg; X-ray, 500 to 600 r; Control, nontreated controls.

4. TEM markedly increased the total incidence of thymic lymphomas, pulmonary adenomas, and lung tumors.

5. HN2 markedly increased the total incidence of pulmonary adenomas and ovarian tumors.

6. X-rays markedly increased the total incidence of thymic lymphomas and ovarian tumors but reduced the total incidence of pulmonary adenomas.

7. All agents caused premature lens opacities, but X-rays alone induced changes of greater severity than those occurring spontaneously in senile controls.

ACKNOWLEDGMENTS

We thank M. A. Kastenbaum for statistical evaluation of data, J. E. Parham for help in data processing, and W. D. Gude for histological assistance.

RECEIVED: October 17, 1962

REFERENCES

1. C. AUERBACH, Radiomimetric substances. *Radiation Res.* **9,** 33–47 (1958).
2. E. BOYLAND and E. S. HORNING, The induction of tumours with nitrogen mustards. *Brit. J. Cancer* **3,** 118–123 (1949).
3. A. C. GRIFFIN, EUGENIA L. BRANDT, and E. L. TATUM, Nitrogen mustards as cancer-inducing agents. *J. Am. Med. Assoc.* **144,** 571 (1950).

4. A. C. Griffin, Eugenia L. Brandt, and E. L. Tatum, Induction of tumors with nitrogen mustards. *Cancer Res.* **11,** 253 (1951).
5. W. E. Heston, Induction of pulmonary tumors in strain A mice with methyl-bis(β-chloroethyl)amine hydrochloride. *J. Natl. Cancer Inst.* **10,** 125–130 (1949).
6. W. E. Heston, Carcinogenic action of the mustards. *J. Natl. Cancer Inst.* **11,** 415–423 (1950).
7. W. E. Heston, Occurrence of tumors in mice injected subcutaneously with sulfur mustard and mustard. *J. Natl. Cancer Inst.* **14,** 131–140 (1953).
8. W. E. Heston, E. Lorenz, and Margaret K. Deringer, Occurrence of pulmonary tumors in strain A mice following total-body X-radiation and injection of nitrogen mustard. *Cancer Res.* **13,** 573–577 (1953).
9. M. B. Shimkin, Pulmonary-tumor induction in mice with chemical agents used in the clinical management of lymphomas. *Cancer* **7,** 410–413 (1954).
10. A. L. Walpole, Carcinogenic action of alkylating agents. *Ann. N.Y. Acad. Sci.* **68,** 750–761 (1958).
11. A. C. Upton, F. P. Conte, G. S. Hurst, and W. A. Mills, The relative biological effectiveness of fast neutrons, X-rays, and γ-rays for acute lethality in mice. *Radiation Res.* **4,** 117–131 (1956).
12. A. C. Upton, A. W. Kimball, J. Furth, K. W. Christenberry, and W. H. Benedict, Some delayed effects of atom-bomb radiations in mice. *Cancer Res.* **20,** (Part 2) 1–62 (1960).
13. G. S. Melville, Jr., K. W. Christenberry, M. Slater, and A. C. Upton, A quantitative grading method for the study of radiation-induced lens opacities. *Radiation Res.* **5,** 605 (1956).
14. H. L. Seal, The estimation of mortality and other decremental probabilities. *Skand. Actuarietdskr.* **37,** 137–162 (1954).
15. H. J. Curtis and Katharine Gebhard, The relative biological effectiveness of fast neutrons and X-rays for life shortening in mice. *Radiation Res.* **9,** 278–284 (1958).
16. H. J. Curtis and K. L. Gebhard, Aging effect of toxic and radiation stresses. In *The Biology of Aging,* (Bernard L. Strehler, ed.), pp. 162–166, Waverly Press, Baltimore, 1960.
17. H. J. Curtis and R. Healey, Effects of radiation on aging. In *Advances in Radiobiology* (G. C. de Hevesy, A. G. Forssberg, and J. D. Abbatt, eds.), pp. 261–265, Oliver & Boyd, Edinburgh, 1957.
18. A. C. Upton, Ionizing radiation and aging. *Gerontologia* **4,** 162–176 (1960).
19. P. Alexander and Dorothea I. Connell, Shortening of the life span of mice by irradiation with X-rays and treatment with radiomimetic chemicals. *Radiation Res.* **12,** 38–48 (1960).
20. H. J. Curtis, Radiation-induced aging in mice. *Proc. 3rd Australasian Conf. Radiobiol. Sydney, 1960.*
21. C. Solomon, A. E. Light, and E. J. DeBeer, Cataracts produced in rats by 1,4-dimethanesulfonoxybutane (Myleran). *Arch. Ophthalmol.* **54,** 850–852 (1955).
22. P. C. Koller and A. Casarini, Comparison of cytological effects induced by X rays and nitrogen mustard. *Brit. J. Cancer* **6,** 173–185 (1952).
23. Irene U. Boone, Betty S. Rogers, J. R. Maxfield, and J. B. Storer, Nitrogen mustard and triethylene melamine content in normal and tumor tissues after intra-arterial and intravenous injection in rats. *Cancer Res.* **17,** 1120–1126 (1957).
24. M. V. Nadkarni, E. I. Goldenthal, and P. K. Smith, The distribution of radioactivity following administration of triethylenimino-*s*-triazine-C^{14} in tumor-bearing and control mice. *Cancer Res.* **14,** 559–562 (1954).
25. H. E. Skipper, L. L. Bennett, Jr., and W. H. Langham, Over-all tracer studies with C^{14}-labeled nitrogen mustard in normal and leukemic mice. *Cancer* **4,** 1025–1027 (1951).

RADIATION RESEARCH **19**, 169–178 (1963)

Mutation and Killing of *Escherichia coli* WP-2 by Accelerated Heavy Ions and Other Radiations[1]

R. A. DEERING[2]

Biophysics Department, Yale University, New Haven, Connecticut

INTRODUCTION

This report is concerned with the genetic and killing effects of 140-Mev accelerated oxygen ions as compared to the effects produced by 40-Mev α-particles, 250-kvp X-rays, Co^{60} γ-rays, and 1-Mev electrons. Heavy ion effects on several biological systems have been discussed by Brustad (*1*) and by Deering *et al.* (*2*). A review of the physics of heavy ion interactions with matter has been published by Hutchinson and Pollard (*3*). Mutational effects in *Saccharomyces* have been studied by Mortimer and Brustad (*4*).

METHODS

Escherichia coli WP-2 (tryptophan-requiring) was used. Unless otherwise noted, the growth medium prior to preparation for irradiation was as follows: tris(hydroxymethyl)aminomethane, 12 gm; KCl, 2.0 gm; $(NH_4)_2SO_4$, 1.0 gm; Na citrate$\cdot 2H_2O$, 0.5 gm; $MgSO_4 \cdot 7H_2O$, 0.1 gm; Na_2HPO_4, 0.14 gm; glucose, 2.0 gm; L-tryptophan, 20 mg; HCl to bring the pH to 7.1; H_2O to volume of 1 liter. For the preparation of starved cells, log phase cultures grown at 37°C were cooled, washed in the above medium with no glucose, tryptophan, or phosphate, and resuspended at a concentration of about 4×10^7 cells per milliliter in a growth medium containing only one-tenth the full amount of Na_2HPO_4. After 9 hours of incubation in this medium, there were about 8×10^8 viable, phosphorus-starved cells per milliliter. These cells were cooled, washed, and concentrated in the growth medium with no glucose, phosphorus, or tryptophan. About 10^9 of these starved cells in 0.015 ml were deposited on the surface of small 0.5-inch agar disks, and the

[1] Work supported by funds provided under Contract AF-41(657)-305 with the School of Aviation Medicine, Randolph Air Force Base, Texas. The heavy ion exposures were supported under Contract AT(30-1)-2052 with the U.S. Atomic Energy Commission.

[2] Present address: Physics Department, New Mexico Highlands University, Las Vegas, New Mexico.

liquid was allowed to soak in. The cells covered an area of about 0.4 cm^2. They were several layers thick, but irradiations done on these samples led to the same results as with thinner layers. The thickness of the cell layer and its stopping power have been introduced as a correction factor in our calculations of rates of energy loss. The starved cells were smaller than log phase cells, and therefore more could be deposited without giving a thickness great enough to seriously alter the beam energy during passage through the sample. A large number of cells per sample was necessary to obtain sufficient reversions for accurate results in the plating techniques. Survival and reversion results obtained from the starved cells were more reproducible over long periods of time than were data obtained from the log phase cells used in some earlier experiments. For the starved cells on agar blocks, no death occurred during storage times of up to 10 days, provided the cells were kept at 4°C in a saturated water atmosphere. Unless specifically noted, starved cells were used in the experiments described here.

Oxygen ion and α-particle (helium ion) irradiations were done with the Yale heavy ion linear accelerator. The initial beam energy from this machine was 10.5 Mev per nucleon. The irradiation apparatus was that described by Dolphin and Hutchinson (*5*) with the modification that the beam passed from the machine vacuum through a nickel foil into the gaseous atmosphere surrounding the agar block samples in the irradiation chamber. The beam current entering a Faraday cup was measured with a vibrating reed electrometer. From a knowledge of the beam area and the integrated charge entering the chamber, it was possible to calculate the incident-particle flux density on the sample.

The stopping material between the full-energy beam and the center of the deposited bacterial samples was equivalent to 14 mg/cm^2 of aluminum. This reduced the oxygen ion beam energy from 168 Mev to 140 Mev and the helium ion beam energy from 42 Mev to 40 Mev. These values were calculated from the range-energy curves of Northcliffe (*6*) and of Schambra *et al.* (*7*). The rates of energy loss, as calculated by the methods outlined by Hutchinson and Pollard (*3*), and the range-energy curves (*6, 7*) were: 140-Mev oxygen ions; charge +8; linear energy transfer (LET), 3400 Mev cm^2/gm;[3] 40-Mev α-particles (helium ions); charge +2; LET, 190 Mev cm^2/gm. From the rates of energy loss and the incident-particle flux densities, it was possible to calculate the absorbed dose in rads. The time-average dose rates for the oxygen and helium ions from the heavy ion accelerator were approximately 30,000 rads/min. Within the machine pulses, which occupied only 2% of the actual irradiation time, the dose rate was of the order of 1,500,000 rads/min.

The X-irradiations were done on samples on agar blocks with a 250-kvp G.E. Maxitron X-ray machine operated at 30 ma and at a distance of 16 cm. The dose rate was 2840 rads/min. Samples were also irradiated with Co^{60} γ-rays at a dose

[3] 10 Mev cm^2/gm is 1 kev/micron for material of density 1 gm/cm^3.

rate of 3820 rads/min. Electrons (1 Mev) from a Van de Graaff were also used, at dose rates of 36,000 and 1,400,000 rads/min. All irradiations were done at room temperature either in air or nitrogen. The dose rates in all cases except for oxygen ion and helium ion runs were determined by $FeSO_4$ dosimetry according to Weiss *et al.* (*8*).

After irradiation, the cells were washed from the agar blocks with 1 ml of growth medium lacking glucose, phosphate, and tryptophan. Platings were performed as described by Doudney and Haas (*9*). Except for special experiments noted below, the plating medium was a salts–glucose medium (M-medium of Haas and Doudney) (*10*), supplemented with 25 ml of standard nutrient broth solution per liter. This amount of broth contained enough tryptophan for limited growth of the tryptophan-requiring cells and enough other amino acids for mutation expression in this strain (*9*). Viable cell count was determined by plating at high dilution on similar plates. At low concentration, tryptophan-requiring cells gave small colonies on this semienriched medium. When larger number of cells were plated and incubated, the tryptophan-requiring cells formed a continuous diffuse background owing to limited growth, whereas any tryptophan-independent reversions showed up as large, dense, white colonies. The tryptophan in 20 ml of the plating medium allowed growth to proceed to a density of about 5×10^9 tryptophan-requiring cells per plate. This upper growth limit did not depend on the number of cells initially plated, provided it was between 10^6 and 10^9 per plate. For the determination of reversions to tryptophan independence, 0.2 ml of the 1-ml suspension of cells was spread on each of three plates and incubated for 72 hours at 37°C. Unirradiated samples were plated as controls with the same numbers of viable cells per plate. Many control plates were done along with each radiation run in order to determine accurately the background mutation rate for that run. The number of spontaneous mutants per plate was subtracted from the reversions obtained with the irradiated samples in order to determine the true number of radiation-induced reversions. The number of spontaneous mutants per plate ranged from 10 to 20, depending on the run. Over the range used in these experiments (10^7 to 2×10^8 viable cells per plate), the number of radiation-induced reversions per 10^8 viable cells proved to be a constant for any given sample and not dependent on the number of viable cells spread on the plate. The growth rate of the cells, as plated on M-medium plus 2.5% broth, might conceivably be different at any given survival level, depending on what radiation was used. This could possibly alter expression of reversions (*11*). This did not prove to be a problem, since experiments showed that, at a common survival level, the lag period and the subsequent growth rate on the plating medum were the same for the heavy ions as for X-rays.

RESULTS

Results for cell survival and reversion to tryptophan independence as a function of radiation dose under aerobic conditions are shown in Fig. 1. The survival curves

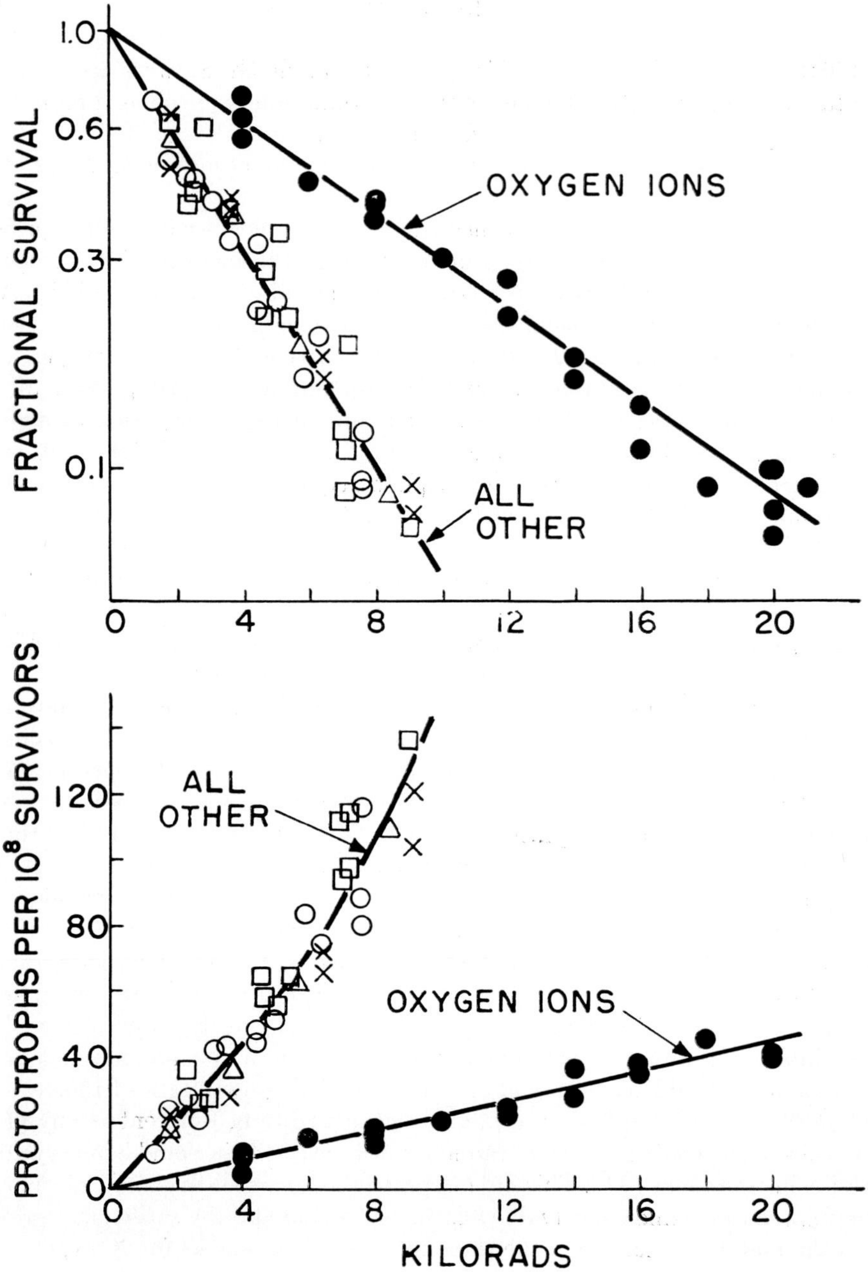

FIG. 1. Survival and reversion to tryptophan independence for *Escherichia coli* WP-2 as a function of dose for various radiations. These irradiations were done under aerobic conditions. *Top:* Survival. *Bottom:* Reversions. ● 140-Mev oxygen ions. × 250-kvp X-rays. ○ 40-Mev α-particles. △ Co^{60} γ-rays. □ 1-Mev electrons.

are of the classical "single-hit" type. The number of reversions produced by the oxygen ions as a function of dose also follows an apparent "single-hit" mechanism (linear curve with dose, as expected from the limiting case of a single-hit requirement). The initial portion of the reversion curve for the other radiations is also linear with dose. At higher doses, however, the number of reversions goes up more rapidly, showing a deviation from a straight line. To determine sensitivity parameters presented later in tables and discussion, only the initial linear portion of this curve was used. Within experimental error, all the radiations except oxygen ions gave the same survival and reversion curves as a function of dose. When compared on the basis of energy absorption (rads), the oxygen ions are less efficient for both killing and production of reversions. These results are later summarized in Table I.

The survival curves are described by the relation $N/N_0 = e^{-k_2 D}$, where N/N_0 is the surviving fraction of cells after a radiation dose D (kilorads are used for evaluating the constants in these experiments), and k_2 is a measure of the sensitivity of the cell to the radiation in question. The oxygen ion reversion curve and the initial linear part of the reversion curves for the other radiations are described by $R/N = k_1 D$, where R/N is the ratio of revertants to viable cells after a dose D in kilorads, and k_1 is a measure of radiation sensitivity for reversion. Average values of k_1, k_2, and k_1/k_2 are shown in Table I.

Kada *et al.* (*12*), using X-rays, showed that only 30% as many reversions appeared when their irradiated cultures were plated on plain minimal medium ("zero-point" reversions) as compared to minimal medium supplemented with 2.5% broth. To compare the relative numbers of "zero-point" reversions and total reversions obtained under our plating conditions for heavy ions versus lower LET radiations, we plated irradiated (aerobic) cultures on both minimal and semi-enriched medium (M plus 2.5% broth). For the oxygen ions, the reversions obtained by plating on minimal medium were about 25% of those obtained when plating was done on M-medium plus 2.5% broth. For γ-rays and α-particles, the same proportion of "zero-point" mutants were obtained, to within experimental error.

Studies of irradiation in nitrogen versus irradiation in air were made. The samples on agar blocks were maintained in circulating moist air or moist purified nitrogen for 8 minutes prior to and during irradiation. Experiments showed that 4 minutes of gassing under these conditions was sufficient to produce the maximum effect due to exclusion of oxygen. Complete survival and reversion curves as a function of dose were obtained for oxygen ion, α-particle, X-ray, and 1-Mev electron irradiations. The survival curves were exponential in all cases, and the reversion curves were the same shape in nitrogen as in air, differing only by a dose factor. For all radiations, the survivals were higher in nitrogen, and a smaller fraction of mutants was found among the survivors. Table I summarizes these results.

The two dose rates associated with the 1-Mev electron irradiations (36,000 and 1,400,000 rads/min) gave the same results for survival and reversion to within experimental error. Therefore, it seems reasonable to assume that the differences observed between the biological effects of oxygen ions (dose rate of about 1,500,000 rads/min within pulses) and the other radiations (about 1,500,000 rads/min within pulses for helium ions; about 3000 rads/min for X-rays; about 4000 rads/min for γ-rays; and about 36,000 rads/min for electrons) cannot be explained on the basis of the difference in the dose rates alone.

Even though no dose-rate effect showed up for the electron irradiations, there is still the possibility that the very high-intensity oxygen ion and helium ion irradiations resulted in "oxygen depletion" in the samples irradiated in air, thus causing them to respond as though they were anoxic. Any anoxia would be expected to decrease the killing and reversion sensitivity of the cells. The observed shift in sensitivity in this direction for the oxygen ion irradiations might conceivably be due to this. Unfortunately for our analysis, the high-intensity irradiations are also higher LET, which could cause a similar response. The high-dose-rate helium ions gave an "oxygen effect" of about a factor of 3 for survival. Therefore, it would seem that little anoxia was being produced due to high dose rate in the aerobic helium irradiations. The dose rates for oxygen ion irradiation were about the same as those for helium ions. Thus, we might assume that the oxygen ions also were resulting in no anoxia. However, some question on this point still exists.

DISCUSSION

From Table I, we see that the relative biological efficiency (RBE) of the oxygen ions for aerobic irradiation as compared to the other radiations is about 0.45 for killing and 0.23 for reversion. An RBE of less than 1 for the heavy ions is not unexpected, since it has also been observed at very high LET with many systems *(1, 2, 4, 13)*. This decrease in RBE at high LET is primarily due to "overkilling"; that is, more energy than necessary is deposited in the sensitive region, thus resulting in a wasting of energy. For the anaerobic irradiations, the RBE of the oxygen ions as compared to the other radiations is about 1 for killing and about 0.3 for reversion. The approximate reliabilities of the data are estimated in Table I.

In order to compare the effectiveness of the radiations for the production of these reversions with the effectiveness for killing, the ratio k_1/k_2 may be used. An interesting comparison appears. In the aerobic case, this ratio for the oxygen ions is only about 50% of that for the other radiations. The electrons, γ-rays, X-rays, and α-particles all give the same result. For the anaerobic irradiations, the ratio k_1/k_2 for the oxygen ions is about 30% of that for the other radiations.

As another way of comparing radiation-induced reversion and killing in these bacteria, we might consider the relative proportion of reversions produced at the

TABLE I

SENSITIVITY PARAMETERS

Radiation	LET (*Mev cm²/gm*)	Reversion, k_1 (*krad*$^{-1}$)	Killing, k_2 (*krad*$^{-1}$)	k_1/k_2
In Air				
1-Mev electrons	~2.5	10×10^{-8} (±7%)	0.29 (±5%)	3.5×10^{-7}
Co^{60} γ-rays	~5.0	10×10^{-8} (±7%)	0.29 (±5%)	3.5×10^{-7}
250-kvp X-rays	~10	10×10^{-8} (±7%)	0.28 (±5%)	3.5×10^{-7}
40-Mev α-particles	190	10×10^{-8} (±7%)	0.29 (±5%)	3.5×10^{-7}
140-Mev oxygen ions	3400	2.3×10^{-8} (±5%)	0.13 (±5%)	1.8×10^{-7}
In Nitrogen				
1-Mev electrons	~2.5	6×10^{-8} (±10%)	0.09 (±10%)	7×10^{-7}
250-kvp X-rays	~10	5×10^{-8} (±10%)	0.07 (±10%)	7×10^{-7}
40-Mev α-particles	190	7×10^{-8} (±10%)	0.10 (±7%)	7×10^{-7}
140-Mev oxygen ions	3400	1.9×10^{-8} (±10%)	0.085 (±7%)	2.2×10^{-7}

same survival levels for different radiations. A plot of reversion frequency among survivors as a function of the survival level for the different radiations (aerobic) is given in Fig. 2. At common survival levels, we see that only one-half to one-third as many reversions are produced among the survivors of oxygen ion irradiations as from the other radiations. This indicates that the heavy ions have a greater tendency to kill a cell rather than leave partial damage manifested as a mutation. The damage to a cell produced by an accelerated oxygen ion is more of an "all-or-nothing" event than for the other radiations used here. This result is not unexpected, since the passage of a very highly ionizing oxygen ion through a cell nucleus could cause tremendous damage resulting in little chance of survival. Partial damage (measured as mutation in our case) might only result from secondary electrons (δ-rays) produced by a heavy ion track passing close to a cell nucleus but not actually hitting it. Some calculations by the author (unpublished) indicate that the killing and reversion rates observed here are compatible with the hypothesis that: (1) A heavy ion passing through the bacterial nucleus has a high probability of killing the cell; and (2) heavy ions passing close to the nucleus but not hitting it can produce partial damage as well as killing, as a result of the δ-rays which extend to a considerable distance to the side of the main track. Mutations among survivors could result from these δ-rays. The other radiations studied here (fast α-particles, X-rays, δ-rays, electrons) have a less positive effect with regard to cell killing, thus leaving more partial damage among the survivors.

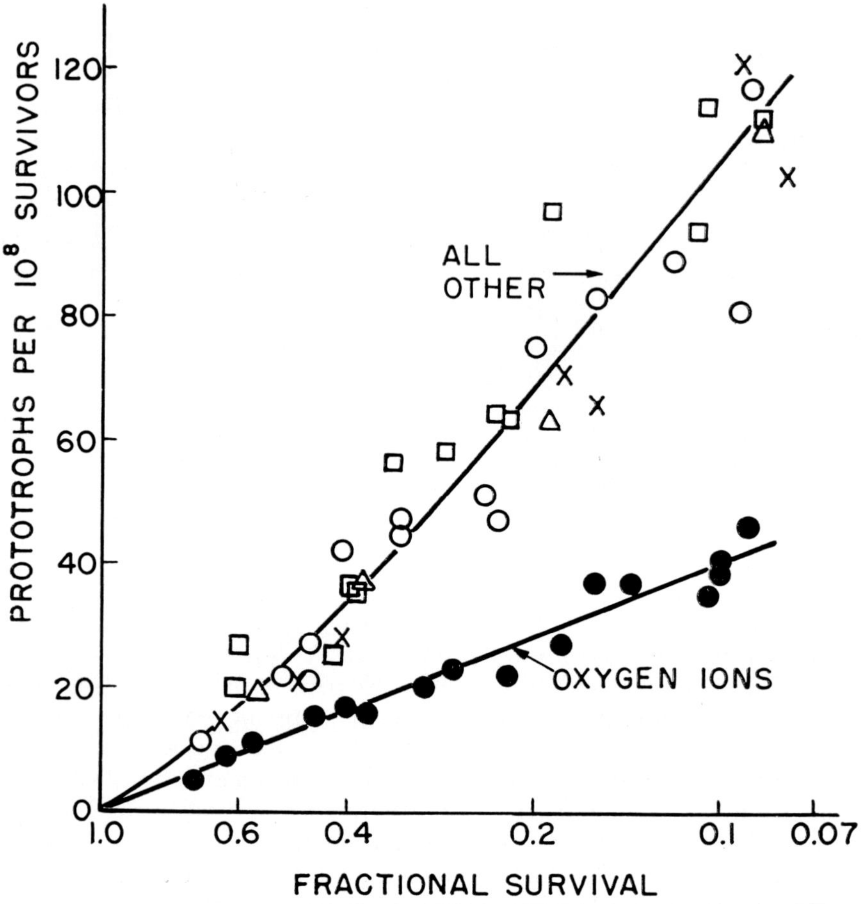

FIG. 2. Comparison of reversion frequencies among survivors as a function of survival fraction for the different radiations (aerobic). The symbols for the different radiations are as designated in Fig. 1.

Table II shows the factors by which the radiation sensitivities are higher in the presence of air than in nitrogen. Ignoring the differences between the results for electrons, X-rays, and α-particles on the assumption that these differences may not be significant, we see an "oxygen effect" for these radiations of about 3 for killing and about 1.5 for reversion. The "oxygen effect" for the accelerated oxygen ions is about 1.5 for killing and about 1.3 for reversion. We see that some "oxygen effect" still exists with the heavy ions, although of a lower magnitude than with the lower LET radiations. These results are in keeping with those of Brustad (*1*) and of Schambra (*14*).

TABLE II
"OXYGEN EFFECT"
(Ratio of effectiveness in air/nitrogen)

Radiation	*Reversion*	*Killing*
1-Mev electrons	1.4–1.6	3.0–3.7
250-kvp X-rays	1.7–2.0	3.5–4.3
40-Mev α-particles	1.3–1.5	2.7–3.3
140-Mev oxygen ions	1.2–1.4	1.4–1.6

For aerobic irradiation, qualitatively similar results were obtained when log-phase cells were used rather than phosphorus-starved cells, although results were not so reproducible.

The oxygen ions are similar in their physical properties to primary galactic cosmic rays. From the practical point of view, with regard to the biological effects of these particles in space, the ratio k_1/k_2 (mutation/killing) is of interest. This ratio is a measure of the ability of the radiation to produce nonlethal genetic effects as compared to its killing ability. Let us make the somewhat dubious assumption that the mutational and killing effects observed in these bacteria can be generalized to include cells of higher organisms. Small numbers of dead cells produced in most tissues of an organism should not be detrimental, provided they are a small fraction of the total cell number. They are generally removed from the system. On the other hand, genetic effects could be of more serious concern to the individual (somatic cell mutation) and certainly to future generations (germ cell mutation). The higher the ratio k_1/k_2, the greater the ratio of viable mutated cells to dead cells. Since k_1/k_2 is *lower* for oxygen ions (see Table I), they should be of less concern with regard to mutations that the usual radiations (X-rays, γ-rays, electrons, fast low-charge particles). Mortimer and Brustad (*4*) have shown that for *Saccharomyces* the RBE for different mutations may vary from 0.4 to 2 in the very high LET region. Thus, extreme caution must be used in making any generalizations from our rather limited results on a single mutation. It is possible that other mutational events in the bacterium could occur with much higher RBE's, thus limiting our conclusions to certain mutations only.

SUMMARY

The Yale heavy ion linear accelerator and other radiation sources have been used to irradiate *Escherichia coli*, strain WP-2 (tryptophan-requiring). Radiations used were: 140-Mev oxygen ions, 40-Mev α-particles, 1-Mev electrons, Co^{60} γ-rays, and 250-kvp X-rays. Cell survival and reversion to tryptophan independence were studied At doses giving common survival fractions there are about one-half as many reversions for the oxygen ions as for the other radiations. Complete curves for survival and reversion as a function of radiation dose are presented. The effect of irradiating in nitrogen versus irradiating in air has been studied for survival and reversion to tryptophan independence. For survival, the nitrogen protective effect is equivalent to a factor of about 3.5 in dose for X-rays and 1.5 for oxygen ion irradiation. For reversion to tryptophan independence, this effect is about 1.7 for X-rays and 1.3 for oxygen ion irradiation.

RECEIVED: June 11, 1962

REFERENCES

1. TOR BRUSTAD, Molecular and cellular effects of fast charged particles. *Radiation Res.* **15,** 139–158 (1961).
2. R. A. DEERING, F. HUTCHINSON, and P. E. SCHAMBRA, Biological effects of accelerated heavy ions. *Aerospace Med.* **32,** 915–920 (1961).
3. F. HUTCHINSON and E. POLLARD, Physical principles of radiation action. In *Mechanisms in Radiobiology* (M. Errera and A. Forssberg),Vol. 1, pp. 1–92, Academic Press, New York, 1961.
4. R. K. MORTIMER and T. BRUSTAD, Mutation induction in *Saccharomyces* using radiations of different linear energy transfer. (Abstract) *Radiation Res.* **12,** 458 (1960).
5. G. W. DOLPHIN and F. HUTCHINSON, The action of fast carbon and heavier ions on biological materials. I. The inactivation of dried enzymes. *Radiation Res.* **13,** 403–414 (1960).
6. L. C. NORTHCLIFFE, Energy loss and effective charge of heavy ions in aluminum. *Phys. Rev.* **120,** 1744–1757 (1960).
7. P. E. SCHAMBRA, A. M. RAUTH, and L. C. NORTHCLIFFE, Energy loss measurements for heavy ions in Mylar and polyethylene. *Phys. Rev.* **120,** 1758–1761 (1960).
8. J. WEISS, A. O. ALLEN, and H. A. SCHWARZ, Use of the Fricke ferrous sulfate dosimeter for gamma ray doses in the range 4 to 40 kr. *Proc. 1st Intern. Peaceful Uses of Atomic Energy, Geneva, 1955* **14,** 179–181 (1956).
9. C. O. DOUDNEY, and F. L. HAAS, Modification of ultraviolet-induced mutation frequency and survival in bacteria by post-irradiation treatment. *Proc. Natl. Acad. Sci., U. S.* **44,** 390-401 (1958).
10. F. L. HAAS and C. O. DOUDNEY, Relation of nucleic acid synthesis to radiation-induced mutation frequency in bacteria. *Proc. Natl. Acad. Sci., U. S.* **43,** 871–883 (1957).
11. E. M. WITKIN, Time, temperature, and protein synthesis: A study of ultraviolet-induced mutations in bacteria. *Cold Spring Harbor Symposia Quant. Biol.* **21,** 123–140 (1956).
12. T. KADA, E. BRUN, and H. MARCOVICH, Comparison de l'induction de mutants prototrophes par les rayons X et U. V. chex *Escherichia coli* B/r Try-. *Ann. Inst. Pasteur* **99,** 547–566 (1960).
13. J. A. SAYEG, A. C. BIRGE, C. A. BEAM, and C. A. TOBIAS, The effects of accelerated carbon nuclei and other radiations on the survival of haploid yeast. II. Biological experiments. *Radiation Res.* **10,** 449–461 (1959).
14. P. E. SCHAMBRA, Thesis, Yale University, 1961 (Present address: Institut fur Strahlenbiologie, Kernforschungszentrum, Karlsruhe, Germany).

Abstracts of Papers for the Eleventh Annual Meeting of the Radiation Research Society, Milwaukee, Wisconsin, May 27–29, 1963

SECTION A. RADIATION CHEMISTRY

A1. *Radiation Chemistry of Tetranitromethane in Air-Saturated Aqueous Solution.* B. J. BIELSKI and A. O. ALLEN, Chemistry Department, Brookhaven National Laboratory, Upton, Long Island, New York.

$C(NO_2)_4$ is a useful reagent for the detection of HO_2 radicals, since the product of their reaction, nitroform anion $C(NO_2)_3^-$, is easily determined by spectrophotometry. Precise yields under gamma rays were obtained by working at very low doses. The reaction with HO_2 is $C(NO_2)_4 + HO_2 = C(NO_2)_3^- + H^+ + O_2 + NO_2$. The NO_2 then disproportionates: $2NO_2 + H_2O = HNO_2 + HNO_3$. The OH radicals all react with HNO_2 and NO_2, oxidizing them to nitrate. At pH 3 or above, $G(C(NO_2)_3^-) = G(-C(NO_2)_4) = G_H$. In more highly acid solutions excess HNO_2 reacts with the molecular peroxide simultaneously formed to give (by a known reaction) pernitrous acid: $HNO_2 + H_2O_2 = ONOOH + H_2O$. Pernitrous acid, unlike H_2O_2, reduces $C(NO_2)_4$: $C(NO_2)_4 + ONOOH + H_2O = C(NO_2)_3^- + 3H^+ + 2NO_3^-$. In acid solutions $G(C(NO_2)_3^-)$ therefore rises above G_H and approaches $G_H + G_{H_2O_2}$. In the presence of added alcohol or H_2O_2, which convert OH into HO_2 or similar reducing radicals, $G(C(NO_2)_3^-)$ increases by the expected amount. (Work supported by the U.S. Atomic Energy Commission.)

A2. *The Radiation Chemistry of Aqueous Ferrous Sulfate-Benzoic Acid Solutions.* JANET GEISSELSODER, MARY JANE KINGKADE*, and JOHN S. LAUGHLIN, Division of Biophysics, Sloan-Kettering Institute, New York, New York; and Department of Chemistry, Hunter College, City University of New York, New York.

A dilute solution of ferrous sulfate and benzoic acid in 1 N H_2SO_4 was first proposed by Adams [*Rad. Research* **7,** 298 (1957)] as a dosimeter. This dosimeter is nearly four times as sensitive as the standard Fricke dosimeter, and its response is quite reproducible. Its response was found to be non-linear, however, in the dose range in which it would have to be used if small volumes of solution are necessary.

Irradiated solutions were analyzed for hydroxy isomers of benzoic acid. Both the efficiency of production, and the ratios of one isomer to another were found to differ significantly from irradiated solutions of benzoic acid with no ferrous ion present.

A3. *Isomerization of Alkyl Halides by Radiation.* MASAAKI TAKEHISA*, GERRIT LEVEY and JOHN E. WILLARD, Department of Chemistry, University of Wisconsin, Madison 6, Wisconsin.

Earlier work in our laboratory [*J.A.C.S.* **83,** 4672 (1961)] has indicated that CH_3CHCH_2Cl radicals produced in the gamma ray radiolysis or the photolysis of liquid n-C_3H_7Cl can undergo a chlorine atom shift to produce $CH_3CHClCH_2$ which reacts with HCl to produce stable

i-C_3H_7Cl. The G-values of i-C_3H_7Cl are proportional to the concentration of HCl, indicating an HCl-catalyzed chain reaction. Further studies now indicate that: (1) this type of isomerization occurs in both the photolysis and radiolysis of gaseous n-C_3H_7Cl, (2) the reverse isomerization of i-C_3H_7Cl to n-C_3H_7Cl is relatively unimportant, (3) n-C_4H_9Cl undergoes HCl catalyzed gamma ray induced isomerization to *sec*-C_4H_9Cl and *iso*-C_4H_9Cl isomerizes to *tert*-C_4H_9Cl, (4) the temperature coefficients for the radiation induced isomerization of liquid normal propyl chloride and liquid normal butyl chloride in the range between $-80°$ and $+100°$ C corresponds to an apparent activation energy of about 3 kcal/mol. The ratio of $G(i\text{-}C_3H_6TCl)/G(n\text{-}C_3H_6TCl)$ for the radiolysis carried out in the presence of tritiated hydrogen chloride changes relatively little over this temperature range, (5) HCl does not catalyze a radiolytic chain isomerization of n-C_3H_7Br to i-C_3H_7Br at 25°, and (6) radiation induced isomerization of n-C_4H_9Cl occurs in both the crystalline and glassy states at -196°C with G values of the order of unity but is not appreciably catalyzed by up to 2 mole % HCl. In conjunction with the isomerization studies analysis of the radiation products from n-C_3H_7Cl has indicated marked changes in G values for dichloropropane and for hexane derivatives when the radiolysis is carried out in the solid state as contrasted to the liquid state. Possible interpretations of the isomerization and phase effects will be discussed.

A4. *Homogeneous Catalysis by OsO_4 in Radiolysis of Aqueous Solutions.* M. HAÏSSINSKY and J.-C. DRAN*, Institut du radium, Paris V^E, France.

When dilute oxygenated 0.8 N H_2SO_4 solutions of Te^{IV} are irradiated with γ rays of Co^{60} the solute is oxidized to Te^{VI} ($G = 3.0$ in 10^{-3} M solution), and H_2O_2, which does not react with Te-compounds in acid solution, is formed with $G = 2.2$. The addition of OsO_4 in amounts 50 to 100 times smaller than those of Te, suppresses the formation of H_2O_2 and the oxidation G value (6.0) becomes slightly greater than $G(Te^{VI}) + G(H_2O_2)$ measured in absence of OsO_4.

The irradiation of Pt^{II} in aerated hydrochloric acid solution by γ rays produces oxidation to Pt^{IV} and the process presents a long after-effect due to the slowness of the reaction with H_2O_2. In 2.10^{-3} M solution of Pt^{II} in 0.8 N HCl $G(Pt^{IV}$, initial$) = 4.2$, $G(Pt^{IV}$, after-effect included$) = 7.8$. Here again the addition of OsO_4 suppresses the after-effect and $G(Pt^{IV})$ immediately after irradiation is 7.8. The presence of H_2SO_4 seems to diminish in this case the catalytic effect of OsO_4. A tentative interpretation of the results will be given.

A5. *The Conversion of Atomic Hydrogen into Electrons**. MAX S. MATHESON* and JOSEPH RABANI* (Introduced by Sheffield Gordon), Argonne National Laboratory, Argonne, Illinois.

In previous work [*J. Phys. Chem.* **66**, 2081 (1962)] H atoms produced in a gas phase electric discharge were introduced into an aqueous solution of chloroacetate ion yielding with increasing pH an increase in the ratio, Cl^- formed to H introduced. A mechanism involving the reaction of H atoms with OH^- to yield probably e^-_{aq} was proposed.

$$H + OH^- \rightarrow e^-_{aq} \text{ (or } H_2O^-) \tag{1}$$

This was confirmed [*J. Phys. Chem.* in press; *Proc. Roy. Soc.* 381 (1962)] by the action of X-rays on water, where H atoms as well as electrons are formed. The electrons were eliminated by using scavengers which do not yield H or H_2 by their reaction with e^-_{aq} (e.g., acetone). H atoms were converted to H_2 by organic scavengers (e.g., formate, methanol). By increasing the pH in such systems, the hydrogen yield is decreased in accordance with the competition in the bulk between reaction (1) and the dehydrogenation. The use of a linear accelerator (a 0.1 A and 0.4 μsec pulse of 15 Mev electrons) yielding a high concentration of radicals ($\sim 10^{-6}$–

10^{-5} *M*) has enabled direct observation of (1). In solutions of ~0.1 *M* H_2 the OH radicals were converted into H atoms, and at a high enough pH, these were converted into electrons by reaction (1). This conversion was confirmed at high pH by following the increased optical absorption of e_{aq}^-. (Based on work performed under the auspices of the U. S. Atomic Energy Commission.)

A6. *A Determination of the Rate Constant for the Reaction of Hydrogen Atoms with Ferrous Ion.*
HAROLD A. SCHWARZ, Chemistry Department, Brookhaven National Laboratory, Upton, Long Island, New York.

The intensity dependence of the radiation-induced oxidation of deaerated ferrous sulfate solutions has been studied using the electron beam from a Van de Graaff accelerator. The ferric yield in 5×10^{-4} *M* ferrous sulfate in 0.4 *M* sulfuric acid decreases from a G value of 7.95 to 4.8 as the intensity increases from 10^4 rads/sec to 2×10^7 rads/sec. The yield depends primarily on the ratio of the radiation intensity to the square of the ferrous ion concentration. The decrease in yield is attributed to a competition between the two reactions (1) $H + FeII \rightarrow FeH^{++}$ and (2) $H + H \rightarrow H_2$. The ferric hydride ion formed in reaction (1) produces ferric ion by $FeH^{++} + H^+ \rightarrow FeIII + H_2$. At high intensities, most of the hydrogen atoms react according to (2) resulting in a decrease in yield. There is a relatively slight acid effect explained by a small contribution from the reaction $H + FeH^{++} \rightarrow FeII + H_2$. When the intensity is kept constant at 2×10^6 rads/sec and the radiation time is varied from 10^{-5} sec to 10^{-3} sec, the yield drops from 7.6 to 5.7. (At the shorter times the pulses were repeated 10 to 1000 times with 10^{-2} to 10^{-1} sec between pulses in order to develop sufficient product). This result allows an estimate of the average lifetime of the hydrogen atom in the solution and hence the rate constants in reactions (1) and (2). In the expressions $R_1 = k_1(H)(FeII)$ and $R_2 = 2k_2(H)^2$ k_1 is 1.7×10^7 M^{-1} sec^{-1} and k_2 is 1.1×10^{10} M^{-1} sec^{-1}. (Research performed under the auspices of the U. S. Atomic Energy Commission.)

A7. *The Rate Constants for Hydrogen Atom and Hydroxyl Radical Reactions in Aqueous Solution.*
J. K. THOMAS*, (Introduced by E. J. Hart), Argonne National Laboratory, Argonne, Illinois.

The irradiation of $10^{-3} \rightarrow 0.8$ *N* sulfuric acid solutions with and without added hydrogen peroxide and oxygen has been carried out under pulsed conditions (1.4 μ second pulses) (Intensity ~10^{26} ev l^{-1}sec^{-1}), on a Linear Accelerator and under approximate steady state conditions on a Van de Graaff. (Intensity range 2.7×10^{22} ev l^{-1}sec^{-1} to 2.7×10^{23} ev l^{-1}sec^{-1}). In the Linear Accelerator experiments as there was no effect of pulse length from $0.4 \rightarrow 5.2$ μsec, no significant chemical reaction occurred during the pulse but only subsequent to the pulse duration. Hence a known concentration of H and OH radicals were produced instantaneously, these then reacted with themselves and/or any solutes present to an extent depending on the relative rates of the reactions. Analysis of the results on an analog computer gave the ratios of the rate constants of the processes occurring in the systems. In the Van de Graaff experiments due to the approximate steady state condition, effectively all the chemical reactions occurred during the irradiation period. Here a steady state concentration of H and OH radicals was set up depending on the rate of production of these species and the absolute rates with which they reacted with themselves and/or any solutes present. With a knowledge of the relative rate constants determined in the Linear Accelerator experiments it was possible to get good agreement between the Van de Graaff experiments and computation of these results with the following rate constants: $2k_{H+H} = 1.2 \times 10^{10}$, $k_{H+OH} = 1.2 \times 10^{10}$, $2k_{OH+OH} = 6 \times 10^9$, $k_{H+O_2} = 1.2 \times 10^{10}$, $k_{H+H_2O_2} = 4 \times 10^7$ M^{-1} sec^{-1}. A summary of the analog computations is included. (Based on work performed under the auspices of the U. S. Atomic Energy Commission.)

A8. *Hydrated Electron Rate Constants of Some Protein and Nucleic Acid Constituents.* EDWIN J. HART, SHEFFIELD GORDON, and J. K. THOMAS,* Argonne National Laboratory, Argonne, Illinois.

Highly significant to chemists and biologists are recent studies indicating that the hydrated electron, e_{aq}^-, is the dominant reducing species in neutral and alkaline aqueous solutions. This species forms by hydration of the thermalized secondary electrons. Utilizing the transient optical absorption band of the hydrated electron [*J. Am. Chem. Soc.* **84,** 4090 (1962); *Nature* **197,** 45 (1963)], rapid reactions of e_{aq}^- with hydrogen ions, hydroxyl radicals, hydrogen peroxide, oxygen and carbon dioxide have been reported [*J. Am. Chem. Soc.* (In press)]. The absolute rate constants for these reactions are in the range 1–3 $\times$ 10^{10} $M^{-1}sec^{-1}$. Equally high rate constants have been found and will be reported for a number of organic compounds, particularly derivatives of the pyrimidine and purine bases. Possible, therefore, are direct reactions of the hydrated electron with biological molecules even in the presence of appreciable concentrations of oxygen and carbon dioxide. The decay of the hydrated electron light absorption is observed at 5850 A. About 3 μM e_{aq}^- are introduced in the aqueous solution by a single 0.4 μsec pulse of 13 Mev electrons. The reaction of the hydrated electron with the added compound is followed by the decay of this absorption over a period of 1 to 20 μsec. The purines, pyrimidines, nucleosides and nucleotides display high reactivity whereas arabinose, ribose, and the proteins; bovine albumin, trypsin, chymotrypsin and lysozyme, and their amino acids except cystine are relatively unreactive. Absolute rate constants of a number of these compounds will be reported and the reactivity of the various chemical linkages with the hydrated electron will be discussed. (Based on work performed under the auspices of the U. S. Atomic Energy Commission.)

A9. *X-Irradiation of Ribonuclease in Aqueous Solution.* T. W. SMITH* and S. J. ADELSTEIN, Departments of Anatomy and Radiology, Harvard Medical School, Boston, Massachusetts.

The effects of X-rays on dilute solutions of bovine pancreatic ribonuclease have been studied with respect to several kinetic and chemical properties. Loss of activity toward the substrate 2′, 3′ cyclic cytidine phosphate results from a decrease in the maximum velocity with no change in substrate affinity. Amperometric titrations with silver showed that no sulfhydryl groups are formed on irradiation and that the number of disulfide bonds determined by sulfitolysis is unchanged. The possibility of disulfide exchange is being explored. The difference spectrum of irradiated vs. unirradiated enzyme has been examined from 220 to 400 mμ. A sharp minimum is observed at 235 mμ as are changes in the region 285 to 295 mμ. The depth of the valley at 235 mμ runs parallel to the decrease in maximum velocity and suggests that the loss of enzymatic activity can be correlated with a change in molecular configuration. This research has been supported by a grant (A-4219) from the U. S. Public Health Service.

A10. *Effects of Several Substances on the Radiation Sensitivity of Catalase.* WOLFGANG LOHMANN, ALFRED J. MOSS*, WILLIAM H. PERKINS*, and CHARLES F. FOWLER*, Radioisotope Service, VA Hospital; and University of Arkansas Medical Center, Little Rock, Arkansas.

Catalase, diluted in an aqueous phosphate buffer solution (pH 7.0), was irradiated with different doses of X-rays (0 to 4 $\times$ 10^6 r) in the presence and absence of different concentrations of glycerol, diglycyl-glycine, fructose, sucrose, glucose, Mn^{++}, and Cu^{++}. The activity of catalase was determined with a Cary 14 spectrophotometer at 240 mμ, using the rate of decomposition of 0.005 M hydrogen peroxide at pH 7.0. The results show that all substances used give an excellent radioprotective effect varying, however, in degree. This protective effect might be due to chelating, in case of glycerol, with the catalase-Fe centres or to radical scavenging in case of diglycyl-glycine. The results will be discussed with consideration of possible complex formation and radical scavenging.

A11. *The Formation of Ribose and Deoxyribose by Ultraviolet Irradiation of Formaldehyde in Water.* CYRIL PONNAMPERUMA* and RUTH MARINER* (Introduced by Robert Painter), Exobiology Division, National Aeronautics and Space Administration, Ames Research Center, Moffett Field, California.

When an aqueous solution of formaldehyde containing 3×10^{-4} moles per liter is exposed to a source of ultraviolet light, a large number of organic compounds is formed. Among these ribose and deoxyribose were identified. Paper chromatography and radioactive tracer techniques were used in the analysis. A similar but less significant result is produced by the use of cobalt-60 γ rays

Ribose and deoxyribose are the sugars in RNA and DNA. Their formation by a simple abiological process has a possible bearing on the hypothesis that life originated on this earth by a gradual process of chemical evolution.

A12. *Synthesis of Porphine-like Substances during Chemical Evolution.* ANTON SZUTKA, Department of Chemistry, University of Detroit, Detroit, Michigan.

According to present theories, the formation of life on the earth and elsewhere was preceded by evolution on a chemical level. The primitive atmosphere subjected to the action of different energies changed its constituents by the formation of more complicated molecules, which then became the building blocks of the living cell. From the evolutionary point of view, porphine-like substances possess the important quality that they are colored substances absorbing the energy of visible light and making it available for chemical transformations. Therefore, at least one-third of the energy of the solar spectrum would become available for selective photochemical reactions. The gain due to the early appearance of porphines, i.e., without aid of living cells, is very considerable, and some facts support the idea that porphines were already active in the very earliest quasi-living organic structures. It was shown in our previous study, that porphine-like substances could be synthesized from simple precursors using gamma-irradiation. The precursors for the synthesis were pyrrole and aldehyde. The availability of these precursors in the primeval earth conditions can scarcely be doubted. In the present study ultraviolet radiation was successfully used as a source of energy. The porphines were identified by visible spectra of the free base, visible spectra of the acid salts, and visible spectra of the zinc complexes. The presence of water and the autocatalytic activity of the systems are discussed. This work is supported by the Grant NsG-226-62 from the National Aeronautics and Space Administration.

SECTION B. CHROMOSOMES AND MUTATIONS

B1. *Studies on Reparable Premutational X-Ray Damage.* R. F. KIMBALL, Biology Division, Oak Ridge National Laboratory, Oak Ridge, Tennessee.

In previous work, the X-ray induced premutational damage leading to lethal and slow-growth mutations in *Paramecium aurelia* has been shown to be of at least two kinds. One kind, presumably chromosomal breakage, can lead to two-hit mutations and has a half-life of the order of minutes. The other kind, possibly alterations of DNA bases, leads only to one-hit mutations and produces them only when the DNA replicates. Before replication, this damage disappears with a half-life of the order of hours. The present paper will review briefly the grounds for these conclusions and report and discuss the following additional properties of the second class damage and of the mutations that it produces: (1) The production of this class is oxygen-dependent to nearly the same extent as other kinds of damage. (2) The phenotypic effect of the mutations that are produced by this class is not greatly different from that of mutations produced by other classes. (3) The question of the number of chromosomal strands affected by this type of damage will be discussed from the distribution of mutations to the products of the first few postirradiation divisions.

B2. *Effects of Radiation on Paramutation.* DUANE B. LINDEN, Agricultural Bio-Sciences Division, Puerto Rico Nuclear Center, Mayaguez, Puerto Rico.

The R locus in maize has been investigated by Brink as the location of a paramutation event. The R^r allele produces purple aleurone, R^{st} and R^{mb} different mottled aleurones. If the heterozygous genotypes R^r R^{st} or R^r R^{mb} are obtained, the R^r alleles then derived from them are found to have undergone a change so that the phenotypes produced by the derived R^r alleles are light purple. This alteration of the R^r allele expression is unidirectional, i.e., only R^r alleles derived from the cross are affected, and occurs 100% of the time.

The sources regulating paramutation change (R^{st} and R^{mb}) were irradiated before crossing to R^r to determine the effects of radiation on paramutation. The R^r stock was also irradiated before crossing with the sources of regulator.

The two regulator stocks had somewhat different radiation responses. The R^{st} source had a low incidence of complete inactivation but a partial alteration to less efficient paramutation expression occurred frequently. The R^{mb} source ordinarily induces a lower degree of alteration in R^r than the R^{st} source. After irradiation some of the R^{mb} crosses resulted in apparent complete inactivation of the paramutation phenomenon. Others however had a more efficient alteration than normal in that change in the R^r allele was greater than in the control.

The irradiated R^r group which were altered had either an apparent complete inactivation of the paramutation alteration or a reduced degree of change in the R^r gene. The frequency of changes to no effect from irradiation in all groups studied indicate that this is more likely to be an inactivation event rather than a gene mutational alteration.

B3. *Coat Color and Behavior Mutations in Inbred Mice under Chronic Low-Level γ-Irradiation.* DOROTHEA STARBUCK MILLER, Whitman Laboratory, University of Chicago, Chicago, Illinois.

Through nine years when the radiation in the animal quarters was at background level, no mutations were observed in our inbred DBA and C57BL mice or in several thousand offspring of crosses between the two strains. Since the mice are handled individually for audiogenic seizure tests at 30 days, each mouse receives moderate scrutiny. Over a five year period, when the colony was exposed to chronic γ-irradiation at a dosage of .2 mrad per hour, a number of alterations in coat color and behavior appeared, which proved to be genetic in origin. (1) Blonde, a gene causing extra dilution in DBA/1. Due to low viability, the mutant type died out before genetic analysis was complete. (2) Cordovan, an allele at the black-brown locus in C57BL/10, recessive to black and dominant over brown. (3) Two alleles of steel in C57BL/6, a dominant gene with pleiotropic effects. In contrast to the original steel mutant in which the homozygote dies in utero, the homozygotes appear as black-eyed white, anemic, sterile progeny, surviving typically from 10 to 40 days. In the second allele, some black-eyed white mice, less severely anemic, survive up to one year; all males have been sterile, but two females have produced one litter each. (4) White diamond on belly in C57BL/6, a dominant gene. The homozygote is dominant pink-eyed albino, viable and fertile. (5) Yellow belly in C57BL/6, a simple dominant, probably an allele of black-and-tan. (6) A series of independent mutations causing heightened susceptibility to audiogenic seizures in C57BL/6 which are normally seizure-resistant. One of these mutations proved to be a single dominant. (Supported by USPHS research grant B-654).

B4. *Is Mutation Rate Significantly Altered by Five-Fold Differences in Natural Background Radiation?* L. W. MERICLE, R. P. MERICLE*, and W. S. OSBURN*, Michigan State University, East Lansing, and University of Colorado, Boulder, Colorado.

Variations in background radiation levels at the earth's surface are often dismissed as being too small to constitute an important environmental differential for the biota. Yet Osburn has observed that *Penstemon* native to a radioactive dike region near Central City, Colorado, exhibits significant differences in the frequency of morphological anomalies, these being correlated with the level of surface radiation present in the various microenvironments. To experimentally evaluate whether the "hot" dike environment would materially affect the mutation rate in a plant known from laboratory experiments to be highly radiosensitive, preliminary experiments were conducted during Summer, 1962. Base-line mutation rates in clones of hybrid *Tradescantia* were first determined at Science Lodge, Colorado (background radiation, 0.05 mr/hr). These same plants were then transferred in the same pots to the radioactive dike where the radiation level was 0.25 mr/hr (other environmental conditions almost identical). At the dike, the incidence of floral anomalies was 9-times that at Science Lodge, increasing from 4.2 to 36.8%, while the somatic mutation rate for flower-color mutants also showed statistically significant increases, e.g., the average number of mutant sectors per petal rose more than 4-fold (from 0.53 to 2.24) and the number of mutant cells, more than 3-fold (from 2.98 to 9.34). Since these effects are typical of responses shown by *Tradescantia* in experiments using higher radiation levels, this implies that the differences observed herein are basically radiation-induced. However, such large increases in mutation rate at such low radiation levels forces the conclusion that strong environmental synergisms must be involved. Controlled laboratory experiments using simulated environmental components, including radiation, are now underway in an attempt to elucidate these relationships. (Supported by USAEC).

B5. *A Study of the* in Vivo *Segregation of Bacterial DNA Using H^3 Thymidine Decays.* MARY OSBORN* and STANLEY PERSON* (Introduced by Ernest Pollard), Graduate School Committee on Biophysics, The Pennsylvania State University, University Park, Pennsylvania.

The segregation of DNA into progeny has been studied using decays from H^3 thymidine that is incorporated into the DNA of the bacterium *E. coli* $15_{T\text{-}L\text{-}}$, an auxotroph requiring thymidine and leucine. Cells were grown in the presence of exogenous H^3 thymidine for several generations and considered fully labeled. These fully labeled cells were transferred to unlabeled medium and reincubated for various times corresponding to 1 to 3 generations in cold medium. Samples were removed, washed, resuspended and stored at 4°C to accumulate H^3 decays. These partly labeled suspensions, and the fully labeled one, were assayed at intervals for colony forming ability to obtain survival curves. All survival curves are of a "single hit" nature. The survival of fully labeled cells decreases exponentially with time. Those for partly labeled cells show two distinct portions: an initial exponential decrease followed by leveling. This is in agreement with the semi-conservative model of DNA segregation.

B6. *The Relationship between Radiation-Induced Chromosome Damage and Loss of Reproductive Integrity.* D. ROY DAVIES* (Introduced by Arnold H. Sparrow), Biology Department, Brookhaven National Laboratory, Upton, New York.

The radiation sensitivity of single meristematic hair cells of *Tradescantia* was determined by direct measurement of their ability to continue dividing at least five or six times. With these particular cells, survival could be followed for two decades. The dose response curve after exposure to 250 kv X-rays was sigmoid, and similar to that reported for a variety of mammalian cell lines, having a D_0 of 149 r and an extrapolation number of 1.6.

Detailed observations were also made of all forms of chromatid and chromosome aberrations induced after irradiating all stages of the mitotic cycle of these same meristematic cells. Doses of 36, 63 and 90 r were used and fixations made at approximately two hour intervals up to 26½ hours postirradiation. Linear or quadratic equations relating the yields of particular aberration types to dose were fitted to the data. Because of the high frequency of aberration induction and the complexity of the configurations induced, much lower doses had to be used in evaluating aberration frequency than in determining reproductive integrity. However, knowing the relation of aberration yield to dose, the frequencies of aberrations which might be expected at the high doses could be calculated. On the basis of these data it proved to be difficult to equate in any simple manner loss of genetic information to loss of reproductive integrity. (Research carried out at Brookhaven National Laboratory under the auspices of the U. S. Atomic Energy Commission.)

B7. *Chromosome Abnormalities after Irradiation of Ascites Tumor Cells in G_2 and S Periods.* TITUS C. EVANS and JAE HO KIM, Radiation Research Laboratory, Iowa City, Iowa.

Ehrlich and S-180 ascites tumor cells were incubated *in vitro* for twenty minutes with tritiated thymidine and exposed immediately thereafter to 500 r of X-radiation. The cells were inoculated into mice and were sampled at two hour intervals thereafter for a thirty hour period. Autoradiographs were prepared from the samples and after proper exposure and photographic development, they were prepared for cytologic study. The unlabeled cells were assumed to be the ones in the G_2 (or premitotic) stage, and the labeled anaphases were assumed to have been in the synthesis (S) period at the time of exposure. There was a postirradiation period of about five hours during which time there was little or no mitosis. Upon recovery of mitosis, abnormalities began to appear both in the labeled and unlabeled cells. From twelve to twenty hours (2 hour samples) after irradiation, cells were scored in anaphase as to whether they were normal or abnormal, labeled or unlabeled. Without considering the absolute numbers involved, a percentage of abnormal anaphases in the unlabeled group was around 30 without much variation in that found for the five periods. The percentage of anaphases that were abnormal in the labeled groups also did not vary extensively in the five groups and averaged around 45%. Therefore, it was concluded that irradiation during synthesis was just as effective, if not more so, than irradiation just before mitosis.

B8. *The Effect of Chronic Neutron Irradiation on the Development of Chromosome Aberrations.* H. J. CURTIS and JOHN TILLEY*, Biology Department, Brookhaven National Laboratory, Upton, New York.

It has long been known that chronic gamma irradiation is about four times less effective in causing life shortening in mice than is acute irradiation, but for neutrons chronic and acute irradiations are equally effective. It was recently shown that chronic gamma irradiation is also about four times less effective in producing chromosome aberrations in liver cells in mice than is acute gamma irradiation, showing that the chromosomes can heal themselves considerably after small doses. The present experiments compare chromosome aberrations following acute and chronic neutron irradiation. They show that with chronic irradiation chromosome damage develops very rapidly. For equal rad dosages of neutrons, chronic is just as effective as is acute irradiation in producing chromosome aberrations. This shows that there is no chromosome healing even after very small doses of neutrons. These experiments give a firm cellular basis for the known differences between the life shortening effects of neutrons and gamma rays. They also add considrable support to the somatic mutation theory of aging. (Research carried out at Brookhaven National Laboratory under the auspices of the U. S. Atomic Energy Commission.)

B9. *Effectiveness of Tritiated Thymidine Compared with Tritiated Water and Cobalt-60 Gamma-Rays for the Induction of Chromosomal Breaks.* W. C. DEWEY, R. M. HUMPHREY, and ANN JONES*, Department of Physics, The University of Texas M. D. Anderson Hospital and Tumor Institute, Houston 25, Texas.

Hamster cells growing *in vitro* were chronically irradiated for 11 hours with either tritiated thymidine (HTdR) incorporated into DNA during a one-hour pulse label, tritiated water ($H_2{}^3O$) contained in the medium, or with gamma-rays delivered from a Co-60 teletherapy unit. The cells were fixed after 11 hours of continuous irradiation, and the number of breaks and exchanges (equivalent to two breaks) were scored in metaphase cells. The number of tritium disintegrations which occurred in cells labeled with HTdR was determined from autoradiographic grain counts compared with liquid scintillation counts. (The film efficiency was 16%.)

The breakage frequency was proportional to the 1.6–1.8 power of the dose, and 20–40% of the breaks were attributed to chromatid exchanges. The amount of radiation required to produce one visible chromosomal break per cell was as follows: 1150 disintegrations from HTdR (with the tritium either in the ring or methyl group) and 380 rads for both $H_2{}^3O$ and gamma-rays. If the DNA were distributed throughout the nucleus (radius of 3.75 μ), the average nuclear radiation dose would have been 310 rads (380 rads to the DNA if it were distributed in a 0.5 μ shell at the surface of the nucleus). In these cells irradiated with HTdR the location of the breaks was not correlated with the distribution of the autoradiographic grains. Therefore, on the basis of energy absorbed in the nucleus, the effectiveness for breaking chromosomes is about the same for HTdR incorporated into DNA as for $H_2{}^3O$ and gamma-rays.

B10. *The Effect of Chronic Gamma Irradiation on Cell Proliferation and Growth Inhibition in Root Meristems of* Pisum. J. VAN'T HOF* and A. H. SPARROW, Biology Department, Brookhaven National Laboratory, Upton, New York.

A series of experiments were performed to determine whether the minimum mitotic cycle time was altered in root meristem cells of *Pisum sativum* by chronic gamma irradiation exposures sufficient to produce growth inhibition. Reduction in cell number per meristem and inhibition of root elongation were used as indices of radiation effect. Colchicine was used to produce a tetraploid population of cells and the minimum cycle time was determined by noting the period of time between the production of tetraploid cells and the time they first appeared in the subsequent mitosis. Cycle time measurements were carried out after 3 successive days of irradiation. At this time the number of cells per meristem was reduced by approximately 5, 25, and 45% of control in roots exposed to 250, 500, and 1000 r per day respectively. Root elongation was also inhibited after 3 days at 500 and 1000 r per day, but there was no difference in the minimum cycle time between irradiated and control roots. Reduction in the number of cells per meristem proved to be a valuable index of radiation effect since the data showed a dose relationship much earlier than did growth measurements. Cytological analysis indicated that the number of abnormal anaphases produced after 3 days of irradiation increased with dose. Since the minimum cycle length was not changed by doses which caused growth inhibitions, it is suggested that cell proliferation was reduced in the exposed meristems by cell death due to chromosome damage or by permanent mitotic arrest and not primarily by an increase in duration of the mitotic cycle. (Research carried out at Brookhaven National Laboratory under the auspices of the U. S. Atomic Energy Commission.)

B11. *Chromosome Analysis in Laboratory Species by Peripheral Blood Techniques.* J. S. BURKLE, C. B. JACOBSON* and I. R. TELFORD,* Radiation Exposure Evaluation Laboratory, U. S. Naval Hospital, Bethesda, Maryland; and Department of Anatomy, George Washington University, Washington, D.C.

The value of peripheral blood chromosome analysis by various modifications of Moorhead's technique has been amply established in man and animal species. Because of the current interest in the effect of radiation on chromosomes, a technique for leukocyte culture and karyotypic analysis has been developed. Success has been effected in dogs, guinea pigs, rabbits, rats, mice and monkeys. To minimize culture variations a prefabricated freeze-dried culture kit is used.

The basic technique used is described. Leukocytes are separated by dextran and inoculated into NCTC 109, 250 μg streptomycin, 500 units penicillin, 0.025 ml Phytohemagglutin-P. Cultures are incubated for 72 hours and 1 μg of colchicine is added to arrest growth in metaphase. 200–500 units human fibrinolysin are added when necessary to break up cellular clumps and sheets. The fixed cellular suspension is placed on a slide, flamed and stained with 8% Giemsa. Chromosome spreads are photographed and enlargements cut up for karyotypic analysis.

Only slight variations of the basic technique are necessary to effect leukocyte growth in various species. Karyotypic analysis of various animals will be shown. Examples of radiation effects, including ring forms, centromere changes, chromatid breaks, deletions, translocations and fragmentation will be demonstrated.

Comparison of karyotypic analysis of peripheral blood leukocyte cultures, *in vitro* bone marrow culture, and short-term *in vivo* marrow preparations show no significant variations.

B12. *Some Properties of DNA Irradiated* in Vitro. HELEN HARRINGTON and MARLENE RICANATI*, Division of Radiation Biology, Department of Radiology, Western Reserve University, Cleveland, Ohio.

DNA, isolated from calf thymus or from mouse leukemic lymphoblasts (L 5178Y) grown in tissue culture, was affected by low doses of X-irradiation. When dissolved in 0.01 *M* phosphate buffer at pH 7.0 at a concentration of 33 μg DNA/ml, the reduced specific viscosity (η sp/C) was 70% and 60% of the sham-irradiated control after 500r and 1000r, respectively. Heating the solution to 100°C decreased the viscosity of the irradiated solution to a greater extent than that of the control. When the concentration of DNA was higher than 100 μg/ml the effect decreased, becoming insignificant at 1 mg/ml. The DNA was not protected when irradiated in an atmosphere of N_2, but no radiation effect was observed when the DNA was dissolved in complete tissue culture medium containing 20% horse serum, in 0.01 *M* phosphate-0.015 *M* sodium citrate, or in 0.01 *M* phosphate-0.13 *M* mercaptoethanol. DNA in which 23–29% of the thymine was substituted with iodouracil was not affected to a greater extent by *in vitro* irradiation than nonsubstituted DNA, in contrast to results obtained in *in vivo* experiments (*Federation Proc.*, In Press). The sedimentation rate of the irradiated DNA was not significantly different from that of the control, but the temperature at the midpoint of the thermal transition (Tm) was about 1° lower for the irradiated DNA. It is possible that radicals formed by irradiation of the aqueous solution produce single-chain breaks in the ribose-phosphate backbone of the DNA molecule and that these breaks are accompanied by a partial collapse of the extended helix in isolated regions.

SECTION C. ENZYMATICS AND BIOCHEMISTRY

C1. *Further Observation on the Radiation Response of Auxin Metabolism in the Animal.* S. A. GORDON and E. BUESS*, Division of Biological and Medical Research, Argonne National Laboratory, Argonne, Illinois.

At the Harrogate Conferences in 1962, we reported on the occurrence and radiation response of auxin biosynthesis in animal tissues. The biosynthetic sequence examined was the conversion of tryptophan to the auxin 3-indoleacetic acid. The titer of this enzyme in the mouse liver was enhanced by dosages of 50 to several hundred r and, to a lesser extent, by stress situations. A hormonal control of the enzyme was inferred from observations on the change in titer of the enzyme in the pre- and postfetal animal, and from finding that the enzyme was amenable to substrate adaptation. Supporting this inference are recent observations on the radiation response of adrenalectomized animals. Adrenalectomy obviates almost completely both the enhancement of enzyme activity following low doses of X-rays and the inhibition of activity following high doses (>1Kr). Experiments will be described which indicate that the tryptophan pyrrolase and serotonin systems are not involved in the biosynthesis of auxin and, by implication, its radiation response. (Work supported by U. S. Atomic Energy Commission.)

C2. *Radiation Physiology of Fruit—Ascorbic Acid, Sulfhydryl, and Soluble Nitrogen Content of Irradiated Citrus.* Roger J. Romani* (Introduced by M. Goldman), Department of Pomology, University of California, Davis, California.

The time course for the postirradiation changes in ascorbic acid, sulfhydryls, and soluble nitrogen may reflect on the nature of radiation stress and subsequent physiological response of the fruit tissues.

Lemons and oranges were exposed to relatively massive doses of ionizing radiation ranging from 200 to 1200 Krads. The lower doses in this range are in the realm of radio-pasteurization treatments, the higher exposures were used to accentuate the radiation effects on quiescent fruit cells. Both sulfhydryl and ascorbate levels are reduced by the irradiation. The decrease continues after the exposure period followed by partial recovery 24 hours later. Increased solubilization of the nitrogenous materials also occurs following the irradiation of lemons at 400 Krad. A similar response was not shown by the oranges correlating with their greater radio-resistance. How the nitrogen release affects the expression and interpretation of the analytical results will be discussed. [Supported by AEC Contract AT (11-1)-34.]

C3. *Lenticular Enzyme Changes in Young Rabbits Following Exposure to 800 r X-Irradiation.* A. A. Swanson* (Introduced by A. K. Davis), Research Unit, Southeastern Radiological Health Laboratory, Division of Radiological Health, U. S. Public Health Service, Montgomery, Alabama.

Six- and eight-week-old New Zealand White male rabbits were exposed to 800 r whole-head X-irradiation. Lenses along with a representative sample of liver were removed 18 hours post-irradiation, homogenized and analyzed by following the kinetics of glucose-6-PO_4 dehydrogenase, TPN isocitrate dehydrogenase, malic dehydrogenase, glutathione reductase, glyceraldehyde-3-PO_4 dehydrogenase, nucleoside phosphorylase, diaphorase and DPN cytochrome *c* reductase. The enzyme proteins were quantitatively measured spectrophotometrically. Decreased glucose-6-PO_4 dehydrogenase, glutathione reductase and glyceraldehyde-3-PO_4 dehydrogenase values were observed in irradiated lens (capsule and epithelium combined) and liver tissues in both groups. Increased values were noted in the irradiated lenticular and liver tissue homogenates for nucleoside phosphorylase, diaphorase and DPN cytochrome *c* reductase in the two age groups studied. TPN isocitrate dehydrogenase and total protein content did not change appreciably in either group. A variable response was detected for malic dehydrogenase in the irradiated lens and liver homogenates when compared with their respective controls for the six and eight week old rabbits. The data in these studies may imply damage to the electron-oxidative transport mechanism suggesting an uncoupling process without the subsequent production of adenosine triphosphate.

C4. *Steroid Biotransformations and Androgen Production by Testes from X-Irradiated Mice.* LeGrande C. Ellis* and David L. Berliner, Department of Anatomy, Division of Radiobiology, University of Utah College of Medicine, Salt Lake City, Utah.

Methods have been worked out for the isolation, purification, and characterization of the intermediates formed when 5-pregnenolone-7α-H^3 and progesterone-4-C^{14} were incubated with mouse testes. With these techniques, it was shown that 17α-hydroxyprogesterone and androstenedione are important intermediates in the biosynthesis of testosterone by normal mouse testes. Total body irradiation of mice with 500 r decreased testicular weight and produced a biphasic response in steroid biotransformation and androgen production. An initial increase in side chain splitting activity was followed by a decreased activity which increased to above normal levels by 30 days post irradiation. An apparent block in the reduction of the oxygen function at carbon-17 was also observed until 20 days post irradiation. There was a direct correlation of the production of progesterone and 17α-hydroxyprogesterone, both of which had an inverse relationship with the production of androstenedione. The syndrome of events observed appears to be mediated by pituitary gonadotropins as well as the availability of metabolic cofactors such as TPN and DPN. Although previous work has indicated that the cells responsible for androgen production are radioresistant, these data indicate that the androgen producing cells are subject to the effect of radiation even through the outward histological appearance of these cells may indicate that they are normal.

C5. *Influence of Radiation on the Development of Microsome Oxidase and Reductase Activity in the Livers of Young Male Rats.* Bernard E. Hietbrink*, Marjorie Keshmiri*, and Kenneth P. DuBois, U. S. Air Force Radiation Laboratory, University of Chicago, Chicago, Illinois.

Studies in this laboratory [*Radiation Research* **16,** 555, (1962)] demonstrated that total-body X-irradiation (100 r to 400 r) inhibits development of enzymes responsible for oxidative desulfuration of a cholinergic phosphorothioate, Guthion (DBD) in livers of young male rats. Our recent stiudies (*Federation Proc.* **22,** 1963, in press) indicated that shielding certain areas and administration of MEA reduce this inhibitory effect. The present study was undertaken to determine the influence of daily doses of gamma radiation on development of microsome oxidases and the effect of X-irradiation on development of reductase activity in livers of young male rats. Young rats (23 days old) received 20 or 40 r of gamma radiation daily. The animals were sacrificed at intervals during 21 days after initial exposure for measurement of phosphorothioate-oxidizing activity of the liver. Exposure to 20 r per day did not affect enzyme synthesis but 40 r per day inhibited normal development of the enzyme activity. Enzymatic reduction of *p*-nitrobenzoic acid to *p*-aminobenzoic acid was used as a quantitative method for measuring TPNH-reductase activity. Reductase activity of livers of 22-day-old male rats was less than half the adult level. It increased to adult levels by 35 days of age. Administration of 400 r of X-ray to 23-day-old rats had no effect on development of reductase activity. Thus, sublethal doses of X-irradiation do not influence synthesis of reductase activity in livers of young male rats in contrast to the marked inhibitory effect of radiation on development of microsome oxidase which also requires a reduced pyridine nucleotide for activity.

C6. *Influence of Early Sublethal Whole-Body Irradiation and of Breeding Status on Thermal Aging of Collagen Fibers in the Mouse.* E. B. Darden, Jr.,* Margaret Bradley,* and A. C. Upton, Biology Division, Oak Ridge National Laboratory, Oak Ridge, Tennessee.

To explore the relation between shortened survival and late effects of ionizing radiation on specific age-dependent processes, the aging of collagen fibers from tail tendons of irradiated and unirradiated mice was investigated. Virgin male and female RF/Up mice, caged separately by sex in groups of 8–10, received a whole-body exposure of 450 r at 2–3 months of age, or in the case of a few animals, a local exposure of 2000 r confined to the tail. At intervals throughout the remainder of the life span the irradiated animals and controls were killed, and the temperature of maximum contraction (TMC) determined for single tail-tendon fibers. In fibers from both irradiated and unirradiated animals the mean TMC increased smoothly with age, with no significant difference in slope between groups. The mean TMC of fibers from mice which were members of actively breeding or formerly breeding pairs showed no significant correlation with age. The observed results indicate that the thermal response of collagen fibers shows an age-dependent relation to temperature which is not appreciably influenced by whole-body X-radiation in life-shortening doses or by larger doses of X rays localized to the tail. The results with breeders imply the influence of other factors on the age-dependent changes in collagen (i.e., sexual, nutritional, or stress variables), the role of which remains to be established.

C7. *Immediate Effects of Radiation on Rat Pituitary Respiration.* MILTON A. LESSLER and RICHARD BUGOCI*, Department of Physiology, The Ohio State University, Columbus 10, Ohio.

These studies were designed to provide information on the sequence of respiratory events which occur immediately after *in vitro* irradiation of the pituitary. Pituitary glands were rapidly removed from decapitated rats, quickly cut into uniformly thin slices, and incubated in Krebs III medium at 37°C. Irradiation of metabolizing tissues was accomplished by means of a modified Warburg apparatus in which individual flasks could be sequentially positioned over the port of an 85 kvp X-ray tube. Paired control flasks were shielded in an adjacent 37°C bath during irradiation of the experimental flasks. A one hour control run, before irradiation of experimental samples, served as a base line for comparison of the initial activity in each flask. Whole rat pituitary showed a marked increase in respiration after an X-ray dose of 1200r. In order to determine the site of this postirradiation increase in metabolic activity, the respiration of posterior and anterior pituitary was studied. Comparison of the respiratory activities indicated that the increased respiration that had been observed following whole pituitary radiation was due primarily to increased respiration of irradiated anterior pituitary tissue. (This study was supported by an Ohio State University Development Fund Grant.)

C8. *Species Difference in Postirradiation Hyperglycemia.* DONALD R. ANDERSON, Bionucleonics Department, School of Aerospace Medicine, Brooks Air Force Base, Texas.

Alteration in carbohydrate metabolism resulting from radiation exposure has been extensively reported in the literature. Kohn [*Am. J. Physiol.* **165,** 27 (1951)] and Kay and Entenman [*Proc. Soc. Exptl. Med.* **91,** 143–146 (1956)] have reported on a plasma glucose elevation in rats which reached a maximum at 2–4 days postirradiation. Other species have been studied with nominal glucose serum elevations and a general result has been the finding of an increase in the level of liver glycogen postirradiation.

In a study concerned with the changes of serum composition following acute radiation in the Macaca Mulatta primate it was found that a marked hyperglycemia was observed within 30 minutes of the radiation exposure. At two hours the glucose level was considerably reduced and had returned to essentially normal at four hours postirradiation. In an attempt to relate this phenomenon with other species previously reported, rats were irradiated, and it was found that they did not respond to this immediate "glucose burst." The rabbit and the dog were then investigated, and it was found that their serum response also did not demonstrate this very early hyperglycemia.

Additional monkeys were then irradiated and in a program utilizing chemical protective compounds it was observed that the preadministration of some of these protective materials modified the hyperglycemic response.

C9. *The Responses of Cellular Ultrastructures to Ionizing Irradiation.* ANNA GOLDFEDER and L. A. MILLER, Cancer and Radiobiological Research Laboratory, Department of Hospitals and New York University, New York City.

Combined studies have been carried out on the effects of X-irradiation on the fine structures and on intracellular enzymatic activity of normal and neoplastic cells. The types of tumors (epithelial, slow-growing and spindle cell, rapidly growing) both isologous to the same inbred strain of mice and normal mouse lymph nodes served as experimental material. The first discernible changes in the cellular ultrastructures, revealed electron microscopically, were: (1) dilatation of vesicles of the endoplasmic reticulum, (2) swelling or shrinkage of mitochondria and the disruption of their cristae, (3) breakages of the plasma membranes, and (4) aggregation of the ribonucleoprotein (RNP) particles. The nuclear membrane and the nuclear sap in these radiation-affected cells remained apparently unchanged. The aforementioned changes in the ultrastructures were more prominent in the spindle tumor cells and in the cells of the lymph nodes following relatively smaller X-ray doses (400 to 3000 rads) than in the epithelial tumor cells following larger doses (5000 rads).

Quantitative determinations on enzymatic activities such as catalase and ATPase in the nuclear, mitochondrial and cell sap fractions isolated from the X-irradiated tumors *in situ* by ultracentrifugation procedures revealed: (1) a displacement of enzymatic activity (particularly of catalase) within the intracellular compartments following various doses of X-irradiation, and (2) initial increases or initial decrease followed by a later increase in ATPase activity to almost normal levels at post-irradiation times up to 144 hours after a fixed dose of 5000 rads. These changes in the enzymatic activities varied in extent between these two tumor-types following irradiation with equal X-ray doses. (Grant from NCI, NIH C2565.)

C10. *Antioxidant Activity in Ascites Tumor Cells.* EDWARD D. LASH* (Introduced by Howard S. Ducoff), Department of Physiology and Biophysics, University of Illinois, Urbana, Illinois.

Lipid peroxides added to Ehrlich ascites tumor cells inhibit respiration and glycolysis, and also cause decreased cell viability. Many tumors and rapidly proliferating normal tissues contain antioxidants which prevent lipid peroxidation *in vitro*. However, peroxidation can occur *in vitro* in brain, adult liver and other organs. It has been reported that cell fractions from several types of rat hepatoma do not themselves form peroxides, but are generally unable to inhibit formation in normal liver homogenates.

The effect of Ehrlich and Krebs-2 ascites tumor cells on lipid peroxidation was studied by means of the thiobarbituric acid assay. Aeration of intact or homogenized tumor cells yielded no detectable peroxidation, whereas liver homogenates produced large amounts of peroxides under the same conditions. Addition of ascitic fluid, or of injured or homogenized tumor cell preparations, prevented peroxidation in the liver homogenate test system; in contrast, addition of intact, washed tumor cells was not inhibitory. Antioxidant activity was found in both the cytoplasmic and nuclear fractions. Ultraviolet irradiation catalyzed peroxide formation in Ehrlich cells and cell fractions, but the amount formed was less than one-tenth that in irradiated liver homogenate. Ultraviolet irradiation also destroyed the antioxidant activity in ascitic fluid. (This work was performed under contract AT (11-1) 878 with the USAEC.)

C11. *Early Alterations in Plasma Proteins in the Gamma-Irradiated Chick.* EMILY J. B. CHRISTIAN and S. PHYLLIS STEARNER, Division of Biological and Medical Research, Argonne National Laboratory, Argonne, Illinois.

Permeability changes leading to lethal circulatory failure can occur within a few hours after irradiation of the 3-day chick. Decrease in blood pressure, hemorrhage, and edema are characteristic features. Alterations in concentration of plasma protein and its principal components have been used as indicators of the permeability changes caused by sublethal and lethal doses.

The normal plasma protein concentration is nearly 4 grams percent, of which 1.5 gm per cent is albumin and about 2.5 gm per cent is the total globulin fraction. Co^{60} γ-irradiation below that which causes early mortality (death within 24 hours) produces little change in the concentration of proteins. After exposure to a minimal lethal dose (700 r delivered in 10 minutes) a slow change occurred in the circulating plasma. A minimum concentration was reached at 6 hours and a gradual return to normal values at 24 hours. Doses in the 90–99% lethal range for early mortality (1200 r to 1400 r delivered in 10 minutes) almost immediately produced drastic changes in the plasma protein concentration. In 2 hours the quantity of albumin decreased by 60% and that of globulin by 45%. Postirradiation increases in the red cell hematocrit values could be correlated with decreased circulating plasma volumes and decreased plasma protein concentrations. (Work supported by U. S. Atomic Energy Commission).

C12. *Effects of Radiation and/or Catalase Inhibitors on Catalase Activity in* Tetrahymena pyriformis *W*. JAY S. ROTH and GAYLA BUCCINO*, Institute of Cellular Biology, University of Connecticut, Storrs, Connecticut.

The protozoan *Tetrahymena pyriformis* is extremely resistant to radiation; it is estimated that the LD_{50} is between 300,000 and 500,000 r. Since in mammals radiosensitive tissues contain low nuclear catalase activity, and this activity is sensitive to radiation [Biochem. J. **77,** 5 (1960)], it is of interest to assess the properties and distribution of catalase activity in *Tetrahymena.*

The protozoa contain considerable enzyme activity; approximately 90% is found in the particulate material sedimenting at 1500*g* or higher. A major portion of the activity may reside, therefore, in the nuclear or mitochondrial fraction, or both. The specific catalase activity in the particulate fraction is in the range of 2000 μM H_2O_2 decomposed/mg N/min at 0°C.

The effect of catalase inhibitors sodium azide, 3-amino-1,2,4-triazole (AT) and allylisopropylacetamide (AIPA) on oxygen consumption and growth will be presented.

When the protozoa are grown in the presence of AIPA and subjected to 500,000 r of γ-irradiation from Co^{60}, growth was inhibited 80% more than the sum of the inhibitions observed on treatment with irradiation or AIPA alone. With AT plus irradiation, the combined inhibition was the same as the sum of the inhibitions of these two agents alone. AIPA may, therefore, sensitize *Tetrahymena* to the effects of radiation. (Supported by the U.S. Atomic Energy Commission and the National Institutes of Health).

SECTION D. HEMATOLOGY AND MARROW TRANSPLANTATION

D1. *Effects of Sublethal Doses of Whole Body X-Irradiation on the Kinetics of More Mature Erythroblasts in the Dog.* N. ODARTCHENKO*, H. COTTIER*, L. E. FEINENDEGEN* and V. P. BOND, Medical Research Center, Brookhaven National Laboratory, Upton, Long Island, New York.

Dogs are given whole body irradiation (50 to 150 r) within 30 minutes after a single injection of tritiated thymidine. The progression of initially labeled erythroblasts through mitosis and into more mature stages corresponding to initially nonlabeling cells, is followed by serial bone marrow sampling and autoradiography. The findings are compared with data obtained from nonirradiated animals. The time of this progression is not modified to a major extent at either of the two dose levels used. The labeling index curve of the most mature erythroblastic mitosis as a function of time after injection of tritiated thymidine, shows evidence of mitotic delay of cells irradiated while in late interphase (end of S and G2). At least a fraction of cells irradiated while in prophase of most mature erythroblastic mitosis progress through anaphase and telophase. The duration of DNA synthesis itself is not markedly modified. Most of the depletion of the more mature erythroblasts as observed at later times after whole body X-irradiation with 150 r appears to originate from radiation damage caused in the less mature erythroblastic precursors. (Supported by the U. S. Atomic Energy Commission).

D2. *Simulation of Extracorporeal Blood Irradiation by the Localized Tail Irradiation of Mice.*
B. CASSEN, M. MOODY* and R. NEFF*, Laboratory of Nuclear Medicine and Radiation Biology of the Department of Biophysics and Nuclear Medicine, School of Medicine, University of California at Los Angeles.

Previous attempts to study the effect of irradiating blood alone in a living animal have required operational procedures with attendant complications as for example, the necessity of heparinization. A method was evolved to give a few hundred to a few thousand rads average dose to the blood of a mouse by irradiating its tail only with about 60 times the average blood dose from a 50 kv beryllium window X-ray tube. Unfortunately, lymphocytosis in mice is normally very variable, but by using a sufficiently large number of irradiated and control mice it was possible to determine with good statistical significance that 7000 r blood irradiation can produce an appreciable lymphopenia in 24 hours, followed by recovery within 72 hours. No long-duration lymphopenia was observed in these experiments. RISA was used to determine the fraction of the animal's blood that is in the tail. The lymphopenia produced is consistent either with the hypothesis of the lymphocytes being injured or killed by the direct action of the radiation or with an alternate hypothesis that the rate of new lymphocyte production by mitotic division of lymphatically recirculating stem-cell large lymphocytes is decreased. (Supported by Contract AT(04-1)GEN-12 between the Atomic Energy Commission and the University of California at Los Angeles).

D3. *The Effect of Total Body Irradiation on the Size Distribution of Circulating Lymphocytes.*
R. D. NEFF* and B. CASSEN, Laboratory of Nuclear Medicine and Radiation Biology of the Department of Biophysics and Nuclear Medicine, School of Medicine, University of California at Los Angeles.

By the use of a method developed in this laboratory for efficiently separating lymphocytes from whole blood, it is relatively easy to determine the size distribution of the separated lymphocytes with a Coulter counter. A complete lymphocyte size distribution curve on rabbit blood can be obtained with a single channel counter in about 90 minutes.

The size distribution in healthy rabbits is reasonably reproducible. It is markedly affected by a few hundred rads total body radiation. The small lymphocytes consistently fall off more rapidly than the larger ones. The fall-off ratio increases with increasing dose. The effect tends to support the hypothesis that the large lymphocytes constitute a stem cell series for continuous production during lymphatic recirculation, of small lymphocytes. The radiation, even less than 100 rads, arrests the mitosis of the large lymphocytes while the already produced small cells are continually leaving the vascular and lymphatic compartments. Other interpretations can be made. Studies are being made of the sensitivity of using the size change distribution as a biological dosimeter. (Supported by Contract AT(04-1)GEN-12 between the Atomic Energy Commission and the University of California at Los Angeles.)

D4. *The Erythropoietin Tolerance Test in Radiation Studies of Plethoric Mice.* CLIFFORD W. GURNEY, Departments of Medicine and Physiology, University of Chicago and the Argonne Cancer Research Hospital, Chicago Illinois.

Radiation damage, recovery, protection, and combination with chemotherapeutic agents have been measured in plethoric mice, in which damage may be determined at low doses of radiation (50–300 r). The cell population under investigation consists of the important radiosensitive cells of the marrow, the stem cells.

Plethoric mice cease erythrocyte production at ambient conditions. A quantitative wave of erythropoiesis, arising from stem cell differentiation, is produced by erythropoietin. This is conveniently measured by the per cent incorporation into newly formed erythrocytes of Fe^{59} administered 48–60 hours after erythropoietin. Stem cell damage is demonstrated by impairment of response to 6 units of erythropoietin. The radiation dose-cell damage curve for stem cells *in vivo* and *in situ* resembles that observed in tissue culture by other investigators.

Stem cell recovery pattern is observed by challenging different groups of animals with erythropoietin at different times after irradiation. At low radiation doses recovery is characterized by instantaneous damage, additional "damage" 24 hours later, a plateau for several days, and finally rapid complete recovery. Protection by MEA or AET administered immediately before irradiation is slight when the stem cell compartment is challenged immediately after irradiation, but increases with time and is maximal if erythropoietin administration is delayed until just before the onset of rapid recovery as observed in nonprotected animals.

Finally, the erythropoietin tolerance test was used to demonstrate the degree to which Actinomycin or nitrogen mustard and irradiation are additive. (Operated by the University of Chicago for the United States Atomic Energy Commission).

D5. *Changes in Peripheral Blood of Female Goats Following Acute, Fractionated or Continuous Gamma Irradiation.* E. W. HUPP*, C. A. O'BRIEN*, H. B. PACE*, J. W. AUSTIN* and G. M. ADAM* (Introduced by G. M. Krise), Radiation Biology Laboratory, Texas A. & M. College, College Station, Texas.

Female Spanish goats were subjected to 300 r Co^{60} gamma radiation. One group of 9 animals received a single acute dose at 100 r/hour; a second group of 6 goats received 3 fractions of 100 r/hour, each fraction was separated by 10 days; the third group of 6 goats received continuous irradiation at the rate of 15 r per 20 hour irradiation day for 20 days. Blood samples were obtained from the jugular vein before and at intervals of 120 days after irradiation. Hematocrit values in the continuous group were slightly but not significantly depressed from the end of irradiation until 28 days after irradiation, hemoglobin and red blood cell count were also slightly depressed in this group. Red blood cell values in the other 2 irradiation groups were very similar to the control. White blood cell counts (WBC) reached a low value 4, 10, and 14 days postirradiation in the fractionated, continuous and acute groups, respectively. By 14 days postirradiation the continuously irradiated group had returned to approximately 75% of the control value of 8500/mm^3 and have remained at that level to 120 days. WBC values in the acute and fractionated irradiation groups have remained about 50% of control from 21 to 120 days after irradiation. Differential WBC counts indicate that the early decrease in leucocytes was due to lymphopenia, but after 4 days postirradiation, both lymphocytes and granulocytes were decreased.

D6. *Some Latent Effects of Chronic Neutron Exposure on Erythropoiesis in the Monkey.* T. P. LEFFINGWELL, G. S. MELVILLE, JR., and R. J. YOUNG*, The Radiobiological Laboratory of the United States Air Force and the University of Texas, Austin, Texas.

Two groups of male *Macaca mulatta* monkeys were exposed to either 583 or 834 rep of Po-Be neutrons on a regular schedule over a period approximating three years. Two of the 834 rep animals died during the irradiation sequence; two died within four days after the sequence was terminated; two died approximately five months later. One of the 583 rep animals died approximately nine months after the exposure was stopped, one currently evidences anomalies which we feel presage death, and four of the irradiation group counterparts evidence clinical good health. All six concurrent controls survive.

Stable and radioiron studies and peripheral hematologic samplings have been employed to study the effects of the irradiation on blood-forming tissues. Patterns have been elicited which developed over a period of several months preceding death. Among changes noted during this period is development of a progressive normochromic macrocytic anemia accompanied by a chronic absolute reticulocytosis. Plasma iron turnover rate, and the specific activity of both the heme and non-heme cell iron is increased in these animals. Lifespan of the mature red cells is essentially normal; however, it would appear that a relatively high percentage of the maturing reticulocytes undergo lysis before reaching maturity. Complementary studies in process will be discussed.

D7. *Long Term Effects of Total-Body X-Radiation on Peripheral Blood Values in the Beagle.* A. C. ANDERSEN, W. GEE*, and L. S. ROSENBLATT*, School of Veterinary Medicine, University of California, Davis; and Biological Frontiers Institute, Livermore, California.

From 354 female Beagles, some 4,400 blood samples taken between one and nine years after irradiation were analyzed statistically for possible long term effects. The dogs had received single or fractionated exposures totaling either 100 r or 300 r (midline air dose). Fourteen different traits were analyzed according to basic experimental design (randomized blocks) to eliminate certain environmental variables insofar as possible. Time trends in erythrocyte values (PCV; RBC; Hgb) were similar in irradiated dogs and sham-treated controls, except in later years when higher exposed subgroups declined below controls. Sedimentation rates increased as a function of time in irradiated dogs and suggested a delayed effect. Leukocytic elements showed either no treatment effect, over-compensation or failure to recover. Monocytes and band cells showed no radiation effect. Eosinophile number was unaffected except for the highest exposed subgroups were elevated values persisted. Heterophils and lymphocytes showed recovery in lower exposed subgroups, but higher exposed subgroups failed to recover. (Supported by the US Atomic Energy Commission).

D8. *Measurement of the Radiation Sensitivity of Mouse Bone Marrow Cells by Use of I^{131}-Labeled Iododeoxyuridine ($I^{131}UdR$).* W. B. STALLCUP,* G. CUDKOWICZ* and W. L. HUGHES* (Introduced by A. C. Upton), Biology Division, Oak Ridge National Laboratory, Oak Ridge, Tennessee.

A quantitative assessment of the proliferative capacity of (BALB/c $\times$ A/He)F_1 marrow cells *in vivo* was obtained by determining the ability of these cells to repopulate the spleen on transplantation into X-irradiated (700 r) syngeneic recipients. The proliferation of the transplanted cells was measured by determining their uptake of I^{131}UdR, a specific deoxyribonucleic acid precursor, in the spleen. The relation between the I^{131}UdR uptake in the repopulated spleen and the number of marrow cells transplanted 5 days earlier was linear over a range from 0.5×10^5 to 16×10^5 normal cells. Curves identical in slope were obtained with marrow cells exposed *in vitro* to 50, 100, 200, and 400 r 300 kvp X rays. From these data, an X-ray dose survival curve was obtained in the usual manner. The advantages of this method for studying the proliferation of marrow cells, as influenced by irradiation, are as follows: (1) the recipient mouse is an optimal medium for growth of transplanted marrow cells and need not be kept alive for more than 5 days, (2) I^{131}UdR labeling is specific for DNA of cells in S phase and, therefore, measures *directly* marrow cell proliferation, (3) five observations, i.e., five recipient mice, are adequate for reproducible assessment of the residual proliferative capacity of a given number of irradiated marrow cells. Hence, since the linear portion of the dose-response curves is very broad and its slope is not affected by irradiation, dose-response curves, X-ray survival kinetics, and LET effects can be established with relatively few animals and with an accuracy comparable to that obtained in studies *in vitro*.

D9. *Fe^{59} Incorporation by Spleens of Lethally Irradiated Mice Injected with Isologous Bone Marrow.* L. H. SMITH, Biology Division, Oak Ridge National Laboratory, Oak Ridge, Tennessee.

Fe^{59} uptake by spleens of lethally X-irradiated mice is a function of the number of isologous bone marrow cells injected. Uptake depends on erythropoietic activity in the spleen which reflects quantitative transplantation of marrow cells. We developed this system as a means of evaluating *in vitro* treatment of cells injured by radiation. (C3H × C57BL)F_1 mice are exposed to 900 r and injected with isologous bone marrow. Eight days after marrow injection, Fe^{59} is given i.p. and spleen removed 6 hours later. Uptake is linear with marrow dose between 0.05 and 0.8 × 10^6 cells. Beyond 0.8 × 10^6 cells, reduction of uptake was observed rather than the expected plateau. Spleen weight is also reduced after high marrow doses. These decreases may represent a physiologic response that signals a shutdown in cell proliferation in the hyperactive spleen which, in mice given 0.8 × 10^6 cells, takes up 4 times the iron as that of a normal mouse. Short-term culture conditions were investigated to obtain an optimal environment for irradiated marrow cells. Initially, we used Tyrode's solution for a 6-hour incubation period, noting both iron uptake of spleen induced by these cells and cell counts in the incubated cultures. Up to 50% variation was observed not only in erythropoietic activity of cells, but also in the number of cells remaining after 6 hours incubation at 23°C. Variation has been reduced by use of 10% calf serum in Tyrode's solution without calcium. Reduction in cell number (10–15%) still is observed, but reduction in erythropoietic activity is minimized.

D10. *A Differential Method for Measuring the Erythropoietic Rates of Donor and Host Marrow in Radiation Chimeras.* D. E. Carlson* (Introduced by K. H. Clifton), Department of Radiology Research Laboratories, University of Wisconsin Medical School, Madison, Wisconsin.

A rapid, accurate method for measuring erythropoiesis in animals possessing proliferative tissues of different antigenic specificities is presented. Using Fe^{59} in tracer amounts and agglutinating reagents specific for one erythrocytic type, it is possible to determine the proportion of the erythrocytes of each phenotype in the circulation, and to measure the quantity of isotope incorporated into each cell type. In the experiments with lethally irradiated rats protected by bone marrow, erythrocytes in the same aliquot were separated by differential agglutination using heteroimmune reagents specific for antigenic specificities C and D. Both fractions thus separated were lysed, assayed spectrophotometrically for oxyhemoglobin, and the radioactivity was measured with a low-background scintillation counter. Data were expressed as specific activities, i.e., as counts per minute per unit of spectrophotometric absorbance. The ratio of the host-cell specific activity to the donor-cell specific activity plotted against time is an indication of the rate at which the grafted marrow is replacing or being replaced by the recovering tissue of the host. The sums of the oxyhemoglobin and radioactivity values for the agglutinated aliquots when compared with the unseparated control samples indicated only slight loss of cellular material during the separation procedure. (Supported by Grant No. G15966 from the National Science Foundation).

D11. *Studies on Differential Radiosensitivity of the Erythropoietic Capacity and Immunologic Competence of Bone Marrow.* Don H. Shaw* (Introduced by K. H. Clifton), Department of Radiology Research Laboratories, University of Wisconsin Medical School, Madison, Wisconsin.

Dove bone marrow is capable of erythrocytic repopulation when transplanted into lethally irradiated pigeons and produces, or directs production of, a potent hemagglutinin which causes "*in vivo* agglutination" of host erythrocytes. In this marrow transplant system erythropoietic capacity is directly measurable by differential agglutination of donor and host type erythrocytes. Immunologic competence of the marrow is also quantitatively measurable, as a function of the titers of anti-host species specific hemagglutinins.

A series of marrow suspensions ranging from 250 × 10^6 to 25.0 × 10^6 nucleated cells were transplanted into 5 groups of lethally irradiated pigeons (2600 r total body). Another series of marrow suspensions containing 125 × 10^6 cells were exposed to X-rays *in vitro* at doses of 1000, 1400, 1800, 2200 and 2600 r and were injected intravenously into lethally irradiated groups.

The circulating donor erythrocytes were measured at intervals after transplantation in all groups and the sera from the grafted birds were tested for titers of anti-host agglutinins.

At radiation doses higher than 1000 r to the marrow there was a negative correlation between the percentage of "*in vivo* agglutination" and survival. The pattern of death of pigeons with irradiated marrow differed from that of the irradiated controls, i.e., irradiated marrow had some protective effect. A negative correlation also existed between the maximum average anti-host agglutinin titers and the dose of irradiation to the marrow. These data imply that irradiation of the marrow prior to transplantation decreased the deleterious immunologic competence of the heterologous marrow to a greater extent than it decreased the beneficial erythropoietic capacity. (Supported by NSF Grant G15966).

D12. *The Effect of Reticuloendothelial Stimulation on Radiation Chimeras and on the Primary and Secondary Response.* W. R. WOOLES* and N. R. DI LUZIO, Department of Physiology, University of Tennessee Medical Units, Memphis, Tennessee.

Our studies have demonstrated a hyperfunctional state of the reticuloendothelial system (RES) enhances rejection of heterologous and homologous bone marrow in irradiated mice. Further studies have demonstrated a relationship between the functional state of the RES at the time of transplantation and survival of lethally irradiated mice treated with homologous bone marrow. In order to evaluate whether rejection can occur after transplantation was achieved, radiation chimeras which had survived 30 days or longer were injected with either saline or glucan, an RE stimulating agent, and survival determined. Saline-treated heterologous chimeras manifested a 58% survival as opposed to 0% in glucan-treated chimeras. No mortality was observed in saline-treated homologous chimeras whereas glucan-treated chimeras manifested 50% mortality. Isologous chimeras were unaffected by either saline or glucan. Since marrow rejection could be due to an enhanced immunological response in the RE hyperfunctional group, primary and secondary hemolysin titers were determined in saline and glucan, normal and irradiated mice. Mean peak primary hemolysin titers of RE hyperfunctional mice were increased 300%. The secondary hemolysin response in glucan-treated mice was elevated 30 fold over the controls and 20 fold when compared to the peak primary response. After 500 r X-ray the secondary response in glucan-treated mice was increased 600% over saline irradiated controls. The results indicate that the failure in heterologous and homologous bone marrow acceptance and rejection in chimeras may be the result of hyperphagocytosis as well as an enhanced immunological response.

SECTION E. RADIATION PHYSICS

E1. *Physical Factors in Cinefluorography. III. Relative Patient Dose for 35 mm and 16 mm Camera Systems.* JOHN HALE, ROBERT EPPERSON*, DAVID L. GEORGE*, and THEODORE A. TRISTAN*, Department of Radiology, Hospital of the University of Pennsylvania, Philadelphia, Pennsylvania.

Within the last few years, cinefluorography (X-ray motion pictures) has become an important technique in diagnostic radiology. Either 35 mm or 16 mm camera systems may be used. One of the factors by which these systems can be compared is the entrance dose to the patient that is required to produce equal motion picture film exposures. Measurements have been made of the characteristics of a cinefluoroscope from which the ratio of patient dose has been calculated for 35 mm as compared to 16 mm camera systems with either variable X-ray tube potential or variable X-ray tube current methods of exposure control. For the variable current method, the 35mm/16mm patient dose ratio was found to be 4.5, in fair agreement with the ratio of the speeds of the lenses used with the two systems. For the variable potential method, the patient dose ratio varied between 2.3 and 2.8. (This work was supported in part by Grant (CA-01984) from the United States Public Health Service, National Institutes of Health).

E2. *Optimization of Crystal Positions in a Total-Body Counter.* CAROL M. NEWTON*, ROBERT J. HASTERLIK, SANDRA J. LARSON*, and DANIEL GARIGAN*, Department of Medicine, University of Chicago, Biological Sciences Computation Center; and Argonne Cancer Research Hospital[1], Chicago, Illinois.

Total-body counters should be insensitive to redistribution of isotope within a subject. Two factors contribute to this sensitivity. (1) The crystal array may count an isolated source with an efficiency sensitive to source position. (2) Distortion of the observed gamma spectrum by Compton and other absorptive effects is sensitive to body build and isotope distribution. This paper describes efforts to minimize the effects of the first factor.

A linear crystal array is considered optimal, with respect to a given linear source locus, whenever the crystals are spaced so that their combined counting efficiency varies minimally when counting a point source at various positions along the source locus. Trial-and-error determinations of the optimal 4-crystal array for one source locus proved time-consuming but clearly worthwhile. We have written a computer program which expedites determination of optimal 2-, 3-, and 4-crystal linear arrays for any specified linear source locus parallel to the array axis, given information about individual crystal counting efficiencies. Degree of optimization for any crystal array is estimated by an error function, and the calculated error is printed for crystal positions near the optimal. Other features of this program and associated experimental findings will be discussed. These findings concern our total-body counter, but might also aid economical designing of other such facilities.

E3. *A New Technique for Determining Quality of X-Ray Beams.* JOHN R. CAMERON* and GORDON KENNEY* (Introduced by Halvor Vermund), Harshaw Chemical Company, Cleveland, Ohio.

The conventional method for determining the quality of an X-ray beam by a half value layer is tedious, time consuming, and subject to a number of errors. The purpose of this report is to suggest an alternative method which appears to have significant advantages. If one measures an X-ray beam with two radiation dosimeters which have markedly different responses for different quality X-rays, the ratio of uncorrected measurements will determine the quality of the X-ray beam. This is true if there are not two energies with the same correction factor. Many common dosimetry materials (e.g., film and glass rods) do not meet this criteria. The thermoluminescent radiation dosimeters constructed of LiF and Al_2O_3 meet this criteria and have markedly different responses in the region below 250 KVP (or 120 Kev effective). The results and accuracy of the technique will be discussed.

E4. *Thermoluminescent Radiation Dosimetry with Lithium Fluoride.* JOHN R. CAMERON*, DAVID ZIMMERMAN* and GORDON KENNEY* (Introduced by Halvor Vermund), Harshaw Chemical Company, Cleveland, Ohio.

An activated LiF material has been developed especially for thermoluminescent radiation dosimetry (TLD-100 and TLD-700 from the Harshaw Chemical Company, Cleveland, Ohio). A report will be given of the characteristics which are important for dosimetry purposes. A "reader" has been developed using readily available components. The heating element is a modified soldering gun, the high voltage supply for the photomultiplier tube consists of 45 v batteries between dynodes and the current from the photomultiplier tube is measured by converting it into pulses with a capacitor in parallel with a neon bulb. The pulses are counted by an inexpensive decade scaler. The reader is satisfactory to a standard deviation of ±3% in the range of 10 r to 10,000 r and can be extended to 100,000 r by a simple modification. Each measurement uses about 35 mg of the loose powder which is reusable after proper annealing. The

[1] Operated by the University of Chicago for the United States Atomic Energy Commission.

response is only 30% greater at 30 Kev effective than for Co^{60} gamma rays. Thermal neutrons give about 50 times greater response than gamma or X-rays. At room temperature the stored thermoluminescense decays at less than 5% per year. The low temperature thermoluminescent peak has been almost completely eliminated by a special annealing procedure prior to irradiation. The dosimeter is being used in routine clinical problems.

E5. *LiF Thermoluminescent Dosimeter System for Radiation Research.* RICHARD C. MCCALL*, LEWIS E. BABCOCK*, and RICHARD C. FIX, Controls For Radiation, Inc., Cambridge, Massachusetts.

A dosimeter system has been developed which has widespread use in radiation research, both in routine and specialized applications. The system is based on the thermoluminescent property of specially activated LiF which causes it to emit an amount of light proportional to the received dose when heated after exposure to radiation. The following response characteristics to X and gamma radiation have been determined: (1) Range: less than 10 mrads to 10^5 rads. (2) Energy Independence: relative response 1.0 from 1.3 Mev to 100 kev; gradual increase to 1.4 (unshielded) or 1.1 (shielded) from 100 kev to 40 kev. (3) Dose Rate Independence: up to at least 2.5×10^5 rad/min. (4) Accuracy: ±5% throughout range. (5) Tissue and Air Equivalence: effective Z for photoelectric absorption of 8.14 compared to 7.42 for tissue and 7.64 for air. (6) Active Volume: 0.06 cm^3 of phosphor.

In addition, the response to betas, protons, and fast neutrons has been measured. A linear relationship was found over the dose ranges studied. Several forms of dosimeters have been developed including types which are permanently encapsulated and those which utilize the loose phosphor. A reader has also been developed which permits rapid readout by relatively unskilled personnel. Because of its response characteristics, small size, and simplicity of use, the dosimeter has *in vivo* applications (depth dose measurement, dose distribution in whole body irradiation, intracavitary dosimetry, dose confirmation for radioactive implants) as well as other uses such as beam calibration, half-value layer determinations, and particle dose measurements.

E6. *The Dose Response of Glass, Thermoulminescent and Film Dosimeters to High Energy Charged Particles.* E. TOCHILIN, J. T. LYMAN, F. H. ATTIX and E. J. WEST, U. S. Naval Radiological Defense Laboratory, San Francisco, California; Donner Laboratory, University of California, Berkeley, California; and U. S. Naval Research Laboratory, Washington 25, D. C.

The wide linear dose range, good storage characteristics, and small size of certain solid state dosimeters have led to their use in measuring radiation fields encountered during space flights. While extensive information is available on the behavior of these systems to electrons and gamma-rays, there is virtually no data on their response to protons and other heavy cosmic-ray particles. A study was made on the response of silver-activated phosphate glass dosimeters and of CaF_2:Mn and LiF thermoluminescence dosimeter to 910-Mev alpha particles and 730-Mev protons from the UCLRL 184-inch cyclotron. Similar data were also obtained for specific photo graphic emulsions. Dosage sensitivity relative to Co^{60} gamma rays was evaluated for the primary particle beams and, by means of absorbers, for various points along the Bragg curve of the alpha particle beam. Dose rate dependence was also investigated. The dependence of dose response upon the linear energy transfer (LET) will be presented for all systems. Pending availability of cyclotron time, additional information will be obtained with protons ranging in energy from 15 to 55 Mev. (Supported in part by USAEC and ONR.)

E7. *Stabilization of a Gamma Scintillation Spectrometer.* ROBERT A. DUDLEY* and REMIGIUS SCARPATETTI* (Introduced by Alan D. Conger), International Atomic Energy Agency, Vienna, Austria.

The principles and performance of a system for stabilizing a gamma ray spectrometer against zero and gain drifts of virtually any origin will be described. The spectrometer consists of a NaI(Tl) crystal and 200 channel analyzer. A reference source emitting gamma rays of 2 energies in coincidence with beta rays is incorporated within a small plastic scintillator, and positioned adjacent to the NaI(Tl) crystal. The channel number of the reference gamma ray pulses as produced in the NaI(Tl) crystal is determined by the analyzer in a manner identical to that for gamma rays from the experimental source. However, the reference gamma pulses, being distinguished by their coincident beta rays, are therafter processed differently from other gamma pulses. First, their channel number is observed by an auxiliary circuit, which controls zero and gain so as to keep the 2 reference peaks in their predetermined channels. Second, the reference pulses are not stored in the memory, and thereby contribute almost no background. Thus by means of a negative feedback loop enclosing the entire analogue portion of the spectrometer, ideal stability is closely approached without significant penalty. This stability greatly increases the power of the spectrometer for many purposes, especially in the unscrambling of mixed spectra such as occur in activation analysis and elsewhere.

E8. *A Precision Cavity Chamber for Measurement of Intermediate Energy X-Rays.* HAROLD O. WYCKOFF and FRANCIS R. SHONKA, National Bureau of Standards, Washington, D. C.; and St. Procopius College, Lisle, Illinois.

The International Commission on Radiological Units Handbook 78 describes a precision cavity chamber constructed by the National Bureau of Standards for comparison of standards with other national laboratories. The outer electrode was a graphite spherical shell. The center electrode was aluminum with dimensions empirically adjusted to minimize the energy dedendence. Later, a chamber of similar design was contructed with parts molded at St. Procopius College of a conducting air equivalent plastic (Second Atoms for Peace Conference, 1958), eliminating the empirical adjustment of the center electrode and resulting in a mechanically stronger instrument. These chambers are now used for comparison of national standards and as standards at other laboratories.

Recently SPC developed a mechanically superior plastic, easily molded and welded even in thin sections. Since the energy dependence of the present chamber results from the excessive thickness required for electronic equilibrium with Co^{60}, it was decided to construct a family of new chambers of several wall thicknesses. Here the spherical chamber and insulated guard ring assembly is a single welded unit. Results obtained for chambers with 0.18 mm and 0.35 mm wall thicknesses show a maximum divergence of 3 or 4 percent in the calibration factor for half value layers from 1.64 mm through 21.5 mm aluminum. We are now completing a design of a chamber for intermediate energies and redesigning the chamber for high energies. The next step will be to design a chamber for softer x-rays than those reported here.

E9. *A Study of Multiplication in Tissue Equivalent Gas Using Radiations of Different LET.* CATHARINE WINGATE and HAROLD H. ROSSI, Department of Radiology, Radiological Research Laboratory, Columbia University, New York, New York.

The measurement of the low doses usually encountered in radiation protection requires inconvenient large chamber sizes. This makes determination of the dose distribution in human phantoms impractical. It is thus very desirable to develop techniques whereby ionization chambers of greatly reduced size can be used. Earlier work by Rossi and Lubert [*Health Phys.* **1**, 46–50 (1958)] has shown that parallel plate ionization chambers can exhibit considerable gas multiplication without loss of linearity. The present study is designed to determine if such muliplication can also be obtained in the more convenient cylindrical geometry, using tissue equivalent gas, and whether the multiplication depends on LET.

Early results indicate a multiplication of at least 10^4, which is independent of both intensity and LET within the limits thus far investigated. These findings will be presented together with a discussion of the implication of this work for radiation protection dosimetry. (Based on work performed under Contract AT-(30-1)-2740 for the U. S. Atomic Energy Commission.)

E10. *Air and* in Vivo *Dosimetry on the Sandia Pulsed Reactor.* CAPTAIN VINCENT T. PENIKAS, Biomedical Branch, Biophysics Division, Research Directorate, Hq AFSWC, Kirtland AFB, Air Force Systems Command, New Mexico.

The Sandia Pulsed Reactor is a bare cylindrical, enriched-uranium metallic assembly similar to the Los Alamos Scientific Laboratory's Godiva II. The reactor was pulse operated producing a 50 microsecond pulse width at half maximum pulse height and a fuel material temperature rise of approximately 100°C. Sheep, dogs and miniature swine were exposed to a mixed neutron-gamma radiation field from the reactor. The air dose, entrance and exit doses were measured. Dosimetry packages were surgically implanted to obtain an estimate of the tissue depth dose in the living animal. The neutron dose was determined by means of threshold foil measurements. Gold and cadmium covered gold were used for determining the integrated thermal flux; plutonium-239, neptunium-237, uranium-238 and sulfur-32 for determining the integrated fast neutron fluxes; and metaphosphate glass rods containing silver for determining the gamma dose. All animals received lateral exposures at a midline distance of two meters from the reactor core center. The neutron rad dose measured in air was 159 ± 6.5 for a burst temperature rise of 100° C. The gamma dose was 32 ± 2.7 r. The entrance and exit doses as well as the dose to the internal package varied among the three species and depended upon the burst temperature rise, distance from the reactor, orientation of the foils with respect to the reactor, and the thickness and composition of the attenuating tissues.

E11. *Satellite Measurements of Space Radiation Doses.* R. A. GLASS, E. E. GAINES,* and W. L. HOLLISTER,* Research Laboratories, Lockheed Missiles & Space Company, Palo Alto, California.

Environmental radiation measurements have been made on board the satellite. These measurements have provided information on the radiation fields experienced in low-altitude satellite orbits (150 to 800 km). The region of space for which integral radiation exposures have been obtained, is that traveled by many instrumented flights and all manned and biological flights.

Radiation monitors included dosimetry films (DuPont 555 and 834) as well as Mg, Ni, Au, and Pb activation foils. Depth-dose information was obtained with the use of Al, Cd, and Pb shields.

The daily radiation doses observed for various flights range from 0.015 to 70 rads (through 1.3 g/cm^2) and can be chiefly attributed to (1) cosmic rays, 0.015 rads for all orbits; (2) Van Allen belt protons, 0.25 rads for 800 km apogee orbit; and (3) artificial belt electrons, 15 rads for 400 km apogee (July 1962), 0.5 rads for 400 km apogee (Jan. 1963), 70 rads for 700 km apogee (Aug. 1962). Presumably, doses from Van Allen protons and artificial electrons are received mainly in the region of the South American anomaly.

The artificial electrons, injected by the high altitude nuclear burst of July 9, 1962, caused the daily radiation dose to undergo the remarkable rise from 0.015 rads to 15 rads for the 400 km apogee orbit. The apparent half life for disappearance of the belt (at low altitude) appears to have lengthened from 15 to 80 days in the period July, 1962 to January, 1963.

SECTION F. CELL DIVISION AND DNA SYNTHESIS

F1. *The Radiation-Induced Depression of Tritiated Thymidine Incorporation into Isolated Nuclei—A Possible Mechanism.* SHIRLEY M. LEHNERT*. (Introduced by S. Okada), Division of Experimental Radiology, University of Rochester School of Medicine and Dentistry, Rochester, New York.

In vitro incorporation of tritiated thymidine into DNA of nuclei isolated from regenerating liver, supplied with an exogenous source of DNA synthesizing enzyme, is depressed when nuclei are taken from whole-body irradiated rats. This depression is not demonstrable immediately after irradiation but develops progressively with time thereafter. In studies of the mechanism of this effect, it was found that reduced incorporation could be separated into two nucleoprotein fractions isolated from nuclei after irradiation. However, incorporation of tritiated thymidine into purified DNA isolated from such preparation did not differ from that into DNA from a nonirradiated source, and it thus appears that the radiation-induced lesion resides in a nucleoprotein complex.

One change to be observed in deoxyribonucleoprotein is that the protein content is increased relative to DNA. This may be demonstrated in irradiated preparations both by direct measurement of protein:DNA ratio, and by a study of the *in vivo* incorporation of DNA and protein precursors into deoxyribonucleoprotein. It is suggested that this relative increase in nuclear protein content is at least partly responsible for the depressed priming ability of nuclear DNA following irradiation.

F2. *The Effect of Whole Body X-Irradiation on Mouse Spleen DNA Synthesis.* NELSON FAUSTO* and J. L. VAN LANCKER, Department of Pathology and Regional Primate Center, University of Wisconsin, Madison, Wisconsin.

X-irradiation (800 r whole body dose) inhibits *in vitro* incorporation of ^{3}H TDR into DNA of mouse spleen homogenates obtained 1, 3, and 6 hours after X-irradiation. The incorporation of labeled precursors into DNA of nuclear preparations obtained from spleen 1 hour after whole body X-irradiation was studied. X-irradiation interferes with incorporation of ^{3}H TDR into nuclei incubated with normal spleen cytoplasm, and of ^{14}C TMP, into nuclei incubated with regenerating liver supernatant. In contrast, the incorporation of ^{14}C TMP into boiled purified DNA in presence of spleen supernatants is not affected in 1 hour, but is reduced approximately 50% six hours after X-irradiation. Measurements of DNase and β-glucuronidase release, 1, 3, and 6 hours after X-irradiation demonstrate a marked increase in nonparticulate enzyme activity 6 hours after X-irradiation. These results suggest (1) that the low incorporation of precursors 6 hours after X-irradiation results from cellular death, and (2) that the block in DNA synthesis observed 1 hour after X-irradiation cannot be explained by alteration of the activity of the enzymes involved in the last steps of DNA synthesis.

F3. *The Immediate Effect of X-Radiation on Deoxyribonucleic Acid Synthesis in Mammalian Cell Cultures.* ROBERT B. PAINTER and RONALD E. RASMUSSEN*, National Aeronautics and Space Administration, Ames Research Center, Moffett Field, California.

Incubation of either HeLa S3 cells or Chinese hamster cells with labeled nucleic acid precursors for one to two hours after X-irradiation resulted in dose-dependent inhibitions of incorporation of these materials into cellular deoxyribonucleic acid (DNA). Semi-log plots of the results show curves which can be resolved into two components. Since these results are evident within an hour after irradiation, the effect is almost exclusively on cells in the DNA synthesis (S) phase at the time of irradiation and contributions from cells entering S after irradiation can be ignored. Estimates of the size of the irradiation-affected components will be given and compared with known and possible participants in the DNA-synthesizing system.

F4. *An Autoradiographic and Biochemical Study of DNA Synthesis in Hepatocytes Following Irradiation.* W. B. LOONEY, L. O. CHANG*, M. L. PARDUE*, and F. W. BANGHART*, Radiobiology and Biophysics Laboratory, University of Virginia School of Medicine, Charlottesville, Virginia.

The dose-response curve for the effect of X-irradiation on DNA synthesis in hepatocytes of regenerating liver has been made following 188, 375, 750, 1500, 3000, 6000, 9000 and 12,000 r of irradiation given locally to the liver at a rate of 300 r per minute. Two-hundred gram male, Lewis strain, rats were used in these experiments. The irradiation was given immediately before the injection of 50μc of tritiated thymidine at 19 hours after partial hepatectomy. The animals were sacrificed one hour later. Quantitative autoradiographic and biochemical analysis of aliquots of the same liver have been used to assess the effects of irradiation on DNA synthesis.

The quantitative autoradiographic results can be expressed as a second order differential equation. The equation can be interpreted as denoting the minimal number of parameters within the system. The equation does not imply that precisely two mechanisms are involved in the decrease in the DNA synthetic rate. However, the suggestion is made that the system is a complex one, all of the parts of which are not equally affected by radiation.

The biochemical results show no significant effects of irradiation at 1500r. At 6000r there is a depression of DNA synthesis to 35% of the control value. The depression at 12,000r was essentially the same as for 6000r. There was a marked variation in the percentage of hepatocytes synthesizing DNA in different animals. A positive correlation was found between the per cent labeled hepatocytes and the tritiated thymidine in the biochemically isolated DNA. No correlation was found between the grain counts per nucleus determined autoradiographically, and the activity of the tritiated thymidine found in the isolated DNA.

The total H^3 activity in the acid-soluble fraction in the liver increases as the radiation dose increases. Since no decrease in per cent labeled hepatocytes, and no decrease in the total DNA content of the liver at 12,000r was found one hour after irradiation, the inverse relationship between the DNA and acid-soluble fractions suggests the accumulation of the precursor substances, rather than the breakdown products, is occurring after irradiation. (Supported in part by AEC Contract AT(40-1)-2889).

F5. *The Kinetics of Tritiated Thymidine Incorporated in Regenerating Rat Liver.* L. O. CHANG* (Introduced by W. B. Looney), Radiobiology and Biophysics Laboratory, Department of Radiology, University of Virginia School of Medicine, Charlottesville, Virginia.

The study of thymidine incorporation into DNA has been made at 19 hours after partial hepatectomy, since this is the time of the maximum rate of DNA synthesis in the first cycle of hepatocytes. Nineteen hours is the midpoint in the 8 hour period for DNA replication, and the per cent of labeled hepatocytes reach a plateau at this time.

Two-hundred gram, Lewis strain, male rats were used in these experiments, and 50 μc of tritiated thymidine was injected at 19 hours. The animals were sacrificed at 2, 5, 10, 15 and 30 minutes, and 1, 2 and 3 hours after administration. A modified Schmidt-Tannhauser method has been used for fractionation. The tritium activity in the DNA, RNA, acid soluble (ASF) and lipid solvent fractions (LSF), has been determined by means of liquid scintillation counting. Aliquots of the sample liver have also been used for the quantitative autoradiographic study.

The tritium activity in the ASF of the liver rises immediately and reaches a maximum at 10 minutes. This gradually declines, reaching a plateau in approximately 1 hour. There is a rapid incorporation of tritiated thymidine into DNA during the first hour. The rate is a slower rate between 1 and 3 hours.

The incorporation of tritiated thymidine into DNA of individual hepatocytes determined by autoradiography also shows a similar pattern of uptake during the first hour. The grain counts per nucleus reach a plateau in 1 hour. However, the per cent labeled hepatocytes continue to rise. This suggests that the results of the biochemical data may need to be adjusted for the change in the cell population during the longer periods of study.

Studies are also being made to determine the time sequence of DNA replication in individual chromosomes between the onset of synthesis at 15 hours after hepatectomy and the onset of mitosis. Preliminary results indicate that relatively few chromosomes are labeled during the beginning part of the synthetic period, 15 hours after partial hepatectomy. The majority of chromosomes are labeled by 17 hours, and almost all of the chromosomes are labeled by 19 hours. This percentage is little changed at 21 hours, but is decreasing by 23 hours. (Supported in part by AEC Contract AT(40-1)-2889).

F6. *DNA Synthesis and Mitotic Activity in Bone Marrow, Intestine, and Mammary Tumors of Mice after X-irradiation.* EMILIA FRINDEL*, ROBERT F. KALLMAN, and HENRY S. KAPLAN, Department of Radiology, Stanford University School of Medicine, Palo Alto, California.

BALB/c female mice were whole-body irradiated with 150 and 300 r of 250 kv X-rays. Six μc of H^3-labeled thymidine was injected intraperitoneally at times between 1 and 72 hours after irradiation. The specific activity was determined in DNA extracted from femoral/tibial bone marrow. Mitotic counts were made on representative smear preparations. DNA synthesis and mitotic activity were both depressed shortly after irradiation. This was followed by an increase to greater than normal levels; then there was a subsequent second depression, and finally a second peak. The first mitotic and DNA synthetic peaks occurred, respectively, at 10 and 18 hours after 150 r, or at 12 and 24 hours after 300 r. The second peak in DNA synthetic activity was higher than the first and was observed at 48 hours (150 r) or 72 hours (300 r). Similar observations were made with bone marrow, small intestine, and isologously transplanted mammary carcinoma of C3H mice after whole body irradiation with 200 r. However, the initial depression and subsequent overshoot in DNA synthetic and mitotic activities occurred at different times in the three different tissues. It is suggested that a partial synchronization of the cells was achieved by irradiation. The biological significance and possible applications to radiotherapy will be discussed.

F7. *Effects of X-Irradiation on Mitosis and DNA Synthesis in Ehrlich Ascites Tumor Cells.* JAE HO KIM* and TITUS C. EVANS, Radiation Research Laboratory, University of Iowa, Iowa City, Iowa.

Incorporation of H^3-thymidine into the cells was studied with autoradiography by determining mean grain count and percentage of cells labeled within a 30 minute period of incubation. These results, together with the mitotic index, were used to determine the periods of the mitotic cycle and to study the effects of irradiation on the various stages. Mitosis (M) was found to be 1 hour; the G_1 period was about 6 hours; synthesis (S) lasted about 8 hours; and G_2 was 4 hours in duration. It was concluded that irradiation (300 r, 500 r, 1000 r) inhibited cell division and caused cells to accumulate late in G_2. Upon recovery of cell division, the mitotic index increased to above control levels for a short period of time. The extent and duration of the overshoot was related to the amount of irradiation and cleavage delay. There was a reduction in rate of synthesis as indicated by decreased grain count and increase in the percentage of cells labeled during the 30 minute incubation period. Cells labeled *in vitro* and then allowed to develop in the body showed a delay (in the irradiated cells) in the appearance of labeled mitosis. In irradiated cells, the G_2 period was about twice as long as in the controls. Likewise, in irradiated cells the duration of time in which labeled mitosis was found (equal to the period of synthesis) was also about twice as long as in the controls. (This work was supported in part by grants from the American Cancer Society and The Division of Biology and Medicine of the U.S.A.E.C.).

F8. *Reutilization of DNA by Ehrlich Ascites Cells.* RENATO BASERGA and WALTER E. KISIELESKI, Department of Pathology, Northwestern University Medical School, Chicago; and Division of Biology and Medicine, Argonne National Laboratory, Argonne, Illinois.

Mice injected with tritiated thymidine were inoculated intraperitoneally with Ehrlich ascites tumor cells at various intervals after the administration of the radioisotope. Radioautographic and radiochemical studies were performed on the nonradioactive tumor cells growing in the radioactive hosts. The results indicated that Ehrlich cells take up radioactive label from the host thus confirming previous results [*J. Natl. Cancer Inst.* **28,** 331 (1962)] that labeled DNA may be reutilized. There was a considerable amount of radioactivity, as tritiated water, in the ascitic fluid, but of the nucleic acid fractions of the tumor cells, only the DNA fraction was found to be radioactive. The pattern of labeling suggested that most of the reutilized label originates from epithelial cells of the small intestine shedded into the intestinal lumen. (Work supported by grants from the NIH, USPHS and by the USAEC).

F9. *The Effect of Cobalt 60 Gamma Irradiation on the Incorporation of Iodine 131-Labeled Iododeoxyuridine (IUDR) into the DNA of the Mouse.* S. L. COMMERFORD* and W. L. HUGHES* (Introduced by Victor P. Bond), Medical Department, Brookhaven National Laboratory, Upton, New York.

Relatively small doses of Co^{60}-gamma radiation will markedly reduce the subsequent incorporation of IUDR into the DNA of 6-10-week-old female Swiss mice. Whole-body irradiation of 18 rads (given 6 hours before intravenous injection of trace labeled IUDR) is sufficient to reduce IUDR incorporation into intestinal DNA to half that of the unirradiated controls. In the range of 0–20 rads, the logarithm of incorporated IUDR decreases linearly with increasing dose, and there is no threshold.

Direct measurements indicate that irradiation produces no significant change in the rate of catabolism of IUDR; therefore the decrease in incorporation of IUDR does not appear to be due to more rapid catabolism. Comparison of the incorporation of high specific activity I^{131}-labeled IUDR (over one curie per micromole) with that of low specific activity IUDR (14 microcuries per micromole) suggests that a large part of the reduction in trace labeled IUDR incorporation at high gamma ray doses is due to an increase in the pool of competing DNA precursors (e.g., thymidine) but that this effect is not important at low doses.

The rate which gamma ray effects on IUDR incorporation develop, and the modifying effect of fluorodeoxyuridine provide further insight into the mechanism of the radiation effect and will be discussed. (Supported by the U.S. Atomic Energy Commission).

F10. *Alterations in the Effect of X-Radiation on DNA Synthesis in Cell Cultures by Oxygen and Bromdeoxyuridine.* RONALD E. RASMUSSEN* and ROBERT B. PAINTER, National Aeronautics and Space Administration, Ames Research Center, Moffet Field, California.

HeLa S3 and Chinese hamster cell cultures have been irradiated in the presence of 5% CO_2 plus 95% O_2, or 95% air, or 95% N_2, and the rates of deoxyribonucleic acid (DNA) synthesis among the various treatments compared. An effect similar to, but apparently not identical with, the classical oxygen effect was observed. In younger HeLa S3 cultures the presence of N_2 during irradiation decreased the depression of rate of DNA synthesis, but in older cultures the radiation-induced DNA synthetic rate depression was unaffected by the gaseous environment during irradiation.

The effect of bromdeoxyuridine (BUdR) on the radiation-induced inhibition of DNA synthesis was also studied. Incubation of cells in the presence of 5 μg/ml BUdR for two days prior to irradiation apparently decreased the inhibition of DNA synthesis caused by low doses of X-rays, but did not affect the inhibition caused by higher doses. The possible mechanism of these effects will be discussed.

F11. *Cytoplasmic Radiation Damage in the Sea Urchin Egg.* RONALD C. RUSTAD, MARY CORABI*, and SHUHEI YUYAMA*, Institute of Molecular Biophysics, Florida State University, Tallahassee, Florida; and Marine Biological Laboratory, Woods Hole, Massachusetts.

Although many examples of cytoplasmic radiation sensitivity are known, the classical experiments on irradiated anucleate sea urchin eggs revealed no mitotic delay following insemination with normal sperm. Since these experiments had been performed at low doses, they were repeated at doses as large as 100 Kr. The possible mitotic delays never exceeded twice the error of estimate of the division time of the control. Hence, the centrifugal anucleate portion of the cytoplasm is effectively insensitive to gamma rays. Anucleate halves prepared from normal eggs by cutting with microneedles were radiation sensitive. Mitotic delay and early blastula death followed insemination with normal sperm.

These observations define a sensitive cytoplasmic system which can be stratified into the centripetal half of the sea urchin egg by centrifugation. The simplest interpretation of the removal of sensitivity from one portion of the cytoplasm is that a toxin is released by the sensitive sites. (This work was supported by contracts with the United States Atomic Energy Commission).

F12. *Ultraviolet Action Spectra for Mitotic Spindle Destruction and Anaphase Delay Following Irradiation of Cytoplasm.* DARRELL Q. BROWN* and RAYMOND E. ZIRKLE, Committee on Biophysics, University of Chicago, Chicago, Illinois.

Ultraviolet irradiation of cytoplasm causes mitotic spindles to diminish or disappear [*Ann. N. Y. Acad. Sci.* **59,** 503 (1955)]. This effect is thought to be mediated by a spindle "poison" produced photochemically from a cytoplasmic precursor. To aid identification of this precursor, an action spectrum was obtained. The cytoplasm of *Amblystoma* tissue-culture cells was irradiated in early metaphase with 8 μ diameter, UV-microbeams of various wavelengths. The power in various microbeams was measured with a photomultiplier which was calibrated against a thermopile. Doses at each wavelength were graded by progressively doubling the exposure time. Spindle destruction was scored by observing the decrease in birefringence with a polarization microscope. In addition, we recorded the time of anaphase, and thereby obtained an action spectrum for anaphase delay. Based on incident energy, the dose-effect curves for spindle destruction showed relative efficiencies of 11200, 4330, 1180, 926, 694, 629, 1010, 1860, 1470, 1080, 294, and 75 at 2250, 2345, 2410, 2480, 2535, 2600, 2655, 2755, 2800, 2895, 2967 and 3025 Å, respectively. Efficiencies for anaphase delay were nearly identical to these. This delay of anaphase could be mediated by a second precursor having an identical absorption spectrum, or it could be a consequence of damage to the spindle. These action spectra are parallel to the absorption spectrum of a tyrosine-containing protein. (Supported by USAEC and USPHS).

SECTION G. RADIUM, STRONTIUM AND CALCIUM METABOLISM

G1. *Comparative Metabolism of Ba^{133} and Ca^{45} by Embryonic Bone Grown* in Vitro. WELLINGTON MOORE, JR.* (Introduced by A. K. Davis), Research Unit, Southeastern Radiological Health Laboratory, Division of Radiological Health, U. S. Public Health Service, Montgomery, Alabama.

This is a report on the comparative metabolism of Ba^{133} and Ca^{45} by embryonic chick bone grown *in vitro*. The uptake of Ba^{133} was influenced by the period of incubation in the labeled medium, age and weight of the bones, and concentrations of calcium and barium ions in the medium. Culturing of embryonic bone *in vitro* showed that chick and rat bone could discriminate against Ba^{133} in favor of Ca^{45}. Heat treating the bones destroyed their ability to discriminate against Ba^{133}. In live bones, the selective mechanism functioned at 37°C but not at 3°C. The results suggested that discrimination against barium in favor of calcium was largely a function of viable bone cells.

G2. *Placental Transfer of Strontium in Rats.* ANN G. RUHMANN*, BETSY J. STOVER, KENNETH R. BRIZZEE*, and DAVID R. ATHERTON, Division of Radiobiology, Department of Anatomy, University of Utah College of Medicine, Salt Lake City 12, Utah.

Several dose levels of Sr^{85} or Sr^{90} were given subcutaneously to adult female rats, both pregnant and nonpregnant. Pregnant rats were injected on the fifteenth, seventeenth, or nineteenth gestational days. Several nullipara of comparable age were injected with each group. The pregnant females were either sacrificed on the twentieth gestational day or allowed to deliver and suckle their young. Fetuses, pups, dams and excreta were analyzed for strontium burden. Analysis of fetuses revealed that gestational injection day was the most important factor governing fetal fractional retention of radionuclide passing the placenta. Litters from dams injected on the nineteenth gestational day contained three times the per cent dose of those injected on day seventeen and sixteen times that of those injected on day fifteen. Retention of Sr^{90} was dose independent. Suckling pups demonstrated a similar dose differential according to gestational injection day, and also showed a continued increase in strontium burden from birth until weaning. There was a marked disparity in strontium metabolism between pregnant and nonpregnant adult rats. The dams retained less strontium than the nullipara which were injected and sacrificed concomitantly. The difference was greater than the fetal retention, and was reflected in a significantly higher urinary excretion by the dams. The fecal to urinary ratios were 0.43 for pregnant and 0.55 for nonpregnant rats, one to five days after injection. (Supported by the USPHS and the USAEC).

G3. *The Transfer of Strontium-90 from the Maternal Skeleton to the Offspring in Monkeys and Rats.* L. W. Tuttle, R. C. Baxter*, and B. J. Hopkins*, Department of Radiation Biology, University of Rochester School of Medicine and Dentistry, Rochester, New York.

Two young adult female Rhesus monkeys having body burdens of Strontium-90 established orally 14 and 25 months prior to parturition, produced viable offspring whose body burdens were measured by bremsstrahlen counting at birth. The offspring of a mother having a body burden of 17.8 microcuries resulting from oral treatment with Strontium-90 14 months earlier had a body burden of 1.14 microcuries or 6.4% of the maternal burden. The offspring of a mother having a body burden of 15.1 microcuries resulting from Strontium-90 treatment 25 months earlier had a body burden of 0.21 microcuries or 1.4% of the maternal burden. The offspring were normal, and with their mothers are being maintained for long-term observation.

In rats, the measurement of the body burdens of 67 newborn in seven litters showed that the average body burden per rat was 0.04% of the mothers' burden or approximately 0.4% per litter when parturition occurred 3 months after intravenous injection of Strontium-90.

G4. *Secretion of Dietary Sr^{90} and Calcium into Beagle Milk.* R. J. Della Rosa and R. Pool*, School of Veterinary Medicine, University of California, Davis, California.

The secretion of dietary Sr^{90} and calcium into beagle milk has been studied in 10 dogs on a continuous ingestion program at 5 different dose levels ranging from 0.007 to 3.3 μc Sr^{90}/gm of dietary calcium. The Sr^{90} was added to a standard balanced diet starting at about 20 days after conception. In the transfer from diet to milk, the mean Sr^{90}/Ca of the milk was 0.24 that of the diet; the mean Sr^{90}/Ca of the plasma was 0.45 that of the diet; and the mean Sr^{90}/Ca of the milk was 0.50 that of the plasma. The value of the Sr^{90}/Ca of the milk relative to the Sr^{90}/Ca of diet was constant during the 35-day lactation period. The calcium concentration of the milk increased slightly during lactation, while the Sr^{90} concentration of milk, as well as the plasma concentration of both Sr^{90} and calcium, remained constant. If milk is considered as the source of dietary Sr^{90}, the Sr^{90}/Ca in bone of the nursing pup relative to milk is 0.8 indicating minimal discrimination against strontium during this period. (Supported by the USAEC).

G5. *Discrimination between Ingested Radium and Calcium by Mice.* Asher J. Finkel and Nancy M. Bergstrand*, Division of Biological and Medical Research, Argonne National Laboratory, Argonne, Illinois.

Newborn mice and their mothers were placed on a diet containing 26 gm Ca and 12.5 μc Ra^{226} per kg. Male and female mice from these litters were sacrificed periodically in groups of three and the eviscerated carcasses were analyzed for calcium and radium. The ratio of radium/calcium in the mice to that in the food increased with early growth of the mice but appeared to become stable between 0.25 and 0.30 after 6 weeks of age. The discrimination value for suckling mice living entirely on mother's milk was much lower and appeared to be the result of double discrimination by virtue of the calcium and radium passing through the mother first. Before the young mice started to eat the radium-containing food, the ratio appeared to be leveling off at 0.07, which is almost exactly 0.27×0.27. The discrimination value of 0.25 to 0.30 found here is much lower than that found by other investigators for Sr^{90} fed to newborn and young adult mice under similar conditions. No attempt was made to distinguish between the roles of gut, kidney, and bone in the discrimination process. (Work supported by U. S. Atomic Energy Commission).

G6. *Changes in Calcium-Strontium Metabolism with Age in Young Miniature Swine*[1]. R. O. McClellan* (Introduced by L. K. Bustad), Biology Laboratory, Hanford Laboratories, General Electric Company, Richland, Washington.

Previous work with miniature swine fed Sr^{90} daily revealed a decreased discrimination against Sr^{90} relative to calcium in the young animal [*Life Sciences* **1,** 669, (1962)]. To define more clearly the influence of age on discrimination against strontium relative to calcium, a double tracer study was performed in miniature swine 15 to 240 days of age. Young animals of suckling age were administered a single dose of Ca^{45} and Sr^{90} in a milk solution via gastric gavage. Older animals were given a single dose of Ca^{45} and Sr^{90} with an aliquot of the normal ration. The highest retention of both radionuclides at ten days after administration was 60–80% and was observed in the youngest animals. Retention of both radionuclides decreased with increasing age at the time of administration, Sr^{90} more markedly than Ca^{45}. The ratio of skeletal Ca^{45}/Sr^{90} to administered Ca^{45}/Sr^{90} approached unity for one very young and changed progressively with age to approximately 0.25 for the older animals. (Work performed under Contract No. AT(45-1)-1350 between the Atomic Energy Commission and the General Electric Company).

G7. *Quantitative Distribution of Radium-226 in Various Sites of the First Molar and Mandible of Adult Beagles.* Webster S. S. Jee, Robert K. Haslam,* Kendrick A. Sears,* and Norman Dockum,* Division of Radiobiology, Department of Anatomy, University of Utah College of Medicine, Salt Lake City, Utah.

A study was initiated to quantitate the distribution of radium in the teeth and mandibles of 28 adult beagles involved in the Utah chronic toxicity program. A single intravenous injection of 10, 3, or 1 μc of radium-226 citrate/kg was given. In the dogs studied to date, the maximum concentration of radium in the dentin was found to be approximately 10 times that of the maximum concentration in acellular cementum and 5 times that of maximum cellular cementum concentration. There was approximately a difference of a factor of 10 between the average maximum to average diffuse (measured at 5 mm from the site of maximum deposition) concentrations of radium in the dentin. "Hot spots" in the mandible have concentrations of radium in the same order of magnitude as those "hot spots" located in the dentin. Diminution of radium-226 by physico-chemical processes from various sites in dental tissues and the mandible will be reported. The relationship of local irradiation dose to damage was investigated and will be discussed. Supported by U. S. AEC Contract AT(11-1)-119 and NIH-2G-958).

[1] Grateful acknowledgement is made of the technical assistance of J. L. Beamer, R. L. McCluskey, and the staffs of the Experimental Animal Farm and Biological Analyses Operation.

G8. *Radium Metabolism in a Man.* CHARLES W. MAYS, RAY D. LLOYD,* WILLIAM R. CHRISTENSEN,* DAVID R. ATHERTON, and GLENT S. PITCHFORD*, Radiobiology Division, Anatomy Department, University of Utah Salt Lake City, Utah.

An 80-year-old man with an epidermoid carcinoma on the face was given 10 μc Sr^{85} plus 1.5 μc Ra^{226} by intravenous injection. At death, 141 days later, biological retention of Sr^{85} was 16.0% (15.6% in bone plus 0.4% in soft tissue). Ra^{226} retention was only 6.5% (5.2% in bone plus 1.3% in soft tissue). Plasma clearance of Sr^{85} was about 1.9 liters/day into the G.I. tract and 2.8 liters/day by the kidney. In contrast, plasma clearance of Ra^{226} was a much higher 69 liters/day into the G.I. tract, but only 0.5 liters/day by the kidney. The lower retention of radium in man is ascribed to its enormous clearance into the G.I. tract. (Supported by the U. S. Atomic Energy Commission).

G9. *Studies of Strontium-85 Kinetics in Patients.* KARIN R. COREY, DAVID WEBER*, PETER KENNY*, ERNEST GREENBERG*, and JOHN S. LAUGHLIN. Divisions of Biophysics and Clinical Investigation, Sloan-Kettering Institute, New York, New York.

Previous studies of strontium and calcium metabolism in man have dealt with the uptake and turnover that occurs within a couple of weeks after an intravenous injection of a tracer. The few available measurements with whole-body counters refer to the skeleton as a whole. The object of this study was to measure the uptake and retention of strontium-85 in various bones by external counting for at least 5 months. Eight patients with breast cancer were given intravenous injections of 100 μc of strontium-85. External counting of the activity in tibia, knee, spine, and trochanter was done repeatedly. In some studies, blood samples and excretions were also assayed for the first 10 or 14 days of the study.

Mathematical analyses were made of data obtained from a few days after the injection to the end of each study. The results from several patients demonstrate the presence of a strontium pool in all healthy bones with nearly the same turnover rate as the serum strontium. This substantiates the assumptions usually made in the calculation of accretion rate. In other cases, deviations from the normal turnover caused by disease will be illustrated. The significance of the break in the serum curve, observed by others using radioactive calcium, will be clarified and discussed.

The information on strontium retention is directly applicable to strontium-90 metabolism and supplements earlier studies with whole-body counting.

G10. *Strontium-90 Metabolism in Young Adults on a Low Calcium Diet.* JOSEPH SAMACHSON*, HERTA SPENCER, EDWARD P. HARDY, JR.*, and JOSEPH RIVERA*, Metabolic Section, Veterans Administration Hospital, Hines, Illinois; and Health and Safety Laboratories, New York Office, U. S. Atomic Energy Commission.

Ten young adult volunteers were studied on a controlled intake which averaged 179 mg of stable Ca and 3.3 $\mu\mu c$ of Sr^{90} per day, and the results were compared with those of volunteers of similar age group previously studied on an intake of 1141 mg Ca and 13.3 $\mu\mu c$ Sr^{90} per day. Intake of the volunteers before controlled conditions was estimated to be about 10 $\mu\mu c$ Sr^{90}/day. On the low Ca diet, urinary Ca was half the value on a high Ca diet, and urinary Sr^{90} values averaged 0.42 $\mu\mu c$/day and 1.13 $\mu\mu c$/day during low and high calcium intake respectively. Although net absorption on the low Ca-low Sr^{90} intake was small, the volunteers were in balance. Calculations showed however that much of the excretion came from the previous intake, so that the body retained a higher proportion of the Sr^{90} content of 3.3 $\mu\mu c$ in the low Ca diet than of the 13.3 $\mu\mu c$ of the high Ca diet.

G11. *Effect of Combined Use of Mercurials and Ammonium Chloride on Radiostrontium Excretion in Man.* JACOB MENCZEL, HERTA SPENCER, and JOSEPH SAMACHSON, Metabolic Section, Veterans Administration Hospital, Hines, Illinois.

Studies performed in this laboratory have shown that an increase of the urinary excretion of calcium induced by ammonium chloride was accompanied by an increase in radiostrontium excretion in man. Sr^{85} was used intravenously and orally as the tracer. In order to investigate whether the excretion of Sr^{85} could be further increased by the additional use of mercurials, studies on the effect of NH_4Cl and mercuhydrin on the enhancement of Sr^{85} were carried out in five patients under controlled dietary conditions on the Metabolic Research Ward. The effect of 2 ml of mercuhydrin given intramuscularly was studied first; thereafter, in a second study the combined effect of NH_4Cl and mercuhydrin was investigated on the excretion of calcium and radiostrontium. Nine grams ammonium chloride were given for 4–5 days, and on the last day of ammonium chloride administration, 2 ml mercuhydrin were injected. The administration of mercuhydrin alone produced an increase of the urinary excretion of calcium and of Sr^{85}, which was further increased when preceded by the use of ammonium chloride. The greater loss of Sr^{85} following administration of ammonium chloride and mercurials is probably due to the concomitant loss of calcium.

G12. *Effect of Corticosteroids on Radiostrontium Metabolism in Man.* HERTA SPENCER, ISAAC LEWIN*, and JOSEPH SAMACHSON*, Metabolic Section, Veterans Administration Hospital, Hines, Illinois.

Since corticosteroids are known to cause demineralization and to increase the excretion of calcium in urine, the effects of three corticosteroids were studied on the excretion of radioactive strontium in man. These studies were carried out under controlled dietary conditions on the Metabolic Research Ward. Tracer doses of Sr^{85} were given intravenously before and during corticosteroid administration. Plasma levels, urinary and fecal excretions of Sr^{85} were determined. An increase in the urinary Sr^{85} excretion occurred when corticosteroids were used, which induced an increase in urinary calcium excretion. On the other hand, the urinary Sr^{85} remained at control levels when corticosteroids were administered which did not change the excretion of calcium. There was no correlation between the negative nitrogen balance induced by corticosteroids and the effect on calcium and strontium metabolism. The effect of one of the corticosteroids was also studied on the intestinal absorption of both Sr^{85} and Ca^{45}. In these studies the radioisotopes were administered orally. The absorption of Sr^{85} and Ca^{45} was somewhat lower during the administration of the corticosteroid than in the control study.

SECTION H. BIOPHYSICS

H1. *Radiation Effects on Brine Shrimp Cysts.* WALLACE SNIPES* and WALTER GORDY, Department of Physics, Duke University, Durham, North Carolina.

Strong ESR signals of free radicals were observed when brine shrimp cysts (eggs) were X-irradiated under vacuum, under pure oxygen, or under dry air; but when the samples were irradiated under moist air or under water vapor, the ESR signals were an order of magnitude weaker for the same dosage (the order of 5×10^6 r). It was found that the signal decayed slowly (lasting for days) under O_2 or under dry air, but somewhat more rapidly than under vacuum (lasting for weeks). When exposed to moist air, the signal decayed in hours. In agreement with Engel and Fluke [*Radiation Research* **16,** 173 (1962)], it was found that the survival or hatching after irradiation in moist air was greater than after irradiation under dry conditions. However, we have found that storage in dry oxygen after irradiation is more detrimental than any other conditions studied. From our results it can be concluded that the water vapor protects from the oxygen effect, probably by neutralizing radiation-induced free radicals before they can interact with O_2 to produce an irreversible damage. No effects were found for H_2. Effects of NO and and N_2 are under study. (Research supported by the Air Force Office of Scientific Research, Grant No. AF-AFOSR-62-327).

H2. *Intermolecular Radiation Effects in Dry Protein Mixtures, and Such Mixtures Containing Cysteine.* JOHN W. PREISS, Physics Department, The University of Delaware, Newark, Delaware.

Small quantities of basic proteins, irradiated in the dried state, alter the turbidity of nucleic acid solutions to which they are added in such a manner that the resulting turbidity-dose function can have one or more maxima. Previous experiments, involving the irradiation of dry protein mixtures, indicate that this effect may be useful in the study of intermolecular radiation effects [*Radiation Research* **18,** 121–132 (1962)]. The present experiments are concerned with the bombardment of such dry mixtures as chymotrypsinogen-invertase, chymotrypsinogen-invertase-cysteine, chymotrypsinogen-cysteine, and ribonuclease-cysteine, with 7 kev electrons. Cysteine always produced an apparent reduction of the enzymatic sensitivity, of any protein with which it was bombarded. It also shifted the characteristic turbidity maxima, of proteins with which it was bombarded, toward higher doses, with either an increase or a decrease of amplitude. The enzymatic sensitivity of invertase was not changed by irradiating it with any quantity of chymotrypsinogen. However, the chymotrypsinogen turbidity maximum was shifted toward higher doses, and nearly extinguished, even when the mixture contained only one invertase molecule for every 20 chymotrypsinogen molecules. The results show that there are at least two kinds of intermolecular radiation effects. (Supported in part by PHS Research Grant CA-06837 from the National Cancer Institute).

H3. *Resonance Radiation Effects of Low Energy Monochromatic X-Rays on the Metalloenzyme Catalase.* HENRY J. BOMBERG* and ROBERT A. LUSE, Puerto Rico Nuclear Center, Mayaguez, Puerto Rico.

To answer the question "what are the unique effects of ionizing radiation on matter?", our present research program has studied X-irradiation effects in the 5-20 Kev energy range upon biological systems. This energy region is of considerable importance since it contains the K-absorption edges of the constituent atoms of most living systems. X-radiation of these energies is produced from incident radiation of much higher energies (as cobalt-60 gammas, 250 Kv X-rays) by degradation through Compton scatter. Biological systems chosen for study were those which are composed primarily of light elements with but traces of medium atomic weight elements. The metalloenzyme catalase has been studied extensively to date by three investigators. For this enzyme, which contains four atoms of iron in its porphyrin ring structure, the question was "does radiation absorbed by the iron atoms produce more damage (inactivation) per electron volt absorbed than radiation absorbed only by the light elements (carbon, hydrogen, oxygen, etc.) which make up the bulk of the catalase molecule?" Experiments were designed to show or disprove the presence of a true action spectrum of radiation in the kilovolt region. The presence of such a spectrum has been shown and indicates unique effects of such radiation, entirely divorced from the general "indirect" effects of radiation (which may be simulated chemically under conditions of far less energy absorption per molecule). (Work supported by U. S. Atomic Energy Commission.)

H4. *Effect of Alpha Particles on Induced Enzyme Formation in* E. coli. HAROLD E. FREY and ERNEST C. POLLARD, Graduate School Committee on Biophysics, The Pennsylvania State University, University Park, Pennsylvania.

An open polonium alpha particle source which can be loaded at the factory, sealed when necessary, and which is normally operated behind a thin mylar foil, has been designed, constructed and put into use. The thin mylar foil permits good penetration by the alpha particles allowing the inactivation of biological samples. The source has been calibrated by inactivating T1 bacteriophage and beta-galactosidase. The flux is 4.8×10^7 alpha particles per square centimeter per second. The source has been used to study the effect of alpha particles on the induction of ML3 *E. coli* bacteria, which are induced with methyl-beta-d-thiogalactopyranoside (TMG). During irradiation, the bacteria are supported on a membrane filter. The time course of induction has been studied and it is obviously very sensitive to alpha particle bombardment. Because of the changes in the actual rates of induction due to radiation, it is not easy to give a figure for sensitivity. It is clear, however, that very low doses, not more than three times those needed to inactivate the colony-forming ability, will produce drastic effects on the ability to become induced. This sensitivity indicates that the process of induction is concerned with some rather large structural entity.

H5. *The Effect of Raditaion on the Production of Lysozyme in T1 Phage.* ERNEST POLLARD and SUZANNE WOODYATT, Graduate School Committee on Biophysics, The Pennsylvania State University, University Park, Pennsylvania.

The action of T1 phage in causing the formation of lysozyme can be studied by using induced bacteria, which contain beta galactosidase which has no access to its substrate unless the bacterial cell wall has become damaged or opened. Using the accessibility of the enzyme to its substrate as a measure of the lysozyme activity, it has been possible to study the effect of cobalt gamma radiation on T1 phage in both the wet state, in broth, and the dry state. It is found that the irradiation in the wet state has a considerable effect on the ability to produce lysozyme, so that the inactivation of the phage and the inactivation of the lysozyme-producing activity seem to go together. On the other hand, when irradiated in the dry state the ability to produce lysozyme is only ⅓ as sensitive as that of the phage as regards the infectivity process. There seems, therefore, to be a difference in the inactivation by free radicals and by the direct effect which show up clearly with these experiments.

H6. *Molecular Damage by Radiation to the Enzyme Ribonuclease.* J. W. HUNT and J. F. WILLIAMS, The Ontario Cancer Institute, Toronto, Canada.

The radiation sensitivity of RNase under a variety of environments has been examined in detail during the past three years [*Radiation Research* **17,** 703 (1962)]. Attempts are now being made to determine the chemical and structural changes which take place within the molecule. The breakage of disulfide bridges has been measured and can be responsible for only a fraction of the total inactive molecules. These results agree with the appearance of cystine-like free radicals in the ESR spectra. The maximum number of broken disulfide bridges which may be observed is an average of one per molecule. Using the technique of Tanford [*J. Am. Chem. Soc.* **77,** 6409 (1955)], the unmasking of hidden tyrosine groups has been observed following the irradiation. This event occurs with a fairly high probability and may be a reflection of a general unfolding of the molecule following the ionizing event.

H7. *On the Nature of Enzyme Inactivation by Radiation.* L. G. AUGENSTEIN and K. L. GRIST, Biophysics Department, Michigan State University, East Lansing, Michigan; and Biology Department, Brookhaven National Laboratory, Upton, New York.

An important mechanism for enzyme inactivation by five-e.v. excitations is the disruption of *specific* S—S and hydrogen bonds. That is, the destruction of trypsin and ribonuclease activity is directly correlated with an increase in the number of titrable SH groups and further impediments on the ability of the products of disrupted S—S and/or hydrogen bonds to re-form increases the measured inactivation yields. However, not all S—S bonds are equally susceptible to radiation disruption. In particular, when ribonuclease samples are irradiated sufficiently to destroy up to 75% of enzymic activity, the increased SH groups which can be titered arise almost exclusively from *only two* of the constituent eight half-cystine. Such preferential localization of radiation effects is consistent with earlier postulates (of L.G.A.) concerning the mechanism of enzyme inactivation by a number of physical agents.

H8. *Comparison of Emission from Excited States Produced by Ultraviolet Light and Ionizing Radiation.* EDWARD YEARGERS, DEVAUGHN NELSON, JAYANTI NAG-CHAUDHURI, JAMES CARTER, and LEROY AUGENSTEIN, Biophysics Department, Michigan State University, East Lansing; Health Physics Division, Oak Ridge National Laboratory.

The emission from powders of the aromatic amino acids and the enzymes trypsin and ribonuclease resulting from excitation with X-rays and ultraviolet light have been compared. The results indicate that not less than 0.03 and probably 0.2 or more of the energy absorbed from X-rays may eventually appear in the lowest excited level of some of the compounds. Further, from all of the compounds the ratio of fluorescence to phosphorescence observed during UV excitation is approximately an order of magnitude greater than occurs during X-irradiation. In general, maxima in the X-ray emission spectra are at longer wave lengths than the corresponding UV fluorescence and phosphorescence peaks. The value of 0.2 is much larger than the fraction of *primary* excitations to the lowest excited level which would be expected to result from interactions with fast electrons. Also, the fluorescence-phosphorescence ratios for ionizing radiation are much smaller than would be expected for *primary* optically-allowed transitions to the lowest excited singlet state with intersystem crossing to the lowest excited triplet state. Thus it is necessary and worthwhile to consider mechanisms to account for these results in condensed systems. (This research was conducted under the auspices of the U. S. Atomic Energy Commission).

H9. *Modifications of Excited States of Amino Acids and Proteins Resulting from Environmental Changes.* JAYANTI NAG-CHAUDHURI and LEROY AUGENSTEIN, Biophysics Department, Michigan State University, East Lansing, Michigan.

Different spectroscopic parameters of the three aromatic amino acids and the enzymes trypsin and ribonuclease (RNase) have been studied in aqueous solutions, in a mixed organic solvent and in crystalline powders. The parameters measured include the wave lengths of the maxima of fluorescence and phosphorescence; the comparison of the relative intensities of the emission occurring as fluorescence and as phosphorescence; and the rates and kinetics of the decay of phosphorescence. With the exception of RNase, the wavelength of the fluorescence maximum is scarcely affected by changing the physical environment. However, the position of the maximum of phosphorescence was red-shifted in the crystal by as much as 500 Å compared to the values obtained in an organic-solid matrix. For the amino acids, the ratio of fluorescence to phosphorescence is greater in crystals than in either of the two types of solvents studied. The reverse seems to be true for the proteins investigated. In all cases, the decay times observed in the crystalline powders were shorter than those observed in the solid solvent system. These results provide knowledge about the environment of individual amino acid residues within a protein molecule. (This work was supported by research contract AT(11-1)1155 between the U. S. Atomic Energy Commission and Michigan State University).

H10. *A Suggested Mechanism for Relative Biological Effectiveness Involving the Participation of the Cellular Environment.* R. J. SHALEK, R. M. HUMPHREY, and S. J. SEDITA*, Department of Physics, The University of Texas M. D. Anderson Hospital and Tumor Institute, Houston, Texas.

Most living organisms show an increasing relative biological effectiveness (RBE) with increasing linear energy transfer (LET) or else pass through a maximum in sensitivity as LET increases. Nonliving pure materials show equal or decreasing radiation sensitivity with increasing LET, whether irradiated in the dry state or dilute solution. It is suggested that a two-step mechanism which has been widely considered as a model for the oxygen effect be extended to account for RBE's in the range 1 to 4. It is postulated that in living cellular material an initial radiation event upon a vital molecule results in a radical which can be (a) restituted by an SH compound, (b) confirmed by reaction with molecular oxygen at the radical site, or (c) confirmed by an additional reaction with a radiation produced radical. As the LET becomes greater, possibility (c) increases in probability resulting in an increasing RBE. At very high LET, the local energy is more than required for the observed effect and the RBE declines.

To test the postulates, the survival of free T2r bacteriophage was measured following anoxic irradiation by gamma-rays, X-rays, and protons in 0.4% broth solution (not capable of O_2 effect at low LET) or in 10^{-2} M cysteine solution (capable of O_2 effect at low LET). According to the model, the RBE in broth should resemble that for pure chemicals and the RBE in cysteine that in living cells. The initial results have been consistent with the model but have not as yet been decisive. (Supported in part by a contract with the United States Atomic Energy Commission).

H11. *Interpretation of the Multi-Hit Curve in Terms of the Theory of Compartments.* ALDO RESCIGNO* (Introduction by Cornelius A. Tobias), Donner Laboratory, University of California, Berkeley, California.

The equation $S = 1 - (1 - e^{-kD})^n$, where S is the standardized response to a dosage D, and k and n are positive constants, is compared with the equation

$$X = \sum_i A_i e^{-\alpha_i t},$$

where X is the amount of a material in a certain compartment, at a time t after the breaking of an essential connection between two precursor compartments. By imposing certain conditions on the structure of a system of compartments, the two previous equations assume the same form, putting $D = Rt$ and $S = KX$, where R and K are positive constants. Some physical interpretations are suggested for these two constants. (This work was supported jointly by NASA and AEC).

H12. *Modification of Radiation Injury with Magnetic Fields.* NABIL M. AMER* (Introduced by Cornelius A. Tobias), Donner Laboratory, University of California, Berkeley, California.

Pupae of *Tribolium confusum* were irradiated with 1200r of 250 kVp X-rays. Following irradiation one group of pupae was placed between the poles of a permanent magnet with a field of 3.6 Kilogauss. A second group was placed between the poles of a *dummy* magnet of the same geometry. Both groups were incubated at 38°C. After 7 days, the time necessary for the pupae to change to adults, the adults were studied in relation to wing abnormality induction, following the methods of Beck *et al.* The group incubated in the dummy magnet had a 93.4% ± 1.4 incidence of abnormal wing development. The group incubated in the magnetic field, exhibited 54.1% ± 5.3 incidence of abnormal wing development. The remaining adults were normal; pupal death did not exceed 3% of the total number of pupae. It was noticed that the wing abnormality in the group exposed to the magnetic field was of a lesser degree of intensity in comparison with abnormals of the control group. The experiment has been repeated four times with a total of 728 pupae.

These results evince that the magnetic field at the strength indicated has a protective effect in modifying the radiation induced damage in this system. A comparative study of free radical content of the magneto-protected group versus the control is being performed. The possible influence of different magnetic field intensities and the effect of time exposure to the magnetic field subsequent to irradiation are being further investigated. (This work was supported by NASA and AEC).

SECTION I. CELLULAR INACTIVATION AND INHIBITION

I1. *A Method for Estimation of the Mean Lethal Dose of Solid Transplantable Tumors* in Vivo. KELLY H. CLIFTON, Department of Radiology Research Laboratories, University of Wisconsin Medical School, Madison, Wisconsin.

Methods for quantitative estimation of the mean lethal dose (MLD) of mammalian cells have, for the most part, depended on cloning procedures *in vitro*, the use of tumor systems which grow as free cell suspensions *in vivo* or tumors from which free cell suspension can readily be prepared. Such suspensions cannot be readily prepared from many solid tumors without resort to prolonged digestion procedures or other methods which almost certainly result in a selected cell population. The method to be described has been developed with a transplantable C3H/WR mammary carcinoma, does not require preparation of free cells, and may be widely applicable.

Grafted tumors are irradiated *in situ*, removed, and crude cell suspensions are prepared with a Snell cytosieve. Serial dilutions are made on the basis of the volume of packed cells after centrifugation of the first suspension, and are grafted in histocompatible recipients. Latency, i.e., the period from grafting until tumors are first palpable, is determined, and is inversely proportional to an exponential function of the packed cell volume injected. The procedure involved in calculation of the MLD and the possible sources of error will be discussed. The MLD of the mammary carcinoma irradiated *in vivo* in these studies was 671 r. (Supported by Grant #T66D, American Cancer Society).

I2. *Relationship between Tumor Growth and Radiosensitivity.* JAMES A. BELLI and J. ROBERT ANDREWS, Radiation Branch, National Cancer Institute, National Institutes of Health, Bethesda, Maryland.

In order to answer certain questions concerning the relationship between tumor growth and radiosensitivity, survival curves for a strain-specific murine leukemia (P-388) were determined with cells irradiated *in vivo, in vitro* and "*in situ*" at various times following the transplantation of 10^6 cells. It was found that the MLD has a value of 110 r for the survival curve of cells of one-day growth; this value increases to about 400 r for cells four and seven days posttransplantation. In addition, variation of the extrapolation number was observed; in general, this variation was inversely related to the rise in MLD. The finding of an extrapolation number for three day tumor cells of <1 (0.6) suggested the presence of a population of cells of heterogeneous sensitivity. This heterogeneity was thought to be due to the presence of a small number of anoxic cells in a population otherwise fully oxygenated. The inverse slope-ratio for the most resistant (seven-day) to most sensitive (one-day) cells was found to be 3.7. Tumor cells were also irradiated *in vitro* or *in vivo* in animals sacrificed 15 minutes prior to exposure (referred to as irradiated *in situ*) at various times post-transplantation. Radiosensitivity of cells irradiated *in vitro* or *in situ* appeared to be independent of growth-stage. The extrapolation number for both conditions was 5.9; MLD *in vitro* = 151r, and *in situ* = 431 r. The inverse slope-ratio (2.8) agrees with the oxygen-enhancement ratio reported for other mammalian cell strains.

I3. *Postirradiation Recovery Processes and Their Dependence on Metabolism in Cultured Mammalian Cells.* M. M. ELKIND and TOMMASO ALESCIO*, National Cancer Institute, Bethesda, Maryland.

Pursuing our earlier studies, we now have information concerning the nature of the processes responsible for the variation of survival with time of cells sublethally damaged by an acute exposure. Asynchronous Chinese hamster cells were exposed to fractionated doses of 55 kv X-rays, and the survival kinetics at room temperature vs. 37° C were measured during the division delay period. The initial part of the recovery curve is largely temperature independent and the remainder of the curve is largely temperature dependent. This suggests that the postirradiation events related to survival may consist of two types: (1) a metabolism independent process(es) which leads to the rapid repair of sublethal damage before sublethally affected cells have had much of a chance to leave the age dependent response states they were in at the time of their first exposure; and (2) a metabolism dependent process(es) which permits surviving cells to progress toward division occupying, thereby, different response states along the way. The latter response states may not be the same as those occupied by asynchronous cells not previously exposed. The foregoing interpretation is supported by measurements of the postirradiation rates of DNA synthesis and is in accord with a model presented by us to explain some of our earlier observations [*J. Cell. Comp. Physiol. Suppl. 1* **58,** 113–134 (1961); see p. 129].

I4. *Variations in X-Ray Response during the Division Cycle of Partially Synchronized Chinese Hamster Cells in Culture.* WARREN K. SINCLAIR and RICHARD A. MORTON*. Division of Biological and Medical Research, Argonne National Laboratory, Argonne, Illinois.

Chinese hamster cells (clone V79-1) grown in culture have been partially synchronized by a combination of cooling, gentle trypsinization and agitation. Studies of the growth of these cells and the percentage of cells pulse-labeled with H^3 thymidine, as a function of time, have enabled the stages in the division cycle to be identified. Exposure at intervals to a single dose of X-radiation (750 r, 250 kvp X-rays, HVL 0.9 mm Cu) showed a single peak of resistance closely correlated with the maximum percentage of labeled cells, i.e., in the S period. This peak is repeated at approximately the same stage in the next cycle. Complete X-ray survival curves taken at intervals during the two cycles showed that the response at each stage can be approximated by the relation $S = 1 - (1 - e^{-D/D_0})^n$ and the data are consistent with almost no change in D_0 but considerable changes in n. Similar experiments are in progress with ultraviolet radiation. (Work supported by U. S. Atomic Energy Commission).

I5. *Change in Radiation Sensitivity during Different Phases of the Cell Cycle for Normal and Bromodeoxyuridine-Treated Mammalian Cells.* R. M. HUMPHREY, W. C. DEWEY, and ANN CORK*, Department of Physics, The University of Texas M. D. Anderson Hospital and Tumor Institute, Houston, Texas.

Chromosomal damage observed at metaphase resulting from 250 rads of Co-60 γ-rays or 100 ergs/mm^2 of ultraviolet (UV) radiation in the Chinese hamster cell in relation to the stage of cell cycle has been described [*Exptl. Cell Res.* **27,** 441 (1962) and *Second Int. Cong. Radiation Research, England,* p. 26 (1962)]. For ionizing radiation, the more sensitive stage was that following DNA synthesis (G_2); whereas, no difference was observed between cells in DNA synthesis (S) or in the pre-DNA synthetic period (G_1). For UV radiation, the most sensitive cells were those in S phase.

In the present experiments, hamster cells were grown in the presence of bromodeoxyuridine (BUDR) for 12 or 48 hours prior to pulse labeling with H^3-thymidine and irradiation. Metaphases were scored at various time intervals after irradiation and by autoradiography were identified as labeled or unlabeled. After 12 hours in BUDR, it was found that the cells in S phase are 6 times more sensitive to ionizing radiation (250 rads) than G_1 cells; furthermore, the G_1 cells did not show an increase in sensitivity over that of non-BUDR treated cells. After 48 hours in BUDR the S cells did not show a further increase in sensitivity, but G_1 cells experienced a two-fold increase in sensitivity. For UV radiation (10 ergs/mm^2) it was found that all phases after 48 hours in BUDR had a three-fold increase in radiosensitivity.

I6. *The Radiosensitivity of Murine Lymphoma Cells* in Vivo *as Determined by a Splenic Colony Method.* R. S. BUSH* and W. R. BRUCE* (Introduced by J. W. Hunt), Department of Medical Biophysics, University of Toronto; and The Ontario Cancer Institute, Toronto.

The spleens of normal or supralethally irradiated AKR/J mice intravenously injected with leukemic cells from adult AKR/J mice with spontaneous or transplanted leukemia contain discrete macroscopic nodules 10 days following the injection. This procedure may be used to assay the fraction of cells in a cell suspension wtih proliferative capacity (*Nature, in press*).

The assay has been used to examine the radiation sensitivity of two transplanted leukemic cell lines with doubling times in the spleen of 12 and 24 hours. The survival curve obtained by irradiation of either line with Co^{60} γ-rays *in vivo* and *in vitro* to doses sufficient to reduce the surviving fraction to 10^{-5} yielded D_0's not significantly different from the D_0 of 115 rads obtained for normal bone marrow cells using the splenic colony method [*Radiation Res.* **14,** 213–222 (1961)]. This is significantly lower than the value of 160 rads obtained by Hewitt and Wilson for mouse lymphoma cells obtained by a limiting dilution method [*Brit. J. Cancer* **13,** 69 (1959)].

I7. *Effects of Cosmic Radiation on Seed Differentiation and Development.* JOHN V. SLATER* and CORNELIUS A. TOBIAS, Donner Laboratory, University of California, Berkeley, California.

Seeds of a variety of plants were flown during the past year in co-operation with NASA by means of high altitude balloons over Labrador. Nuclear emulsions accompanying the seeds showed the presence of approximately 20 heavy ions per square centimeter with various atomic numbers up to and including iron. These flights lasted approximately fifty hours at an altitude of 25 miles. The effects noticed mainly with corn (Golden Bantam) and attributed to cosmic radiation were (a) arrests in pigmentation, (b) irregular morphogenesis, and (c) early cell loss resulting in visible streaks in the leaves.

Seeds of African Daisies exhibited a lowered percentage of germination after the flights. Approximately 6% of the corn seeds flown exhibited some defect. It is expected that satellite flights of the seed material used may result in increased effects especially if flown through radiation belts.

Research with the Berkeley HILAC is currently under way in attempts to evaluate the effects of heavy ions under controlled conditions at sea level on seed development and differentiation. (This work was supported jointly by the National Aeronautics and Space Administration and the U. S. Atomic Energy Commission).

I8. *Survival and Dark-Germination of X-Irradiated* Arabidopsis thaliana, race Estland. SUMANA K. DEVI*, KEDAR N. PRASAD*, and EDGAR F. RILEY, Radiation Research Laboratory, State University of Iowa, Iowa City, Iowa.

Arabidopsis thaliana, race Estland has 5 chromosomes, a short life cycle of about 4 weeks, and an absolute light requirement for germination. The requirement of exposure to light during germination has been considered to be a simple dominant trait. X-ray induced mutations in this variety have been reported and, in 1962, McKelvie described a list of mutant genes. For the present study, wet and air dry seeds were exposed to doses ranging from 1 to 100 Kr of 250 Kvp X-radiation. (Wet seeds were soaked in 10^{-3}M KNO_3 for 10 hours just before irradiation.) In both groups, wet and dry seeds, exposure doses greater than 50 Kr reduced the percentage germinating in light. The percentage of seeds maturing was inversely related to exposed dose. A few seeds (F_1) collected from surviving plants were able to germinate in the dark.

I9. *Some Observations on Two Modes of Radiation Death in Two Ciliate Protozoans.* JOHN CALKINS* (Introduced by R. J. Shalek), Physics Department, The University of Texas, M. D. Anderson Hospital, Houston, Texas.

Ultraviolet light and ionizing radiation may produce death in protozoa with strikingly different symptoms. It has commonly been observed that protozoa irradiated with ionizing radiation show complete repair of the physiological manifestations of radiation damage at the time of the first postirradiation division while the effects of ultraviolet light may be observed, or even be greatest, when one or two divisions have intervened between irradiation and manifestation of the effect. However, by proper manipulation of experimental factors it is possible to control to a certain extent the type of symptoms that radiation exposure will produce. These experimental factors include photo-reactivation, separation of doses, and irradiation at particular times in the interdivision cycle.

Strains of *Tetrahymena pyriformis* and *Paramecium aurelia* that have been isolated and grown in this laboratory for several years are used as experimental subjects. Variation of the above mentioned parameters can shift the symptoms of death in these animals in a striking manner and these shifts are attributed to such factors as the repair rate of the damage and the nature of the principal lesion. (This work was supported in part by Training Grants CRT-5047 and CRT-5099 from the National Cancer Institute of the National Institutes of Health).

I10. *Changes in Dose-Survival Curves during the Division Cycle of* Oedogonium cardiacum. R. J. HORSLEY and L. A. FUCIKOVSKY*, The Ontario Cancer Treatment and Research Foundation, Hamilton, Ontario.

In our previous work, (*Intern. J. Radiobiol.* in publication) we have shown that there is a cyclic fluctuation in radiosensitivity after either 1960 or 3530 rads of Cobalt 60 radiation delivered at different times during the cell cycle. Radiosensitivity, as measured by cell viability, is determined by counting the number of cells in each chain arising from the irradiated spores. Synchronized cell division occurs naturally since large numbers of zoospores, all at about the same age, can be collected in 2 hours or less. Dose-survival curves have been measured at 4 hours after collection and from 11 to 14 hours which is a preprophase period during which the cells are several times more sensitive to radiation. The survival curve at 4 hours is characterized by an initial shoulder followed by an exponential decline. Curves measured at about 13 hours are more complicated. They show an early rapid exponential decline, then level off to form a shoulder followed by a second exponential decline. Slopes and shapes of survival curves measured at different times during the cell cycle will be compared.

I11. *Acute Gamma Radiation Effects upon Growth Rates of* Chlorella pyrenoidosa. O. M. MEREDITH* and J. T. HEINTZELMAN* (Introduced by Lawrence E. Detrick), Research Laboratories, Lockheed Missiles & Space Company, Palo Alto, California.

Co^{60} irradiation, above a threshold exposure level of approximately 500 Krad, sharply slowed growth rates of algal cell suspensions in a metabolically active state. Measurements of induced injury were based upon hemocytometer cell counts, turbidimetry and chlorophyll determinations of rolling tube cultures grown upon a nitrogen-containing media under constant fluorescent lighting for the duration of the observations. At the observed minimally effective radiation level, the cell growth rate was slowed in terms of cell number and of cellular size. The capacity for growth or cell maintenance was restricted at 500 Krad and curtailment of the same capacities appeared to be a function of exposure for observations at 1000 and 1500 Krad. Chlorophyll content of cells remained constant for a few hours and then declined after 500 Krad, while there was an immediate decline on chlorophyll level after 1000 and 1500 Krad. In these instances, there was no coincident decrease in cell number or in turbidity of cell culture. No significant delays in mitosis could be detected at the dose levels employed since cell growth was so sharply curtailed. From these data the mechanism of radiation injury appeared related to a restriction of materials or processes requisite for chlorophyll production and normal cell growth.

I12. *Absence of Radiation-Induced Division Block in the Alga,* Brachiomonas submarina. H. S. DUCOFF and BARBARA D. BUTLER*, Department of Physiology and Biophysics, University of Illinois, Urbana, Illinois.

Among the characteristic responses of irradiated cells is a temporary cessation of division. This is usually manifested as an immediate inhibition of entry into division, and occurs even after doses which produce negligible lethality. Occasional exceptions have been noted but have not received careful study.

Brachiomonas submarina, a free-swinging unicellular green alga, offers a number of advantages for radiobiological investigation: it is large enough for direct microscopic count, forms colonies on agar so that viable counts are easily obtained, and is amenable to division synchronization by manipulation of the light cycle. A 6 kr dose of X-rays (280 kpv) reduces colony formation by 90–98%; nevertheless, the irradiated population continues to increase at the control rate for at least 36–48 hours, or until an approximately 6-fold increase is obtained. This absence of a division block is found whether the cultures are maintained under conditions of illumination or with a cycle of 15 hours of light followed by 9 hours of darkness. Under conditions of cycled illumination, division takes place during the last 4 hours of the dark period. This is true in control cultures, in cultures X-irradiated at the beginning of the light period, and in cultures X-irradiated at the end of the light period. (This work was performed under contract AT (11-1) 878 with the USAEC.)

SECTION J. RADIOISOTOPE TOXICITY AND BONE STRUCTURE

J1. *An Improved Method for the Measurement of Bone Mineral Content* in Vivo. JOHN R. CAMERON* and JAMES A. SORENSON* (Introduced by Halvor Vermund), University of Wisconsin, Madison, Wisconsin.

An improved photon absorption method for the determination of bone mineral content *in vivo* has been developed. Using a collimated beam of monochromatic photons from a radioactive source (I^{125} or Am^{241} at present), and a collimated scintillation detector aligned with this beam, the count rate of the transmitted beam through a thickness of tissue and bone is measured. This is compared with the transmission through an identical thickness of tissue alone. A mathematical relationship gives the equivalent thickness of compact bone mineral at the point of the first measurement. A series of such measurements made at one millimeter intervals across the bone is used to obtain the total bone mineral content of a cross section of the bone. It is in principle possible to obtain information on bone composition, such as the hydroxyapatite to nonmineral ratio, or the calcium to phosphorus ratio, by making duplicate measurements with different monochromatic photon energies. The bone mineral content has been measured on over 200 persons. Repeat measurements have usually given reproducibility within 3%. By using I^{125} (27 Kev) and Am^{241} (60 Kev) the per cent by weight of hydroxyapatite present in the bone has been determined for a number of individuals. The result for these individuals are in the range of 40 to 60% hydroxyapatite. Studies with phantoms gave accuracies of about 3% for both methods. The principal errors are the result of uncertainties in absorption coefficients, and lack of complete monochromaticity of the photon beams. These errors can be reduced with further study.

J2. *Relative Bremsstrahlung Efficiency in Sr^{90} Labeled Bone.* R. D. LLOYD,* C. W. MAYS, and D. R. ATHERTON, University of Utah, Salt Lake City, Utah.

Bremsstrahlung X-rays are produced when energetic β-particles are emitted and absorbed. The number of X-ray photons produced by absorption is proportional to the effective atomic number (Z_{eff}) of the absorber. Body burdens of Sr^{90} can be evaluated by bremsstrahlung counting, but accurate measurements demand that the efficiency of bremsstrahlung production (photons/μc) in the animal relative to that in a standard be known. Beagle bone uniformly labeled with Sr^{90} was provided for this study by Dr. R. J. Della Rosa and Dr. M. Goldman, University of California at Davis. In addition, bones obtained from beagles at various times after a single injection of Sr^{90} were used. Their bremsstrahlung output was compared with that from an aqueous solution of $Sr^{90} + Y^{90}$ in a plastic vial. Individual bones and the standard were centered in water-filled cans 8.5 cm in diameter, and the bremsstrahlung response between 50 and 1000 kev was recorded using an 8 × 4 inch NaI (T1) crystal in a 0.02 inch thick stainless steel housing. Since the gross density of an intact bone reflects its Z_{eff}, an expression describing the bremsstrahlung efficiency relative to that in water in terms of density was determined. The empirical relation obtained from bone uniformly labeled with Sr^{90} was Efficiency = 1 + 0.76 (density-1). Thus, for a beagle whose intact bones average 1.46 gm/cm^3, the $Sr^{90} + Y^{90}$ bremsstrahlung output is about 1.35 times that of a water-filled phantom. (Supported by the U. S. Atomic Energy Commission).

J3. *Osteoarthropathy in Rats Given Calcium^{45}*. J. F. KUZMA* and G. E. ZANDER-PRINCIPATI, Marquette University School of Medicine, Milwaukee, Wisconsin.

"Pulmonary" hypertrophic osteoarthropathy or osteophytosis has been reported in a number of animal species, but its occurrence in the rat has not been noted. In a continuing study of bone tumors induced by calcium^{45}, strontium^{89} and strontium^{90} in animals, ten instances of localized osteoarthropathy have been encountered in female Sprague-Dawley rats, viz: eight with calcium^{45}, one with strontium^{89}, and one control. Site involved included one hindfoot in all, both hindfeet in one, forefoot in two, and tail in one. All lesions initially noted by roentgenograms appeared on the average of 15 months following the administration of the isotope. Pulmonary pathology was present in four, and only one had a coexistent malignant tumor at a distant site.

Osteoarthropathy in the rat is apparently rare. The incidence herein reported (3%) in rats receiving calcium^{45} suggests a causal or potentiating relationship. Radiographic and histologic appearances are to be presented. (Supported by Grants AEC No. A.T. (11-1)-105 and USPHS No. RH-00139-03).

J4. *I^{131} in the Feed, Thyroid, and Milk of Dairy Cows*. L. K. BUSTAD, E. E. ELEFSON*[1], E. C. WATSON*, I. C. NELSON*, D. H. WOOD*[2], and R. O. MCCLELLAN*. Hanford Laboratories, Richland, Washington.

A single I^{131} contamination event of forage was simulated by administering I^{131}-labeled feed to dairy cattle twice daily, each feed sample being spiked on day one with 5 μc per sample. Peak milk concentration in the dairy cattle occurred on the fourth day with about 0.4% of the first day's dose of 10 μc observed per liter of milk. The peak thyroid concentration in the cattle occurred after one week and was 60% of the first day's dose of I^{131}. If one drank one liter of the contaminated milk each day and assumed a 72-hour delay, a 30% uptake and a 7.6 day effective half-life, peak thyroid concentrations would have occurred after two weeks at 0.4% of the first day's dose to the cow. The infinity thyroid dose to such a person would be about 700 mrads. This dose, however, is considerably greater than that described for adults who manifest a 10–20% peak uptake drinking I^{131}-labeled milk. (This work performed under Contract No. AT(45-1)-1350 between the Atomic Energy Commission and the General Electric Company).

---

[1] Present address: College of Veterinary Medicine, Washington State University, Pullman, Washington.

[2] Captain, USAF, VC, assigned to Hanford Laboratories. The experiments described were conducted according to the "Principles of Laboratory Animal Care," established by the National Society for Medical Research. The views expressed herein are those of the authors and do not necessarily reflect the views of the U. S. Air Force or the Department of Defense.

J5. *The Acute Toxicty of Strontium-90 in Gestating Rats.* B. J. HOPKINS*, R. C. BAXTER*, and L. W. TUTTLE, University of Rochester School of Medicine and Dentistry, Rochester, New York.

Some acute effects of strontium-90 upon the developing rat embryo have been observed. Gestating rats were injected intravenously with strontium-90 at two different dose levels. Fetal mortality, growth and hematocrit were measured. Examination of 725 implantation sites showed that the injection of 191 microcuries of strontium-90 on day two postconception produced a significant increase in fetal mortality and growth retardation when observed on the 20th day post conception. The injection of 382 microcuries of strontium-90 on day two produced similar changes of greater magnitude. The injection of 191 microcuries on day 10 postconception produced no significant effect on either fetal growth or mortality. The injection of 382 microcuries on day 10 produced significant growth retardation, but only a slight increase in mortality above control values. The maternal hematocrits were lowered significantly at either gestation age regardless of dose. The difference from control values was greater in those treated on day 2 postconception. Fetal hematocrits of strontium treated rats were decreased slightly below control values.

J6. *Strontium-90 Induced Fetal Anomalies in Rats.* B. J. HOPKINS* and L. W. TUTTLE, University of Rochester School of Medicine and Dentistry, Rochester, New York.

Anomalous development has been produced in rat fetuses by the injection of strontium-90 to the mother. Pregnant Long-Evans rats were injected intravenously with a total dose of 191 or 382 microcuries on day 10 postconception. Gross examination of 164 treated and 159 control embryos on day 20 postconception disclosed a significant incidence of maldeveloped fetuses. Total doses of 191 and 382 microcuries of Strontium-90 produced 17.6% and 55.2% respectively of defective embryos as compared to a 3.1% incidence in controls. The most common defects observed were taillessness, retarded growth, reduced eye volume and skeletal defects in order of frequency observed. The incidence of defective embryos may vary directly with the radiation dose to the fetus.

J7. *Serum Transaminase Levels in Pu^{239} Burdened Beagle Dogs.* WALTER STEVENS and DAVID L. BERLINER, University of Utah College of Medicine, Salt Lake City, Utah.

Serum transaminases (glutamic-oxaloacetic and glutamic-pyruvic transaminase) have been shown to be sensitive indicators of tissue damage in humans, dogs, and other animals. Serum transaminase levels, particularly serum glutamic-pyruvic transaminase (SGPT), can be used to detect early active liver damage before any abnormality is shown by other liver function tests. In general, the extent of the rise reflects the severity and extent of hepatocellular damage. Serum transaminase levels were measured in a group of normal noninjected beagles as well as in dogs burdened with Pu^{239}. The injected doses of Pu^{239} range from 0.016 μc/kg to 2.8 μc/kg and burden times span a period of 12 to 120 months. The normal mean for serum glutamic-oxaloacetic transaminase (SGOT) is 18 Sigma-Frankel units/ml and the normal mean for SGPT is 22 units/ml. A significant number of the Pu^{239} burdened animals had elevated SGPT values and a few of the dogs had elevated SGOT values. Two animals, each injected with 2.8 μc Pu^{239}/kg and burden times of 24 months had greatly elevated SGPT values. These findings will be related to radiation induced liver necrosis and to the distribution of Pu^{239} in these dogs. (Supported by the U. S. Atomic Energy Commission).

J8. *Comparative Toxicity of Pu^{238} and Pu^{239}.* J. E. BALLOU* (Introduced by R. C. Thompson), Hanford Laboratories, Richland, Washington.

Plutonium-238 and Pu^{239} are alpha-emitting radioisotopes having about the same decay energy spectra but different physical half-lives of 89 years and 24,300 years respectively. On the basis of their similar radiation characteristics, the two isotopes would be expected to elicit comparable biological responses when administered in equivalent microcurie amounts. Differences in biological response to the two isotopes would presumably be due to the different mass amounts of plutonium administered in the two instances. In the present study, the acute toxicity of Pu^{239} and Pu^{238} was determined following intravenous administration of the isotopes in citrate buffer solution. Plutonium-239 was significantly more toxic on an equivalent microcurie basis than Pu^{238} over a dose range of about 80 to 140 μc/kg. Toxicity was grossly evidenced by loss of weight and earlier death following Pu^{239} injection. Preliminary histopathological observations showed earlier hepatic damage and recovery in the animals receiving Pu^{238}. Plutonium-239 was, however, more damaging to the spleen. The general pattern of distribution shown by autoradiography suggested Pu^{239} was in the form of small aggregates localized in the reticuloendothelial cells. The Pu^{238} was more diffusely distributed, suggestive of a more ionic nature. The greater toxicity of Pu^{239} was not apparent when lower doses of the isotopes were combined with X-ray exposure. It is probable that the distribution changes associated with the large mass quantities of Pu^{239} contribute to the acute toxicity of this isotope. (This work performed under Contract No. AT(45-1)-1350 between the Atomic Energy Commission and the General Electric Company).

J9. *The Effects of Inhaled $Pu^{239}O_2$ in Adrenalectomized Rats.* G. S. RHYNEER,*[1] H. W. CASEY,*[2] and W. J. BAIR, Hanford Laboratories, Richland, Washington.

Lymphocytopenia is an early response to the inhalation of $Pu^{239}O_2$ by rats and dogs, and is generally unaccompanied by other changes in the circulating blood elements which occur after whole-body irradiation. Since inhaled $Pu^{239}O_2$ is almost entirely found in the lungs and its accumulation in the bronchial lymph nodes does not appear to coincide with the onset of the lymphocytopenia, it is difficult to ascribe the lymphocytopenia to direct radiation effects. To gain a better understanding of the mechanisms involved, the possibility of the lymphocytopenia being associated with an adrenal-cortical response was investigated. Adrenalectomized and sham operated rats were exposed to $Pu^{239}O_2$ aerosol two and one-half weeks after surgery. One group of adrenalectomized rats was maintained on hydrocortisone. Periodic blood samples were taken for total leukocyte counts, differential counts, and hematocrits. At time of sacrifice, about five weeks after exposure to $Pu^{239}O_2$, the lungs contained 1 to 2 μc Pu^{239} and received an average dose of about 10,000 rads. Following exposure to $Pu^{239}O_2$ the lymphocyte counts of the sham operated rats decreased about 60 per cent from the pre-exposure levels, while those of the adrenalectomized rats dropped only 40 per cent. Thus, adrenalectomy decreased the magnitude of the Pu^{239} induced lymphocytopenia response. The greatest drop in lymphocyte level, 90 per cent, occurred in the adrenalectomized, hydrocortisone treated, $Pu^{239}O_2$ exposed rats. These results suggest a possible role of the adrenal in the manifestation of lymphocytopenia following inhalation of $Pu^{239}O_2$. (This work performed under Contract No. AT(45-1)-1350 between the Atomic Energy Commission and the General Electric Company).

SECTION K. ACUTE EFFECTS IN MAMMALS

K1. *Effects of Radiation on a Small South American Primate,* Tamarinus nigricollis. NAZARETH GENGOZIAN and JERRE BATSON*, Medical Division, Oak Ridge Institute of Nuclear Studies, Oak Ridge, Tennessee.

---

[1] Present address: University of Chicago, School of Medicine, Chicago, Illinois.

[2] Captain, USAF, VC, assigned to Hanford Laboratories. The experiments described were conducted according to the "Principles of Laboratory Animal Care," established by the National Society for Medical Research. The views expressed herein are those of the authors and do not necessarily reflect the views of the U.S. Air Force or the Department of Defense.

Studies have been initiated on the feasibility of using a small South American primate, *Tamarinus nigricollis*, as a laboratory animal for radiation research. Several features of this primate recommending that some attempt be made to use it in biological research are (1) its small size, ranging from 250 to 350 grams in adults; (2) low cost in procurement and maintenance; and (3) the occurrence of twins in the litters, a consistent feature in this species. Satisfactory procedures for handling and maintaining the animals in the laboratory have been developed and will be described briefly. Preliminary total-body irradiation (cesium^{137} gamma rays, 4.1 r/min) studies have indicated these small primates to be quite sensitive to ionizing radiation. Thus, mortality has been obtained with radiation doses as low as 100 r and 200 r and preliminary estimates place the 30-day LD_{50} and LD_{100} for these animals at 200 r and 400 r. The profound hematologic effects observed and the relationship of time of death to radiation dose suggest this radiosensitivity to be a real phenomenon. Immunologic studies also indicate the inability to equate mortality (LD_{100}) and immune suppression in these irradiated animals. (Supported by United States Air Force Contract AF 41(657)-398).

K2. *Mortality and Clinical Signs in Swine Exposed to Total Body Co^{60} Gamma Radiation.* F. W. Chambers, Jr., CAPT MSC USN, C. R. Biles*, L. J. Bodenlos, CDR MSC USN*, and J. H. Dowling, LCDR MSC USN*, Naval Medical Research Institute, Bethesda Maryland.

The radiation from a unique 4 π Co^{60} irradiator was used for this experiment. The irradiator is unique in that the air dose is relatively uniform throughout the representative volume of the irradiated animals. Approximately five hundred swine were used, divided as to sex and as to weight (70 pounds and 140 pounds average). Forty-eight animals were the usual number irradiated at each dose level, the doses being increased in 50 r increments in the range of zero to approximately one hundred per cent mortality. Depth dose distributions were determined using miniature tissue equivalent ionization chambers in tissue equivalent phantoms and cadavers. Mortality and clinical sign data are discussed. (The opinions or assertions contained herein are the private ones of the authors and are not to be construed as official or reflecting the views of the Navy Department or the naval service at large).

K3. *$LD_{50/24\ hour}$ Determinations from X-Irradiation of the Chick Embryo.* Neal K. Clapp* (Introduced by William D. Carlson and James N. Shively), Radiology Section, Colorado State University, Fort Collins, Colorado.

$LD_{50/24\ hour}$ estimations for X-irradiation of chick embryos have been made using a machine operated at 280 KVP, 20 Ma, and an HVL of 1.3 mm. copper at 50 cm. distance. Dosages were determined by sealing a 100 r Victoreen r-meter ionization chamber within the egg at the embryo site. The dose rate was measured as 124 r per minute. Randomly selected groups of embryos from 2–19 days of age were irradiated. Ages of embryos were measured at 24-hour intervals of incubation. Embryos were removed from their shells at the end of a 24-hour post-irradiation period. Viability was determined by the presence of a beating heart in the younger embryos. The appearance of a normally functioning extra-embryonic blood vascular system and associated capillary oozing following vessel disruption as well as response to mechanical stimulus were used as criteria in older embryos. The $LD_{50/24\ hour}$ doses have been correlated with age of embryonic development. Histopathologic studies are in progress and will be reported elsewhere.

K4. *Growth Rate Comparisons of Domestic Chickens Irradiated during the Third, Eighth, and Thirteenth Days of Embryonic Development at Three Increments of the LD_{50}.* Harry D. Muller* and Robert E. Moreng, Department of Poultry Science, Colorado State University, Fort Collins, Colorado.

Five hundred chicks surviving single dose irradiation treatments at 50%, 100%, and 150% of the LD_{50}, during days 3, 8, and 13 of embryonic development were raised in conjunction with 200 nonirradiated chicks of the same genetic composition and age. One-third of the control chicks were sham-irradiated concurrent with the administration of each of the irradiation treatments. Body weight measurements of survivors and controls were secured at 14 day intervals for the first 20 weeks of life, and at 28 day intervals thereafter. Analysis of body weights delineated that for both males and females, the nonirradiated controls, and the 50% of LD_{50} survivors exceeded the survivors of the 100% and 150% of the LD_{50} in body weights. These differences continued for the first five months of growth. The magnitude of the differences decreased with increase in age as the heavier groups plateaued in weight gain while the lighter birds continued to increase in body weight. Ovulation rates were observed on a daily basis from the 7th month of age for all surviving females. Nonirradiated controls exhibited significantly greater ovulatory rates than did survivors of irradiation treatments. (Supported by US Atomic Energy Commission).

K5. *Appraisal of Differences in Acute Mortality in the Mouse from X- or Gamma Radiation with Changes in Exposure Configuration.* SYLVANUS A. TYLER and S. PHYLLIS STEARNER, Division of Biological and Medical Research, Argonne National Laboratory, Argonne, Illinois.

Under certain conditions the magnitude of acute lethality in the mouse after exposure to X- or gamma rays differs for protracted, split and fractionated exposures. In the LAF_1 mouse exposed to Co^{60} gamma rays, the $LD_{50/30}$ increases at a constant rate when a single exposure is protracted for periods up to 6 hours as when the exposure is fractionated or split within 6 hours of the conditioning dose. For intervenient times between 6 and 24 hours, split doses consistently gave lower $LD_{50/30}$'s than protracted exposures of the same duration.

These differences are shown to be expected consequences of the model of injury accumulation in which 2 types of lethal mechanisms that independently contribute lethal effects were postulated—a time-dependent (reversible) process that reduces the effectiveness of the dose at a constant rate (linear reversal) during exposure and a time-independent (irreversible) process. The basic assumption that resolves the differences in acute mortality between exposure configurations is that the reversibility of time-dependent effects is time-limited.

Compatibility of the model with experimental results of several investigators is shown. This is accomplished by use of a normalized variable (the ratio of the $LD_{50/30}$ for any exposure or intervenient time and the instantaneous dose $LD_{50/30}$). (Supported by U. S. Atomic Energy Commission).

K6. *Radiation Mortality in the Mouse: Model of the Kinetics of Injury Accumulation for Protracted Doses.* S. PHYLLIS STEARNER, SLYVANUS A. TYLER and MARGARET H. SANDERSON, Division of Biological and Medical Research, Argonne National Laboratory, Argonne, Illinois.

Effects of exposure time on extent of acute radiation injury in the LAF_1 mouse are reported. Exposures to Co^{60} γ-rays are protracted over single periods varying from 60 min to 3 days; doses are in the 30-day lethal range. Most deaths occur between 9 and 30 days.

Dose effectiveness decreases with increase in exposure time up to about 6 hours, but there is little further decrease when doses are protracted over longer periods. A kinematic model is presented that assumes independent action of (1) a time-dependent (reversible) injury process, regulated by a constant linear reversal of effects, expressed in groups exposed for 360 min or less; and (2) a time-independent (irreversible) process predominantly expressed in groups exposed for 960 or 1440 min.

The exposure-time effect is expressed by D/D_0 ratios (relation between dose, D, required when exposure is delivered over some time period and the instantaneously delivered dose, D_0, required for the same effect). The relation between D/D_0 ratios and exposure time is given by the linear expression $(D/D_0) = 1 + (t/\tau)$. The estimate of the time constant γ is 1419 min. For the time-dependent effect 50% of the animals can reverse at a rate equal to or greater than 0.68 r/min. The estimated LD_{50} for an instantaneous dose is 969 r and σ is 82 r. For the time-independent effect the estimated LD_{50} is 1387 r and σ is 155 r. (Supported by U. S. Atomic Energy Commission).

K7. *Semen Characteristics of Spanish Goats Following Exposure to Mixed Neutron and Gamma Radiation.* J. T. MORROW* and E. W. HUPP* (Introduced by S. O. Brown), Animal Husbandry Department and Radiation Biology Laboratory, A. & M. College of Texas, College Station, Texas.

Sixteen male Spanish goats were divided into four groups, three irradiated and one control. Each of three groups was exposed in a swimming pool type reactor for ½, 1, and 2 minutes (groups 1, 2, 3) to mixed gamma and neutron radiation at a rate of 296r/minute and 20r/minute, respectively. The total doses received were 158, 316, and 632 rads, respectively. Weekly semen collections were made on all goats with the aid of an electro-ejaculator. Semen volume, total sperm numbers, sperm motility, per cent alive and per cent abnormal sperm were recorded. Collections began on the fifth week postirradiation and continued through the nineteenth week. The sperm numbers in groups 2 and 3 reached a low point of 61 and 34 per cent of the controls, respectively, the eighth week after irradiation. Group 1 varied only slightly from the controls. Sperm numbers increased steadily after the initial increase was observed on the twelfth week. Irradiation did not have any effect on the volume of the ejaculate. The per cent abnormal sperm in group 3 reached a high of 62 per cent on the fifth week with a sharp decrease in the number of abnormals during the sixth to eighth week. The percentage of abnormal sperm had decreased to less than 5 per cent by the sixteenth week. The number of dead sperm closely followed the per cent abnormal sperm.

K8. *Response Rate Decrement and Recovery Following Gamma Irradiation.* HUGH C. BLODGETT* and W. LYNN BROWN, Department of Psychology, The University of Texas, Austin, Texas.

This paper, the fourth in a series concerned with decrement of response rate during irradiation, and recovery following irradiation examines the influence upon performance attributable to the rate at which radiation is deliveed. Subjects were 42 albino rats pretrained on operant conditioning equipment to approximately 1200 presses/hr. on a 10/1 food reinforcement schedule. Matched groups were I, control (sham-irradiated); II, III, and IV, dosage 200r given at rates of 100r/min., 500r/min., and 1000r/min. respectively; and V, VI and VII dosage 400r given at the above rates respectively. Subjects were irradiated on days 1, 8, and 15 following performance tests. Performance was recorded from day one through 22. The design permitted comparisons of (1) response decrement, and (2) recovery through 7-day cycles following dosages of 200r, 400r, and multiples of these values, and (3) comparisons between groups having equal dosage given at different rates. Tables and graphs will be presented. Findings: (1) significant dosage by rate interaction, and (2) groups receiving 400r show inverse relationship between response rate and irradiation rate. As in studies in the series using X-radiation there was (3) steady performance in sham-irradiated controls, (4) marked decrement 24 hours after irradiation, varying with dosage, and (5) recovery within cycles varying as a function of dosage and of rate.

K9. *Sensitivity of Irradiated Mice to Bacterial Endotoxin.* WILLIE W. SMITH, ILO M. ALDERMAN* and CAROL SCHNEIDER*, National Cancer Institute, National Institutes of Health, Bethesda, Maryland.

In the course of studies on granulocyte mobilization early deaths made it impossible to obtain counts in whole groups of mice given as little as 0.25 μg of endotoxin 3 days after irradiation with 950 rads [*Proc. Soc. Exptl. Biol. Med.* **53,** 182 (1962)]. In controls the LD_{50} of this preparation was ~ 470 μg/20 g (Values are approximate LD_{50} 70 hours after injection, in μg per 20 g. mouse). Three days after irradiation the LD_{50} was found to be 0.8 μg for 1000 rads, 15 μg for 890 rads and 130 μg for 770 rads (Co^{60}; LD_{50} ~ 820 rads). Endotoxin LD_{50}'s were higher 2 and 4 days than 3 days after irradiation. Shielding the hind legs did not significantly alter the 3-day LD_{50} of 2 μg for 850 r, 200 KV X-rays. Shielding the abdomen caused the LD_{50} to return to 420 μg, nearly the control value. With a 32 × 14 mm shield over the back during lateral irradiation the 3-day LD_{50} was 75 μg, an increase over nonshielded attributable to partial gastrointestinal rather than adrenal shielding. The extreme sensitivity to endotoxin appears to be related to gastrointestinal injury.

In dogs and rats with the gastrointestinal syndrome Conard *et al.* [*J. Appl. Physiol.* **9,** 227 (1956)] and Taketa, [*Radiation Res.* **11,** 471 (1959)] have extended survival with therapy which included antibiotics. Germ-free mice were observed by Wilson and Piacsek to live a day or two longer than conventionals (*Abstr. 2nd Intern. Congress of Radiation Res.* 1962, p. 151). The present results suggest that absorption of small amounts of bacterial endotoxin could account for the occurrence of gastrointestinal deaths at 3.5–4.5 days.

K10. *Further Studies on the Fate of Bacteria Injected into Irradiated Mice.* H. E. Walburg, Jr. and E. I. Mynatt, Biology Division, Oak Ridge National Laboratory, Oak Ridge, Tennessee.

Earlier observations have indicated that 24 hours after the injection of *Pseudomonas aeruginosa* into chronically irradiated mice, there is a secondary increase in the concentration of this organism in the liver. This increase is proportional to the accumulated exposure and is not seen in unirradiated mice. It has also been reported that the leakage of bacteria at the site of their intravenous inoculation results in a subcutaneous focus of infection in irradiated mice. The purpose of this study was to investigate the role of such a subcutaneous depot in the secondary increase of hepatic bacterial levels noted earlier. Young adult male CF-1 mice received an X-ray exposure of 50 r every 48 hours. At various accumulated exposures (500–2500r), groups of mice were injected via tail vein with *P. aeruginosa.* Twenty-four hours after injection, the *Pseudomonas* concentration was increased significantly above the control mean both in the liver and at the inoculation site in the tail. The tail values were usually higher than the corresponding liver values. All of the irradiated mice were leukopenic, and *Pseudomonas* could frequently be cultured from their blood. RF mice treated similarly developed the secondary increase in *Pseudomonas* in the liver only after higher higher accumulated X-ray exposures, although the increase was marked after 1000 r given in a single exposure. These results indicate the importance of sources other than the liver itself in the secondary rise of hepatic bacterial concentrations in irradiated mice.

K11. *Autoradiographic Studies on the Proliferative Capacity of Antibody-Producing Cells.* Toshihiko Sado* and Martha R. Leonard* (Introduced by Takashi Makinodan), Biology Division, Oak Ridge National Laboratory, Oak Ridge, Tennessee.

Rabbit spleen cells preimmunized against bovine serum albumin were cultured *in vivo* in diffusion chambers in the sublethally irradiated mice and stimulated with the secondary dose of the same antigen. The proliferative capacity of antibody-synthesizing cells at various stages of antibody response was studied by combined tritiated thymidine labeling and immunofluorescent techniques. Results indicated that prior to the differentiation of antibody-producing cells there was a very active proliferation of blast cells which have a very short generation time. During the log phase of antibody production (day 5) large antibody-producing cells were very active in DNA synthesis and their estimated mean generation time was less than 9 hours. Some of the small antibody-producing cells also incorporated H^3-thymidine at this time. During the stationary and decay phases, proliferative capacity of these cells declined and the mean generation time became much longer. It was also found that small antibody-containing cells recovered from these stages (later than day 7) were terminal, nondividing cells. These data suggest that antibody response is a reflection of proliferation of antibody-producing cells.

K12. *Decrease in Embryonic Splenomegaly by X-Irradiation.* Frank Seto* (Introduced by E. H. Perkins), Biology Division, Oak Ridge National Laboratory, Oak Ridge, Tennessee.

As part of a quantitative study of splenomegaly in the chick embryo, the effect of X-irradiation on the responding system was investigated. Three series of experiments were conducted: (1) the irradiation of host embryos, (2) the irradiation of donor spleen cells, and (3) the combined irradiation of host embryos and donor spleen cells. Following the irradiation, graded doses of adult chicken spleen cells were injected intravenously and the increase in embryonic spleen measured subsequently. In the uninjected control series, the six-day spleen weights of the irradiated embryos were consistently less than those of unirradiated embryos and the per cent decrease was dose-dependent. Among the injected host embryos, the splenic enlargement of irradiated embryos was reduced proportionately as compared to the unirradiated group. On the other hand, the correlation between the dose of irradiation delivered to donor spleen cells and decrease in splenomegaly was not consistent; e.g., at certain doses enlargement greater than with unirradiated cells was obtained. Similar results were obtained when irradiated cells were injected into irradiated host embryos. These data suggest that contrary to the unidirectional graft-versus-host interpretation of embryonic splenomegaly which follows the grafting of immunologically competent tissues, the embryo is competent and can contribute significantly to the splenic enlargement response. (Performed under a Postdoctoral Fellowship, GSP-18,129, USPHS).

SECTION L. PROTECTION

L1. *Toxicity and Radioprotective Effects of Acetyl* p-*Aminopropiophenone in Mice.* V. Plzak and J. Doull, U. S. Air Force Radiation Laboratory, University of Chicago, Chicago, Illinois.

Synthesis of the *N*-acetyl derivative of *p*-aminopropiophenone (PAPP) has permitted a comparison of the effects of this compound with those of the parent compound in control and X-irradiated mice. Using proplyene glycol as the vehicle, the intraperitoneal LD_{50} (10 day) for acetyl PAPP was found to be about 245 mg/kg in male and 470 mg/kg in female CF_1 mice. Acetyl PAPP is thus about one-half as toxic to mice as PAPP on a molar basis. Maximum protection against 30-day lethality in X-rayed male and female mice was obtained when the acetyl PAPP was given at a dosage level of 100 mgm/kgm between 1 and 2 hours prior to the radiation. Although both agents produce methemoglobinemia, the response in acetyl PAPP-treated mice occurs later (maximum at 3 to 4 hours) than in PAPP-treated mice (maximum within 30 minutes). Removal of the spleen or most of the liver did not decrease the PAPP-induced methemoglobinemia in mice but removal of both kidneys reduced the response by about 25%. Neither acetyl PAPP nor PAPP produced methemoglobin when incubated with mouse, rat or human blood but freshly voided urine from mice given either agent produced methemoglobin when added to shed blood. These studies suggest that acetyl PAPP is converted *in vivo* to PAPP which is subsequently converted into the methemoglobin-producing agent. High pressure oxygen exposure (6 atmospheres) which eliminates the radioprotective effect of PAPP increases the methemoglobin response to this agent, which suggests that the effects are not directly related.

L2. *Protection of Proton-Irradiated Mice with* p-*Aminopropiophenone (PAPP) and 2-Mercaptoethylamine (MEA)*. D. G. OLDFIELD*, J. DOULL, V. PLZAK, A. HASEGAWA*, and A. SANDBERG*, U. S. Air Force Radiation Laboratory, University of Chicago, Chicago, Illinois.

Chemical modifiers of radiation effects are known to be LET-dependent in several systems. For this and other reasons, a study of the relative protection effect of PAPP and MEA against 30-day lethality in mice given whole-body doses of 200–1500 rads of either 440-Mev protons or 250-Kvp X-rays was undertaken. Each experimental group consisted of 20–40 adult CF_1 male mice given a single drug (vehicle only for controls) and a single radiation dose. The PAPP (30 mg/kg in 50% propylene glycol) and MEA (225 mg/kg in water) were administered intraperitoneally five minutes prior to the irradiation which was given at the rate of 40–80 rads per minute with the mice confined in vented plastic centrifuge tubes. For the proton irradiation, sets of 9 tubes were slowly and repetitively passed through the beam perpendicular to its axis. For the X-ray exposures, sets of 16 tubes were continuously rotated within the beam. The absorbed dose was calculated for each radiation from water-phantom measurements made with a Victoreen cavity ionization chamber which had been charge-calibrated against a cobalt-60 source producing a known dose rate. The relative biological effectiveness of protons and X-rays in control groups and the dose reduction factors and relative protective effectiveness in protected groups were determined from calculated regression lines. Although PAPP and MEA reduced the 30-day lethality for both radiations, MEA gave somewhat greater protection than PAPP against protons.

L3. *Chemical Protection in Rats with a Combination of Treatments*. GEORGE W. HARRISON JR.*, GEORGE S. MELVILLE, JR., K. MCKINNEY GALLO*, and THOMAS P. LEFFINGWELL, The Radiobiological Laboratory of the University of Texas and the United States Air Force, Austin, Texas.

Previous studies of combinations of drugs in rodents have demonstrated an enhanced radioprotective effect as compared to the drugs when used alone. The present study demonstrates a potentiation of the protective effect afforded by aminopropylisothiuronium dibromide (APT) and cysteine when serotonin and acetylcholine are also given prior to irradiation.

Female Sprague-Dawley (Holtzman) rats were exposed to 1500r of Co^{60} gamma radiation after treatment with either or both of the drug combinations. Part of the animals in each group were given cysteine therapy postirradiation. Untreated irradiates and irradiates given cysteine therapy only serve as controls. APT and cysteine were administered intraperitoneally in a homogeneous solution 35 minutes prior to irradiation. Serotonin and acetylcholine were administered intraperitoneally in a homogeneous solution for 3 consecutive days postirradiation.

100% mortality at 30 days postirradiation was obtained in the control groups and the serotonin-acetylcholine group receiving no cysteine therapy. All animals in the APT-cysteine group receiving cysteine therapy died. Mean survival times were 4, 6 and 8 days respectively. 5% survival (MST 7 days) occurred in the serotonin-acetylcholine group receiving cysteine therapy. 10% survival (MST 11 days) occurred in the APT-cysteine group which did not receive cysteine therapy. 65.7% survival (MST 21 days) was obtained for either group receiving both APT-cysteine and serotonin-acetylcholine. These treatment groups afford significant protection against mortality when compared to all other groups; a full statistical analysis will be presented. (The authors certify that the experiment was conducted according to the "Principles of Laboratory Animal Care" of the National Society for Medical Research.)

L4. *Influence of β-mercaptoethylamine (MEA) on Iron Absorption of Intestine-Irradiated Rats*. KEDAR N. PRASAD* and JAMES W. OSBORNE, Radiation Research Laboratory, University of Iowa, Iowa City, Iowa.

MEA given before X-irradiation of the exteriorized small bowel of rats significantly reduced radiation damage (*Internat. J. Rad. Biol.*, in press). The purpose of the present investigation was to determine the influence of MEA on mucosal uptake and transport of Fe^{59} to the blood of normal and intestine-irradiated rats. The entire exteriorized ileum and jejunum was X-irradiated with 1400 r or 1800 r with or without MEA. MEA (100 mg/kg) was given intraperitoneally 15 minutes before exposure. The solution (pH 6) of Fe^{59} SO_4 with activity of 60 μc/liter was perfused through the entire irradiated gut for one hour with a speed of 0.8 ± 0.06 ml per minute at 1, 3, 6, 12, and 20 days after exposure. The mucosal uptake of Fe^{59} in animals given irradiation with or without MEA was higher at all intervals after exposure than in sham-irradiated controls. Although the intestine which received 1800 r with MEA appeared histologically normal at day 20, the net transfer of Fe^{59} was higher than in sham-irradiated controls. In another series of experiments, MEA (100 mg/kg) was given to normal rats 15 minutes before perfusion. The mucosal uptake was about the same as seen in the normal animals without MEA, but the net transfer of Fe^{59} to blood was approximately five times higher. In a third series of experiments, the mucosal uptake in normal rats perfused at pH 2 was similar to that seen after perfusion at pH 6, but the net transfer of Fe^{59} from mucosa to blood was about 25 times greater at pH 2 than at pH 6. (Supported in part by Grant RH-21, U. S. Public Health Service.)

L5. *The Distribution and the Chemical Forms of AET Administered as Bis(2-Guanidoethyl) Disulfide in Irradiated Mice.* BERNARD SHAPIRO, GEORGE KOLLMANN*, and EMANUEL E. SCHWARTZ, Research Laboratories, Department of Radiology, Southern Division, Albert Einstein Medical Center, Philadelphia, Pennsylvania.

The distribution and the chemical forms of the protective agent in the various tissues of X-radiated C57BL male mice were studied at 20 and 120 minutes after a protective dose of S^{35}-labeled bis(2-guanidoethyl) disulfide (GED). The mice received 1,000 r (200 r/min.) 10 minutes after the intraperitoneal injection of 140 mg GED-S^{35} per kg. At 20 minutes the irradiated mice showed a large amount of protective agent in the stomach and a small amount of protective agent in the excreta as compared with unirradiated animals. At 120 minutes the irradiated mice showed normal amounts of protective agent in the stomach but still showed poor excretion. The major chemical forms in the irradiated as well as in the unirradiated mice are protein-bound protective agent and free GED. The tissues also contained 2-guanidoethanesulfinic acid, taurocyamine, sulfate and *S*-acetyl-2-mercaptoethylguanidine. The protective agent was bound to proteins by thiolester linkage, mixed disulfide bond, and a third unknown type of bond. Some differences were noted in protein-binding in the irradiated as compared with unirradiated animals. These results are interpreted as demonstrating some interesting effects of radiation on the distribution and metabolism of GED.

L6. *Chemical Protection against Lethal X-Irradiation in Rats.* RICHARD I. H. WANG, Department of Anesthesiology, Roswell Park Memorial Institute, New York State Department of Health, Buffalo, New York.

There has been a lack of information regarding the effective chemical protection against lethal X-irradiation in rats. Existing data have shown that some chemical protection in rats can be achieved by the use of 2-aminoethyl-isothiuronium (AET), serotonin, mercaptoethylamine (MEA) or *para*-aminopropiophenone (PAPP) only at high or near toxic concentrations.

In order to find more suitable and effective chemical protection in rats, different concentrations of mixtures of AET, MEA and serotonin were investigated in this laboratory. Male Sprague-Dawley rats weighing 330 gm (about 12 weeks old) were used. The chemical mixture was given intraperitoneally at 15 minutes preceding exposure. The rats were irradiated in pairs, one as chemically treated and the other as control, by the use of a G. E. Maxitron at 250 kvp, 30 ma, 1 mm A1 plus 0.5 mm Cu added filtration and HVL 1.1 mm Cu. The dose rate was 160 r/min. at TSD of 45 cm. It was found that the chemical mixtures that provided 90 to 100% survival in rats exposed to 900 r ($LD_{100/30\ day}$) contain 2 mg of serotonin, 7 to 28 mg of AET and 6 to 17 mg of MEA. At these concentrations toxicity in rats attributable to the radioprotective chemicals was absent. It was noted that chemical protection in rats was more difficult to achieve than in mice.

L7. *Effects of AET and Bone Marrow on Delayed Somatic Effects of Radiation in Mice.* G. E. COSGROVE, A. C. UPTON, C. C. CONGDON, D. G. DOHERTY and D. G. GOSSLEE, Biology Division, Oak Ridge National Laboratory, Oak Ridge, Tennessee.

Young adult female (101 × C3H)F_1 mice were acutely exposed to 350–1800 r of 250 KVP whole-body X-rays. Some mice at each dose level received 8.8 mg of S-2, aminoethylisothiuronium·Br·HBr (AET) just before irradiation, 10 × 10^6 isologous bone marrow (IBM) cells just after irradiation, or both AET before and IBM after irradiation. Survivors and unirradiated controls were observed throughout life and checked periodically for graying of fur and opacities of the optic lens. Although AET and IBM markedly protected against early lethality and against the induction of thymic lymphomas, protection against life-shortening was less pronounced or equivocal; i.e., after 700 r, mean survival time was 608 days with AET treatment, 584 with IBM, 549 with both AET and IBM, and 565 in nonprotected controls; after 500 r, no protected groups outlived nonprotected controls. Radiation-induced graying of the fur, however, was inhibited by AET. The development of other later radiation effects, such as nonthymic neoplasms, nephrosclerosis, and cataracts was not detectably inhibited by AET or IBM. Why AET protected against some delayed somatic effects of radiation but not against others and why the dose reduction factor in no case approached that noted for the LD 50/30 are questions calling for further study. The protection by IBM against induction of thymic lymphomas is likewise unexplained but consistent with earlier observations by other workers.

L8. *Radioprotection of Human Lymphocytes* in Vitro *by Phytohemagglutinin (PHA).* STEFANO STEFANI* and ROBERT SCHREK, Veterans Administration Hospital, Hines, Illinois.

In suspensions of normal human blood leukocytes filtered through glass wool, 94 to 98 per cent of nucleated cells were lymphocytes. Purified suspensions plus PHA (5 to 30 μl/ml) were incubated in small test tubes and the viable cells were studied and counted in slide chambers. In 3 days, the PHA transformed most of the lymphocytes into large blast-like cells and cells intermediate in morphology between lymphocytes and blasts. Irradiation of purified suspensions of lymphocytes with 150 r killed nearly all the cells within 6 days. The same suspension treated with PHA and irradiated with 150 to 2400 r was found to have many surviving blasts, intermediate cells and lymphocytes. The survival time of irradiated lymphocytes was increased whether PHA was added at any time from 5 days before to 2 days after irradiation. An occasional cell in mitotic division was seen in PHA-treated suspensions irradiated with doses up to 600 r.

Incubation with PHA of suspensions of lymphocytes from the blood of 2 patients with chronic lymphocytic leukemia produced in 6 days a few blast-like cells but the rest of the leukemic lymphocytes were not modified morphologically by the reagent. The unaltered leukemic lymphocytes were moderately resistant to irradiation as compared to the cells not treated with PHA.

These experiments indicated that PHA caused changes in the morphology of normal human lymphocytes and increased their resistance to X-rays. PHA caused little or no morphologic changes in leukemic lymphocytes but protected them to a moderate degree from irradiation. (Aided by grant from National Cancer Institute.)

L9. *Germfree Studies of Protection Induced by Bacterial Endotoxin against X-Radiation.* B. RAPHAEL WILSON and TAIJU MATSUZAWA,* Lobund Laboratory, Department of Biology, University of Notre Dame, Notre Dame, Indiana.

The germfree animal, devoid of bacteria and other microorganisms, provides the means of studying radiation syndrome, protection, and recovery without the complications arising from an animal's microbial associates. The LD_{50} X-ray dose for the germfree Swiss-Webster mouse is 705 r; for its conventional counterpart, 660 r. With the administration of 10 μg *S. typhosa* endotoxin i.p. 24 hours before X-irradiation, the LD_{50} is raised to about 1200 r for the germfree mouse, but only to about 850 r for the conventional mouse. Thus bacterial endotoxin gives protection in the germfree mouse in the "gut death" range. Infant mice (1–6 days old) exposed to 400 r exhibit damage to hair follicles by a delay of two weeks in the appearance of hair. With the administration of endotoxin prior to irradiation, protection against follicular damage is conferred although the coat is not as heavy as nonirradiated controls. Other radiation effects, such as the decreased rate of body growth, are also mitigated by endotoxin. In general, the protective effectiveness of bacterial endotoxin is more pronounced in adult germfree mice than in their conventional counterparts. The differences between infant germfree and conventional mice are small. The working hypothesis for the investigation of the mechanism of endotoxin protection is that the endotoxin provokes a decrease in pO_2 of target tissues. A reduction in oxyhemoglobin in peripheral blood has been observed in mice after endotoxin injection. (Supported by the Office of Naval Research.)

L10. *Modification of Radiation Reaction on Human Skin.* Komanduri K. N. Charyulu*, George K. Stamoulas* and Ella B. Tyree, Memorial Sloan-Kettering Cancer Center, New York, N.Y.

The modification of radiation reaction on human skin has been studied in twelve subjects. The effect of variation of skin temperature during irradiation is one of the parameters investigated. Three adjacent areas on the anterior aspect of each thigh were selected. On each thigh one area was irradiated at room temperature; the intermediate areas were designated as the unirradiated controls. The third area was irradiated at increased temperture on one thigh and at decreased temperature on the other. X-rays at 100 Kv, 6 Ma with no added filtration were employed using a field size of 3 cm diameter at 15 cm FSD. The skin temperature was varied by circulating water at a known temperature through a perspex box attached on the skin to be irradiated. The exact skin temperature, approximately 3 mm below the surface layers of skin was determined by an intracutaneous thermometer.

The reflectance spectrophotometer using interference filters was used to determine the degree of erythema quantitatively by measuring hemoglobin, reduced hemoglobin and melanin. Control readings were made before radiation. After irradiation, measurements were made daily during the first week and three times a week thereafter until there was dry or moist reaction or healing of skin. The results are plotted and will be discussed.

L11. *Infrared Reduction of Cutaneous Ultraviolet Damage.* Mark Allen Everett, C. Kendrick Doran*, H. Dean Everett*, and J. H. Anglin, Jr.*, Department of Dermatology, University of Oklahoma Medical Center, Oklahoma City, Oklahoma.

The hair of young adult white male guinea pigs was epilated with calcium thioglycollate and each was wrapped in aluminum foil with a square aperture exposing only the back of the animal. Each pig was irradiated with ten minutes ultraviolet light from a hot quartz mercury vapor lamp filtered through 2 cm. distilled water. The right side of each pig was then exposed to five minutes infrared radiation from a nichrome heater coil at eighteen inches distance. The erythema produced was measured at hourly intervals and biopsies were taken at 12 and 72 hours. A significant reduction in the visible erythema produced was observed on the infrared exposed side at six and twelve hours. The ultraviolet induced increase in epidermal mitotic rate at 72 hours was significantly less on the infrared exposed tissues. Infrared radiation immediately after ultraviolet exposure thus significantly reduces not only visible erythema but also the subsequent burst of epidermal mitotic activity.

SECTION M. MICROORGANISMS

M1. *The Oxygen Effect in Bacteria Sensitized to X-Rays by Sublethal UV-Photoproducts.* J. E. BAPTIST and R. H. HAYNES, Committee on Biophysics, University of Chicago, Chicago, Illinois.

A strong synergism between ultraviolet light and X-rays for bacterial inactivation was reported last year from this laboratory [*Radiation Res.* **16,** 562 (1962)]. Under appropriate growth conditions, the X-ray inactivation kinetics of stationary phase *E. coli* B/r are exponential; after preliminary exposure to 2537A radiation the X-ray sensitivity of the UV survivors may be increased three fold over that of non-UV irradiated controls. About one half of the UV-induced lesions which participate in this X-ray sensitization may be removed by photoreactivation; therefore, it seems likely that sublethal thymine dimers in DNA constitute one major class of UV photoproducts which can serve to sensitize cells to inactivation by ionizing radiation. If the sensitizing lesions can thus be identified in molecular terms, then studies on the other radiobiological properties of such sensitized cells would appear to be worthwhile. Our initial experiments along this line concern the X-ray oxygen effect. Under fully oxygenated conditions, the X-ray sensitivity increases gradually with the preliminary UV dose up to a plateau level of 3 times that of the controls. However, under anaerobic conditions, the X-ray sensitivity increases more slowly with the pre-UV dose, and does not appear to triple in the experimentally accessible region. This suggests that the oxygen-dependent X-ray lesions interact more strongly with the sublethal UV-photoproducts than do the oxygen-independent lesions. (This work was supported by a grant from the National Institutes of Health, U. S. Public Health Service.)

M2. *Photoreactivation and Dark Recovery of Ultraviolet Killing in* Escherichia coli *Strain 15 TAU.* D. M. GINSBERG and JOHN JAGGER, Walter Reed Army Institute of Research, Washington, D. C. and the University of Tennessee, Knoxville, Tennessee; Oak Ridge National Laboratory, Oak Ridge, Tennessee.

In *E. coli* 15 TAU, which requires thymine (T), arginine (A), and uracil (U) for normal growth, it is known that growth of a logarithmic phase culture with thymine, but without arginine and uracil (+T-AU) for 90 min results in (1) resistance to thymineless death ("immune" state), and (2) a 100-fold increase in multiplicity of UV (2537Å) survival curves [*Progr. Photobiology* 305 (1961)].

Examination of +T-AU (immune) cultures reveals that they are physiologically, morphologically, and radiologically indistinguishable from control (+TAU) cultures in the stationary phase. Blockage of protein and ribonucleic acid syntheses in log phase forces the cells into a premature but apparently genuine stationary phase, where they are more resistant both to thyminelessness and to UV.

Comparing UV responses of sensitive (log phase) or resistant (stationary phase or immune) cultures, it is found that (1) the final exponential portions of the survival curves are parallel, (2) the photoreactivable sectors of both cultures have the same constant value for all UV doses, and (3) the photoreactivation rates depend directly on UV dose and only indirectly on survival. It is concluded that, for the same UV dose, photoreactivable damage is qualitatively and quantitatively identical in the sensitive and resistant cultures. Various considerations lead to the tentative conclusion that the nonphotoreactivable damage is also identical. This suggests that both types of damage are subject to a "dark recovery" in the UV-resistant cells.

M3. *Photoreactivation of Killing of* Streptomyces griseus *Conidia by Far Ultraviolet and Vacuum Ultraviolet Radiation (1500–2600 A).* JOHN JAGGER, R. S. STAFFORD*, and R. J. MACKIN,

Jr.*, Biology and Thermonuclear Divisions, Oak Ridge National Laboratory, Oak Ridge, Tennessee.

Conidia were irradiated in vacuum on millipore filters, and were then photoreactivated on the filters after placement on a nutrient agar surface. The inactivating source was a magnetically constrained DC carbon arc in argon at low pressure, emitting principally at 1548 A. Conidia were exposed to the entire spectrum of the arc, limited by various cut-off filters. Photoreactivation (PR) was done with Daylight fluorescent lamps (3500–7000 A). Survival curves were highly sigmoid above 2200 A, but changed to exponential form at lower wavelengths, indicating that the cells are killed primarily by different mechanisms above and below about 2000 A. The chromophore below 2200 A has not been identified. PR is low after vacuum UV killing, dropping to zero for 1548 A. If the chromophore in this region is nucleic acid, then (1) not all nonionizing damage to nucleic acid is photoreactivable, and (2) the photoreactivable lesion is associated primarily with the 2600 A absorption peak of nucleic acid. Constant dose reduction after PR was not observed for killing above 2200 A. The amount of light for maximum PR was found to be proportional to UV dose (rather than to survival) and to photoreactivable sector at all wavelengths, and PR was always single-hit. It is concluded that the nature of the photoreactivable lesion, as well as the mechanism of PR, is the same for all wavelengths below 2600 A.

M4. *Relation between Radiation Sensitivity of Bacteria and Response to Irradiated Bacteriophage.* Ruth F. Hill and Rose R. Feiner*, Radiological Research Laboratory, Department of Radiology, Columbia University, New York, New York.

UV-sensitive mutants of *E. coli* B have been obtained by UV-irradiation followed by examination of colonies formed by surviving cells. The frequency of such mutants among UV survivors is 1–2% and can be increased tenfold or more by postirradiation growth in the presence of crystal violet, an agent to which B is extremely sensitive. Among three mutants isolated without the use of crystal violet, one was as sensitive to this agent as the parent B whereas the other two and all of nine mutants isolated with the use of crystal violet were more resistant than B.

In this total of twelve UV-sensitive mutants, four had a greatly reduced ability to repair UV damage to the DNA of bacteriophage T1. The UV survival curves for the twelve mutants showed a wide distribution but no correlation between the degree of UV sensitivity and reduced ability to repair T1 DNA. Further evidence that these two properties may be dissociated was obtained by selecting for furacin-resistant mutants of the UV-sensitive mutants. Variants were found which, in addition to increased furacin resistance, showed increased resistance to UV but no increase of the ability to repair UV-damaged bacteriophage DNA. The possibility that a level of UV resistance equal to that of the radio-resistant mutant B/r may be present along with inability to repair UV-damaged bacteriophage DNA, remains open. (Work performed under AEC Contract AT(30-1)2740.)

M5. *The Protective Effect of Alcohols on the Lethal Action of Ionizing Radiation in* E. coli. John D. Earle* (Introduced by Henry S. Kaplan), Department of Radiology, Stanford University School of Medicine, Palo Alto, California.

Glycerol and other polyhydroxyl alcohols protect cells against the lethal effects of ionizing radiation [Burnett *et al., Proc. Soc. Exptl. Biol. Med.* **77,** 636 (1951); Marcovich, H., "Organic Peroxides in Radiobiology," p. 117, Pergamon Press, 1958; Alper, T., *Nature* **194,** 1245 (1962); Dewey, D. L., *Nature* **187,** 1008 (1960) and *Nature* **194,** 158 (1962); Erikson, R. L., and Szybalski, W., *Cancer Res.* **23,** 122 (1963)]. Alper, studying the effect of 1 *M* glycerol on *E. coli* B/r with radiations of various LET, suggested that its protective action was independent of the "oxygen effect." Dewey presented data showing that protection increased with increasing concentration up to 1.5 *M* glycerol, at which point a plateau was achieved. We have examined the protective action of glycerol, ethylene glycol, methanol, and other alcohols and sugars in organisms grown in the presence and absence of purine- and pyrimidine-analogue radiosensitizers. Kaplan *et al.* [*Nature* **194,** 662 (1962)] showed that the sensitization by purine analogues was abolished under anoxic conditions, while pyrimidine sensitization was unaffected. The alcohols examined protect, to the same extent, organisms with both classes of analogues incorporated; thus, where anoxia abolishes purine-analogue sensitization, the alcohols do not. This supports Alper's suggestion that glycerol does not protect by a mechanism involving oxygen. At 1 *M* concentration, dose reduction factors of 3.71, 2.03, and 1.42 were obtained in *E. coli* for glycerol, ethylene glycol, and methanol, respectively. This suggests that protection by these agents may be a function of the number of hydroxyls available on the protecting molecule. Other polyhydroxyl alcohols and sugars, including glucose, sorbitol, and erythritol have also been investigated.

M6. *Competition between Oxygen and Sulfhydryls in Effects on the X-Ray Sensitivity of Normal and* N-*ethylmaleimide Treated* E. coli *B/r.* IVAR JOHANSEN* and PAUL HOWARD-FLANDERS, Yale University School of Medicine, New Haven, Connecticut.

The radiosensitivity of microorganisms and the concentration of oxygen are related by: $D_n/D = (K + m\ [O_2])/(K + [O_2])$, where D_n, D, are the irradiation doses required under anoxia and at the oxygen concentration $[O_2]$ to cause a given biological effect, and K and m are constants. The value of K may reflect a competition between sulfhydryls and oxygen for radiation-induced radicals at the sensitive site in bacteria. To investigate this possibility, cells were treated with *N*-ethylmaleimide (NEM), a sulfhydryl binding agent. The amount of acid soluble —SH in the cells was reduced to between 0–10% of the value in untreated cells. As found by Bridges [*J. Gen. Microbiol.* **26,** 467 (1961)], the NEM treated cells were more sensitive to irradiation under anoxia. NEM treatment did not greatly reduce the value of K. The addition of mercaptoethanol at concentrations of 10 and 100 mM increased K approximately 10 and 100 fold respectively. These results suggest that the principal reactions with radiation-induced radicals (R·) at the sensitive sites in the bacteria, presumably the DNA, are: (1) R· + —SH → RH + S· (2) R· + O_2 → R—OO· (3) R· → unknown inactive products in the absence of O_3 or —SH. Reaction (3) is fast enough to predominate in anoxic NEM-treated cells.

M7. *Radiation Sensitivity of Normal and Sulfur Starved Bacteria.* D. C. HUSTON* and S. PERSON* (Introduced by Ernest Pollard), Graduate School Committee on Biophysics, The Pennsylvania State University, University Park, Pennsylvania.

Certain metabolites such as glutathione (GSH) are known to affect radiation sensitivity. Since the major component of the sulfur pool in *E. coli* B is GSH, it is, perhaps, possible to alter the radiation sensitivity by altering the cellular GSH content. Sulfur starvation results in a depletion of the sulfur pool.

We obtained survival curves for loss of colony-forming ability for suspensions of *E. coli* B and sulfur starved *E. coli* B irradiated with Cobalt gamma rays. The survival curves were identical both having a D_{37} of 3,000 r. When dissolved oxygen was replaced by nitrogen (by bubbling nitrogen through suspensions of normal and of sulfur starved cells) the resulting survival curves again were similar and showed a pronounced decrease in sensitivity.

It would appear that cellular GSH does not alter radiation sensitivity. In order to affect sensitivity, GSH may have to be present at the site of the primary radiation damage that leads to loss of colony-forming ability.

M8. *Studies of Radiation Effects in Suspensions of Bacteria Using Radioactive Oxygen*[15]. ARLENE HALKO*, JACQUES OVADIA, and JOHN SADAUSKIS*, Tumor Clinic, Michael Reese Hospital, Chicago, Illinois.

The enhancement of radiation lesions in the presence of oxygen in a wide variety of biological systems is well established. The essence of this investigation is the utilization of a tracer of radioactive oxygen to study the fate of the gas in the normal cell and the oxygen dependent lesion in the irradiated cell. $Oxygen^{15}$ is produced by the reaction O^{16} (gamma, neutron) O^{15} utilizing 30 MeV. bremsstrahlung from an electron linear accelerator on a liquid oxygen target. The oxygen decays with a half-life of 2.2 minutes by emission of a positron which is detected through its associated 0.51 MeV. annihilation gamma ray. The presence of O^{15} as a non-gaseous metabolic product which appears in a bacteria free filtrate was demonstrated in control experiments, with unirradiated *E. coli* B in glucose minimal media. No incorporation of O^{15} could be detected in unirradiated bacteria. However, studies of bacteria irradiated in buffered saline show a dose dependent incorporation of O^{15}.

M9. *The Effect of Degree of Hydration on Oxygen Dependent and Independent Mechanisms of X-Ray Damage in* Staphylococcus aureus. R. B. WEBB, Division of Biological and Medical Research, Argonne National Laboratory, Argonne, Illinois.

The physical and chemical studies previously applied to bacterial spores [E. L. Powers, *J. Cell Comp. Physiol. Suppl. 1,* **58,** 13–25 (1961); A. Tallentire and E. L. Powers, *Abstracts 2nd Intern. Congr. Rad. Res.* p. 197 (1962)] have been extended to the vegetative bacterium *Staphylococcus aureus.* Washed cells were mounted on membrane filters, dried anoxically overnight to a pressure of about 10^{-5} torr and equilibrated under vacuum for one hour to different vapor pressures of water. The cells were X-irradiated (50 kpv, HVL ~.07 mm Al) in the presence of oxygen or nitrogen at a dose-rate of about 16,000 r/min. The three primary components of X-ray damage previously identified in the spore clearly operate in this vegetative system. These are Class I, oxygen-independent either during or after irradiation, Class II, oxygen-dependent during irradiation, and Class III, oxygen-dependent after irradiation. Class I damage is enhanced by the presence of water and is suppressed by the presence of cysteine or glucose. Class II damage is suppressed by water. Class III damage is suppressed by water or nitric oxide. Although water enhances Class I damage, the overall effect of water in *S. aureus,* as in the bacterial spore, is protective. These results suggest that the widely observed oxygen-enhancing effect in biological systems may be caused by organic radicals that damage the cell only in the presence of oxygen (Class III damage). These radicals are long-lived in the dry cell and may be made ineffective by scavenging or annealing in the wet system in the absence of oxygen. (This work supported by the U. S. Atomic Energy Commission.)

M10. *Dose-Response Curves for Diploid Yeast Irradiated with X- and Ultraviolet Radiation.* J. BORSA* and D. V. CORMACK, University of Saskatchewan, Saskatoon, Canada.

Diploid cells of a culture of *Saccharomyces cerevisiae* were irradiated with 200 KVP X-rays. The X-irradiations were carried out both in air and in oxygen-free nitrogen. The following effects were studied as a function of dose: colony-forming ability, mutation to histidine and tryptophan independence and the appearance of abnormal colonies believed due to chromosomal effects. The survival curves for X-rays were sigmoidal with an extrapolation number of *1.5–1.6* whereas the survival curves for ultraviolet irradiation showed an extrapolation number of *20–25.* Mutation induction was found to increase with dose in a nonlinear manner, and appeared to be due to a two-hit effect. The formation of red-sectored colonies followed a saturation-type curve with the maximum value for u.v. somewhat lower than the value for X-rays. The dose-modifying factor of nitrogen for the X-irradiations was found to be *1.3–1.5* for all effects. The shapes of the dose-response curves are compared with predictions based on a form of the target theory.

M11. *Recovery of Yeast Following Heavy Ion Irradiation.* J. T. LYMAN*, R. H. HAYNES and C. A. TOBIAS, Donner Laboratory, University of California, Berkeley, California.

Following exposure of diploid yeast (*Saccharomyces cerevisiae*) to either X-rays, ultraviolet light or nitrogen mustard, a great increase in viability is observed if the irradiated cells are stored in distilled water (30°C) for 1 to 4 days before plating. The results of previous studies of this dark recovery process by Patrick and Haynes (at the University of Chicago) are consistent with the view that these cells possess enzymes which, under appropriate conditions, are capable of modifying a significant fraction of those radiation-induced molecular lesions which would otherwise lead to cellular inactivation. It is of some interest to know whether or not such a recovery mechanism can operate in cells irradiated with heavy ions, since it is not implausible to imagine that more severe local structural damage might be produced within the columns of dense ionization formed along the tracks of these particles. We have found that storage recovery can indeed occur in diploid yeast (strain X841) following irradiation by both carbon and neon ions with an energy of 10 MeV per nucleon. The recovery process appears to act as a constant dose-modifying agent over several decades of survival; the dose-modifying factor is approximately 2 for both ions, which is comparable to that observed for conventional X-rays. Thus, the storage recovery mechanism seems able to function equally well in cells damaged by either high or low LET radiations. (This work was supported jointly by the National Aeronautics and Space Administration and the U. S. Atomic Energy Commission.)

M12. *Modification of the Radiation Response of a Highly Resistant Bacterium.* A. K. BRUCE, Biology Department, State University of New York at Buffalo, Buffalo, New York.

The effect of *p*-hydroxymercuribenzoate (HMB) on the radiosensitivity of the resistant bacterium *M. radiodurans* has been studied and compared with the related organism *S. lutea,* and with *E. coli* B/r. Previous studies have demonstrated that *M. radiodurans* contains an extractable radioprotective compound which behaves similar to β-mercaptoethylamine (MEA). By inactivating the sulfhydryl groups present in the cell with HMB, a drastic increase in radiosensitivity of the cell would be expected, and is found. At a concentration of 0.1 μmol/ml, HMB reduces the LD/99 of *M. radiodurans* from 600 Kr to 80 Kr, a factor of about 8. The corresponding reduction of the LD/99 for *S. lutea* is from 80 Kr to 25 Kr, a factor of about 3.

Suspensions of these organisms have been exposed to 40 Kr of X-radiation while in various concentrations of HMB (10^{-5} -2 μmol/ml) and survival determined. At this dose both *E. coli* and *S. lutea* require 10^{-2} μmol/ml to reduce survival to 0.1%, while *M. radiodurans* requires an extrapolated amount of 50 μmol/ml (necessary due to the solubility limit of HMB at pH 7). At a dose of 300 Kr, the concentration effect of HMB reduces the survivals of *M. radiodurans* to those of *S. lutea* and *E. coli* after exposure to 40 Kr.

These studies suggest that HMB modifies radiosensitivity by reaction with normal radical-trapping mechanisms, as observed in *E. coli* and *S. lutea,* and in addition removes the influence of a normally-occurring radioprotective agent in the organism *M. radiodurans.* By this mechanism the contribution of indirect effects is maximized. (Supported by USAEC.)

SECTION N. TUMORS AND OTHER EFFECTS IN HUMANS

N1. *Radiation Induced Thyroid Dysfunction in the Dog.*[1] SOL M. MICHAELSON, WILLIAM J. QUINLAN, JR.*, GEORGE W. CASARETT, and JOE W. HOWLAND, Department of Radiation Biology, University of Rochester School of Medicine and Dentistry, Rochester, New York.

Exposure of the head, neck, and thorax of the dog to X-irradiation of sufficient intensity re-

[1] This certifies that the experiments described in the paper "Radiation Induced Thyroid Dysfunction in the Dog" were conducted according to the "Rules Regarding Animal Care" as established by the American Medical Association.

sults in thyroid insufficiency after a latent period of time. In these investigations, groups of female beagles were bilaterally exposed to 907, 1215, 1820, and 2125 r midline air dose (MAD) of 1,000 KVP x-rays to the upper part of the body from the xiphoid process cephalad. Animals that survived the acute 60 day postexposure period were retained for observation of late manifestations. Approximately 18 months after exposure, dogs in the 2125 r and 1820 r groups began to appear sluggish and had abnormal weight gain. The skin became thickened with some pigmentation. These animals gave the appearance of clinical canine myxedema. Thyroid function evaluation was instituted at this time. All animals had minimal I^{131} uptake and high serum cholesterol levels (>200 mg/100 ml). Protein bound iodine determinations were depressed (2.21 ± 0.2 mcgm/100 ml). Injection of 12 or 15 units of thyroid stimulating hormone[2] (TSH) resulted in no increase, and in most cases, an actual decrease in protein bound iodine level among the irradiated dogs (1.22 ± 0.1 mcgm/100 ml). Injection of TSH in sham-irradiated controls resulted in a marked increase in PBI level (6.76 ± 0.3 mcgm/100 ml). At necropsy, the thyroids appeared atrophic. Histopathologic examination showed evidence of scarring, acinar destruction, focal calcification, and acute and chronic inflammation. (Work performed under Contract W-7401-Eng-49 with the United States Atomic Energy Commission and Contract DASAMD 960 with the United States Defense Atomic Support Agency.)

N2. *Effects of Whole-Body Irradiation on I-131 Metabolism in the Mouse.* CHANG W. SONG* and TITUS C. EVANS, Radiation Research Laboratory, University of Iowa, Iowa City, Iowa.

The action of whole-body X-radiation on thyroidal I-131 uptake and release was studied in mice. The animals were fed a low iodine diet for seven days before sacrifice. In the thyroidal uptake experiment, mice were exposed to 1000 r of 250 kvp X-radiation and the 6 hour I-131 uptake was measured. The X-irradiated mice showed increased thyroidal I-131 accumulation soon after irradiation but it began to decrease 12 hours after irradiation and was about half of the control value at 48 hours. In the thyroidal releasing experiment, beginning 20 hours after injection of I-131, 1 mg of propylthiouracil (PTU) in 10% gum acacia in saline was given daily to block further accumulation of I-131. Twenty hours after the first PTU injection, one group of mice was exposed to 1000 r and the changes of thyroidal radioactivity were observed. The biological half-life of thyroidal radioactivity was observed. The biological half-life of thyroidal radioactivity after PTU injection was about 16 hours in the control animals. The 1000 r exposure inhibited the decrease in thyroidal radioactivity for about six hours and after that the releasing rate returned to the control value. The earlier increase of thyroidal I-131 activity by X-irradiation may be due to decreased releasing rate. (This work was supported in part by a grant from the Division of Biology and Medicine of the U.S.A.E.C.)

N3. *Effect of Age at Irradiation upon Life Span Functions in the Rat.* D. C. JONES and D. J. KIMELDORF, U. S. Naval Radiological Defense Laboratory, San Francisco, California.

Male rats (average number/group = 127) were exposed to a single whole-body high sublethal (30 day) dose of fast neutrons (220 ± 10 rads) at one of five ages ranging from the juvenile to the late adult stages of life. Life span functions for these groups were compared with those of littermate controls. For nonirradiated control groups of this Sprague-Dawley strain the median life span was 703 days (S. D. = 41 days). In terms of the median or mean survival time, life expectancy, age-specific death rate, and survival curve, there was a marked detrimental effect of irradiation in animals exposed at one month of age. This radiation effect diminished progressively when exposure occurred at 3 or 10 months of age, and was no longer discernible in groups exposed at 15 or 21 months. For those age groups (1, 3, or 10 months) which exhibited

[2] Thyroid Stimulating Hormone kindly supplied by Endocrinology Study Section, Division of Research Grants, National Institutes of Health.

a significant alteration in life span functions, there was a latent period of seven to ten months before the effect became apparent. It appears that age at exposure is an important stipulation for consideration of long-term effects of irradiation. Further, it appears that animals exposed to sublethal (acute) doses of radiation after full adulthood has been attained may show little or no alteration in life span functions.

N4. *A Uniformity of Life-Shortening among Genetically Different Mice under Daily Gamma Radiation.* D. GRAHN, G. A. SACHER and K. F. HAMILTON*, Division of Biological and Medical Research, Argonne National Laboratory, Argonne, Illinois.

Mice of strains BALB/c, A/Jax, $C3H_f$/He and C57BL/6 plus the F_1 and F_2 generations of the BALB/c:C57BL cross have been exposed for the duration of life to Co-60 γ-radiation, beginning at 100 days of age. Time of death and associated pathology were recorded at doses of 56, 43, 32, 24, 12, 5 and 0 r/day where survival is 100 days or more. A detailed companion study on the LAF_1 mouse demonstrated a linear relation between log mean after-survival from start of exposure (MAS) and arithmetic daily dose. The slopes of the ln (MAS)/r/day relation were −0.0363 and −0.0367 for males and females respectively. For the four inbreds and two hybrids noted, the values range from −0.0325 to −0.0403 for males with a common value of −0.0381 ± 0.0017. For females, the values range from −0.0334 to 0.0406 with a common slope of −0.0385 ± 0.0016. Strain and sex differences are not significant indicating an invariance of life-shortening response as reported for these mice following acutely lethal single doses. Compared to the latter, the daily dose condition demonstrates little effective leukemia-induced life-shortening. In this and other studies underway, the dose-response relation does not include the control; predicted control MAS values are above the observed except for the long-lived hybrid. When MAS is 75–80% or more of control, survival is a complex function of genotype, sex, environment and dose. (Work supported by U. S. Atomic Energy Commission.)

N5. *Mammary Neoplasia Dose-Response Data in Partial-Body Irradiated Rats.* C. J. SHELLABARGER and R. W SCHMIDT*, Departments of Zoology and Pathology, University of Michigan, Ann Arbor, Michigan.

Female, Sprague-Dawley, litter-mate rats were exposed on day 42 of age, individually, to 250 kvp X-rays with the posterior half of the animal shielded. Groups of these animals have been studied for one year after being exposed to one of the following doses: none, 222r, 444r, 666r, 888r, and 1110r. None of the 30 nonexposed animals have developed any neoplasms. The number of rats with one or more mammary neoplasms, the starting number of animals, the total number of mammary neoplasms, the number of adenocarcinomas (AC) and the number of adenofibromas (AF) per exposure groups were: 222r 7 of 30, 7 neoplasms, 2 AC, 5 AF; 444r, 7 of 28, 10 neoplasms, 5 AC, 5 AF; 666r, 13 of 29, 20 neoplasms, 10 AC, 10 AF; 888r, 12 of 28, 21 neoplasms, 10 AC, 11 AF; 1110r, 7 of 26, 7 neoplasms, 4 AC, 3 AF. Only one of these 66 mammary neoplasms occurred outside the exposed area; 12 exposed animals have died, and 12 nonmammary neoplasms have been found in the 141 exposed animals. It appears that 666r and/or 888r induced the maximum mammary neoplastic response and that a further increase in exposure dose does not increase the response. It is suggested that the relative lack of response at the highest dose may be due to cell death. (Supported by USPHS Grant NIH CA 05496.)

N6. *Combined Treatment of Supralethal X-Irradiation and Subsequent Late Effects.* ROBERT T. BINHAMMER, Anatomy Department, University of Cincinnati College of Medicine, Cincinnati, Ohio.

Holtzman female rats 160 ± 5 gms were exposed to 1100, 1200, or 1300 r near total-body X-irradiation in a single exposure under nembutal anesthesia. Shielding of the head with ⅛ in.

lead sheet was carried out to eliminate oral complications. Bone marrow (approximately 25 mg) suspended in Tyrode's solution was transfused after removal from donors which had been pretreated with 12.6 mg/kg chlorambucil. Each rat was injected with 40 mg of streptomycin per day for 15 days. Control measures in various groups consisted of exposure without head shielding, infusion of Tyrode's solution and injection of saline daily for 15 days. Survival rates in the combined treatment groups were 85%, 37% and 29% for the 1100, 1200 and 1300 r exposures, respectively. Surviving animals were maintained for study of late effects. Of 85 animals which received 1100r 63 have died averaging a life span of 352 days. They showed a mammary tumor incidence of 42% and at autopsy 22% showed moderate to severe periarteritis nodosa in the mesentery. Of 48 animals which received 1200 r 38 have died with an average life span of 322 days. Mammary tumor incidence was 25% and 34% showed periarteritis. Only 23 animals survived 1300 r. Twenty have died showing an average life span of 315 days. Mammary tumor incidence was similar to the 1200 r group (26%), but the incidence of periarteritis rose to 50%. Mammary tumor incidence was reduced in all groups as compared with that in Holtzman animals receiving sublethal and lethal doses. (Supported by PHS Grant C-3390 from the National Cancer Inst.)

N7. *Studies on the Response of the Tumor Bed to Irradiation.* WILLIAM C. SUMMERS* and H. VERMUND, Department of Radiology Research Laboratory, University of Wisconsin Medical School, Madison, Wisconsin.

Local pretransplant irradiation of the site of inoculation has been shown to increase survival of C3H/WR mice grafted with gastric squamous cell carcinoma G8755, and of BDF_1 and C57BL mice grafted with gastric adenocarcinoma 328, mammary carcinoma 755, and melanoma B-16. The survival increment was proportional to the dose of radiation up to a maximum at 3000 r. For CA755, the maximal average survival was twice the survival of the control animals. This maximum appeared to be related to the growth rate of the tumor, since preirradiated hosts with slowly growing tumors showed a smaller survival increment (in percentage of the unirradiated controls) than preirradiated hosts with rapidly growing tumors. In addition, growth rate depression (ΔB) by pretransplant irradiation was related to the growth rate of the control (B); i.e., $\Delta B = 0.72B–0.013$. This supported the conclusion that survival increment was related to the growth rate of the control tumors. The time interval between irradiation and tumor grafting was varied from 1 to 254 days and no significant difference in survival increment was found. The data indicated that the radiation induced changes in the tumor bed were of a relatively permanent nature. (This work was supported by Grant T-66-D from the American Cancer Society.)

N8. *Local Recurrence Following a Small Dose of X-Radiation to the C3H Mouse Tumor.* W. RODGER INCH and JOHN A. MCCREDIE*, The Ontario Cancer Treatment and Research Foundation, London, Ontario; and Department of Therapeutic Radiology, University of Western Ontario.

The incidence of local recurrence was studied following administration of a one-third curative dose of X-radiation (2000 rads) to an established tumor. A small piece of the spontaneous mammary tumor occurring in C3H/HeJ mice was implanted into the subcutaneous tissues of first generation offspring and allowed to grow until the maximal dimension was 1.8 ± 0.1 cm (about 30 days). Excision of the tumor at this time was followed by a high incidence of local recurrence. Animals (183) were given radiation, using two parallel opposed fields, to the tumor and its bed 24 hours before excision, to the operative site 24 hours after excision, or to the normal tissue in front of the tumor on the day of operation. The incidence of local recurrence by 100 days was found to be decreased by preoperative but not by postoperative radiation. In addition the optimal interval between irradiation and removal of the tumor was studied using 386 animals; the tumor and its bed were given 2000 rads 1, 3, 7 or 13 days before excision. Preliminary results showed that the incidence of local recurrence was least when the tumor was excised three days following irradiation.

N9. *Time-Sequence Studies of Combination 5-Fluorouracil and Radiotherapy in a Transplanted Adenocarcinoma.* RICHARD P. SAIK* and MORTON M. KLIGERMAN, Department of Radiology, Yale University School of Medicine, New Haven, Connecticut.

Does an optimum time-sequence of two treatment modes exist in combination drug and radiotherapy? A mammary adenocarcinoma of the breast which arose spontaneously in our C_3H mouse colony is transplanted in the thigh of 215 mice. To minimize the influence of host factors, only the rate of decrease in size of the tumors is used in comparing the several treatment schedules in a model system. Bias was further reduced by treating tumors of uniform size and randomly assigning mice from all groups to particular cages after treatment to avoid cage effect. The study was composed of a series of 5 "smaller" identical experiments to further avoid chance events. The mice were randomized into 7 groups receiving: X-ray alone; drug alone; drug 15 minutes prior to X-ray; drug 3 hours prior to X-ray; drug 24 hours prior to X-ray; drug 24 hours after X-ray; and no treatment. 5-Fluorouracil was given in single intraperitoneal injection of 125mg/Kg, an LD_{19}. 500r X-ray (250kv, 15ma, 2mm Al filtration) in single dosage represented an ED_{40} for disappearance of tumor without cure.

Results revealed no significant difference between those receiving X-ray alone and any combination of X-ray and drug. This is at variance with previous reports in literature. There was only slight difference in growth rate between the controls and the mice receiving drug alone. Greater variation in response was noted within each group receiving X-ray than between the individual groups. (Work supported by U. S. P. H. S. Grant, C-4391.)

N10. *Mechanisms of Radiation Reduction in Host Resistance to Tumor Implants.* BADI MANSOUR BOULOS* and TITUS C. EVANS, Radiation Research Laboratory, Iowa City, Iowa.

Sarcoma 180 ascites tumor cells kept by serial transplantation in a local strain of Swiss albino mice were occasionally inoculated into C_{57} Black mice. The greater resistance of the C_{57} Black mice was indicated by more frequent failure to take than when Swiss mice were so inoculated. Host resistance of the C_{57} Black mice was also indicated by a greatly reduced growth in those cases in which the take was successful. Host resistance of the Black mice was reduced by giving the animal whole body irradiation 200–300 r, 2–3 days before inoculation. Host resistance was also reduced by local irradiation to the liver (300 r). Following whole body irradiation with liver shielded there was a slight reduction in host resistance. Manipulation of the liver in "sham" irradiated animals also showed a slight reduction in the host reaction. Previous inoculation with lethally irradiated cells (13K rads) especially with two "booster" doses 2–3 days before inoculation with viable cells, was effective in increasing the host resistance to tumor implantation in Swiss strain. Local liver irradiation (500 rads) two days before the "booster" doses was effective in lowering the resistance of the host to tumor implantation in the isologous type experiment. This shows a tendency for the liver irradiation to interfere with the sensitizing effect of the "booster" dose of heavily irradiated cells and as was found for the effect of irradiation on tumor resistance in the homologous type of experiment, the effect of irradiating of the liver was approximately half that of irradiation of the entire body.

SECTION O. EFFECTS ON SINGLE ORGAN SYSTEMS

O1. *Pharmacological Evidence Suggestive of Subtle Alteration in the Blood Brain Barrier of Head X-Irradiated Rats.* V. NAIR and L. J. ROTH, University of Chicago. Chicago, Illinois.

Our previous studies utilizing I^{131}-RISA and S^{35}-sulfate as indicators have shown that the blood-brain barrier (BBB) damage following head X-irradiation in the rat was of a subtle nature, in comparison to other forms of injury such as those following metrazol seizures [*Federation Proc.* (1962)]. It was felt that perhaps pharmacological indices and pharmacological agents might serve as more useful tools to demonstrate the subtle alterations in BBB following irradiation. The anticonvulsant drug, acetazolamide, which has a slow rate of entry into the normal brain, has been used in the present studies. It was found that in head X-irradiated rats (10,000r) anticonvulsant action of the drug was enhanced with respect to the potency, onset and duration of action [*Federation Proc.* (1963)]. These results suggested altered BBB function in the irradiated rat and to obtain more information on this matter the pattern of entry of acetazolamide into the CNS of rat has been studied using S^{35}-acetazolamide. In nonirradiated rats, there was no significant entry of acetazolamide-S^{35} into the brain at 30 min. after injection. Cerebrospinal fluid was not examined. In the irradiated rats (48-hrs. postirradiation) however, in comparison to the nonirradiated controls, increased amounts of the drug were found in the cerebral cortex, hippocampus and cerebellar cortex. This increase is compatible with the effect of enhanced anticonvulsant action of drug in irradiated rats noted by us. These results are suggestive of subtle alterations in BBB following irradiation, allowing increased penetration of drug into the brain. Preliminary studies in the irradiated rat given acetazolamide show EEG changes which are also in agreement with the above interpretation of subtle alterations in BBB.

O2. *Some Effects on Operant Conditioning of Ionizing Radiation to the Head.* W. LYNN BROWN, H. C. BLODGETT*, J. S. PIZZUTO*, and R. M. RITTER*, The University of Texas, Austin, Texas.

This report will examine changes in response rate on operant conditioning equipment following ionizing radiation to the head. Rats were trained to respond at approximately 25 responses/min. on a 10-to-1 food reinforcement schedule and then divided into five matched groups and were then given 0r, 1000r, 2000r, 4000r, and 8000r of X-irradiation to the head. When the performance of each animal is averaged across the six days of posttreatment testing, there is an inverse monotonic relationship between dose received and performance. That is, the higher the dose, the more inferior the performance, and there are no inconsistences in the relationship. The average performance for all groups tends to improve through day 3, then to decline through day 6.

There is a tendency for the performance trends to "fan out" over the six days of posttreatment testing; however, this is not a direct function of dose—the control group improves, the 100r group stays about the same and the other group drop in performance but the degree of drop for the posttreatment measures for these groups is in reverse order of dose. This is because the performance drop for the higher dose groups occurs earlier than for the lower dose groups.

O3. *Central Nervous System Neurotransmitters and Internal Irradiation.* ENRIQUE EGAÑA, School of Medicine, Santiago, Chile.

This paper deals with the results regarding the synthesis of ACh and the 5-HT content of the diverse CNS levels of internal β-(P^{32}) irradiated adult rats, studied in several experimental groups corresponding to different dose-rate, total-dose and experimental lapses which have been reported elsewhere. The ACh synthesis has been assayed by measuring the "diffusible", the "free" and "bound" of the tissue and the total synthesized ("diffusible" plus total of the tissue) in experiments where CNS slices or strips (brain cortex, hypothalamus, cerebellum, rhinencephalon, pons/medulla and spinal cord) were incubated in optimal eserineized medium in a Warburg vessel. Rectus abdominis was used as biological reagent. The 5-HT content of brain cortex, diencephalon, hypothalamus, rhinencephalon, mesencephalon and spinal cord was estimated by means of a modification of Vane technique with a sensitivity of 300–500 pg. The general results show: (1) at low dose of exposure, the synthesis of ACh and 5-HT increases particularly in the hypothalamus and rhinencephalon, during the first 48 hr after P^{32} administration, this phenomenon depending more on the dose-rate than on the total-dose. (2) In the chronic experiments (90–100 days) which correspond to higher total-dose there appears a decrease of the actual neurotransmitter content, this depending more on the total-dose accumulated in the CNS. Further studies are necessary to establish an overall picture of the general effect of irradiation on the metabolic process of central neurotransmitters. Studies on *l*-noradrenaline, GABA must be undertaken in this respect. (This work has been carried out with the aid of a Grant from the I.A.E.A., Vienna, Contract No. 95/RB1).

O4. *d-Glucose-1-C^{14} Uptake by Central Nervous System of Co^{60} Irradiated Rats.* RAMÓN VALDERAS*, SYLVIA FUENZALIDA* and ENRIQUE EGAÑA, School of Medicine, University of Chile, Santiago, Chile.

Groups of rats weighing 200 g are previously whole-body irradiated (Co^{60}) at total doses of 1,000–2,000–3,000 and 4,000 rad respectively. Dose-rate: 60,000 rad/hr. Sixty minutes after the exposure, the animals receive by intraperitoneal injection 5 μc D-glucose-1-C^{14} per 100 g rat. The whole encephalon C^{14} uptake is measured at 2 and 6 hr after C^{14}-glucose administration. To prepare the encephalon extract, Van Slyke Folch-Pi method is used; the radioactivity of the CNS samples is measured with a windowless flowcounter. Also the expiratory $C^{14}O_2$ is collected and sampled at different lapses (every 30 min during 6 hr). Normal rats, used as control, received the same amount of glucose-C^{14}. Up to this stage, results show a greater C^{14} uptake by the encephalon of irradiated rats compared to normal; the differences being more significant at lapses greater than two hours. At the same time, the expiratory $C^{14}O_2$ decreases in the irradiated animals the CNS of which shows higher C^{14} uptake. Chromatographic analyses complete these studies. (Work has been carried out with the aid of a Grant from the I.A.E.A., Vienna; Contract No. 95/RBI).

O5. *P^{32} Uptake by Internal Irradiated Central Nervous System; a Comparative Study between Autoradiographic and Counting Methods.* SYLVIA FUENZALIDA* RAMÓN VALDERAS* and ENRIQUE EGAÑA, School of Medicine, University of Chile, Santiago, Chile.

Adult internally β-irradiated rats (P^{32} given intraperitoneally) are divided in different experimental groups. The details of exposure have been published elsewhere. The P^{32} uptake for the counting studies is measured in the different levels of CNS: brain cortex, subcorticalis white matter, diencephalon, hypothalamus, cerebellum, rhinencephalon, mesencephalon, pons/medulla and spinal cord. The autoradiographic studies have been carried out with a "sagittal section" of the encephalon in a manner so as to include all levels of the encephalon from brain cortex up to the cervical spinal cord; the thickness of the "sagittal" slices being 0.1–0.2 mm. X-ray plates of high sensitivity were used; the specific activity was densitometrically measured. By comparing the uptake results both by simple counting of slices of the diverse CNS levels and by the autoradiographic method, it has been found that they coincide quite accurately. On the other hand, both studies (counting and autoradiographic) conform to the chromatographic results obtained by the authors on the P^{32} uptake by the different phosphorus compound of the whole encephalon and its different levels. Among these, rhinencephalon, hypothalamus and cerebellum are the most active in the P^{32} uptake. (This work has been carried out with the aid of a Grant from the I.A.E.A., Vienna; Contract No. 95/RB1).

O6. *Irradiation of Scotopic Visual Receptor.* WILLIAM W. DAWSON, Psychology Division, U. S. Army Medical Research Laboratory, Fort Knox, Kentucky.

Action potentials were recorded from primary fibers of the optic nerve in *Limulus*. Under scotopic conditions "on" discharges which were related to phosphenes were observed during irradiation. Reductions in the minimal light threshold under stable scotopic conditions were demonstrated to follow cumulative X-ray doses in a linear fashion. Total doses of < 100r normally reduced light threshold by 0.8 log units. Some preparations exhibited 2.0 log unit gains in light sensitivity. Control measures indicated a loss of sensitivity with time which was anticipated with pathology of the system. The hypothesis of photochemical effect was tested and confirmed electrophysiologically.

Extracts and rod fragment suspensions were made from the retinae of *Rana catesbiana*. Difference absorption spectrophotometry of these irradiated solutions was performed. λ Max. absorption points were found at 500 mμ for digitonin bound rhodopsin and at 520 mμ for rod end suspensions. "Tagging" of the suspended samples by cytochrome C indicated that the 20 mμ shift is not due to scatter phenomena. Both types of rhodopsin preparations exhibit transient increases in density following irradiation which support the electrophysiological data. Recent publications which substantiate an enzyme theory of rhodopsin function were discussed in this context.

O7. *Dose-Effect Studies with Tritiated Thymidine.* L. D. SAMUELS, W. E. KISIELESKI and P. C. HILEY*, Division of Radiological Health, Public Health Service, Iowa City, Iowa; and Division of Biological and Medical Research, Argonne National Laboratory, Argonne, Illinois.

Measurement of toxicity of tritiated thymidine is complicated by the difficulty in applying conventional units of radiation measurement to the beta emission from intranuclear tritium, as tritiated thymidine, incorporated into DNA. Using techniques of radiochemical analysis and autoradiography and following the example of Oakberg, who has used mouse testis as a substrate for measuring the cytological effects of X- and γ-rays, we have extended studies on the cytology of mouse testis to several dose levels of tritiated thymidine. Observations of Johnson and Cronkite that a definite cytotoxicity in the mouse testis can be demonstrated following intraperitoneal administration of tritiated thymidine have been confirmed. Correlation of cell death, measured by counting resting primary spermatocytes, with factors influencing total radiation dose has been attempted. The factor best correlated with cell death is the number of disintegrations per cell. Consideration of disintegrations per cell nucleus takes into account not only direct radiation effect but also possible chemical transmutation effects and disruptive effects of recoil energies. We suggest that disintegrations per cell be used to quantitate exposure to tritium incorporated into vital cell molecules. Further work on quantitating cell populations actually incorporating tritiated thymidine is needed to better apply this technique. Factors influencing the labeling index also need further study. (Work supported by U. S. Atomic Energy Commission).

O8. *Cell Division in the Small Intestine of Rats Exposed to Continuous Gamma Irradiation.* S. LESHER, L. F. LAMERTON, and G. A. SACHER, Division of Biological and Medical Research, Argonne National Laboratory, Argonne, Illinois.

Much evidence has accumulated concerning the effects of brief single exposures on all stages of the generation cycle of rapidly dividing cells, but less is known concerning the effects of long-continued periodic exposure. In an earlier experiment it was found that the proliferative cells of the duodenum of mice exposed to 12 r per day (12 hour protraction) for 200 days had a generation cycle with no detectable abnormalities, and generation time equal to or perhaps slightly less than control. In this report data will be presented concerning the effects of continuous gamma irradiation on the generation cycle of the crypts of the rat small intestine. Male and female 42-day-old AMF_1 hybrid rats (August females × Marshall males) were caged separately and positioned in a caesium-137 unit to receive 50 rads per 23-½ hour day. After 12, 35, or 105 days exposure, rats were injected intraperitoneally with 100 μc of tritiated thymidine and returned to the irradiation chamber until sacrificed at intervals from ½ to 30 hours. Two groups of controls were similarly treated at 54 and 147 days of age. From autoradiographs of 3-μ sections, the percentage of mitotic figures labeled was determined and plotted against time. The first generation time following the injection of tritiated thymidine is the same in rats exposed for 12 and 35 days and in the 54-day-old nonirradiated animals but is at least an hour longer in the 105-day exposure group and even longer in the 147-day-old nonirradiated controls. Throughout all groups the first curve produced by the first division of cells labeled at time of injection is well defined and almost identical in shape and duration, but the control animals exhibit a clear deterioration of the second cycle which is not seen in the irradiated animals. The significance of these curves will be discussed with particular reference to the possible toxicity of tritiated thymidine. (Work supported by U. S. Atomic Energy Commission).

O9. *Skin Lesions in the Mouse from Alpha Particle Formation by Thermal Neutron-Boron-10 Reactions.* LEE E. FARR and T. KONIKOWSKI, University of Texas M. D. Anderson Hospital and Tumor Institute, Houston, Texas.

In the early development of neutron capture therapy procedures in patients, necrotizing skin lesions were extremely troublesome. The clinical problem has been skirted by turning a skin flap, but the mechanism and conditions under which the complication appears have remained unclear. The mechanism obviously could not be studied in patients and while the grosser outlines were elucidated by using the pig as the experimental subject, cost, difficulties of management and housing, and inability to carry out sufficient studies for statistical purposes made these animals of only modest usefulness. Better to evaluate the factors by which heavy particles of low penetration may cause this necrotizing skin lesion, we re-examine our extensive data on mice exposed under conditions similar to the patients and the swine to determine if despite histological differences in skin structure of mouse and pig or man, a similar lesion could not be produced in mice, and if it was uniformly produced by the reaction. A lesion has been produced on the leg of the mouse with appearances similar to that of man. Photographs of each will be shown. Vagaries of the production of the mouse lesion in relation to rad dose, and similar vagaries of skin complication in man will be compared and discussed. (Supported by the U. S. Atomic Energy Commission).

O10. *The Reaction of Melanophores to Irradiation in Various Portions of the Body of the Young Axolotl* (Siredon mexicanum). VICTOR V. BRUNST, Laboratory of Radiobiology, Roswell Park Memorial Institute, Buffalo, New York.

Many observations have been accumulated that show diversity in the reaction of melanophores to irradiation. In the tail of the young axolotl, in most cases the melanophores are very sensitive. On the other hand, in the choroid of the eye of the axolotl they are extremely resistant. In the cornea, the development of melanophores is stimulated by radiation. Although they do not occur in the normal cornea, they can be found in appreciable numbers in the irradiated cornea. Stimulation of development of melanophores was also observed in the liver in irradiated animals.

A special investigation was initiated to compare the reaction of melanophores in the posterior and anterior portions of the body of the young axolotl. One month after hatching, 175 axolotls were divided into seven groups. In 3 groups, the anterior portion of the head was irradiated with 500, 1500 and 3000 r respectively; in another 3 groups, the posterior portion of the body was irradiated with the same doses; and one group served as untreated controls. The conditions of irradiation were as follows: 100 kv, 5 mA, 0.25 mm. Al filter, 0.55 H.V.L., T.O. distance 15 cm. In the tail after irradiation, the pigment layer is gradually reduced. After irradiation of the anterior portion of the head with the same doses, in most cases the melanophores do not change at all. This showed that a considerable difference does exist in the reaction of the same cells to irradiation in various portions of the body.

O11. *Further Studies of Kidney Function in Mice as Measured by a Salt-Water Tolerance Test.* JOHN S. KREBS and RALPH W. BRAUER, U. S. Naval Radiological Defense Laboratory, San Francisco, California.

Studies reported at a previous meeting concerning maximum urinary concentrating ability of mice in relation to age and previous radiation history [*Radiation Res.* **12,** 450 (1960)] have been continued. The additional results confirm those originally found, namely that the urinary concentrating ability, as measured by the NaCl tolerance test, depends upon age and irradiation history of the animal. The nature of the test applied raises two important questions: (1) does the measured concentration of solids in urine agree with the results inferred indirectly by the test? (2) Is the assumed response of the animal to the test situation the only one available to it? Question (1) is answered directly. The urinary concentrations of sodium, potassium, and urea in mice required to drink water containing various concentrations of NaCl have been measured, and a satisfactory account can be made of the volume of urine and the concentration of these substances in urine, in relation to the calculated maximum concentration. Question (2) is answered indirectly, in that the consistency of results obtained is far too great to result from random behavior of animals in a free-choice situation. Nevertheless, the test remains a measurement of water conserving ability in a specific environmental situation, and changing the nature of the test may elicit other environmental responses by the animal. The nature and significance of the responses available to the animal will be discussed.

O12. *Angiographic Changes in Irradiated Kidneys in Dogs.* KLAUS RANNIGER* and MELVIN L. GRIEM, Department of Radiology, The University of Chicago, Chicago, Illinois.

Thirty dogs have been irradiated with varying depth doses from 2500 to 3500 r to one kidney in two to three weeks. Prior to and at different time intervals following the irradiation, serial angiograms of both kidneys were performed. Preliminary results show that roentgenologically demonstrable changes in the treated kidney occur at all dose levels over 3000 r depth dose. These are first seen five to seven months following irradiation and consist of changes in the small arteries. Later, cortical atrophy is noted with decrease of the size of the kidney. Urinalysis is performed frequently and blood pressure is recorded. The work is in progress.

RADIATION RESEARCH 19, 247–260 (1963)

Relative Ultraviolet Sensitivity of Different Phases in the Cell Cycle of Chinese Hamster Cells Grown *in Vitro*[1]

RONALD M. HUMPHREY, WILLIAM C. DEWEY, AND ANN CORK

Department of Physics, The University of Texas, M. D. Anderson Hospital and Tumor Institute, Texas Medical Center, Houston, Texas

INTRODUCTION

Investigations of the radiosensitivity of mammalian cells *in vivo* and *in vitro* during different phases of their cell cycle have been made by chromosomal analysis after irradiation with Co^{60} γ-rays (*1, 2*). The deoxyribonucleic acid (DNA) synthetic period (S) is the most sensitive to ionizing radiation for mouse L and ascites tumor cells (*1*), and the post-DNA synthetic period (G_2) is the most sensitive for Chinese hamster cells (*2*). The pre-DNA synthetic period (G_1) was less sensitive in these cell lines.

Investigations of the induction of chromosomal breaks by ultraviolet (UV) radiation have been reviewed recently by Wolff (*3*). Earlier work with *Drosophila* (*4*) and with pollen tubes of *Tradescantia* (*5*) showed that only single chromatid breaks were produced by UV radiation. However, more recent work by Fabergé (*6*) with maize pollen has shown that dicentrics, exchanges, and inversions could be obtained, although simple breaks were the most frequent type of damage observed.

The present study shows that mammalian cells also exhibit chromosomal damage after UV radiation, and that this damage is observed both as single chromatid breaks and as exchanges. More specifically, by pulse-labeling the cells with tritiated thymidine immediately before irradiation, it was possible to observe chromosomal damage in cells irradiated in the various phases of the cell cycle.

EXPERIMENTAL PROCEDURE

The cell line of Chinese hamster (B-14FAF28), culture conditions, labeling procedure, sampling procedure, slide preparation, autoradiography, and microscopic analysis have been described in detail (*1, 2*).

The modifications for UV have been primarily in the growth vessels and irradiation arrangements. The cells (1×10^6) were plated into 60-mm petri dishes and

[1] This work was supported in part by the National Cancer Institute grant No. C-4484.

incubated overnight in a 7% CO_2 atmosphere which maintained a pH of 7.0 to 7.2. After a pulse-label for 10 minutes with tritium-labeled thymidine[2] (HTDR, 0.5 μc/ml and 1.9 c/mM), the cells were washed twice in Hank's balanced salt solution (without phenol red indicator) containing 10 μg of unlabeled thymidine (TDR) per milliliter. The final wash was drained as completely as possible, the lid removed, and the petri dish bottom irradiated immediately with UV (100 ergs/mm^2) in the 2537-A range. The UV source consisted of two 15-watt General Electric germicidal lamps which emitted 8.3 ergs/mm^2/sec at the exposure distance. Calibration was made with a varistor bolometer in a standard bridge circuit, which was calibrated with a National Bureau of Standards standard lamp. The monolayer of cells is believed to have received a uniform dose of UV, since there was relatively little overlapping of cells, and the salt solution, which itself absorbed only 5% of the incident light, had been mostly removed.[3] Immediately after irradiation, conditioned medium containing 10 μg of TDR per milliliter was added to the petri dishes, and incubation in CO_2 was continued. Samples were taken every 2 hours over a 16-hour period by the addition of colcemid (0.06 μg/ml) to the medium. This arrests cells in metaphase 1 hour prior to fixing the cells. The cells were removed from the dish by trypsinization and washed with hypotonic citrate (1%), and the pellet was fixed with 50% acetic acid. Autoradiographs were prepared by applying stripping film (Kodak AR-10) to the slide and exposing it for 7 days, which gave about 30 to 50 grains per cell. It has been shown that this amount of labeling produces less than 0.05 break per cell (unpublished data). Fifty labeled and 50 unlabeled well-spread metaphase figures were scored at each time interval for chromosomal damage, i.e., single breaks and exchanges, which are scored as two breaks.

The mitotic index (metaphase figures per 100 cells) was scored on at least 300 cells at each time interval of the irradiation without regard to label.

RESULTS

The life cycle of control and irradiated cells can be determined from Fig. 1, where the frequency of labeled metaphase figures is plotted against time after labeling and irradiation. Each point is plotted one-half hour before fixing, since colcemid was added to the sample 1 hour prior to fixing. It was previously reported (*2*) that the average generation time in control cells was 11 hours, and the S period was about 6 hours. The present series of experiments indicate an average generation time of 11.5 hours and an S period of 6 hours. At 1 hour only 10% of metaphases were labeled, indicating that most cells entering mitosis at this time were in G_2 at the time of labeling. At 2.5 hours one-half of the cells in metaphase were labeled,

[2] Obtained from Schwarz BioResearch, Inc.

[3] Clone survival measured to values as low as 0.05% after UV radiation has not demonstrated a resistant fraction; this indicates that less than 0.05% of the cells are protected by overlapping.

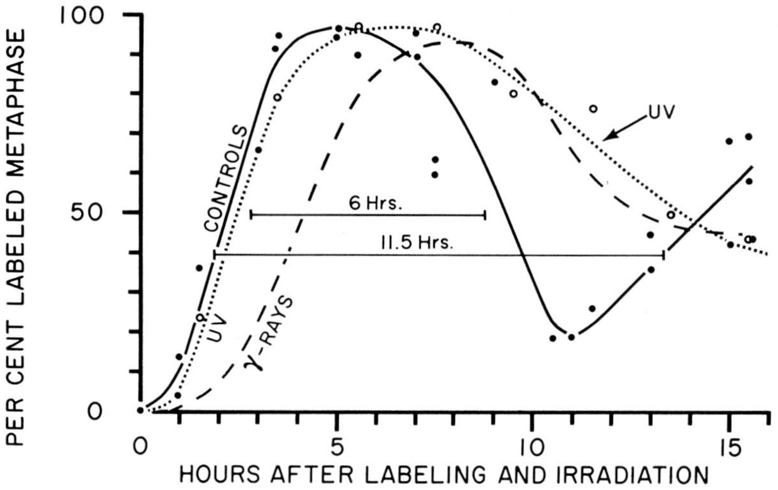

FIG. 1. The percentage of metaphases labeled in the Chinese hamster cells plotted against time in hours after labeling with HTDR and irradiation with 100 ergs of UV per square millimeter. The generation time in the control cells was 11.5 hours. The mitotic delay in cells irradiated with UV was 30 minutes, but was 2.0 hours for cells irradiated with 250 rads of Co^{60} γ-rays. The length of the S phase is indicated as 6.0 hours.

which indicates that the G_2 period, including time to complete mitosis, is about 2.5 hours in duration; this leaves about 3.0 hours for the G_1 period.

A UV dose of 100 ergs/mm^2 was used in the radiation experiments presented here. Ultraviolet survival curves for strain B-14 taken through four decades of survival have yielded a mean lethal dose (D_0) of 50 ergs/mm^2 and an extrapolation number of about 4. Thus, the UV dose of 100 ergs/mm^2 is equivalent to twice the D_0 and results in 40 to 45% survival. This dose of UV produced a mitotic delay of about 30 minutes for cells in the latter part of S phase at the time of irradiation as determined by the delay in reaching the point where 50% of the metaphases were labeled.

It should be noted that, although the ascending portions of the control and irradiated curves in Fig. 1 are quite similar in shape, the descending portion of the irradiated curves does not decrease nearly so rapidly as for the controls. Reasons for this difference can be deduced from the mitotic indices. The mitotic indices of the controls ranged from 4.0 to 6.0, whereas for the irradiated samples they were as follows: 3.2 at 2.5 hours postirradiation, 1.3 to 2.3 at 3.5 to 11.5 hours, and 3.0 to 3.3 at 13.5 to 15.5 hours. This decrease in the mitotic index for irradiated cells must result either from a decrease in the rate at which cells are entering division or from a decrease in the time required to complete mitosis. Since radiation tends to lengthen the mitotic interval, the latter is excluded. Therefore, the dip in the mitotic index which occurred from 3.5 to 11.5 hours after irradiation, when the majority of the dividing cells were labeled, clearly indicates that the labeled cells were progressing through their cell cycle at a reduced rate (a long mitotic lag). Thus, the curve plotting the per cent of metaphases labeled does not dip so rapidly for the irradiated cells as it does for the controls.

It is assumed that the unlabeled metaphases observed prior to 5 hours after irradiation were in G_2 at the time of irradiation, and that the unlabeled cells observed at 11 hours postirradiation were in G_1 phase. This is a reasonable assumption because the curve of labeled metaphases in Fig. 1 rises to 100%, thus indicating that the two populations of unlabeled cells (G_1 and G_2) were separated by the labeled cells which were synthesizing DNA at the time of irradiation. It is probable that the unlabeled metaphases sampled at 14 and 16 hours consisted to a large extent of G_2 cells dividing for the second time.

Cells in different parts of the S phase at the time of labeling can be identified by counting grains in the metaphase cells. Figure 2, which plots for control cells the average grain count per cell as a function of time after labeling, indicates that cells labeled in either early or late S phase have about one-half the grain count of cells labeled in the middle of S phase. This was reported previously by Looney (7)

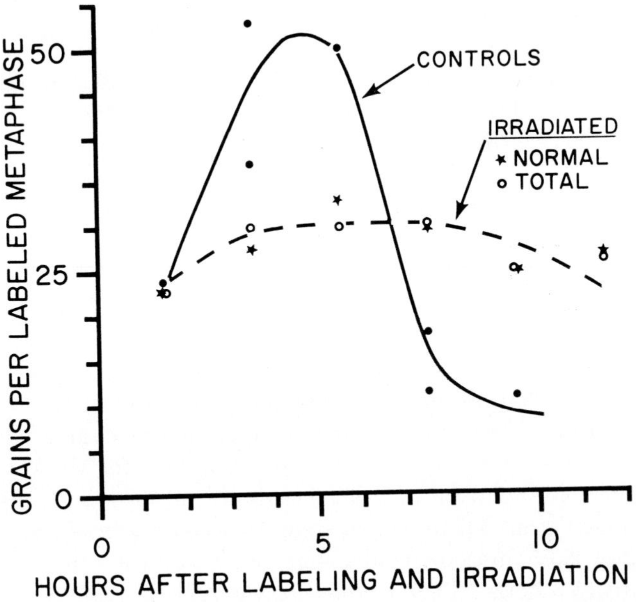

FIG. 2. The grain count per cell at various times after labeling and irradiation with 100 ergs of UV per square millimeter. For grain counts, cells used in the chromosome analysis were chosen. The curve labeled irradiated fits points for both cytologically normal and abnormal cells.

and is attributed to the fact that the rate of DNA synthesis is greatest during the middle of the S phase. For cells irradiated with UV, however, the peak in the grain count curve is eliminated. This indicates that some of the cells which were in late S phase at the time of irradiation were delayed abnormally and thus mixed with cells which were in the middle of the S phase. Furthermore, the plateau in the curve indicates that some of the cells which were in the middle S phase lagged sufficiently in order to mix with cells which were in the early S phase. It should be noted that this mixing in S-phase populations occurred in cells which were both normal and abnormal cytologically.

Figure 3 illustrates the damage observed in labeled and unlabeled Chinese hamster cells at various time intervals after labeling and irradiation with UV. Figure 3*a* shows a metaphase figure (fixed 2 hours after irradiation) which was in G_2 phase at the time of labeling; hence, no grains are found associated with the chromosomes. Figure 3*b* shows a labeled metaphase figure (fixed 2 hours after labeling and irradiation) which was in S phase at the time of labeling. The damage observed is primarily single chromatid breaks. Figures 3*c* and 3*d* are metaphase cells obtained from samples fixed 14 hours after irradiation. Figure 3*c* shows a labeled cell which was in S phase at the time of labeling (S phase sampled late), with gross damage, and Fig. 3*d* shows an unlabeled cell (chromatid exchange, chromatid break, and ring) which was in G_1 phase at the time of irradiation.

Figure 4 represents the frequency of chromosomal damage as a function of time after irradiation for control and irradiated cells. For control cells the damage in labeled and unlabeled cells is not indicated separately, since there was no difference between these two groups with respect to the small amount of spontaneous damage present (0.10 break per cell). The unlabeled cells sampled immediately after irradiation (those in division at the time of irradiation) showed the same amount of chromosomal damage as the controls. During the first 4 hours postirradiation, the UV-induced damage of 0.5 to 1 break per cell in unlabeled cells (cells in G_2 phase at the time of irradiation) is higher than the 0.25 break per cell in labeled cells sampled early (cells in S phase at the time of labeling and fixed at 2, 4, 6, and 8 hours after irradiation). In fact, these S phase cells observed up to 8 hours after irradiation show only slightly more damage than the control cells. In labeled cells sampled late (cells in S phase and fixed at 10, 12, 14, and 16 hours after irradiation), more damage is evident to the extent that it is almost impossible to score some cells (Fig. 3*c*). For example, in the 16-hour sample, the S-phase cells had an average of about 8 breaks per cell, which is eight times that observed in the G_2 cells. The unlabeled cells in the time intervals beginning at 11½ hours consisted of cells which were in G_1 phase at the time of irradiation, and it is probable that cells sampled after 12 hours also consisted of G_2 cells which were in their second division after irradiation. The unlabeled cells sampled at these later time intervals show about

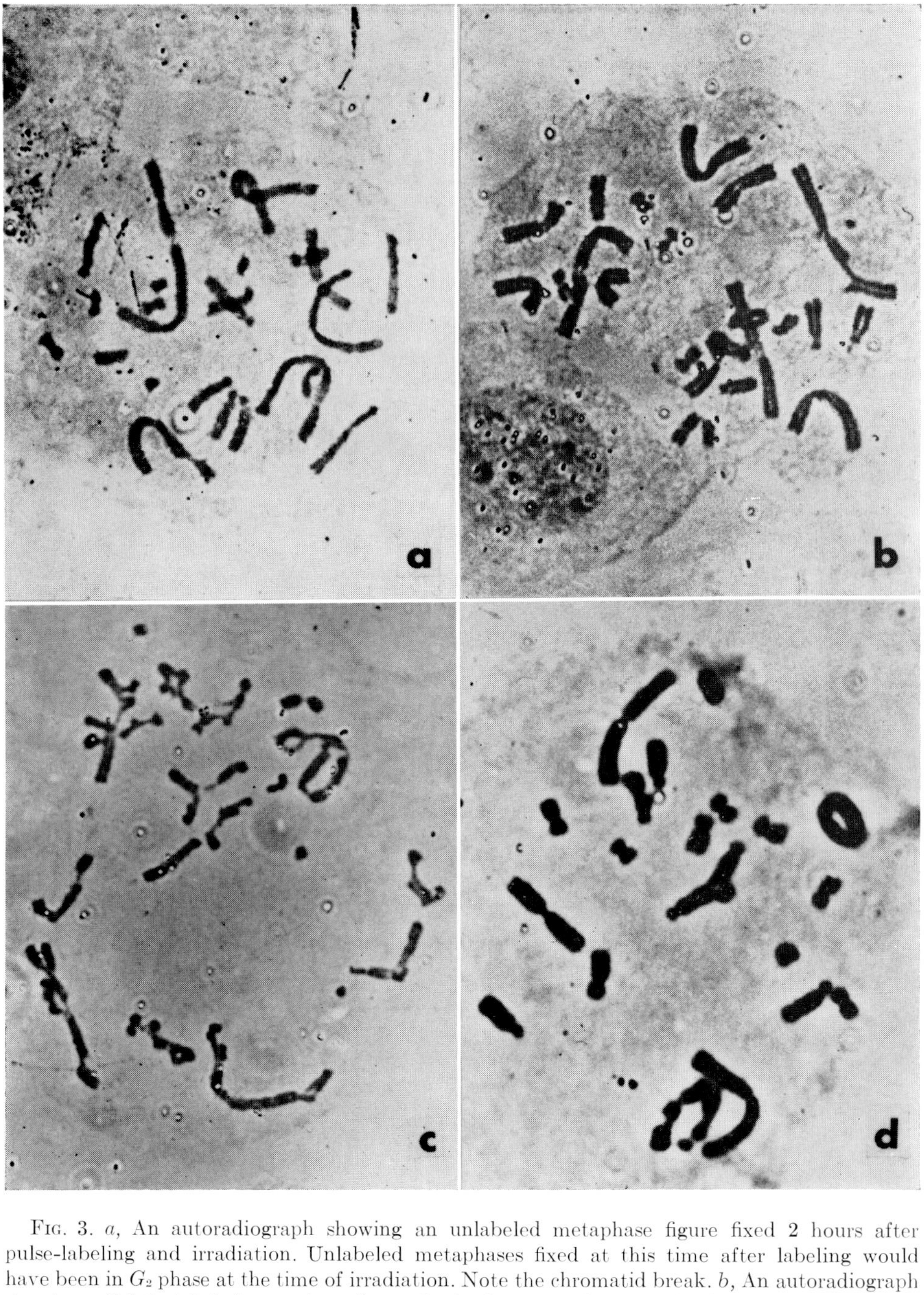

FIG. 3. *a*, An autoradiograph showing an unlabeled metaphase figure fixed 2 hours after pulse-labeling and irradiation. Unlabeled metaphases fixed at this time after labeling would have been in G_2 phase at the time of irradiation. Note the chromatid break. *b*, An autoradiograph showing a lightly labeled metaphase figure fixed 2 hours (early sample) after pulse-labeling and irradiation. Labeled metaphases fixed at this early time interval after labeling would have been in the *S* phase at the time of irradiation. Note the chromatid break. *c*, An autoradiograph showing a labeled metaphase figure fixed 14 hours (late sample) after labeling and irradiation. The cell was in the *S* phase at the time of irradiation. Note the extensive damage due to the chromatid breaks and exchanges. *d*, An autoradiograph showing an unlabeled metaphase figure fixed 14 hours after labeling and irradiation. The cell was in the G_1 phase at the time of irradiation. Note the breaks, exchange, and ring occurring in the same cell.

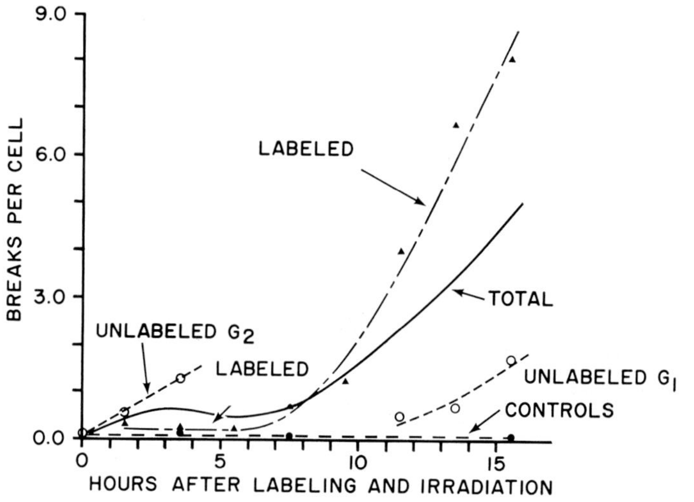

FIG. 4. The frequency of breaks per cell plotted against time after labeling and irradiation with 100 ergs of UV per square millimeter. The total number of breaks (an exchange is scored as two breaks) is divided by the number of cells scored. The unlabeled cells scored up to 4 hours were in the G_2 phase at the time of irradiation; labeled cells were in the S phase at the time of irradiation; and unlabeled cells scored at 11 to 15 hours probably consisted of both G_1 cells in their first division and G_2 cells in their second division after irradiation. The line marked *total* represents the irradiated population when no differentiation is made in regard to labeling; it was obtained by dividing the total number of breaks by the number of cells scored.

the same amount of damage as that seen in the G_2 cells sampled prior to 4 hours (0.5 break per cell).

In Fig. 5 the percentage of cells with at least one abnormality is shown, and the general pattern is similar to that shown in Fig. 4. The per cent of cells showing abnormalities was highest for cells in S phase sampled late (about 70%), less for cells in G_2 phase (about 45%), and least for cells in G_1 and S phases sampled early (about 20%). The cells in mitosis at the time of irradiation show no more damage than the controls (8% abnormal). It is significant to note in Figs. 4 and 5 that labeled cells sampled late have 4 to 8 breaks per cell, whereas 16 to 38% of the cells are normal. This is a significant deviation from the Poisson distribution ($P < 0.001$) in which only 0.03 to 2% should be normal.

Plotted in similar fashion in Fig. 6 is the number of breaks per cell due to dicentrics or chromosome exchanges, which are considered to be exchanges between two chromosome breaks, viz., breaks which involve both sister chromatids at the same locus and are believed to occur when the chromosome is effectively single (*8*). This contrasts with chromatid exchanges, which affect only one of the sister chromatids. The data show that cells irradiated with UV in either G_1, S, or G_2 do

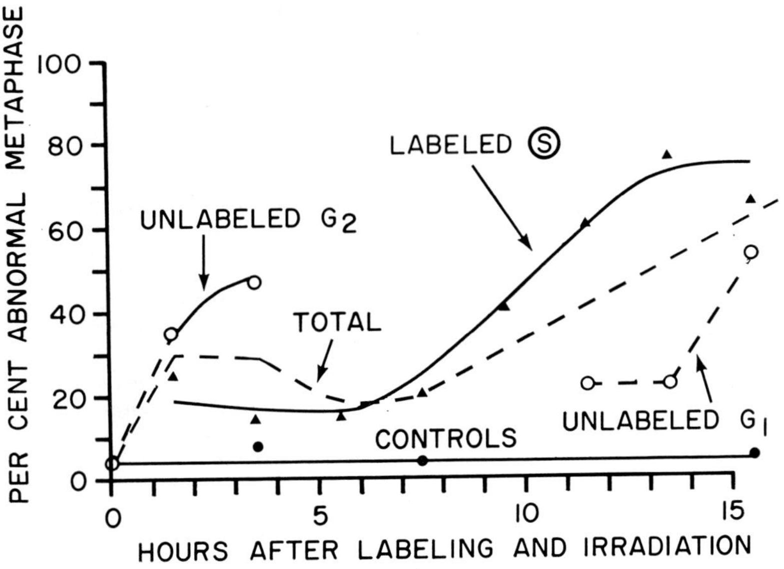

FIG. 5. The frequency of abnormal metaphases containing a minimum of 1 break among cells in different phases of the cell cycle at the time of irradiation. See Fig. 4 for details. The line marked *total* represents the irradiated population when no differentiation is made in regard to labeling; it was obtained by dividing the number of abnormal cells by the number of cells scored.

not differ significantly from each other and from control cells with regard to the frequency of chromosome exchanges.

In Fig. 7, the percentage of total breaks due to chromatid and chromosome exchanges is illustrated. It is obvious that breaks caused by UV radiation in this mammalian cell line are capable of rejoining to form exchanges. In fact, in both the G_1- and S-phase cells sampled late, the greatest fraction of breaks (70 to 90%) is elicited as exchanges. However, in G_2- and S-phase cells sampled early, a smaller fraction of damage (about 40%) results in exchanges. From Figs. 4, 6, and 7 it can be deduced that 70 to 100% of the exchanges are of the chromatid type in cells irradiated in any of the phases of the life cycle; in fact, the frequency of chromosome exchanges in irradiated cells (Fig. 6) is not greatly different from the frequency in control cells.

DISCUSSION

The primary objective of this study was to correlate chromosomal damage induced by UV radiation with the phase of the life cycle that the cell was in at the time of irradiation, and to compare these results with those obtained for ionizing radiation. The results show that UV radiation, like ionizing radiation, causes chro-

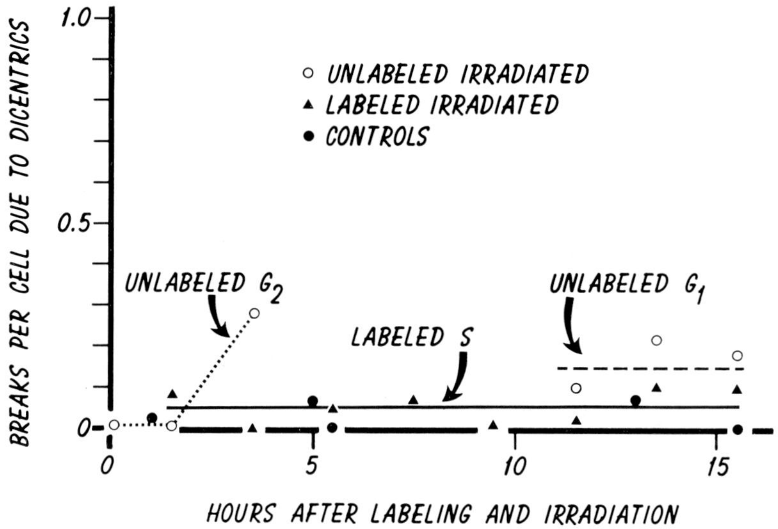

FIG. 6. The frequency of breaks forming dicentrics and chromosome rings among the cells in the G_2, S, and G_1 phases at the time of irradiation. These cells were irradiated with 100 ergs of UV per square millimeter.

mosomal damage in mammalian cells (Fig. 4), and this damage results in chromatid exchanges, as well as in simple chromatid breaks (Fig. 7). The observations were made after a single UV dose (100 ergs/mm^2) equal to two times the D_0 for the Chinese hamster B-14 cell line. The correlation between chromosomal damage, mitotic lag, and cell death after ionizing radiation has been discussed previously (*1, 9*), and these relationships are currently being investigated with different doses of UV. Two times the D_0 dose of UV produces in the S cells sampled early one-half as much chromosomal damage and one-fourth the mitotic lag (30 minutes as shown in Fig. 1) as a dose equal to two times the D_0 dose of ionizing radiation (*2, 10*).

When comparing chromosomal damage at doses around two times the D_0 dose, there are both similarities and distinct differences between UV radiation and ionizing radiation in terms of the cells in the population which are damaged, the level of damage which is expressed, and the type of damage which is observed. Figure 8 summarizes the differences in sensitivity of various stages of the cell cycle to UV and ionizing radiation (data taken from previous paper, *2*). The UV damage of 0.5 to 1 break per cell (Fig. 4) in G_2 cells at the time of irradiation (unlabeled cells of early samples) is two to four times as high as that in S phase cells sampled early, but about the same as that in the G_1-phase cells. After 250 rads of ionizing radiation, about two times the D_0 dose (*10*), there is also four to five times as much damage in the G_2 cells (2.9 breaks per cell) as in the S cells, and the amount of damage is about two to three times as great as for UV. However, S-phase cells sampled late

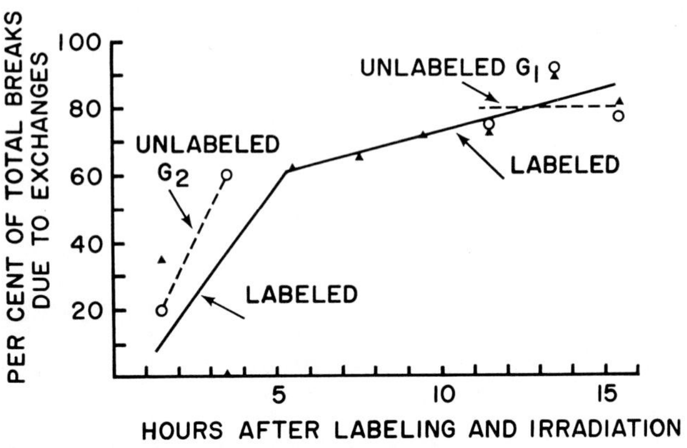

FIG. 7. The frequency of chromatid and chromosome exchanges among the cells in the G_2, S, and G_1 phases at the time of irradiation. These cells were irradiated with 100 ergs of UV per square millimeter.

in time after UV irradiation show an increasing amount of damage (average of 8 breaks per cell), becoming almost impossible to score in some cells (Fig. 4). This contrasts with the results for ionizing radiation in which S-phase cells sampled early and late after irradiation elicit a constant amount of chromosomal damage.

This increase in the amount of damage in the labeled cells which occurs as the cells are sampled at later time intervals after irradiation may be caused by two effects. First, the data in Fig. 2 indicate that there is a mixing of populations; i.e., some of the cells in the latter part of S are delayed in the life cycle to such an extent that they reach division at the same time as cells which were in an earlier part of S phase at the time of irradiation. Second, it may be that heavily damaged cells have a greater mitotic lag and are consequently sampled at later time intervals. However, the data in Fig. 2 also indicate that the mixing of the labeled populations occurs as well for cells which are cytologically normal. Therefore, the increase in the number of heavily damaged cells relative to the normal cells at the later time intervals must be due to a certain extent, at least, to real differences in radiosensitivity during the S phase. The distributions of these S cells deviate greatly from the Poisson distribution in that there are too many cells which are cytologically normal. This may be caused in part by the mixing of the populations, or it may be related to UV's affecting a certain site in the cell (such as the nucleolus), which leads to multiple chromosomal breaks.

An interesting picture is obtained when the frequencies of chromatid and chromosome breaks and exchanges are compared for ultraviolet and ionizing radiation. Chromatid breaks involve only one of the two sister chromatids, and the chromosome breaks involve both sister chromatids at the same locus. Chromosome breaks

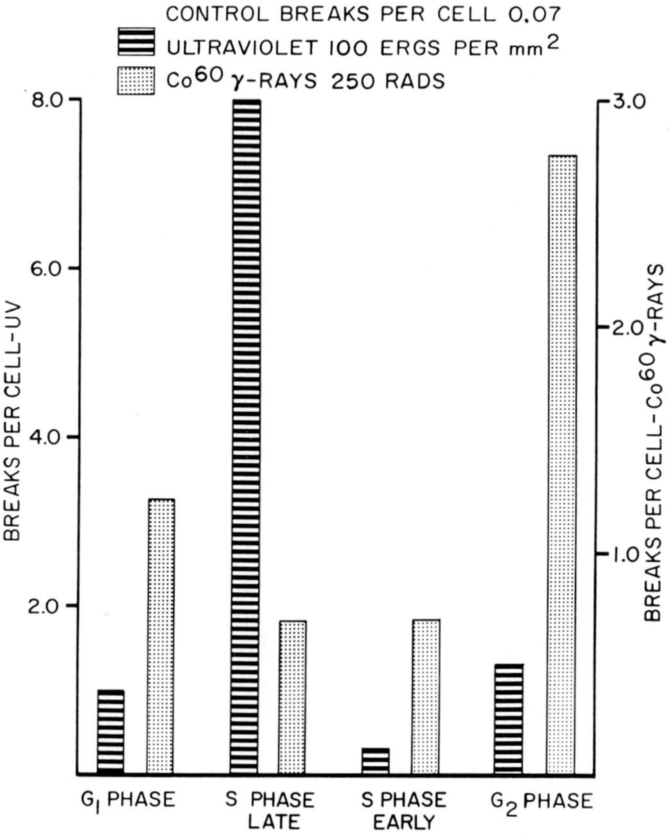

FIG. 8. The average frequency of breaks per cell (exchanges counted as two) in various phases of the hamster cell cycle for 250 rads of Co^{60} γ-rays and 100 ergs of UV per square millimeter.

are generally believed to occur before DNA synthesis when the chromosomes are effectively single (*8*). Earlier work on plant and insect material has shown that UV differs from ionizing radiation in that UV produces only single chromatid breaks and exchanges (*5, 11*), and, even in cases where all types of aberrations are observed, chromatid breaks are still the most prevalent type found (*6, 12*). Ionizing radiation, however, produces both chromatid and chromosome breaks and exchanges. After UV and ionizing radiations, the results show that in mammalian cells the type of break observed depends on the stage of the life cycle the cell was in at the time of irradiation. It has been shown that for ionizing radiation the larger fraction of the breaks in G_1 and S results in exchanges (*2*). Ultraviolet radiation is similar to ionizing radiation in that about 80% of the breaks in G_1 and S cells are also due to exchanges, as shown in Fig. 7. This means that breaks produced both by UV radiation and by ionizing radiation in the hamster cell line are capable of rejoining to form exchanges. In S cells sampled early and in G_2 cells exchanges are also possible but less prevalent; i.e., only 40 to 50% of the breaks are due to exchanges for both UV and ionizing radiation. A significant difference between the effects of the two radiations becomes apparent when the exchanges are classified as chromatid or chromosome (dicentric) exchanges. After ionizing radiation an increase in dicentrics above that seen in the controls is found only in cells which were in G_1 phase at the time of irradition; in fact, about 70% of the exchanges in the G_1 cells were due to dicentrics. However, after UV radiation only about 19% of the exchanges were due to dicentrics, and no significant distinction could be made between control cells and cells irradiated in G_1, S, and G_2 phases in regard to the frequency of dicentrics. This is in confirmation of previous work (*6, 10*) in which UV produced very little chromosome type of damage.

Both the high frequency of chromosome exchanges observed in cells irradiated in the G_1 phase with ionizing radiation and the low frequency after UV radiation are consistent with the chromosome model of Taylor (*13*). In this model the chromosome, although morphologically single, is actually composed of two subunits even at the time prior to DNA synthesis. During the S phase, the two subunits of the chromosome separate into sister chromatids and individually synthesize the complementary subunit. Thus, ionizing radiation apparently breaks with high probability both subunits in the G_1 cell, whereas the chromosome is effectively single, and that break, if it is retained throughout the period of chromosome replication, would be present on both sister chromatids at the same locus (isochromatid break). Two such isochromatid breaks on separate chromosomes with subsequent rejoining could lead to a dicentric. The probability of γ-radiation's inducing breaks at precisely the same locus of the two subunits, once separated, would be extremely low. Therefore, as discussed by Hsu *et al.* (*2*), the complete lack of dicentrics in S cells after ionizing radiation implies that the two subunits in all chromosomes must separate during the interval of a few minutes as the cell leaves the G_1 phase and enters the S phase. It was further postulated, since dicentrics and chromatid exchanges occurred in G_1 cells and even in the same G_1 cell after ionizing radiation, that breakages of the subunits occur as follows: (1) A break may be produced in one subunit but not in the other; (2) both subunits may be broken at the same locus, but one of them may restitute while the other does not; and (3) both subunits may be broken at the same locus, and both breaks remain open. A translocation between two chromosomes having possibilities 1 and 2 would lead to a chromatid exchange, whereas a translocation between two chromosomes having the third possibility would result in a dicentric chromosome exchange. It appears that an energy loss of about 75 to 100 ev per event (*14*) from ionizing radiation is sufficient to break with high probability both subunits at the same locus; therefore, dicentrics resulting from the third possibility are quite prevalent. However, the data indicate that the absorption of UV photons does not cause both subunits to break at the same locus; therefore, possibilities 2 and 3 should occur infrequently, and few dicentrics should be observed after UV irradiation of the G_1 cells.

The observation that cells synthesizing DNA sustain about ten times as much damage from UV radiation as do cells in G_1 and G_2 is also consistent with the model just presented. It is possible that, when the two subunits separate as the cell enters S period, UV is much more effective in producing breaks. As the cell progresses through the S phase, the complementary subunit is synthesized and the UV again becomes much less effective. The reasons that the single subunit is more sensitive to UV than the two-subunit structure are purely speculative. It is possible that chromosomal damage is restituted less rapidly in the single subunits of the S phase cells; however, if this is the case it would apply largely to UV radiation only, because for ionizing radiation a large increase in the radiosensitivity of S-phase cells is not observed. However, it is known that UV photons in the 2600-A range are the most effective in producing chromosomal breaks, probably because they are absorbed preferentially by nucleic acid (*11*). Therefore, it is possible that the structure of the DNA and/or associated nucleoproteins is altered as the subunits separate, which could result in the following: (1) less protection of the DNA by the proteins; (2) preferential absorption of the UV photons by the DNA; or (3) a lowering of the energy required to break the subunit.

SUMMARY

Chromosomal damage after UV irradiation of an *in vitro* mammalian cell line (Chinese hamster) in different phases of the life cycle was determined. The cells were pulse-labeled with tritiated thymidine immediately before irradiation (100 ergs/mm^2), and autoradiographs were prepared from samples taken every 2 hours. Metaphases were classified as labeled or unlabeled and were analyzed for breaks and exchanges. Cells in DNA synthesis at the time of irradiation suffer about ten times the chromosomal damage of cells in G_1 and G_2 phases. Furthermore, for both G_1- and S-phase cells which divide from 10 to 16 hours after irradiation, the greatest fraction of breaks (70 to 90%) is elicited as chromatid exchanges; whereas in G_2- and S-phase cells which divide from 2 to 8 hours after irradiation, a smaller fraction of damage (about 40%) results in chromatid exchanges. The frequency of chromosome exchanges in irradiated cells is not significantly different from that in control cells.

The results were compared with those obtained for ionizing radiation, and significant differences were noted. For ionizing radiation, S-phase cells sampled both early and late after irradiation sustained the same amount of damage, and in G_1 cells 70% of the exchanges were due to dicentrics (chromosome exchanges). For UV radiation cells in S phase which were sampled 10 to 16 hours after irradiation sustained about 25 times as much damage as did cells in S phase which were sampled prior to 8 hours, and in G_1 cells only 19% of the exchanges were due to dicentrics. These findings are consistent with the hypothesis that the chromosome, although morphologically single, consists of two subunits which separate as the cell enters the S phase.

ACKNOWLEDGMENTS

We should like to express our appreciation to Miss Beverly Ann Jones for technical assistance and to Mr. John D. Carnes for the photographs.

RECEIVED: May 28, 1962

REFERENCES

1. W. C. DEWEY and R. M. HUMPHREY, Relative radiosensitivity of different phases in the life cycle of L-P59 mouse fibroblasts and ascites tumor cells. *Radiation Res.* **16,** 503–530 (1962).
2. T. C. HSU, W. C. DEWEY, and R. M. HUMPHREY, Radiosensitivity of cells of Chinese hamster *in vitro* in relation to the cell cycle. *Exptl. Cell Res.* **27,** 441–452 (1962).
3. SHELDON WOLFF, Radiation genetics. In *Mechanisms in Radiobiology* (M. Errera and A. Forssberg, eds.), Vol. I, pp. 419-475, Academic Press, New York, 1961.
4. M. DEMEREC, A. HOLLAENDER, M. B. HOULAHAN, and M. BISHOP, Effect of monochromatic ultraviolet radiation in *Drosophila melanogaster. Records Genet. Soc. Am.* **10,** 139–140 (1941); *Genetics* **27,** 139–140 (1942).
5. C. P. SWANSON, Differential sensitivity of prophase pollen tube chromosomes to X-rays and ultraviolet radiation. *J. Gen. Physiol.* **26,** 485–494 (1943).
6. A. C. FABERGÉ, Ultraviolet induced chromosome aberrations in maize. *Records Genet. Soc. Am.* **20,** 97–98 (1950); *Genetics* **36,** 549–550 (1951).
7. W. B. LOONEY, The replication of deoxyribonucleic acid in hepatocytes. *Proc. Natl. Acad. Sci. U. S.* **46,** 690–697 (1960).
8. N. H. GILES, JR., Radiation-induced chromosome aberrations in *Tradescantia*. In *Radiation Biology* (A. Hollaender, ed.), Vol. I, Part 2, pp. 713–761, McGraw-Hill Book Company, New York, 1954.
9. MASA-ATSU YAMADA and T. T. PUCK, Action of radiation on mammalian cells. IV. Reversible mitotic lag in the S3 HeLa cell produced by low doses of X-rays. *Proc. Natl. Acad. Sci. U. S.* **47,** 1181–1191 (1961).
10. M. M. ELKIND and HARRIET SUTTON, Radiation response of mammalian cells grown in culture. I. Repair of X-ray damage in surviving Chinese hamster cells. *Radiation Res.* **13,** 556–593 (1960).
11. L. J. STADLER and F. M. UBER, Genetic effects of ultraviolet radiation in maize. IV. Comparison of monochromatic radiation. *Genetics* **27,** 84–118 (1942).
12. J. S. KIRBY-SMITH and DORIS L. CRAIG, The induction of chromosome aberrations in *Tradescantia. Genetics* **42,** 176–187 (1957).
13. J. H. TAYLOR, Organization and duplication of genetic material. *Proc. 10th Intern Congr. Genet.* **1,** 63–78 (1958).
14. F. HUTCHINSON and E. POLLARD, Physical principles of radiation action. In *Mechanisms in Radiobiology* (M. Errera and A. Forssberg, eds.), Vol. I, pp. 1–70, Academic Press, New York, 1961.

RADIATION RESEARCH **19**, 261–269 (1963)

Age of the Mother and Previous Breeding History and the Incidence of X-Ray-Induced Congenital Anomalies[1]

ROBERT RUGH AND MARLIS WOHLFROMM

Radiological Research Laboratory, Department of Radiology, Columbia University, New York, New York

INTRODUCTION

There is adequate evidence that X-irradiation of the rodent embryo at any stage of development prior to the completion of organogenesis can produce congenital anomalies (*1–11*). The incidence of such anomalies is roughly correlated with the level of exposure and the specific gestational age. All our previous work was done with young or virgin mice, so that it seemed in order to make a similar study with aged females, particularly those which had been used as breeders for a year but were still fertile. It is known that there is a higher incidence of mongolism among the human offspring born to mothers after the age of 40 years. Such a study with the mouse embryo might reveal the effect of the general aging process of the female and her ovaries on the incidence of congenital anomalies among her offspring, particularly with respect to those induced by ionizing radiations.

MATERIALS AND METHOD

The mice used were exclusively the CF_1 Swiss white strain. The 2-month-old mice were virgins, kept for 2 weeks prior to use in order to condition them to the laboratory environment. The old breeders had been used by Carworth Farms for continuous breeding for 10 to 12 months, during which they produced about nine litters and 100 offspring each. They were approximately 14 months old at the time of this study.

In order to obtain accurately timed pregnancies, a mature and sexually active male was placed with 5 females in their animal box at 5 P.M. and removed at 9 A.M. the next morning. Those females found with vaginal plugs were isolated and used for the experiments. This mating procedure has been used for all prior experiments in this laboratory and has proved satisfactory. It has been found that, although mating normally seems to occur most frequently around midnight,

[1] Based on work under Contract AT(30-1)2740 for the U. S. Atomic Energy Commission and aided by U. S. Public Health Grant RH-00081-02S1.

when the possibility of mating is provided it may occur at any time. The average period between mating and isolation of the mated females is about 12 hours, so that the dating of the gestation ages is by half-days, as 1.5 and 8.5 days.

The X-irradiation facilities consisted of parallel tubes in cross-fire, each at 72 cm from the center of the gravid uterus, and run at 184 kvp, 30 ma, with 0.28 mm Cu and 0.50 mm Al filters, with an aggregate half-value layer of 0.6 mm Cu. The dose rate was 50 r/min in air. It has been found that the slight absorption by the plastic animal cage used for confining the animals during irradiation approximately equals the increase in radiation due to scattering from the 5 females, and the dose delivered to the embryos is very close to 50 r/min. The males were of the same strain, and the controls were identical with those X-irradiated except for the irradiation.

The gestation ages chosen were 1.5 and 8.5 days because these ages had been shown to be particularly radiosensitive. Actually, at 0.0 day (immediately after conception) the zygote is the most radiosensitive, but there is such high mortality at low levels of exposure that the two-cell stage (1.5 days) was chosen along with the stage of active neurogenesis (8.5 days) (*7–13*). The pregnant mice were given a single whole-body exposure of penetrating ionizing radiations (X-rays) ranging from 10 to 200 r. At 18.5 days after conception, shortly before the time of expected delivery at 19.0 days, the data for this paper were collected. The variables were age of female and her ovaries, her previous breeding history, age of the embryos, and the exposure level. These variables were chosen to demonstrate any effect of ionizing radiations on mothers and their ova with different ages and breeding history, specifically as reflected in the production of congenital anomalies.

At 18.5 days postconception the females were killed by cervical dislocation, the gravid uterus was removed, and the position and condition of each implantation were analyzed. Ovulation and implantation number are rarely the same (*14*), so that the base line chosen for this study was the actual implantation, reflecting the actual number of successful fertilizations. Those embryos irradiated at 1.5 days, when they were in the two-cell stage, will generally implant at 4.5 days, but if they are killed the implantation site will be marked only by a residual resorption mass of clotted blood. The fact that no exposure level depressed appreciably the average implantation number indicates that such 1.5-day embryos did in fact implant. They could be killed but would leave at least a hemorrhagic mass and placental remains if not amorphous evidence of some development. Intra-uterine resorptions are found among all matings of normal mice, possibly due to some genetic factors inherent in the stock, so that all data relating to X-irradiation effects must be compared with this base line of normal resorptions.

In addition to the resorptions, the analysis included fetuses with gross central nervous system anomalies such as exencephalia, anencephalia, hydrocephalia, microcephalia, and also included dead fetuses. These latter are identifiable as formed embryos but are dead on examination of the gravid uterus, indicating death sometime after implantation. Other defects were noted, such as microphthalmia, anophthalmia, persistent protruding intestine, and gross but topographically balanced stunting. Stunting has been shown to occur frequently and in many embryos X-irradiated *in utero*. All remaining fetuses were classed as "normal" simply because of the absence of any overt anomaly or death. There is no suggestion that they were in fact normal in the sense of carrying no irradiation damage, but compared with all others they were "apparently normal." It is believed that any embryo in a litter containing embryos with gross irradiation-induced congenital anomalies would itself have some effects, though not necessarily or readily apparent. This might be reflected in mild stunting, effects on ERG or EEG, or other functional tests which will be reported elsewhere.

EXPERIMENTAL DATA

Some 348 pregnancies involving 3705 implantations (average 10.64) were analyzed for this study (see Table I). The average number of implantations for the primipara (virgins) controls and of the old breeders was essentially the same (11.2 and 10.6). Thus, the age of the mother or her ovaries did not appreciably reduce the number of ova ovulated and implantations achieved.

The exposure levels varied with the age of the embryos of both young and old females, since it was found that the earlier stages were more radiosensitive than the older ones. For the 1.5-day-old embryos the exposures were 10 r, 50 r, and 100 r, and for the 8.5-day-old embryos they were 50 r, 100 r, and 200 r. Thus comparisons should be made of embryos exposed at the same gestational age, but developed by the young as opposed to the old mice.

The fetuses of the young mice showed a greater tendency to develop central nervous system anomalies than did those of the old breeders, the difference being 14% and 5.34%. Other congenital defects such as eye anomalies, protruding viscera, cleft palate, anemia, and stunting were found less frequently among the fetuses after 100 r to the young at 1.5 days of gestation or after 200 r at 8.5 days of gestation than to the embryos of the old breeders similarly exposed. Dead fetuses were found slightly more frequently in the young mice exposed to 200 r at 8.5 days. These facts may be explained, at least in part, by the reverse preponderance of a higher resorption rate among the old breeders. Intra-uterine death and resorption after 100 r of exposure to the pregnant young mice at 1.5 days was only slightly above that for their unirradiated controls, whereas for the old breeders it was increased from 16.75% to 25.7%. At higher levels of exposure and at 8.5 days this difference was even greater. The primipara young mice X-irradiated to 200 r at 8.5 days produced 32% resorptions; the embryos of the old breeders, similarly treated, resulted in 65.5% resorptions. This is especially significant, because death, but not resorptions, occurs more often after 8.5 days of development.

TABLE I

AGE OF MOTHER AND PREVIOUS BREEDING HISTORY IN RELATION TO X-IRRADIATION-INDUCED CONGENITAL ANOMALIES[a]

Age of embryo (days)	*Dose of X-rays (r)*	*Pregnancies*	*Implantations*	*Average*	*"Normals" (%)*	*Dead*[b] *(%)*	*Resorptions (%)*	*CNS anomalies (%)*	*Other defects*[c] *(%)*
Young mice									
Controls	0	42	471	11.2	85	0.85	12.7	0	1.7
1.5	10	27	313	11.6	84	1.6	14.0	0	0
1.5	50	22	227	10.3	78	0.88	19.8	0	1.76
1.5	100	27	315	11.6	85	0.32	13.6	0.32	0.32
8.5	50	21	250	11.8	85	0	14.4	0	0.4
8.5	100	21	222	10.5	84	0.45	9.0	4.96	1.35
8.5	200	21	235	11.1	40	12.3	32.3	14.04	1.28
Old breeders									
Controls	00	40	424	10.6	79	1.41	16.75	0	1.81
1.5	10	9	86	9.6	75.6	2.3	19.8	0	2.33
1.5	50	20	234	11.7	77	1.28	18.4	0	2.99
1.5	100	27	241	9.1	69	0.83	25.7	0	4.56
8.5	50	23	226	9.8	83	3.98	11.5	0	1.33
8.5	100	23	255	11.0	73	0.78	22.0	3.53	1.18
8.5	200	25	206	8.2	17.5	8.25	65.5	5.34	3.41

[a] Note that the X-irradiation exposures for the 1.5-day groups were lower than for the 8.5-day groups.

[b] Resorbed and dead embryos are tabulated separately, even though they are all "dead." This is in order to distinguish between those that survive to late fetal life and then die and those that die at an early stage.

[c] Other defects include stunting, often with anemia, eye defects, protruding intestine, and cleft palate.

These figures do not include the "apparently normal" fetuses. Without exception, there were fewer of these "apparently normal" fetuses among the old breeders when the higher levels of irradiation were used than among the similarly treated young mice. The disparity was greatest after 200 r at 8.5 days of gestation, when only 17.5% of the offspring of the old breeders appeared to be "normal," whereas 40% of the offspring of the young mice appeared to be unaffected. This age of gestation and level of irradiation bring out graphically the difference between the reproductive potential of the young and the old mice, showing that the young are apt to produce more fetal deaths, more central nervous system anomalies, and more "normals" than are the older mice, but that the older ones are more likely to produce intra-uterine deaths and resportions.

The data may be further analyzed with respect to the level of risk (Table II).

TABLE II

ESTIMATES OF RISK OF DEATH AND ANOMALIES

Age (days)	*Dose (r)*	*Implantations*		*Normal (%)*		*Risk dead (%)*[a]		*Risk CNS anomalies (%)*[b]	
		Young mice	*Old breeders*	*Young mice*	*Old breeders*	*Young mice*	*Old breeders*	*Young mice*	*Old breeders*
Controls		471	424	85	79	13.5	18.1	0	0
1.5	10	313	219	84	72	15.6	22.1	0	0
1.5	50	227	234	78	77	20.7	19.7	0	0
1.5	100	315	241	85	69	13.9	26.5	0.37	0
8.5	50	250	226	85	83	14.4	15.5	0	0
8.5	100	222	255	84	73	9.5	22.8	5.4	4.6
8.5	200	235	226	40	17	44.6	73.5	26.0	23.4

[a] Percentage risk for the resorptions and dead fetuses is calculated against the total number of implantations.

[b] Percentage risk for the central nervous system anomalies is calculated against the living embryos and fetuses only, since the resorbed or dead could not reveal such anomalies.

The "normals" and the deaths may be tabulated against the total number of implantations, but those with gross central nervous system anomalies should also be calculated against the surviving fetuses only. This difference is shown in Table II, where it is seen that there is practically no risk that X-irradiation at 1.5 days will produce central nervous system anomalies, whereas irradiation to 200 r at 8.5 days will cause 26.0% of the surviving fetuses of the young mice to show these anomalies, as opposed to 23.4% of the surviving fetuses of the older mice. The difference is further emphasized when it is seen that 73.5% of all the embryos of the older mice will be killed by this exposure, and only 44.6% of the embryos of the younger mice will be so killed. These facts are further reflected in the percentage of normals, which was also indicated in Table I.

DISCUSSION

The over-all picture from these data is that the embryos of the young (primipara) mice stand a better chance of developing into "apparently normal" fetuses, but there is also the better general survival which leads to a higher production of gross central nervous system anomalies after X-irradiation, particularly at 8.5 days of gestation. The embryos of the old breeders are so much more radiosensitive that twice as many died and were resorbed as among the younger females, and hence there were relatively fewer left to "appear normal" or to develop anomalies.

There is no question but that ionizing radiations contribute to the aging process (*15–39*). There is also evidence that radiation susceptibility is altered with age (*40*). Few studies have been made on the age of the egg at the time of fertilization and subsequent development (*41, 42*), and none on the relation of age of the animal to the production of congenital anomalies by radiation. There are some recent studies designed to determine the effect on the aging process of embryonic and fetal X-irradiation (*43*), so that this present study of X-irradiation effects on embryos derived from young versus old females is a new contribution in radiobiology.

Rugh (*6*) first described the histological changes in the central nervous system of amphibian embryos after X-irradiation, and this was followed (*8–11*) by a number of studies on the mouse embryo which showed a time-dose relation in the production of congenital anomalies in this mammal. Thus, there is a well-authenticated basis for the present study of the X-irradiation of embryos derived from mice of the same strain, but from females that were aged and reproductively exhausted, as compared with the primipara females, all mated to young and virile males of the same strain. It was not presumed that the ovaries, and their ova, would necessarily show the aging process in advance of other tissues and organs, and this has been supported in a general way by Puck (*44*). Irradiation effects on the brain at or shortly after birth are well-documented (*45*), and the postnatal effects of prenatal X-irradiation are being investigated.

Female mice which have been used for continuous breeding for a year must indeed be tired animals, so that the general physiological condition cannot be ignored in any such study as this. However, such physiological variables should reveal themselves when one compares the production by the controls of the young and old mice. The old breeders showed a base line of only about a 4% increase over the young mice in the intra-uterine deaths and resorptions, and these values were not excessive for mice of any strain. Likewise, there were only 6% fewer "normal" fetuses among the controls of the old breeders, and the average number of implantations was not particularly reduced (11.2 to 10.6). Thus, it seems that production from controls of these two ages of females is not so greatly different as one might expect, making the effect of ionizing radiations the more significant. Exposure at 1.5 days of gestation caused considerably more intra-uterine death and resorption among the old breeders than among the young females, and at 8.5 days the differential was even greater. From this one criterion it seems evident that fertilized eggs developed by the older females are the more radio-vulnerable.

This study was focused particularly on the incidence of the gross central nervous system anomaly known as exencephalia, or brain hernia, the production of which had been shown to be directly correlated with exposure level at 8.5 days of gestation. With exposures of 50, 100, and 200 r at 8.5 days the percentage of "normals" was greater at every exposure level among the fetuses of the young mice than among those of the old breeders, but likewise were the brain anomalies more frequently found. This is explained in part by the fact that the over-all survival among the fetuses of the young mice was better, and such anomalies could develop only among the survivors. As an example, after 200 r at 8.5 days, the old breeders produced 65.5% resorptions, whereas the young mice showed only 32% resorptions.

It should be pointed out that this is a study of the ovum, and therefore only half of the zygote is aged. The sperm were from virile young males, sexually proved, so that any effect demonstrated was due to the aging of the females and their ova only. Such effects as are shown are over and above those that could be attributed to senile physiology of the year-old, reproductively tired female mouse. It has been shown that survival of embryos exposed to X-irradiation is better if the eggs are from younger females, but in consequence the incidence of gross congenital central nervous system anomalies from these younger mice is the greater. The question arises, therefore, as to whether survival is a good thing when it carries with it a greater probability of anomalous development.

SUMMARY AND CONCLUSIONS

1. Ova production as measured by average implantation number in young (primipara) mice as compared with old breeders (of 14± months of age) is essentially the same, when they are mated to young and virile males of the same strain.

2. X-Irradiation of embryos at 1.5 days (two-cell stage) showed a significant difference between fetuses of the young and old females with respect to the percentage of "normals" (higher in the young) and the percentage of resorptions and congenital defects (higher in the older females).

3. X-Irradiation of embryos at 8.5 days of gestation (during neurogenesis) reduced the percentage of "normals" at lower levels of X-irradiation, and to a much greater degree among the old breeders than among the young mice. There were twice as many intra-uterine deaths and resorptions among the older mice after 200 r, but about one-third as many gross central nervous system anomalies among the old breeders. This disparity is reduced when it is emphasized that, since the old breeders lose more embryos, *in utero*, there are fewer survivors to develop persisting congenital anomalies. If the percentage of central nervous system anomalies among survivors only is computed, the disparity still shows a preponderance among the younger mice, but the relation is reduced to 26.0% and 23.4%.

4. Whether the disparity in reaction of embryos of young and old mice is due to aged eggs or to senile physiology of the mother, or to both factors, is not clear. Since the unirradiated controls of these two ages of mice do not show the same degree of disparity, it seems unequivocal that the X-irradiated embryos of the old females are relatively the more radiosensitive, in terms of mortality, but the embryos of the young mice are the more sensitive in terms of surviving morbidity.

RECEIVED: August 17, 1962

REFERENCES

1. S. P. Hicks, Acute necrosis and malformation of developing mammalian brain caused by X-rays. *Proc. Soc. Exptl. Biol. Med.* **75,** 485 (1950).
2. S. P. Hicks, Some effects of ionizing radiations and metabolic inhibition on the developing mammalian nervous system. *J. Pediat.* **40,** 489 (1952).
3. S. P. Hicks, Some effects of ionizing radiation on adult and embryonic nervous system. In *Metabolic and Toxic Diseases of the Nervous System,* Vol. 32, pp. 439–462. Williams and Wilkins, Baltimore, 1953.
4. S. P. Hicks, Mechanism of radiation anencephaly, anophthalmia, and pituitary anomalies. *Arch. Pathol.* **57,** 363 (1954).
5. S. P. Hicks, Radiation as an experimental tool in mammalian developmental neurology. *Physiol. Rev.* **38,** 338–356 (1958).
6. R. Rugh, Histological effects on the embryo following X-irradiation. *J. Morphol.* **88,** 483–501 (1949).
7. R. Rugh, Low levels of X-irradiation and the early mammalian embryo. *Am. J. Roentgenol. Radium Therapy Nucl. Med.* **87,** 559–566 (1962).
8. R. Rugh and E. Grupp, X-irradiation exencephaly. *Am. J. Roentgenol. Radium Therapy Nucl. Med.* **81,** 1026–1052 (1959).
9. R. Rugh and E. Grupp, Exencephalia following X-irradiation of the pre-implantation mammalian embryo. *J. Neuropathol. Exptl. Neurol.* **18,** 468–481 (1959).
10. R. Rugh and E. Grupp, Responses of the very early mouse embryo to low levels of ionizing radiations. *J. Exptl. Zool.* **141,** 571–588 (1960).
11. R. Rugh and E. Grupp, Effect of low level X-irradiation on the fertilized egg of the mammal. *Exptl. Cell Res.* **25,** 302–310 (1961).
12. U. Murakami, Y. Kameyama, A. Majima, and T. Sakurai, Radiation malformations belonging to the cyclopia-archinencephalia-otocephalia group in the mouse fetus. *J. Embryol. Exptl. Morphol.* **10,** 64–72 (1962).
13. A. Majima, Eye-abnormalities in mouse embryos and fetuses caused by X-radiation of mothers. *Nagoya J. Med. Sci.* **24,** 171–186 (1962).
14. E. M. Otis, Prenatal mortality rates of seventeen radiation-induced translocations in mice. U. S. Atomic Energy Commission Report UR-291 (1953).
15. A. Brues, Radiation as a carcinogenic agent. *Radiation Res.* **3,** 272–280 (1955).
16. H. A. Blair, A formulation of the relation between radiation dose and shortening of life span. *Proc. 1st Intern. Conf. Peaceful Uses Atomic Energy, Geneva, 1955* **11,** 118–120 (1956).
17. G. W. Casarett, Acceleration of ageing by ionizing radiation. *J. Gerontol.* **11,** 436 (1956).
18. S. Warren, Longevity and causes of death from irradiation in physicians. *J. Am. Med. Assoc.* **162,** 468 (1956).
19. C. B. Braestrup, Past and present radiation exposures to radiologists from the point of view of life expectancy. *Am. J. Roentgenol. Radium Therapy Nucl. Med.* **78,** 988–992 (1957).
20. P. Alexander, Accelerated ageing—a long term effect of exposure to ionizing radiations. *Gerontology* **1,** 174–193 (1957).
21. P. S. Henshaw, Genetic transition as a determinant of physiologic and radiologic ageing and other conditions. *Radiology* **69,** 30–36 (1957).
22. G. A. Sacher, D. Grahn, and S. W. Lesher, Effect of radiations on ageing and effects of age on radiation sensitivity. *Proc. Am. Inst. Biol. Sci. Symposium on Ageing* (1957).
23. G. Failla, The ageing process and carcinogenesis. *Ann. N.Y. Acad. Sci.* **71,** 1124–1140 (1958).
24. J. B. Hursh, G. W. Casarett, A. L. Carsten, T. R. Noonan, S. M. Michaelson, J. W.

Howland, and H. A. Blair, Observations on recovery and irreversible injury in mammals. *Proc. 2nd Intern. Conf. Peaceful Uses Atomic Energy, Geneva, 1958.*
25. H. J. Curtis and K. L. Gebhard, Radiation induced ageing in mice. *Proc. 2nd Intern. Conf. Peaceful Uses Atomic Energy, Geneva, 1958.*
26. R. F. Kallman and H. I. Kohn, Life-shortening by whole and partial body X-irradiation in mice. *Science* **128,** 301–302 (1958).
27. V. I. Korogodin and G. G. Polikarpov, Biological effects of ionizing radiation on the ageing processes and the span of life. *Med. Radiol.* **3,** 79–85 (1958).
28. J. Storer, Rate of recovery from radiation damage and its possible relationship to life-shortening of mice. U. S. Atomic Energy Commission Report LA-2224, Biol. and Med. 45 pp. (1958).
29. J. L. Tullis, Delayed effects of ionizing radiations in man. *Arch. Pathol.* **66,** 403–417 (1958).
30. H. I. Kohn and P. H. Guttman, Latent period of X-ray induced ageing: A study based on mortality rate and tumor incidence. *Nature* **184,** 735–736 (1959).
31. M. Nakaizuma, Effect of irradiation on the ageing process. *Ronenbya* **3,** 445 (1959).
32. B. L. Strehler and A. S. Mildvan, General theory of mortality and ageing. *Science* **132,** 14–21 (1962).
33. P. Alexander and D. I. Connell, Shortening of the life span of mice by irradiation with X-rays and treatment with radiomemetic chemicals. *Radiation Res.* **12,** 38–48 (1960).
34. L. J. Cole, P. C. Nowell, and J. S. Arnold, Late effects of X-radiation. *Radiation Res.* **12,** 173–185 (1960).
35. G. J. Neary, Ageing and radiation. *Nature* **187,** 10–18 (1960).
36. A. C. Upton, Ionizing radiations and ageing. *Gerontologia* **4,** 162–176 (1960).
37. T. F. Dougherty, Similarities between physiologic and radiologic accelerated ageing. *Federation Proc.* **20,** 3–7 (1961).
38. J. F. Spalding and T. T. Trujillo, Radiosensitivity of mice as a function of age. *Radiation Res.* **16,** 125–129 (1962).
39. G. W. Meier, D. P. Foshee, A. P. Matheny, and F. Carr, Irradiation and aging: Behavioral implications. *Radiation Res.* **16,** 130–137 (1962).
40. P. F. Lindop, F. Rotblat, R. Doll, and R. C. Tudway, The age factor in susceptibility of man and animals to radiation. *Brit. J. Radiol.* **35,** 23–31 (1962).
41. L. Zimmerman and R. Rugh, Effect of age on the development of the egg of the leopard frog, *Rana pipens. J. Morphol.* **68,** 329–346 (1941).
42. E. Witschi, Over-ripeness of the egg as a cause of twinning. *Cancer Res.* **12,** 763–786 (1952).
43. R. Brent and B. T. Bolden, The long-term effects of low-dosage embryonic irradiation. *Radiation Res.* **14,** 453–454 (1961).
44. T. T. Puck, Cellular aspects of irradiation and ageing in mammals. *Federation Proc.* **20,** 31–34 (1961).
45. C. D. Clemente and J. N. Yamazaki, Brain radiation in newborn rats and differential effects of increased age. *Neurology* **10,** 657–669 (1960).

RADIATION RESEARCH 19, 270–276 (1963)

Continuous Low-Dose Radiation Effects on Successive Litters of the Albino Rat[1]

SIDNEY O. BROWN, GEORGE M. KRISE, AND HENRY B. PACE

Radiation Biology Laboratory, Texas Engineering Experiment Station, Texas A. and M. College, College Station, Texas

INTRODUCTION

The aim of this investigation was to study the effect of continuous low-dose γ-radiation on successive litters of albino rats born to mothers who remained continuously in the radiation field. Levels used were 0, 2, 5, 10, and 20 r daily given over a 23-hour period. A secondary aim was to study the effect of this continuous radiation on the fertility of the offspring irradiated *in utero*. The investigations of Bagg (*1*) indicated that continuous radiation influenced primarily the eyes and the circulatory systems of offspring irradiated *in utero* by injections of 5 mc radium but that it did not prevent reproduction. The work of Russell *et al.* (*2*) demonstrated that continuous irradiation during the first 2 weeks of prenatal life of the mouse appeared to have no specific effect other than a decrease in the total reproductive span of the females. In their study the pregnant female mice were subjected to 14 days of continuous Co^{60} radiation at 87 r/week (12.4 r/day). Russell *et al.* (*3*) have reported that females are more sensitive than males to radiation, an observation which in general is in agreement with that of other investigators. The studies of Russell *et al.* (*2*) indicate clearly that continuous γ-radiation cannot be compared with the same radiation administered at a specific stage in the process of embryogenesis.

EXPERIMENTAL PROCEDURES

Radiation Facility

The source consisted of two 1-curie Co^{60} pellets separated by a vertical distance of 6 feet within the source holder. The source holder was so designed that the source could be remotely operated in two positions, storage and radiating. The storage position placed the two Co^{60} pellets behind two lead shields of a thickness calculated

[1] Work supported by Research and Development Division, Office of the Surgeon General, Army Project DA-007-49-MD-957.

to allow minimal exposure for personnel caring for the animals 1 hour each day. In the radiating position the tube containing the sources was wrapped with layers of ⅛-inch lead sheet and 0.005-inch lead foil to allow for maintenance of a constant rate of radiation. When the source decay had reached 5%, sufficient lead foil was removed to return the dose rate to the original value.

Located in concentric circles around the source were cage racks, each accommodating seven cages. The concentric circle of cage racks made use of the inverse square effect to accommodate radiation levels of 2, 5, 10, and 20 r per 23-hour day. The dose rates at the various positions were measured originally by means of Landsverk 200-mr chambers read in a Landsverk Charger Reader. All chambers were calibrated against a standard Co^{60} source. Each rack was positioned in such a way that measurements taken for that rack agreed to within 2% of the other racks already placed. After location of all racks, measurements of the dose for all seven shelf levels were made, and the top and bottom positions were found to be beyond the criterion of accuracy and therefore unusable. Calibrated Landsverk Roentgen Meter Chambers of 10-r and 50-r capacities were used for a final verification as well as subsequent dosimetry after later rate adjustments. This was carried out in various cage positions throughout the 30 × 30-foot room. All cage locations had a maximum allowable dose deviation of 2%. The resulting vertical dose distribution within any given cage rack was less than 2%. The horizontal dose distribution within each cage—that is, from front to back—was less than 5%. All measurements were made in air with energy-equivalent calibrated chambers.

Experimental Animals

This experiment involved 50 female rats of the Holtzman strain, originally derived from the Sprague-Dawley strain. At the initiation of the experiment, the females were 90 days of age. Twenty-five males of the same strain were used to initiate the breeding cycle, and 25 males were employed for each subsequent breeding cycle at 42-day intervals. The animals were maintained in wire cages and fed Purina lab chow as the standard ration. In both the radiation chamber and the control room, the air temperature was maintained between 75° and 80°F throughout the experiment.

In order to obtain a uniformity of mating, the females were placed with the males between 2000 and 2200 hours on the day of the initiation of the experiment and at the same time each day thereafter for 4 days. Females in estrous were allowed to remain overnight with the males, and the following morning the presumably pregnant females were placed in the radiation chamber. (Only when the female is in estrous does she crouch, her ears vibrating, on the approach of the male. On being mounted by the male, she arches her back and stands; also during estrous the vagina opens and presents a dark blue color.) Gestation was assumed to have begun on the morning after the insemination of the females. Gestation of these animals was allowed to proceed in the radiation and control environments. The females were examined daily; when parturition was anticipated, the animals were supplied with shredded paper as nesting material. On the morning after parturition the litters were weighed and examined for externally visible malformations. Weights of the litters were taken twice weekly after the litter size was reduced to 8 animals, and the young were kept with their dam until the time of weaning. Post-weaning weights were recorded at weekly intervals. The growth curves were plotted for 18 weeks of postnatal life. Representative animals of this experiment were X-rayed in order to study bone density, the process of bone growth, and bone maturation.

The influence of radiation on the reproductive capacity of the third litter of offspring born to the irradiated mothers was evaluated by allowing the offspring to remain at their respective radiation levels until 50 days postparturition. Some of the offspring were mated with littermates maintained at the same radiation levels, while others of the same group were bred to unirradiated mates. The litter size and the weights of the offspring of these crosses were recorded, and the young were examined for visible abnormalities.

RESULTS

Effect of Continuous Irradiation on Successive Litters

In these investigations the criteria of reproductive capacity are the production of viable litters, the gross external manifestations of birth anomalies, the number of young born alive, and the average weight of the offspring. From Table I and Fig. 1 it may be observed that radiation doses of 2, 5, 10, and 20 r daily produced no significant alteration in litter size in the first four litters born to females placed in the radiation field at the time of conception. The litters born subsequent to the fourth litter showed a decrease in litter size and considerable variation in the fertility of the females. In the fifth litter one normal, well-developed pup was born to a mother which had received a total of 5530 r at 20 r daily at the time of conception. No young were produced by the two original females still alive after having received 6667 r of total-body continuous radiation. Those mothers receiving 10 r daily showed an apparent decrease in fertility at the time the sixth litter was conceived; however, the controls showed a comparable variation, making it impossible to ascribe these changes to radiation damage. Age is an important factor influencing the size of litters produced near the termination of the reproductive life span of the albino rate.

The total number of offspring born to the mothers on the different levels of radiation showed no significant deviations in successive litters (Table 1, Fig. 1) for the first six gestation periods, except for the fifth litter of those receiving 20 r daily. The total numbers of young produced in all litters considered together by the 10 females on the different daily levels of radiation likewise showed differences that were not significant because of the large variation in the litter sizes.

TABLE I
REPRODUCTIVE HISTORY

Treatment	Litters produced	Avg. litter size	Total number of young	♀ littering (%)	Avg. born per litter		Avg. birth weight (gm)	Avg. 21-day weight (gm)	Surviving ♀ at conception (%)	Dose accumulated at conception (r)
					Alive	Dead				
Control	1	7.3	73	100	6.3	1.0	6.1	47.0	100	0
	2	8.3	67	80	8.1	0.2	7.3	36.0	100	0
	3	9.5	76	80	9.1	0.4	6.3	56.0	100	0
	4	6.4	32	60	5.6	0.8	6.3	76.6[a]	100	0
	5	11.0	23	20	11.0	0.0	6.6	46.0	100	0
	6	10.0	10	10	10.0	0.0	7.5	53.3	80	0
			281							
2 r/day	1	10.3	83	80	9.5	0.8	6.2	43.0	100	0
	2	11.2	90	80	10.1	1.1	6.7	40.0	100	103.2
	3	9.9	89	90	9.8	0.1	6.4	47.0	100	249.7
	4	9.3	65	70	8.7	0.6	6.1	90.4[a]	100	387.1
	5	7.8	39	50	7.6	0.2	6.4	54.3	90	553.0
	6	5.1	19	30	5.1	0.0	6.6	36.0	60	666.8
			385							
5 r/day	1	10.2	82	80	9.2	1.0	6.0	41.0	100	0
	2	10.2	71	70	9.8	0.3	6.5	37.0	100	262.9
	3	9.9	84	90	9.1	0.2	6.7	45.0	100	619.4
	4	10.5	53	60	9.6	0.9	5.9	70.2[a]	100	952.4
	5	4.2	16	40	4.0	0.2	6.7	50.2	70	1382.5
	6	6.2	20	30	6.2	0.0	5.3	50.8	50	1666.9
			326							
10 r/day	1	8.7	70	80	8.7	0.0	5.6	39.0	100	0
	2	11.7	47	40	11.5	0.2	6.0	39.0	90	536.0
	3	9.0	36	40	9.0	0.0	6.5	41.0	90	1268.8
	4	9.3	65	70	9.0	0.3	6.1	82.9[a]	90	1915.0
	5	7.3	44	60	7.3	0.0	6.2	39.7	80	2765.0
	6	5.0	10	20	4.5	0.5	5.2	41.3	50	3333.8
			272							
20 r/day	1	7.8	78	100	6.5	1.3	5.3	40.0	100	0
	2	9.7	78	80	9.6	0.1	5.5	36.0	100	1091.8
	3	10.1	81	90	9.8	0.3	5.9	47.0	100	2517.6
	4	7.6	38	50	7.6	0.0	4.1	64.2[a]	80	3930.6
	5	1.0	1	10	1.0	0.0	7.0	41.0	50	5530.0
	6			0				[b]	20	6667.6
			276							

[a] 25 to 27 days of age.
[b] No litters (all females dead or completely sterile).

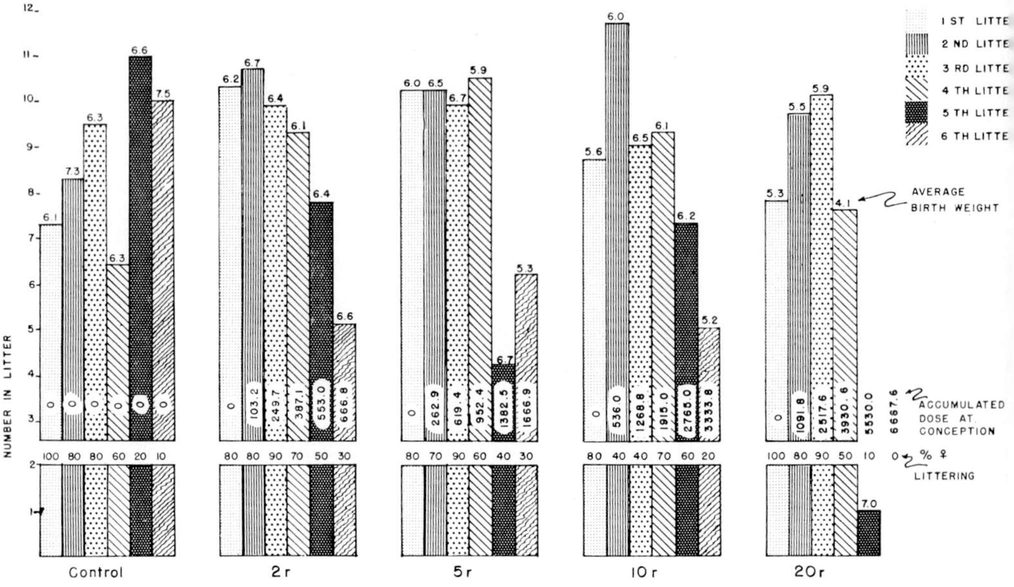

FIG. 1. Litter size as influenced by continuous radiation

Fertility Tests on Irradiated Offspring

Table II shows the results of mating, in various combinations, 10 individuals saved from the third litter of offspring born to mothers in the radiation chamber. These animals were removed from the radiation chamber at the time of mating; thus the F_2 offspring received no radiation. These data show that both males and females which had received 2 r and 5 r daily were fertile; however, the numbers were insufficient to draw specific conclusions as to fertility, litter size, or birth weights. The conclusion suggested, however, is that lifetime continuous irradiation in the albino rat at the level of 2 r and 5 r per 23 hours daily is not incompatible with reproduction of both males and females which were conceived in the radiation field. Continuous doses of 10 r and 20 r daily from the time of conception to the advent of maturity appeared to render both male and female albino rats sterile when mated together or with unirradiated mates.

DISCUSSION

These observations on the effect of continuous radiation on reproduction in the albino rat fall into two distinct categories: first, the effect on the production of functional oöcytes, i.e., the fertility in the albino rat; and, second, the influence of the different continuous radiation levels on fetal morphogenesis and early postnatal life of the rat. A third aspect might be considered in the effect of a continued radia-

TABLE II

THIRD-LITTER F_1 OFFSPRING LITTERING DATA[a]

Treatment	*Number of littering*	*Avg. number per litter*	*Avg. number born*		*Total number born*		*Average birth weight (gm)*	*Genetic radiation accumulated (r)*	*Radiation to offspring (r)*	*Total cumulative radiation (r)*
			Alive	*Dead*	*Alive*	*Dead*				
C♀ × C♂	9/10	8.2	7.2	1.0	65	9	6.4	0	0	0
2r♀ × 2r♂	5/10	8.6	6.8	1.8	34	9	4.4	249.7	112.8	362.5
5r♀ × 5r♂	8/10	8.4	8.1	0.3	65	2	5.6	619.4	282.1	901.5
10r♀ × 10r♂	0/10	0	0	0	0	0	0	1268.8	564.2	1833.0
20r♀ × 20r♂	0/10	0	0	0	0	0	0	2517.6	1128.4	3646.0
10r♂ × C♀	0/10	0	0	0	0	0	0			
C♂ × 10r♀	0/10	0	0	0	0	0	0			
20r♂ × C♀	0/10	0	0	0	0	0	0			
C♂ × 20r♀	0/10	0	0	0	0	0	0			
C♂ × C♀	4/6	7.0	6.9	0.1	30	4	6.0			

[a] No anomalies were observed during the progress of this experiment. Animals with tumors were killed.

tion field on the ability of the mother to lactate and successfully to rear successive litters while remaining continuously in the radiation environment.

During the continuous radiation process the ability to recover or repair the radiation-induced changes within the animal is of sufficient intensity to maintain the functional integrity of the oöcytes during the normal reproductive life span of the albino rat when subjected to 2-r and 5-r daily levels of whole-body chronic γ-radiation from a Co^{60} source. Neither the fertility, i.e., the ability to produce a litter regardless of size, nor the reproductive capacity, based on the total number of offspring produced, was impaired by this radiation level. The 10-r level of continuous radiation did not influence the fertility (total young produced) or the reproductive capacity for five successive litters; however, only two of the five surviving females produced young in the fifth litter. These offspring appeared normal except for decreased weight. When the total reproductive capacity of all 10 test females is considered for all four levels of radiation, no significant effect of continuous radiation may be determined for the albino rat. The only conclusion that our data permit is that for six successive litters with continuous γ-radiation at levels of 2, 5, and 10 r daily neither the fertility nor the reproductive capacity was affected. Radiation at the 20-r level daily did decrease fertility and the total number of litters a female can produce. These data on the rat substantiate the observation of Stadler and Gowen (*4*) on the mouse, i.e., that continuous irradiation up to 2 r/day does not impair reproduction sufficiently to prevent continuation of the germ line.

SUMMARY

Groups of 10 mature female rats of the Holtzman strain were exposed continuously to γ-radiation levels of 0, 2, 5, 10, and 20 r daily after conception. There were no essential differences in litter size, or in number of offspring born, between four succesive litters produced while the mothers remained continuously in the γ-radiation field. There was no significant variation in the first six litters born at the 0-r, 2-r, 5-r, and 10-r daily radiation levels; however, at 20 r daily only one offspring was born in the fifth litter, and none in the sixth. No anomalies were observed at any level of the radiation used in these experiments, except for a slight decrease in average weight of the newborn.

Offspring from the third litter born to mothers continuously in the radiation chamber were shown to be fertile in those groups which received 0, 2, and 5 r of γ-radiation administered over a 23-hour period daily. The corresponding animals receiving daily doses of 10 and 20 r from the time of conception were sterile when bred together or with known fertile unirradiated males.

RECEIVED: June 29, 1962

REFERENCES

1. H. J. BAGG, Disturbances in mammalian development produced by radium emanation. *Am. J. Anat.* **30,** 33 (1922).
2. L. B. RUSSELL, S. K. BADGETT, and C. L. SAYLORS, Comparison of the effects of acute, continuous, and fractionated irradiation during embryonic development. In *Immediate and Low Level Effects of Ionizing Radiation* (A. A. Buzzati-Traverso, ed.), Taylor and Francis, London, 1960.
3. L. B. RUSSELL, K. F. STELZNER, and W. L. RUSSELL, Influence of dose rate on radiation effect on female mice. *Proc. Soc. Exptl. Biol. Med.* **102,** 471–479 (1959).
4. JANICE STADLER and J. W. GOWEN, Patterns of reproductivity of different strains of mice under continuous irradiation. *Records Genet. Soc. Am.* **31,** 118 (1962).

RADIATION RESEARCH 19, 277–285 (1963)

Protein Synthesis in the Irradiated Intestine of the Mouse[1]

MARTIN LIPKIN, HENRY QUASTLER, AND FRANK MUGGIA

Department of Medicine, Cornell University Medical College, 2nd (Cornell) Medical Division, Bellevue Hospital, New York, New York, and Biology Department, Brookhaven National Laboratory, Upton, New York

INTRODUCTION

Protein synthesis in microorganisms is markedly affected only by doses near 100,000 rads (*1*). In the mammal, too, protein synthesis is generally not affected by lethal doses (*2*). However, synthesis of nuclear proteins was found (*3*) to be inhibited in the thymus 3 hours after irradiation with 1000 r, and incorporation of methionine into nondividing nuclei of the tracheal epithelium was depressed 4 hours after irradiation (*4*). It will be reported in this paper that autoradiographic studies of leucine incorporation in the intestine showed no effect for several hours after whole-body irradiation and that a reduced uptake appeared only about 2 to 3 days after irradiation, by which time only severely damaged cells are present.

METHODS

This study was performed on C57 Brown mice of the same strain and general characteristics described in our previous study of protein synthesis in normal intestine; radiochemical and autoradiographic methods were also identical to those previously described (*5*). X-Irradiation was administered to the whole body under the following conditions: 200 kv, 15 ma, inherent filter only, dose rate 250 rads/min. Doses of 160, 320, 640, 800, and 2500 rads were given.

Radiochemical Studies

The animals in the first series received 160, 320, 640, or 2500 rads. They were injected with C^{14}-leucine at the time of irradiation and sacrificed 1 to 72 hours after injection. The second series of animals were injected 1, 2, 3 or 4 days after irradiation with doses of 800 or 2500 rads, and sacrificed 1 to 72 hours after injection.

[1] This project was supported by U. S. Atomic Energy Contract AT-30-1-2179 and U. S. Public Health Service Grants C-3697 and A-3165. A portion of the work was carried out at Brookhaven National Laboratory under the auspices of the U. S. Atomic Energy Commission.

Autoradiographic Studies

Animals were irradiated with 2000 rads. Injection of H^3-leucine was made 1 to 24 hours after irradiation, and animals were sacrificed 2 to 4 hours after injection.

RESULTS

Retention of Labeled Protein in Normal and Irradiated Mice

Figure 1 shows specific activites of protein in the intestine of mice given 0 to 2500 rads, injected with C^{14}-leucine at the time of irradiation, and killed at various times later. It is seen that there is little, if any, difference in uptake and time course of disappearance of labeled protein between the intestines of normal and of irradiated mice. The loss of proliferative cells known to occur largely during the first day after irradiation is not demonstrated by this method. This could be due to masking of a loss in specific tissue elements, by preservation of protein in the bulk of the

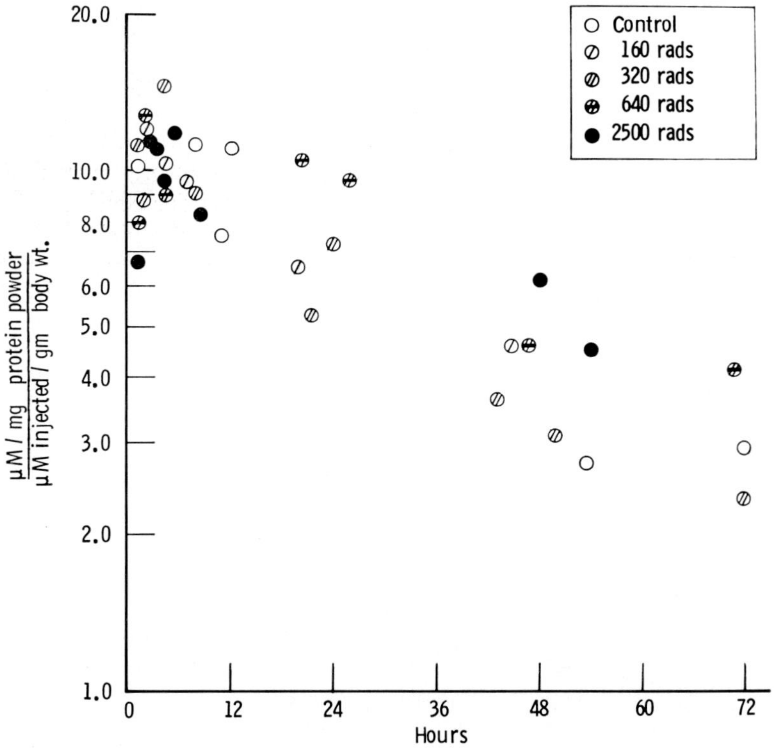

FIG. 1. Specific activity of protein in the intestine of mice given 0 to 2500 rads, injected with C^{14}-leucine at the time of irradiation, and killed various times later. The abscissa records hours after injection.

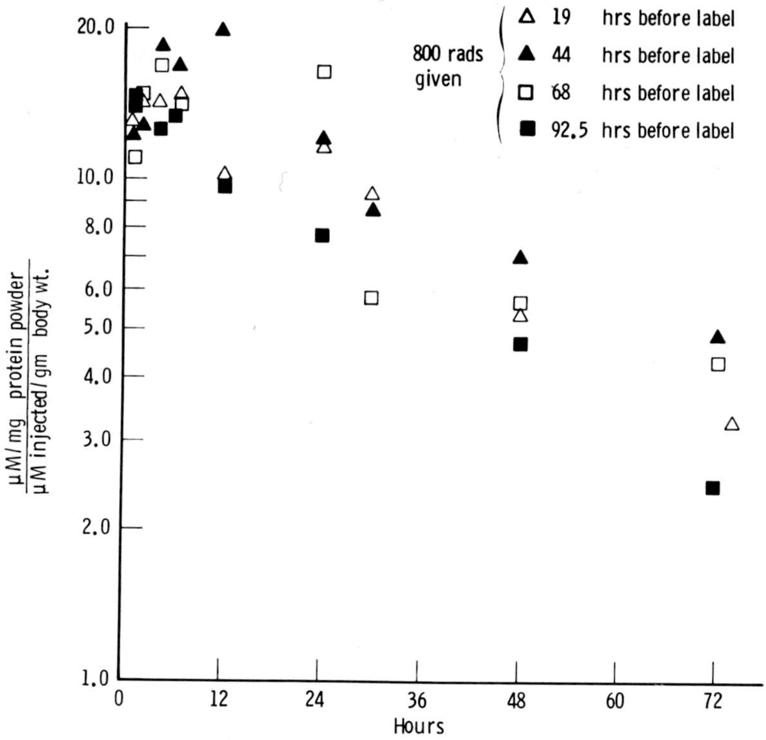

FIG. 2. Specific activity of protein in mice given 800 rads and injected with C^{14}-leucine 19 to 92.5 hours after irradiation. The abscissa records hours after injection.

cells, or to local reutilization of protein from the dead cells, or possibly to a compensatory mechanism, since it appears that at the time when many crypt cells die the normal loss of cells from the villus tips is delayed (*6*).

Labeling of Protein: Chemical Study

Figures 2 and 3 shows data comparable to those in Fig. 1. In Fig. 2, all mice had been given 800 rads, and the injection of C^{14}-leucine was given from 19 to 92.5 hours after irradiation. Figure 3 shows data found after irradiation with 2500 rads. Uptake is definitely reduced 68 hours after irradiation with 2500 rads, and slightly reduced 92.5 hours after irradiation with 800 rads. In all other instances, uptake is normal or slightly higher, and rate of disappearance is unchanged.

Labeling of Protein: Autoradiographic Study.

Figure 4 shows portions of autoradiographs from a normal mouse and from mice labeled 2 and 24 hours postirradiation with 2000 rads. It is seen that protein syn-

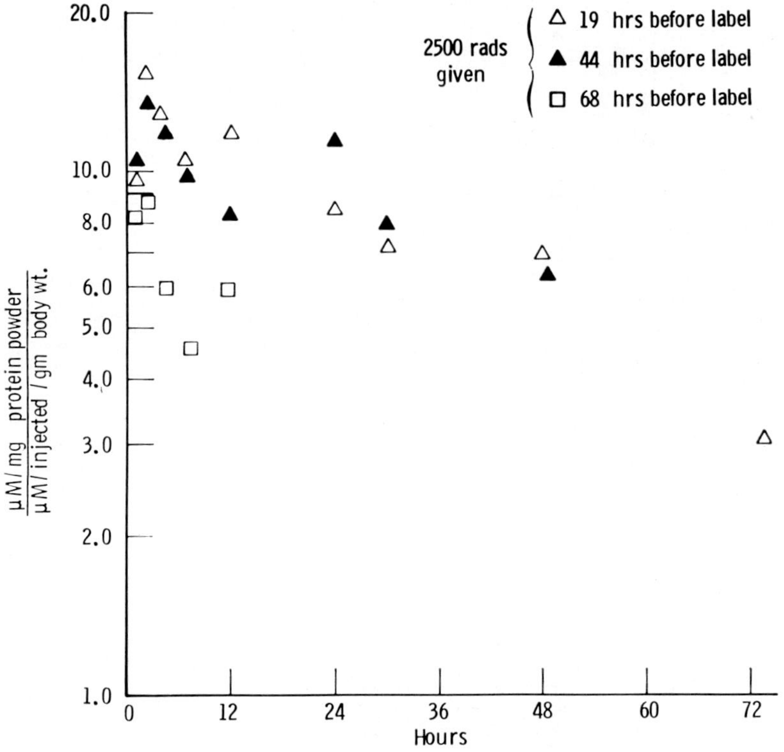

FIG. 3. Specific activity of protein 19 to 68 hours after irradiation with 2500 rads, and injection with C^{14}-leucine.

thesis occurred in the irradiated tissue in every cell and cell component with grain densities similar to those of the controls, even though some of the proliferative cells in the crypts showed gross damage at 2 hours, and considerable loss of cells had occurred at 24 hours. Only obviously dead cells with pycnotic nuclei were free from label. Cells dying or apparently recently dead were still labeled; seemingly protein is not lost during or soon after necrobiosis.

The results of quantitative autoradiographic studies of leucine uptake are shown in Fig. 5 and Table I. Figure 5*A* shows grain densities over nuclei and Fig. 5*B* over cytoplasm of crypt cells in mice injected at various times during the first day post-irradiation (2000 rads) and killed 2 to 4 hours after injection. Little if any change is seen in label incorporation, although all these cells are known to be severely damaged and are not capable of DNA synthesis.

Table I gives grain densities, by location of cell and region within cell, in mice injected with H^3-leucine 1 and 2 days after irradiation with 2000 rads. Specimens

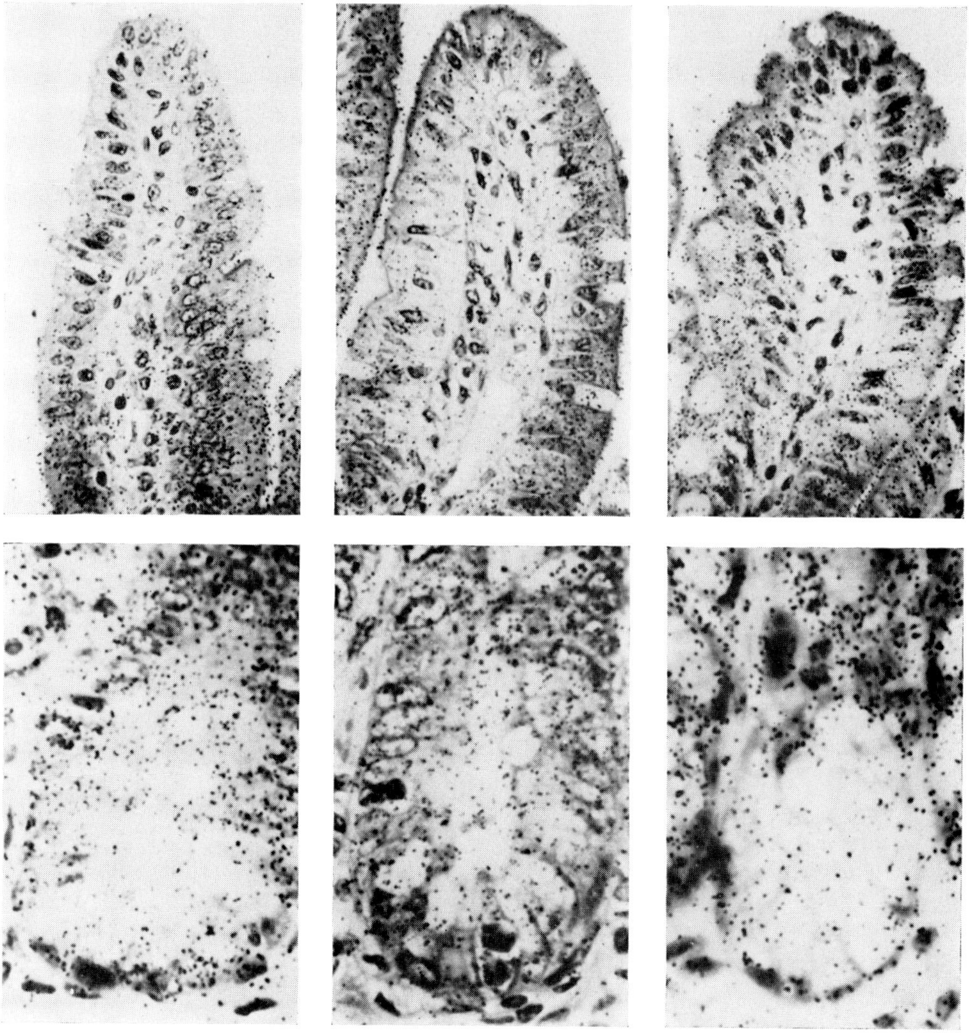

FIG. 4. Intestinal villi (upper row) and crypts (lower row) after injection with H^3-leucine. (*A*) Normal mouse. Protein synthesis is seen in every cell type. (*B*) H^3-Leucine injected 2 hours after irradiation. Leucine incorporation occurs in all cells, even though some of the proliferative cells in the crypt show gross damage. (*C*) H-^{3}Leucine injected 24 hours after irradiation. Leucine incorporation is seen, although considerable loss of cells has occurred. Villi ×700; crypts ×1200.

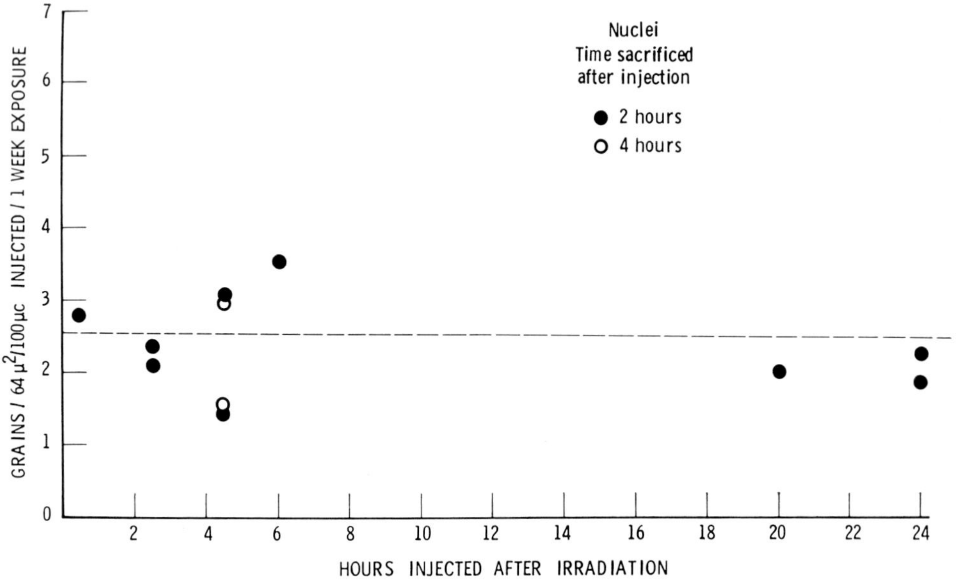

(A)

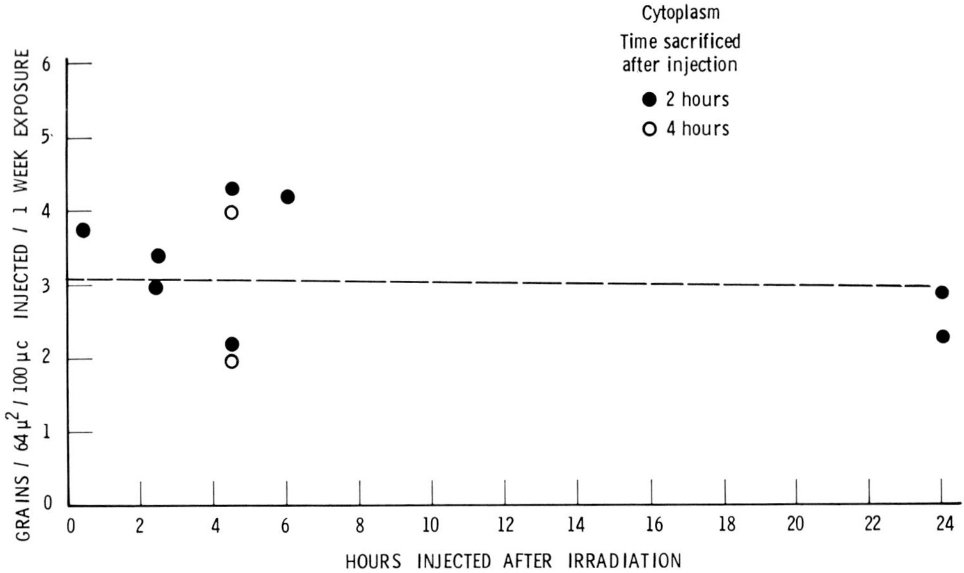

(B)

FIG. 5. Grain densities over nuclei (*A*) and over cytoplasm (*B*) of crypt cells in mice injected at various times after irradiation with 2500 rads and killed 2 to 4 hours after injection. Dotted-line records mean grain density measurements in normal nuclei (*A*) and cytoplasm (*B*) in animals not subjected to irradiation.

TABLE I

GRAIN DENSITIES OF CELLS AND INTRACELLULAR AREAS IN THE INTESTINE AFTER 2000 RADS
(Intracellular gradient)

Cell	Grains/64 μ^2/100μc/1-week exposure					
	1 day after irradiation, villus			*2 days after irradiation, villus*		
	Base	*Middle*	*Tip*	*Base*	*Middle*	*Tip*
Epithelial						
Distal cytoplasm	7.2	6.3	4.6	6.2	5.4	4.0
Proximal cytoplasm	5.8	4.7	3.1	4.3	4.0	2.6
Nucleus	3.6	2.8	1.8	4.6	3.8	2.1
Connective tissue	2.4	2.0	1.8	2.8	2.2	1.9

GRAIN DENSITIES OF CRYPT AND VILLUS EPITHELIAL CELL NUCLEI AFTER 2000 RADS
(Intercellular gradient)

Area	Grains/64 μ^2/100 μc/1-week exposure	
	1 day after irradiation	*2 days after irradiation*
Crypt	6.0	6.1
Villus		
Base	3.6	4.6
Middle	2.8	3.8
Tip	1.8	2.1

Note: Label was injected 3 hours before animal was sacrificed.

were taken 3 hours after injection. The uptake and the gradients within and between cells are very similar to those seen in normal mice (*5*).

At 2 days after irradiation with high doses, leucine uptake in the epithelial cells is reduced, and the reduction is marked at 7 days.

DISCUSSION

It is commonly found that protein synthesis is rather radioresistant. Thus, incorproation of labeled leucine into normal rat liver was slightly increased several hours after X-irradiation, with doses of 1 or 2 kr, although irradiation with 1 kr 2 to 6 hours after hepatectomy in regenerating liver resulted in reduction of uptake by about 30% (*2*). Similarly, incorporation of labeled glycine and lysine into nucleoproteins of normal rat liver and cytoplasmic proteins of liver, thymus, and pancreas was unaffected or slightly increased several hours after 1000 r (*3*). Uptake of methionine-S^{35} into the histone, RNA, and heat-coagulable protein fractions of Jensen rat sarcoma was not affected in any regular manner by irradiation with 2000 r, up to 5 hours after irradiation (*7*). However, tracer incorpation into nuclear protein was reduced after irradiation in the highly radiosensitive lymphocytes (*3*) and the not particularly sensitive cells of the tracheal epithelium (*4*). We found no inhibition of leucine uptake in any of the intestinal cells studied until long after irradiation.

In the intestine, several different kinds of protein are synthesized. The proteins made in the nuclei of proliferative and mature cells are very different from each other and are different from the proteins synthesized in cytoplasms of proliferative and mature intestinal epithelial cells, and from the proteins synthesized in mesenchymal elements. Among the cells of the intestine are some which are highly radiosensitive; in the proliferative cells of the crypt, a dose of a few rads results in noticeable pathological changes in some cells, a dose of 100 rads reduces the rate of tracer incorporation into DNA by about 50% within about 1 hour, a dose of 600 rads causes widespread damage, and a dose of 2000 rads leads to complete destruction of the epithelium. The mature epithelial cells are not killed by radiation in the doses used, but they do show significant functional impairment. Smooth muscles and fibroblasts show no demonstrable radiation effects. Yet in all these cell types, leucine incorporation is equally unchanged for some time after irradiation, as ascertained by autoradiographic analyses after labeling with tritiated leucine.

Beginning 2 days after irradiation with high doses, leucine uptake in the epithelial cells is reduced; the reduction is marked at 3 days. At this time, the epithelial cells are highly pathological, since they were irradiated during their proliferative stage, and have passed through an abnormal development. These cells are impoverished in ribosomes (*8*), which is a morphological expression of reduced ability to synthesize protein.

SUMMARY

Protein synthesis in the irradiated intestine of the mouse was studied. C^{14}-labeled leucine was used for radiochemical investigations, H^3-leucine for autoradiographic studies. No reduction in tracer uptake was found during the first day after irradiation, with doses up to 2500 rads, in any of the cells and cell components studied; however, beginning 2 to 3 days after irradiation with high doses, leucine uptake was reduced.

RECEIVED: July 20, 1962

REFERENCES

1. A. M. BACQ and P. A. ALEXANDER, *Fundamentals of Radiobiology*, pp. 179–186, Pergamon Press, New York, 1961.

2. N. K. SARKER, A. DEVI, and L. H. HEMPELMANN, Effects of irradiation on the incorporation of amino acid into normal and regenerating rat liver. *Nature* **192,** 179–180 (1961).

3. J. E. RICHMOND, M. G. ORD, and L. A. STOCKEN, The effect of X-radiation *in vivo* on protein and nucleoprotein metabolism in the rat. *Biochem. J.* **66,** 123–127 (1957).

4. S. R. PELC, Effects of X-rays on the metabolism of cell nuclei of nondividing tissues. *Nature* **178,** 359–360 (1956)

5. M. Lipkin and H. Quastler, Studies of protein metabolism in intestinal epithelial cells. *J. Clin. Invest.* **41,** 646–653 (1962).
6. H. Quastler and F. G. Sherman, DNA synthesis in irradiated intestinal epithelium. *Exptl. Cell Res.* **19,** 343–360 (1960).
7. B. E. Holmes and L. K. Mee, The incorporation of S^{35} into the proteins of Jensen rat sarcoma cells after irradiation of the tumor. *Brit. J. Radiol.* **25,** 273–278 (1952).
8. H. Quastler and J. C. Hampton, Effects of ionizing radiation on the fine structure and function of the intestinal epithelial of the mouse. I. Villus epithelium. *Radiation Res.* **17,** 914–931 (1962).

RADIATION RESEARCH **19**, 286–297 (1963)

Protein Composition and Growth-Promoting Activity of the Serum after Whole-Body X-Irradiation at Different Ages

ANDRÉ D. GLINOS

Department of Cellular Physiology, Walter Reed Army Institute of Research, Washington, D. C.

INTRODUCTION

Measurements of the growth-promoting activity of blood serum after whole-body irradiation seem to be desirable on two accounts: first, because inhibition of the growth of animal and bacterial cell cultures with serum from irradiated animals has already been reported and attributed to specific radiation-induced humoral toxic factors (*1, 2*); and second, because irradiation has been shown to cause marked changes in the concentration of serum protein fractions (*3–15*), some of which are considered to be involved in cellular growth on the basis of other independent evidence (*16–22*). A meaningful interpretation of any effects that irradiation may have on the growth-promoting activity of the serum would, therefore, require detailed information as to the protein composition of the serum after whole-body irradiation.

Although a rather large number of reports is available concerning radiation-induced changes of the proteins of the sera of monkeys (*3*), dogs (*4*), rabbits (*5–7*), rats (*8–13*), and mice (*14, 15*), there is still considerable uncertainty with respect to the magnitude and time course of the response of the various fractions involved. Both Höhne *et al.* (*8, 9*) and Winkler and Paschke (*10, 11*) described in the rat a decrease in albumin and an increase in the α_2-globulins between 24 and 48 hours postirradiation, with subsequent decrease in the γ-globulins and increase in the α_1- and β-globulins; but, whereas Höhne *et al.* found that the intensity and time course of these changes were not dose-dependent (*9*), the opposite relationship was described by Winkler and Paschke (*10, 11*). In contrast to these results, Fisher *et al.* (*12*) found that albumin and γ-globulin are decreased 7 days after 800 r, but that α- and β-globulins are virtually unchanged, whereas Peters and Bauer (*13*) working with comparable radiation doses described two types of response with prognostic value: a decrease in the albumin and an increase in the α_1-, α_2- and β-globulins, usually associated with lethal injury, and a decrease in the albumin and an increase in the β- and γ-globulins, usually associated with nonlethal injury.

In the present experiments, possible changes in the growth-promoting activity of the serum after acute total-body irradiation were investigated by incorporating sera obtained from irradiated rats into the growth media of replicate cultures of the L strain of mouse fibroblasts. The possible relationship between growth-promoting activity and serum protein changes after irradiation was explored by determining the protein composition of the sera incorporated into the culture media. It is felt that the inconsistencies in the reported behavior of the serum proteins after irradiation are due, at least in part, to individual variation and to fluctuations with time of the values of certain fractions, without any relationship to irradiation. For this reason, instead of the usual single comparison of sera from irradiated and control animals, or of pre- and postirradiation sera from the same animals, an internal standard method combining both these comparisons was used.

EXPERIMENTAL PROCEDURES

Animals

Male Walter Reed-bred rats of the Wistar stock, varying in age from 4 to 40 weeks, were used. Within this range, the following weight-age groups were considered sufficiently uniform to be used as desired in particular experiments: 35 to 65 gm $\approx$4 weeks of age; 100 to 130 gm $\approx$6 weeks; 225 to 275 gm $\approx$10 weeks; 375 to 425 gm $\approx$20 weeks; and 475 to 525 gm $\approx$40 weeks. Depending on the age groups used and in order to obtain a sufficient amount of serum, 5 to 12 experimental or control animals were included in each experiment.

Radiation

Experimental animals were irradiated in a circular Lucite box rotated on a turntable to ensure uniform exposure. An X-ray generator operated at 250 kvp, TSD 80 cm, 30 ma, with a filter of 1 mm Al and 1 mm Cu, and an HVL of 1.93 mm Cu, delivered the radiation. The dose rate was 25 r/min, as measured in air with a calibrated Victoreen thimble ionization chamber. In control experiments, rats were sham-irradiated by placing them in the Lucite box and rotating them for a length of time equal to the exposure time of the irradiated animals.

Blood Sampling

In experiments which included protein determinations, a blood sample of 1 ml was obtained from each experimental or control animal 10 days prior to irradiation. The bleeding was carried out by cardiac puncture under sterile conditions after a 24-hour fast. The blood samples were allowed to clot for 2 hours at room temperature and refrigerated for another 2 hours to aid retraction. The sera were then obtained by "rimming" the clots with a thin glass rod and centrifuging twice at 2000 rpm. After the bleeding, the rats were returned to their cages and allowed food and water *ad libitum*. Ten days later, immediately after being irradiated or sham-irradiated as the case may be, the animals were again fasted for 24 hours, then exsanguinated through cardiac puncture under sterile conditions, and sera were obtained as previously described. After a 1-ml sample from each individual serum had been set aside for protein analysis, the sera were pooled and used in the tissue culture experiments. In experiments where protein determinations were not needed, only the postirradiation bleeding was carried out, as already described.

Protein Determinations

Total protein was determined in individual 10-day preirradiation and 24-hour postirradiation sera from control and experimental rats by the biuret method of Gornall *et al.* (*23*) adapted for 0.1-ml serum samples. Duplicate paper electrophoresis separations on 0.010-ml samples of the same sera were carried out for 16 hours at 12 ma in a barbital buffer at pH 8.6 and ionic strength 0.075 on Whatman 3 MM paper strips. The strips were dried in an oven at 115°C for 30 minutes, then dyed with bromphenol blue. The relative amount of protein in the fractions was determined by using an integrating photometric scanner (*24*).

Tissue Culture

Stock cultures of the strain L-929 of mouse fibroblasts obtained from Dr. Earle several years ago were maintained in Earle's original medium consisting of 40% horse serum, 40% balanced saline solution, and 20% (1:1) chick embryo extract. Only 4-day-old stock cultures were used, to ensure that the cells were in the logarithmic growth phase at the time of harvest. Cells to be used in individual experiments were harvested by trypsinization and resuspended in the experimental medium consisting of 40% pooled serum from irradiated or control rats in Earle's balanced saline solution. The cell density of the suspension was determined by quadruplicate hemocytometer counts. Replicate cultures (*25*) were set up by inoculating T-15 flasks with 3×10^5 cells and bringing the total volume of the cell suspension per flask to 2.5 ml with additional medium. The flasks were then incubated at 37°C for the desired length of time without renewal of the medium. At the end of the incubation period and after microscopic examination of the cells, the flasks were centrifuged at $80 \times g$ for 10 minutes, the medium was decanted, the cells were fixed in citric acid, and the nuclei were counted with a hemocytometer by means of a modification of the original method of Sanford *et al.* (*26*).

RESULTS

Early Effects of Irradiation on Serum Protein Composition

In the first experiment of this series, total serum protein determinations and electrophoretic analyses were carried out on individual serum samples collected from 9 control and 9 irradiated animals before and 24 hours after sham or actual irradiation (600 r) as previously described. In order to minimize individual differences and random time fluctuations, the results of the two analyses of each serum were expressed as the ratio (postirradiation value/preirradiation value). Mean values and standard deviations of these ratios for control and irradiated animals were then calculated and are shown in Table I. On the basis of this internal standard method of comparison, the differences shown at the bottom line of the table express per cent deviations from the norm which can be attributed to the irradiation with reasonable assurance. Evaluation of the significance of these deviations with the t-test shows a small but significant decrease in the total protein and the albumin fraction of the serum. It should be noted that the α_2-globulin fraction increased by almost 30%, although this figure does not appear to be significant because of the large standard deviation associated with this fraction. Table II shows the results of an identical experiment with the radiation dose increased to 1200 r. In this case a significant increase of 50% in the α_2-fraction was found. This partly compensated for the decrease in the albumin, which was the same as with 600 r, and probably accounted for the fact that the decrease in the total protein was less than at 600 r, and not significant.

The approximate age of the rats used in these experiments was 10 weeks. Protein determinations, carried out under similar conditions on sera from rats of the other age groups, showed neither a correlation of the composition of normal serum with age nor any effects of irradiation different from the ones already described.

Growth Rate of the L Strain in Sera from Normal and Irradiated Rats

In the first experiment of this series, replicate cultures of the L strain were set up with an initial inoculum of 3×10^5 cells and sera obtained from sham-irradiated

TABLE I

EFFECT OF 600 ROENTGENS OF WHOLE-BODY IRRADIATION ON THE COMPOSITION OF SERUM PROTEINS 24 HOURS LATER

Rats	*Total protein*[a] *(gm/100 ml serum)*	*Albumin*[a] *(% total protein)*	*Globulin*[a] *(% total protein)*			
			α_1	α_2	β	γ
Sham-irradiated (9 rats)	0.96 0.06	0.96 0.07	1.05 0.10	1.00 0.22	1.04 0.13	1.02 0.18
Irradiated 600 r (9 rats)	0.88 0.07	0.86 0.09	1.11 0.22	1.28 0.38	1.03 0.14	1.12 0.15
Difference	−0.08[b]	−0.10[b]	+0.06	+0.28	−0.01	+0.10

[a] Each set of values represents the mean ratio (postirradiation value/preirradiation value), obtained as described in the text, ± the standard deviation.

[b] t-test: $p < 0.05$.

TABLE II

Effect of 1200 Roentgens of Whole-Body Irradiation on the Composition of Serum Proteins 24 Hours Later

Rats	*Total protein*[a] (*g/100 ml serum*)	Albumin[a] (*% total protein*)	*Globulin*[a] (*% total protein*)			
			α_1	α_2	β	γ
Sham-irradiated (9 rats)	0.97 0.06	1.03 0.03	0.93 0.11	1.14 0.27	1.00 0.18	0.93 0.17
Irradiated 1200 r (9 rats)	0.92 0.05	0.91 0.06	0.92 0.05	1.63 0.46	1.07 0.08	0.91 0.15
Difference	−0.05	−0.12[b]	−0.01	+0.49[b]	+0.07	−0.02

[a] Each set of values represents the mean ratio (postirradiation value/preirradiation value), obtained as described in the text, ± the standard deviation.

[b] t-test: $p < 0.05$.

control and irradiated (600-r) rats. Cell counts were performed in quadruplicate cultures after 2, 4, and 6 days of incubation, without renewal of the medium. The results are shown in Fig. 1, where it can be seen that, for the first 4 days, growth was logarithmic, with a deceleration occurring during the last 2 days, obviously due to the lack of medium renewal. There was no difference in the rates of growth with the two kinds of serum, the mean cell generation time during the logarithmic growth phase being approximately 34 hours for both sera.

The effects of varying the radiation dose were investigated next. In these experiments, replicate cultures of the L strain were incubated for 4 days, i.e., the duration of the logarithmic growth phase, in sera from animals exposed to X-ray doses varying from 600 to 2400 r. Cell counts were performed on quadruplicate cultures at the end of the 4-day incubation period, and the ratio (final cell count/inoculum cell count), i.e., the relative cell number, was used to quantitate growth. The results obtained are shown in Table III, where it can be seen that, within the range of doses investigated, irradiation was without effect.

The age of the rats used in the tissue culture experiments hitherto described was approximately 10 weeks.

Growth-Promoting Activity of Sera from Normal and Irradiated Rats of Different Ages

Since radiosensitivity is known to vary with age (*27–29*), the possible effects of irradiation (1200 r) on the growth-promoting activity of the serum of rats approximately 10, 20 and 40 weeks of age was investigated in the experiments summarized in Table IV. Five control and five irradiation experiments were conducted

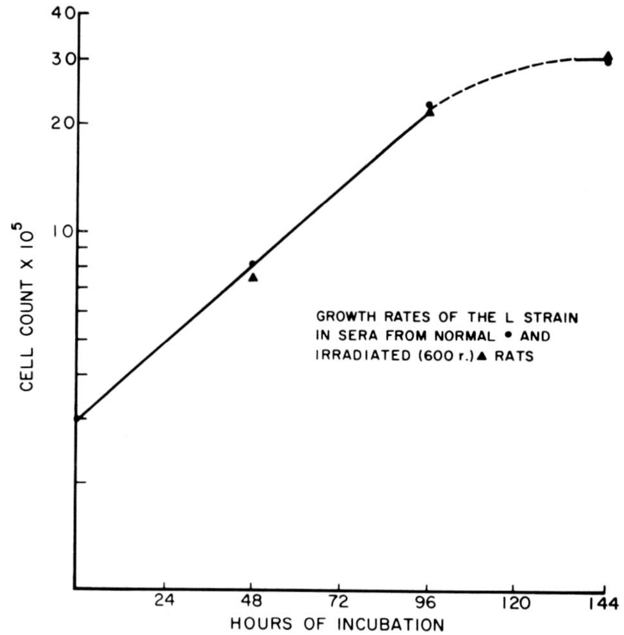

FIG. 1. Cell population kinetics of replicate cultures of the L strain in sera from normal control and irradiated (600-r) rats.

TABLE III

GROWTH OF L STRAIN CELLS IN SERA FROM RATS IRRADIATED WITH DIFFERENT X-RAY DOSES 24 HOURS BEFORE

Radiation dose (r)	*Relative cell number*
600	5.1
1200	5.8
1800	6.9
2400	5.8

with each of the three age groups. As in the previous experiments with various radiation doses, the results are expressed as the relative cell numbers of replicate cultures of the L strain at the end of 4 days of logarithmic growth in sera of control and irradiated rats. No significant differences due to irradiation were found in any of the age groups; the mean relative cell numbers for all control and all irradiation sera were identical.

On the other hand, it was found that, in both control and radiation experiments, relative cell numbers were progressively higher with increasing age. Thus, the mean values of the 10- and 40-week-old groups, calculated on the basis of all con-

TABLE IV

GROWTH OF L STRAIN CELLS IN SERA FROM CONTROL AND IRRADIATED (1200 ROENTGENS) RATS OF DIFFERENT AGES

Rats		*Relative cell number*		
Age (weeks)	*Weight (gm)*	*Control*[a]	*Irradiated*[a]	*Mean*
10	225–275	5.1	4.1	
		4.4	4.5	
		4.9	3.7	4.5[b]
		4.4	4.6	
		4.4	4.4	
20	375–425	5.1	5.2	
		6.0	4.8	
		4.8	6.9	5.2
		4.9	5.9	
		4.1	5.0	
40	475–525	7.3	7.0	
		5.5	5.7	
		6.0	5.8	5.9[b]
		5.6	4.7	
		5.0	6.3	
Mean		5.2	5.3	

[a] Each value represents the ratio (final cell count/inoculum cell count).
[b] t-test: $p < 0.001$.

trol and radiation experiments in each group pooled together, were found to be significantly different from each other when tested with the t-test ($p < 0.001$). Additional experiments with 4- and 6-week-old rats, as reported elsewhere (*30*), showed relative cell numbers 5.7 and 3.2, respectively; radiation was again without effect.

DISCUSSION

The results of the tissue culture experiments of this work indicate a small but significant increase in the growth-promoting activity of the serum with age in normal as well as in irradiated rats, 10 to 40 weeks old (Table IV). This is at variance with the early findings of Carrel and Ebeling on the accumulation of growth-inhibitory factors in the sera of older animals (*31*) but accords with observations of an increase in the growth-promoting activity of the serum with age, within certain limits, by O. A. Trowell (personal communication) in cultures of rat lymph nodes with rat serum, by Penttinen and Saxen in cultures of HeLa cells with human serum (*32*), and by J. M. Bailey (personal communication) in cultures of the mouse lymphoblasts MB III with human serum. Some of the possible theoretical implications of variations in the growth-promoting activity of the serum of rats between the ages of 4 and 40 weeks, found to occur in both the control and irradiated rats in this experiment, have been discussed elsewhere (*30*).

Irradiation with doses varying from 600 to 2400 r was found to be without effect on the growth-promoting activity of the serum, within the entire age range tested. This is at variance with the depression of the rate of growth of chick heart fibroblasts with serum from irradiated rabbits reported by Müller and attributed to the production of a specific humoral factor by the irradiated organism (*1, 2*).

Since its inception, the hypothesis that irradiation induces the production of specific toxic chemical factors (*33*) which can imitate known effects of radiation on cells and tissues (*34*) has generated considerable controversy both among the earlier (see ref. *35*) as well as among contemporary radiobiologists (*36*). Although no such factors have ever been isolated, the argument for their existence has rested on the belief that irradiation can cause a greater effect in some organs with whole-body exposure than with local exposure and that local irradiation elsewhere in the body can result in degenerative changes in nonirradiated tissues (*36*). The demonstration that such distant or abscopal effects of irradiation (see ref. *37*) on lymphoid tissues are secondary to the stress syndrome has led to a questioning of the proposition that there are any such effects that cannot be interpreted on the basis of the known physiological integrative mechanisms of the body or the liberation of nonspecific toxic products from injured or dead cells (*36*).

A comparison of Müller's work with the present experiments, against this background, should begin with a careful examination of similarities and differences in the materials and procedures used. The main similarities are: (1) total radiation dose—900 r in Müller's work and 600 to 2400 r in the present experiments; (2) dose rate—20 r/min and 25 r/min; (3) time of postirradiation blood collection—24 hours in both experiments; and (4) growth period of the tissue cultures—5 days and 4 to 6 days. The most important of these similarities, from the point of view of the physiology of the irradiated organism, is that in both experiments blood was collected only 24 hours after irradiation in anticipation of the subsequent occurrence of extensive cellular death with its concomitant massive release of nonspecific toxic substances in the circulation. The main differences between the two experiments are: (1) animal species—rabbits in Müller's work versus rats in the present experiments; (2) tissue culture system—primary explants of chick heart fibroblasts versus replicate cultures of the L strain cells; and (3) quantitation of cellular proliferation—indirectly, by measuring the radioactivity of the entire explant *in situ* after incubation in the presence of P^{32}, versus directly, by counting cell nuclei. The last two differences render difficult a direct comparison of the results of the two experiments on methodological grounds. From the point of view of the physiology of the irradiated organism, however, the most important difference concerns the animal species used in the two experiments. This is so because the response of the two species with respect to serum protein composition during the first 24 hours after irradiation is strikingly different. In the rabbit, this response is characterized by a marked increase in the β-globulin fraction (*6*) shown to be associated with low-density lipoproteins (*38–40*). In the rat, on the other hand, the results of the present work (Tables I and II) show no change in the β-globulin fraction but a significant increase in the α_2-globulin, known to be associated primarily with glyco- and mucoproteins (*41*).

A high concentration of serum lipoproteins has been correlated with mortality, not only when it occurs early after irradiation, as in the rabbit, but also when it occurs later, as in other species (*4, 40, 42*). In addition, sera with high lipoprotein concentrations have been found to have low growth-promoting activity for mammalian cells (*22*), the general toxicity of lipids in tissue cultures having been demonstrated first by Baker and Carrel (*43*) and subsequently confirmed by others (*44, 45*).

The α_2-serum globulin fraction and associated glycoproteins, on the other hand, have been found to be related to processes of cell growth, both in the organism (*16–20*) and in tissue culture (*21*), although the exact nature of this relationship remains to be elucidated. Some aspects of the latter problem, including the failure of sera with relatively high concentrations of the α_2-globulins to show increased growth-promoting activity, also observed in the present experiments (cf. Tables II and IV), have been discussed elsewhere (*21*).

These considerations make possible an interpretation of differences in the growth-promoting activities of sera from irradiated rabbits and rats on the basis of differences in the concentration of low-density lipoproteins in the two sera. The β-lipoproteins, the α_2-glyco- and mucoproteins, as well as other protein fractions of the serum, are known to respond in a similar manner to insults other than radiation (*46–51*), most probably as a result of tissue injury. It must therefore be concluded that, to the extent that it is mediated through these fractions, any effect that irradiation may have on the growth-promoting activity of the serum will depend on the pattern of the physiological response to nonspecific injury characteristic of the particular organism considered. This conclusion, derived from tissue culture experiments and negative with respect to the hypothesis of specific radiotoxins, is entirely consistent with the findings of Campo *et al.* (*51*) and of Manson and Cloutier (*52*), who were unable to detect by *in vivo* methods the radiotoxic substances reported by Edelmann (*53*) to be present in the serum of irradiated rats.

SUMMARY

1. The composition of the serum proteins of the rat, evaluated 24 hours after irradiation by paper electrophoresis, on the basis of an internal standard of comparison, showed a significant, dose-dependent increase in the α_2-globulin fraction.

2. The growth-promoting activity of the serum, evaluated 24 hours after irradiation by incorporating the serum in the medium of replicate cultures of the L strain

of mouse fibroblasts, did not show any significant difference from the activity of serum from sham-irradiated control rats of the same age.

3. These results were compared with available data pertaining to other mammals, and their implications with respect to the interpretation of the distant, or abscopal, effects of radiation were discussed.

ACKNOWLEDGMENTS

The technical assistance of G. R. Anderson, C. M. Berger, and D. White is greatefully acknowledged.

RECEIVED: July 23, 1962

REFERENCES

1. J. MÜLLER, Influence of ionizing radiation on the appearance in the serum of rabbits of humoral factors slowing down cell division. *Nature* **176,** 43–44 (1956).
2. J. MÜLLER, The influence of ionising radiation on the development of humoral factors which retard cell division in higher organisms. *Physiol. Bohemoslov.* **5,** 337–348 (1956).
3. C. A. LEONE, A. R. HARTNETT, R. CRIST, and C. MCBETH, Paper electrophoretic analyses of sera from irradiated rhesus monkeys. *Radiation Res.* **10,** 357–69 (1959).
4. W. H. GOLDWATER and C. ENTENMAN, Nature of serum protein changes in the X-irradiated dog. *Am. J. Physiol.* **188,** 409–414 (1957).
5. G. MEYNIEL and S. DE MENDE, Étude électrophorétique des protéines du sérum chez les animaux irradiés. *Bull. Sté. Chim. Biol.* **37,** 127–131 (1955).
6. O. ANDREONI, M. DOMPÈ, and A. M. RUSSO, Proteine e lipoproteine seriche in conigli sottoposti a paniradiadiazione. *Ric. Sci.* **25,** 1393–1399 (1955).
7. E. WALDSCHMIDT-LEITZ and L. KELLER, Über den Einfluss der Bestrahlung auf die Zusammensetzung der Serumproteine. *Z. Physiol. Chem.* **323,** 88–92 (1961).
8. G. HÖHNE, R. JASTER, and H. A. KUNKEL, Elektrophoretische Untersuchungen am Serum rontgenbestrahlter Ratten. *Klin. Wochschr.* **39/40,** 952 (1952).
9. G. HÖHNE, H. A. KUNKEL, and R. ANGER, Die Serumeiweisskorper der Ratte nach Röentgenganzbestrahlung mit 3000 r. *Klin. Wochschr.* **11/12,** 284 (1955).
10. C. WINKLER and G. PASCHKE, Serumeiweissveränderungen nach Röntgenganzkörperbestrahlung in Abhängigkeit von der applizierten Dosis. Papierelektrophorese-Untersuchungen an Ratten. *Klin. Wochschr.* **41/42,** 1011 (1955).
11. C. WINKLER and G. PASCHKE, Protein content and composition of rat serum as related to amount of whole-body X-irradiation. *Radiation Res.* **5,** 156–161 (1956).
12. M. A. FISHER, M. Z. MAGEE, and E. P. COUTER, Studies on the serum proteins of the X-irradiated rat. *Arch. Biochem. Biophys.* **56,** 66–75 (1955).
13. K. PETERS and R. BAUER, Untersuchungen über die Wirkung unterschiedlicher Strahlenqualitäten und Strahlendosen auf das Serumeiweiss- und Blutbild von Ratten. *Strahlentherapie* **113,** 553–583 (1960).
14. A. A. WERDER, C. A. HARDIN, and P. MORGAN, The experimental effect of X-irradiation and cortisone on serum proteins. *Radiation Res.* **7,** 500–507 (1957).
15. E. S. GORANSON, E. A. MCCULLOCH, and E. A. CINITS, The effect of whole-body X-irradiation on an alpha-globulin component in the serum of C_3H_f/HeHa Mice. *Radiation Res.* **12,** 560–566 (1960).
16. M. R. SHETLAR, C. P. ERWIN, and M. R. EVERETT, Serum polysaccharide levels in rats bearing the Walker 256 tumor. *Cancer Res.* **10,** 445–447 (1950).

17. P. Bernfield and F. Hamburger, The influence of tumor growth on the plasma proteins in mice. *Cancer Res.* **15,** 359–364 (1955).
18. D. A. Darcy, Immunological demonstration of a substance in rat blood associated with tissue growth. *Brit. J. Cancer* **11,** 137–147 (1957).
19. R. W. Baldwin and H. J. Harries, Serum protein and glycoprotein changes during growth of experimental tumours in the rat. *Brit. J. Cancer* **12,** 99–107 (1958).
20. B. N. White, M. R. Shetlar, and J. A. Schilling, The glycoproteins and their relationship to the healing of wounds. *Ann. N.Y. Acad. Sci.* **94,** 297–307 (1961).
21. A. D. Glinos and W. T. Brown, Quantitative studies on the behavior of the proteins of the medium during the growth of replicate cultures of the L strain. *Exptl. Cell Res.* **27,** 210–220 (1962).
22. E. Saxen and K. Penttinen, Host factors in cell culture: Further studies on the growth-controlling action of fresh human serum. *J. Natl. Cancer Inst.* **26,** 1367–1379 (1961).
23. A. G. Gornall, C. J. Bardavill, and M. M. David, Determination of serum proteins by means of the biuret reaction. *J. Biol. Chem.* **177,** 751–766 (1949).
24. E. L. Durrum and S. R. Gilford, Recording integrating photoelectric and radioactive scanner for paper electrophoresis and chromatography. *Rev. Sci. Instr.* **26,** 51–56 (1955).
25. V. J. Evans, W. R. Earle, K. K. Sanford, J. E. Shannon, and H. K. Waltz, The preparation and handling of replicate tissue cultures for quantitative studies. *J. Natl. Cancer Inst.* **11,** 907–927 (1951).
26. K. K. Sanford, W. R. Earle, V. J. Evans, H. K. Waltz, and J. E. Shannon, The measurement of proliferation in tissue cultures by enumeration of cell nuclei. *J. Natl. Cancer Inst.* **11,** 773–795 (1951).
27. G. A. Sacher, Dependence of acute radiosensitivity on age in adult female mouse. *Science* **125,** 1039–1040 (1957).
28. H. I. Kohn and R. F. Kallman, Age, growth and the LD_{50} of X-rays. Science **124,** 1078 (1956).
29. M. L. Crossfill, P. J. Lindop, and J. Rotblat, Variation of sensitivity to ionizing radiation with age. *Nature* **183,** 1729–1730 (1959).
30. A. D. Glinos, Environmental feedback control of cell division. *Ann. N.Y. Acad. Sci.* **90,** 592–602 (1960).
31. A. Carrel and A. H. Ebeling, Age and multiplication of fibroblasts. *J. Exptl. Med.* **34,** 599–623 (1921).
32. K. Penttinen and E. Saxen, Effect of human sera on cultures of HeLa cells. *Ann. Med. Exptl. Biol. Fenn.* (*Helsinki*) **34,** 22–33 (1956).
33. P. Linser and E. Helber, Experimentelle Untersuchungen über die Einwirkung der Röntgenstrahlen auf das Blut und Bemerkungen über die Einwirkung von Radium und Ultravioletten Lichte. *Deut. Arch. Klin. Med.* **83,** 479–498 (1905).
34. R. Werner, Über die Chemische Imitation der Strahlenwirkung und ihre Verwertbarkeit zur Unterstützung der Radiotherapie. *Strahlentherapie* **1,** 442–498 (1912).
35. J. S. Lawrence, W. N. Valentine, and A. H. Dowdy, The Effect of radiation on hemopoiesis. Is there an indirect effect? *Blood* **3,** 593–610 (1948).
36. G. W. Casarett, S. R. Glasser, E. P. Cronkite, F. Bernheim, V. P. Bond, B. H. Levedahl, O. A. Schjeide, J. R. Totter, T. J. Haley, J. F. Mead, M. Schneider, L. S. Kelly, R. C. Rustad, and H. B. Jones, in *Radiobiology at the Intra-cellular Level* (T. G. Hennessy, B. H. Levedahl, L. S. Myers Jr., D. R. Howton, J. F. Mead, and O. A. Schjeide, eds.), pp. 115–144, Pergamon Press, New York, 1959.
37. Z. M. Bacq and P. Alexander, *Fundamentals of Radiobiology*, p. 451, Pergamon Press, New York, 1961.

38. J. E. HEWITT, T. L. HAYES, J. W. GOFMAN, H. B. JONES, and F. T. PIERCE, Effects of total body irradiation upon lipoprotein metabolism. *Am. J. Physiol.* **172,** 579–587 (1953).
39. T. L. HAYES and J. E. HEWITT, Serum lipoproteins as an indication of survival time in the X-irradiated rabbit. *Am. J. Physiol.* **181,** 280–286 (1955).
40. J. E. HEWITT and T. L. HAYES, X-Irradiation and lipoprotein metabolism in various species. *Am. J. Physiol.* **185,** 257–264 (1956).
41. G. R. COOPER, in *The Plasma Proteins* (F. W. Putnam, ed.), Vol. I, pp. 88–91, Academic Press, New York, 1960.
42. W. H. GOLDWATER and C. ENTENMAN, Effect of X-irradiation on lipid metabolism. III. Dog serum lipoproteins. *Radiation Res.* **4,** 243–256 (1956).
43. L. E. BAKER and A. CARREL, Action des lipoides du sérum sur la multiplication cellulaire. *Compt. Rend. Soc. Biol.* **93,** 79–82 (1925).
44. J. A. JACQUEZ and E. BARRY, Tissue culture media—The essential non-dialyzable factors in human placental cord serum. *J. Gen. Physiol.* **34,** 765–774 (1951).
45. R. CAILLEAU, D. HOARD, and E. ZITCER, Chemical composition of some sera and cells used in tissue cultures. *Texas Rept. Biol. Med.* **15,** 250–259 (1957).
46. L. J. MILCH, R. F. REDMONT, and W. W. CALHOUN, Blood lipoproteins in traumatic injury. *J. Lab. Clin. Med.* **43,** 603–614 (1954).
47. C. HOCH-LIGETI, K. IRVINE, and E. P. SPRINKLE, Investigation of serum protein patterns in patients undergoing operation. *Proc. Soc. Exptl. Biol. Med.* **84,** 707–710 (1953).
48. J. G. ALVAREZ and F. E. DE SALAMANCA, JR., Electroforesis en Papel. IV. Communicacion—Las Variaciones de las Fracciones Proteicas en el Curso Postoperatorio. *Arch. Med. Exptl. (Madrid)* **17,** 555–568 (1954).
49. M. B. WILLIAMSON, Protein metabolism during healing of wounds. *Clin. Chem.* **2,** 1–15 (1956).
50. C. A. HARDIN, A. A. WERDER, and P. MORGAN, The effect of skin transplants on serum proteins in experimental animals. *Surg. Gynecol. Obstet.* **106,** 605–609 (1958).
51. R. D. CAMPO, V. P. BOND, and E. P. CRONKITE, Failure to demonstrate toxic factors in the serum of irradiated rats. *Proc. Soc. Exptl. Biol. Med.* **98,** 440–443 (1958).
52. J. M. MANSON and J. A. R. CLOUTIER, Unsuccessful attempt to detect the presence of a toxic factor in the blood of irradiated rats. *Can. J. Zool.* **37,** 83–85 (1959).
53. A. EDELMANN, Toxicity of serum from irradiated animals. *Science* **121,** 662 (1955).

RADIATION RESEARCH 19, 298–315 (1963)

Analysis of Teeth and Bones for Alpha-Emitting Elements[1]

EDWARD P. RADFORD, JR., VILMA R. HUNT,[2] AND DWYN SHERRY

Department of Physiology, Harvard School of Public Health, Boston, Massachusetts

INTRODUCTION

The important naturally occurring elements accounting for variations in human bone radiation dose are believed to be radium-226 and its daughters, including polonium-210, and the daughters of radium-228. These α-emitting isotopes are present in such small amounts that physical measurements and radiochemical analyses have generally required large bone samples. For purposes of characterizing body burdens of human populations, such samples are not readily available in large numbers. We have developed a method suitable for analysis of samples as small as a single tooth or a comparable piece of bone. Teeth are the only calcified tissues easily available from living individuals of all ages with known residence history and thus may be adequate for population surveys.

With our technique, Ra^{226} is chemically separated and determined in equilibrium with its short-lived daughters, and Po^{210} is measured separately. As an index of Ra^{228} or thorium-228 levels, we have also measured Ra^{224}. All three determinations are done on the same sample. The method is simple to carry out, requiring only 1 day for the chemical separations and preparation for counting. The principal limitation arises from the long counting times required, and the necessity for low-background α-counters. The number of analyses per day depends on the number of counters available.

ANALYTICAL PROCEDURE

Preparation of Samples

Teeth. Remove all filling materials, carious tissue, stained secondary dentin, and calculus. *Bone:* Boil in demineralized water to remove excess fat, then clean

[1] The work reported in this paper was supported by U. S. Public Health Service Grant RG7615 and by the Higgins Fund, Harvard University, in collaboration with the Department of Epidemiology, Harvard School of Public Health.

[2] Scholar, Radcliffe Institute for Independent Study, Radcliffe College, Cambridge, Massachusetts.

thoroughly of any adhering soft tissue. Add 30 ml of concentrated hydrochloric acid, and heat to 60°C until the sample is dissolved. With teeth a clear solution results, whereas considerable undigested fat may remain on the surface of bone solutions. We have found that this fat does not interfere with polonium recovery.

Procedure for Po^{210} separation

Dilute the bone or tooth solution to 100 ml with 0.5 *N* HCl. Place the solution in a modified plating cell made from a commercial baby nursing bottle with the bottom removed. A silver disk (1¼ inches in diameter) is held in the screw top of the bottle by a Neoprene gasket. Thus the plating cell consists of an open inverted bottle with the silver disk at the bottom. A glass cover with a center hole for the stirrer reduces evaporation. Allow Po^{210} to deposit on the silver disk, by the method of Vittum *et al.* (*1*) as modified by Holtzman (*2*). Carry out the plating for 4 hours at 90° to 100°C with continuous stirring. For bone solutions, add 40 mg of ascorbic acid as a reducing agent to prevent any inhibitory effect of ferric ions from blood.

Procedure for Radium Separation

The following is a modification of the coprecipitation method of Goldin (*3*). After plating Po^{210}, filter the bone solutions to remove fat and particulate material. Wash down the filter paper, and dilute to 200 ml with 0.5 *N* HCl (150 ml is sufficient if the samples originally were less than 1 gm). Tooth solutions may be diluted directly after plating without filtration. Add 2 ml of 0.24 *M* lead nitrate and 4 ml of 0.018 *M* barium nitrate (containing 10 mg of Ba). Precipitate lead and barium sulfate with 20 ml of 9 *M* sulfuric acid, and allow the solution to stand for 10 minutes. The solubility factor of calcium sulfate is such that the solution is apt to be nearly saturated. If the solution is allowed to cool, $CaSO_4$ is likely to precipitate, being observed as a more flocculent thick precipitate than the fine, powdery precipitate of barium and lead sulfate. If $CaSO_4$ does precipitate, it can generally be redissolved by heating.

Centrifuge the sulfate solution in a 250-ml centrifuge tube and decant, saving the supernatant solution for calcium determination by the method of Yalman *et al* (*4*). Wash the precipitate into a beaker, using 10 ml of demineralized water, and add 10 ml of 10% disodium EDTA and 2 drops of metacresol purple. Add 4 *N* sodium hydroxide dropwise, and stir the solution until the pH is on the basic side and the precipitate clears. Add 1 ml of 3.8 *M* ammonium sulfate and 2 drops of methyl purple. Reduce the pH to 5 (as determined by the methyl purple indicator), using glacial acetic acid to reprecipitate the barium sulfate. Lead is complexed by disodium EDTA. The final barium sulfate, carrying the radium with it, is then obtained by centrifuging. Transfer as a slurry to a stainless-steel planchet 2 inches in diameter. Use demineralized water to wash out the centrifuge tube, and then evaporate the planchet to dryness under an infrared lamp. This method produces a relatively uniform distribution of the precipitate. Flame the planchet to glowing red to drive off trapped radon and to ignite organic material present. The final precipitate is 25 to 30 mg, consistent with 100% recovery of the barium carrier. Allow the planchet to stand for 2 hours before counting, to eliminate short-lived daughters of Rn^{222} dissolved in the reagent solutions. Store each planchet in a separate envelope in a desiccator.

To avoid contamination of the glassware, use a routine washing system with three soaking solutions: first detergent, then 1% disodium EDTA solution, and finally dilute hydrochloric acid, each for 8 to 12 hours. Rinse with demineralized water.

Determination of Ra^{224} *and* Ra^{223} *in Radium Precipitate*

Radium separated by this chemical method includes Ra^{224} and Ra^{223}, if present. Because these two isotopes have short half-lives, Ra^{226} can be determined separately by allowing the samples to stand for 3 to 4 weeks. We have used two techniques of determining Ra^{224} or Ra^{223} individually. The most generally applicable is a modification of the method of Turner, *et al.* (*5*) for detecting Ra^{224} in the presence of Ra^{226}. In their procedure Ra^{224} is determined from the short half-life decay of its daughter Po^{216}. If a record of individual counts is made with a rate monitor and chart, two counts within 1 second will be registered by Rn^{220} and Po^{216} decay. Because of the 2π geometry of our counters, these double counts will be observed in about one-fourth of the total disintegrations of Rn^{220}. With the low levels of α-activity normally present, such double events occur only rarely by chance.

Radium-223 may be readily detected by decay of Rn^{219} and Po^{215}. In approximately one-eighth of such decays, these two daughters and Ra^{223} will appear as triple counts. In all our records we have seen such a triple count only once, a result which can be explained by chance. We therefore conclude that the Ra^{223} content in our samples is negligible thus far.

Actual analysis of individual counts is made by measuring intervals between counts and fitting their frequency distribution as the sum of two distributions, one nonrandom (arising from Rn^{220} and Po^{216} decay) and the other random (all other events). Details of the theoretical basis for this procedure are given in the Appendix. Because Ra^{224} decays rapidly, it is necessary to make the initial count as soon as possible after chemical separation.

The other method of determining Ra^{224} or Ra^{223} involves the differential decay or growth of the α-activity as shown by Stehney (*6*) and Goldin (*3*). We have found this method to be accurate only if Ra^{224} activity is well above background, that is, greater than approximately 0.10 picocurie, and the ratio of Ra^{226} to Ra^{224} is not greater than 10.

Counting Procedure; Background and Reagent Blank Determinations

All samples are counted for α-activity in windowless gas-flow proportional counters (Nuclear Measurements Corp.), the 2-inch chambers having backgrounds of less than 2 α-counts/hr (generally between 1.0 and 1.8 counts/hr). The Po^{210} samples may be counted in a 1-inch chamber (background approximately 0.7 count/hr). To maintain these low background levels, which are essential to the method, we have had to clean the counters periodically with demineralized water, especially if moderately active radium samples have been counted at any time.

Two reagent blanks for Po^{210} and radium are run once a week and counted for 40 hours. The count above background for Po^{210} blanks has been 0 to 0.5 counts/hr. For radium blanks the count above background was about 1 count/hr, of which about half apparently was from the planchets, as determined from planchet blanks. When radium reagent blanks were counted repeatedly for grow-in of Ra^{226} daughters, little or no increase in activity was found with time, indicating either that the daughters were in equilibrium already (as in the planchets) or that their build-in was small enough to be compensated by a slight amount of Ra^{224} and its daughters which simultaneously decayed out. The constancy of the Ra reagent blanks with time is an important factor allowing improved accuracy of sample counting after Ra^{226} daughters grow in (see below).

For purposes of determining efficiency of chemical recovery, we assume that the counters have 2π geometry, and there is an average backscatter factor of 1.02. It has not been possible to check these assumptions rigorously with our Ra^{226} standard solution (National Bureau of Standards No 4950, accurate to $\pm 0.1\%$), because thin samples made by direct evaporation of the standard do not retain the daughters quantitatively. Early counts on these samples as well as those made from our Po^{210} standard solution (Tracerlab Inc., accurate to $\pm 2\%$) indicate that these assumptions are reasonable. It is possible that the backscatter factor (*7*) is less than 1.02 for radium because of the sample thickness, and greater than 1.02 for Po^{210} because of the semipolished silver surface on which it is plated, but we have arbitrarily retained the single factor. Thus, aside from self-absorption losses, the observed count rate should be 0.51 times the true count rate.

Calculation of Results

All results are expressed as picocuries per gram ash in the sample. Conversion from observed counts to picocuries is based on the recovery data presented below, and on the assumption of 51% counting efficiency exclusive of self-absorption losses. Ash content is calculated from the calcium determination on the basis that the ratio of total ash to calcium is 2.6 (*8*). We have found the calcium content of teeth sufficiently constant ($30\% \pm 2\%$ of total weight) that an average ash content of 78% of the total weight has been assumed for teeth.

RESULTS

Recovery from Spiked Samples

Table I shows recovery data, in all cases with the constant geometry and backscatter correction, for a series of bone and tooth samples spiked with Po^{210} standard solution (Tracerlab Inc., 5.000×10^{-3} μc/liter, accuracy specified within 5%). On plating the standard directly it was found to check within 2% of the supplier's calibration, i.e., within counting statistics in this case. Table I shows that recovery of Po^{210} from these spiked solutions of 22 bones and 13 teeth was 0.99 ± 0.07 (range 0.80 to 1.12). Within the accuracy of the standard, our technique appears to give quantitative recovery of Po^{210}. Some of the variability among the samples may be the result of counting errors due to chance because the total counts observed for each sample were generally 1000 to 2000.

A National Bureau of Standards radium chloride solution ($0.999 \pm 0.001 \times 10^{-9}$ gm in 100 ml), was used to check the efficiency of radium recovery. Table I also shows these results. The recovery from spiked solutions of 11 bones and 15 teeth was 0.65 ± 0.06 (range 0.53 to 0.77). The observed activity of Ra^{226} (Table I) has been converted to the time of flaming of the sample, on the assumption that there is 100% retention of the three short-lived α-emitting daughters. Justification for this assumption is presented below. The loss in processing for Ra^{226}, which on the average is 35%, includes self-absorption of the α's in the sample, and losses of Ra^{226} in the coprecipitation stages. The variability observed among these samples is relatively independent of counting statistics, because each of these samples was counted several times.

Self-Absorption Losses for Radium Measurements

To determine the optimum amount of barium carrier for effective coprecipitation with minimum self-absorption of α's, five samples of the Ra^{226} standard were directly precipitated with varying amounts of barium sulfate. Figure 1 shows the percentage recovery in these samples, corrected for 2π geometry and backscatter, as a function of the amount of barium. It is apparent that, with 5 to 10 mg of barium, radium recovery was maximum; with higher and lower amounts of barium, recovery was less. According to the observations of Nader *et al.* (*9*), one would expect the self-absorption loss to be directly proportional to the thickness of the precipitate for this amount of $BaSO_4$. The dashed line in Fig. 1 represents the self-absorption calculated from their formula, expected on the basis of a uniform precipitate on the planchet. The solid straight line is an empirical representation indicating that self-absorption in our samples is greater than the expected values. We believe that the increased self-absorption loss is a result of nonuniform thickness of the precipitate on the planchet. It is apparent that, if the straight-line relationship shown in the solid line in Fig. 1 does apply, then a sig-

TABLE I

RECOVERY FROM SAMPLES WITH ADDED AMOUNTS OF Po^{210} AND Ra^{226}

(Counts per minute)

Po^{210}			Ra^{226} [a]		
Expected	*Found*	*Found/ expected*	*Expected*	*Found*	*Found/ expected*
		Teeth			
3.34	3.26	0.98	5.66	4.32	0.76
6.68	6.76	1.01	2.83	2.05	0.72
13.35	14.10	1.06	5.66	3.79	0.67
20.01	21.23	1.06	11.32	7.12	0.63
12.64	12.26	0.97	16.98	11.71	0.69
12.14	10.16	0.84	11.32	7.06	0.62
12.14	11.88	0.98	11.32	7.28	0.64
12.14	10.79	0.89	5.66	3.45	0.61
12.14	11.97	0.99	5.66	3.29	0.58
3.14	3.45	1.10	2.83	1.49	0.53
6.28	7.02	1.12	5.66	3.06	0.54
9.42	8.65	0.92	8.49	4.88	0.57
12.56	12.74	1.01	11.32	6.78	0.60
			11.32	7.12	0.63
			11.32	6.30	0.56
		Bones			
13.49	12.54	0.93			
13.49	12.77	0.95			
13.49	13.40	1.00	11.32	7.19	0.64
12.82	12.19	0.95	11.32	6.75	0.60
13.14	12.97	1.01	11.32	7.31	0.65
12.83	12.21	0.95	11.32	7.03	0.62
12.83	12.18	0.95	11.32	7.39	0.65
12.83	11.99	0.93	11.32	7.24	0.64
12.79	12.98	1.02	11.32	6.45	0.57
12.79	11.94	0.93	11.32	8.61	0.76
12.08	12.55	1.04	11.32	8.68	0.77
12.08	12.04	1.00	11.32	8.39	0.74
12.08	12.61	1.04	11.32	8.73	0.77
12.08	12.18	1.01			
10.05	9.65	0.96		Mean ± S.D.	0.65 ± 0.06
10.05	10.07	1.00		Range	0.53–0.77
10.05	9.91	0.99			
10.05	9.36	0.93			
4.08	3.88	0.95			
8.16	7.60	0.93			
12.23	12.68	1.04			
16.31	13.06	0.80			
Mean ± S.D.		0.99 ± 0.07			
Range		0.80–1.12			

[a] Activity corrected to time sample was flamed after plating.

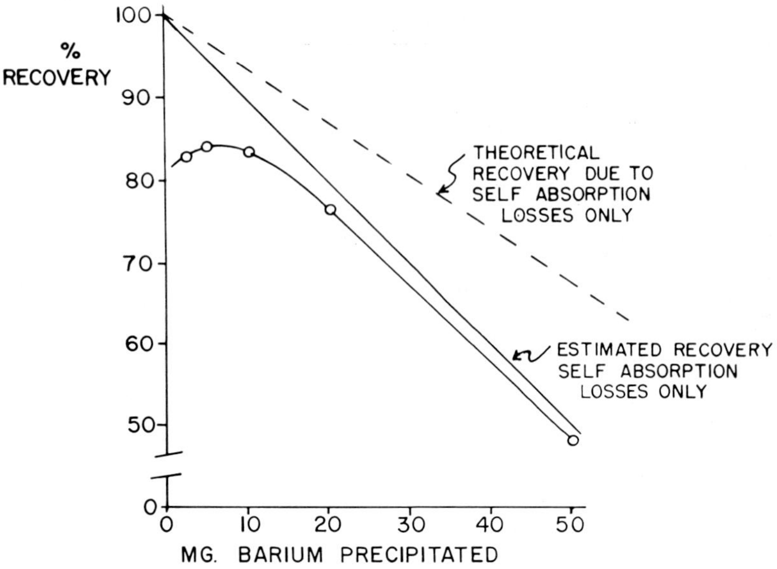

FIG. 1. Recovery of Ra^{226} from solution by a single coprecipitation stage with varying amounts of $BaSO_4$. The dashed line indicates the fractional recovery due to self-absorption of α's based on the formula of Nader *et al.* (*9*) on the assumption that the precipitate is uniformly distributed on the planchet. The solid straight line is an empirical self-absorption line indicating 50% more self-absorption than the theoretical curve would predict, presumably because the precipitate is not uniform. The observed difference between this line and the points is from incomplete coprecipitation.

nificant part of the loss at amounts of barium 10 mg or less must be due to incomplete coprecipitation of the radium.

A series of fourteen experiments was also done by the standard radium separation procedure with bone and tooth samples spiked with Ra^{226}, but with the coprecipitation done in one stage only, that is, with elimination of the lead carrier stage and direct coprecipitation with $BaSO_4$. These experiments gave a mean recovery of 76% (range 69 to 80%). The difference between this result and the two-stage procedure indicates that the omitted stage has an efficiency of about 86%. From Fig. 1 the counting efficiency, considering self-absorption only (solid line), is 90% for 10 mg of Ba precipitated, a figure close to that observed by Stehney (*6*) for a similar thickness of $BaSO_4$. We have, therefore, used these figures to explain the losses of Ra^{226} (Table I). If both coprecipitation stages have a recovery of 86%, then chemical recovery is 74%. The over-all recovery efficiency, exclusive of geometry and backscatter, would be $(0.86)^2 \times 0.90 = 0.665$, very close to the observed value of 0.65.

Retention of Short-Lived Daughters of Ra^{226} on Planchets

Provided that 100% retention of the three short-lived α-emitting daughters of Ra^{226} on the planchet occurs, 99% equilibrium of daughters should be reached in about 25 days. Under these conditions Ra^{226} counted at this time has four α's for every one originally present at zero time, and counting accuracy could be markedly improved, particularly since the reagent blanks show no such change in activity. Repeated counts on samples spiked with Ra^{226} were made to determine if the daughters were completely retained. Figure 2*A* shows a composite build-in curve for 17 bone and tooth samples spiked with Ra^{226} standard. The ordinate represents the ratio of the average count rate at various times to the count rate at zero time calculated from the first count obtained after planchetting. (Since most samples were counted within 1 or 2 hours, these corrections were negligible.) The line drawn in Fig. 2*A* is the theoretical curve for total α-activity on the assumption that the daughters were quantitatively retained. After 3 days the relative count rates were consistently above the theoretical values rather than below. This observation can best be explained by 100% retention of daughters with an increase in counting efficiency for the daughters in comparison with the parent radium α-activity.

To test this possibility more precisely, each count obtained on the 17 samples was converted to zero time by means of standard correction factors (*10*), and the values for all the extrapolated terms were averaged for each sample. Each individual extrapolated value was then compared as a ratio to the mean value thus obtained. This ratio was averaged for all the samples at each time after plating; if no systematic deviation from the theoretical growth curve existed, these ratios should be distributed randomly about 1.0. Figure 2*B* shows a plot of the ratio of the individual extrapolated values to the mean of all determinations as a function of time. The points show a definite rising trend, consistent with increased counting efficiency in the later counts.

This differential counting efficiency presumably depends on greater self-absorption by the parent radium α's in comparison with the daughters, a phenomenon which can only partly be explained by the difference in energy of the α's. Another possible explanation is that the daughter radon is adsorbed on the surface of the precipitate, and thus it and all subsequent daughters are less affected by self-absorption. The solid curve drawn in Fig. 2*B* is based on the assumption that the counting efficiency of the Ra^{226} α's is 90% of the counting efficiency of the three daughters. This approximation appears to fit the data very well, and this correction factor has been applied to all counts on radium samples. Detailed analysis of Figs. 1 and 2 indicates that the self-absorption losses are Ra 16%, daughters 7%.

For the analysis of Ra^{224} decay we have made the same assumptions; the parent radium α-activity counted only 90% as efficiently as the α-activities of the three daughters, and the daughters are 100% retained on the planchet. The assumption

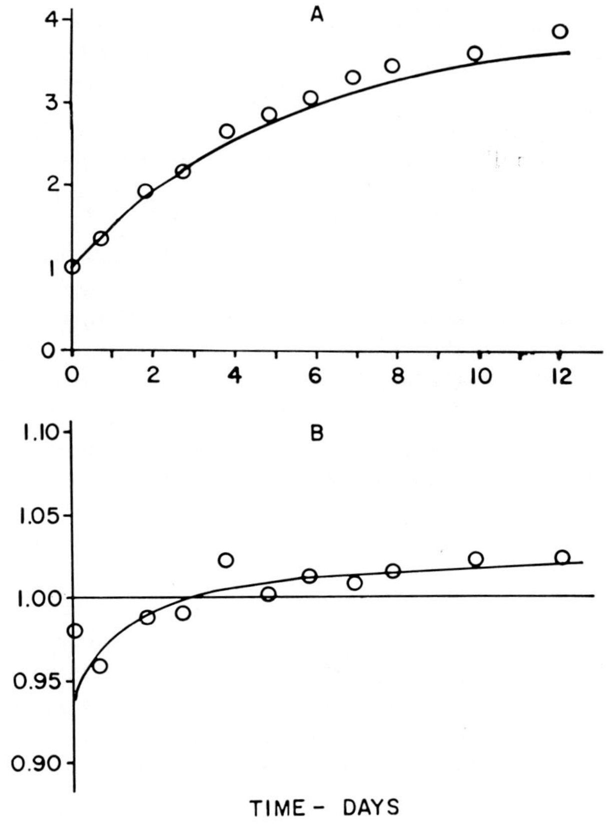

FIG. 2. A, build-up of α-activity in Ra^{226}-spiked bone and tooth samples. Each point is the average of counts made on at least five of seventeen individual samples at varying times after flaming, these counts being related to the zero-time count as determined from the first count on the sample. The line is the expected build-up on the assumption of 100% retention of daughters. B, further analysis of the curve shown in A. Ordinate: ratio of α-activity at time t to mean of all counts on each sample with all counts extrapolated to zero time (see text). The progressive rise in this ratio indicates that the late counts had a higher counting efficiency than the early ones. The line is drawn on the assumption that Ra^{226} α's have a counting efficiency 90% of the three short-lived α-emitting daughters.

of a similar differential efficiency appears reasonable from the standpoint of the α-energies, since the relative energy of parent to daughter α's is similar for both Ra^{224} and Ra^{226}.

Comparison of Our Method with Others

Our chemical separation method of analysis was compared, on a sample of femur from a radium dial painter, with measurements made by a nondestructive method at the Radioactivity Center, Massachusetts Institute of Technology, through the courtesy of Dr. C. J. Maletskos. Measurements of Ra^{224} and Ra^{226} were made at MIT on the whole sample; total Ra^{226} in the bone was obtained by measuring Rn^{222} lost from the bone in an ion chamber, and the Rn^{222} retained in the bone by bismuth-214 γ-rays, by using a scintillation spectrometer. Radium-224 was obtained from thoron determinations by measuring thallium-208 γ-rays. No Po^{210} measurements were done at MIT. The initial weight of the bone sample was 5.470 gm.

Before digestion for our chemical analysis the sample was divided into four quadrants in order to determine possible variations of activity within bone. Due to the loss of bone in the process of cutting, the total bone analyzed from the four quadrants was 4.520 gm, and the final measurements were therefore scaled up to 5.470 gm of bone. Table II shows the comparison of results from the two methods. The agreement between our results and those of the MIT laboratory is excellent, and both Ra results are well within the range of analytical and counting errors for the two methods.

Advantage was taken of the high activity present in this sample to analyze some medullary and cortical sections separately. Although the medullary samples were as small as 10 mg of bone, they could easily be analyzed by our procedure, illustrating the value of the method for quantitative assessment of point-to-point variations of deposition in cases where burdens are high. These results will be presented in detail elsewhere.

Through the generous cooperation of Mr. H. F. Lucas, four samples of bone, adjacent to samples which had been measured at Argonne National Laboratory by different chemical separation methods, were analyzed by our technique. The Argonne procedure for the analysis of Po^{210} is similar to that used by us, except that their samples are initially dissolved in nitric and perchloric acids. For Ra^{226} and Th^{228} analysis, their samples are dry-ashed, and the ash is dissolved in nitric acid. Thorium is extracted into dibutyl phosphate, and Ra^{224} is allowed to grow in.

TABLE II

COMPARISON OF ANALYSIS OF PORTION OF FEMUR FROM RADIUM DIAL WORKER: OUR METHOD, AND ANALYSIS BY MIT RADIOACTIVITY CENTER

	Weight of sample (gm)	*Po^{210}*	*Ra^{226}* (*Total picocuries ± S.D.*)	*Ra^{224}*
Our analysis	4.520	165.0 ± 5.7	414.0 ± 16.9	33.0 ± 1.4
Calculated to 5.470 gm of bone	5.470	199.7 ± 6.9	501.0 ± 20.4	39.9 ± 1.7
Reported by MIT Radioactivity Center	5.470	Not measured	503 ± 18	38 ± 7
Ratio Harvard/MIT			0.996	1.05

The Ra^{224} is extracted and plated on platinum for counting. The Ra^{226} is measured by allowing Rn^{222} to grow in, then adsorbing it on charcoal at dry-ice temperature. The Rn^{222} is then counted in an α-scintillation counter. Note that the Po^{210} and Ra^{226} measurements are not done on the same samples by their method.

Table III shows the results of our analyses compared with the Argonne results. For Ra^{224} the mean recovery from all four samples by the two procedures was within analytical and counting errors; the average ratio of recovery was 1.10, not significantly different from 1.0. The same agreement was found for Po^{210} analyses, our mean recovery being 0.98 times theirs. In one sample (No. 278) our result was significantly higher than theirs, whereas in one (No. 280) our result was significantly lower. We ascribe these differences to local variations of Po^{210} within a single bone. Such local variability was demonstrated in sample No. 278 because we analyzed it in two parts, (278A and 278B in Table III). One part agreed closely with their results; the other did not.

Our results showed an average of 28% more Ra^{226} than was found at Argonne. Two bone samples had a difference in analytical results from the two laboratories greater than could be accounted for by analytical and counting errors, and in all

TABLE III

Po^{210}, Ra^{226}, AND Ra^{224} ANALYSES BY OUR METHOD COMPARED WITH RESULTS FROM ADJACENT BONE SAMPLES BY ARGONNE NATIONAL LABORATORY

(Picocuries/gm ash ±90% error[a])

Sample number		*Po^{210}*	*Ra^{226}*	*Ra^{224}*
120	Harvard	0.105 ± 0.012	0.111 ± 0.017	0.014 ± 0.007
	Argonne	0.102 ± 0.009	0.100 ± 0.008	0.016 ± 0.003
	Harvard/Argonne	1.03	1.11	0.88
276	Harvard	0.094 ± 0.012	0.032 ± 0.006	0.004 ± 0.003
	Argonne	0.109 ± 0.010	0.030 ± 0.004	0.004 ± 0.002
	Harvard/Argonne	0.86	1.07	1.00
278A[b]		(0.173 ± 0.020)	(0.056 ± 0.010)	(0.013 ± 0.006)
278B		(0.256 ± 0.024)	(0.078 ± 0.009)	(0.016 ± 0.009)
Total:	Harvard	0.212 ± 0.017	0.067 ± 0.008	0.014 ± 0.006
	Argonne	0.166 ± 0.009	0.050 ± 0.002	0.010 ± 0.005
	Harvard/Argonne	1.28	1.34	1.40
280	Harvard	0.050 ± 0.008	0.019 ± 0.004	0.008 ± 0.003
	Argonne	0.068 ± 0.008	0.012 ± 0.003	0.007 ± 0.003
	Harvard/Argonne	0.74	1.58	1.14
Harvard/Argonne results				
Average of four samples		0.98	1.28	1.10

[a] Both counting and analytical errors included in Harvard results. Only counting error included in Argonne analysis.

[b] Two separate bone fragments analyzed in our laboratory.

four samples our Ra^{226} results were higher than with the Argonne method. We have no explanation for this difference in results from the two procedures, except possibly to explain the difference by variability between adjacent portions of bone. For the sample (No. 278) analyzed in two parts there was a significant difference in the two pieces by our procedure.

We conclude that, except possibly for Ra^{226} determinations in comparison with the Argonne method, our procedure gave closely comparable results to those obtained in two other laboratories by quite different methods.

DISCUSSION

An important characteristic of a chemical separation technique is the extent to which the procedure discriminates against interfering elements which may be present. Goldin (*3*) investigated the elimination of uranium, thorium, and polonium by his two-stage coprecipitation method, a procedure similar to our radium separation. He found excellent discrimination against all three elements. Since in our procedure Po^{210} is already removed, it is unlikely to contaminate the recovered radium. Petrow *et al.* (*11*) have also reported that interference from other α-emitting elements is eliminated by coprecipitation of radium with lead nitrate, an important point in their processing of mine effluents because of the very high levels of uranium and thorium in comparison with radium. The degree of separation of radium uncontaminated by Pb isotopes was checked in our samples by recounting several months after initial equilibrium was reached. Significant amounts of Pb^{210} are present in samples made from the radium standard as well as from the MIT bone sample. The radium separated from these samples has shown no increase in activity which would be characteristic of the growth of Po^{210} daughter of Pb^{210}. We therefore conclude that no significant amounts of Pb have appeared in the final sample. Discrimination against other elements is the principal reason for using two coprecipitation stages in radium separation; a single $BaSO_4$ coprepicitation stage, although more efficient in radium separation, might permit other elements to be carried down.

Polonium separation depends on electrochemical displacement of silver. There is no other α-emitting element in the electrochemical series which can displace silver in an acid solution (H. G. Petrow, personal communication).

Methods used until now to analyze for these elements include de-emanation techniques (e.g., MIT analytical procedure), chemical separation (e.g., Argonne procedure), and, recently, α-spectrometry (*12*). The latter method could offer many advantages, but it is not yet certain how accurately the radium isotopes can be determined by this method when they are present in amounts less than 0.01 picocurie. The primary advantages of our procedure are the following: (1) It is technically simpler than other methods presently in use. (2) Measurement of the three α-emitting isotopes is done on the same sample at one time. Thus, for example, direct Po^{210}/Ra^{226} ratios can be unequivocally determined. (3) It is suitable for samples as small as a single tooth. (We have been able to measure these elements in deciduous teeth.) (4) Analysis of a large number of samples on a routine basis is possible, the number per day being dependent on the number of counters available. One disadvantage, however, is that the method destroys the sample.

The sensitivity of the method is limited by counting statistics. On the assumption of 24 hours' counting time, and a reagent blank and background of 1 count/hr for Po^{210} and 2 counts/hr for Ra^{226}, the coefficient of variation arising from counting errors can be calculated. With samples of Po^{210} the coefficient of variation exceeds 50% when the total activity of the sample is less than 0.0075 picocurie. For Ra^{226} samples in which daughter equilibrium has been reached, the coefficient of variation exceeds 50% when the Ra activity is less than 0.004 picocurie. The sensitivity of Ra^{224} measurement is limited by the total number of nonrandom events actually observed when the sample is counted and depends also on the absolute level of Ra^{226} (see Appendix). In general, with the levels of Ra^{224} and Ra^{226} we have found in our samples the coefficient of variation of Ra^{224} for a single sample is between 30% and 50% (Table III).

Development of this method raises the question of whether a single tooth or piece of bone is an adequate indicator of whole skeletal burden of these elements. Preliminary studies, which will be reported in detail in a subsequent paper, suggest that a tooth is probably as good as any small sample of bone to estimate human burdens, although variations within the skeleton are present. Also, teeth systematically contain less polonium than bone.

SUMMARY

1. A method for the analysis of a single tooth and small samples of bone for Po^{210}, Ra^{226}, and Ra^{224} is described. It was found to give results in good agreement with those obtained by other laboratories using different methods. Radium-224 was distinguished from Ra^{226} by nonrandom decay of its daughters, or by analysis of the time course of growth or decay of α-activity.

2. There was quantitative chemical recovery of Po^{210} (counting efficiency 51% with 2π geometry and backscatter of 2%). Chemical recovery of radium was approximately 74%; with a self-absorption factor of 0.90, backscatter factor of 1.02, and geometry of 0.50, the combined separation and counting efficiency for radium was 33%. The coefficient of variation for chemical recovery was 7% for polonium and 9% for radium.

3. The chief advantages of the method are its simplicity and the relatively short time necessary for chemical analysis. Simultaneous analyses of Po^{210}, Ra^{226}, and Ra^{224} can be done on the same small sample of calcified tissue. An ash content of 2 gm or less is suitable; for larger samples some modification of the method might be

necessary to avoid $CaSO_4$ precipitation with the initial precipitate in the radium procedure.

APPENDIX

Theory of Analysis of Intervals between Counts To Detect Ra^{224} in the Presence of Ra^{226}

If events in time are stochastically independent (*13*), the probability, $p(t)$, that the waiting time from any arbitrary time to the next event will be less than time, t, is given by equation 1, where b is the reciprocal of the average waiting time.

$$p(t) = 1 - e^{-bt} \tag{1}$$

If the arbitrary reference time immediately follows each preceding event, then $1/b$ is the average interval between events, and b is the rate constant expressing the probability per unit time of the occurrence of any event. Equation 1 may be applied to purely random events, such as decay of Ra^{226}, or to decay of α-emitting daughters after the parent α-decay occurs. In the latter application, b is the decay constant of the short-lived daughter.

Throughout this discussion, events are intended as synonymous with α-emissions, and intervals between events will be governed in some instances by composite decay constants due to intervening β-decay. In the present application, we are concerned with the probabilities of α-emission in a mixture of eight kinds of atoms of widely different decay constants; three daughters and the parent for each of the two chains derived from Ra^{226} and Ra^{224}.

From a record of actual α-activity counts made through a monitoring circuit, the frequency distribution, $I(t)$, of time intervals between counts is determined; discrete values of t, such as 1, 2, 3 minutes and so forth, are chosen for convenience. If all the α-decays were truly random, $I(t)$ could be fitted by an expression based on equation 1, with b the average count rate.

We may now distinguish three types of event applicable to a mixture of radioelements, some of which are daughters of one or more parent elements as seen in the following decay schemes for Ra^{226} and Ra^{224}.

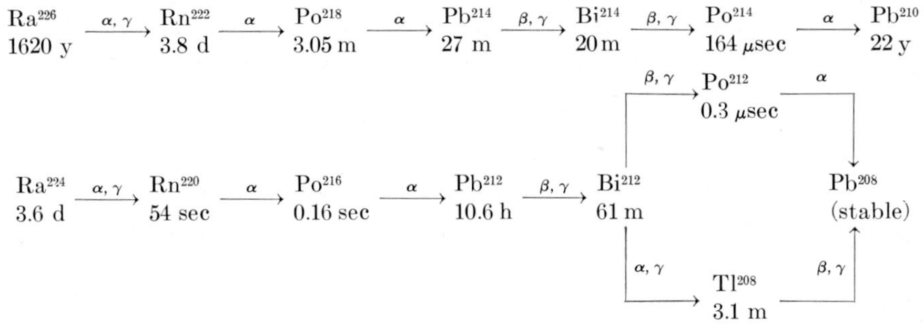

1. Disintegrations in which decay is stochastically independent and does not depend on a previous event (e.g., the parent α-emission from the radium isotopes), or in daughter decays where the decay constant is very small compared with the mean interval between events. Besides the parent radium isotopes, Rn^{222} and Bi^{212}–Po^{212} are also included in this group. Note that the Bi^{212}–Po^{212} decay rate is governed by that of Pb^{212}. Alpha decays from these elements will appear randomly distributed in time.

2. Disintegrations in which the decay constant between α-emissions is very large compared with the time constant of the recording circuit (2 seconds). In this case a double count will be observed, provided both parent and daughter α-activities are counted. Among the daughters of Ra^{224} and Ra^{226}, only Po^{216} (half-life 0.16 second) is in this group.

3. Disintegrations in which the effective α-decay constant is intermediate between disintegrations of types 1 and 2. In this case, coupling of events in a nonrandom pattern may be detectable, but not generally as superimposed double counts. Included in this group are Rn^{220} (thoron) and Po^{218} and Po^{214}, the latter governed by its two parents. Both Po^{218} and Po^{214} can usually be neglected because they do not occur in significant proportions during the first day after plating of the radium. It can be shown, moreover, that even when they are in equilibrium with the parent radium, the effective decay constants of these two polonium isotopes are sufficiently small that with 2π counting geometry little distortion from a random frequency distribution of intervals between counts is detectable from them. It is possible to define rigorously the conditions under which these relatively short-lived polonium daughters may modify the random distribution of counts. Suffice it to say for this discussion, although Po^{218} has a half-life of only 3.05 minutes, we have found that with samples of Ra^{226} in equilibrium with the short-lived daughters the distribution of intervals between counts is not significantly different from random when the total count rate is greater than 4 counts/hr. Thus, the only significant element in his group is thoron (Rn^{220}, half-life 54.5 seconds). The principal addition of the analysis presented here to that of Turner *et al.* (*5*) is the inclusion of Rn^{220} decay in an attempt to improve the accuracy of the Ra^{224} measurement.

Let A be the number of disintegrations of Ra^{224} in a sample during an observation period (16 to 24 hours). The number of α-counts observed from Ra^{224} will be f_1A, where f_1 includes corrections for geometry, backscatter, and self-absorption, and for our counting system is equal to 0.43. Both Rn^{220} and Po^{216} are in equilibrium with Ra^{224} a few minutes after plating; therefore, the number of α-decays from each of these two elements is f_2A, where f_2 is 0.475. (The difference in correction factors is due to less self-absorption by the daughter α's.) A double count will be observed when both α's from these two daughters are counted. The number of double counts observed, N_F, will, therefore, be given by equation 2.

Since all intervals are less than any observable $t(<2$ seconds$)$, the frequency distribution (with respect to time), $F(t)$, will be equal to N_F.

$$N_F = f_2{}^2A = 0.226A \tag{2}$$

The number of counts, N_S, from Ra^{224} followed by either or both counts from Rn^{220} or Po^{216} is

$$N_S = 2f_1f_2(1 - f_2)A + f_1f_2A = 0.312A \tag{3}$$

The two types of paired events (Ra^{224}–Rn^{220} and Ra^{224}–Po^{216}) are indistinguishable from each other because of the short half-life of Po^{216}. The frequency distribution of intervals between two events in this case follows an expression based on equation 1; the total number of intervals, $S(t)$, from Ra^{224}, followed by Rn^{220} or Po^{216} decay, whose duration is less than t, is given by equation 4, where k is the decay constant for Rn^{220}, 0.770 min^{-1}. Note that the number of intervals greater than 5 minutes is generally negligible.

$$S(t) = N_S(1 - e^{-kt}) \tag{4}$$

The total distribution of paired or nonrandom events is the sum of the two distributions (equation 5), representing the number of intervals less than t minutes.

$$F(t) + S(t) = N_F + N_S(1 - e^{-0.770t}) \tag{5}$$

If the nonrandom distribution of intervals, equation 5, is independent of the random distribution, the two may simply be added. At low counting rates, the interaction between distributions can be corrected by the assumption that the random events are distributed over the total observation time less the time intervals occupied by pairs. This latter time is N_S times the average life of Rn^{220}, or 1.31 N_S minutes, generally small enough to be ignored.

On the assumption that the nonrandom pairs do not interfere with the distribution of intervals between random events, the number of random intervals, $R(t)$, with duration less than t is, according to equation 1, given by equation 6, where

$$R(t) = N_R(1 - e^{-(N_R/t_o)t}) \tag{6}$$

N_R is the number of random events, and t_o is the observation time. In samples of low activity, double counts occur rarely by chance. A correction for double counts arising by chance can be made for samples of higher activity. However, we find that, when N_R/t_o (the average count rate for random events) is greater than 0.3 count/min, the method becomes inaccurate as a measure of Ra^{224} activity. As N_R/t_o approaches 0.770 count/min, the distribution, $R(t)$, approaches $S(t)$, and thus these distributions of random and nonrandom events become indistinguishable.

The observed distribution of intervals between counts, $I(t)$, is the sum of the random and nonrandom distributions.

$$\begin{aligned} I(t) &= F(t) + S(t) + R(t) \\ &= N_F + N_S(1 - e^{-0.770t}) + N_R(1 - e^{-(N_R/t_o)t}) \end{aligned} \tag{7}$$

The quantities determined from the moving chart recording the events are $I(t)$, the cumulative distribution of all intervals between events (the time before the first count and after the last is added to make a single interval); t_o, the observation time; N_T, the total counts ($N_T = N_F + N_S + N_R$); and N_F, determined by correcting the observed double counts for those arising by chance from random decays. The observed distribution is fitted to equation 7 by assuming integral values for N_S, within the constraint that the ratio of N_S to N_F should be about 1.38, from equations 2 and 3. When N_S has been estimated by trial-and-error fitting of equation 7 to the observed values, then A can be determined from the sum of equations 2 and 3, and by correction for decay the initial activity of Ra^{224} can be determined.

The accuracy of the determination depends on the number of nonrandom events observed ($N_F + N_S$) corrected for any nonrandom activity due to reagent blanks (essentially zero), and for double counts arising by chance. The greater the Ra^{226} activity, the less accurately is ($N_F + N_S$) determined. This technique is applicable, therefore, only over a restricted range of activity of Ra^{226} and Ra^{224}, up to about 15 counts/hr from each. For more active samples the background and reagent-blank corrections become negligible, and the differential growth and decay method is suitable for separating Ra^{226} and Ra^{224}. If there is a great excess of Ra^{226} over Ra^{224}, neither method of determining Ra^{224} is accurate.

ACKNOWLEDGMENTS

We wish to thank Dr. Brian MacMahon and Dr. A. Segall of the Department of Epidemiology, Harvard School of Public Health, for their encouragement. The radium separation procedure is essentially that originally suggested by Dr. Henry G. Petrow of New York University; his generous assistance and advice have been invaluable. We are also greatly indebted to Dr. C. J. Maletskos of the Massachusetts Institute of Technology, to Mr. H. B. Lucas of Argonne National Laboratory for sending samples for analysis, and to Mr. R. B. Holtzman of Argonne National Laboratory for assistance with the polonium separation method.

RECEIVED: September 13, 1962

REFERENCES

1. E. K. VITTUM, W. L. MINTO, and R. M. FINK, Biological studies with polonium, radium and plutonium. *Natl. Nucl. Energy Ser. Div. VI.* **3,** 8–27 (1950).
2. R. B. HOLTZMAN, Some determinations of the RaD and RaF concentrations in human bone. Argonne National Laboratory Report 6199 (1960).
3. A. S. GOLDIN, Determination of dissolved radium. *Anal. Chem.* **33,** 406–409 (1961).

4. R. G. Yalman, W. Bruegmann, P. T. Baker, and S. M. Garn, Volumetric determination of calcium in presence of phosphate. *Anal. Chem.* **31,** 1230–1233 (1959).
5. R. C. Turner, J. M. Radley, and W. V. Mayneord, The alpha-ray activity of human tissues. *Brit. J. Radiol.* **31,** 397–406 (1958).
6. A. F. Stehney, Radium and thorium X in some potable waters. *Acta Radiol.* **43,** 43–51 (1955).
7. M. L. Curtis, J. W. Heyd, R. G. Olt, and J. F. Eichelberger, Absolute alpha counting. *Nucleonics.* **13,** No. 5, 38–41 (1955).
8. The mean ratio of ash to calcium for teeth and bones. In *Handbook of Biological Data* (W. S. Spector, ed.), p. 73, W. B. Saunders Co., Philadelphia, 1956; also found by R. B. Holtzman (*2*).
9. J. S. Nader, G. R. Hagee, and L. R. Setter, Evaluating the performance of the internal counter. *Nucleonics* **12,** No. 6, 29–31 (1954).
10. H. W. Kirby, Decay and growth tables for the naturally occurring radioactive series. Mound Laboratory, Miamisburg. Report 859 (1953).
11. H. G. Petrow, O. A. Nietzel, and M. A. DeSesa, Radiochemical determination of radium in uranium milling process samples. *Anal. Chem.* **32,** 926–927 (1960).
12. C. R. Hill, An alpha-spectrometer for normal biological levels of radioactivity. *Health Phys.* **8,** 91–92 (1962).
13. W. Feller, *An Introduction of Probability Theory and Its Applications*, Vol. 1, pp. 411–412, John Wiley & Sons, New York, 1960.

RADIATION RESEARCH 19, 316–323 (1963)

Radiosensitivity and Thyroid Function in Mice

TAKEHIKO TSUCHIYA, JUN-ICHIRO HAYAKAWA,[1] SUSUMU MURAMATSU, AND HIDEO ETŌ

Division of Radiation Hazards, National Institute of Radiological Sciences, Chiba, Japan

TSUTOMU SUGAHARA

Department of Experimental Radiology, Faculty of Medicine, Kyoto University, Kyoto, Japan

INTRODUCTION

It is well known that radiosensitivity varies in different inbred strains of mice (*1–3*). It has been reported that the radiosensitivity of animals is also influenced by their basal metabolic rates (*4, 5*) and that hyperthyroid animals are more radiosensitive than normal or hypothyroid animals (*6–8*). However, these hyper- or hypothyroidal animals were produced artificially by the administratioin of thyroid hormone or of antithyroid agents, or by thyroidectomy. In the present investigation, the correlation between radiosensitivity and thyroid function was studied under physiological conditions in different inbred strains of mice. Thus, from a comparison of the three strains it is concluded that physiological variations in thyroid function may influence the radiosensitivity of the animal. The results may explain the differences in the effects of radioprotective agents obtained in different laboratories.

MATERIALS AND METHODS

Animals

Male mice from three strains, CF1, RF, and C57BL/6, were used in this experiment. They were progenies of random matings in breeding stocks maintained by brother–sister matings in the Institute. The ages of mice ranged 60 to 70 days. Mean body weights of these strains of mice, CF1, RF, and C57BL/6, were 29.3 g., 28.2 g., and 22.6 g., respectively. The mice were fed a standard laboratory chow

[1] On leave from Faculty of Agriculture, Nagoya University.

throughout the entire period of the experiment and given tap water ad libitum except in the Mercazole treatment.

Estimation of Thyroid Function

Thyroid uptake of I^{131}. Three microcuries of carrier-free I^{131} solution was injected intraperitoneally into each mouse. The injected dosage of I^{131} was measured for each mouse by total-body counting with a wide-angle scintillation counter immediately after injection. For total-body counting, the mouse was restrained in a cylindrical plastic case. The radioactivity of the thyroid was measured externally by use of a narrow aperture over the scintillation counter. The thyroid region was centered directly above the aperture by restraining the limbs and the incisors of the mouse on a plastic plate. Body background activity was measured over the epigastric region under the same geometrical condition as for the thyroid region. One half of the epigastric region activity was previously found to agree with the thyroid region activity after removal of thyroid tissue. Therefore, the external thyroid count was corrected by one half of body background count. Furthermore, a correction coefficient for the geometrical difference between the total body and thyroid counting was experimentally determined by means of a phantom.

Thus, percentage of I^{131} uptake was calculated by the following formula (*9*):

$$\% \text{ uptake} = \frac{[(T - G) - \frac{1}{2}(B - G)] \times 1.32}{(W - G) \times P} \times 100$$

Where T = thyroid region counts.
B = body background counts.
W = total-body counts.
G = room background counts.
1.32 = correction coefficient of geometrical difference.
P = coefficient of physical decay.

Release rate of thyroid I^{131}. After I^{131} injection, the radioactivities of the thyroid were measured at 24-hour intervals from 24 to 96 hours. Thyroidal retention of I^{131} decreased exponentially with time after injection. The release rate for each mouse is represented by the slope of the regression line plotting the logarithm of the percentage rentention for 4 days after injection. The regression lines were fitted by the method of least squares from the data obtained.

Release rate when reutilization of I^{131} is blocked. Immediately after the initial thyroid activity was measured at 24 hours, oral administration of Mercazole (1-methyl-2-mercaptoimidazole) as a 0.05% aqueous solution was begun. Thyroid activities were measured daily, and Mercazole administration was continued for 4 days. The release rate was calculated in the same manner as described above.

Plasma protein-bound I^{131} conversion ratio. Three microcuries of I^{131} was injected intraperitoneally into each mouse. Twenty-four hours after injection the mouse was sacrificed, and blood was collected from the femoral artery in a syringe containing a small amount of heparin. The blood was lightly centrifuged, and approximately 0.2 ml of plasma was collected in a test tube. The radioactivity in the plasma was measured by use of a well-type scintillation counter. Trichloroacetic acid (10% TCA in water) was used to precipitate plasma protein. The precipitate was washed with 1% TCA, and its radioactivity was measured. The washings with TCA were repeated several times until the radioactivity of the precipitate reached a constant value. The value for the protein-bound I^{131} conversion ratio was obtained by dividing the counts in the final precipitate by the counts in the original plasma.

Rectal Temperature

The rectal temperatures of the three strains of mice were measured with a thermister thermometer. The measurements were made in unanesthetized mice restrained by picking up the tail tip, at approximately the same time each day.

Determination of Lethality after a Single Whole-Body X-Irradiation

The mice of each strain were divided into two groups at random and housed for 1 week in plastic cages (4 to 6 mice per cage), before the experiments were begun. The mice in one group served as untreated controls, and the mice in the other group were treated with either Mercazole or thyroxine. Mercazole administrations were made for 1 week before irradiation in drinking water containing 0.05% Mercazole. For thyroxine treatment, each mouse was injected daily with 6 μg of L-thyroxine in alkaline solution intraperitoneally, for 1 week before irradiation.

The mice were housed individually during irradiation in a cylindrical plastic box, 16 cm in diameter and 3 cm in height, containing eight radial compartments. A Radocon Model 575 dosimeter probe was placed in one of the compartments, and the total dose was checked at every exposure. A deep-therapy standard X-ray machine was operated with the following physical factors: 220 kvp, 8 ma, 0.5 mm Cu plus 0.5 mm Al filter, HVL 1.4 mm Cu, and dose rate of 54 r/min in air at 40 cm.

It has been found previously that these strains of mice, CF1, RF and C57BL, differ from each other in radiosensitivity to single whole-body irradiation; therefore these strains were exposed to their respective near-lethal doses ($LD_{85(30)}$ to $LD_{90(30)}$), i.e., 550 r, 600 r, and 650 r, respectively. After X-irradiation, the mice were housed individually in plastic jars and fed chow and given tap water ad libitum for 30 days or until death. The jars were inspected for dead mice usually twice or at least once each day. Lethality data are presented as per cent mortality during the observation period of 30 days.

RESULTS

Table I shows the per cent I^{131} uptake 24 hours after administration of I^{131}, the conversion ratios (PBI^{131}), and rectal temperatures. The uptakes are significantly different among the three strains studied so far; the values are high in RF, intermediate in CF1, and low in C57BL. A significant difference is observed in the conversion ratios and rectal temperature values between strain C57BL and the other two strains. There seems to be no difference in these characteristics between strain CF1 and RF. In strain C57BL, the conversion ratio and rectal temperature are both low.

Table II shows the release rate of thyroidal I^{131} as defined above with or without Mercazole administration. Mercazole was administered in order to block the reutilization of I^{131} as mentioned above. Thus, the difference in release rate with and without drug administration may correspond to the reutilization rate of I^{131}. The release rate was highest in untreated C57BL, but the difference produced by Mercazole was the smallest in comparison to the other strains. The reutilization rate, therefore, increases in the order C57BL, RF, and CF1, although the difference between strains RF and C57BL is not significant.

Tables III and IV show results of experiments on protection from radiation by Mercazole and sensitization to radiation by L-thyroxine. A part of the experiment with Mercazole was reported previously (*10*).

Because the 1 week treatment with Mercazole was ineffective in affording protection to C57BL mice, a 2 week treatment was also tested. Although the Mercazole

TABLE I

PER CENT I^{131} UPTAKE, CONVERSION RATIO (PBI^{131}) AT 24 HOURS, AND RECTAL TEMPERATURE

Strain	*Percentage I^{131} uptake*		*Conversion ratio*		*Rectal temperature (°C)*	
	Number of animals	*Mean ± S.E.*	*Number of animals*	*Mean ± S.E.*	*Number of animals*	*Mean ± S.E.*
CF1	35	19.9 ± 0.8	5	82.2 ± 1.3	19	38.1 ± 0.2
RF	45	27.2 ± 1.3	5	80.4 ± 0.6	15	38.3 ± 0.2
C57BL	38	13.1 ± 1.1	5	71.0 ± 1.5	15	37.0 ± 0.3

TABLE II

RELEASE RATE (LOG PER CENT RETENTION PER DAY) OF THYROIDAL I^{131} WITH AND WITHOUT MERCAZOLE ADMINISTRATION

Strain	*Untreated*[a] *(mean ± S.E.)*	*Treated*[b] *(mean ± S.E.)*	*Difference (mean ± S.E.)*
CF1	0.0895 ± 0.0053	0.4285 ± 0.0048	0.3390 ± 0.0051
RF	0.0642 ± 0.0046	0.2089 ± 0.0237	0.1456 ± 0.0241
C57BL	0.1217 ± 0.0080	0.2422 ± 0.0283	0.1205 ± 0.0293

[a] Number of untreated animals is 15 mice for each strain.
[b] Number of treated animals is 10 mice for each strain.

TABLE III

THIRTY-DAY MORTALITY OF IRRADIATED MICE WITH OR WITHOUT MERCAZOLE ADMINISTRATION (0.05% in drinking water)

Strain	*Exposure dose (r)*	*Treatment*	*Number of mice used*	*Number of dead mice*	*Per cent of mortality*	*Average survival time (day)*
CF1	550	Treated	48	45	93.8	13.2 ± 1.4[a]
		Untreated	45	45	100.0	13.8 ± 0.5
	600	Treated	28	25	89.3	12.1 ± 2.1
		Untreated	27	27	100.0	13.6 ± 1.1
RF	600	Treated	69	43	62.8	14.1 ± 0.9
		Untreated	86	73	84.9	12.9 ± 0.9
C57BL	600	Treated	34	8	23.5	19.8 ± 3.8
		Untreated	33	7	21.2	9.8 ± 3.3
	650	Treated	69	55	79.7	13.8 ± 1.6
		Untreated	66	60	90.0	13.9 ± 1.4
	650	Treated[b]	29	25	86.2	11.6 ± 0.8
		Untreated	30	27	90.0	11.6 ± 1.7

[a] Mean ±95% fiducial limit.
[b] Two weeks of treatment.

TABLE IV

THIRTY-DAY MORTALITY OF IRRADIATED MICE WITH OR WITHOUT L-THYROXINE (6-μg daily injection for a week)

Strain	*Exposure dose (r)*	*Treatment*	*Number of mice used*	*Number of dead mice*	*Per cent of mortality*	*Average survival time (days)*
CF1	550	Treated	53	42	79.3	14.1 ± 1.8[a]
		Untreated	52	43	82.7	13.8 ± 1.3
RF	600	Treated	39	22	56.4	12.0 ± 1.2
		Untreated	39	29	74.4	12.7 ± 2.0
C57BL	650	Treated	51	42	82.4	14.0 ± 1.6
		Untreated	69	43	62.3	13.7 ± 1.7

[a] Mean ±95% fiducial limit.

treatment is effective for radiation protection in CF1 and RF mice, it was ineffective in C57BL mice even after a 2-week treatment. Mean survival days calculated from the dead during 30 days are not significantly different between control and treated animals at the same dose level. The only exception is the C57BL 600-r group in which the survival time of treated mice was significantly longer than that of the untreated group. A slight protective effect in strain C57BL may be suggested from such data.

TABLE V

Summary of the Properties in Three Strains

Strain	*CF1*		*RF*		*C57BL*
Radiosensitivity	High	$\gtrsim$	High	>	Low
I^{131} uptake	Median	<	High	>	Low
Reutilization rate	High	>	Median	$\gtrsim$	Low
PBI^{131} conversion ratio	High	$\approx$	High	>	Low
Rectal temperature	High	$\approx$	High	>	Low
Protection with Mercazole[a]	+		+		−
Sensitization with L-thyroxine[a]	−		−		+

[a] +, effective; −, not or less effective.

Treatment with L-thyroxine was effective as judged by mortality for radiosensitization of strain C57BL but not in strains RF and CF1. In the latter two strains, mortality was slightly reduced by treatment but this was not statistically significant. The difference observed in the average survival time was also not significant.

DISCUSSION

The above results may be schematically summarized as shown in Table V. I^{131} uptake by the thyroid, reutilization rate of I^{131}, and conversion ratio are all low in C57BL mice as compared with the other two strains. The rectal temperature of strain C57BL mice is lower than in the other strains. The radiosensitivity of C57BL mice as measured by $LD_{50(30)}$ for single exposure is the lowest among others, as reported elsewhere (*11*). The relation between radiosensitivity and strain of mice has not been consistently demonstrable in various institutes; however, the relative differences in radiosensitivity of the three strains used in the present investigation have been confirmed repeatedly. It may be concluded that in C57BL mice the decreased uptake of I^{131}, the decreased reutilization rate, and the low conversion ratio of I^{131} may indicate the low thyroid function which reflects a low basal metabolic rate; this low metabolic rate may play a role in reducing the radiosensitivity of strain C57BL. The higher values for these processes in the other two strains may indicate a higher thyroid function as well as a higher basal metabolic rate. The correlation observed between the I^{131} metabolism in three strains of mice and their radiosensitivity may provide a clue for the interpretation of the nature of the strain difference in response to radiation. Although basal metabolic rates have not been measured as yet, differences in rectal temperatures probably reflect the differences in basal metabolic rates in these strains.

The fact that protection against radiation by lowering the thyroid function with Mercazole was clearly demonstrated in CF1 and RF, but not in C57BL, and that the sensitization to radiation by thyroxine administration was shown in C57BL, but not in CF1 and RF, seems to support the above view. Mice with a physiologically higher thyroid function may be easily affected by Mercazole as compared with those with a physiologically lower function. On the other hand, mice with a physiologically lower thyroid function may be affected more readily by thyroxine administration.

Studies on radiosensitization by thyroxine or radioprotection by antithyroid agents have been reported by several authors (*5–8, 10*), but some of them were unable to show that the treatment affected radiosensitivity. The failures might have been due to the strains or species of animals employed in the work.

It has been reported that radiosensitivity varies in different inbred strains of mice, but the nature of the difference has never been discussed heretofore. The present study on the relation of thyroid function may give some insight to this phenomenon, but this cannot be the only reason for the difference in radiosensitivity. Data on basel metabolic rates and oxygen tension in various tissues will be obtained in future work in order to support the suggested correlation.

SUMMARY

Thyroid function was compared in three inbred strains of mice, RF, CF1, and C57BL/6, whose radiosensitivity was found to be different. The correlation between functional level of the thyroids and radiosensitivity may indicate that the difference in radiosensitivity is due to a physiological difference in the thyroid function and, accordingly, the basal metabolic rate.

Protection against radiation was clearly observed on administration of antithyroid agents in a strain with physiologically high thyroid activity. Similarly sensitization to radiation was demonstrated on the administration of thyroid hormone in a strain with physiologically low thyroid activity.

ACKNOWLEDGMENTS

We are grateful to Dr. S. Tanaka, head of Division of Clinical Investigation in the Institute for his valuable advice, and to Mr. M. Yamada, Chugai Seiyaku Co. Ltd. for furnishing Mercazole.

RECEIVED: September 24, 1962

REFERENCES

1. J. W. GOWEN, Genetic differences in longevity and disease resistance in animals unde irradiation. *Proc. 1st Intern. Conf. Peaceful Uses Atomic Energy Geneva, 1955* **11,** 188-193 (1956).
2. D. GRAHN, Genetic variation in the acute lethal response of four inbred mouse strains t whole body X-irradiation. *Genetics* **42,** 189–198 (1957).
3. H. I. KOHN and R. R. KALLMAN, The influence of death rate studies. *Radiation Res.* **5,** 309-317 (1956).
4. M. KRAHE and H. KÜNKEL, Die Strahlenempfindrichkeit der Ratte bei erhöhtem Grundumsatz. *Strahlentherapie* **106,** 260–262 (1958).
5. T. A. STEIN and M. L. GRIEM, Effect of triiodothyronine on radiosensitivity. *Nature* **182** 1681–1682 (1958).

H. C. Blount and W. W. Smith, The influence of thyroid and thiouracil on mice exposed to roentgen radiation. *Science* **109,** 83–84 (1949).

T. J. Haley, S. Mann, and A. H. Dowdy, The effect of roentgen ray irradiation on normal, hypothyroid and hyperthyroid. *Endocrinology* **48,** 365–369 (1951).

P. V. Vittorio, H. Mars, and M. J. Johnston, Effect of X-irradiation on normal, hypothyroid and hyperthyroid rabbits *Can. J. Biochem. Physiol.* **37,** 1271–1275 (1959).

T. Tsuchiya, J. Hayakawa, and T. Sugahara, Comparison of iodine-131 metabolism in different strains of mice. *Radioisotopes* **11,** 81–85 (1962) (in Japanese).

J. Hayakawa, T. Tsuchiya, and T. Sugahara, Protective effect of Mercazole (1-methyl-2-mercaptoimidazole) against single whole-body irradiations in mice. *Strahlentherapie* **116,** 415–419 (1961).

T. Sugahara, J. Hayakawa, Y. Takeda, and C. Takahashi, Annual Report of National Institute of Radiological Sciences, 101 pp. (1960) (in Japanese).

RADIATION RESEARCH **19**, 324–330 (1963)

Cysteamine Protection of X-Ray-Induced Dysplasia in Mouse Hair[1]

FREDERICK D. MALKINSON, MELVIN L. GRIEM, DAVID M. PHILLIPS, AND PETER H. MORSE

Department of Medicine (Dermatology), Department of Radiology, and Argonne Cancer Research Hospital,[2] University of Chicago, Chicago, Illinois

INTRODUCTION

Previous studies have shown that profound morphological changes in the matri and shaft of actively growing animal and human hair can be induced by irradia tion (*1–3*) or by the administration of certain chemical agents (*4–6*). Microscop examination shows that these induced changes may be remarkably similar in bot forms of injury and that the number of hairs affected is proportional to the dos of radiation or chemical agent received. Recent investigations have revealed th usefulness of hair dysplasia in the mouse as a quantitative biological system fo the demonstration of synergistic effects after the combined use of colchicine (*7, 8* L-triiodothyronine (*9*), or actinomycin D (*10*) and radiation. For observations c other parameters of X-ray-induced changes in hair—especially depigmentation– the reader is referred to the reports by Chase (*11–13*).

The present study was undertaken to determine the value of the hair dysplas technique in assessing the efficacy of radioprotective agents. For this purpos cysteamine (MEA) was chosen as a representative compound of established radi protective potency (*14, 15*).

METHOD

The studies were carried out on young adult female mice of the Carworth Farn #1 strain. Hairs in the resting phase of the growing cycle (telogen) are mitoticall inactive and hence relatively insensitive to irradiation (*2*). Plucking of teloge hairs immediately induces the mitotically active phase of hair growth (anagen which is the radiosensitive stage of the cycle lasting 17 to 20 days in this strain mouse.

[1] Work supported in part by U. S. Public Health Service Grant E-1444 (C6).

[2] Operated by the University of Chicago for the U. S. Atomic Energy Commission.

At the beginning of each experiment, hairs were plucked from the right haunch of all animals. Ten days later, experimental groups of 5 mice were given varying doses of radiation in conjunction with a constant amount of cysteamine. Two series of control groups were run: In one series the animals received cysteamine alone; in the other, radiation alone. Four days later, the newly growing hairs were plucked from the prepared sites and examined microscopically according to the method previously described (*10*).

After irradiation, the cages contained mice from different experimental groups, in an attempt to eliminate "cage" effects.

Previous studies (*7*) have shown that the incidence of dysplasia produced in hairs at different doses of radiation follows a reproducible sigmoid curve. In the earlier as well as in the present investigation, radiation was administered with a Machlett OEG-60 tube operating at 50 kv and 30 ma with 2 mm of aluminum added filtration. This produces a surface dose of 387 r/min at a focal skin distance of 11 cm and a beam quality of 1.2 cm half-value depth in tissue. The animals were adequately shielded and treated individually without anesthesia. Surface doses ranged from 200 to 1600 r, increasing by increments of 100 or 200 r.

Five milligrams of cysteamine hydrochloride (200 mg/kg) was given intra-

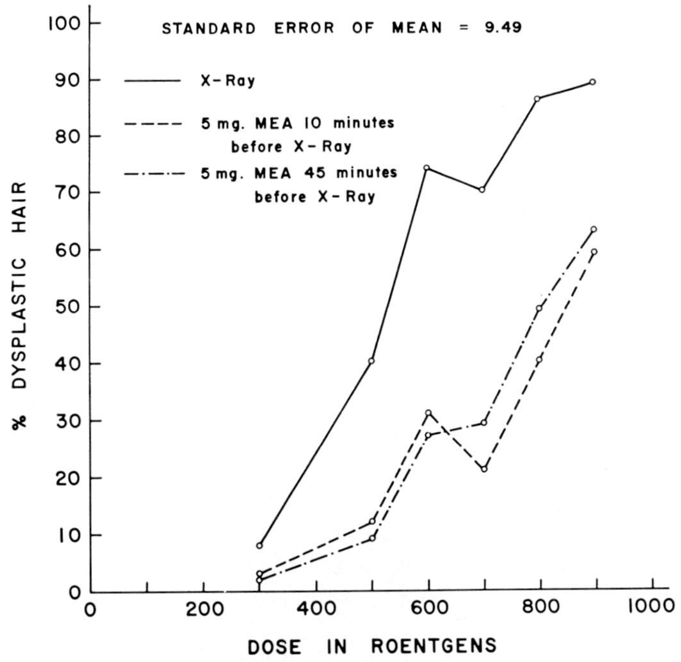

FIG. 1. Lowered incidence of hair dysplasia over a wide dose range after irradiation of mice protected with 5 mg. of cysteamine (MEA).

venously as a freshly prepared solution in 0.5 ml of physiological saline. This was administered 45 minutes before, 10 minutes before, or immediately after irradiation. Initial observations revealed that cysteamine alone produced no significant hair dysplasia in doses ranging from 2 to 10 mg per animal (80 to 400 mg/kg).

Irradiated controls were given intraperitoneal injections of 0.5 ml of physiological saline.

All experimental data have been statistically analyzed by second-order analysis of variance (*16*).

RESULTS

The results of several separate experiments are shown in the accompanying figures, where each point on a graph represents the average per cent of dysplastic hairs from a single group of 5 mice.

Clear-cut protective effects of cysteamine on X-ray-induced dysplasia are demonstrable throughout the dose range of 300 to 900 r (Figs. 1 to 3). The average dose reduction factor is about 1.5, and it appears to make little difference whether drug administration precedes irradiation by 10 minutes or by 45 minutes. No significant protection is seen with doses of 1200 r or higher (Fig. 4).

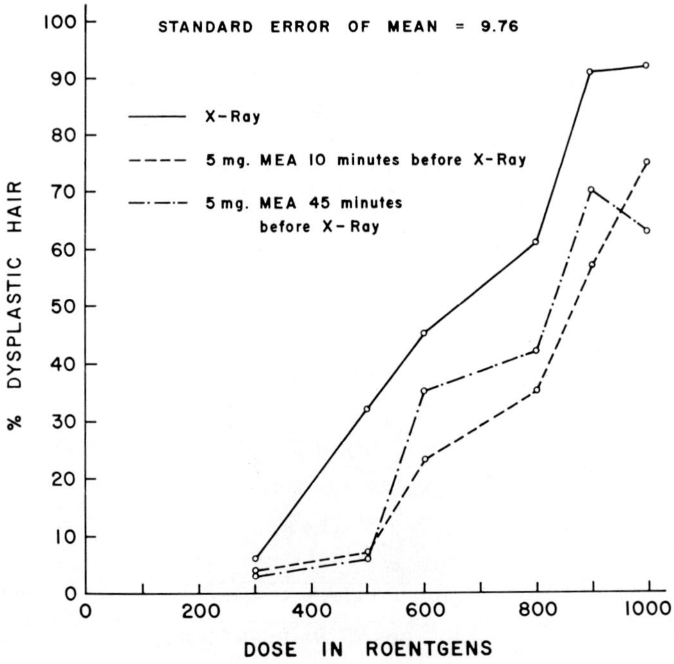

FIG. 2. Lowered incidence of hair dysplasia over a wide dose range after irradiation of mice protected with 5 mg. of cysteamine (MEA). Standard error = 9.76.

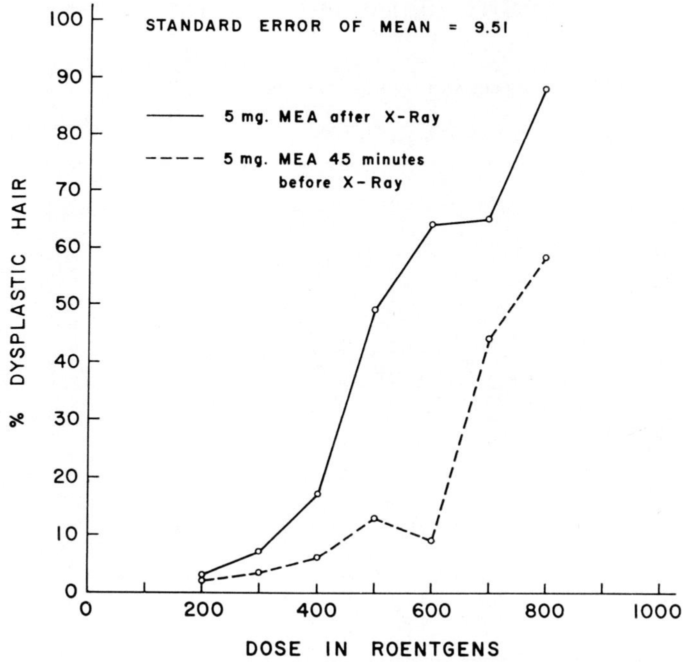

FIG. 3. Lowered incidence of hair dysplasia over a wide dose range, showing significant differences between pretreatment and immediate posttreatment administration of cysteamine in irradiated animals. Posttreatment cysteamine fails to protect against hair dysplasia (see also Fig. 5).

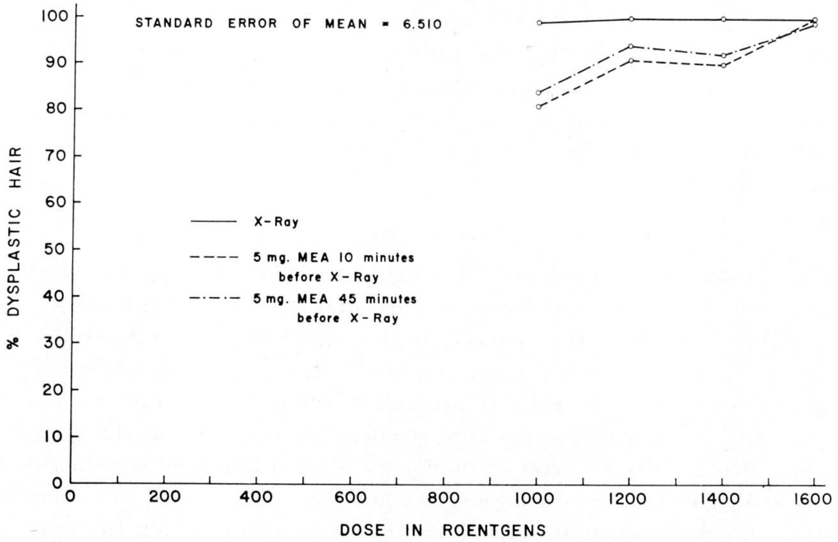

FIG. 4. Failure of pretreatment cysteamine to protect against hair dysplasia in the high X-ray dose ranges.

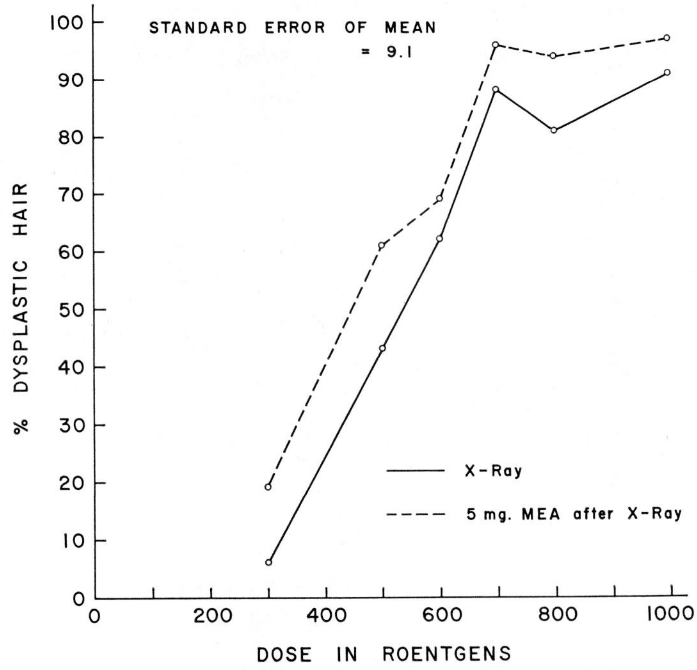

FIG. 5. Moderate potentiation of hair dysplasia in the lower X-ray dose ranges after cysteamine administration immediately post-irradiation.

Figure 5 shows that cysteamine fails to confer any protective effect on hair dysplasia when administered immediately after irradiation. Unexpectedly, some potentiation of hair damage by the drug actually occurs in the lower dose ranges up to 600 r ($P < 0.025$). This result has been confirmed in repeated experiments and is being studied further.

DISCUSSION

The usefulness and sensitivity of the hair indicator technique for assessing protection against the damaging effects of irradiation undoubtedly reflect the high rate of cellular mitosis in the mouse hair matrix, where each epithelial cell divides once every 13 hours (*17*). Since the required rate of cellular replacement is high, damage to relatively few cells is apparently sufficient to produce microscopic morphological abnormalities. In these studies, the few days of the growth period remaining after irradiation were evidently insufficient to permit significant recovery from dysplasia in both cysteamine-protected and unprotected animals. This observation and the striking difference in the incidence of dysplastic hairs in drug-treated and untreated animals seen as early as 48 hours after irradiation suggest that the protective action of cysteamine here lies more in a reduction of the primary irradiation effects than in an acceleration of the recovery processes. However, radiation damage and possible enhanced recovery during the first 48 hours after exposure would not be detectable by this technique.

Previous investigations of protection against hair damage from radiation (*18–22*) have been based solely on observations of subsequent retention or loss of hair. Although this method permits qualitative evaluation of a protective agent—provided anagen has been previously induced—it does not permit quantitative conclusions. Slight or even moderate damage to anagen hairs is often followed by continued growth and will remain undetected by this gross technique. In our current studies, for example, there was no obvious loss of hair despite an incidence of up to 40% dysplasia with X-ray doses as high as 500 r. Only at and above dose levels of 600 r was slower growth apparent and alopecia noticeable. In the cysteamine-protected animals alopecia was not seen at dose levels of less than 800 r, although dysplastic hairs were found after as low a dose as 300 r.

The degree of radioprotection afforded anagen hairs by cysteamine compares favorably with the dose reduction factor of 1.8 for lethal radiation in mice established previously by other investigators (*23*). The reliability, simplicity, and directness of the technique herein described make it generally useful in the evaluation of potential radioprotective agents.

SUMMARY

1. Cysteamine reduces the incidence of radiation-induced dysplasia in the growing hairs of mice.

2. The dose reduction factor of about 1.5 is comparable to the protection afforded by cysteamine in other radiobiological studies.

3. The administration of cysteamine immediately after X-ray exposure results in slightly increased hair dysplasia.

RECEIVED: October 4, 1962

REFERENCES

1. A. W. WILLIAMS, A note on certain appearances of X-rayed hairs. *Brit. J. Dermatol.* **18,** 63–65 (1906).

2. J. R. GEARY, JR., Effect of roentgen rays during various phases of the hair cycle of the albino rat. *Am. J. Anat.* **91,** 51–96 (1952).

3. E. J. VAN SCOTT and R. P. REINERTSON, Detection of radiation effects on hair roots of the human scalp. *J. Invest. Dermatol.* **29,** 205–212 (1957).

4. E. J. VAN SCOTT, R. P. REINERTSON, and R. STEINMULLER, The growing hair roots of the human scalp and morphologic changes therein following amethopterin therapy. *J. Invest. Dermatol.* **29,** 197–204 (1957).

5. F. D. MALKINSON and Y. L. LYNFIELD, Colchicine alopecia. *J. Invest. Dermatol.* **33,** 371–384 (1959).

6. R. G. CROUNSE and E. J. VAN SCOTT, Changes in scalp hair roots as a measure of toxicity from cancer chemotherapeutic agents. *J. Invest. Dermatol.* **35,** 83–93 (1960).

7. M. L. GRIEM, F. D. MALKINSON, and P. H. MORSE, Modification of radiation responses of tissue by colchicine. Effects on mouse hair roots. *Radiology* **77,** 486–492 (1961).

8. F. D. MALKINSON, M. H. GRIEM, and P. H. MORSE, Colchicine synergism of mouse hair root changes produced by X-ray irradiation. *J. Invest. Dermatol.* **37,** 337–344 (1961).
9. M. L. GRIEM, J. A. STEIN, R. P. REINERTSON, R. REINERTSON, and B. R. BROWN, Comparison of effects of I^{131}-induced hypothyroidism and L-triiodothyronine on irradiated hair roots in mice. *Radiation Res.* **15,** 202–210 (1961).
10. M. L. GRIEM and K. RANNIGER, Modification of the radiation effect on the hair roots of the mouse by actinomycin. *Radiation Res.* **17,** 92–100 (1962).
11. H. B. CHASE, Greying of hair. I. Effect produced by single doses of X-rays on mice. *J. Morphol.* **84,** 57–80 (1949).
12. H. B. CHASE, Growth of the hair. *Physiol. Rev.* **34,** 113–126 (1954).
13. H. B. CHASE, Physical factors which influence the growth of hair. In *The Biology of Hair Growth* (W. Montagna and R. A. Ellis, eds.), pp. 435-440, Academic Press, New York, 1958.
14. Z. M. BACQ, A. HERVE, J. LECOMTE, P. FISCHER, J. BLAVIER, G. DECHAMPS, H. LEBIHAN, and P. RAYET, Protection contre le rayonnement X par la β-mercaptoéthylamine. *Arch. Intern. Physiol.* **59,** 442–447 (1951).
15. A. PIHL and L. ELDJARN, Pharmacological aspects of ionizing radiation and of chemical protection in mammals. *Pharmacol. Rev.* **10,** 437–474 (1958).
16. G. W. SNEDECOR, *Statistical Methods,* 4th ed., Chapter 10, Iowa State College Press, Ames, Iowa, 1955.
17. W. S. BULLOUGH and E. B. LAURENCE, The mitotic activity of the follicle. In *The Biology of Hair Growth* (W. Montagna and R. A. Ellis, eds.), pp. 171–186, Academic Press, New York, 1958.
18. A. FORSSBERG, On the possibility of protecting the living organism against roentgen rays by chemical means. *Acta Radiol.* **33,** 296–304 (1950).
19. C. W. WILSON, Effect of pre-irradiation intraperitoneal injection of cysteamine upon the skin and depilatory reactions produced by X-rays in the legs of mice. *Brit. J. Radiol.* **31,** 100–101 (1958).
20. N. V. SAVKOVIC, D. V. RADIVOJEVIĆ, and S. I. HAJDUKOVIĆ, Effet protecteur de la cystéamine administrée localement sur la réaction d'épilation de jeunes rats provoquée par l'irradiation X totale. *Rev. Franc. Etudes Clin. Biol.* **5,** 478-481 (1960).
21. D. RADIVOJEVIĆ, M. L. BEAUMARIAGE, and Z. M. BACQ, Inhibition locale par la cystéamine de l'épilation après irradiation X chez le souriceau. *Compt. Rend. Soc. Biol.* **154,** 422–424 (1960).
22. D. V. RADIVOJEVIĆ, M. L. BEAUMARIAGE, and Z. M. BACQ, Cysteamine et épilation des souriceaux par les rayons X. *Compt. Rend. Soc. Biol.* **154,** 1529–1532 (1960).
23. Z. M. BACQ and P. ALEXANDER, *Fundamentals of Radiobiology.* 2nd ed., Pergamon Press, New York, 1961.

RADIATION RESEARCH **19**, 331–336 (1963)

The Role of Ozone in Radiation Avoidance in the Mouse

DOROTHY C. PETERSON AND HOWARD L. ANDREWS

U. S. Public Health Service, National Institutes of Health, Bethesda, Maryland

INTRODUCTION

Previous work (*1, 2*) has demonstrated that mice recognize an X-ray beam and seek to avoid it at dose rates greater than about 50 r/min. In addition to avoidance, radiation induces a state we have called confusion and reduces the normal spontaneous activity. The magnitude of each of these effects increases with dose rate up to 200 r/min, the highest rate studied.

Indirect evidence appears to exclude visual stimuli as the initiating factor and suggests a direct central action. The radiation-induced products of air, necessary consequences of the whole-body irradiation of breathing animals, may, however, provide clues which trigger the avoidance response. Ozone, in particular, is a radiation product which is irritating and highly toxic. The experiments reported here were designed to assess the role of ozone in the avoidance reaction.

METHODS

A modification of the standard, knife-edge mounted annular cage (*2*) was used to study the effects of ozone on behavior. Normally, fresh air is supplied to the central plenum from which it flows radially outward into the annular space occupied by the test animal. In the present modification, the central delivery tube was divided by a barrier parallel to the line of the knife edges. The inlet tubing was carefully matched to provide two paths of equal resistance to the incoming air streams (Fig. 1).

One blower provided an adjustable supply of fresh air to one-half of the test cage. A second blower supplied the other half of the cage with a blend of fresh air that had passed over a quartz mercury arc. The latter air stream contained a high concentration of ozone and other products formed by the ultraviolet radiation.

Equal total flows to the two halves of the cage were obtained by maintaining equal pressures at points equidistant from the cage. Ozone concentrations were changed by varying the blend of fresh and irradiated air. An adjustable tube was used to withdraw air samples for ozone assays from selected parts of the cage.

Measured air volumes taken from the cage were bubbled through a solution of

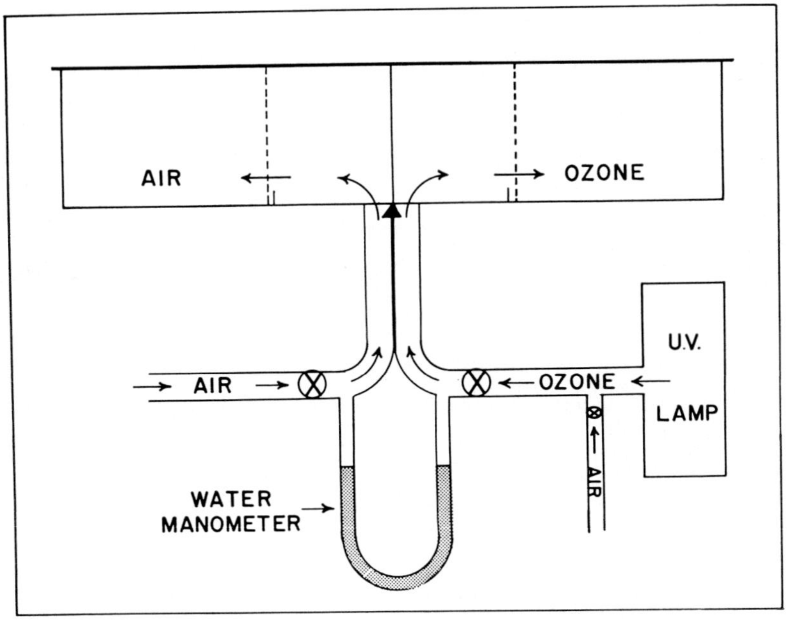

FIG. 1. Modification of annular test cage to permit introduction of ozone into one half. Equal flows are obtained by maintaining equal pressures at two symmetrical points.

potassium iodide which was then titrated with sodium thiosulfate according to the method of Birdsall *et al.* (*3*). With this method, ozone measurements could be made down to 0.5 ppm.

Measurements on samples drawn from various points inside the cage showed that the method of equal pressures was satisfactory for confining ozone to one-half of the test cage. Some mixing by turbulence and diffusion was detected, but this was confirmed to a region about 1 cm on either side of the geometrical boundary.

Studies at high oxygen tension were made by supplying the entire test cage with a mixture of room air and oxygen, blended to obtain the desired concentration. Oxygen concentrations were measured by a modification of the Scholander technique (*4*) on samples withdrawn from the test cage. All gas flow rates were comparable to those used with air alone in previous experiments with the X-ray beam.

Adult male mice of the inbred NIH strain were used as before. In every experimental arrangement, mice were run before the desired environment was established, to ensure the absence of spatial bias. Each test period lasted for 30 minutes after an initial adjustment period of 5 minutes.

As in previous studies, the fraction of the time the animal spent in the "exposure" side of the test cage was determined with an electrical circuit activated by the weight of the animal. Readings were taken at 1-minute intervals throughout the test period.

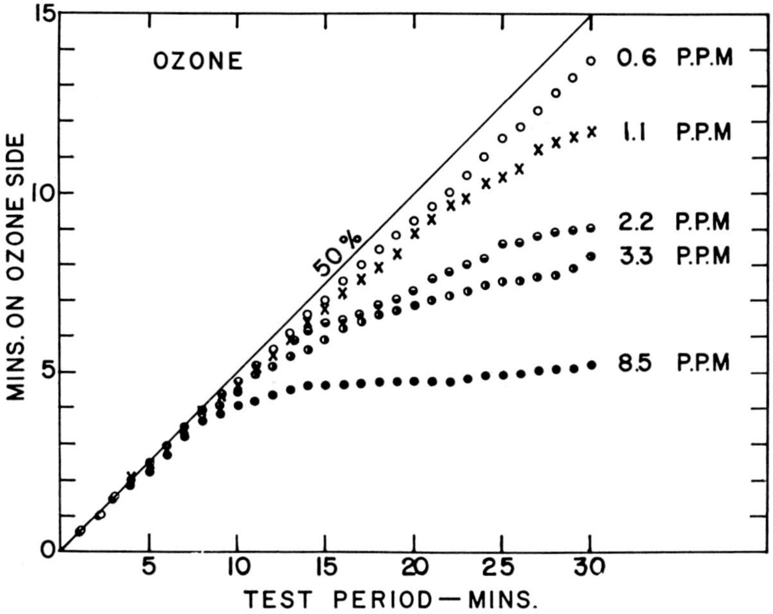

FIG. 2. Development of avoidance to ozone. Each set of points represents the mean behavior of a group of 10 mice. Avoidance becomes more pronounced at the higher ozone concentration. No radiation was involved in these experiments.

Expected occupancy of either half of a clueless environment would be 0.50 of the elapsed time. Any decrease in this factor indicates an avoidance; an increase, a preference.

The phenomenon of confusion previously reported can be demonstrated by calculating the standard deviation of each mean, or by displaying the extreme values observed in groups. All values reported here are based on groups of 10 animals.

RESULTS

The behavior patterns seen in the presence of ozone closely resembled those seen with radiation. A slight avoidance trend appeared at 0.6 ppm, after some 10 minutes of exposure. At 1.1 ppm avoidance was definite (Fig. 2), becoming more pronounced as the ozone concentrations were increased. Time of onset of avoidance was essentially constant, in contrast to the progressively earlier times seen as radiation dose rates are increased.

The presence of a noxious environment greatly enhances the variability of response, or confusion, over that seen in a normal atmosphere. Activity also decreased in the presence of ozone, the effect increasing with ozone concentration.

As with radiation, confusion appeared after about 20 minutes of exposure to 1.1 ppm ozone, appearing earlier and more prominently as ozone concentrations were

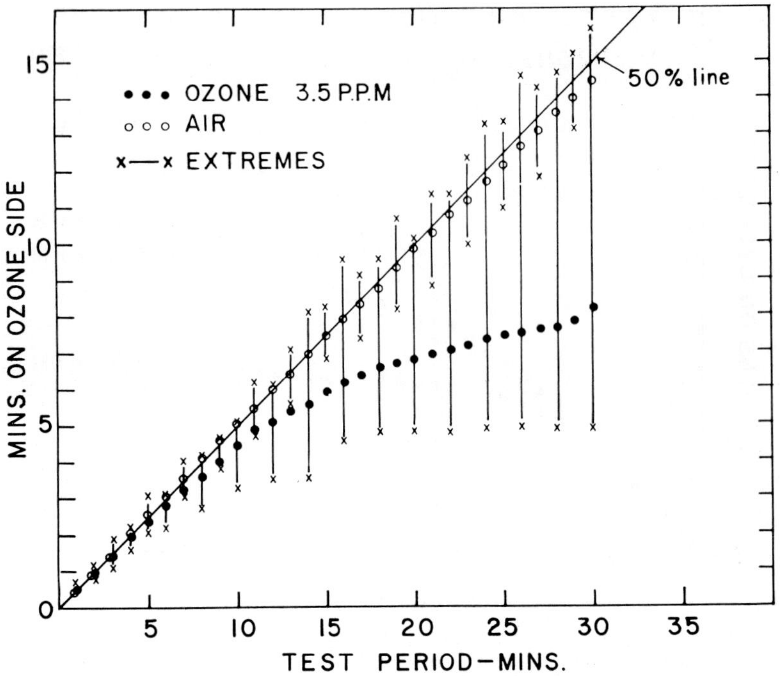

FIG. 3. Development of confusion by exposure to 3.5 ppm ozone. Mean and extreme values are shown for alternate minutes for simplicity.

increased up to 8.5 ppm, the highest concentration studied. Figure 3 shows the mean behavior and the extremes of a group of 10 animals exposed to 3.5 ppm.

Although the effects observed were qualitatively similar to those seen with radiation, they occurred only at ozone concentrations well above those associated with our highest radiation dose rate of 200 r/min. With no animal in the chamber, 200 r/min produced a steady-state ozone concentration of 0.8 ppm. Ozone concentrations at lower radiation dose rates, and with an animal in the cage, were below detection by our analytical method. Linear extrapolation of concentrations obtained at high dose rates cannot be used to estimate concentrations under other conditions. Ozone production rate is very probably proportional to radiation dose rate, but decomposition is a complicated function of concentration, moisture content, and the amount of organic material present. Under our experimental conditions the steady-state concentration will be far from linear with radiation dose rate.

In the absence of radiation there was no detectable difference between behavior in normal air and in 90 to 95% oxygen. Occupancy of each half of the test cage was close to the expected 50%, and the number of excursions from one side to the other was the same in the two environments.

Radiation in the high oxygen atmosphere produced avoidance and confusion with about the same time and dose-rate relations as were seen in room air. Ozone concentrations in 90 to 95% oxygen were below our sensitivity limit, even at a dose rate of 200 r/min. This is presumably due to a considerably increased decomposition rate in the high-oxygen atmosphere.

DISCUSSION

The fact that ozone alone can produce essentially the same reaction as radiation does not necessarily implicate ozone as the pertinent stimulus in the radiation case. Avoidance and perhaps confusion and reduced activity are nonspecific reactions, to be expected when any disagreeable environment is created in one portion of an enclosure with the possibility of escape to a more agreeable situation.

It seems probable that ozone is not involved in the reaction to radiation, since this reaction could be elicited only with ozone externally produced at environmental concentrations several times greater than could have been produced by an effective X-ray beam. However, an environmental ozone concentration may not be representative of the stimulus received by the animal from it. The pertinent concentration is that at the receptors, and this may be considerably lower than that in the environment, since ozone decomposes quite readily, particularly in the presence of organic material and moisture. A penetrating radiation beam, on the other hand, will produce ozone with equal effectiveness wherever free oxygen is available. In the present case, this will be throughout the entire respiratory tract in addition to the general environment. It may well be that, with radiation, ozone concentrations at the receptors are relatively higher than the environmental measurements would indicate.

Although the effectiveness of ozone produced directly at the receptors is not known, it seems doubtful that ozone is the motivating stimulus producing the avoidance reaction. This is in agreement with the previously reported results of irradiation with very soft X-rays, which produce large quantities of environmental ozone, but which are relatively ineffective in producing the avoidance reaction.

Various types of reaction to ionizing have been elicited in several species (*5*). In aquatic animals the stimulus may be chemically mediated (*6*), but ozone can scarcely be involved. Environmental conditions under water are such as to prevent the formation of an effective concentration of ozone. Reaction products of water well, however, be formed in close proximity to chemoreceptors.

The studies on high oxygen concentration provided no conclusive information about the role of ozone. The radiation avoidance reaction was little changed over that seen in normal air, but at the same time there was little environmental ozone, presumably because of the rapid increase of decomposition rate with concentration.

SUMMARY

Mice subjected to ozone in one-half of a test cage show a decreased activity and an avoidance reaction similar to that seen with radiation. With ozone alone, the reaction is elicited only when the environmental concentrations are several times as great as those produced by an effective X-ray beam. No change in the radiation avoidance reaction is observed when the oxygen concentration in the cage is raised to 95%.

RECEIVED: October 8, 1962

REFERENCES

1. H. L. ANDREWS and L. M. CAMERON, Radiation avoidance in the mouse. *Proc. Exptl. Biol. Med.* **103,** 565–567 (1960).
2. H. L. ANDREWS and D. C. PETERSON, Variations in radiation recognition by the mouse. *Radiation Res.* **17,** 514–520 (1962).
3. C. M. BIRDSALL, A. C. JENKINS, and E. SPADINGER, Iodometric determination of ozone. *Anal. Chem.* **24,** 662 (1952).
4. Report No. 57, Committee on Aviation Medicine, National Research Council, Division of Medical Sciences.
5. J. GARCIA, D. J. KIMELDORF, and E. L. HUNT, The use of ionizing radiation as a motivating stimulus. *Psychol. Rev.* **68,** 383–395 (1961).
6. O. D. HUG, Die Auslosung von Fuhlerreflexen bei Schnecken durch Rontgen und Alphastrahlen. *Strahlentherapie* **106,** 155–160 (1958).

RADIATION RESEARCH **19**, 337–344 (1963)

Chromosome Aberrations in Liver Cells in Relation to the Somatic Mutation Theory of Aging[1]

HOWARD CURTIS AND CATHRYN CROWLEY

Biology Department, Brookhaven National Laboratory, Upton, New York

INTRODUCTION

The somatic mutation theory of aging proposes that aging is caused primarily by the gradual accumulation of mutations in the somatic cells of an animal. A direct test of this theory is not now possible, since there is no known method for directly measuring mutations in the somatic cells of animals. However, the problem can be approached by an indirect method by measuring the numbers of microscopically visible aberrations in somatic cells seen at anaphase. The justification for relating this quantity to the numbers of mutations present in these cells comes from work on plants where Caldecott (*1*) and others have shown that for X-ray-induced injury there is a linear relationship between chromosome aberrations in somatic cells and true mutations as scored in the succeeding generation. Heiner *et al.* (*2*) have found that when some chemical mutagens are applied to seeds there are many fewer visible chromosome aberrations in somatic cells, as compared to true mutations, than is the case for X-rays. Thus aberrations are not directly proportional to mutations in all cases, but it seems safe to assume that if a visible chromosome aberration is present there must be mutations present, although the converse is not necessarily true. Thus one can use chromosome aberrations as a rough index of somatic mutations.

Previous work (*3*) has shown that aberrations in liver cells of mice increase linearly with age at least to an age of 12 months. A single dose of X-rays will increase the aberrations to 80% or higher, and these decrease slowly with time over a period of months.

It is well known (*4*) that chronically administered γ-radiation is much less effective in causing life shortening than an equal dose of acute irradiation, whereas for neutron irradiation life shortening is independent of dose rate.

The present work was undertaken in an effort to explain the slow decrease in

[1] Research carried out at Brookhaven National Laboratory under the auspices of the U. S. Atomic Energy Commission.

aberrations after a single dose of X-rays, and to investigate this effect with neutrons. Also, investigations were undertaken with chronic γ-irradiation in an effort to discover a sound cellular basis for the difference between acute and chronic irradiation.

METHODS

The mice used were females of the inbred Charles River strain CDl. They were chosen for these studies because they have a very short life span and die from a wide variety of diseases. The mice were 60 days old at the start of the experiment. Four groups of animals were treated as follows:

Group I. Single total-body dose of 300 rads of fast neutrons from the converter plate at the biology facility of the Brookhaven reactor (*5*).

Group II. Chronic cobalt-60 γ-irradiation of 7.1 rads/day at a rate of 1 rad/hr continued for the duration of the experiment.

Group III. Single total-body dose of 226 rads of X-rays, 250 kvp, 30 ma, ¼ mm Cu and 1 mm Al filtration.

Group IV. Control group.

All mice were kept in the same room in which the chronic irradiation was performed, but the mice not receiving radiation were shielded from the source. All mice were caged in plastic cages, but the mice receiving chronic irradiation were in somewhat smaller cages than the others and possibly did not get quite so much exercise.

Scoring of chromosome aberrations was performed usually at 30-day intervals. Either 5 or 10 mice were selected from each of the groups and injected subcutaneously with 0.005 ml of carbon tetrachloride per gram, which destroys 60 to 70% of the liver. The ensuing liver regeneration reached a peak at 72 hours, at which time the mice were sacrificed by cervical dislocation and decapitation. Portions of the right half of the median lobe of the liver were placed in chilled chromosome fixative consisting of methanol, chloroform, and propionic acid (6:3:2, v/v) and placed in the refrigerator for at least 24 hours.

Squash preparations were made and stained with 1% acetic orcein. They were placed in the refrigerator for 24 hours before scoring. Chromosome aberration percentages were derived from the number of abnormalities encountered in a total of 150 anaphases and telophases. Aberrations were scored as bridges, bridges and fragments, or fragments.

RESULTS

The aberration percentages for the neutron-irradiated mice, the chronic γ-irradiated mice, and the controls are shown in Fig. 1 as a function of time. The increasing aberration percentage after a single dose of neutrons is quite surprising and is certainly a real effect. The mice subjected to chronic γ-irradiation developed chromosome aberrations at a considerably faster rate than the controls.

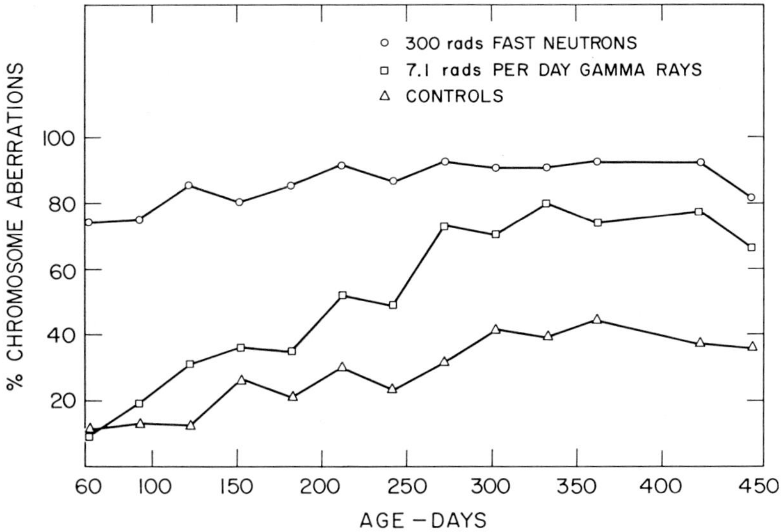

FIG. 1. Chromosome aberrations as a function of age for (1) normal mice, (2) mice receiving a single dose of neutrons, or (3) mice receiving chronic γ-irradiation.

There were not enough mice left at the end of the experiment to construct a significant survival curve. However, at that time mortality in the irradiated groups was not greatly different from that of the controls, in spite of the fact that the neutron-irradiated mice had received an almost lethal dose of neutrons, and the γ-irradiated mice had accumulated about 2850 rads. It is an amazing fact that the irradiated animals can survive apparently quite normally for more than two-thirds of their normal life expectancy after the radiation has severely damaged the chromosomes of a very large majority of all the cells in the body, if liver cells are assumed to be representative of mammalian cells which divide seldom if at all.

The animals in group III, who were given a single dose of 226 rads of X-rays, were scored at the fourth day and again on the day 113 after irradiation. The results are indicated on the graph of Fig. 2. There was relatively little decrease in aberration frequency during this time, as was anticipated from earlier work (*3*). Also plotted on the graph are the results from the chronic irradiation experiment and the controls. At the rate of 7.1 rads/day it took 32 days to accumulate 226 rads in the chronic γ-ray group. If there were no chromosomal recovery, it would be expected that the chronically irradiated mice would have accumulated the same number of aberrations in 32 days as was present in the single-dose animals at 32 days. This theoretical accumulation rate is shown by the dotted line in the figure. Since the experimental points are obviously far from the theoretical line, it follows that there must be chromosome healing from small doses of radia-

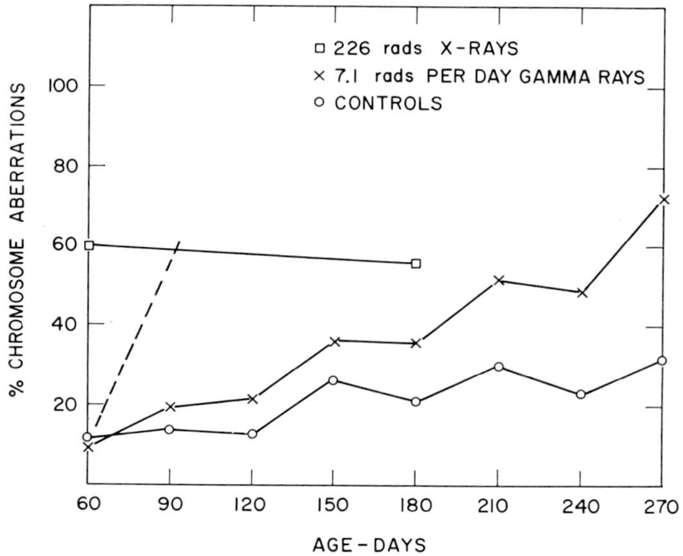

FIG. 2. Chromosome aberrations as a function of age for (1) normal mice, (2) mice receiving chronic γ-irradiation, and (3) mice receiving a single dose of X-rays. If the chromosome aberrations were caused by single-hit events, the chronically irradiated mice would have accumulated aberrations at a rate indicated by the broken line. Since the experimental points are far from the theoretical line, this indicates multihit events and chromosome healing.

tion. Expressed differently, the chromosome aberrations observed here must be due to multihit events.

The types of aberration seen were the same as those previously described (*3*). It was also noted, as before, that in the irradiated groups there was a higher proportion of bridges as compared to the control group. However, the difference was not striking, suggesting that similar mechanisms were causing the aberrations in all cases.

It is interesting to note that, even though the mortality curves were not greatly different for the neutron and chronic γ-ray groups as compared to the controls, these mice were less well able to withstand a stress. This was shown by the fact that the standard dose of CCl_4 killed some of the older mice in the experimental groups but none in the control group (see Fig. 3).

DISCUSSION

These results add greatly to the support for the somatic mutation theory of aging and give an explanation for some of the puzzling aspects of radiation-induced aging.

It is gratifying to substantiate, on a different strain of mouse, the earlier observation (*3*) that chromosome aberrations increase linearly with age, and also that, after a single dose of radiation, the induced mutations disappear very slowly.

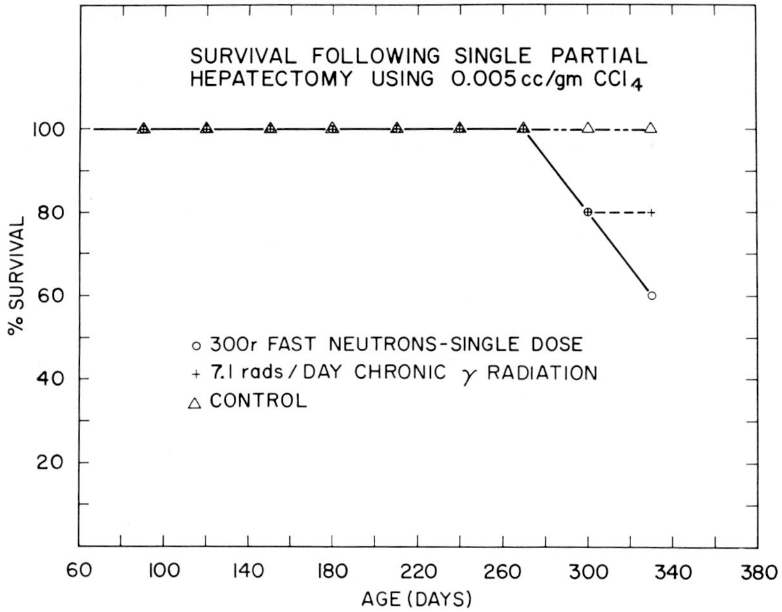

FIG. 3. Groups of mice at the ages indicated were given CCl_4 to cause liver regeneration. The figure shows that as the neutron-irradiated and chronic γ-irradiated mice grew older they were less well able to withstand the stress and some of them died, whereas the normal mice were still able to withstand this stress.

The fact that aberrations actually increase with time after a single dose of neutrons is almost certainly a real effect, since we have observed it in two experiments. The increase is at a much faster rate than would be expected from normal aging. It can be explained by assuming that for some time after the irradiation many of the cells are so badly damaged that they cannot be stimulated to divide and so are not scored. Thus the first readings are too low. As the badly damaged cells recover sufficiently to undergo cell division, more of them are counted, and the percentage of aberrations increases. Apparently, the individual aberrations produced by neutrons are more severe than those produced by X-rays, so they persist much longer. This is consistent with the fact that, as far as aging is concerned, neutron irradiation is completely cumulative, whereas γ-irradiation is much less effective if given in small doses (*4*).

The fact that the aberrations in the chronic γ-irradiation did not increase nearly as fast as one might have predicted from the single-dose results gives even stronger support to the mutation theory, since chronic irradiation is not nearly so effective in causing life shortening as is a single dose. This indicates that in a mammal there can be healing of chromosomes from a small dose of radiation and is in accord with Russell and Russell's finding that there are fewer gene mutations induced in mice by chronic than by acute γ-irradiation (*6*). Puck *et al.* (*7*) found that for mammalian cells in tissue culture the damage from moderate doses of X-ray appears to be genetic in nature and follows a multihit curve.

It is usually found that acute γ-irradiation is about four times as effective, per roentgen, in shortening life span as is chronic γ-irradiation (*4*). Although it is not possible to judge accurately from these data the relative effectiveness of these two modes of irradiation in producing chromosome aberrations, an estimate from the data of Fig. 2 indicates a factor of about 4 between them.

These results correlate well with earlier results (*3*) showing that another mutagenic agent, nitrogen mustard, did not increase the chromosome aberrations and did not cause shortening of the life span.

Thus in all instances so far examined there is an exact correspondence between chromosome aberrations and shortening of the life span, or "aging."

At first glance it would seem that there must be a great deal more to the aging process than the development of somatic mutations, since by irradiation at an early age one can create mutations in virtually every somatic cell, and yet the animal will live an apparently normal life for more than half its normal life expectancy. Obviously if an animal were senescent when a certain number of the somatic cells developed mutations, these irradiated animals would have been senescent at a few weeks of age, and they obviously were not. However, this can be explained in terms of the current ideas of the role of DNA in cell function. If the sole function of DNA in a cell is to synthesize RNA, which in turn synthesizes proteins, then one might expect a nondividing somatic cell to continue to function almost indefinitely with badly damaged DNA, since cell function can be carried on by RNA. Indeed, after cell division in such a damaged cell the two daughter cells would still have half the original concentration of RNA, and it seems reasonable to expect that there is at least a factor of safety of 2 in the RNA concentration in a normal cell. Thus the daughter cells might be expected to function normally. One might even imagine several cell divisions taking place before the concentration of RNA is lowered to the point where the life of the cell can no longer be sustained. Thus one might expect a time delay of the order of several cell divisions between the irradiation of a cell population and the manifestation of the effect. Indeed there is excellent evidence to indicate that this is just what actually happens. Demerec (*8*) found that when a suspension of bacteria is irradiated many of the cells may continue to divide for as many as twelve generations before all the induced mutations become manifest. Newcombe and Scott (*9*) analyzed this phenomenon (phenotypic delay) and concluded that the mutations are indeed induced in the cells, but the influence of the damaged gene can remain dormant for many generations. Furthermore, Puck *et al.* (*7*) showed that mammalian cells in tissue culture continue to divide for three to five cell divisions after a moderate (ca. 150 r) dose of radiation before the daughter cells die or become very bizarre. They find that cells from all organs in the mammal react in this way and have approximately the same radiation sensitivity. Since liver cells undergo cell division, on the average, only about twice after the mouse becomes adult, it would not seem surprising to have the manifestation of genetic damage delayed for a large fraction of the normal life span.

Since some cells, notably brain and muscle cells, never undergo cell division in adults, another explanation for aging in these organs must be found. One might postulate that the endothelial cells of the blood capillaries become nonfunctional because of damage to their chromosomes, and subsequently die, causing capillary stasis and small regions of tissue anoxia. This secondary effect of somatic mutation may be responsible for senescence in these organs, and pathologists have long recognized tissue anoxia caused by inadequate capillary circulation as a concomitant of aging (*10*). This would seem to give a reasonable mechanism for the delayed cell death which is known to be a prominent feature of aging.

This theory is somewhat similar to one put forward by Wulff *et al.* (*11*), who proposed that the somatic mutations produced during aging result in the production of defective RNA and thus defective proteins. They find an increased incorporation of cytidine in certain cells with age, and this presumably means an increased RNA turnover with age. A large turnover of RNA would be inconsistent with the somatic mutation theory of aging, but there may be other explanations. It is quite possible that the cytidine incorporation represents an exchange reaction of some kind which is a normal part of RNA function, and does not represent breakdown and resynthesis of RNA.

These facts seem to fit together remarkably well to give a picture of the basic causes underlying the phenomenon of radiation-induced aging. Since this phenomenon has been found to simulate the natural aging process very closely, it can be taken as strong support for the somatic mutation theory of aging.

SUMMARY

The percentage of cells containing chromosomal aberrations present in regenerating liver of mice has been scored as a function of (1) age in normal mice, (2) age for mice subjected to chronic γ-irradiation, (3) time after a single dose of X-rays and (4) time after a single dose of neutrons. Normal mice develop chromosomal aberrations linearly with age, and mice subjected to chronic γ-irradiation develop them at a greater rate. In comparing acute X-irradiation with chronic γ-irradiation, it is apparent that chromosome aberrations result from multihit events; in other words, chromosome healing is possible after small doses. Chromosomal damage seems more severe for neutrons than for X-rays for equal acute damage, and recovery from neutron irradiation is much slower. These results strongly support the somatic mutation theory of aging, and it is concluded that this theory alone can explain the known facts of aging and radiation-induced aging.

RECEIVED: October 24, 1962

REFERENCES

1. R. S. Caldecott, Seedling height, oxygen availability, storage and temperature; their relation to radiation induced genetic and seedling injury in barley. In *Effects of Ionizing Radiation on Seeds*, pp. 3–24, International Atomic Energy Agency, Vienna, 1961.
2. R. E. Heiner, C. F. Konzak, C. F. Nilan, and R. Legault, Diverse ratios of mutations to chromosome aberrations in barley treated with diethyl sulfate and gamma rays. *Proc. Natl. Acad. Sci. U. S.* **46,** 1215–1221 (1960).
3. K. G. Stevenson and H. J. Curtis, Chromosomal aberrations in irradiated and nitrogen mustard-treated mice. *Radiation Res.* **15,** 774–785 (1961).
4. H. J. Curtis, Radiation induced aging in mice. In *Radiobiology* (P. L. T. Ilbery, ed.) pp. 114–128, 3rd Australasian Conf., Butterworths, London, 1961.
5. H. J. Curtis, S. R. Person, F. B. Olson, J. E. Henkel, and N. Delihas, Calibrating a neutron facility for biological research. *Nucleonics* **14,** No. 2, 26–29 (1956).
6. W. L. Russell and L. B. Russell, Radiation induced genetic damage in mice. *Proc. 2nd Intern. Conf. Peaceful Uses Atomic Energy, Geneva, 1957,* **22,** 360–365 (1958).
7. T. T. Puck, D. Morkovin, P. I. Marcus, and S. J. Cieciura, Action of X-rays on mammalian cells: II, Survival curves of cells from normal human tissues. *J. Exptl. Med.* **106,** 485–500 (1957).
8. M. Demerec, Induced mutations and possible mechanisms of transmission of heredity in *E. coli. Proc. Natl. Acad. Sci. U. S.* **32,** 36–46 (1946).
9. H. B. Newcombe and G. W. Scott, Factors responsible for the delayed appearance of radiation induced mutants in *E. coli. Genetics* **34,** 474–492 (1949).
10. G. W. Casarett, Acceleration of aging by ionizing radiations. In *The Biology of Aging* (B. L. Strehler, ed.), pp. 147–152, American Institute of Biological Sciences, Washington, 1960.
11. V. J. Wulff, H. Quastler, and F. G. Sherman, An hypothesis concerning RNA metabolism and aging. *Proc. Natl. Acad. Sci. U. S.* **48,** 1373–1375 (1962).

RADIATION RESEARCH 19, 345–358 (1963)

The Method of a Competitive Scavenger in Radiation Chemistry

V. N. SHUBIN AND P. I. DOLIN

Radiation Chemical Laboratory, Electrochemical Institute of Academy of Science of U. S. S. R., Moscow

GENERAL DESCRIPTION

The radiation-induced changes in aqueous solutions are determined in principle by the interaction reactions of the solute with hydroxyl radicals and hydrogen atoms—the products of water radiolysis. In order to determine the direction of the radiation-induced process and its kinetics, it is necessary to know the rate constants of the above reactions and of those of radical recombination. But our knowledge about the quantitative characteristics of the reactions of these radicals with the solutes is very scanty, fragmentary, and not always reliable. Evidently, for an accurate determination of such values, we must have a reliable concept about the mechanism of a radiolytic process. It is possible to arrive at this concept only by means of a thorough investigation of the problem.

It is very helpful for this purpose to study radiolysis by using competitive reactions under the conditions of radical transformations. The method is essentially as follows: A transforming scavenger, such as molecular hydrogen, is added to the solution. The hydroxyl radical formed in the process of radiolysis is changed partially or completely (depending on the H_2 concentration) into an H atom by reaction 1. Total transformation, which is possible if the solution is saturated with

$$H_2 + OH \rightarrow H + H_2O \qquad (1)$$

hydrogen under pressure, permits us to study the reactions of atomic hydrogen with various acceptors without having to consider the confusing effect of the OH radical's reaction, which hinders us in obtaining a true picture under usual conditions. Provided the transformation of OH radicals according to reaction 1 is complete, atomic hydrogen is formed with a yield

$$G(H) = G_H + G_{OH}$$

In the systems with a transformation of the radicals, it is possible to study quantitatively the experimental relationships and to obtain reliable evidence on the reaction mechanism. Let us suppose the alternative mechanism of radiolysis to consist in two reactions (reactions 2a and 2b), between which we cannot choose

$$Ac_1 + H \rightarrow \text{Products} \tag{2a}$$

$$Ac_2 + H \rightarrow \text{Products} \tag{2b}$$

a priori. Let us add a competitive scavenger to the solution, which can react with atomic H, as has been proved by special experiments (reaction 3). Now, to estab-

$$Ac_3 + H \rightarrow \text{products} \tag{3}$$

lish the mechanism, it is sufficient to determine in the system obtained the dependence of the radiolysis yield on the concentration of all three scavengers. It is evident that the character of the change in the radiolysis yield, depending on the concentration of competitive scavengers, must be identical, whereas the variation in the concentration of the substance indifferent to a particular radical will not affect the magnitude of the yield. Therefore, from a comparison of experimental relationships obtained it is possible to decide which reactions, 2a or 2b, enters into the true mechanism of radiolysis. Such a qualitative consideration can be confirmed by a subsequent quantitative analysis. For this purpose let us write the following expression:

$$\begin{aligned} G(\mathrm{H}) &= \frac{G(\mathrm{H})}{1 + k_3(\mathrm{Ac}_3)/k_2(\mathrm{Ac})} + \frac{G(\mathrm{H})}{1 + k_2(\mathrm{Ac})/k_3(\mathrm{Ac}_3)} \\ &= \frac{G(\mathrm{H})}{1 + k_3(\mathrm{Ac}_3)/k_2(\mathrm{Ac})} + G(\mathrm{Ac}_3) \end{aligned} \tag{4}$$

Let us rewrite this equation in the form

$$1 + \frac{k_3(\mathrm{Ac}_3)}{k_2(\mathrm{Ac})} = \frac{G(\mathrm{H})}{G(\mathrm{H}) - G(\mathrm{Ac}_3)} \equiv \Psi(G) \tag{5}$$

The consideration of this equation shows that the expression in the right-hand side must be a linear function of the value of the ratio $(Ac_3)/(Ac)$, where (Ac) is the concentration of Ac_1 or of Ac_2. By solving equation 5 graphically, from experimental data on the dependence of the yield on the concentration of all the three scavengers, we shall obtain a sound concept about the mechanism of the process. The values of ψ(G) against the value of the ratio of concentrations of the competitive scavengers must lie on one straight line, for which the tangent of the slope angle is equal to k_3/k_2. An indifferent scavenger will give a different straight line or a curve.

In the radiolysis of substances which act as scavengers of only one of the radicals formed, the transformation yield observed is usually very low, since some of the radicals are recombined back into water (reaction 6). There may be another reason,

$$H + OH \rightarrow H_2O \qquad (6)$$

however, for a decrease in the apparent yield in the water decomposition. This is the back-oxidation (or reduction) of the intermediate products formed. In order to find the true reason for the low radiolysis yield, the method of competitive reactions may be used. For this purpose, it is necessary to produce in the solution the conditions for two reactions which would compete with the recombination process, e.g., reactions 1 and 3, and to determine the experimental relationships between the radiolysis yield and the concentrations of the substances participating in these reactions (H_2 and Ac_3). If the decrease in the yield is due to the back-oxidation (or reduction) of the intermediate products, the yield will depend on the concentration of only one of the scavengers added (in our case, H_2). But if the radiolysis yield is low because of the occurrence of the recombination reaction (reaction 6), the dependence of the yield on the concentration of both scavengers must be approximately identical. Let us write equations 7 and 8 for the consumption and the formation of radicals in this case. The expression for the radiolysis

$$k_1(H_2)\cdot(OH) + k_6(H)\cdot(OH) = MG_{OH} \qquad (7)$$

$$k_3(Ac_3)\cdot(H) + k_6(H)(OH) = MG_H + k_1(H_2)\cdot(OH) \qquad (8)$$

yield will be given by equation 9. By determining with the help of equations 7 to 9

$$k_3(Ac_3)(H) = MG(Ac_3) \qquad (9)$$

the concentrations of H and OH radicals and by substituting them in equation 7

$$\frac{k_6}{k_1\cdot k_3}\,\frac{M}{(H_2)\cdot(Ac_3)} = \phi(G) \qquad (10)$$

or 8, we obtain equation 10, where $\phi(G)$ is a function of the radiolysis yields of the scavenger and of the radical and molecular products of water radiolysis. The graphical solution of this equation is a straight line passing through the origin of coordinate axes. The tangent of the slope angle is equal to $k_6/k_1\cdot k_3$.

RESULTS[1] AND DISCUSSION

The oxidizing properties of atomic hydrogen with respect to the ferrous ion, first observed by Weiss, were initially considered questionable by a number of investigators. To verify the ability of atomic hydrogen to oxidize the Fe^{2+} ion, we studied the effect of molecular hydrogen concentration on the oxidation yield of Fe^{2+} in

[1] Dose rate in our experiments was equal to $(1.75 \div 3) \times 10^{15}$ ev/cm³ sec. The total dose did not exceed 1.5×10^{18} ev/cm³.

solutions saturated with H_2 under pressure. Evidently, if atomic hydrogen is not able to oxidize the ferrous ions, the oxidation yield must fall to very small values with a rise in the H_2 pressure. This would be explained by the fact that the oxidizing components of radiolysis—the OH radicals—being transformed according to reaction 1 into H atoms, do not participate in the oxidation of the ions. Under the saturation conditions at 180 atm (maximum pressure used), the contribution of reaction 1 is ~90%, and the radiolysis yield in this case would be $\leqq G_{H_2O_2}$. In fact (*1*), $G(Fe^{3+}) \simeq G_H + G_{OH} + 2G_{H_2O_2}$. This is a conclusive proof that atomic hydrogen has oxidizing properties with respect to the Fe^{2+} ion.

These experiments, however, do not shed any light on the mechanism of the process in question, about the nature of which so many widely differing hypotheses have been made. In Weiss's opinion, the hydrogen ion is a direct scavenger of the H atom:

$$H + H^+ \rightarrow H_2^+ \tag{11}$$

Then the H_2^+ ion radical, formed according to reaction 11, oxidizes the ferrous ions:

$$Fe^{2+} + H_2^+ \rightarrow Fe^{3+} + H_2 \tag{12}$$

According to the concepts of Davis *et al.* (*2*), Uri (*3*), and Halpern *et al.* (*4*), the ferrous ions are the direct scavenger of H atoms.[2]

Let us add to the solution a competitive scavenger—the ferric ions, which, according to the results of some special experiments, are good scavengers of H atoms. Now it is evident that to determine the mechanism it will suffice to study in the system obtained the dependence of the oxidation yield on the Fe^{3+}, Fe^{2+}, and H^+ concentrations and to compare these data by means of expression 5. It was found in the course of investigation (Fig. 1) that the radiolysis yield changes greatly with an increase in the Fe^{3+} concentration and with decrease in H^+. In both cases the oxidation yield reduces to zero, whereupon the reduction of Fe^{3+} commences. The change in the Fe^{2+} concentration affects the oxidation yield but slightly. A graphical representation of the experimental data (*5*) with the help of equation 5 shows the validity of Weiss's mechanism. From the slope of the straight line we calculated:

$$k_{H+H^+}/k_{H+Fe^{3+}} = 2.8 \times 10^{-3}$$

By using Fe^{3+} as a competitive scavenger, we can obtain a sound concept about the radiolysis mechanism of Fe^{2+} solutions in the presence of oxygen. In Fe^{2+} and Fe^{3+} solutions in sulfuric and perchloric acids saturated with hydrogen and oxygen under pressure, the radiation yields of oxidation are very large and under optimum conditions reach the value of 100 moles per 100 ev and more (*6, 7*). Apparently, it

[2] The fact that the mechanisms suggested by the above authors differ from one another is of no consequence for the purposes of our consideration.

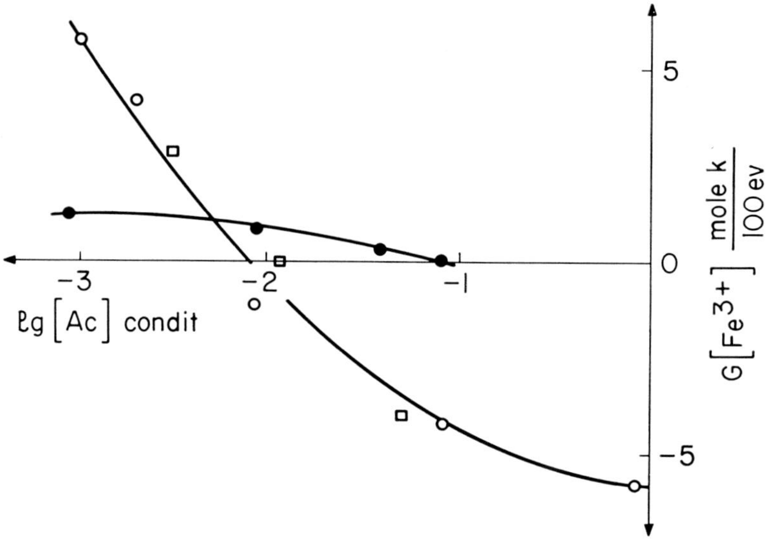

FIG. 1. Dependence of yield of the ferric ion formation on Fe^{3+}, Fe^{2+}, and H^+ concentration. ○, dependence on Fe^{3+} concentration. ●, dependence on Fe^{2+} concentration. □, dependence on acidity.

DEPENDENCE OF $G(Fe^{3+})$ ON CONCENTRATION OF Fe^{3+}, Fe^{2+}, AND H_2SO_4

Scavenger	*Fe^{3+}*					*Fe^{2+}*				*H_2SO_4*			
Concentration (mM)	*1*	*2*	*8.6*	*86*	*860*	*0.115*	*0.23*	*1.05*	*10.5*	*400*	*140*	*29*	*5*
$G(Fe^{3+})$ (moles/100 ev)	5.8	4.2	−1.05[a]	−4.2	−5.8	0	0.3	0.85	1.25	6.5	2.9	0	−4
Concentrations of scavengers	$(Fe^{2-}) = 1.05 \times 10^{-3}\ M$; $(H^+)_{H_2SO_4} = 0.5\ M$; $P_{H_2} = 100$ atm					$(Fe^{3+}) = 8.6 \times 10^{-3}\ M$; $(H^+)_{H_2SO_4} = 0.5\ M$; $(Fe^{2+})/(H_2) \simeq 1.5$				$(Fe^{3+}) = 8.1 \times 10^{-3}\ M$; $(Fe^{2+}) = 1.05 \times 10^{-3}\ M$; $P_{H_2} = 100$ atm			

[a] Minus sign means the reduction takes place.

can be explained by the chain character of the oxidation process. In fact, the reactions 0, 1, and 13 to 19 occur in the course of radiolysis of such solutions. Since,

$$H_2O \xrightarrow{\gamma} H, OH, H_2O_2, H_2 \tag{0}$$

$$OH + H_2 \rightarrow H + H_2O \tag{1}$$

$$Fe^{2+} + OH \rightarrow Fe^{3+} + OH^- \tag{13}$$

$$H + O_2 \rightarrow HO_2 \quad (14)$$

$$Fe^{2+} + HO_2 \xrightarrow{H^+} Fe^{3+} + H_2O_2 \quad (15)$$

$$Fe^{2+} + H_2O_2 \rightarrow Fe^{3+} + OH^- + OH \quad (16)$$

$$Fe^{3+} + H \rightarrow Fe^{2+} + H^+ \quad (17)$$

$$HO_2 \rightleftarrows H^+ + O_2^- \quad (18)$$

$$Fe^{3+} + O_2^- \rightarrow Fe^{2+} + O_2 \quad (19)$$

as the result of the cycle formed by reactions 1 and 14 to 16, some OH radicals are reproduced, the conditions for the development of a chain process are available. The termination of the chain occurs according to reactions 13, 17, and 19. Evidently the conditions for the development of the chain will depend on the ratio of the rates of the chain continuation and termination reactions, i.e., of reactions 1 and 13, 14, and 17, as well as reactions 15 and 19.

If the ferric ions are absent, the only termination reaction will be reaction 13. Under these conditions, the yield increases linearly with a rise in H_2 concentration in the solution (*6*). By means of these data we calculated the ratio of rate constants of reactions 1 and 13: $k_1/k_{13} = 0.135$.

As seen from the reaction scheme, the ferric ion is a competitive scavenger with respect to both O_2 (competition for H atoms) and Fe^{2+} (competition for HO_2 radi-

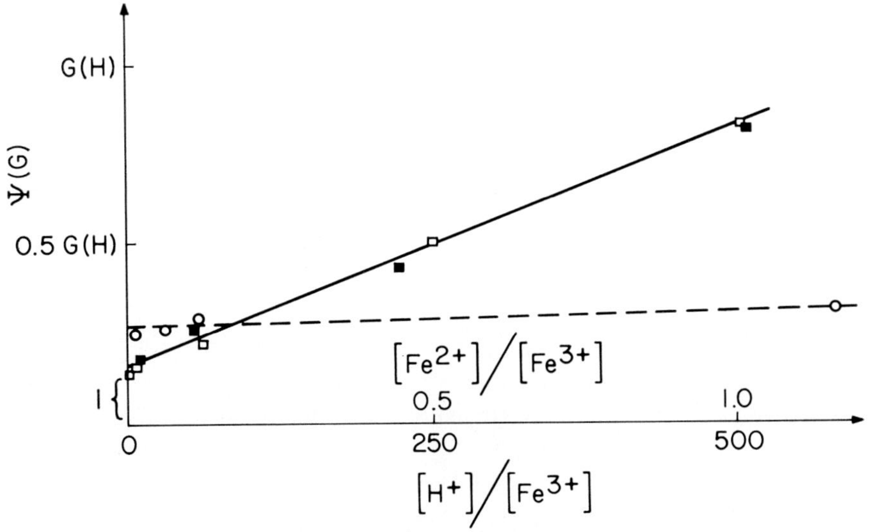

FIG. 2. Graphical solution of equation 5 from data of Fig. 1. □, dependence on Fe^{3+} concentration. ■, dependence on H^+ concentration. ○, dependence on Fe^{2+} concentration.

cal). This permits us to verify the validity of the concept of Krenz and Dewhurst about the mechanism of the Fe^{2+} oxidation process in solutions saturated with air.

Incidentally, a hypothesis has been advanced (*8*) that reaction 20 must be substituted for reaction 15. To verify this hypothesis, we studied the effect of the

$$2HO_2 \rightarrow H_2O_2 + O_2 \tag{20}$$

Fe^{2+} concentration on the oxidation yield, with all other concentrations and the value of the ratio $(Fe^{2+})/(H_2)$ remaining constant. As can be seen from the reaction scheme of the process, if reaction 15 is absent, the yield need not depend on the Fe^{2+} concentration, provided $(Fe^{2+})/(H_2) = $ constant. A considerable increase in the oxidation yield with a rise in the Fe^{2+} concentration experimentally observed (Fig. 3) indicates, however, that the true mechanism includes reaction 15 rather than 20.

Then the effect of the ratio of O_2 and Fe^{3+} concentrations on the oxidation yield, with the value of the ratio $(Fe^{3+})/(Fe^{2+})$ being held constant, was studied (see Table I). The reaction of Fe^{3+} with atomic hydrogen terminates the chain, which results in a decrease in the radiolysis yield. If the concept of the mechanism advanced is correct, the oxidation yield must diminish with a rise in (Fe^{3+}) and increase with a rise in (O_2). In fact, as is seen from Table I, the experimental evidence confirms these hypotheses and, consequently, the mechanism suggested.

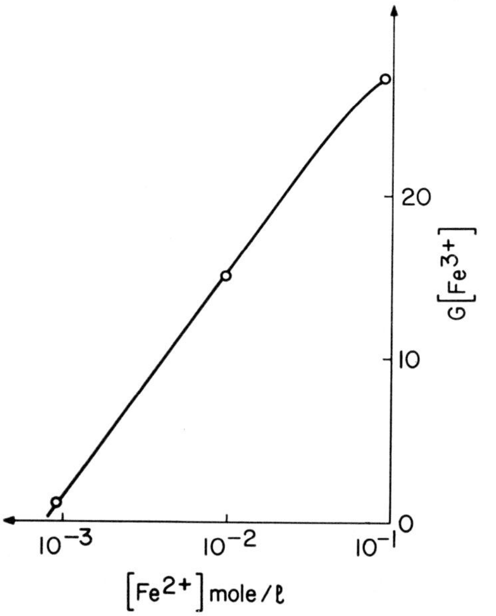

FIG. 3. Dependence of oxidation yield on Fe^{2+} concentration. $(Fe^{3+}) \simeq 10^{-3}\,M$; $(HClO_4) \simeq 10^{-2}\,M$; $P_{O_2} = 10.2$ atm. $(Fe^{2+})/(H_2) \simeq$ constant.

TABLE I

DEPENDENCE OF $G(Fe^{3+})$ ON CONCENTRATION OF O_2 AND Fe^{3+}

(P_{H_2} = 50 atm)

Scavenger	O_2					Fe^{3+}					
Concentration (mM)	*0.28*	*0.98*	*1.68*	*4.48*	*14.3*	*190*	*100*	*39*	*20*	*11*	*9.2*
(H^+) = 0.12 *M*	3.4	11.9	13.5	18.5	21.5	5	6.7	12.2	—	18.5	—
	$(Fe^{3+}) = 1.1 \times 10^{-2}$ *M*; $(Fe^{2+}) = 8.3 \times 10^{-4}$ *M*					(O_2) = 4.48 m*M*; (Fe^{2+}) = 0.83 m*M*					
$(H^+) = 5.10^{-3}$ *M*	6	—	—	6.6	7	—	—	—	6.7	—	6.6
	(Fe^{3+}) = 1.3 m*M*; $(Fe^{2+}) \simeq$ 1 m*M*					(O_2) = 4.48 m*M*; (Fe^{2+}) = 1 m*M*					

TABLE II

DEPENDENCE OF YIELD ON CONCENTRATION OF Fe^{3+}, Fe^{2+}, AND H^+

$[(Fe^{3+})/(O_2) \simeq 3; P_{H_2} = 50$ atm$]$

Scavenger	Fe^{3+}			Fe^{2+}			H^+		
Concentration (mM)	*63*	*8.4*	*1.5*	*0.14*	*0.81*	*8.3*	*5.1*	*45*	*450*
$G(Fe^{3+})$ (moles/100 ev)	3.7	25	43.5	1	17.5	19.5	7.5	17	22
Concentrations of scavengers	(H^+) = 0.1 *M*; $(Fe^{2+}) = 1.5 \times 10^{-3}$ *M*			(H^+) = 0.1 *M*; $(Fe^{3+}) = 9 \times 10^{-3}$ *M*			$(Fe^{2+}) = 9 \times 10^{-3}$ *M*; $(Fe^{3+}) = 2.6 \times 10^{-3}$ *M*		

The ferric ions can be reduced by HO_2 radicals, or by the products of their dissociation according to reactions 18 and 19. Therefore, in the presence of Fe^{3+}, in addition to its competition with O_2 for atomic hydrogen, there must be also a competition between Fe^{2+} and Fe^{3+} for HO_2 radicals. If HO_2 reacts with Fe^{3+} in a dissociated form, the latter competition must depend on pH. For the purposes of qualitative and quantitative verification of these assumptions, the effect of the Fe^{2+}, Fe^{3+}, and H^+ concentrations on the oxidation yield, with the value $(Fe^{3+})/(O_2)$ being constant, was studied. An increase in the Fe^{3+} concentration was found to decrease the yield, whereas for Fe^{2+} and H^+ there is a reverse relationship. These data, presented in Table II, are a qualitative confirmation of the correctness of the mechanism suggested.

The following equation has been deduced on the basis of the mechanism suggested for a quantitative treatment of the experimental data obtained:

$$\left[\left(1 + \frac{k_{17}(Fe^{3+})}{k_{14}(O_2)}\right)\left(1 + \frac{k_{19}}{k_{15}} K_{HO_2} \frac{(Fe^{3+})}{(Fe^{2+})(H^+)}\right)\right] = F(G) \qquad (21)$$

where $F(G)$ is the function of the radiolysis yields of water and scavenger, as well as of the value of the ratio $(Fe^{2+})/(H_2)$:

$$F(G) = \frac{[G(Fe^{3+}) - G_H - G_{OH} - 2G_{H_2O_2}] \dfrac{1}{1 + k_{13}(Fe^{2+})/k_1(H_2)} + 4\left[G_H + \dfrac{G_{OH} + G_{H_2O_2}}{1\, k_{13}(Fe^{2+})/k_1(H_2)}\right]}{G(Fe^{3+}) - G_H - G_{OH} - 2G_{H_2O_2} + 2\left[G_H + \dfrac{G_{OH} + G_{H_2O_2}}{1 + k_{13}(Fe^{2+})/k_1(H_2)}\right]}$$

The consideration of equation 21 shows that if in one of the brackets in the left-hand side of the equation the ratio of concentrations remains constant, while it changes in the other, the expression in the right-hand side must be a linear function of the value of the latter. When equation 21 is solved graphically, the data on the dependence of $G(Fe^{3+})$ on (Fe^{3+}) and (O_2) at $(Fe^{3+})/(Fe^{2+})(H^+) \simeq$ constant, as well as on (Fe^{2+}), (Fe^{3+}), and (H^+) at $(Fe^{3+})/(O_2) \simeq$ constant, give linear dependence of $F(G)$ on the value of the ratio of the corresponding concentrations (see Figs. 4 and 5). This is conclusive proof of the correctness of the oxidation

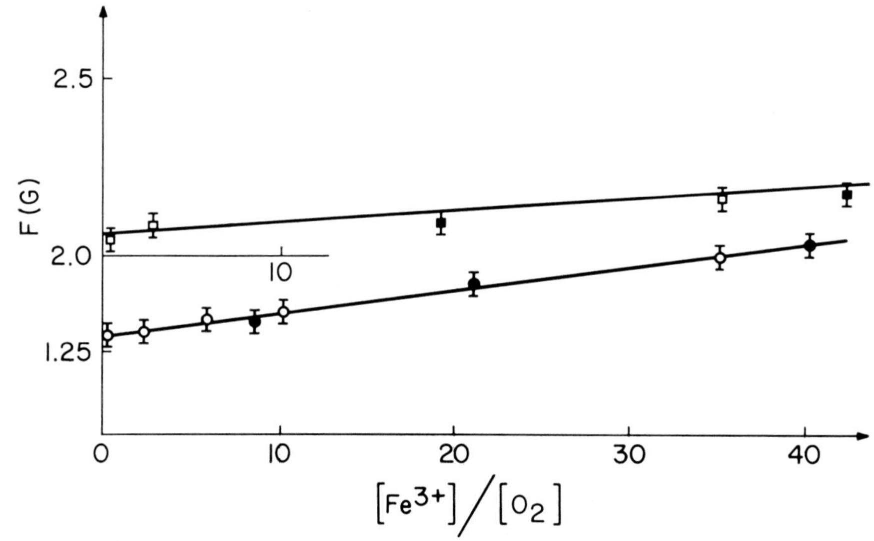

FIG. 4. Graphical solution of equation 21 from data of Table I. *A*, concentration of $HClO_4 \sim 0.12$ *M*: ○, dependence on (O_2); ●, dependence on (Fe^{3+}). *B*, concentration of $HClO_4 \sim 5 \times 10^{-3}$ *M*: □, dependence on (O_2); ■, dependence on (Fe^{3+}).

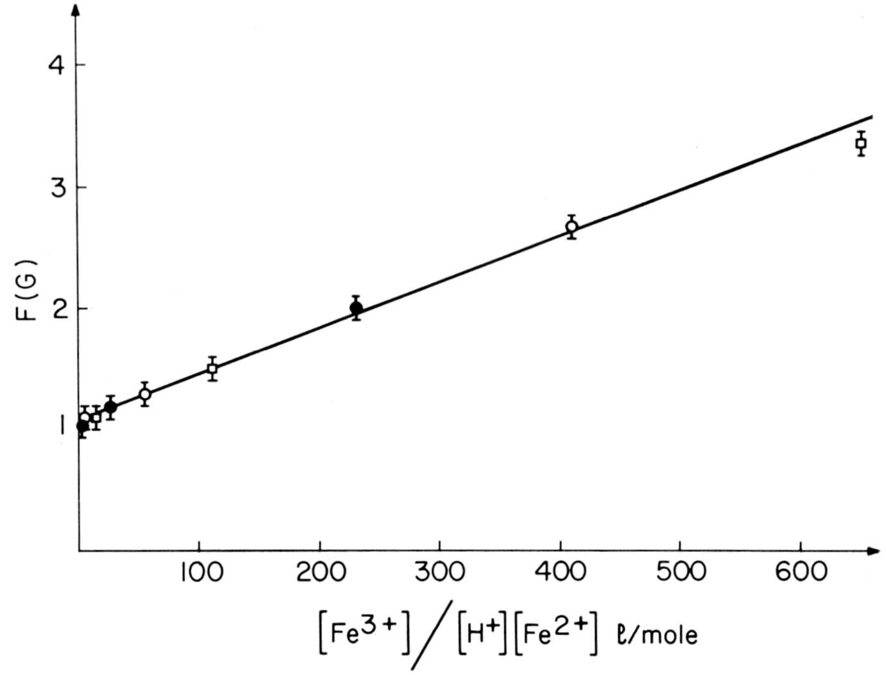

FIG. 5. Graphical solution of equation 21 from data of Table II. □, dependence on (Fe^{3+}). ○, dependence on (Fe^{3+}). ●, dependence on (H^+).

mechanism suggested. From the slope of the straight lines obtained we find $k_{17}/k_{14} = 2.45 \times 10^{-2}$ and $(k_{19}/k_{15})K_{HO_2} = 3.6 \times 10^{-3}$ moles/liter.

The radiation reduction of Fe^{3+} and Cr^{4+} in solutions saturated with air and nitrogen proceeds with a low yield. In strongly acid solutions the ferric ions are not reduced at all. But the reasons for the low radiolysis yields of these ions have not been found as yet. To study the nature of the reaction decreasing the yield, the radiolysis of the ions being considered, in solutions saturated with hydrogen under pressure, was investigated (*9*).

The reduction yield in Fe^{3+} solutions rises with an increase in hydrogen pressure over the solution (Fig. 6) and in the concentration of the ferric ions (Fig. 7). On the basis of these data a conclusion may be drawn that the low radiolysis yields in solutions saturated with air and nitrogen are due to the effective course of the effective course of the recombination reaction in the bulk:

$$H + OH \rightarrow H_2O \tag{6}$$

In addition, as it follows from the results of the experiments on the effect of acidity on the reduction yield, a portion of Fe^{2+} in strongly acid solutions is oxidized again by the H_2^+ ion radicals.

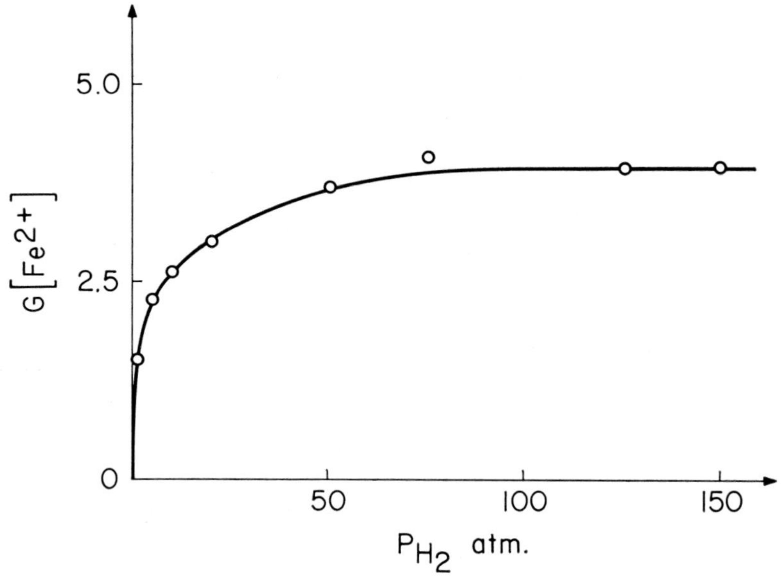

FIG. 6. Dependence of reduction yield of the ferric ions on hydrogen pressure over solution 0.8 *N* H_2SO_4. $(Fe^{3+}) = 2 \times 10^{-3}$ *M*.

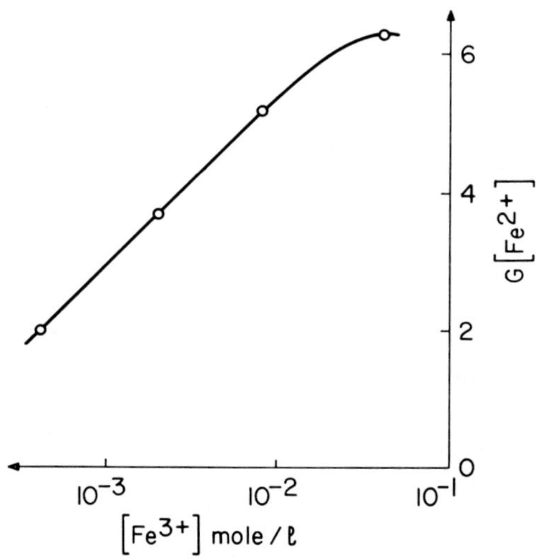

FIG. 7. Dependence of reduction yield on ferric ions concentration. $P_{H_2} = 50$ atm; 0.8 *N* H_2SO_4.

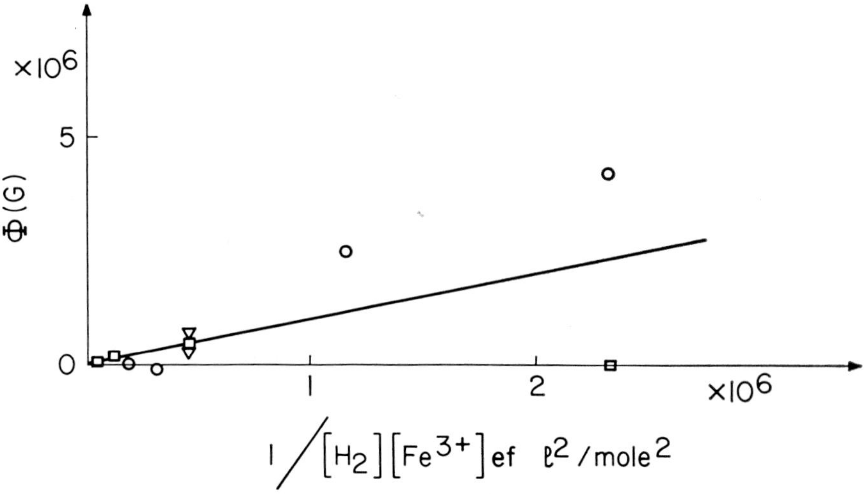

FIG. 8. Graphical solution of equation 10 from data of Figs. 6 and 7. In this case the equation will be

$$\frac{k_6}{k_1 \cdot k_{17}} \cdot \frac{1}{(H_2)(Fe^{3+})} = \frac{1 - Z}{M\left[G(Fe^{2+}) + \dfrac{2G_{H_2O_2}}{1 + 1/Z}\right]} \times \left\{ \frac{2G_{OH}}{\left[G(Fe^{2+}) + \dfrac{2G_{H_2O_2}}{1 + 1/Z}\right]\dfrac{1 + Z}{1 - Z} - (G_H - G_{OH})} - 1 \right\} \equiv \phi(G)$$

where

$$Z = \frac{k_{11}(H^+)/k_{17}(Fe^{3+})}{1 + k_{H_2^+ \to H + H^+}/k_{12}(Fe^{2+})_{ef.}}$$

○, dependence on hydrogen pressure. □, dependence on Fe^{3+} concentration. ▽, dependence on acidity.

A quantitative treatment of the experimental evidence on the effect of the H_2 and Fe^{3+} concentrations on the reduction yield by means of expression 10 made it possible for us to determine the value of the ratio of the rate constants $k_6/k_1 \cdot k_{17} = 10$ moles/sec (Fig. 8).

The saturation of potassium bichromate solutions with hydrogen under pressure considerably increases the radiolysis yield (Fig. 9). It appears, however, that with a change in the bichromate ion concentration from $\sim 2 \times 10^{-5}\ M$ to $\sim 7 \times 10^{-3}\ M$, the reduction yield does not change (Fig. 10). The comparison of these data shows that reaction 6 doesn't occur under these conditions. Consequently, low reduction

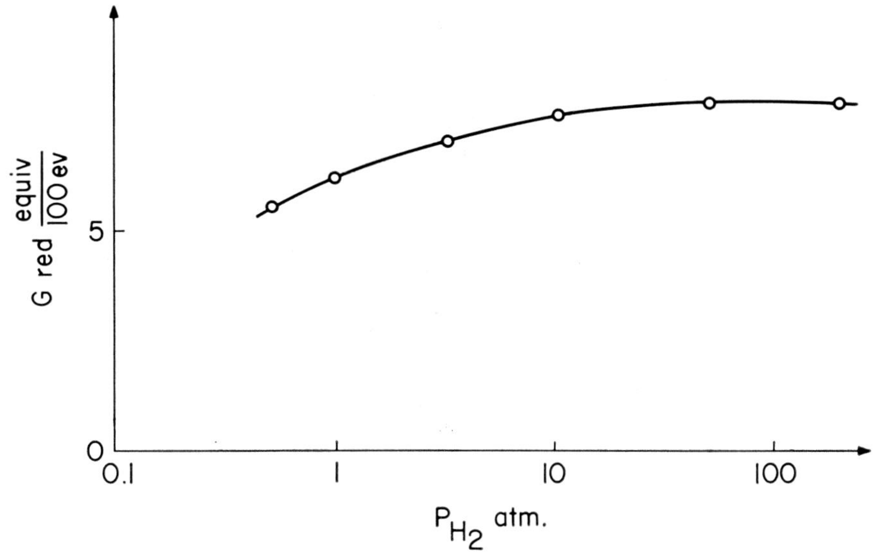

FIG. 9. Dependence of reduction yield of bichromate ions on hydrogen pressure over solution. $pH = 1$.

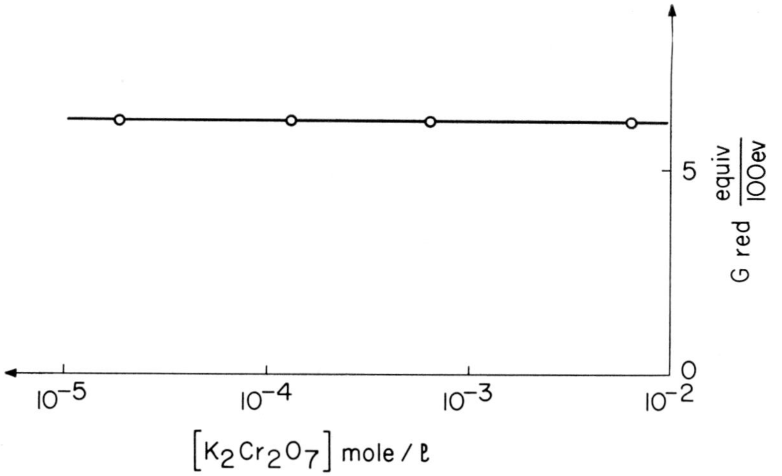

FIG. 10. Effect of bichromate ion concentration on reduction yield. $P_{H_2} = 1$ atm

yields under usual conditions are due to the back-oxidation of one of the intermediate reduction products. The evidence of some additional experiments with Cr^{3+} makes it possible for us to suppose that the ion radical $HCr_2O_7^{2-}$ is such a product.

SUMMARY

The method of a competitive scavenger is described in a general way. The examples given show the great possibilities of this method for the determination of the mechanism of the processes of radiation chemistry. The most reliable results can be obtained when the transformation of the radicals has been carried out. At present, this method is one of the few which can provide a sound concept of the mechanism of the processes occurring in the system on irradiation.

RECEIVED: July 9, 1962

REFERENCES

1. V. N. SHUBIN and P. I. DOLIN, Oxidative properties of atomic hydrogen in the radiation oxidation of ferrous ions. *Zhur. Fiz. Khim.* **34,** 2480–2488 (1960) (in Russian).
2. T. W. DAVIS, S. GORDON, and E. J. HART, Chemical effects of atomic hydrogen in aqueous solutions. *J. Am. Chem. Soc.* **80,** 4487–4491 (1958).
3. N. URI, Inorganic free radicals in solution. *Chem. Rev.* **50,** 375–454 (1952).
4. J. HALPERN, G. CZAPSKI, J. JORTNER, and G. STEIN, Mechanism of the oxidation and reduction of metal ions by hydrogen atoms. *Nature* **186,** 629–630 (1960).
5. V. N. SHUBIN and P. I. DOLIN, Radiation conversions of a mixture of Fe^{++} and Fe^{+++} in an acid solution saturated with hydrogen under pressure. *Dokl. Akad. Nauk SSSR* **138,** 169–172 (1961) (in Russian).
6. V. N. SHUBIN and P. I. DOLIN, The effect of acidity on the yield of radiation-chemical reactions. *Dokl. Akad. Nauk SSSR* **139,** 154–157 (1961) (in Russian).
7. V. N. SHUBIN and P. I. DOLIN, Radiation-chemical transformations of iron ions in $HClO_4$ solutions saturated with hydrogen and oxygen under pressure. *Dokl. Akad. Nauk SSSR* **140,** 1380–1383 (1961) (in Russian).
8. M. A. PROSKURNIN, The relation between the yield of radiochemical reactions and the concentration of dissolved substances. *Dokl. Akad. Nauk SSSR* **135,** 1446–1449 (1960) (in Russian).
9. V. N. SHUBIN and P. I. DOLIN, Radiation reduction of trivalent Fe ions in solutions saturated with hydrogen under pressure. *Dokl. Akad. Nauk SSSR* **134,** 891–894 (1960) (in Russian).

RADIATION RESEARCH **19**, 359–367 (1963)

Radiolysis Products from the X-Irradiation of 2,2,4,6,6-Pentamethylheptane[1]

J. A. KNIGHT AND FRED SICILIO[2]

Nuclear Sciences Division, Engineering Experiment Station, Georgia Institute of Technology, Atlanta, Georgia

INTRODUCTION

Work current in this laboratory is concerned with a study of the radiation chemistry of branched hydrocarbons. Radiolysis products, hydrogen and hydrocarbons through C_7 (*1*) and C_8 and greater (*2*), from the X-irradiation (50 kvp) of 2,2,4-trimethylpentane have been reported. The radiolysis products from the X-irradiation of 2,2,4,6,6-pentamethylheptane (PMH) have been investigated mainly with gas chromatographic techniques, and the results are reported in this paper.

MATERIAL AND METHODS

2,2,4,6,6-Pentamethylheptane

PMH was prepared by hydrogenation of commercially available triisobutylene (*3*). The triisobutylene was hydrogenated in 50-ml batches with glacial acetic acid as a solvent and platinum oxide or 5% platinum on carbon as a catalyst in a Parr hydrogenation apparatus. The crude PMH, after washing and drying, was charged to a total-condensation intermittent-take-off type of distillation column. The packed section, 1 inch by 4 feet, was packed with Podbielniak Heli-Pak No. 2117 stainless-steel packing. The column and take-off valve were designed so that the distillate did not come in contact with stopcock grease at any point. Distillation was carried out at 18 mm pressure. After proper equilibration of the column, fractions of 25 ml or less were taken. The take-off valve was operated by a solenoid and a 30-second cycle timer arrangement so that the valve was open 5% of every 30-second cycle. Approximately 900 ml of pure PMH was obtained from an initial

[1] This research was supported in part by the U. S. Atomic Energy Commission Contract AT (40-1)-2490.

[2] Present address: Department of Chemistry, A. & M. College of Texas, College Station, Texas.

charge of approximately 1600 ml. Gas chromatographic analyses of the purified PMH fractions on a 26-foot column of 20% (by weight) of Dow Corning high-vacuum silicone grease on 30-60 Chromosorb did not show the presence of any impurities (*4*). The purified PMH had a boiling point of 64.5° to 65°C at 18 mm, and 174°C at 740 mm, with $n_D^{25°} = 1.4170$. The reported literature values (*5*) are a boiling point of 178°C at 760 mm, and $n_D^{20°} = 1.4189$.

X-Ray Apparatus and Irradiation Cell

The X-ray apparatus and irradiation cell have been previously described (*1*). All irradiations were performed at 50 kvp and 50 ma, at a dose rate of 1.5×10^{18} ev/gm/min for the volumes of samples studied.

Sampling Technique for Volatile Radiolysis Products

The technique employed for the sampling of the volatile radiolysis products—hydrogen, C_1 through C_4 hydrocarbons, and neopentane—was the same as that used in the irradiation studies of 2,2,4-trimethylpentane, viz., the periodic sampling of the gas phase containing the volatile products, with helium being used as a continuous sweep gas at a known flow rate of 5 to 10 ml/min. (*1*).

Other Hydrocarbon Radiolysis Products

Samples of the irradiated PMH were fractionally distilled with a 1.2×33-cm column packed with Podbielniak Heli-Pak 3013 stainless-steel packing. The distillations were performed very slowly in order to concentrate the radiolysis products of carbon content less than C_{12} in the initial fraction and those of carbon content greater than C_{12} in the final fraction. Chromatograms were obtained on each fraction.

Gas Chromatographic Analysis

Hydrogen and methane were identified and determined quantitatively with a 14-foot column of Linde 13X Molecular Sieve, 50- to 60-mesh. The C_1 to C_4 hydrocarbons and neopentane were analyzed with two columns, one a 28-foot column of 25% (by weight) tri-*m*-cresyl phosphate on 50- to 60-mesh Chromosorb, and the other a 50-foot column of 20% dimethylsulfolane on 30- to 60-mesh Chromosorb. The C_5 to C_8 products were analyzed with two columns, one a 40-foot column of 25% tri-*m*-cresyl phosphate on 50- to 60-mesh Chromosorb, and the other a 29-foot column of 15% isoquinoline on 60- to 70-mesh Chromosorb. The C_8 to C_{11} products were analyzed by utilizing the 40-foot column of 25% tri-*m*-cresyl phosphate mentioned above and a 32-foot column of 15% di-2-ethylhexyl sebacate on 50- to 60-mesh Chromosorb. The C_{12} and greater carbon content radiolysis products were analyzed with three columns, a 10-foot column and a 23-foot column packed with 15% Ucon oil LB-550X on 50- to 60-mesh Chromosorb, and a 20-foot column of 15% Apiezon L on 50- to 60-mesh Chromosorb. All columns were made of ¼-inch o.d. copper tubing. The gas chromatographic unit was calibrated for thermal response to hydrogen and to each of the hydrocarbons identified except as noted in the tables. In the cases of the unknown peaks, the calibration used is given in the tables. Microliter syringes were utilized for injecting samples. Peak areas were measured with a planimeter.

Molecular Weight Determinations

The fraction of higher molecular weight was isolated by removing the parent hydrocarbon, PMH, for about 4 hours at about 0.02 mm Hg at room temperature. Molecular-weight determinations were made on this material with benzene as a solvent on a semimicro scale with a thermistor thermometer (*6*). The molecular-weight determinations of the radiolytic product isolated in this manner were in the range of 298 to 310.

Unsaturation

Unsaturation was determined by measuring volumetrically the amount of hydrogen absorbed by a known amount of the irradiated material. The solvent was glacial acetic acid, and the catalyst was 5% Pt on carbon. The apparatus was very similar to that of Ogg and Cooper (*7*). It was necessary to use fairly large samples for analysis, and the most successful technique for introducing a large sample was by means of a sample holder similar to a separatory funnel with a pressure-equalizing tube.

Measurements were made on irradiated PMH after removal of radiolysis products of carbon content less than C_{12}. The radiolysis products of carbon content less than C_{12} were removed by slowly distilling about one-third of a sample through the distillation column described above. The unsaturation for the C_{12} to C_{24} fraction, expressed in terms of G for carbon–carbon double-bond formation, amounted to 0.6 for a total dose of 1.57×10^{22} ev and to 0.36 for a total dose of 4.27×10^{22} ev. Qualitative infrared evidence for unsaturation in the C^{20} to C^{24} products was obtained with a Perkin-Elmer 221 spectrophotometer with a NaCl prism.

Dosimetry

The method of dose determinations has been described previously (*1*).

RESULTS AND DISCUSSION

The radiolysis products and G values found in this investigation are listed in Tables I and II. The radiolysis products from PMH of carbon content less than C_{12} can be divided into four groups.

Group I. This groups consists of those products that can be related to some structural portion of the parent hydrocarbon, PMH. There are twenty possible

TABLE I

RADIOLYSIS PRODUCTS H_2 AND C_1 TO C_{11} CARBON CONTENT FROM 2,2,4,6,6-PENTAMETHYLHEPTANE

Product[a]	*Group*	G[b]
Hydrogen		1.3
Methane	I	0.74
Ethane and ethylene	II	0.01_5
Propane	IV	0.02
Propylene	IV	0.06
Isobutane	I	0.3_4
Isobutylene	I	1.2
Neopentane	I	0.2_5
2-Methylbutane	III	<0.001
2-Methylbutene-1	III	0.004
2-Methylbutene-2 and/or 2,3-dimethylbutane	III	0.003
2,2-Dimethylbutane	II	0.01_1
2,2-Dimethylpentane	I	0.1_1
4,4-Dimethylpentene-1	I	0.07_6
4,4-Dimethyl-*trans*-pentene-2	I	0.03_1
4,4-Dimethyl-*cis*-pentene-2	I	0.005
2,4-Dimethylpentene-1	IV	0.003
2,2,4-Trimethylpentane	I	1.0_5
2,2-Dimethylhexane	IV	0.01
2,2,3,3-Tetramethylbutane	II	0.01
2,4,4-Trimethylpentene-1	I	0.2
2,4,4-Trimethylpentene-2	I	0.01
2,3,4-Trimethylpentane and/or 2,3-dimethylhexane	III or IV	0.006
2,2,4,4-Tetramethylpentane	II	0.02
2,2,4-Trimethylhexane	II	0.09
2,2,5,5-Tetramethylhexane	II	0.004
2,4,4-Trimethylhexane and/or 2,3,5-trimethylhexane	IV	0.006
Total for C_1 to C_{11} products including eight unknowns		4.93

[a] In addition there were three unknown peaks in the range of C_8 products with G values of 0.008, 0.001, and 0.01, and five unknown peaks in the C_{10} to C_{11} range with G values of 0.15, 0.02, 0.2_6, 0.002, and 0.2.

[b] In molecules/100 ev; for H_2 and methane, total dose for 25-ml samples varied from 4.2×10^{21} ev to 1.57×10^{22} ev; for ethane through neopentane, total dose for 25-ml samples was 4.27×10^{22} ev; and for the remaining products, 1.69×10^{22} ev for 25-ml samples.

TABLE II
RADIOLYSIS PRODUCTS C_{12} AND GREATER FROM 2,2,4,6,6-PENTAMETHYLHEPTANE

Peaks[a]	*G*[b]
1[c]	0.2_3
2[d]	0.05_8
3	0.008
4[d]	0.1_7
5	0.003
6	0.006
7	0.1_4
8	0.04
9	0.02_2
10[d]	0.09_4
11	0.008
12	0.01_4
13	0.09_4
14[e]	0.1_8
15	0.03_2
16	0.07_3
17	0.02_6
18	0.07_2
19	0.03_4
20	0.007
21	0.03_7
22	0.04_2
23	0.1_6
24[d]	0.1_5
25	0.02_9
26	0.04_7
27	0.1_2
28	0.1_3
29	0.02
30	0.01_3
31	0.02_8
32	0.004
33	0.04_4
Total	2.13_5

[a] On the basis of retention times of PMH and 2,2,4,4,6,8,8-heptamethylnonane, and on the grouping of the peaks on the chromatogram, it seems most likely that peaks 1 to 12 correspond to C_{12} and C_{13} compounds; peaks 13 to 18, C_{16} compounds; peaks 19 to 27, C_{20} compounds; and peaks 28 to 33, C_{24} compounds.

[b] In molecules/100 ev; total dose, 1.69×10^{22} ev for 25-ml samples. The values for peaks 1 to 12 and peaks 13 to 33 were calculated by using the thermal responses of PMH and 2,2,4,4,-6,8,8-heptamethylnonane, respectively.

[c] Corresponds to 2,2,4,4,6-pentamethylheptane.

[d] Each of these peaks contains two components.

[e] Contains four components; 2,2,4,4,6,8,8-heptamethylnonane corresponds to one component.

products in this group, taking into account only saturated and olefinic hydrocarbons. Of these twenty possible products, eleven are in the C_1 to C_8 range, and nine are in the C_{11} range. All eleven of the possible products in the C_1 to C_8 range were identified as radiolysis products. (See Table I.) The total G for these products is 4.0, compared with a total G of 4.93 for the C_1 to C_{11} products. It was not possible to identify any of the products in the C_{11} range, since authentic hydrocarbons in this range, of the types expected from the radiolysis of PMH, were not available.

With consideration to the structure of PMH, the precursors leading to the products in group I, in decreasing order of abundance as predicted by the yields, are the t-butyl, 2,2,4-trimethylpentyl, methyl, neopentyl, and 2,2-dimethylpentyl fragments. Scission evidently occurs predominantly at the 2–3 and 5–6 positions of PMH to furnish t-butyl and 2,2,4-trimethylpentyl fragments; ΣG (products for which t-butyl and 2,2,4-trimethylpentyl are precursors) = 2.8, compared to ΣG (group I products) = 4.0.

Group II. This group consists of those products that could form by a combination of two hydrocarbon fragments each of which can be related to some structural portion of the parent hydrocarbon, PMH. If only those products of less than C_{12} carbon content are considered which could form by a combination of two fragments at the original point of fission, then there are seven possible saturated products. Six of these were identified as radiolysis products with a total G of 0.15. (See Table I.) The other possible product in this group is a C_{11} hydrocarbon, 2,2,3,5,5-pentamethylhexane, and no C_{11} products were identified.

Radical combination reactions leading to products in group II probably involve the methyl, neopentyl, 2,2,4-trimethylpentyl, and t-butyl radicals (reaction 1).

$$R_1 + R_2 \rightarrow \text{Product} \quad (1)$$

Yields of products in this group, ΣG (group II products) $\sim$ 0.15, indicate that reaction 1 is relatively unimportant in the radiation chemistry of PMH. The combinations of intermediates leading to products in this group are given in Table III.

TABLE III

PROBABLE INTERMEDIATES LEADING TO PRODUCTS IN GROUP II BY COMBINATION

Product	*G*	R_1	R_2
Ethane and ethylene	0.01_5	Methyl	Methyl
2,2-Dimethylbutane	0.01_1	Methyl	Neopentyl
2,2,4-Trimethylhexane	0.09	Methyl	2,2,4-Trimethylpentyl
2,2,3,3-Tetramethylbutane	0.01	t-Butyl	t-Butyl
2,2,4,4-Tetramethylpentane	0.02	t-Butyl	Neopentyl
2,2,5,5-Tetramethylhexane	0.004	Neopentyl	Neopentyl

Group III. This group consists of those products which could form by rearrangement of one of the primary fission fragments. The neopentyl fragment would seem to be the most likely to rearrange. Three radiolysis products with a total G of 0.008 could form by a rearrangement of the neopentyl fragment followed by either uptake or elimination of hydrogen. (See Table I.)

Group IV. This group, with total $G \sim 0.1$, consists of those products which cannot be accounted for by any of the three ways given above.

Of the twenty-six hydrocarbon radiolytic products identified, twenty are accounted for in groups I, II, and III. There are three unidentified products in the C_8 range with a total $G \sim 0.019$, and five unidentified products in the C_{10} to C_{11} range with a total $G \sim 0.63$. It is likely that the C_{11} radiolysis products were not completely resolved on the gas chromatograph.

There are at least thirty-nine radiolysis products of carbon content greater than C_{12} with a total $G \sim 2.1$. These products arrange themselves on the gas chromatograms mainly into four groups, which most likely correspond to a C_{12} to C_{13} group, $G = 0.79$; a C_{16} group, $G = 0.48$; a C_{20} group, $G = 0.63$; and a C_{24} group, $G = 0.24$. The C_{12} to C_{13} group would contain those C_{12} unsaturates related to the parent compound and those products formed by a reaction of a methyl group with a C_{12} fragment. The C_{16} products could form by a reaction of C_4 and C_{12} fragments and of two C_8 fragments; C_{20} products, by a reaction of C_8 and C_{12} fragments; and C_{24} products, by a dimerization of two C_{12} fragments. The total G of 4.9 for products of carbon content less than C_{12}, as compared with the total of 2.1 for products C_{12} and greater, indicates that the processes leading to the products of carbon content less than the parent hydrocarbon predominate. It might be of interest to note that the ratio $\Sigma G\ (C_1–C_{11})/\Sigma G\ (C_{12}–C_{24})$ for PMH is 2.3, as compared with the ratio of $\Sigma G\ (C_1–C_7)/\Sigma G\ (C_8–C_{16})$ of 2.4 for the X-irradiation of 2,2,4-trimethylpentane (*2*).

Molecular-weight determinations of the higher molecular fraction gave values in the range of 298 to 310. C_{20} and C_{24} saturated hydrocarbons have molecular weights of 282 and 338, respectively. The molecular-weight determinations and the gas chromatographic analyses indicate very strongly that the highest-molecular-weight products, at least in the earlier stages of radiolysis, are those of C_{24} carbon content.

Evidence for unsaturation in the C_{12} to C_{24} radiolysis products has been found by catalytic hydrogenation and infrared measurements. The results in terms of G values for carbon–carbon double-bond formation are 0.6 for a total dose of 1.57×10^{22} ev and 0.36 for 4.27×10^{22} ev. The unsaturation decreases with increasing dose, probably owing to the scavenging action of unsaturated hydrocarbons. Infrared spectra of the radiolytic product of the C_{20} to C_{24} range showed that the most likely carbon–carbon double bonds present are those of the *trans* double bond and the $R_1R_2C = CH_2$ group.

It might be in order to compare some of the G values from PMH with those ob-

TABLE IV

Comparison of Yields from X-Irradiation of 2,2,4-Trimethylpentane (*1*) and 2,2,4,6,6-Pentamethylheptane

Product	G	
	2,2,4-Trimethylpentane	*2,2,4,6,6-Pentamethylheptane*
Hydrogen	2.2	1.3
Methane	1.1	0.74
Isobutane	1.6	0.34
Isobutylene	1.4	1.2
Neopentane	0.2	0.25

tained from the X-irradiation of 2,2,4-trimethylpentane (*1*), as presented in Table IV. The ratio $G(H_2)/G(CH_4)$, r_1, is 2.0 for 2,2,4-trimethylpentane and 1.76 for PMH, whereas the ratio of hydrogen to methyl, r_2, in the parent molecule is 3.6 for 2,2,4-trimethylpentane and 3.7 for PMH. The ratio r_1/r_2 is approximately the same for both compounds; therefore, hydrogen and methyl radicals must undergo the same fate during radiolysis of both compounds.

SUMMARY

In addition to hydrogen, there are at least seventy-three radiolysis products from the X-irradiation of PMH. Thirty-four of these products are in the C_1 to C_{11} range with a total $G \sim 4.9$ and with individual G values ranging from 0.001 to 1.2. Thirty-nine are in the C_{12} to C_{24} range with a total $G \sim 2.1$ and with individual G values ranging from 0.003 to 0.23. Twenty-six of the products in the C_1 to C_{10} range were identified, of which the major ones are methane, isobutane, isobutylene, neopentane, 2,2,4-trimethylpentane, and 2,4,4-trimethylpentene-1. Since authentic hydrocarbon samples of the types expected from radiolysis of PMH are not available, identification of products in the C_{11} to C_{24} range was not possible. In the C_1 to C_{11} range, the processes that lead to a product which can be related to some portion of the carbon skeleton of the parent hydrocarbon predominate. Also, the processes that lead to products of carbon centent less than the parent hydrocarbon predominate over those that lead to products of carbon content equal to or greater than the parent hydrocarbon. Molecular-weight measurements and gas chromatographic evidence indicate very strongly that the highest-molecular-weight products, at least in the earlier stages of radiolysis, are those of C_{24} carbon content. In addition to the identification of unsaturated products in the C_1 to C_{11} range, evidence for unsaturation in the C_{12} to C_{24} range was obtained from H_2 uptake measurements and infrared spectra.

Received: October 1, 1962

REFERENCES

1. J. A. Knight, R. L. McDaniel, R. C. Palmer, and Fred Sicilio, H_2 and C_1–C_7 yields from the radiolysis of 2,2,4-trimethylpentane. *J. Phys. Chem.* **65,** 2109–2110 (1961).
2. J. A. Knight, R. L. McDaniel, and Fred Sicilio, Radiolysis products of C_8 and greater carbon content from 2,2,4-trimethylpentane. *J. Phys. Chem.* April, 1963.
3. P. D. Bartlett, G. R. Fraser, and R. B. Woodward, The isolation and properties of 1,1-dineopentylethylene, a component of triisobutylene. *J. Am. Chem. Soc.* **63,** 495–498 (1941).
4. J. A. Knight, Fred Sicilio, and Neal Houze, Gas chromatographic analysis in fractional distillation of multi-component systems. *J. Chromatog.* **5,** 179–181 (1961).
5. G. Egloff, *Physical Constants of Hydrocarbons,* Vol. V, p. 202, Reinhold Publishing Corp., New York, 1953.
6. J. A. Knight, B. Wilkins, Jr., D. K. Davis, and Fred Sicilio, Semi-micro cryoscopic molecular weight determination with a thermistor thermometer. *Anal. Chim. Acta* **25,** 317–321 (1961).
7. C. L. Ogg and F. J. Cooper, Determination of unsaturation by microhydrogenation. *Anal. Chem.* **21,** 1400–1402 (1949).

RADIATION RESEARCH 19, 368–383 (1963)

Effect of X-Ray on Antigen Metabolism in the Rabbit[1]

H. M. RUBINSTEIN[2] AND H. PERIKH

Department of Experimental Medicine, Michael Reese Hospital, and the Department of Medicine, Chicago Medical School

INTRODUCTION

Large doses of whole-body irradiation can completely inhibit the primary antibody response in the rabbit (*1*). The mechanism of this inhibition remains unknown. Furthermore, the sequence and timing of X-irradiation and antigen injection are important: If the antigen is given before or with the radiation, inhibition of antibody formation is absent or partial, whereas if the antigen is given 12 hours or more after the radiation, inhibition is essentially complete (*1, 2*).

In attempting to study the mechanism of X-ray inhibition of antibody formation, one point that lends itself to experiment is the possibility that the distribution and metabolism of the antigen are grossly altered. The only communication on this subject in the literature is the report of Fitch *et al.* (*3*). They studied the distribution of I^{131}-labeled bacteria in the spleen, liver, and lung of normal and X-irradiated rats. No significant difference in total organ content of I^{131} was found.

Since it is unlikely that the metabolism of bacteria and of soluble foreign proteins are identical, it was felt worth while to restudy the problem with a soluble protein antigen. This paper gives the results of a study of the organ and intracellular distribution of a radioactive protein antigen in normal rabbits and in rabbits receiving 450 r of whole-body irradiation.

METHODS

X-Irradiation

Irradiation was carried out with a conventional 250-kv machine, with the following factors: 200 kv, 75-cm tube-to-target distance, filtration ½ mm Al plus ¼ mm Cu, giving a half-value layer equal to 1 mm Cu. Radiation delivery at the center of the target was 18 r/min. The rabbits were kept in individual aluminum

[1] This study was supported by the National Science Foundation (Grant #G-7602) and the American Cancer Society (Grant #T-175).

[2] Present address: Medical Service, United States Veterans Administration Hospital, Hines, Illinois.

mesh cages, and half the radiation was delivered to each side. The field size was such that two rabbits were irradiated simultaneously.

Antigen

Crystalline bovine serum albumin (Armour) was coupled to S^{35}-sulfanilic acid (Volk, New England Nuclear) by the following method, based on that of Ingraham (*4*): 117 mg of S^{35}-sulfanilic acid was dissolved in 18 ml of cold distilled water with stirring. To this were added 1 ml of 3 *N* HCl and 5.2 ml of 1% $NaNO_2$. After 30 minutes at 4°C, 300 mg of urea was added. After another 30 minutes in the cold, 600 mg of sodium acetate was added. This solution was added slowly with constant stirring to 2 gm of bovine serum albumin dissolved in 20 ml of cold 0.15 *M* NaCl. The pH was adjusted to 8.35 to 8.45 with 12.5% Na_2CO_3, with continuous stirring. Conjugation was allowed to continue overnight at 4°C. The following day, the protein was precipitated at 65% saturation with ammonium sulfate. The precipitate was collected by centrifugation, dissolved in cold distilled water, and dialyzed against cold distilled water until free of sulfate. The solution was again brought to 65% saturation with ammonium sulfate, centrifuged, dissolved in water, and dialyzed until free of sulfate. The conjugated protein was stored at −20° until used. The over-all yield for conjugation was about 80%. By sulfur analysis (kindly performed by Dr. Gershbein of the Illinois Institute of Technology) there were approximately thirteen sulfonate groups per molecule of protein. The radioactivity of the final product at the time of injection varied from 0.2 to 4 μc/mg of protein; most of the preparations used were above 0.9 μc/mg. Preliminary experiments, using the precipitin response, revealed that the material was suitably antigenic in normal rabbits, and that antigen injection 18 hours after 450 r of whole-body irradiation was not followed by detectable precipitins. The conjugated protein was antigenically similar to unconjugated bovine serum albumin: with an antibovine serum albumin serum, at equivalence the native protein and the conjugate precipitated equal amounts of antibody; with an anticonjugated bovine serum albumin serum, at equivalence the native protein precipitated two-thirds as much antibody as the conjugated protein.

Experimental Procedure

The standard dose of antigen employed was 20 mg/kg body weight, given intravenously. The animals were divided into three groups: (A) No X-ray—25 animals; (B) 450 r of whole-body irradiation followed in 18 hours by the antigen (antibody formation inhibited)—21 animals; (C) 450 r of whole-body irradiation followed immediately by the antigen (antibody formation not inhibited)—14 animals. Animals from each of the three groups were sacrificed at 24 hours (group A, 12 animals; group B, 9 animals; group C, 6 animals), 7 days (group A, 7 animals; group B, 7 animals; group C, 6 animals), and 21 days (group A, 6 animals; group B, 5 animals; group C, 2 animals) after antigen injection. When sacrificed at 24 hours, the animals were anesthetized with Nembutal, a blood sample was drawn from the abdominal aorta, and the animals were perfused through the abdominal aorta with 2 liters of cold 0.15 *M* NaCl followed by 2 liters of cold 0.25 *M* sucrose. At 7 and 21 days the perfusion was omitted. Portions of the liver, kidney, spleen, lung, mesenteric lymph node, and appendix were quickly excised and weighed, and homogenates were made in cold 0.25 *M* sucrose with a Potter-type homogenizer with a Teflon pestle. The remainder of the organs were weighed subsequently. All urine was collected from several animals in each group until sacrifice. The homogenates were centrifuged according to the method of Schneider (*5*), and the nuclear, mitochondrial, microsomal, and supernatant fractions were obtained. Protein determinations were done on the homogenates and subcellular fractions of liver, spleen, kidney, and node by the method of Lowry *et al.* (6). Radioactivity determinations on the plasma, urine, homogenate, and subcellular fractions were made with a Packard Tri-Carb scintillation counter. The samples were prepared for counting by the method of Jeffay *et al.* (*7*). At 24 hours, perfusion adequately removed blood from all tissues studied except the lung. The radioactivity of the lung samples was corrected by estimating the lung plasma volume as 76 ml/kg, which, in the absence of direct data for the rabbit, is based on values for other species (*8, 9*). At 1 and 3 weeks the radioactivity in all the tissues was corrected for the radioactivity in the plasma; 38 ml/kg was the factor employed for all tissues except the lung, and 76 ml/kg for the lung. At 1 week, these corrections generally amounted to 2 to 3% or less in the homogenates and fractions, and at 3 weeks the corrections were negligible. The amount of radioactivity in the entire plasma volume was also calculated on the basis of 38 ml/kg.

RESULTS AND COMMENT

Tables I to III present the data on retention of radioactivity by the various tissues studied in all groups of animals. The results are expressed as total-organ radioactivity, radioactivity per 100 mg of wet tissue, radioactivity per milligram of nitrogen, and ratio between the total-organ radioactivity and per cent body weight. All radioactivity is given as per cent of the total injected.

Group A: Control

In addition to Tables I to III, the mean values for the controls at all time periods are presented graphically in Figs. 1 to 4. It may be seen from these figures that the rate of disposal of radioactivity from all the tissues studied decreases with time. This is consistent with the reports of Ingraham (*4*), Haurowitz and Crampton (*10*), and Garvey and Campbell (*11*). Furthermore, as determined from the slopes of the lines, the rate of over-all metabolism of the antigen is fairly uniform in all tissues studied except the lymph node. Although the radioactivity in the

TABLE 1

RETENTION OF RADIOACTIVITY IN TISSUES OF ALL GROUPS OF ANIMALS AT 24 HOURS IN TERMS OF WHOLE-ORGAN CONTENT, ORGAN WEIGHT, AND ORGAN NITROGEN CONTENT

Group	*Organ*	(1) *Organ weight as % body weight* ± *S.D.*	(2) *Whole-organ radioactivity (% injected)* ± *S.D.*	(3) *Per cent radioactivity injected/100 mg* × *10³* ± *S.D.*	(4) *Per cent radioactivity injected/mg N* × *10³* ± *S.D.*	(5) *Column 2/column 1* ± *S.D.*
A	Liver	(11) 2.89 ± 0.64	(11) 6.79 ± 1.46	(11) 9.90 ± 4.77	(11) 4.22 ± 1.54	(11) 2.48 ± 0.90
	Spleen	(12) 0.044 ± 0.014	(12) 0.063 ± 0.026	(12) 5.73 ± 1.80	(12) 2.83 ± 0.92	(12) 1.44 ± 0.30
	Node	(6) —	(6) —	(6) 6.92 ± 2.60	(6) 4.33 ± 1.79	(6) 1.76 ± 0.59
	Kidney	(9) 0.69 ± 0.080	(9) 1.52 ± 0.49	(9) 8.61 ± 2.55	(6) 3.67 ± 0.90	(9) 2.25 ± 0.75
	Appendix	(7) 0.31 ± 0.069	(7) 0.048 ± 0.0066	(7) 0.62 ± 0.17		(7) 0.16 ± 0.040
	Lung	(9) 0.69 ± 0.37	(9) 0.072 ± 0.033	(9) 0.56 ± 0.26		(9) 0.11 ± 0.050
	Plasma		(12) 7.31 ± 2.42			
B	Liver	(8) 3.09 ± 0.37	(8) 6.38 ± 1.03	(8) 7.77 ± 1.43	(8) 3.04 ± 0.75*	(8) 2.07 ± 0.30
	Spleen	(9) 0.034 ± 0.012	(9) 0.070 ± 0.027	(9) 7.59 ± 0.84*	(9) 3.49 ± 1.20	(9) 2.06 ± 0.48**
	Node	(9) —	(9) —	(9) 12.07 ± 6.51*	(9) 8.90 ± 5.37*	(9) 3.22 ± 1.55*
	Kidney	(8) 0.72 ± 0.11	(8) 1.18 ± 0.28	(8) 6.34 ± 1.25*	(8) 3.28 ± 0.56	(8) 1.69 ± 0.35
	Appendix	(9) 0.23 ± 0.055*	(9) 0.042 ± 0.013	(9) 0.72 ± 0.25		(9) 0.19 ± 0.060
	Lung	(9) 0.72 ± 0.29	(9) 0.089 ± 0.039	(9) 0.58 ± 0.25		(9) 0.16 ± 0.076
	Plasma		(9) 7.64 ± 1.44			
C	Liver	(6) 3.52 ± 0.88	(6) 6.91 ± 2.92	(6) 8.20 ± 4.87	(6) 3.26 ± 2.04	(6) 1.92 ± 1.06
	Spleen	(6) 0.052 ± 0.026	(6) 0.089 ± 0.057	(6) 7.42 ± 4.12	(6) 3.62 ± 2.08	(6) 1.76 ± 0.92
	Node	(6) —	(6) —	(6) 8.66 ± 1.52	(6) 5.58 ± 1.02	(6) 2.09 ± 0.48
	Kidney	(6) 0.80 ± 0.15	(6) 1.28 ± 0.98	(6) 6.07 ± 3.50	(6) 3.15 ± 2.01	(6) 1.45 ± 0.88
	Appendix	(6) 0.29 ± 0.081	(6) 0.072 ± 0.045	(6) 1.13 ± 0.73		(6) 0.27 ± 0.18
	Lung	(5) 0.51 ± 0.11	(5) 0.098 ± 0.064	(5) 0.56 ± 0.17		(5) 0.13 ± 0.030
	Plasma		(6) 6.38 ± 2.36			

Notes: *, **, *** indicate, respectively, p less than 0.05, 0.01, 0.001, as compared to controls (group A).
There are no significant differences between group B and group C.
The figures in parentheses indicate the number of animals.
All weights are wet weights.
S.D. = standard deviation.
Group A, controls (no X-ray). Group B, irradiated—antibody formation inhibited. Group C, irradiated—antibody formation not inhibited.

TABLE II

RETENTION OF RADIOACTIVITY IN TISSUES OF ALL GROUPS OF ANIMALS AT 7 DAYS IN TERMS OF WHOLE-ORGAN CONTENT, ORGAN WEIGHT, AND ORGAN NITROGEN CONTENT

Group	*Organ*	(1) *Organ weight as % body weight ± S.D.*	(2) *Whole-organ radioactivity (% injected) ± S.D.*	(3) *Per cent radioactivity injected/100 mg. × 10³ ± S.D.*	(4) *Per cent radioactivity injected/mg N × 10³ ± S.D.*	(5) *Column2/ column 1 ± S.D.*
A	Liver	(7) 3.20 ± 0.35	(7) 0.88 ± 0.12	(7) 1.00 ± 0.15	(7) 0.37 ± 0.051	(7) 0.28 ± 0.057
	Spleen	(7) 0.050 ± 0.023	(7) 0.0075 ± 0.0029	(7) 0.58 ± 0.21	(7) 0.24 ± 0.10	(7) 0.15 ± 0.044
	Node	(7) —	(7) —	(7) 0.97 ± 0.22	(7) 0.58 ± 0.11	(7) 0.28 ± 0.083
	Kidney	(7) 0.60 ± 0.13	(7) 0.16 ± 0.049	(7) 0.96 ± 0.24	(7) 0.35 ± 0.079	(7) 0.27 ± 0.071
	Appendix	(6) 0.31 ± 0.049	(6) 0.0071 ± 0.0028	(6) 0.082 ± 0.020		(6) 0.022 ± 0.0045
	Lung	(7) 0.48 ± 0.095	(7) 0.0094 ± 0.0047	(7) 0.078 ± 0.057		(7) 0.020 ± 0.011
	Plasma		(7) 0.31 ± 0.31			
B	Liver	(7) 2.78 ± 0.69	(7) 0.72 ± 0.16	(7) 1.02 ± 0.29	(7) 0.38 ± 0.11	(7) 0.27 ± 0.085
	Spleen	(7) 0.031 ± 0.014	(7) 0.0081 ± 0.0043	(7) 1.08 ± 0.53*	(7) 0.42 ± 0.22	(7) 0.30 ± 0.17*
	Node	(6) —	(6) —	(6) 2.42 ± 1.08**	(6) 1.36 ± 0.56**	(6) 0.67 ± 0.37*
	Kidney	(7) 0.57 ± 0.096	(7) 0.17 ± 0.052	(7) 1.16 ± 0.25	(7) 0.44 ± 0.11	(7) 0.31 ± 0.091
	Appendix	(7) 0.16 ± 0.040***	(7) 0.0070 ± 0.0036	(7) 0.17 ± 0.088*		(7) 0.045 ± 0.026*
	Lung	(7) 0.49 ± 0.19	(7) 0.013 ± 0.0061	(7) 0.10 ± 0.047		(7) 0.029 ± 0.016
	Plasma		(7) 0.52 ± 0.40			
C	Liver	(6) 2.92 ± 0.34	(6) 0.88 ± 0.44	(6) 1.33 ± 0.69	(6) 0.45 ± 0.25	(6) 0.32 ± 0.16
	Spleen	(6) 0.024 ± 0.0057*	(6) 0.0054 ± 0.0022	(6) 0.94 ± 0.40	(6) 0.32 ± 0.14	(6) 0.23 ± 0.090
	Node	(6) —	(6) —	(6) 1.33 ± 0.35	(6) 0.76 ± 0.20	(6) 0.32 ± 0.072
	Kidney	(6) 0.60 ± 0.063	(6) 0.19 ± 0.083	(6) 1.27 ± 0.51	(6) 0.45 ± 0.19	(6) 0.31 ± 0.12
	Appendix	(6) 0.15 ± 0.049***	(6) 0.0077 ± 0.0027	(6) 0.22 ± 0.057***		(6) 0.052 ± 0.013***
	Lung	(6) 0.41 ± 0.061	(6) 0.013 ± 0.0059	(6) 0.13 ± 0.048		(6) 0.031 ± 0.013
	Plasma		(6) 0.39 ± 0.23			

Notes: *, **, *** indicate, respectively, p less than 0.05, 0.01, 0.001, as compared to controls (group A).
There are no significant differences between group B and group C.
The figures in parentheses indicate the number of animals.
All weights are wet weights.
S.D. = standard deviation.
Group A, controls (no X-ray). Group B, irradiated—antibody formation inhibited. Group C, irradiated—antibody formation not inhibited.

Retention of Radioactivity in Tissues of all Groups of Animals at 21 Days in Terms of Whole-Organ Content, Organ Weight, and Organ Nitrogen Content

Group	*Organ*	(1) *Organ weight as % body weight* ± *S.D.*	(2) *Whole-organ radioactivity (% injected)* ± *S.D.*	(3) *Per cent radioactivity injected/100 mg* × *10*³ ± *S.D.*	(4) *Per cent radioactivity injected/mg N* × *10*³ ± *S.D.*	(5) *Column 2/ column 1* ± *S.D.*
A	Liver	(6) 3.78 ± 0.63	(6) 0.24 ± 0.067	(6) 0.28 ± 0.073	(6) 0.097 ± 0.028	(6) 0.064 ± 0.017
	Spleen	(6) 0.045 ± 0.0080	(6) 0.0016 ± 0.00051	(6) 0.15 ± 0.035	(6) 0.067 ± 0.013	(6) 0.035 ± 0.0084
	Node	(6) —	(6) —	(6) 0.48 ± 0.28	(6) 0.30 ± 0.16	(6) 0.11 ± 0.061
	Kidney	(6) 0.59 ± 0.045	(6) 0.036 ± 0.014	(6) 0.27 ± 0.12	(6) 0.093 ± 0.033	(6) 0.063 ± 0.028
	Appendix	(6) 0.39 ± 0.077	(6) 0.0015 ± 0.00062	(6) 0.016 ± 0.0065		(6) 0.0038 ± 0.0017
	Lung	(6) 0.49 ± 0.050	(6) 0.0013 ± 0.00045	(6) 0.012 ± 0.0030		(6) 0.0027 ± 0.00081
	Plasma		(6) 0.0068 ± 0.0024			
B	Liver	(5) 3.09 ± 0.57	(5) 0.19 ± 0.025	(5) 0.27 ± 0.079	(5) 0.084 ± 0.026	(5) 0.067 ± 0.016
	Spleen	(5) 0.038 ± 0.0081	(5) 0.0016 ± 0.00057	(5) 0.17 ± 0.077	(5) 0.066 ± 0.027	(5) 0.043 ± 0.017
	Node	(5) —	(5) —	(5) 1.29 ± 0.40**	(5) 0.78 ± 0.23**	(5) 0.32 ± 0.080***
	Kidney	(5) 0.59 ± 0.063	(5) 0.041 ± 0.0069	(5) 0.28 ± 0.053	(5) 0.098 ± 0.023	(5) 0.072 ± 0.014
	Appendix	(5) 0.23 ± 0.031**	(5) 0.0018 ± 0.00061	(5) 0.031 ± 0.0064**		(5) 0.0077 ± 0.0020**
	Lung	(5) 0.46 ± 0.039	(5) 0.0016 ± 0.00021	(5) 0.014 ± 0.0019		(5) 0.0035 ± 0.00048
	Plasma		(5) 0.0099 ± 0.0051			
C	Liver	(2) 3.04, 3.47	(2) 0.17, 0.23	(2) 0.21, 0.29	(2) 0.066, 0.092	(2) 0.054, 0.066
	Spleen	(2) 0.029, 0.022	(2) 0.0027, 0.0010	(2) 0.36, 0.20	(2) 0.14, 0.088	(2) 0.091, 0.046
	Node	(2) —	(2) —	(2) 0.45, 0.54	(2) 0.27 0.30	(2) 0.12, 0.12
	Kidney	(2) 0.59, 0.54	(2) 0.063, 0.024	(2) 0.42, 0.20	(2) 0.14, 0.067	(2) 0.12, 0.044
	Appendix	(2) 0.25, 0.20	(2) 0.00095, 0.00067	(2) 0.015, 0.015		(2) 0.0039, 0.0033
	Lung	(2) 0.42, 0.42	(2) 0.0010, 0.00096	(2) 0.0060, 0.010		(2) 0.0024, 0.0024
	Plasma		(2) 0.0065, 0.0059			

Notes: *, **, *** indicate, respectively, p less than 0.05, 0.01, 0.001, as compared to controls (group A).
In group C there were only 2 animals; the values on both are given, and no mean has been calculated.
The figures in parentheses indicate the number of animals.
All weights are wet weights.
S.D. = standard deviation.
Group A, controls (no X-ray). Group B, irradiated—antibody formation inhibited. Group C, irradiated—antibody formation not inhibited.

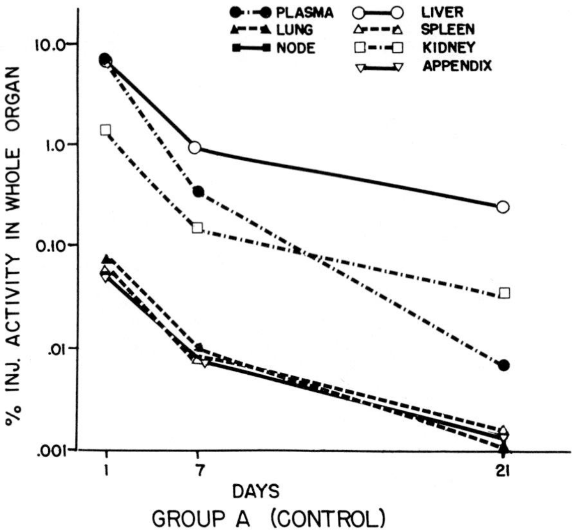

FIG. 1. Whole-organ radioactivity (per cent injected). Control group only.

total-body lymph node tissue cannot be measured, when the radioactivity is expressed in terms of weight, nitrogen content, or per cent body weight of the tissue studied, the curves for the node are flatter than those for the other tissues. This difference in slope for the node in Figs. 2 to 4 is significant at the 5% level. It seems likely, therefore, that the rate of metabolism of soluble foreign protein is slower in lymph node than in the other tissues studied.

It is also clear that, on a weight basis, various tissues vary widely in their capacity to retain antigen. Of the tissues studied, lung and appendix retain the least. Liver, spleen, node, and kidney give similar results. When antigen retention is expressed on a nitrogen basis, these four tissues give results which are similar. Likewise, when the retained antigen is related to the per cent body weight of the tissue studied, lung and appendix give low values, and the remaining four tissues are clustered together.

Although similar studies have been done by others, in most cases the results cannot be compared quantitatively because of differences in amount of protein injected, time of sacrifice, etc. However, several comparisons can be made. Garvey and Campbell (*11*) injected approximately 20 mg of S^{35}-azophenylsulfonate–bovine serum albumin per kilogram intravenously into rabbits. At 24 hours the mean per cent retention of radioactivity in the whole liver was 7.0% of the dose injected. In other experiments, the same authors injected 7 to 10 mg of the same protein per kilogram and assayed the liver at 21 days: the mean per cent retention was 0.35 to 0.36% of the dose injected (*12, 13*). These values are similar to those found in the present study.

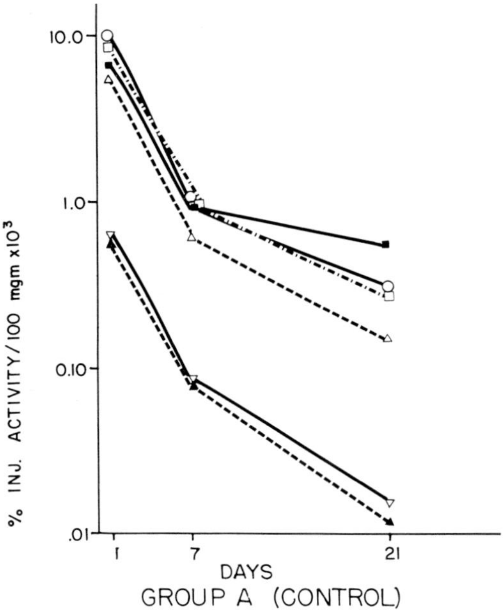

FIG. 2. Tissue radioactivity (per cent injected) related to weight. Control group only.

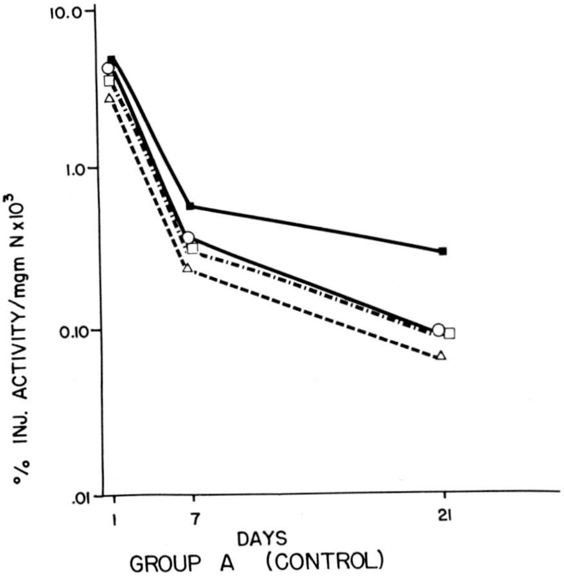

FIG. 3. Tissue radioactivity (per cent injected) related to nitrogen content. Control group only.

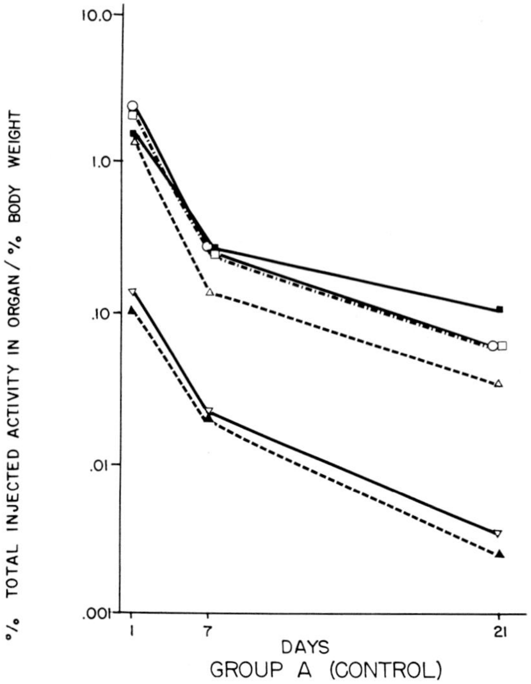

FIG. 4. Relation between tissue radioactivity (per cent injected) and tissue weight (per cent of total-body weight). Control group only.

The plasma antigen content is high at 24 hours but drops rapidly and progressively, only small amounts being present at 21 days. Not given in the tables are the results on cumulative urine collections from the few animals measured. At 24 hours, total urinary radioactivity is 70 to 75% of the amount injected. At 1 week 80 to 85% of the injected radioactivity has appeared in the urine, and at 3 weeks over 90%.

Table IV and Figs. 5 and 6 give the data on the radioactivity content of the subcellular fractions of the various organs. When the radioactivity of the fractions is expressed as per cent of the total homogenate, the various tissues give widely different patterns. In general, the supernatant and mitochondrial fractions contain the most radioactivity. It should be pointed out that the high value for the supernatant fraction of lung at 24 hours may in part be due to the blood within the tissue. When the radioactivity in the various fractions is related to the nitrogen content, a different pattern emerges. The fractions from four tissues were studied by this method: in liver, spleen, and node, the mitochondrial fraction is most active; in the kidney, the nuclear, mitochondrial, and supernatant fractions are about equal. This early predominant localization in the mitochondria was also found by Haurowitz and Crampton (*10*) and by Crampton *et al.* (*14, 15*).

TABLE IV

RADIOACTIVITY IN CELL FRACTIONS AS A FUNCTION OF TIME FOR GROUP A (CONTROLS) ONLY

Time	*Organ*	*Radioactivity in fraction as % homogenate total ± S.D.*				*Ratio: % injected radioactivity/mg N × 10³ in fraction / % injected radioactivity/mg N × 10³ in homogenate* ± S.D.			
		Nuclear	*Mitochondrial*	*Microsomal*	*Supernatant*	*Nuclear*	*Mitochondrial*	*Microsomal*	*Supernatant*
24 hours	Liver	(11) 13.4 ± 4.3	(11) 45.6 ± 16.4	(11) 7.3 ± 3.3	(11) 28.8 ± 17.0	(11) 0.66 ± 0.23	(11) 3.89 ± 1.59	(11) 0.40 ± 0.16	(11) 0.72 ± 0.33
	Spleen	(12) 6.0 ± 2.8	(12) 32.4 ± 10.3	(12) 22.7 ± 11.5	(12) 28.1 ± 14.4	(12) 0.30 ± 0.27	(12) 3.43 ± 0.82	(12) 1.34 ± 0.73	(12) 0.73 ± 0.14
	Node	(6) 12.0 ± 6.2	(6) 19.1 ± 11.2	(6) 5.0 ± 1.1	(6) 59.0 ± 20.7	(6) 0.59 ± 0.25	(6) 2.40 ± 1.70	(6) 0.23 ± 0.040	(6) 1.41 ± 0.47
	Kidney	(9) 17.5 ± 9.0	(8) 27.6 ± 2.9	(9) 4.9 ± 2.8	(9) 43.0 ± 7.8	(6) 0.93 ± 0.51	(6) 1.06 ± 0.39	(6) 0.27 ± 0.054	(6) 1.23 ± 0.33
	Appendix	(6) 8.0 ± 4.2	(6) 10.2 ± 6.9	(6) 10.4 ± 5.3	(6) 63.3 ± 9.7				
	Lung	(9) 3.5 ± 1.5	(9) 4.8 ± 2.9	(8) 6.1 ± 2.1	(9) 72.9 ± 10.3				
7 days	Liver	(5) 18.3 ± 3.3	(5) 52.6 ± 12.5	(5) 10.3 ± 0.83	(5) 22.9 ± 2.8	(5) 0.91 ± 0.36	(5) 3.38 ± 1.17	(5) 0.77 ± 0.12	(5) 0.57 ± 0.092
	Spleen	(5) 23.5 ± 11.4	(5) 43.5 ± 7.3	(5) 15.2 ± 3.5	(5) 28.2 ± 9.0	(5) 0.58 ± 0.29	(5) 3.37 ± 0.31	(5) 1.23 ± 0.48	(5) 1.04 ± 0.53
	Node	(5) 20.9 ± 6.7	(5) 26.6 ± 6.8	(5) 10.5 ± 4.3	(5) 52.9 ± 7.8	(5) 0.74 ± 0.36	(5) 2.48 ± 0.76	(5) 0.71 ± 0.22	(5) 1.22 ± 0.16
	Kidney	(5) 24.4 ± 6.1	(5) 41.6 ± 12.8	(5) 6.5 ± 2.1	(5) 37.2 ± 8.6	(5) 0.98 ± 0.23	(5) 1.72 ± 0.55	(5) 0.55 ± 0.15	(5) 1.13 ± 0.15
	Appendix				(4) 76.5 ± 16.2				
	Lung				(5) 66.9 ± 16.9				
21 days	Liver	(4) 23.3 ± 4.4	(4) 45.9 ± 7.5	(4) 6.5 ± 3.1	(4) 33.9 ± 13.4	(4) 1.28 ± 0.20	(4) 3.24 ± 1.34	(4) 0.76 ± 0.21	(4) 0.63 ± 0.23
	Spleen	(4) 25.3 ± 13.2	(4) 37.4 ± 13.8	(4) 9.4 ± 2.6	(4) 25.2 ± 7.4	(4) 0.83 ± 0.27	(4) 2.92 ± 0.97	(4) 1.27 ±.0.27	(4) 0.50 ± 0.090
	Node	(4) 16.3 ± 10.3	(4) 13.7 ± 3.7	(4) 5.5 ± 1.0	(4) 59.5 ± 11.9	(4) 0.87 ± 0.41	(4) 1.32 ± 0.31	(4) 0.84 ± 0.056	(4) 1.06 ± 0.074
	Kidney	(3) 29.4 ± 6.4	(3) 33.4 ± 1.2	(3) 3.4 ± 0.21	(3) 35.7 ± 6.8	(3) 1.13 ± 0.18	(3) 1.37 ± 0.13	(3) 0.41 ± 0.046	(3) 0.85 ± 0.050
	Appendix				(4) 51.9 ± 14.3				
	Lung,				(4) 50.5 ± 21.2				

Notes: The figures in parentheses indicate the number of animals.
S.D. = standard deviation.

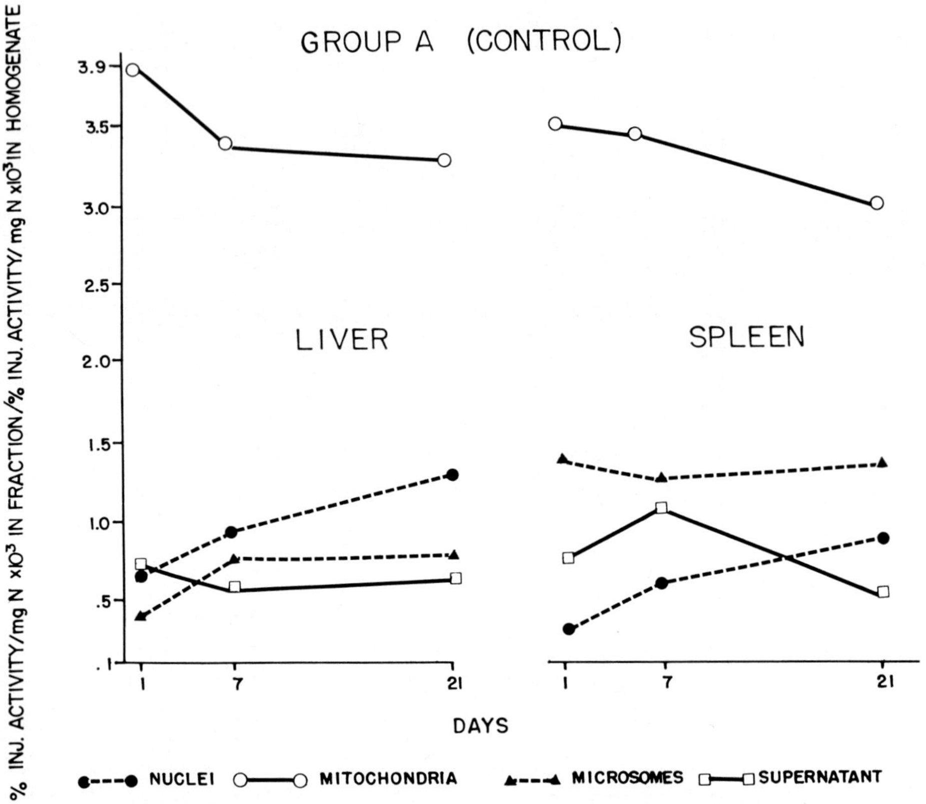

FIG. 5. Relation between fraction radioactivity (per cent injected) and fraction nitrogen content, for liver and spleen. Control group only.

Changes in the distribution of the radioactivity in the various subcellular fractions occur with time. This is well shown in Figs. 5 and 6, which relate the radioactivity of each fraction to the nitrogen content. The most consistent change is a progressive increase in the activity of the nuclear fraction. Less consistently, there are decreases in the activity of the supernatant and mitochondrial fractions, and an increase in the activity of the microsomal fraction. Similar changes with time were also noted by Haurowitz and Crampton (*10*) and by Crampton *et al.* (*15*).

Groups B and C: X-Irradiation

Although not depicted graphically, the over-all rates of metabolism of the antigen by the tissues of irradiated animals of group B (antibody formation inhibited) are similar to those in the controls (Tables I to III). This is also true of the data be-

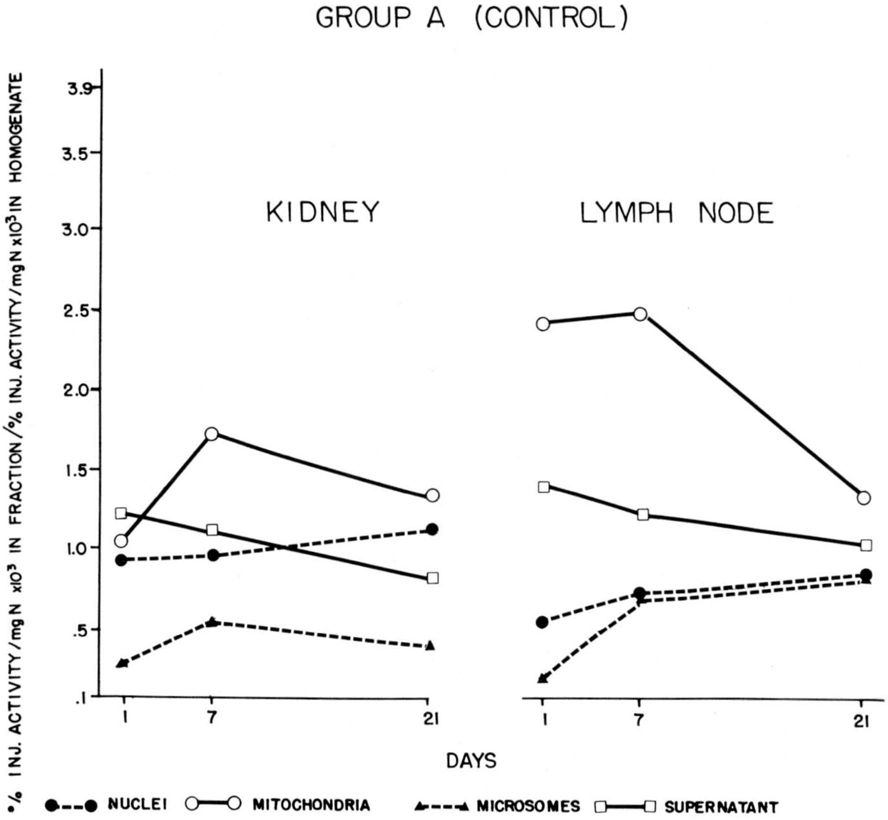

FIG. 6. Relation between fraction radioactivity (per cent injected) and fraction nitrogen content, for kidney and lymph node. Control group only.

tween 24 hours and 7 days from the animals in group C (antibody formation not inhibited); because of the small number of animals sacrificed at 21 days, little can be said of the time period between 1 and 3 weeks in the latter group. The retardation of metabolism of the antigen by the node as contrasted to other tissues is also found in the animals of group B.

Most importantly, whole-organ radioactivity at all periods in all tissues in both groups shows no significant difference from that in the controls.

When the radioactivity is expressed in terms of weight, nitrogen content, or per cent body weight of the tissue studied, certain significant differences emerge when comparison is made with the control figures. In group B, for example, the node shows increased radioactivity by all these criteria at all time intervals. Likewise, in group B, the appendix shows increased antigen retention at 7 and 21 days, and the spleen at 24 hours and 7 days. In group C only the appendix at 7 days demonstrates increased antigen retention. It is noteworthy that these differences occur in organs which decrease sharply in weight after X-irradiation. In consideration of these figures at 24 hours, it must be borne in mind that the animals in group C were sacrificed 18 hours earlier in relation to X-irradiation than the animals in group B, and therefore there was less time for the weight changes to become manifest. Furthermore, when the values for groups B and C are compared, there are no significant differences at all time intervals. It would seem reasonable, therefore, to attribute the differences from the controls in groups B and C entirely to the weight changes of certain organs after irradiation.

The values for plasma antigen content in groups B and C at all time intervals are similar to the control figures. Likewise, the radioactivity excreted in the urine in both groups at all time intervals is not significantly different from that in the controls.

Not presented here are the results on subcellular fractionation of the tissues in groups B and C at all time intervals. Whether expressed as per cent of the homogenate total or in terms of the nitrogen content, the radioactivity retained in the subcellular fractions of the tissues from the animals in groups B and C is not significantly different from control values.

DISCUSSION

A point fundamental to the interpretation of the data presented is the question whether the radioactivity retained in the tissues represents relatively undegraded antigenic material. The consensus of other investigators has been that tagged soluble foreign proteins do remain antigenic for long periods in the tissues, and measurement of the tag (in this case, radioactivity) is a fair measure of the remaining antigen. This conclusion is based on several lines of evidence: (1) the material injected remains in macromolecular form in the tissues for long periods (*4, 11, 13, 16–18*); and (*2*) by using a variety of immunologic methods, such as reversed passive anaphylaxis (*19, 20*), the Schultz-Dale technique (*11*), and the precipitin reaction (*11*), the material found in the tissues has been shown to be antigenic for long periods.

The outstanding finding in the present investigation has been the failure to demonstrate significant differences in whole-organ antigen content of various tissues between normal rabbits (group A) or X-irradiated rabbits in whom the antibody response has not been inhibited (group C) and rabbits in whom antibody formation has been suppressed by whole-body X-irradiation (group B) for periods up to 21 days. When expressed in terms of weight or nitrogen content, certain differences are apparent between the normal and the irradiated rabbits. However, these differences occur principally in organs which show relatively great reductions in weight after irradiation (spleen, lymph node, appendix), and it seems reasonable to ascribe the differences to this cause. Furthermore, analysis of the retained antigen in the subcellular fractions of various tissues also failed to disclose any differences between normal rabbits and rabbits in both irradiated groups.

These results are similar to those of Fitch *et al.* (*3*), who found, at periods up to 6 days, no differences in the total organ content of I^{131}-labeled bacteria in the spleens, livers, and lungs of normal rats and irradiated rats. They also noted increased retention of radioactivity per unit weight in those organs of the irradiated rats which decreased sharply in weight.

Various workers have failed to find differences in total deposition of particulate materials, including colloidal gold (*21*) and thorium dioxide (*22*), in the spleens of normal and irradiated rats and mice. Again the phenomenon of increased retention per unit weight was noted in the spleens of the irradiated animals. Similarly, studies of various enzymes in the tissues, particularly the spleen, of irradiated animals have often shown marked rises in enzyme activity per unit weight, with relatively normal whole-organ content (*23–25*).

All these phenomena suggest that irradiation of a given organ may destroy appreciable numbers of cells but leave intact those cells with certain types of functional activity. This would result in the pattern often found, namely, an increase in the activity in question per unit weight or unit protein, with normal activity in the whole organ.

Applying this concept to the present study, one may conclude that the cells which take up and eventually degrade the bulk of the antigen are relatively little, or not at all, affected by whole-body X-irradiation in doses which inhibit the antibody response.

The present study, therefore, sheds no light on the process of antibody induction. It is possible that injection of much smaller amounts of antigen might lead to different findings. However, with the methods now available, studies can be carried out only with relatively large amounts of antigenic material. The view has been expressed (*10, 26–28*) that, when large amounts of antigen are injected, only a small fraction of the antigen is functional in inducing antibody formation. The present data are consistent with this hypothesis.

Of considerable interest for the present investigation is the observation by Garvey and Smith (*29*) that in newborn rabbits, in which antibody production is absent or retarded, after injection of weight-standardized amounts of tagged antigen, in most of the tissues the whole-organ antigen content is similar to that found in adult rabbits. This is also consistent with the view that the cells necessary for antibody induction account for only a small amount of the antigen when large amounts are injected. In the case of X-ray, presumably the antibody-forming cells are inhibited or destroyed; in the case of the newborn rabbits, presumably the responsive cells have not yet fully populated the lymphatic tissues.

SUMMARY

1. Bovine serum albumin conjugated to S^{35}-sulfanilic acid was injected intravenously in standard doses into three groups of rabbits: Group A (control): nor-

mal rabbits; group B: rabbits injected 18 hours after 450 r of whole-body irradiation (primary antibody response inhibited); and group C: rabbits injected immediately after 450 r of whole-body irradiation (primary antibody response not inhibited). The plasma, liver, spleen, lymph node, kidney, appendix, and lung were studied for radioactivity and protein content at 1, 7, and 21 days after injection.

2. In all groups, the retention of radioactivity in the tissues decreased with time. The over-all metabolism of the antigen by lymph node was retarded when compared to other tissues.

3. There were no differences among all three groups in total-organ retention of antigen at all time intervals. When group A was compared to groups B and C, there were certain differences when antigen retention was expressed in terms of tissue weight or protein content. These differences were attributed to organ-weight changes secondary to irradiation. These differences did not appear when group B was compared to group C.

4. The cells responsible for the retention and degradation of the bulk of injected antigen are not inhibited by irradiation under conditions which inhibit the primary antibody response.

5. When large amounts of antigen are injected, only a small fraction may be important in induction of antibody formation.

ACKNOWLEDGMENTS

We are grateful to Dr. Jack Becktel and Mr. Allen Hoover of the United States Veterans Administration Hospital, Hines, Illinois, for great help in statistical analysis.

RECEIVED: October 10, 1962

REFERENCES

1. F. J. DIXON, D. W. TALMAGE, and P. H. MAURER, Radiosensitive and radioresistant phases in the antibody response. *J. Immunol.* **68,** 693–700 (1952).
2. W. H. TALIAFERRO, L. G. TALIAFERRO, and E. F. JANSSEN, Localization of X-ray injury to initial phases of antibody response. *J. Infect. Diseases* **91,** 105–124 (1952).
3. F. W. FITCH, P. BARKER, K. H. SOULES, and R. W. WISSLER, A study of antigen localization and degradation and the histologic reaction in the spleen of normal, X-irradiated, and spleen-shielded rats. *J. Lab. Clin. Med.* **42,** 598–620 (1953).
4. J. S. INGRAHAM, Artificial radioactive antigens; preparation and evaluation of S^{35}-sulfanilic acid–azobovine gamma globulin. *J. Infect. Diseases* **89,** 109–116 (1951).
5. W. C. SCHNEIDER, In *Manometric Techniques* (Umbreit, Burris, and Stauffer, eds.), p. 188, Burgess Publishing Co., 1957.
6. O. H. LOWRY, N. J. ROSEBROUGH, A. L. FARR, and R. J. RANDALL, Protein measurement with Folin phenol reagent. *J. Biol. Chem.* **193,** 265–275 (1951).
7. H. JEFFAY, F. O. OLUBAJO, and W. R. JEWELL, A new method for the determination of radioactive sulfur in biological materials. *Anal. Chem.* **32,** 306–308 (1960).
8. *Handbook of Biological Data* (Spector, ed.), p. 340, W. B. Saunders, Philadelphia 1956.
9. Biological Handbooks, *Blood and Other Body Fluids* (Dittmer, ed.), p. 9, Federation of American Societies for Experimental Biology,

10. F. HAUROWITZ and C. F. CRAMPTON, The fate in rabbits of intravenously injected I^{131}-iodo-övalbumin. *J. Immunol.* **68,** 73–85 (1952).
11. J. S. GARVEY and D. H. CAMPBELL, The retention of S^{35} labelled bovine serum albumin in normal and immunized rabbit liver tissue. *J. Exptl. Med.* **105,** 361–372 (1957).
12. J. S. GARVEY and D. H. CAMPBELL, Effect of secondary injections of antigen upon the retention in liver of a primary injection. *J. Exptl. Med.* **107,** 497–506 (1958).
13. J. S. GARVEY and D. H. CAMPBELL, The *in vivo* identification in liver tissue of an S^{35}-azo label and its protein carrier. *Arch. Biochem. Biophys.* **73,** 507–508 (1958).
14. C. F. CRAMPTON, H. H. RELLER, and F. HAUROWITZ, Persistence of C^{14}-anthranilazo-ovalbumin in injected rabbits. *Proc. Soc. Exptl. Biol. Med.* **80,** 448–451 (1952).
15. C. F. CRAMPTON, H. H. RELLER, and F. HAUROWITZ, Deposition of beef serum gamma globulin in rabbit organs and subcellular fractions. *J. Immunol.* **71,** 319–324 (1953).
16. F. HAUROWITZ and H. WALTER, Stability of an azoprotein hapten in the organism. *Proc. Soc. Exptl. Biol. Med.* **88,** 67–69 (1955).
17. F. HAUROWITZ, H. H. RELLER, and H. WALTER, The metabolic fate of isotopically labelled proteins, azoproteins, and azohaptens. *J. Immunol.* **75,** 417–422 (1955).
18. A SAHA and J. S. GARVEY, Physical characterization of antigen retained following immunization. *Federation Proc.* **20,** 22 (1961).
19. P. D. MCMASTER and H. KRUSE, The persistence of certain foreign proteins and azoprotein tracer antigens derived from them. *J. Exptl. Med.* **94,** 323–346 (1951).
20. P. D. MCMASTER, H. KRUSE, E. STURM, and J. L. EDWARDS, The persistence of bovine gamma globulin injected as an antigen into rabbits. *J. Exptl. Med.* **100,** 341–362 (1954).
21. L. WISH, J. FURTH, C. W. SHEPPARD, and R. H. STOREY, Disappearance rate of tagged substances from the circulation of Roentgen irradiated animals. *Am. J. Roentgenol. Radium Therapy Nucl. Med.* **67,** 628–640 (1952).
22. D. W. ESPLIN, S. MARCUS, and D. M. DONALDSON, Effects of X-irradiation and adrenalectomy on phagocytic activity. *J. Immunol.* **70,** 454–460 (1953).
23. R. N. FEINSTEIN, Interpretation of some enzyme activity increases after whole-body irradiation. *Radiation Res.* **4,** 217–220 (1956).
24. K. C. SMITH and B. V. A. LOW-BEER, The effect of whole-body X-irradiation on the enzymatic activity of several rat tissues toward uridine, uridylic acid, cytidine, and cytidilic acid. *Radiation Res.* **6,** 521–531 (1957).
25. H. J. EICHEL and S. S. ROTH, Some theoretical consideration of changes in tissue enzyme activity after whole-body irradiation of animals. *Radiation Res.* **12,** 258–265 (1960).
26. F. HAUROWITZ, The immunological response. *Ann. Rev. Microbiol.* **7,** 389–414 (1953).
27. E. H. LEDUC, A. H. COONS, and J. M. CONNOLLY, Studies on antibody production. II. The primary and secondary responses in the popliteal lymph node of the rabbit. *J. Exptl. Med.* **102,** 61–72 (1955).
28. R. G. WHITE, Immune cellular reactions. In *The Scientific Basis of Medicine,* pp. 31–46, Annual Reviews, Athlone, 1961.
29. J. S. GARVEY, D. V. EITZMAN, and R. T. SMITH, The distribution of S^{35}-labeled bovine serum albumin in newborn and immunologically tolerant adult rabbits. *J. Exptl. Med.* **112,** 533–550 (1960).

RADIATION RESEARCH **19**, 384–391 (1963)

Scattering of Gamma Rays in Laminar Media[1, 2]

DOMINIC J. RASO

Technical Operations Research, Burlington, Massachusetts

INTRODUCTION

Extensive Monte Carlo calculations were performed to determine the backscattering of γ-rays from semi-infinite media and the transmission of scattered γ-rays by slabs (*1, 2*). Although the data obtained in these investigations proved useful in the analysis of many radiation transport problems, a number of problems remain that cannot be solved with these programs. Therefore these investigations have been extended in order to make more information available. Results of the scattered energy transmitted were given for normally incident γ-rays on a combination of materials: Pb + Al, Al + Pb, Pb + Fe, Fe + Pb, Fe + Al, and Al + Fe. Also calculations were made to determine the energy backscattered, the energy absorbed,[3] and the energy transmitted in various slabs of water. Results were given for normal incident radiation of energies 1.25 and 0.66 Mev.

METHOD OF CALCULATIONS

Computational techniques are well-developed elsewhere (*3, 4*); only a brief description of them is necessary here. If E_n represents the photon energy, ω_n the angular coordinates describing the direction of motion (the polar and azimuthal angles measured with respect to the z-axis), and z_n the distance from the boundary to the point after the nth collision, then the photon trajectory or history can be described by the set:

$$
\begin{array}{l}
E_0, E_1, \cdots, E_n, \cdots \\
\omega_0, \omega_1, \cdots, \omega_n, \cdots \\
z_0, z_1, \cdots, z_n, \cdots
\end{array}
$$

[1] This work was supported by the Nuclear Defense Laboratory, Army Chemical Center, Maryland.

[2] Preliminary results presented at the Second International Congress of Radiation Research, Harrogate, England, August, 1962.

[3] This is the energy imparted to the secondary electrons rather than the energy deposited by them.

TABLE I

FRACTION OF ENERGY DEPOSITED AFTER ONE INTERACTION

Incident energy, E (kev)	*Probability of Compton scatter*	*Fraction of energy deposited*			
		Compton only	*Expected total*	*By statistical method*	*By analytical method*
200	0.9838	0.215	0.228	0.230	0.227
100	0.8757	0.14	0.247	0.245	0.246
60	0.6142	0.09	0.441	0.440	0.443
40	0.3210	0.06	0.699	0.705	0.700

where E_0, ω_0, and z_0 indicate the initial conditions. The trajectory of each photon is determined by random sampling from the known probability for a given event—photoelectric absorption, Compton scattering, pair production, energy degradation, scattering through an angle, and so forth. The random choice for an event that depends on the previous interaction is determined by the physical laws governing γ-ray transport.

Each collision in the medium is considered to be a Compton interaction or a pair production[4]; photoelectric absorption is taken into account by the introduction of a statistical weight factor that is analytically calculated. The photon history is terminated when (1) the photon passes through the medium without making a collision (unscattered passage); (2) after multiple scattering, the photon energy in the medium is below a cutoff energy (25 kev for water and aluminum, 50 kev for iron, and 100 kev for lead), chosen where photoelectric absorption becomes predominant; (3) after multiple collisions, the photon is backscattered out of the medium, thus contributing to albedo; or (4) the photon passes through the slab after undergoing multiple scattering in the medium. The important parameters of backscattering, absorption, and transmission are summed up in order to estimate albedo, energy deposition in slabs, and transmission.

RESULTS

Table I illustrates the accuracy of taking photoelectric absorption into account analytically when 2000 histories are sampled in concrete. The column heading "By statistical method" refers to the fraction of energy deposited after a single interaction when the photoelectric effects are calculated by random sampling. That is, a random number between 0 and 1 is chosen and compared to P, the probability that an interaction is a Compton scatter (shown in the second column). If the random number is greater than P, then photoelectric absorption is assumed,

[4] The present program follows the history of one 0.511-Mev photon with the statistical weight doubled.

TABLE II

COMPARISON OF RATIOS OF SCATTERED TRANSMITTED ENERGY TO EMERGENT UNSCATTERED RADIATION OBTAINED FOR 1.25-MEV RADIATION IN 1-MFP OF VARIOUS MEDIA

(The first element listed is the one close to the source. The cutoff energies were 0.1 Mev for Pb, 0.05 Mev for Fe, and 0.025 for Al.)

Medium	*Monte Carlo (5000 histories)*	*Experiment (Kimel*[a]*)*
Pb + Al	1.133 ± 0.061	1.3
Al + Pb	0.875 ± 0.061	1.1
Pb + Fe	1.125 ± 0.068	1.3
Fe + Pb	0.845 ± 0.061	0.8
Fe + Al	1.370 ± 0.066	1.6
Al + Fe	1.335 ± 0.067	1.5

[a] L. R. Kimel, Build-up factors for heterogeneous shields, *At. Energ. (USSR)* **10**, 173–175 (1961).

and the total energy, E_n, is deposited. If the random number is less than P, then a Compton scatter is assumed, and a new photon energy, E_{n+1}, is computed by random sampling. The difference, $E_n - E_{n+1}$, is the energy deposited at the point of interaction. The column marked "By analytical method" refers to the results when photoelectric absorption is considered analytically. On the average, $(1 - P)$ collisions deposit energy, E_n, by photoelectric absorption, and P collisions leave $(E_n - E_{n+1})$ behind in the scattered electron. Thus, after each collision, the energy deposited is $(E_n - E_{n+1} P)$. The fourth column in the table is the expected energy absorbed, by using the photoelectric and the integrated Klein-Nishina cross sections per electron. As is seen, the two random-sampling methods give similar results even when as few as 2000 cases are sampled.

Table II compares ratios of scattered transmitted energy to emergent unscattered radiation, a 1.25-Mev source being assumed, with those found by an experiment performed by Kimel *(5)* with a Co^{60} source. Radiation in both cases was normally incident on the various combinations of materials. The thickness of each material was 1 mean free path (mfp). The Monte Carlo data represent an analysis of 5000 photon histories per case. As is seen, the experimental results are on the average about 10% higher than the Monte Carlo results, possibly because of the excessive low-energy response of the detector used in the experiment.

The fraction of energy deposited for normally incident 1.25-Mev photons in various layers of water is shown in Table III. The column headings refer to the total slab thicknesses in centimeters, and the row headings to thicknesses of the subslabs.[5] The results are based on 25,000 histories. Data in the table illustrate that the

[5] To display the distribution of the deposited energy, the physical slab is conceptually divided into a number of regions, briefly referred to as "subslabs." They represent a range of depth inside the actual slab of physical material.

TABLE III

ENERGY DEPOSITION OF 1.25-MEV PHOTONS NORMALLY INCIDENT ON WATER

(Fraction of energy absorbed per incident photon/cm²-sec. The cutoff energy = 0.025 Mev. Based on 25,000 photon histories.)

Subslab thickness (cm)	*Slab thickness (cm)*					
	4	*8*	*12*	*16*	*20*	*24*
0–2	0.0594 ± 0.0015	0.0607 ± 0.0015	0.0614 ± 0.0015	0.0619 ± 0.0015	0.0621 ± 0.0015	0.0623 ± 0.0015
2–4	0.0552 ± 0.0009	0.0575 ± 0.0010	0.0585 ± 0.0010	0.0592 ± 0.0009	0.0596 ± 0.0010	0.0599 ± 0.0010
4–6		0.0568 ± 0.0020	0.0582 ± 0.0020	0.0592 ± 0.0020	0.0597 ± 0.0020	0.0600 ± 0.0020
6–8		0.0512 ± 0.0011	0.0534 ± 0.0010	0.0546 ± 0.0011	0.0553 ± 0.0011	0.0557 ± 0.0011
8–10			0.0508 ± 0.0009	0.0522 ± 0.0008	0.0531 ± 0.0008	0.0536 ± 0.0008
10–12			0.0463 ± 0.0011	0.0486 ± 0.0012	0.0498 ± 0.0012	0.0504 ± 0.0012
12–14				0.0441 ± 0.0003	0.0456 ± 0.0004	0.0464 ± 0.0004
14–16				0.0401 ± 0.0005	0.0424 ± 0.0005	0.0436 ± 0.0005
16–18					0.0400 ± 0.0010	0.0415 ± 0.0010
18–20					0.0352 ± 0.0007	0.0373 ± 0.0007
20–22						0.0345 ± 0.0009
22–24						0.0297 ± 0.0011

TABLE IV

ENERGY DEPOSIITON OF 0.66-MEV PHOTONS NORMALLY INCIDENT ON WATER

(Fraction of energy absorbed per incident photon/cm²-sec. The cutoff energy = 0.025 Mev. Based on 25,000 photon histories.)

Subslab thickness (cm)	*Slab thickness (cm)*					
	4	*8*	*12*	*16*	*20*	*24*
0–2	0.0671 ± 0.0014	0.0696 ± 0.0014	0.0712 ± 0.0014	0.0721 ± 0.0014	0.0727 ± 0.0014	0.0730 ± 0.0014
2–4	0.0655 ± 0.0011	0.0697 ± 0.0012	0.0721 ± 0.0011	0.0734 ± 0.0012	0.0741 ± 0.0012	0.0746 ± 0.0012
4–6		0.0640 ± 0.0013	0.0672 ± 0.0011	0.0690 ± 0.0011	0.0700 ± 0.0011	0.0706 ±0.0011
6–8		0.0561 ± 0.0011	0.0609 ± 0.0010	0.0631 ± 0.0010	0.0644 ± 0.0010	0.0652 ± 0.0010
8–10			0.0561 ± 0.0004	0.0590 ± 0.0004	0.0606 ± 0.0004	0.0616 ± 0.0004
10–12			0.0489 ± 0.0013	0.0532 ± 0.0012	0.0553 ± 0.0013	0.0564 ± 0.0013
12–14				0.0471 ± 0.0009	0.0499 ± 0.0008	0.0514 ± 0.0008
14–16				0.0401 ± 0.0005	0.0440 ± 0.0005	0.0459 ± 0.0006
16–18					0.0381 ± 0.0011	0.0406 ± 0.0011
18–20					0.0329 ± 0.0007	0.0366 ± 0.0008
20–22						0.0323 ± 0.0013
22–24						0.0279 ± 0.0006

absorbed energy density in the first few centimeters of water is almost independent of the thickness of the medium. In other words, increasing the thickness of the medium does not significantly increase the energy absorbed in the subslabs. For a slab thickness of 4 cm, the energy absorbed in the first 2 cm is 5.9%; for a thickness

TABLE V

FRACTION OF ENERGY BACKSCATTERED, ABSORBED, AND TRANSMITTED (WITH AND WITHOUT SCATTERINGS) FOR 1.25-MEV PHOTONS NORMALLY INCIDENT ON VARIOUS SLABS OF WATER (Based on 25,000 photon histories)

Slab thickness (cm)	*Energy albedo*	*Energy absorbed*	*Energy transmitted (scattered)*	*Energy transmitted (unscattered)*	
				Monte Carlo	*Expected* $e^{-\mu x}$
4	0.0117 ± 0.0003	0.1146 ± 0.0016	0.0930 ± 0.0005	0.7807 ± 0.0050	0.7767
8	0.0198 ± 0.0005	0.2261 ± 0.0022	0.1473 ± 0.0011	0.6068 ± 0.0039	0.6033
12	0.0257 ± 0.0004	0.3288 ± 0.0023	0.1751 ± 0.0017	0.4704 ± 0.0033	0.4686
16	0.0292 ± 0.0004	0.4199 ± 0.0023	0.1846 ± 0.0021	0.3662 ± 0.0041	0.3640
20	0.0315 ± 0.0004	0.5028 ± 0.0036	0.1840 ± 0.0026	0.2816 ± 0.0039	0.2827
24	0.0329 ± 0.0005	0.5750 ± 0.0025	0.1720 ± 0.0014	0.2200 ± 0.0028	0.2196
Semi-infinite	0.0340 ± 0.0017[a]				

[a] M. J. Berger and D. J. Raso, Monte Carlo calculations of gamma-ray backscattering. *Radiation. Res.* **12,** 20–37 (1960).

TABLE VI

FRACTION OF ENERGY BACKSCATTERED, ABSORBED, AND TRANSMITTED (WITH AND WITHOUT SCATTERINGS) FOR 0.66-MEV PHOTONS NORMALLY INCIDENT ON VARIOUS SLABS OF WATER (Based on 25,000 photon histories)

Slab thickness (cm)	*Energy albedo*	*Energy absorbed*	*Energy transmitted (scattered)*	*Energy transmitted (unscattered)*	
				Monte Carlo	*Expected* $e^{-\mu x}$
4	0.0278 ± 0.0004	0.1326 ± 0.0012	0.1289 ± 0.0012	0.7107 ± 0.0014	0.7092
8	0.0466 ± 0.0005	0.2595 ± 0.0016	0.1858 ± 0.0018	0.5081 ± 0.0051	0.5029
12	0.0581 ± 0.0008	0.3764 ± 0.0017	0.2048 ± 0.0009	0.3607 ± 0.0026	0.3567
16	0.0651 ± 0.0009	0.4771 ± 0.0022	0.2010 ± 0.0018	0.2568 ± 0.0034	0.2529
20	0.0691 ± 0.0011	0.5619 ± 0.0031	0.1861 ± 0.0028	0.1828 ± 0.0040	0.1794
24	0.0715 ± 0.0012	0.6361 ± 0.0027	0.1626 ± 0.0035	0.1297 ± 0.0042	0.1272
Semi-infinite	0.0740 ± 0.0032[a]				

[a] M. J. Berger and D. J. Raso, Monte Carlo calculations of gamma-ray backscattering. *Radiation Res.* **12,** 20–37 (1960).

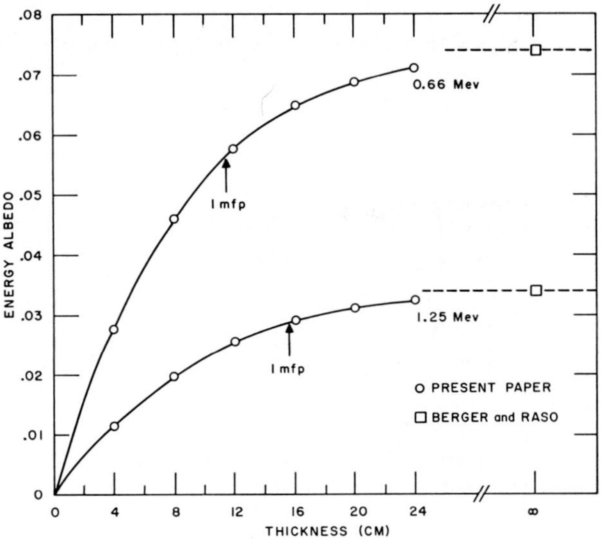

FIG. 1. Energy albedo for 1.25- and 0.66-Mev normally incident photons on various thicknesses of water.

of 24 cm, the energy absorbed in the first 2 cm is 6.2%. The energy absorbed as a result of only single scatterings in 2 cm of water is 5.7%.

Similar results for 0.66-Mev radiation are shown in Table IV. Here, too, the energy density does not vary significantly when the thickness of water is increased. The energy absorbed in the first 2 cm of a semi-infinite medium of water, when we consider only single scatterings, is 6.1%, as compared to 6.7% for 4 cm and 7.3% for 24 cm.

Table V for a 1.25-Mev source and Table VI for a 0.66-Mev source show the energy albedo, the energy absorbed, and the energy transmitted (with and without scatterings) for various slabs of water. The column heading "Energy absorbed" refers to the total energy absorbed in the various thicknesses. The energy albedo for a semi-infinite medium, obtained in a past investigation, shows that 24 cm of water can be considered semi-infinite for the energy albedo.

In Fig. 1, energy albedo for the two energies is plotted against slab thicknesses of water. The figure also shows the results obtained for the semi-infinite case. As can be seen, the fraction of energy backscattered by 1 mfp of water is about 85% of the semi-infinite case for 1.25-Mev photons and about 75% for 0.66-Mev photons.

SUMMARY

A multipurpose γ-ray Monte Carlo program for describing the emergent (backscattering or transmitted) characteristics (E, ω, z) of photons scattered by flat slabs has written. The program is set up to investigate γ-ray backscattering, absorption, and transmission in one, two, or three layers of different materials. The information that may be obtained includes: (1) the number albedo or transmitted; (2) the energy albedo or transmitted; (3) the angular distribution of the emergent number, energy, or dose; and (4) the fraction of energy deposited in layers of the medium.

RECEIVED: October 27, 1962

REFERENCES

1. M. J. BERGER and D. J. RASO, Monte Carlo calculations of γ-ray backscattering. *Radiation Res.* **12,** 20–37 (1960).
2. D. J. RASO, Transmission of scattered γ-rays through concrete and iron slabs. *Health Physics* **5,** 126–141 (1961).
3. H. A. MEYER (ed.), *Monte Carlo Method (Proceeding of a Symposium)*, John Wiley & Sons, New York, 1956.
4. U. FANO, L. V. SPENCER, and M. J. BERGER, Penetration and diffusion of X-rays. *Encyclopedia of Physics,* Vol. 38, Part 2, Springer, Berlin, 1959.
5. L. R. KIMEL, Build-up factors for heterogeneous shields, *At. Ener. (USSR)* **10,** 173–175 (1961).

RADIATION RESEARCH **19**, 392–401 (1963)

The Action of Monochromatic Ultraviolet Radiation on Luminescence in *Armillaria mellea*[1]

MARTHA D. BERLINER

AVCO, Research and Advanced Development Division, Wilmington, Massachusetts

INTRODUCTION

Assay of ultraviolet irradiation damage in microorganisms usually takes several hours to several days. By monitoring changes in the intensity of light emission of cultures of the luminous fungus (basidiomycete) *Armillaria mellea*, immediate effects can be recorded. The bioluminescence of these organisms is interpreted as the result of enzyme-catalyzed oxidations in which sufficient energy is liberated to excite a molecule to an excited state from which it returns to the ground state with the emission of a quantum (*1*).

The investigation follows work previously done on inactivation as a function of wavelength in *Panus stipticus*, another luminescent fungus (*2*). The results reported here indicate that the enzyme system responsible for the light-emitting reaction may be considerably different in these two fungi, and different as well from the luciferin–luciferase complex of other luminescent organisms.

MATERIALS AND METHODS

Dikaryotic mycelial cultures of *Armillaria mellea* were used. Attempts to use the more desirable single-spore cultures were unsuccessful because their light emission was unreliable and short-lived. The method of cultivation and the photometric techniques used for recording light-emission intensities have been described (*3*). Seven-day-old cultures, 0.1 to 0.5 mm thick, approximately 1 cm square, grown on 5-cm petri dishes, were centered, with their lids removed, 4 cm away from the exit of the monochromator. All exposures were made in a dark chamber to eliminate absorption of stray light. The diaphragm of the monochromator was completely open, and the uniform light beam covered an area larger than the colony. The temperature was kept between 22° and 23.5°C, well within the optimum range (*3*).

Ultraviolet source equipment consisted of the following: (1) Osram HBO 200

[1] This work was performed under National Aeronautics and Space Administration Contract NASw-389.

W Super pressure mercury lamp; (2) Farrand grating monochromator #91087; (3) Bausch & Lomb monochromator entrance and exit ultraviolet optics. For the experiments, 70-A half-width entrance and exit slits were used. Ultraviolet energy densities were determined by using a Photovolt photomultiplier with an ultraviolet-sensitive tube. Nominal absolute sensitivities of the photomultiplier tube and read-out instrumentation were obtained from the manufacturers.

Energy densities at the experimental specimen location of the pertinent wavelengths were: 2400 A—3 milliwatts/cm^2; 2540 A—3.2 milliwatts/cm^2; 2650 A—2.7 milliwatts/cm^2; 2800 A—11 milliwatts/cm^2; 2900 A—16 milliwatts/cm^2; 3150 A—120 milliwatts/cm^2; 3660 A—280 milliwatts/cm^2. These energy densities are approximate because of manufacturing variations and aging of the photomultiplier tube.

Uninoculated agar plates were exposed for 30 minutes at all wavelengths tested, and the fungus was then grown on them to see if any of the recorded effects were due to changes in the medium. Cultures grew and luminesced equally well on irradiated and non-irradiated media.

Since the inactivation of pure enzyme systems by ultraviolet light has been shown to depend on the total dose and not on intensity alone or time of irradiation alone (*4*), different doses were obtained by varying the exposure times. Six sets of cultures were exposed for 1 minute, 2.5 minutes, 5 minutes, 15 minutes, 30 minutes, and 1 hour. At 2650 A, cultures were also exposed for 90 minutes and 2 hours. Effects of the following wavelengths, $\pm$35 A, were studied: 2400 A, 2540 A, 2650 A, 2800 A, 2900 A, 3100 A, and 3660 A. After exposure all cultures remained in the dark and were monitored in total darkness to minimize photoreactivation.

Light-emission intensities of the exposed cultures were recorded continuously for 4 hours after exposure and four times daily for the next 7 days to monitor the long-range recovery. All light values were recorded as percentage increases or decreases from the light-emission intensity values immediately prior to exposure. This steady state was arbitrarily set as 100%.

RESULTS

Changes during Irradiation

At certain wavelengths (Figs. 1 to 6) there generally was either an increase or a decrease of more than 10% in the light level during irradiation for the times and exposures investigated. The greatest decline of 40% occurred at 2540 A for a 15-minute exposure. These results are in contrast to our previous experience, under the same experimental conditions, with *Panus stipticus*, where the light intensity decreased at least 50% in 30 minutes at all wavelengths tested.

It is interesting to note that at exposures of 1 hour at 2400 A, 2540 A, 2650 A, and 2900 A, there was an increase in the light emission during exposure rather than an

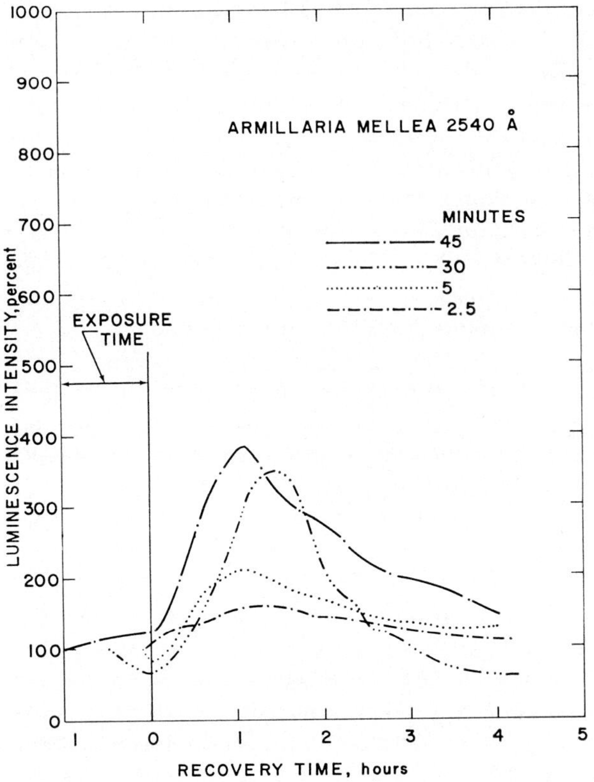

FIG. 1. Light-emission intensities of cultures of *Armillaria mellea* exposed for various times at 2540 A. The preirradiation steady state is set as 100%.

anticipated decrease. The only wavelength at which there was a consistent increase during irradiation was 2800 A, and at 3100 A and 3660 A there was usually a decrease. However, the amounts of increase and decrease were not proportional to the lengths of exposure for any one wavelength or between wavelengths and thus cannot serve as indicators of dosage.

Stimulation after Removal from the Source

Within a short time after removal of the cultures from the ultraviolet source, there was a marked increase in the total light emission over the value prior to irradiation (i.e., 100% level qualified as steady state). The maxima reached are indicated in Table I and Figs. 1 to 6.

At each wavelength there is a dose which produces a maximum increase in bioluminescence. Higher doses do not yield any greater light emission. The maxi-

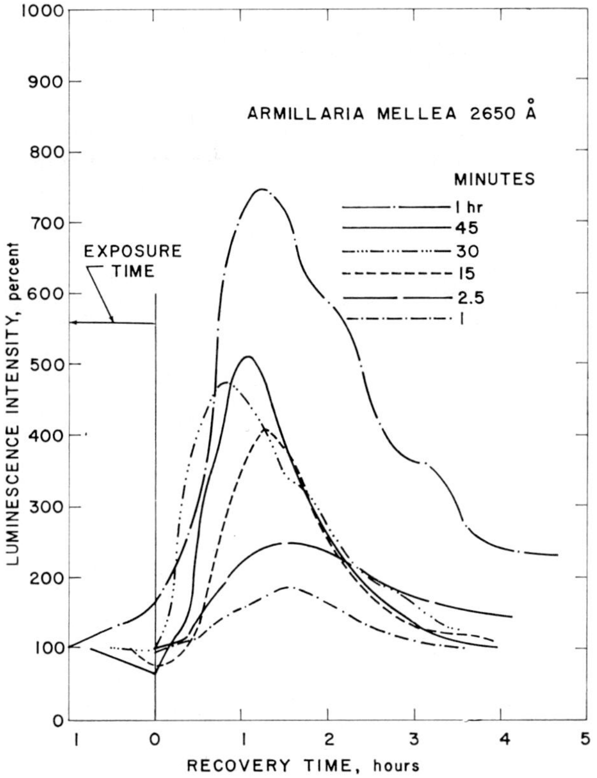

FIG. 2. Light-emission intensities of cultures of *Armillaria mellea* exposed for various times at 2650 A. The preirradiation steady state is set as 100%.

mum light intensity of all samples was reached within 90 minutes of the end of irradiation, regardless of wavelength or total increase. There is no correlation between the dose (energy/cm^2 $\times$ exposure time) and these light-emission maxima. The maximum light emission also increases with the wavelength (Table II).

Long-Term Recovery

Cultures were examined and the light intensities recorded three times daily for a week after exposure to ultraviolet. All cultures, except those exposed at 2800 A, regained light-emission intensities consistent with the controls within 24 hours of exposure. There appears to have been neither permanent damage nor permanent stimulation of either the light-emission intensity or the growth rate.

The long-term recovery of cultures exposed at 2800 A presents a different picture. Twenty-four hours after exposure the light emission of all the cultures was at least

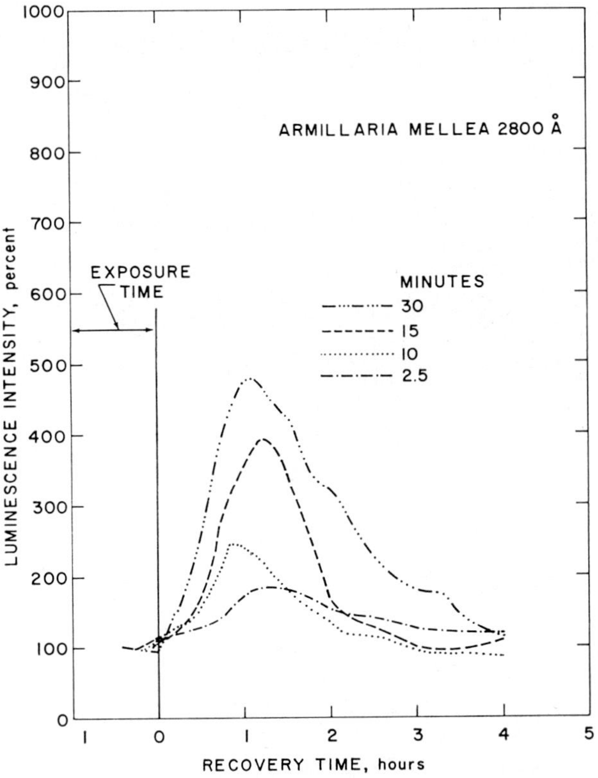

FIG. 3. Light-emission intensities of cultures of *Armillaria mellea* exposed for various times at 2800 A. The preirradiation steady state is set as 100%.

50% or more below the preirradiation values. This was true for cultures exposed as short a time as 1 and 2.5 minutes as well as those exposed for 1 hour. It took between 3 and 5 days for all cultures to regain both the preirradiation light-emission level and the average growth rate. Once established, the subsequent recovery followed the expected pattern.

DISCUSSION

It has been conclusively demonstrated that the luminescent system in *Armillaria mellea* is of the enzyme type, albeit different from that found in other luminescent organisms (*5, 6*). That the effective long-range inactivation is found only at 2800 A suggests a complex system which cannot be interpreted solely on the basis of an action spectrum.

Airth and Foerster (*7*) and Airth (*5, 6*) studied the effect of ultraviolet light at 3660 A on *A. mellea* in both the *in vivo* and the *in vitro* enzyme system. The first *in vivo* report (*7*) indicated a very sharp drop (70%) of the original steady state and a recovery of 40% during irradiation. This recovery was maintained until 90% of the original value was attained and described as a "new steady state." The observations were limited to 90 minutes after removal from the source. In the second *in vivo* report (*6*) Airth observed a 40% drop in the luminescence with no recovery during irradiation. After removal of the ultraviolet source and monitoring for 45 minutes, he observed a "new steady state" 160% higher than the original.

From the long-time observations reported here, it becomes evident that these new light levels are not "new steady states." Instead, they are temporary stimulations of the enzyme systems or some portion thereof. The length of time necessary to reach new maxima is probably determined by the rate of synthesis versus the rate of destruction of photolabile components of the enzyme system (*2, 7*).

The efficiency of inactivation of an enzyme by ultraviolet varies with the wavelength (*8, 9*), and this inactivation occurs when enough chemical changes have

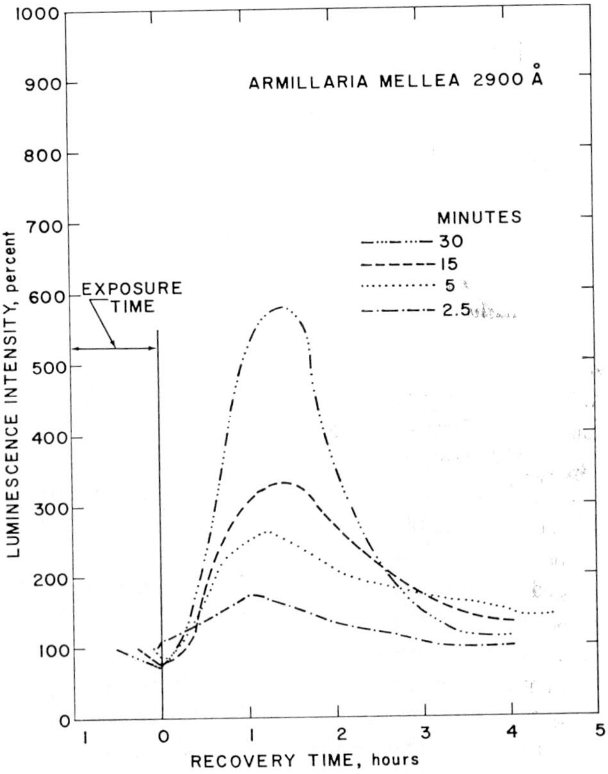

FIG. 4. Light-emission intensities of cultures of *Armillaria mellea* exposed for various times at 2900 A. The preirradiation steady state is set as 100%.

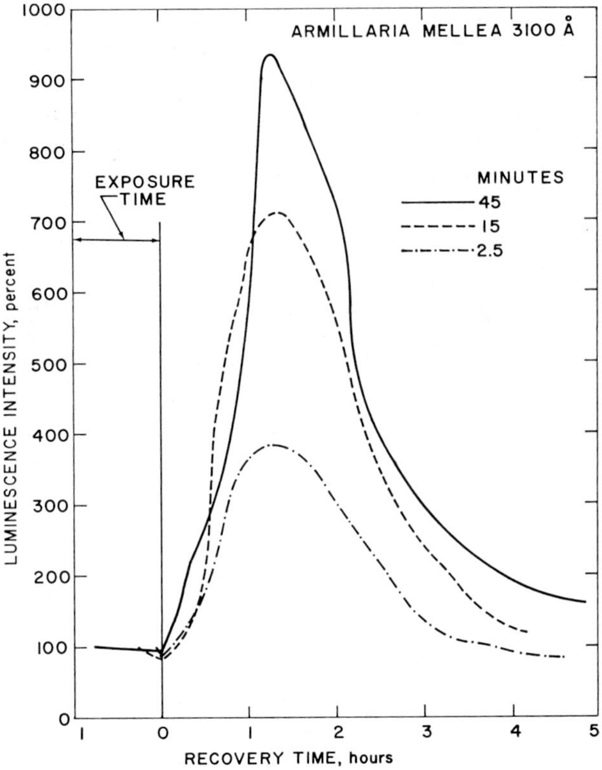

FIG. 5. Light-emission intensities of cultures of *Armillaria mellea* exposed for various times at 3100 A. The preirradiation steady state is set as 100%.

been produced within a fairly restricted portion of the molecule to produce specific alterations in the makeup of the enzyme.

Wavelengths of 2800 A are apparently the most effective in the long term in denaturing and thus inactivating the luminescence enzyme systems of *A. mellea.* The same maximal efficiency of 2800 A was found for quenching the light emission of *P. stipticus,* although the damage was far more extensive (*2*). Even very small amounts of absorbed quanta are effective, since exposures of 1 and 2.5 minutes at 2800 A are sufficient to cause measurable effects.

Many investigators have found a marked stimulation of metabolism in microorganisms after ultraviolet irradiation. Rothstein (*10*) attributed the stimulation of respiration in yeasts to the release of metabolites from cells in which the membranes have been damaged. The probability of the same system's being operative here due to a leakage of substrate and enzyme into the medium is being investigated. At present no gross cytological damage has been found in irradiated cells,

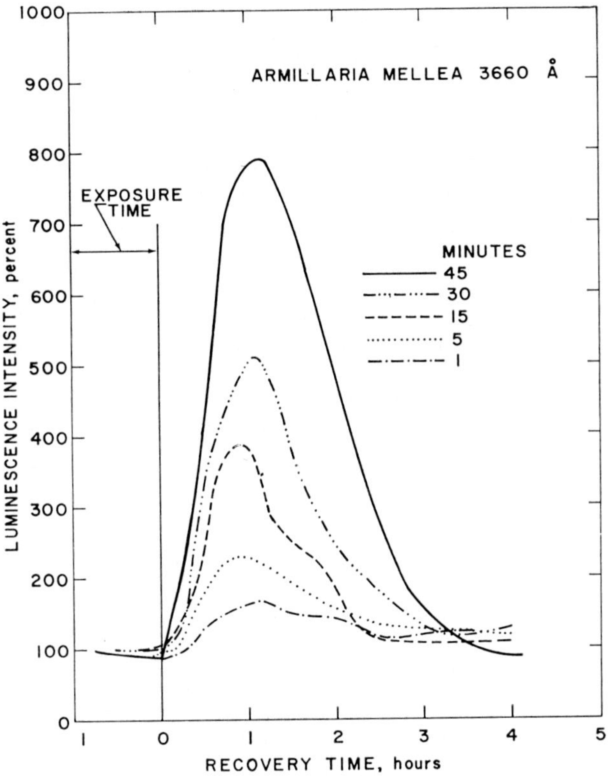

FIG. 6. Light-emission intensities of cultures of *Armillaria mellea* exposed for various times at 3660 A. The preirradiation steady state is set as 100%.

TABLE I

MAXIMUM LIGHT EMISSION AFTER IRRADIATION, EXPRESSED AS PER CENT OF EMISSION BEFORE IRRADIATION

Wavelength	*Exposure time (min)*						
	1	*2.5*	*5*	*15*	*30*	*45*	*60*
2400 A	150	205	245	385	430	340	233
2540 A	160	175	210	220	350	370	220
2650 A	186	244	382	400	495	515	745
2800 A	150	182	244	394	490	398	350
2900 A	173	175	262	330	580	465	316
3100 A	348	385	460	710	860	935	760
3660 A	169	200	228	388	510	790	735

TABLE II

DOSES RECEIVED AS DETERMINED FROM TIMES AND INTENSITIES AT VARIOUS WAVELENGTHS

Wavelength	*Intensity*	*Time*[a]	*Dose*[a]
2540 A	3.2	45	144
2650 A	2.7	60	162
2800 A	11.0	30	330
2900 A	16.0	30	480
3150 A	120.0	45	4,900
3660 A	280.0	45	12,000

[a] For maximum light increase after irradiation.

regardless of wavelength. Cell division does not appear to be affected except at 2800 A where the growth rate is checked for about 3 days, although without killing of the cells.

The luminescence enzyme system of *A. mellea* is much more resistant to equivalent ultraviolet irradiation damage at all wavelengths than that of *P. stipticus* (*2*). The stimulatory nature of these irradiations not only is more effective during exposure but is about ten times as intense during recovery in *A. mellea* as in *P. stipticus*. It may be that *A. mellea* has a peculiarly resistant radiation system because at the longest irradiation time at 2800 A the cultures received a dose of approximately 2×10^8 ergs/cm^2. The mean lethal dose for enzymes averages 10^7 ergs/cm^2, and for various nucleic aids 10^5 ergs/cm^2 (*11*).

Setlow and Doyle (*4*) have pointed out that wavelengths up to 3100 A may inactivate by different mechanisms. Bioluminescence in *A. mellea* as a test mechanism shows interesting results which are now under investigation on the molecular level.

SUMMARY

The effects of different ultraviolet wavelengths and exposures on the light emission of cultures of the fungus *Armillaria mellea* are reported. Irradiation at 2800 A caused the only permanent damage to both respiratory activity and growth. There was a consistent increase in the light emission during irradiation at 2800 A, and a consistent decrease at 3100 A and 3660 A. All wavelengths were effective in causing a temporary intense stimulation of bioluminescence after removal of the ultraviolet source. There is a maximum light increase which varies with the wavelength.
RECEIVED: November 1, 1962

REFERENCES

1. H. H. SELIGER and W. D. MCELROY, Pathways of energy transfer in bioluminescence. *Radia- Res. Suppl.* **2,** 528–538 (1960).

2. M. D. BERLINER and P. B. BRAND, Effects of monochromatic ultraviolet light on luminescence in *Panus stipticus*. *Mycologia* **54,** 415–421 (1962).

3. M. D. BERLINER, Studies in fungal luminescence. *Mycologia* **53,** 84–90 (1961).
4. R. B. SETLOW and B. DOYLE, The action of monochromatic ultraviolet light on proteins. *Biochim. Biophys. Acta* **24,** 27–41 (1957).
5. R. L. AIRTH and W. D. MCELROY, Light emission from extracts of luminous fungi. *J. Bacteriol.* **77,** 249–250 (1959).
7. R. L. AIRTH and G. E. FOERSTER, Some aspects of fungal bioluminescence. *J. Cellular Comp. Physiol.* **56,** 173–182 (1960).
6. R. L. AIRTH, Characteristics of cell-free fungal luminescence. *Light and Life*, pp. 262–273, John Hopkins Press, Baltimore, 1961.
8. L. G. AUGENSTINE, J. G. CARTER, D. R. NELSON, and H. P. HOCKEY, Radiation effects at the macromolecular level. *Radiation Res. Suppl.* **2,** 11–48 (1960).
9. R. B. SETLOW, Ultraviolet wave-length-dependent effects on proteins and nucleic acids. *Radiation Res. Suppl.* **2,** 276–289 (1960).
10. A ROTHSTEIN, Biochemical and biophysical changes in irradiated yeast. *Radiation Res. Suppl.* **1,** 357–371 (1959).
11. A. C. GIESE, Action of ultraviolet irradiation on protoplasm. *Physiol. Rev.* **30,** 431–458 (1950).

RADIATION RESEARCH **19**, 402–408 (1963)

Hydrogen Peroxide Yields from Cobalt-60 Gamma Irradiation of Alkaline Solutions[1]

MARY-LOUISE ROTHSCHILD AND WILLIAM T. TSUKAMOTO

Laboratory of Nuclear Medicine and Radiation Biology of the Department of Biophysics and Nuclear Medicine, School of Medicine, University of California, Los Angeles, California

INTRODUCTION

A considerable number of radiochemical studies have been devoted to determining the products of water decomposition and their yields in acid and neutral solutions, but comparable studies in alkaline solutions are virtually nonexistent (see Allen, *1*, for a discussion). In a previous communication, we reported a value for the observed initial yield of hydrogen peroxide, $G(H_2O_2)_{obs}$, from cobalt-60 γ-irradiation of aerated 0.1 N NaOH based on the reaction of hydrogen peroxide with ferriprotoporphyrin, FPP (*2*). FPP is transformed to another ferriporphyrin compound of unknown structure, FPP′, in a chain reaction initiated by hydrogen peroxide and possible other products of the radiolysis of water. Reported here are the results of the continuation of the study of the transformation reaction of FPP. Values for $G(H_2O_2)_{obs}$ and for the initial yield of total chain-initiating agents, $G(R)$, are presented for alkaline solutions at pH 7.7 to 14. A tentative explanation is given for the values for $G(R)$ based on well-established values for water decomposition products in neutral solution.

EXPERIMENTAL PROCEDURE

Materials. The solutions of ferriprotoporphyrin, FPP, in Clark & Lubs 0.05 M phosphate buffer, pH 8, and 0.05 M borate buffer, pH 8 to 10, 0.05 M phosphate buffer, pH 12 (*3*), and the unbuffered solutions, pH < 13, were prepared by dissolving FPP in the 0.1 N NaOH used to prepare these solutions. The solutions of FPP in 0.05 M carbonate–bicarbonate buffer (*4*) were prepared by dissolving FPP in the 0.2 M sodium carbonate. FPP will not dissolve directly in these buffered and unbuffered solutions. The solutions of higher pH were prepared by dissolving FPP directly in the solution to be used.

[1] These studies were supported by Contract AT(04-1)-GEN12 between the U. S. Atomic Energy Commission and the University of California.

Methods. The methods used here are essentially the same as those described in the previous communication (*2*). Because of the limited solubility of FPP, it was necessary to study the postirradiation reaction by adding 1 ml of FPP dissolved in 0.1 *N* NaOH to the 10 ml of irradiated solutions of lower pH.

A minor modification was made in the butanol extraction technique for separating the transformation product, FPP′, from unreacted FPP. The pH of 5 ml of the reaction mixture was adjusted to 9 to 11 with 5 ml of boric acid, borate, phosphate, or carbonate–bicarbonate buffer and extracted with 10 ml of *n*-butanol.

RESULTS AND DISCUSSION

The mechanism for the transformation of ferriprotoporphyrin, FPP, in aerated buffered and unbuffered solutions at pH 7.7 to 12.3 was examined by studying the effect of initial FPP concentration on the yield of transformation product, FPP′, from the irradiation, postirradiation, and hydrogen peroxide reactions. FPP concentration, hydrogen peroxide concentration, and irradiation dose and intensity were similar to those used in the examination of this reaction in aerated 0.1 *N* NaOH (*2*). The results are similar to those in 0.1 *N* NaOH. The yield of FPP′ increases approximately as the square root of the initial FPP concentration.

The mechanism was further studied by examining the effect of increasing hydrogen peroxide concentration and irradiation dose on the yield of FPP′ from 100 μM FPP in aerated buffered and unbuffered solutions at pH 7.7 to 14. Doses of 0.58 to 2.90 $\times 10^{19}$ ev/l at an intensity of 0.46 $\times 10^{19}$ ev/l-min were used for the irradiation reaction; doses of 1.75 to 8.75 $\times 10^{19}$ ev/l at an intensity of 3.78 $\times 10^{19}$ ev/l-min were used for the postirradiation reaction; and concentrations of hydrogen peroxide of 1 to 5 μM (final concentration) were used for the thermal reaction. The results are similar to those in 0.1 *N* NaOH. The experimental data fit theoretical curves constructed by using equation 19 of reference (*2*) (see footnote 2 of reference *2*), $K = 16\ \mu M$, $B = 1$, and values of A which best fit the data. These results establish the fact that in all the alkaline solutions studied FPP undergoes the same transformation reaction, and the same mechanism is operative. Furthermore, the method used previously for determining the initial yield of FPP′, G(FPP′), the observed initial yield of hydrogen peroxide, $G(H_2O_2)_{obs}$, and the initial yield of all the chain-initiating agents, G(R), formed by cobalt-60 γ-irradiation of aerated 0.1 *N* NaOH can also be used to determine these values in other alkaline solutions.

Values for G(FPP′) were calculated from the values of A determined here for the irradiation, postirradiation, and hydrogen peroxide reactions in buffered and unbuffered solutions at pH 7.7 to 14 by using equations 5, 12, and 15 of reference *2*. G(FPP′) from the thermal hydrogen peroxide reaction is only slightly dependent on pH and solution composition. G(FPP′) from the irradiation and postirradiation reactions is also only slightly dependent on solution composition, but markedly dependent on the pH in strongly alkaline solutions.

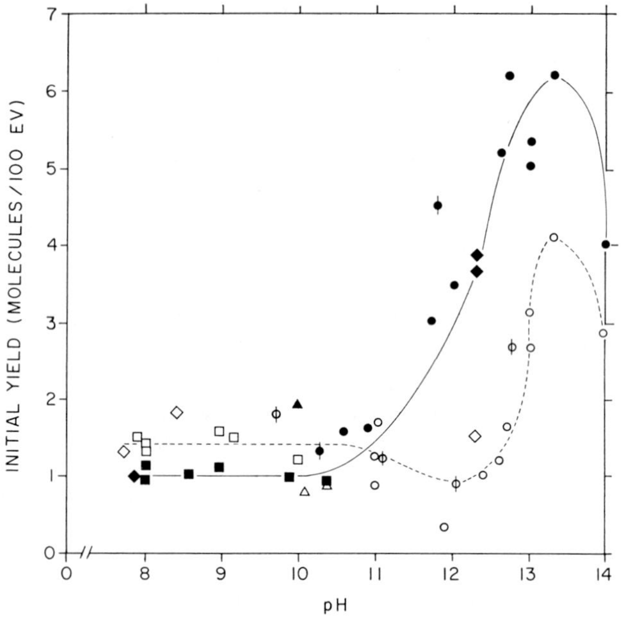

FIG. 1. Effect of pH and solution composition on the initial yields of hydrogen peroxide and chain-initiating agents. G(R),——: ● NaOH solutions, ◆ 0.05 M phosphate buffer, ■ 0.05 M borate buffer, ▲ 0.05 M carbonate–bicarbonate buffer, ⧫ 0.1 N NaOH diluted with 0.1 N H_2SO_4. $G(H_2O_2)$,– – –: ○ NaOH solutions, ◇ 0.05 M phosphate buffer, □ 0.05 M borate buffer, △ 0.05 M carbonate–bicarbonate buffer, ɸ NaOH–H_2SO_4 solutions.

Values for $G(H_2O_2)_{obs}$ and G(R) were calculated by comparing G(FPP′) values from the postirradiation and irradiation reactions respectively, with those from the hydrogen peroxide reaction under the same conditions of pH and solution composition. The results are shown in Fig. 1, where the pH is that of the solution irradiated. The smooth curves were constructed to best fit the experimental points. The significant features of the results are (1) the approximately constant values for G(R) and $G(H_2O_2)_{obs}$ equal to 1.03 and 1.5 molecules per 100 ev, respectively, for aerated alkaline solutions at pH <10.5, excluding carbonate–bicarbonate buffer, and (2) the rapid increase in G(R) above pH 10.5 and in $G(H_2O_2)_{obs}$ above pH 12.5 to maxima of 6.25 and 4.1, respectively, at approximately pH 13.3. The values for $G(H_2O_2)_{obs}$ in weakly alkaline solutions are in agreement with those of Allen and Holroyd (*5*) for aerated neutral solutions irradiated with cobalt-60 γ-rays. They reported a value of 1.23 molecules per 100 ev for preirradiated water but found that the values were larger when the water was not preirradiated, presumably owing to the reaction of OH radicals with a trace of organic impurities which are made unreactive by preirradiation of the water. Although a trace of impurities

TABLE I

EFFECT OF SODIUM HYDROXIDE CONCENTRATION ON THE OBSERVED INITIAL YIELD OF HYDROGEN PEROXIDE

Solution	*pH*	$[Na^+]$	$G(H_2O_2)_{obs}$
Phosphate buffer	8.4	0.047	1.8
$NaOH-H_2SO_4$	9.7	0.049	1.8
$NaOH-H_2SO_4$	11.1	0.050	1.3
$NaOH-H_2SO_4$	12.0	0.055	0.9
$NaOH-H_2SO_4$	12.4	0.057	1.0
NaOH	12.6	0.06	1.2
NaOH	12.7	0.08	1.65
$NaOH-H_2SO_4$	12.8	0.089	2.7
Phosphate buffer	7.7	0.095	1.35
NaOH	13.0	0.100	2.7
NaOH–10^{-3} *M* KBr	13.0	0.100	2.3
Phosphate buffer	12.3	0.15	1.5
NaOH	13.3	0.2	4.1

most likely contributes to the values reported here for $G(H_2O_2)_{obs}$ in aerated alkaline solutions, the rapid increase in these values in sodium hydroxide solutions above pH 12.5 cannot be accounted for entirely by possible impurities in the sodium hydroxide. As shown in Table I, concentrations of sodium hydroxide used to prepare some of the solutions of lower pH are comparable to those in the solutions at pH >12.5.

A comparison of the values for $G(R)$ and those for $G(H_2O_2)_{obs}$ in alkaline solutions at pH <10.5 indicates that when FPP is present during the irradiation it inhibits some reaction(s) which contribute to the observed peroxide yield. The smaller values for $G(R)$ are not an artifact introduced by destruction of the transformation product, FPP′, by cobalt-60 γ-irradiation, because the yield for that reaction is less than 0.3 molecule per 100 ev (M. L. Rothschild, unpublished data), whereas the yield for its formation under the conditions used here is of the order of 5 molecules per 100 ev.

The initial yield of hydrogen peroxide, $G(H_2O_2)$, has been determined for cobalt-60 γ-irradiation of aerated aqueous acid (*6*) and neutral (*5*) solutions and gives the values shown in equation 1, where $F + E$ is the yield of hydrogen peroxide

$$G(H_2O_2) = F + 2E \tag{1}$$

from the decomposition of water, and E is the yield of hydrogen peroxide from the reduction of dissolved oxygen by the H atoms formed from water decomposition in excess of OH radicals. Measurements of $G(H_2O_2)$ in aerated solutions are complicated by the reaction of OH radicals with the molecular hydrogen from water decomposition, which leads to additional hydrogen peroxide formation. To avoid this, Sworski (*6*) and Allen and Holroyd (*5*) irradiated acid and neutral bromide solutions. Bromide ions react with OH radicals to form bromine free radicals which do not react with molecular hydrogen but do react with atomic hydrogen.

The values presented here for G(R) in alkaline solutions at pH $<$10.5 are essentially equal to the value for $F + 2E$ in neutral solution based on Allen and Holroyd's value of $F + E = 0.71$ (see Allen, *1*, p. 46) and the value of Schwarz *et al.* (*7*) of $F = 0.45$ for solutions up to pH 11. It appears, therefore, that G(R) is a measure of $F + 2E$ in aerated alkaline solutions at pH $<$10.5, and that FPP inhibits the reaction of OH radicals with molecular hydrogen.

The differences in the values for $G(H_2O_2)_{obs}$ and G(R) in weakly alkaline solutions are only partially explained by the reaction of OH radicals with molecular hydrogen. Allen and Holroyd's data for hydrogen peroxide yields in neutral solutions in the presence and absence of bromide ions indicate that the peroxide yield from the reaction of OH radicals with molecular hydrogen is of the order of 0.26 molecule per 100 ev. Thus, FPP must also inhibit some other reaction of one of the radicals from water decomposition which leads to hydrogen peroxide formation. As was pointed out above, this might be the reaction of OH radicals with a trace of organic impurities.

A comparison of the values for G(R) and those for $G(H_2O_2)_{obs}$ in alkaline solutions at pH $>$10.5 indicates that at high pH some short-lived radiolysis product(s) is formed which augments the chain-initiation reaction of hydrogen peroxide. The idea of new radical species at high pH is not new. Hart and co-workers (*8, 9*) and Daniels and Weiss (*10*) proposed the formation of O^- and H_2O^-, in lieu of OH and H, respectively, to explain yield changes at higher pH of certain radiation-induced reactions. Presumably, these radical ions react differently from their counterparts, OH and H, at lower pH.

The simplest scheme which would explain $G(R) = F + 2E$, based on the generally accepted reactions for water decomposition,

$$H_2O = H + OH \qquad (R)$$

$$2H_2O = H_2 + H_2O_2 \qquad (F)$$

$$2H_2O = 2H + H_2O_2 \qquad (E)$$

and hydrogen peroxide formation from the radiolysis of aerated aqueous solutions,

$$H + O_2 = HO_2 \qquad (2)$$

$$2HO_2 = H_2O_2 + O_2 \qquad (3)$$

and the previously proposed reaction *2* for the formation of the chain center, C,

$$FPP_n + H_2O_2 = C + Z \qquad (4)$$

is one in which FPP reacts successively with OH and H (or HO_2),

$$FPP + OH = FPP\text{–}OH \quad (5)$$

$$FPP\text{–}OH + H \text{ (or } HO_2) = FPP + H_2O \quad (6)$$

resulting in their recombination and unchanged FPP. According to equations 5 and 6, FPP could inhibit all reactions of OH, but not those of H formed in excess of OH. To satisfy $G(R) = F + 2E$, the reaction product of unknown structure, FPP–OH, can be either associated with the chain-initiation reaction or unrelated to that reaction. However, if FPP–OH is associated with the chain-initiation reaction, this could explain why, based on evidence in the literature that H atoms react with CO_2 in aqueous solutions (*11–13*), $G(R)$ in carbonate–bicarbonate buffer at pH 10 is much larger than $F + 2E$ (see Fig. 1). This scheme, with equation 5 associated with the chain initiation, is also consistent with an increase in $G(R)$ at high pH, based on the pH dependence of OH and H. If, at very high pH, equation 5 is not reversed by equation 6, both radical, or radical ions, O^- and H_2O^- as well as hydrogen peroxide, would lead to chain initiation and thus a large increase in $G(R)$.

SUMMARY

The chain-transformation reaction of ferriprotoporphyrin, FPP, was used to determine the observed initial yield of hydrogen peroxide, $G(H_2O_2)_{obs}$, and the initial yield of total chain-initiating agents, $G(R)$, from cobalt-60 γ-irradiation of aerated alkaline solutions, pH 7.7 to 14, by comparing the initial yields of transformation product from the thermal hydrogen peroxide reaction with those from the postirradiation and irradiation reaction of FPP, respectively. The values for $G(H_2O_2)_{obs}$ and $G(R)$ were found to be approximately constant for alkaline solutions at pH <10.5, with averages of 1.5 and 1.03 molecules per 100 ev, respectively. The values for $G(R)$ above pH 10.5 and those for $G(H_2O_2)_{obs}$ above pH 12.5 were found to increase to maxima at pH 13.3, with values of 6.25 and 4.1, respectively. The values for $G(R)$ in alkaline solutions at pH <10.5 are essentially equal to the value for $F + 2E$ in neutral solution, where $F + E$ is the yield of hydrogen peroxide from water decomposition and E is the yield of hydrogen peroxide from the reduction of dissolved oxygen by the H atoms formed in excess of OH radicals. It is proposed that, in alkaline solutions at pH <10.5, FPP reacts successively with OH radicals and H atoms (or HO_2 radicals), resulting in their recombination and unchanged FPP. It is further proposed that, in alkaline solutions at pH >10.5, new radical species are formed from water decomposition, which presumably do not react in a reversible reaction with FPP, but rather augment the chain-transformation reaction.

RECEIVED: November 19, 1962

REFERENCES

1. A. O. ALLEN, *The Radiation Chemistry of Water and Aqueous Solutions,* D. Van Nostrand Company, New York, 1961.
2. M. L. ROTHSCHILD, Mechanism for the transformation of ferriprotoporphyrin by a cobalt-60 gamma-ray-initiated chain reaction. *Radiation Res.* **17,** 50–62 (1962).
3. W. C. PIERCE and E. L. HAENISCH, *Quantitative Analysis,* 2nd ed., p. 159, John Wiley & Sons, New York, 1940.
4. G. GOMORI, Preparation of buffers for use in enzyme studies. In *Methods in Enzymology* (S. P. Colowick and N. O. Kaplan, eds.), Vol. I, pp. 138–146, Academic Press, New York, 1955.
5. A. O. ALLEN and R. A. HOLROYD, Peroxide yield in the gamma-irradiation of air-saturated water. *J. Am. Chem. Soc.* **77,** 5852–5854 (1955).
6. T. J. SWORSKI, Yields of hydrogen peroxide in the decomposition of water by cobalt-60 gamma-radiation. I. Effect of bromide ion. *J. Am. Chem. Soc.* **76,** 4687–4692 (1954).
7. H. A. SCHWARZ, J. R. LOSEE, JR., and A. O. ALLEN, Hydrogen yields in the radiolysis of aqueous solutions. *J. Am. Chem. Soc.* **76,** 4693–4694 (1954).
8. E. J. HART, S. GORDON, and D. A. HUTCHISON, Free radical initiated $O^{16}O^{18}$-H_2O^{16} exchange reaction in aqueous solutions. *J. Am. Chem. Soc.* **75,** 6165–6169 (1953).
9. S. GORDON and E. J. HART, Gamma-ray induced deuterium gas-water exchange. *J. Am. Chem. Soc.* **77,** 3981 (1955).
10. M. DANIELS and J. WEISS, Chemical reactions of ionising radiations in solution: Part XXII. The radiation chemistry of arsenite solutions: the action of X-rays (200 kv) on aqueous solutions of arsenite. *J. Chem. Soc.* **1958,** 2467–2471.
11. W. M. GARRISON and G. K. ROLLEFSON, Radiation chemistry of aqueous solutions containing both ferrous ion and carbon dioxide. *Discussions Faraday Soc.* **12,** 155–161 (1952).
12. G. STEIN, Some aspects of the radiation chemistry of organic solutes. *Discussions Faraday Soc.* **12,** 227–233 (1952).
13. T. HASSELSTROM and M. C. HENRY, New synthesis for oxalic acid. *Science* **123,** 1038–1039 (1956).

Announcement

The University of Michigan will sponsor a symposium, "Radiation Biology—The Biological Effects of Ionizing Radiation," on July 8–10, 1963. Invited speakers include: P. Alexander, Chester Beatty Research Institute; E. P. Cronkite, Brookhaven National Laboratory; R. F. Kimball, Oak Ridge National Laboratory; and E. L. Powers and W. K. Sinclair, Argonne National Laboratory.

Inquiries may be addressed to C. J. Shellabarger, 7691 Kresge MRB, University of Michigan, Ann Arbor, Michigan.

RADIATION RESEARCH **19**, 409–418 (1963)

Extracorporeal Irradiation of Blood: Calculations of the Radiation Dose[1]

D. N. SLATKIN,[2] C. R. JANSEN,[3] E. P. CRONKITE, AND J. S. ROBERTSON

Medical Research Center, Brookhaven National Laboratory, Upton, New York

INTRODUCTION

The diversion of a portion of the blood flow through an extracorporeal shunt in an irradiation field would be helpful in the study of (1) radiation response of circulating elements in the peripheral blood; (2) radiation injury of circulating plasma proteins; (3) kinetics of blood cell production (particularly the lymphocyte family); (4) therapy of selected leukemias in animals and man; and (5) cardiac output and flow through selected organs by radioisotopic techniques.

A preceding paper demonstrated the induction of a lymphopenia by irradiation of the blood in an extracorporeal field (*1*). A second paper described a heparin lymphocytosis and its mechanism of production (*2*). The third paper of the series will describe the pumping technique in detail (*3*), and this paper considers the radiation dosimetry of partial extracorporeal circulation of blood through a radiation field.

EXPERIMENTAL DESIGN

Details of the experimental setup have been published (*1*, *3*). For orientation, a schematic diagram and photographs of the experimental setup are presented in Fig. 1.

The flow rate through the shunt is 300 ml/min. The transit time through the external circuit is about 3 minutes. The transit dose is about 900 r.

Definitions of Symbols

V = total blood volume within the animal, excluding the volume in the external circuit.

[1] Research supported by the U. S. Atomic Energy Commission.

[2] Present address: Montefiore Hospital, New York 67, New York.

[3] Research Collaborator from the South African Atomic Energy Board, Pretoria, South Africa.

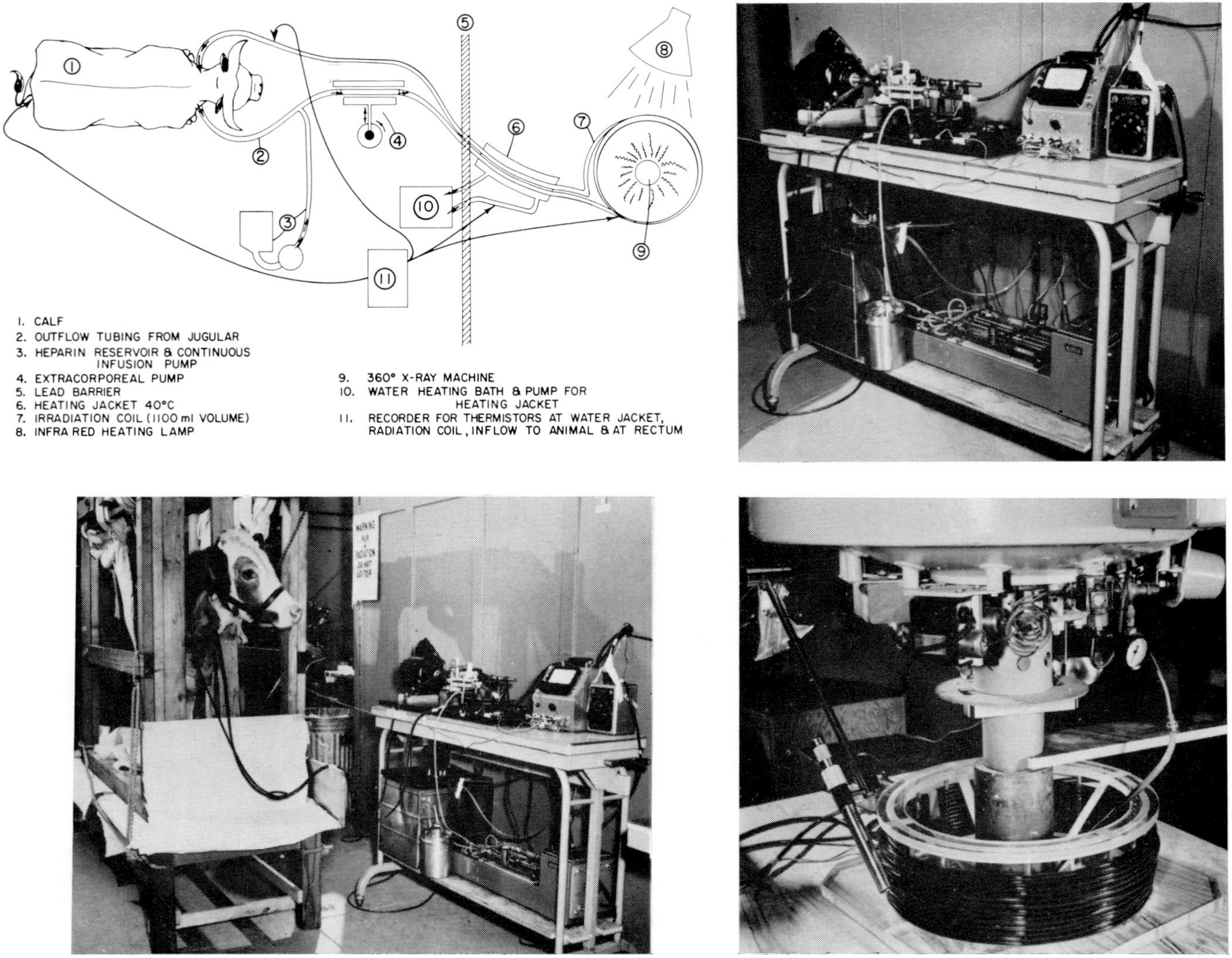

FIG. 1. *Upper left*, schematic diagram of extracorporeal irradiation. *Upper right*, pump, heparin injection water bath. *Lower left*, photograph of calf with blood being irradiated extracorporeally. *Lower right*, 360° X-ray generator and irradiation coil.

R = total cardiac output (volume per unit time).
r = flow rate through the external circuit (volume per unit time).
"n-cells" = cells that have traversed the external circuit n times.
N = the total number of cells per unit volume in the circulation.[4]
$F_n(t)$ = the fraction of cells in the animal at time t that have passed *through* the external circuit n times.

For convenience of mathematical analysis, the time unit taken is that interval of time required for a cell to traverse the external circuits and is denoted by the term "transit." If the flow rate through the external circuit is 300 ml/min and the interval of time to traverse the circuit is 3 minutes, then $r = 900$ ml per transit. It follows, moreover, that the volume of the external circuit is 900 ml. Therefore, r is numerically equal to the volume of the external circuit, provided that the "transit" is the unit of time.

CONSIDERATION I

In the initial consideration of the problem, the following one assumption is made: There is no longitudinal interchange of cells in the external circuit. This is equivalent to postulating that the cells leaving the external circuit at time t are the same that enter at time $(t - 1)$.

The following changes will occur in the small interval of time, Δt, after any time t:

(*a*) $F_n(t) \cdot N \cdot \Delta t \cdot r$: n-cells leave the animal's circulation and enter external circulation. Note that the flow rate is r units of volume per transit, and therefore in Δt transits the flow is $\Delta t \cdot r$ units of volume.

(*b*) $F_{n-1}(t - 1) \cdot N \cdot \Delta t \cdot r$: n-cells enter the animal's circulation from the external circulation. These cells leave the animal's circulation as $(n - 1)$-cells one transit before they re-enter as n-cells.

(*c*) The increase in the number of n-cells in the animal is $F_n(t + \Delta t) \cdot N \cdot V - F_n(t) \cdot N \cdot V$. Since the increment in (*c*) may be attributed to the effects of (*a*) and (*b*), we obtain

$$F_n(t + \Delta t) \cdot N \cdot V - F_n(t) \cdot N \cdot V = F_{n-1}(t - 1) \cdot N \cdot \Delta t \cdot r - F_n(t) \cdot N \cdot \Delta t \cdot r$$

or

$$\frac{F_n(t + \Delta t) - F_n(t)}{\Delta t} = \frac{r}{V} [F_{n-1}(t - 1) - F_n(t)] \tag{1}$$

In the limit, as Δt approaches 0, this becomes the differential equation

$$\frac{dF_n(t)}{dt} + \frac{r}{V} F_n(t) = \frac{r}{V} F_{n-1}(t - 1) \qquad n > 0 \qquad (2)^5$$

[4] It is assumed that N, the number of cells per unit volume, is constant with time and not significantly affected by the mixing of saline from the external circuit.

[5] It has been pointed out by C. W. Gilbert of the Christie Hospitals, Research Physics Department, Paterson Laboratories, Manchester, 20, England, that if N is assumed to

Experimentally the external circuit is filled with physiological saline, and both external circulation of blood and radiation are initiated simultaneously. It is mathematically convenient to adopt as time zero the instant of re-entry of the first irradiated cells into the animal. Under these circumstances the boundary conditions are the following:

$$F_0(0) = 1 \tag{3}$$

$$F_n(n - 1) = 0. \tag{4}$$

For $n = 0$ one may derive the special equation

$$\frac{dF_0(t)}{dt} + \frac{r}{V} F_0(t) = 0 \tag{5}$$

The solution of equation 5 is

$$F_0(t) = \exp\left(-\frac{r}{V}\cdot t\right) \tag{6}$$

The solution of equation 2 is

$$F_n(t) = \frac{r^n}{V^n}\cdot\frac{(t - n + 1)^n}{n!} \exp\left[\frac{r}{V}(n - t)\right] \qquad t \geq n - 1 \tag{7}$$

Equation 7 may be proved by induction as follows: It is of the form

$$\frac{dy}{dt} + P(t)y = Q(t) \tag{8}$$

The solution of this general form is given by

$$y \exp\left(\int P\, dt\right) = \int Q(t) \exp\left(\int P\, dt\right) dt + C \tag{9}$$

where C is a constant. In this particular case,

$$P(t) = \frac{r}{V} \tag{10}$$

$$Q(t) = \frac{r}{V} F_{n-1}(t - 1) \tag{11}$$

Hence the general solution (equation 7) becomes

---

change with time, then equation 2 holds not for $F_n(t)$ but for the function $N(t)\cdot F_n(t)$. If N_0 is the number of cells per unit volume before irradiation starts, i.e., at time -1 on the time scale chosen, then $N(t)\cdot F_n(t)/N_0$ is the chance that a cell has made n transits through the external circuit and is in the animal now.

$$F_n(t) \cdot \exp\left(\frac{rt}{V}\right) = \frac{r^n}{V^n} \cdot \frac{(t - n + 1)^n}{n!} \cdot \exp\left(\frac{r \cdot n}{V}\right) + C \tag{12}$$

But the boundary values are $F_n(n - 1) = 0$. Hence $C = 0$.

Since the solution (equation 7) is true for $n = 1$, it follows that it is true for all integral n. When $dF_n(t)/dt = 0$, $F_n(t)$ has its maximum value,

$$F_n(T_n) = \frac{n^n}{n!} \exp\left(\frac{r}{V} - n\right)$$

at time $T_n = (nV/r) + n - 1$. Moreover, $F_n(T_n)$ is greater than $F_m(T_n)$ for all $m \pm n$, a fact which may be proved as follows: Let p be any negative integer, the absolute value of which is smaller than n, or any positive integer. It suffices to prove that

$$F_{n+p}(T_n) < F_n(T_n)$$

From the general formula of equation 7,

$$F_{n+p}(T_n) = \left(\frac{r}{V}\right)^{n+p} \frac{(nV/r - p)^{n+p}}{(n + p)!} \exp\left(\frac{r}{V} - n + \frac{rp}{V}\right) \tag{13}$$

But

$$\frac{nV}{r} p = \left(\frac{V}{r}\right)\left(n - \frac{pr}{V}\right) \tag{14}$$

$$\therefore F_{n+p}(T_n) = \left[p^n \exp\left(\frac{r}{V} - n\right)\right]\left[\frac{n^p}{(n + p)!}\right]\left(1 - \frac{pr}{nV}\right)^{n+p} \cdot \exp\left(\frac{rp}{V}\right) \tag{15}$$

If p is a positive integer, then

$$F_{n+p}(T_n) = \left[\frac{n^n}{n!} \exp\left(\frac{r}{V} - n\right)\right]\left[\frac{n^p}{(n + 1)(n + 2) \cdots (n + p)}\right] \cdot \left[\left(1 - \frac{pr}{nV}\right)^{n+p} \cdot \exp\left(\frac{pr}{V}\right)\right] \tag{16}$$

But since

$$\lim_{n \to \infty} \left(1 + \frac{z}{n}\right)^n = \exp z$$

then

$$\left(1 - \frac{pr}{nV}\right)^{n+p} < \left(1 - \frac{pr}{nV}\right)^n < \exp\left(-\frac{pr}{V}\right) \tag{17}$$

$$\therefore F_{n+p}(T_n) < F_n(T_n)$$

If p is a negative integer with an absolute value smaller than n, then let $q = p$.

$$F_{n-q}(T_n) = \left[\frac{n^n}{n!} \exp\left(\frac{r}{V} - n\right)\right]\left[\frac{n\cdot(n-1)\cdots(n-q+1)}{n^q}\right]\cdot \left[\left(1+\frac{qr}{nV}\right)^{n-q}\cdot\exp\left(-\frac{qr}{V}\right)\right] \tag{18}$$

Similarly

$$\left(1+\frac{qr}{nV}\right)^{n-q} < \left(1+\frac{qr}{nV}\right)^{n} < \exp\left(\frac{qr}{V}\right) \tag{19}$$

$$\therefore F_{n-q}(T_n) < F_n(T_n)$$

CONSIDERATION II

If one does not assume instantaneous mixing in the animal, the mathematical approach becomes more complex. The work of Nylin and Celander (*4*) describes a method for the determination of the "general dilution curve," $D(t)$, for erythrocytes in the pulmonic portion of the circulation. By analogy, suppose that $D(t)$ represents the general dilution curve for cells in the total circulation, pulmonic and systemic. The circulation time distribution function, $F(t)$, can be derived from the experimentally determined curve $D(t)$ as follows: $F(t)\cdot\Delta t$ is the fraction of cells having circulation time between t and $(t + \Delta t)$. This is identical to the ratio of the number of cells passing the observation point on their first circuit between t and $(t + \Delta t)$ to the total number of cells passing the observation point on their first circuit. Mathematically, this is expressed by

$$F(t)\cdot\Delta t = \frac{D(t)\,\Delta t}{\int_{t=0}^{\infty} D(t)\,dt} \tag{20}$$

Thus $F(t)$ and $D(t)$ differ only by a factor that causes the area under the derived curve $F(t)$ to equal unity.

Let $I(t)$ be the circulation-time distribution function for cells that leave the right ventricle and return to it without traversing the external circuit. Let $J(t)$ be the analogous function for cells that traverse the external circuit. N represents cells per unit volume in right ventricle and in external circuit. $F_n(t)$ is the fraction of all cells in the right ventricle that are n-cells at time t. The total number of n-cells leaving the right ventricle per unit time at time t is $N\cdot R\cdot F_n(t)$. Of these, the number that started in the right ventricle between time $(t - P)$ and $t - (P + \Delta P)$ and did not pass through the external circuit is expressed as follows:

$$F_n(t-P)\cdot(R-r)\cdot N\cdot I(P)\,\Delta P \tag{21}$$

Similarly the number of these cells that started in the right ventricle between time $t - Q$ and $t - (Q + \Delta Q)$ and did pass through the external circuit is

$$F_{n-1}(t - Q) \cdot r \cdot N \cdot J(Q) \, \Delta Q \tag{22}$$

Therefore, by summation,

$$F_n(t) \cdot N \cdot R = \int_{P=0}^{\infty} F_n(t - P) \cdot (R - r) \cdot N \cdot I(P) \, dP + \int_{Q=1}^{\infty} F_{n-1}(t - Q) \cdot r \cdot N \cdot J(Q) \, dQ \tag{23}$$

For convenience, we substitute $Z = Q - 1$, whence

$$F_n(t) = \left(1 - \frac{r}{R}\right) \int_{P=0}^{\infty} F_n(t - P) I(P) \, dP + \frac{r}{R} \int_{Z=0}^{\infty} F_{n-1}(t - 1 - Z) J(Z + 1) \, dZ \tag{24}$$

This is an atypical integral equation for which an explicit solution is not available. An approximate solution, however, may be obtained as follows: The first-order Taylor approximations are

$$F_n(t - P) \simeq F_n(t) - P \cdot \frac{d}{dt} F_n(t) \tag{25}$$

$$F_{n-1}(t - 1 - Z) \simeq F_{n-1}(t - 1) - Z \frac{d}{dt} F_{n-1}(t - 1) \tag{26}$$

Substituting into equation 64, one obtains

$$\frac{d}{dt} F_n(t) + mF_n(t) = mF_{n-1}(t - 1) - mb \frac{d}{dt} [F_{n-1}(t - 1)] \qquad n > 1 \tag{27}$$

where

$$m = \frac{r}{i(R - r)} \tag{28}$$

$$b = \int_{Z=0}^{\infty} Z \cdot J(Z + 1) \, dZ \tag{29}$$

$$i = \int_{P=0}^{\infty} P \cdot I(P) \, dP \tag{30}$$

The exceptional equation is

$$\frac{d}{dt} F_0(t) + mF_0(t) = 0 \tag{31}$$

For simplification, the boundary values chosen are

$$F_0(0) = 5 \tag{32}$$

$$F_n(n) = 0 \tag{33}$$

The solution of equation 31 is

$$F_0(t) = \exp(-mt) \tag{34}$$

The general solution is

$$F_n(t) = \left[\frac{A^n(t-n)^n}{n!} - \frac{mbA^{n-1}(t-n)^{n-1}}{(n-2)!}\right] \exp\,[-m(t-n)] \tag{35}$$

where $A = m + m^2b$. The proof of the above by induction follows: Let $F_n(t) = G_n(S)$, where $S = (t - n)$. Substitution into the right-hand side of equation 27 leads directly to the expression

$$(JS^{n-1} - KS^{n-2} - LS^{n-3}) \exp\,(-mS) \tag{37}$$

where

$$J = \frac{A^n}{(n-1)!} \tag{38}$$

$$K = \frac{A^{n-1}}{(n-2)!} \cdot mb \cdot (n-1) \tag{39}$$

$$L = \frac{(n-2)m^2b^2A^{n-2}}{(n-3)!} \tag{40}$$

Using the Laplace transformation, one obtains

$$L(G_n) \cdot (X + m) = J\left[\frac{(n-1)!}{(X+m)^n}\right] - K\left[\frac{(n-2)!}{(X+m)^{n-1}}\right] - L\left[\frac{(n-3)!}{(X+m)^{n-2}}\right] \tag{41}$$

where X is the transformed variable. Note the Laplace transformation

$$L[S^n \exp\,(-mS)] = \frac{n!}{(X+m)^{n+1}}$$

Hence, from equation 41,

$$G_n(S) = \left(\frac{J}{n} \cdot S^n - \frac{K}{n-1} \cdot S^{n-1} - \frac{L}{n-2} S^{n-2}\right) \exp\,(-mS) \tag{43}$$

$$\therefore F_n(t) = \left[\frac{A^n}{n!}(t-n)^n - \frac{mbA^{n-1}(t-n)^{n-1}}{(n-2)!} - \frac{m^2b^2A^{n-2}}{(n-3)!}(t-n)^{n-2}\right] \exp\,[-m(t-n)] \tag{44}$$

The general formula (equation 35) is therefore valid in so far as the third-order term may be ignored.

DOSE CALCULATION

Equation 7 was used as the basis for programming an IBM-610 computer and the Brookhaven National Laboratory MERLIN computer to generate values of $F_n(t)$. Figure 2 shows the results of calculations when $r/V = 0.0643$. The radiation dose is related linearly to the n value for a group of cells and is indicated on the upper abscissa scale. It is apparent from the graph that about thirty transit times are required to ensure that 50% of the cells have received over 1000 rads, whereas one hundred transit times are needed to ensure that 98% have received 1000 rads. In the latter case some portions of the blood will have received over 10,000 rads.

USEFULNESS OF EXTRACORPOREAL IRRADIATION OF THE BLOOD

In order to interpret the induction of lymphopenia and decreased output of cells in the cannulated thoracic duct during extracorporeal irradiation of the blood, it

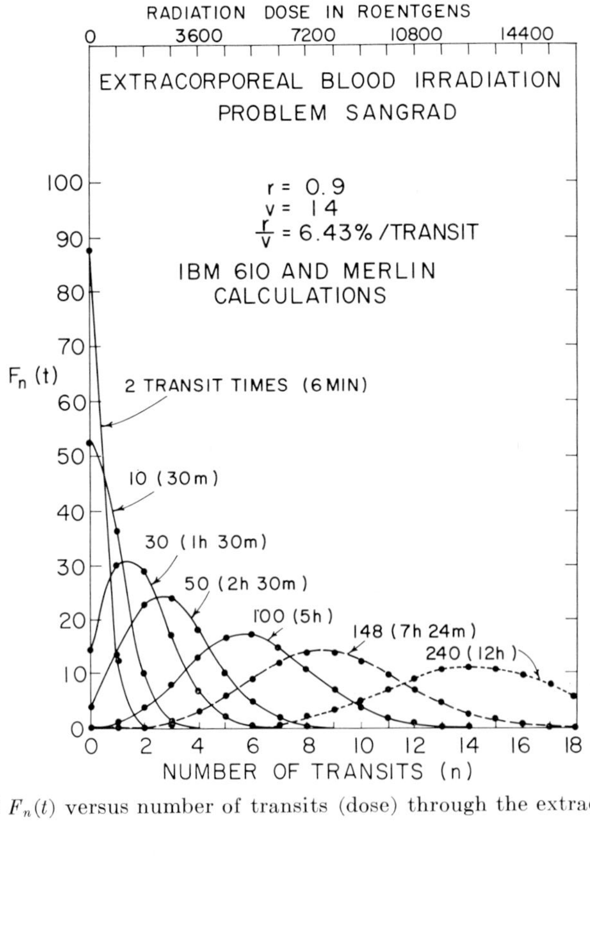

FIG. 2. Graph of $F_n(t)$ versus number of transits (dose) through the extracorporeal shunt.

became necessary to know how long after commencement of irradiation the dose to all cells that remain in the circulation would exceed a minimal lethal dose for lymphocytes. It is quite evident that, after 2 hours of pumping with any r/V ratio that may occur biologically (within limits of variation in blood volume), the vast majority of lymphocytes remaining within the blood stream will have received in excess of a supralethal dose. The dose computations in conjunction with other biologic observations on injury to lymphocytes have made available another potent procedure for the study of kinetics of lymphocyte production, size of lymphocyte mass, etc. (*5*). In addition, other circulating cell types can be studied in respect to radiation injury, kinetics, and control of production. The procedure contributes further techniques for the study of radiation injury and cell proliferation.

SUMMARY

1. Mathematical formulas have been developed and are described which approximate the varying radiation dose delivered to various fractions of blood during continuous extracorporeal irradiation for any time after commencement of the procedure.

2. The fraction of the blood which is irradiated n times in each of several total number of traversals was calculated with a digital computer, and a graph of the results with corresponding radiation doses is presented.

3. This system is analogous to a liquid being pumped through a radiation field from a continuously mixing reservoir and back to the reservoir.

ACKNOWLEDGMENT

We are indebted to Mr. Allen Ashare who programmed the calculation of equation 7 for the MERLIN computer.

RECEIVED: June 27, 1962

REFERENCES

1. E. P. CRONKITE, C. R. JANSEN, G. MATHER, N. NIELSEN, E. A. USENIK, E. R. ADAMIK, and C. R. SIPE, Studies on lymphocytes. I. Lymphopenia induced by prolonged extracorporeal irradiation of the blood. *Blood* **20**, 203–213 (1962).

2. C. R. JANSEN, E. P. CRONKITE, G. MATHER, O. N. NIELSEN, K. RAI, E. R. ADAMIK, and C. R. SIPE, Studies on lymphocytes. II. The production of lymphocytosis by intravenous heparin in calves. *Blood* **20**, 443–452 (1962).

3. E. R. ADAMIK, E. P. CRONKITE, and C. R. JANSEN, The design of a simple non-traumatic pump for extracorporeal circulation. In preparation.

4. GUSTAV NYLIN and HJÖRDIS CELANDER, Determination of blood volume in the heart and lungs and the cardiac output through the injection of radio phosphorus. *Circulation* I, 76–83 (1950).

5. E. P. CRONKITE, C. R. JANSEN, K. RAI, H. COTTIER, and T. M. FLIEDNER. The combined application of lymph duct drainage and extracorporeal irradiation of the blood in the study of lymphopoiesis. Guinnes Symposium on Cell Proliferation, Trinity College, Dublin, Ireland, Aug. 14–15, 1962.

RADIATION RESEARCH **19,** 419–428 (1963)

Influence of X-Irradiation on Zinc-65 Uptake of Testes in Mice[1]

MIKIO SHIKITA AND BUN-ICHI TAMAOKI

National Institute of Radiological Sciences, Chiba-shi, Japan

INTRODUCTION

Testicular zinc metabolism has been shown to be regulated under the control of the pituitary gland (*1*). Hypophysectomy depresses radiozinc uptake of testes, and interstitial cell-stimulating hormone (ICSH) prevents the fall after hypophysectomy. Furthermore, it has been demonstrated that dietary zinc deficiency causes atrophy of testes (*2*) and that administration of cadmium in a sublethal dose has an acute destructive effect specifically on testes, which can be prevented by the simultaneous administration of zinc (*3, 4*). Gunn and Anderson (*5*) reported selective interference of cadmium with radiozinc uptake by only testes and dorsolateral prostate, suggesting that zinc complexes formed in these organs differ from those in other organs. Therefore, zinc seems to have a particular role in the physiological function of testes.

It is well established that the testis is one of the most radiosensitive organs in the body, testicular spermatogenesis being extremely radiosensitive. The production of androgens by interstitial cells, on the other hand, is radioresistant (*6*). It is of interest, therefore, to observe if there would be any change in radiozinc uptake on X-irradiated testes.

EXPERIMENTAL PROCEDURE

Animals. Male black mice of C57-BL strain were employed. Four or five animals were housed in a cage and fed on commercial mouse pellets (Funabashi Farm). At 10:00 A.M. on the day of injection, food was removed. Water was given *ad libitum* throughout the experiment.

X-Irradiation. All irradiations were made with an X-ray generator operating at 200 kvp and 20 ma with added filtration of 0.5 mm copper and 0.5 mm aluminum. The irradiation was always carried out between 10:00 and 12:00 A.M. For whole-body irradiation, 3 or 6 animals were put into a sectioned plastic cage and irradiated

[1] This work was in part supported by Grant (RH-14) of the Division of Radiological Health, Bureau of State Services, U.S. Public Health Service.

at a time at a dose rate of 80 r/min in air. For localized irradiation, the animals were fixed on a wooden board without anesthesia, and head and forelegs or scrotum and hind legs were irradiated, while the other part of the body was shielded with lead plate of 5 mm in thickness. Dose rate was 250 r/min in air, and FSD was 30 cm. Under these conditions, the effective field of the irradiation was 12 cm in diameter, and the shielded area received less than 5 r/min, i.e., less than 2% of the irradiation dose.

Injection of Zinc-65. Zinc-65 was purchased from Oak Ridge National Laboratory as zinc-65 chloride in HCl solution (specific activity, 1511 mc/gm) and diluted with 0.9% NaCl solution to a concentration of 10 or 20 μc per 0.2 ml. All the animals were injected with 0.2 ml of the solution per individual, subcutaneously, between 5:00 and 6:00 P.M. of the same day.

Sacrifice and Autopsy. Between 11:00 and 12:00 A.M. on the following day, i.e., 18 hours after the injection of radiozinc, the animals were sacrificed by a blow on the head. Organs were removed immediately after death, dissected free from surrounding tissues, blotted on paper, weighed with a torsion balance, placed in glass test tubes, and radioassayed. Thereafter, the organs were dried at 110°C in an electric furnace overnight and then left in a $CaCl_2$ desiccator until constant weight was obtained.

Radioassay of Zinc-65. Zinc-65 was determined in a well-type scintillation detector with a medical spectrometer. The radioactivity of the organs is expressed as per cent of the dose injected per unit of wet weight of the organs.

RESULTS

Whole-Body X-Irradiation

Twelve mice, aged 50 days, were used in experiment 1-1. Half of them received a single whole-body X-irradiation dose of 400 r. All the animals were injected with Zn^{65} and killed 24 or 25 hours after the irradiation. A similar experiment was repeated with 6 mice 120 days old (experiment 1-2). Results of the radioassay are shown in Table I. Testicular radiozinc uptake in the irradiated groups was 84.9% (experiment 1-1) and 74.8% (experiment 1-2) of that in their respective controls. These differences are statistically significant at the 1% and 5% level, respectively. Spleen decreased in weight by 53.2% and 41.4%, respectively. Splenic radiozinc uptake, however, increased by 18% in the case of 50-day-old mice and decreased only by 3% in 120-day-old mice. As to other organs examined, no consistent effects of the irradiation was observed. In experiment 1-1, mean dry weight of testes in the irradiated animals and controls was 15.2% and 15.4% of their wet weight. The values for the spleen were 23.2% and 22.7%, respectively. In any case, the decrease in testicular zinc uptake observed in these experiments was statistically significant in terms of either per cent injected Zn^{65} per wet weight or per cent injected Zn^{65} per dry weight.

TABLE I

EFFECT OF WHOLE-BODY X-IRRADIATION ON RADIOZINC METABOLISM IN MICE

Experiment 1-1 (Nov. 8–9, 1961)	*X-Irradiated*		*Controls*	
Age of animals	50 days		50 days	
Number of animals	6		6	
Body weight on day of injection of Zn^{65}	21.8 ± 6.8 gm		22.1 ± 7.3 gm	
	Wet weight mg	*Zn^{65} uptake*[a]	*Wet weight mg*	*Zn^{65} uptake*[a]
Organs examined				
Testes	159 ± 5[b]	1.24 ± 0.03[b]	148 ± 10[b]	1.46 ± 0.04[b]
Seminal vesicle	102 ± 15	2.40 ± 0.44	105 ± 16	2.19 ± 0.50
Spleen	43 ± 5	8.35 ± 0.50	91 ± 9	7.06 ± 0.60
Kidney	137 ± 12	8.49 ± 0.61	144 ± 12	7.74 ± 0.89
Experiment 1-2 (Oct. 6-7, 1961)	*X-Irradiated*		*Controls*	
Age of animals	120 days		120 days	
Number of animals	3		3	
Body weight on day of injection of Zn^{65}	25.3 ± 3.3 gm		26.3 ± 3.3 gm	
	Wet weight mg	*Zn^{65} uptake*[a]	*Wet weight mg*	*Zn^{65} uptake*[a]
Organs examined				
Testes	206 ± 7[b]	0.750 ± 0.039[b]	198 ± 9[b]	1.00 ± 0.05[b]
Seminal vesicle	239 ± 10	0.892 ± 0.054	299 ± 25	1.00 ± 0.05
Spleen	41 ± 3	4.62 ± 0.38	70 ± 6	4.76 ± 0.21
Kidney	315 ± 20	5.70 ± 0.37	333 ± 16	5.55 ± 0.10
Submaxillary gland	139 ± 14	4.41 ± 0.33	158 ± 3	4.55 ± 0.05

[a] Radiozinc in the organs is expressed as per cent injected Zn^{65} per gram wet weight of the organs.

[b] Mean ± standard error.

Local Irradiation to Head or Scrotum

In experiment 2-1, 12 mice 80 days old were divided into three groups of 4 animals each. The first group was X-irradiated locally to the head and forelegs, the second to scrotum and hind legs, and the third served as controls. Total dose of the irradiation was 1000 r. All the animals were injected with radiozinc and sacrificed between 24 and 25 hours postirradiation. Similar experiments were done with mice 110 and 300 days old (experiments 2-2 and 2-3). Table II shows the results of radioassay. Consistent with the results of experiments 1-1 and 1-2, there was a significant decrease in testicular zinc uptake in the animals locally X-irradiated to scrotum. The difference compared to respective controls was statistically significant when the uptake was expressed as per cent of injected Zn^{65} per gram of either wet or dry weight of the testes. In the animals locally irradiated to the head, a similar but less pronounced decrease in testicular zinc uptake was observed. Finally, as to the radiozinc uptake in testes, the results of the experiments of this series were statistically analyzed and are shown in Table III. The term Treatment represents the effect of the X-irradiation, which was found highly significant against the error term due to the variation within group. Further analysis showed that all the differences among the three different treatments are significant, indicating that zinc concentration in locally irradiated testes was significantly low in comparison to that in the controls as well as to that in the head-irradiated group, and that the effect of local irradiation to the head was also significant against the control group. The term Experiment includes the variation caused by the difference both in the age of the animals and in the date of the experiment. This value was also found to be highly significant. The confounding of the age and the date, however, is not resolvable in this case.

Late Effect of X-Irradiation

In experiment 3, 5 mice 90-days-old were X-irradiated (1000 γ) to the head, 5 to the scrotum, and 5 reserved as controls. Eighteen days later, all were injected with radiozinc and sacrificed 18 hours thereafter. As shown in Table IV, the local irradiation to the scrotum markedly decreased testicular weight with damage to seminiferous tubules, but did not significantly change the radiozinc uptake in terms of radioactivity per unit weight of the testes. The irradiation to the scrotum or head had no effect either on the weight or radiozinc uptake of seminal vesicle and spleen.

DISCUSSION

In the experiments reported here, radioactive zinc of high specific activity was used. Thus, the animals received 7 to 14 μg of zinc per individual by the injection of Zn^{65}. Total zinc content of the body of the animals was not measured in our experiment. According to Vallee (7), however, most of the vertebrate organs contain between 20 and 30 μg of zinc per gram of wet tissue. Liver, bone, and voluntary muscle contain about double this amount. Presumably, the animals used in out experiment contained 500 to 1000 μg of zinc per individual in the whole body. Therefore, it seems that the amount of zinc introduced by the injection was about 2% of the zinc pooled in the body. However, most of the zinc is fixed in the body cells, and the zinc concentration in blood serum is very low (7). Here it is to be recalled that the animals were starved in our experiment. From this point of view, it can be assumed that the amount of zinc injected in our experiment was ten or

TABLE II

EFFECT OF LOCAL X-IRRADIATION ON RADIOZINC UPTAKE OF TESTES, SEMINAL VESICLE, AND SPLEEN

Local X-irradiation to:	*Age of animals (days)*	*Body weight (gm) on day of Zn injection*	*Testes*		*Seminal vesicle*		*Spleen*	
			Wet weight (mg)	*Zn^{65} uptake*[a]	*Wet weight (mg)*	*Zn^{65} uptake*[a]	*Wet weight (mg)*	*Zn^{65} uptake*[a]
Experiment 2-1[b]								
Head	80	23.1 ± 0.9[c]	168 ± 9[c]	1.18 ± 0.10[c]	112 ± 23[c]	1.63 ± 0.25[c]	57.1 ± 2.5[c]	5.77 ± 0.87[c]
Testes	80	23.7 ± 0.6	174 ± 5	1.09 ± 0.04	121 ± 8	1.82 ± 0.29	58.8 ± 8.0	7.44 ± 0.22
Control	80	23.4 ± 1.4	173 ± 5	1.44 ± 0.07	118 ± 8	1.91 ± 0.31	57.0 ± 10.4	7.66 ± 0.48
Experiment 2-2[b]								
Head	110	27.9 ± 0.7	190 ± 10	0.913 ± 0.026	198 ± 11	2.33 ± 0.28	56.5 ± 2.6	5.49 ± 0.09
Testes	110	27.9 ± 0.8	183 ± 23	0.761 ± 0.012	188 ± 12	2.08 ± 0.18	64.5 ± 0.4	5.08 ± 0.31
Control	110	27.2 ± 0.6	201 ± 11	1.029 ± 0.052	188 ± 4	1.81 ± 0.12	80.9 ± 10.1	5.25 ± 0.19
Experiment 2-3[b]								
Head	300	30.1 ± 0.4	194 ± 7	0.846 ± 0.027	388 ± 7	0.887 ± 0.050	56.0 ± 5.1	4.49 ± 0.10
Testes	300	30.2 ± 0.6	167 ± 8	0.744 ± 0.025	372 ± 21	0.963 ± 0.102	52.8 ± 1.4	4.96 ± 0.27
Control	300	30.3 ± 1.0	204 ± 30	0.909 ± 0.029	372 ± 19	0.977 ± 0.078	71.5 ± 14.9	4.79 ± 0.26

[a] Radiozinc in the organs is expressed as per cent injected Zn^{65} per gram wet weight of the organs.

[b] Experiment 2-1 was done on July 10–11 in 1962; experiment 2-2 on Dec. 14–15, 1961; and experiment 2-3 on Dec. 20–21, 1961. All groups consisted of 4 mice.

[c] Mean ± standard error.

TABLE III

ANALYSIS OF VARIANCE FOR THE RADIOZINC UPTAKE OF TESTES[a]

Factors	*Sum of squares*	*Degree of freedom*	*Variance*	*Variance ratio*	P[b]
Experiment (Age of animals and date of experiment)	11250	2	5625	57.4	<0.1%
Treatment (X-irradiation)	4128	2	2064	21.1	<0.1%
Interaction of the above	550	4	138	1.4	Nonsignificant
Error	2648	27	98		
Total	18576	35			

[a] The original data are shown in the fifth column of Table II.

[b] Cf. F^2_{27} (0.001) = 9.02; F^2_{27} (0.01) = 5.49; F^2_{27} (0.05) = 3.35; F^4_{27} (0.05) = 2.73.

TABLE IV

RADIOZINC UPTAKE OF TESTES AND SPLEEN 18 TO 19 DAYS AFTER LOCAL IRRADIATION[a]

Local X-irradiation to:	*Body weight (gm)*		*Testes*			*Spleen*		
	Before irradiation	*19 days later*	*Wet weight (mg)*	*Dry weight / Wet weight (%)*	*Zn^{65} Uptake*[b]	*Wet weight (mg)*	*Dry weight / Wet weight (%)*	*Zn^{65} uptake*[b]
	Mean ± standard error							
Head	22.7±1.0	24.8±1.0	151± 9	16.7±0.1	1.17±0.07	81.8± 9.7	26.6±0.4	8.25±0.42
Testes	23.1±0.8	24.5±0.8	48± 1	17.1±0.4	1.25±0.10	98.0±13.4	23.9±1.2	8.45±0.30
Control	23.9±1.5	26.3±1.1	169±13	16.2±0.1	1.23±0.04	89.6± 4.5	25.4±0.2	8.30±0.50

[a] This experiment was done from Feb. 19 to March 10, 1962.

[b] Radiozinc in the organs is expressed as per cent of injected Zn^{65} per gram wet weight of the organs.

twenty times as high as that contained in the blood serum. Therefore, it is suggested that the specific activity of the radiozinc injected was not altered much before it was incorporated into the body organs. Eighteen hours after the injection, Zn^{65} retained by the testes was about 1% of the amount injected per gram of wet tissue. It means that about 0.1 μg of the zinc per gram in the testes was replaced during 18 hours. This calculation is applicable particularly to testes, where Zn^{65}, once incorporated, remains very long (*8, 9*), but it is not applicable to such organs as liver and kidney, where rapid incorporation of Zn^{65} is followed by its rapid departure (*8, 10*). As it was reported that about 30 μg of zinc per gram was present in the testes (*7*), the net quantity of zinc uptake during the period of 18 hours was very small in comparison to the total zinc content in testes, even when one considers the dilution of Zn^{65} by native body zinc before its incorporation into testes.

X-Irradiation, even when localized to the scrotum, resulted in a decreased uptake of Zn^{65} by the testes in our experiment. The results are summarized in a graph and shown in Fig. 1. It seems that the effect was due neither to the decrease in the rate of the diffusion of Zn^{65} from the site of the injection nor to the decrease in the specific activity of Zn^{65} in the blood serum, because the effect was specific on the testes, and no comparable decrease was observed in Zn^{65} uptake by other organs. Matsui *et al.* (*11*) studied the effects of whole-body X-irradiation on the metabolism of Zn^{65} in the mice of CFW strain. In their experiment, the animals were irradiated with 900 r and injected with Zn^{65} subcutaneously. At 3, 6, 12, and 24 hours later, no change was observed in testicular Zn^{65} concentration, in disagreement with our experimental results. Gunn *et al.* (*12, 13*) emphasized the importance of seasonal rhythms to endocrine experimentation in rats. They showed that the capacity of the dorsolateral prostate to concentrate Zn^{65} was much greater in two peak periods than during other periods of the year and that lowering of Zn^{65} uptake of the prostate after irradiation with microwaves occurred only during high phases of the cycle (*14*). It is possible that in the experiment of Matsui *et al.* the mice were in the period of low testicular activity, although it is not clear that there is a similar seasonal variation in testicular zinc metabolism in mice.

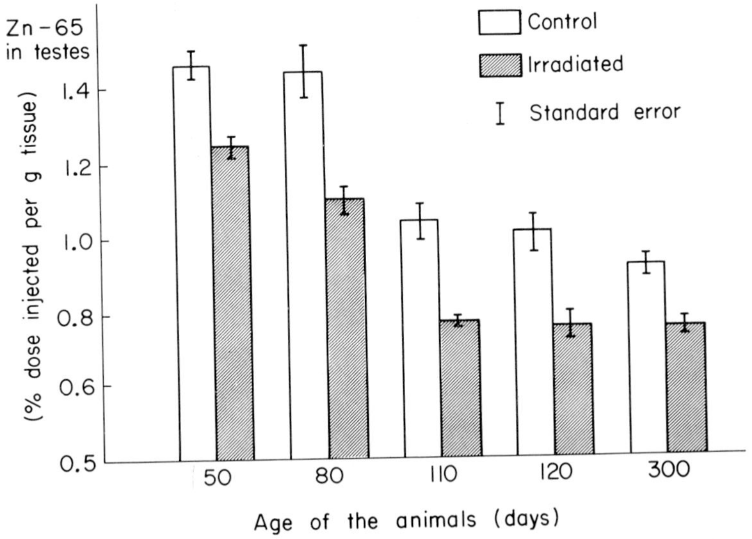

FIG. 1. Effect of X-irradiation on testicular zinc-65 uptake. The animals, 50 and 120 days old, received 400 r of whole-body X-irradiation; those of other ages received 1000 r of localized X-irradiation to the scrotum.

The decrease in radiozinc uptake of the X-irradiated testes observed in the present experiment seems to be mainly due to a direct effect of the irradiation on the testes. Some decrease in testicular zinc uptake was also observed in the animals irradiated to the head. The possibility exists that the testes received some irradiation significant to testicular function, although they were shielded with lead. However, in experiment 2-1 there was a significant decrease in testicular zinc uptake of head-irradiated mice, although there was no decrease in their splenic weight. This observation suggests that there might be an influence of X-irradiation on the rate of secretion of gonadotropin from pituitary glands, as reported by Gunn *et al.* (*15*). It was reported by Rudzik and Riedel (*16*), however, that incorporation of Zn^{65} into testes decreased after adrenalectomy in rats. Therefore, the possibility cannot be excluded that the observed decrease in testicular zinc uptake was mediated through the effect on the adrenals.

Wetterdal (*9*) demonstrated that Zn^{65} taken up by testes was localized mainly in the seminiferous tubules. Furthermore, it has been established that zinc concentration is high in spermatozoa (*17*). In this regard, it is of interest that no change was observed in zinc concentration in testes on the nineteenth day after irradiation. At this time in the experiment, most of the germinal cells in the testes were not present. The unchanged zinc concentration in the damaged testes seems to be unexplicable, if only the germinal cells concentrate zinc. Parizek (*3, 4*) suggested that production of androgen was decreased by cadmium salts, and Gunn *et al.* (*5*) illustrated this. Therefore, it seems probable that zinc has an effect not only on spermatogenesis but also on the function of interstitial cells. It is believed widely that the biogenesis of androgens is performed in the interstitial cells. The processes require the participation of several kinds of dehydrogenases which have been known to be activated by the zinc ion (*18*). It is possible that the decrease in testicular zinc uptake observed here is due to a change in the affinity of interstitial cells to zinc rather than a change in that of germinal cells. Anyway, this could be regarded as one of the very early changes after irradiation, detected by biochemical means.

SUMMARY

1. Twenty-four hours after a single whole-body X-irradiation (400 r), a significant decrease was observed in Zn^{65} uptake of testes in mice. The decrease was statistically significant in terms of percentages of the injected Zn^{65} per unit weight of either wet or dried tissue. Splenic weight decreased approximately by half, but radiozinc concentration in spleen remained unchanged or slightly increased. Radiozinc uptake of seminal vesicles, kidneys, and submaxillary glands was not influenced by the irradiation.

2. Similar depressant effects of X-irradiation on the testicular Zn^{65} uptake was observed after a single local irradiation to scrotum and hind legs (1000 r). Localized irradiation to head and forelegs had less influence on testicular zinc uptake. The

fact suggests that the effect was mainly due to a direct effect of the irradiation on the testes.

3. Nineteen days after the localized irradiation to scrotum and hind legs (1000 r), the weight of the testes decreased markedly. Radiozinc uptake of the damaged testes, however, did not differ from that of the testes in control animals when compared in terms of radioactivity per unit weight of wet or dry organ.

4. The possibility is discussed that the decrease in testicular zinc uptake observed 24 hours after X-irradiation is due to a change in the affinity of the interstitial cells to zinc rather than a change in that of germinal cells in the testes.

ACKNOWLEDGMENTS

Thanks are due to Mr. R. Arai and Miss H. Kakizaki who helped us during the course of the experiment.

RECEIVED: July 23, 1962

REFERENCES

1. S. A. GUNN, T. C. GOULD, and W. A. D. ANDERSON, Hormonal control of zinc in mature rat testis. *J. Endocrinol.* **23,** 37–45 (1961).
2. M. J. MILLAR, M. I. FISCHER, P. V. ELCOATE, and C. A. MAWSON, The effects of dietary zinc deficiency on the reproductive system of male rats. *Can. J. Biochem. Physiol.* **36,** 557–569 (1958).
3. J. PARIZEK, Effect of cadmium salts on testicular tissue. *Nature* **177,** 1036–1037 (1956).
4. J. PARIZEK, The destructive effect of cadmium ion on testicular tissues and its prevension by zinc. *J. Endocrinol.* **15,** 56–63 (1957).
5. S. A. GUNN and W. A. D. ANDERSON, Competition of cadmium for zinc in rat testis and dorsolateral prostate. *Acta Endocrinol.* **37,** 24–30 (1961).
6. C. R. ABBOTT, The effect of X-irradiation on the secretory capacity of the testis. *J. Endocrinol.* **19,** 33–43 (1959).
7. B. L. VALLEE, Biochemistry, physiology and pathology of zinc. *Physiol. Rev.* **39,** 443–490 (1959).
8. J. C. N. WAKELEY, B. MOFFATT, A. CROOK, and J. R. MALLARD, The distribution and radiation dosimetry of zinc-65 in the rat. *Intern. J. Appl. Radiation Isotopes* **7,** 225–232 (1960).
9. B. WETTERDAL, Experimental studies on radioactive zinc in the male reproductive organs of the rat. *Acta Radiol. Suppl.* **156,** 1–83 (1958).
10. G. E. SHELINE, I. L. CHAIKOFF, H. B. JONES, and M. L. MONTGOMERY, Studies on the metabolism of zinc with the aid of its radioactive isotope. II. The distribution of administered radioactive zinc in the tissues of mice and dogs. *J. Biol. Chem.* **149,** 139–151 (1943).
11. K. MATSUI, K. KOMETANI, and K. YAENO, Effect of X-irradiation on zinc-65 metabolism in mice. *Radiation Res.* **15,** 798–809 (1961).
12. S. A. GUNN and T. C. GOULD, Influence of archaic reproduction cycle on sensitivity response of rat dorsolateral prostate to sex hormones. *Proc. Soc. Exptl. Biol. Med.* **100,** 651–653 (1959).
13. S. A. GUNN, T. C. GOULD, and W. A. D. ANDERSON, Seasonal variations in endocrine response to cryptorchidism. *Acta Endocrinol.* **37,** 589–596 (1961).

14. S. A. Gunn and T. C. Gould, The effect of an archaic reproductive cycle on endocrine experimentation in the male laboratory rat. *Acta Endocrinol. Suppl.* **51,** 523 (1960).
15. S. A. Gunn, T. C. Gould, and W. A. D. Anderson, The effect of X-irradiation on the morphology and function of the rat testis. *Am. J. Pathol.* **37,** 203–209 (1960).
16. A. D. Rudzik and B. E. Riedel, The effect of adrenalectomy and cortisone on zinc metabolism in the sex glands and adrenal of the male rat. *Can. J. Biochem. Physiol.* **38,** 845–851 (1960).
17. D. Birnbaumm, T. Hall, and R. Lee, The zinc content of rat sperm cells from ejaculate, vas, epididymis and testis. *Proc. Soc. Exptl. Biol. Med.* **108,** 321–324 (1961).
18. L. T. Samuels, Metabolism of steroid hormones. In *Metabolic Pathways* (D. M. Greenberg, ed.), Vol. I, Chapter 11, Academic Press, New York, 1960.

RADIATION RESEARCH 19, 429–438 (1963)

Effect of Some Metabolites and Antimetabolites on the Breakdown of Deoxyribonucleic Acid and on the Colony-Forming Ability of *Escherichia coli* B after Gamma Irradiation

I. Effect of Citrate, Glutamate, Succinate, Versene and Magnesium Ions

M. DRAKULIĆ AND E. KOS

Department of Radiobiology, Institute "Ruđer Bošković," and Department of Chemistry, Faculty of Agriculture, The University, Zagreb, Yugoslavia

INTRODUCTION

One of the immediate biochemical effects observed in microorganisms after irradiation by X-rays is the breakdown of a part of the intracellular deoxyribonucleic acid (DNA) (*1, 2*). This breakdown is prolonged and more extensive if the irradiated bacteria are incubated in the presence of chloramphenicol (*3*) or under starvation conditions (*1*).

Stuy observed (*1*) that the X-ray-induced breakdown of DNA could be inhibited by a high concentration of citrate. He considered the possibility that the effect of citrate on the DNA breakdown might be related to the inhibition of intracellular deoxyribonuclease (DNase) by this compound. However, he was unable to demonstrate the leakage of this enzyme from the irradiated cells after the breakdown of DNA ceased. Our own efforts to demonstrate the activation of the intracellular (alkaline) DNase in *Escherichia coli* B immediately after irradiation and 15 minutes later were also unsuccessful (*4*).

Although we by no means excluded the possibility that other enzymes involved in the catabolism of DNA were activated by ionizing radiations, we discussed the possibility that an eventual damage to the DNA replication mechanism might be the cause of the observed effect (*4*). In the light of this hypothesis we postulated also that the effect of citrate observed by Stuy (*1*) could be a consequence of some events related to the metabolic role of citrate in the tricarboxylic acid cycle. Therefore, we tested the effects of other metabolites related to this metabolic cycle (succinate and glutamate) on the breakdown of DNA.

The effects of these metabolites were tested by Heinmets and Kathan in ultraviolet-irradiated *E. coli* B/r (*5*).

Both citric and succinic acid have certain structural features which could enable them (especially in the high concentrations used in some of our experiments) to affect the ionic equilibrium in the cells by binding bivalent cations. Therefore their effect was compared with that of the well-known chelating agent Versene (EDTA) and that of magnesium ion which is an activator of DNase.

Further, we verified whether the "stabilization" of DNA by some of the substances we used had any influence on the colony-forming ability of the irradiated cells.

Some results related to this work but obtained with X-rays have been published in the form of a preliminary report (*6*).

MATERIALS AND METHODS

Escherichia coli B was maintained by monthly transfer on agar slants. In each experiment a part of a culture of *E. coli* B grown overnight in a mineral medium (containing $(NH_4)_2 \cdot SO_4$, 1.00 gm; K_2HPO_4, 10.50 gm; KH_2PO_4, 4.5 gm; $Na_3C_6H_5O_7 + 5\frac{1}{2}\ H_2O$, 0.5 gm; 1 ml of a 10% solution of $MgSO_4 \cdot 7H_2O$ and glucose, 4% per 1.000 ml, pH 7.00) was transferred to fresh medium to an optical density of 0.045, as measured with a Unicam S.P. photocolorimeter (red filter). The suspension was incubated with aeration at 37°C until it reached an absorbancy of about 0.200. The cells were harvested by centrifugation in the cold, washed with physiological saline (pH 7.00), and resuspended in acetate buffer (pH 7.00), according to the treatment described by Stuy (*1*).

One half of the suspension was irradiated with a total dose of 16,000 r of γ-rays from a 340-mc Co^{60} source at a dose rate of approximately 1333 r/min, the other half being kept as a control.

Immediately after irradiation, samples for the determination of the DNA content and of the colony-forming ability were taken from both suspensions. The rest was incubated at 37°C with aeration in acetate buffer alone, or with the addition of one of the substances indicated in Figs. 1 to 6. Samples for the determination of DNA and of viability were taken after 30, 60, and 90 minutes of incubation.

Chemical fractionation and the determination of DNA were performed according to the method of Burton (*7*).

The figures represent the mean values obtained from the results of at least three experiments.

For the determination of viability, the cells were plated after a suitable dilution of the suspensions on two series of petri dishes containing Oxo-agar (7.5 gm of agar + 6.5 gm of Nutrient Broth in 500 ml of H_2O) or MA-agar (100 ml of the mineral medium indicated above + 7.5 gm of agar + 400 ml of H_2O). The visible

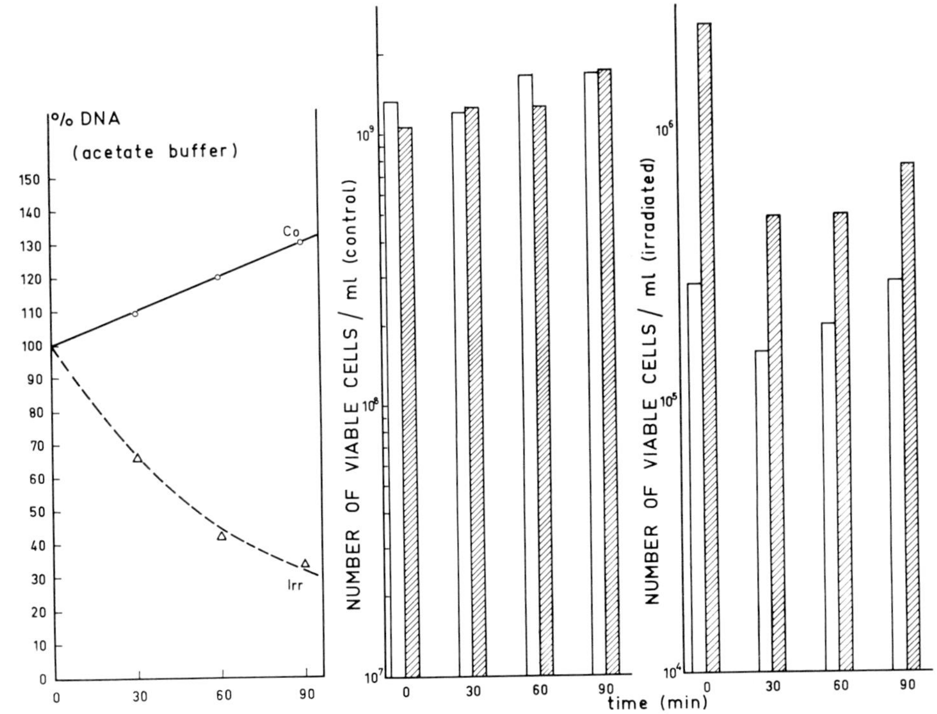

FIG. 1. Percentage of DNA after 30, 60, and 90 minutes of incubation after irradiation in the control (Co) and irradiated (Irr) cultures, as compared to the content at 0 minute (taken as 100%). Incubation in unsupplemented acetate buffer. Number of viable cells per milliliter is indicated in both cultures after plating on Oxo-agar (white columns) and MA-agar (striped columns).

colonies were counted after incubation for 18 to 20 hours at 37°C. The number of viable cells as shown in Figs. 1 to 6 are mean values of the results of at least six independent series of plating.

RESULTS

As seen on Fig. 1, a slow but measurable synthesis of DNA takes place in the unirradiated cells incubated in unsupplemented acetate buffer. Indeed, *E. coli* B is known to be able to utilize acetate as a source of carbon (*8*). These starved cells have not lost the ability to form colonies.

In the irradiated cells incubated under the same conditions, a very extensive breakdown of DNA takes place. More than 80% of the irradiated cells, capable of forming colonies immediately after irradiation, lose this ability after only 30 minutes of incubation in acetate buffer, if they are plated on Oxo-agar.

In unirradiated cells incubated in acetate buffer with 0.5 *M* citrate added, no

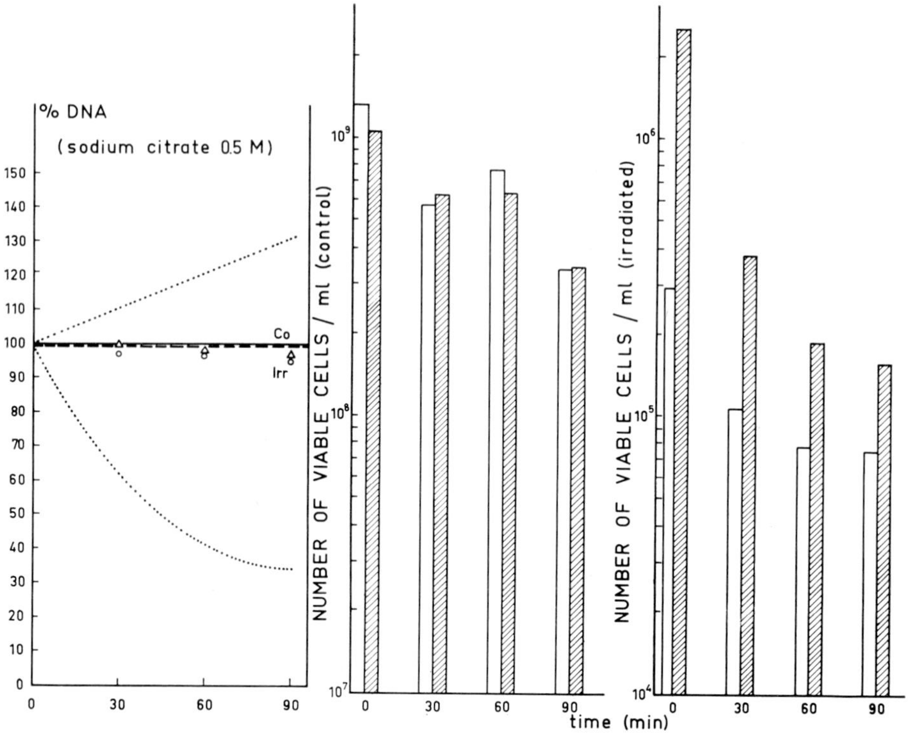

FIG. 2. Percentage of DNA and number of viable cells as indicated on Fig. 1, but after incubation in acetate buffer, with 0.5 *M* sodium citrate added. Dotted lines represent the biosynthetic and the degradative process in acetate buffer, as shown on Fig. 1.

measurable synthesis of DNA takes place (Fig. 2). No measurable breakdown of these macromolecules can be detected in the irradiated suspension under these conditions.

The number of the control cells which give visible colonies diminishes during incubation in this high concentration of citrate, after plating either on Oxo-agar or on MA-agar. As for the survival of the irradiated cells, the lethal effect of this high concentration of citrate is evident, especially after plating on MA-agar (Fig. 2).

As seen in Fig. 3, in unirradiated cells incubated in acetate buffer with added 0.5 *M* succinate, the synthesis of DNA is almost entirely suppressed; the breakdown of DNA in the irradiated cells is also nearly completely inhibited. Both the irradiated and the unirradiated cells incubated in the presence of this high concentration of succinate are unable to form visible colonies.

In the presence of lower concentrations of succinate (10^{-3} *M*), the extremely slow synthesis of DNA in the control is accompanied by an equally slow breakdown

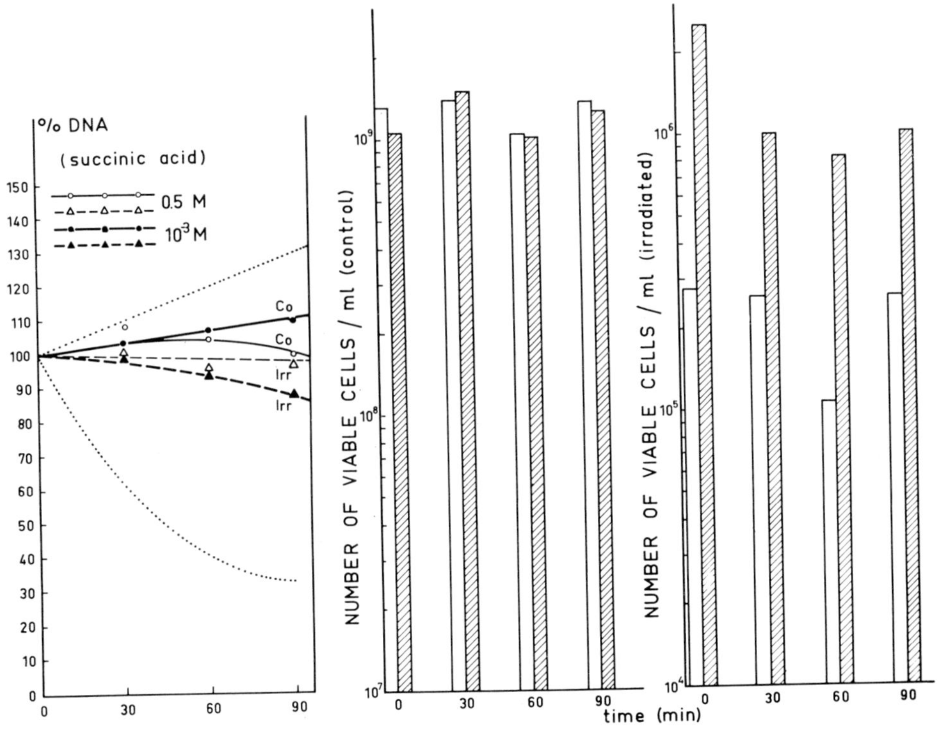

FIG. 3. Percentage of DNA as indicated on Fig. 1, but after incubation in acetate buffer, supplemented with 0.5 M succinic acid (– ○ – ○ – for the control and – –△– –△– – for the irradiated) and 10^{-3} M succinic acid (– ● – ● – for the control and – –▲– –▲– – for the irradiated). The number of viable cells is shown only for the cultures incubated in the presence of 10^{-3} M succinic acid (white columns for plating on Oxo-agar, and striped columns for plating on MA-agar), because those incubated in the presence of 0.5 M succinic acid do not form visible colonies at 30 minutes, nor later.

of DNA in the irradiated suspension (Fig. 3). This concentration of succinate does not affect the colony-forming ability of the unirradiated cells, nor that of the irradiated cells, by comparison with the situation in acetate buffer alone.

The unirradiated bacteria incubated in buffer supplemented with 0.05 M glutamate (Fig. 4) behave very similarly to those incubated in the presence of 0.5 M succinate, as far as the synthesis of DNA is concerned. The situation in the irradiated cells is in this case identical with that in the control. As the incubation of unirradiated cells proceeds, their viability progressively diminishes, after plating both on Oxo-agar and on MA-agar. The colony-forming ability of the irradiated cells decreases quickly; after only 30 minutes of incubation it is completely suppressed after plating on Oxo-agar.

With a lower concentration of glutamate (10^{-3} M), the increase in the DNA

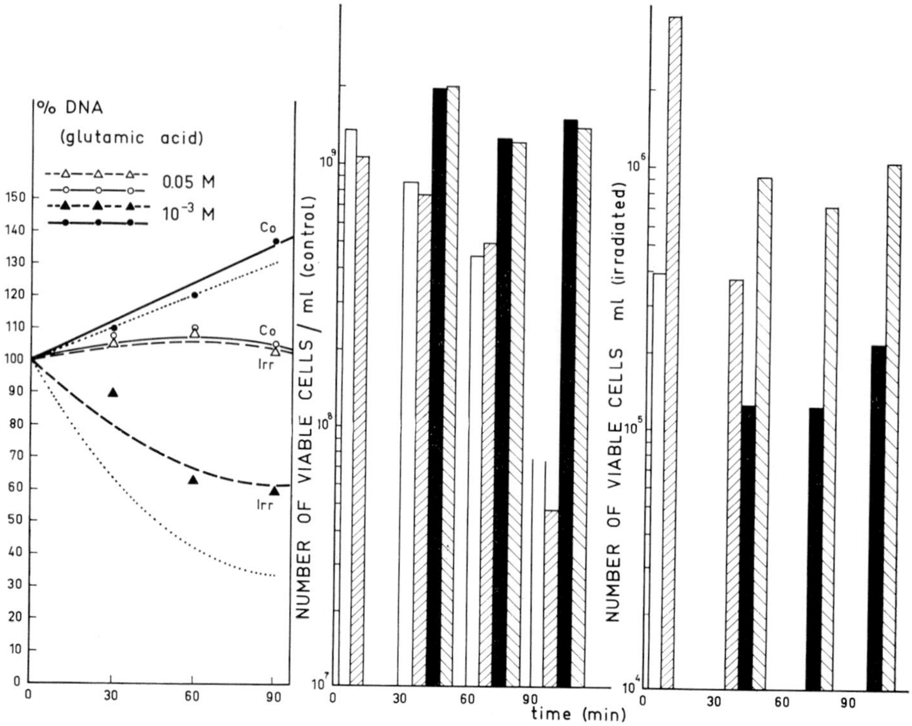

FIG. 4. Percentage of DNA as indicated in Fig. 1. Incubation in acetate buffer, supplemented with 0.05 *M* glutamic acid (–○–○– for the control and ––△––△–– for the irradiated) and 10^{-3} *M* glutamic acid (–●–●– for the control and ––▲––▲–– for the irradiated). Number of viable cells represented for cultures incubated in the presence of 0.05 *M* glutamic acid (*a*, white columns, after plating on Oxo-agar; *b*, striped columns, after plating on MA-agar) and 10^{-3} *M* glutamic acid (*c*, black columns, after plating on Oxo-agar; *d*, columns striped in direction contrary to columns *b*, after plating on MA-agar). The number of irradiated cells capable of colony forming is below 10^4/ml after only 30 minutes of incubation in the presence of 0.05 *M* glutamic acid, after plating on Oxo-agar and is therefore not represented on this figure. During further incubation in this high concentration of glutamic acid, the irradiated cells give no visible colonies at all.

content of the unirradiated cells is accompanied by the breakdown of a similar amount of DNA in the irradiated cells.

During incubation in the presence of 10^{-3} *M* glutamate, the number of viable cells is unaffected in the unirradiated culture but diminishes in the irradiated one in approximately the same way as in acetate buffer alone.

The effect of 10^{-3} *M* Versene (ethylenediaminetetraacetic acid, EDTA) on the content of DNA in both the unirradiated and the irradiated culture (Fig. 5) is

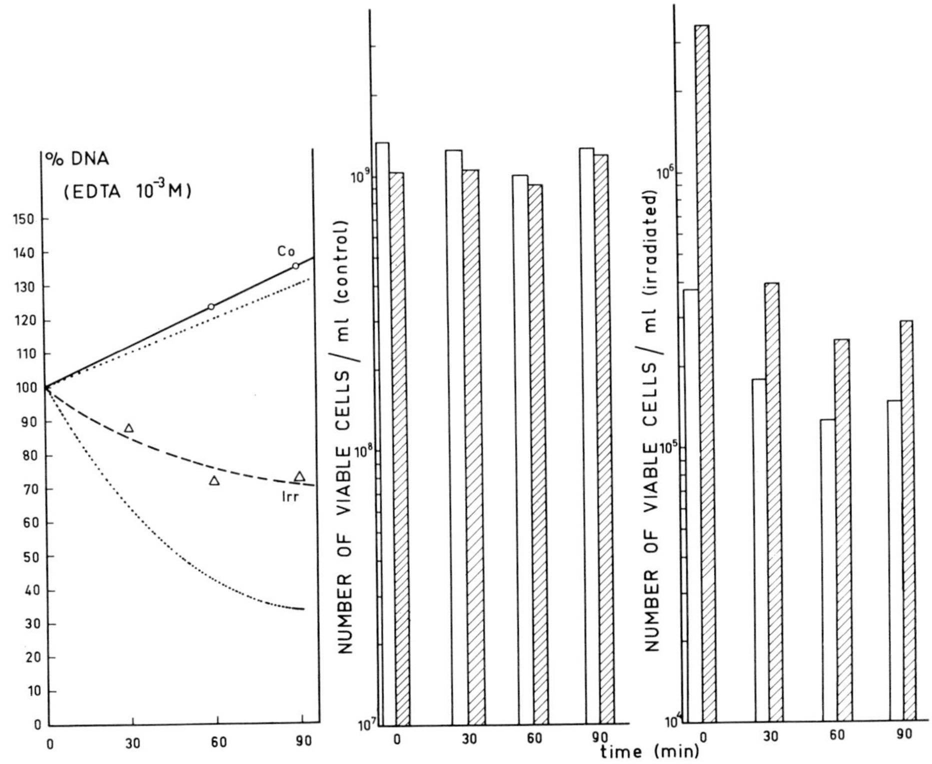

FIG. 5. Percentage of DNA and number of viable cells as indicated on Fig. 1, but after incubation in acetate buffer, supplemented by 10^{-3} *M* EDTA.

similar to that of glutamate used in the same concentration. The colony-forming ability of the control is unaffected. The number of the viable cells in the irradiated suspension diminishes, however, slightly more than in acetate buffer alone.

We tested also the effect of a higher concentration of Versene (10^{-2} *M*). As this concentration causes an extensive lysis of both the irradiated and unirradiated cells, these results will not be described here. According to this observation, Versene seems to enter the cells of *E. coli* B.

The addition of $MgSO_4$ (4×10^{-3} *M*) to cultures incubated in acetate buffer has no effect on the synthesis of DNA in the unirradiated cells, nor on its breakdown in the irradiated bacteria, both of which are going on as in acetate buffer alone (Fig. 6).

The number of viable cells in the unirradiated suspension increases slightly. The addition of Mg^{++} ions has a decidedly beneficial effect on the colony-forming

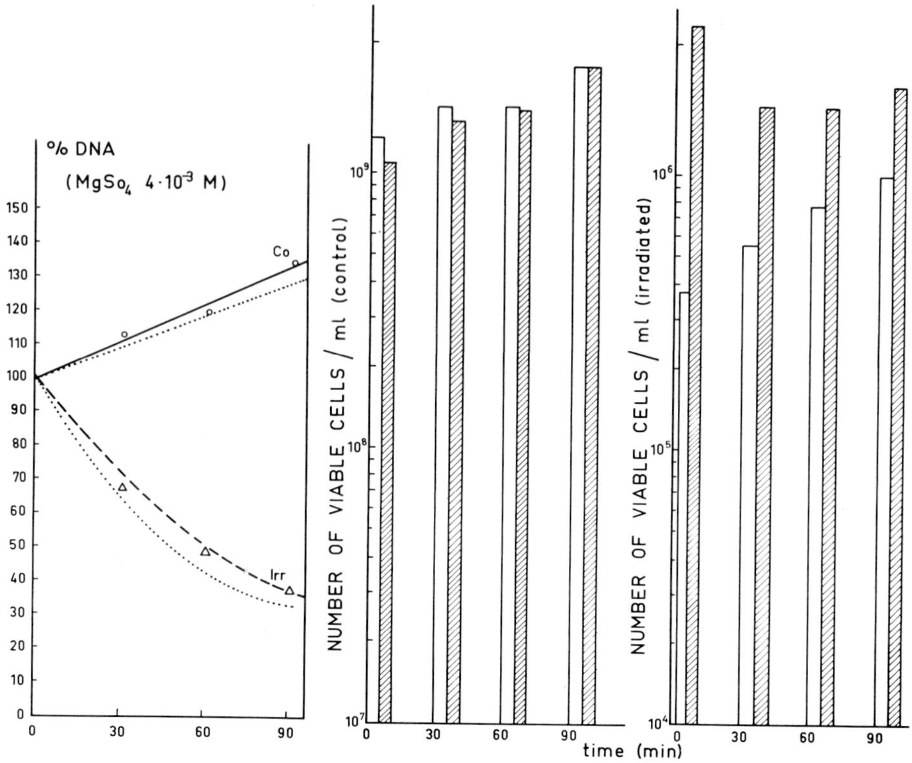

FIG. 6. Percentage of DNA and number of viable cells as in Fig. 1, but after incubation in acetate buffer supplemented by 4×10^{-3} *M* $MgSO_4$.

ability of the irradiated cells plated on Oxo-agar (Fig. 6). The viability of the irradiated bacteria remains approximately on the same level if they are plated on MA-agar.

This is the only case in which we observed a favorable effect on the survival of the irradiated cells in spite of the starvation conditions. It must, however, be stressed that the breakdown of DNA is very extensive in this case.

DISCUSSION

From the results described above, the following facts might be concluded:

1. No correlation has been found between the "stabilization" of DNA by the substances tested in this work and the colony-forming ability of the irradiated cells. This negative results do not, however, permit any conclusion concerning the role of the breakdown of DNA in the lethal effect of γ-irradiation, because the

chemical composition, physical-chemical properties, and biological functionality of the "stabilized" DNA were not studied.

2. A quasi-complete inhibition of the breakdown of DNA in the irradiated cells is observed only under conditions which prevent the increase of the DNA content in the unirradiated cells. This is the case in the presence of citrate (0.5 *M*), succinate (0.5 *M*), and glutamate (0.05 *M*). One could postulate that the high concentrations of these metabolites produce some kind of metabolic block (due, for instance, to an extensive feedback) which prevents some biochemical activities in the cells.

3. In all cases where breakdown of DNA is observed in the irradiated cells, a small but net synthesis of DNA takes place in the controls. The cells presumably utilize for the biosynthesis of DNA precursors from their intracellular pool, or possibly material from a small number of lysed bacteria. It is interesting to note that the amount of DNA broken down in the irradiated cultures at the end of the 90-minute incubation period was either identical to the amount synthesized in the correspondingly treated unirradiated cells (succinate 10^{-3} *M*, glutamate 10^{-3} *M*, Versene 10^{-3} *M*) or approximately double (acetate buffer alone or with added $MgSO_4$, 4×10^{-3} *M*).

These results point to the fact that a breakdown of DNA in the irradiated cells is going on only if some metabolic functions occur which make possible the synthesis of DNA in the unirradiated cells.

Our results do not enable us to draw any conclusion concerning the quantitative relationships existing between the amount of DNA broken down in the irradiated culture in the presence of a given metabolite and the amount of DNA synthesized in the identically treated unirradiated culture. We are also unable to answer the question whether the inhibition of the DNA breakdown, brought about by the substances tested, is a consequence of their action as chelating agents.

In the continuation of this work we tried to verify whether similar relations between the biosynthesis of DNA in the controls and its breakdown in the irradiated cultures could be observed by using a different series of metabolites.

SUMMARY

The effect of a series of metabolites related to the tricarboxylic acid cycle, also of the chelating agent EDTA, and of Mg^{++} ions, on the γ-irradiation-induced breakdown of DNA and viability of *E. coli* B was studied.

High concentrations of citrate, succinate, and glutamate added to acetate buffer in which the cells have been incubated after irradiation inhibit both the biosynthesis of DNA in the controls and its breakdown in the irradiated cells. These substances have, however, a rather unfavorable action on the colony-forming ability of both the unirradiated and irradiated bacteria, causing their decrease, or even complete suppression.

Lower concentrations of succinate and glutamate (10^{-3} M), and the same concentration of EDTA, only partially inhibit the breakdown of DNA in the irradiated cells.

The possible meanings of the above results are discussed.

ACKNOWLEDGMENTS

Our thanks are due to Mr. F. Starček for his unfailing technical assistance.

RECEIVED: July 30, 1962

REFERENCES

1. J. H. STUY, Studies on the radiation inactivation of microorganisms. VII. Nature of the X-ray-induced break-down of deoxyribonucleic acid in *Hemophilus influenzae*. *Radiation Res.* **14,** 56–65 (1961).
2. B. MILETIĆ, Ž. KUĆAN, and LJ. ZAJEC, Synthesis of DNA in X-irradiated *Escherichia coli* B. *Biochem. Biophys. Res. Commun.* **4,** 343–347 (1961).
3. B. MILETIĆ, Ž. KUĆAN, M. DRAKULIĆ, and LJ. ZAJEC, Effect of chloramphenicol on the biosynthesis of DNA in X-irradiated *Escherichia coli* B. *Biochem. Biophys. Res. Commun.* **4,** 348–352 (1961).
4. E. KOS and M. DRAKULIĆ, On the activity of intracellular DNase of *Escherichia coli* B after X-irradiation. *Biochem. Biophys. Res. Commun.* **5,** 152–155 (1961).
5. F. HEINMETS and R. H. KATHAN, Preliminary studies on the mechanism of biological action of ultraviolet irradiation and metabolic recovery phenomenon. *Arch. Biochem. Biophys.* **58,** 205–215 (1954).
6. E. KOS and M. DRAKULIĆ, Inhibition of deoxyribonucleic acid breakdown in X-irradiated *Escherichia coli* by various compounds. *Biochim. Biophys. Acta* **55,** 248–249 (1962).
7. K. BURTON, A study of the conditions and mechanism of the diphenylamine reaction for the colorimetric estimation of deoxyribonucleic acid. *Biochim. J.* **62,** 315–323 (1956).
8. RICHARD B. ROBERTS, PHILIP H. ABELSON, DEAN S. COWLIE, ELLIS T. BOLTON, and ROY J. BRITTEN, Studies of biosynthesis in *Escherichia coli*. *Carnegie Inst. Wash. Publ.* **607** (1955).

RADIATION RESEARCH **19**, 439–446 (1963)

Effect of Some Metabolites and Antimetabolites on the Breakdown of Deoxyribonucleic Acid and on the Colony-Forming Ability of *Escherichia coli* B after Gamma Irradiation

II. Effect of Phosphorylated Derivatives of Adenosine and Pyrophosphate

E. KOS AND M. DRAKULIĆ

Department of Radiobiology, Institute "Ruđer Bošković," and Department of Chemistry, Faculty of Agriculture, The University, Zagreb, Yugoslavia

INTRODUCTION

In the preceding paper (*1*) it was demonstrated that the γ-ray-induced breakdown of deoxyribonucleic acid (DNA) in *Escherichia coli* B can be completely inhibited by the addition of high concentrations of citrate or of succinic or glutamic acid to the bacteria, incubated after irradiation in acetate buffer. A partial inhibition of the DNA breakdown can be attained by lower concentrations of the above metabolites, as well as by the chelating agent Versene (EDTA). The breakdown of DNA which takes place in acetate buffer alone or in buffer supplemented with 4×10^{-3} *M* $MgSO_4$ is very extensive.

No correlation was found between the DNA content and the viability of the irradiated cells.

Most of the compounds tested in the previous work have some structural features which endow them with the characteristics of chelating agents.

In the present paper a series of experiments similar to those performed previously (*1*) will be described. The substances used in this work to influence DNA breakdown in irradiated cells are metabolically related (although rather remotely) to those used in the previous work but have no structural similarities with them. The compounds used were the mono-, di-, and triphosphorylated derivatives of adenosine, and inorganic pyrophosphate.

It is known that the phosphorylated derivatives of adenosine, besides their role in the energetics of living cells, play also an important part as precursors and building blocks of nucleic acids.

We used inorganic pyrophosphate not only for comparison of its effect with that of its adenosyl derivatives but also in view of its possible role in eventual pyrophosphorolysis of DNA in cases where the synthesis of DNA by Kornberg's enzyme is limited or abortive (*2*).

MATERIALS AND METHODS

Maintenance and cultivation of *E. coli* B, irradiation of the suspensions by 16,000 r of γ-rays, and their incubation before and after irradiation were performed exactly as described earlier (*1*). The compounds, indicated in Figs. 1 to 5, were added to the acetate buffer immediately after irradiation.

We used adenosine-3′-monophosphate (AMP-3′) and adenosine-5′-monophosphate (AMP-5′) from Fluka, A.G. Chemische Fabrik, Buchs/S.G., Switzerland. Both adenosine-5′-diphosphate (ADP in the form of sodium salt) and adenosine-5′-triphosphate (ATP in the form of disodium salt) were products of the Sigma Chemical Company. The sodium pyrophosphate ($P - P_i$) was a p.a. product ("Kemika," Zagreb).

Chemical fractionation of the bacteria, the determination of DNA, and the viability of the cells were performed by the methods described earlier (*1*).

RESULTS

As seen in Figs. 1 and 2, both monophosphorylated derivatives of adenosine have somewhat similar effects on the biosynthesis of DNA, in both the unirradiated and the irradiated cultures. After an extremely slow synthesis during the first 30 minutes after irradiation in both the control and irradiated suspensions, the unirradiated cells continue to synthesize DNA slowly, but the DNA in the irradiated cells is broken down at a very low rate.

Neither of the monophosphates has any effect on the survival of the unirradiated cells, but both cause a drop in the number of colony-forming cells in the irradiated cultures during half an hour after irradiation (more than is the case in acetate buffer alone, especially after plating on Oxo-agar; see reference *1*). After this period the number of AMP-3′-treated irradiated cells which are able to form colonies diminishes further, especially after plating on MA-agar. The number of viable cells in the AMP-5′-treated irradiated culture remain about the same, after the initial drop, on both MA-agar and Oxo-agar.

In the presence of ADP (Fig. 3), which is used in a lower concentration than the monophosphorylated derivatives, the synthesis of DNA in the unirradiated cells is accompanied by the breakdown of the same amount of DNA in the irradiated suspension.

This substance has no effect on the viability of the unirradiated bacteria but causes an initial drop in the colony-forming ability of the irradiated cells (again more than was observed in acetate buffer alone; see reference *1*).

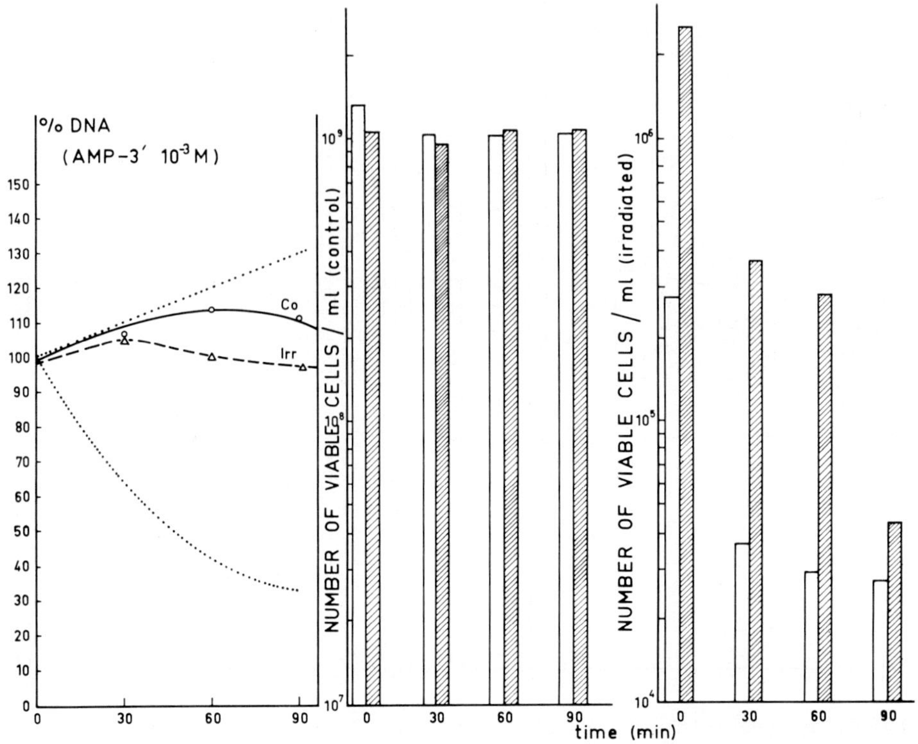

FIG. 1. Percentage of DNA 30, 60, and 90 minutes after irradiation, as compared to the content at 0 minute (taken as 100%) in the control (Co) and irradiated (Irr) culture. Incubation in acetate buffer supplemented with 10^{-3} *M* AMP-3′. Dotted lines represent the biosynthesis and the breakdown of DNA in cultures, incubated in unsupplemented acetate buffer (*1*). Number of viable cells in both cultures is indicated after plating on Oxo-agar (white columns) and MA-agar (striped columns).

As seen in Fig. 4, in the presence of ATP there is neither biosynthesis of DNA in the unirradiated bacteria, nor breakdown of DNA in the irradiated ones.

There is also no change in the colony-forming ability of the unirradiated cells during this experiment. The viability of the irradiated cells diminishes initially after plating both on MA-agar and on Oxo-agar. Furthermore, there is only a slight decrease in the viability on Oxo-agar, but none at all on MA-agar.

The synthesis of DNA in the control culture in the presence of inorganic pyrophosphate (Fig. 5) proceeds at a slightly higher rate than in the acetate buffer alone. Its breakdown in the irradiated cells is also somewhat accelerated.

The number of the colony-forming cells in the unirradiated suspension remains constant during the experiment. The viability of the irradiated cells diminishes,

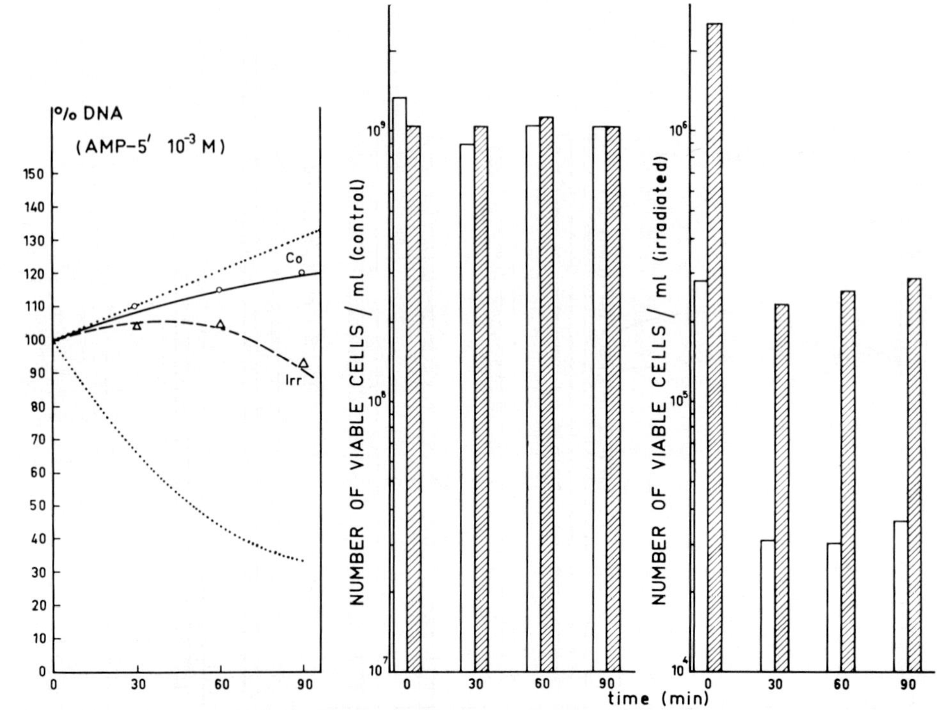

FIG. 2. Percentage of DNA and the number of viable cells as in Fig. 1, but after incubation in acetate buffer in the presence of 10^{-3} *M* AMP-5′.

however, especially after plating on MA-agar, slightly more than in unsupplemented acetate buffer.

DISCUSSION

The results presented here are consistent with the view (*1*) that a breakdown of DNA in the irradiated cells is produced only when some metabolic functions which make possible the synthesis of DNA in the unirradiated cells are occurring.

When no synthesis of DNA takes place in the unirradiated cells, as is the case in the presence of ATP and of high concentrations of citrate, succinate, and glutamate in the previous work (*1*), there is no breakdown of DNA in the irradiated cells.

The results obtained with both monophosphorylated derivatives of adenosine can be compared with those obtained previously (*1*) when 10^{-3} *M* succinate was present during incubation. There is an evident similarity between the changes in DNA content during incubation in the presence of ADP and those observed in the previous work, when glutamate or Versene (both 10^{-3} *M*) was present in the acetate buffer.

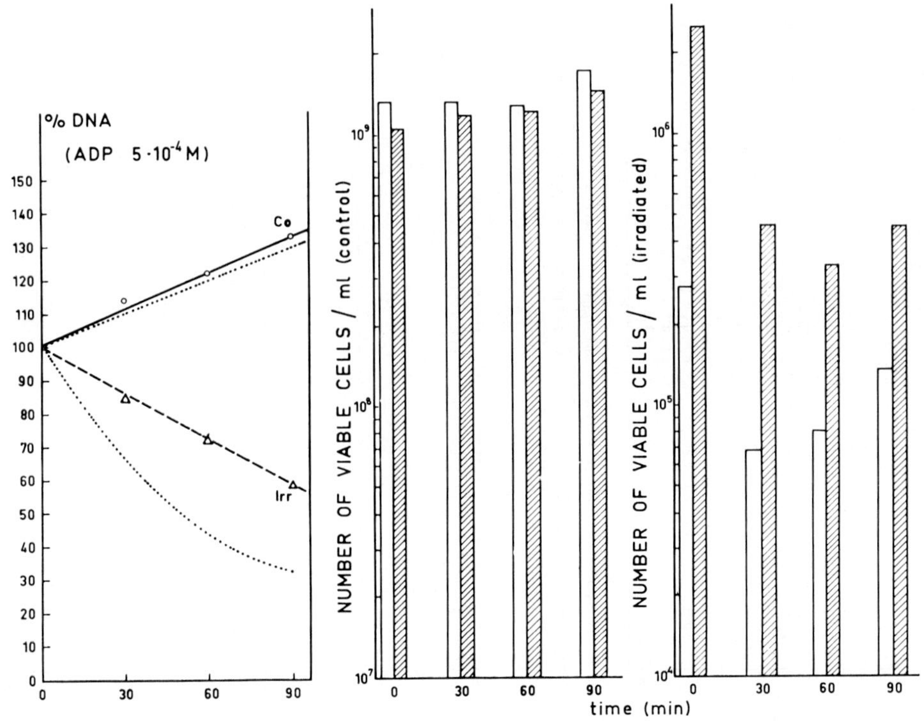

FIG. 3. Percentage of DNA and number of viable cells as in Fig. 1, but after incubation in acetate buffer supplemented by 5×10^{-4} *M* ADP.

If inorganic pyrophosphate is present during the post-irradiation incubation, the amount of DNA broken down in the irradiated culture is twice as great as that synthesized in the unirradiated suspension. Such was the case in the previous series of experiments (*1*) with acetate buffer alone, or when $MgSO_4$ was added. Although the final amount of DNA broken down in the presence of pyrophosphate after 90 minutes of incubation is no greater then the amount broken down in acetate buffer alone, the kinetics is somewhat changed. An acceleration of the breakdown of DNA (and of its biosynthesis in the unirradiated bacteria) is caused by this compound.

These results do not support the hypothesis that the γ- (or X-) ray-induced breakdown of DNA is caused by the activation of DNase, and that it could be consequently inhibited by inhibitors of DNase, for instance by chelating agents. It would be rather difficult to interpret the relations existing evidently between the biosynthetic process in the control and the breakdown of DNA in the irradiated cells on the basis of the action of chelating agents. Our earlier assumption that some of the substances we tested (*3*) cause an inhibition of the DNA breakdown

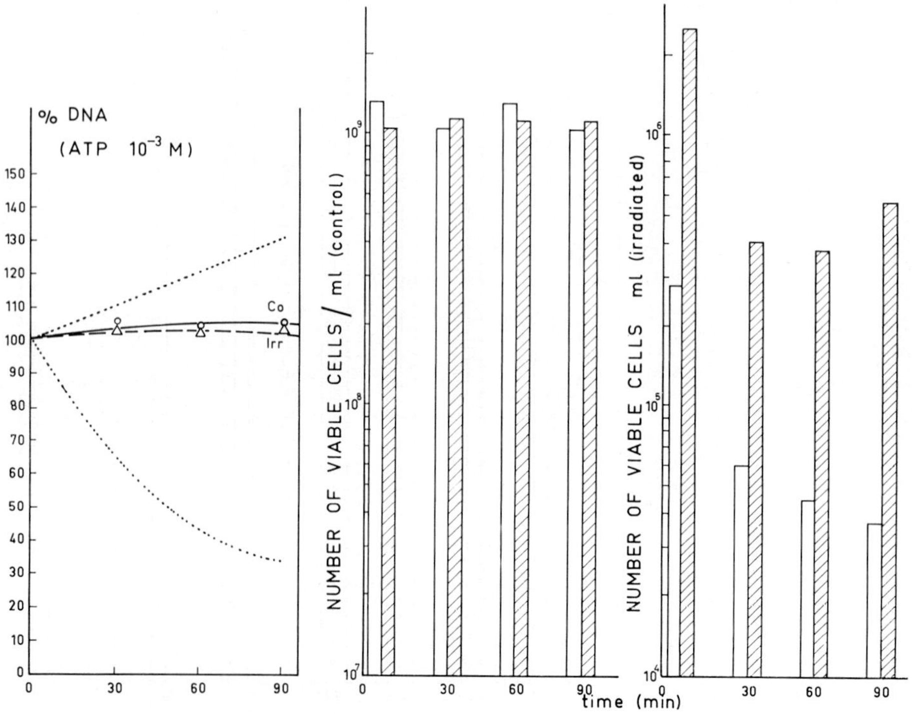

FIG. 4. Percentage of DNA and number of viable cells as in Fig. 1, but after incubation in acetate buffer supplemented by 10^{-3} M ATP.

only through certain physicochemical and structural characteristics becomes, therefore, much less probable.

Although most of the substances which were found to inhibit, partially or completely, the γ-ray-induced DNA breakdown are more or less closely related to certain levels of energy metabolism, we do not think it very likely that the inhibition of DNA breakdown is caused by the stimulation of some energy-yielding processes. We are led to believe that the inhibition of the DNA breakdown is not brought about by just one specific mechanism, but that it can be attained, presumably, by the depression of various metabolic processes (related to DNA replication in different ways) which are going on, although very slowly, in our starving bacteria.

We could verify this hypothesis by testing the effect of such substances which are biochemically and structurally unrelated to those which were shown to inhibit DNA breakdown in the present and in the previous (*1*) work, or which have a metabolically antagonistic action to some of them.

Neither in the previous work (*1*) nor in the present series of experiments could

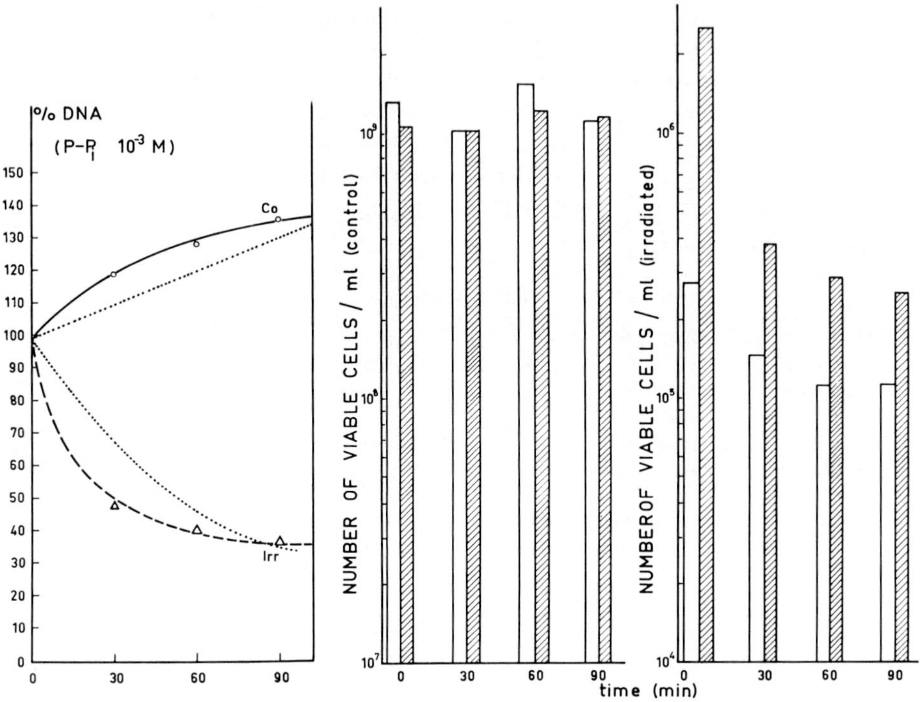

FIG. 5. Percentage of DNA and number of viable cells as in Fig. 1, but after incubation in acetate buffer supplemented by 10^{-3} *M* sodium pyrophosphate.

any positive correlation be established between the DNA content and the viability of the cells during postirradiation incubation. We must, however, stress again, as we did in the preceding paper, that our results by no means permit any conclusion concerning the role of the radiolesion of DNA *in vivo* in the lethal effect of γ-irradiation, because the properties of the DNA "retained" by the irradiated cells were not studied.

SUMMARY

In the preceding paper (*1*) the effect of several substances on the γ-ray-induced breakdown of DNA and the viability of *E. coli* B was described. The general validity of these earlier observations was tested in the present work by using a different series of compounds.

A complete inhibition of the biosynthesis of DNA in unirradiated *E. coli* B as well as a total inhibition of its breakdown in γ-irradiated bacteria was observed if the cells were incubated in acetate buffer in the presence of ATP. In the presence of ADP or of AMP-3′ and AMP-5′, the breakdown of DNA in the irradiated cells is only partially inhibited. If inorganic pyrophosphate is added to the acetate buffer, both the biosynthesis of DNA in the controls and its breakdown in the irradiated suspension are somewhat accelerated.

The effects of the above compounds on the colony-forming ability of *E. coli* B were also studied.

The results of these experiments are compared with those obtained in the previous work, and their meaning is discussed.

RECEIVED July 30, 1962

REFERENCES

1. M. DRAKULIĆ and E. KOS, Effect of some metabolites and antimetabolites on the breakdown of deoxyribonucleic acid and on the colony-forming ability of *Escherichia coli* B after gamma irradiation. I. Effect of citrate, glutamate, succinate, Versene, and magnesium ions. *Radiation Res.* in press.
2. M. J. BESSMAN, J. R. LEHMAN, E. S. SIMMS, and ARTHUR KORNBERG, Enzymatic synthesis of deoxyribonucleic acid. II. General properties of the reaction. *J. Biol. Chem.* **233,** 171–177 (1958).
3. E. KOS and M. DRAKULIĆ, Inhibition of deoxyribonucleic acid breakdown in X-irradiated *Escherichia coli* B by various compounds. *Biochim. Biophys. Acta* **55,** 248–249 (1962).

RADIATION RESEARCH 19, 447–461 (1963)

Electron-Microscopic Changes across Irradiated Rat Intestinal Villi[1]

LAWRENCE E. DETRICK, HARRISON LATTA, HARVEY C. UPHAM, AND RUTH McCANDLESS

Laboratory of Nuclear Medicine and Radiation Biology of the Department of Biophysics and Nuclear Medicine, and the Department of Pathology, School of Medicine, University of California at Los Angeles, California

INTRODUCTION

Absorption is a function of epithelial cells covering the intestinal villi that develop and mature in the germinal crypts, migrate out, over, and off the villi tips with a lifetime of 1.57 days in the rat duodenum (*1*). The effects of ionizing radiation on the mammalian body (*2*) and on the physiology (*3*) and absorption of the intestine (*4–7*) depend on the irradiation dose and species employed, the radiation sensitivity of the cells, and the postirradiation time of study (*5, 8*). Crypt cells were histologically more sensitive to radiation than epithelial cells on the villi (*5, 8*), and information on crypt cell activity has been extended by tagging and autoradiographic methods (*9–11*). Intestinal function was decreased after total-body irradiation. Glucose absorption was decreased 4 and 20 hours after 1410 r (*4*). Intestinal glucose transport accompanied by a high mortality rate was lowest on day 3, made a moderate recovery, only to fall precipitously 11 to 17 days after 600 r (*5*). Glucose absorption after 500 r of total-body (*6*) and 700 r of direct intestinal irradiation (*7*) and thiamine transport (*8*) after 525 r were decreased 72 hours after exposure. The effect of irradiation on intestinal function was attributed, in part, to direct intestinal wall damage (*4, 6–8*). An electron-microscope study has been made of changes in crypt cells and in the mature epithelial cells on the villi of rats after 3000 rads of irradiation (*12*). The fasting rat villus (*13*) and the pathway of fat absorption in the normal rat intestine (*14*) were also studied by this method.

The present experiment employs electron microscopy to obtain more detailed cytomorphology across nonperfused, functionally evaluated, light-microscopically-

[1] Presented at the Federation of American Societies for Experimental Biology, Atlantic City, April 14–19, 1962. These studies were supported by Contract AT(04-1)GEN-12 between the U. S. Atomic Energy Commission and the University of California.

studied irradiated rat intestinal villi (*8*) for a possible morphological explanation of decreased intestinal function on day 3 and delayed functional recovery on days 7 to 17. Tissues from the intestinal thiamine-transport animals (*8*) were used in the present study. Information on tissue source material pertinent to the present study is as follows: Radiation mortality was low, and the physical condition of the remaining animals was good throughout. Mesenteric lymph nodes were mottled on day 6 and irregularly engorged with blood on days 10 and 17. Crypt cell mitosis was distorted at 1 hour, nearly abolished on day 1, and normal in frequency on day 3. Villar epithelium appears recovered on day 5. Methacrylate sections of osmium tetroxide-fixed villi, cut 1 to 2 μ thick, stained with toluidine blue, and examined with a light microscope, showed focal areas of epithelial cell degeneration on days 14 to 17.

MATERIALS AND METHODS

Female CFN strain rats weighing from 155 to 228 gm and fed on an adequate commercial diet were given 525 r of total-body irradiation (*8*). Radiation characteristics were: 250 kvp; 15 ma; FOD 60 cm; filters 0.21 mm Cu inherent, 0.5 mm Cu parabolic, and 1 mm Al; HVL 2.02 mm Cu; rate measured in air, 26.6 to 29.8 r/min. The output was calibrated before and after each experiment with a Victoreen thimble r-meter. Intestinal villi from 8 nonirradiated and 28 irradiated rats were studied with an electron microscope 1 hour and 1, 3 to 7, 10, 14, and 17 days after irradiation. The animals received water, but food was restricted for 24 hours prior to sacrifice. The animals were anesthetized with sodium pentobarbital (30 mg/kg body weight) supplemented with ether. For intestinal thiamine-transport study a 40-cm segment of small bowel was removed through a midline incision, with as little loss of blood as possible (*8*). The nonperfused intact intestinal mucosa in the remaining jejunal stump was fixed *in situ* within 15 minutes of starting the operation. Methods similar to those of Palay and Karlin (*13*) were used with the following modifications: A longitudinal incision 0.5 inch long was made in the center of the intact remaining jejunal stump, and buffered osmium tetroxide was dripped directly on the exposed mucosa and over the serosal surface for 10 minutes (*15*). Transverse intestinal strips 1 mm thick were cut from the fixed area. After further fixation of the strips and dehydration in 95% alcohol, the villi were removed. Dehydration was completed, and separate villi were embedded in methacrylate blocks. Sections were cut with a glass knife (*16*). Sections 1 to 2 μ thick, stained with toluidine blue and examined with a light microscope, were used for orientation (*15*), and sections $\frac{1}{20}$ to $\frac{1}{40}$ μ thick were photographed with an RCA EMU 2B electron microscope. Other animal groups were given corn oil according to the procedure of Palay and Karlin (*14*), and comparative absorption studies were made in control and irradiated rats on days 14 and 17.

RESULTS

Nonirradiated Rat Villi

Simple columnar epithelium covers the villi (Fig. 1).[2] The apical surface contains thin, rod-shaped projections or microvilli. Lateral surfaces show compact interlocking plications. The base is flat or irregular, owing to footlike basal processes. The apical cytoplasm contains a dark band or terminal web with a lateral condensation of fibers or terminal bar. Mitochondria are cylindrical in shape, with a matrix more dense than the cytoplasm, and contain tranverse membranes or cristae. The Golgi reticulum consists of cisternae apical to the nucleus. Centrally located nuclei are filled with granular nucleoplasm and diffuse condensations of chromatin material. Goblet cells have a dark basal nucleus and a characteristic foamlike cytoplasmic mass. Intrusive cells or leukocytes are occasionally observed. Granular and agranular cytoplasmic reticulum is clearly seen at higher magnifications. The cells rest on a thin basal membrane.

Thin independent basement membranes limit the lamina propria laterally and surround the capillaries (Fig. 2). Collagen fibers and various interstitial core cells of the lamina propria occupy the space between the membranes. Capillary walls consist of a single layer of long, flat endothelial cells with a nuclear portion that bulges into the vessel. The lamina propria contains peripheral capillaries, a central arteriole, a central lacteal, nerve fibers, smooth muscle, and core cells of various types. Macrophages are large and ameboid with kidney-shaped nuclei and cytoplasmic inclusion bodies. Mast cell nuclei are large, dense, and irregular, surrounded by cytoplasm containing occasional mitochondria, reticulum, and many large cytoplasmic granules, the majority of which are filled with dense and laminated materials. Long thin cytoplasmic protrusions occur on the surface. Eosinophiles are readily distinguished by large, oval cytoplasmic granules with dark crystal bars across the long axis. Plasma cell cytoplasm contains granular reticulum loosely coiled around the nucleus. Fibroblasts are thin cells with tapering cytoplasmic processes. The thick wall of the central lacteal contains overlapping cells between which a direct channel communicates with the intercellular space. Bundles of nerve fibers and smooth muscle frequently occur in close proximity to the central lacteal.

Changes in Irradiated Rat Intestinal Villi

Morphological lesions are considered in four chronological periods, based on deviations in thiamine transport: (1) unchanged; (2) the lowest; (3) rapid but incomplete recovery; (4) sustained incomplete recovery. The functional correlation is given in the heading of each chronological period studied morphologically.

1. During the first period (1 hour to 1 day), neither function nor morphology

[2] A key to the abbreviations in the figures is given at the end of the article.

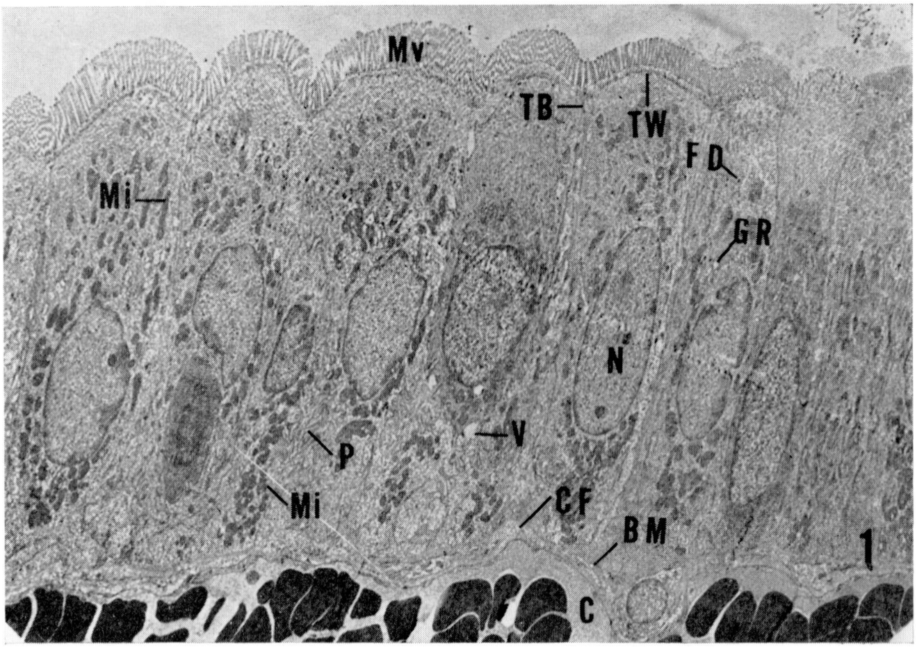

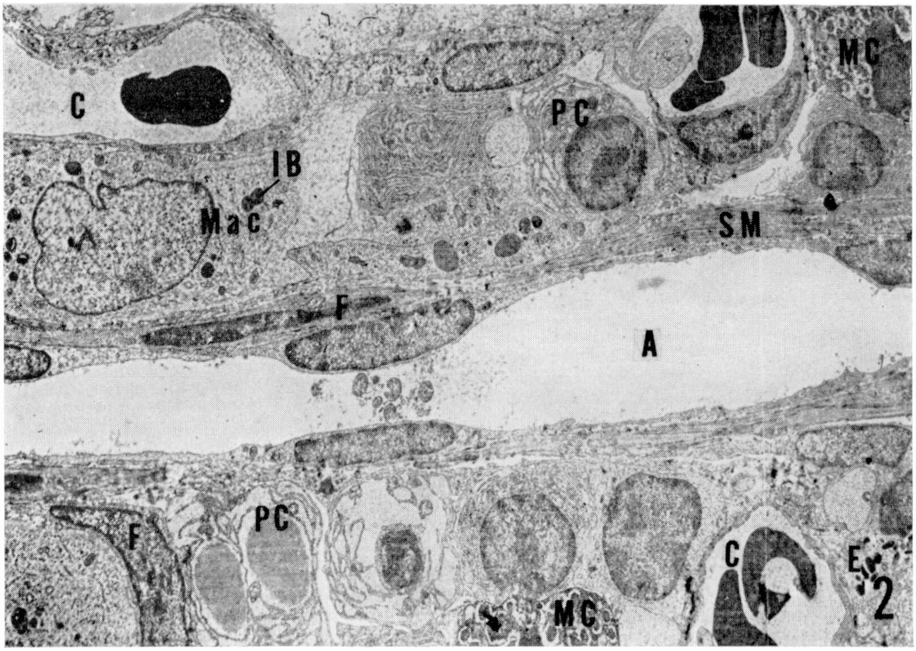

FIG. 1. Longitudinal section of nonirradiated rat epithelium of the villus showing rod-shaped microvilli (Mv), terminal web (TW), terminal bar (TB), oval to cylindrical mitochondria (Mi), nuclei (N), basement membrane (BM), collagen fibers (CF), and peripheral capillary (C). (3200×)

FIG. 2. Longitudinal section of nonirradiated rat lamina propria of the villus showing a peripheral capillary (C), mast cell (MC) with granules filled, plasma cell (PC) with prominent reticulum, macrophages (Mac) containing inclusion bodies (IB), fibroblast (F), eosinophile (E), and smooth muscle (SM). (3200×)

of the epithelium is altered, although crypt damage is greatest, and focal edema occurs across the villi. Epithelial cells on the villi at the time of irradiation are comparatively unaffected at 1 hour (Fig. 3) and on day 1 (Fig. 4). Edematous changes consist of a few fine or several larger cytoplasmic vacuoles (Fig. 4). Occasionally, fluid dilates the intercellular spaces from the basement membrane to the level of the nucleus. Mitochondria are more irregular in shape. Nuclear edges are less rippled. Chromatin is more dispersed. The goblet cells are not changed (Fig. 4). The lamina propria contains focal edematous areas of varying intensities (Fig. 3). Collagen fibers adjacent to the basement membrane are swollen. Eosinophiles are occasionally ameboid in shape, with vacuolated cytoplasm. Mast cells contain much less dark material within the granules. Macrophages are larger and more irregular in shape, with many inclusion bodies and cytoplasmic protrusion. Lymphocytes show moderate vacuolization. Plasma cells frequently show prominent mitochondria and layers of granules in cytoplasmic membranes. Capillaries and the central lacteal are usually dilated.

2. In the second period (day 3), intestinal function is lowest when focal areas of new, abnormal epithelial replacement cells appear on dehydrated villi. The new epithelial replacement cells and villi are smaller than normal (Fig. 5). Microvilli are shorter, thicker, and less numerous. The cytoplasm is of uniform density and contains many fat droplets but few vesicles or vacuoles. Mitochondria are smaller, thicker, and less numerous. The matrix and cristae are intact. Epithelial nuclei are larger and thicker, and the cytoplasm is coarsely granular. Nucleoli are round and dense. The chromatin material is bizarre in shape and distribution. The Golgi vesicles are not dilated. Intercellular fluid, intrusive cells, and epithelial foot processes are not present. The lamina propria of dehydrated villi appears as a compact mass of essentially normal core cells (Fig. 5). Peripheral capillaries and the central lacteal are contracted.

3. In the third period (days 4 to 6), irregular, incomplete functional recovery occurs simultaneously with the reappearance of focal edema and the development of microscopic hemorrhage. The majority of the epithelium on day 4 appear to have recovered (Fig. 6). Microvilli, mitochondria, and epithelial cytoplasm are essentially normal. Basal foot processes are present. Some nuclei are irregular in shape, with coarsely granular nucleoplasm and chromatin that is dense and bizarre in distribution. Edematous changes within and between epithelial cells varied in intensity from comparatively minor (Fig. 6) to more extensive lesions (Fig. 7). Essentially unaltered or moderately vacuolated core cells—eosinophile, mast cell, plasma cell or lymphocyte—are observed migrating through the epithelium as intrusive cells. The lamina propria also contains areas of focal edema of varying intensity (Figs. 6 and 7). Capillaries and the central lacteal are usually dilated. Macrophages contain numerous inclusion bodies and some vacuoles. Extensive peripheral cytoplasmic protrusions are present. Mast cells are scarce or absent, and,

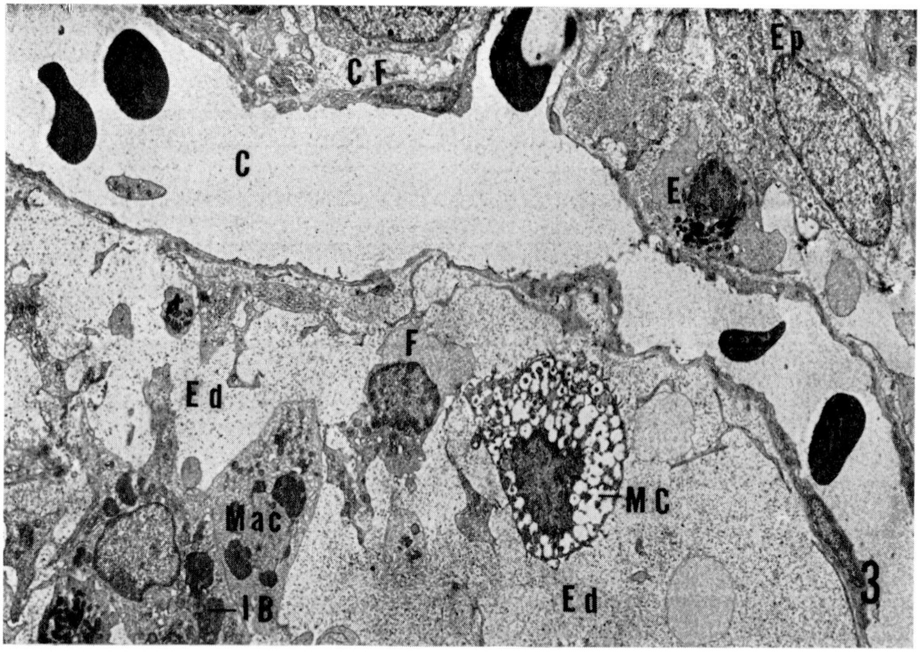

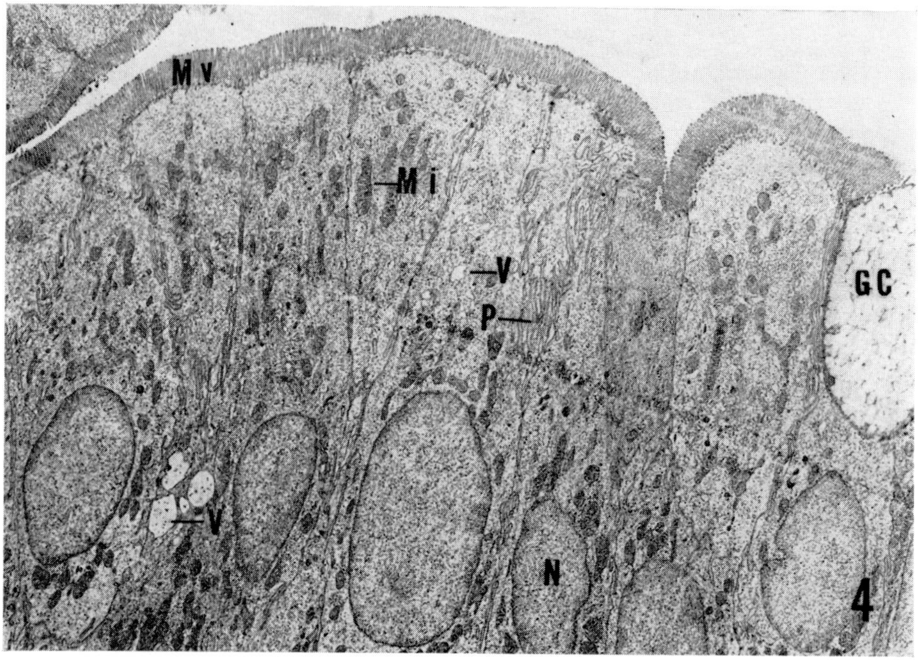

FIG. 3. Longitudinal section of the villus 1 hour after irradiation. Some epithelium (Ep) is shown above. The lamina propria contains swollen collagen fibers (CF), a dilated capillary (C), an ameboid-shaped, vacuolated eosinophile (E), a mast cell (MC) with depleted granules, a macrophage (Mac) with large inclusion bodies (IB), a vacuolated fibroblast (F), and extensive edema (Ed). (4100×)

FIG. 4. Epithelium on the villus 1 day after irradiation is comparatively unchanged. Microvilli (Mv) are long and slender. Goblet cells (GC) are normal. Minor vacuolization (V), variation in shape of mitochondria (Mi), and dispersion of nuclear (N) chromatin appear of little or no functional significance. (4400×)

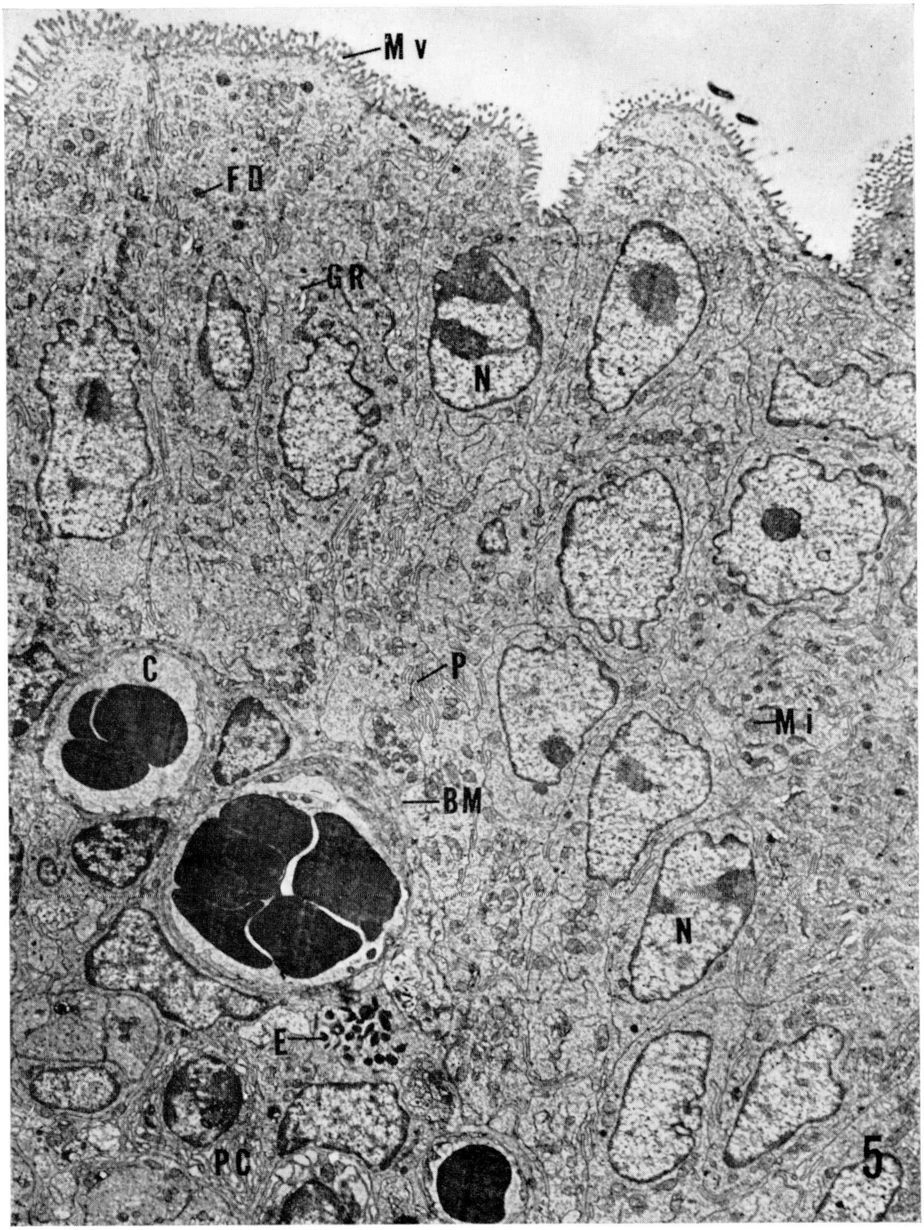

FIG. 5. New abnormal epithelial cells appear on dehydrated villi on day 3. Microvilli (Mv) are shorter and less numerous. Mitochondria (Mi) are fewer, smaller, and less dense. Nuclear (N) chromatin is bizarre in distribution. Edema is lacking in the epithelium above the basement membrane and in the lamina propria around the capillary (C). (4400×)

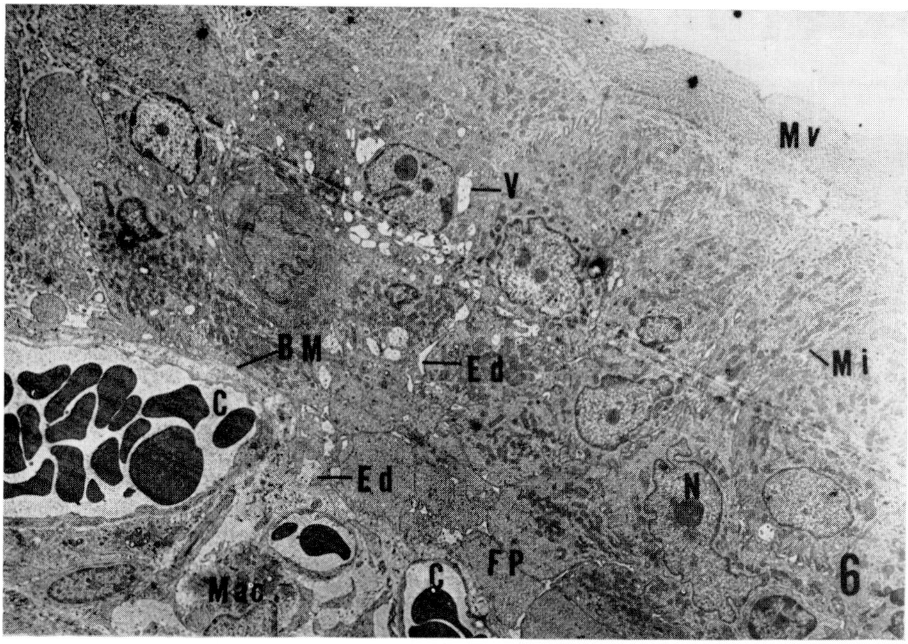

FIG. 6. On days 4 to 6 most epithelium appears essentially normal. Focal areas of edema (Ed) and vacuolization (V) vary in intensity. Comparatively minor lesions occur on day 4. (2300×)

FIG. 7. More marked focal edema (Ed) and vacuoles (V) occur across the villus on day 5. (4900×)

when found, their cytoplasmic granules are nearly depleted of dense material. Eosinophiles in edematous areas are irregular in shape and vacuolated, and the crystals are irregular. Crystal line bars are wider, less dense, irregular in shape, absent or traverse the short axis. Lymphocytes are irregular in shape and vacuolated. Extravascular red blood cells increase in frequency. Endothelial cells occasionally show moderate fine cytoplasmic vacuolization. The collagenous area between the basement membranes is swollen or filled with edema, and fibroblasts in the area are vacuolated.

4. In the fourth period (days 7 to 17), sustained incomplete recovery of intestinal thiamine transport is attributed to focal epithelial degeneration accompanied by edema and microscopic hemorrhage. During this period most epithelium resembles that of the nonirradiated rat villi. Focal vacuolization (Fig. 6) was also present on day 7. In a few villi on day 10, epithelial cells ars narrow and compact, with dense cytoplasm and thin, elongated nuclei (Fig. 8). Microvilli are short. The mitochondria are striking in appearance, owing to swelling, decreased density, and fragmented cristae that occur in the absence of general cytoplasmic vacuolization. An almost immediate transition to less-affected cells takes place. Degenerative lesions in the epithelium on day 14 consist of extensive swelling in a few cells due to edema (Fig. 10). Microvilli are unaffected. The ectoplasm is swollen, and the cytoplasm vacuolated. Some mitochondria are swollen and decreased in number. Nuclei are large and pale, with coarsely granular nucleoplasm. Edema fills the intercellular spaces. On day 17 epithelial degeneration consists of fine, diffuse, cytoplasmic vacuolization, swollen mitochondria, irregularly shaped nuclei, normal nucleoplasm, and dense peripheral chromatin (Fig. 11). Intrusive lymphocytes and migrating red blood cells are present. Intercellular edema is scant. Such lesions may increase until there is nearly complete obliteration of all cellular organelles on days 14 to 17. The lamina propria of most villi is also essentially normal. Focal edema varies in intensity (Fig. 9), shows its greatest frequency on day 10, and then subsides (days 14 to 17). Core cells of the lamina propria are comparatively unchanged, even in the presence of moderate edema (Fig. 9), but become irregular in shape, vacuolated, and granular when focal edema is more severe. Microscopic hemorrhage is most intense on days 10 to 17. Fractured capillaries and escaping red blood cells as well as dumbbell-shaped diapedesing erythrocytes occur. Some endothelial cells contain fine vacuolization. Swelling in the basement membranes beneath the epithelium and around capillaries did not occur in edematous or hemorrhagic areas. Control rat corn oil intestinal epithelium contained small, dense, lipid granules beneath the terminal web. The lipid granules became large irregular masses as the mitochondria increased in number. The granules accumulated in large vacuoles above distended Golgi cisternae, in intercellular spaces, especially above the basement membrane, in the ground substance, and in the lacteal. Unaltered and slightly dilated mitochondria and nuclei in both

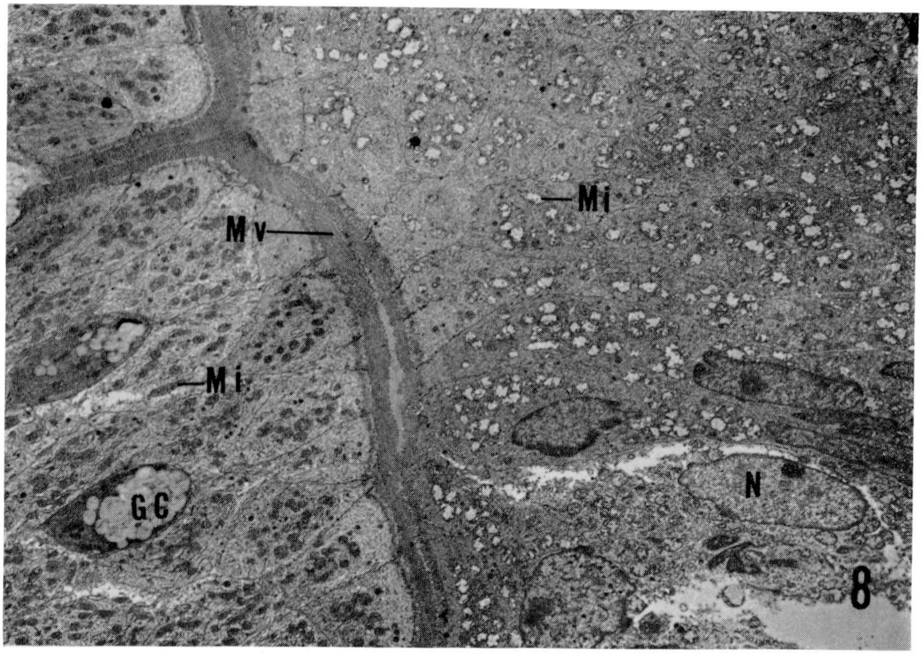

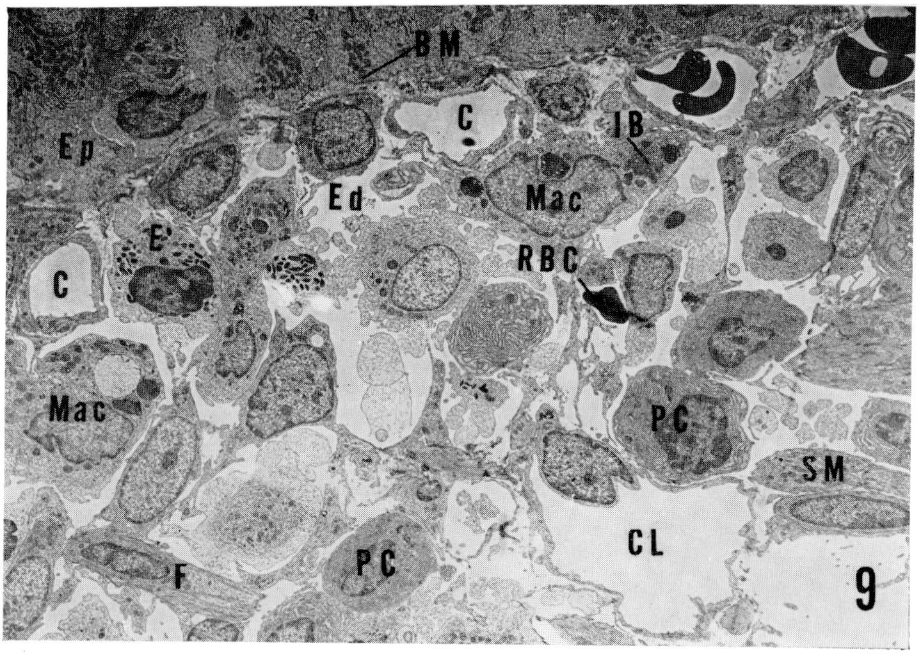

FIG. 8. Longitudinal section of adjacent villi on day 10, showing complete recovery in one villus and extensive alteration in the other. (3700×)

FIG. 9. Recovered epithelium (Ep) above comparatively normal core cells in the lamina propria containing only minor edema (Ed) and microscopic hemorrhage (RBC). Day 10. (2400×)

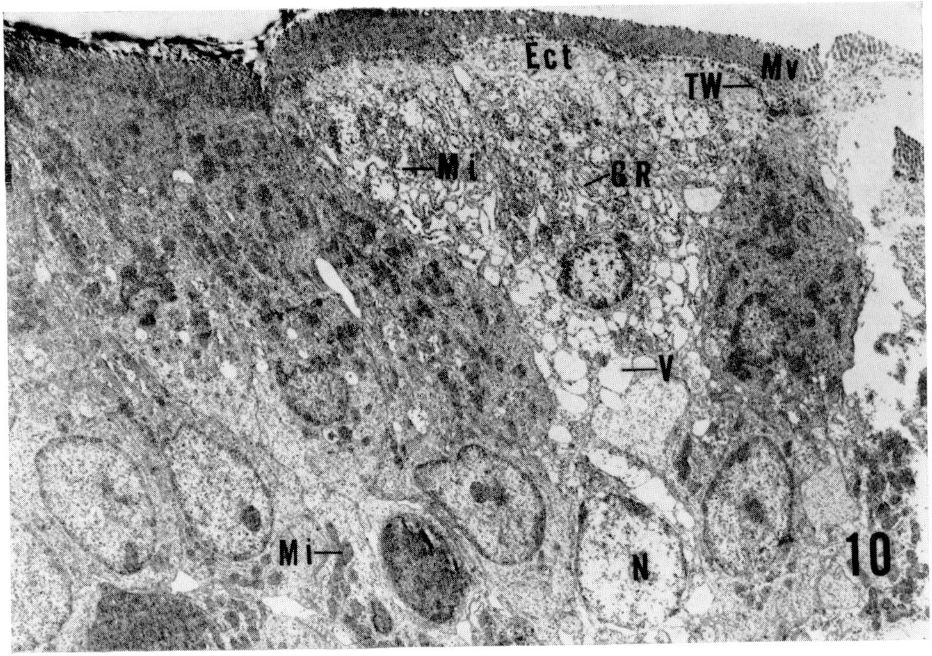

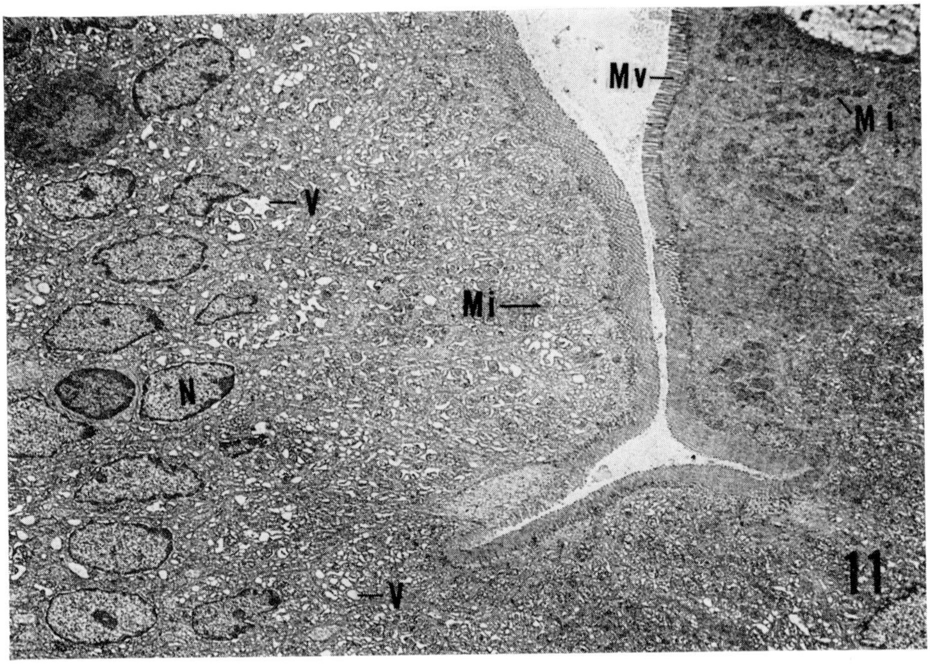

FIG. 10. Focal epithelial cell degeneration on day 14, with swollen pale cells and nuclei (N), ectoplasmic (Ect) and cytoplasmic vacuolization, prominent Golgi reticulum (GR), and mitochondria (Mi) swelling and destruction. (3000×)

FIG. 11. Transverse section of villus on day 17, showing comparatively normal epithelium and microvilli (Mv) below a goblet cell, with an abrupt transition to cells having increased cytoplasmic vacuolization (V) and swollen mitochondria (Mi). (3600×)

the control and irradiated groups were free of lipid granules. Apparently recovered, irradiated corn oil rat intestinal epithelium showed increased cytoplasmic vacuoles, larger lipid masses, and more swollen but fat-free mitochondria on days 14 to 17. Elsewhere, focal epithelial cells showed extensive cytoplasmic vacuolization, the majority of which contained lipid material that varied in size, number, and density. Focal edema, hemorrhage, mast cell degranulation, and lipid granules were present in the lamina propria.

DISCUSSION

The fine structure of control rat intestinal villi is similar to that found by Palay and Karlin (*13*). Epithelial cells of the villi have been frequently implicated in decreased intestinal absorption or transport after irradiation (*5–8*), and the present observations, together with those of Scherer and Vogell (*17*), demonstrate a variety of submicroscopic changes due to radiation. The significance and limitations of electron-microscopic changes for understanding altered cellular function have been emphasized by Schmitt (*19*).

Total-body-irradiation doses of 525 r (*8*) to 600 r (*5*) produce no significant histological changes in epithelium of the villi or functional deviations for 24 hours. Glucose absorption, however, decreased 4 and 20 hours after 1410 r (*4*), and glucose oxidation within the intestinal mucosa increased 3 to 96 hours after 600 r (*20*). Neither the present electron-microscopic examinations nor those of others (*12*) show major changes in the organelles of intestinal epithelium 24 hours after 525 r or after 3000 rads. Variations in the shape of mitochondria (Fig. 4) occur without functional (*8*) or morphological significance (*21*), and the same applies to increased dispersion of nuclear chromatin material (Fig. 4), which has also been previously reported (*22*). Nuclear and mitochondrial changes in the intestinal epithelium reported by Braun (*23*) appear 1 hour after 100 r and are repaired between 3 and 7 days. The present studies were not designed to follow such changes.

Intestinal function measured by thiamine and glucose transport that reached its lowest level 72 hours after irradiation (*5, 8*) was accompanied in the present study by the appearance of new, abnormal epithelial cells on dehydrated villi. No direct effect on intestinal function is attributed to the bizarre distribution of epithelial nuclear chromatin (Fig. 5). Small and less numerous mitochondria frequently appear after renewal of cell division (*21*). The depression of intestinal absorption by radiation (*8*) may be due in part to the initial replacement of villous epithelium by immature and abnormal epithelial cells. The mitochondria in these cells are associated with the phosphorylating mechanism that is essential for glucose (*5*) and thiamine absorption (*8*). The mitochondria may be damaged by irradiation, and the phosphorylating mechanism competitively depleted by glucose (*8*). More extensive morphological lesions are observed in intestinal epithelium 72 hours after 3000 rads of irradiation (*12*).

Morphological changes observed across irradiated rat intestinal villi on days

4 to 6 did not prevent partial recovery of intestinal function (*8*). Focal edema frequently occurred in the epithelium and lamina propria of control rats, and, although increased in frequency and intensity after irradiation, it could not be correlated with functional deviations (*8*). Irradiated rat villi thickened by edema, microscopic hemorrhage, increased core cells, and intrusive cells suggest the presence of extensive trephocytic activity during intestinal recovery. This effect is usually overlooked, but its importance has been reviewed at length by Kelsall and Crabb (*24*).

The terminal period (days 7 to 17) extended beyond that usually studied to determine the effect of radiation on intestinal absorption (*4, 6, 7*). Various stages of epithelial degeneration (Figs. 8 to 11) are considered in part as the morphological explanation of delayed recovery in thiamine absorption (*8*). Furthermore, work in progress reveals rupture of such degenerating cells that leads to complete denudation of the distal villus, thus exaggerating delayed functional recovery. Although microscopic hemorrhage was greatest on days 14 to 17, which is comparable to the results of Ross *et al.* (*25*), intestinal function did not fall further. Sullivan (*26*) has shown that fat absorption was not decreased as a result of exposing the exteriorized intestine to X-irradiation. Results of glucose absorption confirmed previous observations (*5, 8*) on the postirradiation time sequence of decreased intestinal absorption and the onset of recovery. It is of special interest to note that the administration of cysteine or AET presented decreased intestinal absorption of glucose after exposure to 900 r but not after 1500 r. Quastler (*27*) made an electron-microscopic study of corn oil absorption in mice intestine 10 minutes to 5 days after 200, 800, or 3000 rads of total-body irradiation. Absorption and transport were not altered in villar epithelium at the time of irradiation. On days 2 to 5 and after the highest radiation dose, both absorption and transport were decreased, mitochondrial involvement increased, and there was a progressive depletion of ribonucleoprotein granules, and a decrease in mitochondria and membrane-bound vesicles. Corn oil absorption studies (*27*) gave further confirmation of early morphological changes presented as a basis for an explanation of deviations in postirradiation intestinal thiamine transport (*8*). Curran *et al.* (*28*) attributed decreased intestinal transport of sodium and water 6 to 67 hours after 2500 to 3000 rads of abdominal irradiation of rats to a direct radiation effect on the transport process. Intestinal morphology presented and variations in corn oil absorption described show incomplete epithelial cell recovery on days 10 to 17. Such changes may result from submicroscopic premitotic damage at radiation and genetically carried through some ten generations of daughter cells. Epithelial cells not completely recovered at this time may be more susceptible to adverse environmental conditions resulting indirectly from the liberation of mast cell granule contents, increased capillary permeability, fluid, excretion products and hemorrhage in the lamina propria (*29*).

CONCLUSIONS

More detailed information has been sought to explain decreased thiamine transport on day 3 and incomplete functional recovery on days 10 to 17 by an electron-microscopic study of morphological changes in irradiated rat intestinal villi. Neither thiamine transport nor the fine structure in the epithelium of the villi was significantly altered 1 hour or 1 day after 525 r of total-body irradiation, even though focal edema occurred between epithelial cells and between core cells of the lamina propria. On day 3 thiamine transport was lowest when focal areas of new, immature, abnormal epithelial cells appeared on dehydrated villi. A partial recovery of intestinal thiamine transport on days 4 to 6 was not prevented by the reappearance of edematous changes and the development of microscopic hemorrhage. Sustained incomplete recovery of intestinal thiamine transport on days 10 to 17 was attributed to focal areas of epithelial degeneration.

RECEIVED: July 12, 1962

KEY TO ABBREVIATIONS

A	Arteriole	End	Endothelial cell	MC	Mast cell
BM	Basement membrane	Ep	Epithelium	Mi	Mitochondria
BP	Basal processes	F	Fibroblast	Mv	Microvilli
C	Capillary	FD	Fat deoplet	N	Nucleus
CF	Collagen fibers	GC	Goblet cell	P	Plications
CL	Central lacteal	GR	Golgi reticulum	PC	Plasma cell
CP	Cytoplasmic protrusions	IB	Inclusion body	RBC	Red blood cell
E	Eosinophile	IC	Intrusive cell	SM	Smooth muscle
Ect	Ectoplasm	L	Lymphocyte	TB	Terminal bar
Ed	Edema	Mac	Macrophage	TW	Terminal web
				V	Vacuole

REFERENCES

1. C. P. LEBLOND and C. E. STEVENS, The constant renewal of the intestinal epithelium in the albino rat. *Anat. Record* **100,** 357–377 (1948).
2. V. P. BOND and E. P. CRONKITE, Effects of radiation on mammals. *Ann. Rev. Physiol.* **19,** 299–328 (1957).
3. R. A. CONARD, Some effects of ionizing radiation on the physiology of the gastrointestinal tract: A review. *Radiation Res.* **5,** 167–188 (1956).
4. J. T. FARRAR, M. D. SMALL, D. BULLARD, and F. J. INGELFINGER, Effects of total body irradiation on absorption of sugars from the small intestine. *Am. J. Physiol.* **186,** 549–553 (1956).
5. L. E. DETRICK, H. C. UPHAM, D. HIGHBY, V. DEBLEY, and T. J. HALEY, Influence of X-ray irradiation on glucose transport in the rat intestine. *Radiation Res.* **2,** 483–489 (1955).
6. H. M. DICKSON, Effect of X-irradiation on glucose absorption. *Am. J. Physiol.* **182,** 477–478 (1955).
7. W. T. MOSS, The effect of irradiating the exteriorized small bowel on sugar absorption. *Am. J. Roentgenol. Radium Therapy Nucl. Med.* **78,** 850–854 (1957).
8. L. E. DETRICK, H. C. UPHAM, A. K. DUNLAP, and T. J. HALEY, Thiamine transport across the irradiated isolated rat intestine. *Radiation Res.* **15,** 520–526 (1961).

9. H. Quastler, Cell renewal and acute radiation damage. *Radiology* **73,** 161–165 (1959).
10. F. G. Sherman and H. Quastler, DNA synthesis in irradiated intestinal epithelium. *Exptl. Cell Res.* **19,** 343–360 (1960).
11. H. Quastler and F. G. Sherman. Cell population kinetics in the intestinal epithelium of the mouse. *Exptl. Cell Res.* **17,** 420–438 (1959).
12. J. C. Hampton and H. Quastler, Some observations on radiation damage in epithelial cells of the mouse intestine. *Proc. 4th Intern. Conf. Electron Microscopy* **2,** 480–484 (1958).
13. S. L. Palay and L. J. Karlin, An electron microscopic study of the intestinal villus. I. The fasting animal. *J. Biophys. Biochem. Cytol.* **5,** 363–372 (1959).
14. S. L. Palay and L. J. Karlin, An electron microscopic study of the intestinal villus. II. The pathway of fat absorption. *J. Biophys. Biochem. Cytol.* **5,** 373–384 (1959).
15. S. A. Bencosme, R. S. Stone, H. Latta, and S. C. Madden, A rapid method for localization of tissue structures or lesions for electron microscopy. *J. Biophys. Biochem. Cytol.* **5,** 508–509 (1959).
16. H. Latta and J. F. Hartmann, Use of a glass edge in thin sectioning for electron microscopy. *Proc. Soc. Exptl. Biol. Med.* **74,** 436–439 (1950).
17. E. Scherer and W. Vogell, Elektronenoptische untersuchungen zur Strahlenwirkung auf Leber, Milz and Niere. *Strahlentherapie,* **106,** 202–211 (1958).
18. R. A. McGrath, Cell migration and abnormal crypt-cell enlargement in the small intestine of X-irradiated mice. *Intern. J. Radiation Biol.* **2,** 177–185 (1960).
19. F. O. Schmitt, Electron microscopy in morphology and molecular biology. *Proc. 4th Intern. Conf. Electron Microscopy* **2,** 1–16 (1958).
20. R. E. Kay and C. Entenman, Effect of whole-body X-irradiation on glucose oxidation by rat small intestine mucosa *in vitro*. *J. Biol. Chem.* **234,** 1634–1640 (1959).
21. E. W. Dempsey, Variations in the structure of mitochondria. *J. Biophys. Biochem. Cytol.* **2,** 305–312 (1956).
22. Y. S. Lewis, H. Quastler, and G. Svihla, Ultraviolet microscopy of X-irradiated intestine. *J. Natl. Cancer Inst.* **21,** 813–822 (1958).
23. H. Braun, Elektronenoptische untersuchungen an zellen des dunndarmepithels nach rontgenbestrahlung. *Exptl. Cell Res.* **20,** 267–276 (1960).
24. M. A. Kelsall and E. D. Crabb, *Lymphocytes and Mast Cells,* Williams and Wilkins Co., Baltimore, 1959.
25. M. H. Ross, J. Furth, and R. R. Bigelow, Changes in cellular composition of the lymph caused by ionizing radiation. *Blood* **I,** 417–428 (1952).
26. M. F. Sullivan, Absorption from gastrointestinal tract of the rat after X-irradiation. *Am. J. Physiol.* **201,** 1013–1016 (1961).
27. H. Quastler, Effects of ionizing radiation on the fine structure and function of the intestinal epithelium of the mouse. I. Villus epithelium (courtesy of the author).
28. P. F. Curran, E. W. Webster, and J. A. Hovsepian, The effect of X-irradiation on sodium and water transport in rat ileum. *Radiation Res.* **13,** 369-380 (1960).
29. L. E. Detrick, Mucopolysaccharides in postirradiation intestinal absorption studies. In press.

RADIATION RESEARCH 19, 462–473 (1963)

Radiation Chemistry Studies of Water as Related to the Initial Linear Energy Transfer of 11-Mev to 23-Mev Protons[1]

G. L. KOCHANNY, JR.,[2] A. TIMNICK,[3] C. J. HOCHANADEL,[4] AND C. D. GOODMAN[5]

Oak Ridge National Laboratory,[6] Oak Ridge, Tennessee, and Michigan State University, East Lansing, Michigan

INTRODUCTION

The chemical action of high-energy radiations on water is quantitatively interpreted on the basis of the expanding-track (or expanding-spur) model developed by Magee and co-workers (*1*). Calculations of the spatial and temporal distribution of free-radical intermediates are based on an assumed initial distribution of primary species in the tracks (or spurs), diffusion coefficients of the radicals, and rate constants for all pertinent radical–radical and radical–solute reactions. Important measurable quantities which aid in formulating and testing the model are the yields of radical and "molecular" products as a function of LET (linear energy transfer, or energy loss per unit track length) of the radiation. These quantities have been carefully measured for γ-radiation (LET $\sim$ 0.02 ev/A) and for protons and other radiations in the range of LET $>$ 0.4 ev/A (*2*, *3*).

In this paper we report radical and molecular yields for the range of LET 0.2 to 0.4 ev/A, obtained by using protons of various energies in the range 11 to 23 Mev. Initial yields were measured for oxidation of ferrous sulfate and for reduction of ceric sulfate both with and without thallous ion present. These solutes quantitatively scavenge the intermediates produced by decomposition of the water and,

[1] Work performed at the Oak Ridge National Laboratory under the sponsorship of the Oak Ridge Institute of Nuclear Studies. This paper is an abstract from a thesis presented by G. L. Kochanny, Jr., in partial fulfillment of the requirements for the degree of Doctor of Philosophy from Michigan State University.

[2] Present address: The Dow Chemical Company, Midland, Michigan.

[3] Department of Chemistry, Michigan State University, East Lansing, Michigan.

[4] Chemistry Division, Oak Ridge National Laboratory, Oak Ridge, Tennessee.

[5] Electronuclear Research Division, Oak Ridge National Laboratory, Oak Ridge, Tennessee.

[6] Operated by Union Carbide Corporation for the U. S. Atomic Energy Commission.

from proposed mechanisms, allow evaluation of the 100-ev yields G_H , G_{OH} , G_{H_2} , $G_{H_2O_2}$ and G_{-H_2O} .[7] The study entailed accurate measurements of proton energy and proton beam current, for which methods were devised.

EXPERIMENTAL PROCEDURE

Materials and Analytical Methods

Three different dosimeter solutions were irradiated: ferrous sulfate, ceric sulfate, and ceric plus thallous sulfate. All solutions were air-saturated.

The ferrous sulfate dosimeter was 0.002 *M* in ferrous ammonium sulfate, 0.001 *M* in sodium chloride, and 0.4 *M* in sulfuric acid. All materials were Baker and Adamson reagent grade. Laboratory-distilled water was used in the preparation of this solution, since the results were found to be identical when more carefully purified water was used.

Since the ceric sulfate and the ceric plus thallous sulfate dosimeters are particularly sensitive to impurities (*2*), a more carefully designed procedure (*4*) was used in their preparation. G. Frederick Smith reagent-grade ceric bisulfate was heated in a stream of air at approximately 80°C for about 1 hour, or until organic odors originally present were undetectable. A stock solution 0.004 *M* in ceric sulfate and 4 *M* in Baker and Adamson reagent-grade sulfuric acid was prepared with the purified solid in specially purified water. The resulting solution was heated for approximately 12 hours at 100°C and allowed to stand for several days before use. Ceric sulfate solutions were prepared from the stock solution by dilution with nine parts of purified water to one part of stock solution. The ceric plus thallous sulfate dosimeter was prepared in the same manner except that the solution was made 0.002 *M* in A. D. Mackay purified thallous sulfate. The water for preparing these solutions was taken from a Barnstead still and redistilled from acid dichromate, then from alkaline permanganate, and, finally, in an all-silica system. The purified water was stored in silica vessels. The ceric plus thallous sulfate dosimeter undergoes photochemical reaction on exposure to ordinary daylight. For this reason the solution was stored in a brown bottle inside a black bag, and irradiations were performed in semidarkness. Under these conditions photochemical reaction was negligible.

Solutions were analyzed spectrophotometrically with a Cary Model 11 MS recording spectrophotometer. Ferric ion was measured at 3050 A, and ceric ion at 3200 A. The respective molar absorptivities were taken to be 2240 and 5580 liters mole^{-1} cm^{-1} at 25°C (*5*). Peroxysulfuric acid (H_2SO_5) in the ceric sulfate dosimeter was analyzed according to the method described by Boyle (*4*). After the amount of Ce IV remaining after irradiation was measured, a few crystals of Baker and Adamson reagent-grade ferrous ammonium sulfate was added. The amount of ferric

[7] In this paper, an experimentally observed 100-ev yield is denoted by G with the formula of the substance in parentheses, e.g., G(Fe III). The derived yields of substances formed initially from water are denoted by G with the formula as a subscript (e.g., G_{OH}).

ion produced gave a measure of the total oxidizing power of the solution (Ce IV + H_2SO_5). Ce III does not interfere with the measurement of Fe III at 3050 A.

Cobalt-60 Gamma Irradiation

To check the reliability of the dosimeter solutions, yields were measured for each preparation by using cobalt γ-radiation, and compared with reported values. Solutions were irradiated and measured in a stoppered 1-cm silica optical cell provided with noncoloring windows. The dose rate was 6×10^{16} ev g^{-1} min^{-1}. The yield for oxidation of ferrous sulfate, G(Fe III), was taken to be 15.6 (*5*). In six determinations for each of two solutions, the yield for reduction of ceric sulfate, G(Ce III), was 2.48 ± 0.02, in good agreement with the recent value of Boyle (*4*) and with the majority of published values (avg = 2.44 ± 0.03) compiled by Boyle.

In a similar series of measurements, the yield for reduction of ceric sulfate in the presence of thallous sulfate, $G(\text{Ce III})_{\text{Tl}^+}$, was 8.19 ± 0.02, in agreement with a recent value of Boyle and Mahlman (*6*) of 8.18 ± 0.02, but somewhat higher than the value 7.92 originally reported by Sworski (*7*). Sworski's value of 2.39 for G(Ce III) is also somewhat lower than our value. The yields of intermediates derived from our measurements—$G_{\text{H}} = 3.70$, $G_{\text{H}_2} = 0.39$, $G_{\text{OH}} = 2.85$, and $G_{\text{H}_2\text{O}_2} = 0.82$—are in good agreement with generally accepted values (*2*).

Cyclotron Irradiations

Irradiations were performed with the external, deflected beam of the Oak Ridge 86-inch cyclotron. This provided protons at an energy of ~23 Mev and a maximum current of $\sim 10^{-7}$ amp. The beam currents actually employed ranged from 0.5×10^{-9} to 4.0×10^{-9} amp. Irradiation cells were placed at the end of an evacuated tube, approximately 40 feet from the dees. Collimation, as shown in Fig. 1,

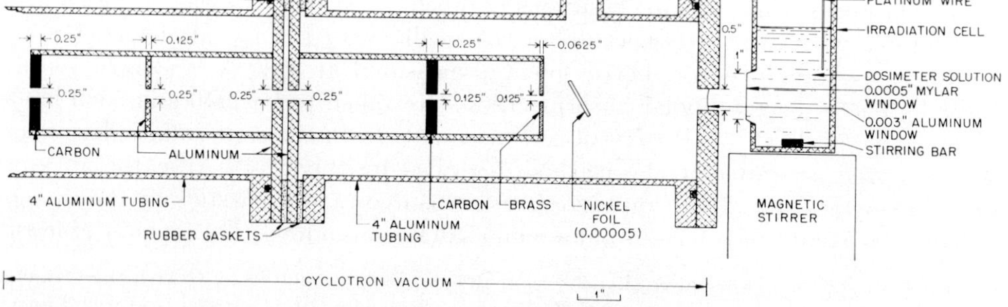

FIG. 1. Experimental arrangement for irradiating solutions with protons from the 86-inch cyclotron.

limited the diameter of the beam emerging through the center of the aluminum window at the end of the beam tube to one-eighth of an inch. Irradiation cells were 250-ml tall form beakers. The proton beam entered the beaker through a 0.5-mil Mylar window cemented (Hysol epoxy resin from Houghton Laboratories) over a 1-inch-diameter opening in the side of the beaker. The solution was stirred by a magnetic stirrer during irradiation in order to prevent depletion of solute in the irradiated zone. The rate of stirring was always maintained well above that at which *G*(Fe III) was found to be independent of stirring speed. The irradiation cells were reproducibly positioned at a measured distance from the window of the beam tube. Also, to ensure that all the beam entered the irradiation cell through the thin Mylar window, the beam pattern was examined periodically with a zinc sulfide phosphor.

Determination of Proton Beam Current Entering the Solution

The proton beam current was monitored by counting the protons elastically scattered by a very thin nickel foil into a scintillation counter. The arrangement is shown in Fig. 1. Since the nickel foil was very thin (0.05 mil, or approximately 1.1 mg/cm^2), most of the proton beam passed through it and into the solution. A small fraction of the protons, proportional to the number which passed through the nickel foil, were elastically scattered into the scintillation counter. The energy spectrum was displayed on a twenty-channel differential pulse-height analyzer. A portion of the spectrum, given in Fig. 2, shows the peak for elastically scattered pro-

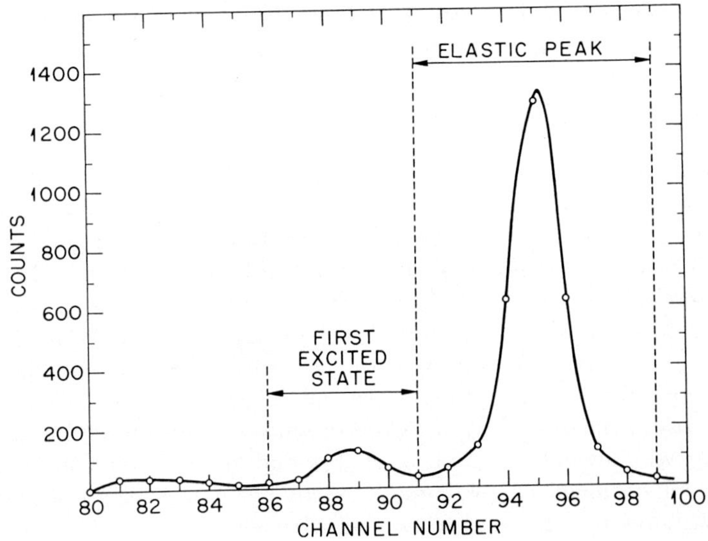

FIG. 2. Portion of nickel scintillation spectrum used in beam-current measurement procedure.

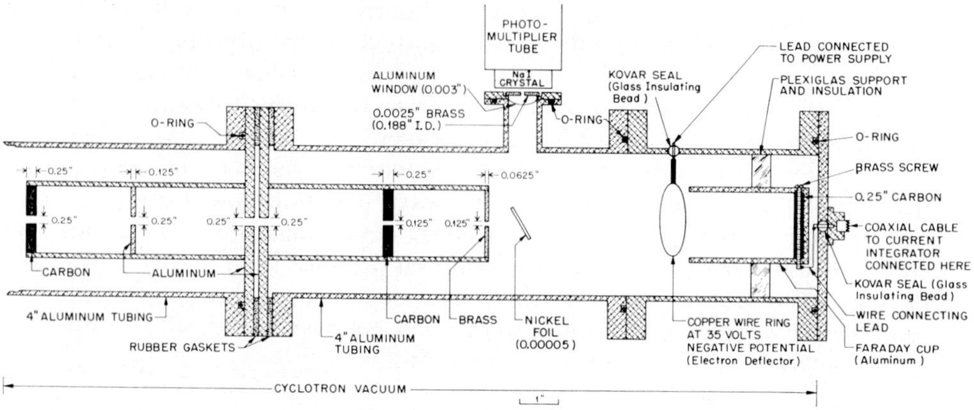

FIG. 3. Experimental arrangement used for measuring beam currents from the 86-inch cyclotron (calibration procedure).

tons (ground state) and also the peak corresponding to the first excited state. The elastic peak was integrated by summing all the counts in channels above the minimum between the first excited state and the elastic peak.

The ratio of the number of protons elastically scattered into the scintillation counter to the number passing through the nickel foil and into the solution was accurately determined by replacing the solution with a Faraday cup, as shown in Fig. 3. This ratio was determined before the runs each day, and it remained constant over at least a 12-hour period, indicating good instrumental stability. The charge collected by the Faraday cup was integrated by means of a condenser-type integrator designed and constructed in the Instruments Division of the Oak Ridge National Laboratory. A current in the range 10^{-12} to 10^{-4} amp can be measured with an accuracy of 1%. The integrator was calibrated before and after each series of experiments against a known current of about 1 μamp. This was provided by a 100-volt source operating through a standard resistance. The potential across the resistance was measured with an accurately calibrated voltmeter.

To produce protons with energy less than the base energy of ~23 Mev, aluminum absorbers were placed in the beam just in front of the beaker. Some secondary electrons ejected from the aluminum absorbers and from the Mylar window enter the solution. The maximum energy of the electrons is 50 kev, and the average energy is considerably less than this. Since the range of a 50-kev electron in Mylar is ~1 mil, most of the secondary electrons produced in the aluminum will be stopped in the Mylar window. The amount of energy deposited in solution (and, therefore, the amount of chemical change produced) by secondary electrons originating in the Mylar window is considered to be negligible (*8*, *9*).

Some preliminary measurements of the proton current were made by dipping a platinum wire into the solution as a charge collector. The wire was connected to a current integrator through a shielded coaxial cable. The proton beam was entirely stopped in the solution, and, in the absence of electrical leaks, all the charge passed to ground through the integrator. This method was found to be accurate to 3% at full beam energy, but when absorbers were placed in front of the irradiation cell to degrade the energy, the error gradually increased to 15% at 11 Mev. As mentioned by Allen (*2*), this method of current measurement is susceptible to such difficulties as scattering of secondary electrons produced by the beam's impinging on any surface, occurrence of electrical pathways from the solution to ground other than through the integrator (e.g., through the ionized air), the *charge displacement effect*, which is the ejection of secondary electrons in the direction of the primary beam from the thin insulating window of the cell into the solution, and other sources of error described in detail in various publications (*2*, *8–13*).

Determination of Beam Energy

Accurate measurement of the proton energy was another problem. Although the Oak Ridge 86-inch cyclotron is designed to operate at a fixed frequency and thus at constant energy, it was found that the beam energy was subject to small variations depending on the operating conditions. For this reason, the beam energy was measured periodically during each series of experiments. The method used was similar to that described previously (*8*, *11*, *13*). An aluminum absorber of known thickness, and of sufficient thickness to reduce the energy to about 6 Mev, was placed in the beam. The beam was then absorbed in ferrous sulfate dosimeter solution, and from the amount of oxidation produced and the known yield versus proton energy in this energy range (results of Anderson and Hart, Fig. 4) the residual proton energy was calculated. The correct energy value was arrived at by a trial-and-error calculation. A base energy in the range 22 to 24 Mev was first assumed. From the known range-energy relationship for protons in aluminum, the residual energy was then calculated. From the measured amount of ferrous oxidation, a yield was calculated for this energy. If this yield was not the correct value for this energy (Fig. 4), the base energy was adjusted, and the calculation was repeated until the correct value of the residual energy was obtained. The estimated accuracy of this method of determining the base beam energy is $\pm 0.3\%$. Since the residual energy is small ($\sim$6 Mev), any error in determination of this residual energy resulting from inaccurate values of G(Fe III), etc., produces a much smaller error in the base beam energy.

Proton beam energies determined in the above manner agreed within 0.5% with independent measurements made by the Nuclear Physics Group at the Oak Ridge National Laboratory (*14*). Briefly, this method involved the degradation of the beam energy with aluminum absorbers until the response of a silicon-surface barrier counter was the same as that produced by α-particles of known energy.

A method commonly used for determining the energy of charged particles is to add increasing amounts of aluminum absorber until the particles are completely stopped in the absorber. However, this method was considered too tedious for the routine measurements required here.

RESULTS AND DISCUSSION

Yields for Oxidation of Ferrous Sulfate

Yields for oxidation of ferrous sulfate by protons of various energies in the range 10.9 to 22.9 Mev are listed in Table I. The values are also plotted in Fig. 4 as a function of particle energy. The reciprocal of the initial linear energy transfer [$1/LET_i$, or $-(dx/dE)_i$] is shown on the scale along the top of the figure. Results of Schuler and Allen (*8*) for deuterons in the energy range 8 to 20 Mev and results of Anderson and Hart (*9*) for protons in the energy range 4 to 11 Mev are shown in Fig. 4 as dashed curves. These were drawn as smooth curves through their ex-

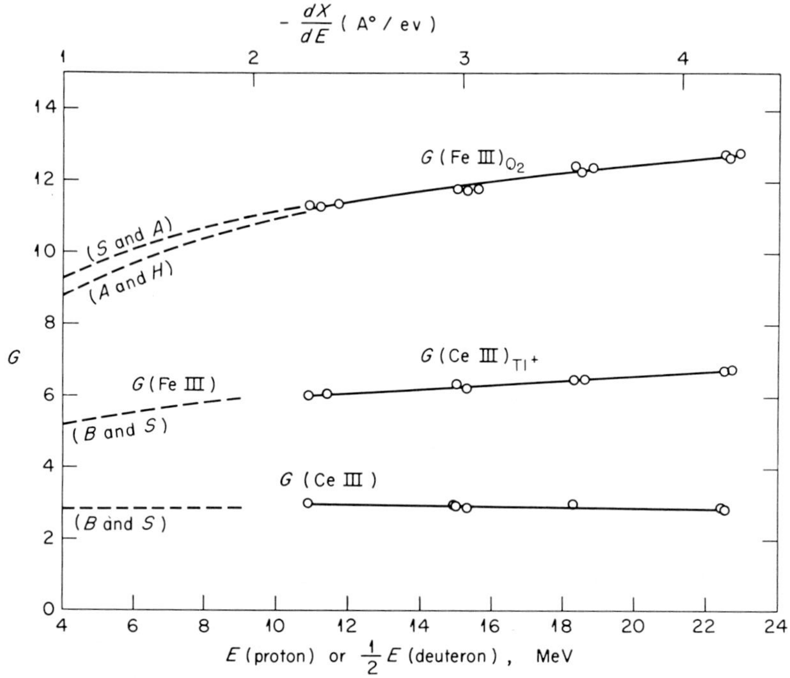

FIG. 4. Yields for oxidation of air-saturated ferrous sulfate solutions, and for reduction of ceric sulfate both with and without thallous ion present, by protons of various energies. The points represent an average of two to four determinations. The upper two dashed curves show results for oxidation of ferrous sulfate by deuterons (Schuler and Allen) and by protons (Anderson and Hart). The lower two dashed curves show results of Barr and Schuler for oxidation of ferrous sulfate and for reduction of ceric sulfate by deuterons.

TABLE I

SUMMARY OF G(FE III), G(CE III), AND $G(\text{CE III})_{\text{Tl}^+}$ VALUES OBTAINED IN THIS INVESTIGATION

Proton energy (Mev)	*G(Fe III)*	*Proton energy (Mev)*	*G(Ce III)*	*Proton energy (Mev)*	$G(Ce\ III)_{Tl^+}$
22.9	12.76	22.5	2.90	22.7	6.77
22.9	12.77	22.5	2.83	22.7	6.71
22.9	12.83	22.5	2.94	22.7	6.78
22.6	12.54	22.4	2.92	22.5	6.77
22.6	12.76	18.3	3.00	22.5	6.67
22.6	12.85	18.3	2.93	22.5	6.72
22.6	12.61	18.3	3.04	18.6	6.50
22.5	12.77	18.3	3.02	18.6	6.46
22.5	12.75	15.3	2.88	18.6	6.43
18.8	12.45	15.0	2.96	18.6	6.48
18.8	12.30	15.0	2.89	18.3	6.45
18.8	12.44	14.9	2.96	18.3	6.45
18.5	12.00	10.9	2.99	18.3	6.56
18.5	12.36	10.9	2.92	15.3	6.22
18.5	12.45	10.9	2.97	15.3	6.19
18.3	12.56	10.9	3.02	15.3	6.22
18.3	12.37			15.3	6.22
15.6	11.99			15.0	6.32
15.6	11.88			15.0	6.36
15.6	11.49			11.4	6.03
15.3	11.52			11.4	6.03
15.3	12.01			11.4	6.07
15.3	11.69			10.9	6.01
15.0	11.77			10.9	6.01
15.0	11.70				
15.0	11.88				
11.7	11.38				
11.7	11.37				
11.7	11.45				
11.2	11.30				
11.2	11.15				
11.2	11.38				
10.9	11.39				
10.9	11.31				
10.9	11.25				

perimental points. In order to make an accurate comparison, their results were adjusted[8] slightly to account for different extinction coefficients used in measuring Fe III, and for a slight influence of ferrous concentration on the yield. Schuler and Allen's results are for 10^{-2} M ferrous sulfate. Their results were adjusted by 0.979 for a difference in ϵ, and by 0.985 for the effect of concentration. Anderson and

[8] We are indebted to one of the referees who suggested making this adjustment.

Hart's values were adjusted by 0.993 for the difference in ϵ. At an energy of 10 Mev, our value is about 1% lower than Schuler and Allen's value, and about 1% higher than Anderson and Hart's value.

As expected, the results indicate that yields for oxidation of ferrous sulfate decreased with increase in LET_i (or with decrease in $1/LET_i$). This is due to the fact that a larger fraction of radicals react with each other at higher LET.

Yields for Reduction of Ceric Sulfate

The yields G(Ce III) for protons in the energy range 10.9 to 22.5 Mev are listed in Table I and plotted in Fig. 4. The yield is essentially constant at 2.95 over the range of LET_i from 0.2 to 0.4 ev/A. Barr and Schuler (*15*) reported a yield of 2.80 $\pm$ 0.04 for 10-Mev deuterons, and of 2.84 $\pm$ 0.05 for 18-Mev deuterons. Their results, extrapolated to the same energy, appear to be about 5% lower than ours.

Yields for Reduction of Ceric Sulfate in the Presence of Thallous Ions

The yields $G(\text{Ce III})_{\text{Tl}^+}$ for protons in the energy range 10.9 to 22.7 Mev are listed in Table I and are also shown in Fig. 4. These values are compared on Fig. 4 with yields obtained by Barr and Schuler (*15*) for the oxidation of ferrous sulfate in the absence of oxygen, for deuterons in the energy range 6 to 16 Mev. These values can be compared, since yields in these two solutions are stoichiometrically equivalent. Their results were adjusted by 0.964, as discussed previously. Their results appear to be about 2½% higher than ours when extrapolated to the same energy.

As expected, the yields $G(\text{Ce III})_{\text{Tl}^+}$ decrease with increase in LET_i (or decrease in $1/LET_i$).

Yields of Peroxysulfuric Acid

As shown by Boyle (*4*), peroxysulfuric acid (H_2SO_5) is produced in small yield in sulfate solutions. This accumulates in the ceric sulfate dosimeter and can be measured. From an average of seven determinations, $G(H_2SO_5)$ was 0.16 $\pm$ 0.04 for 11- to 23-Mev protons. Boyle reported $G(H_2SO_5)$ to be 0.14 $\pm$ 0.02 for cobalt γ-radiation ($LET_i = 0.02$ ev/A). It should be expected that $G(H_2SO_5)$ would increase with increase in LET. The value 0.16 measured here is assumed to be a lower limit.

Molecular and Free Radical Yields

Calculated molecular and free-radical yields are given in Table II. Values listed for G(Fe III), G(Ce III), and $G(\text{Ce III})_{\text{Tl}^+}$ were taken from a plot of the data from Table I in order to obtain the various yields at the same energy. The values G_H, G_{OH}, $G_{H_2O_2}$, G_{H_2}, and G_{-H_2O} in Table II were calculated from G(Fe III), G(Ce

TABLE II

MOLECULAR AND FREE-RADICAL YIELDS FROM THE RADIOLYSIS OF FERROUS AND CERIC SOLUTIONS BY PROTONS OF VARIOUS ENERGIES IN THE RANGE 10.5 TO 22.0 MEV

E_P (Mev)	G(Fe III)	$G(\text{Ce III})_{Tl^+}$	G(Ce III)	G_H	G_{OH}	$G_{H_2O_2}$	G_{H_2}	G_{-H_2O} [a]	G_{HOH} [b]	$G_{-H_2O(T)}$ [c]	X [d]
22.0	12.64	6.71	2.95	2.97	1.88	0.93	0.39	3.74	1.32	5.06	0.48
22.0	12.41	6.58	2.95	2.92	1.82	0.92	0.37	3.66	1.29	4.95	0.48
18.0	12.18	6.46	2.95	2.86	1.76	0.92	0.37	3.60	1.29	4.89	0.47
16.0	11.91	6.33	2.95	2.79	1.69	0.93	0.38	3.54	1.31	4.85	0.46
14.0	11.65	6.21	2.95	2.72	1.63	0.93	0.39	3.49	1.32	4.81	0.45
12.0	11.42	6.07	2.95	2.68	1.56	0.92	0.36	3.39	1.28	4.67	0.45
10.5	11.22	5.98	2.95	2.62	1.52	0.92	0.37	3.36	1.29	4.65	0.44_5

[a] Calculated from equation 1; $G_{-H_2O} = 2G_{H_2} + G_H$

[b] Yield of water from recombination of H and OH; $G_{HOH} = G_{H_2O_2} + G_{H_2}$

[c] Sum of columns 9 and 10.

[d] X equals fraction of radicals combining with solute; $G_H + G_{OH}/2G_{-H_2O(T)}$.

III)$_{Tl^+}$, and G(Ce III) by assuming the following relations between measured yields and yields of intermediates:

$$G_{-H_2O} = G_H + 2G_{H_2} = G_{OH} + 2G_{H_2O_2} \quad (1)$$

$$G(\text{Fe III}) = 2G_{H_2O_2} + 3G_H + G_{OH} \quad (2)$$

$$G(\text{Ce III}) = 2G_{H_2O_2} + G_H - G_{OH} \quad (3)$$

$$G(\text{Ce III})_{Tl^+} = 2G_{H_2O_2} + G_H + G_{OH} \quad (4)$$

In this calculation H_2SO_5 was not considered as an intermediate. If it were assumed to be an intermediate, the stoichiometric relationships would be:

$$G_{-H_2O} = G_H + 2G_{H_2} = G_{OH} + 2G_{H_2O_2} + 2G_{H_2SO_5} \quad (5)$$

$$G(\text{Fe III}) = 2G_{H_2O_2} + 3G_H + G_{OH} + 2G_{H_2SO_5} \quad (6)$$

$$G(\text{Ce III})_{Tl^+} = 2G_{H_2O_2} + G_H + G_{OH} + 2G_{H_2SO_5} \quad (7)$$

In the ferrous sulfate dosimeter and in the ceric–thallous dosimeter, H_2SO_5 acts as an oxidizing agent. In the ceric sulfate dosimeter it does not react. In the absence of direct experimental evidence, it was assumed that H_2SO_5 oxidizes two thallous ions to two Tl^{2+} ions, which in turn reduce two ceric ions. This appears to be a good assumption in view of the fact that $G(\text{Ce III})_{Tl^+}$ is equivalent to $G(\text{Fe III})_{-O_2}$. The yield of H_2SO_5 was 0.16 over the whole range of proton energies. If this were considered as an intermediate, G_H and G_{H_2} would remain the same as in Table II, but the values for G_{OH} would decrease by 0.16 and the values for G_{H_2O} would decrease by 0.08.

Yields for the three dosimeter solutions give a completely consistent set of yields of intermediates. The yields G_H and G_{OH} decrease with increase in LET_i, as expected. However, the molecular yields G_{H_2}, $G_{H_2O_2}$, and $G_{H_2SO_5}$ remain essentially constant over the range of LET from 0.2 to 0.4 ev/A. It was expected that these yields would increase slightly with increase in LET. The magnitude of G_H is very close to the predicted value (*2*). However, G_{H_2} seems to be about 35% lower than the value one would expect (*2*). Also, G_{-H_2O} is lower than predicted. Likewise, G_{OH} is about 15% lower and $G_{H_2O_2}$ about 5% lower than expected (*2*).

We have no good explanation for the low value of the derived hydrogen yield. A small error in a measured yield would be reflected as a large error in the derived hydrogen yield. Also, there may be other reactions of minor importance that should be considered in the mechanisms.

The yield for net water decomposition, G_{-H_2O}, is given by the stoichiometry in equation 1. A yield for total water decomposition, $G_{-H_2O(T)}$, was calculated by assuming that the number of radicals recombining to form water is equal to the number combining to form H_2 and H_2O_2 ($G_{HOH} = G_{H_2} + G_{H_2O_2}$). The yield for total water decomposition, $G_{-H_2O(T)} = G_{-H_2O} + G_{HOH}$, is given in the next to last column of Table II. Both G_{-H_2O} and $G_{-H_2O(T)}$ decrease with increasing LET. The last column in Table II gives the fraction of radicals available for reaction with solute. This fraction, of course, decreases with increase in LET. Variation of yields with LET are generally in qualitative agreement with the diffusion-kinetics model. Also, the results extrapolate smoothly to values obtained by Anderson and Hart (*9*), which were shown to be in accord with the one-radical diffusion model.

SUMMARY

Initial yields were measured for oxidation of ferrous sulfate, and for reduction of ceric sulfate both with and without thallous ion present, by using protons of various energies in the range from 11 to 23 Mev. From these values, yields of the intermediates G_H, G_{H_2}, G_{OH}, $G_{H_2O_2}$, $C_{H_2SO_5}$, and G_{-H_2O} were evaluated.

Over the range of LET covered (0.2 to 0.4 ev/A), G(Fe III) and $G(\text{Ce III})_{\text{Tl}^+}$ decreased with increase in LET_i, whereas G(Ce III) remained constant. The yield G(Fe III) decreased from 12.8 for 23-Mev protons to 11.3 for 11-Mev protons, whereas $G(\text{Ce III})_{\text{Tl}^+}$ decreased from 6.78 to 6.01 in this same range. The yield G(Ce III) remained constant at 2.95 in this range of energy.

The yield G_H decreased from 2.97 at 22 Mev to 2.63 at 10.5 Mev; G_{OH} decreased from 1.88 to 1.52 in this range. G_{H_2} and $G_{H_2O_2}$ remained essentially constant at 0.39 and 0.92, respectively, in this range of energy. The results are generally in agreement with the diffusion-kinetics model.

Methods were devised for measuring accurately both the proton energy and the proton beam current entering the dosimeter solutions.

ACKNOWLEDGMENTS

We wish to express our appreciation to J. W. Boyle, H. A. Mahlman, and J. F. Riley for the numerous discussions which took place throughout the course of this study, and to C. B. Fulmer and J. B. Ball who suggested the method used for measuring beam current.

One of the authors, G.L.K., is grateful to the Oak Ridge Institute of Nuclear Studies for sponsoring the research under the Oak Ridge Graduate Fellowship Program.

RECEIVED: August 22, 1962

REFERENCES

1. A. H. SAMUEL and J. L. MAGEE, Theory of radiation chemistry. II. Track effects in the radiolysis of water. *J. Chem. Phys.* **21**, 1080–1087 (1953).
2. A. O. ALLEN, *The Radiation Chemistry of Water and Aqueous Solutions*, D. Van Nostrand Co., Princeton, New Jersey, 1961.
3. C. J. HOCHANADEL, in *Comparative Effects of Radiation* (M. Burton, J. S. Kirby-Smith, and J. L. Magee, eds.), pp. 151–184. John Wiley & Sons, New York, 1960.
4. J. W. BOYLE, The decomposition of aqueous sulfuric acid solutions by cobalt gamma rays. I. Radical and molecular product yields from Ce(IV) solutions in 0.4 to 18 M H_2SO_4. *Radiation Res.* **17**, 426–449 (1962).
5. C. J. HOCHANADEL and J. A. GHORMLEY, A calorimetric calibration of gamma ray actinometers. *J. Chem. Phys.* **21**, 880–885 (1953).
6. J. W. BOYLE and H. A. MAHLMAN, private communication, Oak Ridge National Laboratory, Oak Ridge, Tennessee, May 8, 1962.
7. T. J. SWORSKI, Mechanism for the reduction of ceric ion by thallous ion induced by cobalt-60 gamma radiation. *Radiation Res.* **4**, 483–492 (1956).
8. R. H. SCHULER and A. O. ALLEN, Radiation chemistry studies with cyclotron beams of variable energy: Yields in aerated ferrous sulfate solution. *J. Am. Chem. Soc.* **79**, 1565–1572 (1957).
9. A. R. ANDERSON and E. J. HART, Molecular product and free radical yields in the decomposition of water by protons, deuterons, and helium ions. *Radiation Res.* **14**, 689–704 (1961).
10. J. SALDICK and A. O. ALLEN, The yield of oxidation of ferrous sulfate in acid solution by high-energy cathode rays. *J. Chem. Phys.* **22**, 438–442 (1954).
11. R. H. SCHULER and A. O. ALLEN, Absolute measurement of beam currents for radiation-chemical studies. *Rev. Sci. Instr.* **26**, 1128–1130 (1955).
12. E. J. HART, W. J. RAMLER, and S. R. ROCKLIN, Chemical yields of ionizing particles in aqueous solutions: Effect of energy of protons and deuterons. *Radiation Res.* **4**, 378–393 (1956).
13. H. A. SCHWARZ, J. M. CAFFREY, and G. SCHOLES, Radiolysis of neutral water by cyclotron produced deuterons and helium ions. *J. Am. Chem. Soc.* **81**, 1801–1809 (1957).
14. J. B. BALL and C. B. FULMER, private communication, Oak Ridge National Laboratory, Oak Ridge, Tennessee, June 19, 1961.
15. N. F. BARR and R. H. SCHULER, The dependence of radical and molecular yields on linear energy transfer in the radiation decomposition of 0.8 N sulfuric acid solutions. *J. Phys. Chem.* **63**, 808–812 (1959).

RADIATION RESEARCH 19, 474–484 (1963)

Comparative Chemical Protection to the Intestinal and Hematopoietic Systems of Whole-Body X-Irradiated Mice

JEAN R. MAISIN[1] AND DAVID G. DOHERTY

Armed Forces Institute of Pathology, Washington, D. C., and Biology Division, Oak Ridge National Laboratory,[2] Oak Ridge, Tennessee

INTRODUCTION

It has already been shown by many authors that MEA (2-mercaptoethylamine) and AET (2-aminoethylisothiourea dihydrobromide) have a marked protective action on the alimentary tract (*1–11*) as well as on the hematopoietic systems of mammals (*6, 12–18*). Maisin and Moutschen (*9*) demonstrated by mitotic counts and chromosome breaks that after a 900-r X-ray exposure APMT (*S*,3-aminopropyl-*N′*-methylisothiourea) and D-2-ABT (D-*S*,2-aminobutylisothiourea) offer some protection to the alimentary tract. Alexander *et al.* (*19*), Langendorff and Koch (*20*), and Langendorff *et al.* (*21, 22*) showed that 5-hydroxytryptamine (enteramine or serotonin) significantly increases the survival time of mice and rats exposed to a lethal X-ray dose. Wang *et al.* (*23*) found that the administration of very small doses of AET or MEA combined with serotonin gives a better survival than the administration of a small dose of each compound alone.

The purpose of this study was to compare the protective activity of MEA, AET, D-2-ABT, APMT, MEA and serotonin, and AET and serotonin combined, on the small intestine and the hematopoietic system.

MATERIALS AND METHODS

Animals

Male and female random-bred A-1 mice, 12 to 14-weeks-old (20 to 28 gm), were used. They were housed 5 to 10 in a cage and had free access to food and water. A Phillips constant-potential X-ray machine was used at 250 kv, 15 ma. Other factors were 1.0 mm Al added filtration; HVL, 0.5 mm of Cu; target-to-object

[1] National Institutes of Health Research Fellow from Louvain, Belgium, World Health Organization Research Fellow while at Oak Ridge. Present address: Radiobiology C.E.N., Mol, Belgium.

[2] Operated by Union Carbide Corporation for the U. S. Atomic Energy Commission.

distance, 60 cm; dose rate in air, 100 r/min. The mice were exposed in groups of 12 in a partitioned, revolving Lucite cage. The $LD_{50(30)}$ days was 650 r.

Preparation of Chemicals

In separate experiments, one of the following compounds was injected intraperitoneally 15 minutes before irradiation: 8.8 mg of AET, 6.0 mg of APMT, 1.5 mg of D-2-ABT, 4.0 mg or 8.0 mg of MEA, or 1.0 mg of serotonin injected 10 minutes before irradiation. In some experiments, 8.0 mg of MEA and 4.0 or 16 mg of AET were given by stomach tube 30 minutes before irradiation. In combined treatment, AET was administered by stomach tube 30 minutes and serotonin intraperitoneally 10 minutes before irradiation.

AET was neutralized with NaOH, and APMT and D-2-ABT were neutralized with $NaHCO_3$. MEA and serotonin were diluted in distilled water.

Mitotic Activity

For the histologic examination and the mitotic activity, two sections were taken from the middle of the duodenum, and two from the last loop of ileum. The tissues were fixed in Zenker-formol and stained with hematoxylin and eosin. Microscopic fields of the crypt region and neck of the small intestinal villus were studied at magnifications of 800× and 700× to obtain mitotic counts. In each section 60 to 120 fields were examined. Cells from late prophase to early telophase were counted.

Nucleated bone marrow cells of one femur were counted in a hemacytometer. The other femur was saved for histologic examination. Two to six mice from each group were killed each day for 8 or 10 days. Normal control mice were also studied.

RESULTS

Mitotic Activity and Survival Time

Figures 1 through 5 show the protective effects of the various compounds on mitosis of intestinal epithelium of mice irradiated at progressively higher doses.

A comparison of AET and MEA administered either orally or intraperitoneally at 900 r (Fig. 1) shows that the most rapid recovery occurred in the orally treated AET animals, the intraperitoneal dose being slightly less effective, whereas no difference was observed between oral and intraperitoneal MEA. A temporary overshoot in mitoses occurred on the fourth day in AET-treated animals and on the fifth day in the MEA-treated animals. In the untreated, irradiated control mice, recovery occurred more slowly, with no overshoot above the normal values. At 1500 r (Fig. 3) the route of administration had no effect on the mitotic recovery time for either compound, the values returning to normal by the fourth day, AET showing a hyper-response in mitotic activity, whereas MEA did not. The total

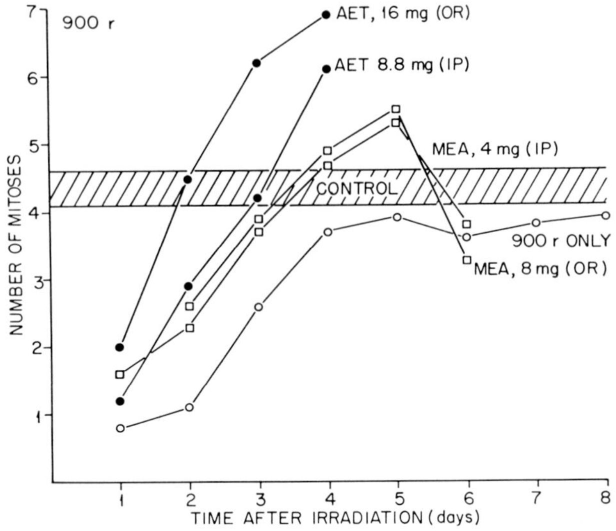

FIG. 1. The protective effect of AET and MEA on mitosis of intestinal epithelium of A-1 mice irradiated with 900 r.

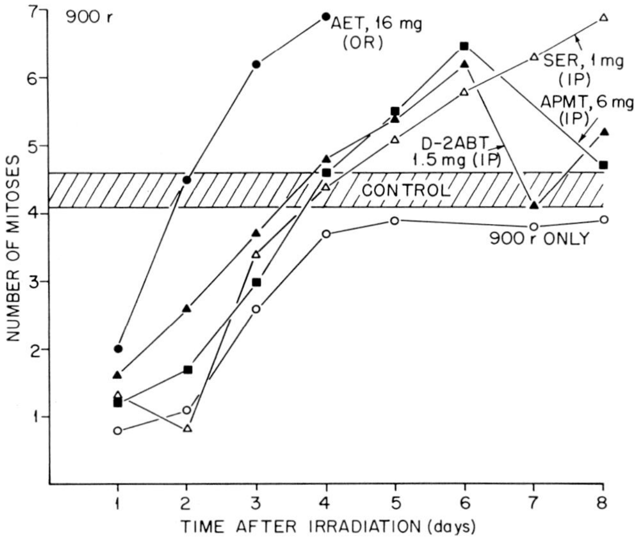

FIG. 2. The protective effect of AET, APMT, D-2-ABT, and serotonin on mitosis of intestinal epithelium of A-1 mice irradiated with 900 r.

number of mitoses in AET-protected mice was higher than in the mice treated with MEA, and some were still alive on day 30, whereas all the MEA-treated mice died by the seventh day. Even at 2000 r (Fig. 5) AET-treated animals showed a recovery to normal by the seventh day, with some overshoot in mitotic activity,

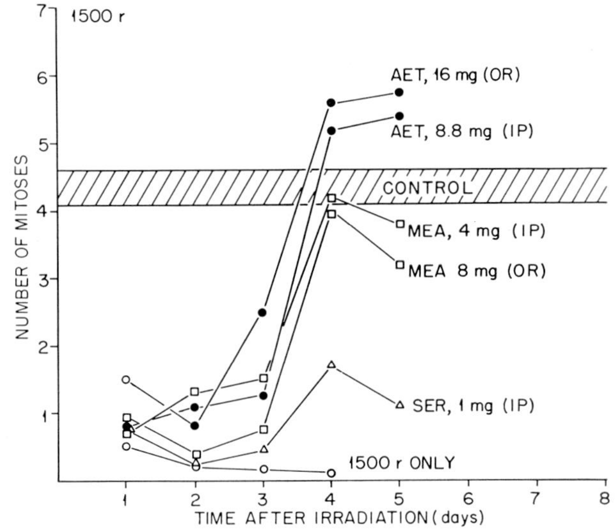

FIG. 3. The protective effect of AET, MEA, and serotonin on mitosis of intestinal epithelium of A-1 mice irradiated with 1500 r.

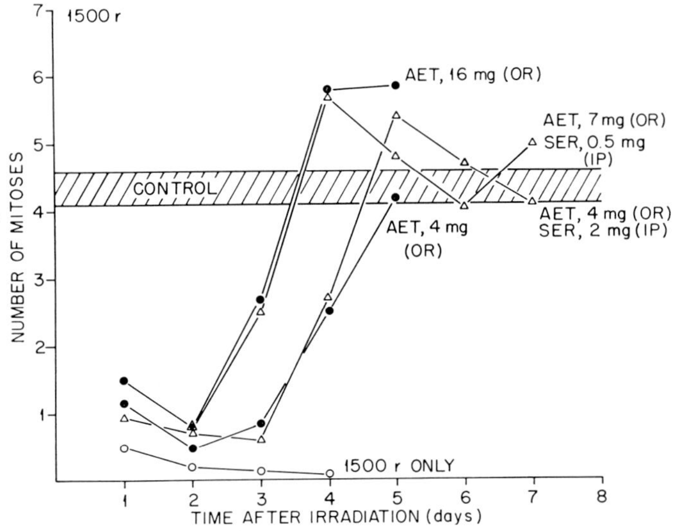

FIG. 4. The protective effect of AET and AET plus serotonin on mitosis of intestinal epithelium of A-1 mice irradiated with 1500 r.

whereas the MEA-treated animals died on the fourth or fifth day before recovery returned to normal. No recovery was obtained at 2500 r.

The response of the intestinal epithelium of mice treated with D-2-ABT, APMT, and serotonin (Fig. 2) at 900 r was about the same as MEA, the maximum response occurring on the sixth day for D-2-ABT and APMT and on the eighth day for serotonin. Some recovery in mitotic count was observed for all three compounds at the 1500-r level, the two isothioureas being a little better than serotonin, although all the mice died by the fifth day.

The combined optimal dose of oral AET and intraperitoneal serotonin proved to be much more toxic than either compound alone, precluding its use in radiation experiments. The results obtained with several nontoxic combinations at lower dose levels of both compounds used before treatment with 1500 r are presented in Fig. 4. AET (4.0 mg) combined with a high dose of serotonin (2.0 mg) yielded about the same intestinal protection as 4.0 mg of AET alone, whereas a combination of 7.0 mg of AET with 0.5 mg of serotonin yielded increased intestinal protection, but not more than that obtained with the optimal dose (16 mg) of AET. Similarly, 12 mg of AET combined with 0.5 or 1.0 mg of serotonin was no better than the 7.0 mg AET–0.5 mg serotonin combination. This latter treatment given before exposure to 2500 r (Fig. 5), however, still promoted a small amount of intestinal recovery by the fifth day—recovery that did not appear in mice treated only with AET.

Hematopoietic Recovery

Figure 6 shows that, after a 1500-r exposure, AET still allowed some bone marrow recovery to take place in a few mice. Areas of nucleated bone marrow

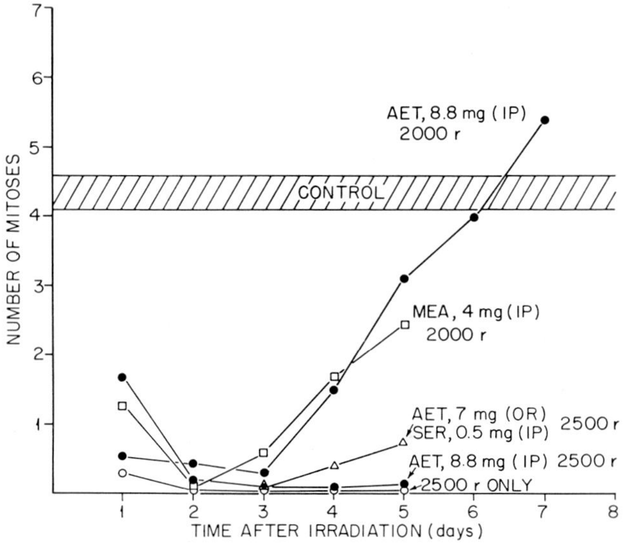

FIG. 5. The protective effect of AET, MEA, and AET plus serotonin on the mitosis of intestinal epithelium of A-1 mice irradiated with 2000 and 2500 r.

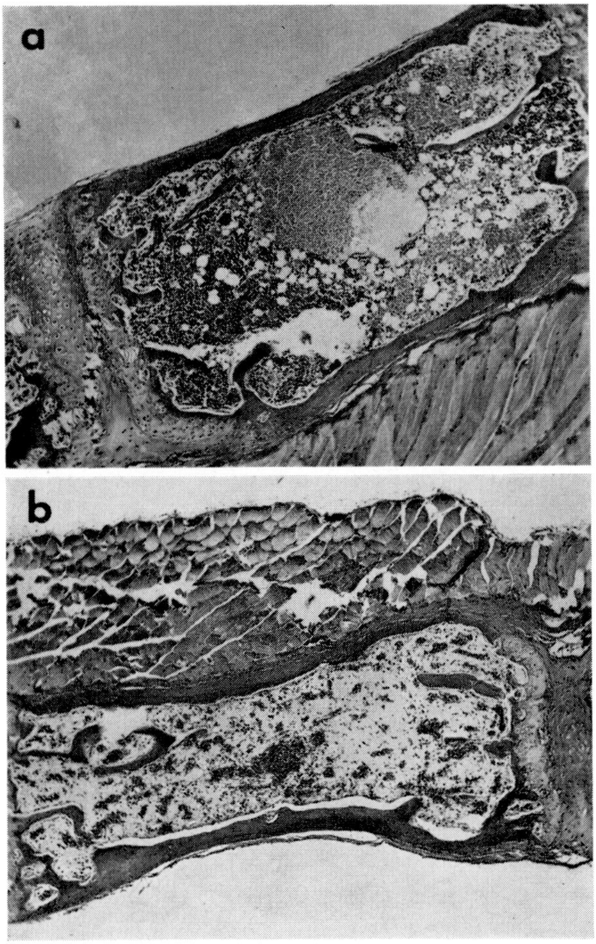

FIG. 6. *a*, Femur of a mouse protected with AET (8.8 mg intraperitoneally) 8 days after 1500 r of X-ray exposure. Note the presence of bone marrow cells and hemorrhage. *b*, Femur of a mouse protected with MEA 6 days after 1500 r of X-ray exposure. Note the hemorrhage and the depletion of the bone marrow.

cells can also be seen. Mice treated with MEA did not show this recovery. Serotonin, D-2-ABT, and APMT also failed to provide bone marrow protection after 1500 r.

Figure 7 shows that bone marrow recovery was actually improved with the combined treatment when compared with the protection offered by the maximum dose of AET and serotonin given separately. It shows clearly, too, that the improvement of the bone marrow recovery depended on the quantity of AET present.

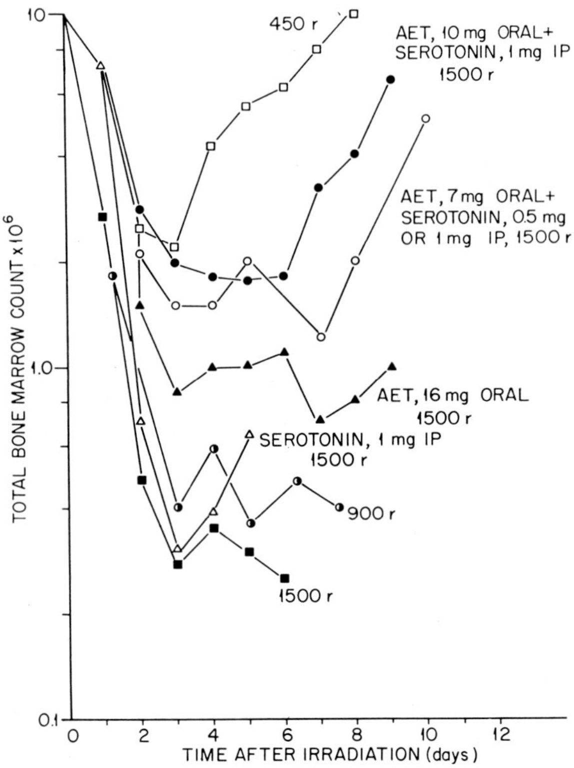

FIG. 7. Bone marrow recovery of mice irradiated with 1500, 900, and 450 r pretreated with AET, serotonin, and AET and serotonin.

Histologic sections revealed that the spleen recovery was also improved by the combined treatment. The recovery started on day 6 and on day 9; large zones of proliferation were seen. In AET-treated mice, the recovery began later and was not so pronounced.

DISCUSSION AND CONCLUSION

Doherty *et al.* (*24*) and Shapira *et al.* (*25*) demonstrated by structural studies of the derivatives of MEA and AET that a combination of a basic and a sulfhydryl group separated by no more than three carbons offers the maximum amount of radiation protection in this class of compounds. They demonstrated, too, that, although *S*,3-aminopropylisothiourea (APT) is more active on a molar basis than AET, it yields about the same radiation $LD_{50(30)}$. Unfortunately, the increased activity of APT is offset by an equal increase in chemical toxicity. The four-carbon compound, *S*,4-aminobutylisothiourea, as well as the corresponding 4-mercaptobutylguanidine is almost completely ineffective in providing radiation protection. Evaluation (in terms of elevation of the radiation $LD_{50(30)}$) of a wide variety of protective compounds related to AET and APT (*26*) revealed that any substitution on the basic structure, although occasionally yielding more active compounds at the 900-r level (*27*), gave compounds with a lower radiation $LD_{50(30)}$ than the parent compounds. The current results suggest that the reduced protective activity at supralethal dose levels of compounds with an alkyl substituent on either the amidine nitrogen-APMT or the carbon chain-D-2-ABT may arise from the lack of protection to the intestinal system. The same degree of protection at 900 r is obtained with the optimal dose of APMT and D-2-ABT, although the latter is more active in that only one-quarter of the amount is necessary (Fig. 1). At 1500 r there is only a small degree of intestinal protection offered by either compound.

Of the five compounds studied, AET offered the best intestinal protection at radiation doses up to 2000 r. The recovery of MEA-treated animals at 900 r and 1500 r is not so rapid, and at 2000 r MEA is ineffective. A partial explanation may be that at 1500 r there is no marrow regeneration in MEA-treated animals, whereas recovery occurs in some AET-treated animals. Serotonin afforded little protection to the small intestine and bone marrow after 900 and 1500 r, in contrast to the results obtained by Langendorff *et al.* (*22*), who believe that serotonin is the best chemical protector known.

We conclude from these results that MEA, in contrast to AET (*11, 18*), protects the small intestine of the mouse to a greater extent than the bone marrow. In the rat given MEA, Maisin (*28*) and Maldague *et al.* (*2*) have previously obtained dose-reduction factors of 1.2 for the bone marrow and 1.5 for the small intestine. AET is more effective in protecting both tissues than MEA, probably because it is a better radical-trapping agent; its two additional nitrogen atoms give it a larger measure of resonance stability (*26*) as well as make it a more reactive sulfhydryl compound.

Many attempts have been made to obtain increased radiation protection by using combined treatments that may be supplementary. Maisin *et al.* (*29*) demonstrated in rats given 700 r that treatment with MEA and liver shielding gave better survival than treatment with MEA alone. Maisin *et al.* (*30*) and Burnett and Doherty (*31*) showed that MEA and AET given before irradiation and followed by isologous bone marrow transplantation, respectively, increased the $LD_{100(30)}$ greater than either alone. Devik (*32*) and Vasilev (*33*) obtained increased 30-day survival with a combination of anoxia with cysteine, MEA, and cystamine pretreatment over chemical alone. Baldini and Ferri (*34*) found increased protection when pantothenic acid was added to MEA pretreatment. Langendorff *et al.* (*35*) reported that gonadectomy of male mice increased their radiation resistance and was additive to MEA treatment. In contrast, Kedrova and Krikhova (*36*) found that combined treatment of rats with ACTH and cysteine accelerated death.

In selecting a combination treatment, we chose the most active sulfhydryl compound, AET, as well as the pharmacologically active agent, serotonin, which provides protection presumably via local tissue anoxia. Intestinal protection after combined treatment was found to be primarily dependent on the dose of AET. At low AET doses the addition of serotonin increased the protective effect, although the maximum possible combined dose was not better than the optimal protection offered by AET alone. A similar dose dependence was observed in the response of the bone marrow, although in contrast to the intestine the combined treatment was more effective than AET alone.

The results obtained in this study illustrate the difficulties involved in the mechanistic interpretation of the biological results obtained with protective agents. With respect to the hematopoietic system, the combined treatment before 1500 r clearly gave better recovery than the optimum treatment with the single compound. These data are similar to the mortality results reported by Wang *et al.* (*23*). In the intestinal system, however, the sulfhydryl compounds alone gave the best protection, the addition of serotonin to a low dose of AET giving only a slight improvement in recovery time. In both systems the degree of protection was dependent on the AET concentration with a definite upper limit of activity. The additivity obtained in the marrow system, as well as the dependence of the intestinal protection on the sulfhydryl compound level, suggests that AET and serotonin act via different pathways. Alternatively, serotonin may produce a greater degree of anoxia in the bone marrow and spleen than in the small intestine. The present data do not permit us to discriminate between these two mechanisms.

SUMMARY

Chemical protection by AET, MEA, D-2-ABT, APMT, serotonin, and a combination of AET and serotonin of the alimentary tracts of mice against 900, 1500, 2000, and 2500 r, and the hematopoietic system after 1500 r has been studied. AET and MEA offered the best intestinal protection, AET being superior to MEA at all dose levels. Doubling the optimal intraperitoneal dose of AET and MEA by oral administration failed to increase the degree of intestinal protection. Combined treatment with AET and serotonin, while providing better protection to the bone marrow than either alone, did not increase intestinal protection beyond that of AET alone.

ACKNOWLEDGMENTS

We wish to thank Dr. C. C. Congdon, Col. C. F. Tessmer, and Dr. D. Mostofi for their interest during this investigation.

RECEIVED: September 4, 1962

REFERENCES

1. P. DESAIVE and J. VARETTO-DENOËL, Influence de la β-mercaptoethylamine sur la response de l'intestin grele du rat à une irradiation roentgenienne localisée. *Experientia* **11,** 242–248 (1955).

2. P. Maldague, A. Dunjic, H. Maisin, and J. Maisin, L'importance de la mercaptoethylamine dans la protection contre le syndrome oesophagien et les lesions cutanées graves. *Compt. Rend. Soc. Biol.* **150,** 1637–1641 (1956).
3. A. Dunjic, J. Maisin, P. Maldague, and H. Maisin, De l'existence de syndromes oropharygne et pulmonaire mortels chez des rats irradiés à fortes doses de R.X. *Compt. Rend. Soc. Biol.* **150,** 587–592 (1956).
4. R. H. Mole and D. M. Temple, Intestinal damage by radiation and its chemical modification. *Nature* **180,** 1278 (1957).
5. R. H. Mole and D. M. Temple, The DNA content of the small intestine as a quantitative measure of damage and recovery after whole body irradiation. *Intern. J. Radiation Biol.* **1,** 28–42 (1959).
6. J. N. Toal, J. C. Reid, R. B. Williams, and J. White, Effect of total-body X radiation from near-threshold to tissue-lethal dose on small-bowel epithelium of the rat. II. Changes in nucleic acid and protein synthesis in relation to cell division. *J. Natl. Cancer Inst.* **21,** 63–76 (1958).
7. R. B. Williams, J. N. Toal, J. White, and H. M. Carpenter, Effect of total-body X radiation from near-threshold to tissue-lethal doses on small-bowel epithelium of the rat. I. Changes in morphology and rate of cell division in relation to time and dose. *J. Natl. Cancer Inst.* **21,** 17–63 (1958).
8. J. R. Maisin, J. Moutschen, G. D. Novelli, and D. G. Doherty, Chemical protection of the intestine against radiation damage. *Radiation Res.* **11,** 453 (1959).
9. J. R. Maisin and J. Moutschen, Chemical protection of the alimentary tract of whole-body X-irradiated mice. II. Chromosome breaks and mitotic activity. *Exptl. Cell Research* **21,** 347–352 (1960).
10. J. R. Maisin and R. A. Popp, Effect of AET on sodium, potassium and esterases of the alimentary tract of irradiated mice. *Am. J. Physiol.* **199,** 251–255 (1960).
11. J. R. Maisin, G. D. Novelli, D. G. Doherty, and C. C. Congdon, Chemical protection of the alimentary tract of whole-body X-irradiated mice. I. Changes in weight, histology, and cell division in relation to nucleic acid and protein synthesis. *Intern. J. Radiation Biol.* **2,** 281–293 (1960).
12. H. M. Patt, D. E. Smith, and E. Jackson, The effect of cysteine on the peripheral blood of the irradiated rat. *Blood* **5,** 758–763 (1950).
13. R. L. Rosenthal, L. Goldschmidt, and B. I. Pickering, Hematologic changes in rats protected by cysteine against total body X-irradiation. *Am. J. Physiol.* **166,** 15–19 (1951).
14. D. F. Peterson and K. P. Dubois, Modification of the radiation-induced increases in phosphatase activity of hematopoietic tissues by chemical agents. *Am. J. Physiol.* **181,** 513–518 (1955).
15. B. G. Crouch and R. R. Overman, Chemical protection against X-irradiation death in primates. A preliminary report. *Science* **125,** 1092 (1957).
16. T. Makinodan, I. C. Shekarchi, and C. C. Congdon, Antibody response of mice treated with 2-mercaptoethylguanidine hydrobromide and lethal doses of X-radiation and its significance to the relation of antigen to host. *J. Immunol.* **79,** 281–287 (1957).
17. L. H. Smith, Protective effect of 2-mercaptoethylguanidine on bone marrow cells X irradiated *in vitro*. *Exptl. Cell Research* **13,** 627–630 (1957).
18. P. Urso, C. C. Congdon, D. G. Doherty, and R. Shapira, Effect of chemical protection and bone marrow treatment on radiation injury in mice. *Blood* **13,** 665–676 (1958).
19. P. Alexander, Z. M. Bacq, S. F. Cousens, M. Fox, A. Herve, and J. Lazar, Mode of action of some substances which protect against the lethal effect of X-rays. *Radiation Res.* **2,** 392–415 (1955).
20. H. Langendorff and R. Koch, Untersuchungen über einen biologischen Strahlenschutz.

XVIII. Die Wirkung zentralerragender Pharmaka auf das bestrahlte Tier. *Strahlentherapie* **102,** 58–64 (1957).

21. M. Langendorff, H. J. Melching, H. Langendorff, R. Koch, and R. Jaques, Untersuchungen über einen biologischen Strahlenschutz. XXI. Weitere Untersuchungen bur Wirkung zentral-erregender und-dämpfender Pharmaka auf die strahlenempfindlichkeit des Tieres. *Strahlentherapie* **104,** 338–344 (1957a).

22. H. Langendorff, H. J. Melching, and H. A. Lander, 5-Hydroxytryptamine as a radiation protective substance in animals. *Intern. J. Radiation Biol.* **1,** 24–27 (1959).

23. R. Wang, J. G. Kereiakes, R. R. Anderson, and A. T. Krebs, Synergistic effect of certain radioprotective compounds. U. S. Army Medical Research Laboratory, Fort Knox, Kentucky, Report No. 407, December 15 (1959); R. Wang and J. G. Kereiakes, Increased radiation protection by combinations of radioprotective compounds. (Abstract) *Radiation Res.* **11,** 476 (1959).

24. D. G. Doherty, W. T. Burnett, Jr., and R. Shapira, Chemical protection against ionizing radiation. II. Mercaptoalkylamines and related compounds with protective activity. *Radiation Res.* **7,** 13–21 (1957).

25. R. Shapira, D. G. Doherty, and W. T. Burnett, Jr., Chemical protection against ionizing radiation. III. Mercaptoalkylguanidines and related isothiuronium compounds with protective activity. *Radiation Res.* **7,** 22–34 (1957).

26. D. G. Doherty, Chemical protection to mammals against ionizing radiation. In *Radiation Protection and Recovery* (A. Hollaender, ed.), Chapter 3, Pergamon Press, London, 1960.

27. R. H. Bradford, R. Shapira, and D. G. Doherty, The intracellular distribution and binding of radiation-protective mercaptoalkylguanides. *Intern. J. Radiation Biol.* **3,** 595–608 (1961).

28. H. Maisin, Contribution a l'étude du syndrome medullaire après irradiation: Étude experimentelle. Editions Arscia S. A., Bruxelles (1959).

29. J. Maisin, M. Mandart, G. Lambert, and H. Maisin, Action curative de la β-mercaptoethylamine chez le rat irradié avec foie protege. *Compt. Rend. Soc. Biol.* **147,** 362–364 (1953).

30. J. Maisin, H. Maisin, and A. Dunjic, Influence de l'injection de mercapto-ethylamine avant l'irradiation sur la survie des animaux injectes après l'irradiation d'une suspension de moelle osseuse. *Compt. Rend. Soc. Biol.* **148,** 1293–1297 (1954).

31. W. T. Burnett, Jr., and D. G. Doherty, Additive effect of S,β-aminoethylisothiuronium·Br·HBr, bone marrow, and streptomycin on irradiated mice. (Abstract) *Radiation Res.* **3,** 217 (1955).

32. F. Devik, Protective effects of combined hypoxia and cysteine treatment on whole-body irradiation of mice. *Brit. J. Radiol.*, **27,** 463–466 (1954).

33. G. A. Vasilev, Acclimatization to hypoxia combined with the introduction of cystamine and cysteamine as a method of radiation sickness prophylaxis. *Med. Radiol.* **4** (1), 41–44 (1959).

34. G. Baldini and L. Ferri, Experimental and clinical research on the radio-protective action of cysteamine and cystamine. II. Experimental research upon mammals. *Brit. J. Radiol.* **30,** 95–98 (1957).

35. H. Langendorff, A. Catsch, and R. Koch, Untersuchungen über einen biologischen Strahlenschutz. XIX. Weitere Untersuchungen über die Strahlenempfindlichkeit und den Cysteaminschutz bei gonadektomierten männlichen Mäusen. *Strahlentherapie* **102,** 291–297 (1957b).

36. E. M. Kedrova and M. A. Krikhova, Absence of summation of protective effects of cysteine and ACTH on irradiation of rats by X ray. *Med. Radiol.* **4** (1), 60–63 (1959).

RADIATION RESEARCH **19**, 485–491 (1963)

Radiation Sensitivity of Mouse Lymph Node Cells Relative to Their Proliferative Capacity *in Vivo*[1]

L. H. SMITH[2] AND O. VOS[3]

Medical Biological Laboratory of the National Defence Research Organization, Rijswijk (Z.H.), The Netherlands, and Biology Division, Oak Ridge National Laboratory,[4] Oak Ridge, Tennessee, U.S.A.

INTRODUCTION

Viability of bone marrow cells irradiated *in vitro* or *in vivo* can be tested according to their ability to transplant and proliferate in lethally irradiated recipients (*1, 2*). The extent to which irradiated bone marrow cells proliferate in the recipient has been measured in terms of 30-day survival (*3, 4*) or the number of spleen nodules formed (*5*). Using the transplantation technique in irradiated recipients, Makinodan *et al.* (*6*) estimated the radiation sensitivity of antibody-forming cells of mouse spleen, and Hodgson (*7*) studied radiosensitivity of erythropoietic tissue of bone marrow. In the present series of experiments we attempted to estimate radiation sensitivity of lymph node cells by using a method similar to the marrow transplantation system. Vos and Weyzen (*8*) have shown that percentage 30-day survival of lethally irradiated (CBA × C57BL)F_1 mice is usually good if they are injected with bone marrow from C57BL mice. Concomitant injection of C57BL lymph node cells, however, reduces 30-day survival in proportion to the number of lymph node cells injected. Presumably, this killing effect results from transplantation of immunologically competent cells that react against host tissue antigens contributed by the other parent, viz., CBA. It seemed feasible, therefore, that reduction in viability of lymph node cells resulting from *in vitro* irradiation would be reflected in a reduction of the killing effect.

METHODS

The recipients were (CBA/Rij × C57BL/Rij)F_1 male mice that weighed 22 to 32 gm and were 11 to 13 weeks old. They were exposed to 912 r of 250-kv whole-body

[1] Investigation was conducted at the Medical Biological Laboratory, The Netherlands, during L. H. Smith's tenure of a National Science Foundation Senior Postdoctoral Fellowship, 1960–1961, in conjunction with support from the Biology Division, Oak Ridge National Laboratory.

[2] Present address: Biology Division, Oak Ridge National Laboratory, Oak Ridge, Tennessee.

[3] Medical Biological Laboratory, The Netherlands.

[4] Operated by Union Carbide Corporation for the U. S. Atomic Energy Commission.

X-rays (HVL = 1.8 mm Cu) as described by Vos and Weyzen (*9*). Within 2 hours after irradiation these mice were injected intravenously with 3.0×10^6 nucleated bone marrow cells from normal C57BL/Rij female mice of the same age or 2 to 3 weeks younger than the recipients. Two to four hours after marrow injection the same mice were injected intravenously with lymph node cells from normal C57BL/Rij female mice. Details of the preparation of the cell suspensions have been published (*9*).

For *in vitro* irradiation of lymph node cells, 2.0-ml aliquots of the suspensions were placed in open petri dishes fitted with Mylar bottoms. Lymph node cell concentration was 30×10^6 cells/ml, and suspension depth at center was about 1.3 mm. The dishes were tilted back and forth several times and covered with Perspex 1 mm thick. Cells were exposed to 100, 200, 300, or 400 r at room temperature (~22°C). Radiation factors were the same as those used for the mice (*4*). The dose was measured during each exposure with a Baldwin Ionex ionization chamber placed on the same level as the cell suspensions. After *in vitro* irradiation, suspensions were diluted to the desired cell concentration, and 0.5-ml aliquots were injected intravenously into the irradiated, marrow-treated mice.

A total of 1450 irradiated F_1 mice were used in fifteen separate experiments. For each experiment, 5 to 11 mice served as X-ray controls. All others were injected with parent (C57BL/Rij) bone marrow cells, and 10 to 25 of these received no further treatment. The remaining mice were given normal or irradiated lymph node cells. Usually one to three different doses of normal cells and two to six doses of irradiated cells were used for each experiment. In eleven of the experiments, one *in vitro* X-ray dose was used; in the other four experiments two to four doses were used. Thirty-day survival was recorded for each group.

RESULTS

The dose of whole-body radiation to which recipient F_1 mice were exposed, i.e., 912 r, corresponds to the 800-r value reported in previous publications of the Medical Biological Laboratory (*10*). Of the 101 irradiated control mice exposed to 912 r, none survived 30 days. From results of previous experiments in which (CBA × C57BL)F_1 hybrids were used (*11*), 912 r appears to be slightly in excess of the 30-day LD_{100}.

Figure 1 shows the effects of injecting normal or irradiated parent lymph node cells on 30-day survival of lethally irradiated F_1 marrow-injected mice. As the dose of normal lymph node cells increased, survival decreased. *In vitro* irradiation of the lymph node cells impaired their ability to reduce 30-day survival. Using the 50% survival point obtained from the fitted lines in Fig. 1, we calculated the per cent surviving cells from the expression

$$\text{Per cent surviving cells} = (ED_{50n}/ED_{50i}) \times 100$$

in which ED_{50n} and ED_{50i} are the number of normal and irradiated cells, respectively, that reduced 30-day survival to 50%. On the basis of these percentages,

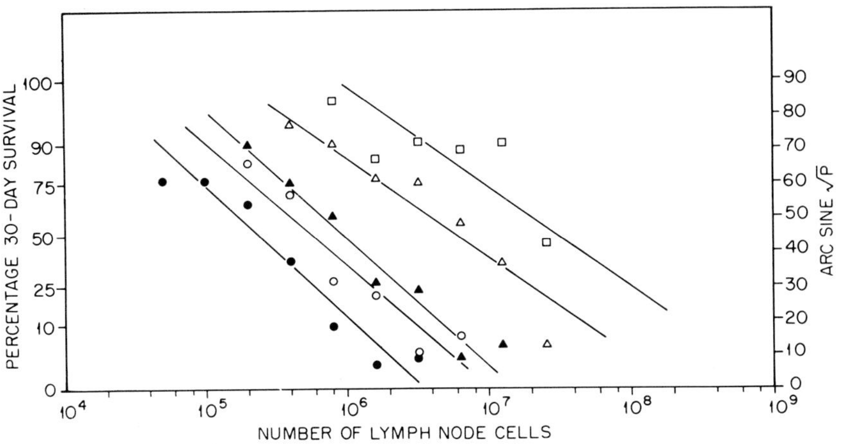

FIG. 1. The 30-day survival of X-irradiated (912 r) (CBA × C57BL)F_1 mice injected with C57BL bone marrow and lymph node cells. Each line is a least-squares fit to percentages transformed to their respective arc sine values. Symbols indicate normal lymph node cells (●), and lymph node cells irradiated *in vitro* with 100 r (○), 200 r (▲), 300 r (△), or 400 r (□). For normal lymph node cells, each point represents 20 to 90 mice (total of 380); and for irradiated cells 10 to 40 mice (total of 160 to 200 per line).

Fig. 2 was constructed. From the exponential portion of this curve, the D_{37} was calculated to be 74 r, with a 95% confidence interval of 51 to 137 r, and the extrapolation number is 2.7 (*12*).

The killing effect of lymph node cells was operative primarily during the 14- to 30-day period after whole-body irradiation, although deaths continued to occur at a reduced rate to day 60, the time when the experiments were terminated. Since use of the 30-day end point was not extremely sharp, calculations of surviving cells based on 35-day and 40-day survivals were made. Results from these calculations indicated that the 30-day end point was best in terms of reproducibility among experiments.

Of the 233 irradiated F_1 mice injected with parent bone marrow only, 78% survived 30 days. This percentage, however, does not represent an average survival for each of the marrow-injected groups, since in eight of the fifteen experiments 30-day survival was 100%.

DISCUSSION

In Table I are summarized data obtained by several investigators who have used the lethally irradiated mouse as a recipient in which proliferation of cells irradiated *in vivo* or *in vitro* was studied. Despite the varied end points used as measures of proliferation, estimates of the radiation sensitivities, in terms of the D_{37}, are reasonably similar for hematopoietic cells. In regard to the present set of data, we have presumably measured radiation sensitivity of immunologically

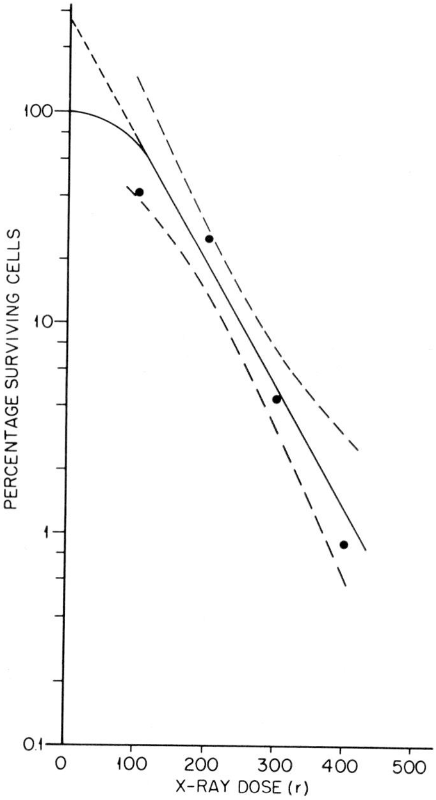

FIG. 2. The effect of *in vitro* X-irradiation on lymph node cells. The line was fitted by the method of least squares. Band denotes 90% confidence limits.

competent cells (IC cells) of lymph nodes. This assumption is supported by a considerable body of evidence obtained from studies on runt disease (*13*) and from results of other experiments in which immunological competency of transplanted cells has been implicated as an etiology of graft-versus-host reaction (14–16). This reaction is also currently considered to be the basis for the killing effect observed when parent spleen (*17, 18*) is injected into lethally irradiated F_1 hybrids treated with parent bone marrow. In some but not all parent–F_1 combinations, injection of parent marrow only into lethally irradiated F_1 hybrids results in the killing effect (*19–21*). This inconsistency is probably associated with variation in experimental methods including X-ray dose and bone marrow dose, as well as with histocompatibility factors. Thus, the variation in methods and animals used by different investigators makes meaningful comparisons of results difficult. In some experiments of the present series, deaths before 30 days occurred in lethally ir-

TABLE I

ESTIMATES OF RADIATION SENSITIVITY OF MOUSE CELLS AS DETERMINED BY VARIOUS INDICES OF THEIR PROLIFERATIVE CAPACITY IN IRRADIATED RECIPIENTS

Cell type	*Index of proliferative capacity*	*D_{37}, X-rays*	*Ref.*
Bone marrow	Per cent 30-day survival	105 rads, *in vitro*	McCulloch and Till (*3*)
Bone marrow	Number of spleen nodules on day 11 after X-ray	115 rads,[a] *in vitro*	Till and McCulloch (*5*)
Bone marrow, erythropoietic	Per cent injected Fe^{59} in RBC on day 10 after X-ray	71 r, *in vitro* or *in vivo*	Hodgson (*7*)
Bone marrow	Per cent 30-day survival	84 r, *in vitro*	Smith and Vos (*4*)
Spleen, antibody-forming	Agglutinin-forming capacity on day 5 or 6 after X-ray	70 r, *in vivo*	Makinodan *et al.* (*6*)
Spleen, antibody-forming	Agglutinin-forming capacity on day 6 after X-ray	47 and 58 r[b], *in vitro*	Celada and Carter (*22*)
Spleen, homograft-reacting	Agglutinin-forming capacity on day 6 after X-ray	78 r, *in vitro*	Celada and Carter (*22*)
Lymph node, immunologically competent	Per cent 30-day survival	74 r, *in vitro*	This article

[a] Co^{60} γ-rays.

[b] Values for two different strains of mice.

radiated F_1 hybrids treated with parent marrow only. This complication could have contributed to the variation encountered in the lymph node cell dose-response curves (Fig. 1).

Although it has not been demonstrated that IC cells form circulating antibodies against host tissue antigens, it is relevant that radiation sensitivity of IC cells, as estimated from data of the present series of experiments, is about the same as that determined for agglutinin-forming cells (*6*). Data of Celada and Carter (*22*) might indicate that radiation sensitivity of spleen cells responsible for homograft rejection is lower than that of spleen cells responsible for agglutinin formation.

Radiation sensitivity of tumor cells has been estimated by several investigators who have also used a method that employs the living mouse as a recipient in which one can compare the reproductive capacity of normal tumor cells and irradiated tumor cells. Data obtained by Hewitt and Wilson (*23*) indicate that for mouse leukemic lymphocytes exposed *in vivo* to γ-rays, the D_{37} is $\sim$162 rads. Similar results were obtained by Berry and Andrews (*24*), who used an ascites form of the leukemia and 3-Mev X-rays.

It is anticipated that this type of experimental approach, which Makinodan has termed *in vivo* tissue culture, will be of value in further studies on mechanisms of radiation damage and on radiation recovery and protection. Although it can be argued that an irradiated mouse does not present an entirely normal environment for cell proliferation, conditions are physiologically better than presently can be attained in tissue culture.

SUMMARY

The 30-day survival of F_1 mice exposed to lethal irradiation (912 r) and injected with parent bone marrow is a function of the number of parent lymph node cells injected. This relationship was used as a calibration curve to determine the surviving proportion of a suspension of lymph node cells irradiated *in vitro*. The radiation response could be represented by a survival curve, the linear portion of which indicated a D_{37} of 74 r and an extrapolation number of about 2.7.

RECEIVED: September 7, 1962

REFERENCES

1. L. H. SMITH, Protective effect of 2-mercaptoethylguanidine on bone marrow cells X-irradiated *in vitro*. *Exptl. Cell Res.* **13,** 627–630 (1957).
2. L. H. SMITH and C. C. CONGDON, Experimental treatment of acute whole-body radiation injury in mammals. In *Radiation Protection and Recovery* (A. Hollaender, ed.), Pergamon Press, New York, 1960.
3. E. A. MCCULLOCH and J. E. TILL, The radiation sensitivity of normal mouse bone marrow cells, determined by quantitative marrow transplantation into irradiated mice. *Radiation Res.*, **13,** 115–125 (1960).
4. L. H. SMITH and O. VOS, Sensitivity and protection of mouse bone-marrow cells X-irradiated *in vitro*. *Intern. J. Radiation Biol.* **5,** 461–470 (1962).
5. J. E. TILL and E. A. MCCULLOCH, A direct measurement of the radiation sensitivity of normal mouse bone marrow cells. *Radiation Res.* **14,** 213–222 (1961).
6. T. MAKINODAN, M. A. KASTENBAUM, and W. J. PETERSON, Radiosensitivity of spleen cells from normal and preimmunized mice and its significance to intact animals. *J. Immunol.* **88,** 31–37 (1962).
7. G. S. HODGSON, Radiosensitivity of marrow cells responsible for re-establishing erythropoiesis in lethally irradiated mice. *Acta Physiol. Latinoam.* in press.
8. O. VOS and W. W. H. WEYZEN, "Killing effect" of injected lymph node cells in homologous radiation chimeras. *Transplant. Bull.* **30,** 111–116 (1962).
9. O. VOS and W. W. H. WEYZEN, A specific immunological tolerance in radiation chimeras. *Transplant. Bull.* **30,** 117–123 (1962).
10. C. VAN DER MEER, O. BROCADES-ZAALBERG, O. VOS, A. J. VERGROESEN, and D. W. VAN BEKKUM, On the mechanism of the radioprotective action of cyanide. *Intern. J. Radiation Biol.* **4,** 311–319 (1962).
11. D. W. VAN BEKKUM and O. VOS, Immunological aspects of homo- and heterologous bone marrow transplantation in irradiated animals. *J. Cellular Comp. Physiol.* (*Suppl. 1*) **50,** 139–156 (1957).
12. T. T. PUCK and P. I. MARCUS, Action of X-rays on mammalian cells. *J. Exptl. Med.* **103,** 653–666 (1956).

13. R. E. Billingham and L. Brent, Quantitative studies on tissue transplantation immunity. IV. Induction of tolerance in newborn mice and studies on the phenomenon of runt disease. *Phil. Trans. Roy. Soc. London Ser. B* **242,** 439–477 (1959).
14. M. Simonsen, On the acquisition of tolerance by adult cells. *Ann. N. Y. Acad. Sci.* **87,** 382–390 (1960).
15. L. J. Cole and R. M. Garver, Abrogation by injected mouse blood of protective effect of foreign bone marrow in lethally X-irradiated mice. *Nature* **184,** 1815–1816 (1959).
16. J. W. Goodman and C. C. Congdon, Blood-marrow mixtures in irradiated mice. *Arch. Pathol.* **72,** 18–26 (1961).
17. L. J. Cole, R. M. Garver, and M. E. Ellis, Transfer of donor immunological reactivity to X-irradiated F_1 hybrid mice by injected parental bone marrow. *Am. J. Physiol.* **196,** 100–104 (1959).
18. E. E. Schwartz, A. C. Upton, and C. C. Congdon, A fatal reaction caused by implantation of adult parental spleen tissue in irradiated F_1 mice. *Proc. Soc. Exptl. Biol. Med.* **96,** 797–800 (1957).
19. D. E. Uphoff, Genetic factors influencing irradiation protection by bone marrow. I. The F_1 hybrid effect. *J. Natl. Cancer Inst.* **19,** 123–130 (1957).
20. G. E. Cosgrove, Jr., A. C. Upton, E. E. Schwartz, and C. C. Congdon, Effects of immunized parental strain bone marrow on lethally irradiated F_1 hybrid mice. *Proc. Soc. Exptl. Biol. Med.* **100,** 417–420 (1959).
21. J. J. Trentin, Tolerance and homologous disease in irradiated mice protected with homologous bone marrow. *Ann. N. Y. Acad. Sci.* **73,** 799–810 (1958).
22. F. Celada and R. R. Carter, The radiosensitive nature of homograft-rejecting and agglutinin-forming capacities of isolated spleen cells. *J. Immunol.* **89,** 161–169 (1962).
23. H. B. Hewitt and C. W. Wilson, A survival curve for mammalian leukaemia cells irradiated *in vivo* (Implications for the treatment of mouse leukaemia by whole-body irradiation). *Brit. J. Cancer* **13,** 69–75 (1959).
24. R. J. Berry and J. R. Andrews, Quantitative relationships between radiation dose and the reproductive capacity of tumor cells in a mammalian system *in vivo*. *Radiology* **77,** 824–830 (1961).

RADIATION RESEARCH 19, 492–511 (1963)

First-Collision Doses Produced by Fast Neutron Fluxes of Wide Energy Distributions

M. L. RANDOLPH

Biology Division, Oak Ridge National Laboratory,[1] Oak Ridge, Tennessee

INTRODUCTION

Although precise fast neutron dosimetry is obtainable by such methods as tissue-equivalent ion chamber measurements, cases arise wherein, for a known neutron spectrum and total fluence,[2] the absorbed dose is desired without recourse to further experimental measurements. The ratio of dose to fast neutron fluence is available in tables and graphs (*2, 3*) for monoenergetic neutrons but not for continuous distributions of neutron energies. We present here methods of calculating the ratio of the average first-collision dose to neutron fluence and give typical results in several media for five particular classes of fast neutron spectra. When the approximate spectrum is known and accurate neutron fluence monitoring is established at a fast neutron facility, as is more frequent than proper dosimetry, this method often becomes either the easiest and sufficiently accurate for many radiobiological studies or is at least a convenient supplement to conventional methods. The method, however, makes no allowance for any γ-radiation which may accompany the fast neutrons.

Our emphasis here is on the calculation of absorbed energy, or dose in rads, unlike some similar calculations (*4, 5*) for fission spectra wherein the emphasis is on dose equivalent in rems or rads times a quality factor (*QF*). This may reflect a difference in the motivation behind calculations: Ours is to help promote quantitative radiobiological studies with fast neutrons from which may result *QF* values

[1] Operated by Union Carbide Corporation for the U. S. Atomic Energy Commission.

[2] The latest terminology recommended by the International Commission on Radiological Units (*1*) is used throughout this text, although the title is in the older, more familiar terminology. Comparison of the new terms with older usage includes: particle fluence, which is the number of particles crossing a unit area and is equivalent to (flux) × (time) in old terms; dose, which is now restricted to the old meaning, absorbed dose; quality factor (*QF*), which is the RBE used for protection purposes; dose equivalent, which replaces the previous term RBE dose; and Kerma (kinetic energy released in material), which is equivalent to the common interpretation of first-collision dose.

for specific effects and hence more general understanding of radiobiology. A different motivation is evaluation of human hazards from fast neutrons for which dose equivalents in rems are indicated. Both motivations are justifiable. Dose-equivalent calculations as presently done involve the added complications (and hence potential sources of error) of determining an average LET for each neutron energy and accepting a *QF*–LET curve. The latter is usually a compromise or "legislated" curve somewhat arbitrarily based on appraisal of still incomplete radiobiological data. An all-embracing *QF*–LET curve is unlikely because of the variety of potential biological effects and their manifestations with other parameters such as dose rate. Nonetheless, calculations of doses in rems have immediate practical value.

METHOD

Calculation of First-Collision Doses in Rads

We follow four principal steps in our calculation of dose to incident neutron fluence: (*1*) Determination of the nuclear (or practically the elemental) composition of the irradiated tissue, a prerequisite because essentially all the energy transferred from neutrons to tissue is by nuclear interactions. (*2*) Calculation from the data of nuclear physics of the ratio, $f_c(E)$, of Kerma (the first-collision dose or kinetic energy per unit mass imparted to irradiated medium of composition c per unit fluence by the first interactions of the incident neutrons each having energy E). This calculation involves obtaining the products of the concentration, n_i, nuclei of isotope i present, times the probability, $\sigma_{ij}(E)$, of the neutron interaction of type j with it, times the average kinetic energy, $\psi_{ij}(E)$, of ionizing particles resulting; and then summing these products for all possible nuclear interactions and nuclei present. The mathematical expression is given by equation 1,

$$f_c(E) = \sum_i \sum_j n_i \sigma_{ij}(E) \psi_{ij}(E) \qquad (1)$$

where the parenthetical E's indicate that the preceding quantity varies with neutron energy E. (3) Determination of the neutron spectrum, or neutron fluence, $N(E)$, as a function of E. The shapes of the more common and more prolific neutron spectra are generally available from the literature of nuclear physics and are applicable provided that reasonable precautions (see Discussion) are taken against degradation of neutron energy and scatter of neutrons. (4) The final step, calculation of the average ratio, F_c, of dose to neutron fluence. The total dose, D_c, delivered to the irradiated medium is the sum, for all neutron energies, of the doses delivered at each neutron energy, or

$$\int_0^\infty f_c(E) N(E)\, dE;$$

and the total neutron fluence, N_t, is

$$\int_0^\infty N(E)\, dE.$$

Hence we have equation 2.

$$F_c = \frac{D_c}{N_t} = \frac{\int_0^\infty f_c(E) N(E)\, dE}{\int_0^\infty N(E)\, dE} \tag{2}$$

Herein we consider primarily the last step and treat the others briefly.

Approximation of f(E)

We calculate for soft tissue (*2*, *6*), bone (*2*, *7*), tissue-equivalent plastic (*2*), some hydrogenous materials, and water. For these compositions, the ratio of Kerma to fluence, based on isotopic elastic scattering alone, has been calculated throughout the energy range 0.01 to 10 Mev (*2*). Since plots of $f(E)$ versus E are rather smooth, $f(E)$ may be approximated in several simple ways, of which we choose the approximation given in equation 3,

$$f'(E) = A + B\sqrt{E} + CE \tag{3}$$

where A, B, and C are empirically determined constants. Our choice of this form is based on its simplicity, amenability to our subsequent calculation, and precision of fit obtainable.[3] For absorbed dose in tissue-equivalent plastic (*2*), tissue-equivalent gas (*2*), water, $(C_2H_2)_n$, and C_2H_4, inspection reveals that mere multiplications of the coefficients for soft tissue by various constants yield satisfactory fits to the National Bureau of Standards calculations for these materials. An empirically determined set of coefficients and the precision of results compared to the *NBS Handbook 75* values are given in Table I. A sharp peak in the curve of cross section versus neutron energy (i.e., a nuclear interaction resonance) for oxygen causes the discrepancies at 1 Mev, and similar ones at 0.44 Mev.

Our approximations to the true ratio, f, are limited to neutron energies less than 10 Mev. However, for many neutron spectra this energy range is sufficient.

Neutron Spectra

We shall consider five analytic approximations for the description of neutron spectra (other than what is here considered the trivial case of monoenergetic neu-

[3] Since about 90% of the value of $f(E)$, for $0.1 \leq E \leq 10$ Mev, results from isotropic elastic scattering by hydrogen, $f(E) \approx 0.55\, n_H E \sigma_H(E)$. Using the theoretical value of $\sigma_H(E)$, one might hope to obtain a more nearly analytic expression for $f(E)$, but the theoretical expression for $\sigma_H(E)$ is so complicated (e.g., see ref. *8*) that a good approximation simpler than equation 12 has not been found.

TABLE I

EMPIRICAL COEFFICIENTS FOR DOSE-TO-NEUTRON FLUENCE RATIO

$(f'(E) = A + B\sqrt{E} + CE)$

Irradiated material and per cent composition by weight	*Coefficients for E in Mev* (*rads per 10^9 n/cm²*)			*Precision of approximation compared to NBS Handbook 75 values*			*Ratio of coefficients to those for soft tissue*
	A	B	*C*	*Maximum deviation, except at 0.44 and 1 Mev (%)*	*Energy range (Mev)*	*Deviation at 1 Mev, 100 (calc.—NBS)/NBS*	
Soft tissue (H, 10; C, 12; N, 4; O, 73)	−0.202	2.757	−0.3245	±3 ±6	0.05–10 0.02–10	−10 −10	1.00
Bone (H, 4; C, 17; N, 5; O, 48; P, 5; Ca, 20)	−0.100	1.209	−0.1293	±4	0.03–10	−15	[a]
Tissue-equivalent plastic (H, 10; C, 86; N, 4)	−0.219	2.991	−0.3521	±4	0.02–10	− 1.5	1.025
Tissue-equivalent gas (H, 10; C, 45.3; N, 4; O, 40.7)	−0.202	2.757	−0.3245	±4	0.02–10	− 8.5	1.00
H_2O	−0.220	3.005	−0.3537	±5	0.02–10	−13	1.09
$(C_2H_2)_n$	−0.168	2.288	−0.2693	±7	0.02–10	− 1.5	0.83
C_2H_4	−0.287	3.195	−0.4608	±4	0.02–10	− 1.6	1.42[b]

[a] No common proportionality of coefficients.

[b] Hurst (*9*) has found the ratio for $C'H_4$ to soft tissue to be 1.45 over a wide range of neutron energies.

trons) which may be substituted into equation 1. These are: (1) the Maxwellian distribution (*10*), used to describe pure fission spectra:

$$N_M(E)\,dE = \left(\frac{2}{\pi^{1/2}T^{3/2}}\right) N_t E^{1/2}\, e^{-E/T}\, dE \tag{4}$$

where T is a nuclear temperature, and N_t is the total neutron fluence; (2) the Watt distribution (*11*), used to describe pure fission spectra:

$$N_W(E)\,dE = N_t \frac{e^{-E_f/T}\, e^{-E/T}}{(\pi E_f T)^{1/2}} \sinh\left(\frac{2(EE_f)^{1/2}}{T}\right) dE \tag{5}$$

where again T is analogous to a nuclear temperature, and E_f is the fragment kinetic energy per nucleon; (3) the evaporation spectrum (*10*), used to describe some spectra produced by charged particle interactions:

$$N_e(E)\,dE = \frac{N_t}{T^2} E e^{-E/T}\,dE \tag{6}$$

(4) the Gaussian distribution about some energy, E^*, used as an approximation to describe some spectra produced by charged particle interactions:

$$N_G(E)\,dE = \sqrt{\frac{K}{\pi}}\,N_t\,e^{-K(E-E^*)^2}\,dE \tag{7}$$

where in order to avoid skew of the distribution and to treat the tails of the spectrum fairly one should impose limits on E^* such as

$$\left(0.01 + \sqrt{\frac{3}{K}}\right) < E^* < \left(10 - \sqrt{\frac{3}{K}}\right) \tag{8}$$

(5) neutron spectra of cosmic-ray origin, which because of their production by knock-on and evaporation processes and subsequent degradation are not simply describable in analytic terms but may be roughly approximated as

$$N_i(E)\,dE = c_i E^{-X_i}\,dE \tag{9}$$

where discrete values of c and X are empirically chosen over wide ranges of E.

Dose Calculations

We undertake the integration of equation 2 for the five classes of neutron spectra mentioned. Our approximations (equation 3 and Table I) are in fair agreement with the best available values of $f(E)$ over the neutron energy range from about 0.03 to 10 Mev, are too small outside of these limits, and are positive only in the energy range from about A^2/B^2 to $(B^2 - 2AC)/C^2$. For tissue and the compounds with proportional coefficients in equation 2 and Table I, the limits of integration between which $f'(E)$ is positive are 0.0054 and 71 Mev. For bone the values are 0.0069 and 85 Mev. Because we wish to obtain approximations suitable for either composition, we choose as our limits of integration $\alpha = 0.0064$ Mev and $\beta = 73.1$ Mev.[4] Although the limits of integration are set this broad, one must still look with suspicion at results for spectra with appreciable tails above 10 Mev or below 0.03 Mev. Because we approximate the true function, $f(E)$, and restrict our limits of integration, we designate our resulting integrations as F' to differentiate them from the exact values of F.

Maxwellian Distribution

Following the previous notation of equations 2, 3, and 4, we have

$$F'(T) = \frac{1.1284}{T^{3/2}} \int_\alpha^\beta (A\sqrt{E} + BE + CE^{3/2})\,e^{-E/T}\,dE \tag{10}$$

The exact solution of equation 10 is quite awkward (see Appendix). However, for

[4] For some calculations, the important quantities are $\sqrt{\alpha} = 0.08$ and $\sqrt{\beta} = 8.55$.

0.2 Mev $< T <$ 2 Mev, the exact result may be approximated, with an error of less than 1% for tissue, by the equation:

$$F'(T) = A + 1.1284BT^{1/2} + 1.5CT \tag{11}$$

Watt Distribution

Starting with equations 2, 3, and 5, we have

$$F'(T, E_f) = C_1 \int_\alpha^\beta (A + B\sqrt{E} + CE)e^{-E/T} \sinh (C_2\sqrt{E})\, dE \tag{12}$$

where

$$C_1 = \frac{e^{-E_f/T}}{(\pi E_f T)^{1/2}} \quad \text{and} \quad C_2 = \frac{2\sqrt{E_f}}{T}$$

The solution to equation 12 is complicated (see Appendix).

$$\begin{aligned} F'(T, E_f) = \frac{1}{\sqrt{\pi}} \Bigg\{ &\left[A + \frac{B}{C_2} + \frac{T}{2}(BC_2 + 3C) + \frac{CT^2C_2^2}{4}\right] \int e^{-y^2}\, dy \\ &- \left(\frac{B}{C_2} + \frac{3CT}{2}\right)(ye^{-y^2}) \\ &+ \left[A - \frac{B}{C_2} - \frac{T}{2}(BC_2 + 3C) + \frac{CT^2C_2^2}{4}\right] \int e^{-z^2}\, dz \\ &+ \left(\frac{B}{C_2} - \frac{3CT}{2}\right)(ze^{-z^2}) \Bigg\} \\ &- \frac{1}{\lambda\sqrt{\pi}} \Bigg\{ \left[A + T(BC_2 + C) + \frac{3CT^2C_2^2}{4}\right] e^{-y^2} + CTy^2e^{-y^2} \\ &- \left[A - T(BC_2 + C) + \frac{3CT^2C_2^2}{4}\right] e^{-z^2} - CTz^2e^{-z^2} \Bigg\} \end{aligned} \tag{13}$$

where $\lambda^2 = C_2^2T$, and the quantities in y and z are to be evaluated at the upper and lower limits of

$$\left(\sqrt{\frac{\alpha}{T}} - \frac{\lambda}{2}\right) \leq y \leq \left(\sqrt{\frac{\beta}{T}} - \frac{\lambda}{2}\right) \quad \text{and} \quad \left(\sqrt{\frac{\alpha}{T}} + \frac{\lambda}{2}\right) \leq z \leq \left(\sqrt{\frac{\beta}{T}} + \frac{\lambda}{2}\right)$$

We cannot here apply the simplifications used with the Maxwellian distribution but do observe that $y_{\max}$ and $z_{\max}$ usually can be treated as infinite.

Evaporation Spectrum

Using equations 2, 3, and 6, we write

$$F'(T) = \frac{1}{T^2} \int_\alpha^\beta (A + B\sqrt{E} + CE)Ee^{-E/T}\, dE \tag{14}$$

For the term in B we set $y^2 = E/T$ and integrate. The result becomes

$$F'(T) = \left|\left[A + \frac{3B}{2}\sqrt{E} + 2CE + \frac{Ef'(E)}{T} + 2CT\right](-e^{-E/T})\right|_{\alpha}^{\beta} + \frac{3\sqrt{\pi T}}{4} B\left[\phi\left(\frac{\beta}{T}\right)^{1/2} - \phi\left(\frac{\alpha}{T}\right)^{1/2}\right] \tag{15}$$

where $f'(E)$ is given by equation 3 and E is to take the values β and α, and $\phi(x)$ is

$$(2/\sqrt{\pi}) \int_0^x e^{-t^2}\, dt$$

For practical purposes, β usually can be taken as infinite.

Gaussian Distribution

From equations 2, 3, and 7, we write

$$F'(E^*, K) = \sqrt{\frac{K}{\pi}} \int_{\alpha}^{\beta} (A + B\sqrt{E} + CE)e^{-K(E-E^*)^2}\, dE \tag{16}$$

By mathematical steps given in the Appendix, we find

$$F'(E^*, K) = f'(E^*) - \frac{B}{16(E^*)^{3/2}K} \tag{17}$$

For spectra with neutron groups of Gaussian distribution having maxima H_i and full widths, w_i, at half-maximum (note $K = 1.386/w_i^2$), we write

$$F' = \sum_i H_i w_i F(E_i^*, w_i) \Big/ \sum_i H_i w_i \tag{18}$$

Since $B\sqrt{E}$ is greater than $f(E)$, the correction term of equation 16 is less than 1% of the value when $w^2 < 0.2E^*$, and

$$F' = \sum_i H_i w_i f'(E^*) \Big/ \sum_i H_i w_i \tag{19}$$

Distribution in Upper Atmosphere and Nearby Space

From equations 2, 3, and 9, we write:

$$F' = \frac{\sum_i \int_{\epsilon_i}^{\epsilon_i'} (A + B\sqrt{E} + CE)c_i E^{-x_i}\, dE}{\sum_i \int_{\epsilon_i}^{\epsilon_i'} c_i E^{x_i}\, dE} \tag{20}$$

$$= \frac{\sum_i \left| c_i \left(\frac{AE^{1-x_i}}{1 - x_i} + \frac{BE^{1.5-x_i}}{1.5 - x_i} + \frac{CE^{2-x_i}}{2 - x_i}\right)\right|_{\epsilon_i}^{\epsilon_i'}}{\sum_i \left| (c_i E^{1-x_i})/(1 - x_i) \right|_{\epsilon_i}^{\epsilon_i'}} \tag{21}$$

and note: (1) if an exponent of E is zero, we replace $E^0/0$ by $\ln E$; (2) the values of c_i and x_i apply between the limits $\epsilon_i \leq E \leq \epsilon_i'$; and (3) by equating successive distributions given by equation 9 at the junction points, $\epsilon_i' = \epsilon_{i+1}$, we find

$$c_{i+1} = c_i \epsilon_i^{(x_{i+1} - x_i)} \tag{22}$$

Calculation of Dose Equivalents

The calculation of dose equivalents for first-collision effects is so similar to those just described for doses that we need give little more than the differences here. For reasons given in the Introduction, approximations are used more freely here than previously. Because the dose equivalent-to-fluence curve becomes almost flat above 1 Mev, it cannot be approximated well by equation 2. However, a satisfactory and convenient fit is afforded by the following bimodal approximation:

$$g_1'(E) = A + B\sqrt{E} + CE \qquad \text{at } E < 1 \text{ Mev} \tag{23}$$

$$g_2'(E) = M + N\sqrt{E} \qquad \text{at } E > 1 \text{ Mev} \tag{24}$$

where $g'(E)$ is our approximation to the dose equivalent per unit fluence arising from first collisions of neutrons with energy E. The coefficients are given in Table II. Since $g(E)$ is positive for all $E > 1$, we may use infinity as the upper limit of integrations, which take the general form

$$G' = G_\alpha^{1'} + G_1^{'\infty} \tag{25}$$

where G' is the ratio of RBE dose per unit fluence, subscripts and superscripts indi-

TABLE II

EMPIRICAL COEFFICIENTS FOR RATIO OF DOSE EQUIVALENT IN TISSUE[a] TO NEUTRON FLUENCE

($g' = A + B\sqrt{E} + CE$ or $g' = M + N\sqrt{E}$)

Neutron energy range (Mev)	*Coefficients for E (Mev)* (rems per 10^9 n/cm²)			*Precision of approximation compared to NBS Handbook 63 values*		
	A or M	*B or N*	*C*	*Maximum deviation, except at 0.44 and 1 Mev (%)*	*Energy range (Mev)*	*Deviation at 1 Mev, 100(Calc.—NBS)/NBS*
(*a*) 0.04–10	− 0.7	31.1	−7.36	±12	0.06–8	−21
(*b*) 0.004–1	− 2.2	34.5	−8.33	± 4	0.03–1	+ 4
(*b*) 1 − ∞	22	4.0	—	± 6	1.5 –9	±13

[a] Composition by weight H, 10%; C, 18%; N, 3%; O, 65%, plus traces of Ca, P, etc. Differences in this composition and tissue used in Table I cause much less uncertainity than QF values employed here.

cate limits of integration, and α is such that $g_1'(\alpha) = 0$ (i.e., $\alpha = 0.0042$ Mev for tissue for coefficients given in Table II).

For the Maxwellian distribution, one combines approximate equation 11 and equations 23, 24, and 25 and obtains

$$G'(T) = (A + 1.5CT - M)\phi(T^{-1/2}) + M + 1.1284T^{1/2}\{B - e^{-1/T}[B + 1.5C - N + T^{-1}(g_1'(1) - g_2'(1))]\} \tag{26}$$

We have not derived the expression in rems for the Watt distribution for two reasons: (1) the result is certainly unwieldy, judging from equation 13; and (2) spectra described by the Watt distribution usually are also adequately described by the Maxwellian distribution.

For the evaporation spectrum we combine equations 15, 23, 24, and 25—note $e^{-\beta/T} = 0$—and obtain

$$G'(T) = \left[A + \frac{3B}{2}\sqrt{\alpha} + 2C(\alpha + T)\right]e^{-\alpha/T} - \left\{(A - M) + \frac{3}{2}(B - N) + 2C(1 + T) + T^{-1}[g_1(1) - g_2(1)]\right\}e^{-1/T} + \frac{3\sqrt{\pi T}}{4}\left[(B - N)\phi(T^{-1/2}) - B\phi\left(\sqrt{\frac{\alpha}{T}}\right) + N\right] \tag{27}$$

For a Gaussian distribution, equation 18 generally suffices.

For upper atmospheric distributions, the previous treatment suffices except that one ϵ_i must be 1 Mev with the g_1' coefficients at lower E values and the g_2' coefficients at higher E values.

RESULTS

All results expressed in rads and most of those expressed in rems were calculated from our most nearly exact equations. Wherever values in rads are given for soft tissue, rad values for several other hydrogenous materials may be calculated by using the last column of Table I.

Using Terrell's (*12*) and Bonner's (*13*) compilations of coefficients for pure fission spectra, we have computed the average dose-to-fluence ratios in soft tissue and bone for several spectra with the Maxwellian and Watt distributions. Numerical values are given in Table III. Furthermore, since the Maxwellian distribution has but one independent parameter, T, the results are also presented graphically in Figs. 1 and 2.

Examples of the evaporation spectra from thin targets are provided by the data of Gugelot (*18*), Albert *et al.* (*19*), and Bramblett and Bonner (*20*). Specific results are given in Table IV for several neutron-producing reactions, and general results are presented graphically in Figs. 2 and 3. For the $Be^9(p,n)B^9$ reaction, Gugelot

TABLE III

DOSE-TO-FLUENCE AND DOSE EQUIVALENT-TO-FLUENCE RATIOS FOR VARIOUS FISSION NEUTRON SPECTRA DESCRIBED BY MAXWELLIAN AND WATT DISTRIBUTIONS

(F_B/F_T Found to be 0.44 in Each Case)

Fission spectrum (thermal neutrons on)	*Coefficients (Mev)*				*Dose/fluence, F′* (rads per 10^9 n/cm²)		*Dose equivalent/fluence, G′ (rem per 10^9 n/cm²)*
	Maxwellian T	*Watt T*	*Watt E_f*	*Ref.*	*Tissue*	*Bone*	
U^{235}	1.236			(11, 12)	2.654	1.177	24.6
		1.0	0.5	(11)	2.741	1.222	
	1.301			(14, 12)	2.711	1.203	24.9
		0.965	0.533	(14)	2.745	1.218	
	1.370			(15, 12)	2.772	1.231	25.1
	1.273			(16)	2.687	1.192	24.8
	1.332			(13)	2.745	1.218	25.0
Pu^{239}	1.517			(15, 12)	2.890	1.286	25.7
	1.247			(16)	2.664	1.181	24.7
	1.385			(13)	2.788	1.239	25.2
U^{233}	1.360			(16)	2.763	1.227	25.1
	1.356			(13)	2.761	1.226	25.1
Cf^{252}	1.567			(17, 12)	2.929	1.304	25.8
		1.136	0.646	(17)	2.938	1.307	
	1.367			(13)	2.771	1.230	25.1
Pu^{240}	1.189			(13)	2.613	1.157	24.3
Jezebel (a critical Pu^{239} assembly)	1.184			(13)	2.608	1.155	24.3

uses different nuclear temperatures below and above 4 Mev. Therefore, we rewrite equation 2 as

$$F' = \frac{\int_\alpha^4 N_1(E) f'(E)\, dE + \int_4^\beta N_2(E) f'(E)\, dE}{\int_\alpha^4 N_1(E)\, dE + \int_4^\beta N_2(E)\, dE} \qquad (28)$$

Using equation 6 and the fit of the two distributions of $N(E)$ at 4 Mev, we obtain a normalizing coefficient ($0.437 T_1^{-2} e^{-4/T_1} = T_2^{-2} e^{-4/T_2}$) and write

$$F' = \frac{\int_\alpha^4 N_1(E) f'(E)\, dE + 0.437 (N_{1,t}/N_{2,t}) \int_4^\beta N_2(E) f'(E)\, dE}{\int_\alpha^4 N_1(E)\, dE + 0.437 (N_{1,t}/N_{2,t}) \int_4^\beta N_2(E)\, dE} \qquad (29)$$

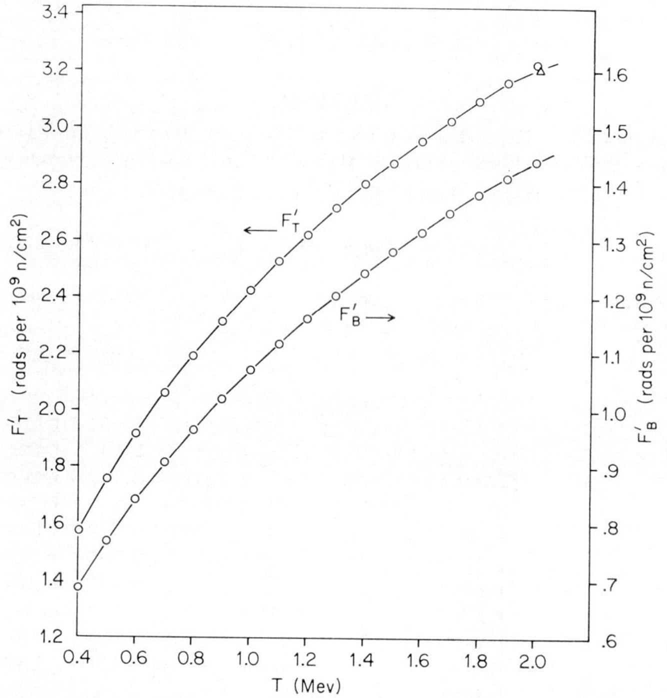

FIG. 1. Plots of dose-to-fluence ratio for standard soft tissue, F_T', and bone, F_B', versus T parameter of Maxwellian distribution of neutron energies. (Note the factor of 2 between scales for F_T' and F_B'.)

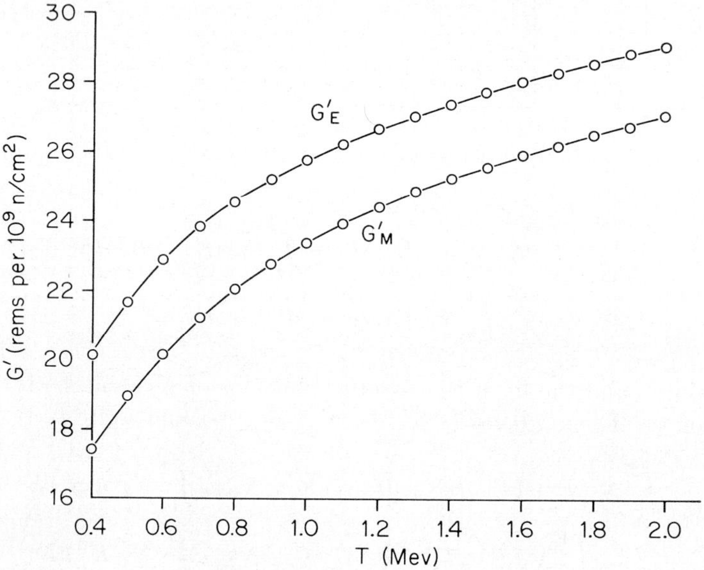

FIG. 2. Plots of dose equivalent-to-fluence ratio versus T parameter of Maxwellian, G_M', and evaporation spectra, G_E', distributions of neutron energies.

where

$$N_{i,t} = \int_\alpha^\beta N_i(E)\, dE$$

For the dose equivalent we take three sets of limits of integration: α to 1, 1 to 4, and 4 to β. Table IV includes this spectrum. About 3% of the total neutrons are above 10 Mev.

Shpetnyi's spectra (*21*) from the prolific $Be^9(d,n)B^{10}$ reaction on a thin (0.1-mg/cm²) target at various bombarding energies and directions of the resulting

TABLE IV

DOSE-TO-FLUENCE AND DOSE EQUIVALENT-TO-FLUENCE RATIOS FOR FAST NEUTRON EVAPORATION SPECTRA PRODUCED FROM THIN[a] TARGETS (F'_B/F'_T about 0.44 in each case)

Target nucleus of (p,n) reaction	*T (Mev)*	*Bombarding energy (Mev)*	*Angle with respect to beam (Degrees)*	*Ref.*	*Dose/fluence* Tissue, F_T' (rads per 10^9 n/cm²)	*Dose/fluence* Bone, F_B' (rads per 10^9 n/cm²)	*Dose equivalent/fluence, G' (rems/10^9 n/cm²)*
Al^{27}	1.3	16	0	(*18*)	3.13	1.39	27.0
Fe^{56}	0.95	16	0	(*18*)	2.76	1.22	25.5
Au^{197}	0.8	16	0	(*18*)	2.56	1.13	24.6
Be^9	0.9–2.3[b]	16	0	(*18*)	2.97	1.33	27.9
Va^{51}	0.78	7	25	(*19*)	2.53	1.12	24.4
	0.98	8	0–120	(*19*)	2.80	1.24	25.7
Mn^{55}	1.1	7	25	(*19*)	2.93	1.30	26.2
	1.1	8	0–120	(*19*)	2.93	1.30	26.2
Co^{59}	0.76[c]	7	25	(*19*)	2.50	1.10	24.3
	0.85[c]	8	0–120	(*19*)	2.63	1.16	24.9
Nb^{93}	0.57	5.3	90	(*20*)	2.20	0.96	22.6
	0.73	8	0–120	(*19*)	2.46	1.08	24.1
Rh^{103}	0.59	5.3	90	(*20*)	2.23	0.98	22.8
	0.70	8	0–120	(*19*)	2.41	1.06	23.8
In^{115}	0.53	5.3	90	(*20*)	2.13	0.93	22.1
	0.65	8	0–120	(*19*)	2.33	1.03	23.4
Ag^{109}	0.56	5.3	90	(*20*)	2.19	0.96	22.4
Sb^{123}	0.51	5.3	90	(*20*)	2.09	0.92	21.8
Cd^{114}	0.49	5.3	90	(*20*)	2.05	0.90	21.5
Sn^{122}	0.46	5.3	90	(*20*)	1.98	0.87	21.1

[a] Energy loss in targets about 1 Mev for ref. *18*; 0.2 Mev for ref. *19*; and 0.3 Mev for ref. *20*.

[b] For $E < 4$, $T = 0.9$; for $E > 4$, $T = 2.3$ (*18*).

[c] Bramblett and Bonner (*20*) find a somewhat different shape distribution at 5.3-Mev bombarding energy.

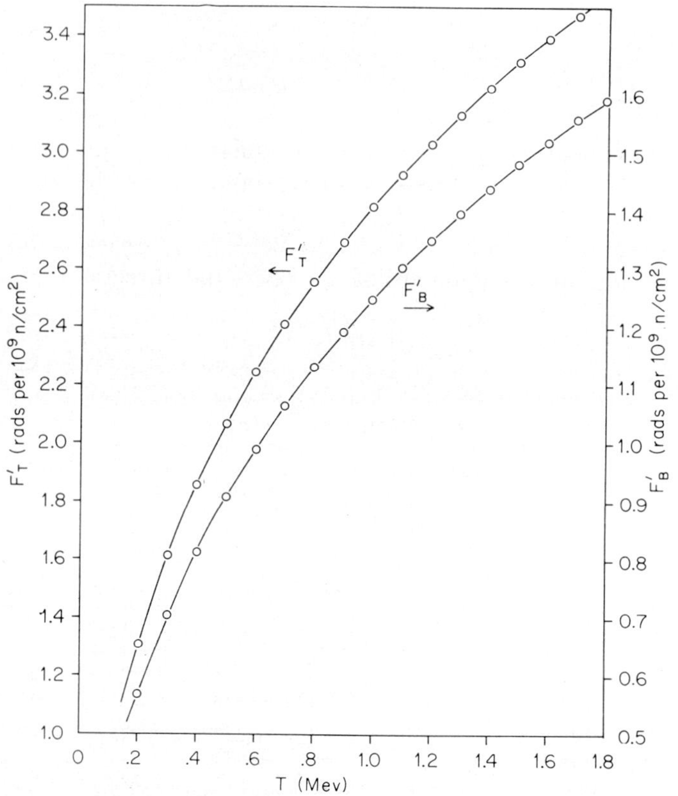

FIG. 3. Plots of dose-to-fluence ratio for soft tissue, F_T', and bone, F_B', versus T parameter of evaporation spectra. (Note the factor of 2 between scales for F_T' and F_B'.)

neutrons furnish examples of Gaussian distributions each with four to six fast neutron groups. Results from his spectra are given in Table V. In these cases of narrow groups, the correction term of equation 17 was seldom, if ever, necessary. However, the final results are not very accurate because the calculations arise from interpolations of E^*, H, and w from graphs.

Hess *et al.* (*22*) describe the energy spectra of neutrons arising from knock-on and evaporation nuclear processes in the upper atmosphere and their degradation. They also describe the spectra of neutrons escaping from the atmosphere to nearby space. In a general way they find that the evaporation source spectrum produces a slight maximum in the spectra near an energy of 600 kev, and that both below 100 kev and above 2 Mev equation 9 applies fairly well with a lower exponent in the low-energy range than in the high-energy range. We have empirically approximated their graphical results with coefficients given in Table VI for three energy ranges

TABLE V

DOSE-TO-FLUENCE AND DOSE EQUIVALENT-TO-FLUENCE RATIOS FOR MULTIGROUP FAST NEUTRONS PRODUCED BY THE $Be^9(d,n)B^{10}$ REACTION ACCORDING TO THE DATA OF SHPETNYI (21)

(F_B'/F_T' between 0.43 and 0.46 in each case)

Bombarding energy, E_d (Mev)	*Direction of neutrons, θ (deg)*	*Dose/fluence* Tissue (rads per 10^9 n/cm²)	*Dose/fluence* Bone (rads per 10^9 n/cm²)	*Dose equivalent/fluence (rems per 10^9 n/cm²)*
0.5	0	3.96	1.72	29.6
0.5	145	3.76	1.68	29.4
1.6	0	4.19	1.86	30.9
1.6	120	3.87	1.76	29.2

TABLE VI

DOSE-TO-FLUENCE RATIOS FOR REPORTED (17) NEUTRON SPECTRA IN THE UPPER ATMOSPHERE AND NEAR SPACE

Spectra Location, elevation, and latitude	*Spectra, Empirical description* X values of equation 9	*Spectra, Empirical description* in Energy range (Mev)	*Dose/fluence* Tissue (rads per 10^9 n/cm²)	*Dose/fluence* Bone (rads per 10^9 n/cm²)	*Dose equivalent/fluence (rems per 10^9 n/cm²)*
200 gm/cm² absorber (i.e., ~12 km) at 44°, geomagnetic latitude	0.941 0 1.467	α–0.08 0.08–0.45 0.45–β	2.57	1.18	28.0
~100 km	0.852 0.335 1.643	α–0.028 0.028–2.8 2.8–β	3.24	1.50	25.3
~26,000 km	0.645 0.320 2.061	α–0.028 0.028–2.8 2.8–β	2.57	1.12	26.3

of three spectra. These approximations differ from curves of Hess *et al.* by as much as ±40%, but averaging should reduce the magnitude of such discrepancies. The resulting values are given in Table VI.

DISCUSSION

We shall discuss our calculation methods generally, associated uncertainties in the input data, and our specific results. Neutron facilities in general emit neutrons and γ-rays, both of which can be biologically significant. Here we discuss only estimation of the neutron dose, but investigators should never ignore the possibility of appreciable γ-radiation. Complexities of mixed radiation dosimetry, such as the fact that many γ-ray detectors are also neutron detectors of a different (usually lower) sensitivity and vice versa, are dealt with elsewhere (*2*).

Almost without exception, the simplifications to the analytic results given as equations 11 and 19 and simplifying remarks that follow equations 13 and 15 are applicable and greatly facilitate the computations. Our approximations $f'(E)$ and $g'(E)$ to the best-known values of $f(E)$ and $g(E)$ are not entirely satisfactory because of resonances in various cross sections for which no very simple expression can entirely compensate. Since we treat distributed spectra, some averaging occurs which tends to diminish the effect of such discrepancies. Therefore, we expect that these considerations cause less than 5% error unless one deals with a Gaussian distribution centering near 1 Mev or 0.44 Mev, for which one could easily make an *ad hoc* correction. Our approximation $f'(E)$ underestimates the true value above 10 Mev where $f(E)$ is relatively large and not accurately known in general. At high neutron energies our approximation $g'(E)$ is more realistic than $f'(E)$. However, for the cases we have evaluated there are relatively few neutrons above 10 Mev. For example, at $T = 2$, 4% of the total neutrons of the statistical model are about 10 Mev, or in the Maxwellian distribution, 1.6% of the neutrons. Calculation of the fraction of the fluence above 10 Mev may be made by using the limits $E = 10$ and ∞ with the A terms of exact equation 10c in the Appendix and equations 13, 15, and 21.

The input parameters, since they all result from experimental measurements, are reviewed somewhat critically. The nuclear data leading to specific calculations of $f(E)$ are under constant refinement. Here we have accepted the concept that all the energy transfers from neutrons to tissue are by isotropic elastic scattering. However, calculation from the $O^{16}(n,\alpha)C^{13}$ reaction data of Walton *et al.* (*23*) suggests that consideration of this reactive collision at neutron energy of 4.2 Mev (where a maximum cross section occurs) would increase the dose contribution for oxygen by about 20%. Such a calculation is suggestive, but not alarming by itself, since oxygen contributes only about 6% of the total dose to tissue at this neutron energy. Two recent compilations (*24*, *25*) of angular distributions indicate that 5- to 10-Mev neutrons elastically scattered by carbon, nitrogen, and oxygen scatter predominately in the forward direction. This tends to decrease the dose-to-fluence ratio. Only because hydrogen, for which the neutron interactions up to 10 Mev are all isotropic elastic scattering, so overshadows the other elements do we presently dare to ignore more refined calculations for other elements as has been done for 14-Mev neutrons (*26*). Although it is the best one can now do, we have mentioned our uneasiness about the presently assigned *QF*–LET curve. A comprehensive analysis of this problem is far beyond the scope of the present paper.

Our calculations have been for Kerma (first-collision dose) in typical soft tissue, bone, and some other more sharply defined compositions and for the dose equivalent arising from first collisions. Of course, for proper evaluation of human hazards one should generally consider a multicollision dose. An unexpected result was that the ratio of dose in bone to that in tissue was nearly 0.44 for all neutron distributions calculated. For specific radiobiological experiments, the composition of the specific tissue in question may be a critical factor. For example, for evaluation of X-ray dose to bone marrow, Epp *et al.* (*27*) give the composition of metaphyseal bone with about 40% more hydrogen than the bone composition used here (*2*, *7*). For Epp's composition (H, 5.6%; C, 12.4%; N, 3.8%; O, 54.7%; P, 7.1%; and Ca, 16.1% by weight) and the neutron energy range considered here, $f(E)$ is 1.28 to 1.37 times that we have used for the bone composition given in Table I. Also Lea (*6*) gives the composition of a dry virus protein as considerably different from typical wet tissue. In the energy range 0.2 to 10 Mev, $f(E)$ for this material varies from 0.7 to 0.8 that for tissue. Elemental compositions of other proteins may be estimated from amino acid compositions tabulated in standard texts, e.g., Mertz (*28*). From the elemental compositions one may then calculate $f(E)$ and $g(E)$ values from the tables in reference *2*.

Although the less experienced reader is referred elsewhere (*29*) for a competent introduction to techniques for fast neutron spectroscopy (and accurate determination of fast neutron fluence), we suggest the following simple tests for prejudging the probable purity of a neutron spectrum. (1) The probability of either absorbing (losing) a neutron or degrading (decreasing) its energy as it goes from source to point of interest is less than

$$\sum_i n_i \sigma_{T,i} ,$$

where n_i is the number of nuclei per square centimeter of any of the i isotopes intervening, and $\sigma_{T,i}$ is the total cross section for neutron interactions. Since σ varies with neutron energy, one uses some average value. (2) For irradiations of materials at a distance r from the source, both in a shield at average distance R from the source, the ratio of direct- to scattered-particle fluence is approximately R^2/r^2. This assumes negligible scatter between source and wall and $r < R$. (3) For neutrons from charged particle accelerators the neutron spectrum will show angular dependence if the beam energy is a major fraction of the neutron energy, and (4) may be less than expected if, in addition, the target is thick enough to absorb a considerable fraction of the beam energy.

For the fission spectra (Table III) the values of F correspond to those of monoenergetic 1.5- to 2-Mev neutrons, i.e., slightly higher than the average neutron energy as usually cited. Of course, our calculations are for unmodified fission spectra, whereas practical cases usually involve modified spectra. From Tables 6 and 7 of Sayeg's experimental results (*30*) for the U^{235} critical assembly Godiva II, we calculate an average F of 2.30×10^{-9} versus our average of 2.72×10^{-9}. The difference of 18% is no larger than would be expected from Sayeg's demonstration that the

Godiva spectrum is considerably softer than the true fission spectrum, presumably because of degradation reactions within the source. Since Godiva is essentially a bare reactor, the degradation of its neutron spectrum will be minimal, and smaller values of F are likely for other kinds of reactors.

As examples of evaporation spectra, we have used Gugelot's results (*18*), although, except for the $Be^9(p,n)B^9$ reaction, they are based on analysis of data only above 2 Mev, which excludes more than half the neutrons predicted.

In calculating for multigroup spectra, wherever possible one should check the shape of each group. For Shpetnyi's data (*21*) all groups so checked were found to fit a Gaussian distribution reasonably well. However, the concept of a multigroup spectrum being the summation of exactly Gaussian distributions is unrealistic and should be regarded only as a useful approximation.

The calculations for neutrons of cosmic-ray origin are probably the least accurate because of the approximations used to describe the spectra and high-energy tails to the spectra. However, the resulting values should be reliable to within perhaps $\pm 40\%$. If the neutron flux in the upper atmosphere is 6 neutrons/cm^2-sec (*22*), the fast neutron dose rate becomes about 16 millirems/day, or 5.8 rems/year, which is in reasonable agreement with the value of 4.5 rems/year at 40,000 feet given by Patterson *et al.* (*31*).

Taking the ratio of dose equivalent to dose, one may obtain a first-collision average QF for a given neutron spectrum. For the spectra considered here, these values range from about 7 to 11, which furnishes a weak justification for taking the QF of all fast neutrons as 10 for quick hazard evaluations. For multicollision dose, this average QF would tend to be somewhat higher.

CONCLUSIONS

Analytic methods for evaluation of the ratios of first-collision dose to fast neutron flux for five classes of neutron spectra have been developed. Results in terms of rads in tissue and bone have been calculated for examples of each distribution and in terms of rems for all but one distribution. Doses for several other hydrogenous materials may be obtained by multiplying tissue doses by stated factors. The neutron distributions describe fission spectra, evaporation spectra, multigroup spectra, and spectra resulting from cosmic rays. Vagaries in this method of dosimetry are discussed briefly. The ratio of dose in bone to that in tissue is found to be 0.44 in every case examined. A fast neutron dose rate of 10 to 20 millirems/day in the upper atmosphere is estimated.

APPENDIX

Here we briefly indicate mathematical steps of the calculations and give some of our most nearly exact F′ values.

1. *Maxwellian Distribution.* Following equation 10 of the text, we set $a^2 = \alpha/T$, $b^2 = \beta/T$, $x^2 = E/T = y$, and write

$$F'(T) = 1.1284 \left[\int_a^b (2Ax^2 + 2CTx^4) e^{-x^2}\, dx + B\sqrt{T} \int_{a^2}^{b^2} ye^{-y}\, dy \right] \quad (10a)$$

Integration by parts yields

$$\begin{aligned} F'(T) = 1.1284 \Bigg\{ & \left| -\left(A + \frac{3CT}{2} + CTx^2\right) xe^{-x^2} \right|_a^b \\ & + \frac{\sqrt{\pi}}{2}\left(A + \frac{3CT}{2}\right)[\phi(b) - \phi(a)] \\ & + B\sqrt{T}\, e^{-\alpha/T}\left(1 + \frac{\alpha}{T}\right) - B\sqrt{T}\, e^{-\beta/T}\left(1 + \frac{\beta}{T}\right)\Bigg\} \end{aligned} \quad (10b)$$

where

$$\phi(z) = \frac{2}{\sqrt{\pi}} \int_0^z e^{-t^2}\, dt$$

and is tabulated in standard reference texts. Rearrangement of terms gives

$$\begin{aligned} F'(T) = {} & (A + 1.5CT)[\phi(\sqrt{\beta/T}) - \phi(\sqrt{\alpha/T})] \\ & + 1.1284T^{-1/2}\{e^{-\alpha/T}[\alpha^{1/2}A + \alpha B + \alpha^{3/2}C + T(B + 1.5\alpha^{1/2}C)] \\ & - e^{-\beta/T}[\beta^{1/2}A + \beta B + \beta^{3/2}C + T(B + 1.5\beta^{1/2}C)]\} \end{aligned} \quad (10c)$$

If our limits of integration are wide enough, we can replace

$$[\phi(\sqrt{\beta/T}) - \phi(\sqrt{\alpha/T})]$$

by 1, $e^{-\alpha/T}$ by 1, $e^{-\beta/T}$ by 0, and, noting that $\alpha \ll T$, we then write the approximation given by equation 11 of the text.

2. *Watt Distribution.* Setting $x^2 = C_2^2E$, and using the exponential form of sinh, for equation 12 we obtain

$$F'(T, E_f) = \frac{C_1}{C_2^2} \int_{C_2\sqrt{\alpha}}^{C_2\sqrt{\beta}} x \left(A + \frac{Bx}{C_2} + \frac{Cx^2}{C_2^2}\right) e^{-x^2/C_2^2T}(e^x - e^{-x})\, dx \quad (12a)$$

Setting

$$\lambda^2 = C_2^2T; \quad y = \frac{1}{\lambda}\left(x - \frac{\lambda^2}{2}\right) \quad \text{and} \quad z = \frac{1}{\lambda}\left(x + \frac{\lambda^2}{2}\right)$$

we write

$$\begin{aligned} F'(T, E_f) = {} & C_1Te^{C_2^2T/4} \\ & \cdot \Bigg\{\int_{y_{\min}}^{y_{\max}} \left[A\left(y + \frac{\lambda}{2}\right) + \frac{B\lambda}{C_2}\left(y + \frac{\lambda}{2}\right)^2 + \frac{C\lambda^2}{C_2^2}(y + \lambda)^3\right] e^{-y^2}\, dy \\ & - \int_{z_{\min}}^{z_{\max}} \left[A\left(z - \frac{\lambda}{2}\right) + \frac{B\lambda}{C_2}\left(z - \frac{\lambda}{2}\right)^2 + \frac{C\lambda^2}{C_2^2}\left(z - \frac{\lambda}{2}\right)^3\right] e^{-z^2}\, dz\Bigg\} \end{aligned} \quad (12b)$$

Integration by parts and considerable algebraic manipulation then yields equation 13 of the text.

4. *Gaussian Distribution.* Starting from equation 16, we change to the variable $y = (E - E^*)\sqrt{K}$ and, relying on the limitation imposed by equation 8, set the limits of integration as $\pm\infty$.

$$F'(E^*, K) = \sqrt{\frac{K}{\pi}}\left[\int_{-\infty}^{+\infty} (A + CE^*)e^{-y^2}K^{-1/2}\,dy + \int_{-\infty}^{+\infty} \frac{C}{K} ye^{-y^2}\,dy + \int_{-\infty}^{+\infty} B\sqrt{yK^{-1/2} + E^*}e^{-y^2}K^{-1/2}\,dy\right] \tag{16a}$$

$$= \frac{1}{\sqrt{\pi}}\left[(A + CE^*)\sqrt{\pi} + B\sqrt{E^*}\int_{-\infty}^{+\infty}\left(1 + \frac{y}{2E^*K^{1/2}} - \frac{y^2}{8E^{*2}K} + \cdots\right)e^{-y^2}\,dy\right] \tag{16b}$$

$$= \frac{1}{\sqrt{\pi}}\left[(A + B\sqrt{E^*} + CE^*)\sqrt{\pi} - \frac{B}{8(E^*)^{3/2}K}\int_{-\infty}^{+\infty} y^2e^{-y^2}\,dy\right] \tag{16c}$$

which readily reduces to equation 17.

ACKNOWLEDGMENT

I am very grateful to Dr. Marvin A. Kastenbaum, Mathematics Division, for conscientiously checking the derivations of equations given here.

RECEIVED: October 10, 1962

REFERENCES

1. Radiation quantities and units. *Natl. Bur. Std. (U.S.) Handbook* **No. 84** (1962).
2. Measurement of absorbed dose of neutrons and of mixtures of neutrons and gamma rays. *Natl. Bur. Std. (U.S.) Handbook* **No. 75** (1961).
3. Protection against neutron radiation up to 30 million electron volts. *Natl. Bur. Std. (U.S.) Handbook* **No. 63** (1957); W. S. SNYDER, Calculation of radiation dose. *Health Phys.* **1**, 55–51 (1958).
4. D. W. JOHNSON and E. J. ROMESBERG, Calculation of flux to dose rate conversion factors for fast and intermediate energy neutrons. *KAPL-2007* (March 20, 1959).
5. J. BRAUN and R. NILSSON, An emergency dosimeter for neutrons. In *Selected Topics in Radiation Dosimetry*, pp. 623–638, International Atomic Energy Agency, Vienna, 1961.
6. D. E. LEA, *Actions of Radiations on Living Cells*, 1st ed., Cambridge University Press, London, 1947.
7. C. A. TOBIAS, H. O. ANGER, and J. H. LAWRENCE, Radiological uses of high energy deuterons and alpha particles. *Am. J. Roentgenol. Radium Therapy Nucl. Med.* **67,** 1–29 (1952).
8. E. M. HAFNER, W. F. HORNYAK, C. E. FALK, G. SNOW, and T. COOR, The total *n-p* scattering cross section at 4.75 Mev. *Phys. Rev.* **89,** 204–222 (1953).
9. G. S. HURST, An absolute tissue dosemeter for fast neutrons. *Brit. J. Radiol.* **27,** 353–357 (1954).

10. J. M. Blatt and V. F. Weisskoff, *Theoretical Nuclear Physics*, John Wiley & Sons, New York, 1952.

11. B. E. Watt, Energy spectrum of neutrons from thermal fission of U^{235}. *Phys. Rev.* **87,** 1037–1041 (1952).

12. J. Terrell, Fission neutron spectra and nuclear temperatures. *Phys. Rev.* **113,** 527–541 (1959).

13. T. W. Bonner, Measurements of neutron spectra from fission. *Nucl. Phys.* **23,** 116–121 (1961).

14. L. Cranberg, G. Frye, N. Nereson, and L. Rosen, Fission neutron spectrum of U^{235}. *Phys. Rev.* **103,** 662–670 (1956).

15. N. Nereson, Fission neutron spectrum of Pu^{239}. *Phys. Rev.* **88,** 823–824 (1952).

16. K. N. Mukhin, L. M. Barkov, and R. I. Gerasimova, quoted by James Terrell, Fission neutron spectra and nuclear temperatures. *Phys. Rev.* **113,** 527–541 (1959).

17. A. B. Smith, P. R. Fields, and J. H. Roberts, Spontaneous fission neutron spectrum of Cf^{252}. *Phys. Rev.* **108,** 411–413 (1957).

18. P. C. Gugelot, Neutron spectra from nuclear reactions induced by 16-Mev protons. *Phys. Rev.* **81,** 51–60 (1951).

19. R. D. Albert, J. D. Anderson, and C. Wong, Evidence for the statistical model obtained from (p,n) spectra of the odd-even elements V, Mn, Co, Nb, Rh and In. *Phys. Rev.* **120,** 2149–2154 (1960).

20. R. L. Bramblett and T. W. Bonner, Neutron evaporation spectra from (p,n) reactions. *Nucl. Phys.* **20,** 395–407 (1960).

21. A. I. Shpetnyi, Energy and angular distribution of neutrons emitted in the $Be^9(d,n)B^{10}$ reaction. *Soviet Phys. JETP* **5,** 357–364 (1957).

22. W. N. Hess, E. H. Canfield, and R. E. Lingenfelter, Cosmic ray demography. *J. Geophys. Res.* **66,** 665–677 (1961).

23. R. B. Walton, J. D. Clement, and F. Boreli, Interaction of neutrons with oxygen and a study of the C^{13} $(\alpha,n)O^{16}$ reaction. *Phys. Rev.* **107,** 1065–1075 (1957).

24. B. R. S. Buckingham, K. Parker, and E. D. Pendleburg, Neutron cross sections of selected elements and isotopes for use in neutromic calculation in the energy range 0.025 eV to 15 Mev. *Atomic Weapons Research Establishment* (*Aldermaston, Berks, England*) *O-28/60* (March, 1961).

25. L. F. Chase, Jr., R. G. Johnson, R. V. Smith, F. J. Vaughan, and M. Walt, Fast neutron cross sections of oxygen and nitrogen. *Air Force Special Weapons Center* (*Kirtland AFB, New Mexico*) *TR-61-15* (February, 1961).

26. M. L. Randolph, Energy deposition in tissue and similar materials by 14-Mev neutrons. *Radiation Res.* **7,** 47–57 (1957).

27. E. R. Epp, H. Q. Woodard, and W. Weiss, Energy absorption by the bone marrow of the mouse receiving whole-body irradiation with 250-kv X-rays or cobalt-60 gamma rays. *Radiation Res.* **11,** 184–197 (1959).

28. E. T. Mertz, *Elementary Biochemistry*, pp. 269–270, Burgess Publishing Co., Minneapolis, Minnesota, 1960.

29. Measurement of neutron flux and spectra for physical and biological applications. *Natl. Bur. Std.* (*U.S.*) *Handbook* **No. 72** (1960).

30. J. A. Sayeg, Revised neutron flux, spectrum, and tissue dose measurements of the Godiva II critical assembly. Los Alamos Scientific Laboratory Report 2432, pp. 1–23 (September 19, 1960).

31. H. W. Patterson, W. N. Hess, B. J. Moyer, and R. W. Wallace, The flux and spectrum of cosmic ray produced neutrons as a function of altitude. *Health Phys.* **2,** 69–72 (1959).

RADIATION RESEARCH 19, 512–525 (1963)

The Dependence of RBE on the Energy of Fast Neutrons[1]

III. Evaluations of Radiation Quality

M. H. BIAVATI,[2] W. ROSENZWEIG,[3] H. H. ROSSI,[2] AND I. MIYANAGA[4]

Radiological Research Laboratory, Department of Radiology, Columbia University, New York, New York

INTRODUCTION

Previous papers in this series have dealt with experimental design and absorbed dose measurement (*1*) and with reduction of mouse spleen and thymus weight (*2*) in studies designed to determine RBE (relative biological effectiveness) as a function of neutron energy. The biological results obtained thus far are consistent with the original hypothesis that biological effectiveness in mammalian systems generally increases if radiation energy is delivered at higher local concentrations, i.e., by particles of higher mean LET. The qualifying term "mean" must be employed, since for all types of radiation the dose is delivered over a wide range of LET values, and hence it cannot be immediately concluded that biological effectiveness is actually greatest for radiation of highest maximum LET.

The test of more specific hypotheses on the relation between biological effectiveness and energy distribution in irradiated tissues requires detailed information on the latter. In the following, such data are presented for the five neutron energies employed in the biological studies which have already been reported (0.43, 0.65, 1.0, 1.5, and 1.8 Mev) (*2*) and for a second set of energies (0.34, 0.58, and 0.76 Mev) utilized in other biological work that will be published later. The information is expressed in terms of a calculated distribution of the absorbed dose due to recoil protons with respect to the LET of the latter, and in terms of experimental determinations of the distribution of absorbed dose with respect to the parameter, Y, for a variety of sphere diameters. The term Y has been defined (*3*) as E_s/d ,

[1] Based on work performed in part under Contract AT(30-1)-2740 for the U.S. Atomic Energy Commission and in part with support of U.S. Public Health Grant RH-99.

[2] Radiological Research Laboratory, Department of Radiology, Columbia University, New York, New York.

[3] Now at Bell Laboratories, Murray Hill, New Jersey.

[4] Now at Health Physics Division, Japan Atomic Energy Research Institute, Tokai-mura. Ibaraki-Pref., Japan.

where E_s is the energy delivered by an *individual* charged particle (and its charged secondaries) to a spherical volume in the irradiated tissue, and d is the sphere diameter. The traversal of such an individual charged particle (together with its δ-rays) is termed an *event*.

A third method (*4, 5*) of specifying energy deposition in irradiated tissues is by means of $P(Z)$, the probability distribution of Z. The term Z is defined as the ratio of E_t, the *total* energy imparted to a spherical volume in the course of the delivery of a given absorbed dose, by the mass, m, of the sphere. This quantity is dimensionally equal to absorbed dose. In the case of large doses and large values of m, the only Z that occurs with significant probability is numerically equal to the absorbed dose. This occurs especially when the LET is low, since in this case for a given absorbed dose a large number of charged particles traverse m, which, in turn, minimizes statistical fluctuations. On the other hand, when the particles are of high LET, when m is small, and when the dose is not too large, it is unlikely that more than one particle traverses m. In this case Z is equal to ΔZ, the increment in energy density for a single event. It has been shown (*3*) that an event of magnitude Y *kev*/μ deposits an increment ΔZ, given by equation 1, where d is expressed in microns.

$$\Delta Z = \frac{30.6Y}{d^2} \times 10^2 \text{ ergs/gm} \tag{1}$$

Since the work reported here involves secondary protons of near maximum LET and sphere diameters of the order of a micron, ΔZ is typically quite large. For instance, for a 1-μ sphere and $Y = 30$ kev/μ, ΔZ is about 10^5 ergs/gm. The LD_{50} for the biological effects on mammalian systems which are of interest here ranges from about 5 to 50 rads or 5×10^2 to 5×10^3 ergs/gm. Thus ΔZ is usually considerably larger than the absorbed doses which are significant. Hence even one event per sphere is rare, and the occurrence of two events is quite unlikely. Under these conditions the probability distribution of local energy density, $P(Z)$, is identical with the distribution due to single events, $P(\Delta Z)$. The latter may be derived from $P(Y)$, the probability distribution of single events in Y, by utilizing equation 1 and performing an appropriate normalization (*3*). However, for the largest sphere sizes investigated (12 μ), ΔZ is considerably smaller (~700 ergs/gm for $Y = 30$ kev/μ), and multiple events are probable at doses of the order of 10 rads (*5*).

CALCULATED LET DISTRIBUTION OF PROTONS

Boag (*6*) has computed the distribution of dose in LET in first collisions by monoenergetic neutrons, using the formula of equation 2, where E_n refers to the

$$D(L) = \frac{2}{E_n^2}(E_n - E_p)\left|\frac{dE_p}{dL}\right| \tag{2}$$

neutron energy, and E_p is the recoil proton energy in the same units. $|dE_p/dL|$ is the absolute value of the slope of the curve relating E_p to LET. The above relation refers to the dose contributed by recoil protons only. This is 90% or more of the absorbed dose at the neutron energies under discussion. However, the compara-

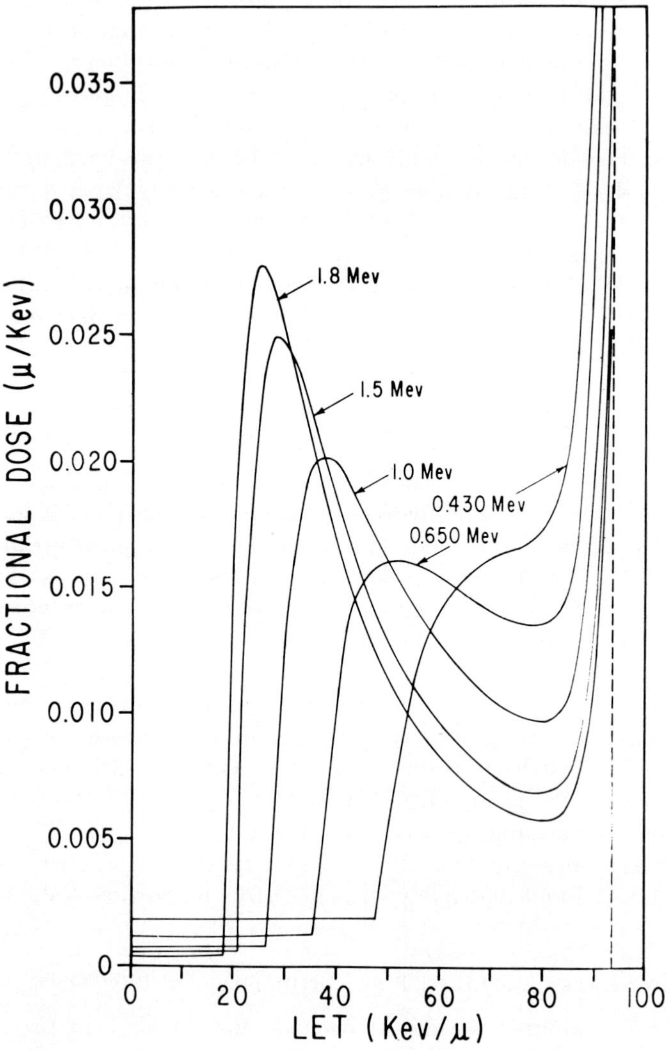

FIG. 1. LET spectra of monoenergetic neutrons ranging from 1.8 Mev to 0.43 Mev as computed from Boag's formula.

tively rare recoiling oxygen, carbon, and nitrogen nuclei have very high LET, and their contribution to the mean LET is not entirely negligible (see below).

In the LET spectra (shown in Figs. 1 and 2), which were computed by utilizing relation 2, the dose deposited by recoiling protons of energy less than that at which the peak of the Bragg curve occurs is of considerable importance. In Boag's compu-

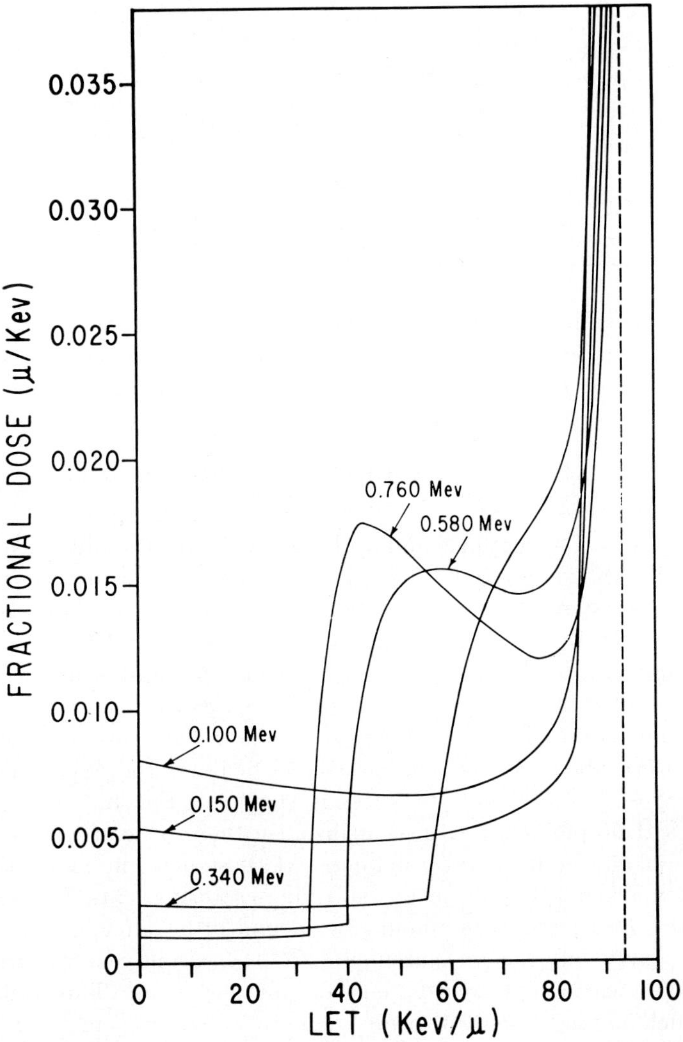

FIG. 2. Let spectra of monoenergetic neutrons ranging from 0.760 to 0.100 Mev as computed from Boag's formula.

TABLE I

CALCULATED DOSE AVERAGE OF LET VERSUS NEUTRON ENERGY

E_n (*Mev*)	$\bar{L}$ (*kev*/μ)
1.8	47.4
1.5	50.6
1.0	58.9
0.760	63.7
0.650	66.7
0.580	70.0
0.430	73.2
0.340	76.0
0.190	73.8
0.150	66.2
0.100	57.1

tations, which pertain to neutron energies that are higher than most of the ones discussed here, this component is negligibly small. The mean value of LET, $\bar{L}$ [the first moment of $D(L)$],[5] for each of the neutron energies is given in Table I, which indicates a maximum value at 340 kev.

EXPERIMENTAL DETERMINATION OF $D(Y)$

Distributions of dose, $D(Y)$, have been previously determined (*7*) for a series of neutron energies. The methods and apparatus used for the present measurements were essentially the same, and the results presented below for the first series of neutron energies are in good agreement with the previous measurements. However, they give more detail in a more restricted energy range and for a larger range of diameters. Figures 3 to 7 show $D(Y)$ distributions for unit-density tissue spheres ranging in diameter from 0.55 to 6 μ for 0.43- to 1.8-Mev neutrons. Experimental points have not been plotted because of the large amount of data. Statistical fluctuations were about 3% or smaller at the peak of the curve. The spread in neutron energies due to target thickness is shown in Fig. 8.

The spherical proportional counter utilized in these measurements has a 4-inch inside diameter and ¼-inch wall thickness. At these neutron energies, such a wall may exhibit marked attenuation or multiple scattering (*1*). Although resultant changes in the $D(Y)$ spectrum should be second-order effects, it was considered advisable to carry out the measurements for the second energy group (0.34 to 0.76 Mev) by means of a counter having minimal mass. This counter was an aluminum shell having a 2-inch inside diameter and a $\frac{1}{32}$-inch wall, lined with 0.01-inch tissue-equivalent plastic. The data obtained with this counter, shown in

[5] Defined as $\int_0^\infty LD(L)\,dL / \int_0^\infty D(L)\,dL$.

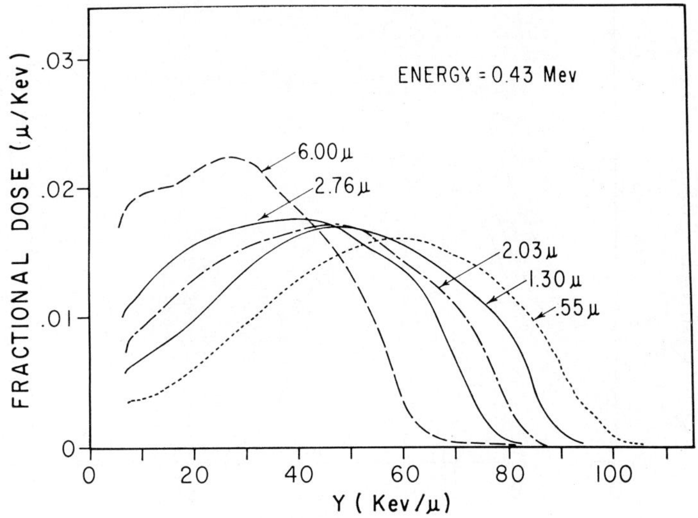

FIG. 3. Experimental $D(Y)$ spectra for 0.43-Mev neutrons

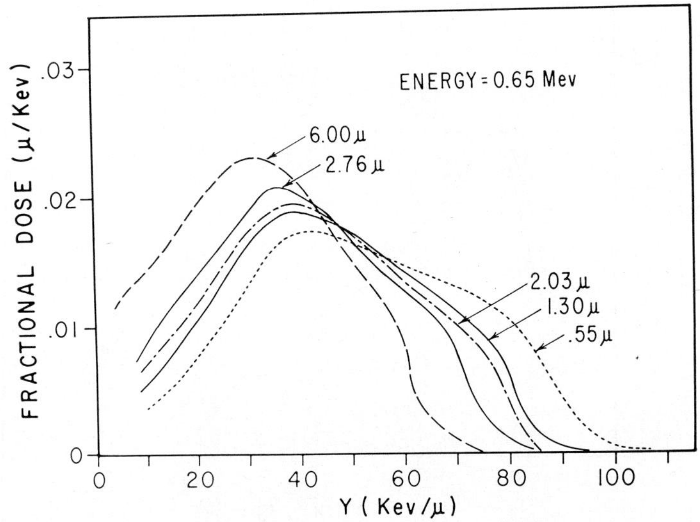

FIG. 4. Experimental $D(Y)$ spectra for 0.65-Mev neutrons

Figs. 9 to 11, fit rather closely to the pattern established at the first group of neutron energies. This indicates that multiple collisions in the thick wall counter probably had little effect on the $D(Y)$ spectrum.

As in previous studies, measurements were also performed by utilizing the

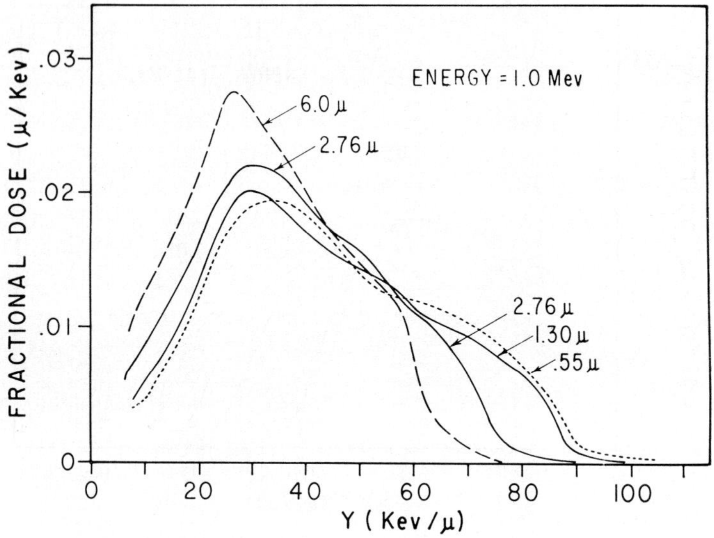

FIG. 5. Experimental $D(Y)$ spectra for 1.0-Mev neutrons

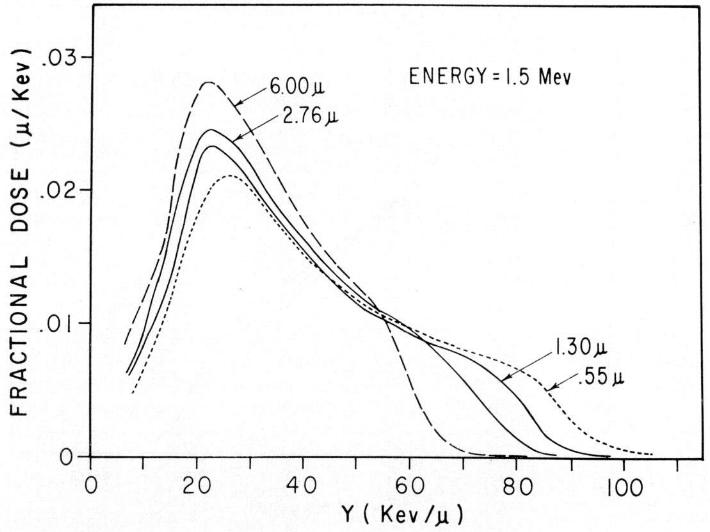

FIG. 6. Experimental $D(Y)$ spectra for 1.5-Mev neutrons

same tissue-equivalent gas filling in aluminum-walled counters in order to evaluate the portion of the $D(Y)$ spectrum due to recoils originating in gas within the sphere. The results were quite similar to the ones reported before (7) and indicated that at the lowest energies and at the largest diameters virtually all the pulses in the counter were due to recoils originating in the gas.

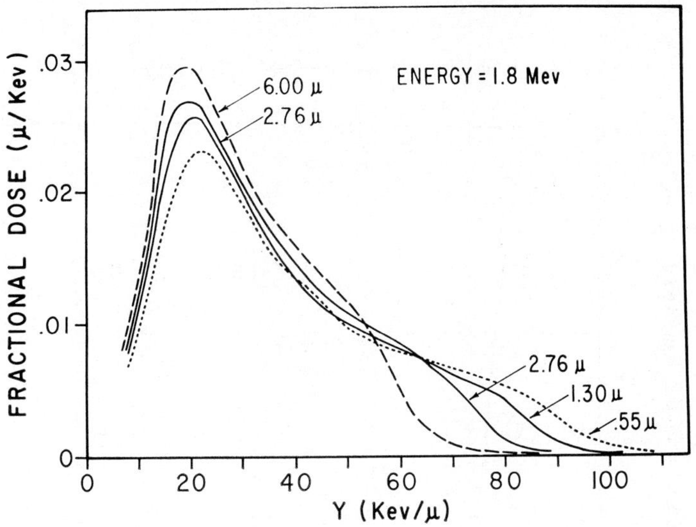

FIG. 7. Experimental $D(Y)$ spectra for 1.8-Mev neutrons

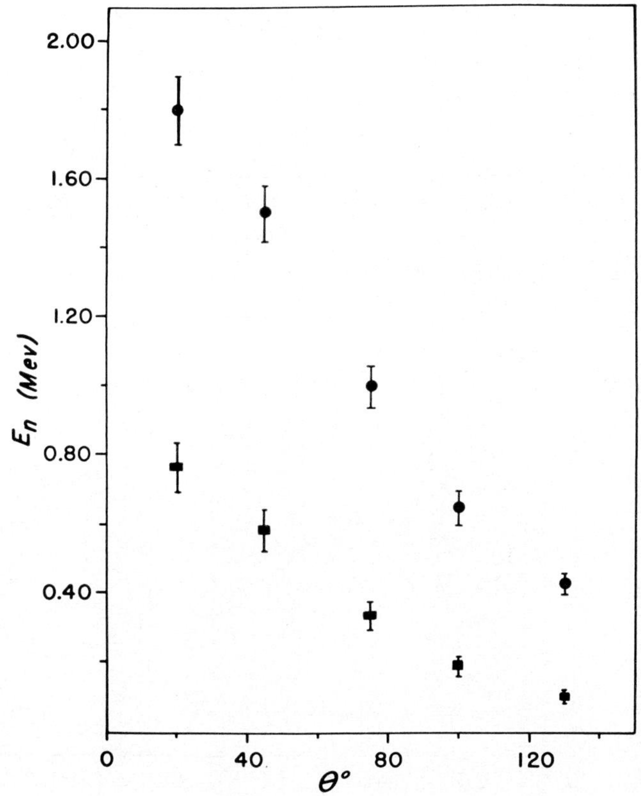

FIG. 8. Neutron energy versus angle between counter and proton beam for both series of measurements. The circles correspond to a proton beam energy of 2.8 Mev, and the squares to a proton beam energy of 1.7 Mev (target: tritium).

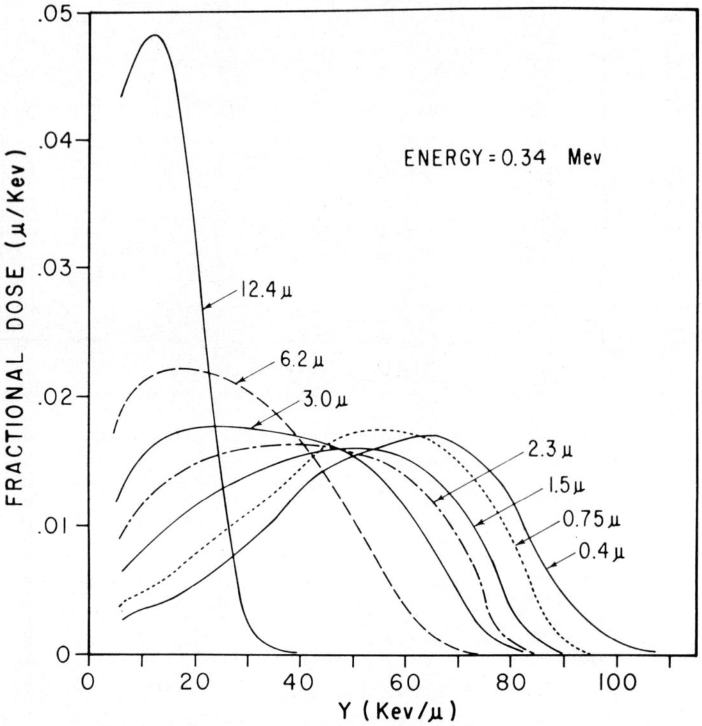

FIG. 9. Experimental $D(Y)$ spectra for 0.34-Mev neutrons

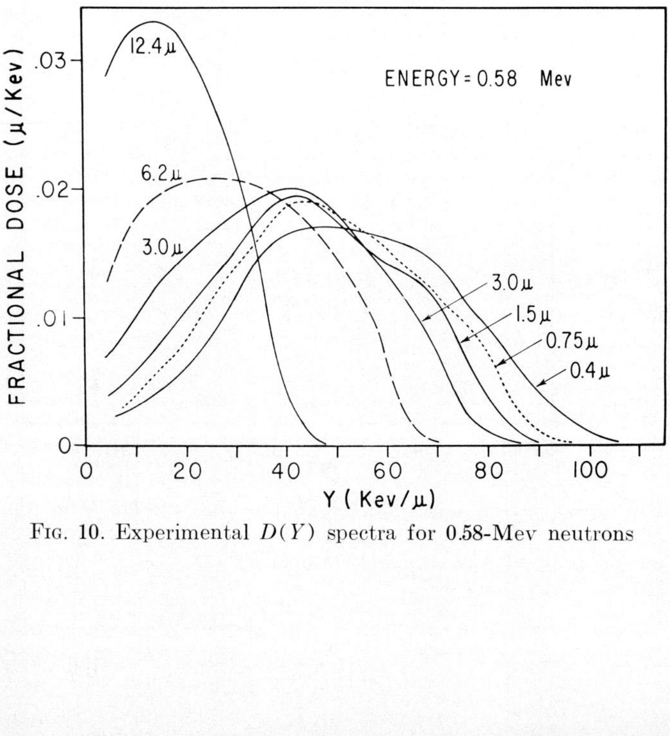

FIG. 10. Experimental $D(Y)$ spectra for 0.58-Mev neutrons

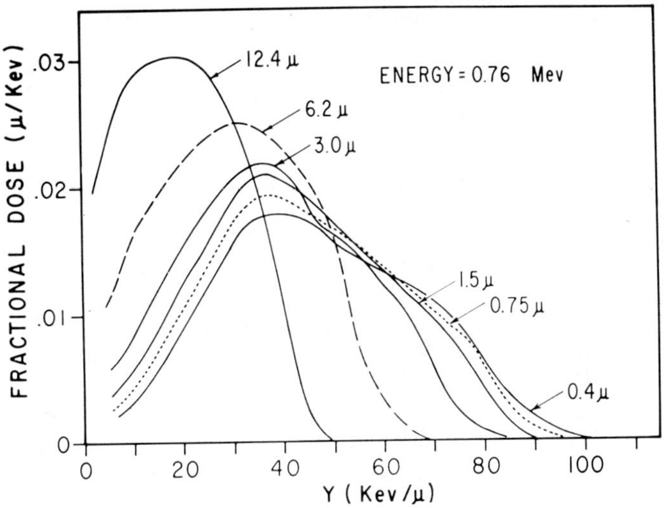

FIG. 11. Experimental $D(Y)$ spectra for 0.76-Mev neutrons

For the low-energy group of neutron measurements, the total doses as measured with a tissue-equivalent ionization chamber (having walls of the same thickness and composition as the counter) and with the proportional counter (for a simulated sphere size of 0.4 μ) are compared with theoretical values in Fig. 12. The theoretical figures were obtained on the basis of proton current, tritium content of target, neutron intensity and energy at the angle of interest (*8*), and first-collision dose per neutron (*9*). The results are in good agreement for 0.34-, 0.58-, and 0.76-Mev neutrons. The measured values at the two lower energies indicate that the dose measured is somewhat greater than that to be expected on theoretical grounds. Figure 13 shows the distribution of dose in Y for a 6.2-μ sphere with the proportional counter located at an angle of 130° with the direction of the proton beam where 100-kev neutrons were expected. At this direction the counter should be exposed to neutrons of a maximum energy of 125 kev which corresponds to a maximum Y value of approximately 20 kev/μ. The curves demonstrate the presence of higher-energy protons. The counter may have been relatively more sensitive to this radiation if it did not originate from the target, because it was placed at about 70 cm from the target, whereas the ionization chamber was only 10 cm away. It has thus far not been possible to identify the contaminating radiation. Because of its presence, the Y spectra obtained at the two lowest neutron energies have been omitted from this report.

MEAN VALUE OF Y

The average Y values, $\bar{Y}$, were computed from the dose distributions for the remaining eight neutron energies. The lower portions of all curves had to be ex-

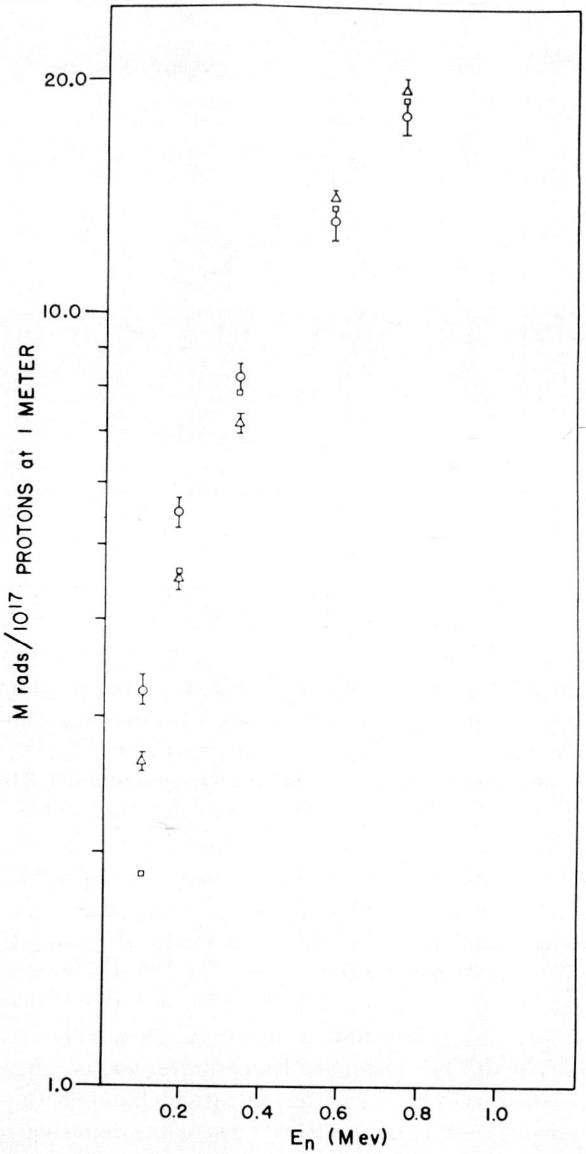

FIG. 12. Experimental and computed absorbed doses for the low-energy group of monoenergetic neutrons. Computed values are surrounded by squares. The circles represent the measurements obtained with the proportional counter simulating a 0.4-μ-diameter tissue sphere, and the triangles represent those obtained with the ionization chamber.

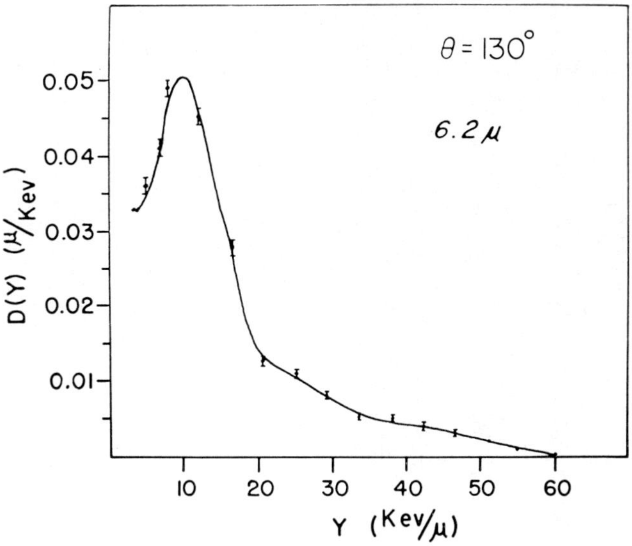

FIG. 13. Distribution of dose in Y for a 6.2-μ-diameter sphere and for the location where 0.100-Mev neutrons were expected.

trapolated, since no measurements were made at Y values below 2.5 kev/μ. To obtain a first approximation for theoretical studies, average values of Y, defined as in equation 3, were plotted versus counter size for each energy. The interpolated

$$\bar{Y} = \frac{\int_0^\infty YD(Y)\,dY}{\int_0^\infty D(Y)\,dY} \tag{3}$$

values at sizes of 0.5, 1.0, 2.5, 5, and 10 μ define a series of curves which are given in Fig. 14.

The figure also shows an idealized relation between $\bar{Y}$ and neutron energy. This may be derived from a determination of $\bar{L}$, which is defined as in equation 4. This was obtained from the curves in Figs. 1 and 2 on the assumption that all

$$\bar{L} = \frac{\int_0^\infty LD(L)\,dL}{\int_0^\infty D(L)\,dL} \tag{4}$$

protons traverse the tissue sphere in straight lines. The results for $\bar{L}$ versus neutron

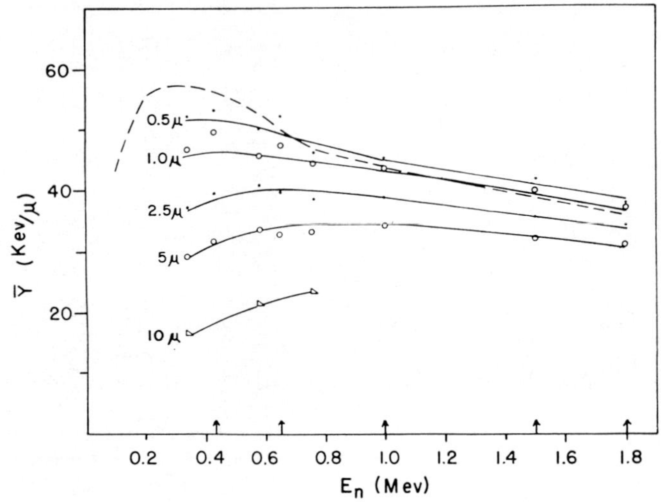

FIG. 14. Dose average Y versus neutron energy for interpolated sphere sizes of 0.5, 1.0, 2.5, 5.0 and 10 μ. The dotted curve represents the theoretical distribution based on the idealization discussed in the text.

energy are given in Table I. In this case the average Y per traversal of secondaries with a LET that is equal to L is ⅔ L and $\bar{Y}$ is equal to ¾ L.

The arrows on the abscissa in Fig. 14 indicate the energies at which the thick-walled counter was used for the measurements. There is some indication at the smaller sizes and lowest energies that the average Y values are somewhat higher for the counter with the ¼-inch-thick wall than for the thin-walled counter. As previously mentioned, this is probably due to multiple scattering of neutrons in the thicker-walled counter, yielding lower-energy protons with higher LET's. For low neutron energies the experimental curves lie considerably below the idealized values, owing to secondary proton tracks which start and end in the gas volume. The computations, however, do not include contributions to the dose by recoiling oxygen and carbon nuclei, and hence the idealized values are lower than the measured values at high neutron energies, where this effect becomes appreciable.

It is evident from the experimental results that, within the range of sphere sizes studied, the maximum average Y occurs at a lower neutron energy as the size decreases. This could conceivably have significant implications in radiobiological studies, since the neutron energy at which the RBE reaches a maximum can be used to select a sphere size for which maximum $\bar{Y}$ is reached at the same energy. This may give an indication of the effective volume from which the energy instrumental in the biological inactivation may be abstracted.

SUMMARY

1. Measurements of the distribution of dose in Y (the energy delivered to tissue spheres divided by sphere diameter) have been carried out at eight neutron energies between 0.34 and 1.8 Mev for a range of sphere sizes.

2. Mean values of Y are compared with idealized values based on calculations of LET spectra.

3. Implications of the results are discussed.

ACKNOWLEDGMENTS

We wish to express our sincere gratitude and appreciation to Drs. V. Bond and J. Bateman for their constant help throughout the experiment. We are indebted to Dr. G. Norris Glasoe for his over-all encouragement and his help in providing the targets for the Van de Graaff generator at Brookhaven National Laboratory. The efforts and cooperation of the Van de Graaff personnel (in particular Dr. David E. Alburger and Mr. R. Lindgren) are greatly appreciated. In addition we thank LCDR James H. Dowling, MSC, USN, of the Armed Forces Radiobiology Research Institute who gave invaluable assistance during the earlier measurements. The help of Mr. L. J. Goodman throughout the experiment is gratefully acknowledged. Mr. J. Penton and Mr. E. Boer assisted with the computations.

RECEIVED: October 13, 1962

REFERENCES

1. H. H. Rossi, J. L. Bateman, V. P. Bond, L. J. Goodman, and E. E. Stickley, The dependence of RBE on the energy of fast neutrons. 1. Physical design and measurement of absorbed dose. *Radiation Res.* **13,** 503–520 (1960).
2. J. L. Bateman, H. H. Rossi, V. P. Bond, and J. Gilmartin, The dependence of RBE on energy of fast neutrons. 2. Biological evaluation at discrete neutron energies in the range 0.43 to 1.80 Mev. *Radiation Res.* **15,** 694–706 (1961).
3. H. H. Rossi, Specification of radiation quality. *Radiation Res.* **10,** 522–531 (1959).
4. H. H. Rossi, Spatial distribution of energy deposition by ionizing radiation. *Radiation Res. Suppl.* **2,** 290–299 (1960).
5. H. H. Rossi, M. H. Biavati, and W. Gross, Local energy density in irradiated tissues. 1. Radiobiological significance. *Radiation Res.* **15,** 431–439 (1961).
6. J. W. Boag, The distribution of linear energy transfer or "ion density" for fast neutrons in water. *Radiation Res.* **1,** 323–341 (1954).
7. W. Rosenzweig and H. H. Rossi, Determination of the quality of the absorbed dose delivered by monoenergetic neutrons. *Radiation Res.* **10,** 532–544 (1959).
8. J. L. Fowler and J. E. Brolley, Jr., Monoenergetic neutron techniques in the 10 to 30 Mev range. *Rev. Modern Phys.* **28,** 103–134 (1956).
9. Radiobiological dosimetry (Report 10e of the International Commission of Radiological Units and Measurements). *Natl. Bur. Std. (U.S.), Handbook.* **88** (To be published).

RADIATION RESEARCH 19, 526–537 (1963)

X-Ray-Induced Incorporation of Tritiated Thymidine into Deoxyribonucleic Acid of Grasshopper Neuroblast Chromosomes

RICHARD A. McGRATH

Institute of Radiation Biology[1] *and Department of Zoology and Entomology, The University of Tennessee, Knoxville, Tennessee*

INTRODUCTION

Most previous studies of the incorporation of precursors into deoxyribonucleic acid (DNA) have shown that irradiation reduces DNA synthesis (*1*). However, Das and Alfert (*2*) have reported an increased incorporation of tritiated thymidine (H^3T) into irradiated onion root tip cells and interpreted this result as evidence for accelerated DNA synthesis in interphase. It has also been suggested (*3*) that H^3T incorporation into mouse intestinal crypt cells which had been blocked mitotically by 5000 r of X-rays could be interpreted as an indication of partial *in situ* repair of damaged DNA. In that study, however, it was not possible to distinguish clearly between normal and abnormal incorporation because: (1) cell stage at the time of irradiation was not known, and (2) individual cells could not be followed after irradiation. In order to study the incorporation of DNA precursors into X-irradiated cells in more detail, the grasshopper neuroblast was selected as experimental material. *Chortophaga* neuroblasts are large cells with a well-defined mitotic cycle. Cell division can be observed in the living cells by bright-field microscopy, all stages of the mitotic cycle can be readily identified, and individual cells can be followed for several hours.

The purpose of this study was to determine whether irradiated neuroblasts that are delayed, stopped, or reverted (see later) mitotically (*4–7*) incorporate H^3T during cell stages which are not usually associated with normal DNA synthesis.

MATERIALS AND METHODS

Embryos of the grasshopper *Chortophaga viridifasciata* (De Geer) at an age equivalent to 14 days of development at 26°C were dissected in isotonic Shaw's

[1] This work was supported in part by a U.S. Atomic Energy Commission Grant AT-(40-1)-2575.

medium (*8*). A piece of mid-ventral tissue was transferred to Shaw's medium which contained 10 μc of (H^3T) [2] per milliliter, and hanging-drop cultures were prepared. Additional details concerning the preparation of cultures have been published (*9*). Yolk was added to all preparations to ensure recovery of mitotic activity after irradiation (*10*). X-Irradiation started 3 ± ½ minutes after tissue was placed in medium which contained H^3T. Hanging-drop preparations were exposed to 32 r of X-rays from a Coolidge tube, operated at 100 kvp and 5 ma (target-to-object distance, 20 cm; 0.28 mm Al filter; about 190 r/min).

Living neuroblasts within the three thoracic segments of the embryo were observed by bright-field microscopy. An incubator which enclosed the lower part of the microscope was used to maintain a temperature of 38° ± ½°C. Cell stages were first identified within 10 minutes after irradiation. Characteristics of the different neuroblast cell stages referred to in this work have been published (*11, 12*). The positions of several early, middle, and late prophase neuroblasts were mapped on the embryo (*9*) to ensure their relocation at a later time. Final identification of cells in living preparations was made within 2 minutes before fixation.

Tissue was fixed with 50% acetic acid, and the fixed hanging-drop preparations then were re-examined. Sketches of the areas to be studied were made which showed the relative locations of enough cells to ensure reidentification of mapped neuroblasts after sectioning. Serial sections, 5 μ thick, were cut parallel to the ventral surface of the embryonic tissue and mounted on subbed (*13*) slides. Slides were treated with 1 *N* HCl at 60°C for 5 minutes to remove cytoplasmic stainability. Autoradiograms were prepared with Kodak NTB-2 emulsion and stained with toluidine blue (*14*).

Sketches, notes, and mapping relationships were used to relocate previously mapped neuroblasts beneath the emulsion. Except where noted otherwise, results reported in this paper are based only on data from neuroblasts which were reidentified. Grain counts were made at a magnification of 1000×.

When the number of grains over a nucleus was less than about 30, the total grain count was recorded. In order to score larger grain numbers, the nucleus was positioned beneath the image of a 5-μ-diameter circle (area = 19.6 μ^2) at the plane of the object, and the number of grains within the circle was either counted or (in the case of very heavy labeling) estimated. Counts per 19.6 μ^2, when multiplied by a factor of about 10, approximate the total counts seen over an average nuclear section area. This factor has also been used when necessary to compare background counts[3] with total counts.

[2] H^3T was obtained from New England Nuclear Corp. at specific activities which ranged from 0.5 to 5.4 curies/mM. Samples of each lot were tested for radioactive contamination by ascending chromatography in a butanol–H_2O (86:14) system followed by gas-flow counting in a strip scanner. Contaminated H^3T was purified chromatographically.

[3] For the determination of background grain numbers, random areas close to but not overlapping the tissue were selected. Total grain number was scored within a circle 22 μ in diameter.

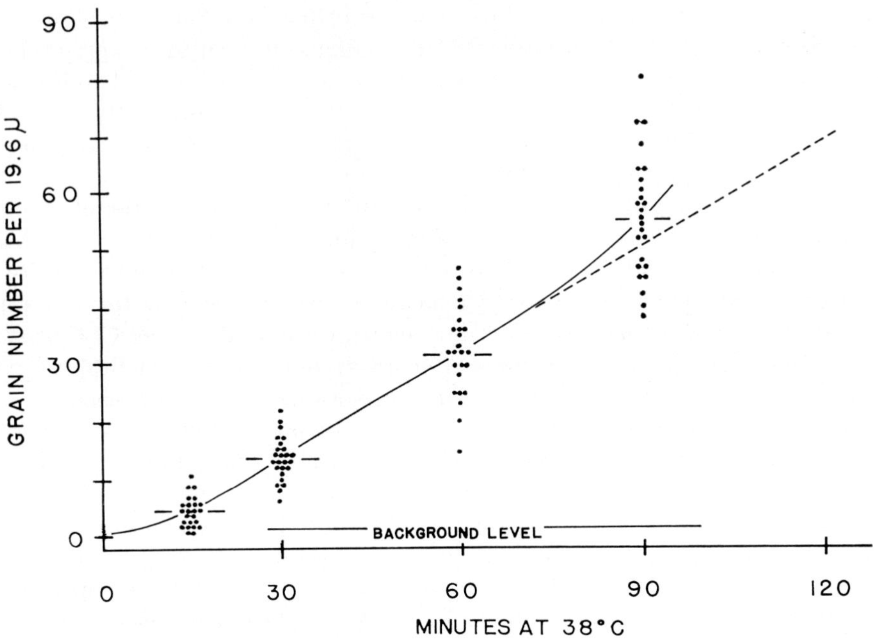

FIG. 1. Relationship between grain number per unit area (19.6 μ^2) and time of incubation in 10 μc of H^3T per milliliter at 38°C. Emulsion exposure time, 5 days. Means indicated by —.

Because of the inaccuracies in grain counting, especially with heavy labeling, and the great variation in grain numbers seen over mitotically affected neuroblasts, counts made over these cells cannot be considered as strictly quantitative. No corrections for section thickness or cross-sectional area were made. Additional technical details are found, where relevant, in the text.

RESULTS AND CONCLUSIONS

Incorporation of H^3T into Nonirradiated Neuroblasts

Time Relationship. Embryos were placed in vials of isotonic medium which contained 10 μc of H^3T per milliliter and left at 38°C for periods of incubation which ranged from 15 minutes to 2½ hours. Individual neuroblasts were not followed. At 30-minute intervals from the start of incubation (one 15-minute interval was used), embryos were fixed, embedded, and sectioned. Autoradiograms were prepared. Grain numbers per unit area were scored over labeled nuclei of interphase and very early prophase neuroblasts. Figure 1 shows the relationship between grain

The average grain number was multiplied by 0.052, the ratio of areas of circles 5 μ and 22 μ in diameter. This value represents the average background within a circle 5 μ in diameter, the unit area used for counting heavily labeled nuclei.

number and time of incubation at 38°C. A curve has been fitted by eye to correspond with the mean grain number at each time. Grain counts at times greater than 90 minutes are not shown because labeling was so heavy that counting was impossible. The straight portion of the curve has been extrapolated to 120 minutes.

Duration of DNA Synthesis. From studies with C^{14}- and H^3-labeled thymidine, Gaulden (*15, 16*) concluded that synthesis of DNA in the grasshopper neuroblast begins in middle telophase and ends in very early prophase. This finding has been confirmed in this investigation by making hanging-drop preparations in H^3T, mapping and following cells in different stages, and making autoradiograms after cells have passed through known mitotic stages. Most cells in stages between middle telophase and very early prophase during the observation period were labeled. Some, but not all, neuroblasts which progressed from very early prophase into later prophase stages were labeled, as were cells which passed from early into middle telophase. No labeling was detected in neuroblasts which were at mitotic stages between early prophase and early telophase during the entire course of the observation period.

On the basis of these results, neuroblasts in very early prophase as well as those in the first part of early prophase have been excluded from further labeling experiments (i.e., approximately 35 minutes were allowed to elapse between the end of the normal DNA synthesis period and the first stages used for these experiments).

Response of Neuroblasts to 32 Roentgens of X-Rays

Effects on Individual Cells. Within 15 minutes after X-ray exposure, the chromatin within some prophase neuroblasts becomes more refractile than normal. This response is characteristic of neuroblasts which stop or revert to an earlier stage. Stopped cells may remain in this condition for about 2 hours without appreciable change in mitotic stage. In neuroblasts which revert, chromosome morphology changes to a condition which resembles an earlier stage. Chromatin which appears highly refractile in the living state appears lumpy or knotted in fixed and stained sections of the same cells.

The average cytological response of neuroblasts which were irradiated in early, middle, or late prophase is shown in Fig. 2. Five points are plotted on each curve: (*A*) the point at which irradiation occurred, (*B*) the first recognition of reversion, (*C*) entrance into maximum reversion, (*D*) departure from maximum reversion, and (*E*) resumption of "normal" appearance. These points are labeled on one curve in the figure. It should be pointed out that the curves are averages of several different kinds of response, and for this reason approximately 50% of the observed points of maximum reversion fall outside the 95% confidence limits.

Response in Relationship to Mitotic Stage. Response of neuroblasts irradiated in any one of the mitotic prophase stages can be grouped into four categories, cells which are: (1) not delayed, proceed through subsequent stages with little or no delay; (2) delayed, take longer than normal in their progress through subse-

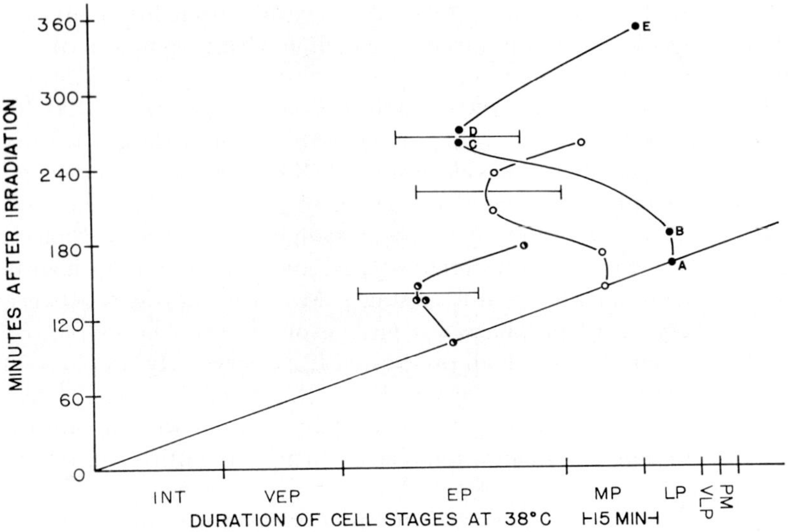

FIG. 2. Extent and duration of reversion and delay of neuroblasts given 32 r of X-rays. Cells which divide with little or no delay (see column 1, Table I) are excluded from these data. Bars indicate 95% confidence limits on the average points of maximum reversion. The sloping base line indicates the progress of an average normal cell at 38°C. INT = interphase, VEP = very early prophase, EP = early prophase, MP = middle prophase, LP = late prophase, VLP = very late prophase, PM = prometaphase. Letters *A* to *E* are defined in text.

quent stages; (3) stopped, retain for a time the characteristics of the stage at which they were treated; (4) reverted, regress to a condition in which chromosome morphology resembles that seen at earlier stages. The percentage of neuroblasts in very early, early, middle, and late prophase, at the time of irradiation, which fall into each of these categories is given in Table I. These data show an increase in types of response after 32 r as the stage of treatment becomes later, up to very late prophase. Cells irradiated in very late prophase divide with little or no delay.

Labeling of Neuroblasts. Within 2 hours after 32 r of X-rays, most early, middle, and late prophase neuroblasts which were either stopped mitotically or reverted to earlier stages were labeled. Early and middle prophase cells which were delayed were also labeled. Delayed late prophase cells were either unlabeled or so lightly labeled that they must be classed as doubtful cases. Cells which divided with little or no delay were not labeled. Figure 3 shows the relationship between stage at the time of irradiation and grain numbers seen over nuclei of delayed, stopped, and reverted neuroblasts. Preparations from which these data were collected were fixed 1½ to 2 hours after irradiation. These data show that labeling of stopped, delayed, or reverted cells is greatest when irradiation occurs in early prophase and is least in cells irradiated in middle and late prophase.

TABLE I

Relation between Stage of Cell at Time of Irradiation and Degree of Mitotic Effect Induced

(Numbers are percentages of cells showing different degrees of effect.)

Prophase stage	*Number of cells*	*Not delayed*	*Delayed*	*Stopped*	*Revert one stage*	*Revert two stages*	*Revert three or more stages*
Very early	9	22	78	0	0	0	0
Early	21	9	43	29	19	0	0
Middle	40	10	8	40	17	25	0
Late	27	41	15	7	15	18	4

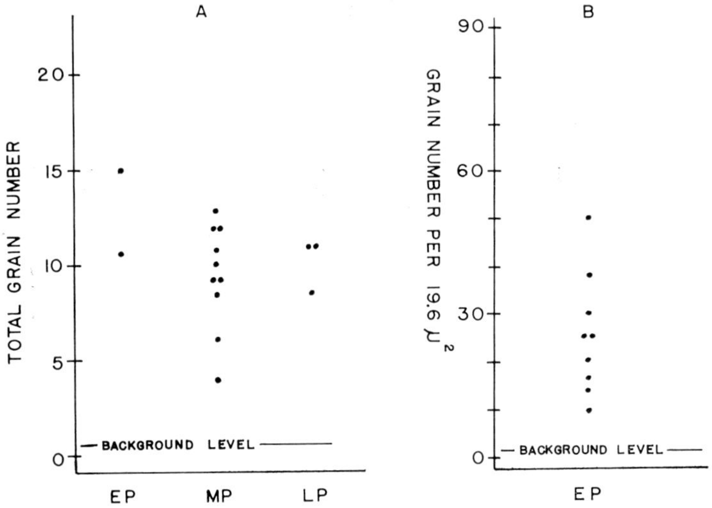

Fig. 3. Grain numbers over sectioned nuclei of neuroblasts which were delayed, stopped, or reverted after 32 r of X-rays in relation to stage at the time of irradiation. Grain numbers represented in *B* were scored over early prophase neuroblasts from the same preparations as cells represented in *A*; grain numbers were so high, however, that a different method of counting was necessary (90-minute controls counted by the same method are shown in Fig. 1). EP = early prophase, MP = middle prophase, LP = late prophase. Emulsion exposure time, 5 days.

No consistent differences in grain numbers could be detected among delayed, stopped, and reverted neuroblasts. Figure 4 shows examples of the degree of labeling seen over nuclei of stopped and reverted neuroblasts. All cells shown in these photomicrographs were at the end of early prophase or the beginning of middle prophase at the time of irradiation. Figure 4*A* shows a cell from a preparation which was fixed 15 minutes after 32 r of X-rays. On the basis of observation of a

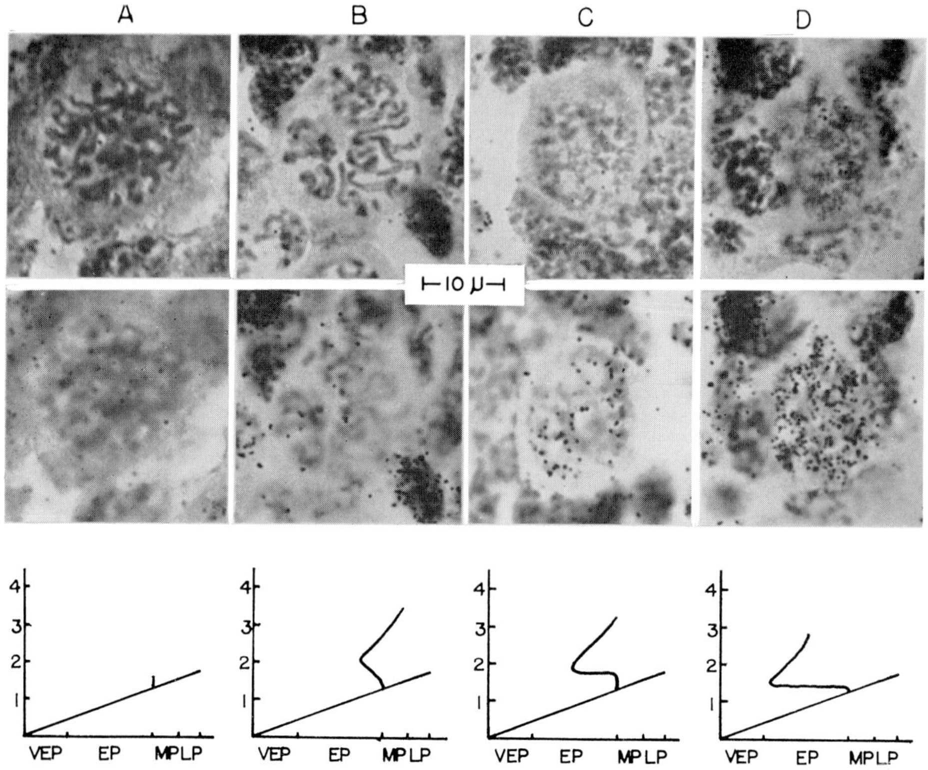

FIG. 4. Prophase neuroblasts which have incorporated H^3T after 32 r of X-rays. Top: Sectioned nuclei in focus. Middle: Grains in the emulsion in focus. Bottom: Charts showing cell stage plotted against hours after start of treatment. The sloping base line indicates the progress of a non-irradiated neuroblast at 38°C. Emulsion exposure time, 5 days. See text for additional details.

number of similarly labeled cells, it is clear that incorporation can be detected in some neuroblasts within 15 minutes after irradiation. Figures 4*B*, *C*, and *D* are photomicrographs of three cells from one preparation which was fixed 2 hours after 32 r. Both the amount of labeling and the mitotic stage which was reached by 2 hours differ in each case.

Response of Neuroblasts to 250 Roentgens of X-Rays

In order to determine whether incorporation of H^3T into prophase neuroblasts occurred after an X-ray dose greater than 32 r, embryos were made in hanging-drop preparations which contained 1 μc of H^3T per milliliter and then exposed to 250 to 256 r of X-rays. Neuroblasts in early, middle, and late prophase were mapped and observed at 38°C for 6 hours. In contrast to the variety of responses

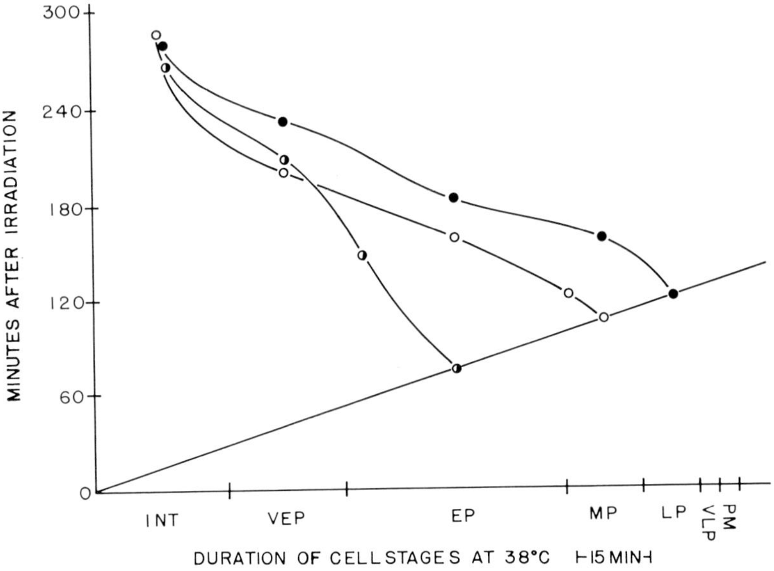

FIG. 5. Average response curves of neuroblasts given 250 to 256 r of X-rays. Cells which divide with little or no delay are excluded. Curves are started at the mid-point of the stage in which the cell was first observed. The sloping base line indicates the progress of an average normal cell at 38°C. Abbreviations same as in Fig. 2.

seen after 32 r, neuroblasts given 250 r in mitotic prophase revert to an interphase-like condition within 5 hours (with the exception only of those cells which divide within about 40 minutes after irradiation). The average cytological response of neuroblasts in each of the prophase stages which were studied is shown in Fig. 5. Points on the curves are averages of eight to ten cells. All cells which were followed during reversion and later reidentified in autoradiograms were heavily labeled. Grain numbers were too high for either total or unit-area counting. Figure 6 shows a photomicrographic field which includes three cells which were in different prophase stages at the time of irradiation. It is clear from these experiments that reversion of prophase neuroblasts in response to 250 r of X-rays is associated with H^3T incorporation.

Deoxyribonuclease and Ribonuclease Digestion after Combined H^3T and X-Ray Treatment

The following experiment was done in order to determine whether the H^3T incorporation which had been detected was associated with chromosomal DNA. Embryos were made into hanging-drop preparations which contained 10 μc of H^3T per milliliter, given 32 or 250 r of X-rays, and then left at 38°C for 3 hours. Squash preparations (*14*) were made in order to ensure maximum possible detection

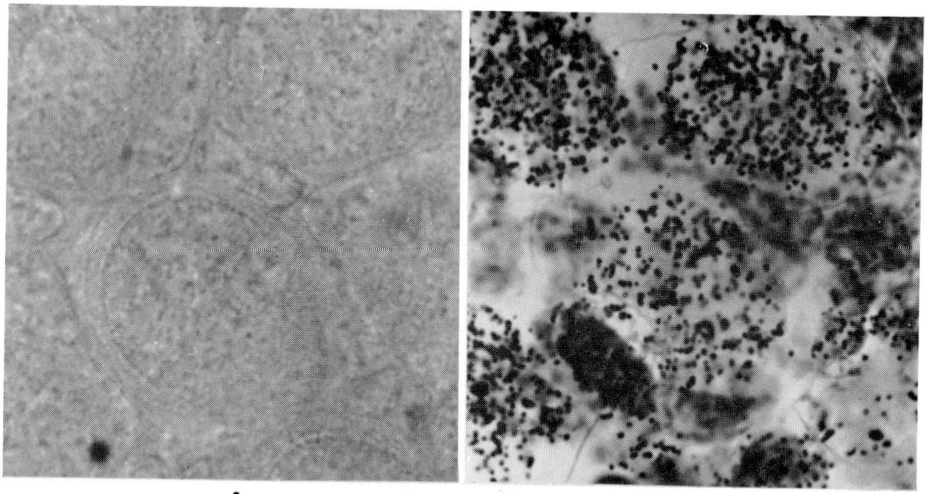

FIG. 6. Photomicrograph of a field which shows neuroblasts which have reverted to an interphase-like condition after 250 r of X-rays. Stages at the time of irradiation: Center: early prophase; upper left: late prophase; upper right: middle prophase. *A*, the fixed hanging-drop preparation. *B*, grains in the emulsion of the corresponding autoradiogram in focus. Emulsion exposure time, 10 days.

of labeling over nuclei. Preparations were treated with 0.01% crystalline DNase (Worthington) in 0.01 *M* phosphate buffer (with 0.123% $MgSO_4$ and 0.1% bovine serum albumin) for 3 hours at 38°C, or with 0.05% RNase (California Biochemical Corporation) in 0.01 *M* phosphate buffer at 38°C for 3 hours. Control squash preparations were incubated in each solution without enzyme for 3 hours at 38°C. No labeling was seen over chromosomes or nuclei in preparations treated with DNase. Control preparations as well as those treated with RNase were heavily labeled. Thus it is clear that H^3T is incorporated into chromosomal DNA under the experimental conditions of this study.

DISCUSSION

Since it is not usually possible to follow individual cells during mitotic reversion, a statistical method which shows a decrease in number of cells in prophase correlated with an increase in interphases has been used in the past. By this technique, Carlson (*4*), Koller (*17*), Darlington and La Cour (*18*), Beatty and Beatty (*19*), and Chandler (*20*) have shown that mitotic reversion occurs in a variety of cell types after X-ray exposure.

Results of this study suggest the possibility that reverted cells which have incorporated H^3T may contribute to a class of "interphase" cells which show high grain numbers when assayed autoradiographically. This possibility should be considered in future experiments of the type reported by Das and Alfert (*2*).

As a result of both statistical analysis and direct observation of hanging-drop preparations, Carlson (*6*) found that after 31 r of X-rays cells near the end of middle prophase or the beginning of late prophase showed maximum sensitivity, i.e., a mitotic delay of about 3 hours. The present study of H^3T labeling after 32 r shows that maximum incorporation of H^3T does not occur during the most radiation-sensitive stage (in terms of mitotic delay) but at early prophase, or possibly sooner.

One explanation of these labeling results is that H^3T incorporation may be an indication of some kind of repair process within X-ray-damaged chromosomes. In this connection, although the relationship may be coincidental, St. Amand (*7*) reported that neuroblast chromosome breakage frequency, when scored at the first anaphase after 32 r of X-rays, was maximum in middle telophase, fell until early prophase, rose during middle prophase, and dropped to near-zero values by prometaphase. If the drop in breakage frequency after middle telophase were correlated with the beginning of DNA synthesis, one might speculate that breakage gradually became undetectable owing to repair during the DNA synthesis period.

The reported H^3T incorporation is probably not a simple result of autoradiation from H^3 (estimated as 0.4 rep/hr[4]). It is possible that association of tritiated compounds with chromosomes can produce autoradiation effects (*22*). In this connection, however, exposure of grasshopper neuroblasts to 50 μc of H^3T per milliliter for 30 minutes has no obvious immediate effect on mitosis, nor is labeling of middle or late prophase cells observed under such conditions (R. A. McGrath, unpublished data).

Cell death is not a factor in this study. Neuroblasts given 32 r or 250 r of X-rays recover from the initial radiation effects and proceed through apparently successful divisions.

Since labeling is not detected after DNase treatment, it seems reasonable to conclude that H^3T becomes associated with chromosomal DNA. From this study, however, it is not possible to determine the nature of this association at the molecular level. An explanation, mainly hypothetical (considering the low X-ray dose), is that irradiation could cause scission of H bonds in the DNA strand and thus provide a template for the addition of H^3T (or possibly other precursors). If a number of adjacent bonds were split, the "synthesis" of small amounts of DNA could possibly result in the formation of multistranded regions on the DNA. It is uncertain, however, whether insertion of H^3T into broken DNA strands, end addition at a site of damage, or true DNA synthesis is involved.

[4] Calculated from $D = 55\ CE$, where D is the dose to water or tissue in rep per day, when it can be assumed that all the energy is dissipated in the volume under consideration; C is the concentration of the isotope in microcuries per gram; E is the energy of the radiation in Mev (*21*).

SUMMARY

The direct observation of irradiated *Chortophaga* neuroblasts at identifiable stages of the cell cycle in the living condition, shows that:

1. Changes in chromosome morphology which are characteristic of mitotic stoppage or delay can be detected within 15 minutes after 32 r of X-rays.
2. Four more or less distinct mitotic responses of irradiated (32 r) prophase neuroblasts can be distinguished: (1) nondelay, (2) delay, (3) stoppage, and (4) reversion.
3. The greatest number of types of response is seen in cells which were irradiated in late prophase, whereas the least variety of responses occurs after treatment of very early prophases.
4. Preparations given 250 r of X-rays show reversion of prophase cells to an interphase-like condition.

The observation of living neuroblasts exposed to tritiated thymidine (H^3T) and then irradiated in hanging-drop preparations and reidentification of the same cells in autoradiograms of sectioned material show that:

1. Prophase neuroblasts which are delayed, stopped, or reverted mitotically in response to 32 r of X-rays incorporate H^3T.
2. Incorporation is greater in cells irradiated in early prophase and less in cells treated in middle or late prophase. No incorporation is seen in cells treated in very late prophase.
3. Incorporation is not seen in preparations treated with DNase before application of autoradiographic emulsion.
4. Labeling can be detected within 15 minutes after X-irradiation of early or middle prophase neuroblasts.
5. After 250 r of X-rays, prophase cells which do not divide within about 40 minutes do incorporate H^3T during reversion to an interphase-like condition.

ACKNOWLEDGMENTS

I am indebted to Drs. J. G. Carlson, M. E. Gaulden, R. F. Kimball, R. B. Setlow, D. Schwartz, and S. Wolf for stimulating discussions of various aspects of the work; to Drs. W. E. Cohn and R. B. Setlow for their help with chromatographic methods; and to W. M. Leach, who helped develop the squash method.

RECEIVED: October 27, 1962

REFERENCES

1. L. A. STOCKEN, Some observations on the biochemical effects of X-irradiation. *Radiation Res. Suppl.* **1,** 53–72 (1959).
2. N. K. DAS and M. ALFERT, Accelerated DNA synthesis in onion root meristem during X-irradiation. *Proc. Natl. Acad. Sci. U. S.* **47,** 1–6 (1961).
3. R. A. MCGRATH, Cell migration and abnormal crypt cell enlargement in the small intestine of X-irradiated mice. *Intern. J. Radiation Biol.* **2,** 177–185 (1960).

4. J. G. Carlson, Immediate effects of 250 r of X-rays on the different stages of mitosis in neuroblasts of the grasshopper, *Chortophaga viridifasciata*. *J. Morphol.* **66,** 11–23 (1940).
5. J. G. Carlson, Effects of X-radiation on grasshopper chromosomes. *Cold Spring Harbor Symp. Quant. Biol.* **9,** 104–112 (1941).
6. J. G. Carlson, Immediate effects of 31 r of X-rays on the different stages of mitosis in neuroblasts of *Chortophaga*. *J. Morphol.* **71,** 449–462 (1942).
7. W. St. Amand, Mitotic inhibition and chromosome breakage induced in grasshopper neuroblasts by X-irradiation at known mitotic stages. *Radiation Res.* **5,** 65–78 (1956).
8. E. I. Shaw, A glutamic acid-glycine medium for prolonged maintenance of high mitotic activity in grasshopper neuroblasts. *Exptl. Cell Res.* **11,** 580–586 (1956).
9. J. G. Carlson, The grasshopper neuroblast culture technique and its value in radiobiological studies. *Ann. N. Y. Acad. Sci.* **95,** 932–941 (1961).
10. M. E. Gaulden and K. L. Kokomoor, Influence of yolk on mitotic rate in untreated and X-rayed grasshopper neuroblasts *in vitro, Proc Soc. Exptl. Biol. Med.* **90,** 309–314 (1955).
11. J. G. Carlson, Protoplasmic viscosity changes in different regions of the grasshopper neuroblast during mitosis. *Biol. Bull.* **90,** 109–121 (1946).
12. J. G. Carlson and A. Hollaender, Mitotic effects of ultraviolet radiation of the 2250 Å region, with special reference to the spindle and cleavage. *J. Cellular Comp. Physiol.* **31,** 149–173 (1948).
13. G. A. Boyd, *Autoradiography in Biology and Medicine*, p. 209, Academic Press, New York, 1955.
14. R. A. McGrath, W. M. Leach, and J. G. Carlson, A squash technique for autoradiography of grasshopper neuroblasts. *J. Royal Microscop. Soc.* **82,** (1963).
15. M. E. Gaulden, DNA synthesis and X-ray effects at different mitotic stages in grasshopper neuroblasts. *Genetics* **41,** 645 (1956) .
16. M. E. Gaulden, In *Mitogenesis* (H. S. Ducoff and C. F. Ehret, eds.), pp. 38–39, University of Chicago Press, 1959.
17. P. C. Koller, The effects of radiation on pollen grain development, differentiation, and germination. *Proc. Roy. Soc. Edinburgh* **B61,** 398–429 (1943).
18. C. D. Darlington and L. F. La Cour, Chromosome breakage and the nucleic acid cycle. *J. Genet.* **46,** 180–267 (1945).
19. A. V. Beatty and J. W. Beatty, Immediate effects of 200 r and 400 r of X-radiation on the microspores of *Tradescantia paludosa*. *Am. J. Botany* **41,** 242–250 (1954).
20. A. C. Chandler, The immediate effects of low doses of X-radiation on the frequency of several mitotic stages in the *Allium* root tip. *Biol. Bull.* **112,** 305–312 (1957).
21. A. M. Brues, Ionizing radiations and cancer. *Advan. Cancer Res.* **2,** 177–195 (1954).
22. M. A. Bender, P. C. Gooch, and D. M. Prescott, Aberrations induced in human leukocyte chromosomes by ^{3}H-labeled nucleosides. *Cytogenetics* **1,** 65–74 (1962).

RADIATION RESEARCH **19**, 538–550 (1963)

The Effect of AET (β-Aminoethylisothiuronium) on Thyroid Function in the Rat[1]

YOSH MARUYAMA[2]

Department of Radiology, Stanford University School of Medicine, Stanford, California

INTRODUCTION

β-Aminoethylisothiuronium (AET) has been shown to reduce the lethal action of X- or γ-radiation in mice, rats, and monkeys (*1–3*). This has been attributed to two primary mechanisms, namely, radical capture (*4*) and tissue hypoxia (*5*). The former mechanism acts by means of an intramolecular transguanylated derivative, mercaptoethylguanidine (MEG), which is able to "trap" reactive free radicals liberated in the cell by radiation. The latter mechanism operates by virtue of a sulfhydryl group on the molecule which can be readily oxidized in the tissues, thereby causing deoxygenation and cell hypoxia (*5*). Maurer and Schreiber (*6*) suggest that sulfhydryl compounds decrease the metabolic activity of the organism. Two studies (*7, 8*) suggest an indirect mechanism by which this can occur, mediated by the thyroid gland and presumably acting through a modification of oxidative metabolism. Both of these studies showed a depression of I^{131} uptake by the thyroid gland. The present experiments are designed to evaluate the effect of AET on thyroid function and to determine wether a true antithyroidal effect obtains.

EXPERIMENTAL PROCEDURE

Male Sprague-Dawley rats weighing between 90 and 250 gm were maintained on Purina laboratory chow and distilled water ad libitum unles otherwise indicated. In the latter case a Remington low-iodine diet (*9*) was given for a 5- to 7-day period prior to the study.

AET obtained as the hydrobromide salt from Schwarz Laboratories[3] was twice recrystallized from isopropanol–ethanol–water; the crystals were collected by filtration, dried over Drierite *in vacuo*, and then stored in a desiccator over Drierite until used. The crystalline material melted sharply at 192° to 194°C. This

[1] Supported by Grants A2958 and RH0024-01, Division of Radiological Health, National Institutes of Health, U. S. Public Health Service.

[2] Advanced Fellow in Academic Radiology of the James Picker Foundation.

[3] Schwarz BioResearch, Inc., Mount Vernon, New York.

purification was performed to eliminate all traces of thiourea which might be present, this being a known antithyroidal chemical and a starting material in the chemical synthesis. For each experiment AET was freshly prepared in 0.1 *N* HCl solution and in the following studies was given either in the acid solution or adjusted to pH 7.0 with either sodium hydroxide or 0.1 *M* sodium phosphate buffer solution.

Carrier-free I^{131} obtained from Oak Ridge was used in these experiments.

Radioactive Iodine Uptake by the Thyroid Gland

Animals were maintained on a Remington low-iodine diet for a 5-day period prior to the uptake study, and all injections were intraperitoneal. The animals were divided into two groups for each time period, with one group serving as controls and the other receiving the chemical. AET was administered in 0.1 *N* HCl, in pH 7.0 solution (neutralized with NaOH, then administered immediately), or after the neutralized solution had stood at room temperature for 15 minutes to ensure complete conversion to mercaptoethylguanidine (MEG). Thirty minutes later, 0.5 to 1.0 μc of I^{131} was given. The animals were sacrificed with chloroform at intervals of 2, 4, 6, and 24 hours; their thyroid glands were excised en bloc with immediate adjacent tissues and individually counted in a well-type scintillation counter. The effect of dose variation was determined by a 4-hour uptake study on five groups of animals, with one serving as controls and the remaining groups receiving doses of 100, 150, 200, or 300 mg/kg. Control groups received either an equivalent dose of physiological saline or, when an acidic solution was given, an equivalent amount of 0.1 *N* HCl.

Determination of Goitrogenic Effect

AET was administered in a single daily dose for 10 consecutive days to animals of starting weight of approximately 100 gm. All doses were given either perorally through a gastric cannula or intraperitoneally. Dose schedules were orally 70 mg/day (about 700 mg/kg) or parenterally 20 mg/day (about 200 mg/kg). Control groups received either physiological saline or 0.1 *N* HCl in equivalent volume. One group was treated with thiourea, 10 mg/day (100 mg/kg), in appropriate form, as this is a known antithyroidal chemical. At the end of this period, the animals were sacrificed, and the thyroid glands were excised, dissected free of adjacent tissue, weighed on a microbeam torsion balance, and fixed in formalin; paraffin sections were stained with hematoxylin and eosin for histological study. All animals were weighed daily in groups.

Intrathyroidal Metabolism of Iodine

Six animals weighing 250 gm were divided into two groups. All doses were intraperitoneal. One group received physiological saline, and the other received AET (300 mg/kg) in phosphate buffer at pH 7.0. Thirty minutes later, 5 or 25 μc of

I^{131}, respectively, was given, and all animals were sacrificed 4 hours after the tracer dose. Their thyroid glands were excised and homogenized in a microglass homogenizer in 1 ml of Hank's balanced electrolyte solution at 0°C. Twenty microliters of the homogenate was spotted on Whatman No. 1 chromatography paper. The homogenates were then enzymatically hydrolyzed for 24 hours under a drop of toluene with 0.005% added propylthiouracil to prevent the oxidation of iodide to iodine [in shaker incubator, 37°C, 10 mg of pancreatin (Merck), 100 μM of phosphate buffer, pH 8.0]. At the end of this period, 20-μl aliquots of hydrolyzate were spotted on Whatman No. 1 paper, and both the hydrolyzed and unhydrolyzed samples were chromatographed in n-butanol–glacial acetic acid–distilled water (78:5:15), and n-butanol saturated with 3 N NH_4OH in a descending chromatographic system. These were dried and then scanned for radioactive peaks by using a gas-flow Geiger-Mueller strip counter. Radioautographs were obtained on Kodak No-Screen film. "Cold" standards of monoiodotyrosine (MIT), diiodotyrosine (DIT), triiodothyronine (T3), thyroxine (T4), and radioactive I^{131} iodide run simultaneously were used to identify the radioactive products and to determine R_f values; these standards were developed with ninhydrin (0.1% in n-butanol saturated with water). The relative proportions of each of the radioactive peaks were determined by planimetric measurement.

Measurement in Vivo of Thyroid Radioiodine Activity

The method of Albert (*10*), Wolff (*11*), and Perry (*12*) was used to determine *in vivo* the release of thyroid radioactivity. A scintillation detector was adapted for direct counting of the thyroid region of the rat. A 0.5-inch lead body shield was provided with a 19-mm opening over which the thyroid region could be reproducibly positioned during brief periods of ether anesthesia. The animals were initially prepared for a 5- to 7-day period on a low-iodine diet to enhance I^{131} uptake. Five microcuries of I^{131} were given, and 40 hours after the dose the first count (zero time) was made with two separate 1-minute counts over the thyroid region. The counts were corrected for decay of the I^{131} ($T_{1/2}$ = 8 days) and, in view of the exponential decline in activity, could be plotted on semilog paper as a per cent of the zero-time count. At the time intervals counted, the major activity resides in the thyroid gland, and no attempt to correct for nonthyroidal activity was made. All injections were intraperitoneal.

In one experiment, two groups of 2 rats weighing 150 gm each were placed on a Purina chow diet. On this diet there is a slow decline of activity corresponding to the normal release rate. After 27 hours, they were treated with either physiological saline or AET in phosphate buffer solution (300 mg/kg), and serial counts were made at intervals for 70 hours. In a second experiment, two groups of 2 rats each were injected at zero time with 10 mg of propylthiouracil (PTU) in a slightly alkaline solution and placed on a diet containing 0.03% PTU. At 27 hours, they received saline or AET and were counted as above. In a third experiment, three groups of 2 animals each were maintained on the Purina chow diet, two being treated with 3 units of thyrotropin (Armour) (TSH) 30 minutes after the saline or AET. This was done 10 hours after the zero-time counts. The third group served as untreated controls. In the latter two experiments, serial counting was continued for 50 to 70 hours.

Measurement of Tissue Distribution of I^{131} after AET

Six animals weighing 150 gm each were divided into three groups in metabolism cages. They were maintained on a low-iodine diet for 7 days prior to the study, and only water was provided during the study period. The groups received saline, thiourea (67 mg/kg), or AET (250 mg/kg), the latter two being equimolar quantities. Thirty minutes later, 5 μc of I^{131} was given. At the end of 4 hours, the animals were anesthetized with ether and bled by cardiac puncture. The blood was collected over heparin, and the plasma was separated by centrifugation at 2500 rpm. Urine was washed from the cages into the collecting vessels and combined with any residual in the bladder. The thyroid, stomach, small bowel, colon, spleen, liver, kidneys, adrenals, and testes were rapidly excised, rinsed with saline, and placed in separate tubes for counting. All samples and a counting standard were counted in a scintillation counter, and the data were calculated as a percentage of the administered dose.

RESULTS

Radioactive Iodine Uptake by the Thyroid Gland

Administration of AET immediately after neutralization (Table IA) or 15 minutes thereafter (Table IB) depressed the uptake of I^{131} by the thyroid. Measurements at 2, 4, and 6 hours show uptakes 8 to 35% of the control groups. By 24

TABLE IA

EFFECT OF AET IN NEUTRAL SOLUTION ON THYROID I^{131} UPTAKE[a]

Uptake period (hr)	*Number of animals*	*Per cent of administered I^{131}, controls*	*Number of animals*	*Per cent of administered I^{131}, AET*[b]	*Per cent of controls*	*t*	*p*
2	8	8.9 ± 3.9[c]	8	0.9 ± 0.2[c]	10	2.05	<0.05
4	7	26.2 ± 5.1	8	2.9 ± 1.6	11	4.35	<0.01
6	8	36.1 ± 6.5	8	8.2 ± 1.6	23	4.16	<0.01
24	8	42.2 ± 7.2	8	31.9 ± 4.0	76	1.26	0.2

[a] Data from Potsaid and Maruyama (7).
[b] Given immediately after adjusting pH to 7.0. Dose = 300 mg/kg.
[c] Standard deviation.

TABLE IB

EFFECT OF MEG[a]

Uptake period (hr)	*Number of animals*	*Per cent of administered I^{131}, controls*	*Number of animals*	*Per cent of administered I^{131}, MEG*[b]	*Per cent of controls*	*t*	*p*
4	6	18.5 ± 4.9[c]	7	1.4 ± 0.5[c]	8	3.42	<0.01
6	8	36.1 ± 6.5	8	12.2 ± 2.8	35	3.37	<0.01
24	7	42.0 ± 8.0	7	26.5 ± 2.5	63	1.84	<0.10

[a] Data from Potsaid and Maruyama (*7*).

[b] Given after adjusting pH to 7.0 and allowed to stand at room temperature for 15 minutes. Dose = 250 mg/kg.

[c] Standard deviation.

TABLE IC

EFFECT OF AET IN ACID SOLUTION ON THYROID I^{131} UPTAKE

Uptake period (hr)	*Number of animals*	*Per cent of administered I^{131}, controls*	*Number of animals*	*AET*[a]	*Per cent of controls*	*t*	*p*
2	8	9.1 ± 4.4[c]	8	4.8 ± 1.6[b]	53	0.91	>0.3
4	8	19.8 ± 4.8	8	8.6 ± 3.6	43	1.87	<0.10
6	8	21.2 ± 4.1	8	8.8 ± 1.8	41	2.76	<0.02
24	8	51.8 ± 14.7	8	47.8 ± 8.8	93	0.23	>0.5

[a] Given in 0.1 *N* HCl solution. Dose = 250 mg/kg. Controls received equivalent volume of 0.1 *N* HCl.

[b] Standard deviation.

hours, there is recovery of both groups to 63 to 76% of the controls. The administration of the chemical as the isothiourea in acid solution (Table IC) shows a less striking effect on the uptake of iodine. This would indicate that the body buffers do not immediately convert AET to MEG, that it is metabolized more rapidly, or that there is less absorption and systemic effect in this form. The depression noted in the early periods is of greatest interest, as it is during the immediate period after injection that the greatest radioprotective action is observed. Uptake depression is maximal with the largest doses of AET and declines considerably as the dosage is decreased (Table II).

Goitrogenic Effect

The results of this experiment are shown in Table III and Fig. 1. The administration of AET over a 10-day period in any of these solutions does not cause any significant effect on the thyroidal mass, whereas the group given thiourea during this period shows, as expected, a doubling of the thyroidal mass (*13*). Histological

TABLE II

EFFECT OF AET DOSE VARIATION ON THE 4-HOUR THYROID I^{131} UPTAKE

AET dose (mg/kg)[a]	*Per cent uptake*	*Percent of controls*
0	24.9 ± 5.7[b]	100
100	16.9 ± 5.6	63
150	9.2 ± 3.8	33
200	5.9 ± 3.2	22
300	2.9 ± 1.6	11

[a] Given immediately after adjusting the pH to 7.0.
[b] Standard deviation.

TABLE III

EFFECT OF AET ON THYROIDAL MASS BY A 10-DAY PERIOD OF ADMINISTRATION

	Number of animals	*Thyroid weight (mg)*	*Thyroid weight × 10⁵ mean body weight*	*t*	*p*
		After oral administration			
Control[a]	9	10.4 ± 0.6[b]	7.7		
AET, 70 mg/day	9	10.6 ± 0.9	8.5	0.19	>0.5
Thiourea, 10 mg/day	9	19.4 ± 2.0	15.5	4.80	<0.01
		After intraperitoneal administration			
Control[a]	5	11.6 ± 1.9[b]	7.3		
MEG, 20 mg/day	5	11.4 ± 0.9	6.7	0.05	>0.5
Control[c]	5	10.9 ± 1.1	7.6		
AET[d]	5	11.4 ± 0.6	7.5	0.40	>0.5
Thiourea 10 mg/day	5	20.4 ± 1.1	13.5	6.13	<0.01

[a] Received normal saline.
[b] Standard deviation.
[c] Received 0.1 *N* HCl.
[d] In 0.1 *N* HCl solution.

study shows no evidence of a hyperplastic gland as is noted with thiourea (Fig. 1). This would also indicate that the degradation of AET does not proceed with significant liberation of thiourea.

Intrathyroidal Metabolism of Iodine

Chromatographic and radioautographic analysis of enzymatically hydrolyzed thyroid homogenates (*14*) shows that the I^{131} in the gland is partitioned between thyroglobulin and free iodide ion in similar amounts in both control and AET-treated animals (Table IV). Furthermore, the organically bound iodine was distributed among the mono-, diiodotyrosines, and coupled thyronine derivatives (T3, T4), which indicates that these reactions are able to proceed in the

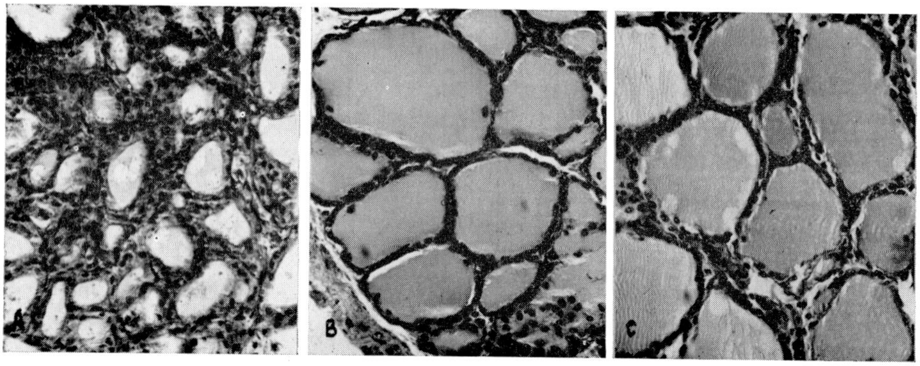

FIG. 1. Histological sections of rat thyroid gland. AET was administered orally in a dose of 700 mg/kg/day (*B*) or intraperitoneally in a dose of 200 mg/kg/day (*C*) for a 10-day period. The glands show no evidence of hyperplasia, whereas the animals receiving thiourea 10 mg/day (*A*) shows clear-cut hyperplasia.

TABLE IV

DISTRIBUTION OF I^{131} IN THE HYDROLYZATE OF THE THYROID GLAND

	Before hydrolysis			*After hydrolysis*	
	Controls	*AET*		*Controls*	*AET*
Iodide	4.1%	4.0%	Iodide	8.3%	2.8%
Thyroglobulin	95.9%	96.0%	MIT	46.2%	58.8%
			DIT	32.1%	30.2%
			T3 + T4	9.1%	4.2%

gland. A larger proportion remains as MIT, and approximately half as much T3 and T4 was present after AET, indicating some depression of the coupling mechanism. However, compared to the striking effect after thiocyanate in which there is a complete failure of organic binding of iodine by thyroid tissue (*15*), or the block of synthesis of higher iodinated tyrosines and thyronines by the thiouracils (*16*), these data show no striking or specific action on the enzymes involved in the intrathyroidal metabolism of iodine.

Release of Thyroid Radioiodine Activity

Direct *in vivo* measurements of the loss of thyroid activity by external counting done in two series of experiments are shown in Fig. 2. In experiments with animals on iodine-containing diets, there is a slow decline in activity corresponding to the normal rate of release of thyroid hormone into the circulation, presumably largely as I^{131} thyroxine (Fig. 2*A*). The administration of AET exerts no effect on the

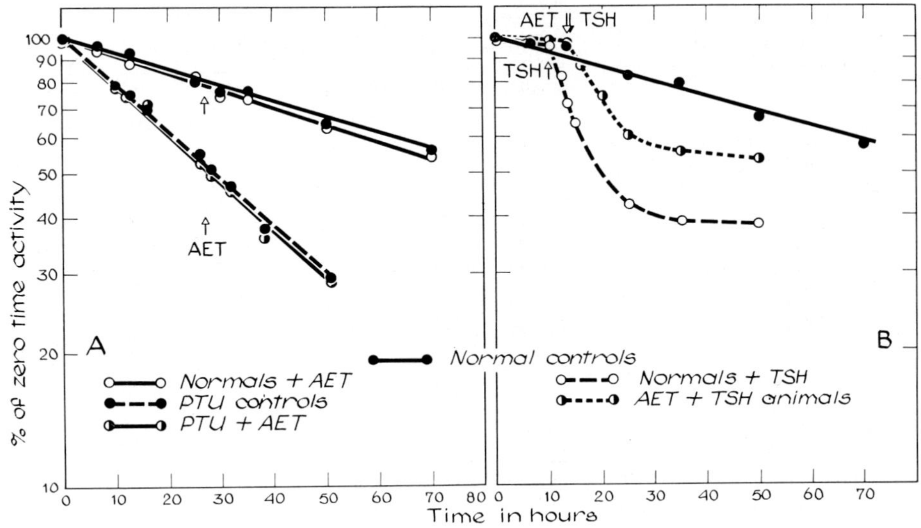

FIG. 2. Release curves of thyroid I^{131} radioactivity beginning 40 hours after the administration of I^{131} (zero time). AET (left) does not alter the release of radioactivity from the thyroid either from those on normal laboratory diets or from those prevented from accumulating iodine by treatment with propylthiouracil (PTU). AET (right) decreases the response to thyrotropin (TSH) and the completeness of the release of iodine from the thyroid gland.

release curve. The $T_{1/2}$ of the decay of activity is approximately 85 hours and compares with that of Wolff ($T_{1/2}$ = 3.3 days, or about 79 hours). Antithyroidal drugs such as thiocyanate, perchlorate, or thiouracil in this situation would lead to a prompt discharge of activity, and thyroxine would promptly inhibit the release of activity through a hypophyseal end-organ mechanism (*11, 17, 18*).

The administration of thyrotropin (TSH) in control animals elicits a prompt and rapid decline in gland activity with a $T_{1/2}$ of 9.5 hours (Fig. 2*B*), (Wolff, $T_{1/2}$ = 8 to 10 hours). In those animals pretreated with AET there is a prompt response to TSH; however, the rate of decline in activity is less ($T_{1/2}$ = 18 hours), and the completeness of the discharge of radioactivity is less. Fifteen hours after a single dose of TSH, controls retain only 42% of their zero-time activity compared to 56% in those animals pretreated with AET. After this period, the effects of TSH decline, and the curve becomes flat.

In animals prevented from further accumulation of iodide by administration of PTU, there is a more rapid decline in radioactivity from the thyroid gland (Fig. 2*A*), and it is a much more sensitive means of detecting alterations in iodide kinetics. Again no detectable change was observed ($T_{1/2}$ = 28 hours; Wolff, $T_{1/2}$ = 1.6 days, about 39 hours). These results indicate that the normal hypophyseal activation of the thyroid gland is not greatly affected, and that AET neither

TABLE V

Distribution[a] of I^{131} in Various Organs after AET Administration

	Control	*Thiourea*	*AET*
Per cent in circulating plasma[b]	1.97	5.81	4.13
Urine	3.56	6.10	12.30
Thyroid	35.70	1.83	8.60
Stomach	1.47	2.24	1.91
Small bowel	1.22	7.48	5.43
Colon	0.16	0.38	0.30
Liver	0.86	2.24	1.91
Kidneys	0.26	0.75	0.50
Spleen	0.06	0.15	0.85
Testes	0.35	0.92	0.62
Adrenals	0.01	0.03	0.02

[a] Per cent of administered I^{131} dose.

[b] Calculated from tables in E. H. Belcher, and E. B. Harriss, Studies of plasma volume, red cell volume, and total blood volume in young growing rats. *J. Physiol.* (*London*) **139,** 64–78 (1957).

accelerates no decelerates the release of radioactive thyroid hormones from the thyroid gland.

Distribution of I^{131} after AET

The data are presented in Table V. Thiourea would be expected to block any accumulation of I^{131} by the thyroid gland, and in this situation the I^{131} should remain in the plasma and be cleared by the kidney. AET should be intermediate in this respect, as it is not nearly so effective an antithyroidal agent. Distribution studies with S^{35}- or C^{14}-labeled AET (*19*) have shown the highest concentrations in spleen, bone marrow, intestine, kidney, and liver, and, if a local toxic effect operates, these should show greater effects than those in which low concentrations are observed (e.g., testes). The data show larger amounts of circulating I^{131} in animals treated with AET or thiourea, and much less of the administered dose in the thyroid. All other sites studied except for spleen show increased amounts of activity of approximately the same degree. The spleen shows a relatively much greater amount of activity. However, the most striking changes are noted in the urinary elimination of I^{131}. AET-treated animals show an over threefold increase in the amount cleared, and this is almost twofold greater than in those animals which received thiourea.

DISCUSSION

The thiourylene group, —NH—CS—NH—, is known to be essential for antithyroidal activity (*13*). Later work has shown that only the thiocarbamide group,

—CS—NH—, is necessary (*20*). The most potent radioprotective chemicals contain a thiol and an amino group in close proximity to each other separated by no more than three carbon atoms (*21*). AET is by far the most potent of the radioprotective chemicals and contains a —CS—NH— group which could exert antithyroidal activity which in turn might contribute to the protective phenomena by depressing the metabolic activity of the organism. The depression of I^{131} uptake has been reported for AET and MEG (*7, 8*) and more recently for mercaptoethylamine as well (*22*). The latter chemical contains no thiocarbamide structure. Nevertheless, these observations raise the possibility that the thyroid and metabolic depression might contribute to the enhanced survivals of irradiated animals.

These experiments show depression of the I^{131} uptake by the thyroid gland; however, the effect drops off rapidly with dose and is altered by injecting in an acid solution. It is not nearly so potent in this action as thiourea. There is no goitrogenic effect, with no significant increase in thyroidal mass or the ratio of thyroidal mass to body weight, and histological examination shows no evidence of hyperplasia of the gland. There is no alteration in the organic binding of iodine or in the biological half-life of radioiodine in the gland, nor is there any marked effect on the release of thyroid hormone from the gland. Experiments measuring the circulating protein-bound iodine (Maruyama, unpublished data) show no significant change from controls. This evidence would preclude any significant direct antithyroidal activity, and therefore the uptake depression should be explained by extrathyroidal factors.

In the distribution experiments, the observation of increased activity in the spleen would be compatible with the possibility that a local toxic effect may permit "pooling" in certain organs; however, such is not supported by the concentration in kidney, liver, or intestines. The most striking action is on the renal elimination, and, in view of the twofold increase even over that eliminated by the thiourea-treated animals, it appears that renal removal is accelerated by AET. This action could be either through an effect on glomerular filtration or through tubular excretion; however, in view of the hypotension reported by DiStefano in cats (*23*), it is probable that glomerular filtration is diminished, and some tubular transport or resorptive mechanism is affected. Hence the probable explanation of the depressed uptake is through multiple diverse and widespread pharmacological and biochemical effects acting through cardiovascular, renal, and perhaps the stress (*24*) caused by the drug's acting through the adrenal gland. In this regard, cortisone has been shown to decrease thyroid uptake of iodide by increasing urinary clearance of iodine (*25*).

Other data indicate that the rendering of an animal to the thyroprivic (and therefore hypometabolic) does not cause significant radioprotection (*26–29*). No true antithyroidal effect has been demonstrated for AET; hence, the intermediation of the thyroid hormones acting through the uncoupling of oxidative phosphorylation between oxygen intake and the synthesis of high-energy phosphate compounds

(*30, 31*) appears unlikely as a significant factor in radioprotection. Nevertheless, AET and similar —SH compounds may affect oxidative metabolism perhaps by combining with enzymes or cofactors which could contribute to the protective phenomena. In this regard, it is known that reduction of general metabolic activity and oxidative processes by anoxia, cold, or chemical inhibitors of respiration produces inhibition of iodide accumulation and transport in thyroid tissue (*32–34*). Barron observes that the dithiol 2,3-dimercaptopropanol (BAL) exerts an inhibitory effect on oxidative metabolism (*35, 36*), and Slater has extensively studied a factor which is inhibited by BAL in hydrogen and electron transport between cytochrome b and c1 (*37, 38*). The effects of —SH reagents are paralleled by properties of active transport in other systems (*39*) and thus could explain the increased loss of iodide in the urine and the depression in certain aspects of iodide accumulation and metabolism in the thyroid gland. In short, our experiments may reflect a generalized effect on active transport acting through interference with aerobic energy metabolism.

Since the radioprotection occurs shortly after administration, any early metabolic depression mediated by the thyroid gland is unlikely, since its effects are much delayed in its appearance. Moreover, any later contribution by metabolic depression which might enhance the survival of irradiated animals is also excluded, since no true antithyroidal action has been demonstrated. The protective action of AET is most likely dependent on its wide tissue, cellular, and subcellular distribution (*19*), both free or as the mixed disulfide (*40*), and on other effects, perhaps hypoxia, that it causes. Further clarification of our understanding of the mechanism of protection by these compounds is necessary, particularly with regard to tissue respiration and oxidative metabolism.

SUMMARY

AET and MEG depress the uptake of I^{131} by the thyroid gland in the rat. It is, however, unassociated with any increase in thyroidal mass in a chronic administration study, shows no evidence of hyperplasia on histological section, and does not affect the release of I^{131} from the thyroid gland. It is concluded that there is no direct antithyroidal activity but a depression of uptake by extrathyroidal mechanisms which have been discussed.

ACKNOWLEDGMENTS

These experiments were largely performed at the Massachusetts General Hospital in Boston, Massachusetts. I wish to acknowledge the facilities made available to me by the Department of Radiology.

RECEIVED: October 30, 1962

REFERENCES

1. D. G. DOHERTY, and W. T. BURNETT, JR., Protective effect of *S*,β-aminoethylisothiuronium·Br·HBr and related compounds against X-radiation death in mice. *Proc. Soc. Exptl. Biol. Med.* **89,** 312–314 (1955).

2. C. C. CONGDON, cited by D. G. Doherty, in *Radiation Protection and Recovery* (A. Hollaender, ed.), pp. 45-86, Pergamon Press, New York, 1960.

3. B. G. CROUCH and R. R. OVERMAN, Chemical protection against X-radiation death in primates. A preliminary report. *Science* **125,** 1092 (1957).

4. D. G. DOHERTY, W. T. BURNETT, JR., and R. SHAPIRA, Chemical protection against ionizing radiation. II. Mercaptoalkylamines and related compounds with protective activity. *Radiation Res.* **7,** 13–21 (1957).

5. L. H. GRAY, A method of oxygen assay applied to a study of the removal of dissolved oxygen by cysteine and cysteamine. In *Progress in Radiobiology* (J. S. Mitchell, B. E. Holmes, and C. L. Smith, eds.), pp. 267–278, Oliver & Boyd, Edinburgh, 1955.

6. H. J. MAURER and A. SCHREIBER, Zur Frage des Schutzmechanismus der Sulfhydryl (—SH) Substanzen. *Strahlentherapie* **108,** 73–83 (1959).

7. M. S. POTSAID and Y. MARUYAMA, Effect of AET and MEG on rat thyroid I^{131} uptake. *Radiology* **74,** 74–76 (1960).

8. R. V. VITTORIO and M. J. CULLEN, The effect of 2-aminoethylisothiuronium·Br·HBr (AET) on thyroid activity in nonirradiated and X-irradiated rats. *Radiation Res.* **13,** 256–262 (1960).

9. R. E. REMINGTON, Improved growth in rats on iodine deficient diets. *J. Nutr.* **13,** 223–233 (1937).

10. A. ALBERT, The *in vivo* determination of the biological decay of thyroidal radioiodine. *Endocrinology* **48,** 334–338 (1951).

11. J. WOLFF, Some factors that influence the release of iodine from the thyroid gland. *Endocrinology* **48,** 284–297 (1951).

12. W. F. PERRY, A method for measuring thyroid hormone secretion in the rat with its application to the bioassay of thyroid extracts. *Endocrinology* **48,** 643 (1951).

13. E. B. ASTWOOD, The chemical nature of compounds which inhibit the function of the thyroid gland. *J. Pharmacol. Exptl. Therap.* **78,** 79–89 (1943).

14. A. TAUROG, G. D. POTTER, and I. L. CHAIKOFF, Conversion of I^{131} to organic I^{131} by cell-free preparations of thyroid tissue. *J. Biol. Chem.* **213,** 119–134 (1955).

15. A. F. FRANKLIN, I. L. CHAIKOFF, and S. R. LERNER, The influence of goitrogenic substances on the conversion *in vitro* of inorganic iodide to thyroxin and diiodotyrosine by thyroid tissue with radioactive iodine as indicator. *J. Biol. Chem.* **153,** 151–162 (1944).

16. D. W. SLINGERLAND, D. F. GRAHAM, R. K. JOSEPHS, A. P. TRAKAS, and E. YAMAZAKI, The effect of propylthiouracil on the conversion of monoiodotyrosine to diiodotyrosine. *Endocrinology* **65,** 178–188 (1959).

17. A. ALBERT and A. TENNEY, Effect of iodide, thiouracil, and thyroxine on the disappearance of thyroidal I^{131}. *Proc. Soc. Exptl. Biol. Med.* **77,** 202–203 (1951).

18. J. E. VANDERLAAN and W. P. VANDERLANN, The iodide concentrating mechanism of the rat thyroid and its inhibition by thiocyanate. *Endocrinology* **40,** 403–413 (1947).

19. R. H. BRADFORD, R. SHAPIRA, and D. G. DOHERTY, The intracellular distribution and binding of radiation protective mercaptoalkylguanidines. *Intern. J. Radiation Biol.* **3,** 595–608 (1961).

20. F. MALOOF and M. SOODAK, The uptake and metabolism of S^{35} thiourea and thiouracil by the thyroid and other tissues. *Endocrinology* **61,** 555-569 (1957).

21. R. SHAPIRA, D. G. DOHERTY, and W. T. BURNETT, Chemical protection against ionizing radiation. III. Mercaptoalkylguanidines and related isothiuronium compounds with protective activity. *Radiation Res.* **7,** 22–34 (1957).

22. P. V. VITTORIO, M. J. ALLEN, and D. L. SMALL, The effects of some radioprotective agents on thyroid activity in nonirradiated and X-irradiated rats. *Radiation Res.* **15,** 625–631 (1961).

23. V. DiStefano, D. E. Leary, and D. G. Doherty, The pharmacology of β-aminoethyliso-thiuronium bromide in the cat. *J. Pharmacol. Exptl. Therap.* **117,** 425–433 (1956).
24. R. H. Williams, H. Jaffe, and C. Kemp, Effect of severe stress upon thyroid function. *Am. J. Physiol.* **159,** 291–297 (1949).
25. S. H. Ingbar, The effect of cortisone on thyroidal and renal metabolism of iodine. *Endocrinology* **53,** 171–181 (1953).
26. H. C. Blount and W. W. Smith, The influence of thyroid and thiouracil on mice exposed to roentgen radiation. *Science* **109,** 83–84 (1949).
27. H. J. Haley, S. Mann, and A. H. Dowdy, The effects of roentgen ray irradiation on normal, hypothyroid and hyperthyroid rats. *Endocrinology* **48,** 365–369 (1951).
28. H. J. Haley, S. Mann, and A. H. Dowdy, A comparison of the response of normal and hypothyroid mice to acute whole body roentgen radiation. *Science* **112,** 333–334 (1950).
29. A. L. Kretschmar, H. J. Gomberg, D. E. Weyant, and F. H. Bethell, The effect of thyroidectomy on the mortality and peripheral blood changes of the rat subjected to whole body irradiation. *Endocrinology* **51,** 59–65 (1952).
30. H. A. Lardy and G. Feldott, Metabolic effects of thyroxine *in vitro*. *Ann. N. Y. Acad. Sci.* **54,** 636–648 (1952).
31. F. L. Hoch and F. Lipmann, The uncoupling of respiration and phosphorylation by thyroid hormones. *Proc. Soc. Natl. Acad. Sci. U.S.* **40,** 909–921 (1954).
32. H. Schachner, A. L. Franklin, and I. L. Chaikoff, The effect of cytochrome oxidase inhibitors on the formation *in vitro* of thyroxine and diiodotyrosine by thyroid tissue with radioactive iodine as indicator. *J. Biol. Chem.* **151,** 191–199 (1943).
33. N. Freinkel and S. H. Ingbar, The relationship between metabolic activity and iodide concentrating capacity of surviving thyroid slices. *J. Clin Endocrinol. Metab.* **15,** 442–458 (1955).
34. N. Freinkel and S. H. Ingbar, Effect of metabolic inhibitors upon iodide transport in sheep thyroid slices. *J. Clin. Endocrinol. Metab.* **15,** 598–615 (1955).
35. E. S. G. Barron, Z. B. Miller, and J. Meyer, The effects of 2:3 dimercaptopropanol on the activity of enzymes and on the metabolism of tissues. *Biochem. J.* **41,** 78–82 (1947).
36. E. S. G. Barron and T. P. Singer, Studies on biological oxidations. XIX. Sulfhydryl enzymes in carbohydrate metabolism. *J. Biol. Chem.* **157,** 221 (1945).
37. E. C. Slater, A respiratory catalyst required for the reduction of cytochrome c by cytochrome b. *Biochem. J.* **45,** 14–30 (1949).
38. E. C. Slater, The constitution of the respiratory chain in animal tissues. *Advan. Enzymol.* **20,** 147–199 (1958).
39. G. H. Mudge, Electrolyte and water metabolism of rabbit kidney slices. Effect of metabolic inhibitors. *Am. J. Physiol.* **167,** 206–223 (1951).
40. L. Eldjarn and A. Pihl, The mode of action of X-ray protective agents. I. The fixation *in vivo* of cystamine and cysteamine to proteins. *J. Biol. Chem.* **223,** 341–351 (1956).

RADIATION RESEARCH **19,** 551–558 (1963)

Radiation-Induced Carboxylation Reactions of Aliphatic Amino Acids and Monocarboxylic Acids

J. LIEBSTER, J. KOPOLDOVA, AND A. BABICKY

Czechoslovak Academy of Sciences, Isotope Laboratory of the Institutes for Biological Research, Prague, Czechoslovakia

INTRODUCTION

In 1960 Weiss *et al.* (*1*) published a paper on the radiation-induced carboxylation of ethanol and methanol to the corresponding monocarboxylic acids and of formic and acetic acid to the corresponding dicarboxylic acids in aqueous deoxygenated solutions (*2*). Parallel with the work in Weiss's laboratory, similar studies were carried out in our laboratory (*3*) on the radiation-induced carboxylation of aliphatic monocarboxylic and α-aminocarboxylic acids. The results obtained confirm the observations of Weiss concerning aliphatic acids and considerably extend our present knowledge of these radiolytic carboxylation reactions. Dose and Ettré (*4*) irradiated alanine in the presence of bicarbonate and observed the formation of aspartic acid; however, they did not give experimental details or quantitative results.

In our present work two types of study were made:

1. The studies of the carboxylation of aliphatic amino acids were carried out with α-aminobutyric acid, norvaline, norleucine, valine, leucine, and isoleucine. The carboxylation products were identified, and the quantitative yield was determined.

A detailed study of the carboxylation of α-aminobutyric acid was made—of the dependence on the radiation dose, the concentration of the irradiated compound, and the ratio of amino acid to CO_2. From the results, certain conclusions concerning the optimum conditions were drawn.

Under the given conditions an exchange reaction on C-1 occurred with all the α-amino acids investigated, yielding the carboxyl-labeled starting material.

2. The carboxylation of aliphatic monocarboxylic acids under the influence of radiation was studied. The optimum conditions for the production of dicarboxylic acids from valeric acid were determined. The carboxylation of the aliphatic acids from C-2 to C-6 were investigated to elucidate the effect of chain length on yield.

The radiation-induced carboxylation could be applicable as a method for the preparation of C^{14}-labeled dicarboxylic amino acids.

EXPERIMENTAL PROCEDURE

Aqueous deoxygenated solutions of the α-amino acids (DL-α-aminobutyric acid, DL-valine, DL-norvaline, DL-leucine, DL-isoleucine, DL-norleucine) and aliphatic monocarboxylic acids (acetic acid, propionic acid, butyric acid, valeric acid, caproic acid as their sodium salts) were irradiated. In our series of experiments 0.05 *M* solutions of the compounds containing 0.02 *M* of $NaHCO_3$ were irradiated for 12 hours, and the yields were compared. In the second series α-aminobutyric acid and valeric acid were irradiated in different concentrations (from 0.05 to 0.25 *M*), $NaHC^{14}O_3$ being added in quantities yielding 0.02 to 0.75 *M* solutions. The ratios of α-aminobutyric acid (or valeric acid) to CO_2 varied from 5:2 to 1:10; the pH of the solutions of the sodium salts of the aliphatic monocarboxylic acids was 9 to 9.7.

Irradiation was carried out with a Co^{60} γ-source at a dose rate of 2.85×10^{17} ev/ml/min for 12, 44, or 96 hours.

The products of irradiation were determined by paper chromatography and comparison of the compounds with standards, or respectively on the basis of the chromatographic behavior, by autoradiography. The quantitative determination of the distribution of the radioactivity was carried out after elution of the identified spots by radiometry. Quantitative analysis was performed by colorimetry after elution.

The localization of C^{14} in glutamic acid was determined by enzymatic decarboxylation and by manometric and radiometric assay of the CO_2 evolved.

The amount of $C^{14}O_2$ fixed was determined by aeration of the acidified irradiated solutions and absorption of the $C^{14}O_2$ in KOH solution, where the amount was determined by titration and radiometry as the difference between the value thus obtained and the amount put in. Simultaneously the acidified irradiated solution was counted on a planchet, thus allowing checking of the results.

RESULTS AND DISCUSSION

Carboxylation of Aliphatic Amino Acids (Table I)

The experiments with α-aminobutyric acid show that at a given concentration of α-aminobutyric acid an increase of the CO_2 concentration leads to a decrease in the percentage of the $C^{14}O_2$ fixed for all the doses investigated.

When the molar fixation of $C^{14}O_2$ is compared, it can be seen that at an α-aminobutyric acid concentration of 0.05 *M* the maximum fixation occurs at an α-aminobutyric acid to CO_2 ratio of 1:5. At the higher α-aminobutyric acid concentrations an increase of $C^{14}O_2$ concentration does not lead to any decisive change in the rate of CO_2 fixation.

From a preparative point of view these conditions appear most advantageous: α-aminobutyric acid concentration 0.25 *M*, ratio 1:1, dose 16.4×10^{20} ev/ml. The amount of glutamic acid-5-C^{14} formed corresponds to 40% glutamic acid of the

TABLE I

FIXATION OF $C^{14}O_2$ (*G* VALUES AND PER CENT OF THE TOTAL ACTIVITY) IN DEPENDENCE ON THE $NaHC^{14}O_3$ CONCENTRATION

(Dose rate 2.85×10^{17} ev/ml/min)

Concentration of α-amino-butyric acid		*Molar concentration of CO_2*							*Dose (ev/ml)*
		0.02 M	*0.05 M*	*0.1 M*	*0.25 M*	*0.35 M*	*0.5 M*	*0.75 M*	
0.05 *M*	*G*	0.2			0.7		0.1		
	%	3.5			1.0		0.07		
0.25 *M*	*G*	0.2							2.05×10^{20}
	%	3.5							
0.5 *M*	*G*	0.2							
	%	2.9							
0.05 *M*	*G*	0.2	0.3		0.6		0.3		
	%	15.5	8.1		3		0.7		7.52×10^{20}
0.1 *M*	*G*			0.8		0.4	0.8	0.6	
	%			10		1.5	1.85	1.0	
0.05 *M*	*G*		0.2						
	%		12.5						
0.1 *M*	*G*			0.5			0.6	0.7	16.40×10^{20}
	%			14.1			3.2	2.55	
0.25 *M*	*G*				1.1		1.0	1.1	
	%				12.1		5.2	4.0	

total amount of $C^{14}O_2$ fixed. Under these conditions the total fixation is 0.03 *M* ($G = 1.1$), i.e., 12%.

For the explanation of these results it is necessary first to consider the mechanism of the carboxylation reaction. For the entrance of CO_2 into an amino acid molecule it is necessary that a radical be formed:

$$HOOC\ CH\ NH_2\ CH_2\ CH_3 + OH \rightarrow HOOC\ CHNH_2\ CH_2\ CH_2 + H_2O$$

This radical reacts according to Weiss:

$$HOOC\ CH\ NH_2\ CH_2\ CH_2 + COO^- \rightarrow HOOC\ CH\ NH_2\ CH_2\ CH_2CH_2COO^-$$

A very interesting and hitherto unknown reaction was observed in these radiation experiments involving an exchange reaction of the C-1 carboxyl group leading to the introduction of a C^{14}-labeled carboxyl group into the originally irradiated compound. For this reaction we are suggesting the following mechanism:

$$\mathrm{HOOC\ CH\ NH_2\ CH_2\ CH_3} + x \rightarrow \mathrm{COO^-} + \mathrm{CH\ NH_2\ CH_2\ CH_3} + y$$
$$\mathrm{^{14}COO^-} + \mathrm{CH\ NH_2\ CH_2\ CH_3} \rightarrow \mathrm{^-OOC^{14}CH\ NH_2\ CH_2\ CH_3}$$

i.e., a decarboxylation of the amino acid yielding CO_2 and the corresponding amine. The radical formed reacts with the radioactive $C^{14}O_2$ from the solution, yielding the carboxyl-labeled original compound.

These reactions then were investigated with other aliphatic amino acids. The results of the experiments are summarized in Table II. In this table the relation of the CO_2 fixation, the exchange reaction, and the formation of α-aminodicarboxylic acids to the chain length from α-aminobutyric acid to norleucine are given. Branching does not have a decisive influence on the degree of the degradation. The degree of CO_2 fixation, on the other hand, increases with these acids in the series with a straight chain almost by 300%; similar conditions prevail with the exchange reaction, where a still greater increase is observed. A similar relation can be seen in the formation of α-aminodicarboxylic acids.

With the branched amino acids the situation is more involved, as the influence of the position of branching is of importance. With valine, an increased fixation, exchange reaction, and formation of dicarboxylic acids against the norisomer are observed, whereas with the higher amino acids the opposite tendency prevails.

In a further study the carboxylation products of the single amino acids were identified. The results are summarized in Table III, where the proportion of the single products to the total radioactivity found in the α-aminodicarboxylic acid is given.

α-Aminobutyric acid gives the lowest yield of α-aminodicarboxylic acid (Table

TABLE II

CARBOXYLATION AND EXCHANGE REACTIONS OF ALIPHATIC AMINO ACIDS
(Amino acid concentration, 0.05 *M*; $C^{14}O_2$ concentration, 0.02 *M*; dose, 2.05×10^{20} ev/ml)

Amino acid	*Fixation of CO_2*		*Exchange on C-1*		*α-Aminodicarboxylic acids*	
	Per cent of total radio-activity	*G*	*Per cent of total radio-activity*	*G*	*Per cent of total radio-activity*	*G*
α-Aminobutyric	3.5	0.21	0.45	0.03	1	0.06
Norvaline	6.0	0.35	1.1	0.07	1.7	0.1
Norleucine	9.6	0.56	1.8	0.11	5.0	0.29
Valine	6.8	0.40	1.3	0.08	3.0	0.18
Leucine	8.2	0.48	1.0	0.06	2.5	0.15
Isoleucine	7.5	0.44	1.0	0.06	2.25	0.13

TABLE III

DISTRIBUTION OF FIXED $C^{14}O_2$ ON THE SINGLE C ATOMS OF THE AMINO ACIDS
(Per cent of the total α-aminodicarboxylic acids formed)

Irradiated amino acid	*Position of fixation*	*Per cent*	*Product*
α-Aminobutyric acid	C-4	100	Glutamic acid
	C-3	traces	Methylaspartic acid
Norvaline	C-5	40	α-Aminoadipic acid
	C-4	60	4-Methylglutamic acid
Norleucine	C-6	8	α-Aminopimelic acid
	C-5	38	5-Methyl-α-aminoadipic acid
	C-4	54	4-Ethylglutamic acid
Valine	C-4	85	3-Methylglutamic acid (2 iso)
	C-3	15	3-Dimethylaspartic acid
Leucine	C-5	45	NH_2-4-methyladipic acid (2 iso)
	C-4	30	4-Dimethylglutamic acid
	C-3	20	3-Isopropylaspartic acid
Isoleucine	C-5	15	NH_2-3-methyladipic acid
	C-4	32	3-Ethylglutamic acid
	C-4	25	3-Methyl-4-methyl-glutamic acid
	C-3	28	3-Methyl-3-ethyl-aspartic acid

II). We have previously reported that the radical formed from α-aminobutyric acid dimerizes easily, which could account for the low yield. Only a very small amount of a radical on C-3 is formed (about 10% of the amount of the radical at C-4); therefore, the potential carboxylation product at C-3, i.e., β-methylaspartic acid, was detected only in traces.

The increased carboxylation reaction observed in norvaline is caused by the participation of C-4 and C-5. With this amino acid, dimerization or recombination, respectively, still occurs; the proportion of the carboxylation reaction therefore does not attain the extent observed with norleucine, where the recombination reaction occurs only in a very reduced extent, the radicals in this case being disposable for the carboxylation reaction.

With norleucine, carboxylation occurs on C-4, C-5, and C-6. Here as well the maximum of the fixation of CO_2 is observed on C-4 in approximately the same proportion as with norvaline, whereas fixation on C-5 is somewhat lower; on the other hand, carboxylation on C-6 occurs.

More complicated relations are observed on comparison of amino acids with a branched chain, as a considerable rupture of C—C bonds occurs besides the generally observed reactions with amino acids with a straight chain. With valine the predominant carboxylation was found on C-4, in agreement with analogous conditions with aminobutyric acid. Simultaneously an addition on C-3 occurred. With leucine the main reactions are addition on C-4 and C-5, the addition on C-5 being higher. Especially complicated conditions are observed with isoleucine, where carboxylation reactions occur on C-4, C-3, and C-5 (their sequence being given according to the importance of the reaction), the carboxylations on C-4 and C-5 being reactions on the end methyl groups and the carboxylation on C-3 on the branching point.

Carboxylation Reactions with Aliphatic Monocarboxylic Acids

In the first experiments the carboxylation of acetic, propionic, butyric, valeric, and caproic acids was studied, the concentration of the acids being 0.05 *M*; ratio of acid to CO_2, 5:2; dose 2.05×10^{20} ev/ml. The results are given in Table IV. An increase of the extent of the carboxylation reaction with chain length was observed. Fifty to seventy per cent of the fixed radioactivity was found in the corresponding dicarboxylic acid. Besides the dicarboxylic acid, the dimerization products were found. The other radioactive compounds were not identified. The exchange reaction observed with the amino acids was not observed in this series.

In another series of experiments the optimum conditions for the carboxylation were investigated with valeric acid in a study similar to that previously performed with α-aminobutyric acid (Table V). The carboxylation reaction increases with the dose. The maximum molar CO_2 fixation occurs with a concentration of 0.1 *M* (ratio of valeric acid to CO_2, 1:7.5 or 1:5). In the single groups (2.05, 7.52, and 16.40×10^{20} ev/ml) the maximum molar fixation was observed with a ratio of valeric acid to CO_2 of 1:5 to 1:7.

TABLE IV

CARBOXYLATION REACTIONS OF ALIPHATIC MONOCARBOXYLIC ACIDS

(Acid concentration, 0.05 *M*; $C^{14}O_2$ concentration, 0.02 *M*; dose 2.05×10^{20} ev/ml)

Acid	*Fixation of CO_2*		*Product of the carboxylation reaction*	*Dimerization product*
	Per cent of total radio-activity	*G*		
Acetic	0.05	0.005	Malonic acid	Succinic acid C-4
Propionic	0.05	0.005	Succinic acid	Adipic acid C-4
Butyric	6.73	0.4	Glutaric acid	Suberic acid C-8
Valeric	16.8	0.99	Adipic acid	Sebacic acid C-10
Caproic	37.2	2.19	Pimelic acid	Decanedicarboxylic acid C-12

TABLE V

FIXATION OF $C^{14}O_2$ (*G* VALUES AND PER CENT OF THE TOTAL ACTIVITY) IN DEPENDENCE ON THE CONCENTRATION OF $NaHC^{14}O_3$

(Dose rate 2.85×10^{17} ev/ml/min)

Concentration of valeric acid (Na)		*Molar concentration of $NaHC^{14}O_3$*										*Dose (ev/ml)*
		0.02 N	*0.05 M*	*0.075 M*	*0.1 M*	*0.15 M*	*0.25 M*	*0.3 M*	*0.35 M*	*0.5 M*	*0.75 M*	
0.05 *M*	*G*	1.0	1.4			1.6	2.2		3	2		
	%	16	9			3.7	2.8		3	1.4		2.05×10^{20}
0.1 *M*	*G*				1.7			2.8		4		
	%				5.8			3.24		2.74		
0.05 *M*	*G*		1.4				2			2		
	%		35.7				10			5.2		7.52×10^{20}
0.1 *M*	*G*				1.5					2.2	2.4	
	%				19					5.7	4.2	
0.05 *M*	*G*		1.1									
	%		56									
0.075 *M*	*G*			1.4								
	%			53								
0.1 *M*	*G*				1.7					2.6	2.1	16.40×10^{20}
	%				47					14	7.9	
0.15 *M*	*G*					1.9						
	%					34.5						
0.25 *M*	*G*						1.5					
	%						16					

The results of these experiments show, besides some theoretically interesting observations, that radiation-induced carboxylations can be employed for the synthesis of specifically labeled aliphatic dicarboxylic acids and α-aminodicarboxylic acids.

SUMMARY

The carboxylation reactions occurring in irradiated aqueous solutions of aliphatic amino acids were investigated for aminobutyric acid, norvaline, valine, norleucine, leucine, and isoleucine. The products of the fixation of $C^{14}O_2$ in these amino acids were identified. The effects of the radiation dose, the concentration, and the ratio of amino acid to $C^{14}O_2$ on the yields of glutamic acid from α-aminobutyric acid as well as the optimum conditions for this reaction were determined. An exchange reaction between the carboxyl group of the amino acid and $C^{14}O_2$ was observed.

A similar study was made for the aliphatic monocarboxylic acids from C-2 to C-6, and the yields of the dicarboxylic acids formed were compared. An increased fixation of CO_2 was observed with growing chain length. The optimum conditions for the carboxylation of valeric acid were investigated.

RECEIVED: October 31, 1962

REFERENCES

1. G. SCHOLES, M. SIMIC, and J. J. WEISS, Radiation induced carboxylation of organic compounds: Formation and Reactions of the carboxyl radical ion. *Nature* **188,** 1019–1020 (1960).
2. A. APPLEBY, J. MOLIAN, G. SCHOLES, M. SIMIC, and J. J. WEISS, *Abstr. 2nd Intern. Congr. of Radiation Res., Harrogate, 1962,* p. 65, Session A-4-1.
3. J. KOPOLDOVÁ, J. LIEBSTER, and A. BABICKY, The mechanism of the radiation chemical degradation of amino acids. II. Degradation of α-aminobutyric acid in aqueous solution and nitrogen atmosphere and comparison with the degradation in oxygen atmosphere. *Intern. J. Appl. Radiation and Isotopes* **13,** 617–622 (1962). III. Radiolysis of norvaline, in aqueous oxygenated and oxygen-free solutions. IV. Radiolysis of valine in aqueous oxygenated and oxygen-free solutions. V. Radiolysis of norleucine, leucine and isoleucine in aqueous solution. *Intern. J. Appl. Radiation and Isotopes* in press.
4. K. DOSE and K. ETTRÉ, Die radiationschemische Synthese von Aminosäuren und verwandten Verbindungen. *Z. Naturforsch.* **13B,** 784–788 (1958).

RADIATION RESEARCH **19**, 559–567 (1963)

Absorption Coefficients of Liquid Water and Aqueous Solutions in the Far Ultraviolet[1]

J. L. WEEKS, G. M. A. C. MEABURN, AND S. GORDON

Argonne National Laboratory, Argonne, Illinois

INTRODUCTION

Renewed interest in the photochemistry of aqueous solutions in the far ultraviolet (below 2000 A) has stimulated activity in determining reliable extinction coefficients in this spectral region. Several conflicting values for the extinction coefficients of liquid water at various wavelengths have been reported (*1–5*). In the present study, extinction coefficients of liquid water have been accurately determined in the region 1900 A to 1700 A, thus extending the measurements of Barrett and Mansell (*1*) and Price *et al.* (*2*). In addition, extinction coefficients have been determined at 1849 A and/or between 1800 A and 1900 A for a variety of compounds in aqueous solution. This included sulfuric acid, sodium sulfate, ethyl acetate, methyl alcohol, formic acid, sodium formate, perchloric acid, hydrogen peroxide, potassium hydroxide, potassium carbonate, and potassium iodide, bromide, and chloride.

EXPERIMENTAL PROCEDURE

Two instruments were used in these studies: a Cary Model 14 spectrophotometer (a double-prism monochromator) and a Jarrell-Ash Model 78-650 spectrophotometer equipped with a 0.5-meter focal-length grating of 30,000 lines per inch. The wavelength scales of both instruments were calibrated by using the 1849-A, 1942-A, and 2537-A emission lines of a low-pressure mercury resonance lamp. Hydrogen discharge lamps were normally used as the sources of radiation for both instruments. However, additional measurements at 1849 A were made with the Jarrell-Ash instrument with the low-pressure mercury lamp as the radiation source.

Two types of absorption cell were used. One was a commercially available variable-space cell lined with Teflon and equipped with Englehard Suprasil quartz windows. Cell depths were accurately determined in the range 10 to 5000

[1] Based on work performed under the auspices of the U. S. Atomic Energy Commission.

μ. The calibration was effected by measuring the optical density at 2268 A of a solution of 3.11×10^{-4} *M* KI. A molar extinction coefficient of 1.28×10^4 liter $mole^{-1}$ cm^{-1} was obtained, in agreement with the results of other investigators (*6*).

The other cell was a thermostated, fixed-space type similar to one previously described (*7*). It was constructed of stainless steel and designed to hold two optically flat and parallel windows of either calcium fluoride or Suprasil separated by a spacer of either gold or platinum. The depth of the empty cell was determined immediately prior to filling by application of the usual techniques of interference spectrophotometry (*8*). Cell depths in the range 1 to 14 μ were used in this work.

Triply-distilled water (*9*) was used in the preparation of all solutions. The best reagent-grade chemicals available were used without further purification, except for formic acid which was purified according to the method described by Hart (*10*). All measurements on solutions were corrected for the absorption of the solvent (triply-distilled water).

RESULTS AND DISCUSSION

Measurements of the extinction coefficients of water between 1942 A and 1730 A were made in the variable-space cell. At each wavelength, readings of the optical density were made at different cell depths, and extinction coefficients were calculated. Corrections were made for reflectance losses of the cell windows and for the scattered light in the Jarrell-Ash instrument. The usual law for absorption in liquids was used:

$$\text{Optical density} = \log_{10} I_0/I = \epsilon cd = kd$$

where ϵ is the molar extinction coefficient, k is the linear extinction coefficient, c is the concentration in moles per liter, and d is the cell depth in centimeters.

Measurements were also made on water by using the fixed-space cell in the region 1850 A to 1700 A, and the extinction coefficients were determined at a number of wavelengths in this region. In addition, measurements were made from 1700 A to 1600 A, but owing to experimental difficulties the data are less reliable in this region. The results for water are shown in Fig. 1. In the wavelength region where both types of cell were used, the data agreed within experimental error. We estimate our error to be ±5% down to 1700 A; below 1700 A the error becomes progressively larger and may be as large as 50% at 1650 A and 100% at 1600 A. The dashed portion of the curve is our estimate of the apparent increase in the linear extinction coefficient.

The effect of temperature on the measured extinction coefficient of water at 1849 A was determined between 21°C and 36°C. These results are shown in Fig. 2, which gives an average temperature coefficient near 25°C of about 0.05 cm^{-1} deg^{-1}. All determinations utilizing the fixed-space cell were made at 25.0° ±

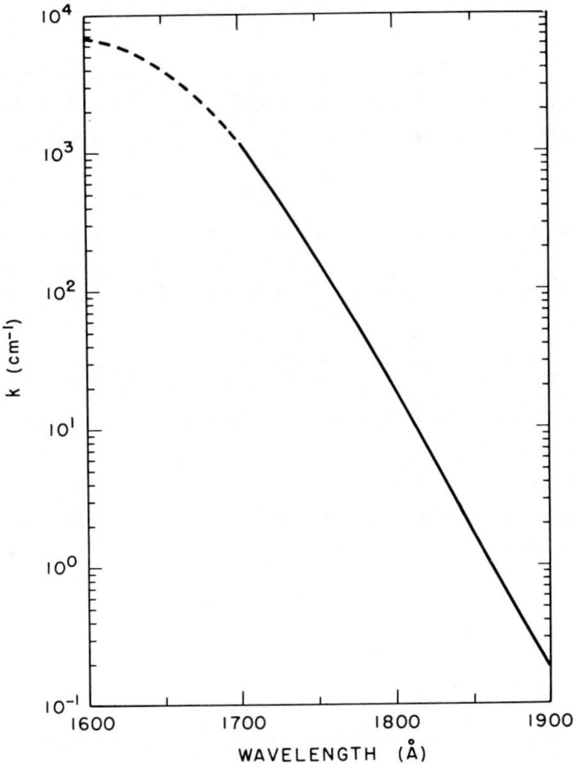

Fig. 1. Linear extinction coefficient of triply-distilled liquid H_2O

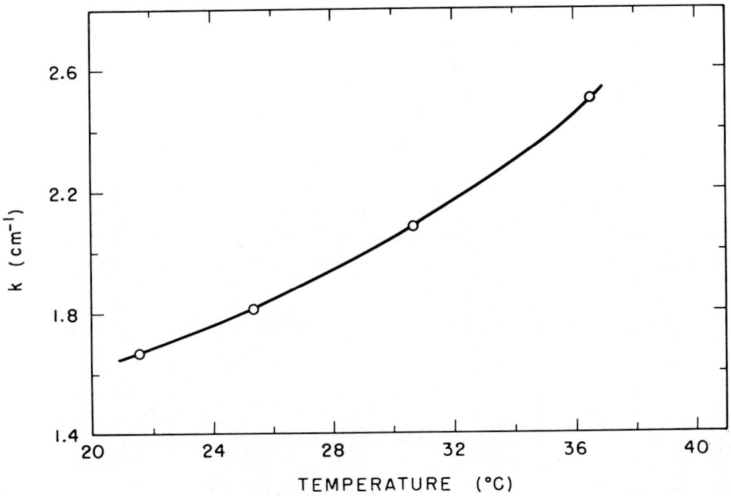

Fig. 2. The effect of temperature on the linear extinction coefficient of triply distilled H_2O at 1849 A.

0.2°C and consisted mostly of the lower-wavelength measurements on water. All other measurements were carried out at room temperature which was 24° ± 1°C.

Several runs were made to compare the observed absorption coefficients of aerated and deaerated water at 1849 A. The effect of dissolved oxygen on the absorption coefficient was found to be less than that of room-temperature variations, so all subsequent measurements were made on solutions which were not especially degassed. Two exceptions were the potassium hydroxide and potassium carbonate solutions, preparations of which were carried out in an atmosphere of helium.

The values obtained for the extinction coefficients of water are 10% higher than those reported by Price *et al.* (*2*) and are approximately 20% higher than those reported by Barrett and Mansell (*1*). At 1849 A and 25°C, they report an extinction coefficient of 1.46 cm^{-1}. We obtain a value of 1.80 ± 0.01 cm^{-1}. There is, however, good agreement between the temperature coefficient obtained above and that determined by Barrett and Mansell. In our determinations, the correction for scattered light is very small. In addition, by use of the variable-space cell and by obtaining straight-line plots, we have minimized any error in cell thickness

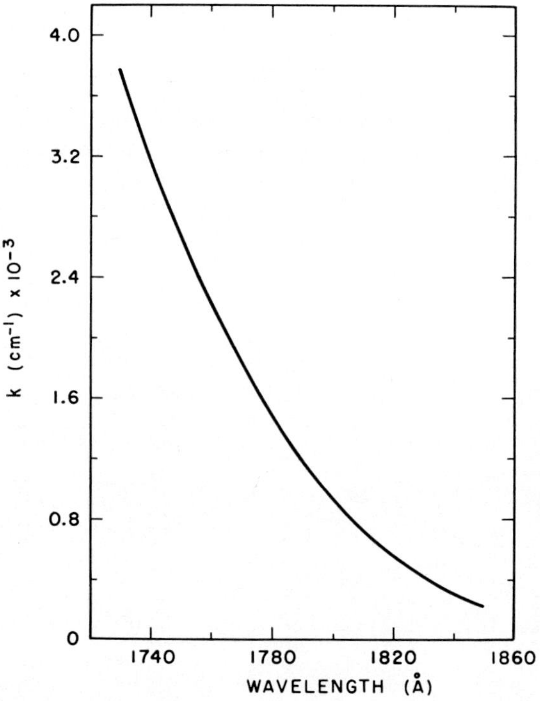

FIG. 3. Linear extinction coefficient of absolute methanol

measurements. We also feel that our wavelength calibrations are more precise than those of Barrett and Mansell. These factors may account for the discrepancy in the results.

Results reported for water vapor (*11, 12*) show a peak in the absorption curve at about 1650 A. Our results in Fig. 1 suggest a shift in this peak to shorter wavelengths, possibly by 100 A or more. However, because of experimental difficulties, we have not yet extended our measurements to low-enough wavelengths to observe the maximum of this absorption band in the liquid phase.

Extinction coefficients for absolute methanol were determined at 25°C between 1730 A and 1850 A, by using the fixed-space cell. Reproducibility was ±2%. The results are shown in Fig. 3. Measurements between 1800 A and 1900 A on several solutions were made with the variable-space cell and the Cary instrument. The results are presented in Figs. 4, 5, and 6. In general, the anions were found to have extinction coefficients which compare favorably at comparable wavelengths with published results of earlier investigations (*5, 6, 13–17*). Our data for iodide ions show a distinct peak near 1800 A of greater magnitude than the other two peaks; in Scheibe's published results (*14*) this additional absorption peak near 1800 A was shown as a slight hump in the absorption curve.

Extinction coefficients of ethyl acetate and hydrogen peroxide solutions at

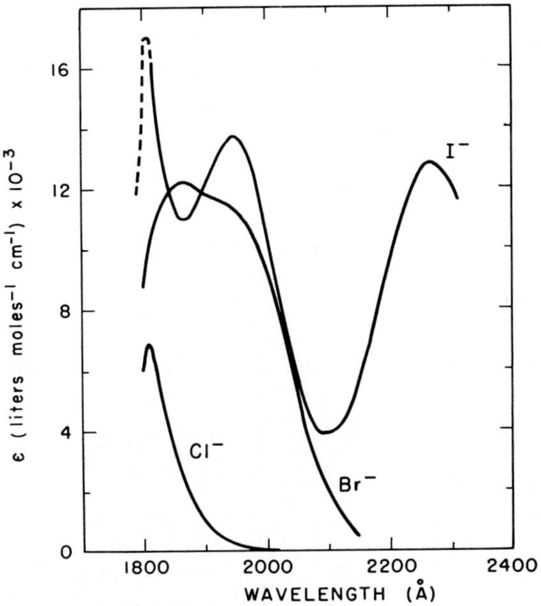

FIG. 4. Molar extinction coefficients of SO_4^{--} (10^{-2} to 2.5×10^{-1} *M* Na_2SO_4), pure HCOOH (26.5 *M*), and ClO_4^- (8.7×10^{-2} to 8.7×10^{-1} *M* $HClO_4$).

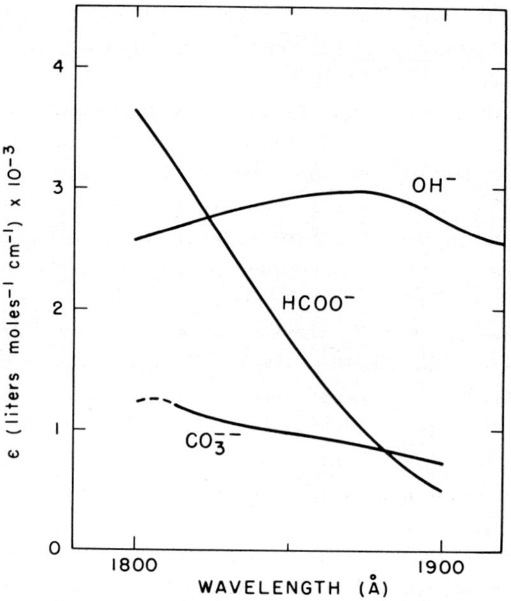

FIG. 5. Molar extinction coefficient of OH^- (1.6×10^{-5} M KOH), $HCOO^-$ (10^{-3} to 10^{-1} M HCOONa), and CO_3^{--} (10^{-2} M K_2CO_3).

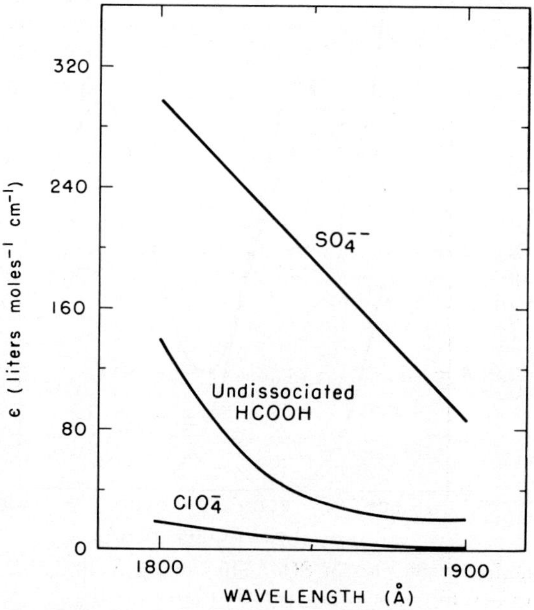

FIG. 6. Molar extinction coefficients of 10^{-3} M solutions of I^-, Br^- and Cl^-

TABLE I

MOLAR EXTINCTION COEFFICIENTS AT 1849 A AND 2537 A OF AQUEOUS SOLUTIONS OF ETHYL ACETATE, HYDROGEN PEROXIDE, AND SULFURIC ACID

Solution	*Concentration (moles liter⁻¹)*	*Wavelength (A)*	ϵ *(liters mole^{-1} cm^{-1})*
Ethyl acetate	0.03	1849	158.0
	0.15	1849	162.0
	0.75	1849	168.0
	0.75	1849	156.0[a]
	0.75	2537	0.013
Hydrogen peroxide	0.007	1849	297.0
	0.07	1849	289.0
	0.07	2537	20.0
Sulfuric acid	0.001	1849	186.0
	0.01	1849	112.0
	0.04	1849	76.0
	0.10	1849	58.0
	0.40	1849	38.0

[a] This value was obtained with the Jarrell-Ash instrument; all others were obtained with the Cary Model 14.

several concentrations were determined at 1849 A and 2537 A and are shown in Table I.

The observed absorption coefficients of three of the solutions studied were markedly dependent on solute concentration. The data for formic acid, when corrected for the absorption of formate ion at the various concentrations studied, yield a constant value of 34.9 at 1849 A for the extinction coefficient of undissociated formic acid. This value was checked by direct measurements on solutions in which the ionization of formic acid was suppressed by addition of known quantities of perchloric acid. The concentration dependence of the extinction coefficient of sulfuric acid, shown in Table I, is due to the contribution of bisulfate ion and sulfate ion. The dependence on concentration of the extinction coefficient of methyl alcohol is shown in Fig. 7, with ϵ having a minimum value at 10 M. An investigation into the possible role of hydrogen bonding on this behavior is contemplated.

SUMMARY

Conflicting values for the extinction coefficient of liquid water have been reported by Barrett and Mansell (*1*), Price *et al.* (*2*), Golding (*3, 4*), and Ley and Arends (*5*). We have redetermined the extinction coefficient of pure liquid water, extending the measurements of Barrett (1900 A to 1850 A) down to 1600 A. Our values in the same region covered are somewhat higher than the most recent meas-

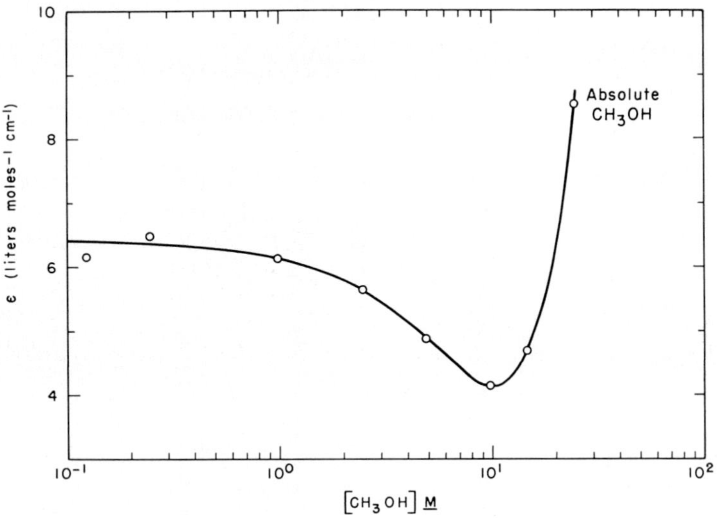

FIG. 7. The effect of concentration on the molar extinction coefficient of aqueous methanol at 1849 A.

urements. At 1849 A and 25°C, we obtain a k (cm^{-1}) of 1.80 (± 0.01); Price *et al.* report a value of 1.6, and Barrett and Mansell obtain a value of 1.46. We find a temperature coefficient of 0.051 ± 0.001 cm^{-1} deg^{-1} between 20°C and 35°C. We have also determined the extinction coefficients of sulfuric acid (0.4 M to 0.001 M), sodium sulfate (0.25 M to 0.010 M), ethyl acetate (0.75 M to 0.030 M), methyl alcohol (24.6 M to 0.12 M), formic acid (26.5 M), sodium formate (10^{-3} M to 10^{-1} M), and perchloric acid (0.087 M to 0.87 M) at 1849 A. The extinction coefficients of sulfuric acid, methyl alcohol, and formic acid show a dependence on concentration, whereas the other solutes studied do not. Two instruments were used in these measurements; a Cary Model 14 spectrophotometer, calibrated with the 1849-A, 1942-A, and 2537-A lines of a low-pressure mercury discharge lamp, and a Jarrell-Ash Model 78-650 spectrophotometer equipped with a 0.5-meter focal length grating with 30,000 lines per inch. Both a Hanovia hydrogen discharge lamp and the low-pressure mercury discharge lamp were used as sources with the Jarrell-Ash instrument.

RECEIVED: November 15, 1962

REFERENCES

1. J. BARRETT and A. MANSELL, Ultra violet absorption spectra of the molecules H_2O, HDO, and D_2O. *Nature* **187,** 138–139 (1960).
2. W. PRICE, P. HARRIS, G. BEAVEN, and E. JOHNSON, Ultra violet absorption spectra of the molecules H_2O, HDO, and D_2O. *Nature* **188,** 45–46 (1960).

3. R. M. GOLDING, Ultra-violet spectra of water solutions. *Nature* **186,** 308 (1960); Ultra-violet absorption spectrum of water. *Ibid.* **189,** 132 (1961).
4. R. M. GOLDING, Ultra-violet absorption spectra of the molecules H_2O, HDO, and D_2O. *Nature* **187,** 139 (1960).
5. A. LEY and B. ARENDS, Absorptionsmessungen Kurzwelligen Ultraviolett. *Z. Physik. Chem.* **B17,** 177–219 (1932).
6. G. STEIN and A. TREININ, Electron transfer spectra of anions in solution. *Trans. Faraday Soc.* **55,** 1091–1099 (1959).
7. V. VON KEUSSLER, UV-Absorptionskuvette für extrem dünne Schichten mit genau messbaren Plattenabstand bis unterhalb 1μ. *Spectrochim. Acta* **6,** 185–193 (1954).
8. ROBERT P. BAUMAN, *Absorption Spectroscopy,* p. 190, John Wiley & Sons, New York, 1962.
9. E. J. HART, S. GORDON, and D. A. HUTCHISON, Free radical initiated $O^{16}O^{18}$-H_2O^{16} exchange reactions for aqueous solutions. *J. Am. Chem. Soc.* **74,** 5548–5549 (1952).
10. E. J. HART, Gamma-ray induced oxidation of aqueous formic acid-oxygen solutions. Effect of oxygen and formic acid concentration. *J. Am. Chem. Soc.* **76,** 4312–4315 (1954).
11. K. WATANABE and M. ZELIKOFF, Absorption coefficients of water vapor in the vacuum ultraviolet. *J. Opt. Soc. Am.* **43,** 753–755 (1953).
12. P. WILKINSON and H. JOHNSON, The absorption spectra of methane, carbon dioxide, water vapor, and ethylene in the vacuum ultraviolet. *J. Chem. Phys.* **18,** 190–193 (1950).
13. A. LEY and B. ARENDS, Die Ultraviolettabsorption des Hydroxylions. *Z. Physik. Chem.* **B6,** 240–246 (1929).
14. G. SCHEIBE, Die Absorption der Halogenionen in wässeriger Lösung im beginnenden Schumann-Ultraviolett (Elektronenaffinitätsspectren). *Z. Physik. Chem.* **B5,** 355–364 (1929).
15. A. LEY and B. ARENDS, Absorptionsspektren von Schwefelverbindungen in verschiedenen Wertigkeitsstufen. *Z. Physik. Chem.* **B15,** 311–324 (1932).
16. A. V. KISS and R. SZABO, Zur Lichtabsorption der polycyclischen innerkomplexen Verbindungen. 4. Nickelkomplexe. *Z. Anorg. Chem.* **252,** 172–184 (1944).
17. L. ORGEL, Charge transfer spectra and some related phenomena. *Quart. Rev.* **8,** 422–449 (1954).

RADIATION RESEARCH **19**, 569–581 (1963)

Effects of X-Irradiation on Cell Differentiation and Morphogenesis in a Developing Beetle Wing

JAMES S. BECK[1]

Donner Laboratory of Biophysics and Medical Physics, University of California, Berkeley, California

INTRODUCTION

In a study of effects of ionizing radiation on development, X-irradiation of the confused flour beetle (*Tribolium confusum*) (*1*) during the first day of the 6-day pupal stage was found to induce a gross deformity of the wings of the adult (imago). The apparent specificity of this deformity, the absence of any other apparent deformities, and the fact that it was grossly evident led to the investigations presented here. The quantitative characterization of such a deformity is quite often a difficult matter. However, this system has characteristics which can be used to advantage in this respect. The deformity studied involves only the wings. These are external and can be isolated reproducibly for chemical measurements and microscopic observation. Furthermore, the membranous wings consist essentially of a single type of cell which can be followed through a consistent course of differentiation and morphogenesis.

Accordingly, the experiments presented below began with the determination of dose-effect relationships and the developmental period of radiosensitivity. The remaining experiments are efforts at chemical, microscopic, and ultramicroscopic characterization of the deformity. These include measurement of phosphorus, an element chosen as an indicator of alterations in cellular state and number and also chosen for its convenience of analysis; light microscopy for morphological effects; and electron microscopy for more refined histological and cytological changes.

The confused flour beetle has two pairs of wings visible externally during the pupal and adult (imaginal) stages. These are the outer elytra and, under them, the membranous (posterior or metathoracic) wings. In the adult, the membranous wings consist primarily of an envelope of cuticle 2 mm long, 1 mm wide and 1 μ thick, weighing about 20 μg. The cuticle has outward projections (spines) a few microns long, arrayed in a pattern such that each spine is the center of a regular

[1] Work done as a postdoctoral research fellow of the National Cancer Institute. Present address: Department of Physiology, University of Minnesota, Minneapolis 14, Minnesota.

hexagon formed by its six nearest neighbors as vertices. A field of view including many spines, then, presents rows in three directions. At the beginning of the pupal stage, when this imaginal wing is yet to be formed, the pupal wing is a flat sac of smooth pupal cuticle containing over half a million hypodermal cells. The members of this population of cells differentiate and construct the imaginal cuticle and spines in strikingly precise synchrony.

The deformity produced by sufficient irradiation during the critical period appears externally as warping of both membranous wings and elytra, displacement of the wings from their normal position on the dorsolateral surface of the abdomen, and failure of the membranous wings to fold normally beneath the elytra. The deformity occurs in degrees over a certain dose range; at lower doses it is seen as a slight lateral divergence of the elytra with extrusion of parts of the membranous wings. A severe deformity typical of that induced by higher doses is shown beside a normal imago in Fig. 1.

FIG. 1. Adult *Tribolium confusum*. Left, wing deformity; right, normal. Scale: smallest division = 0.1 mm.

METHODS

Culturing and Handling

The animals were grown in cultures started from one to two thousand adults in quart jars of glass, with perforated tops, half-filled with culture medium. The medium consisted of about 96% whole wheat flour (without preservatives), sifted to eliminate chaff, and about 4% dry nutritional yeast. These cultures were maintained for a month at 30°C without obvious contamination or overcrowding. New cultures were made by transferring aliquots of pooled adults to new medium. Pupae for the experiments were obtained by removing larvae from the stock cultures and allowing them to develop and pupate on fresh medium. By clearing these larval cultures of pupae and harvesting subsequently developed pupae at a given time after clearing, one can obtain pupae of a known age span. Separation of the animals from the medium was accomplished with 20-mesh/inch soil sieves (0.833-mm openings); separation of larvae from adults and pupae was achieved by allowing larvae to crawl through the sieves; separation of pupae from other forms was done by moving individuals from the mixed group with a camel's hair brush in white enamel trays. During and after irradiation the pupae were kept in glass petri plates. After irradiation these plates were covered with copper wire screens and incubated at 30C°.

Irradiation

The X-irradiation was done with a Machlett OEG 60 tube, at 50 kvp, 25 ma, with an external filter of 0.1 mm Cu and 0.4 mm Al. Dose rate was measured as 86 r/min at the position of the exposed pupae with a 100-r Victoreen chamber on a Plexiglas shelf. For the higher-energy experiment, X-rays were obtained from another machine at 150 kvp, 15 ma, with external filter of 0.25 mm Cu and 1.00 mm Al. Dose rate was from 86 to 92 r/min, and the total dose was monitored by a Radocon integrating dosimeter with a Victoreen chamber placed beside the sample being irradiated. The doses given are not corrected for backscatter from the glass petri plates which held the pupae.

Scoring for Experiments

After eclosion (the final molt and emergence of the imago), the individuals were examined and categorized. In the data which follow, all degrees of wing deformity are consolidated into a single category. Pupae often die or fail to emerge after exposure to doses as high or higher than that which produces very nearly a 100% incidence of the deformity. These individuals are excluded from the analysis and represent the difference between total number in an experiment and the sum of the normal and deformed adults.

Activation Analysis

The technique used in the analysis for phosphorus has been discussed elsewhere (*2*). The activation was produced by exposure for 8 hours to a flux of 5×10^{12} neutrons cm^{-2} sec^{-1}.[2] The nuclear reaction was $P^{31}(n, \gamma)P^{32}$. The induced radioactivity of the wings was measured with a Geiger-Mueller tube. Gamma-ray scintillation spectrometry was done with a 256-channel pulse-height analyzer.

Microscopy

Light microscopy was done by two different methods. Gross sections of whole pupae were prepared as follows: The pupae were decapitated and incised at the posterior end and fixed for 2 days in Helly's fixative or in Lillie's alcohol–acetate–formaldehyde fixative, hydrated with ethanol, kept in methyl benzoate until embedding, and vacuum-embedded in paraffin after 10 minutes in benzene. Sectioning was done with an ordinary microtome, and the sections were mounted on glass slides. The sections of tissue fixed with Helly's fixative were treated with Lugol's solution and thiosulfate before staining. Two staining procedures were used: Groat's hematoxylin (*3*) and Mallory's 1936 method (*4*). Whole mounts of wings, dissected from the pupa or adult, were prepared as follows: With a sharp scalpel blade four or five cuts were made perpendicular to the front edge of the wing and stopped short of the front edge so that the wing remained in one piece. After 24 hours in 10% aqueous solution of formaldehyde, the wings were mounted on albumin-coated glass slides, dried at 50° to 60°C, and stained with hematoxylin (similar to Ehrlich acid hematoxylin, *5*). Staining was continued until the nuclei showed well, usually 2 or 3 days. Then these preparations were dehydrated, and cover glasses were added. For the first 3 days of the pupal stage, whole mounts were made of the whole pupal wing, including pupal cuticle, rather than the free imaginal wing (see below).

Electron microscopy has been done by two methods.[3] Whole mounts were most commonly fixed by floating the cut wings on, or submerging them in, 1% OsO_4 solution for 30 minutes. After fixation, they were washed in H_2O and either put on the Formvar-coated surface of a grid or sandwiched between two uncoated grids in the specimen holder under the dissecting microscope so that the holes of the grids were superimposed. For thin sections the same fixation was used. The specimens were embedded in *n*-butyl methacrylate and cut with a Porter-Blum or an LKB ultratome and put onto Formvar-coated grids. The observations were made with an RCA EMU-2E 50-kv electron microscope.

Isolation of Wings

The usefulness of the measurements of phosphorus depends on the reproducible isolation of wings. In the adult stage the membranous wing was obtained after the

[2] Exposure to neutron flux occurred in the Livermore Pool Type Reactor at the Livermore Division of the Lawrence Radiation Laboratory of the University of California.

[3] Dr. Thomas Hayes of Donner Laboratory collaborated in the electron microscopy.

beetle was killed by decapitation and the elytra were pulled off with very fine forceps. Under the dissecting microscope, the membranous wings were spread and broken off at the hinge point. The breaking point was reproducible. In the pupal stage, the imaginal wing is enclosed within the pupal cuticle. Late enough in the pupal stage the imaginal cuticle is sufficiently strong and separated from the pupal cuticle to permit removal of the imaginal wing from the pupal cuticle. The pupa was killed by decapitation, and the elytra were lifted from over the membranous wings and removed. Then the pupal membranous wings were removed by gentle tension and put onto the surface of distilled water. Under the dissecting microscope, the imaginal wing was pulled out the proximal end of the open pupal cuticular envelope into the surface of the water.

RESULTS

Dose-Effect Relationship

The incidence of the wing deformity as a function of dose was determined by exposure of pupae within the first day of the 6-day pupal stage for both 50-kvp and 150-kvp X-rays at the stated dose rates. Tables I and II give the results. The standard deviations of the fractions affected, f, are computed by the relation

$$\sigma = \sqrt{(1/N)(f)(1-f)}\ ,$$

where N is the number deformed plus number normal. When these data are plotted as survival curves, the curves for 50 kvp and for 150 kvp coincide. On a semi-logarithmic plot this curve has a shoulder to about 1000 r, and for higher doses the logarithm of surviving fraction appears to vary linearly with dose. If this portion of the curve is represented by e^{-D/D_0}, then $D_0 = 100$ r.

Radiosensitive Period

Pupae within 5 and 6 hours of the same age (the final larval molt being used as zero time) were obtained and incubated at 30°C until irradiation at the age to be

TABLE I

FRACTION OF ADULT WING DEFORMITIES AFTER PUPAL EXPOSURE TO GIVEN DOSES OF 50-KVP X-RAYS

Dose (r)	*Number of pupae*	*Number deformed, D*	*Number normal, N*	$\frac{D}{N+D}$	σ
0	451	10	428	0.024	0.007
560	300	13	283	0.044	0.004
1120	303	32	267	0.107	0.018
1400	294	131	156	0.701	0.027
1680	297	265	20	0.930	0.015
1960	299	285	3	0.990	0.006
2240	299	266	2	0.993	0.005

TABLE II

FRACTION OF ADULT WING DEFORMITIES AFTER PUPAL EXPOSURE TO GIVEN DOSES OF 150-KVP X-RAYS

Dose (*r*)	*Number of pupae*	*Number deformed,* *D*	*Number normal,* *N*	$\frac{D}{N+D}$	σ
0	371	6	355	0.017	0.007
500	300	13	275	0.045	0.012
1000	295	26	259	0.091	0.017
1250	298	85	206	0.292	0.027
1500	299	216	74	0.745	0.026
2000	299	283	3	0.990	0.006

TABLE III

FRACTION OF AFFECTED ADULTS AFTER EXPOSURE OF PUPAE TO 2240 ROENTGENS OF 50-KVP X-RAYS AT GIVEN AGES

Age range (*hr*)	*Number of pupae*	*Number deformed,* *D*	*Number normal,* *N*	$\frac{D}{N+D}$
0–6	30	27	0	1.00
17½–23½	29	29	0	1.00
18–23	74	73	0	1.00
23–28	74	70	2	0.97
28–33	76	72	0	1.00
33–38	75	55	19	0.74
38–43	78	23	54	0.30
42–48	29	4	24	0.14
66–72	27	2	21	0.09

tested. The results are presented in Tables III and IV for two different doses, 1540 r and 2240 r. Plotted with linear coordinates, the resulting curves show that incidence of deformity falls steeply at the same developmental time for both doses. The range during which this fall occurs is about 15 hours. The mid-points of the drops in incidence occur at about 37 hours. It may be expected that more homogeneous age grouping would produce a much sharper fall at 37 hours. At any rate, the sharpness of this decline of sensitivity with advancing development suggests that the final larval molt (pupation) is a good marker for physiological age (recall that the pupal stage lasts 6 days), and that the hypodermal cell population is in rather precise synchrony, at least with respect to the actions which control the structures which determine the macroscopic deformity.

Phosphorus Content

The amount of phosphorus in control and experimental wings was determined by counting the P^{32} radioactivity induced by exposure to neutrons. Gamma-ray

TABLE IV

FRACTION OF AFFECTED ADULTS AFTER EXPOSURE OF PUPAE TO 1540 ROENTGEN OF 50-KVP X-RAYS AT GIVEN AGES

Age range (hr)	*Number in pupae*	*Number deformed, D*	*Number normal, N*	$\frac{D}{N+D}$
0–5	230	73	154	0.32
31–36	84	24	58	0.29
32–37	199	53	144	0.27
38–43	200	16	177	0.08
42–47	113	9	94	0.09
48–53	121	5	110	0.04
66–71	120	3	109	0.03

scintillation spectrometry of pooled samples revealed no long-lived γ-emitting nuclides, and the radioactivity 6 days or longer after the activation period decayed with the 14-day half-life of P^{32}. Thus, comparisons based on the radioactivities measured more than 6 days after the end of the activation exposure do indeed reflect the amounts of phosphorus in the wings. In the first experiment, two KH_2PO_4 standards, eight control membranous wings, and ten experimental wings were counted indivdually. The experimental wings were grossly deformed, having been taken from adults developed from pupae exposed to 2240 r of 50-kvp X-rays during the first day of pupal life. These and the control wings were taken from adults 1 day after eclosion. The sensitivity of this determination (*2*) made possible the counting of activities of individual wings. Figure 2 is a semilogarithmic plot of the mean values of the net radioactivities of the individual wings from the two groups at the times of counting. The intervals shown for each point represent two standard deviations for the sample of wings. This does not include counting uncertainty, which is very much smaller than that due to sampling from the biological population. Comparison with the standard gives values of 0.03 μg of phosphorus per control wing and 0.08 μg of phosphorus per experimental wing at 1 day after eclosion.

The finding of this difference between normal and malformed wings after eclosion motivated a more comprehensive experiment to compare the phosphorus content of isolated imaginal wings at different stages of development. The earlier in pupal life that the dissection of wings is done, the more difficult it is to get consistent samples. However, small numbers of wings were obtained at late pupal stages and for some days after eclosion. These were activated with thermal neutrons as before, and the radioactivities were counted for indivdual wings. A convenient zero tme was chosen, and the counts were corrected for decay by use of tabulated values of $e^{-\lambda t}$ for P^{32}, the comparative results being dependent solely on the relative amounts of phosphorus in the individual wings. The means—for groups of the

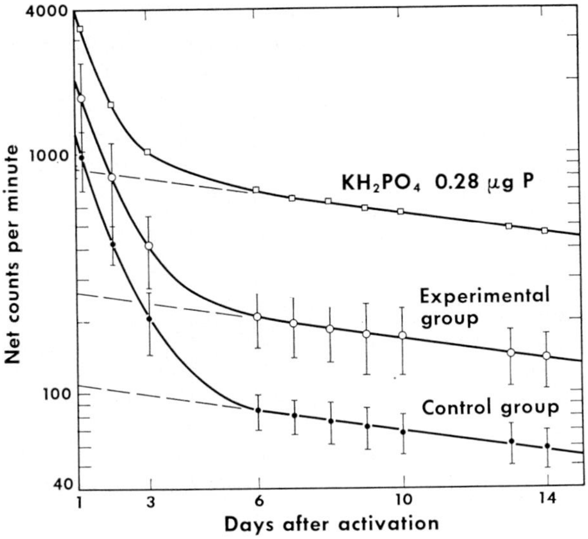

FIG. 2. Decay of neutron-induced radioactivity of normal and deformed wings, plotted as means of counts of individual wings. The intervals represent two standard deviations.

same stage—of these corrected activities are shown in arbitrary units, plotted against the time of sampling in days after pupation, in Fig. 3. The intervals, again, are two standard deviations of the samples. The numbers of wings in the samples varied from 2 to 8.

A delay in eclosion of irradiated pupae is indicated on the graph. (I have studied this delay and found it to be greater for greater doses within the range employed in these experiments.) The loss of phosphorus from the normal wings after eclosion appears to be exponential if the asymptotic value is subtracted from each observed value (*2*). Owing to the greater uncertainty associated with the values for experimental wings, no conclusion can be drawn about the kinetics of the loss of phosphorus from the deformed wings. The maximum value for experimentals is significantly lower than that for controls.

Microscopic Observations

The population of hypodermal cells of the membranous wings are contained in a flat and very thin envelope of cuticle. The cells lie within this container in a double layer, actually a single continuous layer inside the cuticle. These spatial characteristics offer unique opportunities for microscopy. Interference microscopy of whole mounts and electron microscopy of transverse sections have shown the membranous wing to be about 1 μ thick in the adult state. Good images of unsectioned wings can be formed by the electron microscope. Furthermore, selected

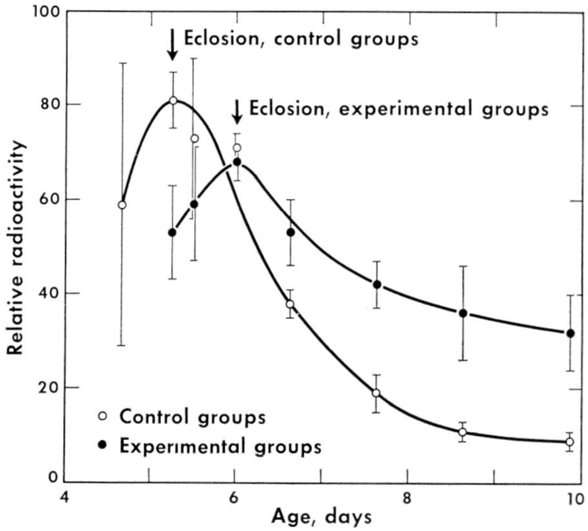

FIG. 3. Phosphorus content of individual control and experimental wings. Mean values of relative P content are plotted as functions of time of development. The intervals are two standard deviations.

areas of the wings can be compared. The following descriptions are the results of observations by light and electron microscopy of sections and whole mounts.

In whole mounts the numbers of nuclei and spines in a given area have been equal where counted in the light microscope. Also, in wings at stages wherein the cells are still present, every spine has been found to be superimposed over a cell nucleus. We have concluded that there is a one-to-one correspondence between hypodermal cells and spines.

The hypodermal cells at the beginning of pupal life have spherical nuclei. They are roughly in a layer adjacent to the cuticle, but in whole mounts no apparent ordered relationship among them exists. In the case of the control wings, near the end of the first day and during the second day the hypodermal cells flatten, their nuclei become discs, and they suddenly appear to be in an orderly layer one cell thick. After this, the imaginal cuticle appears, and quite suddenly, early in the fifth day after pupal life began, the spines appear all at once (by light microscopy) and apparently in final form. Six days after pupation the final molt (eclosion) occurs, and the membranous wing, which has been convoluted within the pupal cuticle, straightens and flattens and then folds within an hour after the shedding of the pupal cuticle. After eclosion the cells disappear from the wing. They are found only rarely in wings isolated 4 days or more after eclosion. The array of spines on the normal wing is neatly ordered, and spines are regular, smooth, and uniform in appearence.

The damage in the wing exposed to X-irraditaion during the critical period of pupal life is manifest in various ways. Many of the normal steps are delayed. (A delay in eclosion was mentioned in connection with the phosphorus determinations.) As soon as 6 hours after irradiation at 1 hour of pupal age, round, dense, basophilic bodies appear among the hypodermal cells of the affected wing. They increase in number until, at 24 hours, they are perhaps half as many as the hypodermal cells; then they decrease in number until they are no longer seen at 113 hours. These bodies appear at 40 hours or so in control wings but are less than one-hundredth as numerous as the hypodermal cells. One is shown in Fig. 4, fixed with OsO_4, sectioned, and viewed by electron microscopy. In the electron microscope, they appear to be transformed hypodermal cells. The appearance of the spines is one of the events delayed by the radiation damage. "Holes" are seen in the final array of spines, and some poorly formed spines are present. In addition, some positions in the array normally occupied by a single spine are occupied by more than one spine. These are usually malformed. Two, three, four, and even five have been seen at a locus. Further, there occur areas where the pattern is in general disorder.

The wings contain organs and tissues other than hypodermal cells. These include tracheae, trachioles, veins, hemolymph, and perhaps others. But all of these together occupy a relatively small volume of the wing and are assumed to be negligible with respect to the measurements done. The adult tracheal system is reduced in the experimental wing in comparison with the control. However, tracheae are present in the pupal stage in both experimental and control wings.

DISCUSSION

In summary, it has been observed that the membranous wings of the confused flour beetle are subject to an apparently specific gross deformity induced by X-irradiation of 1000 to 2000 r during the first 37 hours of the 6-day pupal stage. The survival curve for this effect has a shoulder to 1000 r and a D_0 of 110 r. The membranous wing has been observed to contain a synchronous population of hypodermal cells which form a cuticle with an ordered array of projections (spines) which are in one-to-one correspondence with the cells. The cells—or cellular material—leave the wing, probably randomly, after eclosion. The radiation damage is manifest microscopically and chemically as a morphological transformation of some of the hypodermal cells; disorder of the spine array in regions; malformation, absence, and iteration of spines; delays in some developmental events; and disruption of the normal loss of cellular material from the wing.

In considering analysis of the survival curve, one must recognize the complexity of the system. In particular, two questions must be asked: (1) How many "targets" must be hit before the deformity is scored as such? and (2) How many kinds of "target" are represented by the various kinds and degrees of aberration found? Assuming that the usual analysis applies—a questionable assumption—one finds

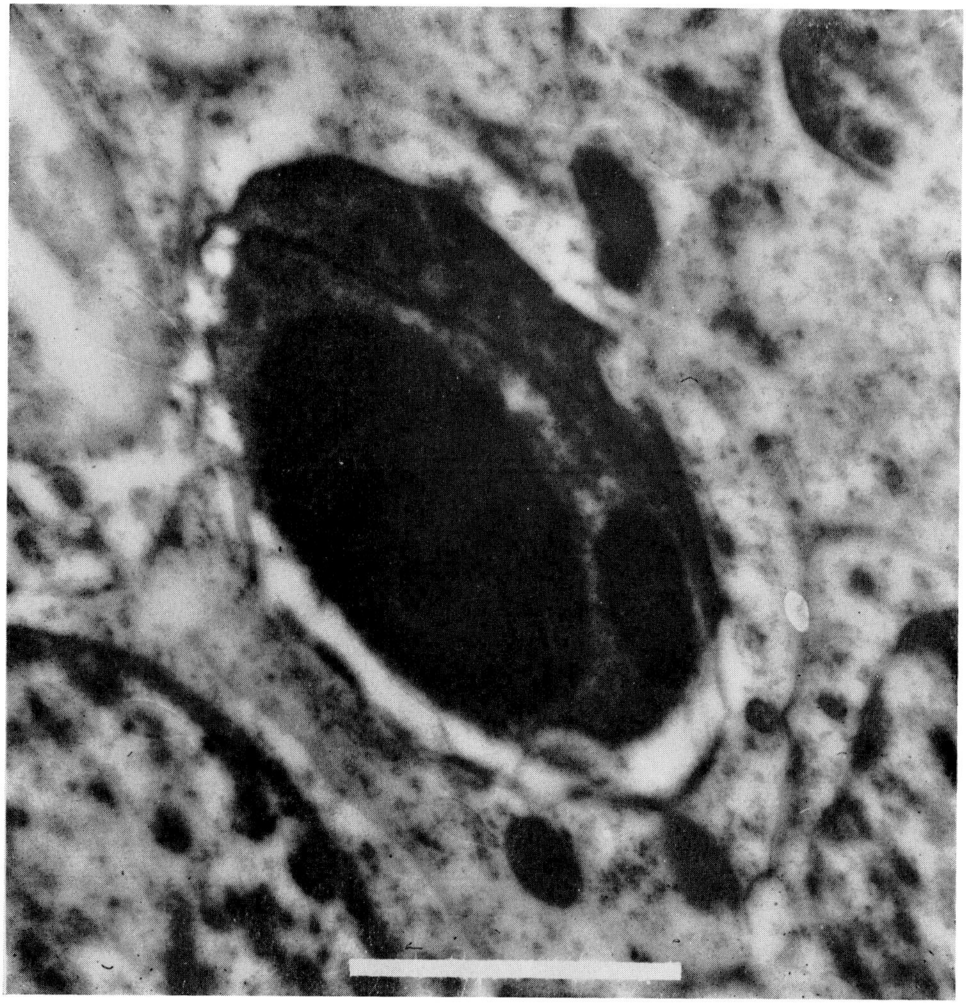

FIG. 4. Electron microgram of transformed hypodermal cell in OsO_4-fixed radiation-damaged wing. Normal nuclei are at lower left and right corners of the figure. Marker represents 1 μ.

that the observed D_0 of 110 r is comparable with the mean lethal doses (D_0 for survival of colony formation) reported for various human cells (*6*) and for Chinese hamster cells (*7*) in tissue culture.

To the interpretations of the findings concerning the critical period stated above may be added the suggestion that the hypodermal cells of the membranous wing—perhaps all hypodermal cells—are in a critical state of activity relatively late in the development of the whole organism. Other deformities have not been seen on external examination. Perhaps we have happened upon the last of the tissues to be in a sensitive state.

The normal variation in phosphorus content as development proceeds is interesting in the contrast between the synchrony preceding eclosion and the randomness after it. Since the cells are known to disappear from the wing after eclosion and since no cell fragments have been observed, one may consider whether these cells are cleared from the wing intact by passive removal, or whether they respond negatively to the number of neighboring cells and actively depart. From this point of view, the retention of phosphorus by the radiation-damaged wing may reflect the final manifestation of cell injury. That is, the damaged cell does not proceed to the final passive unattached state, or does not perform the final act of exodus.

The nature of the cellular change which produces the basophilic and dense-appearing cells after irradiation is still under study. The disappearance of these morphologically altered cells could represent the complete loss of these cells or their return to the morphological state of the unaltered cells. Although I have no cell counts to confirm it, it is my impression that the hypodermal cell population is not diminished enough to account for loss of these cells. The nature of this alteration is interesting; it seems to be a generalized effect on the whole cell, quite unlike anything so limited as a chromosome break. Even metabolic consequences of specific damages may not be expected to produce such uniform and profound changes. The OsO_4-fixed nucleus and cytoplasm alike appear homogeneous and are more dense to electrons.

The multiple structural aberrations produced by exposure to X-rays in this system may be put into three classes: deficiencies, malformations, and iterations. The one-to-one correspondence between hypodermal cells and spines suggests that perhaps a single cell forms a single spine. The "holes" in the array of spines represent the failure of formation of a spine, although cuticle is continuous across the locus. There probably could be different types of damage, all of which result in the inability of a cell to form a spine. Similarly, there may be different injuries resulting in a malformed spine. But I tend to think of a more specific (more refined?) cellular injury when I consider the mechanism by which a cell may be induced to form two or more spines rather than one. Is such a cell one in which the machinery continues to work without the control of some feedback switch?

Clearly, the investigation described here repeats rather than answers some old questions. It is my hope that the wing deformity in *T. confusum*, with its advantages for certain types of study, will help to elucidate the nature of damage to a developing biological system caused by radiation (or toxins). The observations thus far made with this system seem to contradict the concept of the developing tissue as merely a simple amplifier of the same kind of damage as leads to mutation or cell death.

ACKNOWLEDGMENTS

The advice and help of Drs. Rudolph Pipa, Thomas Hayes, and Thomas Manney is appreciated. In particular, Dr. Hayes collaborated in the electron microscopy, and Mr. Manney in the phosphorus determinations. Marian Beck and Robert Padden assisted with technical work.

RECEIVED: October 10, 1962

REFERENCES

1. T. PARK, Observations on the general biology of the flour beetle, *Tribolium confusum*. *Quart. Rev. Biol.* **9,** 36–54 (1934).
2. J. S. BECK and T. R. MANNEY, Neutron activation analysis for phosphorus in a study of development in a beetle wing. *Science* **137,** 865–866 (1962).
3. R. A. GROAT, Initial and persisting power of solutions of iron-hematoxylin lake. *Stain Technol.* **24,** 157–163 (1949).
4. F. B. MALLORY, The anilin blue collagen stain. *Stain Technol.* **11,** 101–102 (1936).
5. R. D. LILLIE, *Histopathologic Technic and Practical Histochemistry*, 2nd ed., Blakiston, New York, 1953.
6. T. T. PUCK, D. MORKOVIN, P. I. MARCUS, and S. J. CIECIURA, Action of X-rays on mammalian cells. II. Survival curves of cells from normal human tissues. *J. Exptl. Med.* **106,** 485–500 (1957).
7. M. M. ELKIND and H. SUTTON, Radiation response of mammalian cells grown in culture. I. Repair of X-ray damage in surviving Chinese hamster cells. *Radiation Res.* **13,** 556–593 (1960).

RADIATION RESEARCH **19**, 582–592 (1963)

Effects of Certain Metal Salts on the Inactivation of Solid Trypsin by Ionizing Radiation

J. A. V. BUTLER AND A. B. ROBINS

Chester Beatty Research Institute, Institute of Cancer Research, Royal Cancer Hospital, Fulham Road, London, England

INTRODUCTION

In a previous paper (*1*) the effect of some additives on the inactivation of trypsin in the solid state by ionizing radiations was examined. It was found that, whereas oxygen had no effect on the sensitiveness of the enzyme when pulsed electrons at high dose rates were used, at low dose rates (Co^{60} γ-rays) it enhanced the degree of inactivation. However, when cysteine, which by itself has a protective effect, was present, oxygen increased the degree of inactivation at the high as well as the low dose rates. For this reason it was thought that the lack of an oxygen effect at high dose rates could be due not to a depletion phenomenon resulting from a low rate of diffusion but to the slowness of reactions in which oxygen takes part.

It was obvious, as had been shown earlier (*2*), that cysteine and oxygen are antagonistic in their action, and that the oxygen effect frequently observed in biological systems could be due not to a direct effect on the main recipient but to the inhibition of the effect of protective agents.

It was therefore desirable to obtain further information about the interactions of oxygen and protective agents. It had been suggested by Howard-Flanders (*2*) that cysteine acts as a protective agent by donating hydrogen to repair the substrate, but, because of the high speed of the reactions, it was thought more likely that it acts by donating or receiving an electron, i.e., by acting as a source or sink of electrons. This suggested that other redox systems would behave similarly, and therefore the effects of adding various metal salts in small quantities to the enzyme were examined, in the presence and absence of oxygen, and also at high and low dose rates. In some cases these were found to have a marked protective effect. A preliminary note dealing with the effects of ferrous and ferric ions has been published (*3*).

EXPERIMENTAL PROCEDURE

The Enzymes

The sources, batch numbers, and details of preparation of the various enzymes are given below. (W) = Worthington Biochemical Corporation. (S) = Seravac Laboratories (Cape Town) Ltd.

Chymotrypsin: (W) CDT 662–65, crystallized, salt-free.

Trypsin: (W) TRL 6112, activated with calcium, adjusted to pH 3.2, dialyzed, and lyophilized.
(W) TRSF 6118, twice-crystallized, washed, and dried (salt-free).
(W) 836–38, twice-crystallized, washed with 0.1 *N* H_2SO_4 insaturated $MgSO_4$, and dried (contained 40% $MgSO_4$).
(S) 80, twice crystallized, activated, lyophilized (salt-free).

Preparation of Samples for Irradiation

Enzyme solutions were made up to a concentration of 5 mg/ml in 10^{-3} *N* HCl. Additives (cysteine, metal salts, etc.) were dissolved in 10^{-3} *N* HCl to such a concentration that the addition of 0.05 ml to 3 ml of enzyme solution gave the required ratio of additive to enzyme. Aliquots (0.2 ml) of the mixed solutions in small tubes were freeze-dried and evacuated for 2½ hours with an oil pump to approximately 0.03 mm Hg. Tubes were either sealed at this points, or air or oxygen was admitted before sealing. In some experiments further evacuation was carried out by using a mercury diffusion pump, when a vacuum of 0.003 mm Hg was reached in a further 4 hours.

Sources of Radiation

High-energy electrons. Irradiations were performed with the 15-Mev linear accelerator at St. Bartholomew's Hospital and with the 4-Mev linear accelerator at the Wantage Research Laboratory (Atomic Energy Research Establishment). Both machines delivered pulsed electrons with a pulse duration of 1.3 and 2.5 μsec, respectively. The samples to be irradiated were arranged on a board so that they all lay in the area of constant dose rate. With the board at 100 cm from the scattering window, the 15-Mev accelerator gave 1 Mrad in 5 minutes. The 4-Mev machine delivered a dose of 1 Mrad/min at a distance of 140 cm.

Details of dosimetry have been given elsewhere (*1*).

Co^{60} γ-rays. Some irradiations were carried out by Dr. A. R. Crathorn of this Institute using a 120-curie cobalt source. Dosimetry was checked by the Fricke dosimeter with $G(Fe^{+++}) = 15.5$ per 100 ev, and the dose rate was 2400 rads/min. Other low-dose-rate irradiations were performed by Miss Burt of the Wantage Research Laboratory using a cobalt source at a dose rate of 4000 rads/min.

Assay Methods

Trypsin was assayed by measurement of the proteolysis of casein solution at pH 7.6; details of procedure have been reported previously (*4*). Some samples of irradiated trypsin were also assayed by measurement of esterase activity, which was found to give the same result as the determination of protease activity. The procedure followed in this case was that due to Geratz using *p*-toluenesulfonyl-L-arginine methyl ester hydrochloride (TAME). The undigested TAME was allowed to react with hydroxylamine, and the resulting derivative was estimated colorimetrically as the ferric ion complex (*5*).

Absorption Spectra

Trypsin TRSF 6118 was incompletely soluble in water, and the insoluble, presumably denatured material from a 2% solution was centrifuged out, leaving a 1.6% (7×10^{-4} *M*) solution at a pH of 5 to 6. (At pH 3 all the trypsin was soluble.) The 7×10^{-4} *M* solution was examined spectrophotometrically between wavelengths 320 and 800 mμ. Copper sulfate or ferric chloride solutions were added in increasing amount, and spectra were obtained for each mixture as well as for the metal ion alone at the same pH. The final concentration of metal ion was about 6×10^{-3} *M* in the case of copper, and 3.5×10^{-3} *M* in the case of iron.

RESULTS

Irradiation of Trypsin without Additives

Observations made with a number of preparations of trypsin, without additives, are shown in Table I. It can be seen that, although the trypsin samples used in the previous investigation were not oxygen-sensitive to high-intensity pulsed radiation, all the trypsin samples reported in this paper are sensitive with a factor

TABLE I

INACTIVATION DOSE OF TRYPSIN SAMPLES *in vacuo* AND IN AIR, WITH 4-MEV ELECTRONS

Sample used	*Treatment*	*D in vacuo*	*D in air*
TRSF 6118	Undialyzed	20	10
TRSF 6118	Dialyzed once	17, 18.2	10
TRL 6112	Dialyzed once	20.4	—
TRL 6112	Dialyzed once	12.5	6.4
TRL 6112	Dialyzed twice	15	9.3, 10, 10
TRL 6112	Dialyzed twice	20.4	—
TRL 6112	Dialyzed against EDTA	12.5	11
Seravac	Undialyzed	15.5, 17, 13.5	11

D_{vac}/D_{air} of about 2.[1] However, it may be noted that in nearly all the present observations D_{vac} of trypsin is higher than the value of approximately 10 Mr previously observed, whereas the values of D_{air} are about the same as those obtained previously. These facts suggest that the present samples contain a protective agent which increases D_{vac} and that the oxygen effect now appearing is mainly or entirely a consequence of the presence of such an agent.

This view is supported by the observation previously made (*1*) that cysteine, which had a marked protective effect on the oxygen-insensitive trypsin *in vacuo*, also produced a marked oxygen effect. The enhancement of the oxygen effect in dilute solutions by cysteine has also been noted by Hutchinson (*6*). Furthermore it can be seen (Table IV) that cysteine had no protective effect on a sample of trypsin which already had a high value of D_{vac}.

Attempts were accordingly made to remove the supposed protective agent. Continued dialysis did reduce the value of D_{vac} somewhat, and dialysis against EDTA reduced it almost to the value of D_{air}. This might suggest that the protective agent is a metal ion; but the behavior of the trypsin is rather different from that found in the presence of added metal ions (see below), and, moreover, on ashing trypsin an insignificant amount of inorganic ash was found.

A possible explanation for the absence of an oxygen effect in earlier experiments is that local heating might occur during irradiation at high dose rates. This would be particularly important *in vacuo* where conduction of heat away from the enzyme would be less than in air or oxygen. In this case a curved plot could be expected, since at the higher doses heating would be more serious, whereas at low doses there should be same observable oxygen effect. However, this kind of behavior was not found. Moreover, the substitution of argon for air in one experiment with the sample of trypsin having no oxygen effect gave the following D values: *in vacuo*, 15 to 16 Mr; in oxygen, 15 to 16 Mr; in argon, 17 Mr. The substitution of argon for vacuum thus had no effect.

Addition of Metal Salts

Table II shows the effects observed with the following additives: ferrous and ferric sulfates, cupric sulfate, cobaltous sulfate, cerous sulfate, zinc sulfate.

In the last column, $(D - D°)/D°c$ gives a measure of the relative protective efficiency of the metal ions under the given conditions. The fact that these values are not constant for a given metal indicates that the relation between protection and metal salt concentration is not linear. However, those figures, especially at the lower concentrations, do give a general impression of the relative effectiveness of the different metals.

The only metal ions which gave a high degree of protection *in vacuo* were copper and iron; zinc was weakly effective, and cobalt, thallium, and cerium almost in-

[1] When not specified, values of D mean D_{37}.

TABLE II

INACTIVATION DOSES OF TRYPSIN (TRL 6112) CONTAINING METAL SALTS

Radiation	*Atmosphere*	$D°$ (*without additive*)	*Additive*	*Amount present in solid* (*w/w*), *c*	*D* (*with additive*)	$\frac{D - D°}{D° c}$
15 Mev	Vacuum	12.5	$CuSO_4$	0.013	35.6	142
4 Mev	Vacuum	14.5	$CuSO_4$	0.0135	25.6	57
15 Mev	Air	6.4	$CuSO_4$	0.013	20	163
4 Mev	Air	7	$CuSO_4$	0.0135	~35.6	~300
15 Mev	Vacuum	12	$Fe_2(SO_4)_3$	0.015	26.5	80
15 Mev	Vacuum	12.5	$FeSO_4$	0.003	18.5	160
15 Mev	Vacuum	12.5	$FeSO_4$	0.01	33.3	167
15 Mev	Air	6.4	$FeSO_4$	0.01	25.6	300
15 Mev	Air	7.0	$FeSO_4$	0.01	22.0	120
15 Mev	Vacuum	14.5	$ZnSO_4$	0.02	25.6	38
15 Mev	Air	7	$ZnSO_4$	0.02	~11.5	~32
15 Mev	Vacuum	12.5	$Ce_2(SO_4)_3$	0.01	12.9	3
15 Mev	Air	6.4	$Ce_2(SO_4)_3$	0.01	7.3	14
15 Mev	Vacuum	12.5	$CoSO_4$	0.011	14.8	17
15 Mev	Vacuum	12.5	EDTA	0.57	11.0	−0.24
15 Mev	Vacuum	12.5	$CuSO_4$	0.013	36	145
15 Mev	Vacuum	12.5	{EDTA + $CuSO_4$}	{0.57, 0.01}	19	— 52

effective. Sulfur was also without effect. The variation of the inactivation dose with concentration of metal ion is shown in Fig. 1, and in general it may be said that the rapid initial increase is followed by a leveling off at 1% to 2% additive. Attempts to add 3% and more of metal ion to trypsin led to poor inactivation-dose plots from which it was difficult to obtain a value of *D*.

The degree of protection afforded by copper ions is influenced by the conditions of evacuation of the samples (Table III). Although exhaustive pumping of the "doped" enzyme had no effect on its activity, the radiation protection by the metal was increased considerably (Fig. 1). This may be the result of removal of residual water from the enzyme which is difficult to reproduce in the different experiments.

Cysteine had a comparatively small effect *in vacuo* in trypsin which was already protected with ferrous salt (Table IV). This shows that the effects of cysteine and iron are to some extent competitive.

Absorption Spectra of Complexes

The optical absorption of trypsin solutions is very low between 320 and 800 mμ, and that of copper sulfate in aqueous solution is also low, up to 600 mμ. However, mixtures of enzyme and Cu^{++} in solution at pH 6 showed pronounced absorption

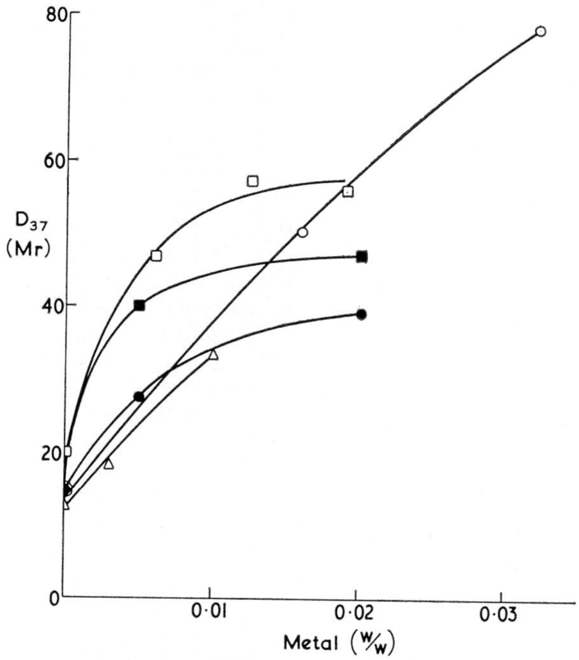

FIG. 1. Protection of solid trypsin by metal ions. Evacuated to 0.02 to 0.04 mm Hg: △ TRL 6112 + Fe^{++}; ○ TRL 6112 + Cu^{++}; ● Seravac + Cu^{++}. Evacuated to < 0.005 mm Hg: □ TRL 6112 + Cu^{++}; ■ Seravac + Cu^{++}.

between 560 and 620 mμ, and to a first approximation this absorption may be taken as that due to the complex. When plotted against the concentration of Cu^{++}, the absorption obtained with a constant quantity of trypsin rapidly approached a limiting value at a copper–trypsin ratio of 4:1 or 5:1, and the complex formation would therefore appear to be complete with this ratio. Figure 2 illustrates the spectrum for the complex obtained by difference, when this ratio is used. The molar extinction coefficient is approximately 180 (1-cm cell), i.e., 35 to 40 per Cu^{++} at the maximum of 670 mμ. When the solutions containing the complex were adjusted to pH 3, the absorption at all wavelengths was merely the sum of copper ion and trypsin contributions. The complex is therefore dissociated at this pH.

Similar curves for the case of Fe^{+++} at pH 5 are given in Fig. 2, but here, because the metal showed pronounced absorption at the low wavelengths, the complexing was regarded as complete when the rate of rise of optical density with added ferric ion at wavelengths from 500 to 580 mμ became equal to that for ferric ion alone. This occurred at a ferric–trypsin ratio of about 2.9:1. The difference spectrum with this proportion is given in Fig. 2. The molar extinction coeffi-

TABLE III

EFFECTS OF COPPER IONS ON SENSITIVITY OF VARIOUS PREPARATIONS OF TRYPSIN TO IONIZING RADIATION

Sample of trypsin	*Treatment*	*Amount of copper ions added*	$D°$	D
TRL 6112	Two dialyses; $P =$	0.016	15.0	50
	0.01 mm	0.031	15.0	78
TRL 6112	Two dialyses; $P <$	0.0062	20.4	47
	0.003 mm	0.0125	20.4	57
		0.019	20.4	~55
TRSF 6118	(Dialyzed);	0.0062	17	48
	$P < 0.003$ mm	0.0125	17	~38
Seravac	$P < 0.003$ mm	0.005	15	40
		0.02	15	47
Seravac	$P = 0.01$ mm	0.005	15	27.2
		0.02	15	39.6
TRSF 6118	Dialyzed; $P \sim 0.01$ mm	0.01	—	25
	Freeze-dried pH 6			

TABLE IV

EFFECT OF MIXTURES OF Fe^{++} AND CYSTEINE ON THE INACTIVATION DOSE OF A TRYPSIN SAMPLE

Additive	*Concentration (w/w)*	D	
		In vacuo	*In air*
Nil	—	21	10
Fe^{++}	0.01	34	22
Fe^{++}	0.01		
+ Cysteine	0.015	39	19
Cysteine alone	0.015	20	10
(Previous result with different sample)	Nil	10	10
Cysteine	0.015	14.6	11

cient of approximately 95 corresponds to 33 per ferric ion, at the maximum of 540 mμ.

In contrast to these results, those for cobaltous ions and trypsin mixtures showed spectra at pH 6 which were virtually the sum of the two constituents, and it is assumed that no complexing occurred. It is not possible to obtain optical evidence of complex formation with colorless ions.

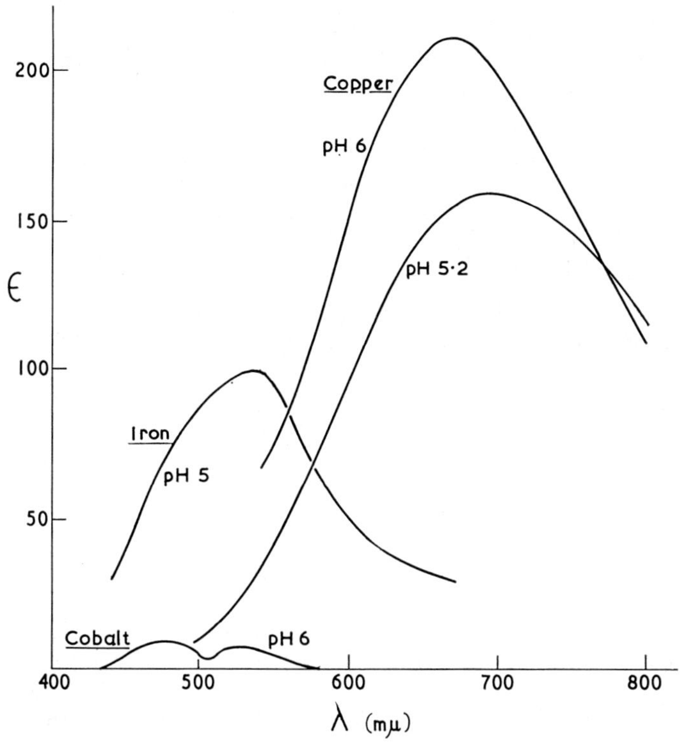

FIG. 2. Absorption spectra of trypsin-metal complexes; ϵ = molar extinction coefficient relative to trypsin.

Effects of the Presence of Oxygen

In all experiments reported here, the D values of *in vacuo* were greater than those in air. This oxygen effect was about twofold but was decreased somewhat by the addition of those metal ions (Table II) which were effective protective agents.

DISCUSSION

In view of the oxygen effects observed in this paper, it is necessary to reconsider the possibility that they may be due to the varying permeability of the solid to oxygen, which might also be affected by the presence of agents like cysteine. If this were the case, it might be expected that the value of D in air would be the variable factor, whereas it is found that the inactivation dose *in vacuo* is variable while its value in oxygen (with one exception) is constant.

Mechanism of Protective Action of Certain Metal Ions

There are two ways in which the presence of metal ions could protect the enzyme from radiation damage:

1. A localization of the primary act by a mechanism such as that envisaged by Fano (*7*), which would diminish the amount of energy deposited in the enzyme, or at least in its active center. Since it has been shown (*8*, *9*) that the —S—S— groups of enzymes are particularly sensitive at least to ultraviolet light, it is possible that the metal ions which are effective are those which are closely associated with —S—S— groups and have a direct protective effect thereon. It has been found that the metal ions which are effective are those in which complex formation with trypsin can be detected, but the sites at which complex (or salt) formation occurs is unknown. Further evidence that complexing is involved in protection is seen in the experiments at the bottom of Table II. These show that the presence of EDTA with copper sulfate markedly reduces the protective action of the copper, and we can conclude that the chelating agent EDTA removes the copper ions from the sites where they effectively protect. It could well be that the complexing occurs at or near the active center, and this results in a stabilization of the enzyme configuration, making it less sensitive to denaturation after the deposition of energy.

It may be noted that the solids containing metal salts have been obtained by freeze-drying from solutions at pH 3. This pH is less favorable to complex formation than pH 6; e.g., in the case of copper, complex formation could be detected at pH 6 but not at pH 3. In an isolated experiment with solids containing 1% copper ion, the preparation at pH 6 was not more sensitive than that prepared at pH 3 (Table III). The conditions operating during the freeze-drying process will, however, be very different from those in dilute solution, and it may be that complexes can be formed under the former conditions which dissociate under the latter.

2. It is also possible that the effective metals act by influencing the processes which occur after the initial ionization. As previously suggested by Butler and Robins (*1*), the initial ionization must be succeeded by processes which lead eventually to the return of electrons to their original or similar sites. Instability occurs in the interval between ionization and neutralization, during which the ionized molecules may undergo changes of configuration. In this view any agent which accelerates the neutralization process will reduce the damage done to enzyme molecules, and metal ions, especially those which have electronic states of not greatly differing energies, might act in this way. A similar mechanism of protection by cysteine has been proposed (*2*), involving the donation of hydrogen atoms from the protective agent to the ionized enzyme, but protection by metal ions cannot be explained in this way.

The oxygen effects provide a possible way of distinguishing between these

TABLE V

VARIATIONS OF OXYGEN EFFECT CAUSED BY THE PRESENCE OF METAL SALTS, DERIVED FROM DATA IN TABLE II

Metal ion added	D_{vac}/D_{air}
None	1.8–2.0
Cu^{++}, 1.3%	1.4–1.8
Fe^{++}, 1%	1.5–1.6
Zn^{++}, 2%	2.2
Tl^{+}, 1%	2.1
Ce^{+++}, 1%	1.8

mechanisms. The protective metals (Table V) decrease the ratio D_{vac}/D_{air} somewhat, whereas the ineffective metals do not change it at all. This would fit in with the first mechanism, according to which it is expected that the effect of the metal ion is to reduce the fraction of the energy deposited in the enzyme, without modifying the conditions under which this fraction acts. On the other hand, as shown previously by ourselves (*1*, *3*) and by other authors (*6*), protection by cysteine is greatly influenced by oxygen.[2] This could easily be explained if cysteine acts as a hydrogen donor, by the supposition that in the presence of oxygen the hydrogen is intercepted.

The effect of the presence of oxygen on the electron-return mechanism is not clear, although it might result in a simple neutralization process's being converted into a peroxidation.

So far the facts have been established, the first mechanism appears to account for the phenomenon adequately.

SUMMARY

1. The samples of trypsin used in this investigation are oxygen sensitive with D_{vac}/D_{air} about 2 for pulsed electrons. As added cysteine has little effect on the inactivation doses, it appears that these samples already contain a protective agent, which, however, is not readily removed.

2. Copper and iron sulfates, when present in the solid enzyme, increase the inactivation dose considerably; but cobalt, thallous, and cerous sulfates are ineffective. Zinc sulfate has a small protective action.

3. Copper and iron sulfates form complexes with trypsin which can be detected by their optical absorption, and the maximum complex formation occurs at about the concentration which gives the maximum protective effect. Cobalt sulfate does not form a complex detectable in this way.

4. The effect of oxygen on the samples containing copper and iron is somewhat

[2] As was pointed out above, cysteine has very little protective effect on the samples of trypsin used here and thus does not modify the oxygen effect already present.

less than on the original trypsin; with the other metal salts, the effect of oxygen is the same as on trypsin alone.

5. There appear to be two types of protective action, in which (*a*) the effect of oxygen is not greatly different from its effect when the agent is absent (metal ions); (*b*) the effect of oxygen is enhanced by the protective agent (e.g., cysteine). Mechanisms of these processes are discussed.

ACKNOWLEDGMENTS

We are very grateful to Miss S. P. Whiting for assistance with the experimental work. We also acknowledge irradiation facilities provided by Dr. R. Roberts, Wantage Research Laboratory, A.E.R.E., Wantage, Berks., and by Professor J. Rotblat, Radiotherapy Department, St. Bartholomew's Hospital, London.

This investigation has been supported by grants to the Chester Beatty Research Institute (Institute of Cancer Research: Royal Cancer Hospital) from the Medical Research Council, the British Empire Cancer Campaign, the Anna Fuller Fund, and the National Cancer Institute of the National Institutes of Health, U. S. Public Health Service.

RECEIVED: October 30, 1962

REFERENCES

1. J. A. V. BUTLER, and A. B. ROBINS, Effects of oxygen on the inactivation of enzymes by ionizing radiations. II. Solid trypsin and deoxyribonuclease. *Radiation Res.* **17,** 63–73 (1962).
2. P. HOWARD-FLANDERS, Effect of oxygen in the radiosensitivity of bacteriophage in the presence of sulphydryl compounds. *Nature* **186,** 485 (1960).
3. J. A. V. BUTLER, and A. B. ROBINS, Metal ion redox systems as radiation protective agents. *Nature* **193,** 673–674 (1962).
4. J. A. V. BUTLER and A. B. ROBINS, Effects of oxygen on the inactivation of enzymes by ionizing radiations. 1. Dilute solutions of trypsin and deoxyribonuclease. *Radiation Res.* **16,** 7–17 (1962).
5. J. D. GERATZ, The effect of aliphatic amino-acids on the activation of trypsinogen and on the stability of trypsin solutions. *Biochim. Biophys. Acta* **56,** 599–601 (1962).
6. F. HUTCHINSON, Sulfhydryl groups and the oxygen effect on irradiated dilute solutions of enzymes and nucleic acids. *Radiation Res.* **14,** 721–731 (1961).
7. U. FANO, Normal modes of a lattice of oscillations with many resonances and dipolar coupling. *Phys. Rev.* **118,** 451–455 (1960).
8. R. SETLOW, A relation between the cysteine content and the ultraviolet sensitivity of proteins. *Biochim. Biophys. Acta* **16,** 445 (1955).
9. L. G. AUGENSTEIN and C. A. GHIRON, The inactivation of trypsin by ultra-violet light. I. The correlation of inactivation with the disruption of constituent cystine. *Proc. Natl. Acad. Sci. U. S.* **47,** 1530–1547 (1961).

RADIATION RESEARCH 19, 593–598 (1963)

The Radiation-Sensitizing Effects of *N*-Ethylmaleimide and Iodoacetic Acid on a Radiation-Resistant *Micrococcus*[1,2]

J. S. LEE, A. W. ANDERSON, AND P. R. ELLIKER

Department of Microbiology, Oregon State University, Corvallis, Oregon

INTRODUCTION

Reagents that combine with sulfhydryl groups have been shown to increase radiation sensitivity of certain microorganisms (*1–3*).

Bridges (*1, 2*) postulated that the sensitization was brought about by the reactions between the sensitizers and the irradiation-activated sulfhydryl groups of vital cellular structures. The results obtained in this laboratory with a radiation-resistant microorganism suggest that other nonspecific reactions may occur as a result of radiotoxic products formed from the test compound. The effects of *N*-ethylmaleimide (NEM) and iodoacetic acid (IAA) added to bacterial suspensions during irradiation were investigated, and the possible mechanisms of their action when exposed to γ-radiation discussed.

MATERIALS AND METHODS

Micrococcus radiodurans was first isolated by Anderson *et al.* (*4, 5*) and is available from the American Type Culture Collection, Washington, D. C. This microorganism has an LD_{50} of 2 to 5 $\times$ 10^5 rads in 0.067 *M* phosphate buffer. This is at least one hundred times as great as the reported LD_{50} of most nonsporulating bacteria when exposed in the presence of oxygen (*6*).

The use of this organism for the investigation of sensitizers is advantageous in that it provides cells of high radiation resistance. This enables application of high radiation intensities which in turn produce basic physicochemical changes within the cell not observed at lower radiation levels. Such information also provides a better approach to the understanding of the mechanism of radiation resistance.

[1] This investigation was supported in part by PHS Grant 00064-06 from Radiological Health Division, U. S. Public Health Service.

[2] Technical Paper No. 1634, Oregon Agricultural Experiment Station. Contribution of the Department of Microbiology.

The cells were grown in a synthetic medium (*7*) cultured at 30°C on a shaker in 100-ml volumes. When the cells approached the terminal logarithmic (log) stage (approximately 48 hours) ten flasks were pooled, and the cells were washed twice by centrifugation in 0.067 *M* sterile phosphate buffer. The cells obtained at this growth stage gave the most consistent radioinactivation patterns. The packed cells were resuspended in buffer to give approximately 6×10^7 cells/ml.

Stock solutions of NEM[3] and IAA[3] were prepared in 0.067 *M* sterile phosphate buffer to give 10,000 μM solutions and stored at 4°C when not used.

The irradiation test vials[4] were filled with 10 ml of cell suspension plus different concentrations of NEM and IAA for the toxicity determinations. A final concentration of 100 μM each of NEM and IAA was used for the sensitization experiments. The final cell population was approximately 3×10^7 per milliliter as determined by plating on Difco standard plate count agar (TGY) and incubating at 30°C for 48 to 52 hours.

The pigments of *M. radiodurans*, zeaxanthin and lycophyll, were identified by their absorption spectra. Several other unidentified carotinoid-like pigments were also observed (*8*). The approximate pigment content was determined by measuring the optical densities at 475 mμ of a crude pigment extract obtained from a packed cell mass suspended in ten times its volume of a 10:10:3 mixture of petroleum ether (boiling range 30° to 75°C), acetone, and absolute methanol. The major portion of the pigment was recovered in the supernatant after storage at 4°C overnight (*8*).

Toxicity determinations of NEM and IAA alone without radiation were carried out by exposing the cells to different concentrations of chemicals at room temperature for 4 hours. Viable counts then were made from each tube and cultured as indicated above.

The irradiation was carried out with a cobalt-60 γ-radiation source at a dose rate of 3×10^5 r/hr.

RESULTS

Toxicity of the Chemicals in Absence of Radiation

Figure 1 shows the decrease of the viability as a function of the chemical concentrations of NEM and IAA. The toxic threshold concentrations were 150 μM for NEM and 350 μM for IAA. It was observed that the toxicity of NEM and IAA increased progressively up to 30 minutes of incubation time, suggesting a cumulative effect. After this time, no further increase in toxicity was observed. In order to eliminate the above effect and to take into account radiation exposure time, all test cells were in contact with the chemicals for 4 hours.

[3] NEM and IAA were obtained from Eastman Organic Chemicals, Rochester, New York.

[4] Thin-walled vials of 20-ml capacity made for liquid scintillation counting by Wheaton Glass Co., Millville, New Jersey.

Effect of Radiation with NEM and IAA

The rate of destruction was increased for the cells irradiated in the presence of IAA, but no effect was observed for NEM (Fig. 2). The above results were obtained for cells irradiated under atmospheric oxygen tension. Nitrogen flushing was carried out by bubbling nitrogen through the suspending medium for 30 minutes and then sealing the tubes. This modification did not change their sensitivities. Cells left in contact with IAA for 4 hours, then centrifuged and resuspended in buffer before irradiation, were not sensitized. The IAA was effective only when present in the suspending medium during the time of radiation exposure. Addition of IAA to postirradiated cells produced no effect. Conversely, suspending the cells in a 100 μM solution of previously irradiated IAA was not toxic, suggesting that most of the toxic products formed during irradiation exposure were short-lived or developed within the cell.

Results shown in Fig. 3 indicate that the total cellular pigment content decreases more rapidly in the cells irradiated in the presence of IAA than in the cells irradiated in phosphate buffer. Results with NEM were comparable to phosphate buffer.

DISCUSSION

The toxicity of NEM and IAA in the presence of radiation has been postulated to be due to the specific combining reactions with vital sulfhydryl groups (*2*). Bridges (*1*) observed that NEM was effective as a radiation sensitizer only in the absence of oxygen, suggesting that the sensitizer was in competition with oxygen. Both NEM and IAA were toxic to *M. radiodurans* at high concentrations. On the

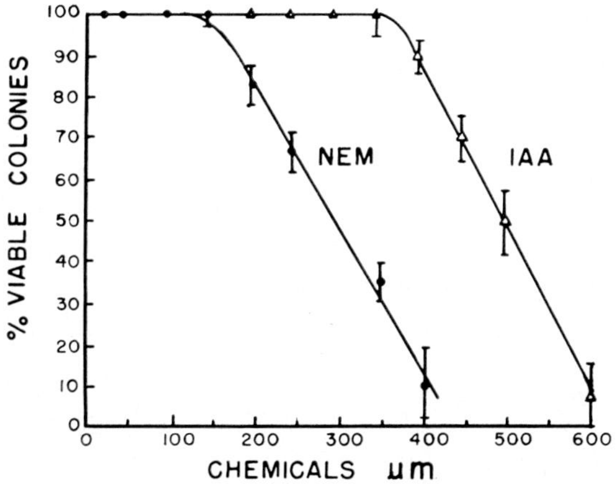

FIG. 1. The effects of NEM and IAA in reducing the viability of *M. radiodurans*, after exposure for 4 hours. The vertical lines represent the range of variations obtained from three separate determinations.

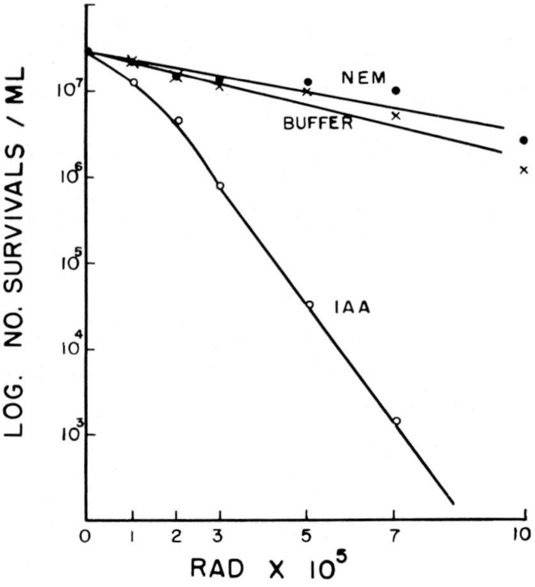

FIG. 2. The radiation-sensitizing effects of NEM and IAA. Cells were irradiated under atmospheric oxygen tension.

basis of Bridges' (*1, 2*) observation, this may be due to blocking of certain sulfhydryl groups essential to the vital processes. The concentrations of NEM and IAA used for irradiation experiments were below the toxic level. The action of IAA under this condition is distinct from that of NEM. Radiation is considered to produce more reactive sulfhydryl groups in the cell; however, the markedly different radiosensitizing effects of NEM and IAA indicate that IAA reacts with other groups in addition to the sulfhydryl.

No sensitization was brought about with NEM either in the presence or in the absence of oxygen. The sensitizing effect of IAA was not influenced by oxygen. This suggests that the mechanism involved with *M. radiodurans* is different from what Bridges (*1, 2*) observed with *Escherichia coli* B/r.

It was also observed that the amount of IAA retained by the cell did not reach the critical sensitizing level and that the free IAA must furnish additional effects during irradiation.

Iodoacetic acid is not highly specific for the sulfhydryl group, and other nucleophilic reagents such as amino and phenolic-hydroxyl groups might have been involved in reactions with IAA (*9*). This may account for some of the sensitizing effects.

A further possibility is the reaction involving the radiolytic products of IAA (*10, 11*). This hypothesis is further substantiated by detecting the release of

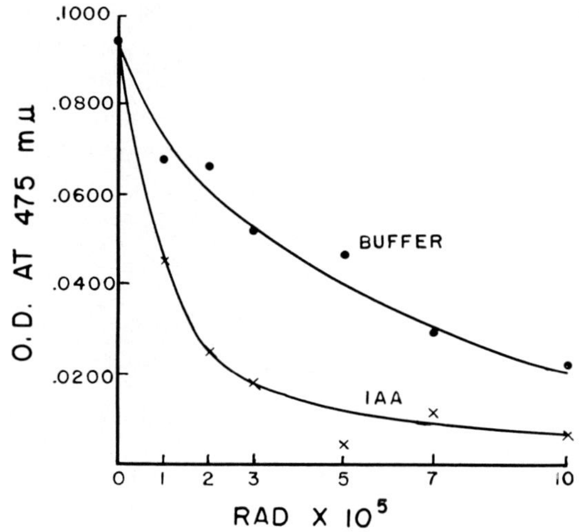

FIG. 3. The loss of pigmentation of irradiated cells with and without IAA. See text for the explanation.

iodide ions or iodide radicals from IAA by irradiating an IAA starch mixture and determining the color intensity of the starch iodide complex. The release of iodide ions or iodide radicals from IAA is dose-dependent and could be used to measure the radiation dose from 3×10^4 to 5×10^5 rads. The presence of starch with IAA is necessary to trap the short-lived radical formed (unpublished observations). The radiolytic products of IAA, the iodide radicals, iodide ions, the alkyl radicals, and ions may play a significant role in sensitization, owing to their high reactivities. They may not only combine with activated sulfhydryl or hydroxyl groups of the cell but may also react with the —C═C— bonds. The rapid loss of pigment color in irradiated cells in the presence of IAA suggests this as a possibility, since the chromophores of the carotenoids are made up exclusively of conjugated carbon double bonds.

The sensitizing effect of irradiated IAA appears to depend more heavily on its highly reactive free radicals and their broadened reactivities than on its sulfhydryl combining action alone. The inability of NEM to sensitize the cell despite its specificity for sulfhydryl groups bears out the above postulation. In the light of the above observations it is more appropriate that IAA should be classed as a radiolethal or radiotoxic compound. This radiolethal effect has also been noted with other halogenated compounds under investigation in this laboratory.

SUMMARY

The sulfhydryl group combining agents, *N*-ethylmaleimide (NEM) and iodoacetic acid (IAA), were investigated for their abilities to enhance γ-radiation inactivation of *Micrococcus radiodurans*. At the nontoxic level of 100 μM, the inactivation by irradiation was accelerated with IAA, but no effect was observed with NEM. The removal of oxygen did not produce any detectable changes in the action of either chemical. The accelerated radiolethal effect appears to be due to the highly reactive radiolytic products of IAA and their nonspecific reactions with various cellular constituents.

ACKNOWLEDGMENT

We are indebted to Miss Diana Fieber for technical assistance.

RECEIVED: November 12, 1962

REFERENCES

1. B. A. BRIDGES, The effect of *N*-ethylmaleimide on the radiation sensitivity of bacteria. *J. Gen. Microbiol.* **26,** 467–472 (1961).
2. B. A. BRIDGES, The chemical sensitization of *Pseudomonas* species to ionizing radiation. *Radiation Res.* **16,** 232–242 (1962).
3. M. KIGA, Y. ANDO, and H. KOIKE, Enhancement of radiobiological effect by malonic and maleic acids. *Science* **122,** 331–332 (1955).
4. A. W. ANDERSON, H. C. NORDAN, R. F. CAIN, G. PARRISH, and D. DUGGAN, Studies on a radioresistant micrococcus. I. Isolation, morphology, cultural characteristics and resistance to gamma radiation. *Food Technol.* **10,** 575–577 (1956).
5. D. E. DUGGAN, A. W. ANDERSON, P. R. ELLIKER, and R. F. CAIN, Ultraviolet exposure studies on a gamma radiation resistant micrococcus isolated from food. *Food Res.* **24,** 376–382 (1959).
6. S. E. GUNTER and H. I. KOHN, The effect of X-rays on the survival of bacteria and yeast. I. A comparative study of the dose survival curves of *Azotobacter agile, Escherichia coli, Pseudomonas fluorescens, Rhodopseudomonas spheroides,* and *Saccharomyces cerevisiae* irradiated in the resting state. *J. Bacteriol.* **71,** 571–581 (1956).
7. H. D. RAJ, F. L. DURYEE, A. M. DEENEY, C. H. WANG, A. W. ANDERSON, and P. R. ELLIKER, Utilization of carbohydrates and amino acids by *Micrococcus radiodurans. Can. J. Microbiol.* **6,** 289–298 (1960).
8. J. S. LEE, Spectrophotometric characterization of carotenoid pigments isolated from *Micrococcus radiodurans.* M.S. Thesis, Oregon State University, Corvallis, Oregon, 1962.
9. P. D. BOYER, Sulfhydryl and disulfide groups of enzymes. In *The Enzymes* (P. D. Boyer, H Lardy, and K. Myrbäck, eds.), 2nd ed., Vol. 1, Chapter 11, Academic Press, New York, 1959.
10. R. H. SCHULER and R. C. PETRY, Decomposition of liquid alkyl iodides by 120 KVP X-irradiation. *J. Am. Chem. Soc.* **78,** 3954–3958 (1956).
11. E. O. HORNIG and J. H. WILLARD, Effects of structure, product concentration, oxygen, temperature and phase on the radiolysis of alkyl iodides. *J. Am. Chem. Soc.* **79,** 2429–2434 (1956).

RADIATION RESEARCH **19**, 599–605 (1963)

Assessment of Actinomycin and Radiation Damage of Stem Cells by the Erythropoietin Tolerance Test

CLIFFORD W. GURNEY AND DIANA HOFSTRA

Argonne Cancer Research Hospital[1] and the Department of Medicine, the University of Chicago, Chicago, Illinois

INTRODUCTION

The damaging effects of actinomycin (*1*) and X-radiation on the bone marrow are well recognized, and the combined use of actinomycin D and radiation has been described on a number of occasions (*2–8*). The additive effects have been well documented, and it is therefore of interest to record the measurement of the damaging effect of actinomycin D alone or in combination with radiation on the primitive, undifferentiated cells of the hemopoietic system, generally considered to be the progenitors of blood formation. For these investigations, the "erythropoietin tolerance test" was employed. The basis of this test is the impairment of response of the hypertransfused mouse to a standard dose of erythropoietin after injury of the primitive cells of the hemopoietic organs (*9–11*).

METHODS

Young virgin Carworth Farms No. 1 female mice, 10 to 12 weeks of age and weighing 20 to 25 gm, were employed in these investigations. Animals were rendered polycythemic by two daily injections of 1 ml of packed homologous mouse red cells given intraperitoneally. Experiments were not begun until at least 5 days after the second transfusion. Eight mice were present in each control and test group.

Solutions of actinomycin D[2] were prepared immediately before injection, the desired amount of antibiotic being dissolved in a volume of saline equal in milliliters to 1% of the weight of the mouse in grams. This material was injected via the tail vein, with a 1-ml tuberculin syringe and a No. 25 needle.

Animals to be irradiated were confined in perforated Lusteroid tubes on a Lucite turntable rotating at the rate of 3½ rpm. They were exposed to a single

[1] Operated by the University of Chicago for the U. S. Atomic Energy Commission.

[2] Actinomycin D was kindly supplied by Dr. Elmer Alpert of Merck, Sharp and Dohme Research Laboratory.

dose of 150 r of X-rays from a General Electric Maxitron 250 machine operated at 250 kvp and 30 ma, with a filter of 0.25 mm Cu plus 1 mm Al, and a half-value layer of 1.04 mm Cu. The target distance was 79 cm, and rate of irradiation was 61 r/min.

A dose of six units of erythropoietin,[3] obtained from anemic sheep plasma and representing 720-fold purification of the raw plasma, was administered subcutaneously in 0.2 ml of normal saline. In experiments which measured the damage of stem cells by actinomycin alone or in combination with irradiation, the erythropoietin was administered within 30 minutes after the actinomycin or irradiation. The erythropoietic response to erythropoietin was measured by administration of 0.5 μc of Fe^{59} chloride intravenously 60 hours after erythropoietin. We have found the interval between 48 and 60 hours to be the optimal time after erythropoietin at which to administer Fe^{59} chloride. Three days after administration of radioiron, the animals were sacrificed, and a measured amount of blood was taken from the cervical vein. Radioactivity in peripheral red cells was determined in a scintillation well counter, and from an estimation of the total blood volume of these animals (approximately 7% of the body weight) and a standard prepared at the time of the injection of the radioiron into the animals, it was possible to calculate the per cent of the injected tracer dose of radioiron incorporated into peripheral red cells. It was not considered necessary to include control groups of plethoric animals not given erythropoietin, since in over 100 such plethoric animals previously studied the 72-hour incorporation of radioiron into peripheral cells was less than 0.3% of the tracer dose administered.

In studying the recovery of the stem cell compartment from the damaging effects of actinomycin, different groups of animals were given actinomycin on different days before administration of erythropoietin. All of them were injected with erythropoietin on the same day and radioiron 60 hours later. All animals were sacrificed 3 days after radioiron injection. In this manner, a single control group serves adequately for all test groups. Forty-seven hours before erythropoietin administration, all mice in the recovery experiment were given a single intravenous booster transfusion of 0.5 ml of packed mouse erythrocytes to ensure maintenance of the plethoric state for the duration of the experiment.

RESULTS

Figure 1 shows the impairment of radioiron incorporation in response to a standard erythropoietin stimulation in the hypertransfused animal as a function of the dose of actinomycin. Mean values, plus or minus the standard deviation of the mean, are plotted. Thirty-six per cent of the tracer was incorporated into newly formed red cells in the saline injected control mice, and 33 μg of actinomycin per kilogram demonstrated very slight impairment of erythropoiesis. From this

[3] Erythropoietin employed in this investigation was made available from the Hematology Study Section of the U. S. Public Health Service.

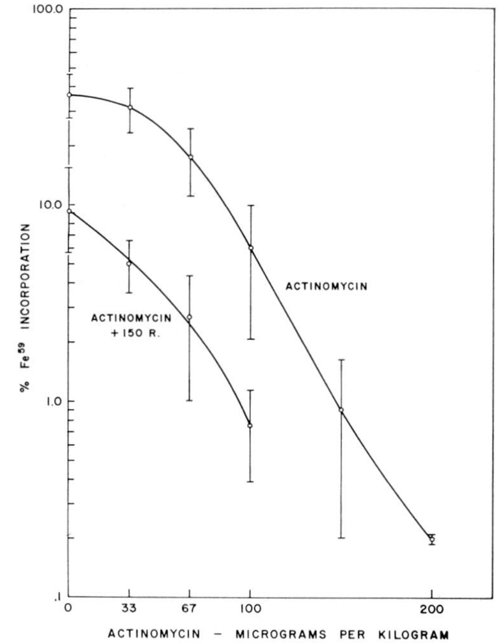

FIG. 1. Impairment of stem cell response to erythropoietin by actinomycin D or actinomycin + 150 r of irradiation in the polycythemic mouse.

point, however, the damage to stem cells, as measured by impaired responsiveness to erythropoietin, increased rapidly with increasing doses of actinomycin. The degree to which 150 r is additive to actinomycin is also indicated. It will be noted that 150 r of radiation is equivalent to approximately 87 μg of actinomycin per kilogram.

Figure 2 records the impairment of response to erythropoietin as a function of administration of 87 μg/kg intravenously at varying times prior to erythropoietic challenge. Little recovery of the "stem cell compartment" from the damaging effect of actinomycin is observed when erythropoietin is administered 24 or 48 hours after actinomycin. When the challenging dose of erythropoietin is administered 96 or 120 hours after actinomycin, the system appears to recover completely; but a group of animals in which actinomycin was administered 6 days before erythropoietin challenge again demonstrates a striking impairment of erythropoietic response to 6 units of erythropoietin.

DISCUSSION

Discussing the synergistic effect of actinomycin D and X-irradiation on the dysplastic changes of growing hairs, Griem and Ranniger recently stated: "The most difficult problem faced by investigators has been the lack of a suitable bio-

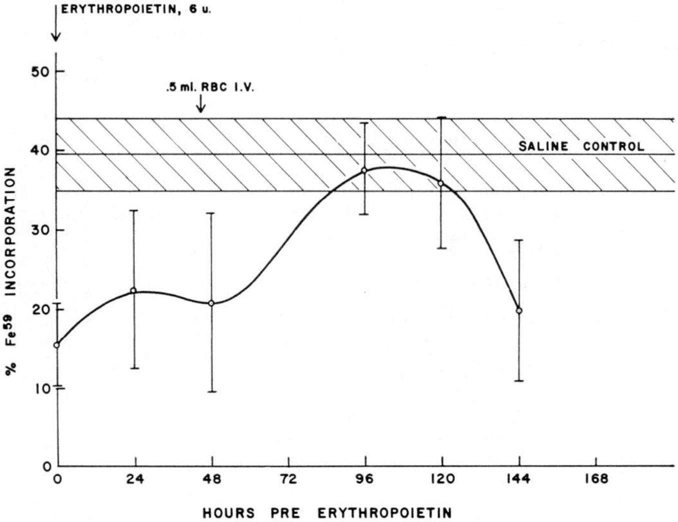

FIG. 2. Stem cell response to erythropoietin after actinomycin D, 87 μg/kg intravenously. Abscissa records the hours before erythropoietin administration when actinomycin D was administered to the various groups.

logical indicator system which could be used for preliminary observations on the combined effects of drug and x-rays for comparison with the effects of either agent alone" (*8*). We report here another system which quantitative measurements of damage of X-irradiation alone or in conjunction with chemotherapeutic agents may be determined. A number of such systems must be devised and explored in great detail, if the combined effects of chemotherapy and X-irradiation are to be investigated intensively. Different systems will afford unique advantages. The present system is of interest to us because the quantity of actinomycin or irradiation which can be tolerated is limited by the bone marrow damage sustained, and the test system employed here yields direct measurement of bone marrow damage. Several investigators have independently concluded that the principal action of erythropoietin is on the stem cell, that is, the primitive, undifferentiated cell of the bone marrow (*12–14*). This is probably the critical cell in determining radiation damage, if the stem cell is multipotential. Although evidence is mounting which indicates that the lymphocytic cells arise from different precursors than the myeloid cells (*15, 17*), there have as yet been no indications that the blood cells produced in the marrow have more than one separate species of precursor. We have described in detail elsewhere the cessation of erythropoiesis in the hypertransfused animal, and the use of this model in the study of the physiology of erythropoiesis (*14, 18*). Erythropoietin initiates a wave of red cell production by differentiation of stem cells into the series of nucleated erythrocyte precursors.

This mechanism of action is suggested by three different methods of investigation (*12–14*) and is considered the primary mechanism of action, although other effects have also been described (*19, 20*). We have concluded that impairment of this response after irradiation or the administration of a chemotherapeutic agent is a manifestation of damage of stem cells (*9, 10*).

Griem and Ranniger found that the number of dysplastic hairs produced as a consequence of actinomycin D administration does not strikingly increase until the dose rate is above 400 μg/kg (*8*). This is in contrast with a striking damaging effect of actinomycin on the stem cell when administered in doses as small as 100 μg/kg. Such a difference in result might well have been predicted, since the production of dysplastic hairs in response to X-irradiation is not noted until doses well in excess of 200 r are administered, whereas 200 r of total-body irradiation has a profound effect on damage of stem cells as measured in the system employed here (*9*).

Recovery of the "stem cell compartment " in the hypertransfused animal after administration of a small dose of actinomycin is of interest. When irradiation producing a comparable initial damage is administered, recovery is not complete until the seventh day (*21*), and the system then remains normal through the fifteenth day (C. W. Gurney, unpublished observations). The pattern of recovery of the stem cell compartment after actinomycin injection is distinctly different, with apparent complete recovery being observed on the fourth day, but with subsequent demonstration of residual damage in the system on the sixth day. In this respect, the pattern of recovery of the stem cell compartment after damage from actinomycin D resembles that obtained with other chemotherapeutic agents (*11*) and is different from that reported by us after X-irradiation. Therefore, although the results of the present experiment indicate the effects of actinomycin and irradiation on a class of primitive erythropoietin-responsive cells of the hematopoietic system are additive, and although dose-response curves relating impairment of response to irradiation or actinomycin make it possible to determine an amount of one which will produce a degree of damage comparable with any dose of the other, the distinctly different patterns of recovery after injury suggest that some basic fundamental difference between the two modes of injury exists. The significance of the early apparent "recovery" after administration of actinomycin, with subsequent demonstration of residual damage, is currently under investigation.

SUMMARY

1. A technique for the measurement of the combined effect of X-irradiation and actinomycin D on the responsiveness of stem cells to erythropoietin has been reported.

2. Findings indicate that, when irradiation is administered immediately after actinomycin injection, deleterious effects on the stem cell, as measured by the

erythropoietin tolerance test, are additive. Approximately 87 μg of actinomycin per kilogram produces the same impairment of response to a standard dose of erythropoietin as does 150 r of total-body irradiation.

3. Although the response to a standard dose of erythropoietin in the hypertransfused animal is normal 4 and 5 days after administration of the 87 μg of actinomycin D per kilogram, residual damage in such animals can be detected when the challenging dose of erythropoietin is delayed until the sixth day.

RECEIVED: November 15, 1962

REFERENCES

1. F. S. PHILIPS, H. S. SCHWARTZ, S. S. STERNBERG, and C. T. C. TAN, The toxicity of actinomycin D. *Ann. N. Y. Acad. Sci.* **89,** 348–360 (1960).
2. R. E. BASES, Modification of radiation response determined by single cell techniques: actinomycin D. *Cancer Res.* **19,** 1223–1229 (1959).
3. P. Y. CHEN and E. J. LIEBNER, *In vitro* effects of X irradiation combined with actinomycin D. *Radiology* **76,** 273–274 (1961).
4. G. J. D'ANGIO, S. FARBER, and C. L. MADDOCK, Potentiation of x-ray effects by actinomycin D. *Radiology* **73,** 175–177 (1959).
5. C. L. MADDOCK, G. J. D'ANGIO, S. FARBER, and A. H. HANDLER, Biological studies of actinomycin D. *Ann. N. Y. Acad. Sci.* **89,** 386–398 (1960).
6. S. FARBER, G. J. D'ANGIO, A. EVANS, and A. MITUS, Clinical studies of actinomycin D, with special reference to Wilm's tumor in children. *Ann. N. Y. Acad. Sci.* **89,** 421–425 (1960).
7. C. T. C. TAN, R. B. GOBBEY, C. L. YAP, N. WOLLNER, C. A. HACKETHAL, L. M. MURPHY, H. W. DARGEON, and J. H. BURCHENAL, Clinical experiences with actinomycins D, KS2, and F_1 (KS4). *Ann. N. Y. Acad. Sci.* **89,** 426–444 (1960).
8. M. L. GRIEM and K. RANNIGER, Modification of the radiation effect on hair roots of the mouse by actinomycin. *Radiation Res.* **17,** 92–100 (1962).
9. C. W. GURNEY and N. WACKMAN, Impairment of erythropoiesis by irradiation. *Nature* **190,** 1017 (1961).
10. C. W. GURNEY, R. DEGOWIN, D. HOFSTRA, and J. BYRON, Applications of erythropoietin to biological investigation. In *Erythropoiesis* (L. O. Jacobson and M. Doyle, eds.), Section 5, Grune and Stratton, New York, 1962.
11. C. W. GURNEY, Dynamics of the stem cell compartment. *Proc. 9th Intern. Congr. Hematol.* In press.
12. E. L. ALPEN and D. CRANMORE, Observations on the regulation of erythropoiesis and on cellular dynamics by Fe^{59} autoradiography. In *The Kinetics of Cellular Proliferation* (F. S. Stohlman, Jr., ed.), pp. 290–300, Grune and Stratton, New York, 1959.
13. A. J. ERSLEV, The effect of anemic anoxia on cellular development of nucleated red cells. *Blood* **14,** 386–398 (1959).
14. E. FILMANOWICZ and C. W. GURNEY, Studies on erythropoiesis. XVI. The response to a single dose of erythropoietin in the polycythemic mouse. *J. Lab. Clin. Med.* **57,** 65–72 (1961).
15. H. S. MICKLEM and C. E. FORD, Proliferation of injected lymph node and thymus cells in lethally irradiated mice. *Transplant. Bull.* **26,** 436–441 (1960).
16. L. O. JACOBSON, E. K. MARKS, E. L. SIMMONS, and E. O. GASTON, Immune response in irradiated mice with Peyer's patch shielding. *Proc. Soc. Exptl. Biol. Med.* **108,** 487–493 (1961).

17. B. M. Gesner and J. L. Gowans, The fate of lethally irradiated mice given isologous and heterologous thoracic duct lymphocytes. *Brit. J. Exptl. Pathol.* **43,** 431–440 (1962).
18. C. W. Gurney, N. Wackman, and E. Filmanowicz, Studies on erythropoiesis. XVII. Some quantitative aspects of the erythropoietic response to erythropoietin. *Blood* **17,** 531–546 (1961).
19. J. Winkert, A. S. Gordon, and E. L. Winkert, Purification and physiological effects of human urinary erythropoietin. *Trans. N. Y. Acad. Sci.* **24,** 135–139 (1961).
20. A. S. Gordon, J. LoBue, B. S. Dornfest, and G. W. Cooper, Reticulocyte and leukocyte release from isolated perfused rat legs and femurs. In *Erythropoiesis* (L. O. Jacobson and M. Doyle, eds.), Section 8, pp. 321–327, Grune and Stratton, New York, 1962.
21. C. W. Gurney, L. G. Lajtha, and R. Oliver, A method for investigation of stem cell kinetics. *Brit. J. Hematol.* **8,** 461 (1962).

RADIATION RESEARCH **19**, 606–620 (1963)

The Linear Energy Transfer Distributions Resulting from Primary and Scattered X-Rays and Gamma Rays with Primary HVL's from 1.25 mm Cu to 11 mm Pb

W. R. BRUCE, M. L. PEARSON, AND HELEN S. FREEDHOFF

Department of Medical Biophysics, University of Toronto and Physics Section, Ontario Cancer Institute, Toronto, Canada

INTRODUCTION

The microscopic spatial distribution of energy absorption in a medium irradiated by ionizing radiation is most easily conceived in terms of linear energy transfer (LET). For X-rays and γ-rays this is the rate at which the electrons that are set in motion by the radiation lose energy along their paths. A number of calculations have been made to determine the LET distributions that result from X-radiation and γ-radiation (*1–3*). The most recent (*4–6*) were made for a wide range of initial energies and included the effects of delta (secondary) electrons. Since these calculations were made, however, theoretical and experimental studies of X-ray penetration (*7–11*) and an extensive tabulation of the spectra of slowed-down electrons based on a more rigorous analysis of electron scattering (*12, 13*) have become available. These developments have made it possible to determine the LET distributions of electrons set in motion in water by X-rays and γ-rays for a variety of radiation geometries and for a wide range of energies. They permit an examination of at least two problems of interest in radiation biology.

Cells exposed to a beam of X-rays or γ-rays at a depth in tissue are subject to a spectrum of radiation that may differ considerably from that of the primary as a result of the contribution of low-energy scattered radiation. The resulting change in the spectrum will give rise to a change in the LET distribution that could well be reflected in the relative biological effect (RBE) of the radiation. A direct comparison of the calculated LET distributions for primary radiation and for radiation at a depth in tissue should show whether the two differ significantly and thus suggest whether there is likely to be a detectable difference in the RBE's of the radiation in these two geometrical situations.

Secondly, in order to interpret the variation of the RBE with the energy of the X-ray and γ-ray energy, it is first necessary to know to what degree the microscopic distribution of the energy absorption varies with the radiation. This information s given by the LET distributions of the radiation.

LINEAR ENERGY TRANSFER DISTRIBUTION

The calculation of the LET distribution of electrons set in motion by X-rays or γ-rays in water was carried out in a series of steps. First, the photon energy spectrum was used to calculate the spectrum of initial electrons—that is, the number of electrons set in motion per cubic centimeter of water. These electrons are slowed down by processes that yield excitations, ionizations, and in some cases energetic secondary electrons. The energy spectrum of all the degraded, scattered, and secondary electrons set in motion by the initial electrons was calculated from the data given by McGinnies (*13*). This procedure yielded a spectrum of slowed-down electrons in units of electrons per energy interval per square centimeter. The LET distribution was finally calculated from this spectrum by assuming that each electron lost energy at a rate characteristic of its energy. The stopping-power equation used to obtain this average energy loss per unit length along the track may include losses up to one-half of the electron's energy in one interaction. The secondary electron resulting from such a process may in fact be more energetic than many primary electrons. It is necessary in calculating LET, therefore, to specify a maximum energy loss that may still be considered to occur "on the track," and to consider losses of energy greater than this as giving rise to electrons that produce tracks of their own. LET distributions have been calculated for two such maximum energy losses.

Four X-ray and four γ-ray spectra were used in these calculations. Each corresponded to the energies and geometries likely to be encountered in a laboratory, and they are listed in Table I. The four measured X-ray spectra were obtained by

TABLE I
RADIATION SPECTRA COMPARED IN THIS INVESTIGATION

A	(1) Primary X-radiation, HVL 1.25 mm Cu	
	(2) Primary and scattered: depth 10 cm, area 400 cm², SSD 50 cm	(*8*)
B	(1) Primary, HVL 3.2 mm Cu	
	(2) Primary and scattered, depth 10 cm, area 400 cm², SSD 50 cm	(*8*)
C	(1) Primary from Cs^{137}, 0.66 Mev	
	(2) Primary and scattered, depth 10 cm, area 400 cm², SSD 35 cm	(*9*)
D	(1) Primary from Co^{60}, 1.25 Mev	
	(2) Primary and scattered, depth 10 cm, area 400 cm², SSD 80 cm	(*10*)

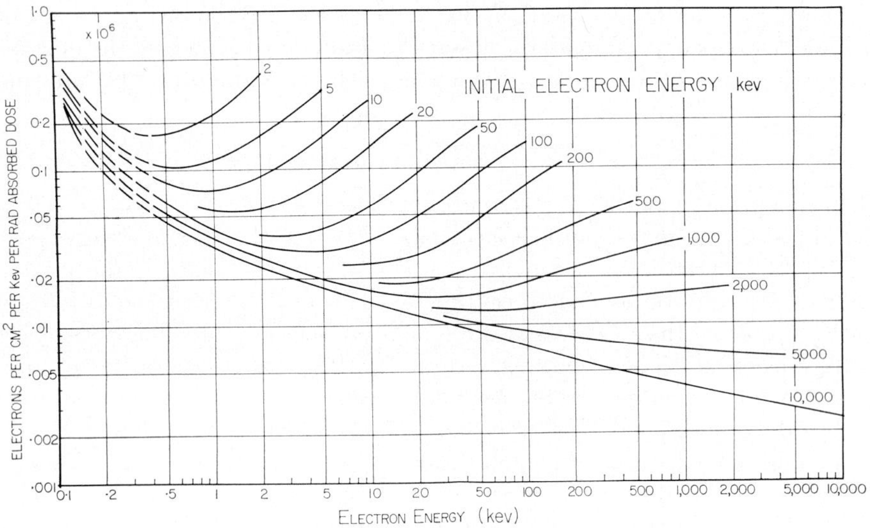

FIG. 1. The energy spectra of slowed-down and secondary electrons in electrons per square centimeter per kiloelectron volt interval from initial electrons with energy from 2 to 10,000 kev, in an infinite water medium. All spectra are adjusted to give an absorbed dose of 1 rad. The solid curve is based on data of McGinnies (*13*). The dashed curves are an extension of these data to lower energies.

scintillation spectroscopy of 250-kv radiation with HVL's of 1.25 and 3.2 mm Cu. The four γ-ray spectra were for Cs^{137} and Co^{60}. The primary radiation was assumed to be monochromatic with an energy of 0.66 Mev and 1.25 Mev. The spectra of scattered γ-rays were calculated by the Monte Carlo method.

The spectra of electrons initially set in motion in water by the X-rays and γ-rays were calculated from the photon spectra and the absorption coefficients for the photoelectric and Compton processes (*14*, *15*). Each electron spectrum was normalized so that $N(E_0)\,dE_0$ represented the number of electrons of energy between E_0 and $E_0 + dE_0$ set in motion in a cubic centimeter of water for *an absorbed dose of 1 rad.*

The spectra of slowed-down electrons were based on tabulations made by McGinnies. Her calculations were made by a method described by Spencer and Fano (*12*) which includes the effects of knock-on collisions but neglects the effects of brehmsstrahlung, which have been shown to be unimportant at these energies. An example of the data that may be obtained from the tabulations is shown in Fig. 1. This graph gives the slowed-down spectra of electrons in water. Each curve corresponds to the spectrum that results when a monoenergetic source of electrons is uniformly distributed throughout the infinite medium, and the curves have been adjusted so that they all correspond to source intensities yielding an absorbed dose of 1 rad.

The abscissa is the energy of the degraded and secondary electrons. The ordinate gives the number of electrons of corresponding energy that pass through an area of 1 cm^2 in the infinite water medium. Each of the curves terminates at an energy corresponding to the energy of the initial electrons, as there are no electrons of higher energy. The number of low-energy electrons set in motion by an absorbed dose of 1 rad is remarkably insensitive to the energy of the initial electrons, as may be seen by the manner in which all the curves converge at low energies. This graph illustrates rather clearly that large differences in quality are likely to produce almost negligible differences in the spectrum of electrons set in motion. This point will be proved by the subsequent detailed calculations.

The function actually tabulated by McGinnies was called $y(E_0, E)$. It is the energy spectrum of electrons per square centimeter that would result when one electron of energy E_0 arises per cubic centimeter in an infinite water medium. The function $y(E_0, E)$ is tabulated for values of E_0 from 6.4 to 6600 kev and for E from 0.45 to 5000 kev. In the present work the tables have been extended for water to values of E_0 down to 1 kev and of E down to 0.11 kev by the use of her initial computer program. These data were further checked by plotting the $\bar{R}$ factor defined by McGinnies (*13*), as a function of energy. At the lowest energies to which these calculations have been extended, the Born approximation is not valid, as the binding energy of the K electrons of the oxygen is 0.48 kev. The remaining eight electrons of the water molecule have lower binding energies, and for this reason, and in the absence of any satisfactory theory for electron scattering at this energy, the calculations were extended to lower energies without any corrections; i.e., it was assumed that the Born approximation still held. The effect of this assumption on the final results will be considered in a later section.

The spectrum of slowed-down electrons that result from the initial electron distribution, $N(E_0)$, may be calculated from the tables of $y(E_0, E)$ by integration as follows:

$$y(E) = \int_0^\infty N(E_0)y(E_0, E)\, dE_0 \qquad (1)$$

where $y(E)$ is now the number of electrons with energy E per energy interval per square centimeter per rad that results from the absorption of the X-rays or γ-rays in water. The value of $y(E)$ calculated in this manner may be used to calculate the distribution in LET.

The LET of an electron along its path through a particular medium depends on its energy, E, and on the maximum energy loss, δ, that may be considered to occur on the track. Although the appropriate choice of δ could be known with certainty only if a microscopic volume sensitive to radiation could be identified, it has become customary in calculations that refer to biological systems to use a value of $\delta = 100$ ev which corresponds to energy dissipation liberated up to something of the order of 30 A from the track (*16*). The degree to which the results of these calculations would be influenced by the choice of δ was tested by using both δ = 100 ev and δ = 500 ev. The latter corresponds to a secondary electron with a range of about 200 A from the track. The function $L(E, \delta)$, which represents the linear energy transfer or the stopping power of these electrons limited to collisional energy losses less than δ, has been shown (*17*, *18*) to be given by

$$L(E, \delta) = \frac{10^4}{m_0c^2} \frac{3N_A Z\phi_0}{4A} \frac{(T+1)}{T(T+2)} \cdot B$$

where

$$B = \ln \frac{\Delta}{\bar{Q}(T)} + \frac{\Delta}{T - \Delta} - \frac{T^2 + 4T + 2}{(T+1)^2} \ln \frac{T}{T - \Delta} + \frac{\Delta^2}{2(T+1)^2}$$

$$\bar{Q} = \tfrac{1}{2} I^2 [T(T+2)]^{-1} \exp [T(T+2)(T+1)^{-2}]$$

$T = E/m_0c^2$, $\Delta = \delta/m_0c^2$, and L is expressed in kiloelectron volts per micron (2)

In these equations, I is the mean excitation potential of the atoms of the medium and has been taken as $0.000145 m_0c^2$ units for water; $\bar{Q}$ is the formal lower limit of electron energy loss that may be lost on the track; and the remaining symbols have their usual meaning. In Fig. 2, $L(E, \delta)$ is plotted for values of δ = 100 and 500 ev and for values of E from 100 ev to 1 Mev. The values of L rise with decreasing electron energy over this range. They are undefined at low energies, as all interactions at these energies will give rise to electrons with energy less than δ.[1]

Equations 2 were used to obtain the LET distribution from the electron spectrum $y(E)$. As $L(E)$ is a monotonically decreasing function of energy, the number of electrons that cross a given surface with LET between L and $L + dL$ is the same as the number between the corresponding energies E and $E + dE$. We may therefore write

$$N(L)\, dL = -y(E)\, dE$$

or

$$N(L) = -y(E) \left(\frac{dL}{dE}\right)^{-1} \tag{3}$$

A more convenient method for presenting the distribution $N(L)$ is as $N(L)L$. This is because $N(L)L\, dL$ is the energy in kiloelectron volts dissipated by electrons with LET from L to dL in a small volume 1 cm^2 in area and 1 μ deep. Figures 3 to 6 give the data for δ = 100 ev, and Fig. 7 gives a typical distribution for δ = 500 ev. Here the abscissa is log LET, and the ordinate has been converted to energy deposited in rads per log LET interval. As the area under the curves is thus the energy deposited by all the electrons, this may be easily compared with the initial

[1] The term $L(E, \delta)$ is undefined at energies below $\Delta + \bar{Q}$, as is shown by Spencer and Attix (*18*).

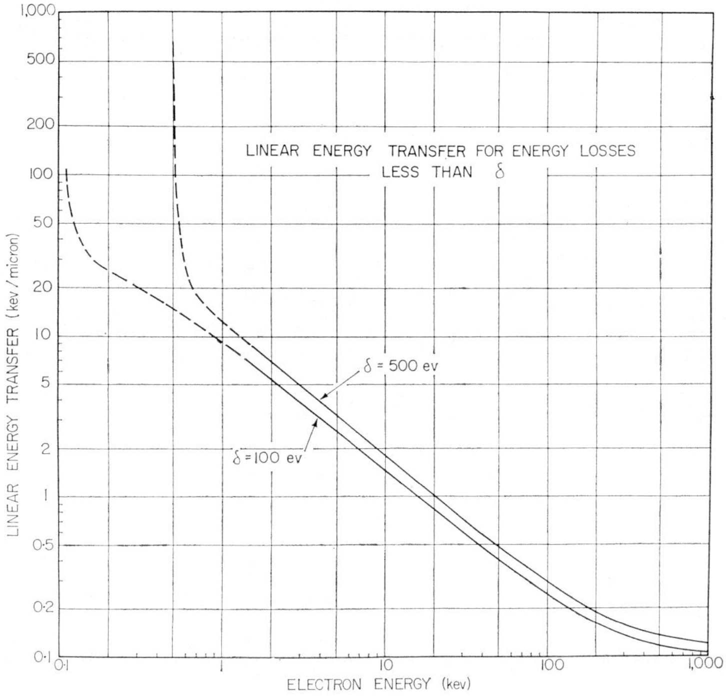

FIG. 2. The linear energy transfer of electrons in kiloelectron volts per micron for electrons of energy from 0.1 to 1000 kev, based on the assumption that energy losses less than $\delta = 100$ ev and $\delta = 500$ ev occur on the track.

absorbed dose of 1 rad in order to check the accuracy of the calculations. In all cases the agreement was to better than $\pm 3\%$. The plot made in this way also facilitates the comparison between the spectra.

All the LET distributions (Figs. 3 to 6) start at values of LET corresponding to the stopping power of the initial electrons with maximum energy and rise as lower initial energy and slowed-down electrons contribute to the dose. A second small rise and maximum occurs at about 30 kev/μ before the curve terminates at a value corresponding to the LET of electrons with energy close to δ. The small maxima are a result of the two factors in equation 3. At low energies and large LET, $y(E)$ increases with decreasing energy. On the other hand, when the energy decreases below 2 δ, $L(E)$ rises rapidly, and the term $(dL/dE)^{-1}$ becomes small. As a result of these two different factors, the product reaches a maximum at a value of LET corresponding to an energy of 2 δ and then decreases.

Each of the Figs. 3 to 6 compares the LET distribution for a primary radiation with that where scatter is important. It is apparent that the effect of scatter in all cases is small. The curves for 1.2 mm Cu HVL and 3.2 mm Cu HVL are also similar, as are those for Cs^{137} and Co^{60}. In fact, the curves for values of LET larger than 2

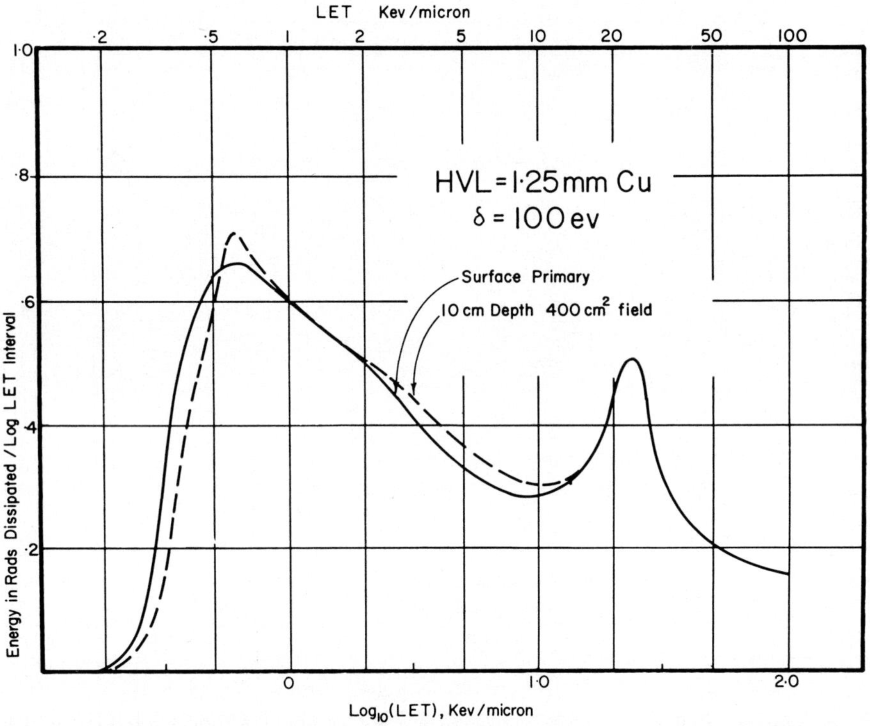

FIG. 3. The linear energy transfer distribution that results from X-rays with an HVL of 1.25 mm at the surface (—) and at a depth (– – –) in a water phantom. Energy losses less than $\delta = 100$ ev are assumed to occur on the track of slowed-down electrons. The total energy dissipated is 1 rad.

kev/μ are remarkably similar for both X-rays and γ-rays. The distributions obtained when energy losses along the track were limited to a value of $\delta = 500$ ev rather than 100 ev were very similar to those obtained in Figs. 3 to 6. An example of the spectra obtained for radiation with an HVL of 3.2 mm Cu is given in Fig. 7. The curves have a similar general shape to the equivalent curves for $\delta = 100$ ev, although the maximum and the termination of the curves are shifted to the higher values of LET calculated when losses up to 500 ev are considered to occur on the track.

AVERAGE LINEAR ENERGY TRANSFER

The detailed LET distributions, although complete, are difficult to use in comparing the effects of various radiations. An average is more convenient, but unfortunately confusion has arisen in the past because the method of averaging has not always been well defined. Three methods of averaging LET will be considered here. The first, which we shall call the *number average LET*, $\bar{L}_N$, is the value of L weighted by the number of electrons in the interval L to $L + dL$ (equation 4).

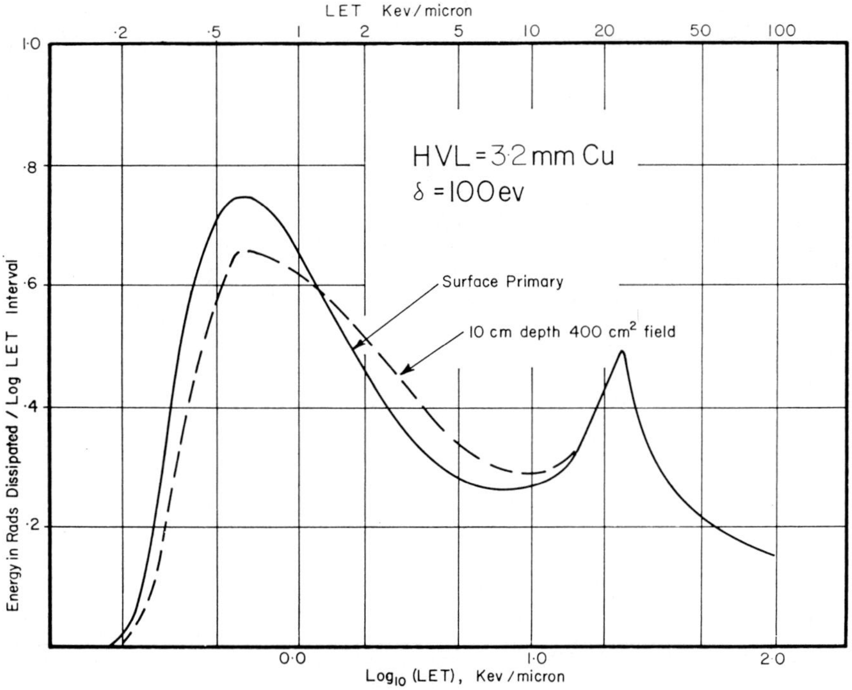

FIG. 4. The linear energy transfer distribution that results from X-rays with an HVL of 3.2 mm Cu at the surface (—) and at a depth (- - -) in a water phantom. Energy losses less than $\delta = 100$ ev are assumed to occur on the track of slowed-down electrons. The total energy dissipated is one rad.

$$\bar{L}_N = \frac{\int_0^\infty LN(L)\, dL}{\int_0^\infty N(L)\, dL} \tag{4}$$

This is just the average LET of electrons passing through a given area. Each of the electron tracks may not be equally effective at producing a particular effect. If each track is weighted by the quantity of energy transferred per micron, we obtain an *energy average LET*, $\bar{L}_E$, given by equation 5.

$$\bar{L}_E = \frac{\int_0^\infty LN(L)L\, dL}{\int_0^\infty N(L)L\, dL} \tag{5}$$

However, as the energy deposited by electrons with one LET will not generally produce the same effect as that at another, this definition is not completely satis-

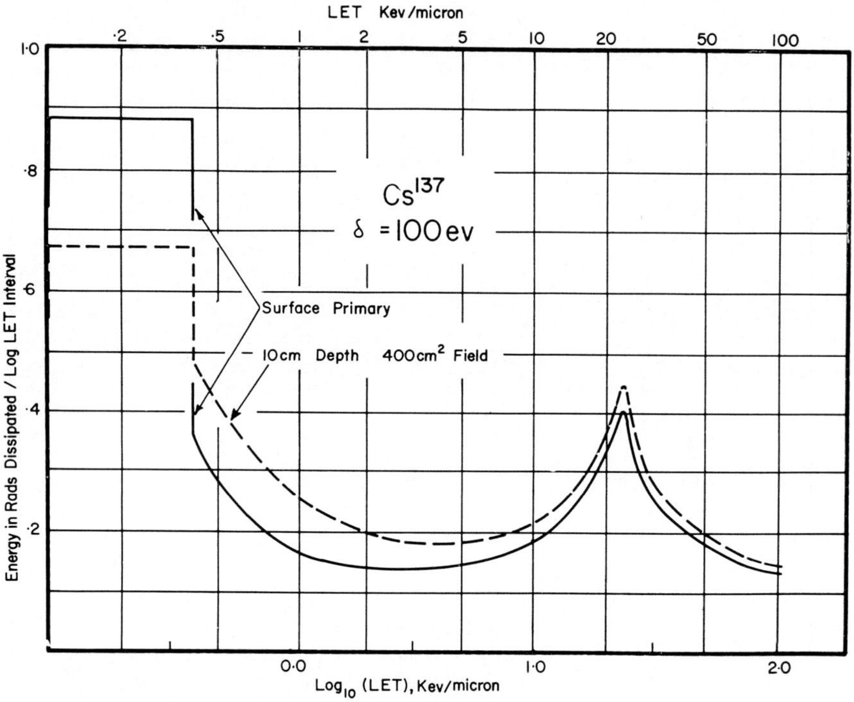

FIG. 5. The linear energy transfer distribution that results from the γ-rays of Cs^{137} at the surface (—) and at a depth (- - -) in a water phantom. The areas under the histograms represent the energy dissipated by electrons with LET from 0.1 to 0.4 kev/μ.

factory. If it were possible to measure the relative effects of the electrons at different LET's and to define a function, $R(L)$, which relates the relative effects to L, a more meaningful average would be possible. The *relative effect average*, $\bar{L}_R$, would be given by equation 6.

$$\bar{L}_R = \frac{\int_0^\infty LN(L)LR(L)\,dL}{\int_0^\infty N(L)LR(L)\,dL} \tag{6}$$

In fact, it is not possible to use this expression, as $R(L)$ is not known.

The number and energy average LET calculated for each of the spectra both for $\delta = 100$ and for $\delta = 500$ ev are given in Table II. Values are given both for the primary radiation and for the primary and scattered radiation observed at a depth of 10 cm in water. In each case the effect of the penetration and scatter produces only a small increase in the average LET's. The choice of δ has little effect

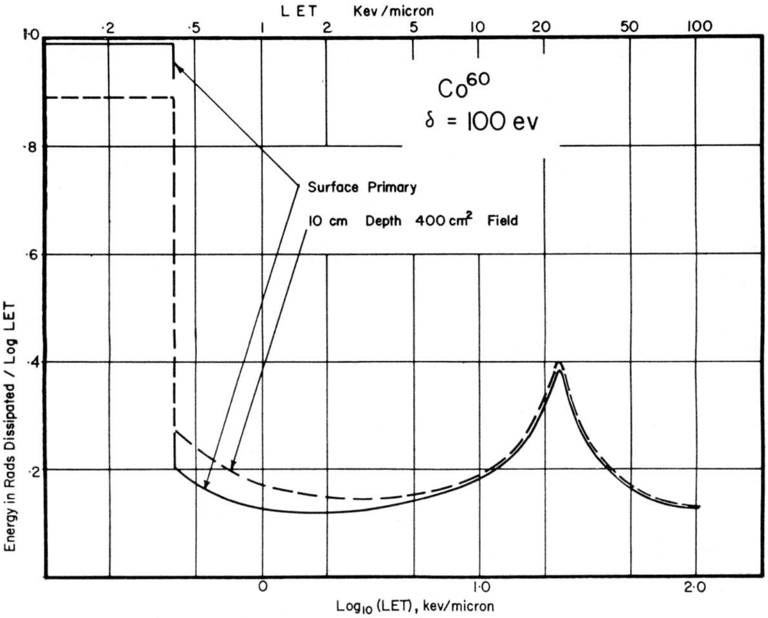

FIG. 6. The linear energy transfer distribution that results from the γ-rays of Co^{60} at the surface (—) and at a depth (- - -) in a water phantom. The areas under the histograms represent the energy dissipated by electrons with LET from 0.1 to 0.4 Kev/μ.

on the number average LET's of the eight spectra, but the energy average for $\delta = 500$ ev was 1.71 to 2.07 times as large as that for $\delta = 100$ ev.

DISCUSSION

The LET distributions presented in Figs. 3 to 6 differ from previous calculations that have included secondary electrons, particularly at high values of LET. This is largely due to the fact that the expression for LET used by Howard-Flanders (*3*), Burch (*4*, *5*), and Danzker *et al.* (Fig. 16 of reference *6*) includes as energy losses along the track only secondary electrons with energy losses less than δ. The primary electrons which drop below this energy and which do not differ from the secondaries they have set in motion must be treated separately and included in the final distribution (*3–5*). Danzker *et al.* have also calculated LET distributions based on an expression for LET that includes all losses less than Δ along the track together (Figs. 9 to 12 of reference *6*). Although the calculations were similar to those presented in this paper, the final distributions differ, as the cutoff energy used was 5.1 kev, which corresponds to the high energy that a secondary electron may dissipate in an ionization chamber.

Average LET values have been calculated by Cormack and Johns (*2*) and by

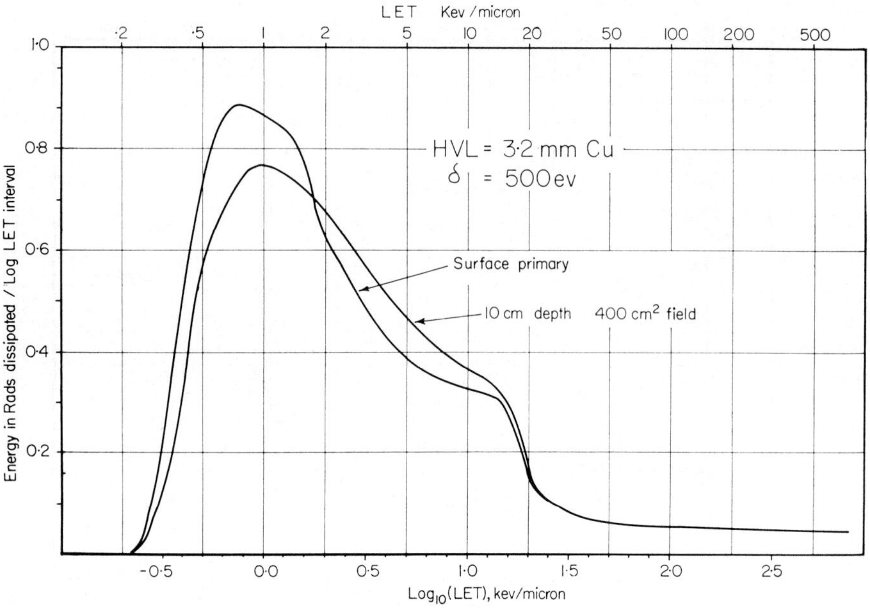

FIG. 7. The linear energy transfer distribution that results from X-rays with an HVL of 3.2 mm Cu at the surface (—) and at a depth (- - -) in a water phantom. Energy losses less than $\delta = 500$ ev are assumed to occur on the track of slowed-down electrons. The total energy dissipated is 1 rad.

Burch (*4*, *5*). The former calculated the mean (number average) linear energy transfer for X-rays and γ-rays without including the effects of secondary electrons. Their results for $\bar{L}_N$ were 1.48 to 1.79 kev/μ for X-rays and 0.254 kev/μ for Co^{60} γ-rays, values very similar to those given in Table II. The similarity is not surprising, as most of the electrons that pass through an area in the irradiated medium have a relatively high energy and low LET. Thus $\bar{L}_N$ primarily depends on the number of primary electrons and is not markedly influenced by the exclusion of secondaries. Burch and Bird calculated a mean (energy average) LET, $\bar{L}_E$, of X-rays as 9.98 to 10.6 kev/μ and of Co^{60} γ-rays as 7.73 kev/μ. The close agreement between these figures and those of Table II was unexpected, when one considers, for instance, the coarseness of intervals used by Burch to calculate the energy spectrum of secondary electrons compared with the complexity of equivalent data for $y(E_0, E)$ handled with computing machines.

It is necessary to ascertain now the degree to which the results obtained depend on the assumptions made in their derivation. Two assumptions warrant particular attention. First is the use of the stopping-power formula at very low energies where it is probably in error and has not been experimentally verified. A correction to this

TABLE II

AVERAGE LINEAR ENERGY TRANSFER RATES FOR X- AND γ-RAY SOURCES

Radiation source		$\bar{L}_N$ (kev/μ)		$\bar{L}_E$ (kev/μ)	
		δ = 100 ev	δ = 500 ev	δ = 100 ev	δ = 500 ev
X-rays					
1.25 mm Cu HVL	P[a]	1.3	1.3	10.4	21.3
	P+S[b]	1.4	1.5	10.7	21.9
3.2 mm Cu HVL	P	1.2	1.2	10.6	21.0
	P+S	1.3	1.4	11.0	21.8
γ-rays					
Cs^{137}	P	0.32	0.30	8.4	14.8
	P+S	0.40	0.40	9.4	17.2
Co^{60}	P	0.30	0.28	7.9	14.4
	P+S	0.32	0.30	8.3	15.0

[a] P signifies primary only.

[b] P+S signifies primary and scattered at a depth of 10 cm in water for a 400-cm^2 field.

formula would be reflected in changes in $y(E_0, E)$ and $y(E)$ at low energies. It would be apparent in the LET distributions for the low-energy high-LET electrons. Thus, if the true value of the stopping power deviated from the assumed value at 1 kev, the LET distribution would be distorted for values greater than 9 kev/μ (see Fig. 2 for $\delta = 100$ ev).

The second assumption also concerns high LET and the calculation of LET for electrons of energy close to the value δ. Because we have assumed losses less than δ to occur on the track, we have the anomalous situation that electrons with energies between δ and 2 δ have a high LET corresponding to the high probability that they may suffer an energy loss that will degrade them to an energy less than δ. They may display this apparent high LET for only a few interactions—hardly what might be considered an energy loss along a line.

The uncertainty introduced by both assumptions concerns particularly the shape of the LET distribution at high LET. It does not influence the energy liberated by these electrons. This is a result of the fact that the total energy transferred by all the electrons represented, for instance, by the area under the curves of Figs. 3 to 6 must be equal to the absorbed dose, which is in this case 1 rad. Although the actual shape of the distributions above LET's of perhaps 10 kev/μ are in considerable question, the areas under the curves at these high LET's must necessarily be unaffected by any modification to the assumptions that have been made. It is at these high LET values that the concept of LET with its implied spatial distribution of energy losses along straight lines becomes tenuous. The limitations, especially when one is comparing the energy losses by electrons with that by heavy particles, has been emphasized by Rossi (*19*), and he has suggested a description of the spatial distribution that circumvents many of these difficulties. However, the comparison of LET distributions for the electrons set in motion by X-rays and γ-rays does ndeed permit the clarification of several problems.

The energy degradation suffered by a beam of X-rays or γ-rays on penetrating water has been shown to influence the LET distributions very little. This is true whether number or energy average LET's are compared and whether δ is taken as 100 ev or 500 ev. Although differences in the RBE's of X-radiation and γ-radiation have been observed, it is unlikely that any biological system is sufficiently sensitive to demonstrate the small effects on LET produced by scattered radiation as demonstrated here. The RBE of a beam of radiation as used in radiotherapy, for instance, may certainly be considered to be unaffected by scattered radiation.

Several factors are responsible for this insensitivity of LET to radiation geometry and photon energy. First, the energy spectrum of X-radiation or γ-radiation that has penetrated and been scattered through even very great depths of water contains very few photons with energies below 20 kev. This is a result of the increase in the probability of photons' being removed by the photoelectric process as their energy decreases, and it leads to an energy spectrum that is not degraded to the degree one might otherwise expect.

The increasing importance of the photoelectric effect at low energies is important for a second reason. Whereas Compton electrons may carry off only a fraction of a scattered photon's energy, the photoelectron usually receives most of it. Consequently the average energy of electrons set in motion by X-rays varies little over a large range of X-ray energies. For instance, photons with an energy of 100 kev give rise to electrons with an average energy of 15 kev; at 50 kev the average is 11 kev; and at 20 kev it is again about 15 kev.

However, perhaps the most important factor is that the number of low-energy secondary electrons does not vary greatly with the energy of the primary electrons. This is clearly demonstrated in Fig. 1. For instance, a given absorbed dose from 10-kev electrons gives rise to only twice as many 1-kev secondary electrons as do electrons with 10,000 kev of energy. As a result of these factors the number of low-energy secondary electrons is not strongly influenced by the X-ray or γ-ray spectrum. Table III, taken from an intermediate step in the calculations, demonstrates this fact for electron energies of 0.11 kev, 0.45 kev, and 1.05 kev for each of the primary spectra.

It has been noted that the relative biological effects of X-rays and γ-rays are quite similar. Many measurements of the RBE's of γ-rays on higher organisms have given values of approximately 0.8 (*20–24*). It is interesting to note that this is approximately the same as the ratio of the number of low-energy electrons for the

TABLE III

NUMBER OF ELECTRONS PER SQUARE CENTIMETER PER KILOELECTRON VOLT PER RAD OF ABSORBED DOSE OF X- AND γ-RAYS

Source	*At 0.11 kev*	*At 0.45 kev*	*At 1.0 kev*
X-rays			
1.25 mm Cu HVL	36.8×10^4	8.1×10^4	6.2×10^4
3.2 mm Cu HVL	37.1×10^4	7.9×10^4	5.7×10^4
γ-rays			
Cs^{137}	30.5×10^4	6.0×10^4	3.76×10^4
Co^{60}	29.6×10^4	5.8×10^4	3.59×10^4

two sources, and it suggests that the low-energy electrons are the biologically important component of the electron spectrum. One might test this theory if it were possible to irradiate the cells with high-energy electrons alone, without secondaries. This is, however, in principle impossible, since, although such electrons have a low LET, this LET is itself an average over many events including the production of low-energy secondaries along the track. Thus there is really no low-LET radiation in the strict sense, as there is always a component of the energy dissipated by high-LET secondary electrons.

CONCLUSION

The LET distribution and the number and energy average LET of electrons set in motion by primary and water-scattered beams of radiation with primary HVL from 1.25 mm Cu to 11 mm Pb are presented. The effect of energy degradation due to scatter in water is very small. Few biological systems are likely to be sensitive enough to changes in LET to make the effect of energy degradation in an absorber biologically significant.

ACKNOWLEDGMENTS

We take pleasure in acknowledging the financial assistance of the National Cancer Institute of Canada and the help of the staff of the Computation Centre of the University of Toronto.

RECEIVED: November 16, 1962

REFERENCES

1. L. H. GRAY, The distribution of the ions resulting from the irradiation of living cells. *Brit. J. Radiol. Suppl.* **1**, 7–15 (1947).
2. D. V. CORMACK and H. E. JOHNS, Electron energies and ion densities in water irradiated with 200 KeV, 1 MeV, and 25 MeV radiation. *Brit. J. Radiol.* **25**, 369–381 (1952).
3. P. HOWARD-FLANDERS, Physical and chemical mechanisms in the injury of cells by ionizing radiations. *Advan. Biol. Med. Phys.* **6**, 553–603 (1958).
4. P. R. J. BURCH, Some physical aspects of relative biological efficiency. *Brit. J. Radiol.* **30**, 524–529 (1957).

5. P. R. J. Burch, Calculations of energy dissipation characteristics in water for various radiations. *Radiation Res.* **6**, 289–301 (1957).
6. M. Danzker, N. D. Kessaris, and J. S. Laughlin, Absorbed dose and linear energy transfer in radiation experiments. *Radiology* **72**, 51–61 (1959).
7. W. R. Bruce, and H. E. Johns, The spectra of X-rays scattered in low atomic number materials. *Brit. J. Radiol. Suppl.* **9** (1960).
8. D. V. Cormack, W. E. Davitt, D. G. Burke, and E. G. Rawson, Spectral distributions of 280 kVp X-rays. *Brit. J. Radiol.* **31**, 565–570 (1958).
9. L. D. Skarsgard, and H. E. Johns, Spectral flux density of scattered and primary radiation generated at 250 kv. *Radiation Res.* **14**, 231–260 (1961).
10. W. R. Bruce, and M. L. Pearson, Spectral distribution of scattered radiation in a water phantom irradiated with cesium-137 gamma rays. *Radiation Res.* **17**, 555–572 (1962).
11. W. R. Bruce, M. L. Pearson, and H. E. Johns, A comparison of Monte Carlo calculations and experimental measurements of scattered radiation produced in a water phantom by primary radiations with half-value layers from 1.25 mm Cu to 11 mm Pb. *Radiation Res.* **17**, 543–554 (1962).
12. L. V. Spencer, and U. Fano, Energy spectrum resulting from electron slowing down. *Phys. Rev.* **93**, 1172–1181 (1954).
13. R. T. McGinnies, Energy spectrum resulting from electron slowing down. *Natl. Bur. Std.* (U.S.) *Circ.* **597** (1959).
14. H. E. Johns, J. E. Till, and D. V. Cormack, Electron energy distributions produced by gamma rays. *Nucleonics* **12**, No. 10, 40–46 (1954).
15. G. W. Grodstein, X-Ray attenuation coefficients from 10 Kev to 100 MeV. *Natl. Bur. Std. Circ.* **583** (1957).
16. D. E. Lea, *Actions of Radiations on Living Cells*, 2nd ed., p. 26, Cambridge University Press, New York, 1955.
17. C. Møller, Uber den Stoss zweier Teilchen unter Berucksichtgung der Retardation der Krafte. *Z. Physik* **70**, 786–795 (1931).
18. L. V. Spencer and F. H. Attix, A theory of cavity ionization. *Radiation Res.* **3**, 239–254 (1955).
19. H. H. Rossi, Specification of radiation quality. *Radiation Res.* **10**, 522–531 (1959).
20. A. C. Upton, F. P. Conte, G. S. Hurst, and W. A. Mills, The relative biological effectiveness of fast neutrons, X-rays, and γ-rays for acute lethality in mice. *Radiation Res.* **4**, 117–131 (1956).
21. J. B. Storer, P. S. Harris, J. E. Furchner, and W. H. Langham, The relative biological effectiveness of various ionizing radiations in mammalian systems. *Radiation Res.* **6**, 188–288 (1957).
22. W. K. Sinclair, S. E. Gunter, and A. Cole, The relative biological effectiveness of 200-kvp X-rays, Co^{60} γ-rays and 22-Mevp X-rays determined from the dose-survival curve of *Saccharomyces cerevisiae*. *Radiation Res.* **10**, 418–432 (1959).
23. E. J. Hall, The relative biological efficiency of X-rays generated at 220 kVp and gamma radiation from a cobalt 60 therapy unit. *Brit. J. Radiol.* **34**, 313–317 (1961).
24. J. E. Till, and J. R. Cunningham, Unpublished data referred to by H. E. Johns, in *The Physics of Radiology*, 2nd ed., p. 673, Charles C Thomas, Springfield, Illinois, 1961.

RADIATION RESEARCH **19**, 621–627 (1963)

Effect of Pretreatment with Colchicine or a Colchicine Derivative on Hemopoiesis in Irradiated Mice

WILLIE W. SMITH, ILO M. ALDERMAN, CAROL A. SCHNEIDER, AND JEROME CORNFIELD

National Cancer Institute and National Heart Institute, National Institutes of Health, Bethesda 14, Maryland

INTRODUCTION

The increase in percentage survival which occurs in mice treated with colchicine and related compounds prior to irradiation (*1–5*) is no doubt the consequence of the early recovery in cellular constituents of the blood (*6*). In the present work studies of bone marrow cellularity and peripheral blood leucocytes have been made in irradiated mice pretreated with colchicine or trimethylcolchicinic acid (TMCA) methyl ether. Results will be presented concerning the times of appearance of treatment effects and their magnitudes.

METHODS

The mice used were (BALB/c × DBA/2)F^1 females 3 to 4 months old weighing approximately 24 gm. They were irradiated with X-rays from a Van de Graaff generator operating at 2.5 Mev and 0.7 ma as in earlier studies, giving an LD_{50} 30 days of 870 r, or γ-rays from a Co^{60} source giving an LD_{50} of 824 rads. The factor 0.95 has been applied to the 2.5 Mev X-ray doses in order to make them equivalent, in terms of LD_{50}, to the Co^{60} doses. Injections were made intraperitoneally 2 days before irradiation for colchicine (40 μg, with one exception which will be indicated) or one day before for TMCA methyl ether (0.5 or 1 mg of the d-tartrate).[1] Bone marrow cellularity was estimated from stained longitudinal sections of femur as previously described (*7*). Granulocyte and lymphocyte counts were made on tail blood and are given as geometric means. The procedure for estimating time of recovery to 1000 cells per cu mm has been described (*6*).

RESULTS

The degree of cellularity of femoral bone marrow, graded from 0 to 4, was estimated for mice given 40 μg of colchicine two days before irradiation with 660 rads

[1] We are indebted to Dr. Joseph Leiter for a supply of this material.

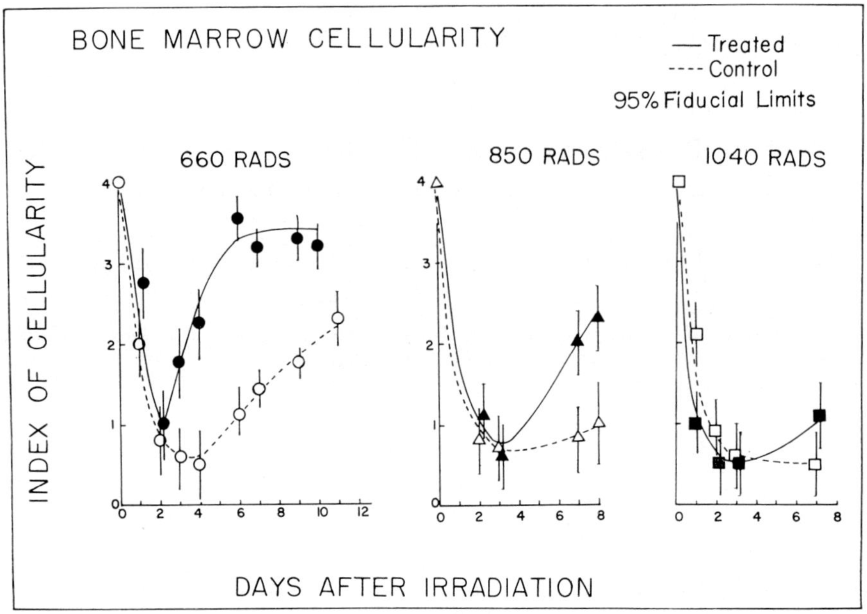

FIG. 1. Estimates of femoral bone marrow cellularity in mice given 40 μg of colchicine two days prior to irradiation with 660 rads or 1 mg of TMCA methyl ether d-tartrate one day before 850 or 1040 rads as compared to irradiation controls.

(LD_5) or 1 mg of TMCA methyl ether d-tartrate one day before irradiation with 850 or 1040 rads, with results as shown in Fig. 1. The effects of the three radiation doses were indistinguishable in sections made two to four days after exposure. Sections from treated mice were indistinguishable from irradiation controls at all dose levels two days after exposure, but on the third day treated mice given 660 rads showed a marked increase in cellularity whereas their controls did not. By the seventh day the marrow of the treated mice given 850 rads was much more cellular than controls. Fig. 2 illustrates the advance in bone marrow recovery seen in mice given TMCA methyl ether prior to irradiation with 850 rads. In mice given 1040 rads the index of cellularity seven days after exposure also was higher in treated than in control mice.[2] Associated with the increase in bone marrow cellularity were increases in leucocyte, platelet and hemoglobin concentrations in peripheral blood (*6*).

Leucocyte counts in colchicine-treated and control mice exposed to 450, 570 and 770 rads are shown in Fig. 3. Mean granulocyte counts in treated mice given 450 or 570 rads exceeded the preirradiation mean at the end of one week, and in the group given 450 rads had risen to twice normal by the tenth day, dropping back to normal at the end of the second week. In control mice these counts first attained

[2] P = 0.02, unicaudal *t* test.

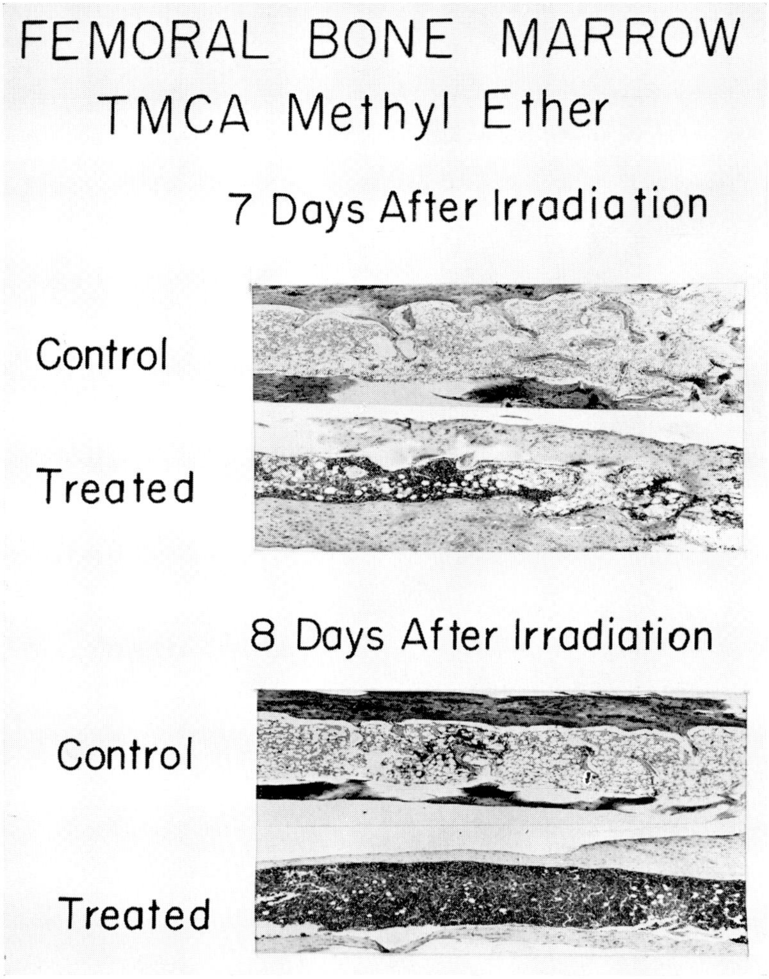

FIG. 2. Sections of femoral bone marrow 7 and 8 days after irradiation with 850 rads in mice pretreated with TMCA methyl ether as compared to irradiation controls.

preirradiation levels about three weeks after exposure. Lymphocyte counts in treated mice had not returned to normal at the end of the three-week observation period but at each dose level the treated mice showed an earlier increase than controls.

The number of days between irradiation and recovery to 1000 granulocytes or lymphocytes per cu mm is shown in Table I for control and treated mice given 770 or 570 rads. It will be noted that colchicine treatment reduced the granulocyte recovery time in mice given 770 rads to the level seen in untreated mice given 570 rads. The effect was thus roughly equivalent to a dose reduction of 200 rads. The mean reduction in recovery time for lymphocytes as compared to granulocytes was

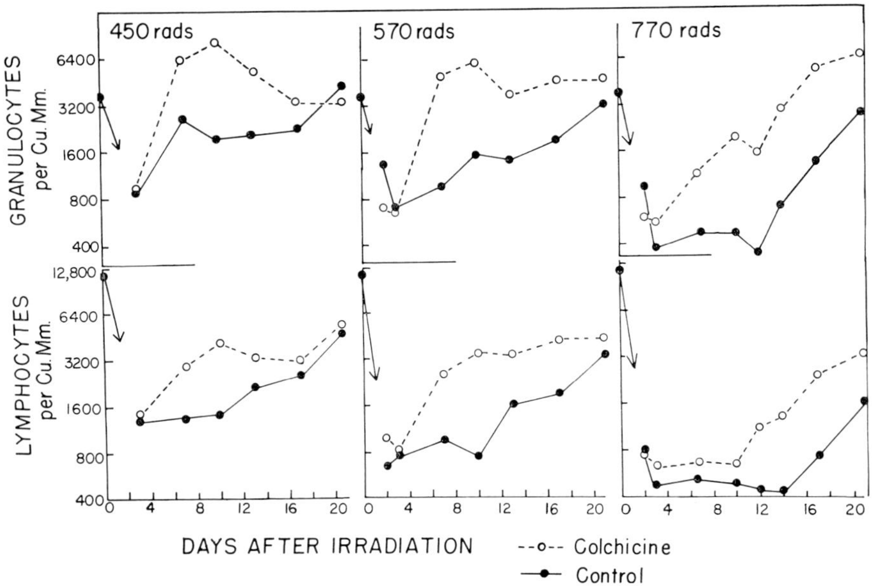

FIG. 3. Granulocyte and lymphocyte counts in mice given colchicine 2 days prior to irradiation with 450 or 570 rads (40 μg) or 770 rads (30 μg) as compared to irradiation controls.

slightly less in the group given 770 rads and slightly more in the group given 570 rads.

The effect of colchicine pretreatment on 28-day survival of lethally irradiated mice is shown in Table II. The colchicine dose of 40 μg gave an effect which was possibly somewhat less than maximum, but colchicine toxicity made higher doses inadvisable. For TMCA methyl ether d-tartrate a dose of 0.5 mg, used for the experiments at 950 rads, gave as good results as 1.0 mg, which was used for the experiments at 1040 rads. The toxicity of this compound was not a problem. The average effect of these treatments on survival was equivalent to that seen with a dose reduction of 180 rads, estimated from our standard dose-survival curve[3] as the difference between the dose given and the dose at which untreated mice have the survival observed in the treated mice.

Counts were made to determine whether or not colchicine treatment affects granulocyte and lymphocyte counts three to four days after irradiation, a time at which definite relationships exist between radiation dose and these counts (*9*). There were 11 experiments in the study (including those of Fig. 3), counts being made on a total of 120 treated mice and an equal number of controls. Radiation doses were 450, 570, 660, 770 and 970 rads for 90 mice pretreated with colchicine and counted on day 3, and 660, 850 and 1040 rads for the remainder, which were given colchicine and counted on day four or TMCA methyl ether and counted on day three or four.

[3] LD_{10}, 700 rads; LD_{90}, 950 rads.

TABLE I

TIME, IN DAYS, BETWEEN IRRADIATION AND RECOVERY TO 1000 GRANULOCYTES OR LYMPHOCYTES PER CU MM OF TAIL BLOOD IN MICE PRETREATED WITH COLCHICINE, AS COMPARED TO THEIR CONTROLS

Dose, rads	*Treatment*	*Time of recovery to 1000 cells per Cu Mm*[a]	
		Granulocytes	*Lymphocytes*
770	Control	15.4 (14.5–16.5)	17.5 (15.7–20.9)
	Colchicine, 30 μg	7.8 (6.7–8.8)	12.5 (11.5–13.5)
570	Control	8.0 (4.5–9.9)	10.9 (9.1–12.5)
	Colchicine, 40 μg	4.0 (3.5–4.5)	3.5 (2.5–4.3)

[a] Values in parentheses represent 95% fiducial limits (*8*).

TABLE II

SURVIVAL OF LETHALLY IRRADIATED MICE PRETREATED WITH COLCHICINE (40 μG, R-2) OR TRIMETHYLCOLCHICINIC ACID METHYL ETHER (0.5–1.0 MG OF THE D-TARTRATE, R-1)

Dose rads[a]	*Number of experiments*	*Number per treatment*	*% Surviving 28 days*		*Approximate dose equivalent*[b]
			Treated	*Control*	
			Colchicine		
950	5	50	84	14	−165
1000	1	20	55	0	−141
1040	2	19	37	0	−138
1090	1	9	44	0	−207
			TMCA Methyl Ether		
950	2	26	92	0	−200
1040	3	87	60	0	−193

[a] 2.5 Mev dose multiplied by 0.95 for equivalence with Co^{60} dose.

[b] Difference, on standard dose-survival curve, between dose given and dose at which control mice have the survival observed in the treated mice.

For the more homogenous set of 90, granulocyte counts for treated mice exceeded controls by an average of 9.1 ± 7.4%[4] and lymphocyte counts by 18.4 ± 5.9%. When the remainder of the experiments were added the granulocyte difference remained essentially the same, 9.2 ± 6.7%, and the mean lymphocyte difference became 16.3 ± 5.0%.

A reduction in radiation dose of 200 rads within the dose range of these experiments is associated with a doubling in the three or four-day granulocyte counts (*9*). The mean effect of colchicine treatment on these early granulocyte counts was not statistically significant. The effect on lymphocyte counts although significant was much smaller than would be expected from a dose reduction of 200 rads.

[4] Standard error.

TABLE III

MEAN GRANULOCYTE COUNTS WITHOUT AND WITH *S. TYPHOSA* ENDOTOXIN MOBILIZATION IN MICE TREATED WITH TMCA METHYL ETHER PRIOR TO IRRADIATION (850 RADS) COMPARED TO UNTREATED CONTROLS[a]

	Day					
	2	*3*	*4*	*6*	*7*	*8*
No Mobilization						
Treated	4010	345	148	354	832	953
Control	5810	494	218	152	185	305
Endotoxin Mobilization						
Treated	19,100	2030	620	2680	7000	8010
Control	21,800	2200	1210	1560	971	1690

[a] Numbers per group were 5 for days 2–6, 10 for day 7, and 9 for day 8. Differences were significant ($P < 0.05$) on day 6 for no mobilization and on days 7 and 8 and for both mobilized and nonmobilized counts.

Additional evidence on the subject of early granulocyte counts was obtained by mobilizing the granulocytes in colchicine-treated and control mice with *S. Typhosa* endotoxin 24 hours before making the counts. Results are shown in Table III. Under these conditions there was a sharp increase in granulocyte count on day 7, while the counts on days 2, 3 and 4 were no higher in treated than in control mice. These results are consistent with the estimates of bone marrow cellularity shown in Fig. 1.

DISCUSSION

The present studies show the times at which certain changes appear in the hemopoietic system of mice treated with colchicine prior to irradiation and, by giving their magnitudes, indicate which changes are consistent with the observed effect on survival.

The appearance of the femoral bone marrow did not vary with radiation dose for the first four days after irradiation, but did show a colchicine effect on the third day in sublethally irradiated mice and on the seventh day in lethally irradiated mice.

Colchicine treatment had no significant effect on granulocyte counts 3 to 4 days after irradiation. If colchicine acts by reducing sensitivity to radiation, only cells released later than this are affected. Such timing would probably be consistent with a reduced sensitivity in the cells undergoing division at the time of injection, one or two days before irradiation. The effect on early lymphocyte counts was significant, though it was only a fraction of the dose-equivalent effect on survival.

The advance in granulocyte recovery was essentially the same as that observed with a comparable reduction in radiation dose. It seems likely that the presence of these granulocytes at a critical time is principally responsible for survival. The advance in lymphocyte recovery was somewhat less at the higher radiation doses and more at the lower doses than observed with this reduction in radiation dose.

We are again reminded of the peculiar species dependence of the colchicine effect on hemopoiesis and survival in the absence of a species dependence of its effect on mitosis, and of the discrepant doses of colchicine and TMCA methyl ether required for the two effects (*5*). Questions related to these facts remain unanswered.

SUMMARY

Treatment of mice with colchicine or trimethylcolchicine acid methyl ether prior to irradiation caused: *1*, an increase in bone marrow cellularity which was apparent 3 days after LD_5 irradiation; *2*, no significant increase in granulocyte counts 3–4 days after irradiation; *3*, a relatively small but significant increase in lymphocyte counts 3–4 days after irradiation; *4* an advance in the time of recovery of granulocyte counts consistent with the effect on survival, which was equivalent to a mean dose-reduction of 180 rads; and *5*, a similar advance in the time of recovery of lymphocyte counts.

RECEIVED: November 19, 1962

REFERENCES

1. W. W. SMITH, Protective effect of a colchicine derivative in mice exposed to X-irradiation. *Science* **127**, 340–341 (1958).

2. W. W. SMITH and J. CORNFIELD, Extending the range of dose-effect curves for irradiated mice. *Science* **128**, 473–474 (1958).

3. W. E. ROTHE and M. M. GRENAN, Radioprotection by mitotic inhibitors and mercaptoethylamine. *Science* **133**, 888 (1961).

4. L. J. COLE and S. R. GOSPE, Increased radioresistance in mice injected with urethan one day before X-irradiation. *Radiation Res.* **15**, 684–693 (1961).

5. W. W. SMITH and I. M. ALDERMAN, Studies on colchicine, colchicine derivatives, and endotoxin in irradiated animals. *Radiation Res.* **17**, 594–607 (1962).

6. W. W. SMITH, R. Q. MARSTON, and J. CORNFIELD, Patterns of hemopoietic recovery in irradiated mice. *Blood* **14**, 737–747 (1959).

7. W. W. SMITH, I. M. ALDERMAN, and R. E. GILLESPIE, Hematopoietic recovery induced by bacterial endotoxin in irradiated mice. *Am. J. Physiol.* **192**, 549–556 (1958).

8. M. A. CREASY, Limits for the ratio of means. *J. Roy. Stat. Soc.*, Series B, **16**, 186–194 (1954).

9. W. W. SMITH, I. M. ALDERMAN, C. A. SCHNEIDER and J. CORNFIELD, Radiation dose-response characteristics of leucocytes in the mouse. *Proc. Soc. Exptl. Biol. Med.* **111**, 182–186 (1962).

RADIATION RESEARCH **19**, 628–635 (1963)

The Generation Cycle of Duodenal Crypt Cells of Mice Exposed to 220 Roentgens of Cobalt-60 Gamma Irradiation per Day[1]

R. J. M. FRY, S. LESHER, A. SALLESE, AND E. STAFFELDT

Department of Physiology, Trinity College, Dublin, Eire, and Division of Biological and Medical Research, Argonne National Laboratory, Argonne, Illinois

INTRODUCTION

In a previous report (*1*) the effects of chronic γ-irradiation, 12 r/day for 200 days, on the generation cycle of mouse duodenal crypt cells were discussed. It has been found (S. Lesher and R. J. M. Fry, unpublished data) that 12 r/day produces a considerable amount of cellular damage to the crypts without an apparent reduction in the mucosal cell population. Theoretically the apparent compensation for cell loss could have been due to either an increased cell life span or a shortening of the cell cycle. It was found that the duration of the generation cycle of the crypt cells of the irradiated animals was approximately 3 hours shorter than in the control mice. Since the result was seen for only one exposure condition, it seems important to check for shortening of the cell cycle with other dose levels and durations of exposure dose. In the experiments to be reported here, estimates were made of the generation time of the duodenal crypt cells of 100-day-old mice exposed to 220 r of γ-irradiation per day for 1, 7, and 14 days and of a similar number of 100-day-old nonirradiated controls.

MATERIALS AND METHODS

At 100 days of age (±5 days), male and female BCF_1 hybrid mice (C57 black females × BALB/c males) were separated as to sex, divided 3 to a cage, and assigned to positions in a Co^{60} γ-ray exposure chamber where they received 220 r/day for 1, 7, or 14 days (*1, 2*). Equal numbers of mice were assigned to unirradiated control groups and maintained in cages and an environment similar to those of the irradiated mice. The γ-rays were delivered in a 10-hour period between 11:00 P.M. and 9:00 A.M. each day by a 100-curie Co^{60} source.

Mice from each of the irradiated groups were removed from the γ-ray room at

[1] This work was performed in part under the auspices of the U. S. Atomic Energy Commission.

9:00 A.M., and both control and irradiated groups were injected with tritiated thymidine between 10:00 and 10:30 A.M. By handling the animals in this manner, the effects of irradiation on incorporation should be similar within each experimental group. Each mouse was injected intraperitoneally with 0.1 ml of sterile distilled water containing 20 μc of tritiated thymidine obtained from Schwarz Bioresearch, Inc., (360 mc/mM). Mice were sacrificed every half-hour for the first 3 hours and at hourly intervals between 3 and 15 hours after injection. Segments of the duodenum approximately 15 mm distal to the pylorus and just beyond the Brunner's gland region were removed, fixed, dehydrated, and embedded in paraffin. Sections (3 μ) were prestained by the Feulgen reaction, and autoradiographs were prepared from them (*3*).

To obtain an estimate of the generation time, the percentage of mitotic figures labeled was determined for each interval after injection of tritiated thymidine on coded and randomized slides. For this determination only metaphase and anaphase figures were scored.

A cell (interphase or dividing) was considered to be labeled when its nucleus showed five or more grains. In a number of animals from each of the experimental and control groups, the following data were determined on sections:

1. Total number of cells (interphase plus mitoses) per crypt section. From these data the mitotic index was determined.
2. The number of abnormal interphase cells per crypt section. The criteria of abnormality were: (*a*) the presence of nuclear material in the cytoplasm, or (*b*) fragmentation of the nucleus.
3. The number of initially labeled cells and total number of cells per crypt section ½ hour after injection of tritiated thymidine. From these data the labeling index was determined.
4. Crypt transit time in the control and 1-day exposure groups. In each animal 50 villi were scored for the presence of labeled epithelial cells on or above the base of the villus. From these data the percentage of labeled villi was determined as a function of time (Fig. 3). Assessments of (1) and (2) were made on sections stained with Feulgen-Fast Green.

RESULTS AND DISCUSSION

Cells in the synthesis stage (*S*) of the generation cycle during the short period in which label is available incorporate the labeled thymidine into DNA. The movement of these initially labeled cells through the stages of the generation cycle can be followed and the duration of the cycle estimated by plotting the percentage of mitotic figures labeled at each sacrifice interval against time (Fig. 1). A cyclic curve is obtained from which an estimate of the generation time can be established by determining the time between homologous points on the two curves.

The curves for the three experimental and the control groups are shown in Fig.

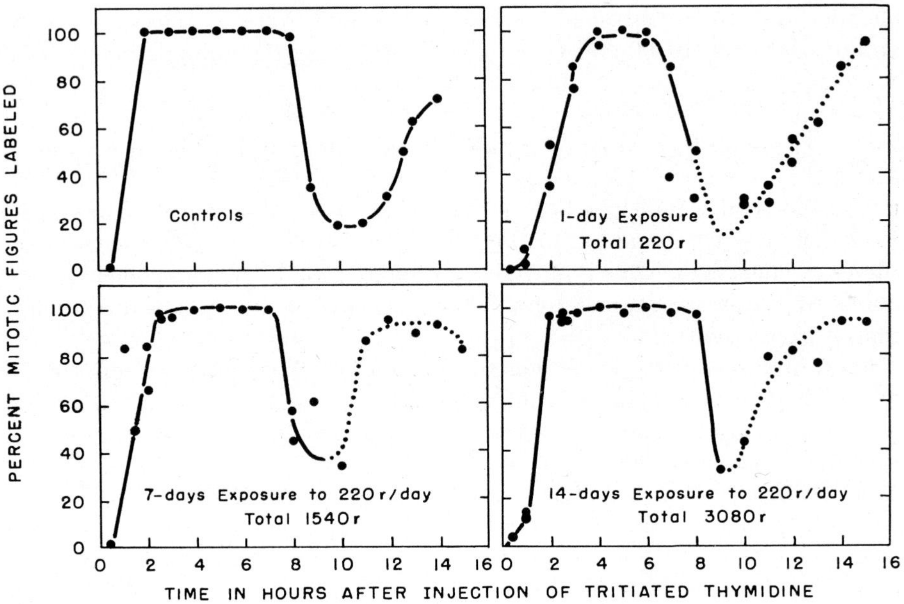

FIG. 1. Percentage of mitotic figures labeled (metaphase and anaphase only) versus time after injection of tritiated thymidine. The positions of the dotted curves appear to be reasonable, although they are drawn more or less arbitrarily according to the authors' interpretation. It is impossible to establish statistically the shape of this segment of the curve, since it represents the interval of greatest interanimal variation.

TABLE I

ESTIMATE OF GENERATION TIME

Exposure group	*Time between troughs (hr)*	*Time between 50% on ascending limbs (hr)*	*Time between 70% on ascending limbs (hr)*
Control	10.5	11	12
1 day	9.0	10	11
7 day	9	9	9
14 day	9	9	9

1, and the estimates of the generation time based on the time elapsed between troughs, 50% points on ascending limbs, and 70% points on ascending limbs are given in Table I.

In the 1-day exposure group it can be seen that the slope of the ascending limb is less than in the controls, and the time at which the maximum fraction of mitoses are labeled is 4 hours, some 2 hours later than in the controls. Therefore some cells which were in the postsynthesis (G_2) stage or in mitosis (M) at the time of the injection of label, and therefore remained unlabeled, had not completed G_2 plus M in 4 hours. This indicates an increase in the duration of G_2 plus M. It is impossible from these data to state whether the delay occurs in G_2 or in M. The duration of the plateau is shortened and the slope of the descending limb is less than in the controls.

These changes in the pattern of the per cent mitoses labeled suggests that the steady flow of cells through the stages of the generation cycle is disturbed, presumably by delay in one or more of the component stages. These results are similar to those reported by Quastler (*4*) for mouse intestine and by Dewey and Humphrey (*5*) studying L-P59 mouse fibroblasts after acute exposure to 250 rads of Co^{60} γ-radiation.

After 7 days of exposure the cyclic curve has a pattern similar to that of the control group. The onset of the plateau is, however, still delayed, and the end of the plateau occurs earlier than in the controls. After 14 days of exposure the duration of G_2 plus M has returned to the control value.

The duration of the S stage for the control group, which may be estimated from the time between the 50% points on the ascending and descending limbs of the curve of Fig. 1, is about 7 hours. The estimates for the 1-day, 7-day, and 14-day exposure groups would be approximately 5½, 6½, and 7 hours. It is doubtful whether the use of this method is valid in the case of the 1-day exposure. The fact that unlabeled mitoses are found again about 7 hours after injection in the 1-day group does, however, suggest that the duration of synthesis may be shortened. These unlabeled mitoses probably arose from cells which were at the end of the presynthesis stage (G_1) and therefore have passed through S, G_2, and prophase in 7 hours, as compared with 8 to 9 hours in the controls.

It can be seen from Table I that the generation time is shorter by approximately 1 hour in the 1-day group and by 2 hours in the 7-day and 14-day groups than in the control group. These estimates apply only to a fraction of the proliferative cell population but indicate that the minimum generation time is decreased.

It should be noted that the pattern of labeled mitoses found in the 1-day exposure group is similar to that which would be recorded if a number of mitoses were falsely scored as negative. There is considerable evidence that irradiation produces a decreased uptake of DNA label (*6–10*). A marked decrease in the uptake of tritiated thymidine, resulting in very light labeling of the cells in the autoradiographs, could cause a confusing incidence of "falsely" unlabeled mitoses. Although the number of grains per nucleus appeared to be lower in the 1-day exposure group than in the control and the other experimental groups, the labeling was sufficiently heavy to make this an unlikely explanation of the results. In the 1-day exposure group the number of cells per crypt section, the per cent mitoses, and the per cent initially labeled cells were all below control values. A reduction in the crypt cell population probably results from loss by death of cells and the reduction in the number of proliferative cells (Fig. 2). The approximately tenfold increase in the

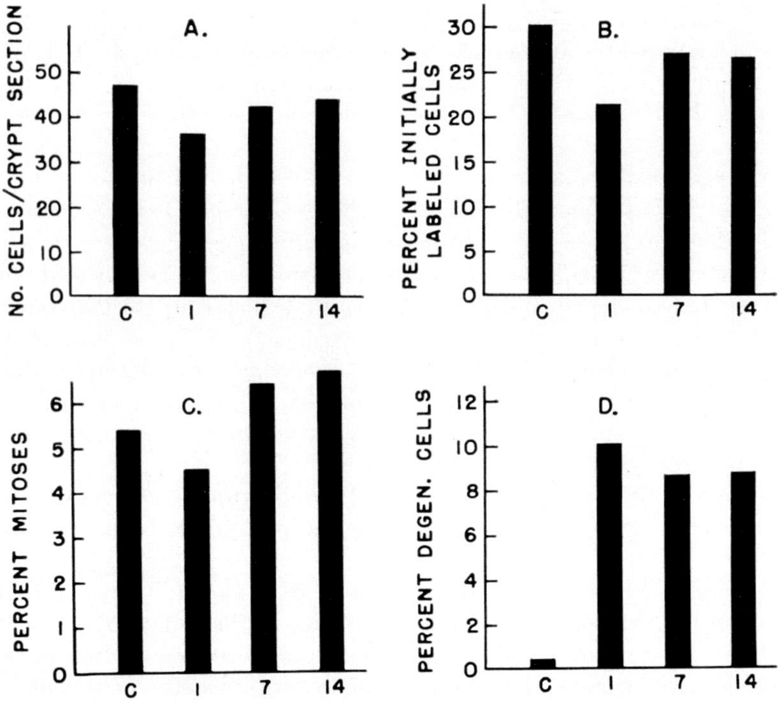

FIG. 2. Histogram to show the average (per 3-μ crypt section) of: *A*, number of cells; *B*, per cent initially labeled cells; *C*, per cent mitosis; and, *D*, per cent degenerated cells. These values were determined in nonirradiated control mice (*C*) and in mice exposed to 220 r/day for 1, 7, and 14 days.

number of interphase cells with marked nuclear abnormalities is an indication of the damage from irradiation (Fig. 2). It is not known how many of the "abnormal" cells succeed in completing one or more divisions or how long an apparently degenerating cell is retained in the crypt. It is, therefore, impossible to correlate this index of damage with actual cell loss.

It can be seen from Fig. 3 that the time at which labeled cells are observed on the villi is later in the 1-day group than in the controls. The decrease in the crypt cell population indicates that the reduced rate of movement of cells out of the crypts is not sufficient to compensate for the decrease in the cell production.

These findings are in general agreement with those of Quastler *et al.* (*11*) and Lamerton *et al.* (*12*).

The results for the 7-day and 14-day groups (Fig. 2) indicate that a considerable degree of recovery from the early effects has occurred. The number of cells per crypt section, although not equal to control values, has increased. Similarly, the number of initially labeled cells has risen. The mitotic index shows an overswing,

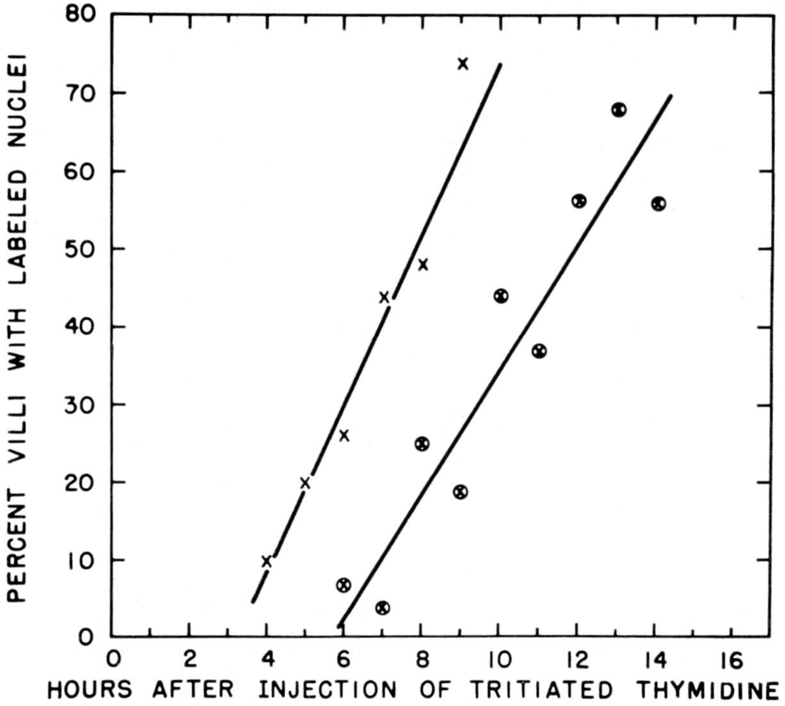

FIG. 3. The movement of labeled nuclei from the crypts onto the base of the villi. Plotted values are the per cent of villi at hourly intervals after the injection of tritiated thymidine which have labeled nuclei on their surface. A least-squares regression line was fitted to these points. × = control; ⊗ = 200 r/day for 1 day.

which has been reported by a number of workers (*12, 13*); however, the actual number of cells in division may not be higher than normal, as the mitotic index is exaggerated by the low crypt section cell count. Furthermore an increased duration of mitosis would also give the false impression of an increase in the number of cells going into division.

The persistence of a large number of degenerating cells is in disagreement with the observations of Quastler *et al.* (*11*), who found that by 48 hours after the onset of 415 rads/day to the rat the amount of nuclear debris corresponded roughly to that found in the crypts of nonirradiated animals. Furthermore, the persistence of large numbers of damaged cells does not support the idea of a development of radioresistance (*14*). The evidence suggests, rather, that there is an adaptation to the environmental stress which compensates for the continued damage. This compensation involves a number of factors. At first the cell death from damage is uncompensated, and the mucosal cell population declines. This decline is halted, at least in part, by the reduction in the generation time, and a reasonably steady state is re-established at a new cell population level. Cell loss by extrusion continues, but the attainment of a new steady state may be aided by an increased life span. Life-span studies are difficult to perform, and therefore the importance of this as a factor in the mechanism of compensation is not known.

The finding that the crypt cell population tends to return to normal levels before there is evidence that the population of the villi increases is consistent with the report of Lamerton *et al.* (*15*) that the diminished proliferation of red cell precursors after 200 rads of acute exposure is accompanied by a retention of mature forms in the bone marrow.

The findings reported here are surprisingly similar to those for the group given 12 r/day for 200 days (*1*), at least in the apparent reduction in generation time of some of the cells and in the compensation for large accumulated radiation doses. Despite the markedly increased cell loss that occurs with 220 r/day, the integrity of the mucosa is maintained after an accumulated dose of 3080 r. However, if there were a small negative balance in cell renewal, the decrease in mucosal cell population would eventually become obvious. It was therefore decided to examine the duodenum after a longer exposure period, close to the time of death.

The mean survival time and the pattern of death of BCF_1 hybrids exposed to 220 r/day has been previously reported (*16*). It was found that the first death occurred after 17 days of exposure and that all the mice were dead by 20 days, with a mean survival of 18 days. Although the pancytopenia found after these periods of exposure indicated that death was primarily a result of damage to the hemopoietic system (G. A. Sacher and M. Miller, personal communication), there was still the possibility that intestinal damage might also have been a contributing factor.

The duodenum of mice sacrificed after 17 and 18 days of exposure were examined microscopically. No quantitative assessments have been carried out, but qualitatively the crypt cells show characteristic evidence of radiation damage, whereas the general appearance of the mucosa suggests that the production of cells has been sufficient to repair lesions and keep mucosal covering intact. The cellularity of the lamina propria appeared to have increased, and there were no apparent lesions of the villi.

SUMMARY

The mucosal epithelium of the duodenum of BCF_1 mice exposed to 220 r/day for 1, 7, 14, 17, and 18 days was studied and compared to that of nonirradiated controls of the same age. The generation time of the duodenal crypt cells of mice irradiated for 1, 7, and 14 days, and of the controls, was determined.

Since it was found that cells are held up between the end of synthesis and the completion of mitosis, the initial effect (at 1 day) may be similar to the effect produced by a single exposure. When exposure is continued, there is an attempt to compensate for cell loss by a speeding up of the generation cycle which is primarily due to a reduction of G_1.

RECEIVED: November 19, 1962

REFERENCES

1. S. LESHER, R. J. M. FRY, and G. SACHER, Effects of chronic gamma irradiation on the generation cycle of the mouse duodenum. *Exptl. Cell Res.* **25,** 398–404 (1961).
2. D. GRAHN, Genetic control of physiological processes: the genetics of radiation toxicity in animals. In *Radioisotopes in the Biosphere*, p. 181, University of Minnesota Press, Minneapolis, Minnesota, 1959.
3. S. R. PELC, The stripping film technique of autoradiography. *Intern. J. Appl. Radiation* **1,** 172 (1956).
4. H. QUASTLER, Cell renewal and acute radiation damage. *Radiology* **73,** 161–165 (1959).
5. W. C. DEWEY and R. M. HUMPHREY, Relative radiosensitivity of different phases in the life cycle of L-P59 mouse fibroblasts and ascites tumor cells. *Radiation Res.* **16,** 503–530 (1962).
6. H. EULER and G. HEVESY, Wirkung der Rontgenstrahlen auf den Umsatz der Nukleinsaure im Jensen-Sarkom. *Kgl. Danske Videnskab. Selskab. Biol. Medd.* **17,** 3–38 (1942).
7. B. E. HOLMES, The inhibition of ribo- and thymonucleic acid synthesis in tumour tissue by irradiation with X-rays. *Brit. J. Radiol.* **20,** *Suppl.* **1,** 450 (1947).
8. L. S. KELLY and H. B. JONES, Effects of irradiation on nucleic acid formation. *Proc. Soc. Exptl. Biol. Med.* **74,** 493–497 (1950).
9. F. G. SHERMAN and H. QUASTLER, DNA Synthesis in irradiated epithelium. *Exptl. Cell Res.* **19,** 343–360 (1960).
10. O. F. NYGAARD and R. L. POTTER, Effect of X-radiation on DNA metabolism in various tissues of the rat. I. Incorporation of C^{14}-thymidine into DNA during the first 24 hours postirradiation. *Radiation Res.* **10,** 462–476 (1959).
11. H. QUASTLER, J. P. M. BENSTED, L. F. LAMERTON, and S. M. SIMPSON, II. Adaptation to continuous irradiation: Observations on the rat intestine. *Brit. J. Radiol.* **32,** 501–512 (1959).
12. L. F. LAMERTON, G. G. STEEL, and D. K. WIMBER, Sensitivity of mammalian tissues to continuous exposure. *Brookhaven Symp. Biol.* **14,** 158–175 (1961).
13. R. B. WILLIAMS, J. N. TOAL, J. WHITE, and H. M. CARPENTER, Effect of total-body X-radiation from wear threshold to tissue-lethal doses on small-bowel epithelium of the rat. I. Changes in morphology and rate of cell division in relation to time and dose. *J. Natl. Cancer Inst.* **21,** 17–61 (1958).
14. M. A. BLOOM, Acquired radioresistance of the crypt epithelium of the duodenum. *Radiology* **55,** 104–115 (1950).
15. L. F. LAMERTON, E. H. BELCHER, and E. B. HARRIS, Blood uptake of Fe59 in studies of red cell production. In *The Kinetics of Cellular Proliferation*, pp. 301–311, Grune and Stratton, New York and London, 1959.
16. D. GRAHN, The genetic factor in acute and chronic radiation toxicity. *Proc. 2nd Intern. Conf. Peaceful Uses At. Energy, Geneva, 1958* **22,** 394–399 (1958).

RADIATION RESEARCH 19, 636–642 (1963)

The Effect of Acidity on the Hydrogen Yield in Gamma-Irradiated Aqueous Solutions

C. H. CHEEK, V. J. LINNENBOM, AND J. W. SWINNERTON
U. S. Naval Research Laboratory, Washington, D. C.

INTRODUCTION

Recent reports on the effect of acidity on the primary hydrogen yield in γ-irradiated aqueous solutions are at variance. Mahlman and Boyle (*1*) reported that G_{H_2} in 0.4 *M* H_2SO_4 equals 0.45, which is the generally accepted value in neutral solutions. Mahlman (*2*) reported that G_{H_2} is independent of acidity up to 0.8 *M* H_2SO_4. Hayon (*3*), however, observed a decrease in G_{H_2} with increasing acidity and reported $G_{H_2} \simeq 0.4$ in 0.4 *M* H_2SO_4, in agreement with the early work of Schwarz *et al.* (*4*).

In view of the discrepancy, it seemed worth while to conduct an additional investigation of the effect of acidity on G_{H_2} by using a method of dissolved-gas analysis developed at this laboratory (*5, 6*).

EXPERIMENTAL PROCEDURE

Baker and Adamson reagent-grade chemicals were used. Water from a Barnstead still was redistilled successively from alkaline permanganate and acid dichromate solutions, with final condensation and storage in quartz apparatus.

The Co^{60} γ-ray source has been described (*7*). An absorbed dose rate of 3.46×10^{20} ev/l-min was obtained in the Fricke dosimeter solution. The absorbed dose rate in each experimental solution was calculated by multiplying the dosimeter value by the ratio between the electron concentrations in the experimental solution and the dosimeter solution. The experimental solutions ranged from neutral to 10 *M* acid, and all contained 10^{-3} *M* potassium bromide.

Experimental solutions were purged with argon and transferred to the irradiation cells by means of the apparatus illustrated in Fig. 1. The apparatus is constructed of Pyrex glass and Teflon-plugged stopcocks. Reservoir *R* is first filled through standard-taper joint *T*, after which the apparatus is assembled and the purging gas routed *ABCDEF*. The solution is purged by the gas emerging from coarse frit *C*. Purged solution may be dispensed through *JF*, while the gas follows either the purging route or the bypass route *AHDEF*. Each irradiation cell, containing a small

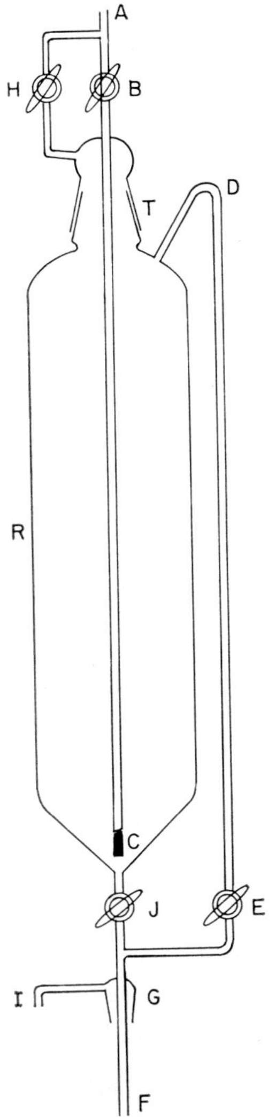

FIG. 1. Purging apparatus

stirring rod, is rinsed with the solution, drained, attached to the 14/35 standard-taper joint *G*, and flushed with the gas which then escapes at *I*. With the gas still flowing, solution is passed into the cell. As the solution overflows, the cell is disconnected and lowered to point *F*, where it is removed and immediately closed with a stopper made by sealing and rounding the narrow end of an inner 14/35 standard-taper joint. This procedure forces out solution which has had momentary contact with the atmosphere and leaves no gas space above the solution. The ir-

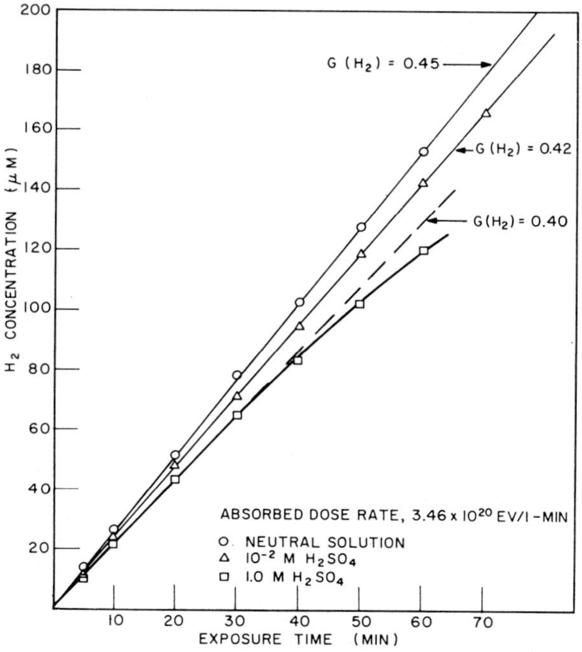

FIG. 2. Variation of H_2 concentration with time of exposure

radiation cells are 2.1 cm in diameter and have a capacity of 26 ml. The capacity of the reservoir is over 700 ml, which permits preparation of over twenty samples from a single filling.

Hydrogen analyses were performed on 8-ml samples of the irradiated solutions by a gas-chromatographic method developed at this laboratory (*5, 6*). Argon carrier gas was used at a flow rate of 50 ml/min, and the instrument was thermostated at 29°C. Daily calibration was performed by injecting 1-ml samples of water equilibrated at 25°C with hydrogen at a partial pressure of 1 atm (total pressure was 1 atm plus aqueous tension). Triplicate calibration runs agreed to within 1%. With a recorder chart speed of 2 inches/min and full-scale response at 1 mv, the sensitivity of the apparatus was 70 $cm^2/\mu M$ of hydrogen.

RESULTS AND DISCUSSION

Graphs of typical runs in neutral solution and at two higher acidities are shown in Fig. 2, and initial yields of hydrogen are presented in Table I. The scatter of results at higher acidity is considerably greater than should be expected from the accuracy of the method, which is reproducible to about 1%. Although the yields diminish more rapidly with dose at higher acidity, the initial yield in 1 M H_2SO_4 can be measured accurately, because the yield curves show no apparent deviation

TABLE I
VARIATION OF H_2 YIELD WITH pH

Solution	*pH*[a]	$G(H_2)$
H_2O	7.0	0.446, 0.449
H_2SO_4	3.6	0.436
H_2SO_4	2.8	0.433
H_2SO_4	2.0	0.420, 0.415
H_2SO_4	1.0	0.409, 0.413
H_2SO_4	0.4	0.410
H_2SO_4	0	0.409, 0.376, 0.395
H_2SO_4	−0.6	0.363, 0.372
H_2SO_4	−1.0	0.29
HCl	0.4	0.413

[a] Values of pH >1 were measured with a meter; values ≦1 are −log *M*, where *M* is the molarity of the acid.

from linearity up to 50 μ*M* H_2. The scatter of results is therefore attributed to impurities in the acid.

Values obtained in this research and those reported by other authors are reproduced in Fig. 3 for comparison. The results obtained at this laboratory are seen to be in substantial agreement with those of Hayon (*3*).

It has been demonstrated that the principal reducing radical produced in water radiolysis bears a unit negative charge (*8*) and exhibits acid-base properties (*9, 10*), with the two forms having distinctly different reactivities toward selected solutes. For the present discussion it is assumed that the basic form is the solvated electron (designated H_2O^-), and the acid form is the H atom.

The processes whereby molecular products are formed in neutral solutions are represented by reactions 1 to 3. It is assumed that hydrogen atoms are formed in

$$2H_2O^- \rightarrow H_2 + 2OH^- \quad (1)$$

$$H_2O^- + OH \rightarrow H_2O + OH^- \quad (2)$$

$$2OH \rightarrow H_2O_2 \quad (3)$$

acid solutions by reaction 4. As the acidity increases, reaction 4 occurs to an in-

$$H_2O^- + H_3O^+ \rightarrow H + 2H_2O \quad (4)$$

creasing extent in the spurs in competition with reactions 1 and 2. H atoms formed in the spurs may undergo the secondary reactions 5 to 7. The probability of occur-

$$H + H_2O^- \rightarrow H_2 + OH^- \quad (5)$$

$$H + OH \rightarrow H_2O \quad (6)$$

$$2H \rightarrow H_2 \quad (7)$$

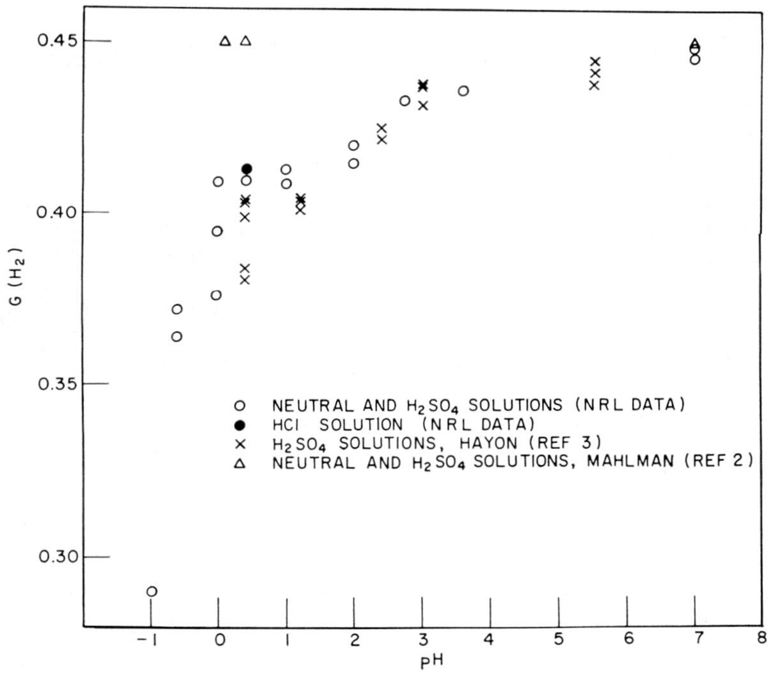

FIG. 3. Variation of H_2 yield with pH

rence of the secondary spur reactions is reduced, since the spurs have become more diffuse during the time required for reaction 4 to occur. The result is an increase in the radical yields at the expense of G_{H_2} and the yield of recombined unlike radicals (designated G_{HOH}). In addition, the ratio between the amounts of H_2 and H_2O formed in reactions 5, 6, and 7 should be different from the corresponding ratio for reactions 1 and 2, because of the altered spatial distribution and the different reactivities of H and H_2O^-.

It is inviting to speculate that k_5 and k_7 are greater than k_1 because of charge repulsion in reaction 1, and that $k_2 > k_6$ because reaction 2 proceeds via electron transfer. On this basis, the compensatory effect of reactions 5 and 7 on G_{H_2} should be relatively greater than that of reaction 6 on G_{HOH}, so that the fractional lowering of G_{H_2} should be less than that of G_{HOH}.

An increase in $G_{H_2O_2}$ with decreasing pH is expected to result from diminished competition of reaction 2 with reaction 3 for OH radicals.

It is well known that the primary yields G_H, G_{OH}, $G_{H_2O_2}$, and G_{-H_2O} increase as the pH decreases below 3. Since G_{HOH}, the sum of the yields of reactions 2 and 6, cannot be measured, its variation with pH is unknown.

By assuming that reactions 1, 2, and 3 proceed with equal facility, Schwarz and co-workers (*11*) estimated from statistical considerations that $G_{HOH} \simeq G_{H_2O_2} + G_{H_2}$. They demonstrated experimentally that the approximation holds well in neutral solution, because the gross yield of water decomposition, $G_{-H_2O} + G_{HOH}$, appears to remain reasonably constant up to high LET when approximated by $G_{-H_2O} + G_{H_2} + G_{H_2O_2}$.

There seems to be no good reason to expect $G_{-H_2O} + G_{HOH}$ to change with pH. The function $G_{-H_2O} + G_{H_2} + G_{H_2O_2}$ increases with decreasing pH (*9*), but it may not be a measure of $G_{-H_2O} + G_{HOH}$ in acid solution because of failure of the relation $G_{HOH} \simeq G_{H_2} + G_{H_2O_2}$ at low pH. If $G_{-H_2O} + G_{HOH}$ is essentially independent of pH, the observed increases in G_{-H_2O}, $G_{H_2O_2}$, G_{OH}, and $G_{H_2O^-}$ (or G_H) must occur at the expense of G_{HOH} and G_{H_2}.

SUMMARY

The initial yield of molecular hydrogen in γ-irradiated aqueous solutions has been measured as a function of acidity in the range from neutral solution to 10 *M* sulfuric acid. The observed decrease in the hydrogen yield with increasing acidity is explained with the assumption that the gross number of radicals formed per unit absorbed dose is independent of pH, so that the increase in measured radical and peroxide yields in acid solutions must occur at the expense of the hydrogen yield and the yield of recombined unlike radicals to form water.

ACKNOWLEDGMENTS

We are grateful to G. R. Gauvin and E. O. Davis for technical assistance.

RECEIVED: November 21, 1962

REFERENCES

1. H. A. MAHLMAN and J. W. BOYLE, Primary cobalt-60 radiolysis yields in heavy water. *J. Chem. Soc.* **80**, 773–774 (1958).
2. H. A. MAHLMAN, Ceric reduction and the radiolytic hydrogen yield. *J. Am. Chem. Soc.* **81**, 3203–3204 (1959).
3. E. HAYON, Effect of solute concentration on the recombination of H and OH in γ-irradiated aqueous solutions. *J. Phys. Chem.* **65**, 1502–1505 (1961).
4. H. A. SCHWARZ, J. P. LOSEE, and A. O. ALLEN, Hydrogen yields in the radiolysis of aqueous solutions. *J. Am. Chem. Soc.* **76**, 4693–4694 (1954).
5. J. W. SWINNERTON, V. J. LINNENBOM, and C. H. CHEEK, Determination of dissolved gases in aqueous solutions by gas chromatography. *Anal. Chem.* **34**, 483–485 (1962).
6. J. W. SWINNERTON, V. J. LINNENBOM, and C. H. CHEEK, Revised sampling procedure for determination of dissolved gases in solution by gas chromatography. *Anal. Chem.* **34**, 1509 (1962).
7. C. H. CHEEK AND V. J. LINNENBOM, The radiation-induced formation of ammonia. *J. Phys. Chem.* **62**, 1475–1479 (1958).
8. G. CZAPSKI and H. A. SCHWARZ, The nature of the reducing radical in water radiolysis. *J. Phys. Chem.* **66**, 471–474 (1962).

9. C. J. Hochanadel, In *Comparative Effects of Radiation* (M. Burton, J. S. Kirby-Smith, and J. L. Magee, eds.), pp. 151–184, Wiley, New York, 1960.
10. N. F. Barr and A. O. Allen, Hydrogen atoms in the radiolysis of water. *J. Phys. Chem.* **63,** 928–931 (1959).
11. H. A. Schwarz, J. M. Caffrey, Jr., and G. Scholes, Radiolysis of neutral water by cyclotron-produced deuterons and helium ions. *J. Am. Chem. Soc.* **81,** 1801–1809 (1959).

RADIATION RESEARCH **19,** 643–654 (1963)

I. Cesium-137 Metabolism in Man[1]

BETTY ROSOFF,[2] STANTON H. COHN,[3] AND HERTA SPENCER[4]

Metabolic Section, Veterans Administration Hospital, Hines, Illinois

INTRODUCTION

The study of the metabolism and distribution of cesium-137 is of particular interest at present because it is a biologically important fission product present in radioactive fallout. Animal experiments have shows species differences in the excretion patterns of parenterally and orally administered Cs^{137}. For example, in rats and rabbits the primary route of excretion is via the kidney, whereas in cows and sheep most of the cesium is excreted in the feces *(1–3)*. In sheep, 50% to 80% of orally ingested Cs^{137} was found to be absorbed *(3)*. Tissue distribution studies in animals have shown that the largest concentration of cesium per gram of wet tissue is found in muscle *(1–3)*.

Previous investigations of cesium in man have been primarily concerned with the measurement of the levels of fallout-produced Cs^{137} in various population groups *(4)*. Recently, with the development of total-body counters, it has also been possible to measure the biological half-life of Cs^{137} in man *(5, 6)*. The results obtained with these measurements are discussed in Part II of this presentation. This report describes a study of the excretion and distribution of Cs^{137} man, after both oral and intravenous administration of tracer doses of this isotope. Attempts to increase the excretion rate of Cs^{137} by various chemical agents are also described.

MATERIALS AND METHODS

The urinary and fecal excretion of Cs^{137} was determined in nine patients with neoplastic disease and in two patients with pulmonary diseases. These patients

[1] Supported by Contract AT(30-1)-1763 from the U.S. Atomic Energy Commission (formerly Montefiore Hospital, New York, New York).

[2] Present address: N.Y.U. Research Service, Goldwater Memorial Hospital and Department of Physiology, Health and Hygiene, Hunter College, New York, New York. For reprints write to Dr. Herta Spencer, Metabolic Section, Veterans Administration Hospital, Hines, Illinois.

[3] Medical Research Center, Brookhaven National Laboratory, Upton, New York.

[4] Metabolic Section, Veterans Administration Hospital, Hines, Illinois.

TABLE I

PATIENTS IN WHOM Cs^{137} EXCRETION AND ENHANCEMENT STUDIES WERE PERFORMED

Patient	*Age*	*Sex*	*Diagnosis*	*Route of administration*	*Study*	
					Type	*Days*
1	46	M	Hodgkin's disease	Intravenous	Excretion	160
2	57	M	Carcinoma of lung	Intravenous	Excretion	60
3	63	F	Carcinoma of colon	Intravenous	Excretion	21
4	45	M	Hodgkin's disease	Intravenous	Excretion Enhancement	42
5	50	M	Chronic pulmonary disease	Oral	Excretion	9
6	57	M	Chronic tuberculosis, inactive	Oral	Excretion	27
7	48	F	Carcinoma of colon with metastases to spine	Oral	Excretion	15
8	59	M	Carcinoma of lung	Oral	Excretion	19
9	55	F	Carcinoma of breast	Oral	Excretion	27
10	53	F	Carcinoma of breast	Oral	Excretion Enhancement	39
11	64	M	Multiple myeloma	Oral	Excretion Enhancement	35

had good nutrition and normal kidney function, and their gastrointestinal tract was not involved in disease (Table I). A single tracer dose of 10 to 50 μc of carrier-free Cs^{137} as chloride was injected intravenously to four patients and administered orally to seven. Blood samples were drawn at frequent intervals on the day of Cs^{137} administration, daily for the following 10 days, and periodically thereafter during the study. The total 24-hour excretion was collected for the duration of the excretion studies, which ranged from 9 to 160 days. In four of these patients, agents which might increase the excretion of cesium were administered at time intervals ranging from 10 to 31 days after the intravenous or oral administration of Cs^{137} (Table II). Normal saline was infused intravenously, and hydrodiuril, ammonium chloride, corticosteroids, the resin kayexalate, and ϵ-aminocaproic acid were administered orally. The tissue distribution of Cs^{137} was studied in four other patients who had expired at various time intervals after administration of the tracer (Table III).

Dose standards for intravenously administered tracers were prepared by quantitatively transferring an equivalent dose from the same syringe and needle into a volumetric flask and diluting with saline to an appropriate volume. Standards for oral doses were prepared by pipetting an equivalent dose into a volumetric flask and diluting in the same manner as above. Aliquots of the standard, whole

TABLE II

Cs^{137} Enhancement Studies

Patient	*Start of treatment after Cs^{137} doses (days)*[a]	*Enhancing agent*	*Dose/day*	*Duration of treatment (days)*
4	13	Infusion of physiologic saline	500 ml	2
4	24	Hydrodiuril	50 mg	3
	31	Ammonium chloride	9 gm[b]	5
10	26	Prednisone	40 mg	14
11	10	Kayexalate	16 gm	5
	21	ϵ-Aminocaproic acid	24 gm	11

[a] A single tracer dose of $Cs^{137}Cl$ was given orally on the first day of the study.
[b] Three grams given three times per day.

TABLE III

Cs^{137} Tissue Distribution Studies

Patient	*Age*	*Sex*	*Diagnosis*	*Days after intravenous injection of Cs^{137}*
1	46	M	Hodgkin's disease	165
12	55	M	Carcinoma of lung	3
13	66	M	Malignant lymphoma	10
14	66	F	Hodgkin's disease	16
15	61	F	Carcinoma of uterus	3

blood, serum, urine, and feces were pipetted directly into counting tubes. Samples of the tissues obtained at autopsy were wet-weighed and placed in counting tubes. The radioassays were performed in a well-type NaI crystal scintillation counter. A single-channel pulse-height analyzer permitted counting at the cesium photopeak. Dose standards were counted at the time the samples were radioassayed. The data are expressed in per cent of the administered dose. For the calculations of the amount of Cs^{137} in whole blood and plasma, the volume of whole blood was assumed to be 5 liters, and of plasma 3 liters.

RESULTS

Excretion Studies

Intravenous Administration. The concentration of Cs^{137} in plasma and in whole blood in a representative study (patient 3) immediately after intravenous injec-

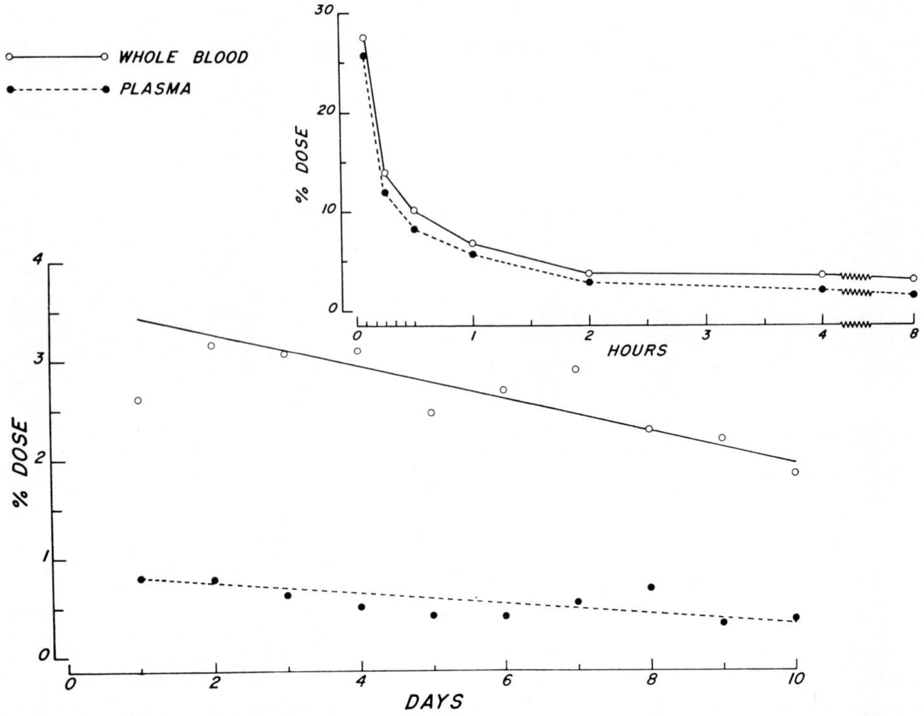

FIG. 1. A single tracer dose of $Cs^{137}Cl$ was injected intravenously. The concentration of Cs^{137} in whole blood and in plasma was determined on the first day of the study at frequent time intervals (see insert) and daily thereafter.

tion is shown in Fig. 1. At 5 minutes after injection of the isotope, the amounts of Cs^{137} in whole blood and in plasma were about equal, 27% and 26%, respectively. These levels decreased in a similar manner over the first 2 hours. The amount of Cs^{137} in whole blood at 2 hours (3.5%) remained the same for several days and then gradually declined to 2% at 10 days. In contrast, the Cs^{137} plasma level continued to decrease from the 2-hour level of 3% to 0.8% at 24 hours and stayed at approximately the same range for the next 10 days.

Most of the intravenously injected cesium was excreted in urine, whereas the fecal cesium excretion contributed only minimally to the total excretion. The excretion curves of patients 1 and 2 who were studied for 160 and 60 days, respectively, are very similar (Fig. 2). The urinary cesium excretion of patient 2 was slightly lower and the fecal excretion was slightly higher than in patient 1, resulting in a similar total excretion for both patients over a 60-day period. The excretion patterns of patients 3 and 4 who were studied for 21 and 11 days, respectively, were similar. Patient 3 excreted 16% of the dose in urine and 4% in stool in the first 11 days, and patient 4 excreted 27% in urine and 2% in stool in the same period of time.

Cs^{137} Body Retention (Intravenous Administration). The amount of cesium remaining in the body was calculated from the total excretion data for patients 1 and 2 (Fig. 3). Each point represents the retention at consecutive 10-day intervals after the intravenous injection of Cs^{137}. Approximately 50% of the dose was present in the body of patient 1 at 50 days, and of patient 2 at 60 days.

Oral Doses. The amount and distribution of Cs^{137} in whole blood and in plasma after the oral administration of Cs^{137} were comparable to those found after the intravenous dose (Fig. 4). In patient 6, the amounts of Cs^{137} in whole blood and in plasma were equal at 1 hour, and at 4 hours there was less in plasma than in whole blood. From 4 to 96 hours, the Cs^{137} level remained relatively constant in whole blood but continued to decrease in plasma. A 4:1 ratio of blood to plasma was reached in 24 hours. In patient 5, the amount of cesium in plasma was already less than in whole blood at 1 hour, and, although both continued to decrease, the

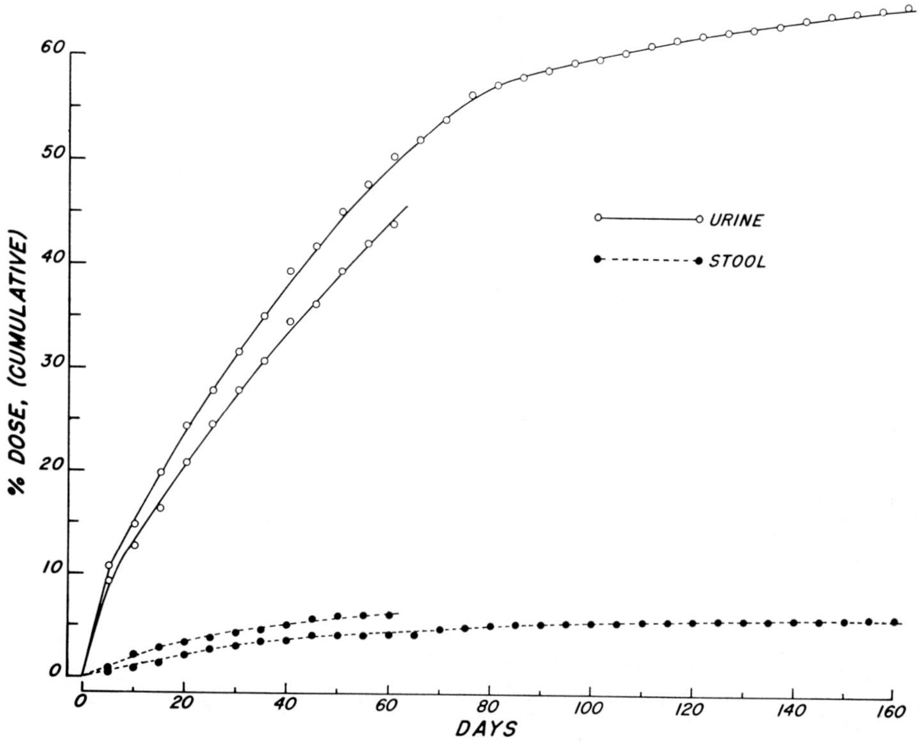

FIG. 2. Urinary and fecal Cs^{137} excretions of patients 1 and 2 after a single intravenous injection of $Cs^{137}Cl$. Patient 1—160-day study; patient 2—60-day study.

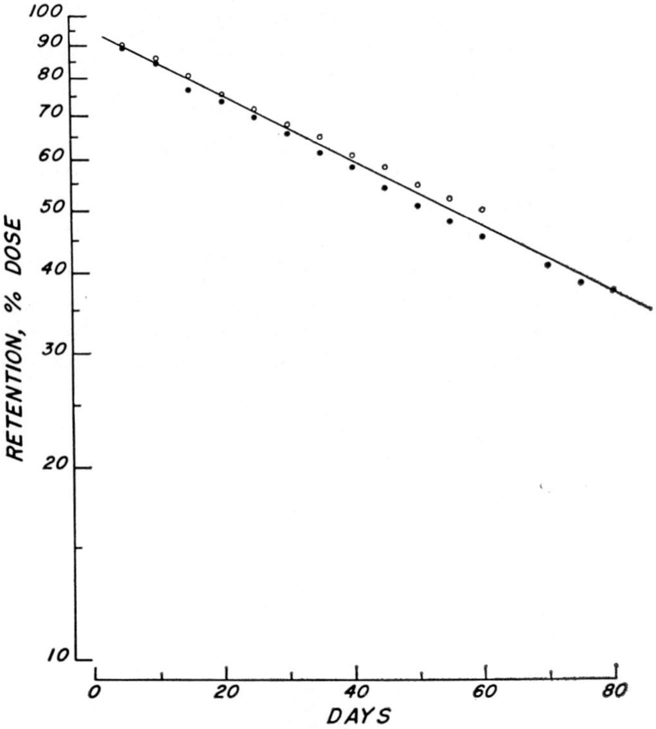

FIG. 3. Cesium-137 whole-body retention of patients 1 and 2. Closed circles, patient 1; open circles, patient 2. A single tracer of $Cs^{137}Cl$ was given intravenously on the first day of the study. The body retention was determined from the excretion data.

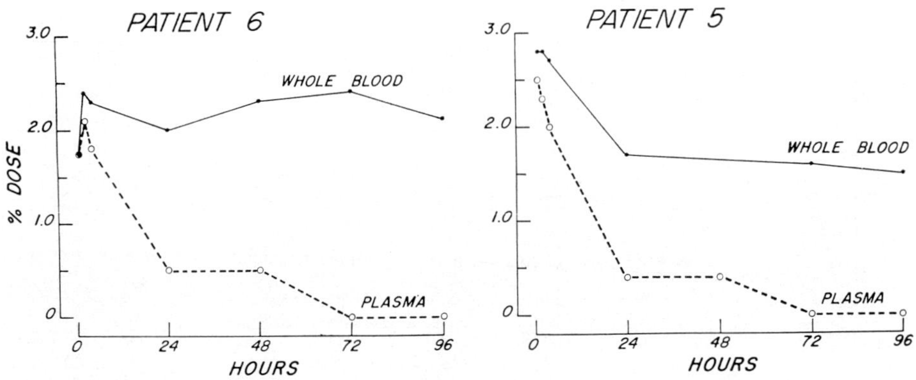

FIG. 4. Cesium-137 concentration in whole blood and in plasma after oral administration of $Cs^{137}Cl$ (patients 5 and 6).

TABLE IV

EXCRETION OF THE TRACER Cs^{137} AFTER ORAL ADMINISTRATION

Patient	*Cumulative excretion for 7 days (% of Administered Dose)*		
	Urine	*Stool*	*Total*
5	7.6	1.8	9.4
6	5.0	2.0	7.0
7	15.7	1.6	17.3
8	12.4	2.1	14.5
9	11.1	1.5	12.6
10	14.5	2.0	16.5
11	7.0	1.8	8.8

plasma levels decreased at a faster rate. At 24 hours the amount of cesium in whole blood was 1.7% of the administered dose, and 0.4% in the plasma.

The 7-day cumulative urinary and fecal Cs^{137} excretions of seven patients who received the tracer orally showed that the total Cs^{137} excretions varied from patient to patient (Table IV). The fecal Cs^{137} excretion was low in all cases and ranged from 1.5% to 2.1% of the administered dose. In each of these patients the urinary Cs^{137} excretion was two and one-half to ten times as high as the fecal Cs^{137} excretion.

The cumulative Cs^{137} excretions over different time intervals after the intravenous and oral administrations of the tracer are compared in Fig. 5. These data show that the urinary and fecal Cs^{137} excretions after oral administration were

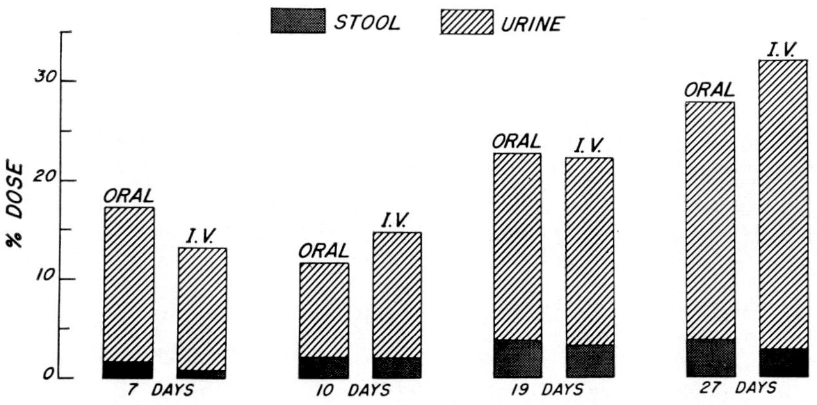

FIG. 5. Cumulative excretion of $Cs^{137}Cl$ after oral and intravenous administration of a single tracer dose given on the first day of the respective studies.

similar to those after intravenous injection. The main pathway of excretion was via the kidney subsequent to the Cs^{137} entry into the body by either route.

Enhancement Studies

Infusions of 500 ml of physiologic saline given on the thirteenth and fourteenth days after the administration of Cs^{137} were ineffective in increasing the urinary or fecal cesium excretion in patient 4 (Table II). Similarly, the administration of 50 mg of hydrochlorothiazide given orally on three consecutive days (days 24 to 26 of study) and of 9 gm of ammonium chloride given daily for 5 days (days 31 to 35 of study) was of no avail in enhancing the Cs^{137} excretion. The administration of 40 mg of prednisone per day given for 14 days (days 26 to 39 after injection of Cs^{137}) was also ineffective in raising the urinary Cs^{137} excretion. A potassium ion-exchange resin, kayexalate, (16 gm/day), given orally from the tenth to the fifteenth day and ϵ-aminocaproic acid (24 gm/day) given orally for 11 days starting on the twenty-first day after the ingestion of Cs^{137} were ineffective in increasing the urinary or fecal Cs^{137} excretion in patient 10.

Tissue Distribution Studies

Cesium-137 tissue distribution studies were performed on five patients described in Table III.

The tissue distribution of Cs^{137} at 3, 10, 16, and 165 days after the administration of the dose is presented in Fig. 6. At 3 days the level of Cs^{137} in per cent of dose per gram of wet tissue was highest in liver (8×10^{-3}). The concentration of both spleen and psoas muscle was slightly lower (7×10^{-3}). The concentration of Cs^{137} was still lower in the following organs, in decreasing order: pancreas, heart muscle, skeletal muscle, rib, adrenals, and lung. The concentration in lung was the lowest of all the tissues analyzed (3×10^{-3}). The tissues of two patients obtained 10 and 16 days after Cs^{137} administration had a concentration about one-half those of the 3-day study. Here again, the concentration in liver and skeletal muscle was highest (3×10^{-3}), with that of spleen, heart muscle, kidney, and lung being similar and slightly lower than that of liver and skeletal muscle. Pancreas showed a concentration of 2×10^{-3}, and rib and adrenals were 1.5×10^{-3}, one-half that of liver. In patient 1, 165 days after Cs^{137} administration all tissues showed a much lower concentration of Cs^{137}. Liver and kidney contained 2×10^{-4}, and the other tissues contained about 1×10^{-4} of the injected dose.

DISCUSSION

Cesium, like potassium, disappears rapidly from the blood stream when injected intravenously. The ratio of whole blood to plasma was 4:1 at 24 hours, and this difference was maintained for several days. Cesium may exchange for potassium in erythrocytes or may be taken up by a similar mechanism as potassium.

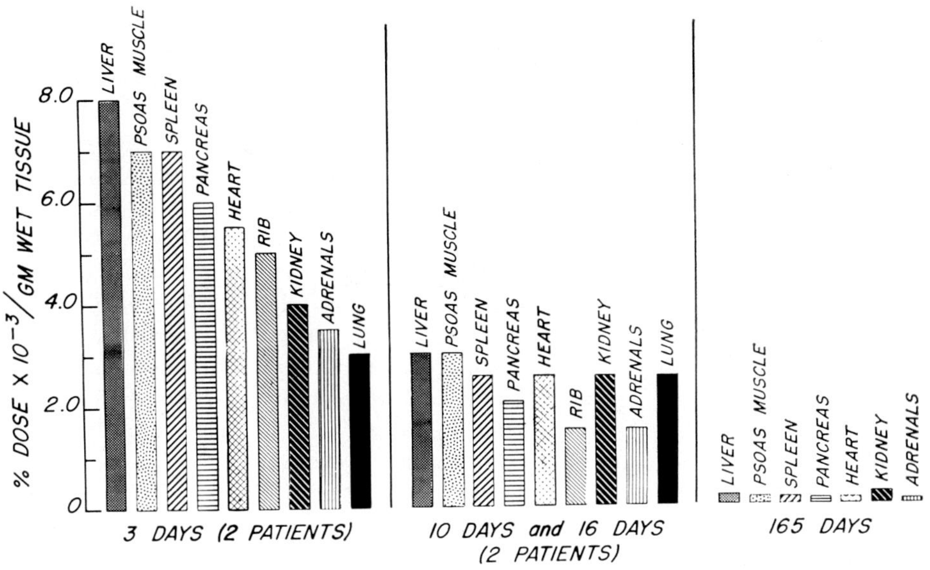

FIG. 6. A single tracer dose of $Cs^{137}Cl$ was injected intravenously to five patients. Tissue samples were obtained at autopsy in two patients 3 days after the injection of the tracer. In one patient each, the samples were obtained at 10, 16, and 165 days after the injection of the tracer.

Relman (*7*) has shown that cesium accumulates preferentially to potassium in muscle tissue, and the same may be true for red blood cells. The rapid and almost complete absorption of orally administered cesium is indicated by the fact that 2% to 3% of the dose is present within 1 hour in whole blood, and a fairly constant level is reached in whole blood in less than 24 hours, similar to the results obtained after the intravenous injection. The cesium accumulation in red blood cells and in other tissues does not seem to be due to passive diffusion between plasma and cells, but the cellular uptake may take place against a concentration gradient. For instance, a 20-fold differential exists between tissues and plasma concentration 3 days after the administration of Cs^{137}.

The results of Cs^{137} excretion studies in man are in good agreement with previously reported findings in animals (*1–3*), the main pathway of excretion being via the kidney. However, the urinary–fecal Cs^{137} excretion ratio of 10:1 in man is considerably higher than in animals. For instance, this ratio was reported to be 3:1 in mice (*8*). Since the soft-tissue concentration decreases with time, the low but continuous urinary Cs^{137} excretion in man is most likely due to a slow release of cesium from cells into the extracellular space and excretion via the kidneys. Some of the loss of cesium from the tissues might be due to exchange with potassium.

It is also possible that the excretion of cesium in man represents a release of cesium from tissues due to cell catabolism. Mraz *et al.* (*9*) suggest that cesium is released from tissues only as a result of catabolism. The fecal excretion might in part be due to excretion via the biliary system into the intestine, since the concentration of cesium is very high in the liver. Hood and Comar (*1*) found that the Cs^{137} level in the liver of rats decreased fairly rapidly with time, and Nelson *et al.* (*10*) reported similar results in mice.

The tissue distribution studies in man reported here reveal that the concentration decreased with time and that the distribution of cesium in soft tissues was uniform by 10 days. Nelson showed in autoradiographic studies in mice that the uptake in liver and spleen was not so high as in muscle and cartilage and that the concentration decreased at a much faster rate (*10*). The tissue analyses in man, however, indicate a fairly uniform concentration in soft tissues at 10 days. The relatively high Cs^{137} concentration in the rib was unexpected in view of the uniform soft-tissue distribution of this isotope. However, no attempt was made to remove the bone marrow from the rib samples, and therefore the concentration in rib may indicate either bone uptake or uptake of cesium in the blood-forming cells of the bone marrow. Further investigations are necessary to verify these observations. The complete absorption of orally administered Cs^{137} in man suggests that the tissue distribution after this route of administration would be similar to that after the intravenous dose. This is also suggested by the work of others in animals (*3*).

The biological half-life of Cs^{137} in man assumes importance in view of the fact that the tissues are exposed to both γ- and β-radiation. Cs^{137} is a β-emitter, but its daughter Ba^{137m} decays by γ-emission to stable Ba^{137} (*11*). Recent studies in dogs exposed to Cs^{137} have shown that in most cases the contribution of the β-radiation to the tissue exposure is considerably greater than that of the γ-radiation (*12*). In the patients studied, 50% of the intravenously administered Cs^{137} was excreted in urine and stool in time ranging from 50 to 60 days. These data are in agreement with the body retention determined by whole-body counting of five other patients who received Cs^{137} intravenously and/or orally. (See Part II of this presentation.)

Enhancement studied in man reported here and elsewhere and those carried out in animals underscore the difficulty in removing Cs^{137} from the body once the radioisotope is deposited in the tissues. Mraz *et al.* (*9, 13*) have shown that an increase of potassium in the diet increases the excretion of acutely administered Cs^{134} in rats and sheep. Richmond and Furchner (*14*) using Cs^{137} confirmed these results in rats. Wasserman and Comar (*15*) found in studies of chronic ingestion of Cs^{137} that the retention of cesium did not appreciably decrease when the dietary potassium intake was increased, and that a 9-fold increase in dietary potassium resulted in only a 2-fold decrease in cesium concentration in muscle. Similar results were reported for man (*16*). Increasing the potassium intake had no significant long-term effect on the excretion of chronically ingested Cs^{137}. It has been suggested that stable cesium might be effective in washing out Cs^{137} from tissues, but recent studies in rats indicate that orally administered cesium chloride does not enhance Cs^{137} excretion, and the toxic effects, in fact, reduce the normal excretion rate (*17*). These reports suggest that further studies with potassium in man under carefully controlled conditions seem to be indicated. Different doses of orally administered diamox were shown to enhance the excretion of Cs^{137} in rats (*18*). To date, the use of catabolic agents which cause a release of tissue potassium and of ion-exchange resins was ineffective in our hands.

SUMMARY

1. The main pathway of Cs^{137} excretion in man after either intravenous or oral administration is via the kidney; the ratio of urinary to fecal excretion is approximately 10:1.

2. Orally administered Cs^{137} is rapidly and almost completely absorbed. The metabolism of the radioisotope was shown to be similar after either intravenous or oral administration.

3. Cs^{137} disappears very rapidly from plasma and is taken up by red blood cells.

4. The biological half-life of cesium in man, determined by analyses of excreta of 2 patients, was found to be 50 and 60 days, respectively. These values are similar to the biological half-lives obtained by long-term whole-body counting studies.

5. The tissue distribution of Cs^{137} in man decreases with time, and the concentration is fairly uniform in the soft tissues by 10 days.

6. Attempts to enhance the excretion rate of Cs^{137} with diuretics, corticosteroids, and ion-exchange resins were unsuccessful.

RECEIVED: December 5, 1962

REFERENCES

1. S. L. HOOD and C. L. COMAR, Metabolism of $cesium^{137}$ in rats and farm animals. *Arch. Biochem. Biophys.* **45,** 423–433 (1953).

2. L. G. WILLIAMS and H. PATRICK, Metabolism of $cesium^{134}$ in rabbits. *Arch. Biochem. Biophys.* **70,** 464–468 (1957).

3. R. O. MCCLELLAN, J. R. MCKENNEY, and L. K. BUSTAD, Metabolism and dosimetry of $cesium^{137}$ in male sheep. Hanford Atomic Production Operation AEC Report, Richmond, Washington. HW-72511 (TID-4500, 17th ed.) (February 1962).

4. J. RUNDO, Radiocaesium in human beings. *Nature* **188,** 703–706 (1960).

5. C. R. RICHMOND, J. E. FURCHNER, and W. LANGHAM, Longterm retention of radiocesium in man. *Health Phys.* **8,** 202 (1962).

6. S. H. COHN, ROSOFF, R., GUSMANO, E. A., and SPENCER, H. H. Long-term Cs^{137} turnover in man as measured by a whole-body counter. *Radiation Res.* **19,** 655–658 (1963) (This issue).

7. A. S. RELMAN, The physiological behaviour of rubidium and cesium in relation to that of potassium. *Yale J. Biol. Med.* **29,** 248–262 (1956).

8. B. Rosoff, A. Feldstein, F. Stand, G. Williams, and H. Spencer, Cesium^{137} excretion and distribution in man. (Abstract) *Radiation Res.* **14,** 495 (1961).
9. F. R. Mraz, M. LeNoir, J. J. Pinajian and H. Patrick, Influence of potassium and sodium on uptake and retention of cesium^{134} in rats. *Arch. Biochem. Biophys.* **66,** 177–182 (1957).
10. A. Nelson, S. Ullberg, H. Kristoffersson, and C. Rönnbäck, Distribution of radiocesium in mice. *Acta Radiol.* **55,** 374–384 (1961).
11. R. H. Wasserman, A. H. Twardock, and C. L. Comar, Metabolic dissociation of short-lived barium^{137} from its cesium^{137} parent. *Science* **129,** 568–569 (1959).
12. M. M. Nold, D. N. Tapper, and C. L. Comar, Cs^{137} dose measurements in tissue II. *Health Phys.* **8,** 217–229 (1962).
13. F. R. Mraz, Influence of dietary potassium and sodium on cesium^{134} and potassium^{42} excretion in sheep. *J. Nutr.* **68,** 655–662 (1959).
14. C. R. Richmond and J. E. Furchner, The enchancement of cesium^{137} excretion by rats fed potassium-supplemented diets. *Proc. Soc. Exptl. Biol. Med.* **108,** 797–798 (1961).
15. R. H. Wasserman and C. L. Comar, The influence of dietary potassium on the retention of chronically ingested Cs^{137} in the rat. *Radiation Res.* **15,** 70–77 (1961).
16. K. G. McNeill, R. M. Green, and A. Rapoport, Influence of increased potassium intake on the excretion of radioactive cesium (Cs^{137}) in humans. *Can. Med. Assoc. J.* **85,** 1377–1380 (1961).
17. J. E. Furchner and C. R. Richmond, The effect of stable cesium on the retention of cesium^{137} by rats. *Proc. Soc. Exptl. Biol. Med.* **110,** 185–187 (1962).
18. C. R. Richmond and J. E. Furchner, Effect of a carbonic anhydrase inhibitor (diamox) on Cs^{137} excretion by rats. *Health Phys.* **6,** 36–40 (1961).

RADIATION RESEARCH 19, 655–658 (1963)

II. Long-Term Cs^{137} Turnover in Man as Measured by a Whole-Body Counter[1]

STANTON H. COHN, BETTY ROSOFF,[2] ERNEST A. GUSMANO, AND HERTA SPENCER[3]

Medical Research Center, Brookhaven National Laboratory, Upton, New York

INTRODUCTION

In order to assess the radiation hazard of the fission product Cs^{137}, it is necessary to determine its long-term turnover rate in man. Part II of the report describes a long-term study of Cs^{137} made on five patients. Measurements of whole-body retention were made with the Brookhaven whole-body counter. It has been found that the technique of radiochemical analysis of excreta is of limited sensitivity for determining whole-body retention at very long periods of time after isotope administration.

In order to assay the radiation hazard, it is further necessary to estimate the retention over the normal life span of man on the basis of the data obtained. Thus a mathematical model must be developed from which long-term extrapolations can be made. In this study, data analysis was carried out with the use of a computer in order to determine the parameters of the mathematical functions that best describe these data.

METHODS

The Brookhaven whole-body counter used in this study has been previously described (*1*). The counter consists of an 8 × 4-inch NaI(Tl) crystal detector with three 3-inch photomultiplier tubes. The detector is suspended 19 inches over the adjustable cot holding the patient. A 400-channel transistorized RIDL (Model 34-12) pulse-height analyzer is employed.

$Cs^{137}Cl$ was administered intravenously as a single dose to two patients and orally to three patients. The descriptions of the patients and details of the isotope

[1] Research supported by the U. S. Atomic Energy Commission.

[2] Present address: N. Y. U. Research Service, Goldwater Memorial Hospital and Department of Physiology, Health and Hygiene, Hunter College, New York City.

[3] Present address: Metabolic Section, Veterans Administration Hospital, Hines, Illinois.

TABLE I

Description of Patients

Patient	*Dose of Cs^{137} Cl (μc)*	*Route of administration*	*Age (years)*	*Sex*	*Diagnosis*
GAR	50	Oral	57	M	Pulmonary tuberculosis, inactive
POS	25	Oral	73	M	Hypopituitarism secondary to pituitary tumor
MAT	10	Intravenous	45	F	Carcinoma of colon
KAU	10	Intravenous	70	M	Malignant lymphoma
BER	10	Oral	60	F	Malignant lymphoma

administration are presented in Table I. All subjects were outpatients and were counted on the average of three times a month.

The variation in the counting rate for the photopeak of a point source of Cs^{137} is $\pm 0.24\%$. The precision of the counter for Cs^{137} in man is 0.36 mμc. The per cent standard deviation of the count rate in a patient for a 10-minute count one year after the oral administration of 50 μc of Cs^{137} is ± 0.27. The variability of the 10-minute background over a 30-day period is $\pm 1.10\%$. The variation in the count rate due to reproducing the patient's position on the cot is less than 2%. The Brookhaven-Merlin computer was programmed to determine the best least-squares fit for the curves and the standard errors.

RESULTS AND DISCUSSION

The whole-body retention data for intravenously-administered Cs^{137} for a representative patient (GAR) are shown in Fig. 1. The biological retention of Cs^{137} for all patients can be described by a sum of a number of exponential functions. However, only the final exponential component is considered in this report, as it represents 85 to 95% of the administered dose and thus accounts for practically all the radiation dose in all patients studied. The intercepts (A) and rate constants (λ) of this major exponential component for each patient, along with their standard errors, as determined by computer analysis, are presented in Table II.

In order to eliminate the effect on the geometry, and thus on the counting, of the initial variations in distribution of the administered isotope, Cs^{137} retention values were obtained from the excretion data for the first few weeks of the study. Thus, the curves were normalized to the retention values obtained by analysis of excretion in patients GAR, MAT, and KAU over the first 3 weeks.

The values for the biological half-life reported here range from 54 to 114 days, with a mean of 75 days. This value is in agreement with that obtained by Lidén (*2*), who reported a biological half-life of 74 days in one male injected intravenously. A similar spread in the values for biological half-life in a situation of

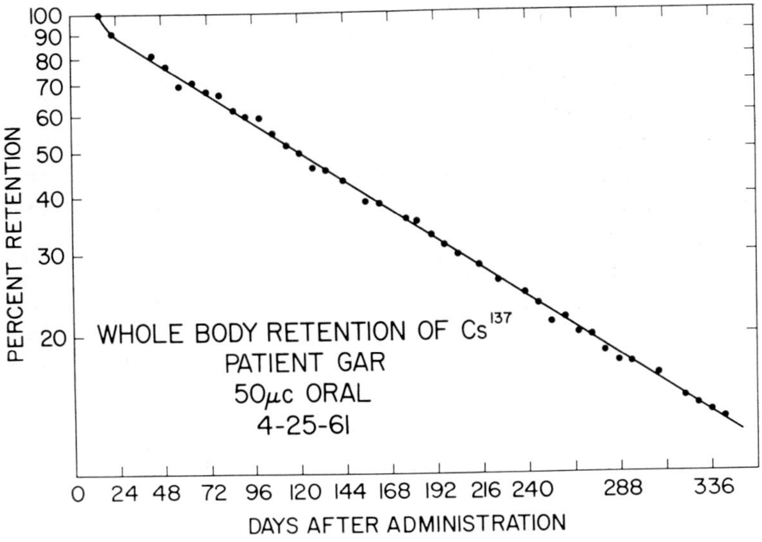

FIG. 1. Whole-body retention of Cs^{137}

TABLE II

LONG-TERM WHOLE-BODY RETENTION OF CESIUM-137

Per cent retention $(R) = Ae^{-\lambda t}$

Patient	*Period of study (days)*	*Number of counts*	A *(intercept) (% injected dose)*	λ *(slope) (day⁻¹, × 10⁴)*	*Biological half-life (days)*
GAR	22–343	41	94.47 ± 0.66[a]	60.72 ± 3.57[a]	$113.99 + 0.67$ $- 0.66$
POS	28–181	16	—	90.39 ± 1.08	$76.65 + 0.90$ $- 0.84$
MAT	9–128	14	85.91 ± 0.90	120.53 ± 1.35	$57.50 + 0.65$ $- 0.64$
KAU	23–239	17	86.67 ± 1.10	127.41 ± 0.90	$54.39 + 0.39$ $- 0.38$
BER	14–106	10	—	96.49 ± 1.97	$71.82 + 2.49$ $- 1.44$

[a] Standard error of the estimate of the coefficients of the line of regression: See Y. Beers, *Theory of Error*, Addison-Wesley Publishing Co., 1957.

chronic exposure was also noted by Rundo (*3*), who obtained values from **48** to **126** days and a mean of **87** days. These values can be compared to the mean value of **135** days as reported by Richmond *et al.* (*4*) and **115** days as reported by McNeil and Green (*5*). The wide variations in biological half-life reported may be due to the effects of age, or possibly metabolic variations or differences in diets of the subjects studied. In the present study the ages of the subjects were from **45** to **73** years, whereas in the other studies the subjects were generally young males. However, even in dogs of the same age and nutritional background, widespread differences in the Cs^{137} turnover rate still occur (*6*).

A single exponential term was sufficient to describe the data for the longest study in the present series, **343** days. Richmond *et al.* (*4*) in a study covering a period of **940** days also found that a single exponential term satisfactorily described the data. On the basis of these findings, it would appear that the data may be extrapolated over considerably longer periods of time. These findings also suggest that Cs^{137} is excreted primarily from one large compartment or, alternatively, is quite uniformly distributed throughout the body, as discussed in Part I.

It will be of interest to investigate, in future studies, the effects of such factors as age, diet, and metabolic disorders on the turnover rate, inasmuch as the present data suggest possible variations in the turnover on the basis of these factors.

RECEIVED: December 5, 1962

REFERENCES

1. S. H. COHN, S. W. LIPPINCOTT, E. P. CRONKITE, and P. G. REIZENSTEIN, Application of whole-body gamma spectrometry to clinical tracer studies. *Proc. Whole Body Counting Symposium, I.A.E.A., Vienna* pp. 469–486 (1962).

2. K. LIDÉN, Cesium 137 burdens in Swedish Laplanders and reindeer. *Acta Radiol.* **56,** 237 (1961).

3. J. RUNDO, *Proc. Whole Body Counting Symposium, I.A.E.A., Vienna* p. 362 (1962).

4. C. R. RICHMOND, J. E. FURCHNER, and W. H. LANGHAM, Long term retention of radiocesium by man. *Health Phys.* **8,** 201 (1962).

5. K. G. MCNEIL and R. M. GREEN, The effective half-lives of Cs and I in the body. *Can. J. Phys.* **37,** 528 (1959).

6. M. N. NOLD, D. N. TAPPER, and C. L. COMAR, Cs^{137} dose measurements in tissue. II. *Health Phys.* **8,** 217 (1962).

RADIATION RESEARCH 19, 659–669 (1963)

Effect of Partial Hepatectomy on Nucleic Acid Metabolism of Regenerating Thymus[1]

A. O. SMOOT[2] AND J. L. VAN LANCKER[3]

Department of Pathology, University of Utah, Salt Lake City, Utah

INTRODUCTION

After the administration of sublethal doses of X-irradiation to unprotected mice, or of lethal doses to protected animals, the damage to lymphoid tissue and bone marrow is repaired (*1–6*). The regeneration of different organs occurs simultaneously, or in sequence, but the effect of regeneration of one organ on another is not known. Studies concerning the restoration of lymphopoietic tissue after total-body doses of X-irradiation to spleen-shielded animals indicate that regeneration of the thymus lags behind that of other lymphopoietic tissues (*4*). Repeated total-body doses of X-irradiation lead to an increase in the incidence of tumors that originate in the thymus (*7*). The induction period of these tumors is characterized by retarded regeneration of the thymic cells (*8*). These observations suggested that thymus may constitute favorable material for the study of the interference between regenerating tissues. Such studies could, however, best be conducted if the metabolic alterations of one of the regenerating tissues could be controlled; this control is possible with regenerating liver. Indeed, after partial hepatectomy, the metabolic steps that culminate in mitosis occur simultaneously in a large number of cells (*9*). The purpose of this study was to investigate the effect of liver regeneration induced by partial hepatectomy on thymus regeneration induced by irradiation of that organ.

METHODS

Three hundred roentgens was administered to the thymus area of 6-week-old C57BL mice with a collimating tube (1 cm in diameter). The distance between

[1] This work was supported by grants No. C 3873 and No. C 3052 of the National Institutes of Health.

[2] Part of this work was performed while Dr. Smoot was the tenant of a Medical Student Fellowship of the National Foundation.

[3] Dr. Van Lancker is a Career Investigator of National Institutes of Health, Department of Pathology, University of Wisconsin, Madison, Wisconsin.

the skin and the X-radiation source was 15 cm. The X-ray generator was operated at 100 kv, 5 ma (HVL 1.5 mm Al), with added filtration of 1 mm Al. Six-week-old C57BL mice were partially hepatectomized under ether anesthesia according to the method of Higgins and Anderson (*9*). Each animal received 5 μc of orotic acid-C^{14} 6 hours before sacrifice. The animals were sacrificed by decapitation and thoroughly bled at various times after X-irradiation or partial hepatectomy. The tissues were homogenized, the nucleic acid extracted, and their specific activities determined as described previously (*10*). The thymus glands used for histological examination were fixed in Bouin's solution, embedded in paraffin, cut, and stained with hematoxylin and eosin.

RESULTS

Because thymus morphology was not qualitatively different in hepatectomized and irradiated animals, and since the changes observed after localized X-irradiation differ from those described after the administration of similar whole-body doses (*11*) only by their intensity and by the rapidity of their restoration, a complete description of the histological changes need not be included. Thus, only a few salient points relative to the discussion will be presented.

Changes in Thymus after Local Irradiation and after Partial Hepatectomy

Because partial hepatectomy itself affects nucleic acid metabolism of mouse thymus, it was necessary to investigate separately the effect of local X-irradiation and partial hepatectomy.

For the sake of clarity, the sequence of the alterations induced in the thymus by local irradiation or by partial hepatectomy will be divided in periods of 0 to 12 hours, 12 to 48 hours, 48 to 96 hours, and 96 to 108 hours.

Changes between 0 and 12 hours. The weight loss (Fig. 1) suggests a decrease in the total cellular population of both hepatectomized and irradiated animals. The low specific activities (Figs. 2 and 3) indicate that the nucleic acid metabolism is altered in each of these groups of animals. These findings may result either from cellular death or from a shift in the cellular population in favor of cells with low metabolic activity. Although there is a loss in both deoxyribonucleic (DNA) and ribonucleic (RNA) content (Figs. 2 and 3) of irradiated animals, there is no immediate change in the nucleic acid content of the hepatectomized animal. The difference could be explained by the appearance of a higher proportion of dead thymic cells in the irradiated animal, a finding which is in agreement with the histological observation.

Changes between 12 and 48 hours. A marked loss of weight (Fig. 1), associated with low specific activities (Figs. 2 and 3) of the nucleic acids, suggests that extensive cellular depopulation has occurred in the thymus of irradiated animals. This probably results from cellular degeneration, an observation in agreement with the marked degree of cellular necrosis observed histologically. The temporary

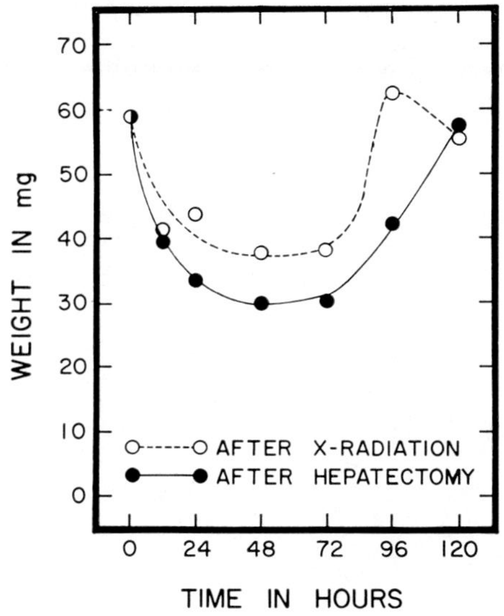

FIG. 1. Changes in thymus weight at various times after partial hepatectomy or local irradiation of the thymus. Each point corresponds to the mean value calculated from six individual determinations. The 0 point refers to the DNA content or specific activity in thymus of untreated mice.

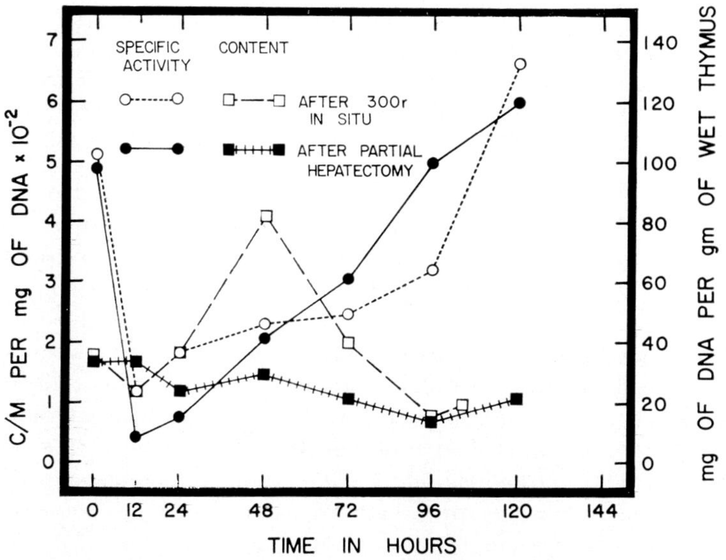

FIG. 2. Changes in thymus DNA content and DNA specific activity in mouse thymus irradiated *in situ* or in nonirradiated mouse thymus after partial hepatectomy, versus the time elapsed after X-irradiation or partial hepatectomy. Specific activities are presented in counts per minute per milligram of DNA, and the DNA content in milligrams of DNA per gram of wet thymus. Six thymus glands were pooled to determine each point of the curves. The 0 point refers to the DNA content or specific activity in thymus of untreated mice.

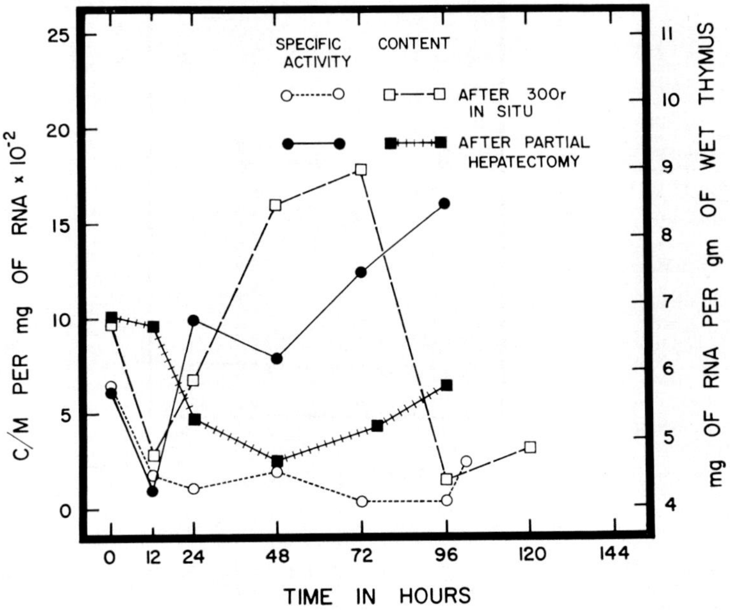

FIG. 3. Changes in thymus RNA content and RNA specific activity in either mouse thymus irradiated *in situ*, or in nonirradiated mouse thymus after partial hepatectomy versus the time elapsed after X-irradiation or partial hepatectomy. Specific activities are presented in counts per minute per milligram of RNA, and the RNA content in milligrams of RNA per gram of wet thymus. Six thymus glands were pooled to determine each point of the curves. The 0 point refers to the RNA content or specific activity in thymus of untreated mice.

increase in nucleic acids is not surprising, because it has been demonstrated, at least in the case of DNA, that this nucleic acid is more resistant to the action of hydrolytic enzymes than other biochemical components in the course of autolysis (*12*). The drop in thymus weight (Fig. 1) and the decrease in nucleic acid content suggest a decrease (Figs. 2 and 3) of thymic cell population in hepatectomized animals. The rising specific activities (Figs. 2 and 3) of the two nucleic acids indicate that, in contrast to the irradiated animals, the remaining cells are actively synthesizing DNA and turning over RNA. These biochemical findings are also in agreement with the histological observations which demonstrate only a mild degree of necrosis and marked cellular depopulation. In the absence of extensive cellular degeneration, it is possible that the reduced cellular population results from migration of thymic cells to other tissues.

Changes between 48 and 96 hours. There is a slow rise in DNA and decrease in RNA specific activities (Figs. 2 and 3) in thymus of irradiated animals, associated with a rapid increase in weight (Fig. 1) starting 72 hours after X-irradiation. These observations suggest that the thymus is slowly repopulated by cells actively synthesizing DNA, but with low RNA turnover. In the absence of quantitative histological studies, these changes could not be demonstrated. The decrease in DNA and RNA contents probably results from the elimination of necrotic remnants; indeed, little cellular degeneration is observed. In hepatectomized animals, RNA content and specific activity increase together; in contrast, DNA content drops slowly, and its specific activity increases slightly. The biochemical changes are accompanied by a moderate increase in thymus weights. These results suggest a shift in the cellular population in favor of cells with a high RNA content and turnover. This may result from a progressive decrease in the proportion of migrating cells, associated with a relative increase in the proportion of fixed cells of the thymus.

Changes after 96 hours. In both irradiated and hepatectomized animals, a slow increase in DNA and RNA contents is observed, associated with a rapid increase in nucleic acid specific activities, and a rapid weight gain. These findings are in agreement with the repopulation of the thymus by lymphoid cells seen histologically.

Changes in Liver after Partial Hepatectomy

The DNA content and the incorporation of orotic acid-C^{14} into liver DNA (Fig. 4) of regenerating mouse liver is similar to that previously observed in rats. There is little or no incorporation between 12 and 24 hours after partial hepatectomy; the specific activity then increases steadily to reach a maximum between 48 and 72 hours after operation. Since the DNA concentration increases steadily from 24 to 108 hours after hepatectomy, and since there is little incorporation in normal liver, it can be assumed that the specific activity measurements reflect *de novo* DNA synthesis.

The results of both RNA specific activities and contents (Fig. 5) of mouse regenerating livers are those expected from previous studies (*13*). Thus, after a temporary depression in RNA per gram of tissue, which reaches a minimum 24 hours after hepatectomy, there is a rapid return to normal concentrations. A high specific activity (100% higher than normal) is observed between 12 and 24 hours after hepatectomy. This high uptake of the isotope probably can be partially explained by the high rate of RNA synthesis at that time.

Experiments in Which Maximum DNA and RNA Synthesis in Regenerating Liver Are Arranged to Coincide with Maximum DNA or RNA Synthesis in the Irradiated Thymus

Two groups of 6 mice were used in each of these experiments. Thirty-six hours after irradiation of one group, all animals were partially hepatectomized. All mice received a single injection of orotic acid-C^{14} 6 hours prior to sacrifice. All animals were killed 72 hours after hepatectomy. The irradiated and nonirradiated thymus glands were then pooled and used for specific activity determinations.

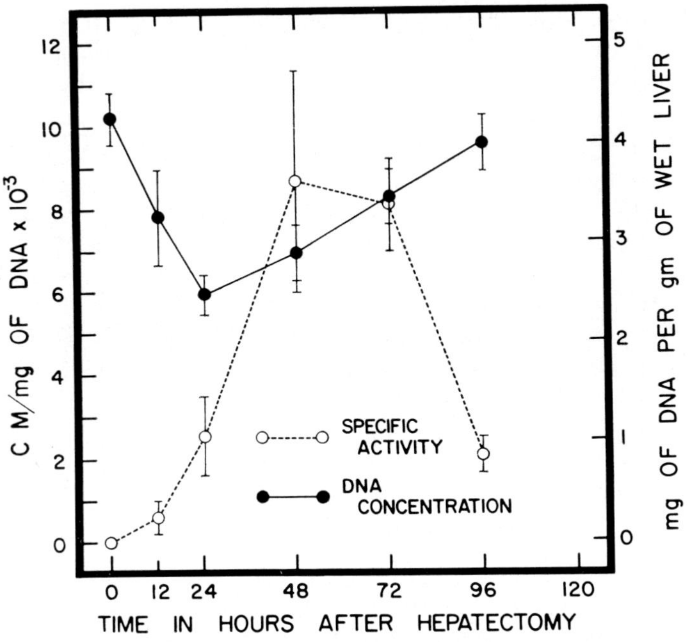

FIG. 4. Liver DNA specific activity expressed in counts per minute per milligram of DNA, and the DNA content in milligrams of DNA per gram of wet liver versus the time elapsed between sacrifice and partial hepatectomy. Each point refers to the mean of values obtained on four individual livers, and the vertical bars refer to the standard deviation calculated according to the formula:

$$\sigma = \sqrt{\Sigma\ (x - \bar{x})^2/(n - 1)}.$$

The 0 point refers to the DNA content or specific activities determined on livers obtained from untreated mice.

The results of this experiment are illustrated in Figs. 6 and 7. The thymus DNA specific activities are expressed as a percentage of the controls. Thus, the 100% value in that graph refers to the thymus DNA specific activity of the hepatectomized animals whose thymus was not irradiated. It is thus a measure of orotic acid-C^{14} incorporation in thymus of partially hepatectomized animals 72 hours after the operation, a situation in every respect identical to the 72-hour point of Fig. 2. It is clear from these results that the specific activity of the irradiated thymus DNA is depressed by 40%. Inasmuch as the results of Fig. 2 indicate that 120 hours after local X-irradiation the thymus DNA specific activity is equal to or higher than that of the nonirradiated thymus, the depression in specific activity observed in irradiated thymus of hepatectomized animals cannot be di-

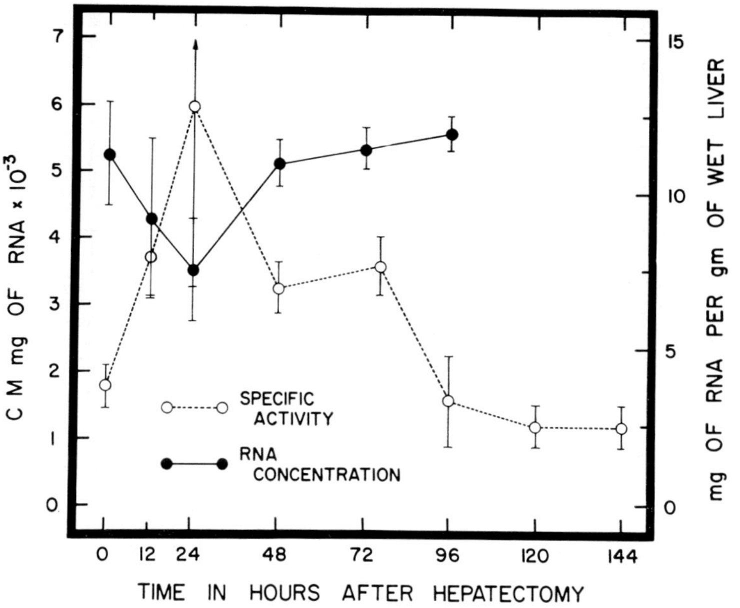

FIG. 5. Liver RNA specific activity is expressed in counts per minute per milligram of RNA, and the RNA content in milligrams of RNA per gram of wet liver versus the time elapsed between sacrifice and partial hepatectomy. Each point refers to the mean of values obtained on four individual livers, and the vertical bars refer to the standard deviation calculated according to the formula

$$\sigma = \sqrt{\Sigma\ (x - \bar{x})^2/(n - 1)}.$$

The 0 point refers to the RNA content of specific activities determined on livers obtained from untreated mice.

rectly ascribed to radiation damage. This experiment suggests, therefore, that the decrease of orotic acid-C^{14} incorporation measured in the irradiated thymus of animals hepatectomized 36 hours after X-irradiation results from the interference of liver regeneration with thymus regeneration.

In a second group of experiments, the animals were hepatectomized 96 hours after X-irradiation, injected with the isotope 6 hours later, and sacrificed 12 hours after hepatectomy, a time when incorporation of orotic acid-C^{14} into DNA of the regenerating liver had not yet started. Consequently, under these conditions, there can be no interference from liver regeneration with thymus regeneration. It is, therefore, interesting that the incorporation of orotic acid-C^{14} in the irradiated thymus (Fig. 6) is very similar to that of the nonirradiated thymus (100% values). Figure 7 demonstrates that the alterations in specific activities are paralleled by alterations in the DNA content of the thymus, thus suggesting

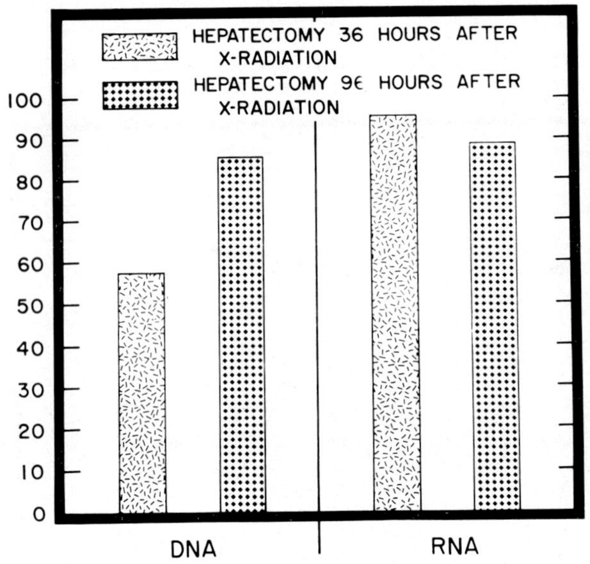

FIG. 6. Specific activity of the irradiated thymus DNA or RNA in animals partially hepatectomized 36 hours (72 hours before sacrifice) or 96 hours (12 hours before sacrifice) after X-irradiation, and sacrificed 108 hours after X-irradiation. The results are expressed as the percentage of the specific activity measured in nonirradiated thymus DNA of mice hepatectomized either 72 or 12 hours before sacrifice.

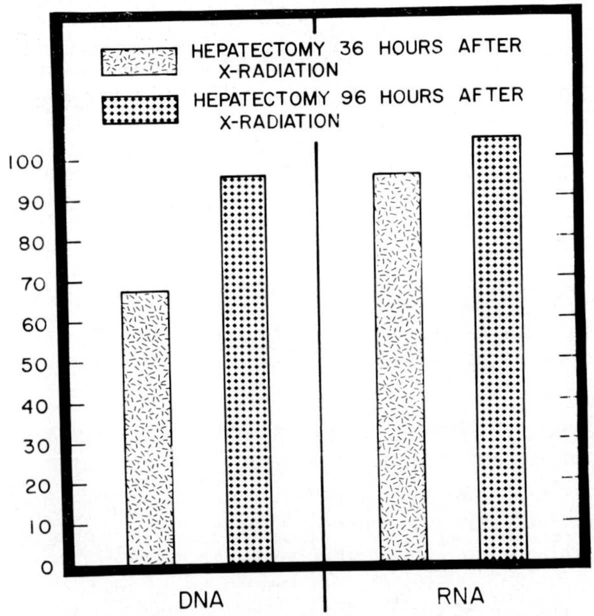

FIG. 7. Total DNA and RNA synthesized in six irradiated thymus glands of partially hepatectomized mice 36 hours (72 hours before sacrifice) after X-irradiation and sacrificed 108 hours after X-irradiation. The results are expressed as the percentage of the DNA determination measured in nonirradiated thymus of mice hepatectomized either 72 or 12 hours after sacrifice.

that the reduced specific activity reflects a retardation in the rate of DNA synthesis.

Finally, columns 3 and 4 of Figure 7 indicate that active RNA synthesis in regenerating liver does not significantly influence the incorporation of orotic acid-C^{14} in thymus RNA, even when hepatectomy is performed **96** hours after X-irradiation, a situation in which the rate of incorporation of orotic acid-C^{14} into RNA is high both in liver and thymus.

DISCUSSION

Although the changes observed in thymus weight and in DNA and RNA contents and specific activities after localized irradiation are not surprising, those found in the nonirradiated thymus glands after partial hepatectomy remain unexplained. It is, indeed, not clear if they result from an effect of liver regeneration per se or from a nonspecific response to stress (*14*). Further experimentation is required for the adequate interpretation of the alterations of the normal thymus after partial hepatectomy.

The goal of this study was to investigate the effect of regenerating liver DNA and RNA synthesis on thymic nucleic acid biosynthesis. The pertinent observation in this respect is the effect of partial hepatectomy on the recovery of the irradiated thymus when the operation is performed **36** hours before thymic X-irradiation. At that time, there is a decrease in the incorporation of orotic acid-C^{14} in the thymus, suggesting that active regeneration of one organ may interfere with the regeneration of another. However, liver regeneration affects regeneration of irradiated thymus only when maximum DNA synthesis in liver occurs simultaneously with maximum DNA synthesis in thymus. Furthermore, the competition between the two regenerating organs interferes only with DNA synthesis, and no changes are detected in RNA synthesis. These results suggest that the regenerating thymus and the regenerating liver compete for some unknown factor directly or indirectly necessary for DNA synthesis. In view of the distance separating the two organs, it is clear that the factors should be present in a pool accessible to both and might therefore be of a humoral nature. The experiment sheds no light on the chemical nature of the factor involved in the competition, nor does it suggest which metabolic pathway is involved in the competition, except that those leading to RNA synthesis can probably be excluded. These results may aid in explaining some of the effects of whole-body irradiation on the thymus glands. The delay in thymus regeneration (*4, 7, 8*), compared to that of other hematopoietic tissues, and the alteration in thymic DNA/RNA ratio (*15*) observed under these conditions could indeed result from the interference of other regenerating tissues with thymic regeneration. It is thus interesting that thymic DNA/RNA ratios remain unaltered if bone marrow is shielded during exposure to whole-body X-irradiation.

SUMMARY

The incorporation of orotic acid-C^{14} was investigated in C57BL mouse thymus DNA and RNA after local irradiation with 300 r, and in liver regeneration after partial hepatectomy.

The effect of DNA synthesis in regenerating liver on DNA synthesis in regenerating thymus was further investigated by arranging the time sequence of the irradiation of the thymus and of the partial hepatectomy so as to make maximum DNA synthesis in liver coincide with maximum DNA synthesis in thymus. It was observed that, under these conditions, the incorporation of the precursor into the irradiated thymus was reduced 40%, suggesting a competition between liver and thymus for factors necessary for regeneration.

RECEIVED: December 5, 1962

REFERENCES

1. M. A. BLOOM, Bone marrow. In *Histopathology of Irradiation from External and Internal Sources* (Wm. Bloom, ed.), Chapter VI, pp. 162–242, McGraw-Hill Book Company, New York, 1948.
2. R. G. MURRAY, The spleen. In *Histopathology of Irradiation from External and Internal Sources* (Wm. Bloom, ed.), Chapter VII, pp. 243–347, McGraw-Hill Book Company, New York, 1948.
3. R. H. MOLE, In *Modern Trends in Pathology* (D. H. Collins, ed.), Chapter VI, pp. 91–105, Paul B. Hoeber, New York, 1959.
4. L. O. JACOBSON, E. L. SIMMONS, E. K. MARKS, M. J. ROBSON, W. F. BETHARD, and E. O. GASTON, The role of the spleen in radiation injury and recovery. *J. Lab. Clin. Med.* **35,** 746–779 (1950).
5. C. C. CONGDON, D. UPHOFF, and E. LORENZ, Modification of acute irradiation injury in mice and guinea pigs by injection of bone marrow: A histopathologic study. *J. Natl. Cancer Inst.* **13,** 73–107 (1952).
6. J. L. VAN LANCKER and J. MAISIN, Le role de la beta-mercaptoethylamine dans la protection et la regeneration des tissus chez les animaux irradies in toto. *Compt. Rend. Soc. Biol.* **148,** 2057 (1953).
7. H. S. KAPLAN, Comparative susceptibility of the lymphoid tissues of strain C57 black mice to the induction of lymphoid tumors by irradiation. *J. Natl. Cancer Inst.* **8,** 191–197 (1948).
8. W. H. CARNES, H. S. KAPLAN, M. B. BROWN, and B. B. HIRSCH, Indirect induction of lymphomas in irradiated mice. III. Role of the thymic graft. *Cancer Res.* **16,** 429–433 (1956).
9. C. M. HIGGINS and M. R. ANDERSON, Experimental pathology of the liver. Restoration of the liver in the white rat following partial surgical removal. *Arch. Pathol.* **12,** 186–202 (1931).
10. J. L. VAN LANCKER and D. G. SEMPOUX, Incorporation of orotic acid C_{14} in rat liver DNA after partial hepatectomy of one partner of a parabiotic pair. *Arch. Biochem. Biophys.* **80,** 337–345 (1959).
11. R. G. MURRAY, The thymus. In *Histopathology of Irradiation from External and Internal Sources* (Wm. Bloom, ed.), Chapter IX, pp. 446–501, McGraw-Hill Book Company, New York, 1948.
12. J. L. VAN LANCKER and R. L. HOLTZER, The release of acid phosphatase and beta-glucuroni-

dase from cytoplasmic granules in the early course of autolysis. *Am. J. Pathol.* **35,** 563–573 (1959).

13. C. D. JARDETZKY and C. P. BARNUM, Metabolic activity and intracellular distribution of nucleic acid phosphorus in regenerating liver. *Arch. Biochem. Biophys.* **67,** 350–365 (1957).

14. M. BLECHER and A. WHITE, *Recent Progr. Hormone Res.* **15,** 391–417 (1959).

15. P. P. WEYMOUTH N. E. DELFEL, R. J. DOELL, H. L. STEINBOCK, and H. S. KAPLAN, Nucleic acid content of the thymic cells of normal and irradiated C57 BL mice. *J. Natl. Cancer Inst.* **15,** 981–990 (1955).

RADIATION RESEARCH 19, 670–675 (1963)

Prevention of Death in Mice after Lethal Irradiation of the Head

ROBERT A. GOEPP[1] AND FRANK FITCH[2]

Walter G. Zoller Memorial Dental Clinic, the Department of Pathology, University of Chicago, and the Argonne Cancer Research Hospital,[3] Chicago, Illinois

INTRODUCTION

Several species of laboratory animals die 9 to 14 days after irradiation of the head with 2000 to 4000 r. Such death is preceded by a progressive weight loss starting about 5 days after irradiation and has been termed by Quastler *et al.* "oral radiation death" (*1*). Previous studies on mice in this laboratory have indicated that starvation and dehydration play a major role in the death of the animals (*2*). Changes in the mucosa of the posterior dorsum of the tongue and of the soft palate became evident about 5 days after irradiation, the mice began to lose weight, and the water intake and urine output decreased markedly. The weight loss was progressive, amounting to about 39% at the time of death 9 to 11 days after irradiation. The changes in the mucosa progressed to frank ulceration about 8 to 9 days after irradiation. These ulcerations, occurring always in the same place, apparently interfered with the normal ingestion of food and water. It appeared that, if nutrition and hydration could be maintained in some manner other than the normal way of feeding, death might be prevented. The present study was undertaken to investigate the effects of liquid diets, parenteral feedings, and gastrostomy tube feedings.

MATERIALS AND METHODS

Male C57Bl mice were given radiation at 250 kv with a standard therapy machine.[4] Mice, anesthetized with Nembutal, were placed in lead shields which permitted irradiation of the head only. Details of the radiation and shielding technique have been described previously (*2*).

[1] Walter G. Zoller Memorial Dental Clinic, and the Department of Pathology, University of Chicago.

[2] Department of Pathology, University of Chicago, and the Argonne Cancer Research Hospital.

[3] Operated by the University of Chicago for the U. S. Atomic Energy Commission.

[4] General Electric Maxitron.

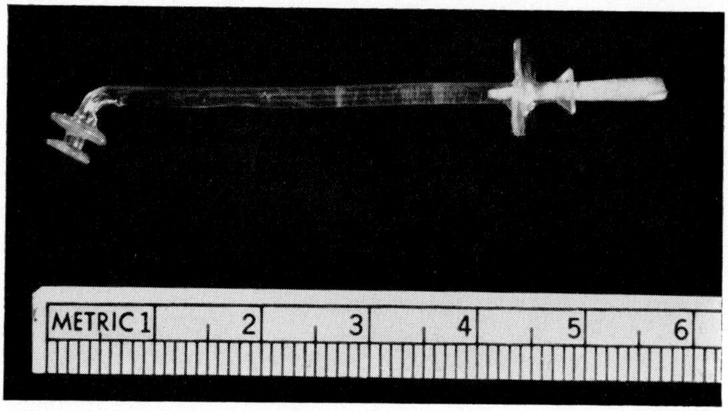

FIG. 1. The polyethylene gastrostomy tube. At the left is the end which was placed in the squamous portion of the stomach. At the right is the external end of the tube which was kept closed between feedings.

Various methods were used in an attempt to maintain adequate nutrition. Some mice were fed a liquid diet of equal volumes of evaporated milk and water with the addition of 40 gm of glucose per liter. Others were given subcutaneous injections of a solution of 5% glucose and 0.9% NaCl, aminosol,[5] or a mixture of penicillin and streptomycin.[6]

Other mice were fed by means of indwelling gastrostomy tubes (Fig. 1) of polyethylene tubing, i.d. 0.055 inch and o.d. 0.075 inch. The tube was heat-fashioned over a Bunsen burner and spun on a wire lathe to produce the flanges. One end of the tube was placed surgically in the squamous portion of the stomach, and the gastric wall was sutured between the flanges. The mid-portion of the tube was bent to lessen tension on the gastric wall. The tube was brought through the muscular layer of the abdominal wall and subcutaneously to the back of the neck where it was passed through the skin, and the large terminal flange was sutured. A toothpick was used to close the external end of the tube between feedings. The mice were caged separately to prevent damage to the tubes. One milliliter of a liquid diet was injected through the tube every hour for 12 hours a day from the fifth to the twentieth day after irradiation. The diet was specially prepared to satisfy the nutritional requirements of mice described by Morris (*3*) and was a modification of that employed by Moskowitz *et al.* (*4*). It consisted of defatted dehydrated eggs 32%, vitamin–dextrin mix 10.8%, dextrin 10.2%, alphacel 6.0%, salts 4.0%, and corn oil 37%. An equal volume of water was added to make the consistency satisfactory for gastrostomy feeding.

[5] A hydrolized protein made by Abbott Company.
[6] Combiotic made by Pfizer Company.

RESULTS

Twenty-four mice irradiated with 2000 r to the head were given the sweetened milk diet starting the fifth day after irradiation. The survival rate 20 days after irradiation was approximately 18%, and the peak incidence of death was 1½ days later than that of nontreated irradiated controls. The weight loss in the surviving mice was nearly as great as in those that died. The surviving mice appeared sick until about the eighteenth day after irradiation, after which time their weight increased. After the twentieth day they seemed nearly normal. Of 12 mice similarly irradiated and fed a chow-and-water diet *ad libitum*, there were no survivors after the eleventh postirradiation day.

In a group of mice receiving 4000 r to the head and fed the sweetened milk diet, there were no survivors and there was no difference in the time of peak incidence of death as compared to controls.

In another group of 12 mice irradiated with 2000 r to the head, receiving subcutaneous injections of 2 ml of a solution of 5% glucose in 0.9% NaCl eight times a day starting the fifth day after irradiation, the survival rate was about 18%. The behavior of the mice during the experiment was similar to that of the mice on the milk diet.

Other mice given 2000 r to the head were treated with subcutaneous injections of aminosol, 2 ml eight times per day; and others similarly irradiated were given 2-ml subcutaneous injections of a mixture of penicillin and streptomycin eight times per day for a total dose of 8000 units of penicillin and 5000 μg of streptomycin per day. In all cases weight loss was similar to that of nontreated irradiated control mice, and the survival rate was not more than 18%. There were never any survivors in control groups of 12 mice irradiated and kept on a chow-and-water diet.

Although these treatments resulted in a few mice surviving a dose of radiation which was lethal to controls, it was evident by the rather marked weight loss, even in the survivors, that replacement of fluid and nutritional requirements was inadequate. For this reason attempts were made to accomplish feeding by means of an indwelling gastrostomy tube.

To determine whether mice could be maintained adequately by gastrostomy feeding alone, several groups of otherwise normal mice were fed by this method only for 15 days. The mortality rates ranged from 60 to 94%, but in individual survivors the weight loss was never more than 23%. All dead mice were autopsied, and the reasons for gastrostomy failure were found to be that the tube came out of the stomach, became plugged, or developed a leak, allowing the diet mix to spread under the skin or into the peritoneal cavity. The cause of death could usually be predicted. When the tubes were plugged, the animals lost weight and died. In the case of a tube leak, the mouse often gained weight, the abdomen became distended, the skin was fixed to the underlying structures, and food leaked out around the external end of the tube. After about 12 days of tube feeding, subcutaneous abscesses often developed at the external site of the tube, although the tube was intact and functioning.

The survival rate of normal mice fed by gastrostomy tube could be maintained at 40% by certain technical improvements, such as placing a bend in the mid-portion of the tube near the internal end in order to lessen tension on the stomach wall; double suturing of the stomach wall around the internal end of the tube; the use of blunted needles for injecting the diet mix into the tube; the use of a reamer to unplug tubes; injecting no more than 1.0 ml of diet mix at one time; and using a special mouse holder during feeding in order to control sudden movements which tended to pull the tube loose. The subcutaneous abscesses were treated by incision and drainage, and irrigation with an antibiotic solution.[6]

A total of 101 gastrostomized mice were irradiated with 2000 r to the head and were fed the diet mix through the gastrostomy tubes from the fifth day after irradiation until the twentieth day, or until death. The experience with nonirradiated controls indicated that it was possible to establish with reasonable certainty whether death was due to technical difficulties with the tubes. All animals dying after irradiation were autopsied, and the functional state of the gastrostomy was determined. If deaths due to gastrostomy failure were excluded, the survival rate after 2000 r of irradiation to the head was 94% (Table I). In these animals the weight loss averaged 21% and never exceeded 25%. If all deaths, including gastrostomy failures, are accepted, the survival rate was 40%. Occasionally death occurred in a mouse where the gastrostomy appeared intact, but these deaths did not exceed 6% of the total group. At autopsy these mice were found to have pneumonia. Many of these deaths occurred before or after the usual survival time for "oral radiation death." By the eighteenth day after irradiation the surviving mice began to eat and drink again, and by the twentieth day the mice were able to maintain themselves by oral ingestion of food and water.

TABLE I

EFFECT OF GASTROSTOMY FEEDING ON "ORAL RADIATION DEATH"

Group	*Number of animals*	*Per cent survival*	*Per cent survival excluding gastrostomy failures*
Irradiated mice, 2000 r to the head	24	0	—
Irradiated mice, 2000 r to the head, gastrostomy-fed	101	40	94
Normal mice, gastrostomy-fed	39	41	100

DISCUSSION

Irradiation of the head of mice with 2000 r without postirradiation nutritional treatment consistently produced 100% mortality. Parenteral feedings resulted in the survival of some mice receiving 2000 r to the head, but this manner of feeding does not supply all the nutritional requirements. The survival of a few such mice treated with antibiotic injections was more likely due to the administration of fluid than to the antibiotics, since earlier studies (*1*, *2*) have demonstrated that infection does not play a major role in the mechanism of "oral radiation death."

The feeding of a more complete diet through gastrostomy tubes resulted in a 94% survival rate in mice receiving 2000 r to the head. This indicated that mice can survive such lethal irradiation if nutrition and hydration are maintained. The surviving mice lost no more than 25% of their original weight during the experiment. Normal mice handled frequently every day will have 10 to 15% variation, usually a loss, in weight.

The observation that the mice began to eat again about 18 days after irradiation implies that the lingual and palatal ulcerations, described in an earlier paper (*2*), must have healed sufficiently by that time to permit oral ingestion. The tongues of irradiated mice dying as a result of technical failure of the gastrostomy tube revealed that healing was evident at 13 to 14 days, and completed before or at least by 20 days after irradiation. Renewal of the tongue epithelium in the guinea pig was reported by Platt to take about 8.4 days (*5*). This is consistent with our observation that thinning of the lingual epithelium was evident about 5 days after irradiation, with frank ulceration occurring at 8 to 9 days. The lingual ulceration apparently forms because of the lack of repopulation of the epithelial tissue. Toto and Ojha reported the epithelial generation cycle in the mouse tongue to be 100 hours (*6*). Since healing was not evident until about 13 days after irradiation, the implication is that mitotic activity may be inhibited for about 9 days after irradiation in the epithelium of the posterior dorsum of the tongue.

SUMMARY

Irradiation of the heads of mice with 2000 r resulted in a severe weight loss and death of all irradiated animals 9 to 14 days after irradiation. The partial maintenance of nutrition and hydration by means of varied parenteral feedings produced a few survivors. The feeding of a more complete diet through indwelling gastrostomy tubes resulted in more than 90% survival. Thus death can be prevented after X-irradiation of the head with doses usually producing "oral radiation death," if nutrition and hydration are adequately maintained. This was most effectively accomplished by feeding through indwelling gastrostomy tubes.

RECEIVED: December 12, 1962

REFERENCES

1. H. Quastler, M. K. Austin, and M. Miller, Oral radiation death. *Radiation Res.* **5,** 338–353 (1956).
2. R. Goepp and F. Fitch, Pathological study of oral radiation death in mice. *Radiation Res.* **16,** 833–845 (1962).
3. H. P. Morris, Nutritional requirements of the mouse. *J. Natl. Cancer Inst.* **5,** 115–141 (1944).
4. M. S. Moskowitz, A. A. Moskowitz, W. L. Bradford, Jr., and R. W. Wissler, Changes in serum lipids and coronary arteries of the rat in response to estrogens. *Arch. Pathol.* **61,** 245–263 (1956).
5. H. Platt, Renewal times of some squamous epithelia in the guinea pig. *Nature* **184,** *Suppl.* **21,** 1654–1655 (1959).
6. P. D. Toto and G. Ojha, Generation cycle of oral epithelium in mice. *J. Dental Res.* **41,** 388–391 (1962).

RADIATION RESEARCH **19**, 676–681 (1963)

Modification of Irradiation Response of Female Rats by Population Density[1]

E. W. HAHN AND J. W. HOWLAND

Department of Radiation Biology, University of Rochester School of Medicine and Dentistry, Rochester, New York

INTRODUCTION

Several reports have been published which suggest that animals are adversely stimulated when group-housed, as evidenced by pathological social behavior (*1*), enlarged adrenal glands (*2, 3*), eosinopenia (*4*), increased adrenal output (*5*), abnormal reproductive function (*6–8*), and growth suppression (*9, 10*).

The objective of this experiment was to study the effect of population density on survival of the rat after varying levels of whole-body X-irradiation.

MATERIALS AND METHODS

Young adult female rats (200 gm) of the Wistar strain (Charles River) were placed in a Lucite exposure wheel, which was radially divided into sixteen compartments, each accommodating 1 rat. The exposure wheel was rotated slowly at a constant speed under the X-ray beam. The animals received 500 r, 750 r, or 1000 r of whole-body X-irradiation and were randomly assigned to groups with 1, 2, 4, or 6 animals to a cage. All animals were uniformly housed in groups prior to irradiation from the day when received from the supplier until the day of exposure (4 to 5 days). On the day of irradiation, all groups were housed in cages measuring 7 × 10 × 7 inches. The source of radiation was a 250-kvp 15-ma X-ray industrial unit, and the dose was delivered at a rate of approximately 18.5 r/min with a target-to-skin distance of 25 inches.

Feed (Purina lab or fox chow) and water were given ad libitum with care taken to assure that sufficient quantities of each were available at all times. Body weights were recorded every other day except weekends. The slopes and standard deviations of the mortality curves were calculated according to the method described

[1] This paper is based on work performed under Contract W-7401-eng-49 between the U. S. Atomic Energy Commission and the University of Rochester, administered by the Department of Radiation Biology of the School of Medicine and Dentistry, Rochester, New York.

by Litchfield and Wilcoxon (*11*). Differences were statistically validated by the *t*-test.

RESULTS

The mortality rate from the various groups given 500 r, 750 r, and 1000 r may be found in Table I in Figs. 1 and 2.

Up to 18.7% of the animals exposed to 500 r and housed either 2, 4, or 6 to a cage died within 30 days after exposure (Table I). However, this level of radiation did not produce any mortality in the singly-housed group.

Table I and Fig. 1 contain the mortality data obtained from animals exposed to 750 r and housed either 1 or 4 animals per cage. Approximately 94% of the animals housed 4 to a cage died within 30 days postirradiation, which is a significantly higher value than the 56% mortality exhibited by the singly-housed animals. One-half of the group-housed animals died significantly sooner than one-half of the individually-housed animals (11 versus 22 days).

The data from the animals exposed to 1000 r may be found in Table I and Fig. 2. All groups, regardless of housing regimen, exhibited 100% mortality. Fifty per cent of the multiply-housed animals in each group, regardless of whether they were housed 2, 4, or 6 to a cage, died significantly sooner than 50% of the singly-housed

TABLE I

Mortality of Rats Subjected to Varying Population Densities and Levels of X-Irradiation

Dose	*Number per cage*	*Number of rats*	*Day first death occurred*	*Per cent dead day 30*	*Day at which 50% died*
500 r	1	16	—	0	—
500 r	2	16	26	12.5	—
500 r	4	32	13	18.7	—
500 r	6	48	15	10.4	—
Controls	6	48	—	0	—
750 r	1	16	8	56.3	22 ± 3.8^{a}
750 r	4	32	5	93.8^{b}	11 ± 1.0^{b}
Controls	4	32	—	0	—
1000 r	1	16	7	100	10 ± 0.3
1000 r	2	16	5	100	8.0 ± 0.8^{b}
1000 r	4	32	4	100	7.6 ± 0.5^{b}
1000 r	6	48	4	100	8.2 ± 0.5^{b}
Controls	6	48	—	0	—

[a] ± the standard deviation.

[b] Significantly different from 1-per-cage group ($P \leq 0.05$).

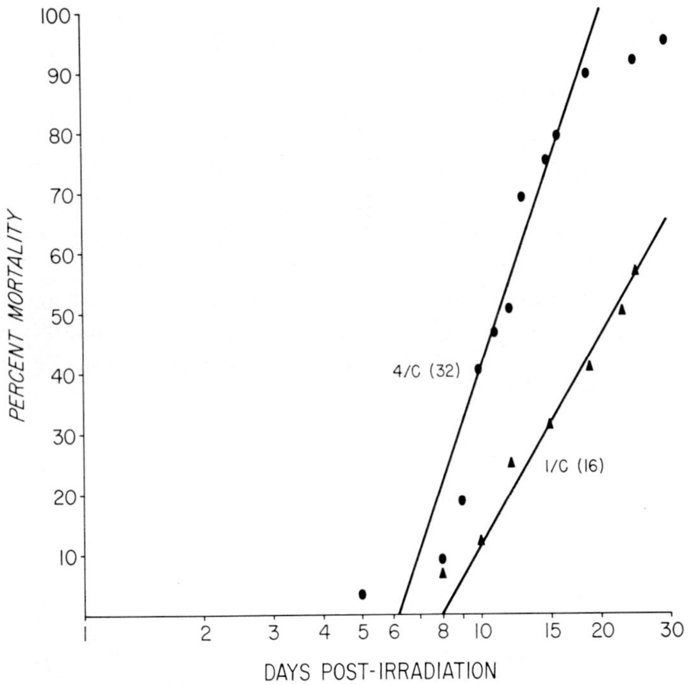

FIG. 1. Mortality of rats subjected to varying population densities after 750 r of X-irradiation. 1/c = 1 animal per cage; 4/c = 4 animals per cage. Numbers in parentheses indicate number of animals per treatment.

animals (8 versus 10 days). Population density pressures thus appear to have caused a significant shift of 2 days in the mortality curve. It is interesting to note that the slopes of the mortality curves are all similar for the group-housed treatments and differ from the singly-housed group. Once the effects of radiation could not be overcome, the singly-housed females died quite rapidly, as indicated by the small standard deviation of the slope of 1.2 days, and the cumulative per cent mortality approximates that of the group-housed data on the eleventh day. In comparison, the standard deviations for the group-housed data ranged from 3.4 days for the 2-per-cage treatment to 2.8 days for the 6-per-cage treatment with 3.3 days for the 4-per-cage treatment. These data could be interpreted to mean that the more radiosensitive animals expired sooner under the social pressures caused by crowding. Consistently, it has been noted in the three exposure trials that the time of death of the first animal always occurs in the group-housed treatments (Table I).

The effect of crowding on food intake was another factor considered in this study.

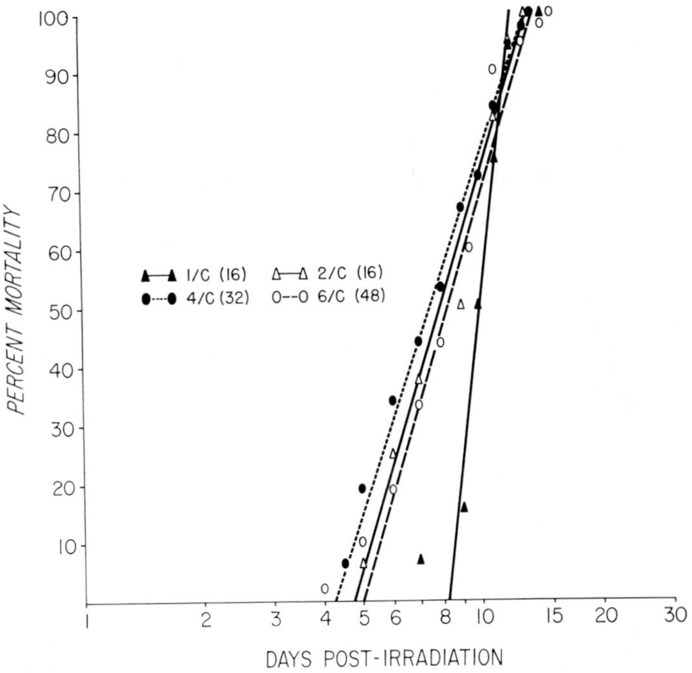

FIG. 2. Mortality of rats subjected to varying population densities after 1000 r of X-irradiation. 1/c = 1 animal per cage; 2/c = 2 animals per cage; 4/c = 4 animals per cage; 6/c = 6 animals per cage. Numbers in parentheses indicate number of animals per treatment.

One might assume that, since the animal housed individually has complete freedom to the food and water facilities, without competition, it would grow and gain weight more rapidly than the group-housed animals. According to the data, however, this is not the case. The irradiated animals, regardless of housing regimen, exhibited body-weight changes of equal magnitude within exposure levels (Fig. 3). The controls housed 4 or 6 per cage exhibited steady weight gains.

DISCUSSION

Raventos (*12*) reported that there was a cage effect which significantly affected the outcome of radiation mortality experiments. No such effect was observed in this experiment. A possible reason for this might be that survivors were constantly recombined to maintain the numbers in each cage for that particular group, and any cross-contamination factor unique for one cage would be spread to other cages. Raventos (*12*) also reported no difference in mortality for singly-housed and multiply-housed irradiated mice. This may be a species difference and requires further study.

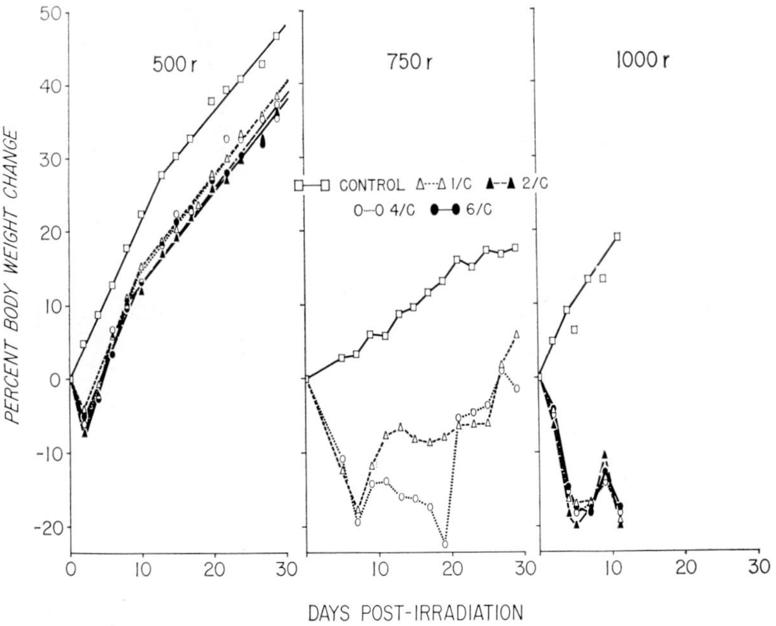

FIG. 3. Body-weight changes of rats under varying population densities after X-irradiation. 1/c = 1 animal per cage; 2/c = 2 animals per cage; 4/c = 4 animals per cage; 6/c = 6 animals per cage.

Many factors, such as competition for space, food, and social rank, along with a decreased resistance to disease and infection, may be producing these differences. Group-housed animals have less resistance to some diseases (*13, 14*), and, therefore, cross-contamination with a cage or cages might be a contributing factor. Competition for living room may also be considered. However, subsequent data collected in this laboratory indicate that these are probably not significant factors (*15*). Another factor might be competition for food, although according to Strecker and Emlen (*16*) limited food supply did not increase competition among house mice. Emotional interactions, such as huddling and fighting to attain a social rank, possibly contribute significantly to the modifications observed in this experiment.

SUMMARY

In summary, the 30-day survival of lethally X-irradiated rats was influenced by the number housed per cage after irradiation. The percentage of animals surviving 500 r and 750 r was higher in singly-caged groups than in groups caged in lots of 2 to 6 per pen. The onset of mortality after 750 r and 1000 r was, likewise, later in singly-caged than in multiply-caged animals.

ACKNOWLEDGMENT

We are indebted to Dr. Arthur Dutton, Associate Professor, Department of Radiation Biology, University of Rochester, for the advice given on the statistical design and analysis of this study.

RECEIVED: December 15, 1962

REFERENCES

1. J. B. CALHOUN, Population density and social pathology. *Sci. Am.* **206,** 139 (1962).
2. D. E. DAVIS and J. J. CHRISTIAN, Relation of adrenal weight to social rank of mice. *Proc. Soc. Exptl. Biol. Med.* **94,** 728 (1957).
3. S. A. BARNETT, Physiological effects of "social stress" in wild rats. I. The adrenal cortex. *J. Physiol. Res.* **3,** 1 (1958).
4. C. H. SOUTHWICK, Eosinophil response of C57BR mice to behavioral disturbance. *Etiology* **40,** 156 (1959).
5. J. W. MASON, Central nervous system factors in the regulation of endocrine secretion. *Recent Prog. Hormone Res.* **15,** 345 (1959).
6. E. G. RETZLAFF, Studies in population physiology with the albino mouse. *Biol. Generalis* **14,** 238 (1938).
7. F. A. CREW and L. MIRSHAIA, The effects of density on an adult mouse population. *Biol. Generalis* **7,** 239 (1931).
8. J. J. CHRISTIAN and C. D. LEMUNYAN, Adverse effects of crowding on lactation and reproduction of mice and two generations of their offspring. *Endocrinology* **63,** 517 (1959).
9. J. J. CHRISTIAN, Effect of population size on the adrenal glands and reproductive organs of male mice in populations of fixed size. *Am. J. Physiol.* **182,** 292 (1955).
10. T. VETULANI, Untersuchungen Über das Wachstum der saugetiere in Abhängigkeit von der anzahl zusammengehaltener tiere. *Biol. Generalis* **7,** 71 (1931).
11. J. T. LITCHFIELD and F. WILCOXON, A simplified method of evaluating dose-effect experiments. *J. Pharmacol. Exptl. Therap.* **96,** 99 (1949).
12. A. RAVENTOS, A factor influencing the significance of radiation mortality experiments. *Brit. J. Radiol.* **28,** 410 (1955).
13. D. E. DAVIS and C. P. READ, Effect of behavior on development of resistance in trichinosis. *Proc. Soc. Exptl. Biol. Med.* **99,** 269 (1958).
14. R. D. STONER and J. T. GODWIN, The effects of ACTH and cortisone upon susceptibility to trichinosis in mice. *Am. J. Pathol.* **29,** 943 (1953).
15. R. ADER and E. W. HAHN, The effects of social environment on mortality to whole body X-irradiation in the rat. *Psychol. Rept.* (1963) In press.
16. R. L. STRECKER and J. T. EMLEN, Regulator mechanisms in house mouse populations and the effect of limited food supply in a confined population. *Ecology* **34,** 375 (1953).

RADIATION RESEARCH 19, 682–700 (1963)

Effect of X-Radiation on DNA Metabolism in Various Tissues of the Rat[1]

V. DNA Metabolism in Regenerating Thymus

YUKIO SUGINO,[2] EUGENE P. FRENKEL,[3] AND RICHARD L. POTTER[4, 5]

Biological Effects of Irradiation Laboratory, The Department of Biological Chemistry and Simpson Memorial Institute of the University of Michigan, Ann Arbor, Michigan, and The Department of Internal Medicine, The University of Texas Southwestern Medical School, Dallas, Texas

INTRODUCTION

In previous studies (*1, 2*) the inhibition and recovery of deoxyribonucleic acid (DNA) synthesis in various rat organs after sublethal total-body X-irradiation was described. By day 1 after 400 r, the thymus gland revealed marked depression of labeled 2-C^{14}-thymidine (C^{14}-Tdr) incorporation into DNA (expressed in terms of the specific activity of isolated DNA 1 hour after the injection of C^{14}-Tdr). This was followed by a tenfold increase in incorporation by day 4. The increased incorporation, suggesting rapid DNA synthesis, occurred in spite of an absence of detectable increase in total DNA. In light of this apparent discrepancy it was deemed desirable to extend the previous observations on DNA metabolism and to attempt to correlate morphological changes in the gland with the observed biochemical changes. Also, since the thymus contains significant amounts of pyrimidine deoxynucleotides (diphosphates and triphosphates), as evidenced by the previously described pools of acid-soluble forms (*3–5*), it is possible that it serves as a significant endogenous source of nucleotides for the rest of the body. The present report con-

[1] This work was supported by U. S. Atomic Energy Commission Contract AT (11-1)-75.

[2] Present address: Department of Medical Chemistry, Faculty of Medicine, Kyoto University, Kyoto, Japan.

[3] Present address: Department of Internal Medicine, The University of Texas Southwestern Medical School, Dallas, Texas.

[4] Deceased—September 26, 1960.

[5] Requests for reprints should be addressed to: Eugene P. Frenkel, M.D., Department of Internal Medicine, The University of Texas Southwestern Medical School, 5323 Harry Hines Boulevard, Dallas 35, Texas.

cerns the incorporation of radiocarbon-labeled thymidine (C^{14}-Tdr), tritium-labeled thymidine (H^3-Tdr), H^3-labeled deoxycytidine (H^3-Cdr), and radiophosphorus (P^{32}) into DNA and the relationships of the pertinent enzymes to pyrimidine nucleotide metabolism. It also describes correlative histological studies, although the more extensive morphologic observations will be reported subsequently (*6*).

EXPERIMENTAL PROCEDURE

Materials

C^{14}-Tdr (specific activity 0.3 μc/μM) is the same as was used in the previous experiment (*1*). Tritiated deoxycytidylic acid (H^3-dCMP), obtained from Schwarz Laboratories, was purified by successive ion-exchange chromatography on Dowex 1 and Dowex 50-W columns (*7*). H^3-Cdr was prepared from the purified H^3-dCMP by phosphomonoesterase action and treated by ion-exchange chromatography on Dowex 1 and Dowex 50-W (*7*). Specific activity of H^3-dCMP and H^3-Cdr was 1 mc/μM. Specific activity of H^3-Tdr was 0.35 mc/μM. Radiophosphorus (P^{32}), as disodium orthophosphate, was obtained from Volk Radiochemical Company. C^{14}-Formaldehyde, obtained from New England Nuclear Corporation, was diluted with nonradioactive formaldehyde to yield an aqueous solution of 2.74 million cpm and 2.5 μM/ml. Deoxyuridylic acid (dUMP) was prepared by chemical deamination of dCMP (*8*) and purified by chromatography on Dowex 1 with a formic acid system. Tetrahydrofolic acid (THFA) was prepared by catalytic hydrogenation of folic acid and stored in vials with nitrogen (N_2) gas (*9*). When used, it was dissolved in N_2-saturated Tris buffer, pH 7.5. Tritiated cytidylic acid (H^3-CMP) was obtained from Schwarz Laboratories and purified in the same manner as H^3-dCMP. All other nonradioactive deoxynucleotides except dUMP, deoxynucleosides, and DNA used as standards were the products of California Corporation for Biochemical Research. Male rats were used in these studies under conditions previously described (*1*).

Methods

Irradiation. Animal maintenance and the conditions of irradiation were as described previously (*1*), except that only the 400-r dose was used, and the duration of irradiation was 11.5 ± 0.5 minutes at a distance of 75 cm.

Administration of precursors. Radioactive precursors were dissolved in a neutral solution of physiological saline, and a 1-ml aliquot was administered intraperitoneally or intravenously per animal. The route of administration is indicated in each experiment.

Analysis of DNA. The amount of DNA in the thymus was determined as previously described (*1*).

Isolation of DNA and determination of specific activity. One hour after the injection of radioactive material, rats were sacrificed by decapitation, and the thymus was quickly removed and frozen in liquid nitrogen.

The method of extraction and counting of DNA radioactivity was essentially that described by Hecht and Potter (*10*), except that a self-absorption correction to infinite thinness was made when the tritiated precursor was employed. The specific activity data were normalized by conversion to "biological concentration coefficients," as described (*1*), except that DNA-P instead of DNA-T was used as the basis of calculation, and all the results were expressed as per cent of normal (non-irradiated) thymus values:

Biological concentration coefficient (BCC)

$$= \frac{\text{Cpm/mM DNA-P}}{\text{Cpm injected/body weight (gm)}} \times 100$$

Isolation of pyrimidines of DNA and determination of their specific activities. DNA, labeled by H^3-Cdr injection, was isolated as usual and hydrolyzed by formic acid to give free purines and pyrimidines, which were then separated by paper chromatography with an isopropanol–HCl solvent system (*11*). Similar treatment of tritiated cytidine monophosphate (H^3-CMP) yielded H^3-cytosine of the same specific activity as that of H^3-CMP, suggesting that there was no loss of tritium during the hydrolysis procedure. Spots of cytosine (R_f about 0.8) and thymine (R_f about 0.4) were cut from the paper and eluted by 0.1 N HCl. An aliquot was used to read the optical density at 260 mμ and 280 mμ, and another aliquot was used for the radioactivity measured by the Packard Tri-Carb liquid scintillation counter, 314 dc, with a high-voltage tap setting of 8 (1200 volts) and discriminator settings of 10–15–50–100 volts. The scintillator mixture used in the system (*12*) consisted of xylene, 500 ml; dioxane, 500 ml; ethyl alcohol, 300 ml; with the addition of naphthalene, 80 gm/l; 2,5-diphenyloxazole (PPO), 5 gm/l; and α-naphthylphenyloxazole (ANPO), scintillation grade, 50 mg/l.

Samples for counting were then prepared by the addition of 10-ml amounts of the mixture to the specimen for counting in 5-dram low potassium-40 glass screw-top vials. Internal standards were employed. The counting efficiency of H^3 in this mixture was about 8%. The specific activity was expressed as counts per minute (cpm) per micromole-base. This value cannot be directly compared to that obtained by windowless counting in the gas-flow counter.

Enzyme Determinations

Assay of dCMP deaminase. Fresh thymus was prepared in a Potter-Elvehjem homogenizer and suspended in isotonic potassium chloride (0.154 M) at 4°C to yield a 20% concentration and then centrifuged at 25,000 × g for 30 minutes. The supernatant was used as the enzyme preparation.

The incubation mixture, similar to that used by Maley and Maley (*13*), contained 20 μM of Tris, pH 8.0, 20 μM of potassium fluoride, 30 μM of potassium chloride, and 3 μM of dCMP made to a final volume of 0.5 ml. After a 20-minute incubation at 37°C, the reaction was stopped by adding 1.0 ml of 0.3 *N* perchloric acid (PCA), and the resulting protein and K-PCA precipitates were removed by centrifugation. A 1.0-ml aliquot of the supernatant was passed through a Dowex 50-W (H^+) column (0.5 × 5 cm) to absorb unreacted dCMP, the column was washed twice (each with 1.0 ml of water), and these washings were combined with the first effluent. The optical density of this solution, which contains newly formed dUMP, was read at 260 and 280 mμ.[6] A blank experiment was carried out in the same manner except that the substrate, dCMP, was added after the 0.3 *N* PCA. The specific enzyme activity was calculated as micromoles of dUMP formed per gram of wet tissue per hour, and all the results were expressed in terms of per cent of normal (nonirradiated) thymus values.

Simultaneous assay of dCMP deaminase and dCMP kinase. With 0.05 ml of the thymus supernatant prepared as above, 20 μM of Tris buffer (pH 7.5), 20 μM of $MgCl_2$, 10 μM of 5′-(pyro)triphosphate of adenosine (ATP), and 2 μM H^3-dCMP were added to a final volume of 0.5 ml. This mixture was incubated for 10 minutes at 37°C, and then 1.0 ml of 1.5 *N* cold perchloric acid (PCA) was added to the reaction mixture and maintained in the ice bath for 10 minutes. After centrifugation, two 0.5-ml aliquots were removed from the supernatant. One aliquot was heated in a boiling-water bath for 15 minutes to hydrolyze dCDP and/or dCTP to dCMP and then was neutralized by 1.0 ml of 0.4 *N* KOH. Centrifugation separated the resulting potassium perchlorate precipitate from the supernatant, and 1.0 ml of the latter was applied to a Dowex 50-W (H^+) column (0.5 × 5 cm). The column was washed twice (with 1.0 ml of water each time), and the washings and effluent were combined to yield a final 3.0-ml volume. Counting was then done on 0.5-ml aliquots of this solution in a Tri-Carb liquid scintillation counter.

As reported by Maley (*14*), dCMP and Cdr remained on the column, and dUMP and Udr passed through the column under these conditions. Moreover, any dDCP or dCTP formed by the action of dCMP kinase would pass through the column in the case of the unhydrolyzed sample, but in the hydrolyzed aliquot they would be converted to dCMP and remain on the column. The counts per minute in the eluate from the hydrolyzed sample represented dUMP and Udr and were referred to as t. This number was proportional to the dCMP deaminase in the tissue. The counts per minute in the unhydrolyzed sample represented dUMP, Udr, dCDP, and dCTP and were referred to as u. Since u minus t equaled dCDP plus dCTP, the resulting figure was proportioned to the dCMP kinase in the tissue,

[6] At days 2 to 4, the ratio of optical density at 280 mμ to that at 260 mμ was slightly higher than that expected for dUMP. This indicated the presence of contaminating dCMP and/or dCTP in the dUMP fraction, the amount of the latter being very small during this period. Therefore, during days 2 to 4, the amount of dUMP was calculated from the two optical density values at 260 mμ and 280 mμ.

if the dephosphorylation of dCDP and dCTP during the reaction can be neglected. Since the amount of these compounds formed during the reaction time of 10 minutes was quite small, the back reaction was not taken into consideration. Spectrophotometric assay of dCMP deaminase, as described by R. Huntington, Y. Sugino, and R. L. Potter (unpublished data), was also performed on separate aliquots of thymus supernatant.

Assay of CMP kinase. In determining CMP kinase, H^3-CMP (2 μM) was employed instead of H^3-dCMP, and the procedure was carried out as above. In this case u was always equal to t, suggesting the lack of CMP deaminase. Therefore, for routine assay, the acid hydrolysis procedure was omitted, and u was considered CMP kinase activity.

Assay of thymidylate (TMP) synthetase. The assay method is essentially the same as that of Maley and Maley (*13, 14*). A 50% homogenate of thymus was prepared as above and centrifuged at 25,000 × g for 40 minutes, and the supernatant was used as the enzyme preparation. A reaction mixture of 100 μM of the THFA in Tris, pH 7.5, 50 μM of $MgSO_4$, 2 μM of C^{14}-formaldehyde (137,000 cpm), and 0.15 ml of the enzyme preparation was incubated under N_2 at 37°C for 1 hour. The reaction was then stopped by heating in a boiling-water bath for 3 minutes, and the denatured protein precipitate was removed by centrifugation. To a 0.2-ml aliquot taken from the supernatant, 0.1 ml of snake venom solution (fresh *Crotalus adamanteus* venom, 10 mg/ml of water) and 0.1 ml of Tris buffer (0.2 M, pH 8.5) were added and incubated at 37°C for 1 hour. After heating in a boiling-water bath to destroy the venom enzyme, protein precipitate was removed by centrifugation. From the supernatant, a 0.3-ml aliquot was added to 0.3 ml of 0.2 N $NaHSO_3$, and the pH was adjusted to 5 to 7 with methyl and phenol red as internal indicators. This solution was then passed through a double column of Dowex 1 (formate, 0.5 × 6 cm) over Dowex 50-W (H^+, 0.5 × 6 cm), the resins being separated by glass wool. The column was washed with water until the total volume of effluent plus water washing was 10 ml, from which 1.0 was used for counting C^{14} activity in a gas-flow counter. Specific enzyme activity was calculated and then expressed as per cent of normal (nonirradiated) thymus values.

Autoradiographic studies. Simultaneous autoradiographic studies were performed, as will be described and discussed in detail (*6*).

RESULTS

Incorporation Studies

Radiation reaction period. During the first 2 days after 400 r of total-body X-irradiation, a marked decrease in the total DNA content of the thymus was noted (Fig. 1) as well as a sharp decrease in total weight of the gland as previously noted (*1*). However, refinement of the methods and study of more points in time have yielded clearer definition of the changes. During this same time there

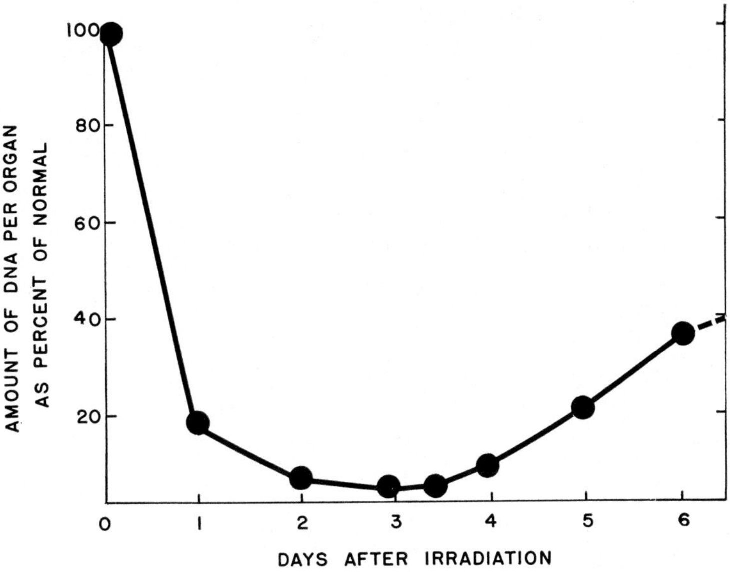

FIG. 1. Amount of DNA at varying times postirradiation. The change in wet weight of the gland reveals an identical pattern, as does the amount of DNA if expressed in terms of concentration of DNA per unit of the gland. Each point represents the mean of 10 animals.

was a sharp decrease in the rate of incorporation of the labeled pyrimidine nucleosides (C^{14}-Tdr, H^3-Tdr, H^3-Cdr) and P^{32} into DNA (Fig. 2 and Table I).

Regeneration period. Two and one-half days postirradiation a change in the rate of incorporation of labeled precursors, in terms of specific activity of DNA, was seen (Table II). The rate of incorporation of H^3-Tdr and P^{32} showed a marked increase (Fig. 2), reaching a maximum peak at day 3½. At this time the increased incorporation rate of H^3-Tdr ranged up to almost twenty times normal (a tenfold increase at day 4 was previously reported; *2*), whereas the P^{32} rate of incorporation increased to only four times the normal level. A very slight increase in net DNA was seen during this initial phase.

The increased rate of incorporation of labeled Cdr lagged somewhat behind that of Tdr, but then rose to six times normal, reaching a peak at day 4½ (Fig. 2). A more evident increase in total DNA became apparent during this phase (Fig. 1), although incorporation rates of labeled Tdr and P^{32} decreased to normal or subnormal levels at this time. By the sixth day, increase in net amount of DNA again ceased.

Comparison of efficiency of labeling by H^3-Cdr of thymine and cytosine of DNA. DNA samples labeled by 1-hour incorporation of H^3-Cdr were hydrolyzed to constituent bases to determine their specific activities. Only pyrimidine bases, thymine (T) and cytosine (C), were labeled. The results are summarized in Table III as

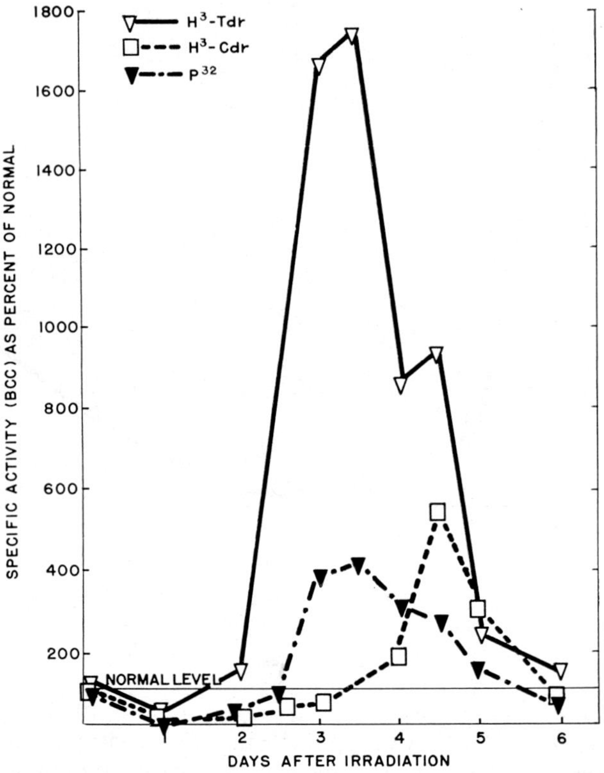

FIG. 2. Composite pattern of labeled precursor incorporation into DNA. Each point represents the mean for at least 10 animals. The Tdr study was carried out first with the C^{14} label (3.0 μc per animal) and then again with the H^3 (100 μc per animal). In each case a 1-hour period of incorporation was permitted prior to sacrifice. The results of these two studies were identical. Ten microcuries of the H^3-Cdr was used. Thirty microcuries of P^{32} was employed.

the ratio of specific activity of thymine to that of cytosine. As demonstrated, the ratio is highest at day 3½, a time at which Tdr incorporation is also at its peak (see Fig. 2).

Table IV reveals the effect of the injection of unlabeled Tdr on the incorporation of H^3-Cdr into DNA-T and DNA-C. Both the normal and the irradiated rats at day 3½ demonstrated a marked depression of the incorporation of H^3-Cdr into DNA-T. No depression of incorporation into DNA-C was noted.

Enzyme Studies

Figure 3 demonstrates the change in concentration of protein noted in the supernatant (25,000 × *g*) of thymus homogenate. This supernatant was employed as

TABLE I

COURSE OF EVENTS DURING THE IMMEDIATE POSTIRRADIATION PERIOD DESCRIBING THE BIOCHEMICAL AND ANATOMICAL CHANGES[a]

Correlative Morphologic and Biochemical Findings: Effect of X-Radiation at Days 0–2	
Biochemical	*Morphological*[a]
1. Sharp decrease in total weight of the gland	1. Marked decrease in total number of cells
2. Sharp decrease in amount of total DNA	2. Marked lysis of lymphocytes
3. Sharp decrease in incorporation rate of precursors: Tdr, Cdr, and P^{32}	3. Some probable reversible cloudy swelling of reticular cells (R.C.) and a large primitive monocytoid reticular lymphoblast type of cell
4. Sharp decrease in dCMP deaminase and thymidylate synthetase	4. Absence of evidence of radioactive label on autoradiography with Tdr
5. Slight decrease in dCMP kinase and CMP kinase	5. Evidence of "basket" cells without radioactive label

[a] See Frenkel *et al.* (*6*).

TABLE II

EARLY EVENTS IN THE PERIOD OF REGENERATION

Correlative Morphologic and Biochemical Findings: Pattern of Regeneration at Days 2½–3	
Biochemical	*Morphological*
1. Onset of reappearance of dCMP deaminase and thymidylate synthetase	1. Relative absence of lymphocytes
2. Onset of incorporation of Tdr, P^{32} and, more slowly, Cdr	2. Occasional labeling of reticulum cells (average 4 gr/cell)
	3. Marked hypocellularity

the enzyme preparation. The pattern of enzyme changes is demonstrated in Figs. 4, 5, and 6 as expressed in terms of nitrogen, DNA-P, and wet weight of tissue, respectively.

Radiation reaction period. During days 0 to 2 postirradiation, a very sharp and marked decline in the levels of dCMP deaminase (Figs. 4, 5, and 6) was seen, reaching a minimum at the second day. Thymidylate synthetase demonstrated a similar pattern. Only moderate decreases in dCMP kinase and CMP kinase were seen (Figs. 4, 5, and 6).

Regeneration period. After day 2½ there was a reappearance of dCMP deaminase and thymidylate synthetase, with progressive recovery to normal values by day 5. The levels of dCMP kinase and CMP kinase remained fairly constant until after day 4, at which time dCMP kinase slowly returned toward normal levels.

TABLE III

COMPARISON OF SPECIFIC ACTIVITIES OF THYMINE AND CYTOSINE OF DNA LABELED BY H^3-DEOXYCYTIDINE INCORPORATION

Rats	Ratio of specific activity of thymine to that of cytosine			
	Thymus		Spleen	
		Average		Average
Controls	0.47, 0.48, 0.53, 0.53 0.78, 0.79	0.60	0.23, 0.34	0.29
Irradiated				
Days: 3.5	0.95, 1.2, 1.2	1.1	0.55, 0.78	0.67
4.0	0.83, 0.72, 1.1	0.89		
4.5	0.56, 0.69, 0.68	0.62		
5.0	0.69, 0.72, 0.95	0.79		
6.0	0.68, 0.77, 0.80	0.75		

TABLE IV

SUPPRESSION OF INCORPORATION OF H^3-CDR INTO THYMINE OF DNA BY NONRADIOACTIVE TDR

Rats	Ratio of specific activity of thymine to that of cytosine			
	Without cold[a] Tdr		With cold[a] Tdr	
		Average		Average
Controls	0.47, 0.48, 0.53, 0.53, 0.53, 0.78, 0.79	0.60	0.04, 0.07, 0.27	0.11
Irradiated 3.5 days	0.95, 1.2, 1.2	1.1	0.04, 0.13	0.09

[a] Nonradioactive: 50 μM of "cold" Tdr was injected into each animal.

DISCUSSION

The course of the biochemical events in the rat thymus after sublethal total-body irradiation (400 r) was studied from the point of view of DNA metabolism (principally that of pyrimidine deoxynucleotide metabolism). As shown in Tables I, II, VI, VII, and VIII, these events can be divided into two periods, the radiation reaction period and the regeneration period. The radiation reaction period is characterized by cellular death with the resultant decrease in the weight of the thymus and a decrease in the total DNA content (Fig. 1). During this same period, the rate of the synthesis of DNA, expressed as the specific activity of DNA labeled after 1 hour of incorporation of C^{14}-Tdr or H^3-Tdr, was greatly decreased,

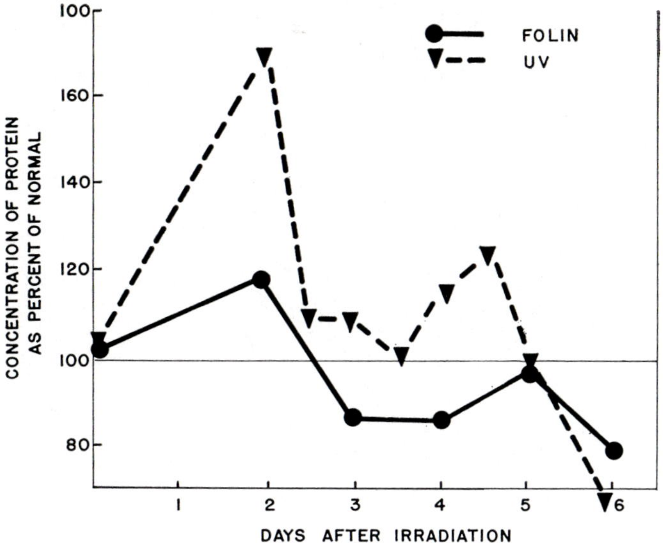

FIG. 3. The concentration of protein in the supernatant (25,000 × g) of thymus homogenate as determined by both Folin and ultraviolet techniques.

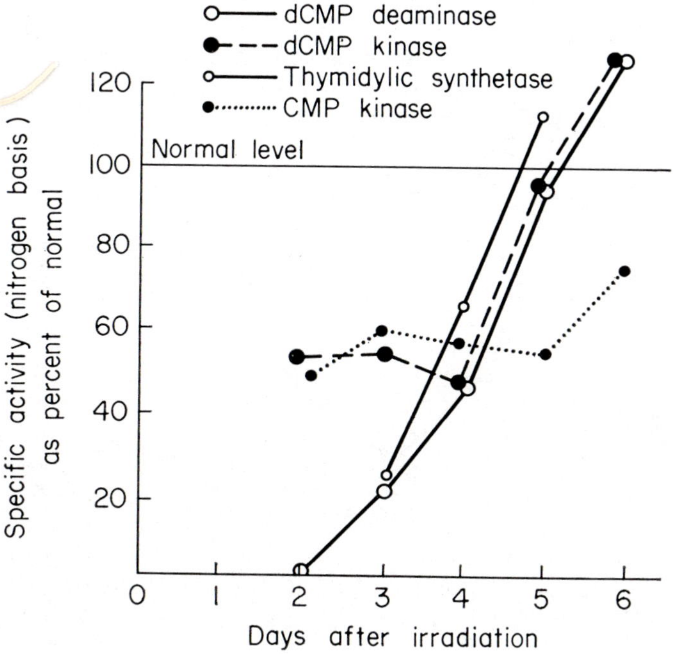

FIG. 4. Enzyme determinations expressed on the basis of nitrogen. Thymidylate synthetase paralleled dCMP deaminase between days 2 and 3.

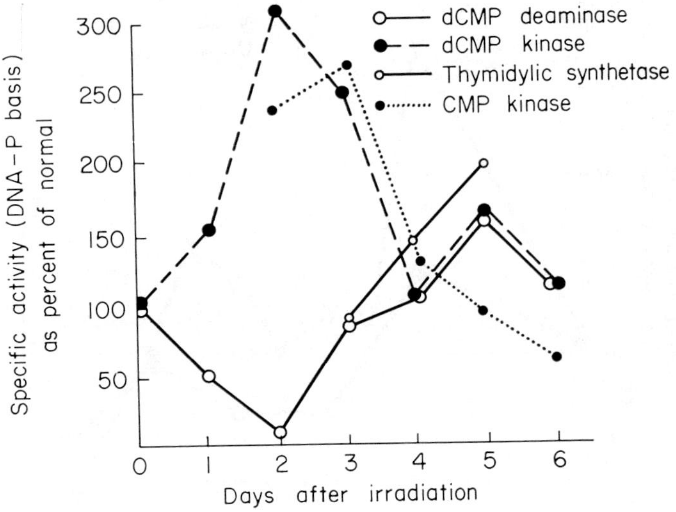

FIG. 5. Composite pattern of the enzymes studied expressed in terms of DNA-P. Thymidylate synthetase completely paralleled dCMP deaminase during days 0 to 3.

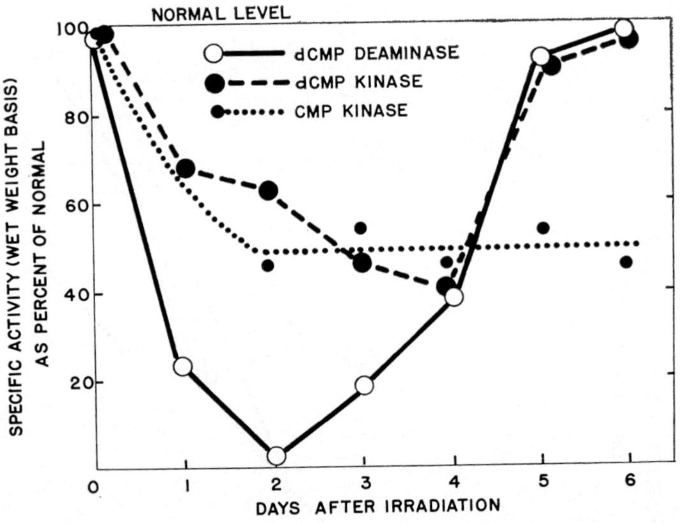

FIG. 6. Composite pattern of enzymes expressed in terms of wet weight of tissue. dCMP deaminase activity was measured both spectrophotometrically and by H^3 radioactivity simultaneously with dCMP kinase in the presence of ATP. Both methods yielded essentially identical results.

approximating a zero level (Fig. 2).[7] As far as this specific period is concerned, the change in the rate of incorporation of the various precursors such as C^{14}-Tdr, H^3-Tdr, H^3-Cdr, and P^{32}-orthophosphate showed nearly the same pattern (Fig. 2) which is consistent with the rapid decrease in the amount of DNA (Fig. 1) and with cellular death (*6*).

During the regeneration period, a complex course of interrelated events is noted (Tables II, VI, VII, and VIII). A dual-phased pattern of precursor incorporation into DNA can be recognized in this period. During the initial phase—that is, the period of days 2½ to 4 (Tables II and IV)—a very marked increase in the rate of incorporation of labeled Tdr is seen. This experiment, which was repeated with more time points to reconfirm the result previously reported by Nygaard and Potter (*2*), demonstrated that the peak of the rate of the incorporation of labeled Tdr is seen at 3½ days postirradiation (Fig. 2) instead of 4 days described in the previous paper, and that the maximum value at day 3½ is twenty times as high as the normal value (Fig. 2). During this same period there is little increase in the amount of DNA (Fig. 1).

When H^3-Cdr, instead of labeled Tdr, is used as the precursor, this abrupt increase in the rate of incorporation is not seen at the same point in time, but it does, in fact, show a peak of activity which is not more than six times normal some 24 hours after the Tdr incorporation peak (Fig. 2). Thus, the second phase (days 4 to 5, Table VII) is characterized by the increased incorporation of H^3-Cdr into DNA. During this second phase, a rapid and continued increase in the amount of DNA is observed (Fig. 1).

When P^{32}-orthophosphate is used as the precursor, the pattern of change in the rate of the incorporation into DNA does not show a sharp peak. Instead, a broad peak is seen between days 3 and 4½, covering both the Tdr and the Cdr peaks (Fig. 2). In this case the maximum value is only four times the normal level (Fig. 2), whereas the maximum value of Tdr incorporation was twenty times as high as the normal value.

This discrepancy in the temporal relationships of these incorporation peaks (Fig. 2) and the greatly enhanced incorporation of Tdr during the initial phase of the regeneration period led to an evaluation of the activity of thymus tissue to synthesize thymidine nucleotides endogenously at various stages of regeneration.

In Table V, the synthetic pathways of DNA pyrimidines are shown. In both the normal (*4*) and the irradiated (*15*) rats, there is a considerable amount of circu-

[7] It is important to emphasize the fact that total-body irradiation was employed and that the response in the thymus may have been indirect. R. K. Boutwell and J. Hofert (University of Wisconsin, unpublished) have obtained data very similar to that shown in Fig. 2 when mice were fasted for 2 days and subsequently fed again. The sharp increase in the specific activity of DNA 40 minutes after injection of radioactive Tdr reached a maximum in 2 days and declined to normal during the following week.

TABLE V

METABOLIC MAP OF THE SYNTHESIS OF DNA CYSTEINE AND DNA-THYMINE

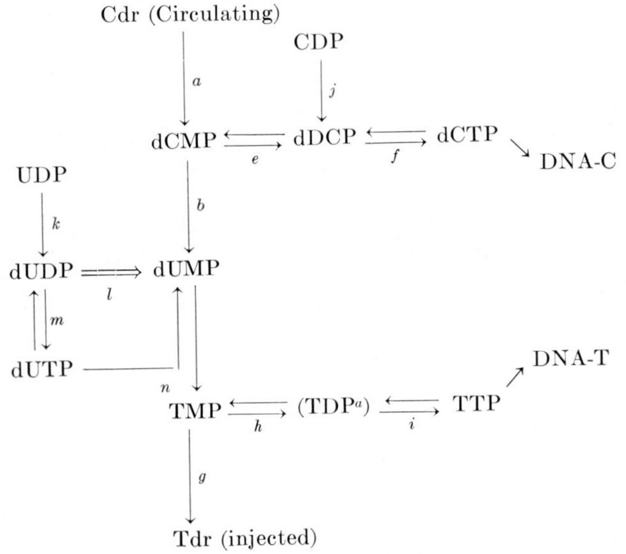

[a] Bianchi *et al.* recently reported that TTP is directly formed from TMP by pyrophosphorylation (*17*).

lating Cdr, whereas the amount of Tdr in the circulation is negligible. It will be worth while to emphasize here that neither is Tdr circulating in a measurable amount in the blood nor is it a normal intermediate in the *de novo* synthesis of TMP. However, Tdr, if injected, can be utilized effectively via a salvage pathway *g* (Table V) (*16, 18*). Cdr utilization can extend into DNA-C and DNA-T via the pathways shown in Table V, the first step being via Cdr kinase (*a*). It is highly probable that the major route of supply of endogenous TMP is predominantly through the dCMP deaminase (*13, 19, 20, 21*) (*b* in Table V) and TMP synthetase (*21–23*) (*c* in Table V) pathways, at least in thymus gland (*13*), although the formation of dUMP from UDP via pathways *k, l, m*, and *n* (Table V) was recently demonstrated with cellfree extract of *Escherichia coli* (*24*).

TMP synthesized endogenously via these pathways can dilute injected radioactive Tdr which is utilized via pathway *g* (Table V). Therefore, it is conceivable that the activities of the enzymes which are concerned with pathways *b* and/or *c* greatly affect the rate of incorporation of injected labeled Tdr into DNA-T.

The interpretation of enzyme changes after irradiation often critically depends on the parameters on which such activities are determined and the manner in which the results are expressed (*25*). Smith and Low-Beer (*25*) and subsequently Eichel

TABLE VI

FIRST PHASE OF REGENERATION

Correlative Morphologic and Biochemical Findings: Pattern of Regeneration at Days 3–4

Biochemical	*Morphological*
1. Onset of increase in net DNA	1. Continued relative absence of lymphocytes
2. Sharp increase of incorporation of Tdr and P^{32}, reaching maximum at day 3½	2. 25% of all cells labeled, the majority being reticulum cells (average 25 gr/cell) with some early labeling of the monocytoid reticular lymphoblast cells (average 4 gr/cell)
3. Ratio of the specific activity of DNA-T to specific activity of DNA-C, 1:1 (T/C ratio)	3. Presence of "basket" cells, some of which demonstrate active labeling
4. Continued recovery of dCMP deaminase and thymidylate synthetase	
5. Progressive increase in incorporation of Cdr	
6. Constant levels of dCMP kinase and CMP kinase	

TABLE VII

SECOND PHASE OF THE REGENERATIVE PERIOD

Correlative Morphologic and Biochemical Findings: Pattern of Regeneration at Days 4–5

Biochemical	*Morphological*
1. Continued increase in net DNA	1. Marked increase in monocytoid reticular lymphoblast cells with over 50% of the cells labeled (average 60 gr/cell), reaching a peak at day 4½
2. Rapid, progressive, sharp increase in incorporation of Cdr, reaching a peak at day 4½	2. Slight continued labeling of reticlum cells (average 4 gr/cell); no label after day 4½
3. Continued rise of dCMP deaminase and thymidylate synthetase activity, attaining normal levels by day 5	3. Initial reappearance of lymphocytes at day 4½
4. Return to normal levels of rate of incorporation of Tdr and P^{32}	4. Progressive increase in total cellularity, especially due to increase in lymphocytes
5. T/C ratio returns to normal 0.6	
6. Return to normal of dCMP kinase and CMP kinase	

TABLE VIII

FINAL RECOVERY PERIOD

Correlative Morphologic and Biochemical Findings: Pattern of Regeneration at Day 6

Biochemical	*Morphological*
1. Continued return of all above parameters toward normal levels, except the incorporation rates of the labeled precursors	1. Continued increase in net cellularity
	2. Progressive increase in percentage of lymphocytes
	3. Only slight labeling of about 10% of cells predominantly of the monocytoid lymphoblast type (average 10 gr/cell)

and Roth (*21*) clearly demonstrated that one must consider total organ activity as well as specific activity of any enzyme measured after irradiation, in light of the loss of tissue weight and nitrogen content of a variable degree. This is especially important in a structure such as the thymus in which considerable cellular destruction occurs and a shift in the cellular population results (*6*). Multiple parameters are therefore reported to demonstrate that a decrease in the specific activity as well as in the total activity of dCMP deaminase and TMP synthetase occurs postirradiation.

It has been shown that dCMP deaminase and TMP synthetase demonstrate a remarkable decrease in activity after irradiation, reaching a minimum value of (or almost) zero at day 2, and then increasing to the normal level by day 5. Thus, at least by day 3½ or 4, these enzymes still reveal much less activity than normal and may limit the endogenous supply of TMP. The factor of limited dilution of the injected labeled Tdr by endogenously formed TMP can account for the markedly enhanced (to twenty times normal) Tdr incorporation at 3 and 3½ days postirradiation. After day 3½, the rate of incorporation of Tdr into DNA-T decreases very rapidly, reflecting the rapid return of dCMP deaminase and TMP synthetase activities (Figs. 5 and 6), through which enough TMP to dilute the injected labeled Tdr can be supplied. As the enzyme activities increase, they are no longer rate-limiting for DNA synthesis, and a rapid and continued increase in the net amount of DNA becomes detectable (Fig. 1). The pattern of labeled Cdr incorporation into DNA is consistent with this increase in the net amount of DNA, which increase ceases at day 6 (Fig. 1).

In light of the decrease in both the specific activity and the total activity of these two enzymes, one can conclude that irradiation causes either a selected destruction of these enzymes or a selective destruction of the specific cells containing these enzymes (*21*). Our morphologic observations (*6*) suggest that the latter explanation is the situation in the thymus.

Field *et al.* have reported that the administration to mice of 5-fluorouracil, which is a known inhibitor (in the form of 5-fluorodeoxyuridylic acid) of TMP synthetase, doubles the incorporation of Tdr into DNA in the bone marrow but has a negligible effect on incorporation into DNA in the intestinal mucosa (*26*). Bone marrow is one of the tissues which has high dCMP deaminase activity (*13*). According to Maley and Maley, TMP synthetase activity is associated with dCMP deaminase in various tissues so as to allow effective synthesis of DNA-T from dCMP (*13, 27*). If this is the case in the bone marrow of the mouse, the observation made by Field *et al.* is in strong support of our explanation for the enhanced incorporation of labeled Tdr into DNA in the irradiated rat thymus. At 3 to 3½ days postirradiation, the enzyme activity for the synthesis of TMP from dCMP is very low, the situation thus being similar to that in the bone marrow of the 5-fluorouracil-treated mouse (*26*). It should be emphasized that the greatly enhanced incorporation peak of Tdr at 3 to 4 days postirradiation was seen only in the thymus (*2*) and the bone marrow (*5*) but not in intestine or spleen (*2*), and that strong dCMP deaminase activity is associated with the former tissues but not with the latter tissues (*13*).

Further support for the concept that the enzymes concerned with TMP synthesis from dCMP are rate-limiting for DNA specific activity in the initial phase of the regeneration period in the irradiated rat thymus was obtained by comparing the relative rates of the incorporation of H^3-Cdr into DNA-C (via pathway *a–e–f* in Table V) and DNA-T (via pathway *a–b–c–h*[8]*–i* in Table V). As already discussed, if the endogenous supply of TMP through pathways *b–c* (Table V) is rate-limiting for DNA synthesis, the pool of thymidine nucleotides must be so small that very little or no dilution is expected in H^3-Cdr incorporation into DNA-T, resulting in the effective incorporation of H^3-Cdr into DNA-T. If these pathways are not rate-limiting, there must be a pool of thymidine nucleotide(s) which can dilute the injected H^3-Cdr before it is incorporated into DNA-T, resulting in the lowered incorporation of H^3-Cdr into DNA-T.[9] The results summarized in Table III as the ratio of specific activity of DNA-T to that of DNA-C, which was labeled by a 1-hour incorporation of H^3-Cdr, demonstrate that the ratio is highest at day 3½, where a maximum incorporation of H^3-Tdr (or C^{14}-Tdr) is observed.

Activity of two other enzymes, CMP kinase and dCMP kinase, which are not directly involved in TMP synthesis, were measured for comparison. These enzymes did not show the significant change in specific activity (Figs. 4, 5, and 6) observed in the case of dCMP deaminase and TMP synthetase.

Simultaneous injection of 50 μM of nonradioactive Tdr with H^3-Cdr almost completely reduced the incorporation of H^3-Cdr into DNA-T, whereas the incorporation into DNA-C was not affected (Table IV), indicating again the significance of the pool of thymidine nucleotide(s), which, in this case, is derived via pathway *g* (Table V). Since this dilution effect produced by the simultaneous injection of nonradioactive Tdr was seen both in the irradiated (3½ days postirradiation) and in the normal thymus, it is inferred that there is no significant difference between the normal and the irradiated rat thymus in the activities of Tdr and TMP kinase (*g–h–i* in Table V). Experiments are presently in progress to clarify this point.

All these results, which strongly suggest that dCMP deaminase and TMP synthetase function as rate-limiting enzymes in the initial phase of the regeneration period of irradiated rat thymus, are in harmony with the observations made by Maley and Maley (*13, 27*) and by Scarano (*20*), who discovered dCMP deaminase and emphasized its physiological importance in DNA synthesis, and by Friedkin's

[8] See footnote in Table V.

[9] A report on the size of the pools and their metabolic significance will be published by O. F. Nygaard and R. L. Potter (submitted to *J. Biol. Chem.*).

(*28*) concept that TMP synthetase may be one of the key enzymes in the control of DNA synthesis.

The physiological importance in DNA synthesis of other thymidine nucleotide-synthesizing enzymes, i.e., Tdr kinase (*g* in Table V) and TMP kinases (*h–i* in Table V), has also been emphasized by several investigators (*17, 29–32*). In the initial phase of the regeneration period of the irradiated rat thymus, however, these enzymes do not seem to be rate-limiting because of two reasons: (1) In this phase, very effective incorporation of Tdr into DNA-T is seen (Fig. 2); and (2) depression of the incorporation of H^3-Cdr into DNA-T produced by the simultaneous injection of nonradioactive Tdr is seen (3½ days postirradiation) as well as in normal thymus (Table V).

The present study began as an attempt to correlate *in vivo* studies of Tdr incorporation (*2*) with assays for individual enzymes by using the 25,000 × *g* supernatant of whole-tissue homogenates. The peculiar increase and decline in the apparent rate of Tdr incorporation has been explained by the demonstration that this peak at 3 to 3½ days postirradiation occurs at a time when the *de novo* synthesis of TMP (via *b–c* in Table V) is very limited, as judged by *in vivo* incorporation of Cdr, and by assays for dCMP deaminase and TMP synthetase. The decline in the apparent rate of Tdr incorporation is explained by the marked increase in activities of *de novo* TMP synthesis. These changes demonstrate a changing enzyme pattern in the tissue as a whole, but in view of the known cell heterogeneity in the thymus it is equally possible that different cell types are characterized by different ratios between enzymes for *de novo* synthesis and enzymes for salvage pathways. An example for dCMP deaminase is suggested by the data of Pitot and Potter (*33*), who showed that dCMP deaminase is present in the Novikoff hepatoma but was low or absent in the Dunning hepatoma. These tumors were thought to be derived from different liver cell types.

The succeeding paper (*6*) will present the results of morphologic experiments carried out with autoradiographic techniques to correlate changes in enzyme patterns with the changes in cell populations, and to study the trigger mechanism(s) for DNA synthesis in regenerating rat thymus.

SUMMARY

The effect of sublethal total-body X-irradiation on DNA synthesis has been studied in the thymus of the rat. The rate of pyrimidine nucleoside precursor incorporation has been followed during the postirradiation period and has been correlated with the related enzymes and with the morphologic events during this period.

The postirradiation period can be divided into a period of radiation reaction followed by a period of tissue regeneration. During the period of radiation reaction, markedly decreased precursor incorporation is noted as well as a decrease in the related enzymes (dCMP deaminase and thymidylate synthetase).

The period of regeneration appears to consist in two discrete phases. The first phase (days 2½ to 3½) reveals a return of the dCMP–dUMP–TMP enzymes and a markedly increased rate of labeled thymidine or radiophosphorus incorporation. During this phase a change in the ratio of DNA-T to DNA-C is present. The second phase (days 4 to 5) is highlighted by a markedly increased rate of labeled deoxycytidine incorporation.

Adequacy of dCMP deaminase and thymidylate synthetase and the endogenous pool size of TMP appear to be crucial factors in this dual-phased recovery period of postirradiation injury.

ACKNOWLEDGMENTS

We wish to express our most sincere appreciation to Professor Van R. Potter, McArdle Memorial Laboratory, Medical School, University of Wisconsin, Madison, Wisconsin, for his advice, suggestions, and assistance in the preparation for publication of this manuscript.

The assistance of Mr. F. Brohn, Mrs. N. Morrison, and Mrs. D. Stead in this work is gratefully acknowledged.

RECEIVED: April 7, 1962

REFERENCES

1. O. F. NYGAARD and R. L. POTTER, Effect of X-radiation on DNA metabolism in various tissues of the rat. I. Incorporation of C^{14}-thymidine into DNA during the first 24 hours postirradiation. *Radiation Res.* **10,** 462–476 (1959).
2. O. F. NYGAARD and R. L. POTTER, Effect of X-radiation on DNA metabolism in the rat. II. Recovery after sublethal doses of irradiation. *Radiation Res.* **12,** 120–130 (1960).
3. R. L. POTTER, S. SCHLESSINGER, V. BUETTNER-JANUSCH, and L. THOMPSON, The isolation of pyrimidine deoxynucleotides from the acid-soluble extract of thymus. *J. Biol. Chem.* **226,** 381–394 (1957).
4. W. C. SCHNEIDER, Deoxyribosides in animal tissues. *J. Biol. Chem.* **216,** 287–301 (1955).
5. R. L. POTTER and O. F. NYGAARD, Effect of X-radiation on DNA metabolism in various tissues of the rat. IV. Early effects. In preparation.
6. E. P. FRENKEL, Y. SUGINO, R. C. BISHOP, and R. L. POTTER, Effect of X-radiation on DNA metabolism in various tissues of the rat. VI. Correlative morphologic and biochemical changes during the regeneration of the thymus. In press.
7. P. REICHARD, Chromatographic separation of cytosine-containing compounds. *Acta Chem. Scand.* **12,** 2048 (1958).
8. L. SHUSTER and N. O. KAPLAN, A specific b nucleotidase. *J. Biol. Chem.* **201,** 535–546 (1953).
9. Y. HATEFI, P. T. TALBERT, M. J. OSBORN, and F. M. HUENNEKENS, Tetrahydrofolic acid. *Biochem. Prep.* **7,** 89–92 (1960).
10. L. I. HECHT and V. R. POTTER, Nucleic acid metabolism in regenerating rat liver. I. The rate of deoxyribonucleic acid synthesis *in vivo. Cancer Res.* **16,** 988–994 (1956).
11. G. R. WYATT, The purine and pyrimidine composition of DNA. *Biochem. J.* **48,** 584–590 (1951).
12. F. E. KINARD, Liquid scintillator for analysis of tritium in water. *Rev. Sci. Instr.* **28,** 293–294 (1957).
13. G. F. MALEY and F. MALEY, Nucleotide interconversions in embryonic and neoplastic tissues. I. The conversion of deoxycytidylic acid to deoxyuridylic acid and thymidylic acid. *J. Biol. Chem.* **234,** 2975–2980 (1959).
14. F. MALEY, The synthesis of 5-methyluridine 5′-phosphate in rat embryo extracts. *Proc. Natl. Acad. Sci. U. S.* **46,** 632–636 (1960).

15. J. PARIZEK, The excretion of deoxycytidine in the urine after irradiation. The cell nucleus. *Proc. Faraday Soc. (Aug. 31–Sept. 1, 1959)* pp. 82–88 (1960).
16. P. REICHARD and B. ESTBORN, Utilization of deoxyribosides in the synthesis of polynucleotides. *J. Biol. Chem.* **188,** 839–846 (1951).
17. P. A. BIANCHI, J. A. V. BUTLER, A. R. CRATHORN, and K. V. SHOOTER, The thymidine phosphorylating kinases. *Biochem. Biophys. Acta* **48,** 213–214 (1961).
18. L. A. ROSE and B. S. SCHWEIGERT, Incorporation of C^{14} totally labeled nucleosides into nucleic acids. *J. Biol. Chem.* **202,** 635–645 (1953).
19. E. SCARANO and R. MAGIO, The enzymatic deamination of 5′-deoxycytidylic acid and of 5-methyl-5′-deoxycytidylic acid in the developing sea urchin embryo. *Expt. Cell Res.* **18,** 333–346 (1959).
20. E. SCARANO, The enzymatic deamination of 6-aminopyrimidine deoxynucleotides. I. Enzymatic deamination of deoxycytidine 5′-phosphate and of 5-methyldeoxycytidine 5′phosphate. *J. Biol. Chem.* **235,** 706–713 (1960).
21. H. J. EICHEL and J. S. ROTH, Some theoretical considerations of changes in tissue enzyme activity after whole-body X-irradiation of animals. *Radiation Res.* **12,** 258–265 (1960).
22. G. K. HUMPHREYS and D. M. GREENBERG, Studies on the conversion of deoxyuridylic acid to thymidylic acid by a soluble extract from rat thymus. *Arch. Biochem. Biophys.* **78,** 275, 298 (1958).
23. M. FRIEDKIN and A. KORNBERG, The enzymatic conversion of deoxyuridylic acid to thymidylic acid and the participation of tetrahydrofolic acid. In *Chemical Basis of Heredity* (W. D. McElroy and B. Glass, eds.), pp. 609–614, Johns Hopkins Press, Baltimore, 1957.
24. E. BERTANI, A. HAGGMARK, and P. REICHARD, Synthesis of pyrimine deoxyribonucleoside diphosphates with enzymes from *Escherichia coli. J. Biol. Chem.* **236,** 67–68 (1961).
25. K. C. SMITH and B. V. A. LOW-BEER, The effect of whole-body X-irradiation on the enzymatic activity of several rat tissues toward uridine, uridylic acid, cytidine, and cytidylic acid. *Radiation Res.* **6,** 521–531 (1957).
26. E. O. FIELD, J. P. KRISS, and L. A. TUNG, Turnover of thymidine in the DNA of marrow and intestinal mucosa in mice, and its response to administration of 5′-fluorouracil. *Cancer Res.* **21,** 2–8 (1961).
27. F. MALEY and G. F. MALEY, Nucleotide interconversions. II. Elevation of deoxycytidylate deaminase and thymidylate synthetase in regenerating rat liver. *J. Biol. Chem.* **235,** 2968–2970 (1959).
28. M. FRIEDKIN, Speculation on the significance of thymidylic acid synthesis in the regulation of cellular proliferation. In *The Kinetics of Cellular Proliferation* (F. Stohlman, Jr., ed.), pp. 97–103, Grune and Stratton, New York and London, 1959.
29. R. MANTSAVINO and E. S. CANELLAKIS, Studies on the biosynthesis of deoxyribonucleic acid by soluble mammalian enzymes. *J. Biol. Chem.* **234,** 628–635 (1959).
30. F. J. BOLLUM and V. R. POTTER, Nucleic acid metabolism in regenerating rat liver. VI. Soluble enzymes which convert thymidine to thymidine phosphates and DNA. *Cancer Res.* **19,** 561–565 (1959).
31. F. J. BOLLUM, J. W. ANDEREGG, A. B. MCELYA, and V. R. POTTER, Nucleic acid metabolism in regenerating rat liver. VII. Effects of X-radiation on enzymes of DNA synthesis. *Cancer Res.* **20,** 138–143 (1960).
32. E. D. GRAY, S. M. WEISSMAN, J. RICHARDS, D. BELL, H. M. KEIR, R. M. S. SMELLIE, and J. N. DAVIDSON, Studies on the biosynthesis of deoxyribonucleic acid by extracts of mammalian cells. V. Factors interfering with biosynthesis. *Biochem. Biophys. Acta* **45,** 111–120 (1960).
33. H. C. PITOT and V. R. POTTER, An enzymatic study on the cellular origin of the Dunning and the Novikoff hepatomas in the rat. *Biochem. Biophys. Acta* **40,** 537–539 (1960).

RADIATION RESEARCH 19, 701–716 (1963)

Effect of X-Radiation on DNA Metabolism in Various Tissues of the Rat[1]

VI. Correlative Morphologic and Biochemical Changes during the Regeneration of the Thymus

EUGENE P. FRENKEL,[2] YUKIO SUGINO,[3] RONALD C. BISHOP, AND RICHARD L. POTTER[4, 5]

Biological Effects of Irradiation Laboratory, The Department of Biological Chemistry and Simpson Memorial Institute of the University of Michigan, Ann Arbor, Michigan, and Department of Internal Medicine, The University of Texas Southwestern Medical School, Dallas, Texas

INTRODUCTION

Necessary for a clearer intrepretation of biochemical data derived from the studies after sublethal total-body irradiation (*1–3*) is the understanding of the correlative morphological changes noted during this period. Previous observations (*3*) emphasized the significance of the evidence of a two-phased pattern of deoxyribonucleic acid (DNA) synthesis and the changes in some of the enzymes [deoxycytidylic monophosphate (dCMP) deaminase and thymidylate (TMP) synthetase] required for DNA [actually thymidylic monophosphate (TMP)] synthesis. The present report concerns the morphologic and autoradiographic patterns observed in the thymus of the rat after 400 r of total-body irradiation and the correlation of these changes with the observed biochemical events. The thymus was selected for study because of the relative homogeneity of cell population and its previously described characteristics of biochemical behavior (3).

[1] This work was supported by U.S. Atomic Energy Commission Contract At(11-1)-75.

[2] Present address: Department of Internal Medicine, The University of Texas Southwestern Medical School, Dallas, Texas.

[3] Present address: Department of Medical Chemistry, Faculty of Medicine, Kyoto University, Kyoto, Japan.

[4] Deceased—September 26, 1960.

[5] Requests for reprints should be addressed to: Eugene P. Frenkel, M.D., Department of Internal Medicine, The University of Texas Southwestern Medical School, 5323 Harry Hines Blvd., Dallas 35, Texas.

The immediate question concerned the possibility of the correlation of an individual cell type with the specific biochemical events during the postirradiation period (*3*).

EXPERIMENTAL PROCEDURE

Material and Methods

The experimental conditions and procedures were as previously described (*3*). The same samples of thymus used for some of the tritiated thymidine (H^3-Tdr) incorporation studies were employed here for the morphologic studies. All autoradiographic studies reported herein were carried out with H^3-Tdr as the label. The labeled precursor (0.3 μM; specific activity 0.35 mc/μM) was given intravenously per tail vein 1 hour prior to sacrifice.

Autoradiographs of touch imprints of thymus were prepared with NTB-3 Kodak Dipping Emulsion. After air drying of the touch preparations there was a 5-minute fixation period in absolute methyl alcohol, and the slides were then stored for dipping in black bakelite slide boxes (Clay-Adams Company). The NTB-5 Kodak Dipping Emulsion (obtained from the Special Sensitized Products Division of Eastman Kodak Company, Rochester, New York) was then softened at 45°C in a water bath in a dark room with a Wratten-Red No. 2 Dark Room Filter. The emulsion was poured, without dilution, into a 50-ml beaker, and the prepared slides were dipped for 30 seconds and permitted to drain onto a towel. The back of the slide was wiped clean, and the slides were kept in a horizontal position until the emulsion hardened. The slides were then replaced in the black bakelite slide boxes, and the boxes were appropriately labeled and stored in a photographic paper safe. Placing an open dish of saturated solution of KNO_2 in the safe helped to maintain a constant humidity of 47%. The exposure time was 24 to 30 days, during which period the slides were maintained in a refrigerator at 5° C. A D-19 developing solution (Eastman Kodak Company) was employed in the manner described by the manufacturer. Prior to developing, the slides were warmed toward room temperature, and the developing and fixation (with Fixer-Hardener, Eastman Kodak Company) were carried out at 15° C. A 2-minute developing time was employed. The slides were then washed briefly, and a 4-minute fixer-hardening time was permitted. After a second brief washing (30 seconds), the slides were dried. The slides were then strained with Wright's or May-Grunwald–Giemsa stain at room temperature.

The touch imprints of the thymus were used for the morphologic studies. At least 500 cells were counted, and in most cases 2000 cells, in each imprint, and the differential percentage of cells was determined. In the autoradiographs the percentage of each type of cell that demonstrated labeling was determined in addition to counting the number of granules such labeled cells contained. Total nucleated cell counts and studies of viable cells were also done. Correlative

DNA analysis was done on the same fraction, performed by the method of Schneider (*4*). This study was performed by gently homogenizing the thymus gland in four volumes of isotonic sucrose solution in a glass homogenizer with a Teflon pestle. After satisfactory dispersion of cells, paired total nucleated cell counts were performed both with dilute acetic acid (2% solution) dilution and by direct phase-contrast microscopy without diluent. The cell counts were performed in a Neubauer Bright-Line hemocytometer chamber. Repeat cell counts were performed with the eosin technique of Schrek (*5*) for the determination of "viable cells." Simultaneous smears were also prepared and strained with Wright's strain for comparison. Total DNA content was determined (*4*) on the same aliquot of the homogenate.

RESULTS

Radiation Reaction Period

During the first 24 hours after 400 r of total-body X-irradiation, a moderate decrease in cellularity of the thymus was noted. Table I outlines the morphologic observations postirradiation. Serial sampling during the first day demonstrated marked involvement of the lymphocytes. Early prominent cloudy swelling was seen, followed by intranuclear vacuolization, pyknosis, and, finally, frank fragmentation of the lymphocytes.

The differential cell counts are demonstrated in Table I. By the criteria of Schooley *et al.* (*6*), cells demonstrating less than 3 silver grains above representative background areas were arbitrarily considered to be unlabeled. Equal sampling of cortex and medulla was attempted. During the first 24 hours there was very marked destruction and removal of lymphocytes from the sampled cortical areas. Lymphocytes in the medullary areas remained and largely accounted for the numbers noted. Also, by employing the eosin technique of Schrek, it was noted that the lymphocytes present at the end of 24 hours even those in the medullary areas, were largely nonviable. By day 2 evidence of marked hypocellularity was apparent, due to disappearance of the population of lymphocytes. "Basket cells" or apparent broken cells were noted in abundance. Autoradiographic studies failed to reveal any demonstrable radiographic label in any of the cells during this period. Differential cell counts (Table I) revealed a relative increase in reticulum cells (see Fig. 1) and prominence of a large "monocytoid reticular lymphoblast" (see Fig. 2). This cell was a large cell with deep blue frothy cytoplasm and a large nucleus which almost completely filled the cell and had reticular characteristics of the chromatin. This cell has been variously called monocytoid lymphoblast, reticular lymphoblast, monocytoid reticulum cell, and lymphocyte precursor cell. Table II demonstrates the correlation of biochemical events with the morphological observations during this period.

TABLE I

CORRELATIVE MORPHOLOGIC OBSERVATIONS

Day	General cellularity	Differential cell counts			Percentage of cells labeled	Type of cell labeled and per cent of these total cells labeled			Number of granules per labeled cell[a]			Basket cells	
		Reticulum cells	"Monocytoid lymphoblasts"	Lymphocytes		Reticulum cells	"Monocytoid lymphoblasts"	Lymphocytes	Reticulum cells	"Monocytoid lymphoblasts"	Lymphocytes	Present	Labeled
Control	Normal[b]	1.0–3.2% (2)°	4–6% (5)	86–95% (93)	3%	5%	Rare	0	3–5/cell (av = 4)	1–2/cell	0	0	0
1	Generally decreased with prominent cloudy swelling, intranuclear vacuolization, pyknosis, and fragmentation of lymphocytes (↓ ↓)	28–37% (35)	13–24% (20)	40–61% (45)	None	0	0	0	0	0	0	++ +0 +++	0
2	Markedly decreased cellularity with some continued evidence of dying lymphocytes (↓ ↓ ↓ ↓)	25–40% (35)	43–68% (50)	8–14% (10)	Rare	1%	0	0	1–3/cell (av = 1)	0	0	++++	0
3	Very hypocellular (↓ ↓ ↓ ↓)	16–24% (18)	70–88% (77)	1–10% (5)	15–18%	15–20%	3–6%	0	20–70/cell (av = 25)	1–3/cell (av = 2)	0	+++	+++
3½	Very hypocellular (↓ ↓ ↓ ↓)	15–25% (18)	85–88% (77)	1–10% (5)	25–30%	12–20%	6–12%	0	15–50/cell (av = 25)	2–6/cell (av = 5)	0	+++	+++
4	Moderately hypocellular (↓ ↓ ↓)	10–19% (15)	70–90% (80)	1–10% (5)	40–50%	5–10%	35–45%	0	6–15/cell (av = 10)	(30–100/cel av = 45)	0	+	+
4½	Moderately hypocellular (↓ ↓ ↓)	5–10% (8)	60–85% (82)	5–15% (10)	50–65%	3–8%	45–55%	0	4–10/cell (av = 5)	40–100/cell (av = 60)	0	0	0
5	Hypocellular (↓ ↓)	5–10% (8)	25–50% (42)	45–60% (50)	25%	Rare	20–40%	Rare	4–6/cell (av = 4)	10–40/cell (av = 20)	1–2/cell	0	0
6	Hypocellular (↓–↓ ↓)	8–14% (10)	15–35% (25)	60–80% (65)	8–20%	2–4%	14–28%	Rare	3–5/cell (av = 4)	3–20/cell (av = 10)	0	0	0

[a] Represents counts above background.

[b] Six animals studied in the normal group.

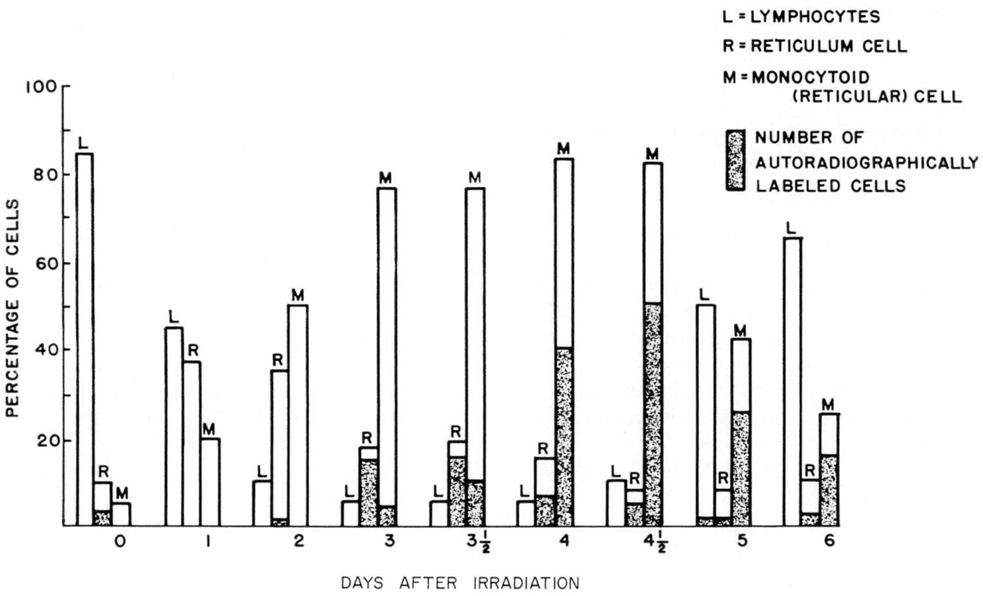

FIG. 1. Differential cell counts and percentage of autoradiographically labeled cells. Counts represent average counts of a 500-cell differential. Variation in cell distribution between medullary and cortical areas occurs as noted in the text. The temporal relations on the abscissa represent days after the single dose of irradiation.

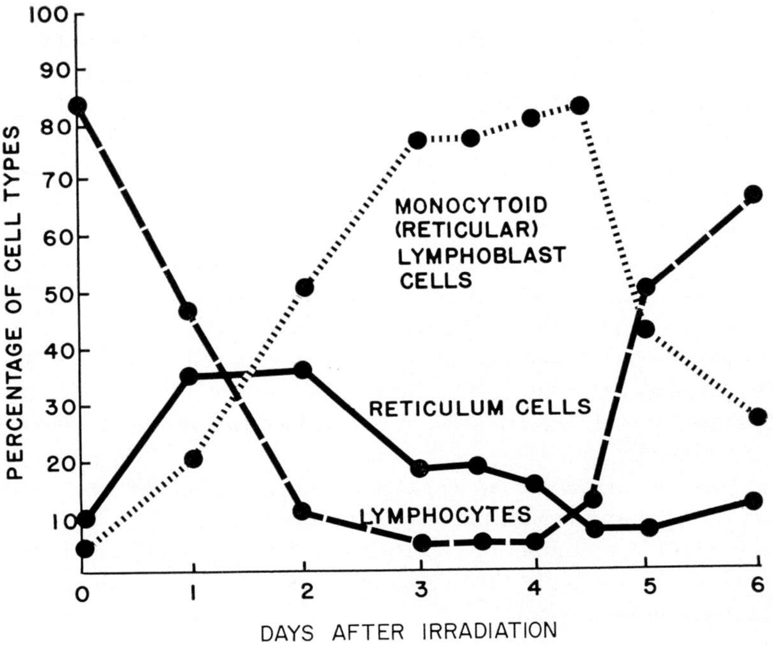

FIG. 2. Differential of cell types noted during the postirradiation period. The abscissa represents days after the single dose of irradiation.

TABLE II

COURSE OF EVENTS DURING THE IMMEDIATE POSTIRRADIATION PERIOD DESCRIBING BOTH THE CORRELATIVE BIOCHEMICAL AND ANATOMICAL CHANGES

Correlative Morphologic and Biochemical Findings: Effect of X-Radiation at Days 0–2	
Biochemical	*Morphological*
1. Sharp decrease in total weight of the gland	1. Marked decrease in total number of cells
2. Sharp decrease in amount of total DNA	2. Marked lysis of lymphocytes
3. Sharp decrease in incorporation rate of precursors: Tdr, Cdr, and P^{32}	3. Some probable reversible cloudy swelling of reticulum cells and evidence of a large primitive "monocytoid reticular lymphoblast" type of cell
4. Sharp decrease in dCMP deaminase and thymidylate synthetase	4. Evidence of "basket cells" without radioactive label
5. Slight decrease in dCMP kinase and CMP kinase	

Regeneration Period

Although a definite change in the pattern of the biochemical events was apparent at 2½ days (*3*), no morphologic changes could be demonstrated until day 3. The glands were very hypocellular at this time, and for the first time autoradiographic examination revealed the presence of cells containing granules. The labeled cells were largely reticulum cells (see Tables I and IV and Figs. 4, 5, and 6). "Basket cells" were prominent, and many revealed very marked labeling by autoradiographic techniques.

Small groups (five per determination) of animals handled in the same manner, except for administration of the labeled precursor, were studied to evaluate the amount of DNA present per cell (see Table III). With the eosin stain of Schrek as a determinant of viability, it was apparent that many cells which had no overt morphologic abnormalities were actually nonviable.

By day 4 a shift in the cellular population was seen (Table I and Figs. 3 and 7). Prominent labeling of the "monocytoid lymphoblasts" was suddenly apparent, and over the subsequent 24 hours almost 50% of this cell type demonstrated the label. By day 4½ an initial reappearance of mature lymphocytes was noted (Table I; Figs. 8 and 9). A correlation of the biochemical and morphological events is shown in Table V.

Beyond this time a rapid reappearance of mature lymphocytes was seen, and the glands revealed an over-all increase in cellularity.

With the increase in number of mature lymphocytes, the differential cell counts returned toward normal, and the degree of autoradiographic labeling also slowly returned toward normal.

Similar sequential morphologic observations made on Wright's and May-Grun-

TABLE III

DETERMINATION OF AMOUNT OF DNA PER CELL

Days post-irradiation	*Total volume of homogenate (ml)*	DNA-P (*μg/ml*)	*Number of nucleated cells/ml*		*DNA-P per nucleated cell*[b] (*pg*)[c]
			Total × *10*^{6}	*Total* × *10*^{6a}	
Normal	2.5	456	66.3		6.9
	2.5	567	92.0		6.2
3	1.6	29.8	3.20	0.80	9.3
	1.6	36.1	4.45	1.13	8.1
4	1.6	59.9	3.60	1.35	16.6
	1.6	35.8	3.42	1.5	10.4
5	2.0	209	24.0	21.6	8.7
	2.0	265	23.0	22.5	11.5

[a] After Schrek (*5*).

[b] Normal rat values (*7*): Liver = 8.2, 10.7; spleen = 6.5; WBC's = 6.6; lung = 6.7; bone marrow = 6.9; heart = 6.5.

[c] Picrograms (or 10^{-12} gm).

TABLE IV

FIRST PHASE OF REGENERATION

Correlative Morphologic and Biochemical Findings: Pattern of Regeneration at Days 3–4

Biochemical

1. Onset of increase in net DNA
2. Sharp increase of incorporation of Tdr and P^{32}, reaching maximum at day 3½
3. Ratio of the specific activity of DNA-T to specific activity of DNA-C, 1:1 (T/C ratio)
4. Continued recovery of dCMP deaminase and thymidylate synthetase
5. Progressive increase in incorporation of Cdr
6. Constant levels of dCMP kinase and CMP kinase.

Morphological

1. Continued relative absence of lymphocytes
2. 25% of all cells labeled, the majority being reticulum cells (average 25 gr/cell), with some early labeling of monocytoid reticular lymphoblast cells (average 4 gr/cell)
3. Presence of "basket cells," some of which demonstrate active labeling

wald–Giemsa strained touch imprints of thymus corroborated the autoradiographic results. Sharper morphologic clarity in these preparations permitted more detailed classification of cell types. However, the significant cellular activity was the same as that demonstrated by autoradiography.

TABLE V

SECOND PHASE OF THE REGENERATIVE PERIOD

Correlative Morphglogic and Biochemical Findings: Pattern of Regeneration at Days 4–5

Biochemical	*Morphological*
1. Continued increase in net DNA	1. Marked increase in monocytoid reticular lymphoblast cells with over 50% of the cells labeled (average 60 gr/cell) reaching a peak at day 4½
2. Rapid, progressive, sharp increase in incorporation of Cdr, reaching a peak at day 4½	2. Slight continued labeling of reticulum cells (average 4 gr/cell); no label after day 4½
3. Continued rise of dCMP deaminase and thymidylate synthetase activity, attaining normal levels by day 5	3. Initial reappearance of lymphocytes at day 4½
4. Return to normal levels of rate of incorporation of Tdr and P^{32}	4. Progressive increase in total cellularity especially due to increase in lymphocytes
5. Return to normal T/C ratio of 0.6	
6. Return to normal of dCMP kinase and CMP kinase	

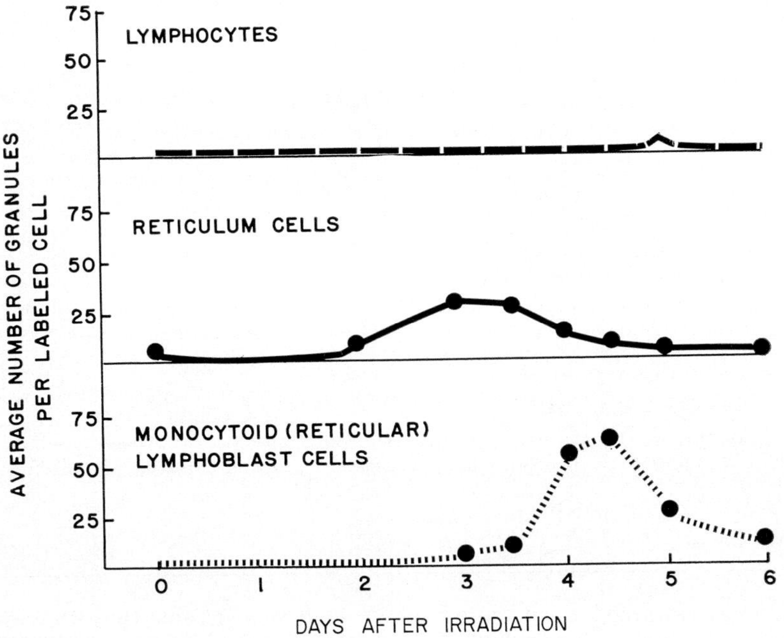

FIG. 3. Number of granules (above background) in the labeled cells. The abscissa represents the days after the single dose of irradiation given on day 0.

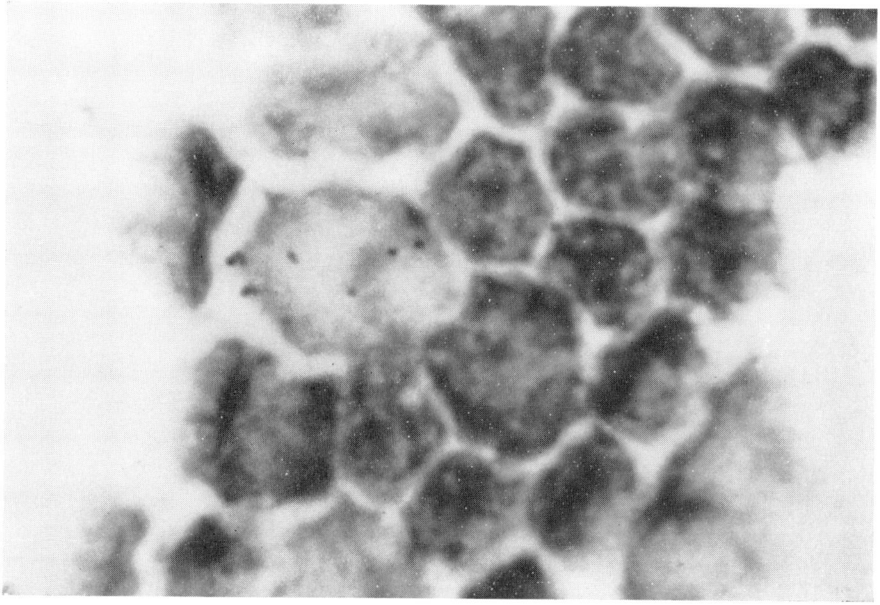

Fig. 4. Imprint of autoradiographically labeled normal (control) thymus, demonstrating some labeling of a reticulum cell. No significant labeling of the lymphocytes is present, and background is very minimal. Magnification 1650×.

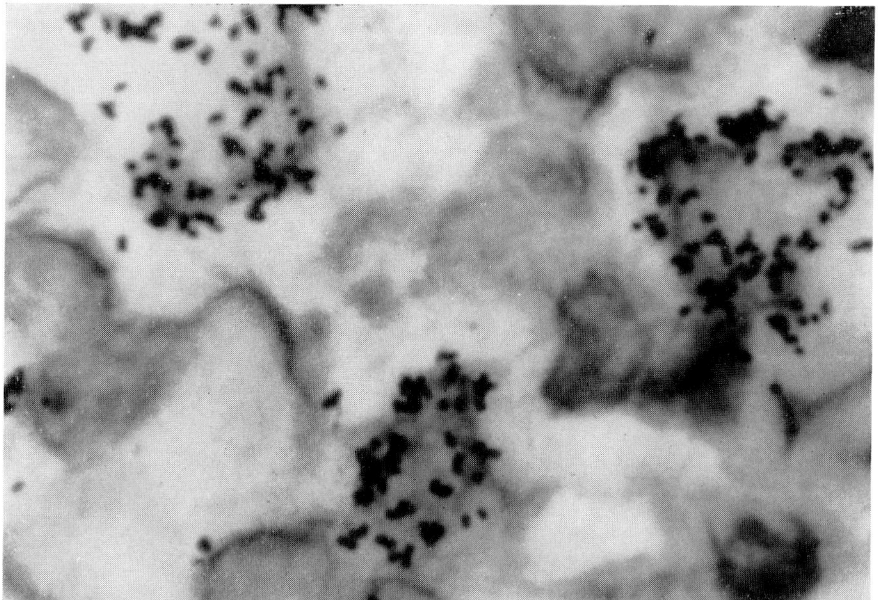

Fig. 5. Autoradiograph of imprint of thymus at day 3, demonstrating considerable labeling of the reticulum cells. Magnification 1650×.

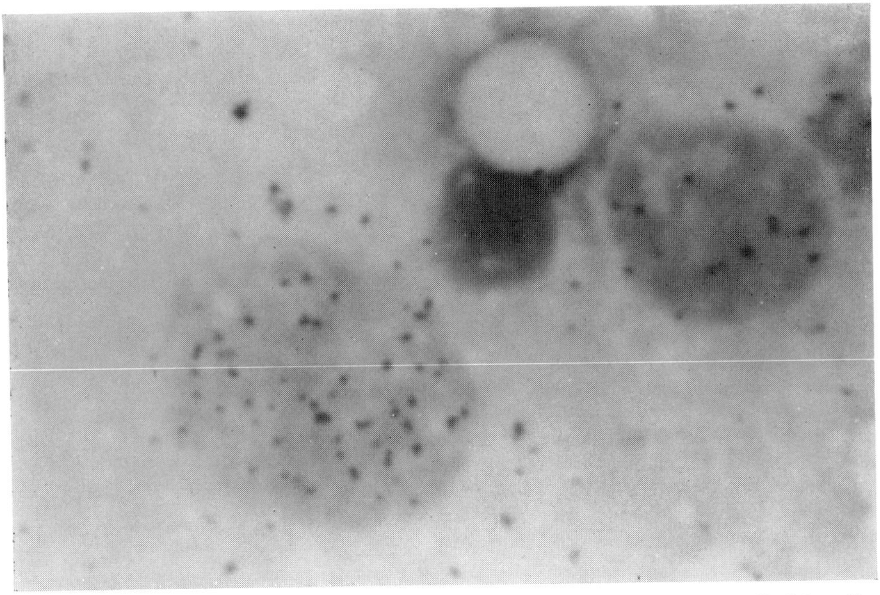

FIG. 6A. Autoradiograph at day 3½, demonstrating a labeled reticulum cell. Magnification 2000×.

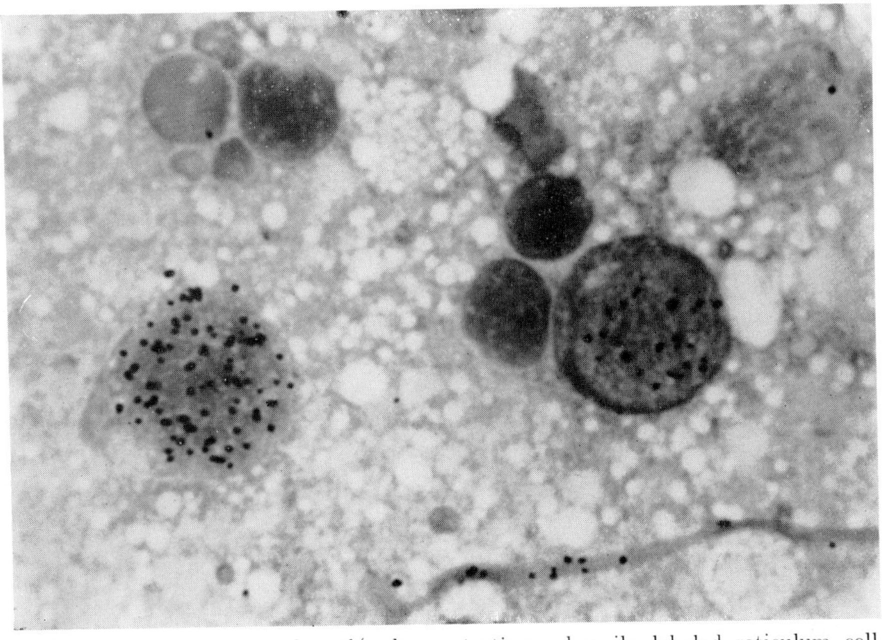

FIG. 6B. Autoradiograph on day 3½, demonstrating a heavily labeled reticulum cell and early labeling of a "monocytoid reticular lymphoblast." Magnification 1650×.

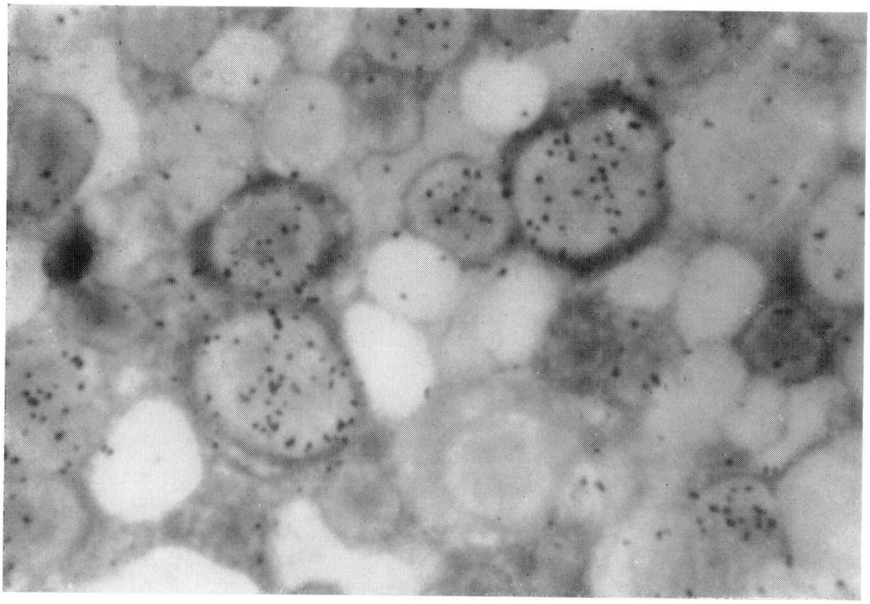

FIG. 7. Uptake at day 4, demonstrating labeling of the monocytoid reticular lymphoblast. Magnification 1650×.

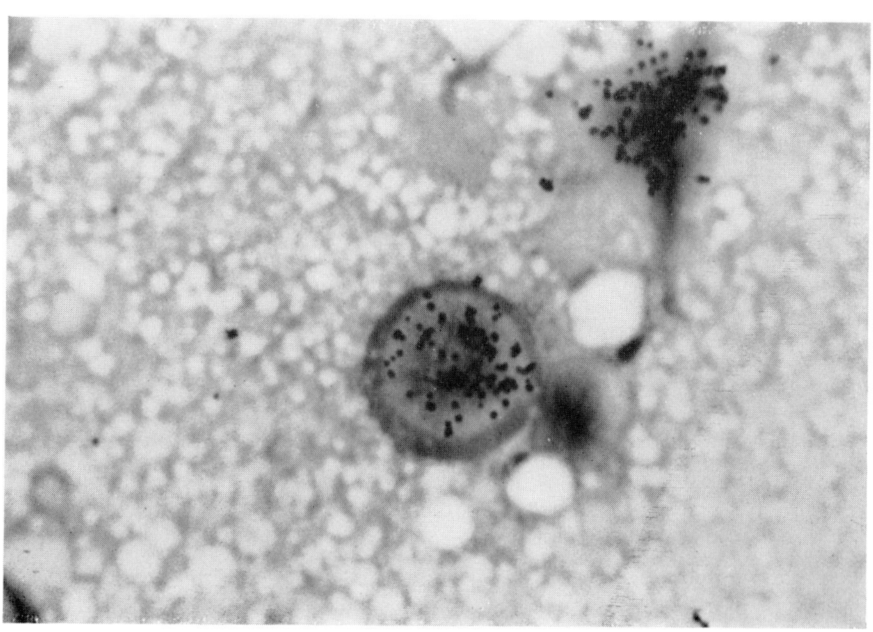

FIG. 8. Well-labeled monocytoid reticular lymphoblast at day 4½. Magnification 1650×.

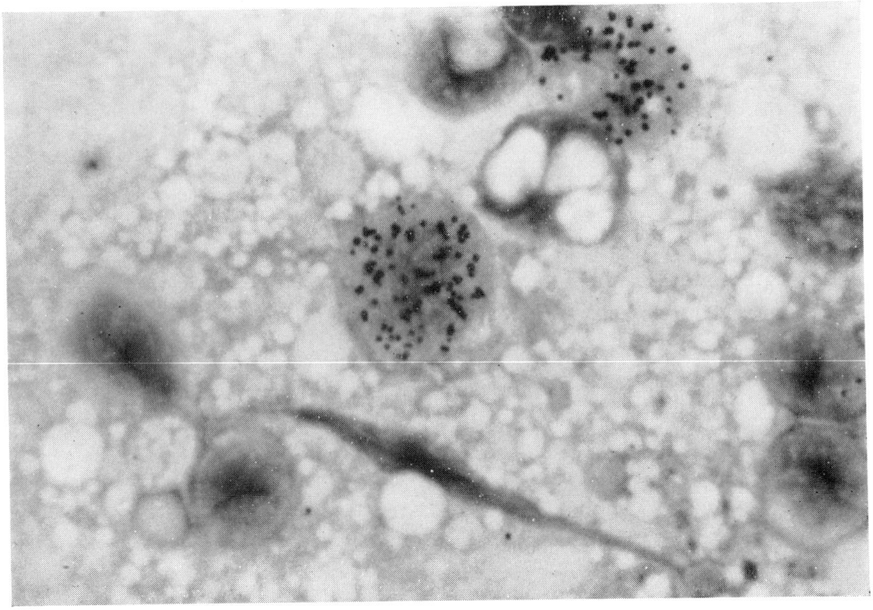

FIG. 9. Well-labeled monocytoid reticular lymphoblast and early emergence of more mature lymphocyte population at day 4½. Magnification 1650×.

DISCUSSION

Lymphoid tissue, the basic cellular mass of the thymus gland, has certain unique biologic responses. One such prominent response is that of the marked sensitivity of lymphoid tissue to X-radiation (*8*). Furthermore, if one accepts the current hematologic concept that the lymphocyte, the predominant cell of lymphoid tissue, is an "end stage" with a finite life span and without the potential for mitosis, then it is the only nonmitotic cell with such great sensitivity to X-radiation (*9*).

The lymphoid tissue of the thymus gland can be morphologically divided into medullary and cortical areas. Within each area, however, the heteroplastic formation of lymphocytes from reticulum cells is well established (*10*), and mitotic count studies (*11, 12*) have led to the conclusion that the thymus is a very active producer of lymphocytes, at least in the rat. Considerable mitotic activity is present in this gland in the progression of maturation from the basic stem cell or reticulum cell to the end stage lymphocyte (often termed thymocyte). Sainte-Marie and Leblond estimated the occurrence of eight mitoses in the cycle of development (*13*). Another anatomical feature that may relate to the response of the thymus to X-radiation is that of a greater number of lymphocytes per reticulum cell (a ratio of 90:1) present in the cortex in contrast to a smaller ratio (20:1) in the medulla (*14, 15*).

Trowell (*16*) has clearly demonstrated a differential sensitivity of lymphocytes in thymus depending on the dosage of irradiation and the location of the cell. Cortical lymphocytes were demonstrated to be four times as sensitive as medullary lymphocytes (*16*), and Trowell has related this to some protective influence of the adjacent reticulum cells. In touch imprint preparations one does not obtain the pattern of structural relationships noted in tissue sections, but sharper morphologic detail is apparent. Thus, clear delineation of the medullary area from the cortical area is not noted, and this may account for some of the differences in our normal ratios of reticulum cells from lymphocytes. However, the clearer morphology permits greater evaluation of stages of cellular maturation between the primitive reticulum cell and the mature lymphocyte.

Previous observations of biochemical events (*3*) have permitted a tentative demarcation of the period of radiation reaction from the period of regeneration, and a similar separation is apparent on morphological grounds. During the first 24 hours postirradiation, cloudy swelling, intranuclear vacuolization, pyknosis, and, finally, fragmentation of the lymphocytes are readily apparent. The lymphocytes in the cortical area are most rapidly destroyed, whereas the medullary lymphocytes are still apparent at the end of 24 hours with 400 r of total-body irradiation, although these cells may also be dying. It has been postulated that the relatively greater numbers of reticulum cells in the medullary region in some manner "protect" adjacent lymphocytes from the effects of irradiation (*14, 16*), thus accounting for these differences. The reticulum cells and large "monocytoid lymphoblasts" become apparent amid the macrophages and debris, and the resistance of such cells to irradiation has been well demonstrated in the past (*9, 17*).

During the first 2 days postirradiation, autoradiographic studies with labeled (H^3) Tdr failed to reveal any uptake of precursor in any of the cells. Besides the frankly fractured and dying cells, many so-called "basket cells" or "degenerating nuclei" were noted, but none of these manifested radioactive labeling.

On strictly morphologic ground the onset of the regenerative period can be identified on day 3. At this time initial radioactive labeling is apparent on autoradiography, and this is largely limited to the primitive reticulum cells (see Table I and Fig. 1). Also, for the first time, the "basket cells" or degenerating nuclei demonstrate labeling. Such labeling has been considered a demonstration of very active metabolic function and has been demonstrated in situations of active cellular proliferation (*18*). Little active labeling is noted in the other cell types present. The previous biochemical observations (*3*) (see Table IV) suggested the possibility that the reticulum cell might be capable of reproduction were it to contain Tdr kinase and were it to have sufficient concentration of preformed Tdr locally. Tdr kinase studies are at present under way to further elucidate this point.

Very little labeled precursor incorporation can be seen autoradiographically in the "monocytoid lymphoblasts" until 24 hours after the reticulum cells manifest their activity—i.e., day 4. At this point, however, very intense labeling is seen in these cells. It has been postulated (*3*) that these cells have the potential for *de novo* synthesis. Should they contain dCMP deaminase and thymidylate synthetase, they would be capable of prominent early precursor incorporation from labeled Cdr, but the present autoradiographic study employed only H^3-Tdr. Serial studies with H^3-Cdr are at present in progress.

Rapid emergence of a large lymphocyte population is noted after the activity in the "monocytoid lymphoblasts." It seems quite justifiable to state that these latter cells are the precursors of the large lymphocyte in the thymus.

Touch imprint stained preparations corroborated the autoradiographic findings. These observations, as well as those of Yoffey (*19*) and many others (*10, 13, 20, 21*) attest to the concept that the reticulum cell gives rise, by a variable number of mitoses, to the lymphocyte.

Thus, as previously mentioned (*3*), tissue injury which results in significant breakdown in DNA could serve to stimulate the production of reticulum cells because of their probable capacity to use local Tdr.

It must be pointed out, as well emphasized by Kelly *et al.* (*6*) and by Cronkite *et al.* (*22*), that interpretations of autoradiographic results on a quantitative basis must be conservative in light of the numerous technical factors that can influence one's results. Even with this perspective our studies seem to indicate a sequential pattern of cell maturation from the primitive reticulum cell to the mature lymphocyte. Others (*23–25*) have suggested that a complete circular pattern of lymphocyte maturation may be present, with the pattern of development from reticulum cell to mature lymphocyte (thymocyte), and that the dying lymphocyte may then provide the protein to the potentially phagocytic reticulum cells to renew this cycle. Thymocytes isotopically labeled *in vitro* were introduced into irradiated mice by Hill and Drášil (*26*), and they were able to demonstrate uptake of the labeled material in the nuclei of the reticulum cells of the thymus, spleen, and bone marrow. Thus the reticulum cell may be provided with preformed DNA from dying lymphocytes and in the presence of its own Tdr kinase is able to replicate nuclear protein and proceed to division. Pertinent to this we observed the marked fall in lymphocytes in the tissue (during day 2) just prior to evidence of synthesis in the reticulum cells. Prior to this point in time synthetic activity in the reticulum cells could not be demonstrated. The availability of increased local concentration of Tdr from dead or dying lymphocytes, presumably in a form in which it may be phagocytosed, may serve as the "trigger" for replication of the reticulum cells.

SUMMARY

Correlative morphologic observations by means of routine cytologic and autoradiographic techniques were made in the thymus of the rat after sublethal total-body X-irradiation. As with the biochemical observations, a period of radiation reaction can be differentiated from the period of tissue regeneration.

A sequential pattern of morphologic and synthetic (incorporation of labeled precursors of DNA) events was demonstrated. These occurred first in the reticulum cells, then in the monocytoid reticular lymphoblasts, and finally in an emerging population of young lymphocytes.

The studies suggest that the primitive reticulum cells reproduce with the available preformed Tdr (from the injured lymphocytes) and that these cells probably contain Tdr kinase but lack dCMP deaminase and TMP synthetase. The breakdown or death of lymphocytes may provide the Tdr to the reticulum cell which is capable of phagocytosis, and thus serve as the "trigger" to synthesis of protein in the reticulum cell and then replication of that cell. It is postulated that the "monocytoid lymphoblasts" are capable of *de novo* synthesis and thus contain dCMP deaminase and TMP synthetase. Finally, mature lymphocytes may demonstrate little or no synthesis because of lack of a rate-limiting enzyme such as TMP kinase or DNA-primer formation.

ACKNOWLEDGMENT

We wish to express our most sincere appreciation to Professor Van R. Potter, McArdle Memorial Laboratory, Medical School, University of Wisconsin, for his advice, suggestions, and assistance in the preparation for publication of this manuscript.

RECEIVED: April 7, 1962

REFERENCES

1. O. F. NYGAARD and R. L. POTTER, Effect of X-radiation on DNA metabolism in various tissues of the rat. I. Incorporation of C^{14}-thymidine into DNA during the first 24 hours post-irradiation, *Radiation Res.* **10,** 462–476 (1959).
2. O. F. NYGAARD and R. L. POTTER, Effect of X-radiation on DNA metabolism in various tissues of the rat. II. Recovery after sublethal dose of irradiation, *Radiation Res.* **12,** 120–130 (1960).
3. Y. SUGINO, E. P. FRENKEL, and R. L. POTTER, Effect of X-radiation on DNA metabolism in various tissues of the rat. V. DNA metabolism in regenerating thymus. In press.
4. W. C. SCHNEIDER, Phosphorus compounds in animal tissues. I. Extraction and estimation of desoxypentose nucleic acid and of pentose nucleic acid *J. Biol. Chem.* **161,** 293–303 (1945).
5. R. SCHREK, Studies *in vitro* on the physiology of normal and of cancerous cells, *Arch. Pathol.* **35,** 857–868 (1943).
6. J. C. SCHOOLEY, B. J. BRYANT, and L. S. KELLY, Preliminary autoradiographic observations of cellular proliferation in lymphoid tissues, using tritiated thymidine. In *The Kinetics of Cellular Proliferation* (F. Stahlman, Jr., ed.), pp. 208–217, Grune and Stratton, New York, 1959.
7. R. VENDRELY, The deoxyribonucleic acid content of the nucleus. In *The Nucleic Acids* (E. Chargaff and J. N. Davidson, eds.), Vol. II, p. 159, Academic Press, New York, 1955.
8. M. ERRERA, Effects of radiation on cells. In *The Cell* (J. Brachet and A. E. Mirsky, eds.), pp. 695–740, Academic Press, New York, 1959.
9. R. SCHREK, Radiation effects on lymphocytes. In *The Lymphocyte and Lymphocytic Tissue* (J. W. Rebuck, ed.), pp. 125–145, Paul B. Hoeber, New York, 1960.

10. A. Downey and F. Widenreich, Ueber die Bildung der Lymphocytes in Lympdrusen und Milz. *Arch. Mikroskop. Anat.* **80,** Abt. 1, 306–394 (1912).
11. J. E. Kindred, A quantitative study of the hemopoietic organs of young albino rats. *Am J. Anat.* **67,** 99–149 (1940).
12. E. Andreasen and S. Christensen, The rate of mitotic activity in the lymphoid organs of the rat. *Anat. Record* **103,** 401–412 (1949).
13. G. Sainte-Marie and C. P. Leblond, Tentative pattern for renewal of lymphocytes in cortex of the rat thymus. *Proc. Soc. Exptl. Biol. Med.* **97,** 263–270 (1958).
14. O. A. Trowell, The sensitivity of lymphocytes to ionising radiation. *J. Pathol. Bacteriol.* **64,** 687–704 (1952).
15. O. A. Trowell, M. J. Corp, and W. R. Lush, Paradoxical resistance of thymus lymphocytes to high doses of X-radiation. *Radiation Res.* **7,** 120–128 (1957).
16. O. A. Trowell, Radiosensitivity of the cortical and medullary lymphocytes in the thymus. *Intern. J. Radiation Biol.* **4,** 163–173 (1961).
17. J. L. Tullis, Radioresistant cells in certain radiosensitive tissues of swine exposed to atomic bomb radiation. *Arch. Pathol.* **48,** 171–177 (1949).
18. D. R. Korst, E. P. Frenkel, and J. E. Wilhelm, Study of "basket cell" metabolic activity in human leukemia by tritiated thymidine radioautography. (Abstract) *J. Clin. Invest.* **40,** 1055 (1961).
19. J. M. Yoffey, *Quantitative Cellular Haematology,* pp. 1–16, Charles C Thomas, Springfield, Illinois, 1960.
20. A. A. Maximow, Bendegewebe und blutbildende Gewebe. In W. von Mollendorff's *Handbuch der mikroskopeschen Anatomie des Menschen,* Vol. 2, Part I, pp. 232–583, Julius Springer, Berlin, 1927.
21. E. Grundmann, Die Bildung der Lymphocyten und Plasmazellen im lymphatischen Gewebe der Ratte, *Beitr. Pathol. Anat. Allgem. Pathol.* **119,** 217–262 (1958).
22. E. P. Cronkite, V. P. Bond, T. M. Fliedner, and J. R. Rubini, The use of tritiated thymidine in the study of DNA synthesis and cell turnover in hemopoietic tissues. *Lab. Invest.* **8,** 263–277 (1959).
23. O. A. Trowell, Re-utilization of lymphocytes in lymphopoiesis. *J. Biophys. Biochem. Cytol.* **3,** 317–318 (1957).
24. O. A. Trowell, Some properties of lymphocytes *in vivo* and *in vitro*. *Ann. N. Y. Acad. Sci.* **73,** 105–112 (1958).
25. R. D. Sundberg, Lymphocytes: origin, structure and interrelationships. In *The Lymphocyte and Lymphocytic Tissue* (J. W. Rebuck, ed.), pp. 1–21, Paul B. Hoeber, New York, 1960.
26. M. Hill and V. Drášil, Nuclear uptake of DNA fragments after injection of P^{32}-labeled thymocytes in lethally irradiated mice. *Exptl. Cell Res.* **21,** 569–582 (1960).

Announcements

The National Academy of Sciences—National Research Council is accepting applications for fellowships and grants in the field of radiology and nuclear medicine on behalf of the James Picker Foundation. Support is not restricted to citizens of the United States or to institutions within this country. Applications for the fiscal year 1964–65 should be submitted by October 1, 1963. Application blanks and further details may be obtained from the Committee on Radiology, National Academy of Sciences—National Research Council, 2101 Constitution Avenue, N.W., Washington 25, D. C.

An International Symposium on Biological Effects of Neutron Irradiations will be held at the Brookhaven National Laboratory, Upton, New York, during October 7–11, 1963. Inquiries with reference to participation should be directed to John H. Kane, Chief, International Conferences Branch, Division of Special Projects, United States Atomic Energy Commission, Washington 25, D. C.

AUTHOR INDEX

A

Alderman, Ilo M., 621
Anderson, A. W., 593
Andrews, Howard L., 331
Armstrong, W. A., 120

B

Babicky, A., 551
Beck, James S., 569
Berliner, Martha D., 392
Bewley, D. K., 50
Biavati, M. H., 512
Bishop, Ronald C., 701
Brown, Sidney O., 270
Bruce, W. R., 606
Butler, J. A. V., 582

C

Cheek, C. H., 636
Christenberry, K. W., 156
Cohn, S. H., 104, 643, 655
Conklin, J. W., 156
Cork, Ann, 247
Cornfield, Jerome, 621
Cress, Edgar A., 129
Cronkite, E. P., 409
Crowley, Cathryn, 337
Curtis, Howard, 337

D

Deering, R. A., 169
Detrick, Lawrence E., 447
Dewey, D. L., 64
Dewey, William C., 247
Doherty, David G., 474
Dolin, P. I., 345
Drakulić, M., 429, 439

E

Elliker, P. R., 593
Etō, Hideo, 316

F

Facey, R. A., 120
Fitch, Frank, 670
Freedhoff, Helen S., 606
Frenkel, Eugene P., 682, 701
Fry, R. J. M., 628

G

Glinos, André D., 286
Goepp, Robert A., 670
Gold, Ruth, 88
Goodman, C. D., 462
Gordon, S., 559
Grant, D. W., 120
Griem, Melvin L., 324
Gurney, Clifford W., 599
Gusmano, E. A., 104, 655

H

Hahn, E. W., 676
Hanna, Calvin, 1
Hayakawa, Jun-Ichiro, 316
Hilton, Sylvia, 42
Hochanadel, C. J., 462
Hofstra, Diana, 599
Hornsey, S., 50
Howland, J. W., 676
Humphrey, Ronald M., 247
Humphreys, W. G., 120
Hunt, Vilma R., 298

J

Jansen, C. R., 409
Jones, David C. L., 142

K

Kimeldorf, Donald J., 142
Knight, J. A., 359
Kochanny, G. L. Jr., 462
Kopoldova, J., 551
Kos, E., 429, 439
Krise, George M., 270

L

Lee, J. S., 593
Lesher, S., 628
Liebster, J., 551
Linnenbom, V. J., 636
Lipkin, Martin 277
Lippincott, S. W., 104

M

McDonald, T. P., 156
McGrath, Richard A., 526
Maisin, Jean R., 474
Malkinson, Frederick D., 324
Maramatsu, Susumu, 316
Maruyama, Yosh, 538
Meaburn, G. M. A. C., 559
Miyanaga, I., 512
Morse, Peter H., 324
Muggia, Frank, 277

O

O'Brien, James E., 1

P

Pace, Henry B., 270
Pearson, M. L., 606
Perikh, H. 368
Peterson, Dorothy C., 331
Phillips, David M., 324
Phillips, Richard D., 142
Pihl, Alexander, 12, 27
Potter, Richard L., 628, 701

Q

Quastler, Henry, 277

R

Radford, Edward P., Jr., 298
Randolph, M. L., 492
Raso, Dominic J., 384
Robertson, J. S., 104, 409
Robins, A. B., 582
Rosenzweig, W., 512
Rosoff, Betty, 643, 655
Rossi, H. H., 512
Roth, Jay S., 42
Rothschild, Mary-Louise, 402
Rubenstein, H. M., 368
Rugh, Roberts, 88, 261
Rupkey, A. Katherine, 88

S

Sallese, A., 628
Sanner, Tore, 12, 27
Schneider, Carol A., 621
Sherry, Dwyn, 298
Shikita, Mikio, 419
Shubin, V. N., 345
Sicilio, Fred, 359
Silini, G., 50
Slatkin, D. N., 409
Smith, L. H., 485
Smith, Willie W., 621
Smoot, A. O., 659
Snyder, Fred, 129
Spencer, Herta, 643, 655
Staffeldt, E., 628
Sugino, Yukio, 628, 701
Swinnerton, J. W., 636

T

Tamaoki, Bun-Ichi, 419
Timnick, A., 462
Tsukamoto, William T., 402
Tsushiya, Takehiko, 316

U

Upton, A. C., 156

V

Van Lancker, J. L., 659
Vos, O., 485

W

Wang, S. C., 88
Weeks, J. L., 559

SUBJECT INDEX

A

Age and breeding history, effect on X-ray induced congenital anomalies. RUGH AND WOHLFROMM, 261
Alpha-emitting elements, analysis of teeth and bones. RADFORD *et al.*, 298
Amino and monocarboxylic acids, radiation induced carboxylation reaction. LIEBSTER *et al.*, 551
Antigen metabolism in rabbit, effect of X-irradiation. RUBINSTEIN AND PERIKH, 368

B

Bacteria, *E. coli*, effect of gamma irradiation on breakdown of DNA. KOS AND DRAKULIC, 439
 mutation and killing with heavy ions. DEERING, 169
 radiation sensitivity. DEWEY, 64
 radioresistant, effect of —SH combining chemicals. LEE *et al.*, 593
Beetle wing, effect of X-irradiation on developing cells. BECK, 569
Behavior, radiation avoidance of mouse, role of ozone. PETERSON AND ANDREWS, 331
Biological half life of cesium in man. ROSOFF *et al.*, 643
Bioluminescence, effect of UV radiation fungus. BERLINER, 392
Blood, extra corporeal irradiation, calculation of dose. SLATKIN *et al.*, 409

C

Calcium benzoate dosimeter, salicyclic acid yield. ARMSTRONG *et al.*, 120
Cataracts, radiation, lens epithelial cell proliferation and migration. HANNA AND O'BRIEN, 1
Cell culture, ultraviolet sensitivity. HUMPHREY *et al.*, 247
Cesium metabolism in man. ROSOFF *et al.*, 643
Cesium—137 turnover in man as measured by whole-body counter. COHN *et al.*, 655
Chromosomes aberrations in regenerating rat liver as function of age and type of irradiation. CURTIS AND CROWLEY, 337
Collison doses produced by fast neutron fluxes of wide energy distribution. RANDOLPH, 492

D

Deoxyribonucleic acid, breakdown following gamma irradiation. DRAKULIC AND KOS, 429
 of grasshopper neuroblasts, radiation induced incorporation of tritiated thymidine. McGRATH, 526
 metabolism, regenerating rat thymus, effect of X-irradiation. FRENKEL *et al.*, 701, SUGINO *et al.*, 682
Dose equivalent calculations for fast neutrons. RANDOLPH, 492
Dosimetry, salicyclic acid yield in calcium benzoate dosimeter. ARMSTRONG *et al.*, 120
Duodenal crypt cells of mice, generation cycle, effect of daily gamma irradiation. FRY *et al.*, 628

E

Electron irradiation, inactivation of solid trypsin, effects of metal salts. BUTLER AND ROBINS, 582
Enzyme(s), inactivation by ionizing radiations, kinetics. SANNER AND PIHL, 12
 spleen, effect of X-irradiation. ROTH AND HILTON, 42
Erythropoietin test, assessment of actinomycin and radiation damage of stem cells. GURNEY AND HOFSTRA, 599

F

Fast neutron flux, analytical evaluation of the first collison dose. RANDOLPH, 492
Fungus, *Armillaria mellea*, action of UV radiation. BERLINER, 392

G

Gamma irradiation, of alkaline solutions, hydrogen peroxide yields. ROTHSCHILD AND TSUKAMOTO, 402
of amino acids and monocarboxylic acids. LIEBSTER *et al.*, 551
aqueous solutions, effect of acidity on hydrogen yield. CHEEK *et al.*, 636
bacteria, enhancement of inactivation by chemicals. LEE *et al.*, 593
effect on breakdown of DNA of *E. coli*. KOS AND DRAKULIC, 439
generation cycle of mouse duodenal cyrpt cells. FRY *et al.*, 628
lens epithelial cell proliferation and migration. HANNA AND O'BRIEN, 1
Gamma ray scattering in laminar media. RASO, 384
Gamma-rays, primary and scattered, LET distribution. BRUCE *et al.*, 606
Grasshopper neuroblast chromosomes, and radiation induced incorporation of tritiated thymidine. MCGRATH, 526
Guinea pigs, relative potency of X-rays and fast neutrons. PHILLIPS *et al.*, 142

H

Hamster cell cultures, ultraviolet sensitivity. HUMPHREY *et al.*, 247
Hemopoiesis in irradiated mice, effect of pretreatment with colchicine. SMITH *et al.*, 621
Hydrogen peroxide yields from irradiated alkaline solutions. ROTHSCHILD AND TSUKAMOTO, 402
Hydrogen yield in gamma irradiated solutions, effect of acidity. CHEEK *et al.*, 636

I

Ionizing radiations, kinetics of enzyme inactivation. SANNER AND PIHL, 12
Irradiation, continuous low dose, of rats, effect on successive litters BROWN *et al.*, 270
with heavy ions, mutation and killing of *Escherichia coli*. DEERING, 169
whole-body, effect on bone marrow lipids of rats. SNYDER AND CRESS, 129

L

Linear energy transfer distributions resulting from primary and scattered X- and gamma rays. BRUCE *et al.*, 606
Lipids of bone marrow, rat, effect of whole-body irradiation. SNYDER AND CRESS, 129
Litters, rat, effect of continuous low dose irradiation. BROWN *et al.*, 270
Lymph node cells, radiation sensitivity relative to proliferative capacity. SMITH AND VOS, 485

M

Man, cesium metabolism. ROSOFF *et al.*, 643
cesium—137 turnover. COHN *et al.*, 655
kinetics of skeletal metabolism of Sr^{85} and Ca^{47}. COHN *et al.*, 104
Mice, chemical protection of intestinal and hematopoietic systems. MAISIN AND DOHERTY, 474
daily gamma irradiation, generation cycle of duodenal crypt cells. FRY *et al.*, 628
effect of age and breeding history on congenital anomalies. RUGH AND WOHLFROMM, 261
hair, cysteamine protection of radiation induced dysplasia. MALKINSON *et al.*, 324
irradiated, effect of pretreatment with colchicine on hemopoiesis. SMITH *et al.*, 621
irradiation of intestine and protein synthesis. LIPKIN *et al.*, 277
partial hepatectomy, effect on nucleic acid metabolism of regenerating thymus. SMOOT AND VAN LANCKER, 659
prevention of death after lethal irradiation of the head. GOEPP AND FITCH, 670
radio sensitivity of lymph node cells. SMITH AND VOS, 485
and thyroid function. TSUCHIYA *et al.*, 316
role of ozone in radiation avoidance. PETERSON AND ANDREWS, 331

sterility induced by X-irradiation, protection. RUPKEY *et al.*, 88
testis, effect of X-irradiation on zinc uptake. SHIKITA AND TAMAOKI, 419
effect of X-ray and neutron dose fractionation. SILINI *et al.*, 50
Microscopic changes following X-irradiation of rat intestinal villi. DETRICK *et al.*, 447
Monte Carlo program for gamma ray backscattering. RASO, 384

N

Neutrons, dependence of RBE on energy. BIAVATI *et al.*, 512
Neutrons and X-rays, relative potency in guinea pigs. PHILLIPS *et al.*, 142
Nucleic acid metabolism of regenerating thymus, effect of partial hepatectomy. SMOOT AND VAN LANCKER, 659

O

Oral irradiation death, prevention in mice· GOEPP AND FITCH, 670

P

Pentamethylheptane, radiolysis products. KNIGHT AND SICILIO, 359
Photons characteristics, multi purpose Monte Carlo program. RASO, 384
Population density, effect on radiation response. HAHN AND HOWLAND, 676
Portein synthesis in irradiated mouse intestine. LIPKIN *et al.*, 277
Proton, initial LET, radiation chemistry of water. KOCHANNY *et al.*, 462

R

RABBIT, antigen metabolism, effect of X-irradiation. RUBINSTEIN AND PERIKH, 368
Radiation chemistry, absorption coefficients of liquid water. WEEKS *et al.*, 559
amino and monocarboxylic acids. LIEBSTER *et al.*, 551
gamma irradiated aqueous solutions. CHEEK *et al.*, 636
hydrogen peroxide yields from irradiated alkaline solutions. ROTHSCHILD AND TSUKAMOTO, 402
method of a competitive scavengers. SHUBIN AND DOLIN, 345
Radiation dose, calculation, excorporeal irradiation of blood. SLATKIN *et al.*, 409
Radiation quality of fast neutrons, evaluation. BIAVATI *et al.*, 512
Radiation sensitivity, bacteria, *Serratia marcessens*. DEWEY, 64
Radical scavenger, method in radiation chemistry. SHUBIN AND DOLIN, 345
Radiolysis of pentamethylheptane. KNIGHT AND SICILIO, 359
of water with 11–23 Mev protons. KOCHANNY *et al.*, 462
Radiomimetic agents and X-rays, comparative late effects. CONKLIN *et al.*, 156
Radioprotection, AET, effect on thyroid function in the rat. MARUYAMA, 538
against sterility in mice. RUPKEY *et al.*, 88
chemical, of intestinal and hematopoietic systems of irradiated mice. MAISIN AND DOHERTY, 474
cysteamine, against dysplasia of mouse hair. MALINSON *et al.*, 324
Rat and mouse, radiation cataracts. HANNA AND O'BRIEN, 1
Rats, age and effect of irradiation on serum proteins. GLINOS, 286
continous irradiation, effect on litters. BROWN *et al.*, 270
intestinal villi, electron microscopic changes after X-irradiation. DETRICK *et al.*, 447
modification of radiation response by population density. HAHN AND HOWLAND, 676
regenerating liver, somatic mutation theory of aging. CURTIS AND CROWLEY, 337
thymus, correlative morphologic and biochemical changes during regeneration. FRENKEL *et al.*, 701
regeneration, effect on DNA metabolism. SUGINO *et al.*, 682
thyroid function, effect of AET. MARUYAMA, 538
X-irradiation, effect on spleen lysosomal enzymes. ROTH AND HILTON, 42
whole-body, effect on bone marrow lipids. SNYDER AND CRESS, 129
Relative biological efficiency, dependence on energy of fast neutrons. BIAVATI *et al.*, 512

of ionizing radiations on bacteria. DEERING, 169

S

Serum proteins, effect of X-irradiation. GLINOS, 286
Skeletal metabolism of Sr^{85} and Ca^{47} in man. COHN *et al.*, 104
Somatic effects, comparative, X-rays and radiomimetic agents. CONKLIN *et al.*, 156
Somatic mutation theory of aging. CURTIS AND CROWLEY, 337
$Strontium^{85}$ and $calcium^{47}$ in man, skeletal metabolism. COHN *et al.*, 104
Sulfhydryl combining agents, radiation sensitizing effect on resistant bacteria. LEE *et al.*, 593

T

Teeth and bones, analysis for alpha emitting elements. RADFORD *et al.*, 298
Testis, mice, effect of X-irradiation. SHIKITA AND TAMAOKI, 419
effect of X-ray and neutron dose fractionation. SILINI *et al.*, 50
Thyroid function, mice, and radiation sensitivity. TSUCHIYA *et al.*, 316
rat, effect of AET. MARUYAMA, 538
Trypsin inactivation by ionizing radiations. BUTLER AND ROBINS, 582

U

Ultraviolet radiation, action of luminescent fungus. BERLINER, 392
Ultraviolet sensitivity of hamster cell culture. HUMPHREY *et al.*, 247

W

Water, liquid and aqueous solutions, absorption coefficients in for UV. WEEKS *et al.*, 559
radiolysis with 11–23 Mev protons. KOCHANNY *et al.*, 462

X

X-irradiation, bacteria, sensitivity of, *Serratia marcescens*. DEWEY, 64
blood, calculation of dose. SLATKIN *et al.*, 409
congenital anomalies, effect of age and breeding history. RUGH AND WOHLFROMM, 261
effect on cells of developing beetle wing. BECK, 569
effect on DNA metabolism, correlative morphological and biochemical changes. FRENKEL *et al.*, 701
of regenerating rat thymus. SUGINO *et al.*, 682
incorporation of tritiated thymidine ino. DNA of grasshopper neuroblast. McGRATH, 526
mice cysteamine protection of induced dysplasia in hair. MALKINSON *et al.*, 324
effect of pretreatment with colchicine on hemopoiesis, SMITH *et al.*, 621
induction of sterlity, protection. RUPKEY *et al.*, 88
intestine, and, protein synthesis. LIPKIN *et al.*, 277
lethal, of head, prevention of death, GOEPP AND FITCH, 670
mice, role of ozone in avoidance behavior. PETERSON AND ANDREWS, 331
nucleic acid metabolism in thymus. SMOOT AND VAN LANCKER, 659
sensitivity of lymph node cells. SMITH AND VOS, 485
testis, effect on zinc uptake. SHIKITA AND TAMAOKI, 419
and thyroid function. TSUCHIYA *et al.*, 316
whole-body, chemical protection of intestinal and hematopoietic systems. MAISIN AND DOHERTY, 474
of pentamethylheptane products. KNIGHT AND SICILIO, 359
rabbit, effect on antigen metabolism. RUBINSTEIN AND PERIKH, 368
rats, effect on distribution of spleen enzymes. ROTH AND HILTON, 42
intestinal villi, electron microscopic changes. DETRICK *et al.*, 447
modification of response by population density. HAHN AND HOWLAND, 676
of varying ages, protein composition and

growth promoting activity of serum. Glinos, 286
X-irradiation and actinomycin D, erythropoietin tolerance test. Gurney and Hofstra, 599
X-ray and neutron dose fractionation, effect on mouse testis. Silini *et al.*, 50
and radiomimetic agents, comparative late somatic effects. Conklin *et al.*, 156
X-rays primary and scattered, LET distribution. Bruce *et al.*, 606
250 KV and fast neutrons, relative potency in guinea pigs. Phillips *et al.*, 142